ELECTRICITY AND ELECTRONICS FOR THE MICROCOMPUTER AGE

ELECTRICITY AND ELECTRONICS FOR THE MICROCOMPUTER AGE

STANLEY L. ROSEN

COORDINATOR, AVIONICS
TULSA AREA VO-TECH SCHOOL / TULSA, OKLAHOMA

JOHN WILEY & SONS
NEW YORK CHICHESTER BRISBANE TORONTO SINGAPORE

Text design by Karin Gerdes Kincheloe.
Cover design by Steve Jenkins.
Production by Cindy Funkhouser.
Cover photo by Paul Steel / The Stock Market.

Library of Congress Cataloging in Publication Data:

Rosen, Stanley L.
Electricity and electronics for the microcomputer age.

Bibliography: p.
Includes index.
1. Electric engineering. 2. Electronics. I. Title.
TK146.R537 1987 621.38 86-15912
ISBN 0-471-88195-3

Printed in the United States of America

10 9 8 7 6 5 4 3 2 1

TO MY WIFE, NANCY, AND CHILDREN,
SACHA AND MIRIAM, WITH LOVE
AND APPRECIATION.

PREFACE

In the earliest days of radio and electronics, the jobs of equipment design, construction, troubleshooting, and operation were frequently performed by the same person. Later, as the importance of electronics grew, these tasks came to be performed by specialists. It is no longer necessary for the operator of most electronic equipment to understand the principles of electronic component operation. Nor is it necessary for the operator to perform any but the simplest maintenance procedures. A similar division has occurred between the responsibilities of the design engineer and those of the maintenance technician.

Judging from present trends, it seems likely that this trend toward greater specialization will continue. For example, the introduction of modular assemblies and built-in diagnostic programs has created a need for "front-line" maintenance personnel who can effect field repairs by swapping faulty modules for operating ones. It is worth stressing, however, that although the modularized approach to unit construction and built-in diagnostic programs has created a new classification of technicians, the need for "depot-level" troubleshooting has not diminished. In fact, more jobs are available each year for individuals with a thorough grounding in electronic technology.

Further, it is clear that technological advances are taking place at an increasing rate, and greater demands are being made on the skills and background of technical employees. In recent years, digital technology and more particularly microprocessors have been incorporated into many areas of electronics. Today, digital circuitry is found in nearly every application. In the near future, fiber optics can be expected to show substantial growth as well. Other advances in components and techniques can be expected as the result of satellite communications and space exploration. Since industry is no longer able to wait for the maturation and training of a new generation of engineers and technicians to match each step forward, technical education will have to provide each future job holder with not only the practical skills necessary at this moment but also with sufficient analytical ability to keep current of this changing technology. It is in the light of these developments in the electronics industry that this book was written.

Some of the characteristics of this book were suggested by the military training manuals of the 1940s and 1950s. These manuals were usually well illustrated and attempted to provide all the material necessary to perform specific jobs in a clear manner. In comparison with these manuals, many modern textbooks say very little about troubleshooting or the components used in electronics and concentrate student efforts on substituting numbers into various formulas. I thought it would be a good idea to write a book that would stress troubleshooting and the analysis of component failures and that would show real-world applications for the theories presented. A modern textbook, I decided at the beginning of the writing, should have detailed material on the components covered in the theoretical text, as well as instruction in the composition and operation of multimeters, oscilloscopes, and signal sources. Further, there should be enough illustrations and figures included to show the reader how the components and test equipment used in electronics look.

Naturally, there were certain failings in the military manuals that it was wise to avoid. Once a bit of information was presented, for example, it was rarely reviewed or explained again from a different point of view. In addition, the manuals were purposely limited in their goals. Their object was to provide all the training necessary for a specific job, as that job was then defined. Little effort was invested in preparation for work on the next generation of equipment. Other failings were terseness and a common lack of self-evaluation materials and exercises, which later military texts did provide.

As the writing progressed, I became increasingly aware that the modern engineer or technician had to be able to do things that were not dreamed of when those military manuals were written. Certain technical jobs had become incredibly more complex due to the introduction of integrated circuits. With the rise of the microprocessor, the engineer and technician have been called upon to deal with design and repair problems such as electromagnetic interference, circuit timing, and previously noncritical static conditions and power line transients. This brought about the fogging of certain time-honored trade and professional distinctions. Once, it was easy to distinguish electricians, electronic technicians, and engineers: electricians used multimeters, electronic technicians used meters and oscilloscopes, while engineers relied on mathematical analysis.

There are those who maintain that these distinctions are still true, but they are fighting a losing battle. With such tools as scientific calculators and small computers replacing the cumbersome slide rules of the last generation, mathematical analysis of circuits has become a practical tool for circuit troubleshooting as well as circuit design. To support circuit analysis, each chapter of this book includes a mathematical section designed to introduce certain concepts as they will be needed or to provide practice in their application. Even if you have studied these topics in a formal math course, it is recommended that these sections be used to provide practice in the application of mathematics to the solution of problems in electronics.

Each chapter of this book also contains a programmed review section designed so that a progress check and review can be accomplished after each chapter. These, along with the problems included in each chapter, provide a means for checking your understanding of the material as you progress. Correct use of this material will ensure you a thorough foundation of theory and practice and will make your studies easier.

ACKNOWLEDGMENTS

The author wishes to thank the corporations and individuals who supplied photographs or materials used for illustrations:

Biddle Instruments
Bird Electronic Corporation
Hickok Teaching Systems, Inc.
John Fluke Mfg. Co., Inc.
Kulka Smith, Inc.
Sencore
Simpson Electric Corp.
Tektronix, Inc.
Triplett Corp.
3M, Static Control Systems Division

The photographs have been used with permission and all rights, including patent and copyright, are reserved for their holders. Particular thanks are due to Tektronix and the Static Control Systems Division of 3M Corp. for supplying a large number of excellent photographs. Additional photographs were designed and taken by Mr. Mike Hermes of Tulsa, Oklahoma.

Valuable advice was obtained from the following reviewers:

Ron Gamel
Tulsa Area Vo-Tech School

Marion Caryl and Harold Drain
Tektronix, Inc.

Jack Barkley
Practical Schools

William H. Blanton, Jr.
Delta-Quachita Vo-Tech

Lawrence A. Ezard
Pennsylvania State University–The Capital Campus

Paul D. Fouts
Indiana Vocational Technical College

Don Grob
Salina Vo-Tech

Thomas Harden
Northern Kentucky University

John Hoeft
Austin Vo-Tech Institute

Karl Hunter
Florida Junior College

William Perkins
ITT Technical Institute

Robert Reaves
Durham Technical Institute

William A. Scott, Jr.
Hobson State Technical College

Art Seidman

Howard C. Shehane
Columbus Tech

Robert E. Smith
Hillsborough Community College

John Wardell
Spoon River College

The author wishes to thank the staff of John Wiley & Sons for their help, suggestions, encouragement, and patience. I owe a particular debt of gratitude to Mr. Al Lesure, Mr. Joe Morse, and Mr. Hank Stewart who provided encouragement and guidance from the outset, and to Mr. Joe Keenan, Mr. Kieran Murphy, Ms. Karin Kincheloe, and Ms. Cindy Funkhouser for their hard work.

Finally, I would like to express my appreciation to Mr. Richard Garretson, my agent, who kept the whole thing rolling, and to my wife, Nancy, who typed and proofread the manuscript.

Stanley L. Rosen

CONTENTS

1 ELECTRICITY AND THE ATOM

A CHAPTER PREVIEW 1

B PRINCIPLES 1

B.1 INTRODUCTION: THE BASIC TASKS OF TECHNOLOGY 1
B.2 ENERGY AND WORK 1
B.3 ELECTRICAL EFFECTS: A BIT OF HISTORY 1
B.4 FRANKLIN'S DISCOVERIES 1
B.5 FRANKLIN'S MISTAKES 2
B.6 CONVENTIONAL CURRENT AND ELECTRON FLOW 2
B.7 ATOMS, ELEMENTS, AND COMPOUNDS 3
B.8 THE MOLECULE 3
B.9 BEGINNINGS OF MODERN ATOMIC THEORY 3
B.10 BOHR'S MODEL OF THE ATOM 4
B.11 THE BEHAVIOR OF CHARGE CARRIERS IN ATOMS 6
B.12 CONDUCTION ELECTRONS 7
B.13 BEHAVIOR OF CHARGE CARRIERS IN SUBSTANCES 7
B.14 INSULATORS, CONDUCTORS, AND SEMICONDUCTORS 7

C EXAMPLES AND COMPUTATIONS 7

C.1 THE CALCULATOR 7
C.2 DECIMALS 9
C.3 ARITHMETIC WITH DECIMALS 10
C.4 CHANGING COMMON FRACTIONS TO DECIMALS 12
C.5 THE SMALL COMPUTER AND THE STUDY OF ELECTRONICS 13

D APPLICATIONS 13

E PROGRAMMED REVIEW 15

INSTRUCTIONS FOR USING PROGRAMMED REVIEW MATERIALS 15

F PROBLEMS FOR SOLUTION OR RESEARCH 18

2 THE ELECTRIC FIELD AND ELECTRIC CURRENT

A CHAPTER PREVIEW 20

B PRINCIPLES 21

B.1 THE ELECTRIC FIELD 21
B.2 MAPPING AN ELECTRIC FIELD 21
B.3 MEASUREMENT OF CHARGE 22
B.4 THE PRODUCTION OF STATIC CHARGES 23
B.5 THE BEHAVIOR OF CHARGED OBJECTS 24

B.6 CHARGING BY CONTACT 24
B.7 GROUNDING 25
B.8 CHARGING BY INDUCTION 25
B.9 STATIC CHARGE EXISTS ONLY ON THE SURFACE OF OBJECTS 26
B.10 MOVEMENT OF ELECTRICAL CHARGE CARRIERS 27
B.11 POTENTIAL DIFFERENCE 27
B.12 THE CIRCUIT 28

C EXAMPLES AND COMPUTATIONS 28

C.1 SIGNED NUMBERS 28
C.2 EXPONENTS AND SCIENTIFIC NOTATION 31
C.3 SCIENTIFIC NOTATION 32
C.4 ENGINEERING NOTATION 32

D APPLICATIONS 33

D.1 STATIC ELECTRICITY 33
D.2 DANGERS OF STATIC ELECTRICITY TO ELECTRONIC COMPONENTS 34
D.3 METHODS OF STATIC ELECTRICITY PREVENTION IN THE ELECTRONICS INDUSTRY 34

E PROGRAMMED REVIEW 37

F PROBLEMS FOR SOLUTION OR RESEARCH 40

3 CURRENT, POTENTIAL DIFFERENCE, AND CELLS

A CHAPTER PREVIEW 42

B PRINCIPLES 43

B.1 SOURCES AND LOADS 43
B.2 FUNCTIONS OF A LOAD 44
B.3 DEFINITION OF THE AMPERE 45
B.4 CURRENT DIRECTION, ELECTRIC FIELD DIRECTION, AND DIRECT CURRENT 46
B.5 MEASURING CURRENT: DEVICES AND METHODS 46
B.6 MEASURING POTENTIAL DIFFERENCE: DEVICES AND METHODS 50
B.7 READING ANALOG MULTIMETER SCALES 52

C EXAMPLES AND COMPUTATIONS 55

C.1 REVIEW OF THE METRIC SYSTEM AND METRIC PREFIXES 55
C.2 ROUNDING OFF 57
C.3 ADDING AND SUBTRACTING NUMBERS IN SCIENTIFIC OR ENGINEERING NOTATION 59
C.4 MULTIPLYING AND DIVIDING NUMBERS IN SCIENTIFIC OR ENGINEERING NOTATION 60
C.5 ENGINEERING AND SCIENTIFIC NOTATION ON A CALCULATOR 61
C.6 ENGINEERING AND SCIENTIFIC NOTATION COMPUTATIONS ON A CALCULATOR 62
C.7 ENGINEERING AND SCIENTIFIC NOTATION IN BASIC 62

D APPLICATIONS: CHEMICAL CELLS AS CURRENT AND POTENTIAL SOURCES 63

D.1 HISTORY OF CHEMICAL CELLS 63
D.2 PRACTICAL CELLS 64
D.3 CHARACTERISTICS OF CHEMICAL CELLS 64
D.4 THE LECLANCHÉ OR CARBON–ZINC CELL 66
D.5 THE ZINC CHLORIDE CELL 67
D.6 THE ALKALINE CELL 67
D.7 MERCURIC OXIDE AND SILVER OXIDE CELLS 68
D.8 LITHIUM CELLS 69
D.9 SECONDARY CELLS 69
D.10 THE LEAD–ACID, OR PLANTÉ, CELL 69
D.11 THE SEALED LEAD–ACID, OR GELLED ACID, CELL 70
D.12 THE MAINTENANCE AND RECHARGING OF LEAD–ACID CELLS 71
D.13 NICKEL–CADMIUM SECONDARY CELLS 72

E PROGRAMMED REVIEW 73

F PROBLEMS FOR SOLUTION OR RESEARCH 76

4 SOURCES IN SERIES, PARALLEL, AND SERIES-PARALLEL

A CHAPTER PREVIEW 78
B PRINCIPLES 79
B.1 ELECTRICAL AND ELECTRONIC DIAGRAMS 79
B.2 SOURCES IN SERIES 82
B.3 SOURCES IN PARALLEL 84
B.4 SERIES–PARALLEL CONNECTION OF SOURCES 85
B.5 CIRCUIT EQUIVALENTS 87
B.6 GROUNDED CIRCUITS 88
C EXAMPLES AND COMPUTATIONS 89
C.1 FORMULAS AND EQUATIONS 89
C.2 CHECKING SOLUTIONS BY UNIT ANALYSIS 92
C.3 FORMULAS FOR METRIC EQUIVALENTS 92
C.4 CONVERSIONS USING A COMPUTER PROGRAM 93
D APPLICATIONS 94
D.1 FAILURE MODE ANALYSIS 94
D.2 VARIATIONAL ANALYSIS 95
E PROGRAMMED REVIEW 96
F PROBLEMS FOR SOLUTION OR RESEARCH 98

5 RESISTANCE, OHM'S LAW, AND WIRE

A CHAPTER PREVIEW 102
B PRINCIPLES 103
B.1 RESISTIVITY 103
B.2 OHM'S LAW 103
B.3 MEASURING RESISTANCE 105
B.4 WHY MEASURE RESISTANCE? 107
B.5 THE EFFECT OF TEMPERATURE ON RESISTANCE 108
C EXAMPLES AND COMPUTATIONS 109
C.1 OHM'S LAW CALCULATIONS 109
C.2 EXERCISES IN VARIATIONAL ANALYSIS 111
C.3 RECIPROCAL QUANTITIES AND CONDUCTANCE 112
D APPLICATIONS 113
D.1 WIRE GAUGE SIZES 114
D.2 SOLID AND STRANDED WIRE 116
D.3 INSULATION 118
D.4 CABLE 119
E PROGRAMMED REVIEW 120
F PROBLEMS FOR SOLUTION OR RESEARCH 122

6 POWER: RESISTANCES IN SERIES, PARALLEL, AND SERIES-PARALLEL

A CHAPTER PREVIEW 124
B PRINCIPLES 125
B.1 WHAT IS POWER? 125
B.2 ELECTRIC POWER 125
B.3 MEASURING ELECTRIC POWER 127
B.4 RESISTANCES IN SERIES 128
B.5 RESISTANCES IN PARALLEL 130
B.6 RESISTANCE, CONDUCTANCE, AND EQUIVALENT CIRCUITS 132
B.7 SERIES–PARALLEL CIRCUITS 133
C EXAMPLES AND COMPUTATIONS 133
C.1 SQUARE AND SQUARE ROOT COMPUTATIONS 133
C.2 SQUARE AND SQUARE ROOT CALCULATIONS ON A SMALL COMPUTER USING BASIC 136

C.3 REVIEW OF OHM'S LAW, POWER, AND RESISTANCE/CONDUCTANCE COMPUTATIONS 136
C.4 VARIATIONAL ANALYSIS OF SERIES AND PARALLEL CIRCUITS 137

D APPLICATIONS 139

D.1 POWER DISSIPATION IN WIRES 139
D.2 INCANDESCENT AND NEON LAMPS 139
D.3 FUSES 142
D.4 SWITCHES 146

E PROGRAMMED REVIEW 154

F PROBLEMS FOR SOLUTION OR RESEARCH 156

7 CIRCUIT ANALYSIS AND PRACTICAL RESISTORS

A CHAPTER PREVIEW 158

B PRINCIPLES 159

B.1 INTRODUCTION TO CIRCUIT ANALYSIS 159
B.2 NETWORK GRAPHING 159
B.3 VOLTAGE RISES AND VOLTAGE DROPS 161
B.4 KIRCHHOFF'S VOLTAGE LAW 162
B.5 KIRCHHOFF'S CURRENT LAW 166

C EXAMPLES AND COMPUTATIONS 167

C.1 GRAPHS 167
C.2 ANGLES 171
C.3 SIMULTANEOUS EQUATIONS 174
C.4 TOLERANCE CALCULATIONS 179

D APPLICATIONS 182

D.1 WHAT IS A RESISTOR? 182
D.2 WHY RESISTORS ARE USED 182
D.3 TYPES OF FIXED RESISTORS 183
D.4 STANDARD RESISTOR VALUES 185
D.5 THE COLOR CODE 186
D.6 RESISTOR SIZE AND POWER DISSIPATION 188
D.7 OTHER ENCODING SYSTEMS 189
D.8 VARIABLE RESISTORS 189

E PROGRAMMED REVIEW 192

F PROBLEMS FOR SOLUTION OR RESEARCH 196

8 NETWORK THEOREMS AND PRACTICAL RESISTOR CIRCUITS

A CHAPTER PREVIEW 198

B PRINCIPLES 199

B.1 NETWORK THEOREMS: THE Δ–Y EQUIVALENCY THEOREM 199
B.2 IDEAL VOLTAGE AND IDEAL CURRENT SOURCES 203
B.3 THE SUPERPOSITION THEOREM 204
B.4 THEVENIN'S THEOREM 206
B.5 NORTON'S THEOREM 207
B.6 THE RELATIONSHIP BETWEEN THEVENIN AND NORTON EQUIVALENTS 209
B.7 MILLMAN'S THEOREM 210

C EXAMPLES AND COMPUTATIONS 211

C.1 SIMULTANEOUS EQUATIONS ON A SMALL COMPUTER USING BASIC 211
C.2 Δ–Y AND Y–Δ EQUIVALENCY USING A SMALL COMPUTER 214
C.3 COMPARISON OF KIRCHHOFF'S LAW ANALYSES AND NETWORK THEOREMS 216

D APPLICATIONS 216

D.1 SHUNTS 216
D.2 RANGE MULTIPLIERS 218
D.3 THE BRIDGE CIRCUIT 218
D.4 VOLTAGE DIVIDERS 220
D.5 MAXIMUM POWER TRANSFER AND RESISTIVE NETWORKS 222

E PROGRAMMED REVIEW 225

F PROBLEMS FOR SOLUTION OR RESEARCH 227

9 MAGNETISM AND ELECTROMAGNETIC COMPONENTS

A CHAPTER PREVIEW 228
B PRINCIPLES 229
B.1 WHAT IS MAGNETISM? 229
B.2 THEORY OF MAGNETISM 230
B.3 THE MAGNETIC FIELD AROUND A CURRENT-CARRYING WIRE 232
C EXAMPLES AND COMPUTATIONS 239
C.1 FUNCTIONS USED IN ELECTRONIC TECHNOLOGY 239
C.2 GRAPHING THE FUNCTIONS USED IN ELECTRONIC TECHNOLOGY 240
C.3 TRIGONOMETRIC FUNCTIONS 242
D APPLICATIONS 247
D.1 ELECTROMAGNETIC COMPONENTS 247
D.2 CIRCUIT BREAKERS 247
D.3 RELAYS 249
E PROGRAMMED REVIEW 256
F PROBLEMS FOR SOLUTION OR RESEARCH 259

10 WAVEFORMS AND THE OSCILLOSCOPE

A CHAPTER PREVIEW 260
B PRINCIPLES 261
B.1 RELATIONSHIP BETWEEN A MAGNETIC FIELD AND AN ELECTRIC FIELD 261
B.2 CONDUCTORS, FORCES, AND MAGNETIC FIELDS: THE GENERATOR EFFECT 262
B.3 GENERATOR OUTPUT 264
B.4 WAVEFORMS 266
C EXAMPLES AND COMPUTATIONS 269
C.1 RESOLVING VECTOR QUANTITIES 269
C.2 COMPUTATIONS WITH SINE WAVES 273
C.3 COMPUTATIONS WITH SQUARE WAVES AND PULSES 275
D APPLICATIONS 277
D.1 THE OSCILLOSCOPE 277
D.2 THE DISPLAY SECTION 278
D.3 THE VERTICAL SECTION 280
D.4 THE HORIZONTAL SECTION 281
D.5 OSCILLOSCOPE PROBES 283
D.6 THE DUAL-TRACE, TRIGGERED OSCILLOSCOPE 285
D.7 OBSERVING WAVEFORMS AND MAKING MEASUREMENTS WITH AN OSCILLOSCOPE 288
E PROGRAMMED REVIEW 293
F PROBLEMS FOR SOLUTION OR RESEARCH 296

11 AC MEASUREMENTS AND WAVEFORM GENERATION

A CHAPTER PREVIEW 298
B PRINCIPLES 299
B.1 MEASUREMENT OF CURRENT AND POTENTIAL DIFFERENCE IN AC, SQUARE WAVE, AND PULSE CIRCUITS 299
B.2 OHM'S AND KIRCHHOFF'S LAWS IN AC CIRCUITS 301
B.3 POWER IN AC CIRCUITS 303
B.4 MEASURING FREQUENCY 304
B.5 SIGNAL SOURCES 307
B.6 SIGNAL SOURCE CONNECTORS AND CABLES 314
C. EXAMPLES AND COMPUTATIONS 316

C.1 PHASE AND PHASORS 316

D APPLICATIONS 320

D.1 TYPES OF ELECTROMAGNETIC METERS AND THEIR APPLICATIONS 320
D.2 ELECTROMAGNETIC METER MOVEMENT SUSPENSIONS AND MAINTENANCE 324
D.3 ELECTROMAGNETIC METER SENSITIVITY, ACCURACY, AND EFFECT ON A CIRCUIT 325

E PROGRAMMED REVIEW 327

F PROBLEMS FOR SOLUTION OR RESEARCH 329

12 INDUCTION AND PRACTICAL INDUCTORS

A CHAPTER PREVIEW 332

B PRINCIPLES 333

B.1 MUTUAL INDUCTION 333
B.2 SELF-INDUCTION 336
B.3 THE UNIT OF INDUCTANCE 337
B.4 POTENTIAL DIFFERENCE ACROSS AND CURRENT THROUGH AN INDUCTOR 338
B.5 INDUCTIVE VOLTAGE SURGES 341
B.6 INDUCTORS AND RESISTORS IN AC CIRCUITS 341
B.7 INDUCTIVE REACTANCE 343
B.8 INDUCTANCES IN SERIES AND PARALLEL 344
B.9 IMPEDANCE 346

C EXAMPLES AND COMPUTATIONS 347

C.1 INTRODUCTION TO LOGARITHMS 347
C.2 USING LOGARITHMS IN INDUCTANCE CALCULATIONS 348

D APPLICATIONS 350

D.1 PRACTICAL INDUCTORS 350
D.2 COIL CHARACTERISTICS: *Q* 353
D.3 COIL CHARACTERISTICS: POWDERED IRON AND FERRITES 354

E PROGRAMMED REVIEW 357

F PROBLEMS FOR SOLUTION OR RESEARCH 360

13 INDUCTIVE CIRCUITS AND TRANSFORMERS

A CHAPTER PREVIEW 362

B PRINCIPLES 363

B.1 COMPOSITE AC AND DC SOURCES IN *RL* CIRCUITS 363
B.2 SQUARE WAVES AND PULSES IN INDUCTIVE CIRCUITS 365
B.3 *Q* IN CIRCUITS AND CIRCUIT BRANCHES 369
B.4 COUPLING AND MUTUAL INDUCTANCE 371
B.5 THE TRANSFORMER EFFECT 372
B.6 REAL TRANSFORMERS 376
B.7 TRANSFORMERS FOR IMPEDANCE MATCHING 378

C EXAMPLES AND COMPUTATIONS 380

C.1 WHY USE SINE-WAVE ANALYSIS? 380
C.2 MUTUAL INDUCTANCE AND TRANSFORMER CALCULATIONS 381
C.3 RECTANGULAR COORDINATES, POLAR COORDINATES, AND THE *j* OPERATOR 381

D APPLICATIONS 386

D.1 TRANSFORMER TYPES: CHARACTERISTICS AND FAILURE MODES 386
D.2 TRANSFORMER FAILURE MODES AND TROUBLESHOOTING 392

E PROGRAMMED REVIEW 394

F PROBLEMS FOR SOLUTION OR RESEARCH 398

14 CAPACITANCE IN DC CIRCUITS AND CAPACITORS

A CHAPTER PREVIEW 400
B PRINCIPLES 401
B.1 WHAT IS CAPACITANCE? 401
B.2 CAPACITORS IN DC CIRCUITS 405
B.3 THE TIME CONSTANT IN *RC* CIRCUITS 409
B.4 PARALLEL AND SERIES–PARALLEL *RC* CIRCUITS 411
B.5 CAPACITORS IN PARALLEL AND SERIES 414
C EXAMPLES AND COMPUTATIONS 416
C.1 EXERCISES IN CAPACITOR CALCULATIONS 416
C.2 COMPUTATIONS WITH RECTANGULAR AND POLAR COORDINATES 418
D APPLICATIONS: PRACTICAL CAPACITORS 423
D.1 CAPACITOR TYPES AND CHARACTERISTICS 423
D.2 CODING OF CAPACITOR CHARACTERISTICS 430
E PROGRAMMED REVIEW 431
F PROBLEMS FOR SOLUTION OR RESEARCH 435

15 CAPACITANCE IN AC CIRCUITS: ELECTROLYTIC AND VARIABLE CAPACITORS

A CHAPTER PREVIEW 436
B PRINCIPLES 437
B.1 THE CAPACITOR IN CIRCUITS WITH CHANGING POTENTIAL DIFFERENCES 437
B.2 CAPACITORS IN AC CIRCUITS: CAPACITIVE REACTANCE 441
B.3 CAPACITIVE REACTANCE AND IMPEDANCE 444
B.4 ANOTHER WAY OF LOOKING AT CAPACITIVE REACTANCE 448
B.5 PARALLEL *RC* CIRCUITS 450
B.6 OPERATION OF THE DIELECTRIC IN A CAPACITOR 451
C EXAMPLES AND COMPUTATIONS 454
C.1 REVIEW OF SERIES AND PARALLEL *RL* CIRCUITS 454
C.2 SOLVING SERIES AND PARALLEL CIRCUIT *RC* PROBLEMS 454
D APPLICATIONS 455
D.1 ELECTROLYTIC CAPACITORS 455
D.2 VARIABLE CAPACITORS 461
D.3 TESTING CAPACITORS 464
D.4 REPLACEMENTS FOR FAULTY CAPACITORS 465
E PROGRAMMED REVIEW 466
F PROBLEMS FOR SOLUTION OR RESEARCH 469

16 POWER IN RC AND RL CIRCUITS: PRACTICAL RC CIRCUITS

A CHAPTER PREVIEW 472
B PRINCIPLES 473
B.1 POWER AND REACTIVE POWER IN CAPACITIVE AC CIRCUITS 473
B.2 REACTIVE POWER, TRUE POWER, AND APPARENT POWER IN *RC* CIRCUITS 475
B.3 POWER AND REACTIVE POWER IN INDUCTIVE AC CIRCUITS 477

B.4 REACTIVE POWER, TRUE POWER, AND APPARENT POWER IN *RL* CIRCUITS 479
B.5 POWER FACTOR 481

C EXAMPLES AND COMPUTATIONS 483

C.1 PRACTICE IN AC CIRCUIT ANALYSIS 483
C.2 DECIBELS 487
C.3 DECIBELS AND POTENTIAL DIFFERENCE AND CURRENT RATIOS 489

D APPLICATIONS 491

D.1 TYPES OF PRACTICAL *RC* CIRCUITS 491
D.2 *Q* IN CAPACITIVE CIRCUITS 497
D.3 TROUBLESHOOTING *RC* CIRCUITS 498

E PROGRAMMED REVIEW 500

F PROBLEMS FOR SOLUTION OR RESEARCH 502

17 RCL AND TUNED CIRCUITS

A CHAPTER PREVIEW 504

B PRINCIPLES 505

B.1 SERIES *RCL* CIRCUITS 505
B.2 PARALLEL *RCL* CIRCUITS 508
B.3 SERIES–PARALLEL *RCL* CIRCUITS 510
B.4 SERIES RESONANT CIRCUITS 514
B.5 PARALLEL RESONANT CIRCUITS 521
B.6 COMPARISON OF SERIES-TUNED AND PARALLEL-TUNED CIRCUITS 530

C EXAMPLES AND COMPUTATIONS 530

C.1 MATHEMATICAL ANALYSIS AS AN EXPLANATION OF CIRCUIT BEHAVIOR 530
C.2 USING THEVENIN'S AND NORTON'S THEOREMS TO ANALYZE RESONANT CIRCUITS 535

D APPLICATIONS 537

D.1 PRACTICAL SERIES RESONANT CIRCUITS 537
D.2 PRACTICAL PARALLEL RESONANT CIRCUITS 539
D.3 FILTERS 540

E PROGRAMMED REVIEW 544

F PROBLEMS FOR SOLUTION OR RESEARCH 548

GLOSSARY 551

ANSWERS TO SELECTED PROBLEMS 567

TABLE OF TRIGONOMETRIC FUNCTIONS 575

INDEX 579

ELECTRICITY AND ELECTRONICS FOR THE MICROCOMPUTER AGE

CHAPTER 1

ELECTRICITY AND THE ATOM

A. CHAPTER PREVIEW

1 This chapter begins with an analysis of the three basic tasks of technology: obtaining energy, controlling it, and applying it to do useful work. Remembering these tasks will help you understand and solve the problems that are an important part of the work of engineers and technicians.

2 People observed the effects of electricity long before much was understood about it. Learning how certain confusions came into being will clarify your understanding of this subject.

3 You will learn about electrical energy and the nature of matter, including molecules, atoms, and atomic particles.

4 This chapter contains an explanation of the atom. Using this explanation, you will learn how electrical charges behave in an atom.

5 Because electrical effects are based on the behavior of electrical charges in substances, you will learn how atoms are held together, and what this has to do with the electrical nature of substances.

6 The Examples and Computations section provides an introduction to the selection and use of a scientific calculator as an aid to technical problem solving. Calculator skills are practiced in a review of decimal operations. You will also learn to use a small computer and a popular form of the BASIC programming language to perform certain calculations.

7 In the Applications section, you will learn about two modern electronic devices, the light-emitting diode (LED) and the laser, which make use of the principles of electron energy levels.

B. PRINCIPLES

B.1 INTRODUCTION: THE BASIC TASKS OF TECHNOLOGY

Humpty Dumpty sat on a wall
Humpty Dumpty had a great fall
All the king's horses and all the king's men
Couldn't put Humpty together again.

This little poem, which isn't nonsense, by the way, but a very old political joke, summarizes the difference between a technological and a nontechnological world. If there is a job to be done in a nontechnological world, it gets done by muscle power. In a technological world such as ours, work is done through the use of many sources of energy. The energy from a controlled explosion of gasoline in an automobile engine is only one of the kinds of energy used to do work in a technological world.

Regardless of the type of energy, the basic requirements for using it fall into three categories: obtaining the energy, controlling it, and applying the controlled energy to do some sort of work. These jobs are also basic considerations in the field of electrical and electronic technology. A specific kind of energy, electrical energy, is obtained from a source, controlled in special ways, and supplied to do work.

Keeping these considerations in mind can make the job of the technician easier. Suppose that you have been asked to repair an electronic unit. You might begin by comparing the work the unit is supposed to do and what it is actually doing. Clearly, if the unit is doing the work that it was designed to do in the way that it is supposed to, there may not be anything wrong with it. If the unit will not do the work it was designed to do, you might consider the source of the energy used by the unit. Is it getting enough of the right sort of energy? Lastly, you may have to trace the control of energy through the unit, step by step, in order to find those parts which are not working. Answering questions of this sort is called "troubleshooting," and it is the major job of the maintenance technician.

B.2 ENERGY AND WORK

In the above paragraphs, the words *work* and *energy* were used in the general sense, but because this book considers electricity as *electrical energy*, the two words require a scientific definition. Energy, in the scientific sense, is the ability to do work. This is not much of an improvement upon the everyday definition of energy, and it does little more than relate the terms energy and work. It is hard to define energy specifically because there are a number of different kinds of energy. A rock balancing at the top of a mountain has one kind of energy, while that same rock rolling down the mountain has another.

Work, on the other hand, is easier to define. One scientific definition states that work is done when a force moves an object some distance in the direction of the force. The key word in this definition is *movement:* work is done only when there is movement. This does not agree with the usual sense of the word work. Lifting a heavy book up from a table is work in both the scientific and in the everyday senses, but holding it in the air is *not* work in the scientific sense, regardless of how tiring it might be. As peculiar as it seems, this definition of work will be developed as this book proceeds and will serve to simplify many complex concepts.

B.3 ELECTRICAL EFFECTS: A BIT OF HISTORY

People have known certain things about electrical energy for a very long time. Almost all ancient peoples feared and respected the power of lightning. In addition to this, the ancient Greeks learned something peculiar about amber, a hard, stonelike material. They found that rubbing it with a cloth gave the amber the power to attract small bits of wood or feathers. In some way, the amber changed the space around it so that materials a small distance away behaved in a curious manner. Proof that these early discoveries influenced the entire history of electricity and electronics can be found in the word *electricity* itself. The Greek word for amber is *electrum.* Both lightning and the power of the amber are effects of electricity, although how these things are related was not discovered until much later.

It was not until 1650, more than 2000 years after the first written reference to the effect of rubbed amber, that a German inventor built a machine that produced reasonable amounts of electrical energy. This machine produced small lightning-like sparks, but the operation of the machine itself was little understood until the American Benjamin Franklin performed many experiments to find out more about the nature of electricity.

B.4 FRANKLIN'S DISCOVERIES

Franklin thought that electricity was an invisible fluid which could be removed from or added to substances by rubbing them with certain kinds of cloth. Glass, for

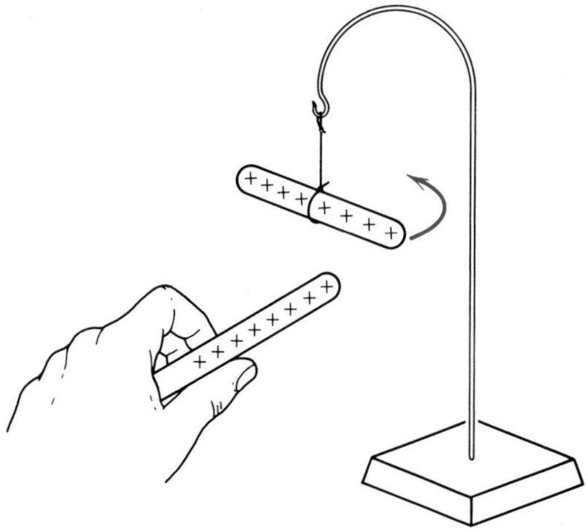

Figure 1.1 Two glass rods rubbed with a silk cloth repel each other.

example, had to be rubbed with a silk cloth. Franklin found that there were two classes of substances. When two objects belonging to the same class were "electrified," the objects repelled each other, as shown in Figure 1.1. Two rods belonging to different classes attracted each other, as shown in Figure 1.2. Franklin thought that the rubbing process added electric fluid to one class and removed it from the other. The substances to which rubbing added the electric fluid he called "positively charged"; those that he imagined to have lost electric fluid he called "negatively charged." Two substances with the same charge, he noted, repel each other. Substances with opposite charges attract each other.

Figure 1.2 A glass rod rubbed with silk attracts a rubber rod rubbed with fur.

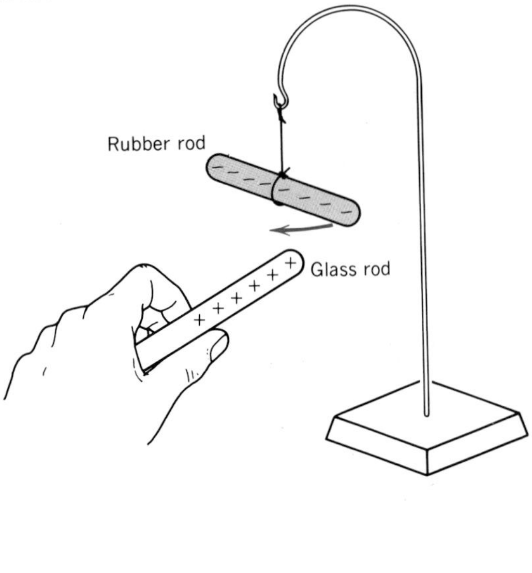

B.5 FRANKLIN'S MISTAKES

Using these ideas, Franklin was able to explain a number of electrical effects. Unfortunately, his work also caused problems that still linger. One of the problems has to do with comparing the nature of electricity to a liquid. Although it was very helpful in the early days of investigation, and may even be of use to beginning students, comparing electricity to the flow of a liquid tends to hide certain important characteristics of electricity and to make others harder to understand.

The second problem came about because Franklin thought that if a wire is connected between oppositely charged objects, the electric fluid would flow from the positively charged object, where there was too much of it, to the negatively charged object, where there was not enough. This grew into the concept of a *current*, or flow of electricity, from an area with a positive charge to an area with a negative charge. Today, we know that the opposite is true. Electrons, tiny parts of atoms, are added to substances to give them a negative charge. Removing electrons from a piece of material gives the material a positive charge. If oppositely charged objects are connected by a wire, electrons will move from the negatively charged object, through the wire, to the positively charged object.

Unfortunately, this was learned after many important discoveries were made. Franklin's theory of a flow, called *electric current*, from areas of positive charge to areas of negative charge, had become built into electrical theory in spite of the fact that it was wrong.

B.6 CONVENTIONAL CURRENT AND ELECTRON FLOW

A number of textbooks tried to correct Franklin's error by speaking of current flow from negative to positive, the actual direction of electron movement. The result of this was to introduce more confusion and to create a division between books meant for engineers and books meant for technicians. Franklin's definition of current direction, now called *conventional current*, was thought to be better for engineers, while electron movement was supposed to be better for technicians.

Recently, some people have felt that technicians who work with engineers should also use the conventional current method. All the effects of electricity discussed in this book can be explained equally well using either method. Both methods will be used in this book, with a preference given to the electron flow explanation.

B.7 ATOMS, ELEMENTS, AND COMPOUNDS

In the last section, electrons and atoms were mentioned briefly. In order even to begin to understand modern electricity and electronics, you have to break away from the 100-year-old explanations that treated electricity like water flowing in pipes and relate electricity to the nature of matter, that is, to how things are composed.

The concept of the atom was a philosophical notion for a long time before it had any practical meaning. It was not until the science of chemistry began to develop that the atomic theory began to be studied seriously, and early chemists explored the concepts of elements and compounds. Most of the materials in the world were found to be made up of various combinations of a few basic substances. These basic substances came to be called *elements*, and as time passed, some 90 of them were discovered existing in nature. Several more have been manufactured in modern laboratories. Elements may be found in uncombined form in nature. An example is the gas helium, which does not combine with other elements. For the most part, however, matter is made up of *compounds*, that is, combinations of two or more elements.

Chemists also discovered that a certain weight of one element would combine with a certain weight of another element to produce a compound whose weight was the sum of the two. For example, 2 grams (g) of the gas hydrogen would combine with 16 g of oxygen to produce 18 g of water, with no hydrogen or oxygen left at the end. This fact provided evidence for the theory of the atom. The oxygen atom of the previous example weighed 16 times as much as a hydrogen atom, and to manufacture water, two hydrogen atoms joined with each oxygen atom. A single unit of the compound water, then, might be expected to have a weight 18 times greater than a hydrogen atom.

B.8 THE MOLECULE

A single unit of any compound is called a *molecule*. Even the earliest chemists were able to take the molecules of some compounds apart to determine which elements the compound was composed of. In most cases, a limited amount of energy, such as the heat from a charcoal fire, was enough to do this. But the methods used by chemists were not sufficient to take atoms apart. In fact, for a long time it was believed that atoms could not be taken apart at all.

B.9 BEGINNINGS OF MODERN ATOMIC THEORY

Further progress in our knowledge about the structure of matter had to wait until the beginning of our century, when the British physicists Thomson (1856–1940) and Rutherford (1871–1937) performed experiments to show that an atom is not as solid and indivisible as had been thought. The results of these experiments showed that atoms were mostly empty space. Figure 1.3 is what Rutherford saw as the model of an atom. Instead of a solid object, the atom was found to be composed of a massive central part, called the *nucleus*, which is surrounded by a cloud of lighter particles spinning around it. These lighter particles were called *electrons*.

Rutherford's theory of the atom was not completely in agreement with all that was known at the time, but his ideas made it possible to explain many observations about the world in the fields of chemistry and physics. In particular, the negatively charged electrons provided the missing part needed for an explanation of electrical effects. In fact, as Rutherford pointed out, the atom is held together by electrical forces, the force of attraction between the positively charged nucleus and the negatively charged electrons. This attraction, he thought, exactly balanced the outward force on the spinning cloud of electrons and kept each atom a stable system.

Thirty-five years ago, before the tremendous rise of solid-state electronics and the introduction of the transistor as a basic component, a textbook could have stopped after explaining Rutherford's model of the atom and identifying the electron. Instead of talking about electricity as though it were like water flowing through pipes, you might have learned about tiny electrons flowing through the spaces between atoms in a wire. But such explanations are too simple to be of much use today. Remember what was said in the first section. The basic topic with which you must deal is energy,

Figure 1.3 The Rutherford model of the atom.

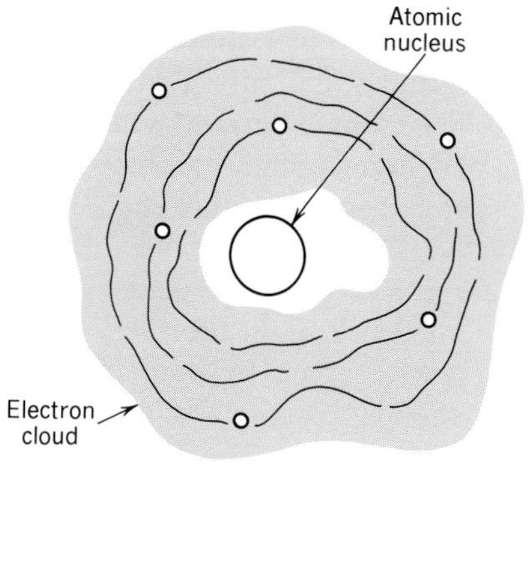

and Rutherford's theory of the atom did not take into account the concept of energy.

The place of energy in atomic theory is the subject of a branch of physics called *quantum mechanics*, which began to be studied at about the time Rutherford performed his experiments. In 1913, the Danish physicist Neils Bohr suggested a number of changes and additions to Rutherford's model of the atom that added the findings of quantum mechanics to atomic theory. Much has been learned since Bohr's ideas were put forth, but his explanation of the structure of matter prepared the way for understanding the effects of electricity used in modern technology.

B.10 BOHR'S MODEL OF THE ATOM

Taken together, Thomson's, Rutherford's, and Bohr's concepts of the atom call for a fairly dense central portion called the nucleus. The nucleus of every atom is composed of one or more positively charged particles called *protons*. In addition to the protons, in all elements except the lightest, there are one or more particles without electric charge called *neutrons*. The nucleus of the hydrogen atom, which is the simplest, has only one proton and no neutrons. On the other hand, the nucleus of uranium, one of the most complex occurring in nature, has 92 protons and 146 neutrons.

Modern scientific experiments have enabled us to weigh and measure such tiny objects as atoms, electrons, and protons. Atoms, for example, are so incredibly small that it would take

602,000,000,000,000,000,000,000,000

atoms of the element hydrogen to weigh 1 kilogram (kg). Each hydrogen atom, then, weighs about

0.000 000 000 000 000 000 000 000 001 67 kg.

Since the weight of a hydrogen atom is almost completely concentrated in its nucleus, which consists of a single proton, this is also the weight of a proton. This is quite a small number, but remember, an electron weighs only $\frac{1}{1850}$ as much. The atom is not only incredibly light, it is also incredibly small, the diameter of an average atom being only about 0.000 000 000 2 or 0.000 000 000 3 meter (m). (If you have forgotten the meaning of decimal notation, refer to the Examples and Computations section of this chapter. In the next chapter, you will learn to write very large and very small numbers in a more convenient form.)

the charge of the protons in the nucleus of an atom would tend to break it apart. In some way, the presence of the neutrons tends to serve as a kind of "glue" and holds the nucleus together. There is a minimum number of neutrons necessary for a given number of protons in an atomic nucleus. If this number of neutrons is not present, the nucleus will be unstable and break apart, releasing a relatively vast amount of energy for such a small object. Only the atomic nucleus of hydrogen, consisting of a single proton, does not need any neutron glue.

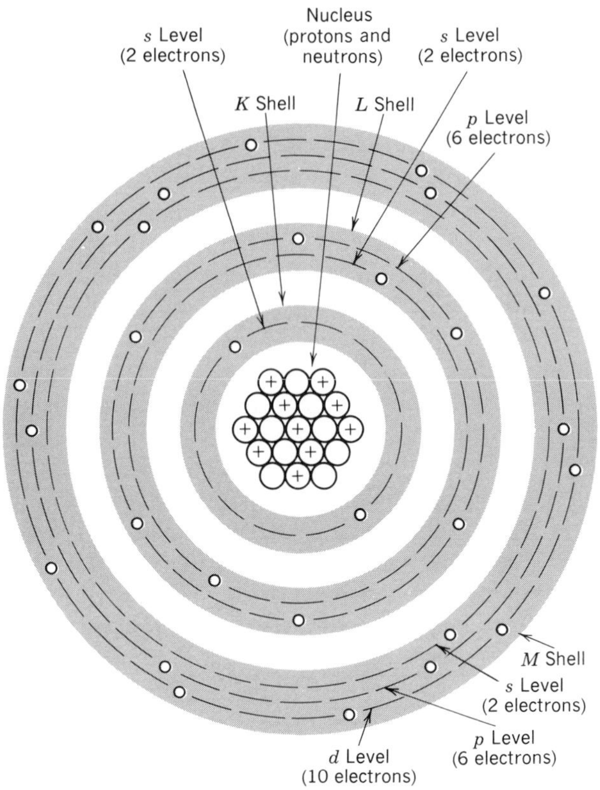

Figure 1.4 The Bohr model of the atom.

The positive charge of the protons in the nucleus of the atom is balanced by the negative charge of the electrons that circle the nucleus, spinning around it in specific paths that form what are called *shells*, or *energy levels*. Just as in the case of the electrically charged piece of amber, the space around the charged particles is changed by the electric field caused by the charge.

The differences between the Bohr and Rutherford–Thomson descriptions of the atom can be seen in part by comparing Figures 1.4 and 1.3. In Figure 1.4 you can see that the electrons move about the nucleus in paths or energy levels that are grouped into shells. Electrons are never found between energy levels or between shells. The energy level represents two things: a particular distance from an atomic nucleus and a particular amount of energy possessed by an electron. The energy levels closest to the nucleus are the lowest, and those further away are occupied by electrons with more energy.

So far, the Bohr model of the atom does not seem too far distant from the world of our experience, but

Table 1.1 Shells, Energy Levels, and the Maximum Number of Electrons in Each Level

Shell	*Energy Level*	*Maximum Number of Electrons*
K	*s*	2
L	*s*	2
	p	6
M	*s*	2
	p	6
	d	10
N	*s*	2
	p	6
	d	10
	f	14
O	*s*	2
	p	6
	d	10
	f	14
	g	18
P	*s*	2
	p	6
	d	10
	f	14
	g	18
	h	22
Q	*s*	2

things are more complex than this. First, each energy level of each shell cannot hold more than a certain number of electrons. As shown in Figure 1.4, the shells, beginning with the one closest to the nucleus, are labeled *K*, *L*, *M*, and so on, while the energy levels in each shell are labeled *s*, *p*, *d*, *f*, and so on, again starting closest to the nucleus.

Table 1.1 shows the shells, the energy levels found in each shell, and the maximum number of electrons that can exist in each level. The simplest atom, that of hydrogen, has a nucleus that contains one proton. Since the number of electrons in an atom tends to equal the number of protons in the nucleus, you would expect to find one electron circling around the single proton in the hydrogen atom in the *s* energy level of the *K* shell. (This is true, as we shall see in Section B.11 of this chapter, only in what is called the *ground state*, that is, when no additional energy has been added to the electron.) The atom of the element helium is somewhat more complex than the hydrogen atom. The nucleus of the helium atom is made up of two protons and two neutrons. Two electrons circle the nucleus in the *s* level of the *K* shell. This means that the *s* energy level is filled (see Figure 1.5).

The next element, lithium, has three protons and three neutrons in its nucleus. Two of its three electrons fill the *s* level of the *K* shell. Since the *K* shell

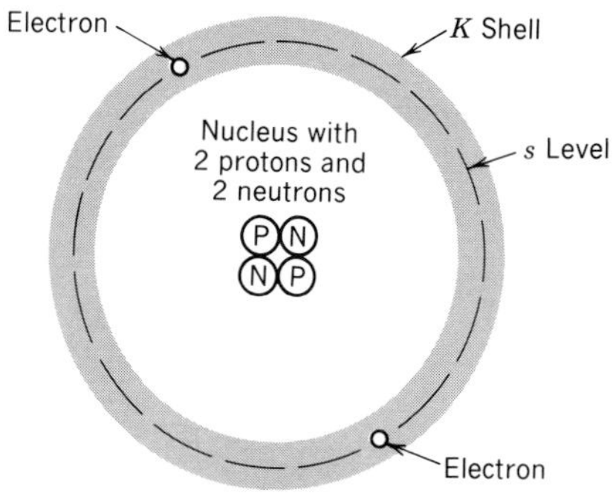

Figure 1.5 Symbolic representation of a helium atom.

has only one energy level, the third lithium electron occupies the *s* level of the second, or *L*, shell. The *L* shell has two energy levels, the *s* level with a capacity of two electrons and the *p* level with a capacity of six (see Figure 1.6). This means that the *L* shell will be filled with eight electrons before the next shell is started.

The element whose number of electrons fills the *L* shell is neon, with 10 electrons in all—2 in the *s* level of the *K* shell, 2 in the *s* level of the *L* shell, and 6 in the *p* level of the *L* shell (Figure 1.7, on p. 6). It is an interesting and important point that the neon atom, which just fills its *L* shell, like the helium atom, which just fills its *K* shell, shows very little chemical activity and clings to its electrons strongly. The filled shell seems to be a preferred, stable state.

Lithium, on the other hand, which has filled its *K* shell and has a single electron in the *L* shell, enters eagerly into chemical activity with other elements. The outer electron, called the *valence electron*, can be given up to another atom that needs a single electron to complete a shell.

For example, lithium forms a compound with hydrogen, called lithium hydride. In this compound, the

Figure 1.6 Representation of a lithium atom.

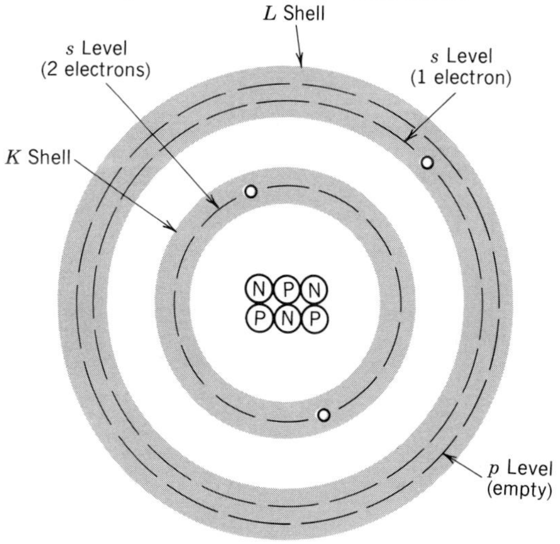

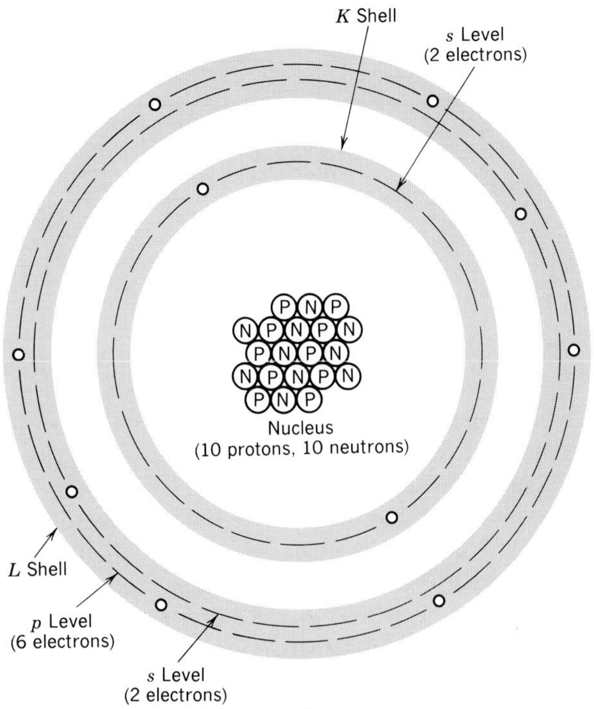

Figure 1.7 Representation of a neon atom.

outer lithium electron is transferred to the *K* shell of the hydrogen atom, making the charge of the lithium atom as a whole +1 and the charge of the hydrogen atom −1.

These charges hold the two atoms together to form a single molecule of the compound lithium hydride. Compounds held together in this fashion are said to have an *electrovalent*, or *ionic*, *bond* (Figure 1.8).

In nature, these substances, such as ordinary table salt, often form crystal structures consisting of intermingled charged atoms, or *ions*, as they are called.

Another sort of bonding can take place when an outermost shell is partially filled. For example, two hydrogen atoms will position themselves so that their valence electron energy levels overlap, as shown in

Figure 1.8 Single molecule of lithium hydride, showing an ionic or electrovalent bond.

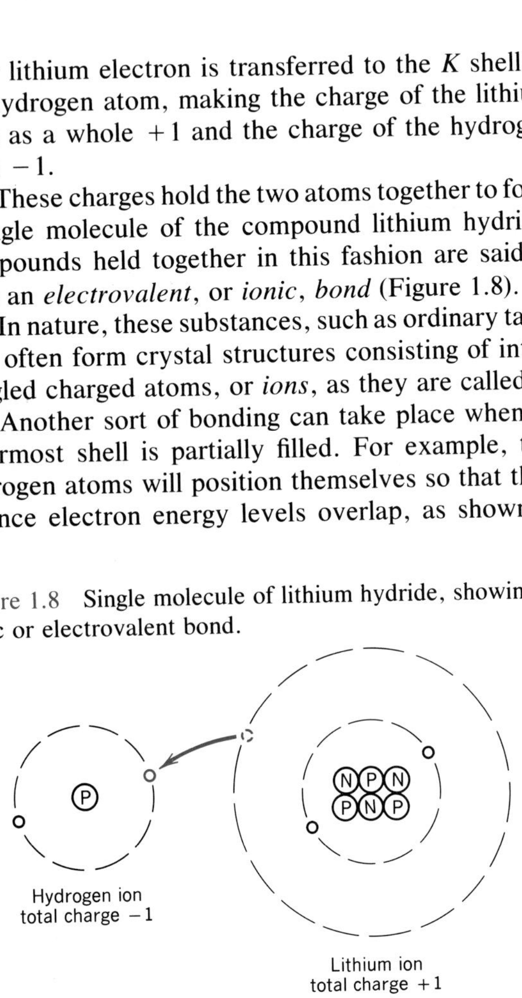

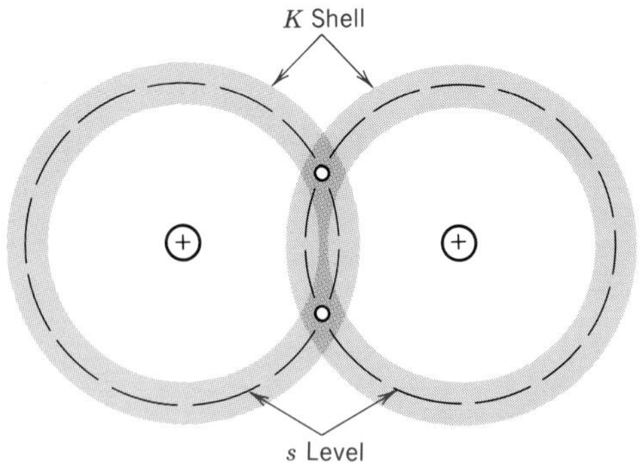

Figure 1.9 Covalent bonding in hydrogen atoms.

Figure 1.9. In this way, both atoms share their valence electrons, and both now have completed the *s* level of the *K* shell. This sharing of electrons between atoms is called *electron pair bonding*, or *covalent bonding*. The molecules of common gases such as oxygen and nitrogen normally contain two atoms held together by covalent bonds. In addition, carbon, silicon, and germanium, elements that are important in electronics, also tend to form complex covalent bonds.

Since covalent bonding brings the outermost shells of the atoms into contact, the bond is usually closer and stronger than an electrovalent bond.

B.11 THE BEHAVIOR OF CHARGE CARRIERS IN ATOMS

So far, two charged particles existing inside the atom have been discussed, the proton and the electron. Although the proton weighs about 1850 times more than an electron, the proton is less interesting for the study of electricity. The movement of electrons accounts for most of the electrical and electronic effects used today. As stated earlier, the electron in an atom always occupies some energy level, which means that it possesses a certain amount of energy. When an electron possesses a minimum amount of energy and is found on the lowest available energy level of a shell, it is said to be in its *ground state*. An electron may absorb energy from a source outside the atom. If it does this, it is no longer in the ground state, and it can no longer exist on its previous energy level. It must exist on a higher energy level, spinning around the nucleus on a path further away. Note that nothing has been said about the electron moving from one energy level to another. On the atomic level, things do not happen in the same way that they do in the familiar world of freeways, motorcycles, and toothpaste ads. The electron simply ceases to exist on one energy level and begins existing on another. Similarly, an electron may give off a specific amount of energy and occupy a lower energy level closer to the atomic nucleus. This, in fact, is the source of all light, as will be discussed in the Applications section of this chapter. In this respect, an electron does not act as a solid particle but rather as a package of energy.

B.12 CONDUCTION ELECTRONS

If an electron absorbs enough energy, it may occupy an energy level so far from its nucleus that the positive charge on the nucleus no longer has much effect on the electron. An electron of this kind is called a "free" electron, or a *conduction electron*. It is a simplification, but still quite true, to say that the study of electronics is a study of the movement of conduction electrons. When an electron escapes from the immediate vicinity of the atom, the atom itself becomes positively charged, but it will capture another electron in time, at which point the process will begin again.

B.13 BEHAVIOR OF CHARGE CARRIERS IN SUBSTANCES

Although based in part on what goes on inside an atom, electricity and electronics deal more directly with the effects found in collections of atoms, particularly with the movement of conduction electrons through metals. Ions, atoms that have gained or lost a number of electrons and are therefore no longer uncharged, do provide the electrical effects connected with the production of electrical energy in cells and batteries, but they are not of primary concern in our field of study. In general, the movement of ions takes place only in substances that are in the form of a liquid or a gas.

B.14 INSULATORS, CONDUCTORS, AND SEMICONDUCTORS

The electrical characteristics of the materials used in electronic components depend on the energy levels of the valence electrons in the atoms that make up the materials. In certain materials, the energy levels of the valence electrons are so low that these electrons are tightly held by the positive charges of atomic nucleii. Materials of this sort have few free electrons at conduction energy levels. If an electron should happen to absorb enough energy to exist at a conduction energy level, it gives up this energy very quickly and is recaptured by an atom. These materials are called *insulators* and are valuable in technology precisely because they do not permit an easy passage of charge carriers.

In some materials, particularly silver, copper, gold, and aluminum, the atoms of the material form tightly packed structures in which the valence electron energy levels of adjacent atoms actually overlap. In materials of this sort, it is possible to consider the valence electrons of the atoms as belonging to the entire mass of the material rather than to individual atoms. The conduction electrons may be thought of as a cloud or fog drifting between the atoms of the material. But this does not mean that the conduction electrons can possess any amount of energy. As in the case of electrons orbiting the nucleus of an atom, the laws of quantum mechanics limit the energy possessed by conduction electrons to specific energy levels. The energy a conduction electron may possess depends on a number of things, including the way in which the atoms of the material are arranged. In contrast to insulators, in which the individual atoms or molecules of material possess valence electrons that are well below conduction energy levels, metals like silver, copper, gold, and aluminum possess conduction electrons at certain specified energy levels. These materials are called *conductors*. A third class of materials has become very important in the field of electronics. This group of materials presents a condition in which the energy level of the valence electrons is close to a permissible conduction energy level. These materials are called *semiconductors*. In its natural state, there are few conduction electrons present in a lump of semiconductor material, but it is relatively easy for valence electrons to absorb enough additional energy to become conduction electrons. Electronic components using this characteristic of semiconductor materials presently provide most of the devices used to control electrical energy.

C. EXAMPLES AND COMPUTATIONS

C.1 THE CALCULATOR

Working with numbers is an important part of both the study and practice of electronic technology. Electrical and electronic principles are easier to understand and use if they are stated in mathematical form, and effective troubleshooting requires the ability to perform mathematical calculations quickly and accurately. Years ago, engineers used devices called *slide rules* to help make calculations, but these were neither accurate nor easy to use. The students, engineers, and technicians of today have a much better aid to calculation—the electronic calculator.

Electronic calculators come in a confusing variety of styles ranging from the simple four-function type to the portable computer. Since your calculator will be used throughout your studies, it must be purchased with an eye toward the needs of more advanced courses. There are two main types of calculators, programmable and nonprogrammable. Programmable calculators may be set up to do certain series of calculations and may be quite useful. On the other hand, programmable calculators are less powerful than small computers. This book will provide exercises and explanations using nonprogrammable calculators. Where increased calculating power is necessary, methods of using a small computer will be shown.

On the other end of the scale from the programmable calculators are the simple, four-function calculators that can be purchased for less than $10, often considerably less. These devices can add, subtract, multiply, and divide—the four arithmetic functions. Some models will do percentages as well. Although calculators of this type are fine for balancing a checkbook or totalling up grocery purchases, the four-function calculator is not sufficient for technical work. Table 1.2 lists some of the functions and shows the function keys that are used in technical work. You may not recognize some of these functions at the moment, but you will be using these and perhaps a few others before your course of study is completed.

Another important feature to look for in your calculator is the presence of memory keys. These keys allow you to store some numbers in the calculator for later work. A technical calculator should allow you to store at least one number for future use, although the ability to store three or four is even better. You should look for keys that enable you to store a number in the memory, recall it from the memory, and add or subtract a number to or from the stored number.

Most calculators on the market today use what is called *algebraic notation*. This is a fancy way of saying that they work in the order that most people write operations. That is, if you want to add 3 and 4, you push the key for 3, then the key for +, then the key for 4, and finally, the key labeled =. At this point, the number 7 appears on the calculator. A few calculators, however, use a system called "Reverse Polish Notation." In this system, to add 3 and 4, you would first push the key 4, then the ENTER key, then the 3 key, and finally the + key. At this point the sum 7 would appear on the calculator. It is said that the Reverse Polish system is able to do calculations with fewer key pushings, but it is not as popular as the algebraic system. Therefore, this book will provide examples only in the algebraic system.

In addition to these important points, there are a number of physical features that you should think about before choosing your calculator, since they are critical

Table 1.2 Calculator Functions Used in Electricity and Electronics

Function Name	*Typical Key Markings*	*Use*
Essential Functions		
Addition,	+	
Subtraction,	−	
Multiplication,	×	The four standard functions, equals sign and decimal point
Division	÷	
Decimal point	.	
Equation	=	
Change Sign	+/− or CHS	Allows the sign of a number to be changed
Parentheses	[,] , (,)	Allows complex calculations.
Exponential Functions	EEX or EE	Permits calculations in scientific notation.
Trignometric and Inverse Functions	SIN, COS, TAN, ARC	Needed for work with ac circuits.
Powers and Roots	y^x	Permits calculation of the power or root of a number.
Pi	π	Very useful key for computing ac quantities.
Logarithmic Functions	LOG, 10^x	Useful for decibel ratios.
Natural Logarithmic Functions	ln, e^x	Essential for work with capacitance and inductance.
Useful Functions		
Inverse	1/x	Found on most technical calculators, speeds calculations
Square and Square Root	x^2, $\sqrt{\ }$	Speeds calculations, y^x may be used if these are not present.
Rectangular to Polar, Polar to Rectangular	R → P P → R	Useful for engineering computations in ac theory.

for the comfortable operation of the device. First, is the calculator of a handy size? Some are too big to fit conveniently in a pocket, toolbox, or book bag, while others are so small that they tend to slide off a desk. Another consideration is the number of functions controlled by each key. In order to make the devices smaller, most manufacturers require each key to perform at least two functions. On the other hand, if too many functions are performed by each key, operation gets confusing. The ideal is two functions for each key; four or more is just too much. Finally, how do the keys feel when they are pressed? If they feel mushy and there is no solid tactile click to the keyboard when it is new, you may be sure that it will get worse as time passes. There is nothing more annoying than trying to work a complicated calculation on a calculator and not being sure that the last key you pressed actually entered a number into the machine.

Saving time and effort in calculations depends on your ability to use the calculator in an efficient manner. Forgetting how to do a particular kind of operation or making mistakes in entering numbers can render the calculator more of a handicap than a help. It is important to study the instruction manual that came with your calculator thoroughly and to practice entering numbers until you can be sure that you will not make careless errors.

Some of the worked examples in this book will be based on the use of a calculator. In order to follow these examples, you will have to understand the keystroke notation used. When directions are given, the words on the left side of the column will describe what you are doing, while the numbers, symbols, or words in squares represent the keys that must be pressed in order from left to right. For example, these might be the steps in solving a problem:

Enter length of wire in meters.	[3] [6]
Select multiplication.	[×]
Enter weight of 1 m (meter) of wire in kilograms.	[.] [0] [0] [6]
Display result.	[=]

Often, all the keystrokes for a single calculation will be listed in a single step:

Calculate total weight of wire by multiplying weight of 1 m by length of wire.	[3] [6] [×] [.] [0] [0] [6] [=]

Once you have become familiar with this notation, you will find it helps you to follow the steps in problem solving.

C.2 DECIMALS

Since the study of electricity involves incredibly tiny objects such as electrons, you need to be able to use very small numbers easily. The Romans were excellent civil engineers, but they did not have a number system that allowed them to calculate with small parts of a unit. Fortunately, the number system we use, called the *Arabic system*, is well fitted to express small numbers in a convenient way. Each part of a number, called a *digit*, has two values. In the number 387, the digit 8 has an *intrinsic value*, that is, the value of the number by itself, 8 in this case. It also has a *place value*, which is determined by the position of the digit in the number. The place value of the 8 in 387 is 80, or 8 times 10, because the 8 appears in the tens place in the number 387. Figure 1.10 shows some of the place values for digits used in large numbers.

The number 387 is composed of three different place value digits:

3 in the hundreds place	300
8 in the tens place	80
7 in the units place	7
or, adding them up,	387

Now, although this elegant system was used to express numbers greater than 1 for a long time, fractions are still being used to express numbers that are less than 1, that is, parts of a unit. In common speech, we talk about half a cup or three-quarters of an hour. This does not cause too much trouble as long as the parts you are talking about are fairly large. But can

Figure 1.10 Place values for digits used in large numbers.

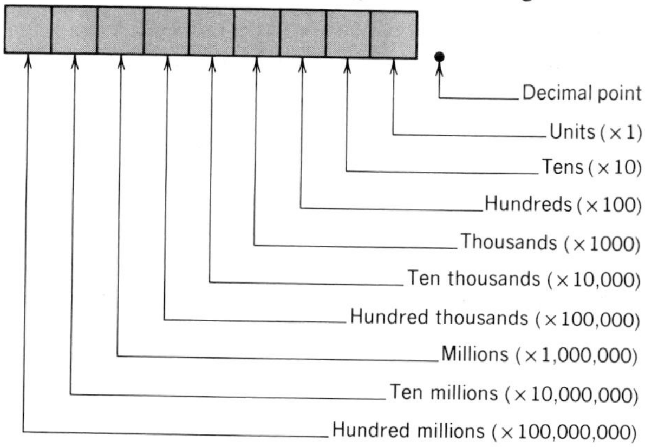

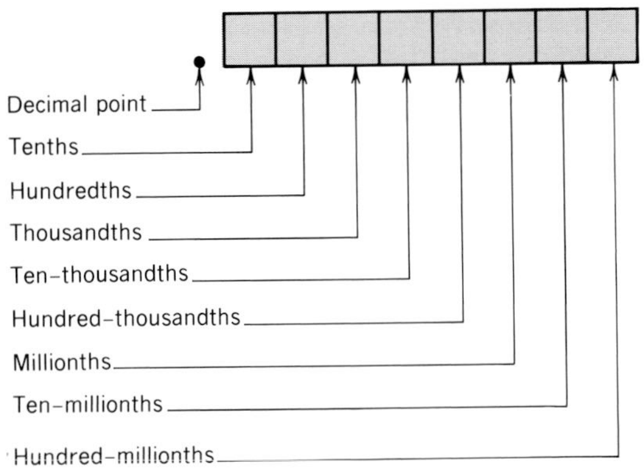

Figure 1.11 Place values for decimal places.

you imagine the problem of dealing with portions like one five hundred and seventy-third of a meter? In order to deal with parts of a unit that are this small, people working in the sciences use special forms of fractions called *decimals*. Decimals are easier to write and much easier to use with a calculator. Decimals use the positional character of the Arabic number system to provide place values that are less than 1. This is done by placing a period immediately to the right of the units digit and reading everything to the right of this point as a tenth, hundredth, thousandth, and so on, part of a unit. The period is called the *decimal point*, and numbers to the right of the decimal point are called *decimal places*. Figure 1.11 shows the values of some decimal places. For example, the number 387.6 means

3 in the hundreds place	300
8 in the tens place	80
7 in the units place	7
and 6 in the tenths place	0.6
or	387.6

Everyone is familiar with decimal notation in reference to money. For example, the price $3.05 means three dollars and five-hundredths of a dollar, but since a hundredth of a dollar is a cent, you get accustomed to saying three dollars and five cents and tend to forget what that decimal point actually means.

In the field of electronics, it is necessary to be able to think in terms of and to read decimal values automatically. A number of examples are given below. Note that when the entire number is less than 1, an additional zero has been added to the left of the decimal point. This is done in most technical material to emphasize the decimal point and assure that the number is read properly.

8.6	eight and six-tenths
0.05	five-hundredths
0.73	seventy-three hundredths

C.3 ARITHMETIC WITH DECIMALS

One of the best reasons to use decimals instead of fractions in your calculations is the ease with which arithmetic operations may be accomplished, particularly with a calculator. Decimal numbers may be added in the same way as whole numbers, provided you are careful about the decimal point. For example, add the following weights of electronic units to see if a shelf that is supposed to support 29 kg can support the entire system.

Unit 1 weighs 15.6 kg.

Unit 2 weighs 3.25 kg.

Unit 3 weighs 0.75 kg.

Unit 4 weighs 10 kg.

If you were doing this on paper, you ought to write the weights down in column form, being careful to keep the place values lined up to avoid confusion. It would look like this:

Unit 1	15.6
Unit 2	3.25
Unit 3	0.75
Unit 4	10
Total	29.60

In fact, just as an extra zero is added in 0.75 to help, extra zeros can be added to the right of the last decimal digit as place keepers to keep the decimal points lined up and the columns straight. If this is done, the column addition will look like this:

Unit 1	15.60
Unit 2	3.25
Unit 3	0.75
Unit 4	10.00
Total	29.60

Your calculator will be able to keep the columns straight without the addition of any extra zeros, and the problem may be entered directly like this:

Weight of unit 1	[1] [5] [.] [6]
Add	[+]
Weight of unit 2	[3] [.] [2] [5]
Add	[+]
Weight of unit 3	[.] [7] [5]
Add	[+]
Weight of unit 4	[1] [0]
Sum	[=]

At this point, you should be able to read the answer 29.6 in the display.

Try adding the following decimals both on paper and with your calculator, reading the numbers aloud as you write or enter them. Even if you are familiar with decimals, this additional practice will help you in later chapters.

a. 0.096 + .003 + 36.9 + 18.05
b. 1037.98 + 68.3 + 560
c. 19.03 + 8.005 + 2.24 + 3.166 + 15.333
d. 0.004 + 1.125 + .02 + .0617
e. 4.425 + 3.82 + 2.09 + .107
f. 9372.6 + 875.32 + 9.1804
g. .1 + .05 + .005 + 0.03
h. 0.00637 + .0425 + 0.9034

The subtraction of decimals is very nearly identical to the subtraction of whole numbers, but again it is important to keep the decimal points lined up and the columns straight when working with pencil and paper. When working with a calculator, the device itself will keep them straight for you. For example, subtract 3.97 from 4.058:

Enter minuend (the number from which you are going to subtract).	[4] [.] [0] [5] [8]
Select subtraction.	[−]
Enter subtrahend (the number to be subtracted from the minuend).	[3] [.] [9] [7]
Display the answer.	[=]

After the equals key is pressed, the answer, 0.088, will be displayed.

In order to see how much time your calculator can save in the calculation of problems, try the following subtractions with paper and pencil, noting the time it takes to finish all the problems. Then do the same calculations with your calculator, again noting the time needed to complete. Compare the two times.

a. 12.25 − 9.057
b. 1.333 − 0.1667
c. .053 − 0.038
d. 137.96 − 108.179
e. 15.05 − 12.978
f. Subtract .000675 from 0.01385.
g. Subtract 909.93 from 1001.8.
h. 12.35 − 7.75

Decimals are multiplied in the same way as whole numbers, except that it is necessary to determine where to place the decimal point in the answer if you are working on paper. As in the case of addition, the calculator will do this for you, but the calculator's results can be misleading in some cases, even though the answer will always be correct. The number of decimal places in the answer to a decimal multiplication on paper will always be equal to the sum of the number of decimal places of the two numbers being multiplied. For example, multiply the two numbers 3.25 and 2.6. This is done on paper by writing the numbers in column form:

$$\begin{array}{r} 3.25 \\ \times 2.6 \\ \hline 1950 \\ 650 \\ \hline 8450 \end{array}$$

Since there are two decimal places in the multiplicand and one in the multiplier, the answer should have three decimal places in it. It should read 8.450.

With the calculator, this example becomes a simple exercise in entering numbers:

Enter the multiplicand.	[3] [.] [2] [5]
Select the operation.	[×]
Enter the multiplier.	[6] [.] [2]
Calculate answer.	[=]

At this point, the answer, 8.45, should appear on the display. Note that the final zero has been dropped. This is done automatically, because $\frac{450}{1000}$ is the same as $\frac{45}{100}$. Try the following multiplications for practice, both with paper and pencil and on the calculator.

a. 42.3 × 6.8
b. 4.57 × 0.20
c. 1.2 × 0.0065
d. 27 × .0062
e. 9.01 × 1.09
f. 30.01 × 10.65
g. 0.0038 × .00125
h. 83.69 × 100

Like multiplication, the division of decimals requires one step more than the division of whole numbers, since it is necessary to place the decimal point. On paper, this is done by moving the decimal point in the divisor (the number you are dividing by) to the right until it is to the right of the number. The decimal point in the dividend (the number being divided) is then moved the same number of places to the right, and division is performed in a normal manner, with the decimal point in the quotient (the answer) being placed directly above the decimal point in the dividend. What this actually does is to multiply the divisor by a whole number large enough to make the divisor a whole number. When the dividend is multiplied by this same number, the actual quotient is *not* changed. For example, to divide 6.2 by 3.25, the division is written in the standard manner

$$3.25\overline{)6.2}$$

To make the divisor 3.25 a whole number, it is necessary to move the decimal point two places to the right. Doing this to the dividend 6.2 is a bit of a problem, since there are not enough decimal places in the dividend. This is easily solved, however, by adding a zero, as shown below. Once this is done, the division can proceed normally.

```
       1   R 295
  325)620
      325
      ---
      295
```

Since this division does not come out evenly, that is, there is a remainder, you might want to add several more zeros, so that the decimal part of the quotient can be calculated.

```
        1.907
  325)620.000
      325
      ---
      295 0
      292 5
      -----
        2 500
        2 275
        -----
          225
```

It is possible to keep on adding zeros, but there is a limit to how many decimal places are actually needed in any application. This subject will be discussed in the next section.

With the calculator, the job is considerably easier.

Enter the dividend.	[6] [.] [2]
Select the operation.	[÷]
Enter the divisor.	[3] [.] [2] [5]
Display the answer.	[=]

At this point, the answer 1.9076923 is displayed.

Division is generally the most time-consuming of the arithmetic processes if done with pencil and paper. Try doing the following eight examples, first with pencil and paper and then with your calculator. Keep track of the time it took with each method.

a. 12946.378 ÷ 396.52
b. 55.778 ÷ 6.68
c. 3.7125 ÷ 2.25
d. 8.851 ÷ 3.34
e. 0.001575 ÷ 0.0063
f. 9.5625 ÷ 2.55
g. 12.49625 ÷ 9.997
h. 0.146 ÷ 36.5

C.4 CHANGING COMMON FRACTIONS TO DECIMALS

Because our number system can express decimals in an easier to use form than the fraction notation, it is sometimes necessary to change a fraction to a decimal. This is easily done by using your calculator to perform the division indicated by the fraction, that is, dividing the numerator of the fraction by the denominator. For example, $\frac{3}{4}$ is the same as the decimal 0.75. Enter this on your calculator:

Enter numerator.	[3]
Select division.	[÷]
Enter denominator.	[4]
Display answer.	[=]

The decimal form of $\frac{3}{4}$, 0.75, will then be displayed.

Use your calculator to obtain the decimal equivalents for the following common fractions:

a. $\frac{1}{4}$	b. $\frac{1}{2}$	c. $\frac{3}{8}$
d. $\frac{5}{16}$	e. $\frac{3}{32}$	f. $\frac{5}{64}$
g. $\frac{1}{8}$	h. $\frac{1}{16}$	i. $\frac{17}{32}$
j. $\frac{9}{16}$	k. $\frac{1}{3}$	l. $\frac{11}{32}$

Note that some of these common fractions can be converted to fairly short decimals. For some, however, like $\frac{1}{3}$, the display fills up with digits. This is because a fraction is always an exact number, while a decimal may not be. In the case of $\frac{1}{3}$, for example, the decimal equivalent is 0.333333 . . ., for as long as you care to go on writing more digits. A number like this, which can be written as an exact number as a common fraction but can be carried out to an infinite number of decimal places is called an *infinite decimal*. In most cases, you do not have to carry decimal calculations out to as many decimal places as your calculator will display. In fact, in many practical applications, using too many decimal places is really a form of error, since it implies a level of accuracy that might not really exist. An example of this would be calculating the circumference of a circle. This is done by multiplying the diameter of the circle by π (pi). On your calculator, π is probably displayed as 3.1415927, but it is unlikely that you can measure the diameter of a fair sized circle to better than two decimal places without using very special measuring devices. If the diameter of the circle is 3.12 m, then π times the diameter would be displayed as 9.8017692 m. But this is really not true, since you do not know the actual diameter of the circle to a ten-*millionth* of a meter. A more meaningful answer would be obtained by *rounding off*, that is, eliminating the extra decimal places. When this is done, the circumference is accurately represented as 9.80 m, accurate to the same two decimal places, or hundredths of a meter, to which the diameter was measured. The actual rules for rounding off will be given in Chapter 3, since these are frequently used in converting from the familiar system of customary units, such as inch, foot, and so on, to the metric system used in technology.

C.5 THE SMALL COMPUTER AND THE STUDY OF ELECTRONICS

In addition to the calculator, you might also learn to use a small computer to solve some of the more complex problems you will come across in electronics. The price of small computers is dropping quickly, and the ability to use them in technical applications is an important skill. Most small computers use an operating language called BASIC, which stands for Beginners All-purpose Symbolic Instruction Code.

The computers themselves vary greatly in size and features, but they are similar in that most use the form of BASIC distributed by Microsoft, Inc. or an equivalent. The examples in this book will be modeled on this form of BASIC. There will be no attempt to teach either computer programming or computer operation. If you own or have access to a small computer, you will have to study its instruction manual. On the other hand, the examples and programs given will be fully explained, so that if you can get a computer running, you should be able to use them.

At this point, it is a good idea to read the instructions on how to start up a typical computer and how to enter the BASIC language. Since every computer has slightly different start-up procedures, you will have to learn the procedure for the computer you are using.

Did you know that a computer with BASIC can be used as a calculator? It can, if you learn a few very simple differences. BASIC uses the same plus (+) and minus (−) signs as your calculator, but the symbol for multiplication in BASIC is the asterisk, or star (*), and the symbol for division is the slash (/). For example, 8*4 means 8×4, and 9/5 means $9 \div 5$.

When your computer is operating in BASIC, you will see some sort of character on your screen. This character is called a *prompt*, and it signals that the computer is ready to receive commands or information from its keyboard. The prompt may be OK or ⟩ or something of that sort. Once you have gotten the prompt on the screen, type in PRINT 4+18 and then push the RETURN or ENTER key. In a fraction of a second, the answer 22 appears, and then the computer-ready prompt is repeated. This mode of operation in BASIC is called the *immediate* or *command mode*, and it is different from the mode of operation in which a program is entered. In the immediate mode, a calculation is performed every time the RETURN or ENTER key is pressed. This means that a series of numbers may be added in the immediate mode of BASIC in the same way that this is done on a calculator. For example, type in the following:

```
PRINT 183 + 96 + 217 + 418
```

As soon as the RETURN key is pressed, the answer, 914, appears on the screen. By the way, this is why the command PRINT has to be entered. If you omit this command, the answer will not be printed on the screen. When the answer to a calculation is printed on the screen in the immediate mode, there is no record of the calculation or the steps required to get there in the computer. Nothing has been stored in the computer memory.

Try performing the simple exercises in this section using a computer. Remember to use the * for multiplication, the / for division, and the RETURN or ENTER key in place of the = used to display an answer on the calculator.

D. APPLICATIONS

You do not have to look far to find examples of the absorption and reradiation of energy by electrons. In fact, all visible light, whether natural or artificial, is produced when electrons absorb energy from some source and then return it as light. In the sun and other stars, matter is changed directly to energy, and this energy is absorbed by electrons in the photosphere, the glowing region of the sun. This also explains why

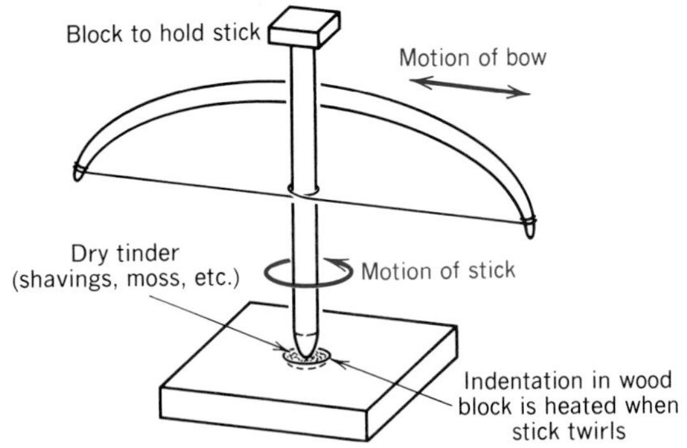

Figure 1.12 A fire bow.

materials glow when they get hot, that is, when the atoms and electrons absorb heat energy.

The earliest form of artificial light, fire, was sometimes started in just this way. The fire bow pictured in Figure 1.12 was an early machine for adding enough heat energy to a piece of wood to make it start burning. The heat energy released by the burning wood was then radiated as both heat and visible light.

The incandescent light bulb, another source of artificial light, uses much the same principle of operation as a fire, except that the source of energy is electricity rather than burning wood. A fine wire called the *filament* is heated by the electrical energy, and it is this portion of the lamp that produces the light. Unlike the wood, the filament does not burn. It does, however, boil away at a slow rate.

When electrical energy is directly absorbed by electrons, without the intermediate step of producing heat, white light is rarely produced. More usually, it is red, green, yellow, or blue, as in the glowing tubes of "neon" signs. The color depends on the difference between the energy level of the electrons that have absorbed the energy and the energy level the electrons occupy after giving up this energy. Figure 1.13 shows a gas discharge tube. It is a glass tube from which air is pumped out and then a small amount of a single gas is added. When this tube is connected to a source of electrical energy, some electrons of the atoms of the gas pick up enough energy to temporarily move to a conduction band. An individual electron tends to give up this energy and emit a small amount of light. Since the source of electrical energy is constantly supplying more energy, this process continues, converting electrical energy to light.

Figure 1.13 A gas discharge tube.

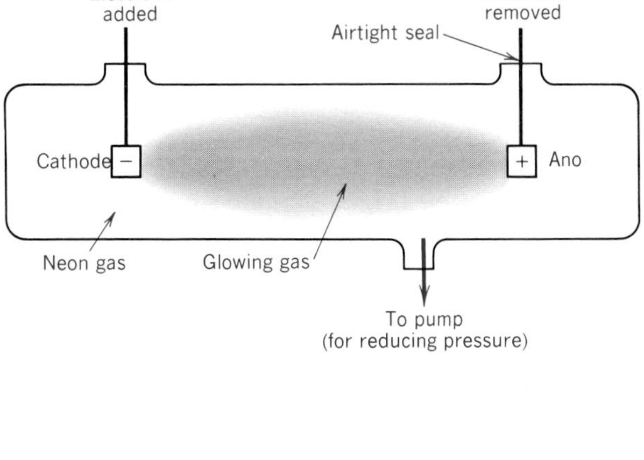

This is the same process that takes place in the fluorescent lamp. In fact, the real operating portion of a fluorescent lamp looks like a gas discharge tube. The gas in the tube is mercury vapor. In order to produce a light that resembles daylight to the human eye, the inside of the tube is coated with a material called a *phosphor*. The phosphor coating absorbs the mercury vapor light and, using the same principle, radiates a cool blue white or warm reddish white light, depending on the phosphor used.

Modern technology has given us two new sources of artificial light, the LED, or light-emitting diode, and the laser. The LED is an electronic component designed to produce little heat in operation and therefore may last much longer than a light bulb. Because of their long life expectancy and low cost, LEDs are widely used in the electronics industry. Figure 1.14 shows some LEDs.

The laser is another example of the technological application of energy levels. Those who have seen lasers in operation find it hard to describe the intense beams of light emitted. In a simple form, the principle of laser operation is to pump energy in some form into a material or a gas until a large number of the electrons in the material are in a high energy state. Then, a great many of the high-energy-state electrons drop into low-

Figure 1.14 Typical light-emitting diodes (LEDs). (Photo by M. Hermes.)

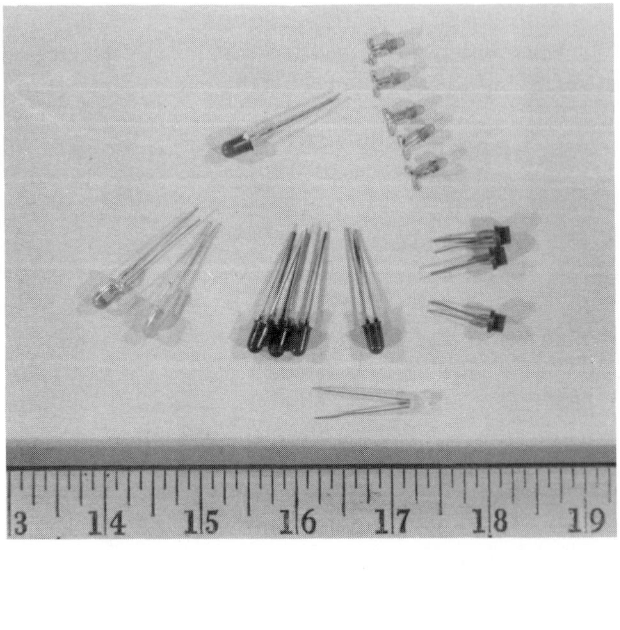

energy orbits at once. This releases a burst of high energy in the form of a beam, due to the shape of the "lasing" material and the way in which a triggering impulse is distributed through it.

E. PROGRAMMED REVIEW

INSTRUCTIONS FOR USING PROGRAMMED REVIEW MATERIALS

Each chapter in this book contains a programmed review section made up of a number of frames. The purpose of this material is to summarize certain key information contained in the chapter, to help you remember this information, and to point out facts that you may have missed. Each frame contains a question designed to test your understanding. Below the question are several possible answers. When you are reading the statement and trying to answer the questions, cover these answers with a piece of paper or a card. Jot your answer to the question down on a separate piece of paper. (Writing the answer is frequently an important aid in remembering information.) Uncover the answers and check your answer to the question against those given in the frame. If your answer is correct, you will be directed to another frame whose number is given in parentheses after the answer you have chosen. Sometimes, you will be directed to review a part of the chapter. Unless otherwise instructed, read through the sections listed and return to the same review frame.

FRAME 1

In contrast to the simple calculators used to add up grocery slips or balance check books, scientific or technical calculators provide a number of functions. Two kinds of scientific or technical calculators are:

a. Programmable and nonprogrammable. (2)
b. Any other answer, review Section C.1.

FRAME 2

BASIC is a programming language used by computers. It stands for Beginners All-purpose Symbolic Instruction Code. Although almost as small as a calculator, a device that uses BASIC is considered to be:

a. A computer. (3)
b. Any other answer, review Section C.5 and go on to Frame 3.

FRAME 3

The scientific definition of *work* states that work is done when a force moves an object some distance in the direction of the force. Which of the following activities would *not* be work in the scientific sense:

Rolling a rock up a mountainside.

Holding a rock that would otherwise roll down a mountainside.

Rolling a rock along level ground.

Pushing a rock off a cliff.

a. Holding a rock that would otherwise roll down a mountain. (5)
b. Any other answer, (4).

FRAME 4

Your answer was not correct; the correct answer was "holding a rock." Remember that in order for work to be done in the scientific sense, the force must result in a movement of an object. For example, if you tried to push a truck that was stuck in the mud, your effort could not be considered work, in the scientific sense, unless you were actually able to move the truck. Go on to Frame 5.

FRAME 5

The American scientist and inventor Benjamin Franklin did much early theoretical and practical work in the field of electricity. One of his most important contributions is listed below. Which one is it?

The invention of the battery.

The idea of positive and negative charges.

The discovery of lightning.

A useful description of the atom.

a. The idea of positive and negative charges. (7)
b. The discovery of lightning. (6)
c. Any other answer, review Section B.4.

FRAME 6

Franklin's experiment of flying a kite during a thunderstorm was useful and important, although he could hardly be credited with the discovery of lightning. What this experiment did was to help show that lightning is one of the effects of electricity. With this understanding, Franklin developed ways of protecting buildings from damage during thunderstorms. Go on to Frame 7.

FRAME 7

Franklin's conception of electricity as a kind of fluid led to a comparison between the "flow" of electricity and the flow of ___________. This comparison is called the *hydraulic analogy* and is widely found in many textbooks. Although it can be helpful to beginning students, it must be kept in mind that this analogy does not represent physical reality. What word belongs in the space in the above paragraph.

a. A liquid, or water. (8)
b. Any other answer, review Section B.5.

FRAME 8

Since Franklin thought of electricity as a kind of fluid, he used the term ___________ to describe the passage of electric charge from one point to another.

a. Electric current. (10)
b. Flow. (9)
c. Any other answer, review Section B.5.

FRAME 9

Franklin used the words *electric current* to describe the passage of electricity from one charged, or "electrified," body to another. Today the words *flow* or *electron flow* are also widely found, as is the phrase *current flow*. Current flow is really two words that say the same thing, but this phrase has become so popular that this has generally been forgotten. Go on to Frame 10.

FRAME 10

In the late nineteenth and early twentieth centuries, three basic atomic particles were discovered and studied. These are the ___________, ___________, and the ___________.

a. Electron, proton, and neutron (order is not important). (12)
b. Any other answer, (11).

FRAME 11

The correct answer is the electron, proton, and neutron. Review Sections B.9 and B.10 and answer the following question. Question: State the charge of the electron, proton, and neutron.

a. The electron is negatively charged, the proton is positively charged, and the neutron has no charge. (12).
b. Any other answer, reread Sections B.7 through B.10.

FRAME 12

Most materials have been found to be made up of combinations of certain basic substances. Some 90 of these basic substances were discovered in nature, while several others not found in nature have been manufactured in laboratories. What are these substances called?

a. Elements. (14)
b. Any other answer, (13).

FRAME 13

The correct answer is elements. The atoms of each element are different from the atoms of any other element. Elements combine to form compounds. Go on to Frame 14.

FRAME 14

Every element is different from every other element in the structure of its ___________.

a. Substances, review Section B.7 and try Frame 14 again.
b. Compounds. (15)
c. Atoms. (16)
d. Any other answer, review Sections B.7 to B.10.

FRAME 15

Compounds is not the correct answer. Although compounds do have particular chemical properties, by definition, compounds are made up of at least two different elements. Go back to Frame 14.

FRAME 16

An electron, whether attached to a particular atom or existing independently in a piece of material, has a particular energy. This is why we can refer to both the orbits of an electron around the atomic nucleus and the amount of energy possessed by an electron as an __________ __________.

a. Energy level. (17)
b. Any other answer, review Section B.10.

FRAME 17

The ability of atoms to bond together to form molecules depends on the giving up, adding, or sharing of outer energy level electrons. An element that readily gives up, adds, or shares outer energy level electrons is considered chemically active. These outer energy level electrons are called __________ electrons.

a. Valence electrons. (18)
b. Any other answer, review Section B.10.

FRAME 18

It is a natural tendency for the number of electrons in the energy levels surrounding an atomic nucleus to equal the number of protons in the nucleus. When, for any reason, the number of electrons is greater or smaller than the number of protons, the atom is referred to as an __________.

a. Ion. (19)
b. Any other answer, review Sections B.10 and B.11.

FRAME 19

When one atom gives up a valence or outer orbit electron to another atom, both atoms become ions. The atom that gained the electron now has an electrical charge of -1, while the atom that gave up the electron now has an electrical charge of $+1$. What will be the result of the electrical charge on the two atoms?

a. The atoms will attract each other. (20)
b. Any other answer, review the effects of electric charge, Section B.4, and then go on to Frame 20.

FRAME 20

When oppositely charged ionized atoms are held together, they form a molecule. What is the technical term for the bond between the atoms?

a. Ionic bond or electrovalent bond. (21)
b. Any other answer, review Section B.10.

FRAME 21

When two or more atoms share electrons so that the outer, or valence energy band of each atom is filled, the bond between the atoms is referred to as a _____ bond.

a. Covalent (22)
b. Any other answer, review Section B.10.

FRAME 22

When an electron possesses the minimum amount of energy necessary to exist in the lowest available or unfilled energy level around an atom, it is said to be in a ground state. However, an electron may absorb energy and assume a higher energy level. If an electron absorbs enough energy, it will exist on an energy level so far from its nucleus that the atom then becomes a positive ion. What is the technical term for an electron that occupies an energy level that is not close to an atomic nucleus?

a. Conduction electron. (24)
b. Free electron. (23)
c. Any other answer, review Section B.12 and go on to Frame 23.

FRAME 23

The technical term for an electron occupying an energy level high enough for it to be considered as belonging to the entire piece of material rather than to a specific atom is conduction electron or conduction band electron. Often, the potentially confusing term "free electron" is used. Although this is not actually wrong, it also implies that the electron is completely free to occupy any point within the material and to have any energy whatsoever. This is not true. There are specific conduction energy levels for a material just as there are specific allowed energy levels around the nucleus of an atom. Go on to Frame 24.

FRAME 24

One of the most important applications of the notion of electron energy levels is its ability to explain the difference between materials that are good conductors of electricity and materials that do not conduct electricity, which are called ____________.

a. Insulators. (end)
b. Any other answer, review Section B.14.

E. PROBLEMS FOR SOLUTION OR RESEARCH

1. Using a calculator, fill in the following table of fraction–decimal equivalents.

FRACTION	*DECIMAL*	*FRACTION*	*DECIMAL*
$\frac{1}{32}$		$\frac{5}{16}$	
$\frac{1}{16}$		$\frac{1}{3}$	
$\frac{3}{32}$		$\frac{1}{2}$	
$\frac{1}{8}$		$\frac{9}{16}$	
$\frac{5}{32}$		$\frac{5}{8}$	
$\frac{3}{16}$		$\frac{3}{4}$	
$\frac{7}{32}$		$\frac{15}{16}$	
$\frac{1}{4}$			

2. Perform the following calculations:

a. $1.4142 \div 2$
b. 0.866×3.1416
c. $1.05 \div 4.3$
d. $15.79 + 3.18 + 9.2 + 0.037$
e. $1.0 \div 3.0$
f. $87.5 - 9.96$
g. $1.0 \div .707$
h. 9.01×1.09
i. $15.05 - 12.978$
j. $\frac{1}{6.283}$
k. $30.01 \times .0062$
l. $0.01385 - 0.000675$
m. $1 \div 0.00628$
n. $87.5 \div 1000$

3. Using pliers or other tool to protect your hand, hold a piece of iron wire in a gas flame and allow it to heat slowly. Observe the color changes in the wire as it becomes heated. Which color suggests that the most energy is being emitted by the wire? Which color would be associated with the least amount of energy?

4. When sunlight is allowed to pass through a triangular glass prism, the white light is broken up into color segments like a rainbow. These colors are of extreme importance to the student of electricity and electronics not only because they are an example of the way in which energy affects electrons but also because they are used as a code in industry. Draw a diagram of the color segments, or *spectrum*, as it is normally called, and memorize the colors. You will need this information later in your studies.

5. Look up the terms *spectrum* and *spectrograph* in a good encyclopedia. Does the existence of bright spectrum lines support the theory that light is emitted when electrons change energy levels?

CHAPTER 2 THE ELECTRIC FIELD AND ELECTRIC CURRENT

A. CHAPTER PREVIEW

1 In this chapter you will learn that an electrical charge creates an *electric field* in the space around it.

2 You will learn how the electric field causes the energy possessed by charge carriers to change, depending on their place in the field. You will also learn how an electric field can be mapped by lines of force.

3 This chapter will consider the subject of electrostatics, that is, what happens when there is a surplus or deficiency of charge carriers in an object. Such important topics as potential difference, voltage, electromotive force, and potential gradient will be defined.

4 You will learn what a circuit is, and some of the characteristics of closed circuits and open circuits.

5 The Examples and Computations section introduces four topics necessary for an understanding of the electric field and the behavior of charged objects. These are signed numbers, exponentials, scientific notation, and the International System of Units.

6 The Applications section contains important information on the dangers of static electricity to modern electronic components.

B. PRINCIPLES

B.1 THE ELECTRIC FIELD

In Chapter 1 it was pointed out that a charge carrier modifies the space around it so that a force of attraction or repulsion is exerted on nearby objects, particularly other charged objects. Figure 2.1 shows two negatively charged objects, either electrons or objects to which additional electrons have been added. Using a sensitive balance like the one pictured in Figure 2.2, the French physicist Charles Coulomb (1736–1806) was able to study the force existing between the two charged objects. He learned that if the amount of charge on one or both of the objects is increased, the force produced will also increase. If the charge on one of the objects is doubled, the force will be doubled.

On the other hand, if the distance between the two charge carriers is increased, the force between them decreases. If the distance is doubled, the force decreases by a factor of 4. But if the distance is halved, the force increases by a factor of 4, and so on.

What really causes the force between the two charge carriers is not important, and attempts to study this question quickly move from the area of technology to philosophy. It is enough to say that a charge carrier changes the quality of the space around it by producing what is called an *electric field*. Another charge carrier brought into an electric field experiences a force of attraction or repulsion and, if able, will move in the direction of the force.

You will recall that work is done when something moves in the direction of a force. Figure 2.3 shows how a charge carrier that is free to move is brought into the neighborhood of a fixed charge carrier. It takes an external force to push the mobile charge carrier into this position against the force of repulsion between the two identical charges. This work may be considered as a certain amount of energy added to the mobile charge carrier or to the system composed of both.

The second charge carrier, pictured in Figure 2.4, possesses a certain amount of energy by reason of its position in the electric field of the first. If this second charge carrier then moves to position *B*, in the direction of the force of repulsion, some of the energy it possessed at point *A* will have been converted to work, that is, the work necessary to move the object from *A* to *B*. At point *B*, the object possesses less energy than it did at point *A*. As you can see, it is the position of object 2 in the electric field of object 1 that determines the energy of object 2.

Figure 2.1 The force between two charge carriers.

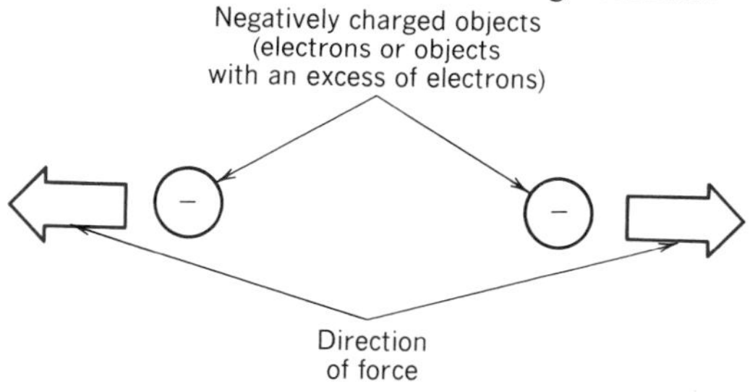

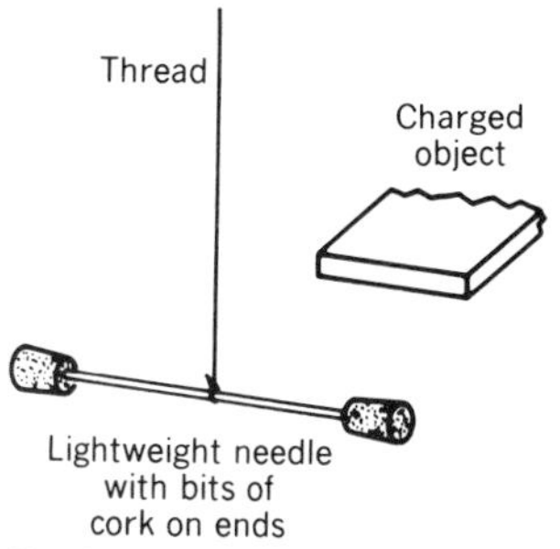

Figure 2.2 A Coulomb balance.

B.2 MAPPING AN ELECTRIC FIELD

Michael Faraday (1791–1867) devised a way to map the electric field around charged objects. Faraday's method was to draw a series of lines representing the electric field around a charged object to show the direction of the force that the field would exert on a small *positively* charged object. This method enabled him to picture the direction and shape of complex electric fields caused by a number of neighboring charged objects. An application of Faraday's method is shown in Figure 2.5, where the shape of the electric field around a spherical object, such as a spherical piece of amber, is shown. The direction of the arrowheads shows the direction in which a small positive test charge would move if placed on the line. Because the lines in a Faraday diagram show the direction of force, they are called *lines of force*. It is important to understand that these lines have no real existence. They cannot be cut,

Figure 2.3 A force is required to bring a charge carrier into the neighborhood of a fixed object with a similar charge.

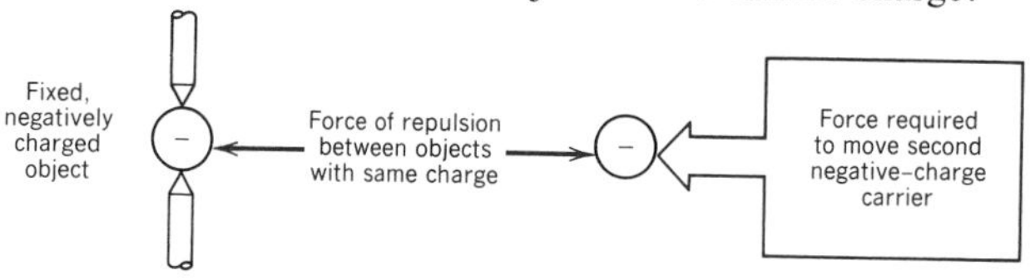

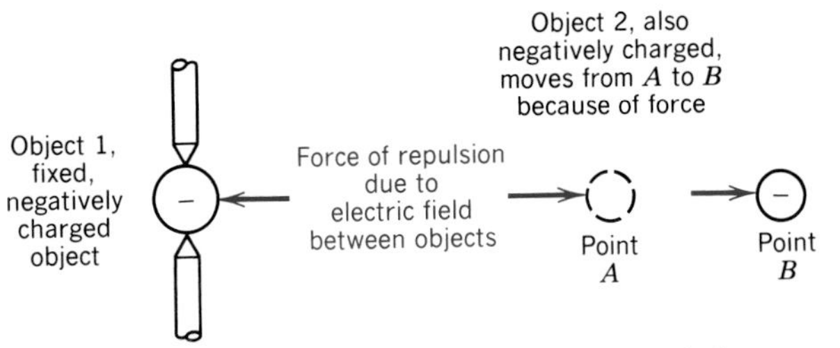

Figure 2.4 If a charge carrier moves under the influence of an electric field, some of the energy it possessed has been turned into work.

moved, or otherwise touched or felt. Many textbooks refer to the cutting of lines of force. This is no more real than saying that you cut the lines of longitude as you sail or fly around the world. What is real is the electric field. Cutting lines of force actually means movement across rather than in the direction of an electric field.

A further refinement of Faraday's method of charting the electric field was to vary the number of lines drawn through an area in the field to suggest the strength of the force exerted on a test charge located in that area. In electric field diagrams, such as that of Figure 2.6, areas of greater force, that is, of greater field strength, are shown by a bunching of the lines of force. Areas of weak force, or field strength, are shown by spreading the lines of force so that fewer of them are shown in an area.

Typical electric field diagrams are shown in Figures 2.7 and 2.8. In Figure 2.7, the lines of force between a positively charged sphere and a sphere with an equal negative charge are shown. Note that the lines are closer together between the spheres and further apart to the sides. This means that the field is strongest between the objects. In figure 2.8, the field between two spheres with identical negative charges is shown.

Figure 2.5 A map of the electric field around a charged sphere.

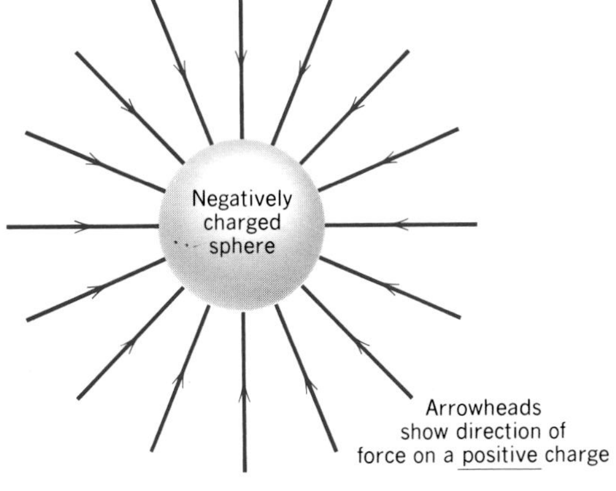

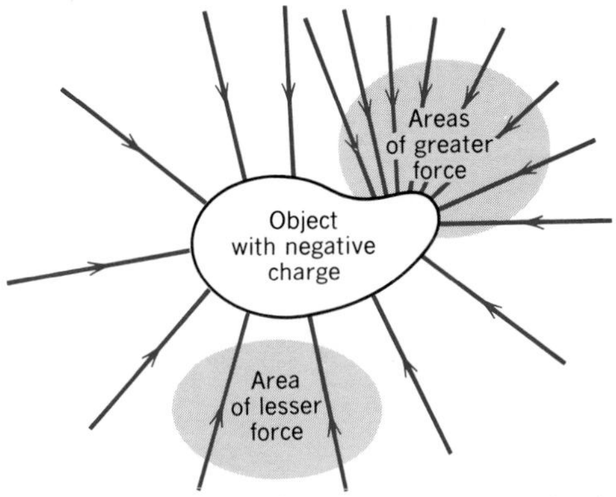

Figure 2.6 Areas of greater force are shown by bunching the lines of force.

In this instance, the field between the spheres is relatively weak. Both of these diagrams are idealizations because they leave out the influence of other objects in the neighborhood, which would change the shape of the fields in complex ways. Remember that it is customary to draw the arrowheads in these figures to show the direction of the force on a positive test charge.

B.3 MEASUREMENT OF CHARGE

The electron was unknown in Coulomb's day, so he defined a basic unit of electric charge in terms of distance and the force exerted on a test charge. These were quantities that he could measure directly with a

Figure 2.7 Lines of force between positively and negatively charged spheres.

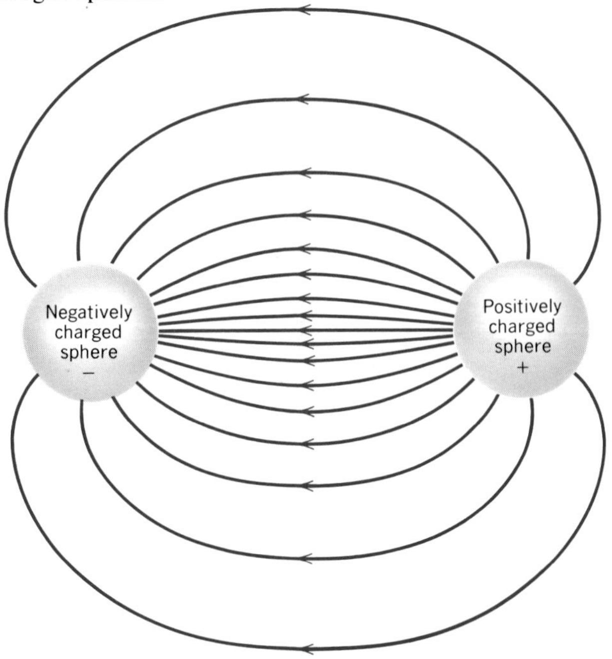

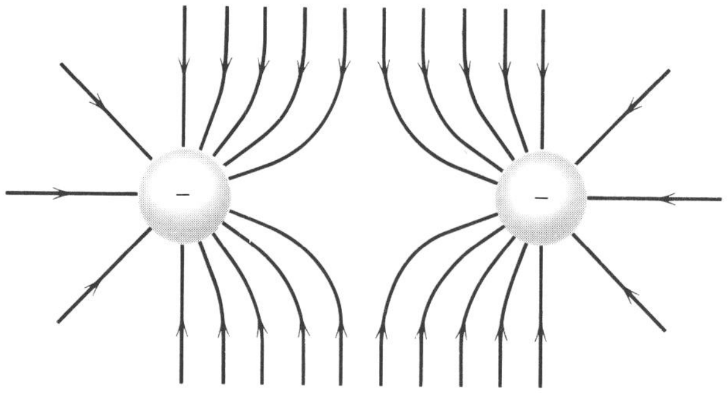

Figure 2.8 Lines of force between two negatively charged spheres.

ruler and his balance. This unit, called the *electrostatic unit of charge*, or esu, is not used in technology today. Instead, a more precise unit based on the charge of the electron, which was measured fairly accurately during the first part of this century, has become the unit of electric charge. This unit is called the coulomb and is abbreviated with a capital C. The coulomb is the charge possessed by 6,250,000,000,000,000,000 electrons. (This looks like an impossibly large number, but remember that an electron is incredibly small and has a very small charge. You will learn an easier way to write such very big numbers in the Examples and Computations section of this chapter.)

An object will have a negative charge of one coulomb if 6,250,000,000,000,000,000 electrons are added to it. Most materials have no net charge, since the number of negative electrons balances the number of positively charged protons in the atoms of the material. If instead of adding 6,250,000,000,000,000,000 electrons to an uncharged object, that many are removed, the object would have a positive charge of one coulomb. The symbol used to represent the electrical quality of charge is the capital letter Q, so that a diagram like Figure 2.9 means that the charge on the sphere is negative (minus) and is 2 C.

B.4 THE PRODUCTION OF STATIC CHARGES

In the last chapter, you learned that the earliest experiments produced electricity by rubbing different materials together. The production of charge by this method is technically referred to as *triboelectricity*. What the rubbing actually does is bring the materials into close contact with the addition of the heat energy caused by the rubbing. If the materials are then separated quickly, one of them will be found to be negatively charged, while the other will have an equal positive charge. That is, one of the materials took a certain number of electrons from the other, and both materials are charged. It is important that the two materials are separated quickly. If not, the electrons in the negatively charged material will move back to the positively charged material, neutralizing the charge on both.

Early experimenters tried all sorts of materials to generate electric charge, and it was found that some combinations work much better than others. Some materials are apt to give up electrons more easily than others and are referred to as *positively triboelectric*, while some materials are more likely to take electrons and are called *negatively triboelectric*. Table 2.1 is a triboelectric series table. It lists materials from the most positively triboelectric at the top to those that are most negatively triboelectric at the bottom. For a particular sized piece of material and a "standard" amount of rubbing, the greatest amount of charge can be produced by using materials that are furthest apart

Figure 2.9 A sphere with a negative charge of 2 C.

$Q = -2$ C

Table 2.1 Triboelectric Series

Air		
Human hands		↑
Rabbit fur		
Glass		
Human hair		
Nylon		Increasingly
Wool		Positive
Lead		↑
Silk		
Aluminum		
Paper		
Cotton	—	Neutral
Steel		
Wood		
Amber		
Hard rubber		
Copper		↓
Silver		Increasingly
Gold		Negative
Rayon		
Polyester		
Orlon		
Polyethylene		
PVC		
Silicon		
Teflon		↓

on the list. For example, a larger electrical charge would be produced by rubbing your hand across a sheet of Teflon® plastic than would be produced by rubbing it across a glass window. This does not mean, for example, that you cannot create an electrical charge by rubbing your hands on rabbit fur. A certain amount of charge will be developed. The material closest to the top of the list will possess a positive charge, while the material closer to the bottom of the list will have the negative charge. However, the closer together the two materials are on the triboelectric series table, the smaller the charge, measured in coulombs, that will be produced.

It is interesting to note that some of the insulators used in modern electronic components are strongly triboelectric. This causes many problems in industry, as will be discussed in the Applications section.

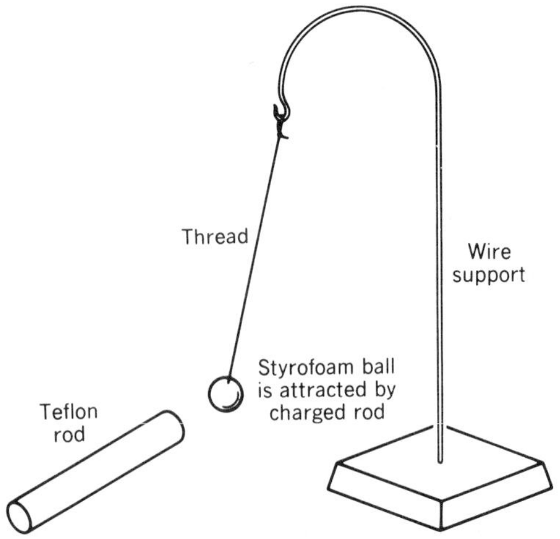

Figure 2.10 A charged rod attracts small pieces of plastic.

B.5 THE BEHAVIOR OF CHARGED OBJECTS

One basic principle of the behavior of charged objects that can be illustrated using only simple equipment is *charging by contact*. If a Teflon® rod is rubbed with wool or fur, it will develop a negative charge. That is, it will obtain a number of additional electrons from the wool or fur. The electric charge produced by rubbing different materials together results from the gain or loss of electrons by the materials. The materials are no longer electrically neutral, that is, the number of electrons in each material is no longer roughly the same as the number of protons in the atoms of the material. A charge of this type is called a *static charge*, and the effects of static charges are considered in a subject called *static electricity*. It has become customary to talk about the effects of static electricity and the effects of electrons moving through materials that possess a large number of conduction electrons as though two different subjects were involved. This is not the case at all. The only difference is that static electric effects result from the addition or removal of electrons, while *current electricity*, as it is sometimes called, consists of effects that result from the presence of electrons in conduction energy levels.

If a charged rod is brought near a small piece of plastic material, such as the styrofoam ball shown in Figure 2.10, this bit of material will be attracted to the rod. After touching the rod, however, the styrofoam will jump away, and a force of repulsion will be found to exist between them.

The reason for this is the transfer of charge carriers by contact between charged and uncharged objects. When the rod comes into contact with the suspended material, the two form a single system, and some of the extra electrons in the rod tend to move into the sphere. Because the styrofoam ball provides a poor path for the movement of electrons, it takes an observable amount of time for the electrons to enter it. Eventually, the excess charge that was formerly on the rod is shared by the rod and the styrofoam. Once this happens, the styrofoam is repelled by the rod.

B.6 CHARGING BY CONTACT

Charging a piece of material by touching it with a charged object is called *charging by contact*, in contrast to the original charging of the rod by rubbing, which is called triboelectricity. The important feature of charging by contact is that there is a path for the charge carriers to follow between the two objects. Once the charged rod and the styrofoam come into contact, the transfer of electrons begins.

After a few minutes, if the rod is rubbed again and brought near the styrofoam, the suspended ball will again be attracted to the rod, showing that the ball is no longer charged. During the time between the initial contact of the rod and the ball, the excess electrons in the styrofoam distributed themselves into other nearby objects, either through the thread supporting the styrofoam or through the air itself, particularly if it is fairly humid. This is why you do not normally experience a shock upon touching a metal doorknob after walking across a rug in the summer. In summer, there is much more water vapor in the air, and this water vapor provides a path for objects to lose an electric charge by giving up electrons to or obtaining them from nearby objects.

B.7 GROUNDING

The effects of charging by contact are much more noticeable when the object charged is rather small. If, as shown in Figure 2.11, a much larger piece of styrofoam touches a charged rod, the system composed of the rod and styrofoam has a much larger surface area. (It is actually the surface area rather than the volume that is important in static electric effects.) This means that the charge must be distributed over a much larger area, and its effects are therefore considerably weaker.

This can be illustrated quite dramatically by charging a styrofoam ball by contact and then touching it to a piece of copper wire that is connected to a water pipe running through the ground. Once the wire touches the styrofoam, the ball will be found to be completely uncharged. This process is called *grounding*. In effect, grounding connects the charged object to the largest piece of material that you can conveniently reach, the entire planet Earth. The Earth is so huge in comparison with any charged object that may be touched to it that it is capable of absorbing any number of electrons or making up a deficiency of any number. This means that no charge will be left on a grounded object.

The effects of grounding are shown quite clearly through the use of a device like that pictured in Figure 2.12. This device is called an *electroscope* and is very simple to construct. As shown in the figure, it consists of two light metal foil strips suspended so that they are free to move. The strips are usually placed in a glass jar so that they may be observed without the possibility of disturbance by air currents. If the loop at the top of the electroscope is touched with a charged rod, the strips will be charged by contact, since they are connected to the loop. This means that both strips will have the same charge. This will cause a force of repulsion between them, and the two strips will be forced apart, as shown in Figure 2.13. If the electroscope is properly constructed and the humidity is low, the two strips will remain separated for a fairly long time. If, however, a grounding wire is touched to the loop on the top of the electroscope, the strips will immediately hang straight down, showing that the system composed of the loop, connecting wire, and strips no longer has an electric charge. Or to put it more precisely, the negative charge of the electrons remaining in the system is balanced by the positive charge of the protons.

Figure 2.11 The effects of charging by contact are easier to see if the object charged is small.

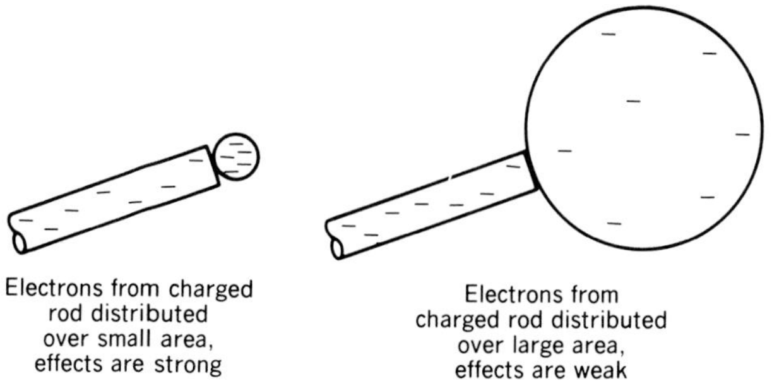

Electrons from charged rod distributed over small area, effects are strong
Electrons from charged rod distributed over large area, effects are weak

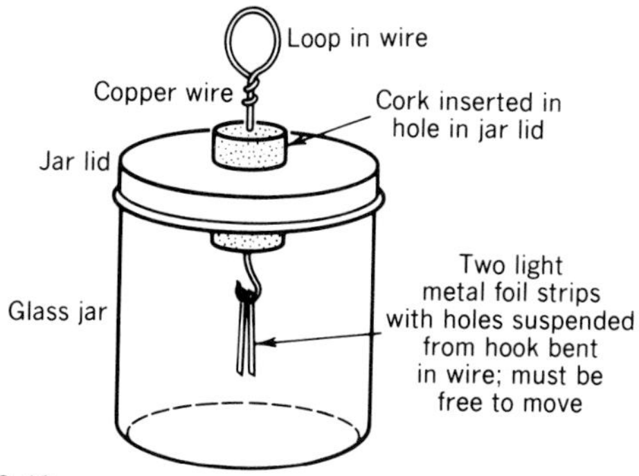

Figure 2.12 A homemade electroscope.

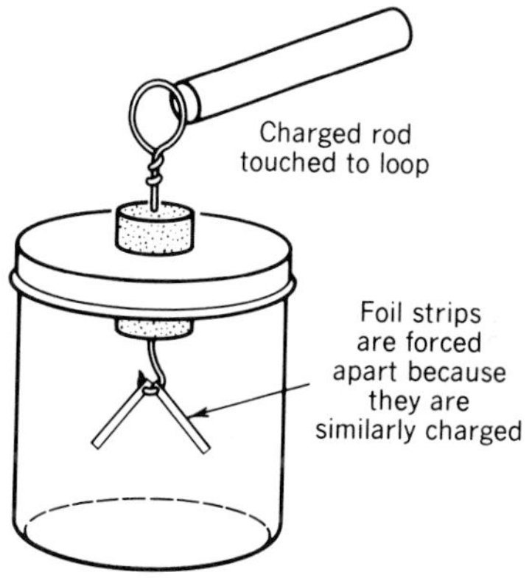

Figure 2.13 If a charged object is touched to the electroscope top, the strips will be forced apart.

B.8 CHARGING BY INDUCTION

The effect of grounding also permits an object to be charged without actually touching it to a charged object. This is called *charging by induction* and is illustrated in Figure 2.14. A charged rod is brought close to a suspended styrofoam ball, and a grounding wire or finger is touched to the side of the ball opposite the charged rod. The grounding wire is then withdrawn and the charged rod removed. The styrofoam ball will then be found to be charged. Curiously enough, however, it will have a charge opposite to that of the rod used. Charging by induction can be explained by the fact that the charged rod will repel electrons in the

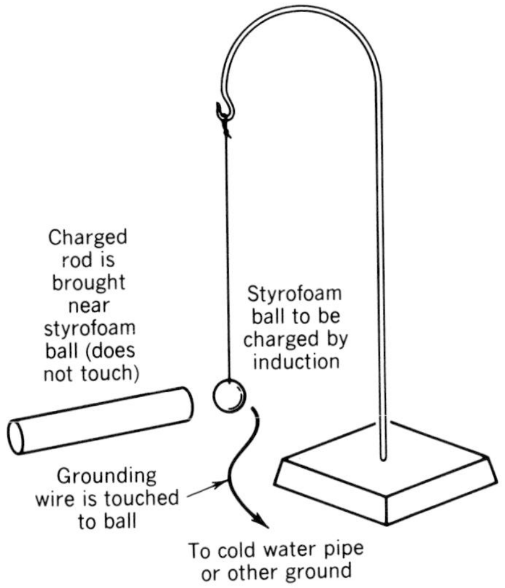

Figure 2.14 Charging by induction.

styrofoam ball if it is negatively charged and will attract them if it is positively charged. In spite of the fact that few conduction electrons are present in styrofoam in its normal state, the approach of the charged rod will provide enough energy to raise some electrons to a conduction level. These electrons will then move in response to the electric field from the charged rod. If the rod is negatively charged, these electrons will tend to move toward the opposite side of the styrofoam ball, as shown in Figure 2.15, and will be transmitted to the Earth through the grounding wire. If the wire is removed before the charged rod is withdrawn from the neighborhood of the ball, a net positive charge will remain on the styrofoam. As soon as the charged rod is withdrawn, the positive charge will distribute itself evenly on the surface of the styrofoam.

If the rod used is positively charged, as in Figure 2.16, a number of electrons will be attracted to the point at which the rod approaches the styrofoam. The rest of the styrofoam will then appear to have a net positive charge, and electrons will move from the Earth, through the grounding wire, to the styrofoam. When

Figure 2.15 Detailed view of charging by induction with a negative charged rod.

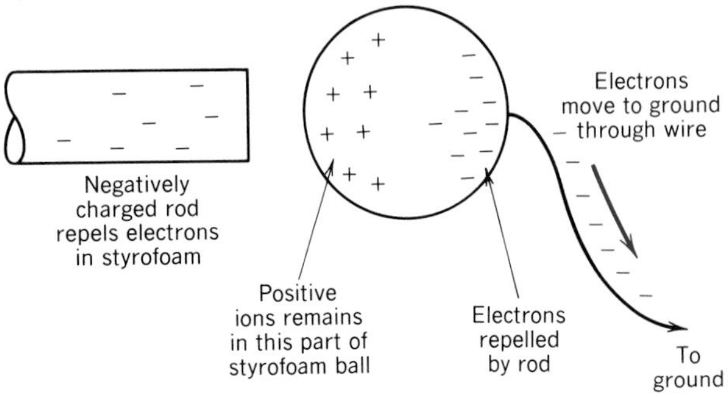

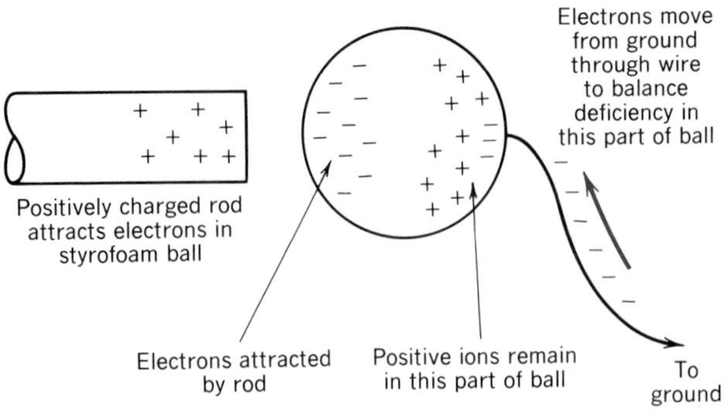

Figure 2.16 Detailed view of charging by induction with a positively charged rod.

the grounding wire and rod are then removed, the styrofoam will have a negative charge.

B.9 STATIC CHARGE EXISTS ONLY ON THE SURFACE OF OBJECTS

Another interesting characteristic of static electricity is that electric charges distribute themselves only on the outside surface of an object. This can be shown through the use of a hollow sphere (Figure 2.17) or other hollow container. An electroscope with an insulated wire serves to detect the presence of charge. If the sphere is given a strong charge and the uninsulated end of the electroscope wire is carefully touched to a point on the inside of the sphere, no charge will be detected. Touching the wire to the outside of the sphere, however, shows the presence of a charge. Because there is no charge on the inside of the sphere, there is also no electric field inside it. This is why it is relatively safe to remain inside a closed automobile during a thunderstorm. If lightning should happen to strike the automobile, the effects will tend to be isolated to the outside surface.

Figure 2.17 Experiments with a charged, hollow sphere show that electric charges are distributed only on the outside sur-

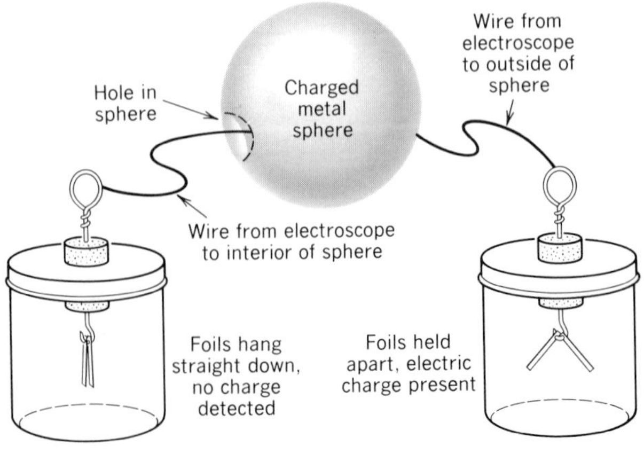

B.10 MOVEMENT OF ELECTRICAL CHARGE CARRIERS

In the above discussion of the distribution of charge carriers, you learned that excess electrons added to an object tend to distribute themselves on the outside surface. This is easier to visualize when electrons have been added but it is also true when a number of electrons have been removed from an object. The deficiency exists on the outside surface and tends to be equally distributed on the entire surface. That is, if there are no other factors, such as the presence of another charged object nearby, a static electric charge at one point on the surface of an object will be the same as that at another point. The reason for this is that the charge carriers move because of the force exerted on them when they are in each other's electric field.

A charge carrier in an electric field, then, is like a weight in the gravitational field around the Earth. At any point in the field, the charge carrier or the weight has a force acting on it that tends to make it move. In the first chapter, you learned that work is defined as movement in the direction of a force. The ability to do work is defined as energy. This means that a charge carrier in an electric field and a weight in a gravitational field both possess a certain amount of energy at any point in the electric or gravitational field. If the charge carrier or the weight are at rest in the field, this energy is called *potential energy*. The charge carrier will move in the direction of the force due to the electric field to a point where it will have less potential energy than before. In the same way, a weight that is not held in place will fall. In electronics, potential energy is referred to by the shortened form *potential*. For example, the potential energy, or potential, of an electron near another negative charge is greater than the potential energy at a point further away. Since all charge carriers tend to move into the Earth, the potential of the Earth, or ground, is considered to be zero, and all other points are compared to the Earth when speaking of their potential.

B.11 POTENTIAL DIFFERENCE

The difference in potential between two points is a very important concept in electronics and is called the *potential difference* between the two points. When referring to potential difference, the term *voltage* is also used. The voltage between two points is just another way of referring to the difference in potential energy of a charge carrier at the two points.

The term *electromotive force* (abbreviated *emf*)

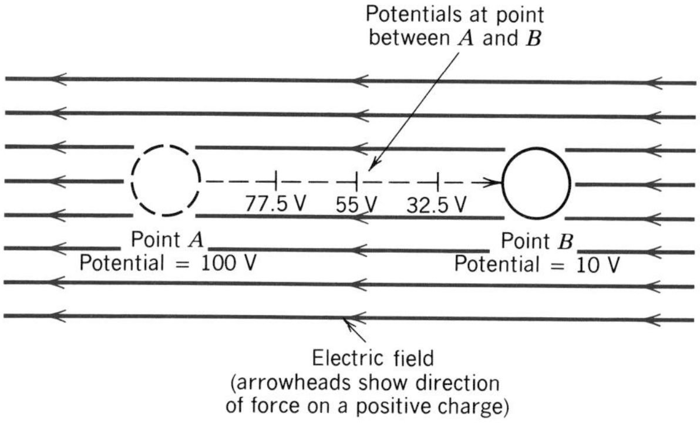

Figure 2.18 Potential gradient: the potential of the electron changes gradually between point *A* and point *B*.

is frequently found in textbooks and is used to mean the same thing as voltage. Technically, it is incorrect to call potential energy a force. But since an electric field exerts a force on a charge carrier, the two terms came to be associated.

Another concept that is frequently used in technology is that of the *potential gradient*. Simply stated, this refers to the fact that the potential difference in an electric field varies smoothly and continuously between points that have greater potential and points with less energy, that is, those at a lower potential. If, for example, an electron moves from point *A* to point *B* in Figure 2.18, and if the potentials shown represent the energies possessed by a negative charge at each of the points, the change in the potential energy of the electron will be gradual and constant. This is in contrast to the change in the *force* on the electron, which will decrease more rapidly as the electron moves away from the negative charge that causes the field.

The examples used so far have illustrated the electric field and potential gradient between opposite charges, but as shown in Figure 2.19, a field and potential gradient will also exist between two bodies with similar charges of unlike magnitude. Suppose *A* and *B* are the same physical size but that *A* has a negative charge of 2 C and *B* has a charge of 1 C. If a wire is connected between the two objects, a certain number of electrons will cross the wire to *B* until the charges

Figure 2.19 A field and potential gradient exist between objects with similar charges when there is a difference in the magnitude of the charge.

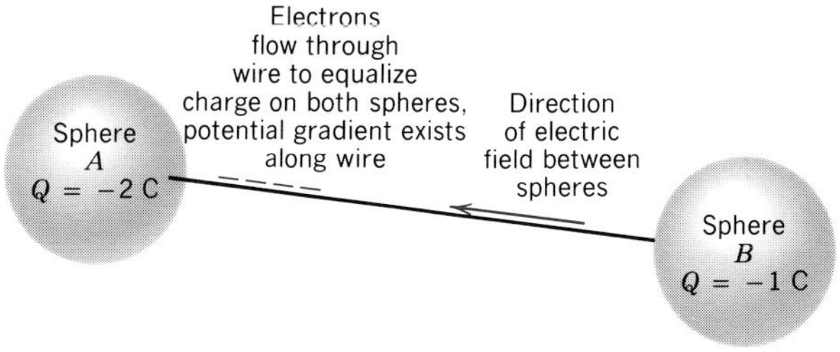

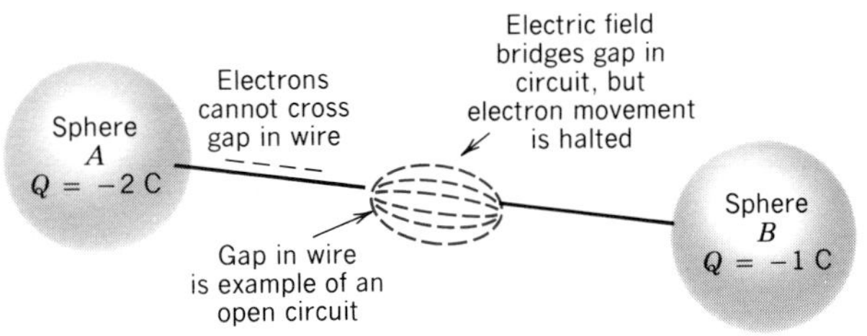

Figure 2.20 A gap in the wire from A to B in Figure 2.19 would be an open circuit.

on both objects are equal, or 1.5 C on both. During the first instant that the wire is connected, an electric field through the wire is established, and some of the additional electrons on the surface of object A move under the force generated by this field. When enough electrons have entered object B so that both A and B have the same charge, there is no longer such a movement of charge carriers.

B.12 THE CIRCUIT

The wire in the above explanation provided what is called a *closed circuit*, that is, a path between a point of higher potential or voltage and a point of lower potential. The definition of a closed circuit is a path that charge carriers can follow in moving in an electric field. The opposite of a closed circuit is an *open circuit*. In general, an open circuit is a path that is very difficult or impossible for charge carriers to follow from a point of higher to a point of lower potential. For example, air does not provide a very good path for charge carriers, so if the wire connected between A and B in Figure 2.19 had a gap in it, we would say that there was an open circuit at the gap. Note that the electric field still bridges the gap, as shown in Figure 2.20, but the path for the movement of charge carriers has been broken.

C. EXAMPLES AND COMPUTATIONS

C.1 SIGNED NUMBERS

The existence of protons and electrons with equal and opposite electrical charges leads naturally to the use of *signed numbers*, that is, numbers prefixed by either a positive or negative sign, such as +3 and −5. In addition to using signed numbers to identify positive and negative charges, these numbers are frequently used in electronics to mark other opposite quantities that cancel each other if they are combined. Examples of this are electron flows in opposite directions in the same conductor and the forces due to electric fields in opposite directions. Normally, only negative numbers are marked with a sign. It is usual to omit the plus sign with positive numbers, so that the bare number 6, for example, means +6.

When adding signed numbers, you must pay attention to the signs. If the numbers to be added have the same sign, they may be added directly. The sign of the sum will be the same as the sign of the numbers added.

EXAMPLE:
Add the following:

$$\begin{array}{r} 6 \\ 27 \\ 43 \\ \underline{+18} \\ +94 \end{array}$$

In the case of the sum of negative numbers, the minus sign is assigned to the sum. ■

EXAMPLE:
Add the following:

$$\begin{array}{r} -\ 6 \\ -27 \\ -43 \\ \underline{-18} \\ -94 \end{array}$$

■

When the numbers to be added have different signs, the matter becomes a bit more complicated. The easiest way to add a series of numbers with differing signs is to add all the numbers with positive signs and all the numbers with negative signs and then to calculate the *difference* between the positive and negative sums. Assign the sign of the largest of the partial sums to this difference.

EXAMPLE:
Add the following:

$$\begin{array}{r} -12 \\ +\ 8 \\ -\ 9 \\ +\ 6 \\ -\ 3 \\ \underline{-\ 2} \end{array}$$

■

SOLUTION:
In order to do this, first add together all the positive numbers:

$$\begin{array}{r} 8 \\ \underline{6} \\ 14 \end{array}$$

and all the negative numbers:

$$\begin{array}{r} -12 \\ -\ 9 \\ -\ 3 \\ \underline{-\ 2} \\ -26 \end{array}$$

Find the difference of the positive and negative partial sums:

$$\begin{array}{r} -26 \\ \underline{+14} \\ -12 \end{array}$$

Notice that the sign of the difference of the partial sums is the same as that of the larger of the two partial sums. ■

When using a calculator, it is not necessary to calculate the partial sums, the machine itself will keep track of the sign, as long as you are careful to enter the sign of each negative number. ■

EXAMPLE:
Add the following numbers using a calculator: 8, −14, −21, 36, −3. ■

SOLUTION:
There are several ways to do this, but one of the most direct methods is to use the change sign key on your calculator. This key is frequently marked +/− or CHS and is pressed *after* a negative number is entered.

Enter each of the numbers in turn, and press the change sign key if the number is negative. Select addition.	[8] [+] [1] [4] [+/−] [+] [2] [1] [+/−] [+] [3] [6] [+] [3] [+/−]
Press equals key to display the sum.	[=]

Your calculator display should read 6. ■

Perform the following additions with pencil and paper and then with your calculator. Compare the results. Which method was quicker? Which was more accurate?

a. −14, 38.5, 6.47, −9.3
b. 3.75, −6.28, −6.253, −3.93
c. −42, −14, −6, −18.75
d. 0.003, +.052, −0.0301, −.006
e. 8.86, −14.33, +3.75, +9.01
f. 6.67, −3.25, −9.33, −2.25
g. −9, 6, 5, −13, −27
h. 85.2, 19.6, −27.33, +8.3
i. −.093, −0.37, −.065, +1.05
j. 12,537, −6,840, −4,231, +8,365

To subtract signed numbers, a simple rule is followed. Change the sign of the subtractor and add the subtractor and the subtrahend. For example, subtract −14 from 32. Writing this out you get:

$$\begin{array}{rr} & 32 \\ (-) & \underline{-14} \end{array}$$

Now change the sign of the subtractor and add:

$$\begin{array}{r} 32 \\ \underline{+14} \\ +46 \end{array}$$

As in the case of addition, subtracting signed numbers with a calculator is a simple task if you are careful to enter the sign of the negative numbers.

EXAMPLE:
The following example is worked for both pencil and paper and a calculator. Subtract −82 from 96. ■

SOLUTION 1 (pencil and paper):
First write the problem

$$\begin{array}{rr} & 96 \\ (-) & \underline{-82} \end{array}$$

Change the sign and add:

$$\begin{array}{r} 96 \\ \underline{+82} \\ 178 \end{array}$$

SOLUTION 2 (using a calculator):
When using a calculator, the change sign key should be pressed after each negative number is entered.

Enter the subtrahend.	[9] [6]
Select subtraction.	[−]
Enter the subtractor.	[8] [2] [+/−]
Press equals key to display difference.	[=]

Your calculator display should now read 178. ■

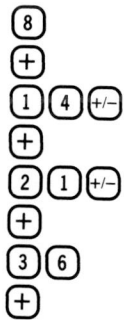

Try the following exercises with both pencil and paper and a calculator so that you develop the habit of working with signed numbers. An error in using signed numbers is difficult to spot when you are checking work, so accuracy is important.

a. Subtract −82 from 136.
b. Subtract 18 from −42.
c. Add −27, 13, −9, and 4.
d. Subtract 18 from 12.
e. Subtract 6 from −4.
f. Add 29, −3, +6, and subtract −7.
g. Subtract +4.937 from 5.02.
h. Subtract −19.375 from 8.27.
i. Subtract 6.932 from 4.226.

The multiplication of signed numbers with pencil and paper also follows a simple rule, but it is one that is sometimes hard to remember and seems a little illogical. It is this: if the two numbers to be multiplied have the same sign, whether it is negative or positive, multiply the numbers and assign a plus sign to the product. If the numbers have different signs, multiply them and assign a negative sign to the product.

EXAMPLE:
Multiply +35 by −15 using paper and pencil. ■

SOLUTION:
Write the problem in the normal way and multiply:

$$\begin{array}{r} 35 \\ \times\ 15 \\ \hline 175 \\ 35 \\ \hline 525 \end{array}$$

Since the multiplicand and the multiplier have different signs, the product will be a negative number. The full answer, then, is −525. ■

EXAMPLE:
Multiply −16 by −12 using pencil and paper. ■

SOLUTION:
Write the problem in the normal way and multiply:

$$\begin{array}{r} 16 \\ \times\ 12 \\ \hline 32 \\ 16 \\ \hline 192 \end{array}$$

Since the multiplicand and the multiplier have the same sign, a plus sign should be assigned to the product. The answer is +192, or just 192, since the plus sign is assumed if no sign is present. ■

With a calculator, it is again not necessary to keep track of the signs as long as they are properly entered with the change sign key as required. The calculator itself will provide the correct sign for the product.

EXAMPLE:
Multiply −42 by −18 using a calculator. ■

SOLUTION:

Enter multiplicand. [4] [2] [+/−]
Select multiplication. [×]
Enter multiplier. [1] [8] [+/−]
Press equals key to display answer. [=]

Your calculator display should now read 756. ■

The calculator will assign a negative sign when the product requires it, as in the following example.

EXAMPLE:
Multiply −17 by +13, using a calculator. ■

SOLUTION:

Enter multiplicand. [1] [7] [+/−]
Select multiplication. [×]
Enter multiplier. [1] [3]
Press equals key to display answer. [=]

Your calculator should now read −221. ■

The same rule for the determination of sign is used in division. If the divisor and the dividend have the same sign, the quotient (the answer) will be a positive number. If the divisor and the dividend have differing signs, the quotient will be a negative number.

EXAMPLE:
Divide −64 by −13 using pencil and paper. ■

SOLUTION:
Perform the division in the normal manner, adding zeros after the decimal point in the dividend so that the quotient will have three decimal places to the right of the decimal point.

$$\begin{array}{r} 4.923 \\ -13\overline{)-64.000} \\ \underline{52} \\ 120 \\ \underline{117} \\ 30 \\ \underline{26} \\ 40 \\ \underline{39} \end{array}$$

Since the divisor (−13) and the dividend (−64) have the same sign, the answer, 4.923, will be a positive number. ■

Using a calculator for dividing signed numbers differs from multiplication only in that the function selected is division. All other operations are exactly the same.

EXAMPLE:
Divide 875 by −14 using your calculator. ■

SOLUTION:

Enter dividend.	[8] [7] [5]
Select division.	[÷]
Enter divisor.	[1] [4] [+/−]
Press equals key to display answer.	[=]

Your calculator should now display −62.5. ■

Perform the following multiplications and divisions of signed numbers first on paper and then with your calculator. Compare the results. Which method showed the smaller number of errors?

a. Divide +3 by −3.
b. Multiply −85.2 by −3.7.
c. Divide −9.5 by 18.2.
d. Divide 8 by 3 and then multiply by −2.
e. Divide +54 by +8.
f. Multiply −256.3 by +9.25.
g. Multiply −16 by 34.
h. Divide −91.336 by −19.6.
i. Multiply 96.95 by −8.3.
j. Divide −25 by −6.25
k. Divide 700.14 by 42.
l. Divide −168.75 by 75.
m. Multiply −24.6 by −6.2.
n. Divide 93.9 by 18.
o. Subtract −14 from 9 and then multiply by −8.25.
p. Multiply 64.5 by −1; multiply the result by −1 again.

C.2 EXPONENTS AND SCIENTIFIC NOTATION

Although the use of decimals helps, the writing and use of very large and very small numbers remains a problem. In order to use such numbers, scientists, engineers, and technicians make use of a system called *scientific notation*.

Scientific notation is based on a type of mathematical shorthand called *exponentials*. Exponentials are really a simple way of writing a number multiplied by itself a number of times. For example, you can write two times two as 2×2, or, using the exponential method, you can write 2^2, which also means two times two. The little 2 written above and to the right of the number is called the *exponent*, and the other number is called the *base*. The exponent tells you how many times to multiply the base number by itself. In the same manner, 4^6 means $4 \times 4 \times 4 \times 4 \times 4 \times 4$, or four times itself six times. The number 4^6 is read as *four to the sixth power*. In general, if A is any number, A^n means the number A times itself n times.

In reading exponents, 3^2 is read as three squared, while 3^3 is read as three cubed. For that matter, any number or letter with an exponent of 2 is read as that number or letter squared.

EXAMPLES:
16^2 is read as "sixteen squared."
D^2 is read as "D squared."
Similarly,
16^3 is read as "sixteen cubed."
D^3 is read as "D cubed."
$2M^3$ is read as two M cubed." ■

Try reading the following exponential forms for practice, writing them out, and calculating them, as has been done in a.

a. $3^3 = 3 \times 3 \times 3 = 27$
b. 2^4
c. 8^2
d. 10^3
e. d^2, where $d = 5$
f. 1.414^2

Since you have just read something about negative numbers, you might wonder if negative numbers can be used as exponents. The answer is yes, and the meaning attached to such forms is the number one divided by the base number times itself as many times as the exponent indicates. For example, 2^{-2} means one divided by two times two, or $\frac{1}{4}$. Exponents are frequently used in the sort of mathematics you will need to solve problems and make calculations in electronics, and they will be covered in greater detail in later chapters, but for the moment, it is the exponents of the base number 10 that will be discussed.

EXAMPLES:

$$3^{-2} = \frac{1}{9}$$

$$A^{-3} = \frac{1}{A^3}$$

C.3 SCIENTIFIC NOTATION

Multiplying or dividing numbers by 10 is a very simple thing to do, since all that is involved is moving the decimal point. When you write 35, this is actually 35.0000000. . . . To multiply 35.00 by 10, all you have to do is move the decimal point one place to the right, resulting in 350.0. To divide 35.00 by 10, all you have to do is move the decimal point one place to the left, getting 3.500.

This is the basis of the scientific notation used to write large or small numbers. In this notation, each number is written in two parts. The first part is called the *significant digits*, and the second part is called the *exponent*. The exponent tells you how many places to the right or left to move the decimal point in the significant digits. For example, 3.5×10^2 means to move the decimal point in 3.5 two places to the right. You will have to put in an extra zero to mark the second place, and when this is done, you get 350.

Try evaluating 8.3×10^3. In this case, the exponent tells you to move the decimal point three places to the right, making 8300. You will see the use of this system when you try to write out the number 6.2×10^{26}. It would look like this:

620,000,000,000,000,000,000,000,000.

As you can see, 6.2×10^{26} is a lot easier to write.

Similarly, you can use negative exponents of 10 to write very small numbers. The number 6.5×10^{-3} means that you move the decimal place three places to the left, getting 0.0065. Try writing out 3.62×10^{-9}. Isn't the exponential system easier? For practice with this system, write out the following numbers expressed in scientific notation.

a. 6.02×10^4
b. 8.30×10^6
c. 1.99×10^{-2}
d. 4.00×10^8
e. 4.56×10^{-9}
f. 2.06×10^{-18}
g. 7.07×10^1

Note that in all the above numbers there is one number or decimal place to the left of the decimal point, and one, two, or more to the right of it. This is the form of the significant digits in scientific notation. You may sometimes see something like 68.75×10^3, but this is not true scientific notation. It would be more correct to move the decimal point one more place to the left and add one to the exponent. The correct form would be 6.875×10^4. From this example, you can see that it is an easy matter to write numbers in scientific notation. For example, suppose that you want to write 365.85 in scientific notation. To do this you would have to move the decimal point *two* places to the left. Therefore, 2 is the exponent, and the number is then written 3.6585×10^2 in scientific notation.

Write the following numbers in scientific notation:

a. 83.2
b. 620
c. 333.33
d. 5000
e. 62,000,000
f. 183,620
g. 21
h. 3.33

Did you have a problem with the last one? The problem was that you didn't want to move the decimal point at all. You could write this by writing 3.33×10^0. This is true because 10^0 is equal to 1.

Decimals may also be converted to scientific notation by counting the number of places you have to move the decimal point to the right. for example, convert 0.0039 to scientific notation. It is necessary to move the decimal point three places to the right

$$0.0_1 0_2 3_3 9$$

In this case, the exponent is written as *minus* three, because you are moving the decimal point to the right, or 3.9×10^{-3}. Convert the following decimals to scientific notation:

a. 0.00375
b. .08002
c. 0.000000000998
d. .0000000000000005
e. 0.33333333
f. .707

C.4 ENGINEERING NOTATION

Once you have understood scientific notation, it is quite easy to work with *engineering notation*. Engineering notation is really only a special case of scientific notation. In engineering notation, the exponents are always positive or negative multiples of three, that is, 3, 6, 9, and so on, or −3, −6, −9, and so on. So that the exponent can always be expressed as a multiple of 3, the significant digits must be allowed to range from 1 to 999.

This is in contrast to scientific notation, where the range of the significant digits is limited to a number from 1 to 9.99. . . . For example, the number 820,000 would be written as 8.2×10^5 in scientific notation but as 820×10^3 in engineering notation. Some numbers,

6250, for example, are written in the same way in both scientific and engineering notation. In both notations this number is 6.25×10^3.

In order to write a number that is greater than 1 in engineering notation, it is only necessary to move the decimal point in groups of three digits to the left. The left-most group or groups then become the significant digits.

$$6/\underbrace{250}_{6}/\underbrace{000}_{3}. = 6250 \times 10^3 = 6.25 \times 10^6$$

With numbers smaller than 1, the decimal point is moved to the right, three places at a time, and a negative exponent is used:

$$0.000\ 063 = 63 \times 10^{-6}$$

In some cases, it is necessary to place additional zeros to the right of the last digit to complete a group.

Convert the following numbers to engineering notation.

a. 1800
b. 0.001
c. 0.00025
d. 22,560,000,000
e. −0.00693
f. 250,000
g. .627
h. 1627000
i. .3652
j. 999000
k. 0.000 000 006 5
l. 1,200,000
m. 1000
n. 0.006325

One of the principal reasons for the use of engineering notation is that it is an essential part of the metric system, or International System of Units (SI), which defines the units to be used in technology in the world. Today, there is a great deal of pressure on American and British industry to use the metric system instead of the traditional units such as the inch, foot, yard, and mile. This debate has nothing to do with the use of the SI, or metric, system for electrical units, as the decision to use metric quantities in electronics has already been made and these metric units are now regularly used. One of the strengths of the metric system is its use of engineering notation in the names of units. Table 2.2 gives the names of some of the exponents that are used as unit name prefixes. For example, 0.001 V (volt) is called a millivolt (mV), while 1,000,000, or 10^6, ohms (Ω) is called a megohm (MΩ). You will have to memorize these exponent prefixes and learn to use them in order to work in the field of electricity or electronics. These prefixes will be studied again in the next chapter.

It should be noted that some scientific calculators and BASIC language computers work in scientific notation and not in engineering notation. That is, significant digits range from 1 to 9.99. . . and exponents are

Table 2.2 Unit Name Prefixes in the Metric System

Prefix	*Abbreviation*	*Decimal Value*	*Exponential Value*
pico-	p	0.000000000001	10^{-12}
nano-	n	0.000000001	10^{-9}
micro-	μ	0.000001	10^{-6}
milli-	m	0.001	10^{-3}
centi-	c	0.01	10^{-2}
deci-	d	0.1	10^{-1}
deka-	D	10	10^{1}
kilo-	K or k	1,000	10^{3}
mega-	M	1,000,000	10^{6}
giga-	G	1,000,000,000	10^{9}

not necessarily multiples of 3. This can be something of an annoyance to the beginning student, but after some experience with conversion from decimal to engineering notation, the problems disappear.

The use of scientific and engineering notations on a calculator or small computer will be discussed in the next chapter, along with exponential computations.

D. APPLICATIONS

D.1 STATIC ELECTRICITY

As pointed out in this chapter, most of the modern applications of electricity involve the movement of charge carriers from a place where they have more energy to a place where they have less. Moving charge carriers can be made to do useful work. Recently, a number of important applications for static charges have been invented. Among these is the *cathode-ray tube*, similar to the devices used as the picture tube in television sets and computer monitors. The construction of these tubes is illustrated in Figure 2.21. A coated

Figure 2.21 The cathode-ray tube (CRT) uses static charges to direct a stream of electrons.

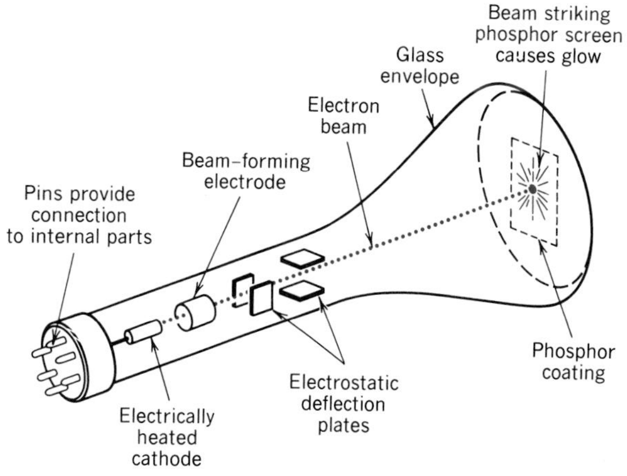

metal sleeve is electrically heated. This forces a large number of electrons into a conduction level in the coating and literally boils them off into the tube, from which almost all the air has been removed. A hollow cylinder in this tube is given a very high positive charge, strongly attracting the electrons, which are formed into a thin beam. This beam can be aimed to strike a particular part of the screen by a series of deflection plates, whose charges are controlled so as to move the point of impact across the screen rapidly. The screen itself is coated with a *phosphor*, that is, a material that gives off light when struck by the electron beam. By varying the intensity of the beam and moving it so quickly that the human eye blends the combination of dots produced on the screen, an entire picture can be formed.

Another application of static electricity is the removal of dust and smoke particles from the air, particularly in factory smokestacks. Highly charged metal plates attract small dust and smoke particles in the same way that a charged rod attracts small bits of paper. The dust and smoke particles may then be trapped before they can reenter the air around the plates.

D.2 DANGERS OF STATIC ELECTRICITY TO ELECTRONIC COMPONENTS

Thirty-five years ago or so, static electricity was commonly thought of as the annoying sparks produced in dry weather when one touched a doorknob after walking across a rug. Of course, there were some exceptions to this; people who worked in areas with explosive fumes or a lot of fine dust were aware of the danger of a static electric spark setting off an explosion. But except for these individuals, static electricity was nothing more than a dry winter annoyance and a laboratory phenomenon.

The reason that static electricity could be ignored by most people a few years ago is twofold. First, most of the clothing worn then was cotton, woolen, or nylon. Referring back to the triboelectric series of materials given in Table 2.1, you can see that these are all neutral or positive, so that the amount of static electricity generated was not overly great. Still referring to the table, you can see that the worst condition generally occurred when hard rubber shoe heels were rubbed across woolen rugs. Second, with the exception of the hazardous areas mentioned, there was not much damage that a static charge could do, except sting fingers and scare pets. Today, the situation is very different. Millions of dollars have been spent to eliminate the dangers of static electricity in electronics plants, and even more millions have been lost because of inadequate static prevention.

Orlon, polyester, and acetate rayon rank as highly negative on the triboelectric table, while human hands are nearly the most positive. The act of smoothing polyester slacks or an orlon sweater generates a large static charge. Even more serious than this change produced by the popular fabrics used in clothing is the greatly increased sensitivity to static damage of the solid-state electronic components used in industry today. Transistors and integrated circuits used in computers and other applications can easily be destroyed or damaged by static discharges. During the last few years, it has been discovered that static electricity damage is the prime cause of equipment failure in the field.

The destruction of components by static electricity is bad enough, but it has also been discovered that the function of certain kinds of components is impaired by even a single static discharge. Often this impairment of function will not result in a recognizable failure, and the unit containing the component will be left in service for a long time, causing minor, intermittent problems that are very hard to correct because they are very hard to track down. In addition to this impairment of function, static discharge will frequently reduce the useful life of some components, even those that were once thought of as being fairly resistant to any sort of damage.

D.3 METHODS OF STATIC ELECTRICITY PREVENTION IN THE ELECTRONICS INDUSTRY

The prevention of static electric damage to electronic components and units is a new subject, and new equipment and methods are frequently introduced. In general, it is expensive to protect components, and this protection is needed at every step of the way from the manufacture of the components through their shipment, handling, assembly, and even to the operation of the completed units.

Protection of electronic equipment, both components and completed units, falls into three categories. Simplest and least expensive is protecting the components or units in shipment. The components or units are protected by packing them in conductive plastic envelopes. This is done even when it is only necessary to move them from one part of a plant to another. Since the component is inside the protective shield, all parts of it will be at the same potential, eliminating most of the danger. Most of the damage to components and units occurs when different parts of the component or unit are at different potentials. In cases where any change in potential can damage a component or unit, the plastic envelope or carrying case can be grounded.

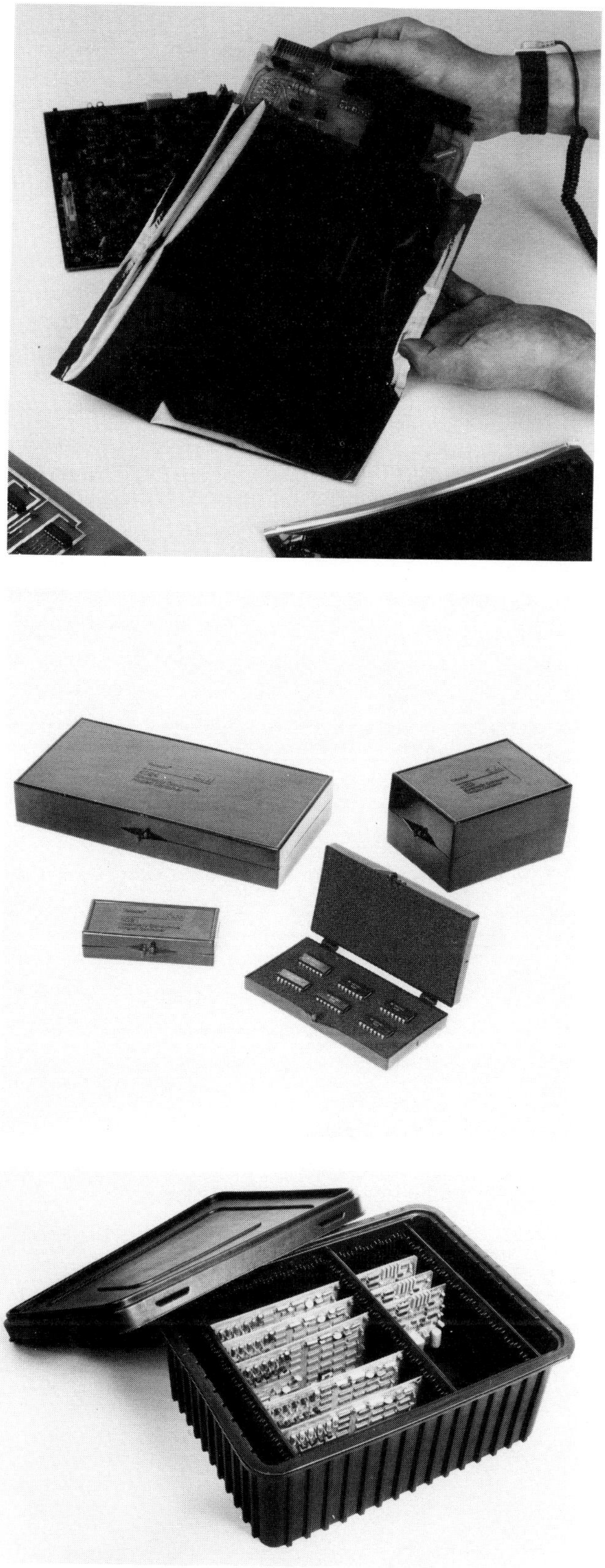

Figure 2.22 Conductive packaging materials used to prevent damage to components during shipment. (Photo courtesy of 3M/Static Control Systems Division.)

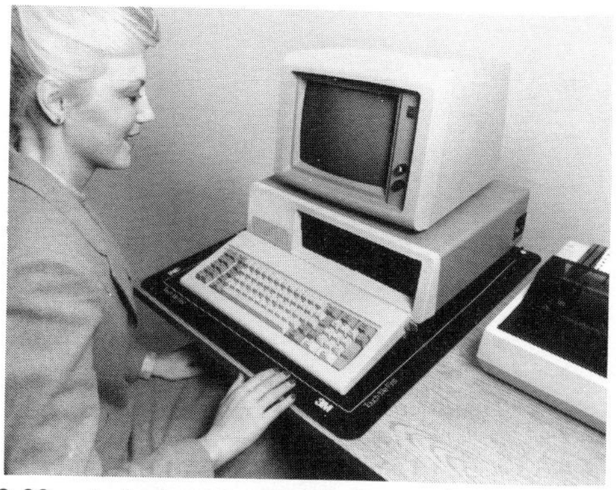

Figure 2.23 A desk pad suitable for static-free operation of a microcomputer. (Photo courtesy of 3M/Static Control Systems Division.)

Figure 2.22 shows some of the envelopes, antistatic pads, and carryalls frequently used in industry. Any field service technician is expected to carry a few of these envelopes along on a service call in case a subassembly has to be removed from a piece of equipment and carried back to the home office.

The operation of static-sensitive equipment presents a major problem in many offices and factories today. The problem is particularly serious when computer equipment is being operated in front offices, where the operators are dressed in fashionable clothing often made of synthetic fabrics. Nylon hose or underwear in contact with polyester slacks or dresses is frequently a problem, although almost any combination of modern underwear and outer clothing will produce triboelectricity. If this were not enough, the synthetic fabrics used in office furniture and carpeting will provide serious static charges.

At one time, special conductive floors were built into all rooms in which computers were housed. These floors, along with special metal furniture and conductive cloth upholstery, grounded static charge quickly. Today, however, almost every room in a modern business may have a microcomputer in it. Instead of the computer flooring, desk-top pads and underdesk runners of grounded, conductive plastic are widely used. Figure 2.23 shows a desk with a desk pad suitable for static-free operation.

Another problem that can occur in offices and factories is the problem of static surges caused by nearby lightning strikes. Since Benjamin Franklin's invention of the lightning rod, few buildings are damaged, but unless special precautions are taken, the enormous discharge of a lightning strike can severely damage sensitive electronic components connected to a power line during a severe storm. The lightning protection devices that were used to protect standard industrial equipment such as motors are not generally sufficient to protect

Figure 2.24 Power line conditioning equipment (Photo by M. Hermes.)

modern electronic equipment, and an entire industry has grown around the production and installation of power line conditioning equipment needed for modern units. Figure 2.24 illustrates some of this equipment.

Electronic components and subassemblies are most open to damage by static discharge during assembly and repair, and assemblers and technicians must be aware of the methods used to protect against damage. Three methods are in common use. The first is to ensure that the person touching the components or assemblies is at ground potential at all times and that any static charge that might tend to build up due to clothing friction is sent to ground. This is done by the use of grounded wrist straps, as shown in Figure 2.25. You must become accustomed to wearing such straps (usually one is sufficient, although in extreme cases, two may be worn), and you must make it a habit to put them on and ensure that they are properly grounded before starting to work on static-sensitive assemblies. Many older technicians, particularly those trained in television repair, do not like to use grounding straps, since older textbooks stressed the danger of being grounded while working on live equipment. Modern grounding straps have been designed to prevent the possibility of accidents, however, and only provide a path for the gradual escape of a static charge. On the other hand, it is dangerous to substitute a bare wire wrapped around the wrist and connected to ground for a commercial grounding strap. Grounded floor mats are also used when working on sensitive components.

Another caution for the technician is to ensure that the hands and the equipment being worked on are at about the same potential. This is done by using a conductive plastic bench mat that is grounded. The wrist strap may be connected to the bench mat to ensure that both are at the same potential. Figure 2.26 shows a modern industrial work station with wrist straps, bench, and floor mats.

In many cases, the grounded work station is suf-

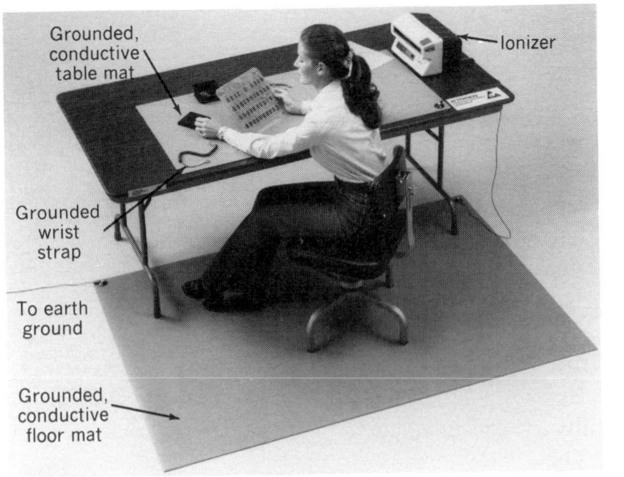

Figure 2.26 A modern industrial work station for static-sensitive component assembly or repair. (Photo courtesy of 3M/Static Control Systems Division.)

Figure 2.25 A grounded wrist strap. (Photo courtesy of 3M/ Static Control Systems Division.)

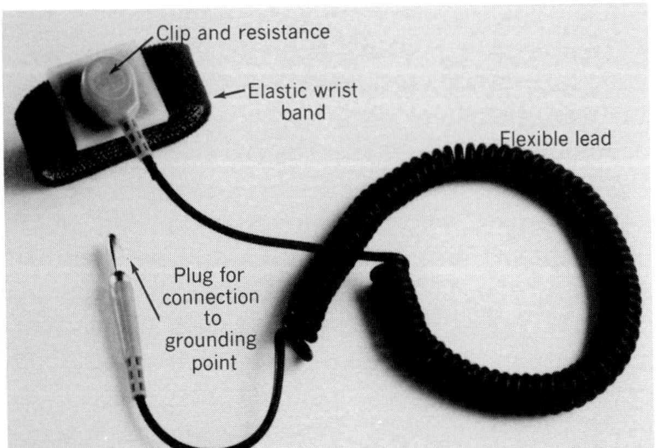

Figure 2.27 An ion source neutralizes static charges. (Photo courtesy of 3M/Static Control Systems Division.)

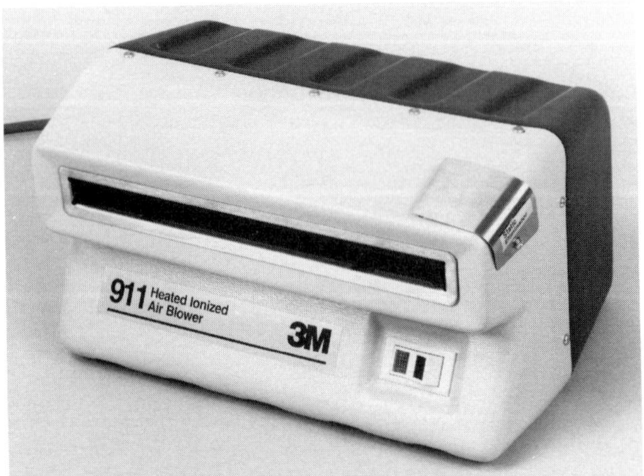

ficient to protect against static discharge damage. In situations where insulated plastics are involved or highly sensitive components are being installed, it is sometimes necessary to provide a stream of ionized air in the work area. A device like that pictured in Figure 2.27 produces both negative and positive ions, which are repelled from objects with the same charge but are attracted to objects with the opposite charge. When a stream of ions comes into contact with an object with opposite charge, it eventually neutralizes it completely. It should be noted that uncharged objects tend to attract equal numbers of positive and negative ions and so remain uncharged. A small ion generator is usually sufficient for a single work station.

Other precautions include the use of grounded soldering irons and special tools.

E. PROGRAMMED REVIEW

FRAME 1

In Chapter 1, *work* was defined as what happens when a force moves an object some distance in the direction of the force. The definition of "energy" given was ________.

a. The same as gravity. (3)
b. Sometimes produced by electricity. (3)
c. Equivalent to movement. (2)
d. The ability to do work. (4)
e. Any other answer, review Chapter 1, Section B.1.

FRAME 2

Work was defined in terms of force and movement. Although certain kinds of energy involve motion, others do not. Review section B.1 and go on to Frame 4.

FRAME 3

Do not confuse energy with the electric or gravitational fields that may define the amount of energy an object has at a particular point in the field. Review Section B.1 and go on to Frame 4.

FRAME 4

During the nineteenth century, the British scientist and experimenter Michael Faraday devised a way of mapping an electric field using ________. They would show the direction of the force on a small, positively charged object placed in the field and could be grouped to show the strength of the field as well.

a. Lines of potential. (6)
b. Lines of force. (5)
c. Pieces of amber. (6)
d. None of the above. (6)

FRAME 5

A charge carrier modifies the space around it to produce an electric field. The field produces ________ a charge carrier placed in it.

a. A force on. (8)
b. A charge on. (7)
c. A movement of. (8)
d. Any other answer, review Section B.1.

FRAME 6

Review Section B.2 and return to Frame 4.

FRAME 7

The charge carrier already has a charge on it. You are confusing the effects of an electric field with charging by induction. Return to Frame 5 and choose another answer.

FRAME 8

A *force on* or a *movement of* are both correct. The force is the result of the electric field. The motion is actually the result of the force and is the work that the field does on the charge carrier. Go on to Frame 9.

FRAME 9

The unit of charge used in technology is the ________. One ________ is the charge possessed by 6.25×10^{18} electrons.

a. Coulomb. (11)
b. esu. (10)
c. Any other answer, review Section B.3.

FRAME 10

The electrostatic unit of charge, abbreviated esu, is not widely used in technology today because it is based on measurements of force and distance. These quantities are harder to measure accurately than the charge on an electron. For this reason, the unit of charge used in technology is the coulomb, abbreviated C. Go on to Frame 11.

FRAME 11

The method of producing an electric charge by rubbing two objects together is called ________.

a. Triboelectricity, or triboelectric generation. (12)
b. Any other answer, review Section B.4 and go on to Frame 12.

FRAME 12

If a charged object is touched to a wire that is connected to a rod driven into the soil or to a metal water pipe, the charge on the object will ________. This process is called ________.

a. Disappear; grounding. (13)
b. Any other answers, review Section B.7 and repeat Frame 12.

FRAME 13

Describe, in a step-by-step manner, what happens when a charged object is brought into contact with an uncharged object which is free to move.

a. The correct answer should have the following points:
   i. Uncharged object is attracted.
   ii. After contact, the charge is distributed on the outside of both objects.
   iii. After charge is distributed, the object which is free to move is repelled. (14)
b. If any of the above points is omitted, review Sections B.6 and B.9.

FRAME 14

In electronics, the potential energy of a charge carrier in an electric field is called the ________ or the ________ of that point.

a. Potential; voltage. (15)
b. Any other answer, review Section B.10.

FRAME 15

The potential or voltage at a point in an electric field is also called ________ force, which is abbreviated ________.

a. Electromotive; emf. (16)
b. Any other answer, review Section B.11 and try this frame again.

FRAME 16

The difference in the energy possessed by a charge carrier at two different points in an electric field is called the ________ between the two points.

a. Potential difference. (17)
b. Any other answer, review Section B.11.

FRAME 17

A path which charge carriers may take to move from a point at which they have a higher potential energy to a point where they have less is called a ________ ________.

a. Closed circuit. (18)
b. Any other answer, review Section B.12 and go on to Frame 18.

FRAME 18

Numbers prefixed with either a positive or negative sign, such as +3 and −5, are called ________ ________.

a. Signed numbers. (19)
b. Positive and negative numbers. (19)
c. Any other answer, review Section C.1 and go on to Frame 19.

FRAME 19

Subtract 18 from 12 without the use of calculator.

a. 30 (20)
b. 6 (21)
c. −6 (22)
d. Any other answer, check your arithmetic or review Section C.1.

FRAME 20

The number 30 is not the correct answer. You made

one of two mistakes: either you added the two numbers or you changed the sign of the subtractor twice.

$$\begin{array}{r} 12 \\ (-)\ \underline{18} \\ -6 \end{array}$$

Go on to Frame 22.

FRAME 21

The number 6 is not the correct answer. You correctly changed the sign of the subtractor to -18 and added $+12$ and -18, but you should have assigned the same sign to the difference as the larger of the two terms, $-$ in this case. Go on to Frame 22.

FRAME 22

Multiply -16 by -4 without using your calculator.

a. -64 (23)
b. $+64$ (24)
c. Any other answer, check your arithmetic.

FRAME 23

The number -64 is not correct. You forgot the basic rule of multiplying signed numbers. That is, multiply the two numbers together. If the two numbers have the same sign (even if both are negative), the product is a positive number. If the signs of the multiplier and the multiplicand are different, assign a minus sign to the product. Try the following problems with pencil and paper.

$$\begin{array}{r} -37.9 \\ \underline{\times\ 4.6} \end{array} \qquad \begin{array}{r} -82.23 \\ \underline{\times\ -4.67} \end{array} \qquad \begin{array}{r} 18.93 \\ \underline{\times -6.63} \end{array}$$

a. -174.34, $+384.0141$, -125.5059 (24)
b. If you have made errors in arithmetic, check your work and correct it. If you have errors in the sign of the answers, review Section C.1, paying close attention to the examples and exercises, and then try Frame 23 again.

FRAME 24

Divide 42.75 by -3.

a. 14.25 (25)
b. -14.25 (26)
c. Any other answer, review Chapter 1, the discussion on division of decimals.

FRAME 26

The rule for the division of signed numbers is similar to that used for multiplication. For division, it reads: if the divisor and the dividend have the same sign (whether positive or negative), assign a plus sign to the quotient; if the divisor and dividend have different signs, assign a minus sign to the quotient. Perform the following divisions with paper and pencil.

$$-17.94 \div 3.25$$
$$-17.28 \div -4.8$$
$$334.5993 \div -36.33$$

a. -5.52, $+3.6$, -9.21 (27)
b. If you have any other answers, check your arithmetic or review Chapter 1 and Chapter 2, Section C.1 and try Frame 26 again.

FRAME 27

The expression 16^3 is read ___________, and the number 3 is called the ___________.

a. Sixteen cubed or sixteen to the third power; exponent. (28)
b. Any other answer, review Section C.2.

FRAME 28

The expression 4^2 is read ___________, and it is equal to ___________.

a. Four squared or four to the second power; 16. (29)
b. Any other answer, review Section C.2.

FRAME 29

In scientific notation, there is always ___________ digit to the left of the decimal point. In engineering notation there is/are ___________ digit(s) to the left of the decimal point and the exponent is always divisible by ___________.

a. One; one, two, or three; three. (30)
b. Any other answer, review Sections C.3 and C.4 and repeat Frame 29.

FRAME 30

Convert the following numbers to scientific notation without using a calculator.

0.00365   182,000   7,935,800,000

a. 3.65×10^{-3}; 1.82×10^{5}; 7.9358×10^{9} (31)
b. Any other answer, review Section C.3.

FRAME 31

Write the following terms in decimal form:

$$9.75 \times 10^{-4}$$
$$8.636 \times 10^{5}$$
$$6.50 \times 10^{-6}$$

a. 0.000975; 863,600; 0.0000065 (32)
b. Any other answer, review Section C.3 and return to Frame 30.

FRAME 32

Write the following numbers in engineering notation:

1.73×10^{4} 0.06 184,000 −0.1

a. 17.3×10^{3}; 60×10^{-3}; 184×10^{3}; -100×10^{-3}
b. Any other answers, review Section C.4.

FRAME 33

State two reasons for the increased danger to electronic components from static electric discharge during assembly and testing.

a. Two reasons that should come to mind are the increased sensitivity to static damage of modern components and the use of more highly triboelectric materials in modern clothing. (34)
b. If your answer did not include at least one of those stated above, review Section D.2. Go on to Frame 34.

FRAME 34

Cite three methods used in modern industry to reduce the danger to electronic components from static discharge during assembly and testing.

a. Working on special, grounded, antistatic mats; requiring workers to wear grounded wrist straps; using air ionizers to remove built-up charges. (end)
b. If your answer did not include at least two of the three methods cited above, review Section D.3.

E. PROBLEMS FOR SOLUTION OR RESEARCH

1. Add:

a. −43, 19, 22
b. +0.03, 9, .62
c. 410,628, −632,030, 211,092
d. −87.65, −4.06, −16.1
e. −9.23, +16.4, −8.007, 8.41
f. 0.00365, −.0125, .9010, −.02
g. 41.25, −36.9, −70.035, 18.83, −9.993
h. −85.37, 16.94, 12.86, 38.53
i. 128,000, −67,425, −53,120, 2,700
j. 4.653, −3.764, −2.983, −1.448

2. Subtract:

a. −18.9 from −3.63
b. .006 from −0.1
c. 8 from −14
d. −4.302 from 18.90
e. −0.061 from −.005
f. −6.75 from 3.26
g. 2.28 from 1.414
h. −27.22 from −54.68
i. 4 from −1.53
j. −28,503 from 17,295

3. Multiply:

a. −18.475 by 16.28
b. 1.01 × −9.37
c. 2.1 by 0.0068
d. −3.33 × −1.87
e. +36.05 by −9.009
f. 42.06 by .06
g. −8.320 × 0.1200
h. 0.0067 × −0.0124
i. 6427 × −901
j. −6.1 × 7.05
k. −.01 × −.0015
l. −9.315 × −6.4

4. Divide:

a. −.011 by −.015
b. 868.75 by −3
c. −11.5 by 36
d. −18 by −.015
e. −275.0335 by +62.65
f. −134.725 by −42.5
g. +872 by +9
h. −.00167 by .05678
i. −1.14714 by −0.06
j. +403.087 by −3.62
k. −10,546.624 by −11.36
l. −.000536 by +.08

5. Convert the following decimal numbers to scientific notation:

a. 86,430,000
b. 0.15
c. 0.0000013
d. 927
e. 41.116
f. 11
g. 90.01
h. 0.00068
i. .2060
j. 186,000
k. 89,200
l. −0.0673

6. Convert the following numbers in scientific notation to decimal number form:

a. 3.1×10^{8}
b. 1.02×10^{-6}
c. 1.762×10^{3}
d. 4.02×10^{-1}
e. 6.28×10^{-7}
f. 5.05×10^{4}
g. 9.29×10^{-5}
h. 3.28×10^{12}
i. 4.305×10^{4}
j. 1.006×10^{1}
k. 8.4×10^{5}
l. 1.045×10^{2}
m. 9.3×10^{10}
n. 8.85×10^{-5}
o. 1.637×10^{4}
p. 8.53×10^{-12}

7. Convert the following numbers to engineering notation:

a. 1001
b. 118,000
c. .1
d. 12,750
e. 430,000,000
f. .667
g. 0.000142
h. 93,000,000
i. 0.03
j. 1,650,000,000
k. 0.000000045
l. .004675
m. 300000
n. 1252.9
o. −.4753
p. 180,000,000,000

8. Convert the following numbers in engineering notation to decimal form:

a. $3.2 \times 10^{+3}$
b. 4×10^{-3}
c. 1×10^{9}
d. 8.5×10^{-6}
e. 4.56×10^{-3}
f. 865×10^{-9}
g. 4.75×10^{-3}
h. 3.27×10^{-6}
i. 640×10^{12}
j. 11.221×10^{3}
k. 8.06×10^{6}
l. 998×10^{-18}
m. 1.25×10^{-9}
n. 47.653×10^{3}
o. 8×10^{-9}
p. 84×10^{-3}

9. Convert the following numbers to engineering notation. Some of them are already in the correct form.

a. 1.04×10^{3}
b. 6550.7×10^{-3}
c. 67.3×10^{-4}
d. 9×10^{-3}
e. 1.07×10^{-18}
f. 1993×10^{-6}
g. 36.05×10^{-9}
h. 1.25×10^{17}
i. $8{,}350 \times 10^{3}$
j. 357×10^{12}
k. 24×10^{4}
l. 5.56×10^{-2}
m. 18.9×10^{-11}
n. 850×10^{9}
o. 62×10^{-6}
p. 3.35×10^{-1}

10. Clarissa Cascode is working as an electronic component assembler to help pay for her technical education. Four months ago, in September, her employers were satisfied with her work, but now she is beginning to get complaints that too many of her units fail the quality control test after she has finished them. Clarissa knows that she is working as carefully as she did before. Could static electricity be a cause of the problem?

a. How could Clarissa check to see if this is a possible cause of the trouble?
b. What solutions might she suggest to her employers?

11. Sphere *A*. has a negative charge, $Q = 2$ C, while sphere *B* has a positive charge, $Q = 3$ C. If the two spheres touch, what will be the charge on each sphere?

12. Fill in the table below:

Exponent	Symbol	Prefix
_____	_____	milli
_____	_____	giga
10^{-6}	_____	_____
_____	_____	kilo
_____	p	_____
_____	_____	mega
10^{-9}	_____	_____

13. Provide the correct unit prefix in the following expressions. The first one has been done as an example.

a. 4×10^{6} watts $= 4$ megawatts
b. 2×10^{-3} seconds
c. 6×10^{-9} seconds
d. 850,000 volts
e. 5.42×10^{-6} ampere
f. 2.24×10^{-8} seconds
g. 5,000,000 ohms
h. 2700 meters
i. 0.75 watt
j. 8.5×10^{-3} volt
k. 18×10^{6} ohms
l. 25000 ohms
m. 0.001 volt
n. 0.000000000073 second
o. 173×10^{-6} second
p. 8×10^{4} ohms
q. 4×10^{-2} ampere
r. 0.453 meter
s. 0.0001 volt

14. Some home computers are particularly sensitive to static electric discharge. Write a brief report on practical and inexpensive ways to protect a computer from damage or faulty operation due to static buildup.

15. Discuss the similarities of and differences between the electric field and the gravitational field.

CHAPTER 3 CURRENT, POTENTIAL DIFFERENCE, AND CELLS

A. CHAPTER PREVIEW

1 In this chapter you will learn about sources and loads. Sources are devices that supply electrical energy, and loads are devices that transform electrical energy into some form of useful work. Among other things, you will learn that sources supply electrons with high potential energy and also provide a potential difference that forces these electrons to move through a circuit.

2 You will learn the definitions of current and direct current, and their relationship to an electric field.

3 The devices that technicians commonly use to measure electric current will be discussed, and you will learn to identify the common types of meters.

4 You will learn to measure the current, or flow of electrons, in a closed circuit.

5 Common potential or voltage measuring devices will be illustrated and discussed. You will learn to identify and describe the important characteristics of each type.

6 The Examples and Computations section reviews the mathematical techniques for addition, subtraction, multiplication, and division of exponentials and numbers in scientific or engineering notation. These skills are applied to the calculation of current and charge in circuits.

7 You will learn to use calculators and small computers with scientific and engineering notation problems.

8 Building on your knowledge of the International System of Units (the metric sytem), this section explains the difference between some of the metric units and the customary units which are still widely used in English-speaking countries. Also included are a set of rules for rounding off unit conversions as well as other numbers.

9 After learning the material presented in the Applications section, you will be able to identify the principal types of cells. The section covers most of the portable, chemically-operated sources of electrical energy in use today. You will also learn the details of construction and the advantages and disadvantages of each type.

B. PRINCIPLES

B.1 SOURCES AND LOADS

The principles of triboelectricity described in the last chapter are useful for defining the electric field and potential, but the applications for triboelectric energy are limited. In fact, as shown in the Applications section, the very high potentials produced can damage electronic components. In order to obtain useful work from electrical energy, an electric field and a supply of charge carriers at a high potential level must be present. A device that provides these conditions is called a *source*. There are many kinds of sources, but all have one thing in common: as a part of a circuit, they all inject charge carriers, almost always electrons, into the circuit at high potential and remove the low-potential charge carriers from the circuit. This is done by producing an electric field and potential gradient in the circuit. In the source itself, some other form of energy, either chemical, mechanical, or heat, is utilized to raise the energy level of the low-potential charge carriers that enter the source from the circuit.

Figure 3.1 is a symbolic view of the operation of a source. The source produces an electric field through the external path or closed circuit, and a high potential electron moves along the circuit because of the force produced on it by the field. Similarly, low-potential electrons drift into the source. If the circuit is made of a material that contains a large number of electrons in the conduction energy level, the material composing the circuit will tend to remain electrically neutral. For every electron that moves from the source into the circuit, one electron will drift into the source.

Figure 3.1 Representation of a potential gradient created by the electric field produced by a source.

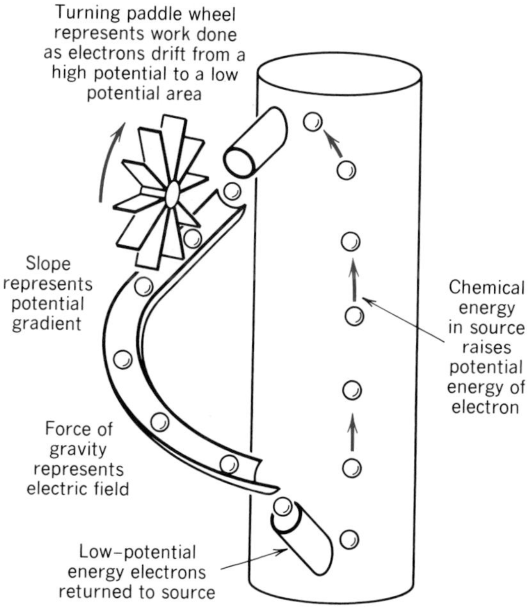

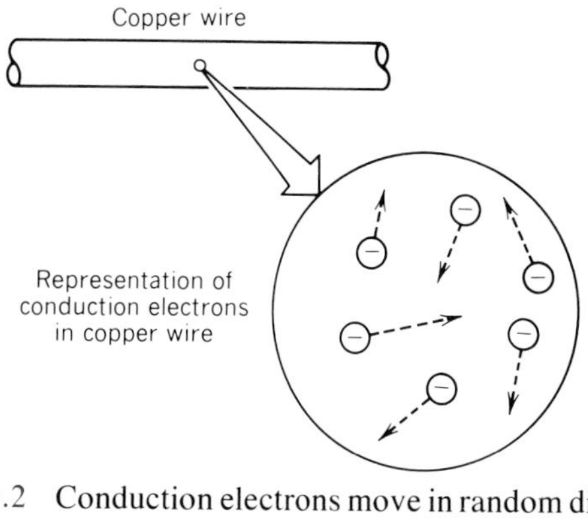

Figure 3.2 Conduction electrons move in random directions unless they are subjected to an external electric field.

Notice that the word *drift* is used to describe the motion of electrons. This choice is deliberate, for electrons do not move in only one direction or in lock-step, like a column of soldiers. The conduction electrons in a piece of material like a wire are constantly moving in various directions and at various speeds, depending on the amount of energy they have absorbed and the crystalline structure of the material within which they are found. Figure 3.2 illustrates the way in which conduction electrons move if they are not subjected to an electric field.

However, when a source that produces an electric field is connected, there is a constant force on the conduction electrons so that whatever direction they may be moving in, there is a gradual drift along the lines of force of the field. This is shown in Figure 3.3. In this figure, you see that the conduction electrons are still moving in all directions, some of them with

Figure 3.3 When an electric field exerts a force on conduction electrons, there is a gradual drift in the direction of the force in addition to the random movement.

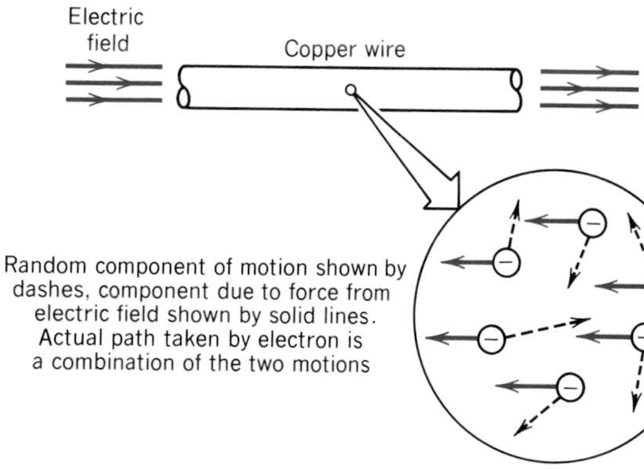

speeds greater than that of the drift velocity produced by the electric field, but the general tendency is to drift from a point of high potential to a point of low potential in the direction of the field.

Depending on what book you are looking at, this drift of electrons is called flow, current, or electron flow. In order to minimize confusion between the electron drift direction and the direction of conventional current, which explains electrical effects as though the charge carriers were positively charged, this book will use the terms *electron drift direction, electron flow,* or *current,* even though only the first is a technically correct description of what happens.

In Chapter 1 it was stated that charge carriers could be made to do useful work in passing from a point of high potential to a point of lower potential. In order to benefit from the work done when the charge carriers move, some sort of device is needed that converts the movement into another form of energy, into a means for storing information, or into a form suitable for controlling something. This device is called a *load.* There are many kinds of load, for the work done by moving charge carriers can be put to many uses. Figure 3.4 shows a general sort of load inserted into a circuit consisting of a wire and two charged spheres.

When the wires in Figure 3.4 are first connected, electrons begin to drift from the negatively charged sphere to the positively charged one. During the first instant of connection, the electric field through the wire will be strong, and a large number of electrons will be drifting through the load and on to the positively charged sphere. However, as these arriving electrons distribute themselves on the surface of the positively charged sphere, the potential difference between the two spheres will decrease. The strength of the electric field and the force on the drifting charge carriers will also decrease. Because we are dealing with a general drift of electrons, each of which is moving in an erratic manner, the actual velocity of the drift will not vary much as the strength of the electric field decreases. On the other

Figure 3.4 A load inserted between two charged spheres.

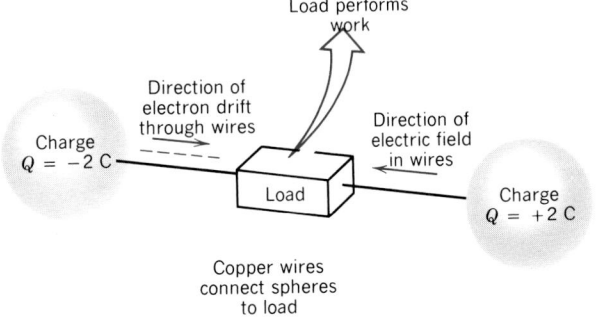

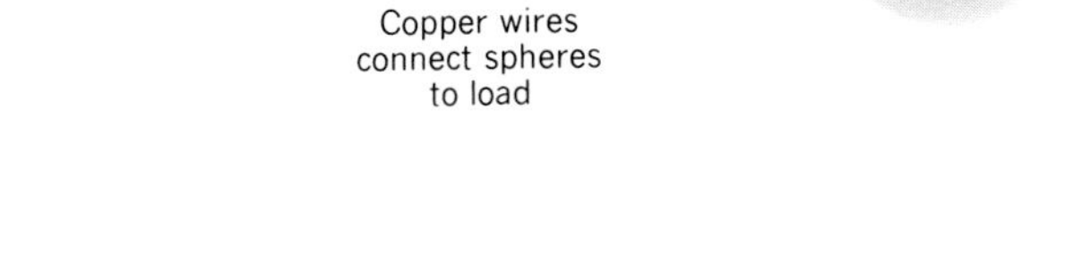

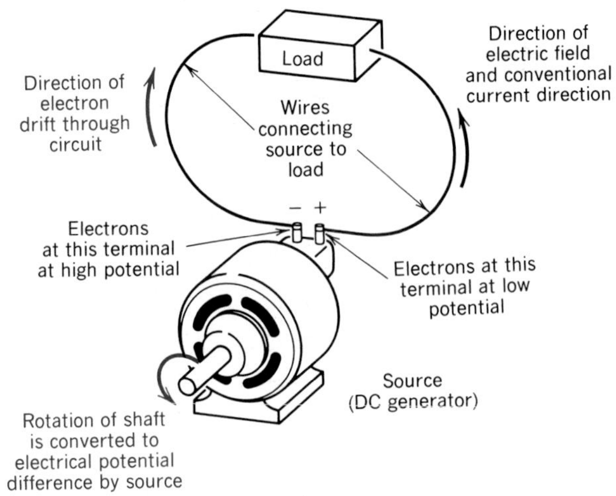

Figure 3.5 A true source uses some sort of energy to maintain a potential difference between its terminals.

hand, the number of electrons will decrease, and since the potential difference between the two spheres is becoming smaller, the amount of work that is done in the load drops quickly.

Most of the work that we want to have done by electrical energy has to be done over a period of time, and so a static electric charge on a sphere that does not sustain a potential difference between two points in a closed circuit cannot operate as a source.

A true source operates as shown in Figure 3.5. It uses some sort of energy to maintain a potential difference across its terminals. That is, an electron at one of its terminals will have a higher potential than an electron at the other terminal. If a closed circuit is connected between the terminals, low-potential electrons will drift into the terminal marked with the plus sign and will be raised to a higher potential level by the energy utilized by the source and reinjected into the circuit through the source terminal marked with the minus sign.

B.2 FUNCTIONS OF A LOAD

A closed circuit like that of Figure 3.6 consists of a source, a load, and a path through which the electrons can travel from the source to the load and back to the source. In some applications, the path is considered to be a part of the load, although this is generally more common in the field of electric power distribution than in electronics. This is because most of the potential energy supplied by the source is utilized in the load in electronic equipment. Very little of this energy is lost or used in other parts of the circuit. In the field of electric power distribution, the path between source

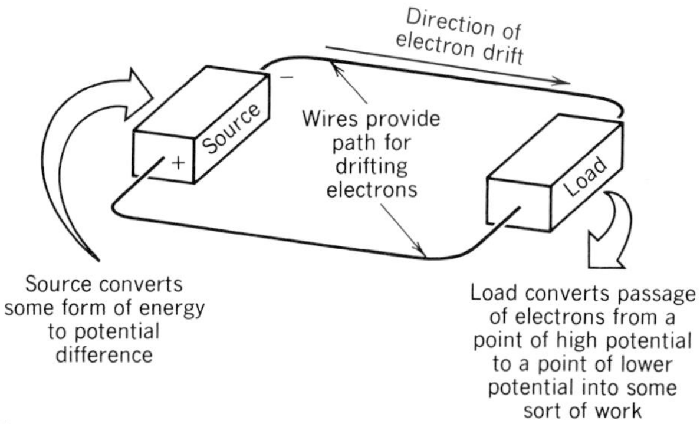

Figure 3.6 A closed circuit consists of a source, a load, and a path through which electrons can travel from the source to the load and back to the source.

and load tends to be long, and a fair amount of the potential energy of the drifting electrons is consumed in the path rather than in the load.

Among the more common loads are those that convert the potential energy of drifting electrons to heat, light, and mechanical force. Although these loads are constructed and operate in different ways, all have the common characteristic of requiring a continued supply of energy from the drift of electrons.

B.3 DEFINITION OF THE AMPERE

Since the steady drift of electrons through a circuit is important to the proper operation of many load devices, a measure of the current, or drift of electrons past a point in the circuit, is one of the vital pieces of information you need to know about a circuit. If the number of charge carriers drifting past a point in a circuit is fairly constant, the drift or flow is symbolized by the capital letter I. If you are interested in the flow at only one instant of time, with the implication that the number of electrons passing a point in the circuit changes in some way, the lowercase letter i is used. The symbol I represents the *current,* or *steady-state current,* while i is referred to as the *instantaneous value* of the current at some point in time.

Regardless of which value is referred to, steady state or instantaneous, the current is measured in *amperes*. One ampere signifies a drift or flow of 6.25×10^{18} electrons past a point in a circuit in one second. Since one coulomb is the same as the charge on 6.25×10^{18} electrons, one could say that there is a current of one ampere or, as it is usually abbreviated, 1 A, in a circuit in which one coulomb of charge passes a point each second. The abbreviation Amp or AMP is also used. If twice the number of electrons, that is, 12.50×10^{18}, passes through a point in a second, the current I in the circuit is 2 A.

The relationship between the current in a circuit, the charge in coulombs passing through a point, and the amount of time it takes for that charge to pass can be written in a form that is easy to remember and more useful than a statement in words. This form is called a *mathematical formula* or *an equation*. The formula showing the relationship among the quantities of current, charge, and time is written like this:

$$I_{(\text{amperes})} = \frac{Q_{(\text{coulombs})}}{t_{(\text{seconds})}} \qquad \text{FORMULA 3.1}$$

This means that the current I through a circuit is equal to the charge Q passing a point divided by the time t that it takes the charge to pass the point.

EXAMPLE:
A charge of 3 C passes through a point in the circuit shown in Figure 3.6 in 2 s. What is the current in the circuit? ■

SOLUTION:
Since you know the charge Q passing a point and the time that it takes, you can calculate the current in the circuit using Formula 3.1.

a. First write the formula,

$$I_{(\text{amperes})} = \frac{Q_{(\text{coulombs})}}{t_{(\text{seconds})}}$$

b. Next substitute the values that you know for the letters that represent these values,

$$I_{(\text{amperes})} = \frac{3}{2}$$

c. Perform the indicated arithmetic,

$$I_{(\text{amperes})} = 1.5$$

d. Assign the correct unit to the answer,

$$I = 1.5 \text{ A}$$ ■

Using the methods of algebra introduced in Chapters 4 and 5, it is possible to write Formula 3.1 in two additional ways. Using these formulas sometimes makes it easier to solve problems. The forms are:

$$Q = It \qquad \text{FORMULA 3.2}$$

and

$$t = \frac{Q}{I} \qquad \text{FORMULA 3.3}$$

Remember that these are rearrangements of Formula 3.1, and the letter symbols represent the same quantities they did in that formula.

EXAMPLE:
A current I of 2.5 A flows through a circuit for 8 s. What quantity of charge passes through a point in the circuit during that time? ■

SOLUTION:
This problem gives both the circuit current and the time during which this current flows. The unknown quantity, that is, the quantity you are asked to calculate, is Q, the amount of charge that passes through a point in the circuit. Formula 3.2, in which the unknown quantity Q appears alone on the left side of the equals sign, is the easiest to use.

a. Write the formula

$$Q_{\text{(coulombs)}} = I_{\text{(amperes)}} t_{\text{(seconds)}}$$

b. Remember that It means I *times* t, and substitute the known values in the formula:

$$Q_{\text{(coulombs)}} = 2.5 \times 8$$

c. Perform the arithmetic and assign the correct unit to the answer:

$$Q = 20 \text{ C}$$ ■

B.4 CURRENT DIRECTION, ELECTRIC FIELD DIRECTION, AND DIRECT CURRENT

Formula 3.1 enables you to calculate the size of the current in a circuit, but it says nothing about which way the charge carriers are drifting. This is important in electronics, for some circuits have more than one source in them, and it is not always easy to see which is the direction of the current. Quantities like current, which have both a magnitude and a direction assigned to them, are called *vector quantities*. Force is also a vector quantity.

Two things are always true about the direction of electron drift in a closed circuit. The first is that the electrons will always tend to drift along lines of force, in the direction opposite to that shown by the arrowheads on the lines of force that map the field. Remember that the arrowheads are drawn to show the direction of the force on a positive charge carrier, not on an electron. The second fact is that an electron in the circuit outside the source will tend to drift from a point of high potential to a point of lower potential.

The direction of the electric field in a particular circuit depends on the source, as does the direction of the current. Some sources keep the direction of the field in the circuit constant. A source of this type is called a *direct current source*, or *dc source*, to distinguish it from sources that change the direction of the field. You will study such more complex sources later in this book. For now, however, it is easier to visualize the effects of current if only dc sources are considered.

B.5 MEASURING CURRENT: DEVICES AND METHODS

Since the current through a circuit is so important, the devices and methods used for measuring it require careful attention. Roughly speaking, nearly all the measurement devices used in electricity and electronics are called *meters*. A device that measures only current is called an *ammeter*, a combination of the words ampere and meter. Meters able to measure more than one quantity are called *multimeters*.

Figure 3.7 is representative of a large class of ammeters. These meters are electromechanical devices that draw the energy they require to function from the circuit whose current is being measured. This kind of meter is frequently built into a unit, so that the current in a particular circuit may be constantly monitored. Further, this meter belongs to the group called *analog*

Figure 3.7 A typical ammeter. This is an analog meter and is designed to be built into the front panel of an electronic unit. (Photo by M. Hermes.)

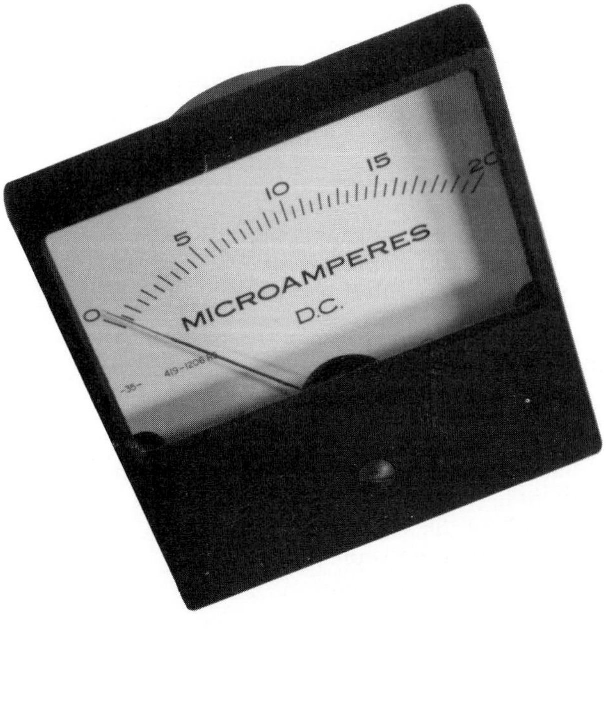

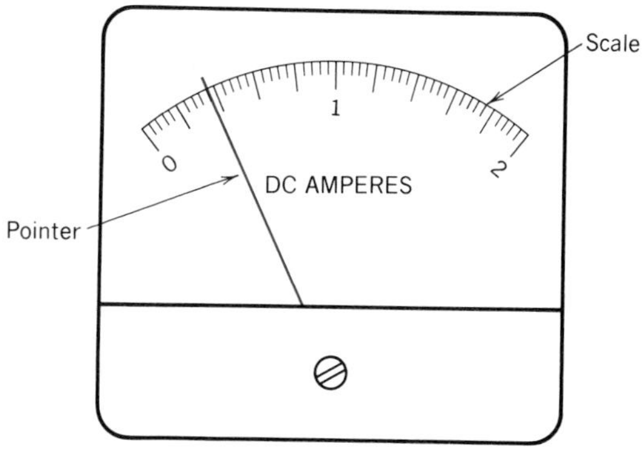

Figure 3.8 The pointer and scale of an analog meter.

meters. In an analog meter, a pointer is made to move over a scale, as seen in Figure 3.8. The distance that the pointer moves from its zero position, technically referred to as the *deflection* of the pointer, is proportional to the amount of current through the meter. The greater the current, the greater will be the deflection of the pointer. The scale enables the deflection to be read with a fair amount of accuracy. For example, the meter in Figure 3.8 shows a reading of about 0.36 A.

Ammeters of this kind are limited in that they accurately measure current only in a specific range of values. The meter in Figure 3.8 could not be used to measure a current of 20 A, for example, and might easily be destroyed if that much current were allowed to flow through it. The *range* of this meter is 0 to 2 A, and the meter should not be required to measure currents higher than 2 A.

This particular meter is not practical for measuring small currents, either. For example, a current of 0.001 A or 1 mA would cause scarcely any pointer deflection. For such small currents, an ammeter with a range of 0 to 1 mA or, better still, 0 to 10 mA would be used. Meters with current ranges in the milliampere range are called *milliammeters*. *Microammeters*, measuring currents as small as one-millionth of an ampere, are common.

Regardless of its range limitations, however, the analog ammeter is still a relatively inexpensive and accurate way to measure currents within a specific range. Table 3.1 gives the ranges of some commercially available meters. Ammeters with ranges greater than 100 A are usually not available as "off-the-shelf" items. They are made up from meters with lower ranges by means of a range multiplier called a *shunt*.

The analog ammeter, like almost all of the dc ammeters used today, measures current in a circuit only when it is acutally inserted into the circuit. Figure 3.9 shows how a circuit is broken and an ammeter is inserted between the source and the load in one part of the path. It does not matter where this kind of simple

Table 3.1 Ranges of Some Commercially Available DC Ammeters

Type	*Range*
Microammeters	0–10 μA
	0–25
	0–50
	0–100
	0–200
Milliameters	0–1 mA
	0–3
	0–5
	0–10
	0–15
	0–20
	0–25
	0–100
	0–200
	0–250
	0–300
	0–500
Ammeters	0–1 A
	0–1.5
	0–2
	0–3
	0–5
	0–10
	0–15
	0–25
	0–30
	0–50
	0–100

Figure 3.9 In current measurements, the ammeter is inserted into the circuit.

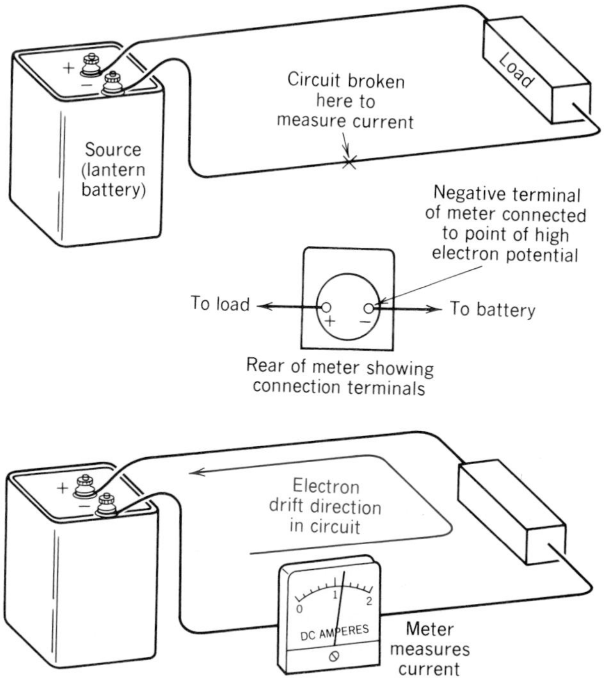

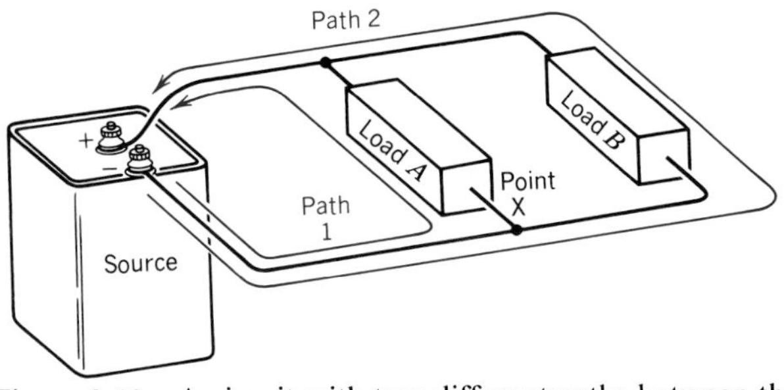

Figure 3.10 A circuit with two different paths between the two terminals of the source.

circuit is broken and the ammeter is put because the electron drift is the same in every part of the circuit. This is not always true, however. Compare the circuits shown in Figures 3.9 and 3.10. In Figure 3.10 there are actually two different paths from the negative terminal of the source, where the electrons enter the circuit, to the positive terminal, marked with a plus sign, where the electrons reenter the source. One path goes through load A, while the second path goes through load B. If the ammeter is placed at point X in the circuit, it would only measure the current through load A.

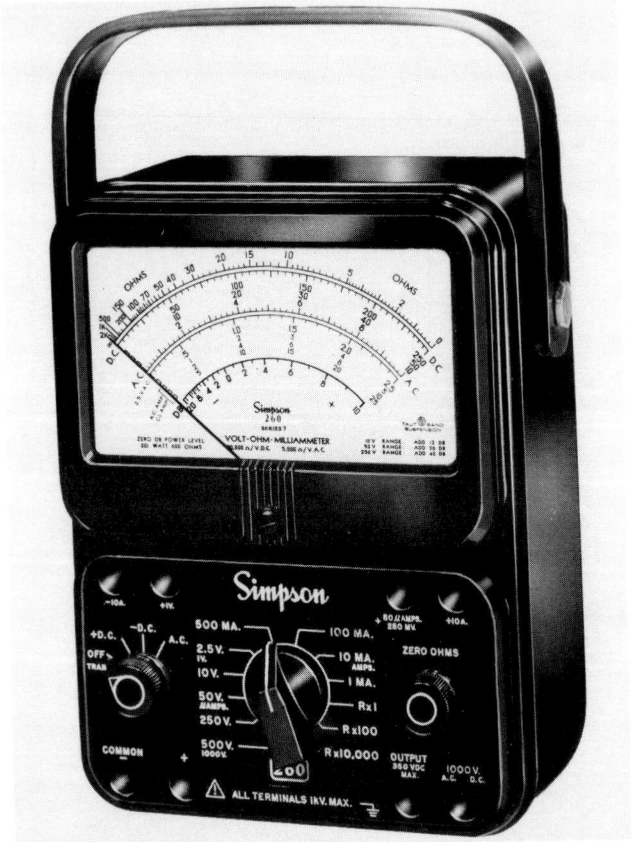

Figure 3.11 A multimeter (an analog VOM). (Photo courtesy of Simpson Electric Co.)

Since it would be inconvenient for a technician to carry a collection of ammeters about, a device called a *multimeter* was invented. In the multimeter, a switch enables the user to select the range of current that is going to be measured. The meter face is supplied with several scales, as seen in Figure 3.11, which correspond to different range selector switch settings. In almost all cases, this kind of multimeter can be used to measure current and other electrical quantities. There are a number of related devices that resemble the one shown in Figure 3.11, and it is sometimes difficult to distinguish one from another. With the one pictured here, called a *VOM,* or *volt-ohmmeter,* measurements of current and potential difference can both be made. There is a source of electric power in the device, but this source is *not* used for current or potential difference measurements. The VOM is used in the same way as the ammeter. That is, the circuit in which the current is to be measured is broken at a point, and the meter is inserted in the circuit by means of test leads.

One of the two test leads used for multimeter connections shown in Figure 3.12 is red and the other black. One end of each lead has a plug designed to fit into a jack on the multimeter, the other end has some sort of probe or gripper for connecting to the circuit being measured. When using a VOM, ammeter, or any sort of analog multimeter, it is important to hook the meter up correctly. That is, the meter pointer must deflect in the proper direction (up the scale). If the meter is connected incorrectly, damage can result. The pointer could be bent, or the meter itself could burn out. This is why meter leads are red and black. The red lead is conventionally plugged into the meter jack marked with a plus sign or a red marking, and the black lead goes to the jack marked with a minus sign, the word *COMMON*, or a black marking. When used to measure current, it is important that the electron drift

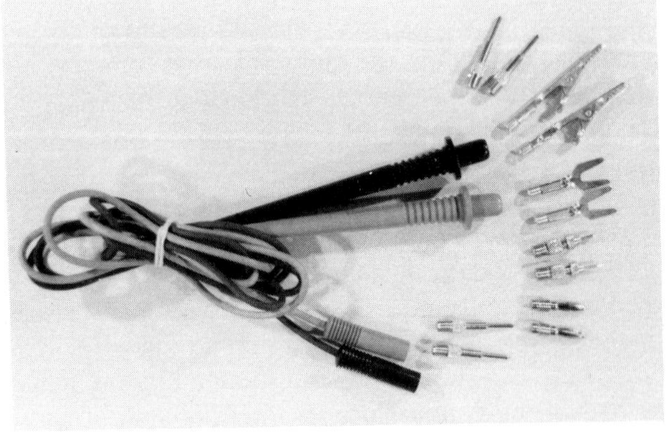

Figure 3.12 Multimeter test leads can have a variety of probes and clips for making connections to circuits. (Photo by M. Hermes.)

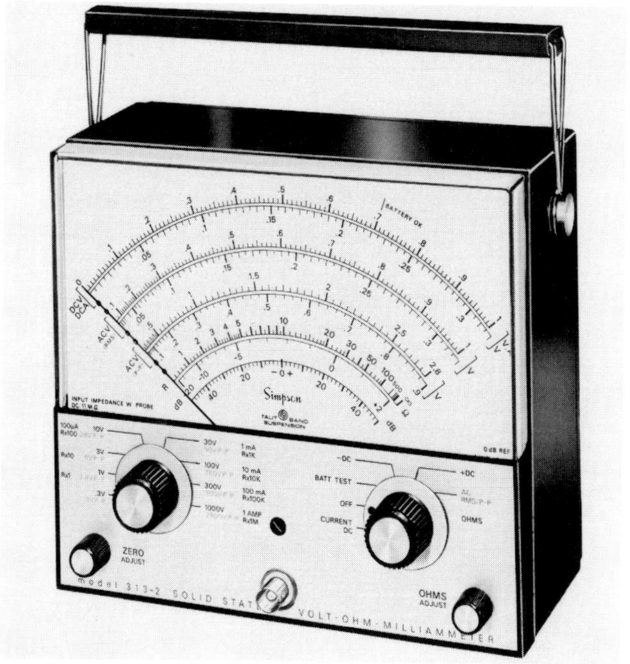

Figure 3.13 A typical EVM (electronic voltmeter), actually a multimeter. (Photo courtesy of Simpson Electric Co.)

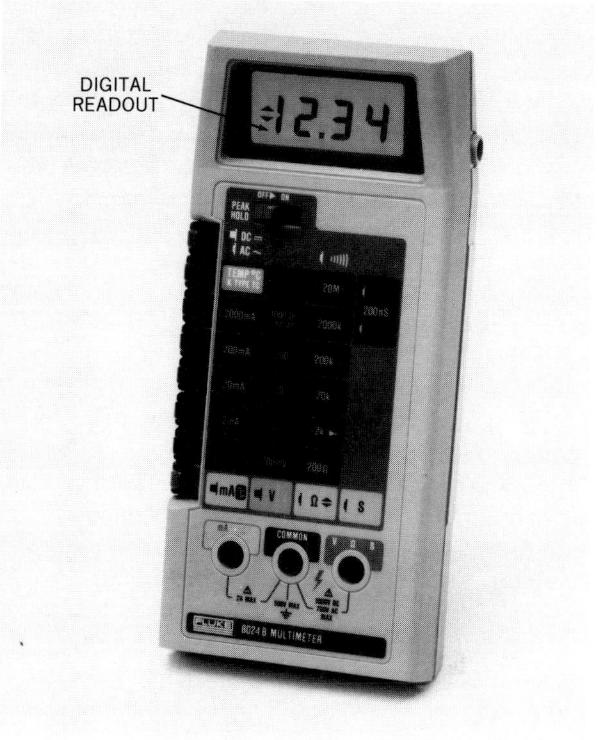

Figure 3.14 A digital multimeter is not built around an analog meter. (Reproduced with permission of the John Fluke Mfg. Co., Inc.)

enters the meter through the black lead and *leaves* it through the red lead.

A third type of current-measuring device includes the meter shown in Figure 3.13. This type has various names, such as TVM (transistor voltmeter), but the most general term is EVM, electronic voltmeter. Many of these devices are multimeters. These devices all have one thing in common that distinguishes them from a VOM. All EVMs use some sort of electric power, whether from an internal source or from the mains, in order to operate. This is in addition to the power they draw from the circuit being measured. As in the case of the VOM, the EVM is used by breaking the circuit and connecting the meter leads correctly. Most EVMs, however, contain components to provide some protection in case of improper connection of the meter leads.

Figure 3.14 illustrates a fourth kind of current-measuring device. Unlike the other three, these *digital multimeters,* or DMMs, are not built around an analog meter. Instead of the deflection of a pointer, the numerical value of the quantity being measured is displayed in the same way in which numbers are displayed on a calculator. The digital multimeter seen in Figure 3.14, like the VOM, is designed to be completely portable and uses an internal source as shown in Figure 3.15. Note that in some units, the selector switches have been replaced by pushbuttons along the side of the meter. Some technicians prefer this arrangement since it makes it possible to hold and operate the device with one hand.

You will have to learn to operate all the various types of meters and understand the applications, advantages, and disadvantages of each kind.

One of the things you will have to learn, particularly when using any kind of analog meter, is how to recognize and avoid subjecting your meter to an overload condition, that is, attempting to measure a current

Figure 3.15 A hand-held DMM is powered by an internal battery. (Photo by M. Hermes.)

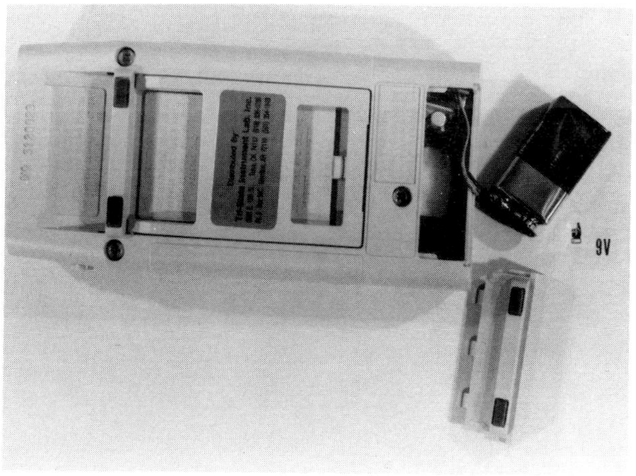

or voltage beyond the range or setting of the meter. Most problems occur when measuring current. For example, a milliammeter with a 0- to 10-mA range or a VOM set to this range is placed in a circuit with a circuit current of 1 A. The result is awful. The pointer slams into a stop at the right end of the scale, bending badly and sometimes breaking. If there is no internal protection for the meter, it will probably also burn out. With a digital meter, an OR (overrange) indication may appear on the display, or if the overload is severe enough (and this is easy to produce if you are not careful), a fuse inside the meter may be disabled. The only way to prevent such things from happening is to calculate, or at least estimate, the circuit current *before* connecting your meter. If the calculated current is well within the range of your meter and you are using any sort of multimeter, be sure to set the meter to the highest available current range before connecting it to the circuit. Also be sure that the current path between the terminals of the source includes some load other than the meter. If the range setting is too high, the indication will be very low or the pointer deflection will be small. In this case, it is easy to select the next lower meter range. Finally, be sure that analog meters are connected so that the pointer will deflect up the scale.

Figure 3.16 is a step-by-step flow diagram for making current measurements using a typical multimeter. If your meter is an *autoranging* model and selects its own range setting, ignore the range-setting steps in the diagram. It is important to follow the steps in order from the START block at the top of the page to the bottom, following the flow arrows. A rectangle contains a particular step, while a diamond represents a choice. A choice means that there are two or more ways to proceed, depending on your answer to the question in the diamond. Follow only the path that corresponds to your answer.

B.6 MEASURING POTENTIAL DIFFERENCE: DEVICES AND METHODS

In addition to measuring the current through a circuit, it is frequently necessary to measure the potential difference between two circuit points, for example, the potential difference between the two terminals of a source. Potential difference is symbolized by the capital letter E when the potential difference is fairly constant over a period of time. As in the case of current, a lowercase letter, e for potential difference, is used

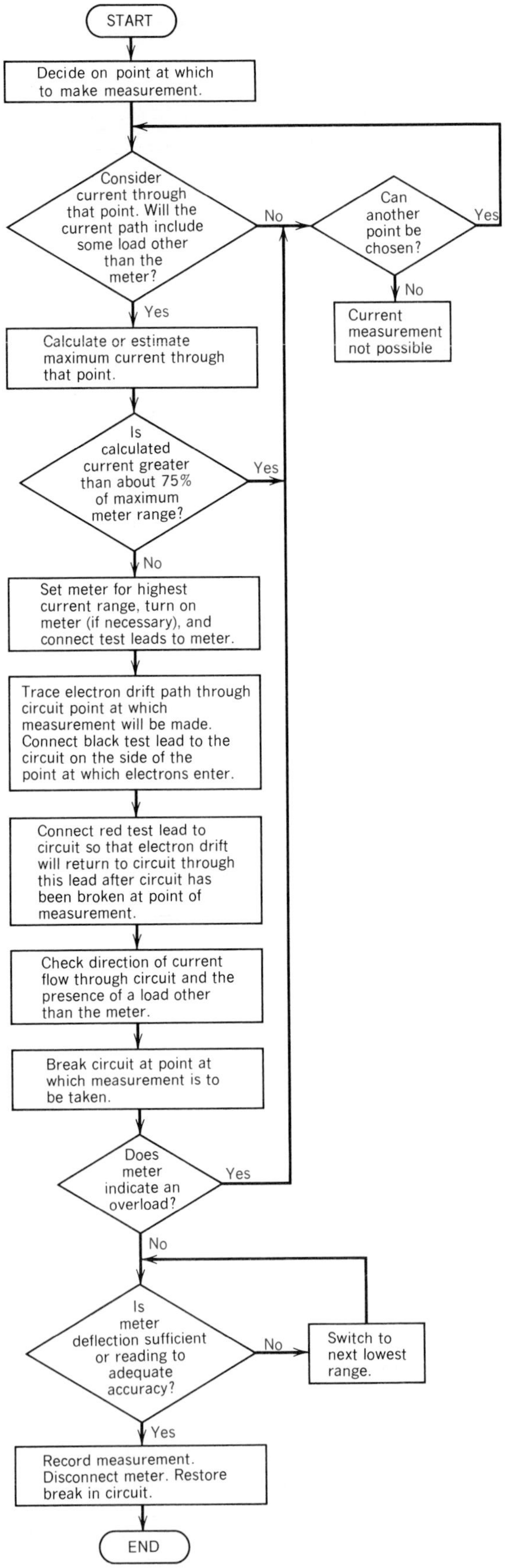

Figure 3.16 Flow diagram for making current measurements using a multimeter.

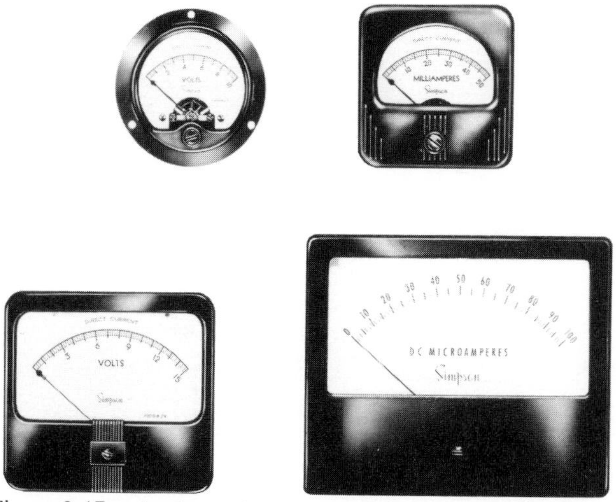

Figure 3.17 Analog voltmeters closely resemble analog ammeters in form. (Photo courtesy of Simpson Electric Co.)

to represent the instantaneous value of a changing quantity. Sometimes you will see the letter *V* used to represent potential or potential difference.

Potential difference is measured in volts. The volt, like the ampere, is named after a pioneer in the study of electricity, in this case Alessandro Volta (1745–1827), an Italian experimenter who built an early practical current source. The volt in the meter-kilogram-second (mks) system is theoretically defined in terms of work and charge. For the moment, it is sufficient to point out that potential difference measurements are the most important and easily made in the process of troubleshooting. All the multimeters described in Section B.5 also perform potential difference or voltage measurements. In fact, an older form of multimeter, the VTVM (vacuum tube voltmeter), which is now considered obsolete, made voltage measurements but was not equipped to make current measurements. Simple analog voltmeters (Figure 3.17) closely resemble analog ammeters. In point of fact, they *are* ammeters to which an additional component has been added. The principal difference between current- and voltage-measuring devices lies in how they are used. Current in a circuit is usually measured by breaking the circuit and connecting the meter so that the electron drift takes place through it. This is often inconvenient, so much so that certain current-measuring devices use methods to eliminate the need for breaking the circuit.

By comparison, potential difference measurements are easy to make. Since voltage, or potential difference, is actually a comparison of the difference in energy of charge carriers at different points, all that is necessary is to connect the two terminals of the voltmeter or the two leads of the multimeter to the two points whose potential difference is required.

Table 3.2 Ranges of Some Commercially Available Voltmeters

Type	*Range*
Voltmeters	0–1 v
	0–2
	0–5
	0–10
	0–15
	0–25
	0–30
	0–50
	0–100
	0–300
	0–500

When voltage measurements are made with an analog voltmeter, VOM, or EVM, it is necessary to connect the meter so that the pointer will deflect up the scale, as in the case of current measurements. This is done by connecting the black test lead, or minus terminal, of the meter to the point at which the electrons will have greater potential energy. The red test lead, or plus terminal, may then be connected to the second point on the circuit. The potential difference between the two points can be read on the meter.

When using an analog voltmeter to measure potential, it is important to select a meter whose operating range is correct for the measurements intended. Microvoltmeters and millivoltmeters are generally not commercially available, as shown in Table 3.2, but are made up using microammeters or milliammeters.

As in the case of current measurement, you will have to learn to avoid subjecting your meter to an overload condition when making potential difference measurements. This is somewhat easier to do than in the case of current measurements. First, the potential difference supplied by the source in a circuit is generally known. Only certain circuits contain points with potential differences greater than that provided by their source or sources. These circuits are not difficult to recognize. Second, even inexpensive multimeters possess high-voltage ranges. Ranges that measure up to 1000 or 1500 V are typical. The majority of the electrical and electronic units in operation today operate on potential differences well below these levels.

Still, it is wise to set your meter to its highest range before connecting it to the circuit. You can switch to a lower range if necessary. Note that the overload and wrong range indications are the same as for current measurement. There are fewer protective devices for overload conditions during voltage measurement than there are for current measurement, so be careful at all times. Figure 3.18 is a flow diagram for measuring potential difference.

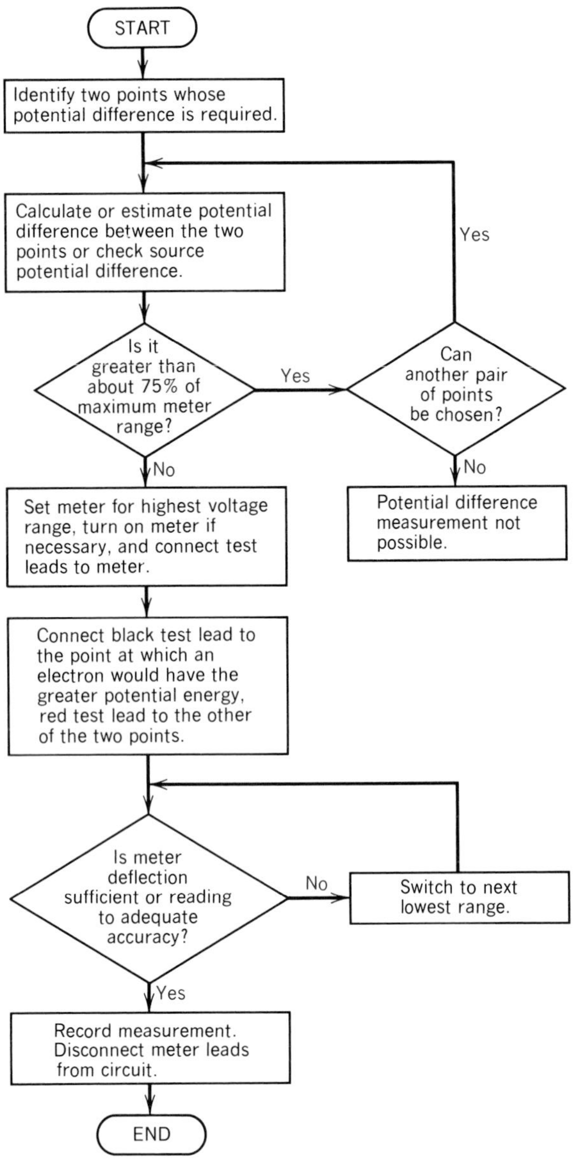

Figure 3.18 Flow diagram for making voltage measurements.

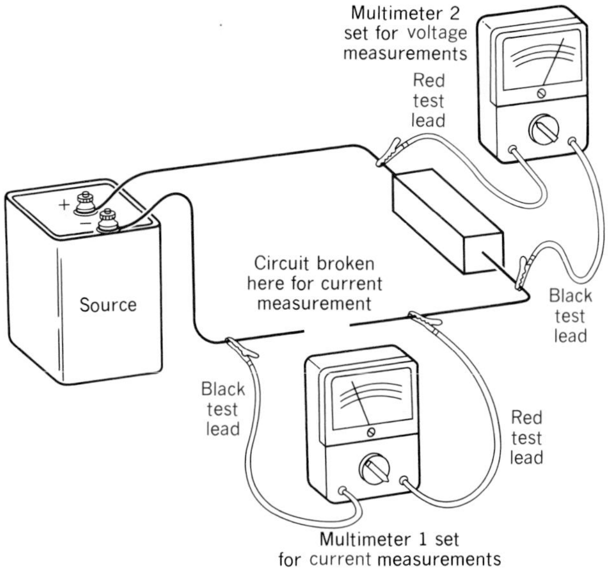

Figure 3.19 A circuit with both a voltmeter and an ammeter connected.

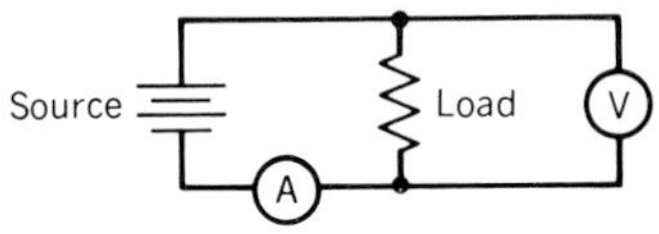

Figure 3.20 The schematic diagram of the circuit shown in Figure 3.19.

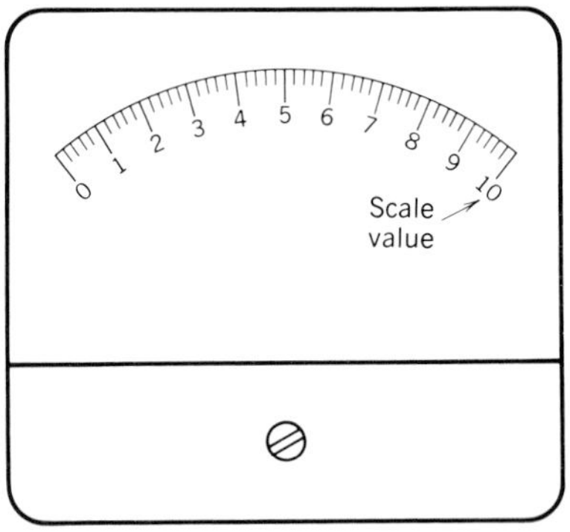

Figure 3.21 A simple analog scale. Each scale line corresponds to a single value.

Figure 3.19 shows a circuit with both an ammeter and a voltmeter connected. This same arrangement is shown in a symbolic form called a *schematic diagram* in Figure 3.20. Schematics are easier to draw and to follow than the diagrams used to this point, and you will learn to use them as your work progresses.

B.7 READING ANALOG MULTIMETER SCALES

Reading analog meter scales is something that has to be learned, like telling time on a watch with a mechanical movement, even though continuing progress suggests that digital displays will replace most analog devices in the not too distant future. Analog scales may be simple, like that shown in Figure 3.21, or multiple, as in Figure 3.22. Simple scales are used on all single-range meters and on some meters that have a range selector that operates by selecting multipliers for the scale on the meter. For example, in Figure 3.23, the meter pointer is on 2 and the range selector is turned to $V \times 10$. This then represents a measurement of 20 V.

Multiple scales can be confusing, even when the range selector switch indicates which of the scales or ranges is selected at the moment. The scale selected

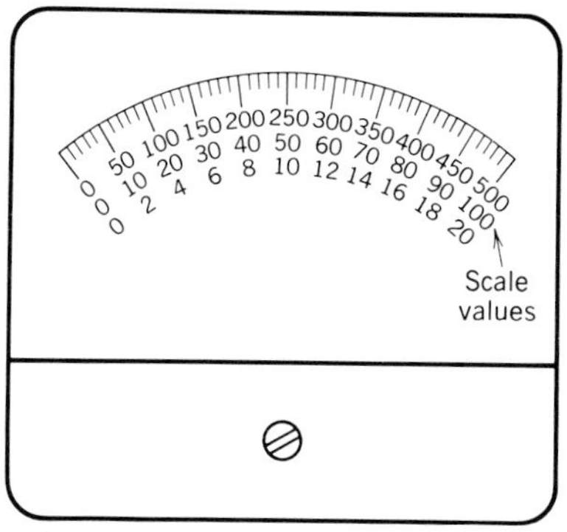

Figure 3.22 A multiple scale. The value of each scale line depends on the setting of the range selector.

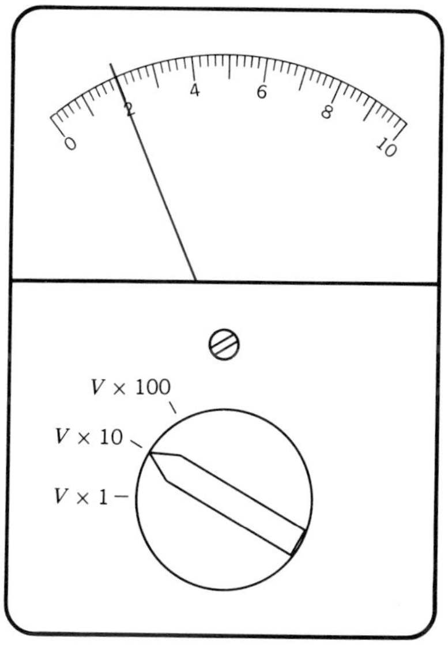

Figure 3.23 A simple scale with a multiplier range selector. This reading is 20 V.

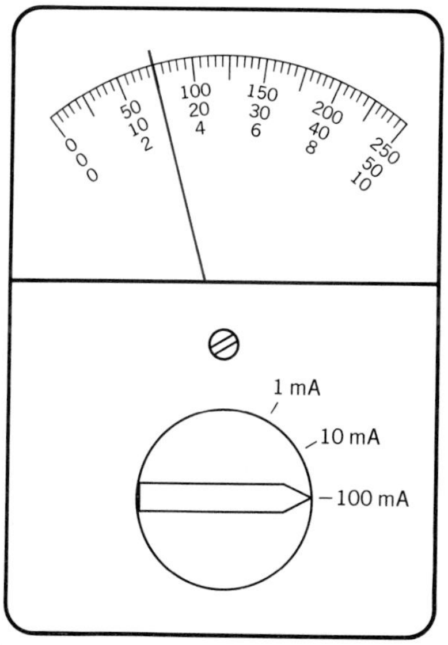

Figure 3.24 The scale selected is 10 times 0 to 10, so 30 mA is indicated.

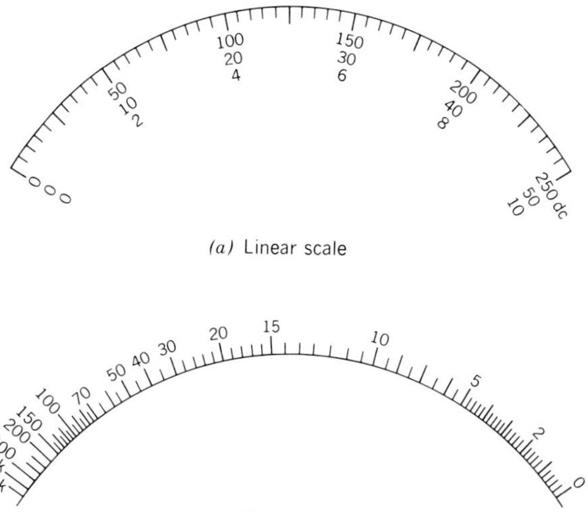

(a) Linear scale

(b) Nonlinear scale

Figure 3.25 Two types of scales.

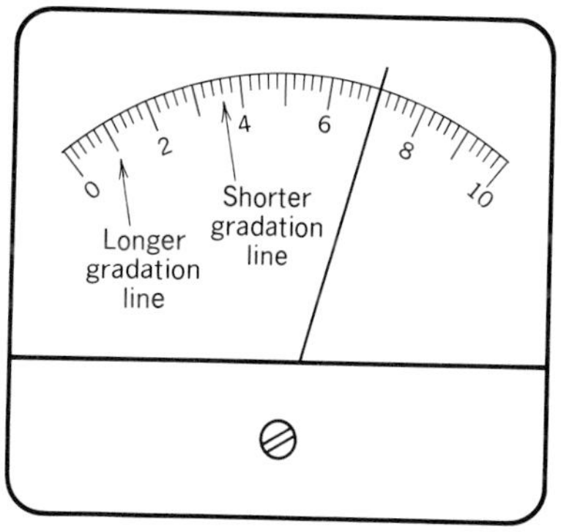

Figure 3.26 This scale has two types of gradation lines.

in Figure 3.24 is 10 times 0 to 10, so the indication is 30 mA.

Another feature that makes meter scales hard to read is that there are two types. In the first type, shown in Figure 3.25*a*, referred to as *linear,* the scale divisions are equally spaced. There are four smaller lines of equal length between each of the longer divisions. This is not true, however, of the nonlinear scale seen in Figure 3.25*b*. Here, the spacing between 0 and 15 occupies half the scale, while the indications from 15 through 2K (2000) are crowded into nearly all the other half. Only a tiny space at the extreme left of the scale remains for indications from 2000 to infinity. As strange as it looks, this is a common scale found on VOMs.

Determining what a particular pointer deflection actually means can be a problem, especially if the meter uses multiple scales. The first thing to do is to determine which scale is actually selected by the range selector or to note the multiplier if the scale is a multiplier type. The next thing to do is to determine the kinds and number of the division lines on the scale. On the 0- to 10-V scale in Figure 3.26, there are two

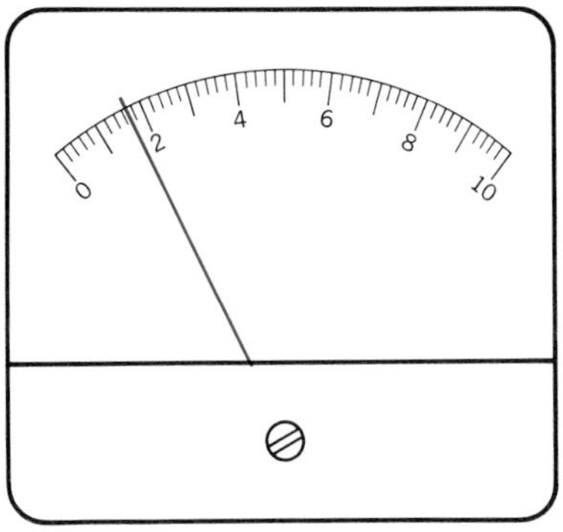

Figure 3.27 The total deflection of the pointer is 1.6.

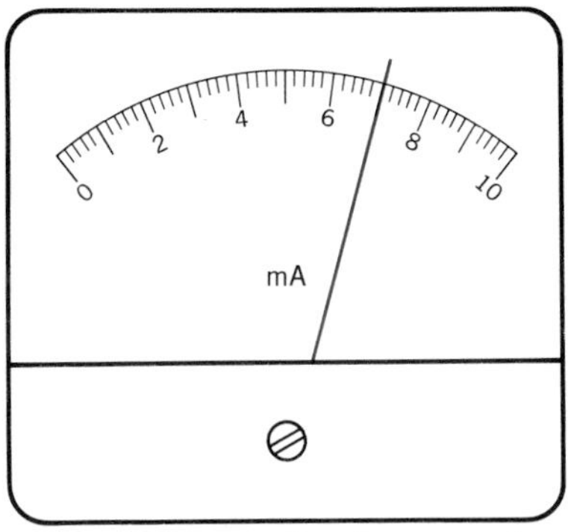

Figure 3.29 Milliameter reading for example.

line lengths, longer and shorter. The second longer division line from the left is labeled 2, the fourth 4, and so on. This indicates that the value of *each* longer division line, counting from zero at the left, is 1. The pointer reading in Figure 3.26 is therefore 7. Four shorter lines divide the space between each longer division line into five parts. Each part, then, is $\frac{1}{5}$, or 0.2. The total deflection of the pointer in Figure 3.27 is 1.6. That is, one long division line, valued at 1, plus three shorter lines, each valued at 0.2. As a check, you can count all the spaces between division lines of any size between 0 and the pointer. There are eight of them:

$$8 \times 0.2 = 1.6$$

The 0-to-250 scale in Figure 3.28, on the other hand, assigns another value to the spaces between the dividing lines. Counting the spaces between 0 and 50,

Figure 3.28 The 250-V scale assigns a value of 5 to each of the small divisions.

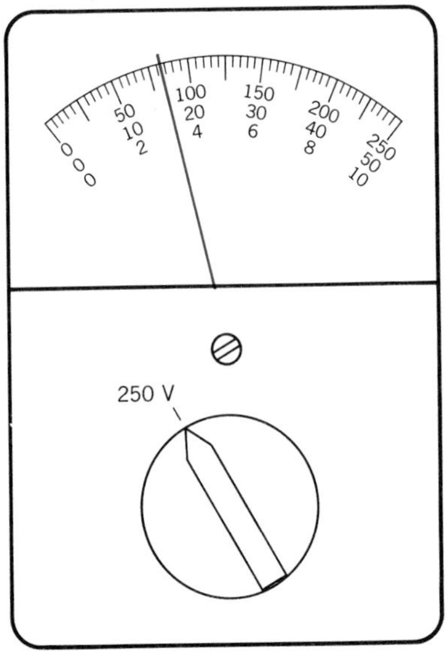

you see that there are 10. Each one represents a deflection of $\frac{50}{10}$, or 5. The pointer in Figure 3.28 indicates 80, since the 0-to-250 range is selected. On some meters, it is possible to estimate when the pointer is halfway, a quarter of the way, or three quarters of the way between the lines.

EXAMPLE:
What is the reading of the analog multimeter in Figure 3.29? ■

SOLUTION:
Each of the longer division lines represents a value of 1 mA, and each shorter line represents a value of 0.2 mA. The pointer has deflected through six longer lines, four shorter ones, and about half of a fifth. The indication is

$$(6 \times 1) + (4 \times 0.2) + \left(\frac{1}{2} \times 0.2\right) = 6.9 \text{ mA} \quad ■$$

There are two additional points that will help you to read meters accurately. Both these points involve the position of the meter. First, it is a good idea to keep the meter either standing upright or lying on its back during a series of measurements. Changing the position of the meter may change the deflection slightly, especially when a relatively massive pointer is used in the meter. It certainly will change the position of your eyes with respect to the meter. The position of your eyes is the second point of importance in reading a meter. If you are to one side or the other of the meter face, an error called *parallax error* will result. This is shown in Figure 3.30 and occurs because there is an appreciable distance between the pointer and the scale card. The figure is a top view of a person looking at an exaggeratedly large meter. You can see that the

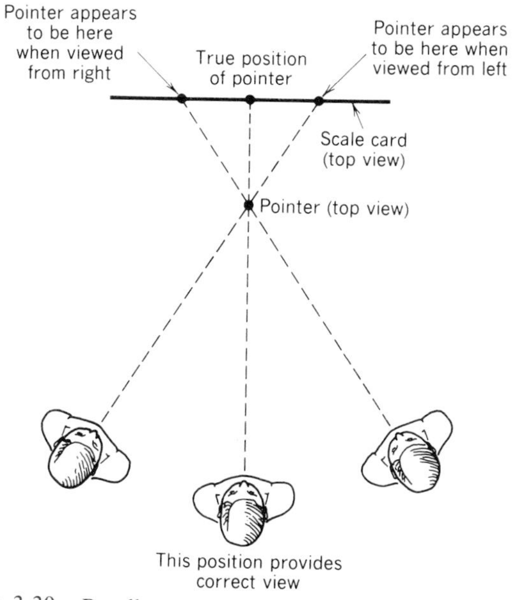

Figure 3.30 Parallax error occurs because there is a distance between the pointer and the scale card.

position of the pointer is only seen properly when the head is directly in front of the meter. Better quality multimeters reduce parallax error by mounting an arc-shaped mirror segment on the scale, as shown in Figure 3.31. If the person viewing this type of scale sees two pointers, the real pointer and the image in the mirror, it means that the head is off to one side. Moving the head so that only the pointer itself is seen and the mirror image is hidden by the pointer indicates that the scale is being viewed properly, and no parallax error exists.

Practice your skill by interpreting the meter deflections shown in Figure 3.32 (page 56).

Figure 3.31 An arc-shaped mirror segment shows when parallax error exists.

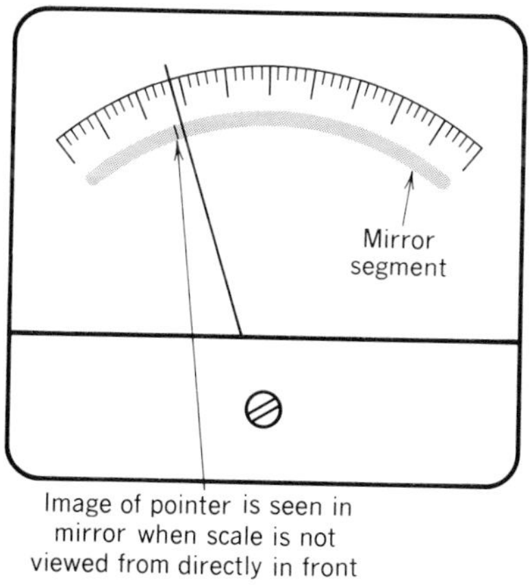

C. EXAMPLES AND COMPUTATIONS

C.1 REVIEW OF THE METRIC SYSTEM AND METRIC PREFIXES

In Chapter 2, you began a study of the metric system and metric prefixes, which are used along with engineering notation to express very large and very small quantities. Table 3.3 repeats the commonly used metric prefixes introduced in the last chapter. Table 3.4 lists some of the metric units frequently used in electronics. You are probably familiar with the meter as a measurement of distance, but there may be some confusion with the use of the kilogram as the unit of mass if you are not familiar with the difference between the metric, or SI, system and the U.S. Customary Units. In the U.S. Customary System, there is no unit of mass. The familiar unit, the pound, is really a measurement of force. Since the grocer is measuring the force that a sack of potatoes exerts on a scale, there is nothing wrong with the use of a force unit instead of a mass unit in daily life. For scientific purposes, however, it is better to separate the concepts of mass and force. For this reason, the kilogram is the unit of mass in the mks system used today in science and engineering, while the unit of force is the newton, the amount of force exerted by a one-kilogram mass on the surface of the Earth. Work, or energy, which is the capacity to do work is measured in foot-pounds in the U.S. Customary System. In the metric system, it is measured in newton-meters or joules. You will remember from Chapter 1 that work is defined as a force operating through a distance. Therefore, the base unit of work in the metric system is the operation of a force of one newton operating through a distance of one meter. One newton-meter is called a joule, abbreviated J.

Table 3.3 Unit Name Prefixes in the Metric System

Prefix	*Abbreviation*	*Decimal Value*	*Exponential Value*
pico-	p	0.000000000001	10^{-12}
nano-	n	0.000000001	10^{-9}
micro-	μ	0.000001	10^{-6}
milli-	m	0.001	10^{-3}
centi-	c	0.01	10^{-2}
deci-	d	0.1	10^{-1}
deka-	D	10	10^{1}
kilo-	K or k	1,000	10^{3}
mega-	M	1,000,000	10^{6}
giga-	G	1,000,000,000	10^{9}

Write the following quantities using metric prefixes in both the prefix and abbreviated forms. The first has been done as an example.

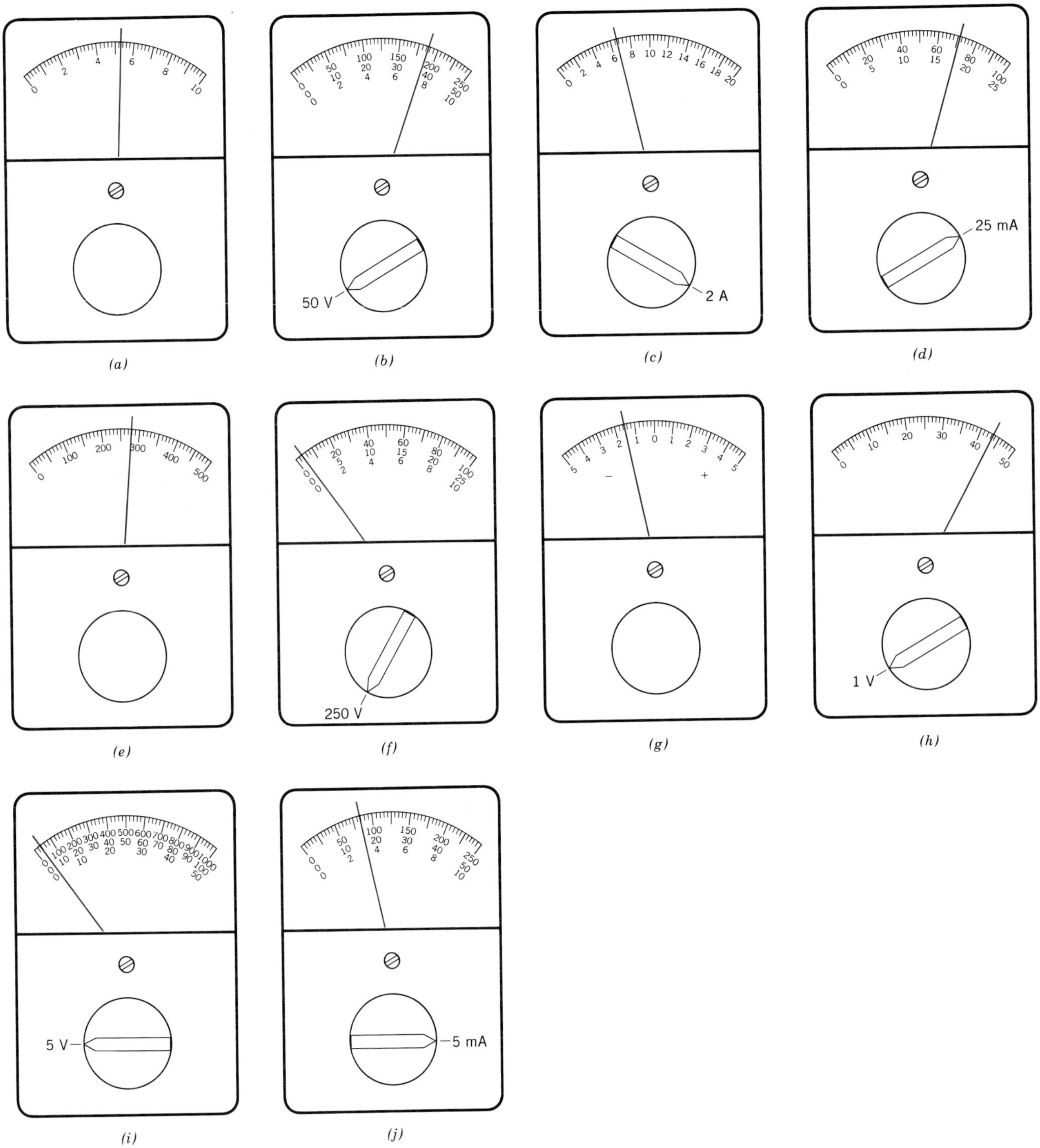

Figure 3.32 Figures for exercise.

a. 1000 volts
prefix form: 1 kilovolt
abbreviated form: 1 kV
b. 0.001 ampere
c. 3×10^{-9} seconds
d. 1,000,000 ohms
e. 0.03 meters
f. 0.015 seconds
g. 8×10^{-6} seconds
h. 1.85×10^{3} ohms
i. 0.0000033 A
j. 3500 meters
k. 6.72×10^{6} volts
l. 0.0004 amperes
m. 900 ohms
n. 450,000 watts
o. 8.85×10^{-12} seconds
p. 42×10^{-6} volt
q. 6.2×10^{4} ohms
r. 3.67×10^{-3} meter
s. 1,300,000 watts
t. 4280 ohms

C.2 ROUNDING OFF

Rounding off numbers, that is, reducing the number of significant figures for the sake of practicality and sometimes truth, is a common activity in daily life. For example, the actual distance between two points that have to be connected with a wire, if measured with a ruler, might be 200 mm. Using highly sophisticated measuring devices, you might find that the distance is actually closer to 199.9675 mm, but in most cases this increased accuracy is worthless. The difference between 200 mm and 199.9675 mm is only 0.0325 mm and is meaningless in comparison with the total length of the wire needed. In fact, the difference between the rough and accurate measurements is only 0.016 percent of the total distance. In practical electronics, decimal places representing less than about 0.1 percent of the whole number being considered are usually not important. For example, a 100-kV source may actually produce a potential difference of 100,000 + (0.001 × 100,000) or 100,100 V, without making any significant difference. This extra hundred volts would be very difficult to measure and would not affect the behavior of the source or a circuit connected to it. On the other hand, 100 V represents 10 percent of the potential difference of a 1-kV source, and this kind of difference can be measured and might well make a significant difference in the operation of a circuit. It would be correct, therefore, to round off 100,100 V to 100,000 V, or 100 kV, but it would be incorrect and misleading to round off 1100 V to 1 kV.

Since zero is used both as a place keeper and as a number in the Arabic number system, it is frequently difficult to tell which function a particular zero fulfills. In the quantity 100,000 V, for example, does the zero immediately to the right of the numeral 1 mean that the voltage is greater than 99,000, or that the zero in the ten thousands place represents an actual measurement? Unless there are other nonzero digits involved, or a decimal point is shown, there is no way of knowing. The number 100,000, therefore, is said to contain only one *significant figure* or *digit,* the number 1. A significant figure or digit is defined as a number considered to result from an accurate measurement or a mathematical computation. The five zeros to the right of the numeral 1 in 100,000 are called *trailing zeros*

Table 3.4 Metric Units Frequently Used in Electronics

Name	*Unit of*	*Abbreviation*	*Equivalent U.S. Customary Unit*
Meter	Length	m	Foot 1 foot = 0.304 meter 1 meter = 3.28 feet
Kilogram	Mass	kg	Pound 1 pound = 0.454 kilogram 1 kilogram = 2.2 pounds
Second	Time	s	Same
Volt	Potential Difference	v	Same
Ampere	Current	A	Same
Ohm	Resistance		Same
Joule	Work, energy	j	Foot-pound 1 foot-pound = 1.356 joules 1 *j* = .737 foot-pounds

and may or may not be the result of measurement or computation. In the number 240, there are two significant figures or digits and one trailing zero.

One or more zeros are considered significant figures or significant digits when they are found between two nonzero figures. For example, 9080 contains three significant digits, and 400,100 contains four. Use of decimals is another way in which zeros can be shown to be significant figures. In the number 300.0, there are four significant figures, as signaled by the use of the zero to the right of the decimal point.

In decimals less than 1, the leading zeros, that is, the zeros to the left and right of the decimal point are not considered significant digits. In the number 0.00015, there are only two significant figures, 1 and 5. A zero between two nonzero digits or zeros to the right of a nonzero digit, on the other hand, are considered significant. Thus, 0.0304 contains three significant figures, and 0.00090000 contains five.

Note that if the number or numbers to the *left* of the decimal point are not all zero, any zeros immediately to the right of the decimal point are significant. There are four significant figures in 7.007 and five in 30.004.

Practice your understanding of these ideas by stating the number of significant figures in the following numbers.

a. 370,000,000	g. 0.0013
b. 4020	h. 2.006080
c. 700.9	i. 10
d. 0.040	j. 100.0150
e. 1.001	k. 60801
f. 080	l. 1.00

The conversion from U.S. Customary Units to metric units frequently results in longer than justified decimal numbers. For example, if you convert 59.6 in. to meters by multiplying 59.6 by 0.0254, you obtain 1.51384 m as an answer. This figure contains five places to the right of the decimal point and suggests that the equipment used measured accurately to 0.00001, or 10×10^{-6} m (ten millionths of a meter). The truth of the matter was that the tape or yard stick used could only measure to the nearest tenth of an inch (59.6 in.). The closest practical conversion of inch to meter values occurs when the meter value shows two more significant figures to the right of the decimal point than the inch value. For example,

$$59.6 \text{ in.} = 1.514 \text{ m}$$

The figure 1.514 is obtained from 1.51384 by the use of round-off rules. These rules should be memorized and used without exception to give consistency to your work. Banks, computers, and math teachers have different round-off methods. The following are drawn from those recommended by the American National Standards Institute, an organization whose job it is to minimize confusion in industry by suggesting standard ways of doing or saying things.

ROUND-OFF RULE 1. When the number immediately to the right of the right-most digit or place to be kept is less than 5, the number in the right-most digit or decimal place to be retained remains unchanged.

EXAMPLES:

1.1234 rounded to three decimal places (four significant figures) is 1.123.

1.1234 rounded to two decimal places (three significant figures) is 1.12.

1.1234 rounded to one decimal place (two significant figures) is 1.1.

4321 rounded to three significant figures is 4320.

4321 rounded to two significant figures is 4300.

4321 rounded to one significant figure is 4000. ■

ROUND-OFF RULE 2. When the number immediately to the right of the right-most digit or decimal place to be kept is more than 5, the number in the right-most digit or decimal place to be kept is increased by 1.

EXAMPLES:

1.5678 rounded to three decimal places (four significant digits) is 1.568.

1.5678 rounded to two decimal places (three significant digits) is 1.57.

1.5678 rounded to one decimal place (two significant digits) is 1.6.

1567 rounded to three significant digits is 1570.

1567 rounded to two significant digits is 1600.

1567 rounded to one significant digit is 2000. ■

ROUND-OFF RULE 3. When the number immediately to the right of the right-most digit or decimal place to be kept is 5 and there are no numbers or only zeros to the right of this 5, then if the number in the right-most digit or decimal place to be kept is odd, it is increased by 1, and if it is even, it is left unchanged.

EXAMPLES:

1.15 rounds to 1.2.

1.3500 rounds to 1.4.

1.65 rounds to 1.6.

1.8500 rounds to 1.8.

27,500 rounds to 28,000.

36,500 rounds to 36,000. ■

ROUND-OFF RULE 4. If the 5 immediately to the right of the right-most digit or decimal place to be kept is followed by any numbers other than zero, the number in the right-most digit or decimal place to be kept is increased by 1 whether the number is even or odd.

EXAMPLES:

1.2501 rounds to 1.3.

1.4599 rounds to 1.5.

3501 rounds to 4000.

67,851 rounds to 67,900. ■

ROUND-OFF RULE 5. The final rounded value of a number must be obtained by rounding off the most precise value available and not from a series of successive roundings. For example, 0.5499 should be rounded off to 0.550, 0.55, or 0.5 and not to 0.6 since the most precise value available is less than 0.55.

Try rounding off the following numbers to three significant figures and to two significant figures.

a. 67.324	i. 155,000
b. 0.09443	j. 155,075
c. 1876.35	k. 25,003
d. 143.5	l. 355.55
e. 0.01343	m. 0.10941
f. 1,287,593	n. 0.00360
g. 284.50	o. 1.009
h. 399.25	p. 302.953

C.3 ADDING AND SUBTRACTING NUMBERS IN SCIENTIFIC OR ENGINEERING NOTATION

Computations in electricity and electronics frequently require the addition or subtraction of numbers that have been written in engineering or scientific notation. Of course, it is always possible to write the numbers out in normal form and perform the required operation. In fact, if the exponents are between +3 and −3, this is probably the easiest method.

EXAMPLE:
Add 1.126×10^{-2} and 628×10^{-3}. ■

SOLUTION:
Write the numbers out and add:

$$1.126 \times 10^{-2} = 0.01126$$

$$628 \times 10^{-3} = 0.628$$

$$\begin{array}{r} 0.01126 \\ +0.628 \\ \hline 0.63926 \end{array}, \text{ or } 639.26 \times 10^{-3}$$ ■

If the exponents are large, however, it is easier to add or subtract numbers by adjusting the position of the decimal point, as required, in one of the numbers to be added or subtracted until the exponents of both numbers are the same. The numbers can then be added or subtracted directly.

The key to this method is realizing that if you multiply a number by 10 and then divide it by 10, you have not changed the number at all. Moving the decimal point one place to the right in a number is the same as multiplying it by 10; moving it one place to the left is the same as dividing it by 10. Also, adding 1 (that is, +1) to the exponent of a number in engineering or scientific notation is the same as multiplying the number by 10, and subtracting 1 from the exponent is the same as dividing by 10.

EXAMPLE:
Express the number 18.35×10^{-7} as a number with an exponent of −6. ■

SOLUTION:
In order to do this, you have to add 1 to the exponent of 10^{-7}. This is the same as multiplying by 10. Therefore, if you multiply by 10, you will have to *divide* by 10 in order to keep the value the same. That is, you will have to move the decimal point one place to the left:

$$18.35 \times 10^{-7} = 1.835 \times 10^{-6}.$$ ■

EXAMPLE:
Add the numbers 1.65×10^5 and 8.36×10^3. ■

SOLUTION:
One way to solve this problem is to write 8.36×10^3 as a number with an exponent of 5, by *adding* 2 to the exponent. This means that you will also have to move

the decimal point two places to the *left* to keep the value of the number the same. Note that you have to put in an extra zero as a place keeper: $8.36 \times 10^3 = 0.0836 \times 10^5$. The two numbers may then be added normally

$$\begin{array}{r} 1.65 \quad \times 10^5 \\ +0.0836 \times 10^5 \\ \hline 1.7336 \times 10^5 \end{array}$$

This problem should be completed by making use of the rounding-off rules. Both 8.36×10^3 and 1.65×10^5 have three significant figures, so the answer 1.7336×10^5 should be rounded off to 1.73×10^5. ■

Try the following addition and subtraction problems without using a calculator. Use the rounding-off rules as necessary. Round off to as many significant figures as the least accurate of the numbers given.

a. $18.3 \times 10^5 - 1.77 \times 10^6$
b. $697 \times 10^9 + 1.25 \times 10^{12}$
c. $83 \times 10^{-3} + 1.42 \times 10^{-1}$
d. $3.008 \times 10^{-6} - 9.2 \times 10^{-8}$
e. $19293 \times 10^2 - 0.468 \times 10^3$
f. $2.7 \times 10^{-6} + 560 \times 10^{-9}$
g. $0.82 \times 10^2 - 4700 \times 10^{-3}$
h. $11.04 \times 10^{-4} + 0.91 \times 10^{-3}$
i. $63.71 \times 10^0 - 63.71 \times 10^{-2}$
j. $4700 \times 10^{-9} - 39 \times 10^{-6}$
k. $0.027 - 1.84 \times 10^{-2}$
l. $6800 \times 10^{-12} - 5.1 \times 10^{-9}$

C.4 MULTIPLYING AND DIVIDING NUMBERS IN SCIENTIFIC OR ENGINEERING NOTATION

The multiplication of two numbers in scientific or engineering notation is extremely simple if you remember one rule:

To multiply two numbers in scientific or engineering notation, multiply the significant figures together and determine the exponent of the product by adding *the exponents of the two numbers.*

EXAMPLE:
Multiply 8.37×10^3 by 1.06×10^2. ■

SOLUTION:
First multiply the significant figures together (if negative numbers are involved, watch the signs carefully):

$$\begin{array}{r} 8.37 \\ \times\ 1.06 \\ \hline 5022 \\ 000\ \\ 837\ \ \\ \hline 8.8722 \end{array}$$

Then add the exponents to determine the exponent of the product (again, pay attention to sign), $2 + 3 = 5$. The answer is 8.8722×10^5. Since both the multiplier and the multiplicand have three significant figures, the product should also be rounded off to 8.87×10^5. ■

In cases where either or both the significant figures and exponents have negative signs, extreme care must be taken to multiply or add the signed values correctly. Try the following without the use of a calculator:

a. $8.3 \times 10^2 \times 5.2 \times 10^3$
b. $21 \times 10^{-1} \times 6 \times 10^2$
c. $-36 \times 10^6 \times 8 \times 10^{-2}$
d. $14 \times 10^{12} \times 3.2 \times 10^{-3}$
e. $1.03 \times 10^3 \times -6.28 \times 10^{-3}$
f. $2.2 \times 10^{-6} \times 1.5 \times 10^{-3}$
g. $-6.3 \times 10^2 \times -2.14 \times 10^{-3}$
h. $-34.2 \times 10^4 \times 6.2 \times 10^0$
i. $-1.006 \times -4.2 \times 10^{-3}$
j. $9.91 \times 10^3 \times 2.7 \times 10^2$
k. $3.6 \times 10^{-12} \times -2.2 \times 10^6$
l. $-7.5 \times 10^{-3} \times -1.5 \times 10^{-2}$

The rule for the division of one number in scientific or engineering notation by another requires not only careful attention to sign but also that you keep track of which number is the divisor and which is the dividend:

To divide one number in scientific or engineering notation by another, first divide the significant figures portion of the dividend (the number to be divided) by the significant figures portion of the divisor (the number you are dividing by). Then determine the exponent of the quotient by subtracting *the exponent of the* divisor *from the exponent of the* dividend.

EXAMPLE:
Divide 6.24×10^3 by 2.4×10^{-2}. ■

SOLUTION:
The dividend is 6.24×10^3 and the divisor is 2.4×10^{-2}. First divide the significant figure portion of the dividend by the significant figure portion of the divisor.

```
      2.6
24.)62.4
    48
    14 4
    14 4
       0
```

Then determine the exponent of the quotient by subtracting the exponent of the divisor from the exponent of the dividend:

```
       3
(−)   −2
       5
```

The quotient is then 2.6×10^5. ■

Try the following division problems without using a calculator. Where necessary, use the rounding-off rules to round off to as many significant figures as the least accurate of the numbers given.

a. $2.074 \times 10^6 \div 3.4 \times 10^3$.
b. $2.73 \times 10^{-6} \div 2.1 \times 10^2$.
c. $38.08 \times 10^{-4} \div 5.6 \times 10^{-3}$.
d. $4.05 \times 10^3 \div -1.5 \times 10^{-1}$.
e. $18.33 \times 10^{-2} \div 4.7 \times 10^3$.
f. $9.84 \times 10^3 \div 8.2 \times 10^4$.
g. $-7.5 \times 10^{-5} \div 2.25 \times 10^{-6}$.
h. $31.28 \times 10^{-9} \div 6.8 \times 10^{-6}$.

C.5 ENGINEERING AND SCIENTIFIC NOTATION ON A CALCULATOR

Although it takes a few extra keystrokes, almost all scientific calculators are equipped to operate in scientific notation. In fact, they will switch to scientific notation automatically if the result of a calculation would result in a number that would not fit the normal eight-digit display. For example, enter 99999999 and add 1 to it. Pressing the equals sign key will display the answer 1.   08. Notice the space between the decimal point and the 08. This tells you that the number displayed is 1×10^8 and not 1.08. Now enter the number 0.0000001 and divide it by 2. Pressing the equals sign key will then display 5.   −08, or 5×10^{-8}.

In addition to this automatic conversion to scientific notation for numbers of more than eight digits or decimal places, it is possible to enter numbers into the calculator in engineering or scientific notation and to perform calculations through the use of the key [EE] or [EEX]. In order to enter a number in scientific or engineering notation, all that is necessary is to enter the significant figures, press the [EE] or [EEX] key, and enter the exponent. The [+/−] or [CHS] key may be used to enter negative exponents.

EXAMPLE:
Enter the number 245.39×10^6 into a calculator. ■

SOLUTION:

Enter the significant figures.	[2] [4] [5] [.] [3] [9]
Select scientific notation.	[EEX]
Enter the exponent.	[6]

The calculator will now display the number in engineering notation 245.39   06. This is, however, only a temporary display. The calculator will convert the displayed number to scientific notation or, if it is within the range that can be displayed, to standard form. For example, enter 245.39×10^6 as above. Now press one of function keys (+, −, ×, ÷, or =), and the display automatically shifts from 245.39   06 to 2.4539   08, which is the same number but now in scientific notation. The same changing of form takes place when decimals are keyed in. ■

EXAMPLE:
Display 3.7×10^{-2} on a calculator. ■

SOLUTION:

Enter significant digits.	[3] [.] [7]
Select scientific notation.	[EEX]
Enter exponent.	[2]
Change the sign of the exponent.	[+/−]

The calculator will now display 3.7   −02, or 3.7×10^{-2}. Once you become accustomed to these forms, they will not cause any difficulty, and you will be able to use your calculator for computations involving engineering or scientific notation. ■

One odd point in the last example is worth noting, that is, the change in the function of the [CHS] or [+/−] key after the [EE] or [EEX] key has been pressed. After the [EE] or [EEX] key has been pressed, only the sign of the exponent is affected by the [CHS] or [+/−] change sign key until one of the function keys has been pressed.

EXAMPLE:
Enter 2.456×10^{-2} and observe the function of the change sign key. ■

SOLUTION:

Enter significant digits.	[2] [.] [4] [5] [6]

At this point, the change sign key will place a minus sign

to the left of the significant digits.	
Try it.	[+/−]
The display should now read:	−2.456
The significant digits can be again made a positive number by pressing the change sign key again.	[+/−]
The display should now read:	2.456
Select scientific notation.	[EEX]
Pressing the change sign key will now change the sign of the exponent. The minus sign will appear to the *right* of the significant digits.	
Try it.	[+/−]
The display should now read:	2.456 −00
Enter the exponent.	[2]
The display now reads:	2.456 −02

Pressing the change sign key will now change the sign of the exponent only. ■

C.6 ENGINEERING AND SCIENTIFIC NOTATION COMPUTATIONS ON A CALCULATOR

After you have learned the material in the previous section, you should be able to use your calculator for computing the answers to problems involving engineering or scientific notation. If your calculator displays answers in their written-out form or in scientific notation, you may have to reconvert the answers, particularly if you want them to be in engineering notation. In spite of this, the ability of the calculator to keep track of the location of the decimal points reduces any computation to an exercise in correct number entry. It should be noted that some calculators permit a selection of either scientific or engineering notation.

EXAMPLE:
Add 641.75×10^{-6} to 8.43×10^{-4} using your calculator. ■

SOLUTION:

Enter significant digits of first number.	[6] [4] [1] [.] [7] [5]
Select scientific notation.	[EEX]
Enter exponent.	[6]
Enter correct sign for exponent.	[+/−]
Select addition.	[+]
Enter significant digits of second number.	[8] [.] [4] [3]
Select scientific notation.	[EEX]
Enter exponent.	[4]
Enter correct sign for exponent.	[+/−]
Press equals key to display answer.	[=]

The display should now indicate the correct answer, 1.48475 −03, or in actual notation 1.48475×10^{-3}. ■

Even such sign-filled problems as multiplying 18.3×10^{-7} by -9.3×10^{-4} can be carried out easily:

Enter significant digits of multiplicand.	[1] [8] [.] [3]
Select scientific notation.	[EEX]
Enter exponent and correct sign.	[7] [+/−]
Select multiplication.	[×]
Enter significant digits of multiplier.	[9] [.] [3]
Enter correct sign for multiplier.	[+/−]
Select scientific notation.	[EEX]
Enter exponent of multiplier and its sign.	[4] [+/−]
Press equals key to display product.	[=]

Your calculator should now display the correct answer, −1.7019 −09, or -1.7019×10^{-9}. Try the exercises in Sections C.3 and C.4 on your calculator.

C.7 ENGINEERING AND SCIENTIFIC NOTATION IN BASIC

The standard BASIC language uses scientific notation in much the same way a calculator does to express very large and very small numbers. Like most calculators, BASIC uses scientific rather than engineering notation and switches to this notation automatically when it is dealing with a number with more digits or decimal places than BASIC recognizes. This can be shown by entering the following program:

```
10 INPUT "WHAT NUMBER SHOULD I
     PRINT"; N
20 IF N = 0 GOTO 50
30 PRINT N
40 GOTO 10
50 END
```

Run the program that you just keyed in and enter the number 999,999 when the prompt appears on the screen. Note that the number is reproduced exactly by the computer. Now enter 27,000,000 and note that your form of BASIC probably converts this to scientific notation and prints 2.7 E 07, which means 2.7 with a base 10 exponent of 7, or 2.7×10^7, using the notation with which you are familiar. Now type in the number 0.00000085 when the prompt appears. Again the same thing happened. BASIC automatically converted this to 8.5 E −07 or, in more familiar form, 8.5×10^{-7}.

Use the program that you entered to find the largest and the smallest numbers that BASIC will print without the automatic conversion to scientific notation. If your BASIC is typical, it will print numbers between 999,999 and 0.0000001 without conversion to scientific notation. This is because BASIC stores numbers as seven-digit information words, although it only prints six digits of whole numbers.

BASIC calls six-digit whole numbers and seven-place decimals *single-precision* numbers. Single precision is more than adequate for computations in technology, and it is doubtful that you will ever need any more than this. For those who might need more accuracy, some forms of BASIC permit the printing of *double-precision* numbers, which have up to 16 significant figures.

In addition to the automatic conversion to scientific notation, you may also enter numbers directly in engineering or scientific notation. For example, typing in PRINT (265.3 E-03 * 1.82 E 05) followed by pressing the ENTER or RETURN key will cause the computer to display 48284.6, which is the product of 265.3×10^{-3} and 1.82×10^5. Note that the computer automatically converts back to decimal form when the number to be printed is within the range 0.0000001 to 999,999.

D. APPLICATIONS

D.1 HISTORY OF CHEMICAL CELLS

In order to provide the energy required by modern technology, a source of electric current and an electric field is required, and it must be a source that can do a moderate amount of work in a controlled manner over a period of time. As in many cases in the pioneering days of electricity, the discovery of a practical device was made before it was understood how the device actually worked. The first chemical cell was discovered, although not recognized for what it was, by the Italian scientist Galvani in 1786. Galvani's friend, the physicist Alessandro Volta, for whom the quantity the volt has been named, began to study the effect that his friend noticed. Volta, giving full credit to his friend for the discovery, called the effect "Galvanism" and pushed his research to surprising lengths in a short time.

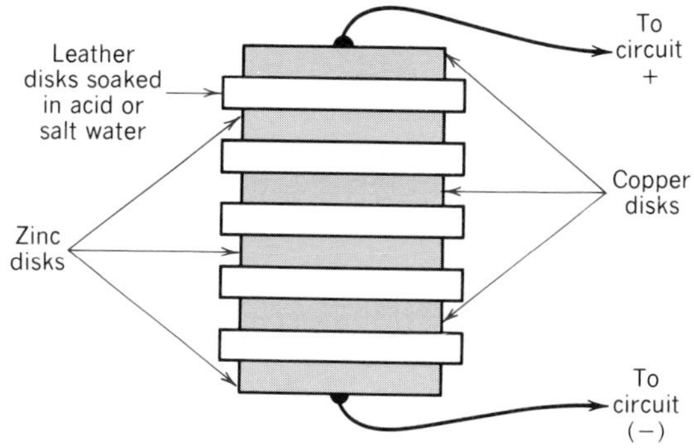

Figure 3.33 A form of the voltaic pile or voltaic battery.

Volta's research led to his building the first modern electric battery. Similar to that shown in Figure 3.33, this device is called a *voltaic pile* or *voltaic battery*. It is composed of a stack of alternating disks of two different metals separated by spacers made of leather soaked in an ionized solution. When the top and bottom disks are connected to a circuit, the pile acts as a source.

Today, it is possible to explain the function of Volta's device and to relate its operation to the effects of triboelectricity. If you had not begun by studying electricity in terms of the electric field and energy, it would be hard to see what a battery has to do with a glass rod that is rubbed with a silk cloth. As explained earlier, however, the electrons in the silk cloth are at a lower energy level than those in the glass rod. If the two are brought into close contact, a certain number of electrons will drift into this lower energy level and enter the cloth. The drift will continue until the electric field caused by the excess electrons in the cloth exactly balances the difference in the energy levels between the rod and the cloth. In the pile, an ionized liquid like salt water, which is able to conduct electrons easily, is in contact with two different metals. The metals are chosen so that there is a large difference in the potential energies of their electrons. Because of this, the metal whose electrons are at a higher potential will give up electrons to the liquid, while the metal with the lower potential energy electrons will gain them from the liq-

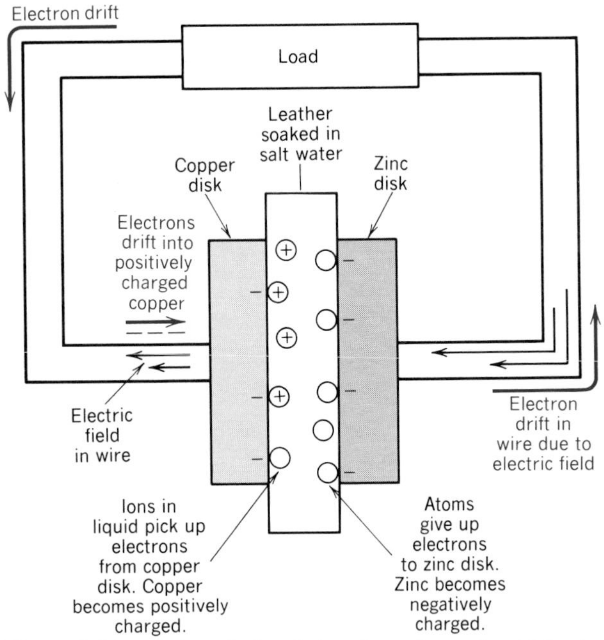

Figure 3.34 A closed circuit is a loop through which electrons move.

uid. The actual chemical process involved is more complicated than described here. In general, one of the metals is dissolved to furnish ions in the liquid. The ions act as charge carriers. As in the case of the glass rod and silk cloth, this process will continue until there is a negative charge on the metal receiving the electrons from the liquid. When this negative charge balances the difference in potential between the two metals, further electron transfer stops. If this chemical cell is connected to an external circuit, however, the electrons in the negatively charged metal will create an electric field that will cause a drift of electrons from the negatively charged metal, through the circuit, to the metal with the deficiency of electrons. But the effect of this current is to reduce the negative charge on the metal whose electrons have less potential energy. This means that more electrons will be transmitted from the liquid. In fact, as you can see in Figure 3.34, there is a closed loop through which the electrons drift. In the external circuit, they are driven by the electric field. In the source itself, it is the difference in potential energy of electrons in different metals that makes them move. One of the ways of viewing a source is to consider it an *electron pump* which uses chemical energy to "pump" electrons through a circuit.

D.2 PRACTICAL CELLS

Before the days of power networks that make it possible for all but the most isolated places to be connected to commercial electric power, many isolated farmhouses and field equipment sites used a combination of water- or wind-powered generators and storage cells for electric power. With the development of commercial power networks, however, chemical cells remained in use only for starting automobile engines and for providing power for portable equipment. Recently, the use of chemical cells has had a comeback. New solid-state electronic units require so little power that they may be efficiently operated from chemical sources. Also, the rise in the manufacture and sale of electronic toys has provided a huge market to the manufacturers of small chemical cells.

Today, a great deal of the test and troubleshooting equipment used by technicians can operate from chemical sources. In addition, many computer installations also contain chemical power sources as standby power to prevent the loss of information if there is a failure of commercial power. Because of their wide use, it is important that you learn to recognize, test, and understand the advantages and weaknesses of the various chemical cells on the market.

D.3 CHARACTERISTICS OF CHEMICAL CELLS

Chemical cells differ in a number of ways. These differences fit them to different applications and also require different methods of testing. Even the checkout counter of the average supermarket or variety store is decorated with a bewildering variety of shapes and sizes. Basically, however, there are only cells and batteries, although cells are normally also called "batteries." To be more correct, a battery is a *combination* of cells packaged in a single container, while a cell is a device made of two dissimilar metals and contains some sort of ionized fluid. (In modern cells, this fluid is often not actually in liquid form.)

D.3.1 PRIMARY AND SECONDARY CELLS

There are two broad categories of cell. The *primary* cell is a chemical cell that furnishes a certain amount of energy to a circuit, and it is then thrown away. *Secondary cells,* on the other hand, are designed to be reenergized. They can be restored to an almost new condition by the addition of electrical energy from an external source. This is why secondary cells used to be called "accumulators." They are capable of storing electrical energy for use at a later time. The reenergizing of secondary cells or batteries composed of secondary cells is called *recharging,* and it is accomplished by forcing a charging current through the cell or battery in the direction opposite the normal direction of electron movement in the cell or battery. This reverses the chemical state within the cell, restoring it to a condition close to its original.

Primary and secondary cells resembling those in use today were invented at about the same time in France. In 1860, Gaston Planté presented a paper to the French Academy of Sciences in which he described the construction of a cell that used lead and lead dioxide as the dissimilar metals and a mixture of water and sulfuric acid as the liquid. The familiar lead–acid storage battery used in automobiles is composed of secondary cells of this type.

At the same time, Georges Leclanché was at work developing a primary cell that is still named after him in Europe. Leclanché was trying to perfect a *dry* cell that would eliminate the hazards and inconveniences of a chemical cell using a liquid. In 1868, he was awarded a patent on a primary cell in which the ionized liquid, called the *electrolyte,* and one of the two metals were actually combined in a paste form. Most of the cells used in portable radios, flashlights, and toys today are only slight improvements on the Leclanché design.

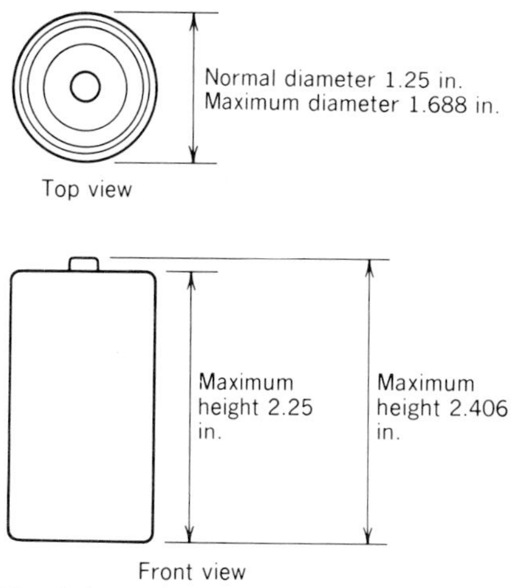

Figure 3.35 A large flashlight cell can have an A-h rating of 5 A-h.

D.3.2 POTENTIAL DIFFERENCE AND CURRENT PRODUCED BY A CELL

Regardless of whether the cell is a primary or secondary cell, it is important to know the potential difference produced by the cell, the amount of current that the cell can produce, and the length of time that the cell will operate at this level before it has to be recharged or replaced. Unfortunately, these are by no means simple questions. For some chemical cells, the potential difference produced by the cell remains fairly constant for the usable lifetime of the cell and then decreases sharply if the cell is used beyond this point. Other sorts of chemical cells show a steady, slow decline in their potential difference. This situation is further complicated by the fact that some chemical cells will recover a part of their original potential difference if allowed to rest for a period of time.

In general, the potential difference produced by each type of cell in its new condition or by each cell in a new battery of cells depends on the two metals involved in its chemical process. For a Leclanché cell, 1.55 V is typical. Cells using other combinations of metals produce potentials varying from about 1 V to more than 3 V. Chemical cell manufacturers usually select an *end voltage* for each of their product lines. When the potential difference across the cell or battery reaches the end voltage, the component must be replaced or recharged. For example, the end voltage for the Leclanché cell is generally considered to be 0.8 V. This end voltage is a manufacturers' convention, and it is quite possible that a piece of equipment powered by such a cell will not get sufficient energy to operate long before the potential difference produced by its source falls to 0.8 V.

Knowing the end voltage is only one part of understanding how much energy a chemical cell may be expected to deliver. Manufacturers also specify the amount of current produced by a particular type of cell or battery by giving each of their products an *ampere-hour* rating, often abbreviated *A-h.* The ampere-hour rating is obtained by connecting a sample cell to a circuit and measuring the current produced while keeping track of the time elapsed and the potential difference produced by the cell. When the potential difference of the cell falls to the end voltage value, the test is halted and the current and time are tabulated. For example, a large flashlight cell such as that pictured in Figure 3.35 may have a rating of 5 or 6 A-h. This would mean that the cell delivered a current of about 0.1 or 0.12 A for a period of 50 hours. The 50-hour discharge rate is one commonly used by manufacturers.

There is a point of confusion that is common, however. The 50-hour rate will not tell you directly about the 10-hour rate or the 100-hour rate. If the cell will deliver 5 A-h during 50 hours, it is probable that it will deliver less if it is discharged over a shorter time, say 10 hours. In fact, the 10-hour rate of the cell may only be 2 or 3 A-h. On the other hand, if the cell is permitted to discharge over a longer period, the energy obtained from it may be greater, depending on the time and the type of cell.

Another important characteristic of different chemical cells is the manner in which the potential difference produced by the cell changes as its ampere-hour capacity is used up. Figure 3.36 is a graph showing the potential difference across two different types of cell as they approach the end of their useful life. The

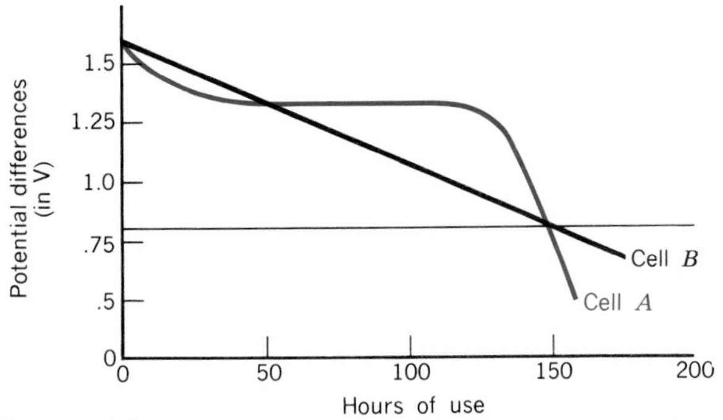

Figure 3.36 The potential difference across two different types of cells when they are in use.

potential difference of cell *A* is fairly constant over its useful life but drops sharply after a certain time. Cell *B*, on the other hand, shows a gradual drop in potential difference for a long period of time. Some circuits require the use of type *A* cells, since they might function improperly if the potential difference drops during operation. In other circuits, it is preferable to use type *B* cells, since the gradual change would allow cell replacement before the potential difference dropped below a critical point.

D.3.3 SENSITIVITY TO TEMPERATURE AND SHELF LIFE

Two other characteristics of cells are important to know. These are *sensitivity to temperature* and *shelf life*. Many chemical cells, including the most common flashlight cells, do not function well at low temperatures. Some types do not function at all if they get too cold. This is one of the reasons it is harder to start a car in cold weather. The shelf life of a cell is the time a cell can be kept in storage without being used without significant loss of ampere-hour capacity or usable life. This generally refers only to primary cells, since secondary cells may be recharged after they have begun to lose their charge. It is surprising that many who buy cells expect that they are ''new'' if they are in sealed packages. This is definitely not the case. Cells stored for a long time, particularly if they have been kept at room temperature, show a significant loss of usable capacity. Most cells have a longer shelf life if they are stored at low temperatures, just above the freezing point, 0°C. For this reason, it is a good idea to store flashlight cells under cold, but not freezing, conditions. This can be done by placing them in a sealed plastic bag in the refrigerator. Before the cells are used, they should be allowed to warm up gradually, keeping them in the sealed bag to prevent water condensation inside the cells.

D.4 THE LECLANCHÉ OR CARBON–ZINC CELL

One of the most common primary cells in use today is the carbon-zinc cell, which differs only a little from the ''dry'' cell patented by Leclanché in 1860. It is called a *dry* cell because it does not contain a liquid electrolyte, as does the lead–acid secondary cell found in automobiles. Instead, the electrolyte contains a water solution electrolyte that has been mixed with a powder to form a paste. In one sense, it is dryer than a lead–acid cell, but if the paste actually dries out completely, the cell will cease to function.

Figure 3.37 shows a cutaway view of a carbon–zinc cell. Actually, the carbon rod through the center of the cell does not enter into the chemical reaction that produces the potential difference. It is used only to provide a contact to the manganese dioxide powder that is one of the active metals in the cell. The other metal is the zinc can that encloses the inner portion. The electrolyte is a paste of ammonium chloride, zinc chloride, starch, and water between the manganese dioxide and the zinc can. The manganese dioxide is mixed with powdered carbon to provide a good electrical contact and to absorb the gas that is produced when the cell is providing an electric current. If the carbon powder were not present, tiny bubbles of gas would form inside the cell and interrupt the current path from the manganese dioxide particles to the zinc. This would stop the operation of the cell in a short time. The actual chemical processes that go on inside an operating carbon–zinc cell are complex and have little bearing on the subject of electricity. It is enough to say that electrons are transferred from the carbon–manganese dioxide powder through the electrolyte to the zinc can and that some of the zinc is dissolved in this process. This is why the cell has a steel

Figure 3.37 Cutaway view of a Leclanché or carbon–zinc cell.

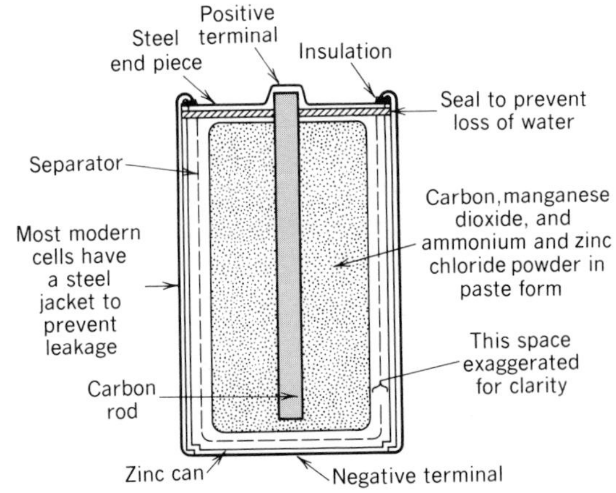

Table 3.5 Dimensions and Service Capacities of Leclanché Cells

Cells Designation	*Length (m)*	*Diameter (m)*	*Average Service Capacity at 20°C. (A-h)*
AAA	0.043	0.01	0.2
AA	0.048	0.014	0.6
C	0.046	0.024	1.6
D	0.057	0.032	4.0
F	0.087	0.032	7.0

outer jacket. Early cells had only a paper wrapping around the zinc can and would sometimes leak as the zinc can dissolved.

The ampere-hour, or service, capacity of a chemical cell depends, among other things, on its size. Since the carbon–zinc, or Leclanché, cells were the first to become popular, their standardized sizes have influenced the shapes and sizes of other types. Table 3.5 gives the physical shapes, sizes, and service capacities for some of the most commonly used Leclanché types.

The carbon–zinc cell is particularly troubled by constant operation, primarily due to the formation of gas bubbles inside the cell. As explained above, these gas bubbles interrupt the current path through the cell. This process is called *polarization*. For this reason, the full ampere-hour capacity of the cell can best be realized if it is used in intermittant service and allowed to rest between uses. A Leclanché cell may provide *twice* the service life if it is allowed to rest between uses, allowing sufficient time for the powdered carbon to absorb the gas produced during operating periods.

The potential difference produced by a new carbon–zinc cell is 1.55 V, and this will decline gradually as the cell is used. Table 3.6 shows the potential difference and condition of D size cells specifically, although other Leclanché cells are comparable. It is a handy thing to post somewhere so that you can check the condition of flashlight and transistor radio cells periodically.

The carbon–zinc cell is inexpensive, but it has two big disadvantages in addition to the problem of polarization. Cells of this sort should not be used under low- or high-temperature conditions. At temperatures below freezing, 0°C, or above 54°C, carbon–zinc cells will quickly lose their service capacity. Also, they tend to have a rather short shelf life if stored at room temperature. After two years at room temperature, a Leclanché cell is generally dead even if it has never been used.

Table 3.6 Potential Difference and Condition of Leclanché Cells

Potential Difference (D size cell measured with digital multimeter in no-load condition)	*Condition*
1.55	New
1.49	Good
1.41	Poor
1.24	Replace (Cell dead)

D.5 THE ZINC CHLORIDE CELL

The zinc chloride cell is actually an improved version of the Leclanché cell. The difference is that it uses only zinc chloride in its electrolyte in place of the mixture of zinc chloride and ammonium chloride. Although this seems only a small difference, it changes the operating reaction of the cell considerably. In the zinc chloride cell, the gases produced by operation are recombined to form water, so that polarization does not occur at as high a rate as it does in the carbon–zinc cell. Part of the chemical process also breaks down water, however, so that the cell actually dries out while in operation. In fact, the zinc chloride cell is actually a dry cell at the end of its life.

Because of the lessened polarization, it is possible to obtain more current from a zinc chloride cell than from a carbon–zinc cell of equal size. Currents as much as 50 percent higher may be expected from zinc chloride cells without a shortening of service life.

The shape of the discharge curve of the zinc chloride cell is the same as that of the Leclanché cell. The potential difference drops gradually from its beginning 1.55 V. Zinc chloride cells are generally more expensive than carbon–zinc cells, but they are somewhat less bothered by heat and cold and may be used at temperatures ranging from 0 to 71°C.

D.6 THE ALKALINE CELL

Another improvement of the Leclanché cell is the alkaline cell. Actually, alkaline manganese dioxide would be a better name because a variety of cells use an alkaline solution or paste as the electrolyte. As you can see in Figure 3.38, the structure of the alkaline cell differs considerably from that of the carbon–zinc cell. First of all, the solid zinc can that formed the negative plate in the carbon–zinc cell has been eliminated. A layer of powdered zinc is used, since the particles of powder have a larger surface area for the chemical reaction than a solid can. Contact with the powdered zinc is provided by a brass cylinder that contains additional electrolyte to counteract the loss that occurs

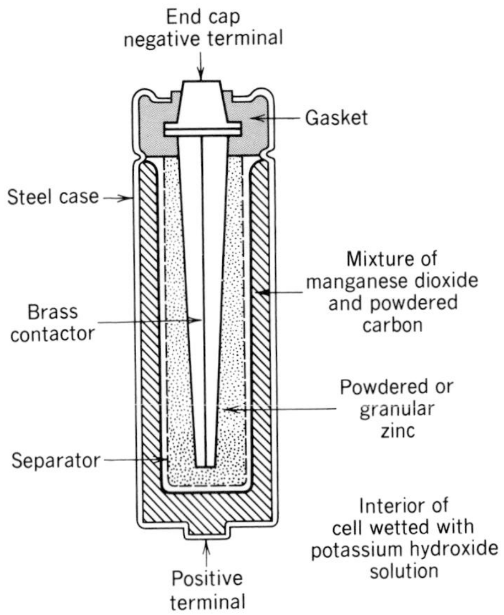

Figure 3.38 Cutaway view of a size AA alkaline cell.

through gas formation while the cell is operating. As in the Leclanché cell, the positive plate is formed of a powder mixture including manganese dioxide. The electrolyte used is a water solution of potassium hydroxide, commonly called lye.

Because of its construction, the alkaline cell has much greater ability to provide high current service, without much loss of service capacity, than the Leclanché cell or the zinc chloride cell. The potential difference produced by all three, since it depends on the metals used rather than on the details of construction, is 1.55 V for a new cell.

An overall comparison of the more expensive alkaline cell with the carbon–zinc type shows the relative superiority of the alkaline cell. Under conditions of relatively high current flow, the alkaline cell may provide up to seven times the service life of the carbon–zinc cell. Although the ampere-hour capacity of the alkaline cell is only twice that of a carbon–zinc cell of comparable size, the alkaline cell is much more likely to deliver a higher proportion of its capacity than the carbon–zinc cell. Both the low-temperature performance and the shelf life of the alkaline cell are considerably better than the carbon–zinc cell and somewhat better than the zinc chloride cell. The high-temperature characteristics of alkaline cells are about the same as those of the carbon–zinc cell and somewhat poorer than those of zinc chloride cells. According to one manufacturer's specifications, the operating temperatures for alkaline cells are from −28.9 to 54.4°C. The shelf life of alkaline cells at normal room temperature is estimated to be about four years, or twice that of Leclanché cells.

D.7 MERCURIC OXIDE AND SILVER OXIDE CELLS

Until recently, cells using mercuric oxide as one of the active metals were the most stable and most compact primary cells commercially available. Although they were fairly expensive, their small size made them a natural choice for miniature equipment, including hearing aids and some portable test equipment. In general, *mercury cells,* as they are commonly called, provide nearly three times more energy per unit of weight than Leclanché cells and four times the energy per unit of volume. Figures 3.39 to 3.41 show the physical construction of common mercury cells. Those shown in Figures 3.39 and 3.40 are "button" cells. In the cell shown in Figure 3.39, the potassium hydroxide electrolyte is absorbed by pads. In the type shown in Figure 3.40, the negative plate (powdered zinc) is mixed with the electrolyte and a gelling compound. The cylindrical mercury cell shown in Figure 3.41 is manufactured in the same sizes as Leclanché and alkaline cells.

The standard mercury cell produces a potential difference of 1.35 V when new since it uses mercury and zinc rather than manganese dioxide and zinc as its active metals. One of the characteristics of this kind of cell is that it has a rather flat discharge curve. This means that the potential difference across the cell will remain fairly constant until the service life is over. Mercury cells are not capable of delivering as high a current as alkaline cells, but their overall service capacity is nearly twice that of equal-sized alkaline cells. A size AA mercury cell will provide 2.4 A-h, while a size D cell will deliver 14 A-h. The shelf life of mercury

Figure 3.39 Cross-section of typical mercury cell.

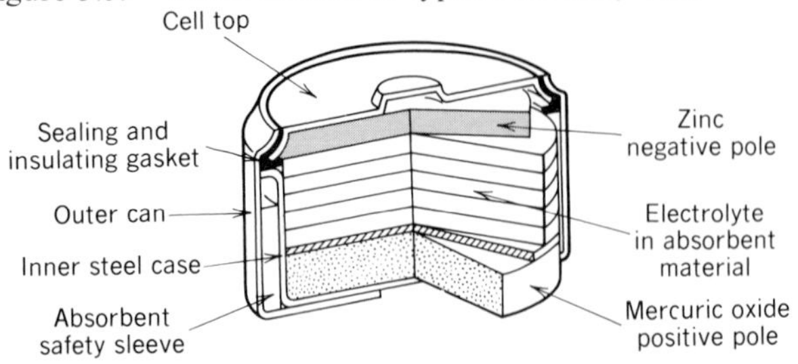

Figure 3.40 Cross-section of mercury cell with gelled electrolyte.

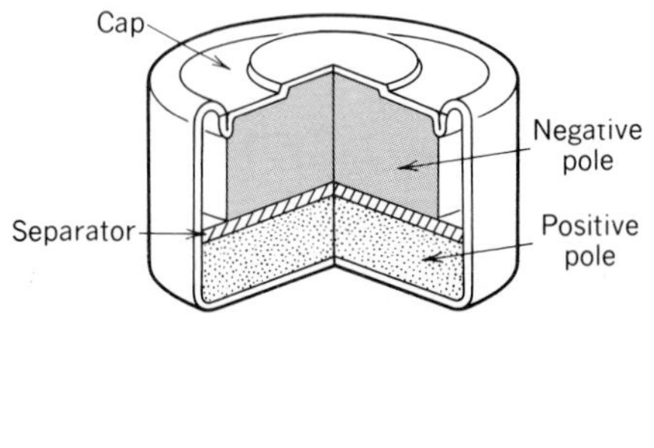

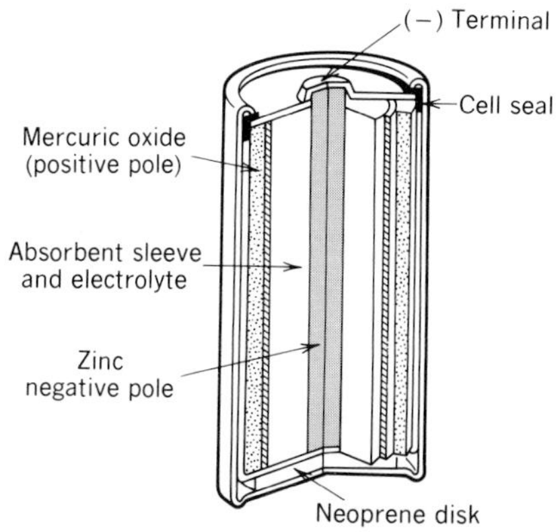

Figure 3.41 Cross-section of cylindrical mercury cell.

cells is better than that of Leclanché cells, averaging two to four years. On the other hand, the low-temperature performance of mercury cells is poor, and they should not be used at temperatures around 0°C.

Similar in appearance to the mercury cell is the silver oxide cell. Instead of mercuric oxide, the silver cell uses silver oxide as an active metal. This combination of active metals produces a potential difference of 1.6 V, which is slightly higher than that of the Leclanché cell. In other characteristics, the silver oxide cell is similar to the mercury cell, although it is reputed to be able to function somewhat better at low temperatures.

D.8 LITHIUM CELLS

Although there are many other types of primary cells that have not been discussed, only the newly invented lithium cells are popular enough to justify study. The lithium cell is a fairly new product, and there are presently several different combinations of electrolyte and active metals being produced. All lithium cells produce a potential difference that is considerably higher than that of any other commercially available cells. The two most popular systems use a lithium metal negative cylinder and a positive connection formed by a gas dissolved in the electrolyte. These systems produce potential differences of 2.8 and 3.7 V, respectively. The discharge curve of these cells is quite flat, although there is a slight *rise* in the potential difference across the cell during a short break-in period. After that, the lithium cell will produce its rated potential difference almost until it stops working completely.

In addition to delivering more energy per weight and volume than any other cell except the mercury and silver oxide cells, the lithium cell can deliver heavy currents until its ampere-hour capacity is used up. Although the characteristics vary according to the type of cell, lithium cells are also capable of operating at extreme temperatures. Some lithium cells will function at temperatures as high as 73°C, with full voltage and current output. At low temperatures, their performance is usually much better than any other type of cell. At −28°C, a temperature at which Leclanché, alkaline, and mercury cells are useless, some lithium cells will deliver up to 96 percent of their rated capacity and will even function at temperatures as low as −40°C. The shelf life of lithium cells is also superior to any other primary cell. The principal drawbacks to the use of lithium cells as backup power in computer equipment is their cost and the fact that lithium metal will burn when exposed to air. The cells themselves may explode if heated to too high a temperature.

D.9 SECONDARY CELLS

Unlike primary cells, which are used to produce electrical energy, secondary cells are used to store it. The chemical process that goes on inside a secondary cell is reversible. This means that by applying a potential difference derived from some other source across the terminals of the cell and forcing a *charging current* through it, the cell may be returned to its original (or nearly its original) condition. There are presently only four types of secondary cells in wide use, the liquid-filled lead–acid, or Planté, and nickel–cadmium cells and the smaller, gelled lead-acid and gelled-electrolyte ni-cad cells.

D.10 THE LEAD–ACID, OR PLANTÉ, CELL

The lead–acid cell, sometimes referred to by the name of its inventor Planté, has proved itself so successful that only in the last few years have serious efforts been made to improve the basic design. All lead–acid cells use the same chemical system. A positive plate of lead dioxide and a negative plate of porous sponge lead are suspended in a solution of water and sulfuric acid. At the positive plate, the lead dioxide reacts with the acid to produce lead sulfate. This releases negatively charged oxygen ions into the electrolyte. At the negative plate, sponge lead is converted to lead sulfate. The oxygen ions combine with hydrogen in the electrolyte to form water, giving up their excess electrons to the negative plate. The chemical action dilutes the electrolyte. The process produces a potential difference of about 2 V across the plates of the cell and will provide a gradually decreasing voltage to an external circuit until both the positive and negative plates are coated with lead sulfate, and the electrolyte solution becomes too dilute to support the chemical action.

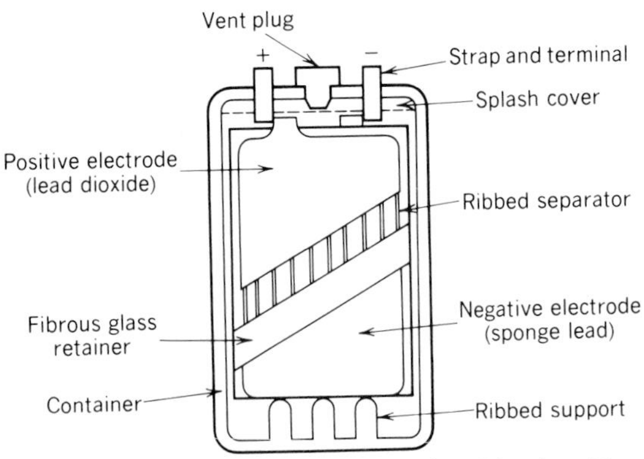

Figure 3.42 Construction of a conventional lead–acid cell.

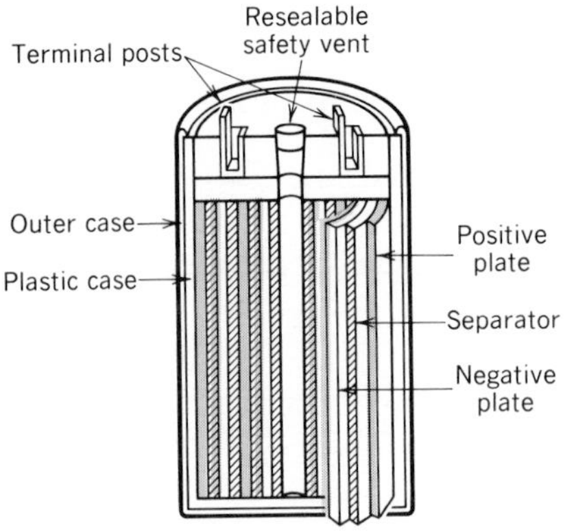

Figure 3.43 Cutaway view of a sealed lead–acid cell.

When the chemical action has stopped, the cell is said to be fully discharged. When a lead–acid cell has reached its fully discharged state or before, when it is only partially discharged, a charging current may be sent through the cell in the direction opposite to that of the normal current flow when the cell is acting as a source. This reverses the chemical activity of the cell. If carried on long enough, the lead sulfate will be completely removed from the plates, restoring the cell to an almost new condition.

As shown in Figure 3.42, a commercial lead–acid, or Planté, cell is composed of interleaved positive and negative plates attached to positive and negative bus bars. Since the ampere-hour capacity of a cell depends on the area of its plates, such close packing will produce a cell with a large energy-to-volume ratio.

The potential difference across a lead–acid cell decreases gradually as the service capacity is used, but this is not a serious problem, since the cell may be recharged many times. Eventually, however, the growth of lead sulfate crystals, called *dendrites,* within the cell causes contact between the negative and positive plates. Once this happens, the cell is said to be *shorted out* and can no longer be used or recharged. The lead–acid cell exhibits good low-temperature performance at low to moderate currents. The difficulties that motorists encounter during winter mornings arise because a cold automobile engine requires a large starting current. High-temperature conditions, on the other hand, support the growth of lead dendrites within the cell, so a lead–acid cell should not be stored at temperatures above 54°C.

D.11 THE SEALED LEAD–ACID, OR GELLED ACID, CELL

Recently, some automobile manufacturers have started to market "sealed, maintenance-free" storage batteries. These units have no provision for the addition of water to replace the water normally lost through evaporation or through overcharging. Instead, a sufficient amount of extra water is designed into the electrolyte system so that the addition of water is not required through the projected life of the battery. This type of cell should not be confused with a true sealed lead–acid cell.

The internal construction of a typical sealed lead–acid cell is shown in Figure 3.43. Thin lead dioxide and sintered lead strips are rolled to produce a cell with a large effective plate area in a relatively small volume. The sulfuric acid and water electrolyte is absorbed in porous separator strips or mixed with a gelling solution that prevents leakage and enables the cell to be used in any position. Since the cell is completely sealed (except for a safety vent in some models), the gases formed during charging cannot escape. The cell acts as a closed system, and the gases are recombined to form water. Because of this, however, it is necessary to control the charging rate carefully, so that the rate of gas production does not exceed the rate at which the gases recombine to form water. If the charging rate is too high, gas will escape through a safety vent or puncture the case. Table 3.7 lists the dimensions and ampere-hour capacities of two popular models of sealed lead–acid cell.

Like the Planté cell, the sealed lead–acid cell can produce very high currents for a very short time without permanent damage to the cell. A size D cell, for example, may supply a surge current of 100 A for a fraction of a second. After the service capacity of the

Table 3.7 Two Popular Models of the Sealed Lead-acid Cell

Cell Size Designation	*Length (m)*	*Diameter (m)*	*Service Capacity in A-h (20 hour rate)*
D	0.06	0.034	2.7
X	0.072	0.044	5.2

sealed lead–acid cell is used up, as in the case of the Planté cell, it should be recharged immediately. An uncharged cell is liable to form lead sulfate dendrites between the positive and negative plates, making it impossible to use or recharge the cell.

The low-temperature characteristics of sealed lead–acid cells are good, and they may be used at temperatures as low as −40°C, some 20 degrees lower than the lowest temperature at which Planté cells are generally used. Sealed cells may be used at temperatures as high as 60°C, and the service capacity actually increases slightly to that point. At normal room temperatures, a sealed cell not connected to a load can be expected to retain a safe level of charge for up to three years. If regularly recharged, the cell can be stored for a much longer period without the formation of dendrites.

D.12 MAINTENANCE AND RECHARGING OF LEAD–ACID CELLS

The life of lead–acid cells can be protected by attention to two details. The Planté-type cells must have sufficient water added regularly to keep the acid concentration in the electrolyte within operating limits, and both Planté and sealed lead–acid cells must be recharged when their service capacity begins to be used up. It is a relatively simple matter to add water to a Planté cell, but knowing when and how to recharge deserves explanation. There are two ways to determine the remaining service capacity in a lead–acid cell. The first, which involves measuring the concentration of the sulfate ions in the electrolyte, can be applied only to Planté cells. A device called a *hydrometer,* pictured in Figure 3.44, is used to measure the density of the electrolyte solution. A lower concentration of sulfate ions in the electrolyte means that appreciable amounts of lead sulfate have formed on the plates and the cell is nearing the point at which it must be recharged. Table 3.8 lists the specific gravity readings of a hydrometer used to measure the condition of a typical Planté cell.

Figure 3.44 A typical hydrometer (Photo by M. Hermes).

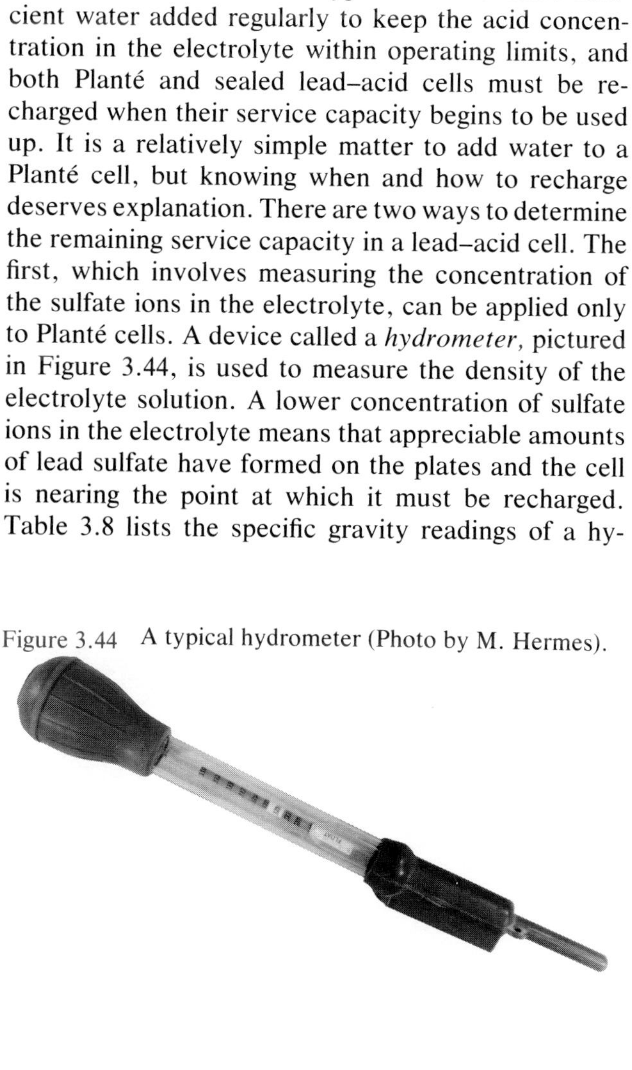

Table 3.8 Specific Gravities of Lead–Acid Cells

Specific Gravity of Electrolyte at 20°C	*Service Life Remaining*
1.275	Fully charged
1.245	75%
1.215	50%
1.185	25%
1.155	Little charge remaining
1.125	Fully discharged

The values in Table 3.8 are intended for use at room temperature, 20°C. Since the specific gravity of the electrolyte depends not only on the concentration of sulfite ions but also on the temperature of the liquid, it is necessary to change the given figure according to the temperature. This is a fairly easy process, if the temperature range is not too extreme. For every degree centigrade above 20, add 0.0007 to the specific gravity figures read on the hydrometer. For every degree centigrade below 20°, subtract 0.0007. For example, if the temperature of the electrolyte was 26°C, the true specific gravity of the electrolyte would be six times 0.0007, or 0.0042 higher than the hydrometer reading.

Clearly, it is not possible to take specific gravity readings on the electrolyte in sealed lead–acid cells, nor is a hydrometer as common a device in a technician's tool kit as a good digital multimeter. If, for any reason, the specific gravity method cannot be used, or if the cell to be checked is a sealed type, the potential difference across the cell may be measured and compared to the figures given in Table 3.9 to determine the state of the cell.

There are various ways of recharging lead–acid cells. Because the sealed lead–acid cells has to be charged at a slower rate than the Planté cell, any method safe for use on a sealed cell will also work on a Planté cell.

In general, charging consists of forcing a current through the cell in the direction opposite to that in which the current flows when the cell is acting as a

Table 3.9 Potential Difference and Service Capacity of Sealed Lead-acid Cells

Potential Difference Across Cells (Without Load)	*Remaining Service Capacity (Approximate)*
2.2	100%
2.15	90%
2.10	60%
2.05	40%
2.0	15%
Under 2.0	Little charge remaining

source. The positive terminal of the charger is connected to the positive plate of the cell and the negative terminal of the charger is connected to the negative plate. The potential difference produced by the charger must, of course, be greater than the potential difference produced by the cell being charged; otherwise the cell will discharge itself through the charger circuit.

Have you ever brought an automobile to a garage to have the battery recharged? If so, you will remember that the attendant opened the battery vent caps before connecting the charger. When the charger was turned on, the electrolyte solution in the battery boiled vigorously, producing a great deal of gas.

The production of gas in a cell being charged results because the typical garage battery charger is a device that applies a constant potential difference of 2.55 to 2.6 V across each cell of the automobile battery. This potential difference produces a current through each cell that will recharge it to 95 percent of its rated service capacity in half an hour. This is called the *fast charge rate*. Charging at the fast charge rate puts a great deal of strain on cells, however, and is not recommended as a regular method. A sealed lead–acid cell normally has to vent quantities of gases before they are recombined into water if it is fast charged. This loss of water can considerably shorten the life of the cell.

A gentler method of recharging a lead–acid cell is to apply a constant potential difference that is less than 2.4 but greater than 2.3 V across the cell. This rate is called the *float charging rate* or *float charging potential*. At this rate, it takes about 16 hours to recharge a lead–acid cell to 100 percent of its service capacity. Recharging at the float charging rate instead of the fast charge rate can extend the useful life of a sealed lead–acid cell by a factor of seven times or more.

Industrial and computer installations that must be protected from power failure frequently use lead–acid or sealed lead–acid cells as standby sources. These cells are constantly charged at the float charging rate while the commercial power is operating. If commercial power from the mains is interrupted, the fully charged secondary cells are automatically switched into the circuit.

Both the above methods of recharging cells specified a constant potential difference applied across the cell. It is also possible to recharge a cell by passing a constant current through it. In most cases, a charging current equal to the current that may be drawn for 10 hours from a fully charged cell is used. This constant current charging rate is called the *C/10 charge rate*. A fully discharged cell must be recharged at a C/10 rate for 14 to 16 hours in order to return to 100 percent of its rated service capacity. Constant-current charging has a number of advantages over constant-voltage charging, particularly when several cells or a battery is being charged.

The C/10 charging rate is not as suitable for the constant-charge maintenance of standby cells as a constant current rate equal to the 500-hour discharge rate of the cells. Use of the 500-hour discharge rate, or C/500, is called *trickle charging*. Cells may be trickle charged for long periods of time without loss of useful life.

D.13 NICKEL–CADMIUM SECONDARY CELLS

Presently available in cell sizes ranging from tiny "button" models to giant cells equivalent to the lead–acid cells used on submarines, nickel-cadmium, or ni–cad cells, represent a serious competition to the lead–acid secondary cells that had previously dominated this market. The structure of a typical prism-shaped ni–cad cell is similar to that of a Planté cell, except that the plates are not made of lead. The active metals in a ni–cad cell, regardless of shape and construction details, are metallic cadmium in the negative plates and nickelic hydroxide in the positive. In some cells, the active metals are embedded in a porous nickel matrix for support. The separators are made of an absorbant, nonwoven fabric and absorb the potassium hydroxide and water solution that is the electrolyte in all ni–cad cells.

Typical button and cylindrical ni–cad cells frequently used as sources in portable electronic equipment and calculators are shown in Figures 3.45 and 3.46. Regardless of its shape, the potential difference across the plates of a fully charged ni–cad cell is about 1.25 V, which explains why rechargeable ni–cad cells of similar size usually cannot be interchanged with

Figure 3.45 Typical button ni–cad cells are frequently used in portable equipment (Photo by M. Hermes).

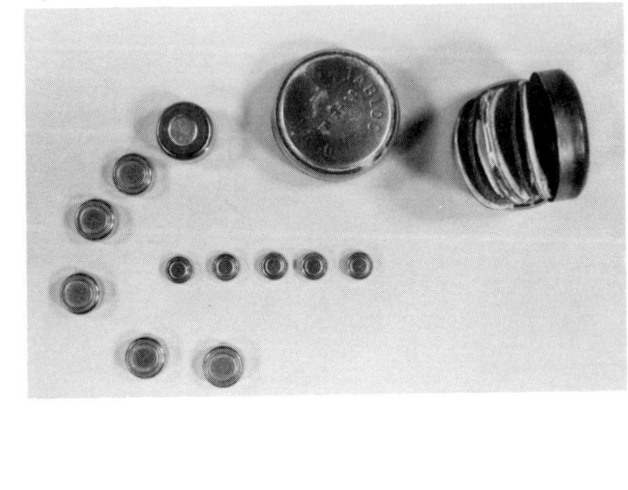

Figure 3.46 Cylindrical ni–cad cells used to power calculators (Photo by M. Hermes).

1.5 V Leclanché cells in many electronic devices. Of special interest in computer and industrial applications are the small, encapsulated cells designed to be built permanently into electronic units to provide standby power for critical circuits. Built-in trickle charge circuits keep the cells fully charged until they are needed.

Ni–cad cells, unlike lead–acid cells, have a rather flat discharge curve, that is, the potential difference across a nearly discharged cell will be almost the same as that across a fully charged cell. This is an advantage if the cell is serving as a power source for electronic components, but it makes it extremely difficult to tell when a cell needs to be recharged. For this reason, ni–cad cells are best put in a float charge or trickle charge circuit to bring them up to full capacity after each use. Fortunately, also, ni–cad cells are better able to tolerate storage in an uncharged condition than lead–acid cells.

Ni–cad cells provide good performance at both high and low temperatures and may be used as sources at temperatures ranging from -20 to 45°C. High temperatures tend to reduce the ampere-hour capacity of ni–cad cells, however, and charge will be lost even if the cell is only stored. Low-temperature operation is normal, except that the cells should not be recharged at temperatures below 0°C.

Because of their light weight, reliable service, and good temperature characteristics, ni–cad cells have gained wide acceptance in industry. There are, however, three problems associated with the use of ni–cad cells that every technician should know and understand. The first problem is a condition called *thermal runaway*. It can occur when a cell is charged at too high a rate. This condition causes the charging current to increase steadily, overheating the cell, and may even lead to explosion. Thermal runaway is best prevented by careful attention to the charging of ni–cad cells.

Another problem is a curious condition known as the *memory effect*. This condition occurs when a cell, particularly a cell used as a standby source, is repeatedly discharged only slightly, say, to 80 percent of its service capacity, and then recharged again. If this happens often, the cell seems to take on almost human characteristics. It somehow "remembers" its earlier exertions and will refuse to provide more service capacity than previously drawn. The only way to prevent memory effect is to periodically discharge ni–cad cells completely (called *deep discharge*) and then to recharge them.

The third problem occurs when a number of ni–cad cells are connected to form a battery. When a battery is used as a source, the cell with the smallest service capacity will discharge first. If the other cells in the battery still retain significant portions of their service capacity, the discharged cell will begin to recharge with opposite polarity! This condition, called *reversal of polarity,* causes large amounts of potentially explosive hydrogen gas to be produced. Reversal of polarity can be avoided by periodically deep discharging all the cells in the battery and then recharging them completely.

In general, the ni–cad cell is more sensitive to damage through faulty charging than the Planté or sealed lead–acid cell. Manufacturers' recommendations for the recharging of each cell type should be followed carefully.

E. PROGRAMMED REVIEW

FRAME 1

An electric source is the part of a circuit that supplies electric energy. The source provides a __________ between its terminals.

a. Potential difference (3)
b. Flow of electrons. (2)
c. Any other answer, review Section B.1.

FRAME 2

Your answer, a current or flow of electrons, is only correct if the circuit in question is a closed circuit and there is a current. A source always supplies a potential difference, even if an open circuit is involved. Go on to the next frame.

FRAME 3

The drift of electrons under the influence of an electric field is called a __________.

a. Current, flow, or electron drift. (4)
b. Any other answer, review Section B.1.

FRAME 4

A load is defined as the portion of a circuit that converts the movement of electrons to another sort of ____ .

a. Energy, or work. (5)
b. Any other answer, review Section B.2.

FRAME 5

A closed circuit consists of a ________ , a ______ , and a __________ through which charge carriers may travel.

a. Source; load; path. (6)
b. One or more answers incorrect, review Section B.2.

FRAME 6

Electron drift, or current, is measured in ________ . The letter symbol for a steady-state current is _____ , while __________ signifies the value of a changing current at a particular instant.

a. Amperes; *I*; *i*. (7)
b. Any other answer, review Section B.3.

FRAME 7

If a charge of 6 C passes through a point in a circuit in 1.5 s, the current through that circuit is ________ .

a. 4 A. (9)
b. 9 A. (8)
c. Any other answer, check your arithmetic and, if necessary, review Section B.3.

FRAME 8

Instead of *dividing* the charge passing through a point by the time, you multiplied the two quantities. Go on to the next frame.

FRAME 9

The current through a circuit is related to the amount of charge that passes through a point in the circuit in 1 s. This can written as a mathematical formula $I =$ __________ .

a. $\frac{Q}{t}$ (10)
b. Any other answer, review Section B.3.

FRAME 10

Quantities like force and current, which have both a magnitude and a direction assigned to them, are called __________ quantities.

a. Vector. (11)
b. Any other answer, review Section B.4.

FRAME 11

A source that tends to keep both the direction and the amount of current constant in a given circuit is called a __________ __________ __________.

a. Direct current source. (12)
b. Any other answer, review Section B.4.

FRAME 12

A device which measures only current is called an __________ . Meters able to measure more than one quantity as well as different ranges of a quantity are called __________ .

a. Ammeter; multimeters. (13)
b. Any other answer, review Section B.5.

FRAME 13

The type of meter in which a mechanical pointer is made to move over a scale is called an __________ meter.

a. Analog. (14)
b. Any other answer, review Section B.5.

FRAME 14

When measurements are made with an analog meter, VOM, or EVM, it is necessary to connect the meter so that the pointer will deflect up the scale. This is done by connecting the black test lead, COMMON, or negative terminal of the meter to the point at which the electrons in the circuit being tested have the __________ potential energy.

a. Most. (15)
b. Any other answer, review Section B.5.

FRAME 15

Potential difference is symbolized by the letter ___ when the potential difference is fairly constant over a period of time; ___ is used to represent the instantaneous value of a changing potential. The letter ___ is sometimes also used.

a. *E*; *e*; *V*. (16)
b. Any other answers, review Section B.6.

FRAME 16

Current in a circuit is usually measured by _______ the circuit and connecting the meter so that the electron drift takes place through it.

a. Breaking. (17)
b. Any other answer, review Sections B.5 and B.6.

FRAME 17

The potential difference between two points in a circuit can be measured with a multimeter set for voltage measurement by __________.

a. Connecting the meter leads to the two points. (19)
b. Breaking the circuit and connecting the meter. (18)
c. Any other answer, review Section B.6.

FRAME 18

It is not necessary to break the circuit to make potential difference (voltage) measurements. It is only necessary to break a circuit and connect the meter if current measurements are made. To measure potential difference, it is only necessary to connect the leads of a properly set meter to the two circuit points whose potential difference is required. Go on to the next frame.

FRAME 19

When making either voltage or current measurements, it is a wise precaution to set the meter to the ______ range available first and then select __________ ranges if necessary.

a. Highest; lower. (20)
b. Any other answer, review Sections B.5 and B.6.

FRAME 20

When making either voltage or current measurements with an analog meter, it is important that the meter pointer will deflect up the scale. This will happen if the __________ test lead or the terminal marked _____ is connected to the point at which the electrons have the least potential energy.

a. Red; +. (21)
b. Any other answer, review Sections B.5 and B.6.

FRAME 21

Match the following quantities with their correct metric units

length	joules
potential difference	kilograms
time	meters
mass	amperes
current	newtons
force	seconds
work	volts

a. length, meters
   potential difference, volts
   time, seconds
   mass, kilograms
   current, amperes
   force, newtons
   work, joules (22)
b. More than two wrong, review Table 3.4.

FRAME 22

8.3450 rounded off to three significant digits is __________ .

a. 8.34 (23)
b. 8.35, review Section C.2, Rule 3.
c. Any other answer, review Section C.2.

FRAME 23

A chemical cell that serves as a source of electrical energy generally consists of two __________ separated by an __________.

a. Metals; electrolyte. (24)
b. Any other answer, review Section D.1.

FRAME 24

What is the key difference between primary and secondary cells?

a. Secondary cells can be recharged. (25)
b. Any other answer, review Section D.3.1.

FRAME 25

The carbon–zinc cell is also called the ________ cell.

a. Leclanché. (26)
b. Any other answer, review Section D.3.1.

FRAME 26

The potential difference that exists across the terminals of a chemical cell when the cell must either be recharged or replaced is called the ________ ________ .

a. End voltage. (27)
b. Any other answer, review Section D.3.2.

FRAME 27

The total current that a cell is supposed to be able to deliver is called its ________ rating. Service capacity is another name for this.

a. Ampere-hour. (28)
b. Any other answer, review Section D.3.2.

FRAME 28

The length of time during which an unused cell (or any other component, for that matter) may be stored without severe deterioration before use is called its ________ ________.

a. Shelf life. (29)
b. Any other answer, review Section D.3.3.

FRAME 29

Because its electrolyte is in a paste form, the Leclanché cell as well as the later versions of this design are called ________ cells.

a. Dry. (30)
b. Any other answer, review Section D.4.

FRAME 30

The active metals in a Leclanché cell are ________ and ________ ________.

a. Zinc and manganese dioxide. (31)
b. Any other answer, review Section D.4.

FRAME 31

The active metals in an alkaline cell are ________ and ________ ________. The elecrolyte is ________ ________, commonly called lye.

a. Zinc; manganese dioxide; potassium hydroxide. (32)
b. Any other answers, review Section D.6.

FRAME 32

The lithium cell produces a higher ________ than any other type.

a. Potential difference or voltage. (33)
b. Any other answer, review Section D.8.

FRAME 33

A potential difference of 2 or 2.2 V is produced by ________ or ________ cells, a potential difference of 1.3 V is typical of a freshly recharged ________ cell.

a. Lead–acid or Planté; ni–cad. (34)
b. If all answers are not as above, review Sections D.12 and D.13.

FRAME 34

Name three problem or danger conditions that must be watched for when using or recharging ni–cad cells.

a. Thermal runaway; memory effect; reversal of polarity. (End)
b. Any other answer, review Section D.13.

E. PROBLEMS FOR SOLUTION OR RESEARCH

1. Round off the following numbers to three significant digits and to two significant digits.

a. 8.722	c. 5.5678	e. 1.3500
b. 11.5614	d. 1.725	f. 9.3350

g. 1.1398　　i. 1,253,749　　k. 73.15
h. 4.6451　　j. 6.453　　l. 86550.0

2. Perform the following computations without using a calculator. Round off your answers to three significant digits.

a. -16.12×-4.2
b. $63.2 \times 10^3 + 7.05 \times 10^4$
c. -15×10^6 divided by 5×10^3
d. $-8.25 \times 10^4 \times -1.16 \times 10^{-2}$
e. $-6.28 \times 10^{-3} - (-1.64 \times 10^{-2})$
f. 104×10^{-3} divided by 8×10^3
g. $18.33 \times 10^{-2} - 4.7 \times 10^{-3}$
h. $14 \times 10^{12} \times 3.2 \times 10^{-3}$
i. $-6.18 \times 10^2 + 45.28 \times 10^1$
j. 4.05×10^3 divided by -1.5×10^{-1}
k. $-93.25 + 1.5 \times 10^3$
l. $-16.82 \times 10^{-2} - (-486.7 \times 10^{-4})$

3. Perform the following computations with a calculator or small computer. Round off your answers to three significant digits.

a. $9.84 \times 10^3 - 8.2 \times 10^4$
b. $3.6 \times 10^{-12} \times -2.2 \times 10^6$
c. 31.28×10^{-9} divided by -6.8×10^{-6}
d. $64 \times 10^{-3} - (+8.2 \times 10^{-2})$
e. $8.65 \times 10^4 + 42.785 \times 10^3$
f. $-1.006 \times (-4.2 \times 10^{-3})$
g. $-14.765 \times 8.23 \times 10^{-4}$
h. -32.78×10^{-3} divided by -1.53×10^{-2}
i. $-85.04 \times 10^6 + 19.65 \times 10^7$
j. -19.75×10^3 divided by -3.26×10^{-4}

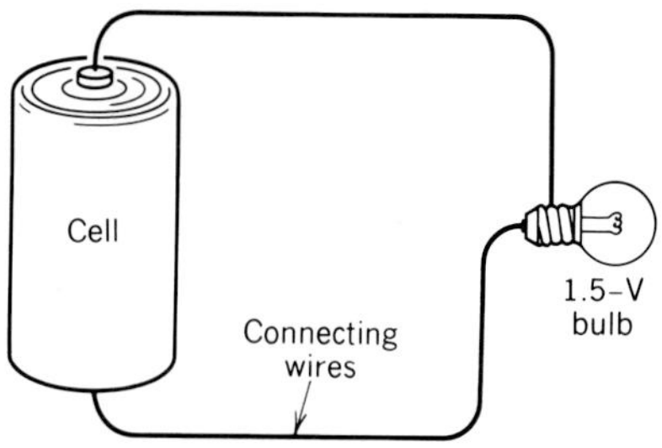

Figure 3.47 Circuit for Problem 7.

k. $-4.825 \times 10^{-3} - (-6.3 \times 10^{-2})$
l. $8.85 \times 10^{-6} + 432 \times 10^{-7}$

4. If 1 C of charge is produced by an excess or deficiency of 6.25×10^{18} electrons, what is the charge in coulombs of 7.8125×10^{17} electrons?

5. If the amount of charge found in problem 4 passes a point in a circuit in 4 s, what is the current through the circuit?

6. Certain electronic components called capacitors store charge. If a capacitor has been charged by a current of 150 mA for 8 s, how many coulombs of charge are stored in it?

7. In order to test a cell, you have constructed the circuit shown in Figure 3.47. What should you have to do to measure the potential difference across the cell with a VOM? What changes would have to be made to measure the current produced by the cell?

8. Complete Table 3.10.

Table 3.10

Cell Name	*Active Metals*	*Electrolyte*	*Potential Difference of New Cell (V)*	*Approximate Shelf Life (Years)*	*Low-Temperature Performance*
Sealed lead–acid	Lead, lead oxide	Sulfuric acid solution	______		Fair to good
______	Manganese dioxide, zinc	Ammonium chloride and zinc chloride paste	1.55	About 1	Fair
Planté cell	______	______	______		______
______	______	Water solution of potassium hydroxide	1.55	4	Good
______	Depends on type	Depends on type	2.8 to 3.7	As long as 10	Excellent
______	Cadmium and nickelic hydroxide	______	1.25		Good

CHAPTER 4

SOURCES IN SERIES, PARALLEL, AND SERIES-PARALLEL

A. CHAPTER PREVIEW

1 Since this chapter will deal with more complex arrangements of sources and loads, you will begin by learning how such arrangements can be symbolized on paper. You will learn the characteristics and applications of pictorial, wiring, interconnect, and schematic diagrams.

2 You will learn why sources are connected in series, parallel, or series–parallel, and how to determine current and potential difference in these circuits. You will also learn how to simplify these calculations in complex circuits through the use of the principle of equivalency.

3 The Examples And Computations section considers formulas and equations. You will learn how to use and to solve simple equations for unknown electrical quantities and metric unit conversions.

4 The Applications section illustrates two methods of analysis that are useful in troubleshooting.

B. PRINCIPLES

B.1 ELECTRICAL AND ELECTRONIC DIAGRAMS

The typical electrical or electronic circuit in modern equipment frequently has several components acting as loads, and may have several sources. Electronic units have become a maze of wires, connectors, and printed circuit boards as shown in Figure 4.1. Repair or modification of such units would be totally impossible without some sort of guide to identify the individual parts and to indicate their functions. In order to find a way through a jungle of wires and components, technicians and engineers use a variety of maps or diagrams. Like the road maps that help a driver find a way across an unfamiliar town or across the country, electrical and electronic maps use symbols drawn or printed on paper to represent what exists in the real world. The ability to use the various sorts of circuit maps is critical for anyone in the field of electricity or electronics today, and a large part of this consists of memorizing the symbols and understanding what they represent.

Figure 4.1 Modern electronic units have become a maze of wires, connectors, and circuit boards (Reproduced with permission from the John Fluke Mfg. Co., Inc.).

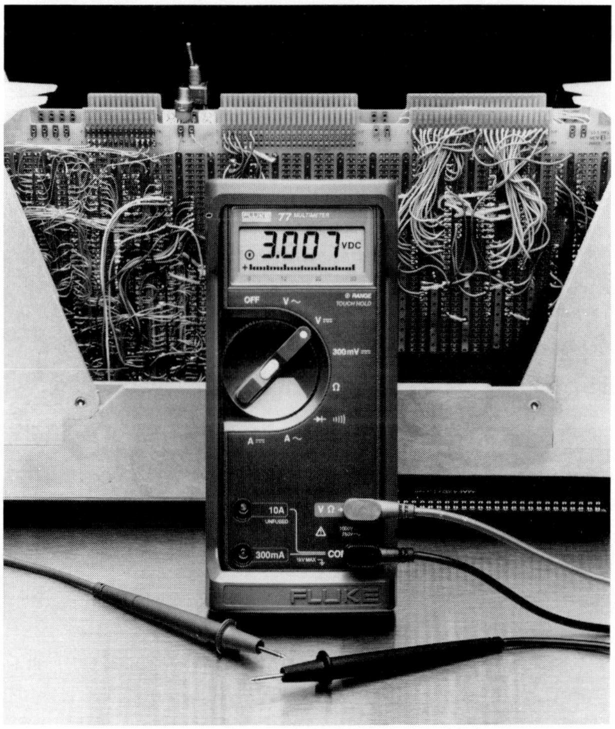

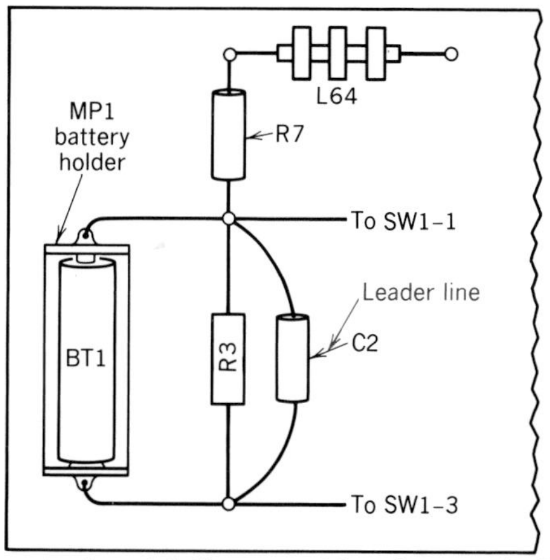

Figure 4.2 A pictorial diagram with reference designators.

B.1.1 PICTORIAL DIAGRAMS

Just as there are specialized maps for pilots, motorists, weathermen, and generals, there are a number of different kinds of diagrams used in electronics, depending on the sort of information about the circuit or unit that is required. The simplest to read is called the *pictorial diagram*. The pictorial diagram may be a line drawing (sometimes with shading to emphasize the shapes) or even a photograph of a piece of equipment. The names of the components, part numbers, or what are called *reference designators* are shown on the diagram, either lettered on the components themselves or connected to them by thin lines called *leader lines*.

Reference designators, which generally consist of a combination of letters and numbers, are used to uniquely identify the component or assembly to which they are assigned. In Figure 4.2, the component BT1 is uniquely identified by this reference designator. No other component in this unit is called BT1, so that if the repair manual tells you to replace BT1, there will be no confusion. The reference designator also tells you the class or type of this component. In this case, the letters BT signify that the component is a cell or battery of cells. Each class of electrical or electronic components has its own group of widely recognized reference designator letters. If this unit contained a second cell, it would be referred to as BT2 in order to eliminate any confusion. Reference designators are stackable. This means that if you are working on a system composed of several units, each of which has its own source cells, each of these cells could be identified in a specific manner. For example, a large computer might consist of a large cabinet with three power supplies, each of which had several sealed lead–acid cells to furnish backup power. The entire cabinet might have the reference designator A1, and its three power supplies would be referred to as PS1, PS2, and PS3.

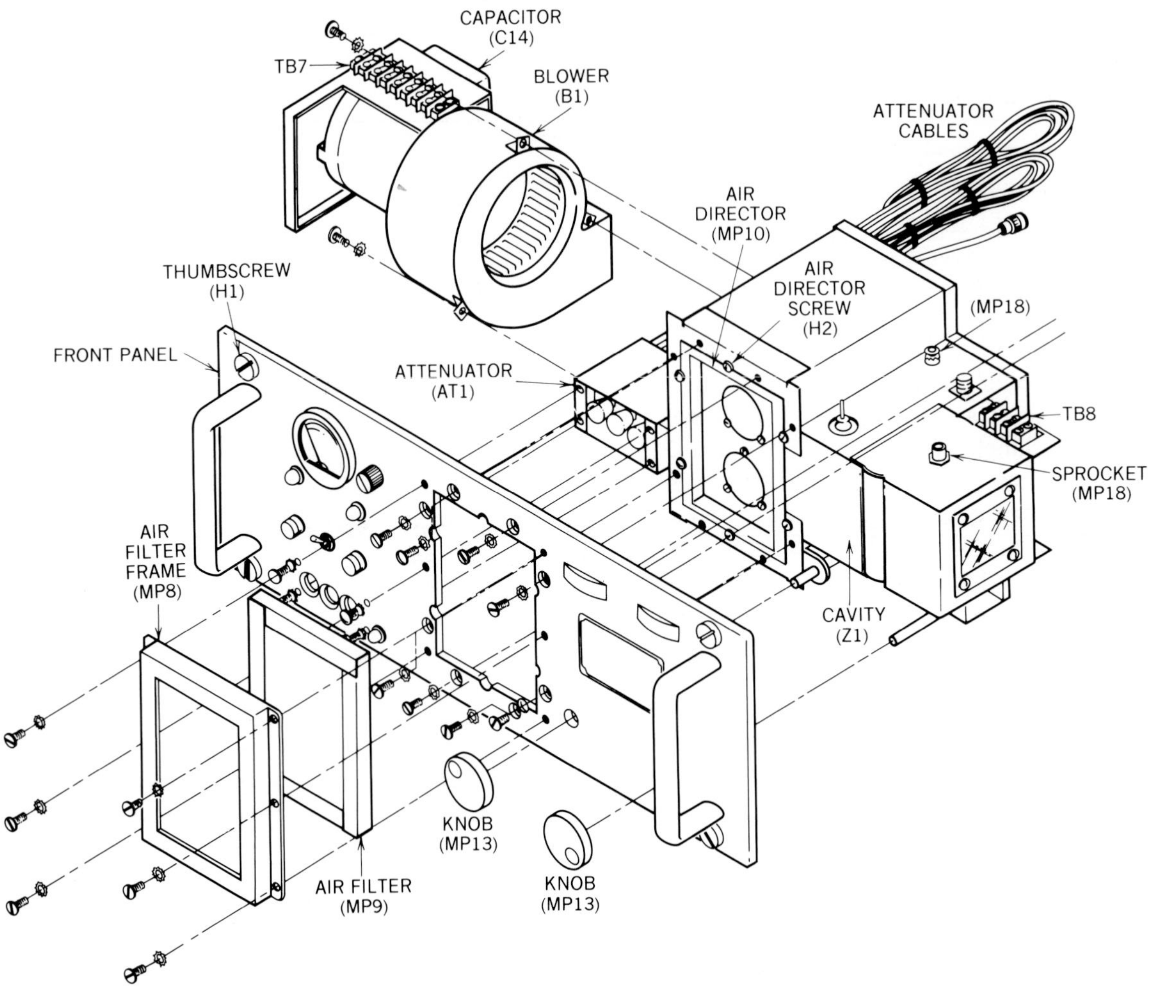

Figure 4.3 A parts blowup is one form of pictorial diagram.

Therefore, the first cell of power supply #3 would be uniquely identified by the reference designator A1PS3BT1. Although such reference designators are more frequent in military than in industrial or commercial pictorial diagrams, they are becoming more common as the complexity of industrial and commercial electronic equipment increases. Using such reference designators, an instruction manual can simply say "replace A1PS1BT1 and A1PS3BT1."

A pictorial diagram provides information concerning the appearance of a unit, the shapes, relative sizes, and locations of components, and the positions of the interconnecting wires. It frequently names the components in such a way as to permit using a parts list to obtain further information about a particular component. However, the pictorial diagram does not provide much information about the function of a particular component, and if the diagram pictures a unit composed of a great many circuits, it is often impossible to determine to which circuit a particular component belongs.

A strikingly odd form of the pictorial diagram, used when mechanical as well as electronic components are involved, is the *assembly* or *parts blowup*, shown in Figure 4.3. This diagram shows each component or part of the unit connected to its eventual place on a main assembly by a dotted line. The overall appearance is as though an explosive charge had gone off inside the unit and reduced it to individual parts. In spite of its curious appearance, this sort of diagram is particularly useful for showing otherwise hidden components or assemblies. It may, if carefully drawn, greatly help in the disassembly or reassembly of a unit.

B.1.2 INTERCONNECT OR WIRING DIAGRAMS
The diagram shown in Figure 4.4 is particularly helpful to those who must troubleshoot or assemble a *system*, that is, a group of units that function together. In general, the wiring or interconnect diagram uses squares or rectangles to represent the various parts of a unit or system and is detailed only in specifying wires, connectors, and connection points. The colors and sizes

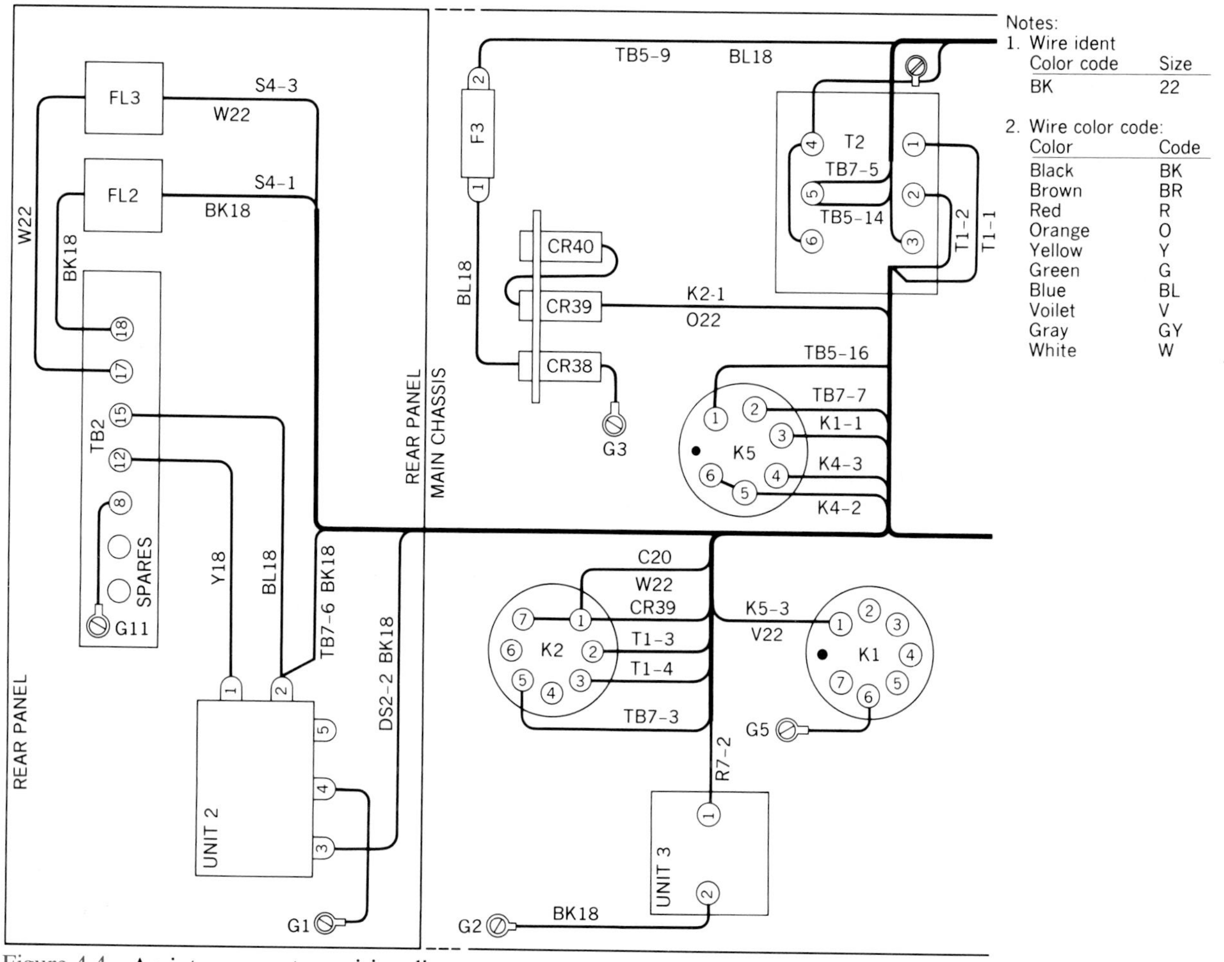

Figure 4.4 An interconnect or wiring diagram.

of the various wires that interconnect the assemblies are frequently given. The wiring or interconnect diagram makes no effort to give information about the sizes, shapes, physical locations, or functions of units or components. Its main purpose is to describe the electrical interconnections within a system.

B.1.3 SCHEMATIC DIAGRAMS

Among the most widely used electrical and electronic diagrams are *schematic diagrams*. This form of diagram is used to impart information about the electrical interconnection of components. It is drawn in such a way as to also provide information about the function of the individual components and the subassemblies they compose. The schematic diagram (see Figure 4.5) is an arrangement of standardized symbols for the various components used in a unit. The symbols are connected by solid lines representing current paths between the components (these paths are frequently wires, but this is not necessarily so). The symbols should be arranged in such a manner as to group the symbols for the parts that function together in the actual unit. This makes it possible for an engineer or technician to interpret the function of a particular circuit or component by examining the schematic diagram. Reference designators are assigned to all the symbols, and characteristic values for components are usually placed on the schematic as well.

The schematic diagram gives no indication of the physical size or location of components. Two parts shown next to each other on a schematic may be on opposite sides of a unit. Nor is there any indication of how two connected parts are actually joined. They may be connected by means of a wire or be joined together in other ways; the diagram makes little or no distinction.

Frequently, when a schematic diagram would be difficult to follow because of the large number of components involved, a *simplified schematic* is used. This diagram purposely leaves out some of the essential parts of the circuit or unit in order to illustrate the principles of operation more clearly. Figure 4.6 is a simplified schematic of the same circuit whose schematic is shown in Figure 4.5.

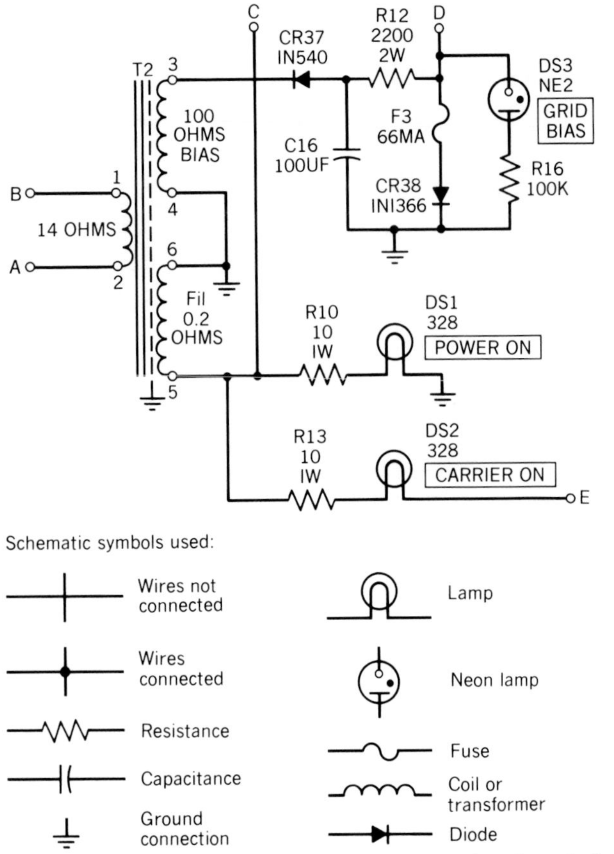

Figure 4.5 A schematic diagram uses conventional symbols to represent the components in a unit.

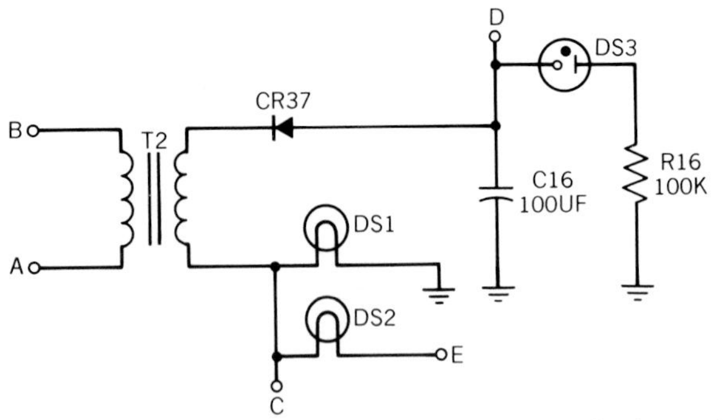

Figure 4.6 A simplified schematic of the circuit shown in Figure 4.5.

B.1.4 BLOCK DIAGRAMS

A fourth type of diagram is the *block diagram* shown in Figure 4.7. The block diagram usually uses labeled rectangles to symbolize circuits and shows only the generalized paths of signals between the blocks. Diagrams of this kind are frequently used in textbooks and instruction manuals to explain how a unit functions or to help in reading a complex schematic diagram. Sometimes the block and schematic diagrams are combined so that the operation of a particular circuit can be illustrated in detail or as an aid in troubleshooting. The lines drawn between the blocks in a block diagram represent the flow of information or signals, rather than actual wires, and are therefore drawn with arrowheads to show the destination of the signals.

B.2 SOURCES IN SERIES

Figure 4.8 shows a line drawing of a typical AA size cell and the schematic symbol for a cell. Note that the longer line in the symbol always represents the more positive terminal of the cell, even when the tiny plus sign is omitted, as is frequently the case. If the cell is a new Leclanché type, the potential difference across the terminals will be 1.55 V. When this cell is connected to a load, the amount of energy delivered depends on the potential difference and the current produced. If the particular load in question requires more energy than can be supplied by a single cell, two

Figure 4.7 A block diagram. Note that the lines between the blocks represent signals rather than current paths.

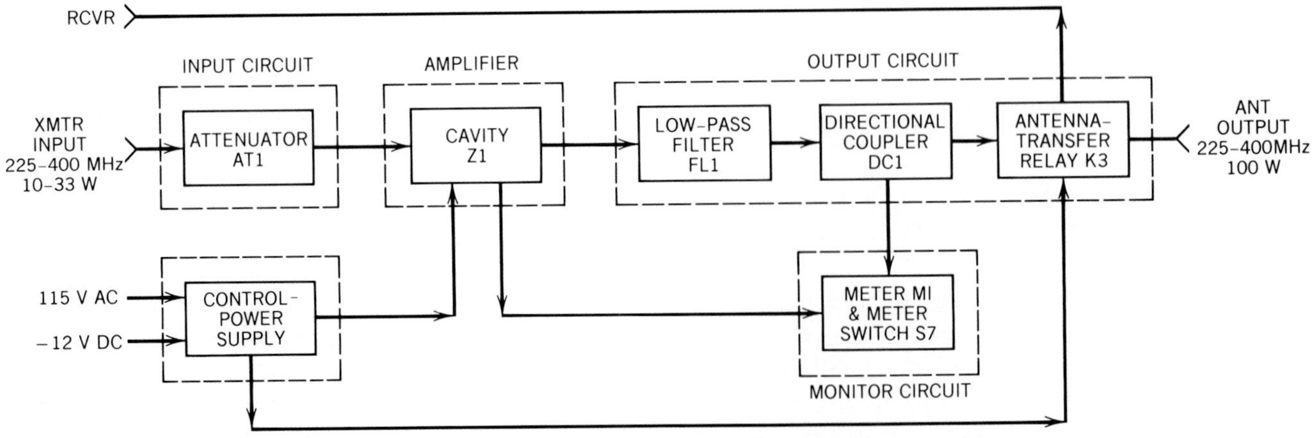

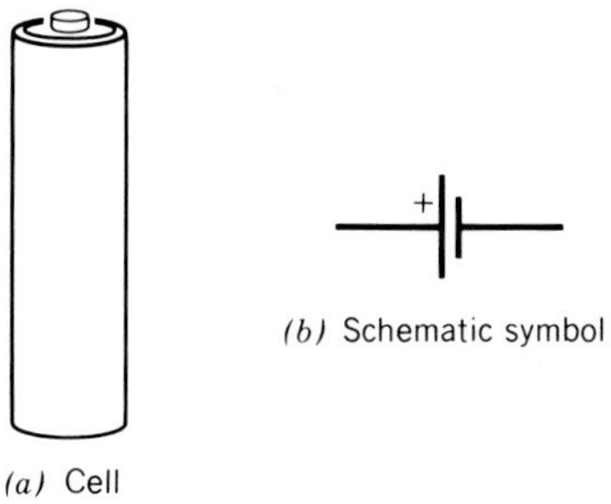

Figure 4.8 A typical AA size cell and its schematic symbol.

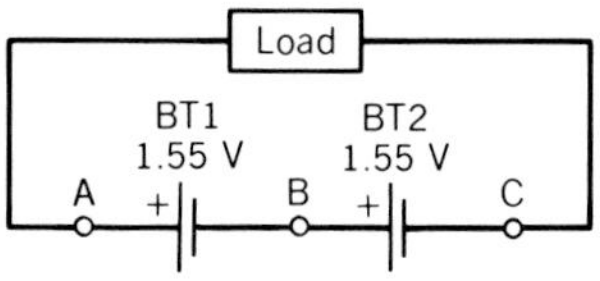

Figure 4.9 A series circuit.

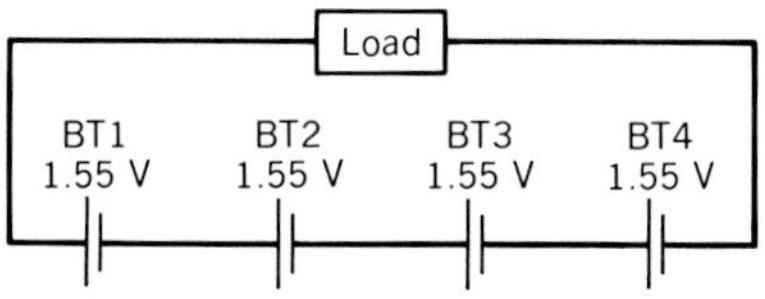

Figure 4.10 Additional cells may be added to a series circuit.

or more cells may be used. The cells and load shown in Figure 4.9 are connected in what is called a *series circuit*. There is only one current path, without branches, and the component parts are connected like beads on a string. If we consider point C as the reference point from which potential differences will be measured, point B will be at a potential of 1.55 V when compared to point C. Similarly, point A will be at a potential of 1.55 V when compared to point B.

As you might expect, the potential difference between points C and A will be 3.1 V, or the sum of the potential between C and B and B and A. This is true because the electric field from cell BT1 and the field from BT2 are operating in the same direction through the circuit. The fields produced by the cells aid each other, so the full description of this arrangement would be *series-aiding*.

Additional cells might be added to the series string, as shown in Figure 4.10, with each cell contributing another 1.55 V of potential difference to the sum, if each cell is connected so as to add its electric field to that produced by the other cells. If the cells are connected in this way, the potential difference across the series connection is the sum of the potential differences produced by each cell. This can be written as a formula:

$$E_{\text{total}} = E_{\text{BT1}} + E_{\text{BT2}} + \cdots \qquad \text{FORMULA 4.1}$$

(a) (b)

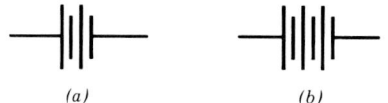

Figure 4.11 Schematic symbols for batteries.

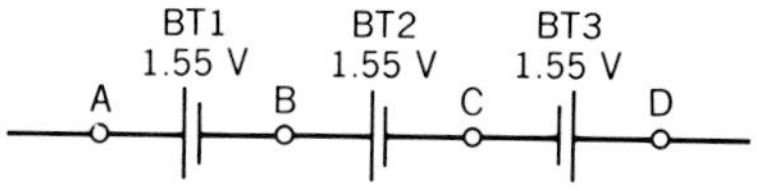

Figure 4.12 Cell BT3 is connected in series opposing.

In this formula, the dots after the last plus sign mean that you could continue adding more factors until the potential differences of all the cells have been added. If the potential difference produced by each cell is the same, all that is necessary to calculate the potential difference across the series string is to multiply the potential difference produced by one cell by the number of cells in series:

$$E_{\text{total}} = E_{\text{cell}} \times \text{number of cells} \qquad \text{FORMULA 4.2}$$

Although each cell in a series string adds its potential difference to the circuit, the circuit current will not be greater than the current that can be produced by one of the cells. This is true because all the current in a series circuit will pass through each cell.

Groups of cells are packaged in various shapes as batteries by manufacturers. Most batteries are built up of Leclanché, Planté, or ni–cad cells. The most common symbol for a battery, regardless of the number of cells it contains, or the potential difference produced, is shown in Figure 4.11*a*. Occasionally, the symbol is made up of three cell symbols as in Figure 4.11*b*.

If one of the cells in a series string is connected as in Figure 4.12 so that the electric field it produces is in the opposite direction of that produced by the other cells, the potential difference produced by the cells is still the sum of the individual potential differences of each cell, but the directions of the fields must be taken into account. In this case, the potential at point A with respect to point B is $+1.55$ V (the cells are again Leclanché types). Likewise, the potential difference from C to B is $+1.55$ V, and so the potential difference from C to A is 3.1 V. From D to C, on the other hand, the potential difference using D as the reference is -1.55 V. It is still the potential difference produced by a single cell, but point C is connected to the negative rather than the positive terminal of the cell. The electric field of BT3 *opposes* that of BT1 and BT2. Adding the potential difference between points D and A (-1.55, $+1.55$, $+1.55$) results in a potential difference of $+1.55$ V between these points. In other words, connecting BT3 in an opposite or *opposing*

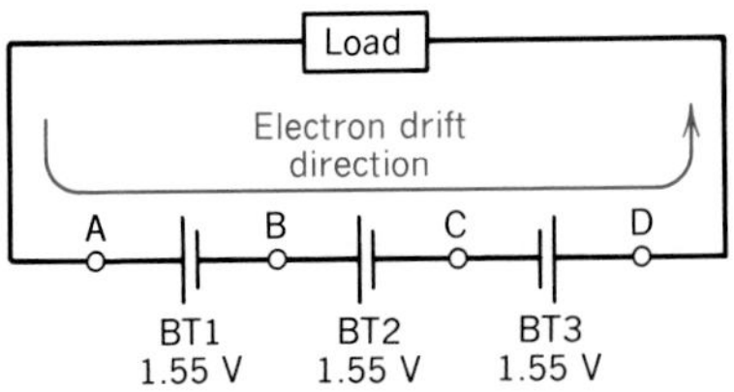

Figure 4.13 Electron drift in the circuit of Figure 4.12 when a load is connected.

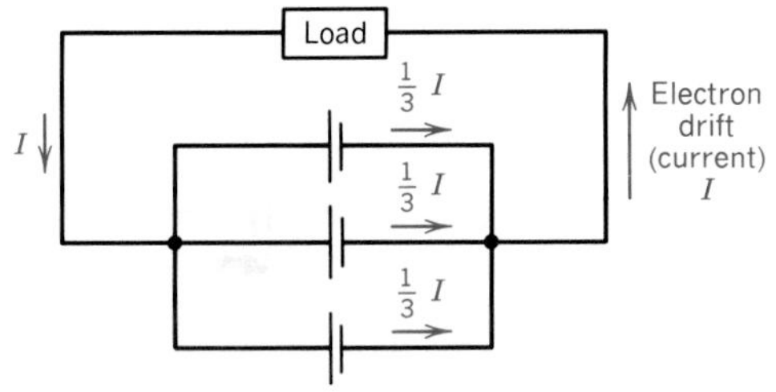

Figure 4.15 Electron drift (current) in a parallel circuit.

manner has the effect of canceling out the potential difference produced by one of the other two cells.

From this example, you can see that the electric field produced by one or more sources is a vector quantity, having both magnitude and direction, and that it is necessary to consider the direction of the field when adding the potential differences produced by a group of cells in series.

If a load is connected to the cells of Figure 4.12, the direction that the electrons will take in drifting through the circuit is as shown in Figure 4.13. Notice that the electrons move through BT3 in the direction opposite to that normal for a cell acting as a source. Such a reverse current will produce large quantities of gas in a Leclanché cell, and, if the current is great enough or flows for a long enough time, the cell will be destroyed.

B.3 SOURCES IN PARALLEL

The amount of energy delivered by a source to a load depends not only on the potential difference produced by the source but also on the current through the circuit. In the previous chapter, you probably noticed that cells with larger plate areas had a larger service capacity than smaller ones of the same type. The maximum current that a cell can produce in a closed circuit, without a severe decrease in the cell potential difference, depends on the area of its plates. However, you cannot always expect to find commercial cells of the size necessary to produce exactly the current required by a particular load. This problem is solved by connecting several cells as shown in Figure 4.14. This arrangement is called a *parallel connection*. In this arrangement, each cell produces an amount of current, and the total current through the load is equal to the sum of the currents produced by all of the cells. If each of the cells is capable of supplying a current of 0.1 A, the three cells in parallel can supply up to 0.3 A without a serious decrease in the potential difference. Note that this arrangement still provides the potential difference of only one cell across the load. Unlike the case of the series connection, the potential differences do not add up. The arrangement of cells shown in Figure 4.14 operates as though it was a single Leclanché cell with a plate area three times that of a single cell.

In Figure 4.15, you can see that although all the circuit current goes through the load and through the wires connected to the load, only one-third of the total current is produced by and flows through each cell. If all the cells produce the same potential difference across their positive and negative terminals, any number of them can be connected in parallel to increase the circuit current.

When connecting cells in parallel, it is important that the potential differences produced by the cells are the same. If this is not the case, the condition shown in Figure 4.16 will exist. In this circuit, cell BT3, which produces a potential difference of only 0.8 V, actually acts like a second load in the circuit. Notice the direction of the electron drift through BT3. It is in the direction opposite to that of the other cells. As explained in Chapter 3, this would tend to recharge the cell, producing large quantities of gas that would de-

Figure 4.14 A parallel circuit.

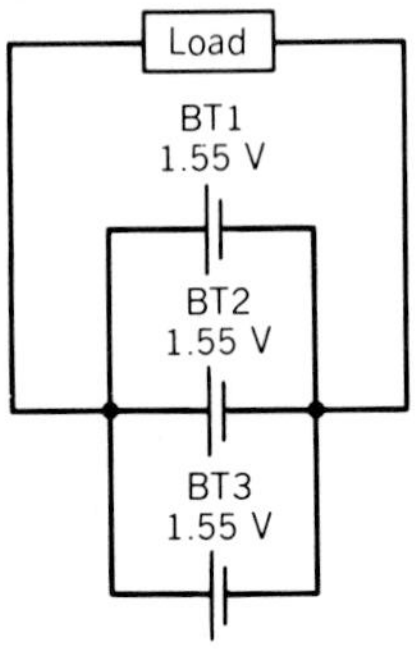

Figure 4.16 Electron drift (current) in a parallel circuit when one source produces a smaller potential difference than the others.

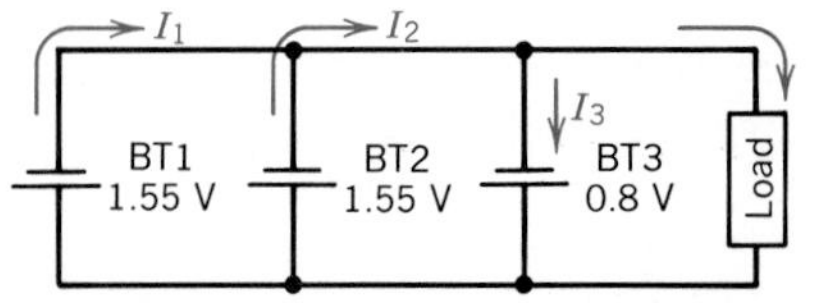

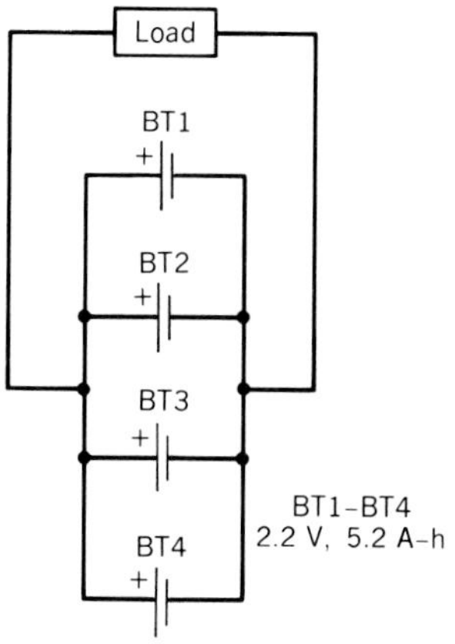

Figure 4.17 The service capacity of four identical cells connected in parallel is four times the service capacity of a single cell.

stroy it, even if the cells were secondary cells, since the charging rate would be very high.

The amount of current that can be produced by a number of similar cells connected in parallel without a serious drop in the potential difference can be determined by multiplying the current that a single cell could deliver in the circuit by the number of cells in the parallel connection. Mathematically this is written:

Total Current = Current Produced By One Cell × Number of Cells

Or, using letter symbols:

$$I_{\text{total}} = I_{\text{single cell}} \times \text{Number of Cells}$$

FORMULA 4.3

Similarly, the service capacity in A-h of a number of cells connected in parallel can be determined by multiplying the service capacity of a single cell by the number of cells in the parallel connection. Or, using mathematical form:

$$\text{Service capacity} = \text{Service capacity}_{\text{one cell}} \times \text{Number of Cells}$$

FORMULA 4.4

For example, each of the sources in the parallel circuit in Figure 4.17 is a size X sealed lead–acid cell at full charge, with a service capacity of 5.2 A-h. The service capacity of the four cells connected in parallel is 4 × 5.2, or 20.8 A-h.

B.4 SERIES–PARALLEL CONNECTION OF SOURCES

Some circuits require both more current and more potential difference than can be produced by either a series or parallel connection of individual cells. In circuits of this kind, a combination of series and parallel connections can be used to provide more potential difference *and* more current. A series–parallel connection of four source cells is shown in the schematic diagram of Figure 4.18. In this arrangement, two groups of two parallel-connected cells are in series. If the cells are Leclanché types, the potential difference between points *A* and *B* will be 1.55 V, and the potential difference between *B* and *C* will also be 1.55 V. This means that the potential difference between *A* and *C* is 3.1 V. Figure 4.19 shows the electron drift paths through the series–parallel connection. Each cell has exactly one-half of the total circuit current through it. The total circuit current is twice that through any cell of the arrangement.

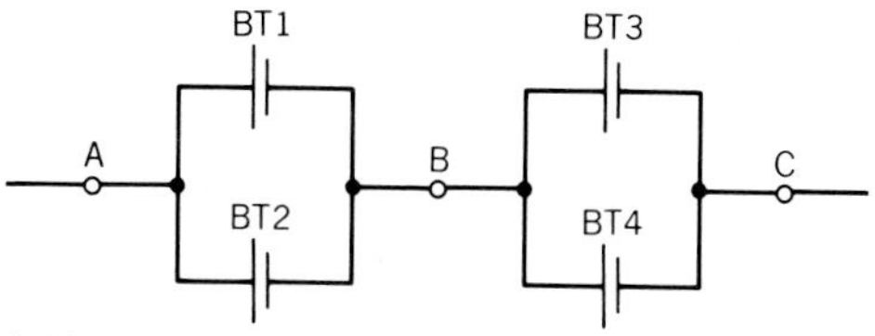

Figure 4.18 A series–parallel connection. Two groups of two parallel-connected cells are in series.

Although some might be impractical, there is no limit to the possible number of different series–parallel arrangements of sources. Because of this, the calculation of the potential difference and current in a series–parallel circuit may become difficult or complicated. There is a way, however, to simplify things through the use of *equivalent* circuits. The principle of equivalent circuits is so simple that some books say very little about it, but it is one of the most powerful methods for finding out what goes on in a particular electronic circuit. The principle is based on the fact that when the operation of a part of a circuit is being analyzed, it is possible to redraw the schematic of the circuit, substituting simpler arrangements of parts for more complex arrangements in a different portion of the circuit. This can be done provided that the electrical characteristics of the two arrangements are the

Figure 4.19 Electron drift (current) paths through the series–parallel connection of Figure 4.18.

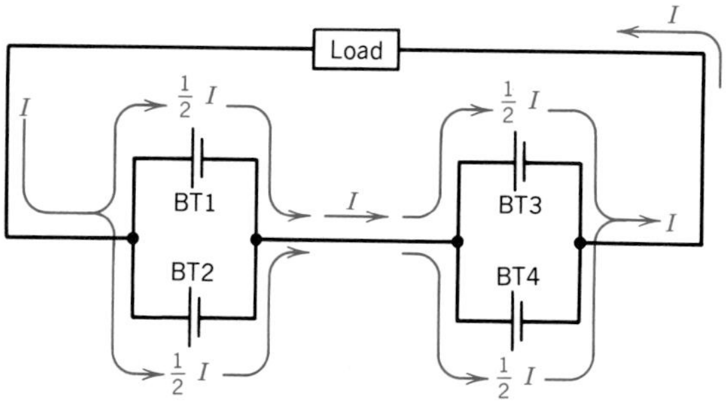

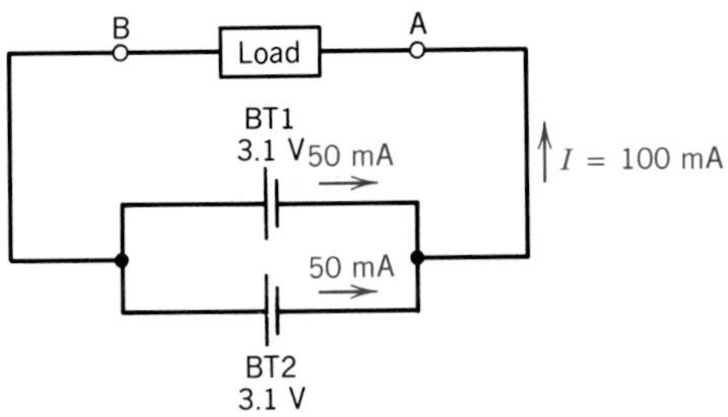

Figure 4.20 Two cells in parallel.

same. Consider the circuit of Figure 4.20. If you are interested in the potential difference between points *A* and *B*, you can redraw this schematic as shown in Figure 4.21, for purposes of analysis. As far as the load is concerned, the sources provide a potential difference of 3.1 V and a current of 100 mA, whether one or two source cells are involved. In the circuit of Figure 4.20, not much is gained by redrawing the two cells as a single equivalent cell with a potential difference of 3.1 V, but you can see that Figure 4.22*b* is going to be easier to work with than 4.22*a*.

There are methods of analysis that permit differing sources to be redrawn as a single equivalent source. But for the moment, if the sources are not too different, sufficient accuracy is provided by the two following approximations. The order in which they are applied does not matter.

APPROXIMATION A. Two or more sources connected in series may be replaced by a single equivalent source by adding the potential differences produced (paying attention to the directions of the electric fields, of course). In cases where the current or service capacity of the sources is not exactly the same, the current production capabilities or service capacity assigned to the equivalent source is the same as that of the replaced source producing the smallest current or having the smallest service capacity. This is necessary to avoid creating a situation in which *real* sources would be so overloaded that an explosion could result.

EXAMPLE:

What is the potential difference between points *A* and *E* in Figure 4.23*a*? What is the maximum safe current? ■

Figure 4.21 Equivalent circuit of Figure 4.20, the two cells in parallel have been redrawn as a single equivalent cell.

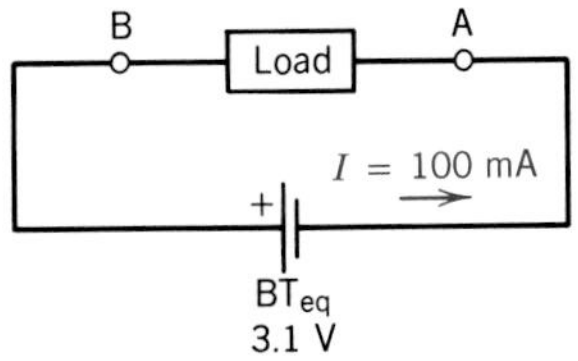

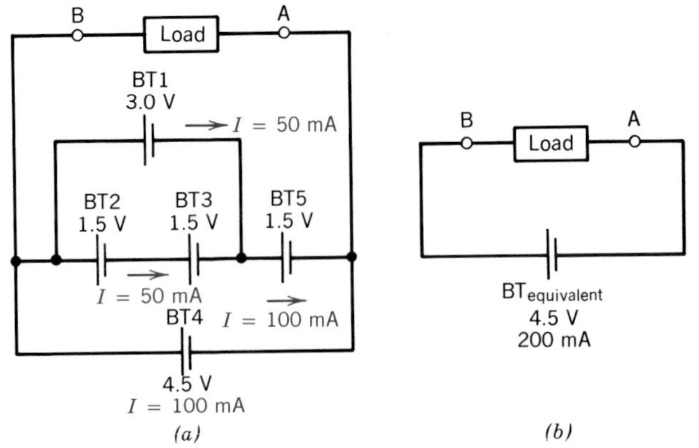

Figure 4.22 An equivalent circuit makes it easier to visualize the function of a circuit.

SOLUTION:

Redraw the schematic replacing the four source cells with an equivalent source by calculating the potential difference supplied by each of the cells.

BT1	1.55 V
BT2	2.2 V
BT3	1.3 V
BT4	2.2 V
Total	7.25 V

The safe current or maximum service capacity of the equivalent source should be the same as that of the cell which produces the smallest current or has the smallest service capacity. In this case, the cell with the smallest current capability is BT3. The equivalent source produces a potential difference of 7.25 V at a maximum current of 65 mA, as shown in Figure 4.23*b*. ■

APPROXIMATION B. Two or more sources connected in parallel may be redrawn as a single equivalent source with a current-producing capability or service

Figure 4.23 A series circuit and its equivalent circuit.

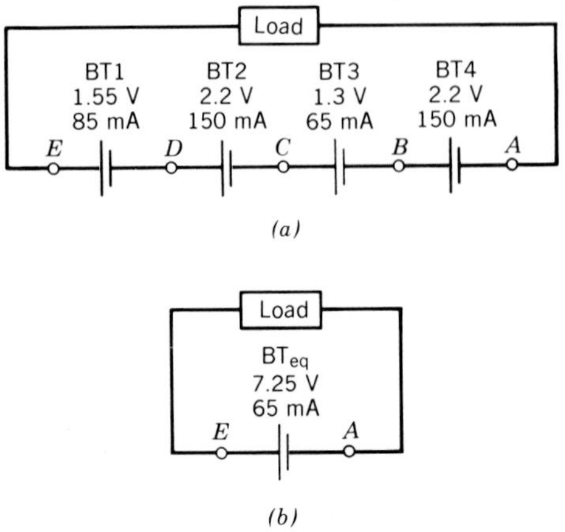

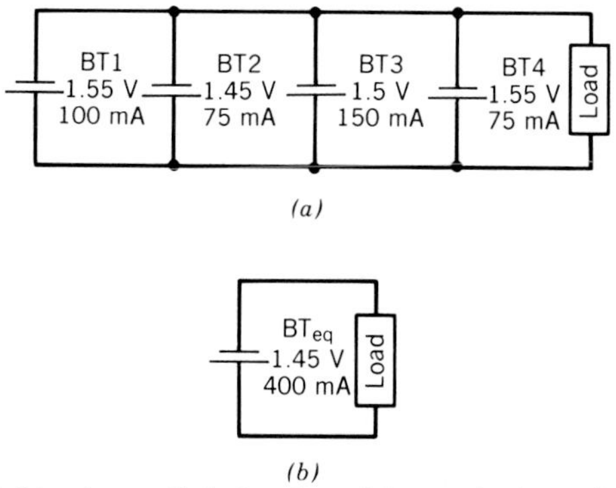

Figure 4.24 A parallel circuit and its equivalent circuit.

capacity obtained by adding the current produced or the service capacity of each of the parallel-connected sources. In cases where the potential difference produced by the individual sources is not exactly the same, the equivalent source is assigned the smallest of the potential differences produced by the parallel sources, although the true potential difference will be somewhat greater than this. (In the case of chemical cells, this difference has to be small or serious conditions may occur.)

EXAMPLE:

What is the potential difference between points *A* and *B* in Figure 4.24*a*? How much current can flow through the load without a serious drop in potential difference? ■

SOLUTION:

Redraw the schematic diagram, replacing the four parallel sources with a single equivalent source. According to Approximation B, the current delivered by the equivalent source will be the sum of the currents actually produced by the sources in parallel. The potential difference across the equivalent source will be the same as the smallest of the potential differences of the parallel sources. The equivalent circuit is shown in Figure 4.24*b*. The potential difference across the load is 1.45 V, and the current through it will be 400 mA. ■

You can continue to combine sources into equivalents until all have been replaced by one equivalent source. Do not, however, confuse the equivalent circuit with reality. You have drawn an equivalent circuit as an aid in analyzing the behvior of a real circuit, but the equivalent circuit is only a tool, a mathematical abstraction of a real circuit. It may or may not actually function if built, and in most cases, the components called for in equivalent circuits are not actually available commercially. In the next section, you will see one of the important differences between equivalent and actual circuits.

B.5 CIRCUIT EQUIVALENTS

Compare the series–parallel arrangements of Figures 4.25 and 4.26. In the first of these, two groups of two parallel-connected cells are connected in series. In the second circuit, two groups of series-connected cells are connected in parallel. The two circuits appear to be quite different, in spite of the fact that they are both series–parallel combinations of four cells. But when circuit equivalents are drawn for each of the two, certain similarities become evident.

In the first circuit, the parallel combinations of BT1 and BT2, as well as BT3 and BT4, may be replaced by equivalent sources producing a current of 200 mA and a potential difference of 1.55 V, as shown in Figure 4.27*a*. As a second step, the two equivalent sources connected in series may be replaced by a single equivalent source producing a potential difference of 3.1 V and a current of 200 mA. This equivalent circuit is drawn in Figure 4.27*b*.

In the circuit of Figure 4.26, each of the two series arrangements, BT1–BT2 and BT3–BT4 may be re-

Figure 4.25 Two groups of two parallel-connected cells connected in series.

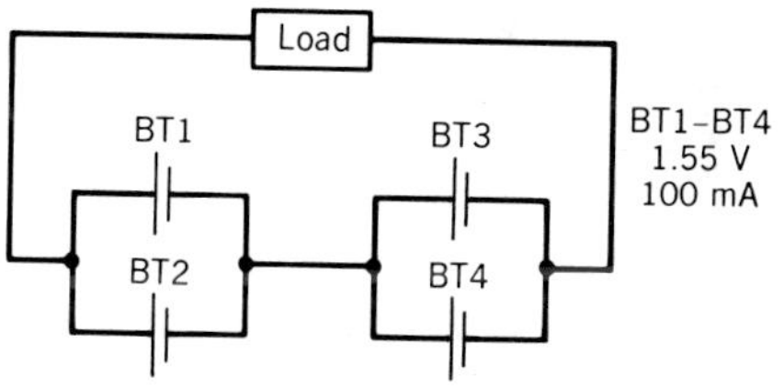

Figure 4.26 Two groups of series-connected cells connected in parallel.

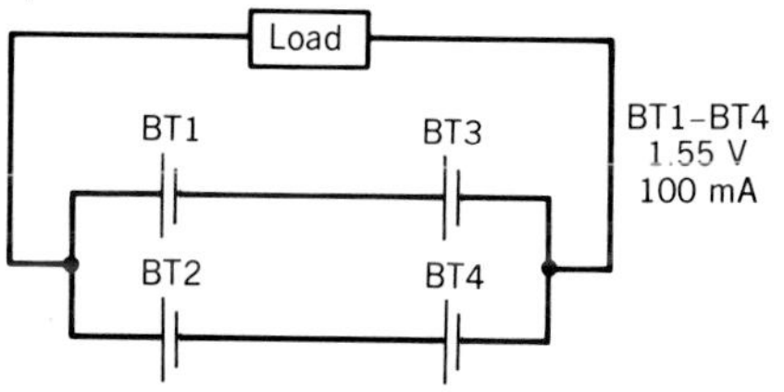

Figure 4.27 Redrawing of the schematic of Figure 4.25 to obtain an equivalent circuit.

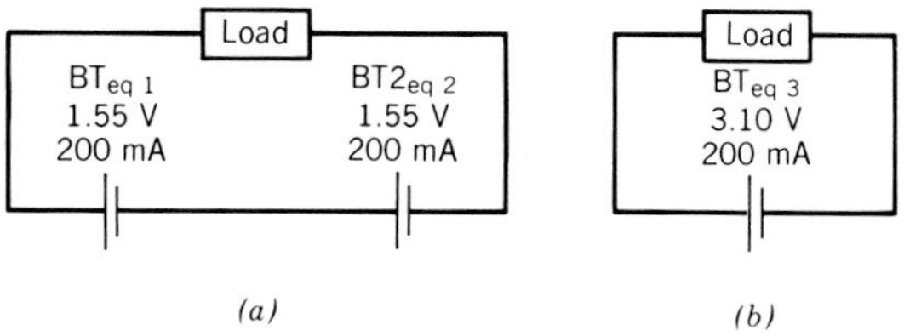

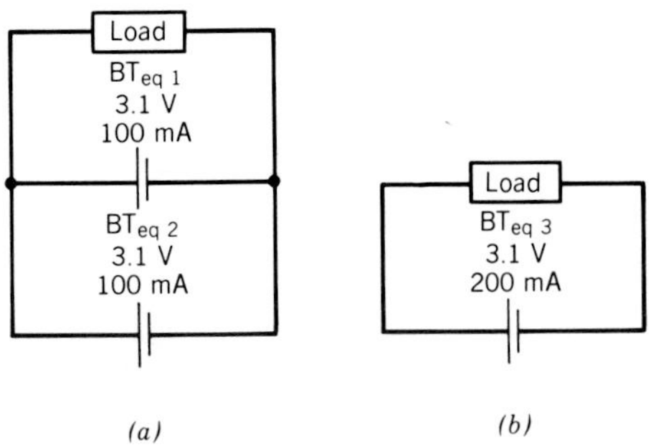

Figure 4.28 Redrawing the schematic of Figure 4.26 to obtain an equivalent circuit.

placed with an equivalent source producing a potential difference of 3.1 V and a current of 100 mA. This replacement is shown in Figure 4.28*a*. As a second step, the two parallel equivalent sources may be replaced with a single equivalent source producing a potential difference of 3.1 V and a current of 200 mA, as seen in Figure 4.28*b*.

B.6 GROUNDED CIRCUITS

Beginning students should be aware of the practice of *grounding* sources. This is the connection of one of the source terminals to a metal frame or network of interconnected ground points. Usually, the frame or ground point network is also connected to the Earth by the electrical distribution system or other means of connection. Although almost any point in a circuit or any terminal of a source can be grounded, it is generally the most negative source terminal that is connected to ground. Since this represents the point at which electrons furnished by the source have the most potential energy, and require distribution to most parts of an electronic unit, grounding frequently results in a saving in the amount of wire needed. Another advantage of grounding one terminal of a source, when connection to the earth is used, is the prevention of static charge damage to components in the circuit. Earth grounding of electronic unit panels and cabinets also serves to prevent the possibility of electric shock to individuals operating the equipment. Figure 4.29 shows a schematic diagram of a power source composed of three carbon–zinc cells connected in series. The negative terminal of BT3 is connected to ground, as shown by the presence of the ground symbol.

In the earlier discussion of sources in series, parallel, and series–parallel, the potential differences between pairs of points in the circuits were determined. When a source terminal or any other circuit point is grounded, a reference is established for potential measurements. Such measurements are taken with the common, or black meter lead connected to the grounded point of the circuit. Since potential indications can be either positive or negative with respect to ground, a digital multimeter is preferred for this type of measurement. An analog meter can easily be damaged by incorrect connection.

When the common probe of a digital multimeter is connected to the grounded point in the circuit of Figure 4.29, it is then possible to measure the potential of any point in the circuit with respect to the ground reference. Point *E* in the diagram is an isolated, grounded terminal. If the red (positive) meter probe tip is touched to point *A* in the circuit, the meter reading will be nearly zero. This is true because point *A* is at a potential of zero with reference to the circuit ground. In theory, all circuit points shown connected by a solid, straight line in a schematic diagram are assumed to be at the same potential. Similarly, if the red probe tip is moved to point *E*, an isolated, grounded point, the meter reading will still be zero (ideally) since all grounded points are at the same potential. In other words, there is no potential difference between two grounded points. The ground, then, acts like a conductor between the point of the circuit ground and point *E*.

If the red probe tip is moved to point *B*, there will be a meter reading of +1.5 V due to the existence of a source. In effect, the meter is now measuring the potential difference across BT3. When the red probe is touched to point *C*, the meter reading will be +3 V

Figure 4.29 A circuit with the most negative source terminal grounded.

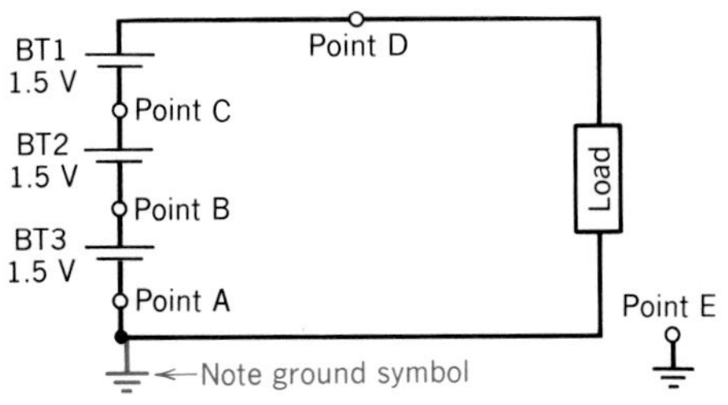

Figure 4.30 Circuit with the most positive source terminal grounded.

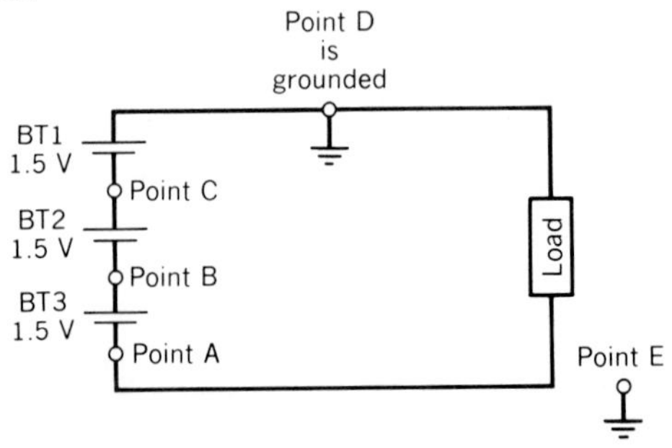

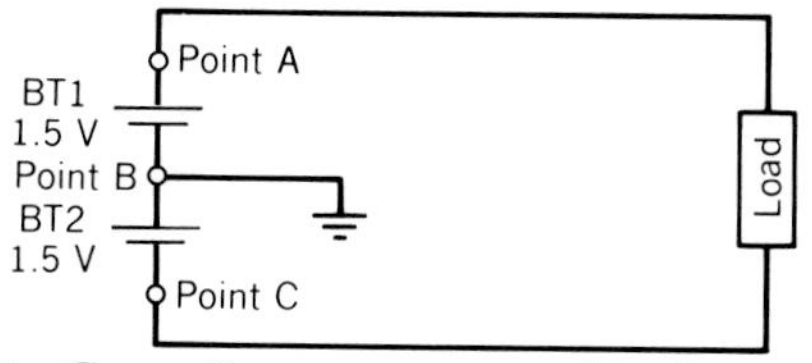

Figure 4.31 Grounding at a source midpoint terminal.

since the potential difference across the series combination of BT2 and BT3 is being measured. Finally, touching the red probe tip to point *D* will indicate a potential of +4.5 V at that point with respect to ground.

Although the grounding of the most negative source terminal is usual, sometimes it is the most positive terminal that is grounded, as shown in Figure 4.30. Here the circuit is the same as in the previous figure, except that the ground connection has been moved to point *D*. This in no way affects the function of the circuit but does change the potential measurements at the various points in the circuit with respect to the new reference. Connecting the common probe tip to the ground at point *D*, and touching the red probe tip to point *E* produces a meter reading of zero. This is true because both points are at the same potential. Moving the red probe tip to point *C*, on the other hand, produces a meter reading of −1.5 V. Since point *D*, which is now the reference, is connected to the positive terminal of BT1, point *C*, connected to the negative terminal of BT1, will be at a more negative potential with respect to the reference. Similarly, points *B* and *A* will show measured potentials of −3 and −4.5 V, respectively.

Figure 4.31 shows another way of grounding a source terminal. With the ground reference connected to point *B*, point *A* will show a potential of +1.5 V and point *C* a potential of −1.5 V. This grounding arrangement is becoming increasingly more common in modern units, and many power supplies produce +15 and −15 V with respect to a ground reference.

C. EXAMPLES AND COMPUTATIONS

C.1 FORMULAS AND EQUATIONS

By now you have learned a number of formulas, that is, mathematical ways of stating relationships among electrical quantities in simple terms that make it easier to calculate quantities that are not directly given.

EXAMPLE:
You know that a charge of 3 C passes a point in a circuit in 2 s. What is the circuit current? ■

SOLUTION:
The answer to this question can be found by using Formula 3.1. This formula is:

$$I = \frac{Q}{t}$$

or, in words, the current is equal to the charge in coulombs divided by the time required for this charge to pass a point in the circuit. The formula is used by *substituting* the known values for their letters in the formula

$$I = \frac{Q}{t} = \frac{3}{2}$$

and then performing the indicated arithmetic. The answer is written, $I = 1.5$. ■

A formula consists of some letters that represent quantities, numbers, and an equals sign. The letters used in formulas are the standard quantity symbols like *I*, *E*, and *Q* that you have previously used, while the numbers and mathematical signs specify certain arithmetic operations.

EXAMPLES:
I means the current through a particular part of a circuit.
$I + 4$ means the current through a particular part of a circuit plus 4.
$2I$ means two times the current through a particular part of a circuit. ■

Sometimes, when it is necessary to distinguish among a number of different components or quantities, additional numbers or *subscripts* are used. You have previously seen how individual cells may be distinguished in a complex circuit by calling them BT1, BT2, and so forth. Subscripting is nothing more than putting this additional identifying number below the line, BT_1, BT_2, and so forth.

Although a formula uses several quantity symbols, in most cases the actual numerical values of these quantities are known. They have been measured, or calculated previously, or are simply given in the statement of a problem. These quantities are called *given* or *known* quantities. There is always, however, at least one quantity whose numerical value is not known. It is called the *unknown quantity*, and the formula is used to describe the arithmetic operations required to calculate the unknown using known or given quantities.

This is done through the use of the equals sign (=). The equals sign is a symbolic way of saying that the arithmetic value of all the numbers and letters to the left of the equals sign is the same as the arithmetic value of all the terms to the right of it. For example, it is possible to write

$$3 \times 2 = 5 + 1$$

A formula that uses an equals sign is called an *equation*. Equations are used by performing certain mathematical operations that permit all the unknown quantities to be placed on one side of the equals sign and the known quantities to be placed on the other side. This permits *solving* the equation by carrying out the arithmetic functions required by the side of the equation containing the known quantities.

These arithmetic functions are usually rather simple. On the other hand, the operations that permit the unknown quantities to be collected on one side of the equation and the known quantities on the other are sometimes more complicated. In general, you should think of the equation as a balanced see-saw. In both the equation and the see-saw, it is possible to add or subtract something from the balancing weights, but in order to preserve the balance, you must add or subtract the same weight or quantity from both sides of the balance point. In an equation, the equals sign can be thought of as the point of balance. For example, in the equation $E + 3 = 15$, E is the unknown quantity, and 3 and 15 are known quantities. To solve this equation, that is, to determine the value of E, the quantity $+3$ has to be removed from the left side of the equation. This can be done by subtracting 3 from *both* sides of the equation:

$$\begin{aligned} E + 3 &= 15 \\ -3 \quad &\quad -3 \\ E \quad &= 12 \end{aligned}$$

Performing this solves the equation for the unknown quantity E. This can be stated as a general rule.

The same quantity can be added to or subtracted from both sides of an equation without disturbing the balance of the equation.

Solve for the unknown quantity in the following equations:

a. $Q + 15 = 27$
b. $2 + A - 5 = 6$
c. $3 + X = 6 + 4$
d. $E - 6 = 7$
e. $15 - R = 10$
f. $18 - E = 3$
g. $H + 0.0037 = 0.083$
h. $Z - 9 = 6 + 5$
i. $3 + X = \frac{3}{2}$
j. $A - 2 = B + 5$, where $B = 7$

Similarly, both sides of an equation can be multiplied or divided by the same number without disturbing the equation. This is frequently a very useful method for solving an equation, but care must be taken that both *sides* of the equation are multiplied or divided.

EXAMPLE:
Solve for the value of R in the following equation:

$$2R + 8 = 18$$

■

SOLUTION:
Recall that $2R$ means 2 *times* R. Therefore, to solve for R, it is necessary to divide by 2. But this does NOT mean

$$\begin{aligned} 2R + 8 &= 18 \\ \div 2 \quad &\quad \div 2 \\ R + 8 &= 9 \end{aligned} \qquad \text{THIS IS NOT CORRECT!}$$

It is necessary to divide every term of the equation by 2,

$$\begin{aligned} (2R + 8) &= 18 \\ \div 2 \quad &\quad \div 2 \end{aligned}$$

or, $R + 4 = 9$, in order to preserve the balance of the equation, and to obtain the answer.

$$\frac{2R + 8}{2} = \frac{18}{2}$$

$$\begin{aligned} R + 4 &= 9 \\ -4 &\; -4 \\ \hline R \quad &= 5 \end{aligned}$$

■

Notice that in adding or subtracting quantities from both sides of an equation, it is only necessary to add or subtract from each *side* of the equation; but when multiplying or dividing, it is necessary to multiply or divide each term of the equation.

EXAMPLE:
Solve the following equation for Q:

$$\frac{1}{7}Q + 2 = 3$$

■

SOLUTION:
In its present form, this equation is in terms of $\frac{1}{7}$ Q rather than Q. In order to solve the equation for Q it is necessary to multiply both sides by 7.

$$\left(\frac{1}{7}Q + 2\right) = 3$$

$$\times 7 \qquad \times 7$$

$$Q + 14 = 21$$

Subtracting 14 from both sides of the equation yields

$$Q = 7$$

Instead of multiplying first, 2 could have been subtracted from both sides

$$\frac{1}{7}Q + 2 = 3$$

$$\underline{\quad -2 \quad -2}$$

$$\frac{1}{7}Q = 1$$

At this point, the multiplication by 7 produces the solution

$$\frac{1}{7}Q = 1$$

$$\underline{\times 7 \qquad \times 7}$$

$$Q = 7$$

■

The general rule for this mathematical operation is:

An equation remains unchanged if both sides are multiplied or divided by the same number. Note that this means that each term in the equation must be multiplied or divided by the same number.

For practice, solve the following equations for the value of the unknown quantity.

a. $6Y + 12 = 18$

b. $\frac{8 + Z}{2} = 7.5$

c. $3X + 7 = 16$

d. $\frac{Z}{3} + \frac{Z}{2} = 36$

e. $\frac{5}{9}C + 32 = 6$

f. $3.75X = 4$

g. $\frac{J}{2} + 3 = 7$

h. $\frac{15}{32}X - 2 = 7$

i. $0.035Y = 0.15$

A third method of isolating all the unknown quantities on one side of an equation is referred to as *transposition and collection of terms*. Collection of terms is merely the grouping and simplification of terms. It is done by rewriting both sides of the equation so that all similar terms, that is, all terms involving the same unknown, and all the number terms, are grouped together.

EXAMPLE:
Rewrite the following equation to collect the terms:

$$-3 + A + 2A + 7 - A = 9B - 6 + 3B + 4 - 2$$

■

SOLUTION:
Begin by rewriting to group similar terms on one or the other side of the equation

$$+A + 2A - A - 3 + 7 = 9B + 3B - 6 - 2 + 4$$

Then simplify the terms by combining

$$2A + 4 = 12B - 4$$

■

Collection of terms is one of the most common tasks connected with the use of formulas. It has to be done when the known quantities have been replaced by their values in a formula.

Transposition is also a simple process. Consider this equation:

$$3A + 1 = A + 15$$

It would be easy to determine the value of A if all the terms involving A were on one side of the equation and all the pure numbers on the other. Transposition makes this possible. Recall that it is possible to add or subtract the same quantity from both sides of an equation. It does not matter whether this quantity is a number, or a letter representing a number. For instance, it is possible to "remove" the A term from the right side of the above equation by subtracting A from both sides:

$$3A + 1 = A + 15$$

$$\underline{-A \qquad\quad -A}$$

$$2A + 1 = 15$$

Now, subtract 1 from each side

$$2A + 1 = 15$$

$$\underline{\quad -1 \quad -1}$$

$$2A = 14$$

and divide by 2 to obtain the value of A

$$\frac{2A}{2} = \frac{14}{2}$$
$$A = 7$$

The following problems provide review of the methods of solving equations presented so far:

a. $3.5X = 4 - X$
b. $a + 6 = 16 - 5(a + 24)$
c. $B + C = 6B$, where $C = -2$
d. $3(2 + a) - 4a = 0$
e. $0.75D + 2 = 3$
f. $0.065Y + \frac{Y}{2} = 0.25$
g. $\frac{3E + 7}{9} = 6E - 1$
h. $3X + 7 = 16 - 3X$
i. $\frac{Z}{2} + 3 = 7 - Z$

C.2 CHECKING SOLUTIONS BY UNIT ANALYSIS

When the solution of a practical problem involves one or more formulas, it is a good idea to check your recollection of the formulas. One way to do this is to use a process called *dimensional analysis*. This is done by substituting the measuring units for the unit symbols in the formula.

EXAMPLE:
You seem to remember that the formula relating speed (V), distance (D), and time (T), is $V = \frac{D}{T}$. Use dimensional analysis to check this formula. ■

SOLUTION:
Dimensional analysis is performed by substituting the measuring units for the unit symbols in the formula. The measuring unit for speed (V) is meters per second or $\frac{\text{m}}{\text{s}}$, for distance ($D$) it is meters (m), and for time, it is seconds (s). Substituting, $\frac{\text{m}}{\text{s}} = \frac{\text{m}}{\text{s}}$. The measuring units on the left side balance those on the right side, showing that the dimensions, that is, the units of measurement, are correct. This does not necessarily mean that the formula is actually correct. For instance, $V = \frac{D}{T}$, $V = 3\frac{D}{T}$, and $V = 3\frac{D}{T} + 16$, all provide the same balance of measuring units. It does, however, show whether all the required quantities have been considered. ■

C.3 FORMULAS FOR METRIC EQUIVALENTS

In addition to the formulas that relate electrical quantities, the following common formulas can be of value in technical work.

LENGTH (L)

$$L_{\text{meters}} = 0.9144003 \times L_{\text{yards}}$$
$$L_{\text{yards}} = 1.093613 \times L_{\text{meters}}$$
$$L_{\text{meters}} = 0.3048 \times L_{\text{feet}}$$
$$L_{\text{feet}} = 3.280840 \times L_{\text{meters}}$$
$$L_{\text{meters}} = 0.0254 \times L_{\text{inches}}$$
$$L_{\text{inches}} = 39.3700787 \times L_{\text{meters}}$$

AREA (A)

$$A_{\text{square meters}} = 0.8361274 \times A_{\text{square yards}}$$
$$A_{\text{square yards}} = 1.195990 \times A_{\text{square meters}}$$
$$A_{\text{square meters}} = 0.092903 \times A_{\text{square feet}}$$
$$A_{\text{square feet}} = 10.76391 \times A_{\text{square meters}}$$
$$A_{\text{square meters}} = 0.00064516 \times A_{\text{square inches}}$$
$$A_{\text{square inches}} = 1550.003 \times A_{\text{square meters}}$$

VOLUME (V)

$$V_{\text{cubic meters}} = 0.7645549 \times V_{\text{cubic yards}}$$
$$V_{\text{cubic yards}} = 1.3079506 \times V_{\text{cubic meters}}$$
$$V_{\text{cubic meters}} = 0.028316 \times V_{\text{cubic feet}}$$
$$V_{\text{cubic feet}} = 35.31467 \times V_{\text{cubic meters}}$$
$$V_{\text{cubic meters}} = 0.000016387 \times V_{\text{cubic inches}}$$
$$V_{\text{cubic inches}} = 61023.74 \times V_{\text{cubic meters}}$$

LIQUID MEASURE (V)

$$V_{\text{liters}} = 3.7854125 \times V_{\text{gallons}}$$
$$V_{\text{gallons}} = 0.264172052 \times V_{\text{liters}}$$
$$V_{\text{liters}} = 0.946353 \times V_{\text{quarts}}$$
$$V_{\text{quarts}} = 1.05668820 \times V_{\text{liters}}$$
$$V_{\text{liters}} = 0.473177 \times V_{\text{pints}}$$
$$V_{\text{pints}} = 2.1133741 \times V_{\text{liters}}$$

MASS (M)

$$M_{\text{kilograms}} = 0.4535924 \times M_{\text{pounds}}$$
$$M_{\text{pounds}} = 2.20462262 \times M_{\text{kilograms}}$$
$$M_{\text{kilograms}} = 0.028349 \times M_{\text{ounces}}$$
$$M_{\text{ounces}} = 35.2739619 \times M_{\text{kilograms}}$$

FORCE (F)

$$F_{\text{newtons}} = 4.4482225 \times F_{\text{pounds}}$$
$$F_{\text{pounds}} = 0.22480894 \times F_{\text{newtons}}$$

Using these formulas requires you to choose the correct form and to substitute the known value to the right of the equals sign. The arithmetic can then be performed with a calculator and the round-off rules can be applied.

EXAMPLE:
The Little Gem Computer Company has received an order for ten of its DUMBO-1 computers from the French government. Since France uses the metric system, the shipping papers will have to list the weight of the units in kilograms. Each DUMBO-1 (fully packed) weighs 1756 pounds. What will be the weight of the shipment in kilograms? ■

SOLUTION:
To convert from pounds to kilograms, use the formula:
$M_{\text{kilograms}} = 0.4535924 \times M_{\text{pounds}}$
Ten computers weigh 10 × 1756 lb, or 17,560 lb.
Substituting,
$M_{\text{kilograms}} = 0.4535924 \times 17{,}560$
$M_{\text{kilograms}} = 7965.0825$
Since the original measurement is given to four significant places, the answer should be rounded off to 7965 kg. ■

C.4 CONVERSIONS USING A COMPUTER PROGRAM

In cases where it is necessary to perform many conversions from one system to the other, a simple BASIC program can be used to save time and increase accuracy. The program given here is an example. Better-designed programs can easily be written, but this one will work on most small computers. It will convert the following units:

YARDS to METERS
METERS to YARDS
FEET to METERS
METERS to FEET
INCHES to METERS
METERS to INCHES
SQUARE YARDS to SQUARE METERS
SQUARE METERS to SQUARE YARDS
SQUARE FEET to SQUARE METERS
SQUARE METERS to SQUARE FEET
SQUARE INCHES to SQUARE METERS
SQUARE METERS TO SQUARE INCHES
CUBIC YARDS to CUBIC METERS
CUBIC METERS to CUBIC YARDS
CUBIC FEET to CUBIC METERS
CUBIC METERS to CUBIC FEET
CUBIC INCHES to CUBIC METERS
CUBIC METERS to CUBIC INCHES
GALLONS to LITERS
LITERS to GALLONS
QUARTS to LITERS
LITERS to QUARTS
PINTS to LITERS
LITERS to PINTS
POUNDS to KILOGRAMS
KILOGRAMS to POUNDS
OUNCES to KILOGRAMS
KILOGRAMS to OUNCES
POUNDS to NEWTONS
NEWTONS to POUNDS
...

PROGRAM 4.1 UNIT CONVERSION

```
10   REM: PROGRAM FOR CONVERTING
       UNITS
20   RESTORE: INPUT "I WANT TO CONVERT
       FROM ", J$
30   INPUT "TO ",K$
35   FOR N = 0 TO 29
40   READ A$, B$,C
50   IF A$ = J$ AND IF B$ = K$ THEN GOTO
       80
60   NEXT N
70   PRINT "TRY ENTERING UNITS AGAIN":
       GOTO 20
80   PRINT "ENTER VALUE IN ",J$
85   INPUT J
90   K = C*J
100  PRINT J;J$ " = "K;K$
110  INPUT "DO YOU WISH TO CONVERT
       ANY OTHER UNITS? Y/N",Q$
120  IF Q$ = "Y" THEN GOTO 20
130  PRINT "GOODBYE": END
140  DATA METERS,YARDS,1.093613,YARDS,
       METERS,0.9144003
150  DATA METERS,FEET,3.280840,FEET,
       METERS,0.3048
160  DATA METERS,INCHES,39.3700787,
       INCHES,METERS,0.0254
170  DATA SQUARE METERS,SQUARE
       YARDS,1.195990,SQUARE YARDS
180  DATA SQUARE METERS,0.8361274,
       SQUARE METERS,SQUARE FEET
190  DATA 10.76391,SQUARE FEET,SQUARE
       METERS,0.092903
200  DATA SQUARE METERS,SQUARE
       INCHES,1550.003,SQUARE INCHES
210  DATA SQUARE METERS,0.00064516,
       CUBIC METERS,CUBIC YARDS
220  DATA 1.3079506,CUBIC YARDS,CUBIC
       METERS,0.7645549
```

```
230 DATA CUBIC METERS,CUBIC FEET,
      35.31467,CUBIC FEET
240 DATA CUBIC METERS,0.028316,CUBIC
      METERS,CUBIC INCHES
250 DATA 61023.74,CUBIC INCHES,CUBIC
      METERS,0.000016387
260 DATA LITERS,GALLONS,0.264172052,
      GALLONS,LITERS,3.7854125
270 DATA LITERS,QUARTS,1.05668820,
      QUARTS,LITERS,0.946353
280 DATA LITERS,PINTS,2.1133741,PINTS,
      LITERS,0.473177
290 DATA KILOGRAMS,POUNDS,2.20462262,
      POUNDS,KILOGRAMS
300 DATA 0.4535924,KILOGRAMS,OUNCES,
      35.2739619,OUNCES
310 DATA KILOGRAMS,0.028349,NEWTONS,
      POUNDS,0.22480894
320 DATA POUNDS,NEWTONS,4.4482225
```

Be sure to enter the unit names exactly as above when using this program, otherwise the program will cause "TRY ENTERING UNITS AGAIN" to be printed. This will continue to happen until the unit names you type in are exactly the same as those stored in the DATA statements beginning in line 140.

EXAMPLE:
Convert 33.75 inches to meters. ■

SOLUTION:
After loading and running Program 4.1, type INCHES (RETURN) in answer to the question "I WANT TO CONVERT FROM." The program will display "TO," signaling you to enter the unit you wish to convert to. Enter

METERS (RETURN)

The program then begins reading the DATA statements in line 140 to determine the correct formula to use. The formula consists of the names of two units and a number by which the first unit must be multiplied in order to convert to the second unit. Once the unit names you have entered have been matched with those in the DATA statements, you will be asked to supply the actual measurement that has to be converted, "ENTER VALUE IN INCHES." The program then performs the substitution and the multiplication and prints the solution

33.75 INCHES = 0.85725 METERS. ■

Lines 35 and 60 of the program set up what is called a "for-next" loop. This ensures that the computer will stop looking for DATA statements after it has tried all the comparisons stored in the program. If this feature is not present, and if a unit not stored in the program (miles, for example) is entered, the program will stop itself after it has run through all the DATA statements.

Notice that this program does not perform the rounding-off operation, although this feature could be added. The conversion factors have been given to a much greater accuracy than is normally required, so you will usually have to round off after a conversion.

D. APPLICATIONS

D.1 FAILURE MODE ANALYSIS

The two circuits shown in Figures 4.32 and 4.33 are those previously studied in Section B.5. You will recall that the two circuits were shown to have the same equivalent circuit, and it was pointed out that the two were exactly the same as far as the load was concerned. But is this exactly true? That depends on the state of the components that make up the circuit. There is no difference between the two series–parallel arrangements as long as all is functioning normally, but is this still true if one of the more probable kinds of failure occurs? The ability to answer this question is important to the work of both circuit designers and maintenance personnel. There are really three questions involved:

1. In what ways do the components used in a circuit fail?

Figure 4.32 Two groups of two parallel-connected cells connected in series.

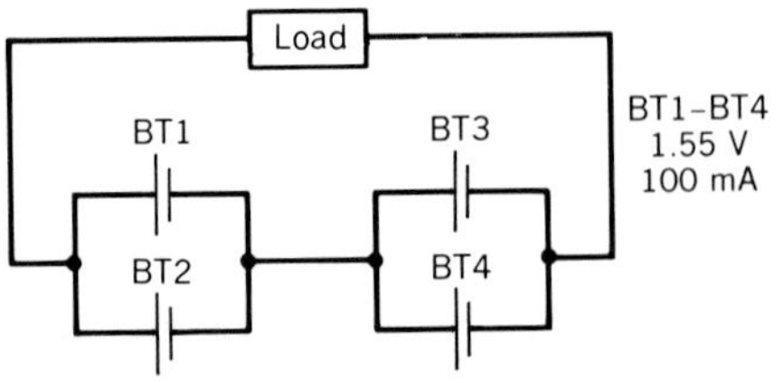

Figure 4.33 Two groups of series-connected cells connected in parallel.

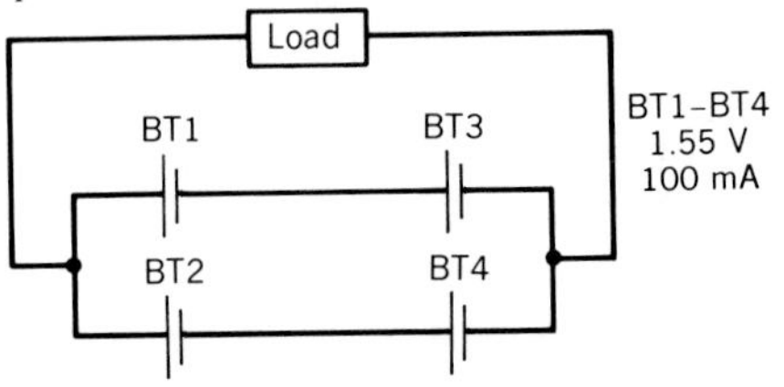

2. What are the probabilities of the various kinds of failures happening in the circuit under discussion?

3. What will happen in the circuit under discussion when one of the components fails in one of its more common failure modes?

If the cells in Figures 4.32 and 4.33 are Leclanché cells, the answers to questions 1 and 2 would be:

a. Highest probability mode of failure is a drop in the potential difference produced by a cell.

b. A low probability mode of failure for Leclanché cells in the kind of circuit shown is short-circuiting.

Now, what would happen if one of the cells, say BT1, in each of the circuits had a sudden drop in its produced potential difference to 1.1 V. In the circuit of Figure 4.32, the potential difference produced by the parallel combination of BT1 and BT2 would drop significantly. In series with the 1.55-V potential difference produced by the parallel combination of BT3 and BT4, this results in a potential difference less than the 3.1 V normally produced across the series–parallel combination.

In the circuit of Figure 4.33, the potential difference produced by BT1 in series with BT2 is going to be less than the normal 3.1 V, while the potential difference produced by the series combination of BT3 and BT4 is 1.55 + 1.55, or 3.1 V. The potential difference of the parallel combination of BT1–BT2 and BT3–BT4 will then be less than 3.1 V because of the smaller potential difference produced by one of the two circuit branches. Note that this is the same as the potential difference produced by the series–parallel combination shown in Figure 4.32.

This *failure mode analysis* shows that the circuits react in the same way for the highest probability failure in one of the cells. In the presence of a short circuit, however, which is not one of the standard failure modes for Leclanché cells, the behavior of the two arrangements will be different. A short circuit, that is, a direct current path as shown by the dotted lines in Figure 4.34 results in the two circuits producing two different potential differences. In the circuit of Figure 4.34*a*, a short circuit in BT1 also provides a direct path from the negative to the positive terminal of BT2. This will quickly cause a complete discharge of BT2, and perhaps damage to it. This is not exactly the case in the circuit of Figure 4.34*b*, where the damaged cell will be BT3.

Figure 4.34 The circuits of Figures 4.32*a* and 4.33*b* with BT1 short-circuited. In this condition the two circuits do not behave in exactly the same way.

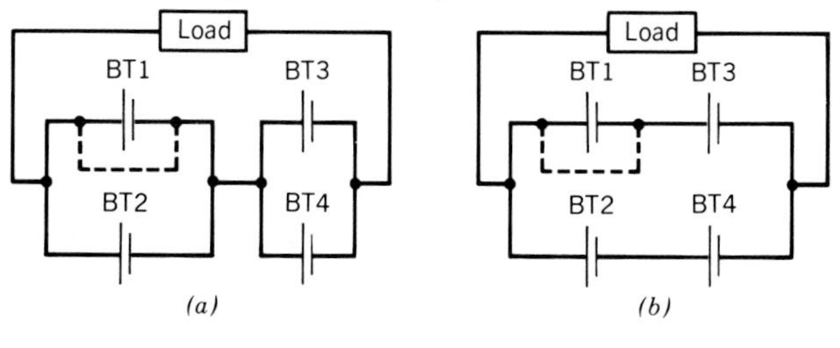

D.2 VARIATIONAL ANALYSIS

The technique of failure mode analysis described above is a very powerful tool for troubleshooting electronic units. It has the disadvantage, however, of requiring you to know quite a bit about the ways in which components fail when they are used in a particular way. This knowledge is hard to get unless you have a certain amount of experience with real equipment and components. Like medicine, electronic troubleshooting is part science and part personal skill.

There is another form of analysis, however, that the student can master completely. It is called *variational analysis* and can be of use in predicting which component in a circuit is faulty. More specifically, it will show you what will happen in a circuit when a particular component fails. Variational analysis is based on the fact that the potential and current at points in a circuit may be described mathematically through one or more equations. Although it is sometimes difficult to determine the equations that describe the potential and current in a complex circuit, once this has been done, it is rather easy to see what will happen if one or more of the quantities in the mathematical description are changed. This will enable you to compute the current and potential at various points in the circuit when everything is functioning properly and to understand how the potential and current will change as other circuit values change. Comparing the values of current and potential actually measured in a given circuit with those calculated from the mathematical description will tell you if there is something wrong. Noting what will happen to the value of the potential and the current in the mathematical description as certain quantities are varied will often point to a faulty component.

For example, the method of variational analysis can be applied to the circuit whose schematic is shown in Figure 4.35. This circuit is a series–parallel arrangement of several kinds of cells with different potential differences and current capacities. Although you are not yet able to write the mathematical description of this circuit, the rules that you have learned concerning series and parallel cells will enable you to answer the

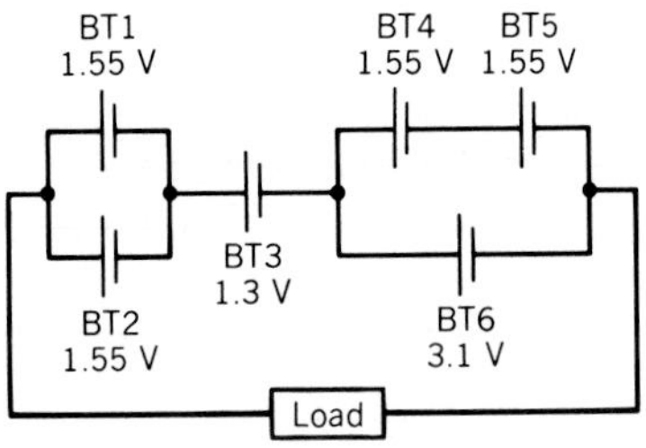

Figure 4.35 A series–parallel circuit.

following questions concerning the potential difference across the load and the current through it.

EXAMPLE:
What will happen to the potential difference across the load if the potential difference supplied by BT3 increases? ■

SOLUTION:
In order to apply the rules for the behavior of series and parallel circuits more easily, it is a good idea to reduce the complexity of this circuit by combining some of the cells to form equivalents, using the approximations given in Section B.4. Cells BT4 and BT5 can be combined into an equivalent cell BT7, as in Figure 4.36*a*. The arrangement is now somewhat easier to deal with, but it is also possible to combine BT1 and BT2 into one equivalent cell and BT7 and BT6 into another, as shown in Figure 4.36*b*. The original series–parallel circuit has now been reduced to a simple series circuit made up of three cells, although only one of these is actually a real component. It is easy to see that if the potential difference supplied by BT3 increases, the potential difference across all three cells and the load will also increase. ■

This example shows how variational analysis and the principle of equivalent circuits can be used to provide information useful for troubleshooting circuits. In the following chapters, these methods and principles will be put to increasing use.

Figure 4.36 Equivalent circuits of the circuit shown in Figure 4.35.

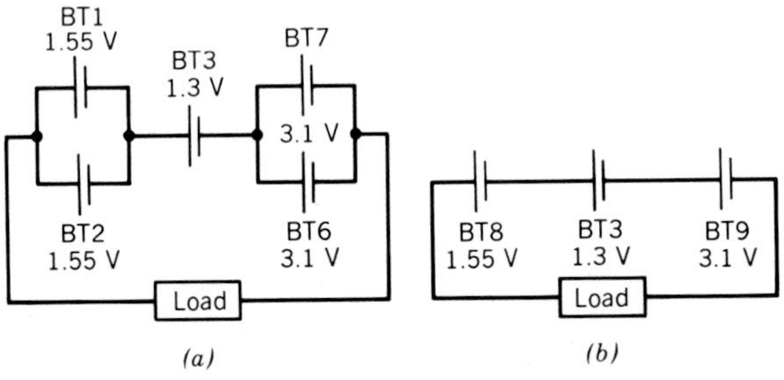

E. PROGRAMMED REVIEW

FRAME 1

Electrical and electronic diagrams use symbols to represent electrical components and units. Four major types of diagrams are pictorial, interconnect or wiring, block, and __________ diagrams.

a. Schematic. (2)
b. Any other answer, review Section B.1.

FRAME 2

The names of components, part numbers, or what are called __________ are usually shown in pictorial diagrams.

a. Reference designators. (3)
b. Any other answer, review Section B.1.1.

FRAME 3

Reference designators are used to uniquely identify the components in an electrical or electronic assembly. They also identify the __________ of the component.

a. Class or type. (4)
b. Any other answer, review Section B.1.1.

FRAME 4

The type of diagram that provides the most information about the function of individual electrical components in an assembly is the __________ diagram.

a. Schematic. (5)
b. Any other answer, review Section B.1.3.

FRAME 5

A type of diagram that is particularly helpful in troubleshooting or assembling an entire system is the __________ diagram. This type of diagram is detailed only in specifying wires, connectors, and connection points.

a. Interconnect or wiring. (6)
b. Any other answer, review Section B.1.2.

FRAME 6

The block diagram uses lines drawn between the blocks to represent the flow of ____________ or ____________ rather than wires or current paths.

a. Information; signals. (7)
b. Any other answer, review Section B.1.4.

FRAME 7

The arrangement of cells in Figure 4.37 is called ____________. If the three cells are Leclanché types, the potential difference across the load will be ____________ V.

a. Series or series-aiding; 4.5 or 4.65. (8)
b. Any other answer, review Section B.2.

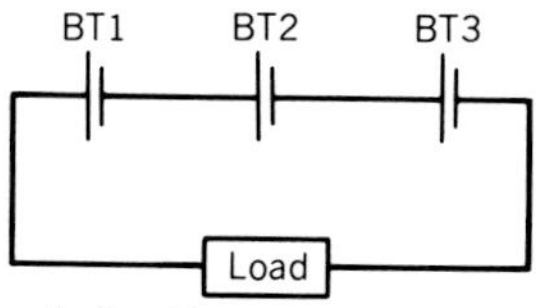

Figure 4.37 Circuit for Frame 7.

FRAME 8

If one of the cells in the diagram of Frame 7 is inserted backward, resulting in the circuit of Figure 4.38, the reversed cell is said to be in ____________. The potential difference across the load will now be ____________ V.

a. Series-opposing or series-bucking; 1.5 or 1.55. (9)
b. Any other answer, review Section B.2.

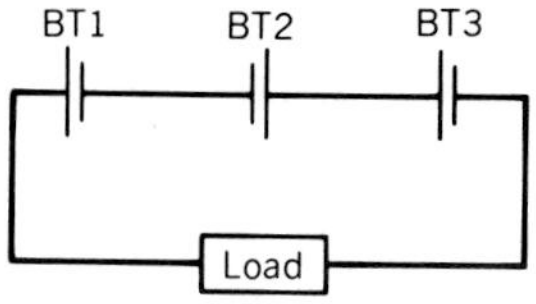

Figure 4.38 Circuit for Frame 8.

FRAME 9

In a series circuit there is only one current path without any branches. The current through any component is ____________ as that through any other component.

a. The same. (10)
b. Any other answer, review Section B.2.

FRAME 10

The circuit whose schematic is shown in Figure 4.39 is referred to as a ____________ circuit. The current through each of the cells ____________.

a. Parallel; may be different. (11)
b. Any other answer, review Section B.3.

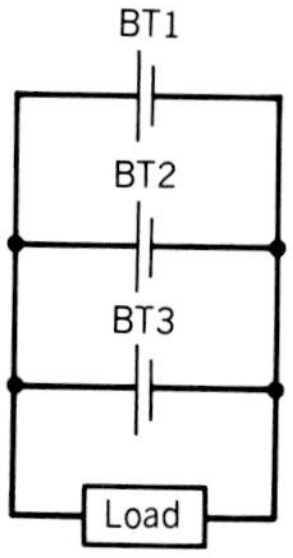

Figure 4.39 Circuit for Frames 10 through 12.

FRAME 11

The circuit of Figure 4.39 is used when it is necessary to furnish more ____________ to a load than can be supplied by a single cell without a serious drop in the potential difference.

a. Current. (12)
b. Any other answer, review Section B.3.

FRAME 12

In the circuit of Figure 4.39, each cell produces a potential difference of 2.2 V, can supply a current of 100 mA to the load, and has a service capacity of 4 A-h. What are the potential difference across and the current supplied to the load? What is the service capacity of the battery composed of BT1, BT2, and BT3?

a. 2.2 V; 300 mA; 12 A-h. (13)
b. Any other answer, review Section B.3.

FRAME 13

In order to calculate the current through a load, it is frequently useful to combine a series–parallel combination of source cells into a single, equivalent source. Draw the schematic of the equivalent circuit of Figure 4.40, showing the potential difference.

a. Potential difference is 3.1 V. (14)
b. Any other answer, review Section B.5.

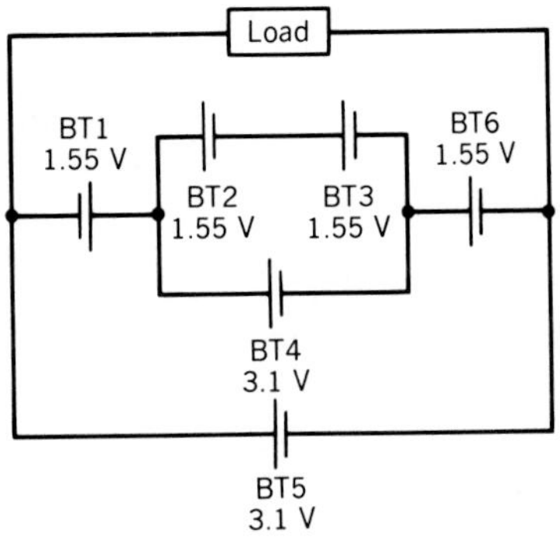

Figure 4.40 Circuit for Frame 13.

FRAME 14

A formula uses several letters to represent quantities. In most cases the values of these quantities have been measured or stated in the problem, but the value of at least one quantity must be calculated. It is called an __________ quantity.

a. Unknown. (15)
b. Any other answer, review Section C.1.

FRAME 15

A formula is frequently called an __________ because there is an "equals" sign in it.

a. Equation. (16)
b. Any other answer, review Section C.1.

FRAME 16

Solve the following equation for the value of P. $Q = 6$ and $W = 27$.

$$3P = \frac{W + 1}{Q}$$

a. $P = 1.556$. (17)
b. Any other answer, review Section C.1.

FRAME 17

Solve the following equation for the value of E.

$$\frac{1}{8} = \frac{1}{2E + 2}$$

a. $E = 3$. (18)
b. Any other answer, review Section C.1.

FRAME 18

Failure mode analysis can frequently help find the fault in a circuit or unit. This kind of analysis is based on three questions. These are:

1. __________
2. __________
3. __________

a. 1. In what ways do the components used in a circuit fail?
   2. What are the probabilities of the various kinds of failures happening in the circuit under discussion?
   3. What will happen in the circuit under discussion when one of the components fails in one of its more common failure modes? (19)
b. Any of the three incorrect, review Section D.1.

FRAME 19

Variational analysis can be of use in predicting what will happen when a component in a circuit fails. It is based on the fact that the potential and current at points in a circuit can be described by one or more __________.

a. Equations. (END)
b. Any other answer, review Section D.2.

E PROBLEMS FOR SOLUTION OR RESEARCH

1. The cells shown in the schematic of Figure 4.41 are lithium cells, each producing a potential difference of 2.8 V. What is the potential difference across the load? If the circuit is cut at point B, what is the potential difference across the load?

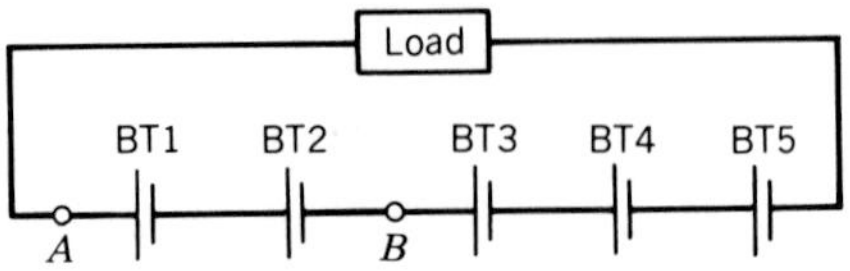

Figure 4.41 Circuit for Problem 1.

2. What is the technical term for the circuit shown in the schematic of Figure 4.42? If the three cells are identical and if the sum of the currents passing through the two loads is 150 mA, what is the current supplied by each source cell?

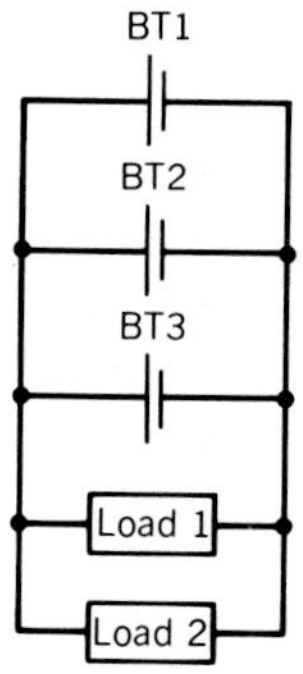

Figure 4.42 Circuit for Problem 2.

3. Draw a single-cell equivalent circuit for the series–parallel arrangement of Figure 4.43. Show the potential difference across the load.

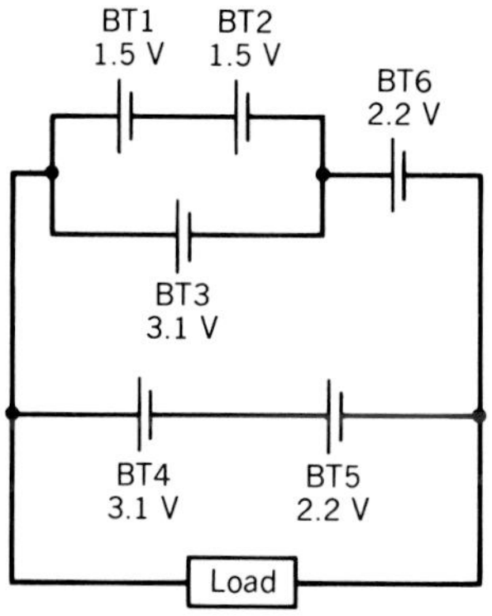

Figure 4.43 Circuit for Problem 3.

4. The circuit shown in Figure 4.44 is composed of sealed lead–acid cells, each of which has a potential difference of 2.2 V and furnishes a current of up to 100 mA in this circuit. What is the potential difference across the load?

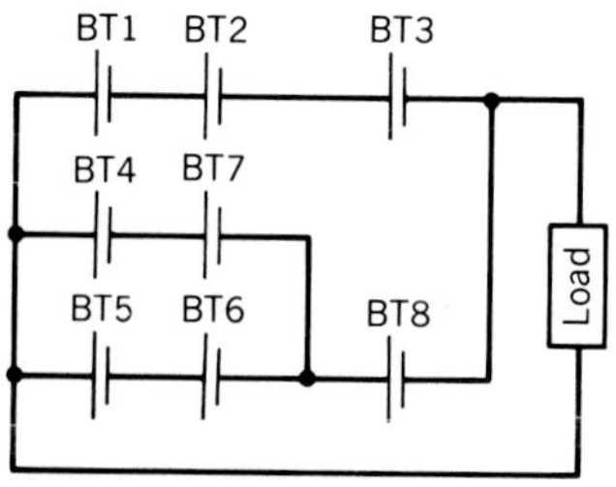

Figure 4.44 Circuit for Problem 4.

5. Which cells in Figures 4.41 and 4.42 could be replaced by an open circuit without changing the potential difference across the load? Could any of the cells be replaced with a short circuit without affecting the potential difference across the load?

6. What kind of diagram is shown in Figure 4.45? What kinds of information are given in it?

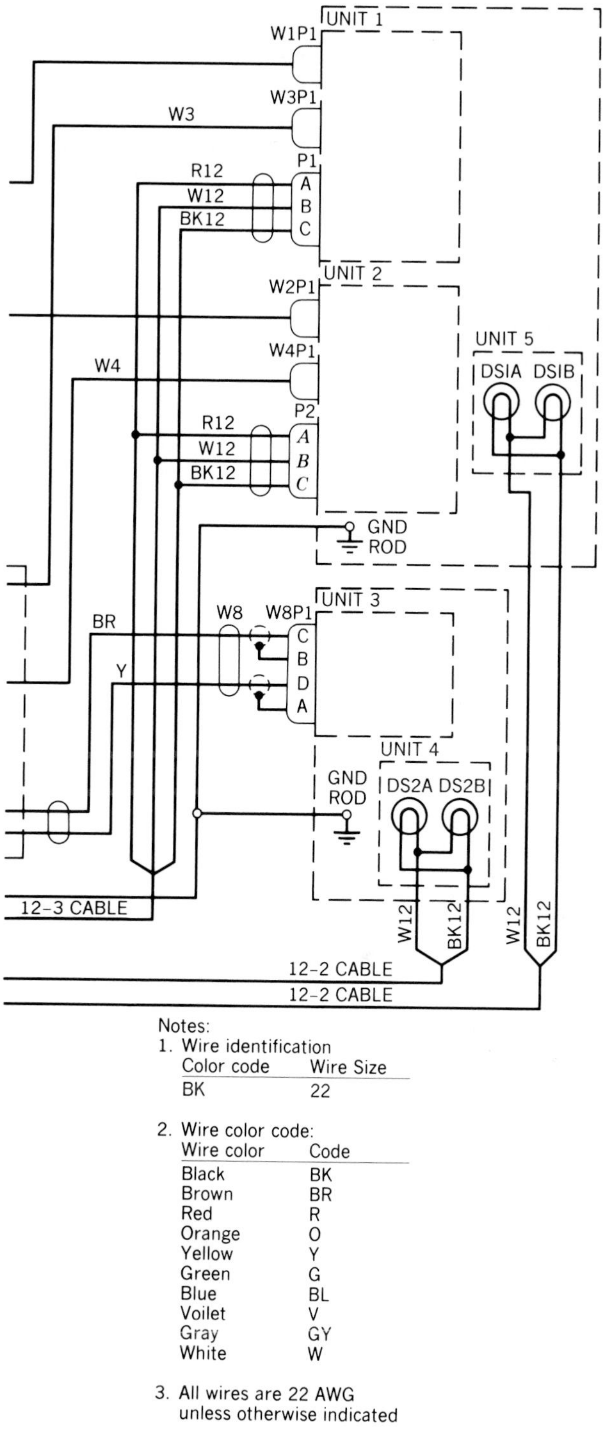

Figure 4.45 Figure for Problem 6.

7. The unit conversion formulas given in Section C.2 are too accurate to be easily remembered. Round off the multipliers to the number of significant figures shown below and perform the following conversions:

a. 1.75 feet = ______ m
b. 3.6 lb (force) = ______ N

c. 16 cubic feet = _______ cubic meters
d. 1.125 liters = _______ pints
e. 4.28 m = _______ inches
f. 6.65 quarts = _______ liters
g. 0.03 square meters = _______ square inches
h. 16.03 lb = _______ kg
i. 3.25 gallons = _______ liters
j. 16 in = _______ m

8. Solve the following equations:

a. $16A + 9 = 44$

b. $+3A + 7 - 2 - A = 6 - A$

c. $\frac{1}{9}(A + 3) = 5$

d. $\frac{1}{2}(A + 7) = 2A + 6$

e. $j - 4 = 7 - j + 6$

f. $\frac{c}{2} + \frac{c}{4} = 3$

g. $0.35Z + \frac{Z}{6} = 1.25$

h. $X + 7 - (3X + 9) = 8$

i. $\frac{1}{P} + 3 = 9$

j. $Z + \frac{1}{3}Z + 1 = Z + 2$

k. $\frac{P}{2} + \frac{P}{3} = 6$

l. $2A + 4 = -2(3A - 6)$

9. Up to this point, you have been required to solve equations involving a single unknown quantity. The following equations have two or more unknown quantities, and an exact numerical answer is not possible. The object of this exercise is to express one of the unknown quantities in terms of the others. The first exercise has been done as an example.

a. $2P + 3 = Q - J$

$P = ?$

ans. $2P + 3 = Q - J$

$- 3 \qquad\qquad -3$

$2P = (Q - J - 3)$

$\div 2 \qquad\qquad \div 2$

$$P = \frac{Q - J - 3}{2}$$

b. $3P = J - 2$
$P = ?$

c. $a + b = 4b - 1$
$a = ?$

d. $\frac{1}{x} = \frac{2}{J + 3}$
$x = ?$

e. $Q(2a + 7) = 3$
$a = ?$

f. $I = \frac{E}{R}$
$R = ?$

g. $P = EI$
$E = ?$

h. $X = 2\pi FL$
$L = ?$

i. $X = \frac{1}{2\pi FC}$
$C = ?$

CHAPTER 5

RESISTANCE, OHM'S LAW, AND WIRE

A. CHAPTER PREVIEW

1 This chapter defines electrical resistivity and electrical resistance and explains why it takes a source of energy to make electrons drift through a conductor.

2 You will learn to use an important formula called Ohm's law, which shows the relationship of potential difference, current, and resistance.

3 You will learn to measure resistance using modern multimeters.

4 The effect of temperature on resistance will be covered, along with a way to calculate how the resistance of copper wire changes with changing temperature.

5 In the Examples and Computations section you will practice using the three forms of Ohm's law to calculate potential difference, current, and resistance in circuits. The use of variational analysis with Ohm's law will be presented.

6 The concept of conductance will be introduced to simplify the study of parallel resistances, which is discussed in Chapter 6.

7 The Applications section provides an introduction to various sizes and types of wire and cable commonly used in electricity and electronics.

B. PRINCIPLES

B.1 RESISTIVITY

In Chapter 2 you learned that an electric field will cause a drift of conduction electrons, otherwise known as a current, through a conductor. When this happens, the electric field is supplying energy to the electrons. This supply of energy is necessary because the atoms of the conductor impede the drift of conduction electrons by capturing and holding them for a brief time. When a conduction electron is captured by an atom, it gives up a small amount of energy, usually in the form of heat, and assumes a lower energy level, revolving around the capturing atom. Since the number of conduction electrons in a piece of material tends to remain constant at a given temperature, the capture of a conduction electron by an atom is usually balanced by an electron of a different atom entering the conduction level. When a valence electron absorbs energy, it then exists on a conduction level. The energy absorbed by valence electrons is derived from the electric field, while the energy released when electrons drop from a conduction to a valence level is usually converted into heat.

The effect of this capture of electrons is called the *resistivity* of the material.

The resistivity of a material is a measurement of how well the atoms of the material block the drift of electrons through it.

Resistivity is a property of the atoms in a material and also depends on how these atoms are arranged in the material. Resistivity is symbolized by the Greek letter ρ (rho). Table 5.1 gives the resistivity of some of the materials commonly used in electronic equipment. Note that the figures given for resistivity in Table 5.1 do not have any units. This is because the table provides figures based on a comparison with the resistivity of silver, the best of the conductors commonly used in electricity and electronics. The resistivity of copper is only slightly higher than that of silver.

The concept of resistivity is useful for providing better definitions of conductor and insulator than were used earlier in the text.

Materials that have low resistivity are considered to be good conductors.

Table 5.1 Resistivity of Some Metals Commonly Used in Electronics Related to Silver (Silver = 1)

Material	*Resistivity at 0 °C*
Aluminum	1.69
Carbon	23,000.00
Copper	1.07
Gold (99% pure)	1.49
Gold (14 K)	1.02
Iron	6.67
Nichrome V	7,680.00
Nickel	3.50
Silver	1.00

High resistivity means that the atoms of the material tend to capture and hold drifting electrons, or that there are few or no conduction electrons present in the material. Materials with high resistivity are called non-conductors *or* insulators.

B.2 OHM'S LAW

Resistivity is not hard to understand because you know about atoms, electrons, and energy levels. Unfortunately, the resistivity of a material is not as important to the technician as the opposition to an electric current caused by a particular electronic component or a conductor such as a piece of wire. The opposition to the drift of electrons in a particular piece of material of a certain length and thickness is the *resistance* of that piece of material.

In 1827, Georg Simon Ohm, a German scientist, discovered the way in which potential difference and current through a conductor are related. Ohm knew nothing about atomic structure, but he was able to describe the relationship between the potential difference between the ends of a conductor and the current through it in mathematical terms. He found that the potential difference measured in volts divided by the current measured in amperes was equal to some constant. In other words, Ohm found that for a particular length and thickness of a conductor, the ratio of the potential difference and the current was constant. This can be written in mathematical terms as:

$$\frac{\text{Applied potential difference}}{\text{Current through the conductor}} = \frac{E}{I} = \text{a constant}$$

This constant, which depends among other things on the resistivity of the material, is the resistance of that particular piece of material.

Resistance is a measure of the ability of a certain length and thickness of material to oppose the flow of an electric current.

The symbol R is used for resistance, and its basic unit has been named the ohm, in honor of the man who discovered the simple relationship of potential difference, current, and resistance. The symbol used for ohms is the Greek letter omega, Ω. In a schematic diagram, the symbol for a component that supplies resistance is -ʌʌʌ-.

The relationship of potential difference, current, and resistance is shown in the formula called Ohm's law. It is written as:

$$R \text{ (ohms)} = \frac{E \text{ (volts)}}{I \text{ (amperes)}} \qquad \text{FORMULA 5.1}$$

Using Formula 5.1, you can find the resistance of a length of conductor by dividing the measured potential difference between its ends by the current through it.

EXAMPLE:
When a length of wire is connected to the terminals of a 12-V battery, a current of 0.5 A flows through it. What is the resistance of the wire? ■

SOLUTION:
Formula 5.1 (Ohm's law) shows how potential difference, current, and resistance are related. Writing the formula $R = \frac{E}{I}$, and substituting the known values for E and I, $R = \frac{12}{0.5}$, or $R = 24$. The resistance of the wire is 24 ohms, or 24 Ω. ■

In this example, you found out something about this piece of wire. The resistance is as much a property of this piece of wire as its length, weight, and shape. The resistivity of the material of which the wire is made is another matter. It is a property of the material, regardless of its shape or form.

For most of the materials used in electronics, the resistance of a particular piece of material DOES NOT depend on the potential difference between the ends of the material or the amount of current through it. This is fairly accurate for metals such as copper, silver, aluminum, or iron. Therefore, if a length of wire has a resistance of 24 Ω when a 12-V battery is connected to it, the wire will also have a resistance of 24 Ω when a 6-V source is connected.

EXAMPLE:
The length of wire of the previous example is now connected to a 6-V battery. The current through the wire now measures 0.25 A. Is the resistance still 24 Ω? ■

SOLUTION:
As in the previous example, the resistance of the wire is calculated by using Formula 5.1 and substituting the new values of potential difference and current.

$$R = \frac{E}{I} = \frac{6}{0.25} = 24$$

Yes, the resistance of the wire is still 24 Ω. ■

In addition to the comparative resistivities given in Table 5.1, it is also possible to express resistivity in absolute terms, that is, without comparison to silver. In this case, resistivity is measured in ohm·meters. Table 5.2 lists the resistivity of some materials frequently used in electricity and electronics. Knowing the absolute resistivity of a material makes it possible to better state the relationship between resistance and resistivity.

The relationship between the resistivity of a material and the resistance of a piece of material, if temperature effects are ignored, is given by

$$R \text{ (ohms)} = \frac{\rho l}{A}$$

where ρ is in ohm·meters, l is in meters, and A is the cross-sectional area in square meters. It is unlikely that you will ever have to calculate the resistance of a length of material from the resistivity. On the other hand, it is useful to know the relationship between resistance

Table 5.2 Resistivities of Materials

Material	*Resistivity in ohm·meters at 0 °C*
Conductors	
Aluminum	2.49×10^{-8}
Carbon	3.4×10^{-5}
Copper	1.58×10^{-8}
Gold (pure)	2.19×10^{-8}
Gold (14K)	1.5×10^{-8}
Iron	9.8×10^{-8}
Nichrome V	1.13×10^{-6}
Silver	1.47×10^{-8}
Insulators	
Amber	5×10^{14}
Glass	1×10^{10} to 1×10^{14}
Rubber	1×10^{13} to 1×10^{16}
Mica	1×10^{11} to 1×10^{15}
Wood	1×10^{8} to 1×10^{11}

and resistivity, and that the resistance of a piece of material is proportional to its resistivity and length and

The resistance of a piece of material depends on the material, its temperature, length, and thickness. The resistance (in most cases) DOES NOT change if a different potential difference is applied to the ends of the material. The current, however, DOES change if the potential difference is changed.

B.3 MEASURING RESISTANCE

There are three methods for measuring resistance in use by technicians today. The *bridge method* of measuring resistance is a bit like using a laboratory balance scale (see Figure 5.1) to weigh something. To use this balance, the object to be weighed is put in the pan on one side and known weights are added to the pan on the other side. When the indicator points straight down to show that both pans are at the same level, the weights added exactly equal the weight of the object. The bridge method of measuring resistance operates by creating an electrical circuit with the resistance to be measured in one "arm" of the circuit. Precisely known resistances are added to the other "arm" until a balance is reached. This method is very accurate because the flow of electrons through the bridge is only used to show when the two arms balance. It is not necessary to know either the potential difference across the bridge or the current through it. Because it uses high-precision components, however, the bridge method of resistance measurement is generally found in a science laboratory, an instrument repair shop, or in a quality control section.

Figure 5.1 Laboratory balance scale.

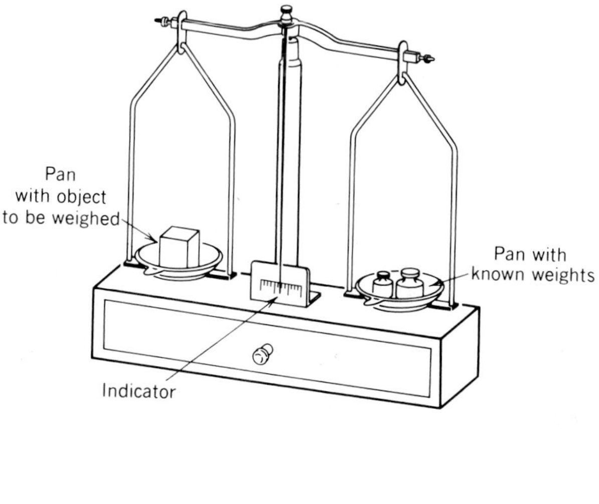

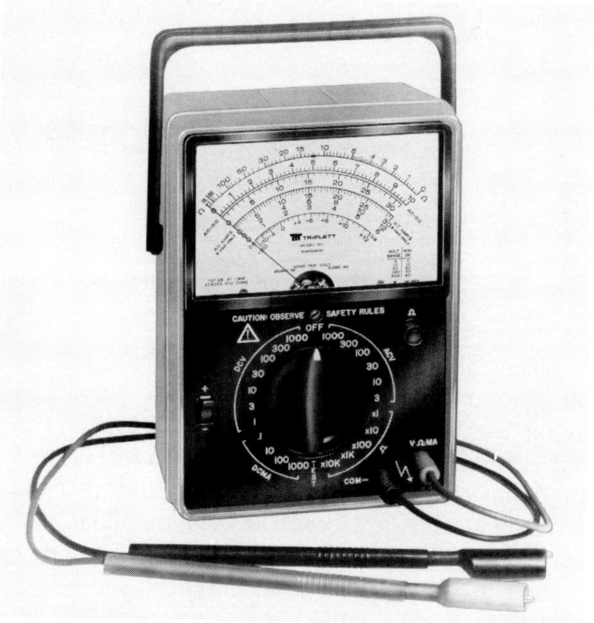

Figure 5.2 An analog multimeter. (Photo courtesy of the Triplett Corp.)

The second way to measure resistance uses Ohm's law. Almost all analog multimeters, like the one pictured in Figure 5.2, work in this way. One or more cells provide a potential difference across the resistance to be measured, and the current through that resistance causes the indicator needle of an analog meter to move. This method is less accurate than the bridge method because the potential difference across the unknown resistance must be controlled and the meter must be extremely accurate. In order to control the potential difference, analog multimeters have an OHMS ADJUST control placed so that it can be adjusted as the source cells get used up. If you use this type of multimeter, you must check and, if necessary, adjust the OHMS ADJUST control before making resistance measurements. This adjustment is performed by touching the tips of the two meter leads together and adjusting the OHMS ADJUST control until the meter pointer indicates 0 Ω. As the service capacity of the cells is used, this checking becomes more important.

Another difficulty in using some analog multimeters is the OHMS scale on the meter face. Notice that the scale pictured in Figure 5.3 is nonlinear, that is, the distance between the numbers becomes smaller as the numbers increase. This makes it hard to read the meter accurately. In some cases, this can make it hard to use an analog multimeter for certain kinds of testing. Some meters also have the scale reversed, with zero on the right-hand side rather than on the left side of the meter.

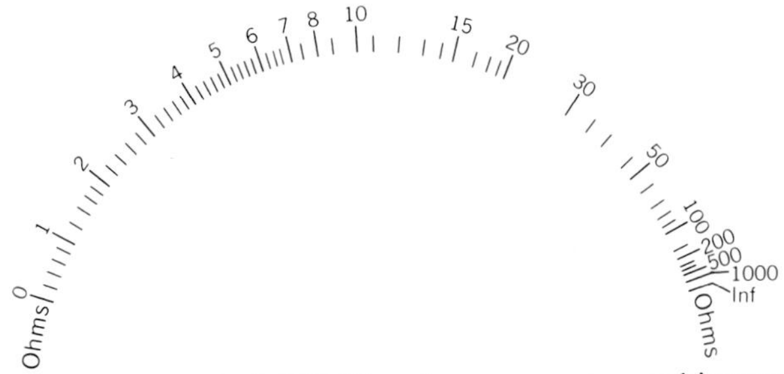

Figure 5.3 Typical OHMS scale on an analog multimeter.

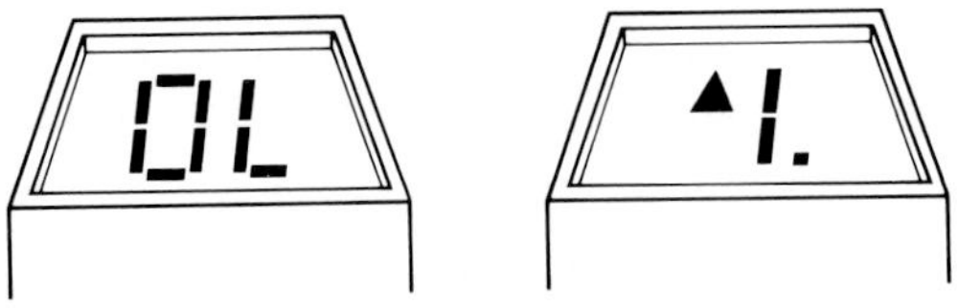

Figure 5.5 Typical out-of-range or overrange indications.

The third method of measuring resistance is to compare the effect of the unknown resistance on a circuit with the effect of an accurately known resistance. In the digital multimeters shown in Figure 5.4, this comparison is done by a tiny computer that shows the result in numerical form. The accuracy of this method can be very high, and the meters are easy to read. This method does not require the frequent setting of an OHMS ADJUST control. Also, because these meters are easier to read and are better protected from damage if accidentally connected to a powered circuit, they are a good choice for use in the field.

Before making resistance measurements, it is important to make sure that the components measured are not connected to any sort of electric power. Some multimeters can be damaged if they are connected to a power source when they are set up to measure resistance. Even if your multimeter is protected from damage, the resistance measurements will have no meaning if there is a power source in the circuit.

Unlike potential difference and current measurements, polarity generally makes no difference in resistance measurement. That is, it does not matter which meter lead is connected to a particular end of the component to be measured. (This is not true in the case of semiconductor components, however.) Selecting the right measurement range is of the same importance as in voltage and current measurements. As in the case of voltage and current measurements, some modern multimeters select their own range, depending on the value measured. These multimeters are called *autoranging* meters.

If you are not using an autoranging multimeter, the most accurate results are obtained by using the lowest range value that will work, and there is no danger in guessing too low a range. The use of too low a range when measuring voltage or current might damage a meter, but when measuring resistance, the meter itself will signal you to select a higher range. For example, if you are trying to measure the resistance of a component that has a resistance of 20,000 ohms, or 20 kΩ, and you select the 200 Ω range, some sort of "out-of-range" or "overrange" indication will appear on a digital meter. Figure 5.5 shows some typical overrange indications. On an analog meter, the meter needle will either swing all the way over or will hardly move. In either case, it will be very hard to read the resistance value.

When an overrange indication is given on a digital meter, or when the value can not be read on an analog meter, you should switch to the next highest range. Repeat this switching until an accurate reading is possible. Note that it may be necessary to adjust the OHMS ADJUST setting every time the position of the RANGE switch is changed. (For some of the poorer quality analog meters, there are resistance values that will be difficult to read regardless of the scale selected.) Make your readings quickly and do not allow the meter leads to remain connected to the component being measured for longer than necessary. Also, do not allow the tips of the test probes to touch each other for any length of time, except when checking the OHMS ADJUST setting. A multimeter set to measure resistance supplies power through its leads. Wasting this power will use up the service capacity of the multimeter cells more quickly. When a multimeter is not in use, it is a good idea to set it to measure high-voltage AC and to switch it off. This will ensure that the cells are not connected to the test leads, and will also protect the meter from damage if connected to a circuit and turned on before it is set correctly.

Figure 5.4 Digital multimeters indications. (Reproduced with permission from the John Fluke Mfg. Co., Inc.)

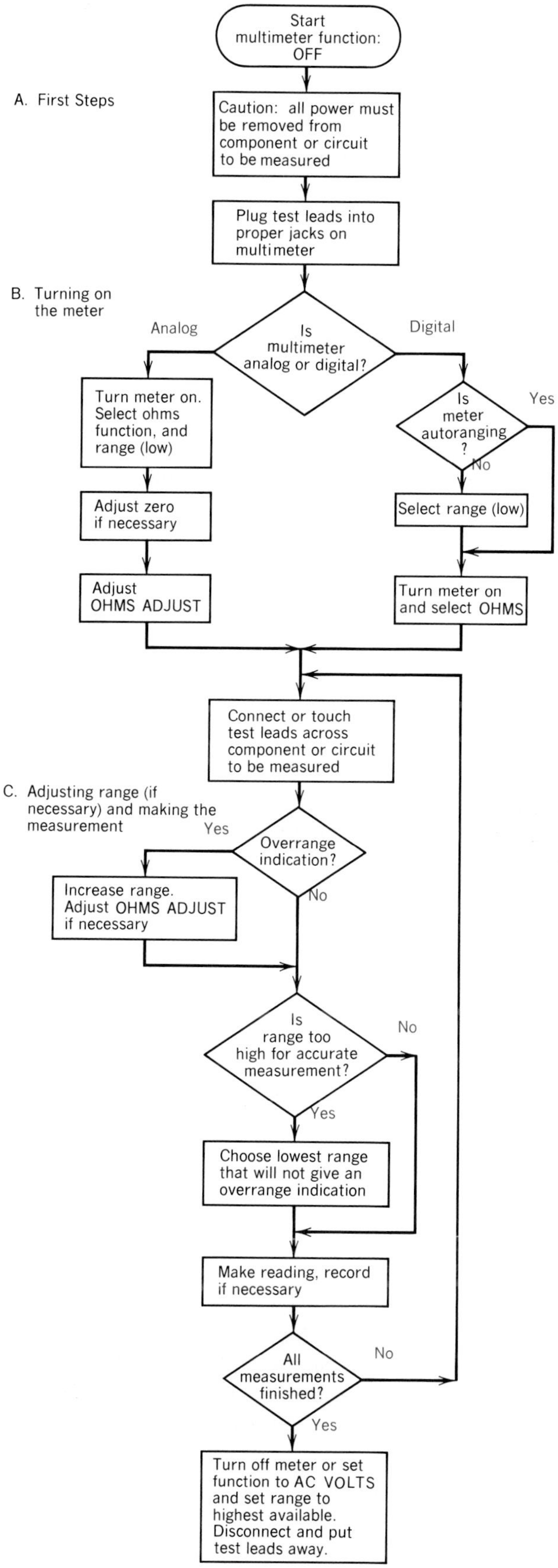

Figure 5.6 Flow diagram for making resistance measurements.

Figure 5.6 is a step-by-step flow diagram for making resistance measurements using a modern multimeter. As in the flow diagrams in the previous chapter, it is important to follow the steps in order from the START block at the top of the page to the bottom, following the flow arrows. A rectangle ▭ contains a particular step, while a diamond ◇ represents a choice. A choice means that there are two or more ways to proceed, depending on your answer to the question in the diamond.

B.4 WHY MEASURE RESISTANCE?

Resistance measurements are one of the simplest ways to find the cause of certain kinds of trouble in electrical and electronic equipment. Current measurements, you will recall from Chapter 3, are difficult to make. In order to make current measurements, you have to break a circuit and place the meter in series with the source and the load. In simple circuits, however, once power has been shut off, resistance measurements can be made by connecting the measuring instrument *across* the component whose resistance is to be measured. Resistance measurements are therefore as easy to make as voltage measurements. In fact, it is often simplest to make voltage measurements, shut off the power, and make resistance measurements, and then use Ohm's law to calculate the current through a component, rather than to break the circuit and make current measurements directly.

The most important function of resistance measurements in troubleshooting is to determine if there actually is an electrical connection or current path between two points in a circuit or between the two ends of a component. Testing for a low-resistance current path or closed circuit between two points is called *continuity checking*. Many problems caused by broken wires, poor electrical contact, or burned-out or short-circuited components are easily found by continuity checking.

Figure 5.7 shows one common check to see if electric power is actually getting to a unit. With the unit line plug removed from the wall outlet, and the unit power switch set to OFF, the multimeter test leads are connected to the blades of the line plug. The resistance shown on the meter will probably be well over a megohm, and perhaps overrange even on the highest range setting. If the unit power switch is now set to ON, a closed circuit with a resistance of between 50 and 300 Ω is usually indicated. If an overrange con-

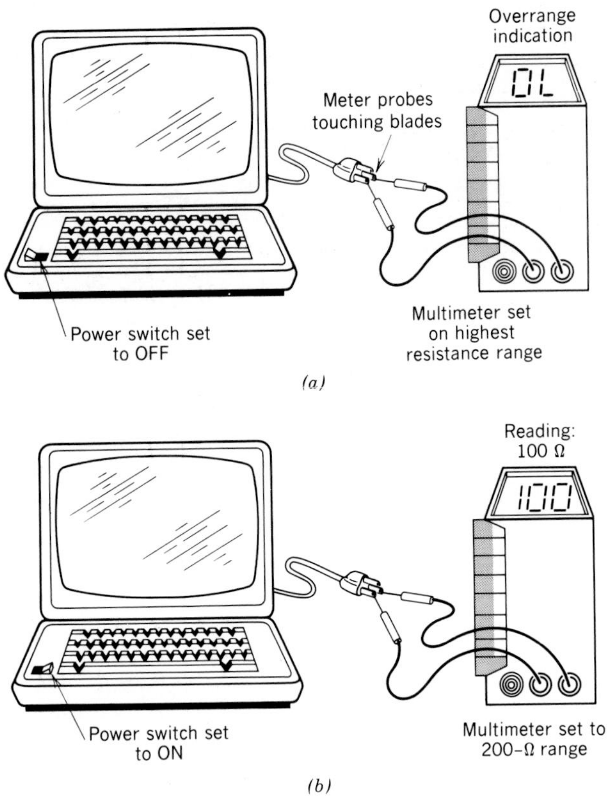

Figure 5.7 Using continuity checks in troubleshooting.

dition is still shown, it is possible that the unit fuse, power cord, or the power switch may be faulty.

Resistance measurements can also reveal if electronic components are no longer functioning well. You will learn to make these measurements as you become familiar with the construction, applications, and failure modes of electronic components.

B.5 THE EFFECT OF TEMPERATURE ON RESISTANCE

In learning about resistance, you found out that the resistance of a component or a wire was determined by the resistivity of the material, its length, and its thickness. This is true, but if you are going to be a good technician, you have to learn how electronic components behave in the real world. In the real world, everything operates at some temperature. The resistivities of materials and the resistances of components are generally calculated at room temperature, 20°C. Much electronic equipment *does not* operate at room temperature. Some equipment is located in the field, while other units heat up because they use electric power. Heating can be an important problem in small units such as microcomputers.

For most materials, the resistance of a particular length and thickness of material increases as the temperature of the material increases. This is explained by going back to the discussion of the structure of matter in Chapter 1. In that chapter, it was pointed out that the atoms are held in a crystal structure, in most solid materials. As a material gets hotter, the atoms absorb energy and vibrate. A vibrating atom takes up more space than an atom at rest. Because of this, atoms in a warmer material are bigger obstacles to drifting electrons. This makes it easier for the atoms to capture the conduction electrons.

The increased vibration of the atoms as a material gets hotter means that the resistance of most materials used in electronic components will increase as the temperature increases. Semiconductor materials used in transistors are an important exception to this. Semiconductor materials and some insulators actually show a lower resistance as their temperature increases, and serious problems may result. In these materials, in their pure state, there are few or no conduction electrons at normal temperatures. However, if they are heated, enough energy is added to the material to raise some of the valence electrons to a conduction band, and the passage of an electric current through the material is made easier.

An example of increased resistance at high temperature that is sometimes seen by technicians is the change in the resistance of coils of copper wire. These coils are used in relays found in many industrial machines. The manufacturer usually marks the resistance on these coils, along with the operating current, or the operating voltage. But this is generally the resistance measured at room temperature, 20°C.

A relay is a kind of switch that operates when the current through its coil is at a certain level. A typical example is a relay that operates with a potential difference of 5 V DC across its coil and has a coil resistance of 50 Ω. Using Ohm's law in the form

$$I = \frac{E}{R},$$

it is possible to calculate the operating current of this relay. It is 0.1 A, at room temperature. But what will happen if this relay is placed in a unit that is operating at 60°C? That is a fairly high, but not unusual, operating temperature. At this temperature, the resistance of the relay increases to 57.85 Ω, and if the potential difference across the coil remains 5 V DC, the current through the coil will be

$$I = \frac{E}{R} = \frac{5}{57.85} = 0.08 \text{ A}$$

The current through the relay coil is therefore much less than the 0.1 A required by the manufacturer. Will the relay work properly? There is a chance that it will not.

Problems of this sort are not frequent, but they happen often enough to repay learning how to calculate the resistance change in copper, which is the most frequently used conducting material in electrical and electronic components. In order to do this, you must know that the conductor in question is copper, and you must be able to measure or calculate its resistance at some known temperature, perhaps 20°C, although any temperature at which electronic components normally function can be used. Formula 5.2 can then be used to calculate the resistance of the copper at a second temperature:

$$R_{T2} = R_{T1} \times \frac{234.5 + T2}{234.5 + T1} \qquad \text{FORMULA 5.2}$$

where $T1$ is the temperature at which the resistance is known, usually room temperature, and $T2$ is the other temperature, which may be higher or lower than $T1$.

EXAMPLE:
The manufacturer's catalog tells us that the relay we have just been talking about will operate if the coil current is 0.09 A or greater. What is the maximum temperature at which this relay will operate reliably? ■

SOLUTION:
In order to solve this problem, it is necessary to calculate the resistance of the coil when the potential difference across it is 5 V DC and the current is 0.09 A. Using Ohm's law, Formula 5.1,

$$R = \frac{E}{I} = \frac{5}{0.09} = 55.56\ \Omega$$

From this you know that the resistance of the coil will be 55.56 Ω at the maximum temperature. You also know that the resistance of this coil was 50 Ω at room temperature (20°C). These values can then be substituted into Formula 5.2 in order to calculate $T2$, the temperature at which the resistance of the relay coil will be 55.56 Ω.

$$55.56 = 50 \times \frac{234.5 + T2}{234.5 + 20}$$

This can be simplified by adding the 234.5 and 20 and then by dividing both sides of the equation by 50.

$$1.11 = \frac{234.5 + T2}{254.5}$$

Now multiply both sides by 254.5 to get 282.49 = 234.5 + $T2$. Subtracting 234.5 from both sides of the equation, the answer is

$$T2 = 47.99°\text{C}$$

This is the highest temperature at which the relay can be expected to operate reliably. If this relay had been in a piece of equipment that operated normally when first turned on, but failed after a few minutes of operation, the alert technician would measure the operating temperature of the unit to see if the problem might be the buildup of too much heat in the unit. Perhaps the whole problem might be caused by a poorly operating cooling fan, or a dirty air filter. ■

C. EXAMPLES AND COMPUTATIONS

C.1 OHM'S LAW CALCULATIONS

Formula 5.1, Ohm's law, shows how the resistance of a piece of material can be computed if you know the potential difference between the ends of the material and the current through it. In this form

$$R = \frac{E}{I}$$

the quantity on the left side of the equation (R) is the unknown, while the quantities on the right side are known (E and I). With the formula in this form, the resistance R is expressed in terms of potential difference and current. This form of the equation is easy to use if the resistance is the unknown quantity, but if the resistance is known and either the current or potential difference is the unknown quantity, it is frequently easier to transpose Formula 5.1 and isolate a different quantity on the left side of the equation.

EXAMPLE:
A piece of wire with a resistance of 24 Ω is connected across a 5-V power source. What will be the current through the circuit? ■

SOLUTION:
This question may be answered by substituting the known values in Formula 5.1.

$$R = \frac{E}{I} \qquad 24 = \frac{5}{I}$$

As you learned in Chapter 4, this equation can be simplified by multiplying both sides of the equation by the unknown value, I:

$$I \times 24 = \frac{5}{I} \times I \quad \text{or} \quad 24I = 5$$

Solving, $I = 0.208$ A. ■

Another way of dealing with this question is to transpose equation 5.1 so that the unknown quantity is isolated on one side of the equals sign. Solving for E is simply a matter of multiplying both sides of the equation by the same value, I, as in the previous example.

$$I \times R = \frac{E}{I} \times I \quad \text{or} \quad E = IR \qquad \text{FORMULA 5.3}$$

Dividing both sides of this equation by R provides a solution for I:

$$\frac{E}{R} = \frac{IR}{R} \quad \text{or} \quad I = \frac{E}{R} \qquad \text{FORMULA 5.4}$$

The three forms of Ohm's law are:

$$R = \frac{E}{I} \qquad \text{FORMULA 5.1}$$

$$E = IR \qquad \text{FORMULA 5.3}$$

$$I = \frac{E}{R} \qquad \text{FORMULA 5.4}$$

An easy way of remembering the three forms of Ohm's law is to use the Ohm's law wheel shown in Figure 5.8. To use the wheel in solving a problem, first determine which of the three quantities, either potential difference, current, or resistance, is unknown. Then cover the letter symbol for that quantity with your thumb. The physical position of the other two letter symbols will then show the form of the Ohm's law formula.

For example, if a problem gives both the potential difference and the resistance, the current is the unknown quantity. Write $I =$. Now cover the symbol I in Figure 5.8. The remaining symbols are E over R. Fill in $I = \frac{E}{R}$. It is now a simple matter to replace E and R with their given values and to calculate I.

Figure 5.8 Ohm's law wheel.

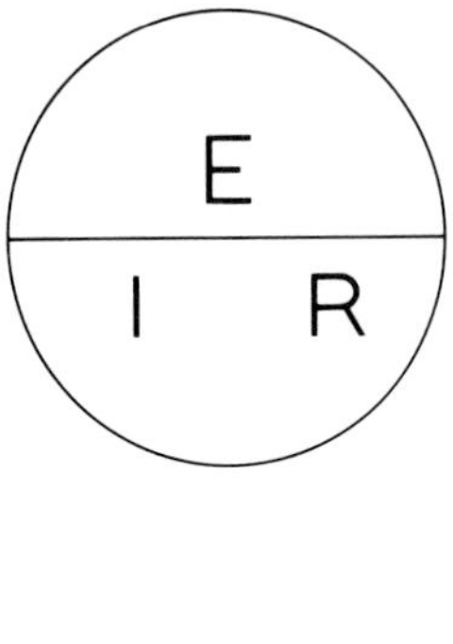

Table 5.3 Metric Prefixes Generally Used With Resistance Values

Numeric Value	*Metric Prefix*	*Long Form*	*Symbol Form*
0.001	milli-	milliohm or m ohm	m
1,000	kilo-	kilohm or K ohm	K or k
1,000,000	mega-	megohm or M ohm	M

Similarly, if the current and resistance are known, it is the potential difference that must be computed. Write $E =$, and cover the letter E. The two remaining symbols, I and R, are on the same line, therefore, $E = IR$.

In practical circuits, resistances ranging from a few thousandths of an ohm to several million ohms are found. The metric prefixes that you learned in Chapter 2 are used to make it easier to write resistance values. Table 5.3 lists the prefixes generally used for resistances. The long form is frequently used in text, while the symbol form is usually found in schematic diagrams and parts lists. For example, the resistance of a component is 2200 Ω. This would be written as 2.2 kilohms or 2.2 K ohms. A schematic diagram would use the symbol form 2.2K Ω or, if it was clear that resistance was the quantity, just 2.2K.

Use the Ohm's law wheel to obtain the required formula and fill in the blanks in the following table. Round your answers off to two significant figures:

Required Form of Ohm's Law Formula	*I*	*E*	*R*
______	9 mA	27 V	?
______	?	8 V	40 kΩ
______	0.33 A	?	1.2 Ω
______	200 mA	5 V	?
______	?	10 V	2.5 Ω
______	65 mA	18 V	?
______	?	64 V	18 K
______	0.0122 A	?	2.2 K
______	0.029 A	18 V	?
______	?	3.5 V	150 Ω
______	0.125 A	?	1200 Ω
______	?	34 V	6.8 K
______	1.54 mA	6 V	?
______	3.33 mA	13 V	?
______	0.0027 A	?	18,500
______	?	120 V	1 MΩ

C.2 EXERCISES IN VARIATIONAL ANALYSIS

The three forms of Ohm's law, Formulas 5.1, 5.3, and 5.4, describe a relationship among electrical quantities that is particularly useful as a basis for variational analysis. Writing the form

$$I = \frac{E}{R}$$

you can see that if the resistance in the circuit is kept the same, any increase in the potential difference will cause an increase in the circuit current. For example, in Figure 5.9 the potential difference supplied by the battery is 5 V, and the resistance is 100 Ω. Using Ohm's law, the circuit current is calculated to be 0.05 A. If the resistance is kept constant at 100 Ω, and the potential difference is doubled to 10 V, the new circuit current will also be doubled

$$I = \frac{E}{R} = \frac{10}{100} = 0.1 \text{ A}$$

Halving the potential difference, to 2.5 V, will halve the current to 0.025 A. This relationship is referred to by saying that the current is *directly proportional* to the potential difference.

If, on the other hand, the potential difference supplied by the source is kept constant and the resistance is changed, a different sort of change occurs in the circuit current. You have seen that a potential difference of 5 V and a circuit resistance of 100 Ω results in a circuit current of 0.05 A, or 50 mA. Doubling the resistance to 200 Ω while the potential difference remains constant at 5 V results in a current of

$$I = \frac{E}{R} = \frac{5}{200} = 0.025 \text{ A}$$

This is *half* the current in the original circuit. Halving the circuit resistance, as you might guess, results in a *doubling* of the current

$$I = \frac{E}{R} = \frac{5}{50} = 0.1 \text{ A}$$

This relationship is exactly the opposite of the relationship between the potential difference and the current. If the resistance increases, the current will *decrease*; a decrease in resistance will cause an *increase* in current. The current is referred to as *inversely proportional* to the resistance.

Figure 5.9 Simple circuit for variational analysis.

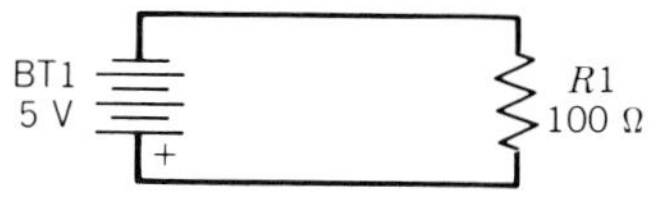

Table 5.4 Variational Analysis with Ohm's Law

I_{new}	E_{new}	R_{new}
______	$2E$	Same
______	Same	$0.5R$
$2I$	Same	______
$\frac{1}{4}I$	______	Same
$2I$	$2E$	______
$\frac{1}{4}I$	______	$\frac{1}{4}R$
______	Same	$1.5R$
$\frac{1}{2}I$	______	$2R$
$1.8R$	$0.3I$	______
______	$2E$	$2R$

The use of variational analysis and Ohm's law provides a powerful method for troubleshooting electrical or electronic equipment since it will suggest possible causes for changes in circuit quantities. For example, it is noted that the current through a poorly operating circuit is now less than it was when previously measured. Using the information in the above paragraph, you can see that a decrease in circuit current would result from either a decrease in potential difference or an increase in circuit resistance or both. It is easy to measure the potential difference across the circuit power source. If the voltage is found to have decreased by about the same percentage as the decrease in current, it is clear that the source is faulty. If, on the other hand, the decrease in potential difference is small or nonexistent, an increase in circuit resistance must be the problem. Poor or corroded connections or broken wires are likely faults.

Table 5.4 provides an exercise in the use of variational analysis with Ohm's law. Each line of the table gives the values for two of the three electrical quantities with respect to previous measurements. For example, $2I$ means twice the last measured value of the current. In every case, some of the values have changed. Fill in the blanks to show the new value for the quantity that is not given.

The use of variational analysis with Formula 5.2, the formula used to determine the resistance of copper at temperatures other than 20°C, is not as direct as its use with one of the three forms of Ohm's law. Observe that there is a large constant term, 234.5, in both the numerator and denominator on the right side of the equation:

$$R_{T2} = R_{T1} \times \frac{234.5 + T2}{234.5 + T1}$$

Changing $T2$ from 40 to 80°C is not going to double the resistance. In equations of this type, where proportionately large constant terms are involved, doubling one of the quantities on the right side of the equation will not double the quantity on the left side. All that can be said is that increasing the value of the numerator or decreasing the value of the denominator of the fraction

$$\frac{234.5 + T2}{234.5 + T1}$$

will make the entire term larger and will result in an increase of R_{T2}. Decreasing the value of the numerator or increasing the value of the denominator will have the opposite effect. Similarly, increasing the value of R_{T1} will increase the value of R_{T2}. These directions of change are easily summarized as in Table 5.5.

Such tables are useful for gaining experience with the behavior of electrical quantities in circuits and for relating abstract mathematical expressions to measureable effects in circuits.

Try to produce variational tables for the following formulas. In some cases it is not easy to see what will happen if certain values are changed. In these situations, try substituting various values for the terms on the right side of the equation and see how the left side changes.

a. $U = \frac{B}{11}$

b. $X_c = \frac{1}{2\pi FC}$

c. $R_T = \frac{1}{\frac{1}{R1} + \frac{1}{R2}}$

d. $X_1 = 6.28FL$

e. $C = \frac{0.159}{FX_c}$

f. $P = EI$

Table 5.5 Variational Analysis Tables Showing How R_{T2} Changes When the Other Quantities in Formula 5.2 are Changed

If R_{T1}	$T2$	$T1$	*Then* R_{T2}
Up	Same	Same	Increases
Down	Same	Same	Decreases
Same	Up	Same	Increases
Same	Down	Same	Decreases
Same	Same	Up	Decreases
Same	Same	Down	Increases

C.3 RECIPROCAL QUANTITIES AND CONDUCTANCE

This chapter has stressed resistance, the opposition to the flow of current through a particular component or piece of material. For certain applications, however, it is the ability of a component or piece of material to *permit* the drift of conduction electrons that is important. This quality is called *conductance*, and is symbolized by the letter G. Conductance is defined as the opposite of resistance. Mathematically, this is written

$$R = \frac{1}{G} \qquad \text{FORMULA 5.5}$$

That is to say, resistance is the *reciprocal* of conductance. Multiplying both sides of Formula 5.5 by G and dividing both sides by R, it is also possible to write

$$G = \frac{1}{R} \qquad \text{FORMULA 5.6}$$

In other words, the conductance of a component or piece of material is the reciprocal of its resistance. Formerly, the unit of conductance was the *mho* ("ohm" spelled backward), but this has been changed to the *siemens*, in honor of the German inventor Ernst von Siemens (1823–1883). From Formulas 5.5 and 5.6, you can see that an increase or decrease in the resistance of a component or piece of material will have an opposite effect on its conductance. The two quantities are inversely proportional.

If you know the resistance of a piece of material, the conductance can easily be calculated with your calculator using the reciprocal key, [1/x].

EXAMPLE:
The resistance of a certain component is 6.8 kΩ. What is its conductance? ■

SOLUTION:
If the resistance is known, Formula 5.6 permits the calculation of the conductance.

Enter the resistance value	[6] [8] [0] [0]
Select reciprocal	[1/x]
Read answer	0.000147

The conductance is 0.000147 S. ■

As practice, calculate the following resistances or conductances, as required. Round off to three significant figures.

a. $R = 100, G =$
b. $G = 0.0196\ S, R =$
c. $R = 0.18, G =$
d. $R = 3.9\ k\Omega, R =$
e. $R = 9.1, G =$
f. $G = 0.298\ S, R =$
g. $G = 100\ S, R =$
h. $R = 200, G =$
i. $G = 10^{-3}\ S, R =$
j. $R = 18, G =$

In addition to conductance, there are several reciprocal quantities that are used in electronics, so that it is worth exploring the mathematical characteristics of reciprocals.

FACT 1:
The reciprocal of any number, quantity, or collection of terms that is not zero or equal to zero is defined as a fraction with the number, quantity, or collection of terms as the denominator and the number 1 as the numerator.

EXAMPLES:

The reciprocal of 8 is $\frac{1}{8}$

The reciprocal of a is $\frac{1}{a}$

The reciprocal of $\frac{1}{4}$ is $\frac{1}{\frac{1}{4}}$ or 4

The reciprocal of a + b is $\frac{1}{(a + b)}$ ■

FACT 2:
Any quantity times its reciprocal is equal to 1.

EXAMPLES:

$$4 \times \frac{1}{4} = \frac{4}{4} = 1$$

$$(a + b) \times \frac{1}{a + b} = \frac{a + b}{a + b} = 1$$ ■

FACT 3:
The reciprocal of zero or any collection of terms equal to zero is meaningless.

EXAMPLES:
0 has no reciprocal
$a - a$ has no reciprocal ■

FACT 4:
The reciprocal of the reciprocal of a number, quantity, or collection of terms is equal to the number, quantity, or collection of terms itself.

EXAMPLES:

$$\frac{1}{\frac{1}{2}} = 2$$

$$\frac{1}{\frac{1}{x}} = x$$

$$\frac{1}{\frac{1}{R1 + R2}} = R1 + R2$$ ■

FACT 5:
Forming the reciprocal of both sides of an equation does not change the truth of the equation.

EXAMPLES:

If $2 + 2 = 4$, then $\frac{1}{2 + 2} = \frac{1}{4}$.

If $Y = X + 10$, then $\frac{1}{Y} = \frac{1}{X + 10}$. ■

Simplify the following terms using your knowledge of reciprocals.

a. $\frac{1}{\frac{1}{6}}$

b. $\frac{1}{\frac{1}{\frac{1}{X}} + X}$

c. $Z = \frac{1}{\frac{1}{G} + \frac{1}{G}}$; $\frac{1}{G} = ?$

d. $\frac{1}{a - \frac{1}{\frac{1}{a}}} = ?$

e. $J = \frac{1}{Q} \times \frac{1}{\frac{1}{Q}}$

D. APPLICATIONS

It is hard to find an electronic unit or electrical machine that does not contain some form of wire, but many introductory textbooks say little about this widely used component. The following sections are intended as a

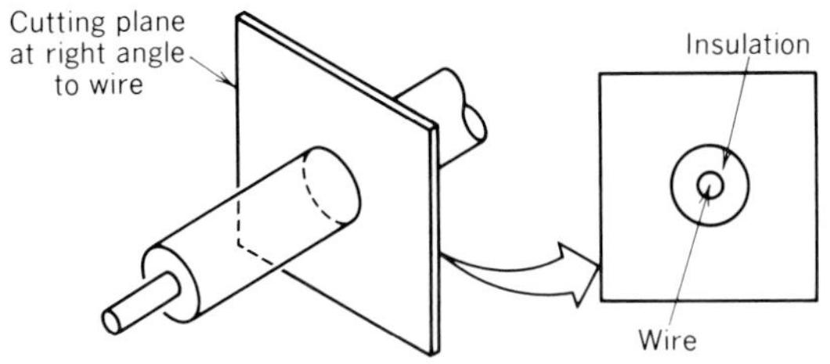

Figure 5.10 Most wire has a circular cross section.

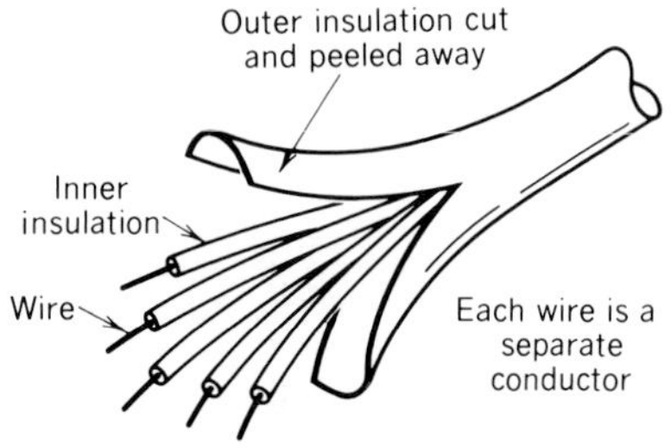

Figure 5.11 A cable consists of two or more conductive paths bound into a single package.

general introduction to the kinds of wire and cable you can expect to see frequently.

First, it is important to distinguish between wire and cable. In everyday language the word *cable* refers to almost any heavy electrical conductor. To be precise, however, a *wire* is a single conductive path made of a length of solid metal or a number of metal strands twisted together. Most wire has a circular cross section, as shown in Figure 5.10, although square and rectangular cross sections may be used for special purposes. An electrical cable consists of two or more separate conductive paths bound into a single package, as shown in Figure 5.11.

D.1 WIRE GAUGE SIZES

Earlier in this chapter, you learned that the resistance of a length of conductive material depends in part on the thickness of the conductor. Wire thickness is measured in a number of ways. In the metric system, the diameter of a conductor is given in millimeters, but in the U.S. customary system two different measurements and units are used. One measurement gives the diameter of the wire in thousandths of an inch, or mils (1 mil = 0.001 in.). To convert from an inch measurement to mils, simply multiply the measurement in inches by 1000:

$$D \text{ (mils)} = 1000 \times D \text{ (inches)} \qquad \text{FORMULA 5.7}$$

Similarly, dividing by 1000 will convert from mils to inches:

$$D \text{ (inches)} = \frac{D \text{ (mils)}}{1000} \qquad \text{FORMULA 5.8}$$

EXAMPLE:
A piece of wire measures 0.0201 in. in diameter. What is its diameter in mils? ■

SOLUTION:
Substituting in Formula 5.7,

$$D \text{ (mils)} = 1000 \times 0.0201 \text{ in.}$$
$$D \text{ (mils)} = 20.1$$

The diameter of the wire is 20.1 mils. ■

The second measurement used to measure wire thickness in the U.S. customary system is the *circular mil*. This unit is obtained by multiplying the diameter of the wire *in mils* by itself. The measurement of the cross section of a wire in circular mils is related to the cross-sectional area of the wire. This is why the measurement in circular mils is often called the "area in circular mils." In your study of the nature of resistance and resistivity, you learned that the resistance of a length of wire depends upon its cross-sectional area. For this reason, the "area" in circular mils gives a better idea of the comparative resistance of two equal lengths of wire than does the diameter.

EXAMPLE:
Two equal lengths of round wire with diameters of 0.03196 and 0.02257 in., respectively, are used as loads in a circuit. Which wire will have the smaller resistance? How much more current will flow through the smaller resistance than the larger one? ■

SOLUTION:
The first part of this problem is easy. If the lengths of the wires are the same and if they are made of the same material (that is, if the resistivities are the same), the thicker wire will have less resistance since the formula relating resistance and resistivity is

$$R = \frac{\rho l}{A}$$

That is, the resistance *decreases* when the area increases. Because the area of the cross section is proportional to the length of the diameter, the wire with the larger diameter also has the larger cross-sectional area and the smaller resistance. The second part of the problem can be solved by comparing the cross-sectional area of both wires in circular mils. First, it is necessary to convert the wire diameter to mils. (Always convert diameter measurements to mils before trying to compute the area in circular mils, otherwise an error might occur.) Using Formula 5.7:

$$\begin{aligned} D \text{ (mils)} &= 1000 \times D \text{ (inches)} \\ &= 1000 \times 0.02257 \\ &= 22.57 \text{ mils} \end{aligned}$$

Now calculate the area in circular mils by multiplying the diameter in mils by itself, that is, square the diameter:

$$\begin{aligned} A \text{ (circular mils)} &= D \text{ (mils)}^2 \\ &= 22.57 \times 22.57 \\ &= 509.4049 \end{aligned}$$

For the second wire,

$$\begin{aligned} D \text{ (mils)} &= 1000 \times D \text{ (inches)} \\ &= 1000 \times 0.03196 \\ &= 31.96 \end{aligned}$$

The cross-sectional area in circular mils is

$$\begin{aligned} A \text{ (circular mils)} &= D \text{ (mils)}^2 \\ &= 31.96 \times 31.96 \\ &= 1021.4416 \end{aligned}$$

Comparing the areas in circular mils of the two wires, $\frac{1021.4416}{509.4049}$ is about equal to $\frac{2}{1}$. The thicker wire has about twice the area of the thinner. This means that the thicker wire will have about half the resistance of the thinner wire. According to Ohm's law, Formula 5.4,

$$I = \frac{E}{R}$$

if the same potential difference is applied across both loads, roughly twice the current will pass through the thicker wire. ■

Figure 5.12 A standard wire gauge. (Photo by M. Hermes.)

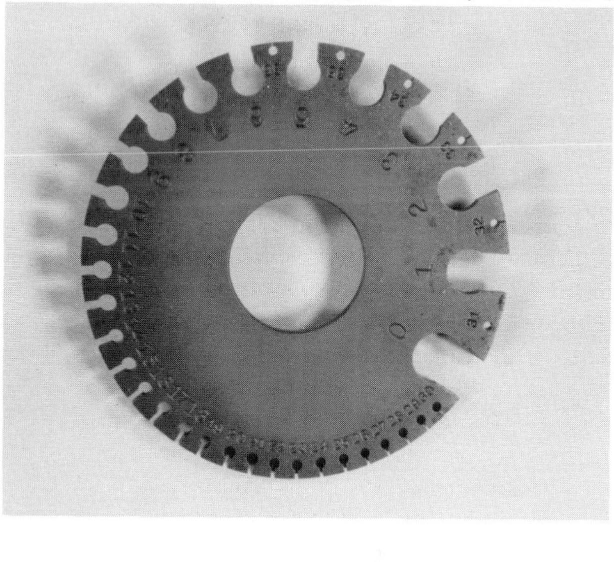

The most common way of describing wire size in the United States is to refer to a gauge number. A gauge, pictured in Figure 5.12, is actually a sizing device that assigns a particular gauge number to wire of a particular diameter. The most widely used gauge for electricity and electronics is the American Wire Gauge, abbreviated AWG. It is identical with the Brown and Sharpe (B&S) gauge. Table 5.6 lists the AWG numbers most commonly used in electricity and electronics, wire diameters in both U.S. customary and metric units, cross-sectional area in circular mils, and the resistance of a 1-m length. You can see that as the gauge number *increases*, the thickness of the wire *decreases*. As might be expected, the AWG sizes are based on U.S. customary units. The gauge sizes are calculated so that an increase of three gauge numbers is an almost exact halving of the cross-sectional area in circular mils. A decrease in the gauge number by three, say from AWG 20 to 17 means a doubling of the cross-sectional area in circular mils.

This bit of information can be of more use than you might expect. For example, suppose that you have to modify a system composed of several units interconnected by cables, each composed of 10 separate AWG No. 24 wires. New units have been installed in the system to provide four times the number of circuits. This means that new cables will have to be installed. Each new cable will have to be composed of at least 40 separate wires. You have been given the job of making the necessary changes. Now your common sense and knowledge of wire sizes will be tested. A 40-wire cable composed of AWG No. 24 wires will be roughly four times thicker than a 10-wire cable, assuming that the thickness of the insulation can be neglected. Will this require drilling larger holes in the system enclosure? How much time would it take to do this? Might it not be better to use cables composed of thinner wires that would fit through the same holes as the original 10-wire cable? Since you remember that an increase of three in the AWG number is equivalent to a halving of the wire cross section, you know that an increase of six in the gauge number would mean a decrease in the cross-sectional area by a factor of four. A 40-wire cable composed of AWG 30 wires would be about the same thickness as a 10-wire cable made up of AWG No. 24 wires. But before you order or begin to build 40-wire cables, it is necessary to find out if AWG 30 wires can be used in this system. Remember, the resistance of a wire depends on its cross-sectional area. All other things being equal, a length of AWG 30 wire will have four times the resistance as a length of AWG No. 24 wire—an increase of six in the gauge number means a decrease in the area by a factor of four. In the following chapter, you will learn about the safe

Table 5.6 AWG Gauge Numbers Most Commonly Used in Electronics and Electricity

AWG Gauge No.	Diameter *m*	Diameter *Mils*	Cross-sectional Area in Circular Mils	Resistance of 1m at 20°C
4/0 or 0000	0.01168	460.0	211,600	0.0001608
2/0 or 00	0.009266	364.8	133,100	0.0002557
1/0 or 0	0.008251	324.9	105,500	0.0003224
1	0.007348	289.3	83,690	0.0004065
2	0.006543	257.6	66,370	0.0005126
3	0.005827	229.4	52,640	0.0006464
4	0.005189	204.3	41,740	0.0008151
5	0.004621	181.9	33,100	0.001028
6	0.004115	162.0	26,250	0.001296
7	0.003665	144.3	20,820	0.001634
8	0.003264	128.5	16,510	0.002061
9	0.002906	114.4	13,090	0.002599
10	0.002588	101.9	10,380	0.003277
11	0.002305	90.74	8,234	0.004132
12	0.002052	80.81	6,530	0.005210
13	0.001828	71.96	5,178	0.006570
14	0.001628	64.08	4,107	0.008285
15	0.001450	57.07	3,257	0.01045
16	0.001291	50.82	2,583	0.01317
17	0.001150	45.26	2,048	0.01661
18	0.001024	40.30	1,624	0.02095
19	0.0009116	35.89	1,288	0.02641
20	0.0008118	31.96	1,022	0.03331
21	0.0007230	28.46	810.1	0.04200
22	0.0006438	25.35	642.4	0.05296
23	0.0005733	22.57	509.5	0.06678
24	0.0005106	20.10	404.0	0.08421
25	0.0004547	17.90	320.4	0.1062
26	0.0004049	15.94	254.1	0.1339
27	0.0003606	14.20	201.5	0.1688
28	0.0003211	12.64	159.8	0.2129
29	0.0002859	11.26	126.7	0.2685
30	0.0002546	10.02	100.5	0.3385
31	0.0002268	8.928	79.7	0.4269
32	0.0002019	7.950	63.21	0.5383

current capacity of wires and power transfer. This information will help you make the decisions required by this kind of job.

From this example, you can see the value of the AWG system. Because of its usefulness and familiarity, this book will continue to use the AWG number system along with wire diameter dimensions in metric units.

D.2 SOLID AND STRANDED WIRE

The wire used in electricity and electronics today is either composed of a single piece of metal with a circular cross section as shown in Figure 5.13*a*, or it is made up of a number of thinner strands twisted together as pictured in Figure 5.13*b*. In Figure 5.13*b* you can see that there is some space between the strands of the stranded wire. This means that for equal cross-sectional areas of conductor material, the solid wire will take up less space than stranded wire. Solid wire is also easier to use. When making connections with stranded wire, it is necessary to ensure that *all* the strands are involved in the connection, and that there

Figure 5.13 Solid conductor and stranded wire.

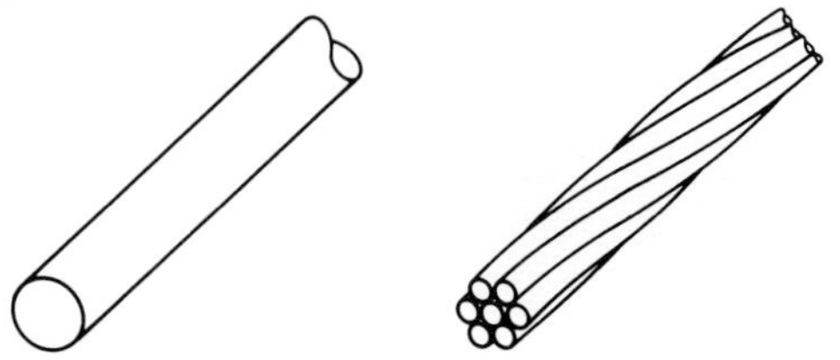

(a) Solid conductor *(b)* Stranded wire

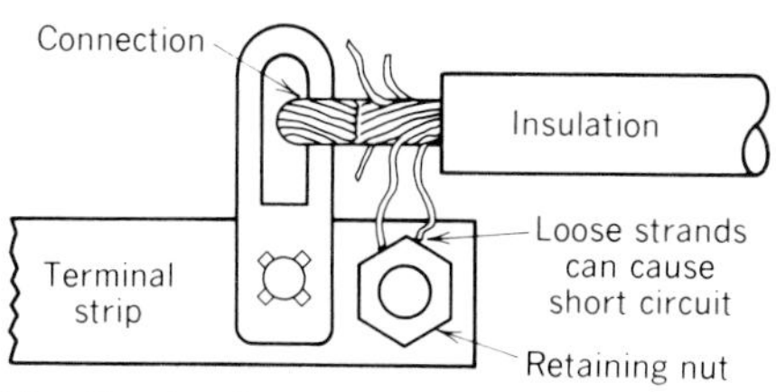

Figure 5.14 Caution is necessary when using stranded wire.

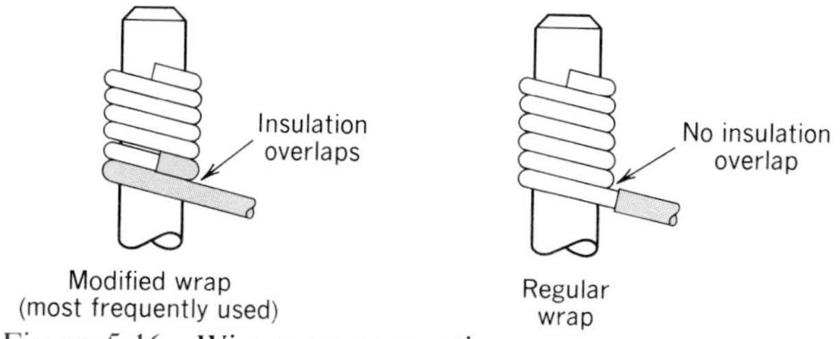

Figure 5.16 Wire-wrap connections.

are no loose strands that could cause a short circuit as seen in Figure 5.14.

Solid wire is not as strong as the same AWG number stranded wire. Nor is it as flexible. Vibration and flexing cause the formation of tiny cracks in solid wire as shown in Figure 5.15. This type of crack formation is called *metal fatigue* and will result in an increase in wire resistance and the eventual breaking of the wire. For this reason, solid wire is generally used only for short connections such as component leads, or where adequate support can be provided. One such use of solid wire is in electronic components that contain coils of wire. Relays and transformers are members of this group, and solid wire is preferred in their construction since the smaller space required for a given cross-sectional area in solid wire makes it possible to pack a larger number of turns of wire into a small space. A further saving in space is obtained by using a thin varnish or lacquer coating to insulate the wire rather than a thicker material. Wire of this type, that is, solid copper insulated with a thin coating of varnish, is commonly called *magnet wire* or *transformer wire*. Magnet wire is commercially available in spools in sizes from AWG 12 to AWG 40. Because the insulating lacquer coating is difficult to remove from the ends of the wire, it is usually not used for anything but the winding of coils.

Since copper corrodes quite easily and forms an oxide coating that complicates electrical connections, it is common to coat bare copper with a thin plating of tin, tin alloy, or silver. This thin coating protects the wire from corrosion and makes it much easier to form connections.

Figure 5.15 Formation of metal fatigue areas.

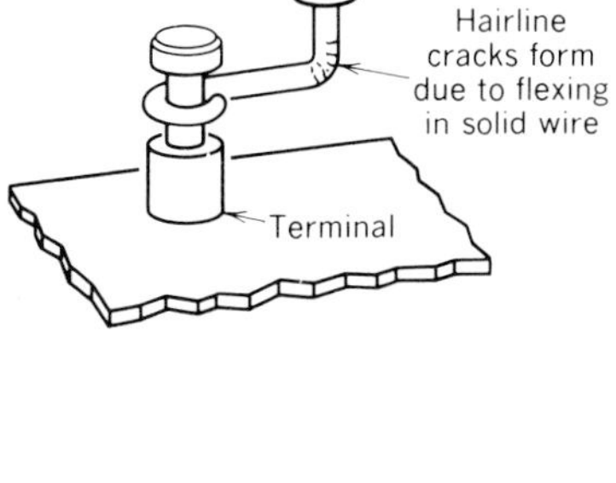

Aluminum wire is sometimes used instead of copper wire. Aluminum is much lighter than copper and does not corrode as readily, but copper is a better conductor than aluminum. This means that thicker aluminum wire would have to be used to provide as low a resistance as a copper wire. Aluminum is also hard to solder, so that more sophisticated methods would have to be used to form connections. For these reasons, aluminum wire is found only in applications where weight is the most important consideration.

Silver-plated wire is used in radar and similar applications because silver is even a better conductor than copper. Silver-plated wire is also used in a construction technique called *wire-wrap*. Wrapped connections like those shown in Figure 5.16 are strong and have low resistance. Wire-wrap is becoming a popular method for building the first models of new designs. These first models, called prototypes, must be constructed in such a way as to allow changes to be made easily. Since ease of change is one of the features of wire-wrap technology, this method can save time and effort in the early stages of product development. Figure 5.17 is a photograph of a wire-wrapped circuit board. All the components are mounted on the top of the board, while the bottom consists of a maze of wires connecting pins that make contact with the components on the other side. Wire-wrap wire is generally AWG 30, although AWG 28 and 26 are sometimes found.

Figure 5.17 A Wire-wrapped circuit board (Photo by M. Hermes).

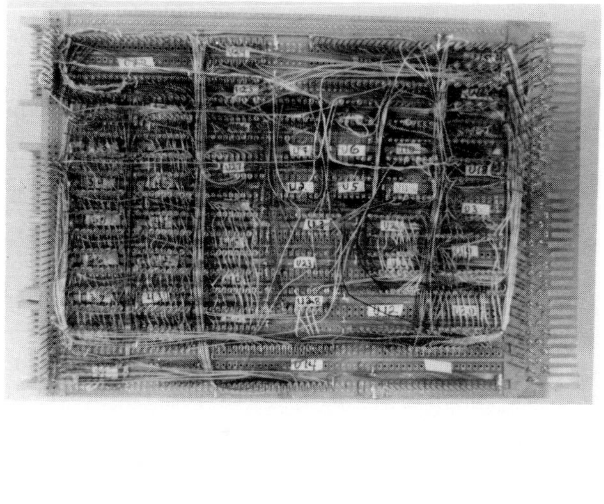

Table 5.7 Number of Strands and Single Strand Gauge in Stranded Wire

AWG No. of Stranded Wire	*Number of Strands*	*AWG No. of Single Strand*
8	84	28
10	65	28
12	65	30
14	41	30
16	26	30
18	16	30
20	7	28
22	7	30
24	7	32
26	7	34
28	7	36
30	7	38

A widely used type of solid "electronic" wire is solid copper, which has been coated with a tin alloy and covered with an insulating plastic layer. It is sometimes called *hook-up wire*, although stranded wire is most commonly understood when hook-up wire is referred to. It is available in gauge sizes from AWG 20 to 30. Previously, most of the component connections within electronic units were made with solid or stranded wire. Today, the use of printed circuits, strips of conductive copper deposited on boards of fiberglass or epoxy, have replaced much of the hook-up wire connection in units.

Because solid wire is not as strong or flexible as stranded wire, stranded wire is used where unsupported lengths of more than a few centimeters are needed. Table 5.7 lists the number of strands and single-strand gauge numbers commonly used in AWG stranded wire. For special purposes, stronger wire is produced by replacing a number of the tinned copper strands with nickel-plated copper, or with steel. This does increase the resistance of the wire, however. The major disadvantage of stranded wire is that it is somewhat harder to work with than solid wire, particularly in the preparation of wire ends for joining. Figure 5.18 shows the steps involved in preparing stranded wire for soldering. *Tinning*, that is, melting a thin film of tin alloy (solder) onto the strands, keeps them together and prevents accidental short circuiting.

D.3 INSULATION

In most applications, it is necessary to insulate conductive wire to prevent short circuits or contact with other conductors. This is done by covering the wire with a uniform coating of insulating material. Bare wire and component leads can be covered with a plastic

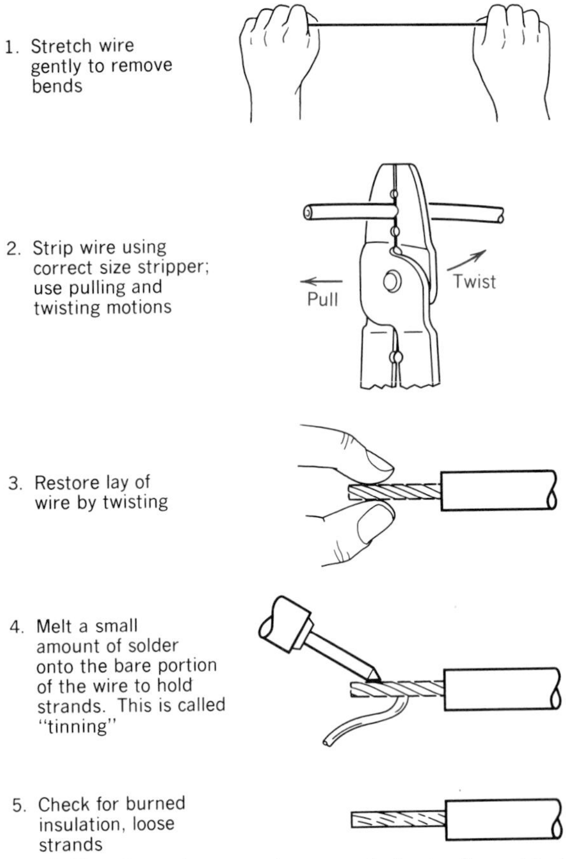

1. Stretch wire gently to remove bends
2. Strip wire using correct size stripper; use pulling and twisting motions
Pull
Twist
3. Restore lay of wire by twisting
4. Melt a small amount of solder onto the bare portion of the wire to hold strands. This is called "tinning"
5. Check for burned insulation, loose strands

Figure 5.18 Steps in preparing stranded wire for soldering.

sleeving, commonly called *spaghetti*, before installation. See Figure 5.19. In installations where extra mechanical strength is needed, a special form of sleeving is used. This sleeving shrinks when heated and moulds itself to grip connections and wires firmly. The steps in using heat-shrink tubing to insulate a wire and strengthen a connection are shown in Figure 5.20.

Most of the wire used in electricity and electronics

Figure 5.19 Insulating bare wire with plastic sleeving.

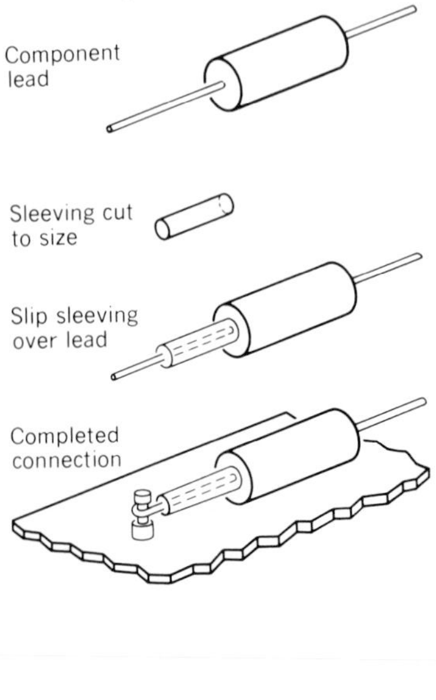

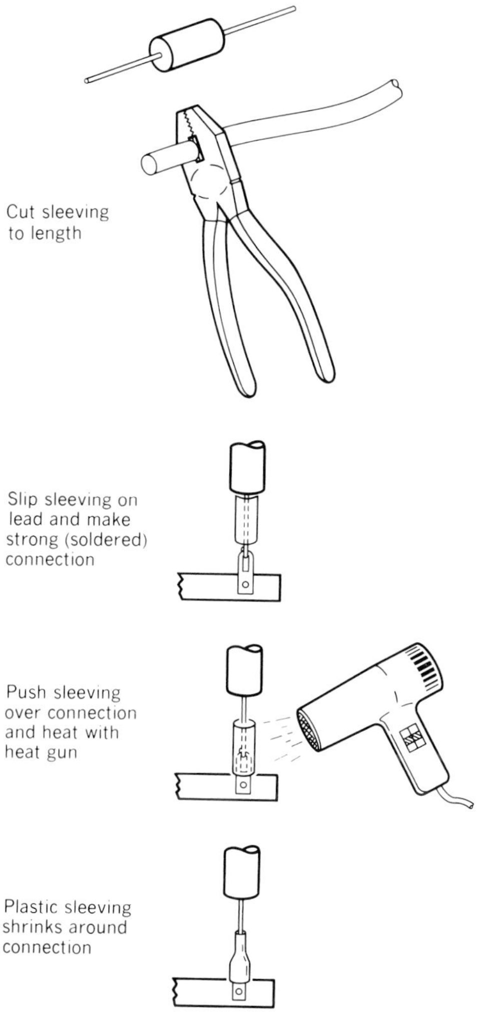

Figure 5.20 Steps in using heat-shrink tubing to insulate and strengthen a connection.

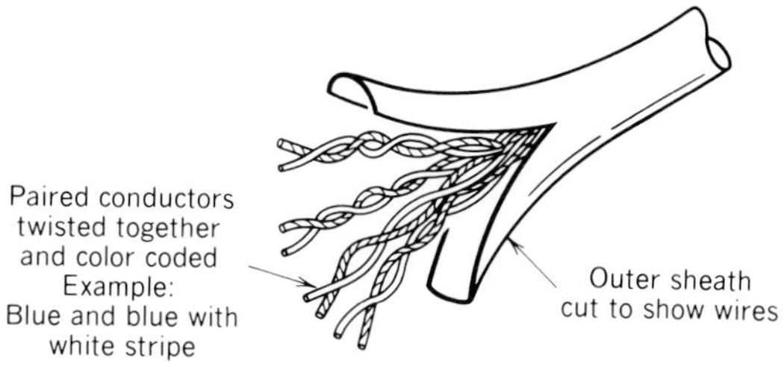

Figure 5.21 A paired conductor cable of the sort commonly used in telephone service.

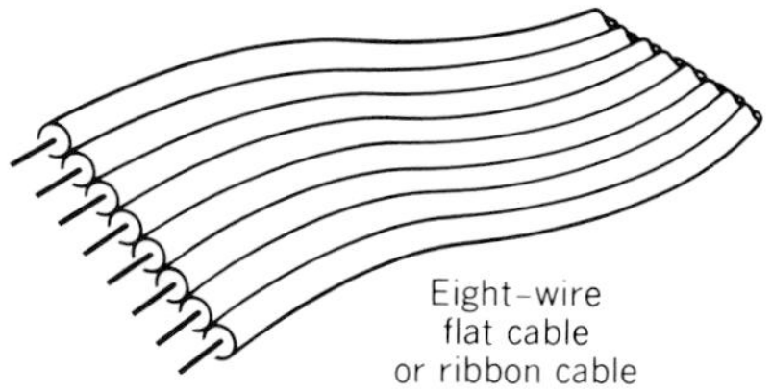

Figure 5.22 Ribbon cable is widely used in the computer industry.

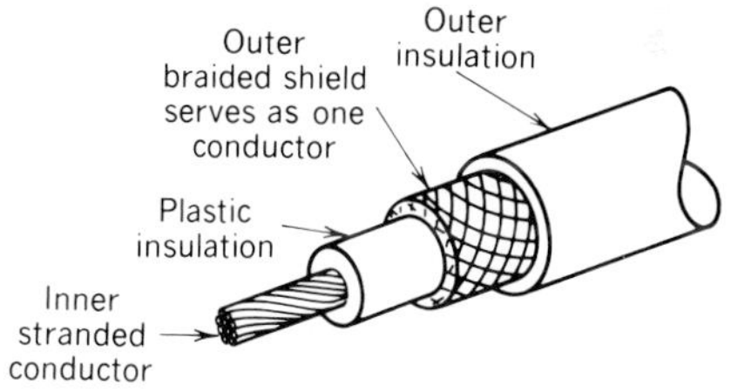

Figure 5.23 Coaxial cable.

is manufactured with a uniform covering of insulating material over the conductive metal. Over the years, wire manufacturers seem to have tried nearly every possible insulating material for their products. Still, no all-purpose insulation has been discovered. Today, the most widely used insulation materials are plastic, either polyvinyl chloride (PVC) or some form of fluorine compound (Teflon®). Other plastic and synthetic rubber compounds are used in special-purpose cables and wires. Insulating materials are selected on the basis of their ability to withstand high potential differences, heat, and their overall physical qualities such as flexibility, resistance to cracking, and so on.

D.4 CABLE

Earlier in this section, a cable was defined as two or more separate conductive paths bound into a single package. In some cables, such as that shown in Figure 5.21, individual conductors are paired, either through the use of colored insulation or by some other means, so that each pair may serve as the positive and negative leads of a separate circuit. Most cables of this sort have a circular cross section; but flat, ribbon-type cable shown in Figure 5.22 is also used, particularly in the computer industry. Although ribbon cable occupies more space than round cable, it provides greater flexibility and can be used with connectors that attach to the cable easily.

One of the most familiar sorts of cable used in electronics work is coaxial cable, usually called *coax* (pronounced 'cō-ax). It is used when it is necessary to minimize interference or loss of power. Referring to Figure 5.23, you can see that a coaxial cable consists

Table 5.8 Some Popular Types of Coax

Type	*Diameter*	*AWG Stranding or Inner Conductor Diameter*
RG-59U	6.12	Solid, 0.58 mm
RG-58U	4.95	Solid, No. 20
RG-58A/U	4.95	19 Strands of No. 32 = No. 20
RG-174U	2.54	7 Strands of No. 34 = No. 26
RG-8U	10.2	7 strands of No. 21 = No. 13

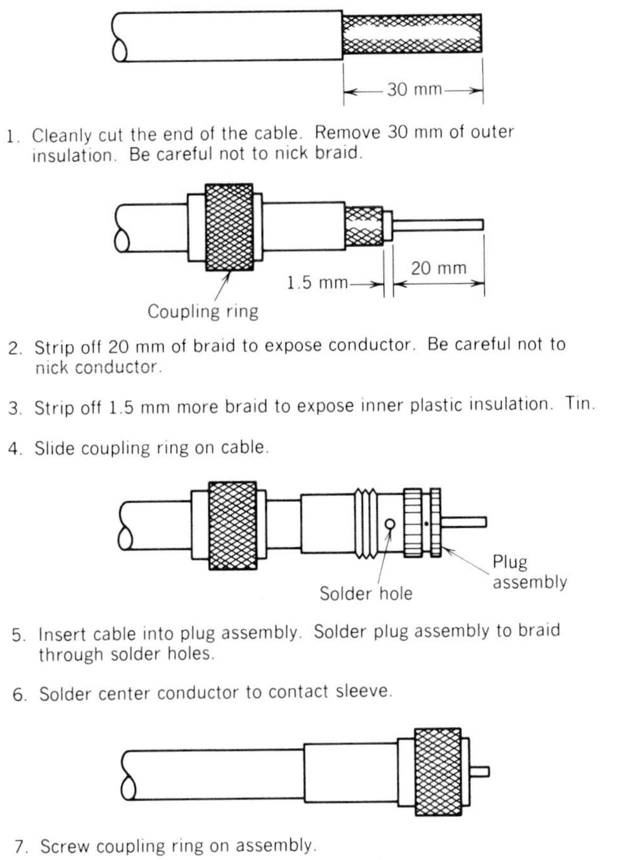

30 mm
1. Cleanly cut the end of the cable. Remove 30 mm of outer insulation. Be careful not to nick braid.
1.5 mm
20 mm
Coupling ring
2. Strip off 20 mm of braid to expose conductor. Be careful not to nick conductor.
3. Strip off 1.5 mm more braid to expose inner plastic insulation. Tin.
4. Slide coupling ring on cable.
Plug assembly
Solder hole
5. Insert cable into plug assembly. Solder plug assembly to braid through solder holes.
6. Solder center conductor to contact sleeve.
7. Screw coupling ring on assembly.

Figure 5.24 Steps followed in attaching a connector to coaxial cable.

of an inner conductor, plastic insulation, a conductive metal braid that acts as the second conductor, and an outer sheath of insulation. In spite of the fact that it is difficult to make connections with coax, the electrical characteristics of this cable are so valuable that it is frequently used. Table 5.8 lists some of the coax types frequently found, and Figure 5.24 shows the steps followed in attaching one form of connector to the end of a coax cable.

E. PROGRAMMED REVIEW

FRAME 1

The resistivity of a substance is a measurement of how well the atoms of this kind of substance oppose the drift of conduction electrons. Materials with high resistivity are good *conductors/insulators/semiconductors*. (Choose one.)

a. Conductors, review Section B.1.
b. Insulators. (2)
c. Semiconductors, review Chapter 1, Section B.14.

FRAME 2

The resistance of a piece of material is a measure of how much opposition this piece of material provides to electric current. Resistance depends on ________, ________, ________, and ________.

a. resistivity; length; cross-sectional area; temperature. (4)
b. Any other answer (3).

FRAME 3

Resistivity depends on the structure of the atoms of a type of material and how these atoms are bound together in the material. Resistance, on the other hand, does not refer to a type of material in general, but to a specific piece of material that has resistivity, length, and a cross-sectional area. It is also at some temperature. All these factors affect resistance. Go on to Frame 4.

FRAME 4

Ohm's law is a mathematical way of stating a relationship that exists in a closed electric circuit. Ohm's law describes how the current is *the same as/greater than/related to/none of these/* the potential difference across a conductor and the resistance of the conductor.

a. Related to. (6)
b. Any other answer. (5)

FRAME 5

Recall that potential difference is the difference in the ability of an electron to do work at two different points in an electric field. The potential difference between the two points is measured in volts. Current is the drift of conduction electrons through a conducting, closed circuit under the influence of an electric field. Go on to Frame 6.

FRAME 6

Ohm's law states that the resistance of a piece of material in ohms is equal to the applied potential difference in volts divided by the resulting current in amperes. How would you write this as a formula?

a. $R = \frac{E}{I}$. (8)
b. Any other answer. (7)

FRAME 7

If you know the potential difference between the ends of a wire or other conductor *and* the current through the conductor, you can use Ohm's law to find the resistance of the conductor. The formula for Ohm's law is

$$R = \frac{E}{I}$$

That is, the resistance of a piece of material is equal to the potential difference across the material divided by the resulting current. Go on to Frame 8.

FRAME 8

In order to calculate the resistance of a long wire, you have made the setup shown in the schematic diagram in Figure 5.25. The voltmeter shows a potential difference of 12 V, while the ammeter indicates 300 mA. What is the resistance of the wire?

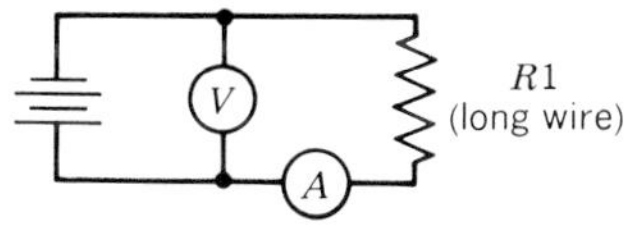

Figure 5.25 Schematic of circuit for Frame 8.

a. 40 Ω. (9)
b. Any other answer, review Section B.2.

FRAME 9

In most digital multimeters, a tiny computer is used to compare the effect of the unknown resistance on a circuit with the effect of a known resistance. The first step before making resistance measurements with a digital multimeter is to __________.

a. Make sure that the power in the circuit to be measured is off. (10)
b. Any other answer, study Figure 5.6.

Figure 5.26 Schematic diagram for Frame 12—using continuity measurements in troubleshooting.

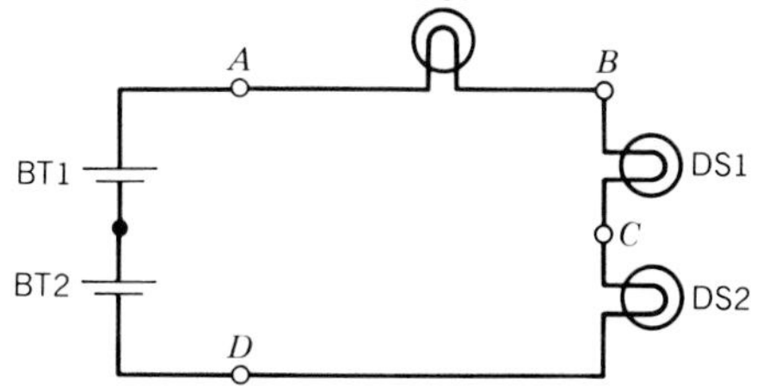

FRAME 10

Usually, the most accurate resistance measurements are obtained by using the lowest multimeter range that will work. If the range selected is too low, the scale on an analog multimeter will be difficult to read; a digital multimeter will indicate __________.

a. Out-of-range or overrange. (11)
b. Any other answer, review Section B.3.

FRAME 11

Regardless of which method is used to measure resistance, the measuring device furnishes electric power to the component or circuit whose resistance is being measured. The source of this power is one or more cells located in the meter. The power is furnished to the component or circuit through __________.

a. The meter leads. (12)
b. Any other answer, review Section B.3.

FRAME 12

Figure 5.26 is the schematic diagram of a simple circuit that you are troubleshooting. You suspect that one of the components is burned out (open-circuited). Which steps would you follow to use continuity measurements to check pilot lamp DS2?

a. 1. Connect a jumper wire between points *A* and *D*.
   2. Connect leads of multimeter set for resistance measurement to points *A* and *D*.
b. 1. Disconnect cells from points *A* and *D*.
   2. Connect leads of a multimeter set for resistance measurement to points *A* and *D*.
c. 1. Disconnect cells from points *A* and *D*.
   2. Connect leads off a multimeter set for resistance measurement to points *C* and *D*.
d. Connect leads of a multimeter set for resistance measurements to points *C* and *D*.

   a. or b. (13)
   c. (14)
   d. Repeat Frame 9, then go to Frame 14.

FRAME 13

Your answer is not quite correct. You were right to disconnect the cells first, but if the multimeter leads are connected to points *A* and *D*, you will be checking the continuity of all three bulbs, not DS2. Go on to Frame 14.

FRAME 14

A certain coil is composed of 15,000 turns of thin copper wire and has a resistance of 1 kΩ at room temperature (20°C). What will be the resistance of this coil at an operating temperature of 40°C?

a. About 1080 Ω. (15)
b. Any other answer, review Section B.5.

FRAME 15

The formula $R = \frac{\rho l}{A}$ states that the __________ of a material is directly proportional to its __________ measured in __________ and its __________ measured in meters, and __________ to its __________ measured in square meters.

a. resistance; resistivity; ohm·meters; length; inversely proportional; area. (16)
b. Any other answer, review Section B.2.

FRAME 16

Give the reciprocals of the following terms, simplify where possible

a. $1 + \frac{1}{2}$

b. $X - \frac{1}{\frac{1}{X}}$

c. $\frac{1}{G} \times \frac{1}{\frac{1}{G}}$

a. $\frac{2}{3}$; no reciprocal; 1. (17)
b. Any other answer, review Section C.3.

FRAME 17

The resistance of a component is 4.7×10^3 Ω. Calculate its conductance.

a. 4.7×10^{-3} S. (18)
b. 0.00021 S or 2.1×10^{-4} S. (19)
c. Any other answer, review Section C.3.

FRAME 18

Your answer is not quite correct. You did calculate the reciprocal of 10^3, but not of 4.7. The correct answer is 2.1×10^{-4} S. Go on to Frame 19.

FRAME 19

The diameter of AWG 24 solid copper wire is about 0.02 in. What is its cross-sectional area in circular mils? What approximately is the cross-sectional area of AWG 21?

a. About 400 circular mils; about 800 circular mils. (END)
b. Any other answers, review Section D.1.

E. PROBLEMS FOR SOLUTION OR RESEARCH

1. Complete the following sentences by filling in the blanks.

a. __________ is a mathematical statement of the relationship among potential difference, current, and __________ in an electric circuit.

b. __________ is provided by an electric field in order to cause electrons to drift through a conductor.

c. If two wires are made of the same material and have the same thickness but different lengths, the __________ wire will have the higher resistance.

d. If two wires are made of the same material and have the same lengths, but are of different thicknesses, the __________ will have the higher resistance.

e. A 3-m piece of copper wire has *more/less/the same* resistance *than/as* an equal length of iron wire of the same thickness.

f. A conductor has __________ resistance, an insulator has a very __________ resistance.

g. The lower the __________ of a material, the better it is as a conductor of electricity.

h. If you increase the potential difference across the ends of a conducting wire, its resistance will __________.

i. If you increase the potential difference across the ends of a conducting wire, the current will __________.

2. A conductor with a resistance of 10 Ω is connected across the terminals of a 1.5-V cell. What is the resulting current through the conductor?

3. If a second 1.5-V cell is placed in series with the cell in the circuit of Problem 2, the potential difference across the conductor will be doubled. How will this change the resistance of the conductor and the current through it?

4. Figure 5.27 is the schematic diagram of a simple circuit, showing the resistance of the load and the current through it. What is the potential difference of the battery?

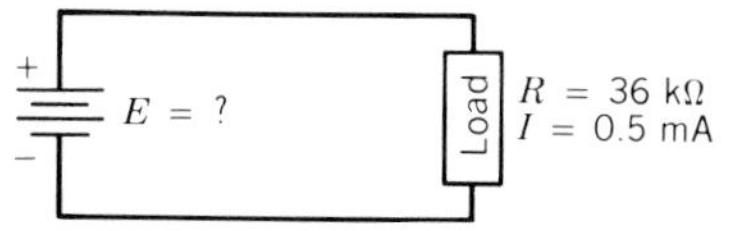

Figure 5.27 Schematic diagram for Problem 4.

5. Solve for the unknown quantities:

a. $E = 12$ V, $R = 100\ \Omega$, $I = ?$
b. $E = ?$, $R = 100$ kΩ, $I = 50$ mA
c. $E = 5$ V, $R = ?$, $I = 25$ mA

6. An extension cord composed of three insulated wires (Figure 5.28) has been crushed and may have been damaged. Explain how you could use a multimeter to check the cord to see if it is safe for use.

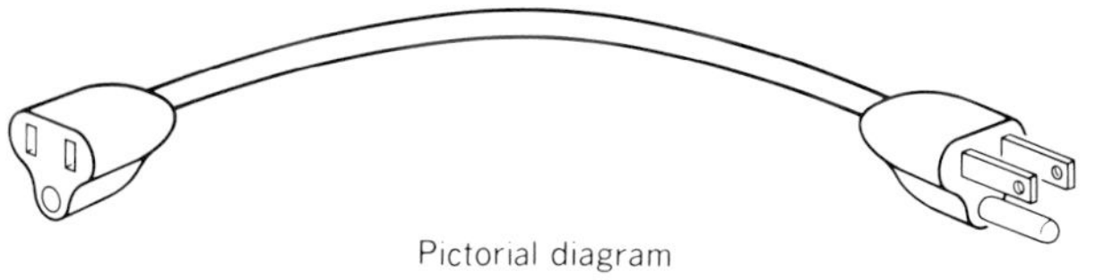

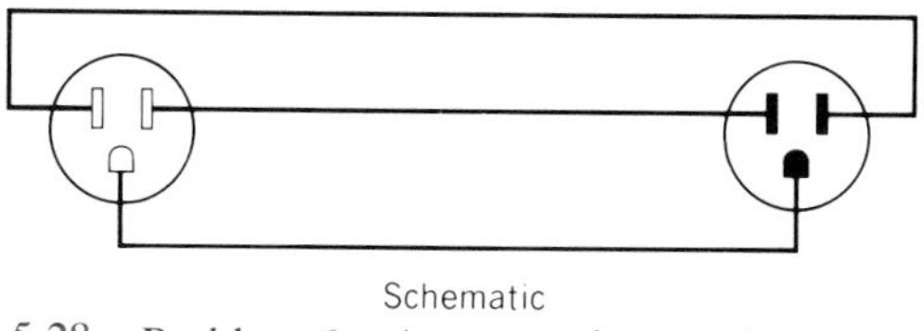

Figure 5.28 Problem 6—An extension cord.

7. What is the difference between resistivity and resistance? Which does a multimeter measure?

8. A painful shock may be felt when a current of 1 mA passes through the body. A person leaning against a grounded bench feels such a shock when accidentally touching a 120-V power line terminal. What is this person's body resistance?

9. List the steps required to measure resistance using an analog multimeter; using a digital multimeter with autoranging.

10. A coil of copper wire has a current of 15 mA through it and a resistance of 2 kΩ at a temperature of 20°C. What will be the current through this coil at a temperature of 50°C if the potential difference across the coil remains the same?

11. List three ways in which resistance measurements can be used in troubleshooting.

12. Question for thought: What happens to the energy supplied by the electric field when a current flow is produced through a conductor?
Hint: What happens to a wire through which a large current is flowing?

CHAPTER 6

POWER: RESISTANCES IN SERIES, PARALLEL, AND SERIES-PARALLEL

A. CHAPTER PREVIEW

1 In previous chapters, the electrical quantities charge, current, potential difference, and resistance were presented. In this chapter you will learn about power, a quantity based on work and time, and how to measure electric power.

2 You will also learn how to calculate the total resistance of circuits consisting of more than one resistive element. Ohm's law is used to calculate the potential difference and current through parts of complex circuits.

3 The Examples and Computations section introduces square and square root computations required to calculate circuit power. Calculator and small computer methods of solving power law formulas are shown.

4 Additional exercises related to the use of variational analysis are illustrated as an aid to working with Ohm's law and power formulas.

5 The Applications section of this chapter is an introduction to three important components: lamps, fuses, and switches. You will learn to recognize the most common forms of these components as well as their characteristics.

B. PRINCIPLES

B.1 WHAT IS POWER?

The first chapter of this book was based on the importance of viewing electricity as one form of energy. It was shown that an electric field performed work on conduction electrons in order to create a current. An electron moving in an electric field can be compared to a weight falling in the gravitational field of the earth. In both cases, the amount of work done by the field is equal to a change in potential—voltage in the case of electrons, height above ground in the case of the weight—times a quantity value, either the charge of the electrons moved or the mass of the weight. In many real-world situations, however, it is not the total amount of work that is important but the rate at which the work is done.

Power is the rate at which work is done. Although the horse is no longer an important source of power in our society, mechanical power is still measured in horsepower (hp). Automobile and small engine manufacturers have complex ways of measuring horsepower, but the scientific definition of one horsepower is the power necessary to lift 550 pounds a distance of one foot in one second. As a formula, this is written:

$$P_{\mathrm{hp}} = 0.001818 \times \frac{f \times d}{t} \qquad \text{FORMULA 6.1}$$

where f is the force in pounds, d is the distance in feet, and t the time in seconds.

In the scientific mks system used in this book, power is measured in joules per second, or watts. Recall that a joule is a force of one newton operating through a distance of one meter. One horsepower is equal to 746 joules per second:

$$1 \text{ hp} = \frac{550 \text{ ft lbs}}{\text{s}} = \frac{746 \text{ J}}{\text{s}} \qquad \text{FORMULA 6.2}$$

See Figure 6.1 for a pictorial representation of this equality. Solving the above equation for the metric unit, it is also possible to write:

$$1 \text{ J/s} = 1 \text{ W} = 0.00134 \text{ hp} = 0.737 \text{ ft lb/s} \qquad \text{FORMULA 6.3}$$

Figure 6.1 The unit of power in the U.S. customary system is the horsepower: 1 HP = 746 Newton meters/second.

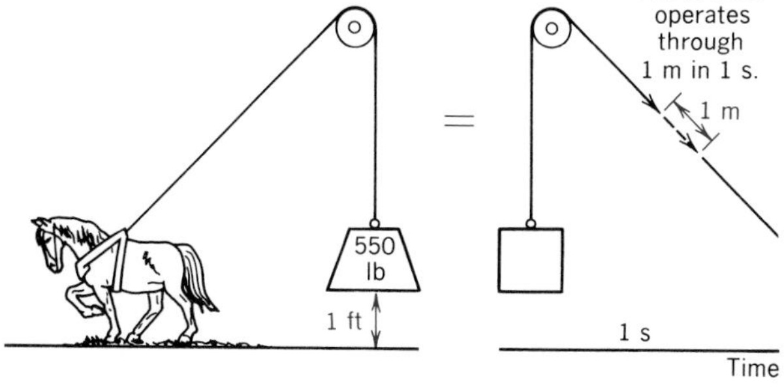

B.2 ELECTRIC POWER

The unit of electric power is defined as the power used when the field caused by a potential difference of one volt moves an electrical charge of one coulomb past a point in one second. It is also equivalent to one joule per second. This unit is called the *watt* (W) in honor of the British inventor James Watt (1736–1819). In mathematical terms this is written as:

$$P = \frac{EQ}{t} \qquad \text{FORMULA 6.4}$$

where P is the power in watts, E is the potential difference in volts, Q is the charge moved in coulombs, and t is the time in seconds.

Note that the quantity P in Formula 6.4 may be thought of in several ways. It is the amount of power supplied by the electric field to move a certain amount of charge from one point to another in a certain time. It also includes the amount of power that is added to the system when the charge is moved. For example, suppose that you have a system like that pictured in Figure 6.2 consisting of two metal spheres connected by a copper wire. If the system is placed in an electric field, electrons in the wire and in sphere B will begin to drift toward sphere A (recall that negatively charged electrons move in the direction opposite to that indicated by the arrowheads). In their drift, the electrons moving along the surface of sphere B and through the wire are being captured by the atoms of the material and giving up some energy as heat radiation. Electrons are also absorbing energy from the field, breaking away from atoms, and reentering the conduction band. This is the power supplied by the field that is required to overcome the electrical resistance of the conductors. In addition to this, as sphere A becomes negatively

Figure 6.2 Electrons move from sphere B through wire to sphere A.

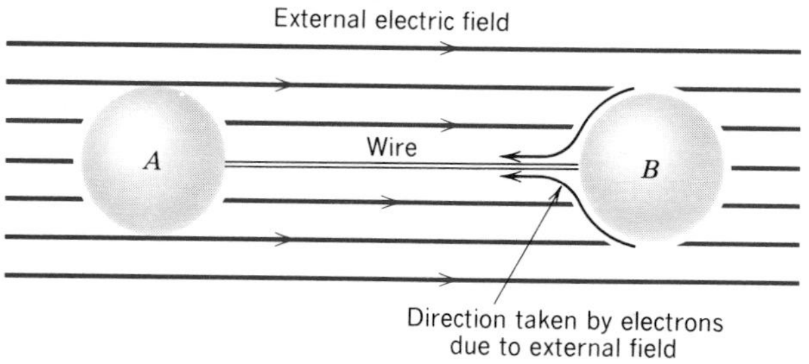

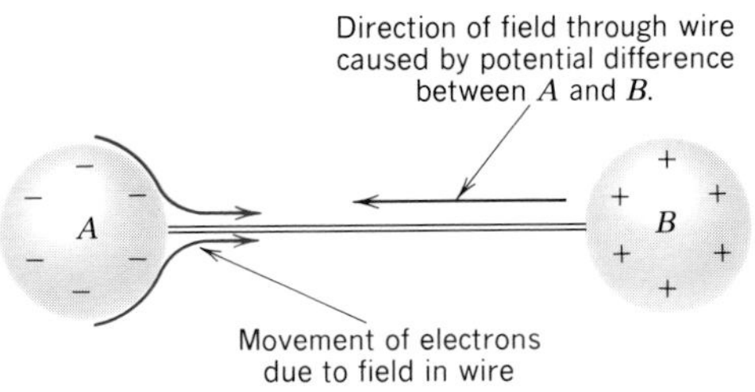

Figure 6.3 When the external field is removed, the imbalance of charge between the two spheres causes a current.

charged, it actually repels the electrons and resists the tendency of the field to force the conduction electrons into sphere A. Therefore, the electric field must also provide the force necessary to overcome the repelling force produced by the increasing negative charge on sphere A. The total power supplied by the field can be divided into two portions.

Total power supplied by field = power used up in causing electrons to move through wire + power required to move electrons against the increasing negative charge of sphere A

If the electric field is now removed, the situation is as shown in Figure 6.3. A potential difference now exists between sphere A and sphere B. This potential difference is actually stored electrical energy and will cause an electric field between spheres A and B. Part of the power provided by the original field was converted into heat, while the remaining portion was turned into the potential energy stored in the potential difference between the two spheres. This is true in every application of electricity; some of the power is converted into heat, while the rest is converted into some other form of energy or stored temporarily as in the potential difference produced in this example. The power converted into heat is usually referred to as the *power dissipation*.

Figure 6.4 shows a simple circuit consisting of a chemical cell and a load. The load in this case is a 10 Ω resistance. The electric field produced by the potential difference of the cell will set up a current through the resistance. Unlike the previous example, where the flow of conduction electrons was impeded by the increasing negative charge of sphere A, in this case the chemical energy of the cell moves conduction electrons from its positive to its negative terminal. The electric power supplied by the potential difference is required only to sustain the flow of electrons through the resistance, that is, the power is dissipated in the resistance.

It is not a difficult matter to calculate the power dissipated in the 10 Ω resistance. Start with Formula 6.4, $P = \frac{EQ}{t}$. But $\frac{Q}{t}$ is actually the current in the circuit, so the symbol I can be substituted for $\frac{Q}{t}$, producing a formula for the power used in this circuit in terms of the applied potential difference E and the current I.

$$P = EI \qquad \text{FORMULA 6.5}$$

This formula is a basic statement of the power law and can be thought of as expressing two ideas:

1. The power supplied to the circuit by the source is equal to the potential difference supplied by the source times the circuit current.

2. The power dissipated as heat by the load resistance is also equal to the potential difference across the load times the current through it.

EXAMPLE:
Calculate the power dissipated by the resistance in Figure 6.5 ■

SOLUTION:
In order to use Formula 6.5, it is necessary to calculate the current through the resistance. For this purpose, Ohm's law can be used since both the potential difference and the circuit resistance are given:

$$I = \frac{E}{R} = \frac{12}{24} = 0.5 \text{ A}$$

The current value may then be substituted in Formula 6.5,

$$P = EI = 12 \times 0.5 = 6 \text{ W} \quad ■$$

In the previous example, two steps were required to calculate the power dissipation. Ohm's law was used to calculate the circuit current, and then the power law formula was used to calculate the power dissipated. Actually, the process can be reduced to one step by

Figure 6.4 In a closed circuit with a source and a resistance as a load, no power is stored; it is all dissipated in moving electrons through the circuit.

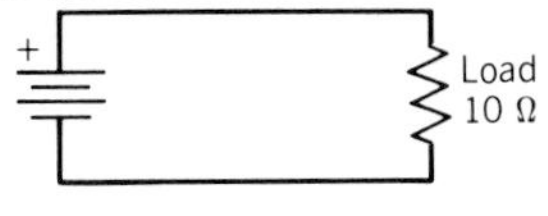

Figure 6.5 Calculating the power dissipated by a resistor.

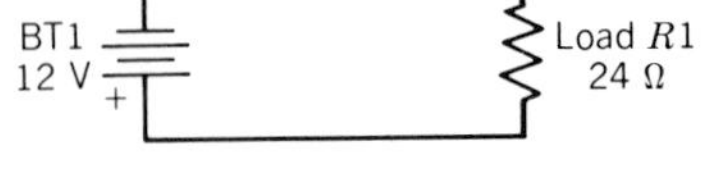

combining the power and Ohm's law formulas. In the above example, $P = E \times I$, but neither P nor I are given. On the other hand, you know from Formula 5.4 that $I = \frac{E}{R}$. Substituting $\frac{E}{R}$ for I in Formula 6.5 gives

$$P = E \times I = E \times \frac{E}{R} \text{ or } \frac{E^2}{R}$$

Then, for cases where power is required and the potential difference and resistance are known

$$P = \frac{E^2}{R} \qquad \text{FORMULA 6.6}$$

may be used.

Similarly, Formula 5.3, $E = IR$, may be substituted for E in Formula 6.5, yielding $P = E \times I = IR \times I = I^2R$ or

$$P = I^2R \qquad \text{FORMULA 6.7}$$

The three forms of the power law formula,

$P = EI$,

$P = \frac{E^2}{R}$,

and $P = I^2R$,

rank second in importance after the Ohm's law formulas in electrical and electronic technology.

EXAMPLE:
A 5-W light bulb, that is, a bulb that dissipates 5 W of power, operates at a potential difference of 12 V. What is the operating current of the bulb? ■

SOLUTION:
Since both P and E are known, and I is required, Formula 6.5 can be used:

$$P = E \times I$$

$$5 = 12 \times I \quad \text{or} \quad I = \frac{5}{12} = 0.417 \text{ A}$$ ■

Formula 6.4 is frequently used to calculate the power dissipation of a known resistance when the current through it is also known.

EXAMPLE:
What is the power dissipation of a 150 Ω resistance when the current through it is 0.01 A? When the current is increased to 0.02 A? ■

SOLUTION:
Using Formula 6.7, you can perform the required calculations easily:

$$P = I^2R = (0.01)^2 \times 150 = 0.0001 \times 150 = 0.015 \text{ W} \quad \text{or} \quad 15 \text{ milliwatts (mW)}$$

When the current is increased to 0.02 A

$$P = I^2R = (0.02)^2 \times 150 = 0.0004 \times 150 = 0.06 \text{ W} \quad \text{or} \quad 60 \text{ mW}$$

Notice that doubling the current from 0.01 to 0.02 A increases the power dissipated in the resistance by *four* times, from 15 to 60 mW. ■

Formula 6.6 is useful for calculating the power that a source will furnish to a load resistance.

EXAMPLE:
What power will a 1.5-V cell furnish to a load of 1000 Ω? ■

SOLUTION:
The power may be calculated directly using Formula 6.6.

$$P = \frac{E^2}{R} = \frac{1.5^2}{1000} = 0.00225 \text{ W} \quad \text{or} \quad 2.25 \text{ mW}$$ ■

B.3 MEASURING ELECTRIC POWER

Although engineers and technicians frequently calculate the power supplied to or dissipated in circuits, power measurements are rarely made in dc circuits where power calculation is easy. For scientific laboratories, a wide variety of equipment is used to measure power and power dissipation. These range from thermometers that record the amount of heat dissipated to elaborate energy-sensing devices. Engineering and technical power measurements are for the most part limited to two types of wattmeter. One is the device pictured in Figure 6.6, which contains two coils of wire, one of which is connected in series with the load, the other in parallel. Based on magnetic principles, this device is capable of reasonably good measurements for power distribution. In communications technology, a second type of wattmeter, shown in Figure 6.7, is sometimes used. It is referred to as a *Thruline® Wattmeter*. This device absorbs some of the power in the circuit to which it is connected and produces an easily measured current proportional to the power in the circuit.

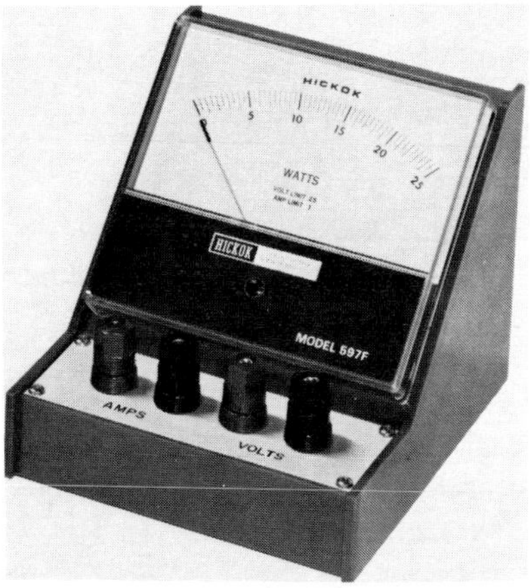

Figure 6.6 A wattmeter used to measure dc power. (Photo courtesy of Hickok Teaching Systems, Inc., Woburn, Mass.).

More common than true power measurements are comparative measurements. These are made in decibels rather than watts, and will be considered in detail later in this book.

Figure 6.7 A thru-line® wattmeter of the type used in communications technology. (Photo courtesy of Bird Electronic Corp.)

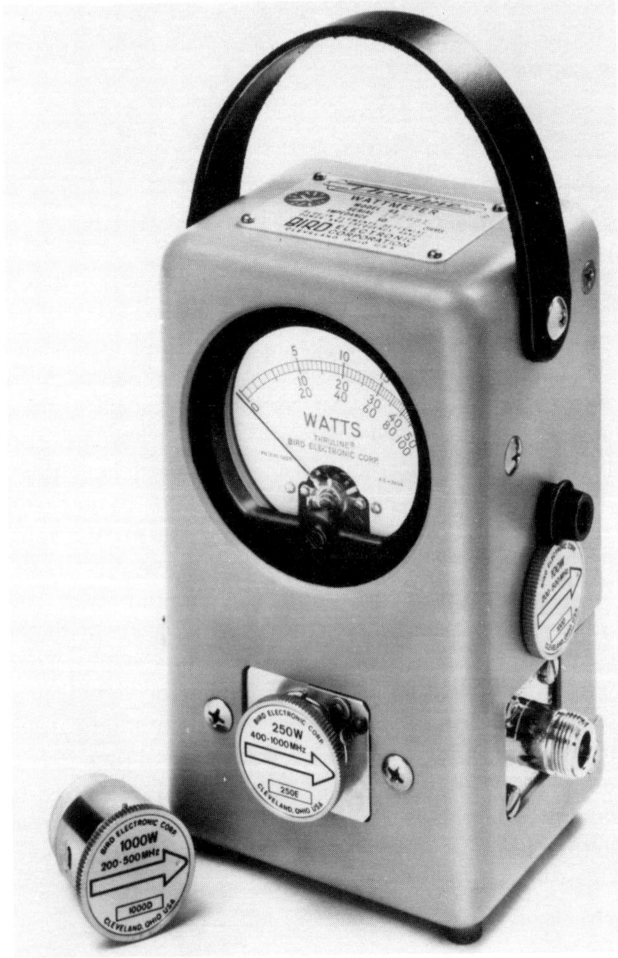

B.4 RESISTANCES IN SERIES

The discussion of circuits and Ohm's law in Chapter 5 proceeded as if all the resistance in each circuit was lumped into one load and that the wires used to connect the load to the circuit source were without resistance. Of course, this is not strictly true. Practically, however, the resistance of the wires used in electronic circuits is much lower than the resistance of the loads. When the resistance of the connecting wires is less than 1 percent of the load resistance, the wires are usually ignored for purposes of Ohm's law calculations.

In electric power distribution circuits, it is frequently not possible to ignore wire resistance. Figure 6.8*a* is a pictorial diagram of such a circuit where the load is a low-resistance lamp and the connecting wires possess an appreciable resistance. The most common way to deal with circuits of this sort is to represent the resistance of each of the connecting wires as a separate load, in series with the lamp as shown in the schematic diagram in Figure 6.8*b*. In electronics, circuits with several loads in series are very common, and the ability to calculate the total resistance of a number of loads connected in series or to apply Ohm's law to a whole series circuit or to parts of it is essential.

In Figure 6.8*b*, load DS1 represents a lamp. Notice that the schematic symbol and reference designator for a lamp are used, while the resistance symbol is used for R_A and R_B, the resistances of the two wires. If the resistances of the wires were zero, the current through

Figure 6.8*a* The load is a low-resistance lamp and the connecting wires possess an appreciable resistance.

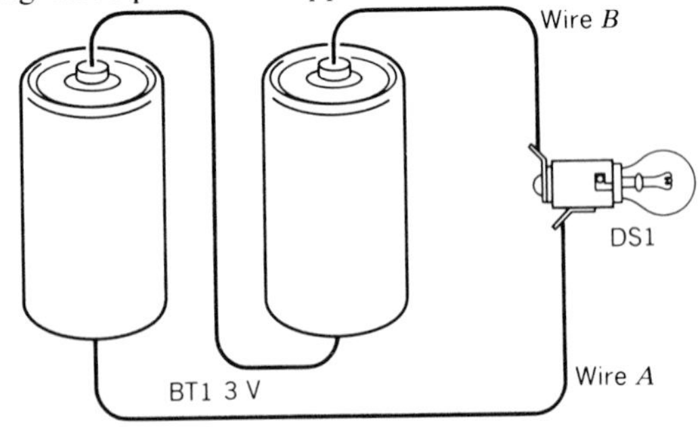

Figure 6.8*b* The resistance of each of the connecting wires is represented as a separate load.

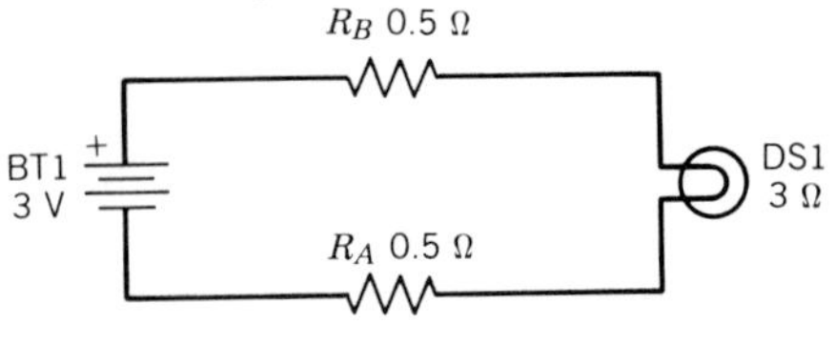

DS1 would be

$$I = \frac{E}{R} = \frac{3}{3} = 1 \text{ A}$$

But this can not be the circuit current since the 3-V potential difference must actually force the current through two additional loads, R_A and R_B. Using a bit of analysis and Ohm's law, it is possible to see what happens in this circuit and to determine its total resistance.

First, the potential difference supplied by the source is given. Since there is no other source of potential difference in the circuit, it is clear that 3 V of potential difference is the total change in the potential of an electron moving through the circuit from the negtive terminal of the source to its positive terminal. The resistances of the loads are also known. Further, it is clear that any current through R_A also flows through DS1 and R_B since there are no branches or alternate paths from the negative to the positive terminal of the source. The circuit current and the total resistance of the circuit are not known. Let these be called I_t and R_t, respectively. According to Ohm's law,

$$E = I_t \times R_t \quad \text{or} \quad 3 = I_t \times R_t$$

Now Ohm's law is also true for each part of the circuit. Therefore, the change in potential, or potential drop, across each resistance in the series string is equal to $I_t \times R$, where R is the resistance of each load in the string. The difference in potential across R_A is

$$E_A = I_t \times 0.5 \quad \text{or} \quad 0.5I_t$$

The difference in potential across DS1 is

$$E_{\text{DS1}} = I_t \times 3 \quad \text{or} \quad 3I_t$$

and the potential drop across R_B is

$$E_B = I_t \times 0.05 \quad \text{or} \quad 0.5I_t$$

Now, since an electron drifting from the negative terminal to the positive terminal of the source passes through each of these changes in potential, or potential drops, its total loss in potential is

$$E_A + E_{\text{DS1}} + E_B = 0.5I_t + 3I_t + 0.5I_t = 4I_t$$

But the total loss in potential through the circuit between the negative and positive terminals of BT1 is 3 V, so

$$3 = 4I_t \quad \text{or} \quad I_t = 0.75 \text{ A}$$

You also know that $3 = I_t \times R_t = 0.75R_t$. Dividing both sides of this equation by 0.75 yields

$$R_t = 4\ \Omega$$

This is exactly the same result that would have been obtained if the three series load resistances had simply been added:

$$R_A + R_{\text{DS1}} + R_B = 0.5 + 3 + 0.5 = 4\ \Omega$$

Mathematically stated,

$$R_{\text{total}} = R_1 + R_2 + \cdots \qquad \text{FORMULA 6.8}$$

The total resistance of several resistances in series can be obtained by adding the individual resistances. The total circuit current and the change in potential, or voltage drop, across the individual resistances can then be calculated using Ohm's law.

EXAMPLE:

Figure 6.9 shows the schematic diagram of a series circuit with the connecting wires represented by low-value resistances (0.1 Ω). What is the circuit current and how much potential difference and power is lost to the resistance of the connecting wires? ■

SOLUTION:

The simplest way of solving this problem is to determine the circuit current first. Since all the resistances are in series, the total circuit resistance can be found by using Formula 6.8.

$$R_T = R_1 + R_2 + \cdots + R_N$$

or

$$R_T = R_A + R1 + R_B + R2 + R_C + R3 + R_D + R4 + R_E$$

$$R_T = 0.1 + 2 + 0.1 + 2 + 0.1 + 4 + 0.1 + 1.1 + 0.1$$

$$R_T = 9.6\ \Omega$$

With the total resistance known, Ohm's law gives the circuit current

$$I = \frac{E}{R} = \frac{12}{9.6} = 1.25 \text{ A}$$

Figure 6.9 A series circuit. The 0.1 Ω resistances represent the resistance of connecting wires.

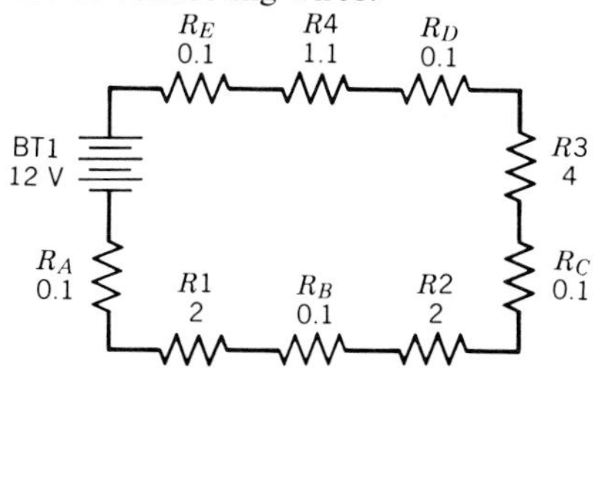

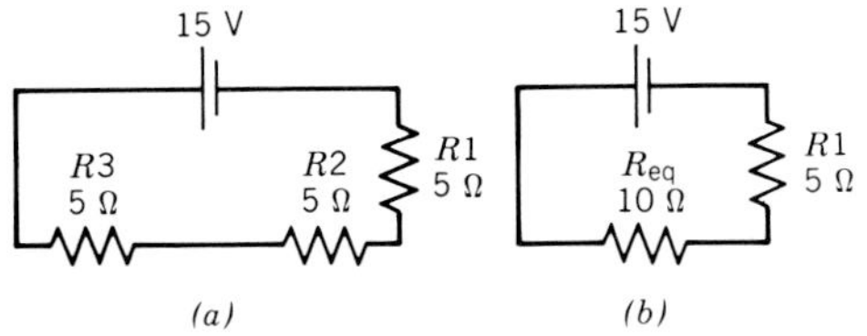

Figure 6.10 Equivalent resistances.

The potential difference or voltage drop across each of the 0.1 Ω resistances is

$$E = IR = 1.25 \times 0.1 = 0.125 \text{ V}$$

Since there are five of them, the total is 5×0.125, or 0.625 V. The power dissipated by one length of wire is given by Formula 6.7:

$$P = I^2R = 1.5625 \times 0.1 = 0.15625$$

Five such resistances will dissipate 0.78125 W. Alternately, since the potential difference or voltage drop across all five wires is known and the total resistance of all five wires is 0.5 Ω, Formula 6.6 can also be used

$$P = \frac{E^2}{R} = \frac{(0.625)^2}{0.5} = 0.78125 \text{ W}$$

■

Just as a circuit containing a number of source cells can be redrawn with a single equivalent cell to aid in calculating circuit quantities, a series string of resistances may be redrawn as a single equivalent resistor whose value is the sum of the resistances replaced by the equivalent. The potential difference or voltage drop across the equivalent resistance and its power dissipation will also be the sum of the voltage drops and dissipations of the resistances replaced by the equivalent resistance. Figure 6.10*a* is the schematic of a series circuit containing three resistances. If your interest in this circuit is focussed only on *R*1, it might be helpful to redraw the schematic as shown in Figure 6.10*b*, replacing *R*2 and *R*3 with a single equivalent resistance, R_{eq}.

B.5 RESISTANCES IN PARALLEL

In the discussion of series circuits in the previous section and in Chapter 5, you learned that the current through all parts of a series circuit is the same. This is understandable since there is only one possible current path from the negative to the positive terminal of the source in a series circuit. In the parallel circuit shown in Figure 6.11, there are two possible paths from the negative to the positive terminal of BT1. From the diagram, you might guess that there are important differences between series and parallel resistances. For

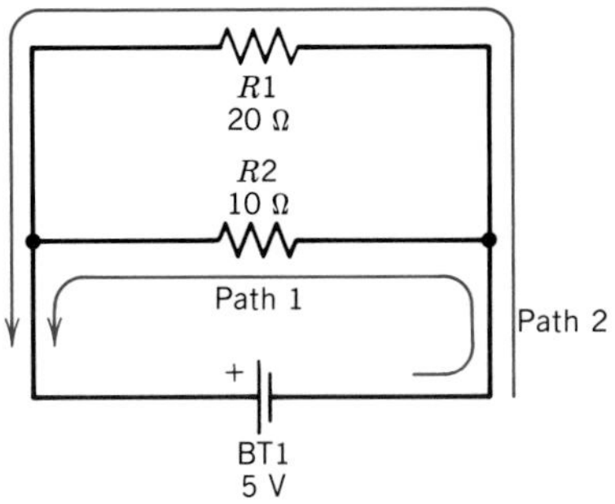

Figure 6.11 There are two paths from the negative to the positive terminal of BT1 in this parallel circuit.

one thing, it is unlikely that the current through the two resistances is the same since *R*1 represents a higher resistance and therefore more difficult path for conduction electron drift. Notice, however, that the potential difference across both resistances is the same, since one end of each resistance is connected to a terminal of the source. From Ohm's law, you also know that

$$R_{total} = \frac{E}{I_{total}}$$

Since Ohm's law also applies to each part of the circuit, and the potential difference across each resistance is known, it is a simple matter to calculate the current through each branch:

$$I_{R1} = \frac{E_{total}}{R1} = \frac{5}{20} = 0.25 \text{ A}$$

$$I_{R2} = \frac{E_{total}}{R2} = \frac{5}{10} = 0.5 \text{ A}$$

The total current, I_{total}, supplied by the source is then $0.25 + 0.5 = 0.75$ A. Substituting these values in

$$R_{total} = \frac{E}{I_{total}} = \frac{5}{0.75} = 6.67 \ \Omega$$

This is a curious value for the total resistance of the circuit composed of a 10 and 20 Ω resistance in parallel. It is neither the sum of the two resistances nor their difference nor their average. How this curious figure is obtained can be seen if we go back to

$$R_{total} = \frac{E_{total}}{I_{total}}$$

But $I_{total} = I_{R1} + I_{R2}$, or

$$R_{total} = \frac{E_{total}}{I_{R1} + I_{R2}}$$

Above, you saw that

$$I_{R1} = \frac{E_{total}}{R1} \quad \text{and} \quad I_{R2} = \frac{E_{total}}{R2}$$

Substituting these values gives

$$R_{total} = \frac{E_{total}}{\frac{E_{total}}{R1} + \frac{E_{total}}{R2}}$$

Dividing the numerator and the denominator of this fraction by the same value E_{total} yields the general formula for calculating the total resistance of two resistances in parallel

$$R_{total} = \frac{1}{\frac{1}{R1} + \frac{1}{R2}} \qquad \text{FORMULA 6.9}$$

You can verify this by substituting the values of 20 and 10 Ω for $R1$ and $R2$:

$$R_{total} = \frac{1}{\frac{1}{20} + \frac{1}{10}} = 6.67$$

the same value obtained from the Ohm's law analysis.

With a calculator, it is easy to calculate and add the reciprocals of any two resistances, and the answer will appear as the $1/x$ key is pressed. Before calculators became common, engineers and technicians used slide rules for calculation. Because of the difficulties in calculating with slide rules, a little trick was invented to determine the total resistance of two parallel resistances. It is worthwhile to learn this trick since it permits many calculations to be worked out by inspection with significant savings in time. The trick involves the simplification of the denominator of Formula 6.9 $\frac{1}{R1} + \frac{1}{R2}$ by multiplying the first term by $\frac{R2}{R2}$ and the second term by $\frac{R1}{R1}$. Since $\frac{R2}{R2}$ and $\frac{R1}{R1}$ are both equal to one, only the appearance of the fraction has been changed, so that the right side of the equation is now

$$\frac{1}{\frac{R2}{R1R2} + \frac{R1}{R1R2}}$$

At this point, multiplying both the numerator and denominator of this fraction by $R1R2$ provides an easy-to-use formula for the total of two resistances in parallel

$$R_{total} = \frac{R1R2}{R1 + R2} \qquad \text{FORMULA 6.10}$$

In other words, the total resistance of two resistances in parallel is equal to the product of the two resistances divided by their sum.

EXAMPLE:

Calculate the total resistance of the parallel arrangement pictured in Figure 6.12. ■

SOLUTION:

Using Formula 6.10, the solution can be obtained by observation:

$$R_{total} = \frac{R1R2}{R1 + R2} = \frac{100}{20} = 5\ \Omega$$ ■

Notice that when two *identical* resistances are in parallel, the resulting resistance is half the value of one of the resistances. Two 120 Ω resistances in parallel would result in a total resistance of 60 Ω.

In Figure 6.13, a third load, resistance $R3$, has been added to the two parallel resistances in Figure 6.12. Using the same method used to obtain Formula 6.9,

$$R_{total} = \frac{E_{total}}{I_{total}} = \frac{E_{total}}{\frac{E_{total}}{R1} + \frac{E_{total}}{R2} + \frac{E_{total}}{R3}}$$

Dividing the numerator and denominator of this fraction by E_{total} gives a form of Formula 6.9 for use with three parallel resistances

$$R_{total} = \frac{1}{\frac{1}{R1} + \frac{1}{R2} + \frac{1}{R3}}$$

Similarly, this method may be used to obtain a formula to find the total resistance of a parallel circuit with any

Figure 6.12 The product-over-sum formula makes it easy to calculate the total resistance of two parallel resistances.

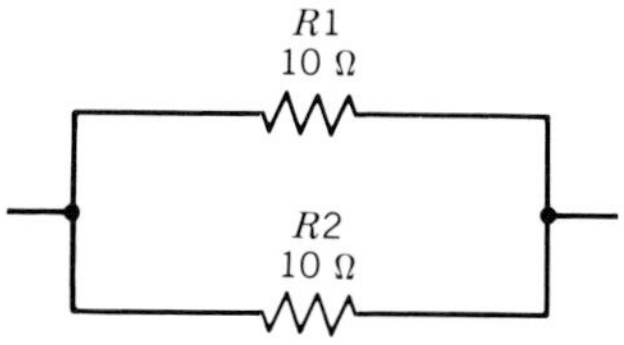

Figure 6.13 A third load, resistance $R3$, has been added to the two parallel resistances in Figure 6.12.

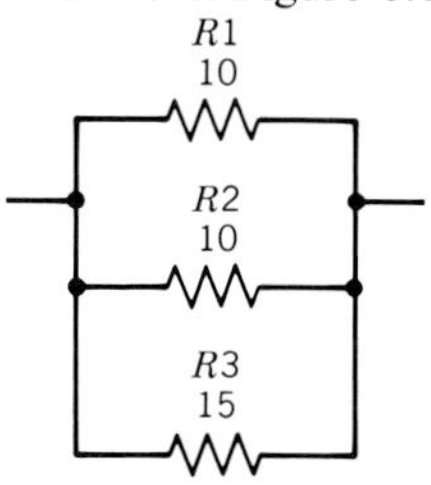

number of resistance terms:

$$R_{\text{total}} = \frac{1}{\dfrac{1}{R1} + \dfrac{1}{R2} + \cdots + \dfrac{1}{R_N}} \qquad \text{FORMULA 6.11}$$

The three dots represent any number of terms, which have been left out for ease in writing. R_N is a symbol used to represent the last term.

Unfortunately, there is no easy *product-over-sum* formula for more than two resistances, but there are two ways to simplify the calculation of the total resistance of three or more parallel resistances. The first method only applies when all the parallel resistances have the same values: the total resistance of N parallel resistances of R ohms each is $\frac{1}{N} \times R$, or

$$\text{The total of } N \text{ equal resistances} = \frac{1}{N} \times R \qquad \text{FORMULA 6.12}$$

For example, five parallel resistances of 20 Ω each have a total resistance of 4 Ω

$$R_{\text{total}} = \frac{1}{5} \times 20 = 4\ \Omega$$

When the resistances are not all equal, a second method, the concept of equivalence, can be used. If there are three resistances, for example, the total resistance of the first two can be calculated using the product-over-sum formula. Once the total resistance of the first two loads has been found, the circuit schematic can be redrawn substituting an equivalent resistance for the first two resistances. Then, the product-over-sum formula can be applied again to obtain the resistance of the equivalent and the remaining load.

EXAMPLE:
Calculate the total resistance of the three parallel loads shown in Figure 6.14.

Figure 6.14 The product-over-sum formula can be used for calculating the total resistance of three or more loads in parallel through the use of the principle of equivalence.

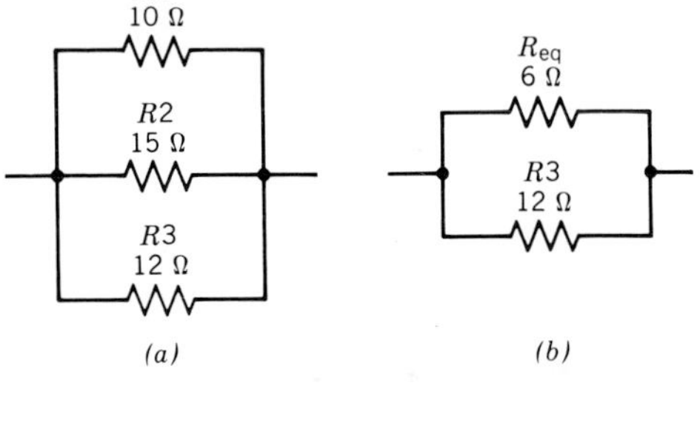

SOLUTION:
This problem can be solved easily, almost without paper and pencil or calculator computation using Formula 6.10 and the principle of equivalency. First use Formula 6.10 to compute the value of an equivalent resistance to replace $R1$ and $R2$

$$R_{\text{eq}} = \frac{R1R2}{R1 + R2} = \frac{150}{25} = 6\ \Omega$$

A redrawing of the schematic diagram to replace $R1$ and $R2$ with R_{eq} is shown in Figure 6.14*b*. The same process can be repeated to compute the total resistance of R_{eq} and $R3$.

$$R_{\text{total}} = \frac{R_{\text{eq}}R3}{R_{\text{eq}} + R3} = \frac{72}{18} = 4\ \Omega$$

The resistance of the parallel combination is 4 Ω. ■

B.6 RESISTANCE, CONDUCTANCE, AND EQUIVALENT CIRCUITS

The difference in the mathematical treatment of series and parallel circuits can be better understood in terms of the part played by each component. In the series circuit shown in Figure 6.15, each of the loads or resistances acts to impede the drift of electrons through the circuit. After passing through $R1$ and losing some potential energy, the electrons must then pass through $R2$ and $R3$. In a parallel circuit, such as that of Figure 6.16, on the other hand, each of the loads or resistances provides another branch or conducting path for the drifting electrons. It is helpful to consider this circuit in terms of conductance rather than resistance. Load A possesses a conductance, $G1$, of $\frac{1}{R}$ or 0.1 S, load B has a $G2$ of 0.05 S, and load C, a conductance $G3$ of 0.04 S. Each load adds its conductance to the circuit, so that the total conductance, G_{total}, between the two terminals of BT1 is $G1 + G2 + G3$ or 0.19 S. This conductance, according to Formula 5.5, is equivalent to a total circuit resistance of 5.26 Ω. Note that this is

Figure 6.15 In a series circuit, each load in turn impedes the passage of electrons from the negative to the positive terminal of the source.

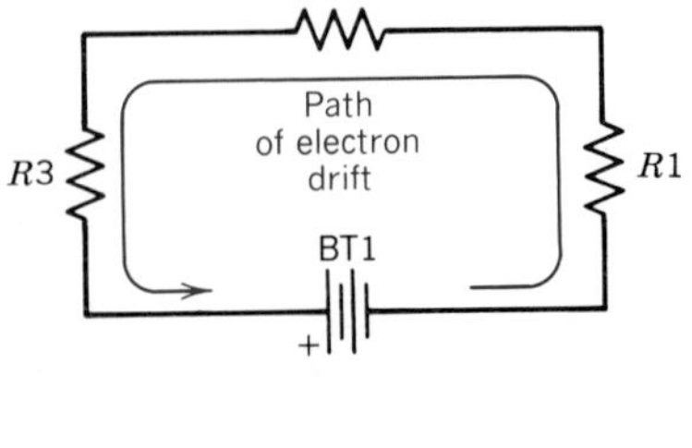

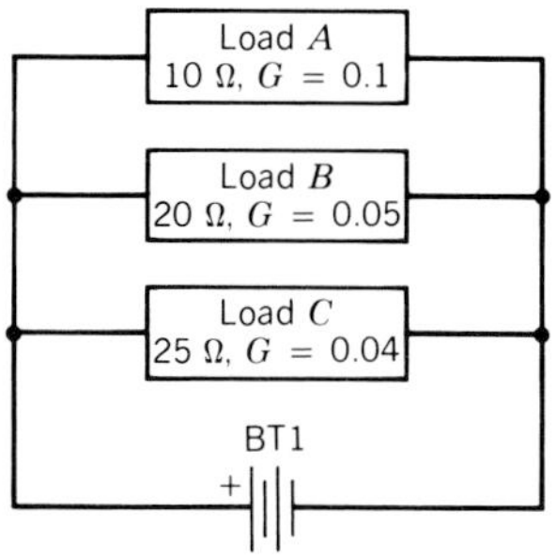

Figure 6.16 In a parallel circuit, each load may be thought of as an additional conductive path, or conductance, between the negative and positive terminal of the source.

the result obtained if you calculate the circuit resistance using Formula 6.11.

$$R_{\text{total}} = \frac{1}{\frac{1}{R1} + \frac{1}{R2} + \frac{1}{R3}} = \frac{1}{\frac{1}{10} + \frac{1}{20} + \frac{1}{25}} = 5.26$$

In a series circuit, the resistances of the loads can be added to obtain the total resistance; in a parallel circuit, the conductances of the loads can be added to obtain the total conductance.

B.7 SERIES–PARALLEL CIRCUITS

Many circuits are neither purely series nor purely parallel in form. They combine both series and parallel components to form complex or, as they are usually called, *series–parallel* circuits. Figure 6.17*a* is the schematic of a typical series–parallel circuit.

Using Ohm's law and the principle of equivalence, it is possible to calculate the current through and the potential difference across any resistance in a series–parallel circuit with only one power source. The general method of doing this is to calculate the total circuit current by replacing all the resistances in the circuit with a single equivalent resistance and using Ohm's law. Once this has been done, it is possible to calculate the potential differences (voltage drops) across the individual loads in the circuit and to redraw the schematic so as to isolate a particular section of the circuit.

Figure 6.17 A series–parallel circuit combines both series and parallel components.

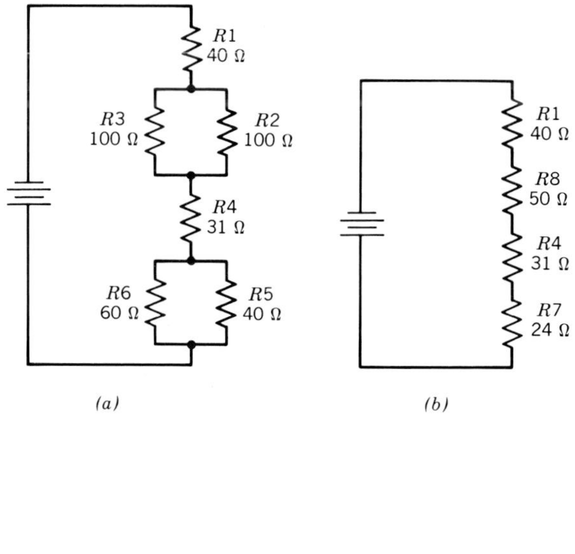

EXAMPLE:
Calculate the current through and the potential drop across the load represented by $R2$ in Figure 6.17*a*. ■

SOLUTION:
The total current through this circuit may be calculated by replacing all six resistances with a single equivalent load. The easiest way to do this is to first reduce the entire circuit to a series string. Using Formula 6.10,

$$T_{\text{total}} = \frac{R1R2}{R1 + R2}$$

resistances $R5$ and $R6$ can be replaced by $R7$, a single 24 Ω load, and loads $R2$ and $R3$ can be replaced by $R8$, a 50 Ω load. This enables the circuit to be redrawn as shown in Figure 6.17*b*. The total resistance of the series string is

$$R_{\text{total}} = R1 + R8 + R4 + R7 = 145\ \Omega$$

Using Ohm's law, the circuit current, rounded off to two significant figures, is 0.069 A. After the circuit current has been determined, the potential difference across $R8$ can be calculated.

$$E = IR = 0.069 \times 50 = 3.45\ \text{V}$$

Since $R8$ is the equivalent of $R2$ and $R3$ in series, $R2$ must have a potential difference of 3.45 V across it. Again using Ohm's law, the current through $R2$ is easily found.

$$I = \frac{E}{R} = \frac{3.45}{100} = 0.0345\ \text{A} \quad \text{or} \quad 34.5\ \text{mA}$$

■

C. EXAMPLES AND COMPUTATIONS

C.1 SQUARE AND SQUARE ROOT COMPUTATIONS

The square of a number or quantity was mentioned in Chapter 3. Recall that it is defined as that number or quantity times itself and is symbolized by placing a small 2 above and to the right of the quantity to be squared.

EXAMPLES:

3^2 means 3×3, is read as "3 squared," and is equal to 9

a^2 means $a \times a$ and is read as "a squared"

ab^2 means $a \times b \times b$ and is read as "a times b squared"

a^2b^2 means $a \times a \times b \times b$ and is read as "a squared times b squared." ■

The inverse operation of squaring a number or a quantity is called *finding the square root*, and the square root of a number or quantity is defined as a number or quantity that will equal the original number or quantity when it is squared.

EXAMPLES:

2 is the square root of 4 since 2^2, or 2×2, $= 4$

a is the square root of a^2 since $a \times a = a^2$. ■

The symbol $\sqrt{\ }$, called a *radical sign*, is used to symbolize square root.

EXAMPLES:

$\sqrt{9}$ is read as "the square root of nine" and is equal to 3 or -3

$\sqrt{a^2}$ is read as "the square root of a squared" and is equal to a or to $-a$

$\sqrt{ab}$ is read as "the square root of a times b"

Although the radical sign is the most common way of symbolizing the square root of a number or a quantity, a fractional exponent of $\frac{1}{2}$ is also used. This symbolism is much more flexible than the radical sign and can be used to express very complex quantities.

EXAMPLES:

$9^{\frac{1}{2}}$ is the same as $\sqrt{9}$ and is equal to 3 or -3;

$a^{\frac{1}{2}}$ is the same as $\sqrt{a}$. ■

The use of a negative exponent means the reciprocal of the number or quantity, so that

$$9^{-\frac{1}{2}} = \frac{1}{\sqrt{9}} = \frac{1}{3} \quad \text{or} \quad \frac{1}{-3}$$

and

$$a^{-\frac{1}{2}} = \frac{1}{\sqrt{a}}$$

Notice that in these examples every number or quantity has two possible square roots, one a positive quantity, and one negative quantity. This is true because the product of two negative numbers or quantities is positive. This curious fact can lead to some confusion when real-world problems are being worked, but in most instances the sign of the square root is either obvious or not important.

EXAMPLE:

A certain light bulb has a power dissipation of 50 W, and an operating resistance of 2 Ω. What is the current through the bulb when it is operating normally? ■

SOLUTION:

Formula 6.7 directly relates power, resistance, and current, $P = I^2R$ or $50 = I^2 \times 2$. $I^2 = 25$. Since I^2 is equal to 25, I is equal to $\sqrt{25}$, or 5. But $\sqrt{25}$ is equal to 5 and to -5. Does this actually mean anything in electrical terms? You learned that a current is a drift of electrons in one direction through a wire. So, if a solution of 5 refers to a current of 5 A in one direction through a circuit, a solution of -5 would refer to a current of 5 A in the opposite direction. In this instance, the fact that both $+5$ and -5 are possible answers to the equation is in keeping with the physical reality of the situation, the fact that the lamp is dissipating 50 W of power is independent of the direction of the current through it. ■

You will become accustomed to the fact that every positive number has both a positive and a negative square root. But it is much harder to get used to the concept of the square root of a negative number. What number multiplied by itself is equal to -4? It is mathematically possible to give meaning to $\sqrt{-4}$, and in fact it is extremely useful to do this in the analysis of electrical and electronic circuits. For the moment, however, it would be better to consider the square root of a negative number as a meaningless concept:

$$\sqrt{16} = +4 \text{ or } -4, \text{ and}$$

$$16^{-\frac{1}{2}} = \frac{1}{4} \text{ or } -\frac{1}{4},$$

$$\text{but } \sqrt{-16} = ?$$

Although it is a relatively easy task to find the square of a number by simple multiplication, there is no simple, short arithmetic process for calculating the square root of a number. Paper-and-pencil methods do exist, but they generally require a number of calculations to be made and are too cumbersome for practical work. For this reason, square root calculations should be done with the help of a calculator. Most scientific calculators have function keys labeled (x^2) and ($\sqrt{x}$), so that a number can be entered and its square or square root calculated directly.

EXAMPLE:
Calculate the square of 6.28. ■

SOLUTION:

Enter number [6][.][2][8]
Select square [x^2]
The answer, 39.4384, is displayed. ■

EXAMPLE:
Calculate the square root of 42.75. ■

SOLUTION:

Enter number [4][2][.][7][5]
Select square root [$\sqrt{x}$]
The answer, 6.5383484, is displayed.

Of course, the full answer is +6.5383484 *and* −6.5383484. As in the case of other calculations, the answer can be rounded off according to the accuracy required. ■

Calculate the following squares or square roots, round off your answer to three significant figures.

a. 5.12^2
b. $\sqrt{64}$
c. 3.1416^2
d. $\sqrt{2}$
e. $2^{-0.5}$
f. 15^2
g. $\sqrt{13.34}$
h. $12^{-0.5}$
i. $53^{-\frac{1}{2}}$
j. $(ab)^2$ where $a = 2$ and $b = 5$
k. $\sqrt{71.9}$
l. -8.4^{-2}
m. 41.6^2
n. -16^2
o. ab^2, where $a = 3$ and $b = 4$
p. $\left(\frac{1}{3}\right)^{-2}$

Technical calculators have a powers and roots key in addition to the square and square root keys. This key is often marked y^x, and can be used to calculate powers and roots in general, including reciprocal quantities. Use of the y^x key takes a few additional keystrokes; it is capable of complex calculations that required significant time before the invention of calculators. Even with the use of a slide rule, a calculation like $1.17^{-\frac{3}{5}}$ was a chore.

EXAMPLE:
Calculate the square root of 1.235 using the y^x key. ■

SOLUTION:
In order to do this, it is necessary to recall that the square root of a number is equal to that number with an exponent of $\frac{1}{2}$. $\sqrt{x} = x^{\frac{1}{2}}$. Since it is not possible to enter fractions into a calculator, the decimal equivalent of $\frac{1}{2}$, that is, 0.5, must be used.

Enter number [1][.][2][3][5]
Select power/root key [y^x]
Enter exponent [0][.][5]
Press equals key to obtain answer [=]

The display should now indicate the answer 1.1113055. Again, both the positive and negative roots are implied. ■

The reciprocals of powers or roots can also be calculated using negative exponents.

EXAMPLE:
Calculate 6.3^{-2}.

SOLUTION:

Enter number [6][.][3]
Select power/root key [y^x]
Enter exponent [2]
Change sign for negative exponent [+/−]
Press equals key to read answer [=]

The answer is now displayed: 2.5195 −02, or 0.025195. This is $\frac{1}{6.3^2}$. ■

Use the power/root key y^x on your calculator to calculate the following:

a. $\sqrt{3}$
b. $13^{-\frac{1}{2}}$
c. 2×0.707^2
d. $\sqrt{84}$
e. $2^4 + 2^3$
f. $19^2 \times 12^{.5}$
g. $\dfrac{1}{6.28\sqrt{4.25}}$
h. $19^{0.01}$
i. $\dfrac{1}{\sqrt{6.28}}$
j. $2ab^2$, where $a = 3$, $b = 4$
k. $256^{0.05}$
l. $\sqrt{.0036}$
m. $19^{1.5}$
n. $\pi^{-\frac{1}{2}}$
o. 1.41^3
p. $3.937^{-\frac{1}{2}}$

C.2 SQUARE AND SQUARE ROOT CALCULATIONS ON A SMALL COMPUTER USING BASIC

BASIC uses a method for symbolizing roots and powers that is like the y^x key on a calculator. The up arrow symbol (↑) or a double caret (/\/\) is used to represent an exponent, so 3 ↑ 2 or 3/\/\2 is the BASIC way of writing 3^2. The following short program can be used to calculate a number to any power within the range of your computer's BASIC.

```
10  INPUT "THE BASE NUMBER IS. . .",X
20  INPUT "THE EXPONENT IS. . .",Y
30  Z = X ↑ Y
35  PRINT "THE BASE NUMBER TO THAT
      EXPONENT IS. . .",Z
40  INPUT "DO YOU HAVE ANOTHER
      CALCULATION/ Y/N" A$
50  IF A = "Y" THEN GO TO 10
60  PRINT "GOODBYE" : END
```

C.3 REVIEW OF OHM'S LAW, POWER, AND RESISTANCE/CONDUCTANCE COMPUTATIONS

Because it is important that you can work Ohm's law, power, and resistance/conductance problems with confidence, the following exercises have been included in this section.

The three forms of Ohm's law are:

$$R = \frac{E}{I} \qquad \text{FORMULA 5.1}$$

$$E = IR \qquad \text{FORMULA 5.3}$$

$$I = \frac{E}{R} \qquad \text{FORMULA 5.4}$$

Since Ohm's law relates the quantities of current, potential difference, and resistance in a circuit or part of a circuit, one of these forms can be used to calculate one of the quantities if the other two are known.

a. A lamp filament has a resistance of 0.3 Ω and is designed to operate from a 1.5-V cell. What is the value of the current when the lamp is connected to the cell?

b. A 24-V lamp normally operates on a current of 150 mA. What is the operating resistance of the lamp?

c. The current through the circuit shown in Figure 6.18 is 250 mA. Calculate the potential differences (voltage drops) across $R2$, $R3$, and $R4$. Is enough information given to do this?

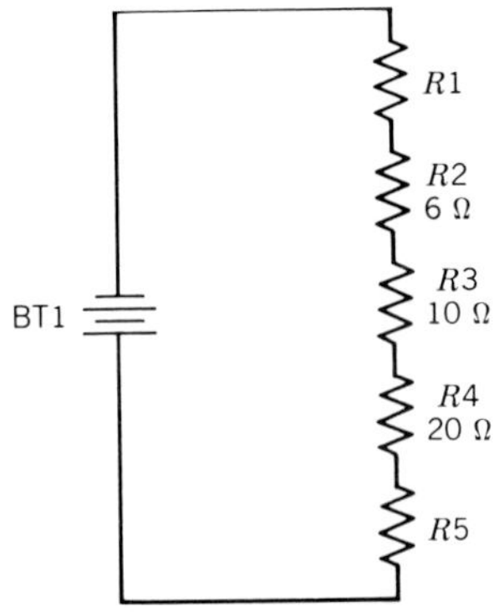

Figure 6.18 Series circuit for problems C.3.c, d, and e.

d. After 12 hours of operation, the potential difference of BT1 in Figure 6.18 is found to have decreased by 10 percent. Do you have enough information to calculate the new voltage drop across $R3$? If so, what will it be?

e. Adding a sixth resistance, $R6$, of 48 Ω to the circuit of Figure 6.18 changes the circuit current to 125 mA. Do you now have enough information to calculate the potential difference supplied by BT1? If so, what is it?

In order to use Ohm's law in many circuits, it is necessary to know how to calculate the total resistance of series, parallel, and series–parallel combinations of resistances and conductances. The general rules for this are:

The total resistance of a series string of resistances is

$$R_{\text{total}} = R1 + R2 + \cdots + RN$$

The total resistance of parallel resistances is

$$R_{\text{total}} = \frac{1}{\frac{1}{R1} + \frac{1}{R2} + \frac{1}{R3} + \cdots + \frac{1}{RN}}$$

For two resistances in parallel, an easier formula is

$$R_{\text{total}} = \frac{R1R2}{R1 + R2}$$

Resistance is the reciprocal of conductance

$$R = \frac{1}{G} \quad \text{and} \quad G = \frac{1}{R}$$

Conductances in parallel can be added like resistances in series

$$G_{\text{total}} = G1 + G2 + \cdots + GN$$

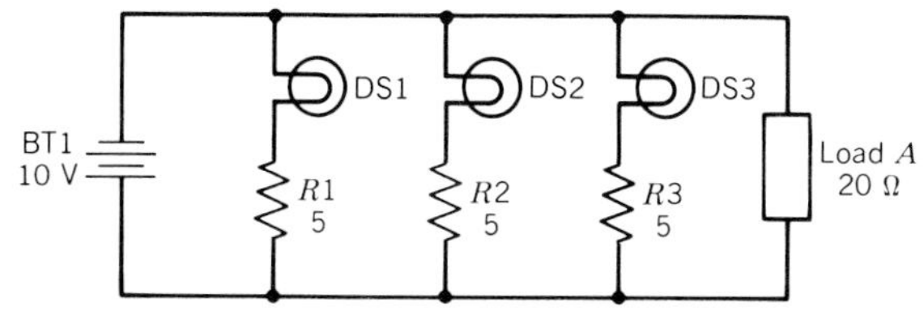

Figure 6.19 Circuit for problems C.3.f and g.

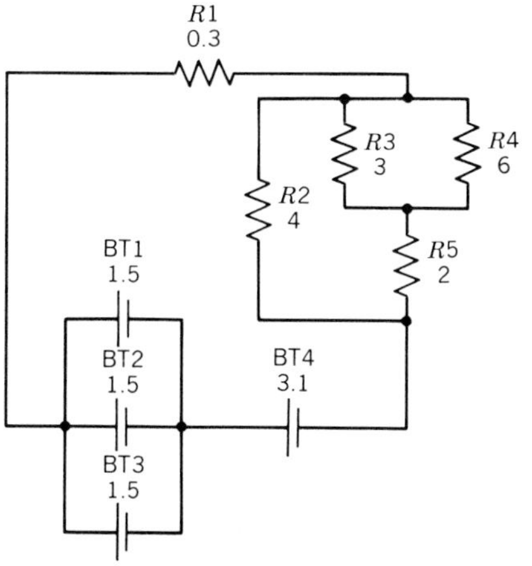

Figure 6.20 Circuit for problem C.3.h.

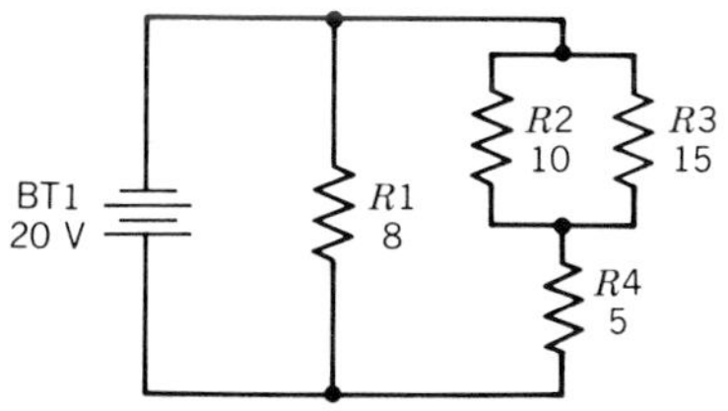

Figure 6.21 Circuit for problem C.3.j.

f. The resistance of each lamp DS1, DS2, and DS3 in Figure 6.19 is 15 Ω. How much current will the source be required to furnish during normal operation?

g. When BT1 is first connected to the circuit shown in Figure 6.19, the resistance of the lamps is practically zero. As the lamps begin to glow, their resistance increases to 15 Ω. What current is supplied by BT1 when it is first connected to the circuit?

h. What is the total circuit current in the circuit shown in Figure 6.20?

i. Calculate the potential difference across each resistance in Figure 6.20.

j. Calculate the current through each resistance in the circuit of Figure 6.21.

C.4 VARIATIONAL ANALYSIS OF SERIES AND PARALLEL CIRCUITS

The methods of variational analysis can be used to demonstrate the striking differences between series and parallel circuits made up of the same components. Figure 6.22*a* shows two 10 Ω resistances connected in series across a 10-V battery. The total resistance of the circuit is

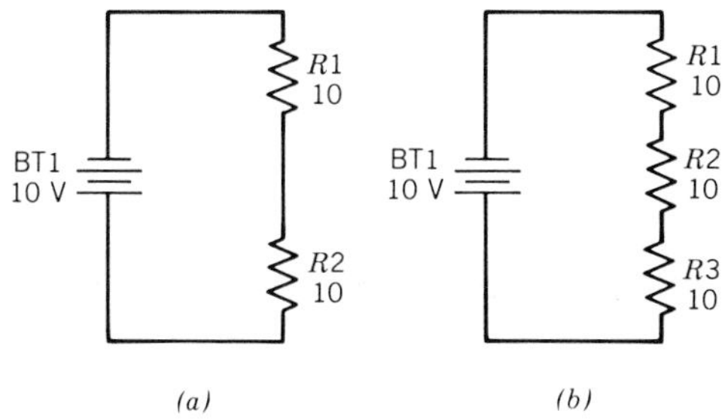

Figure 6.22 Variational analysis of a series circuit.

$$R_{total} = R1 + R2$$

or 20 Ω, and the current through the circuit is $I = \frac{E}{R}$ or 0.5 A. Since this is a series circuit, I_1, the current through $R1$, is equal to I_2, the current through $R2$. It is also equal to the total circuit current provided by the source.

In a series circuit with two or more loads, the current through all the loads is the same, regardless of the difference in the resistance of the loads. The current through any of the series resistances is also the same as the current provided by the source.

The potential difference, or voltage drop, across each resistance in a series circuit depends on the value of the resistance and on the current through it. In Figure 6.22*a*, the potential difference across each of the resistances is 5.0 V.

If a third 10 Ω resistance, $R3$, is added to the circuit of Figure 6.22*a*, as shown in 6.22*b*, the total resistance of the circuit is *increased* by 10 Ω to 30 Ω since

$$R_{total} = R1 + R2 + R3$$

The total current through the circuit, which is the same as the current through each of the series resistances, is *decreased*. The new circuit current is

$$I = \frac{E}{R} = \frac{10}{30} \quad \text{or} \quad 0.33 \text{ A}$$

The potential difference, or voltage drop, across each resistance also decreases, although the total voltage drop across all the loads, which must be equal to the potential difference of the source, remains the same.

The voltage drop across each resistance is

$$E = IR = 0.33 \times 10 = 3.3 \text{ V}$$

The sum of the voltage drop is $3 \times 3.3 = 10$ V.

Adding another series resistance or increasing the total resistance in a series circuit results in a decrease in the circuit current and a decrease in the voltage drop across the loads whose resistance has not changed.

This information can be shown in a variational analysis chart. Table 6.1 is such a chart based on the circuit of Figure 6.22. The letter *d* is used to indicate a decrease in a quantity, an up-arrow to indicate an increase.

This series circuit is a sharp contrast to the parallel circuit in Figure 6.23*a*. The parallel circuit also has a 10-V battery and two 10 Ω loads. The important difference is that the resistances are connected in parallel. The total circuit conductance, then, is $G_{R1} + G_{R2} = 0.2$ S, and the total circuit resistance is $1/G$, or 5 Ω. In general, combining two or more resistances in parallel produces a total resistance that is *less* than the lowest resistance in the parallel combination. The total current supplied by the battery is

$$I = \frac{E}{R_{\text{total}}} = \frac{10}{5} = 2 \text{ A}$$

This is four times the current in the series circuit of Figure 6.22*a*.

The current through each resistance in a parallel circuit is the same only if all the loads have the same resistance, as in this case,

$$I_{R1} = I_{R2} = \frac{E}{R1} = \frac{10}{10} = 1 \text{ A}$$

This means that exactly half the total circuit current of 2 A, or 1 A, flows through each of the parallel resistances. The voltage drop, or potential difference, across each resistance, as you can see from the diagram without any calculation, is exactly the same as the potential difference of the source, 10 V. You will recall that the potential difference across a load in a series circuit depends on the product of the circuit current and the resistance of the load.

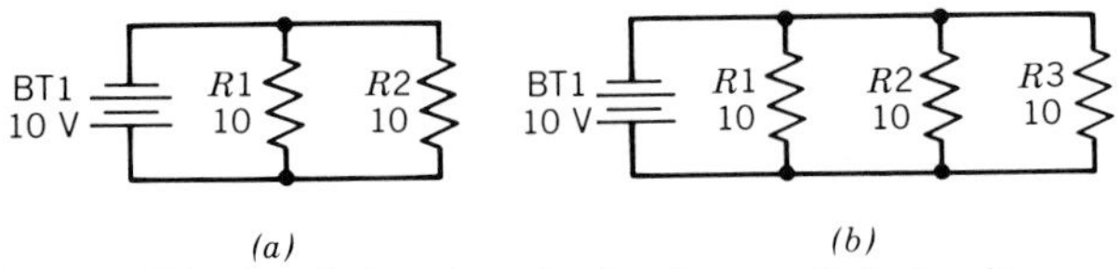

Figure 6.23 Variational analysis of a parallel circuit.

Adding a third 10 Ω resistance, $R3$, in parallel to the circuit of Figure 6.23*a* results in the circuit shown in Figure 6.23*b*. Since another conductance of 0.1 S has been added to the circuit, its total resistance is now smaller:

$$G_{\text{total}} = G1 + G2 + G3 = 0.3 \text{ S}$$

The total resistance of the circuit $R = \dfrac{1}{G_{\text{total}}}$ or 3.33 Ω.

Adding another resistance to a parallel circuit decreases *the total resistance of the circuit. The total resistance is always less than the resistance of the smallest parallel load.*

With three 10 Ω resistances in parallel, the total circuit current, I_{total}, is

$$I_{\text{total}} = \frac{E}{R_{\text{total}}} = \frac{10}{3.33} = 3 \text{ A}$$

In contrast to the series circuit, the addition of another load (that is, another conductance) in a parallel circuit *increases* the total circuit current. The voltage drop across each of the loads is equal to the potential difference supplied by the source. The current through each of the identical resistances $R1$, $R2$, and $R3$ is 1 A, as in the case of the circuit shown in Figure 6.23*a* because neither the source potential nor the resistance of the individual loads has changed.

A variational analysis chart of the circuit in Figure 6.23*a*, Table 6.2, provides an interesting contrast with that given for a series circuit, Table 6.1.

Table 6.1 Variational Analysis of Circuit Shown in Figure 6.22

If	*Then*					
	I_{total}	I_{R1}	I_{R2}	E_{R1}	E_{R2}	R_{total}
$R1\uparrow$, $R2$ same	d	d	d	↑	d	↑
$R1$d, $R2$ same	↑	↑	↑	d	↑	d
$R3$ is added	d	d	d	d	d	↑

Table 6.2 Variational Analysis of the Circuit Shown in Figure 6.23

If	*Then*					
	I_{total}	I_{R1}	I_{R2}	E_{R1}	E_{R2}	R_{total}
$R1\uparrow$, $R2$ same	d	d	same	same	same	↑
$R1$d, $R2$ same	↑	↑	same	same	same	d
$R3$ is added	↑	same	same	same	same	d

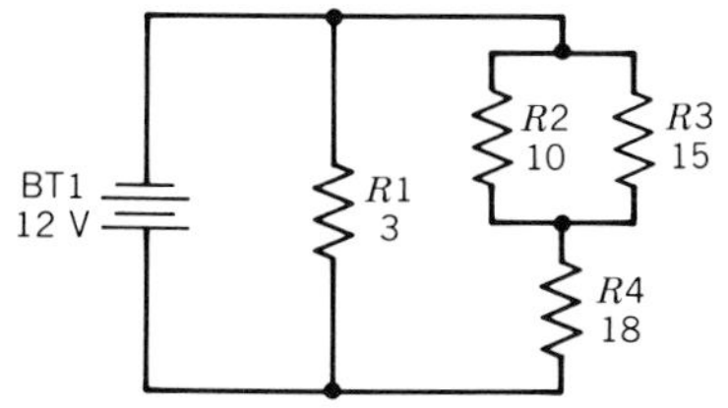

Figure 6.24 Circuit for variational analysis of a series–parallel circuit.

Variational analysis is particularly useful in analyzing series–parallel circuits. Try your hand at preparing such charts for the following changes to the circuit shown in Figure 6.24. Your chart should show the total current and total circuit resistance, as well as the current through and voltage drop across each load.

a. *R*1 increases
b. *R*3 burns out (open circuit)
c. *R*3 decreases
d. *R*3 is short circuited

D. APPLICATIONS

D.1 POWER DISSIPATION IN WIRES

In Chapter 5 you learned that the resistance of a piece of wire depends on its length, cross-sectional area, the resistivity of the wire material, and, to a certain extent, the temperature. Because it has resistance, a length of current-carrying wire dissipates a certain amount of energy in the form of heat. If the current through the wire is large enough, this heat can cause the wire insulation to char or melt, and may even be great enough to melt the wire or cause a fire.

These dangers have led to the publication of tables listing the maximum safe current for AWG gauge wires by various insurance groups and electrical code organizations. Table 6.3 is a sample of current capacity tables. Sometimes, two table columns are necessary, one for a wire mounted alone so that it is cooled by the surrounding air, and a second column for wires found in cables or bundles. Wires that can not be cooled by the surrounding air must have a greater cross-sectional area and a lower resistance so that they will dissipate less energy and remain at a lower temperature.

Both design engineers and maintenance technicians should try to determine wire gauge size carefully when designing or rewiring power-carrying equipment. If you calculate the maximum current that a wire might be required to carry, then you can consult a wire table to determine the gauge size to be used. Usually a wire gauge number one or more smaller (corresponding to a wire with a *greater* cross-sectional area) is selected to provide a safety factor. This is particularly important when the wire is in the interior of a unit near other heat-dissipating components.

Table 6.3 Copper Wire Sizes and Current Capacity

AWG No.	*General Purpose Safe Current (A)*
0000	214.4
00	134.9
0	107.0
1	84.82
2	67.27
3	53.34
4	42.30
5	33.55
6	26.60
7	21.10
8	16.73
9	13.27
10	10.52
11	8.345
12	6.618
13	5.248
14	4.162
15	3.300
16	2.618
17	2.076
18	1.646
19	1.300
20	1.04
21	0.82
22	0.65
23	0.52
24	0.41
25	0.32
26	0.26
27	0.2
28	0.16

D.2 INCANDESCENT AND NEON LAMPS

Although the heat dissipated by conductors possessing resistance is often a problem, some loads are designed specifically to produce heat, such as the electric heater pictured in Figure 6.25*a*. An electric heater is usually nothing more than a length of high-resistance wire connected through a switch to the power mains. Figure 6.25*b* shows the schematic diagram of the heater. Notice the schematic symbol for a switch, wall plug, and resistance heating element. When the switch is closed, the relatively low resistance heater wire is connected directly to the source. It heats quickly, becoming red hot. Some heaters incorporate a small fan to distribute

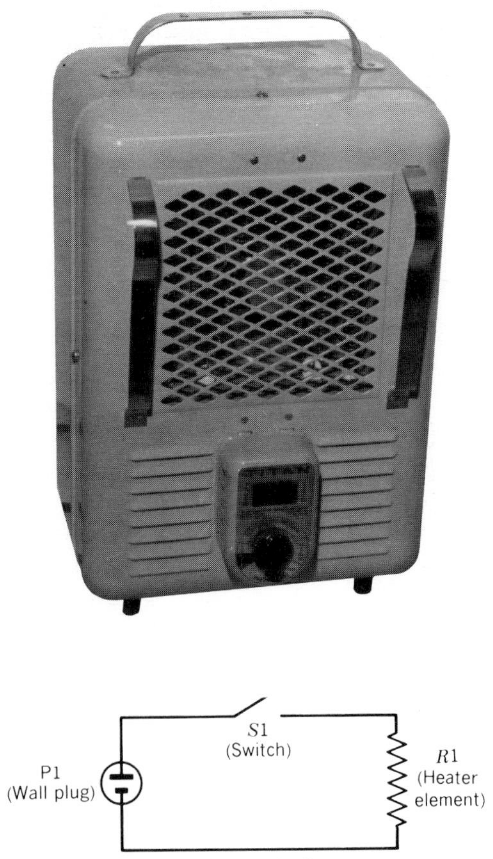

(b) Schematic diagram

Figure 6.25 An electric heater is a load designed specifically to produce heat. (Photo by M. Hermes.)

the heat, and thermostat devices to shut the heater off when the room air temperature reaches a certain level.

The ability of an electric current to make a wire glow is the basis for one of the principal uses of electricity today—electric lighting. You are doubtless familiar with the standard light bulb shown in Figure 6.26. Notice that the functional part of the bulb, the filament, is the only part that actually glows. It is made of a thin tungsten wire in modern lamps, although various other materials, including carbonized thread, were once used. Before the lamp is sealed, the air is pumped out of the bulb, and a small amount of inert gas such as argon or krypton is pumped in. This protects the white hot filament since the inert gas will not combine chemically with the filament, as will the oxygen in air.

Most people accept the wattage ratings of light bulbs, such as 60, 75, or 100 W, without knowing what these ratings mean. They are the power dissipated by the bulb filament as heat. An automobile bulb operating from a 12-V battery may be rated at 5 or 10 W, for

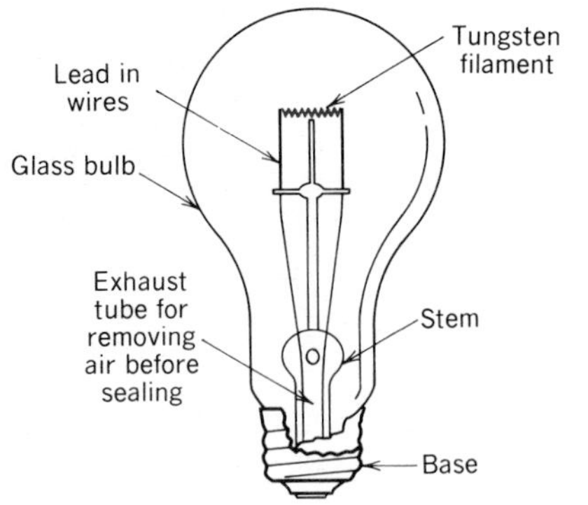

Figure 6.26 The structure of a standard light bulb.

example. Using the power law, Formula 6.5, it is a simple matter to calculate the current through a lamp.

$$P_{\text{diss}} = E \times I, \quad \text{or} \quad I = \frac{P}{E}$$

$$I = \frac{5}{12} = 0.417 \text{ A}$$

Many electrical and electronic units contain light bulbs. These bulbs, once commonly called pilot lamps, are not designed to provide large quantities of light in an area; they serve as indicators to show conditions such as POWER ON in operating units. Formerly, there were two main categories of indicator lamps, filament lamps, which are miniature versions of household light bulbs, and neon lamps, which do not possess filaments. Today, both filament and neon indicator lamps are giving way to the LED, or light-emitting diode, a solid-state device that produces light directly, without the dissipation of large amounts of heat. Since the LED is a solid-state device, a detailed discussion has been left for a later book.

Although they are manufactured in a confusing variety of shapes and sizes, all incandescent and neon lamps have one thing in common. After a certain amount of service, they must be replaced. Aside from accidental breakage of the glass bulb, the most common failure mode of incandescent lamps is "burn out." This means that the thin tungsten wire filament has broken.

Since it is made of a thin wire, the incandescent lamp filament is very sensitive to damage by high voltage or current, shock, vibration, too frequent off-on cycling, and the heat generated by the lamp itself. Even a small increase in the potential difference across the lamp, say 5 percent above its design value, can reduce the life of the lamp by 50 percent. The fact that the resistance of a lamp filament increases with age makes it extremely difficult for circuit designers to control the potential difference across the lamp closely. In the past, radio pilot lamps usually operated with alternating current. Today, however, most equipment indicators run on direct current. Direct current has been found to be much harder on lamp filaments. Ac-operated lamp filaments can last from 2 to 10 times longer than those operated with dc. This is particularly true when the lamps are operated at high temperature. Long-life lamps, those with average life expectancies of from 10^4 to 10^5 hours, operate at low temperatures, and are less affected by this. Standard life expectancy lamps, those with an average usable life of from 1000 to 5000 hours, operate at higher temperatures.

Shock and vibration are also enemies of the indicator lamp filament. Since filaments may be as thin as 3×10^{-5} m, about one thousandth of an inch, filament breakage frequently takes place when a unit is in a vibrating vehicle or when the unit is being moved, even when it is turned off. Many tungsten filaments are actually more brittle when not operating than when white hot.

The current surge that occurs when a lamp is first turned on also results in some failures. A current surge is a sudden increase in circuit current for a brief period of time. Such a surge occurs when a lamp is first turned on because the cold resistance of the tungsten filament is quite low. The resistance of tungsten, like that of copper, increases when the temperature of the material increases. The first in-rush of current heats the filament quickly and increases its resistance so that the surge may only last a few thousandths of a second. Even in this short time, however, there may be damage to both the lamp filament and to other components in the circuit. The surge current is frequently *10 times* or more the normal operating current of the lamp.

Remember that the power dissipated by a component is given by $P = I^2R$. Therefore, the power dissipated by a component in a lamp circuit may be 10^2 or 100 times greater than normal during the current surge. Besides blowing fuses and damaging other components in the lamp circuit, these surges hasten the evaporation of part of the filament. Evaporation of filament material damages the lamp in two ways: it weakens the filament, and the metal vapor deposits itself on the coolest part of the interior of the glass bulb, darkening it, and reducing the amount of light produced by the lamp.

The final problem that plagues indicator lamps is the buildup of heat. Normally, the lamp holder has been selected or designed to channel heat away so that the lamp operates at a safe temperature. In order to provide a better flow of heat away from the lamp, professional maintenance personnel apply a bit of silicon heat-sink compound to the base of the new lamp when making a replacement. Although this material is

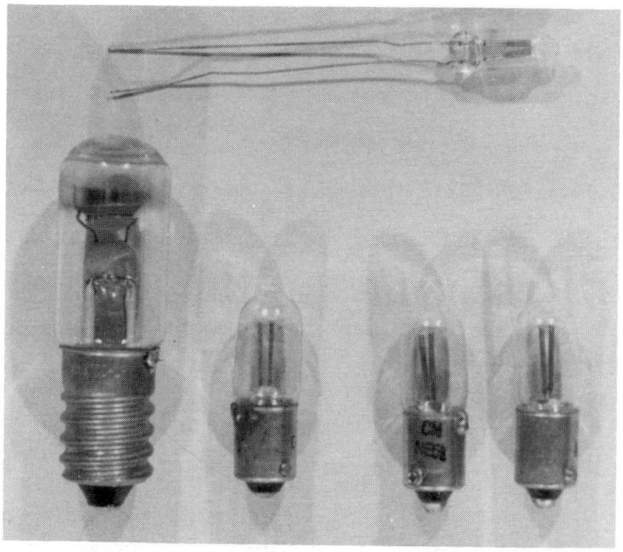

Figure 6.27 Some varieties of neon lamps. (Photo by M. Hermes.)

a good conductor of heat, it is an electrical insulator, so there is no danger of a short circuit.

In spite of the many problems of incandescent lamps, they are widely used since they provide a much greater amount of light than either neon lamps or LED devices. The average standard lamp can be expected to burn for from 1000 to 5000 hours, while a useful life 10 times as long can be expected with long-life bulbs.

Neon lamps (see Figure 6.27) do not contain a filament. Instead, they operate because a small amount of neon or other inert gas has been placed into the bulb from which all the air has been removed. When a potential difference on the order of 65 to 135 V exists between the two electrodes, some of the gas atoms are ionized; that is, valence electrons gain enough energy to enter a conduction band. When these electrons are recaptured by ionized atoms, they give up their energy in the form of light. The neon lamp is a low-current device. Operating current for standard lamps is about 0.5 mA at 95 V for standard models and 2 mA at 120 V for high-intensity bulbs, which produce more light than standard models.

Although they produce less light than incandescent bulbs, neon lamps use less current, less power, and are much more rugged. Shock, vibration, and current surge are not serious problems since there is no delicate filament to break. On the other hand, neon lamps have failure modes that limit their useful life as effectively as the existence of a filament in an incandescent lamp. Neon lamps tend to darken with age, producing less light, and their operating voltage increases as well. After an average of 2.5×10^4 hours, the potential difference required to operate the lamp

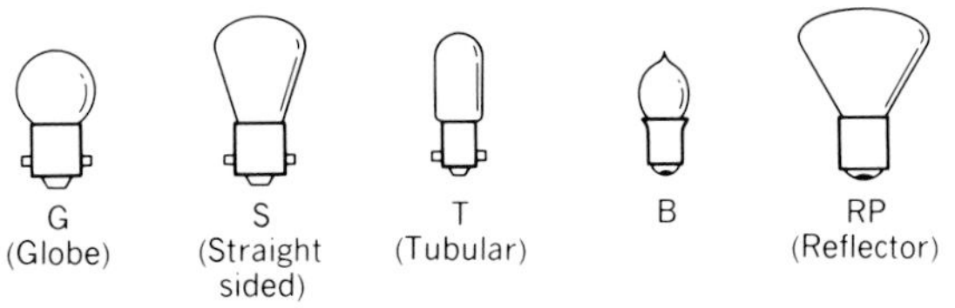

Figure 6.28 Standard bulb shapes for both neon and incandescent lamps.

has risen so high that the light output is either too feeble or not visible at all. At this point the lamp is considered burned out.

Neon lamps are somewhat less sensitive to excessive voltage and current than incandescent lamps, but a 25 percent increase in voltage over the rated value will still reduce the life expectancy of a bulb from 25,000 to 8700 hours. Excessive current will have a similar effect. Neon lamps are more sensitive to high operating temperatures than incandescents, and manufacturers' data sheets often recommend a maximum operating temperature of 75 to 80°C since higher temperatures cause chemical changes inside the lamp that permanently modify its operating characteristics.

Both incandescent and neon lamps are manufactured in a large variety of bulb shapes and base styles. A glass bulb is designated by a combination of letters and numbers. The letter or letters refer to one of the standard bulb shapes shown in Figure 6.28. The numbers give the maximum diameter of the bulb in eighths of an inch. For example, an S-5 bulb indicates a straight side shape with a maximum diameter of five-eighths of an inch. Bulb shape should not be confused with base style. Some popular base styles are illustrated in Figure 6.29. Screw-type bases, sometimes called candelabra bases were once the most popular. Lamps with this sort of base are easy to remove from their sockets, simply by unscrewing them. For equipment subject to vibration, however, screw-type bases are unsuitable since the vibration tends to loosen the lamp and may

Figure 6.29 Popular base styles of lamps.

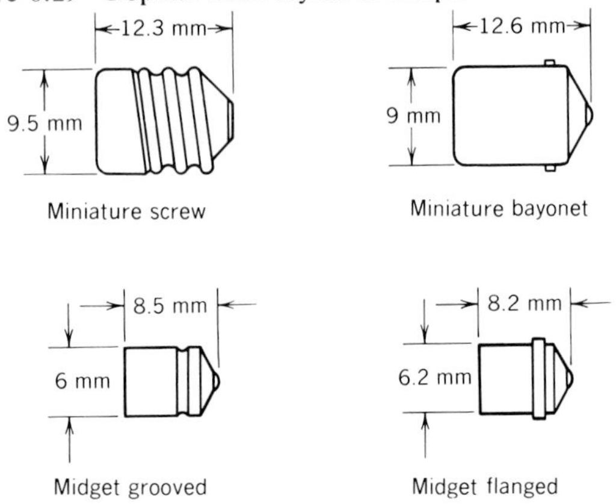

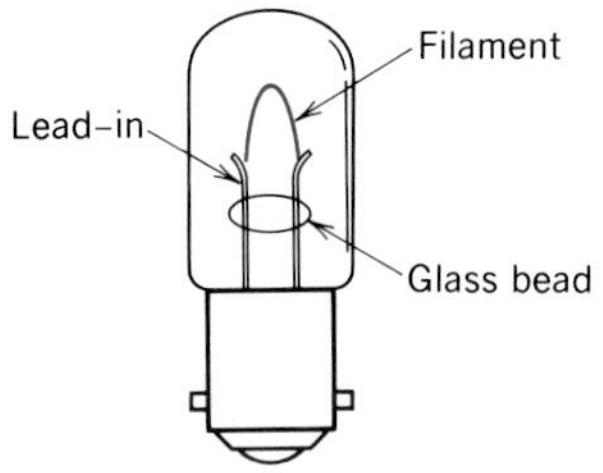

Figure 6.30 Some popular lamps can be identified by the color of the glass bead used to support the lead-in wires.

actually unscrew it completely. In these applications, bayonet, flanged, or grooved bases are usually used. The bayonet is the most common of the three. Pressure from a spring in the lamp socket holds the lamp firmly in place. In order to remove the lamp, it must be pressed in gently and turned slightly before it is withdrawn. Flanged and grooved bases, which are frequently found in industrial equipment, are held in their sockets by means of spring retainers. A special tool is required to remove these lamps for replacement.

To confuse bulb and base styles further, some of the most widely used lamps are known by industry numbers, and are frequently unmarked. The only way of distinguishing these unmarked lamps is by the color of the glass bead used to support the lead-in wires (see Figure 6.30). Table 6.4 gives the essential information about some of these commonly used lamps.

D.3 FUSES

The same physical principle that causes a wire that is carrying too much current to get hot is the basis for another familiar component, the fuse. Everyone is fa-

Table 6.4 Commonly Used Lamps Which Are Recognized by Bead Color

	Lamp Type		*Bead*	*Rating*	
Number	*Base*	*Bulb*	*Color*	*V*	*A*
40	Screw	T-3 $\frac{1}{4}$	Brown	6–8	0.15
47	Bayonet	T-3 $\frac{1}{4}$	Brown	6–9	0.15
50	Screw	G-3 $\frac{1}{2}$	White	6–8	0.2
53	Bayonet	G-3 $\frac{1}{2}$	—	14	0.12
55	Bayonet	G-4 $\frac{1}{2}$	White	6–8	0.4
1487	Screw	T-3 $\frac{1}{4}$	—	12–16	0.2
1815	Bayonet	T-3 $\frac{1}{4}$	—	12–16	0.2

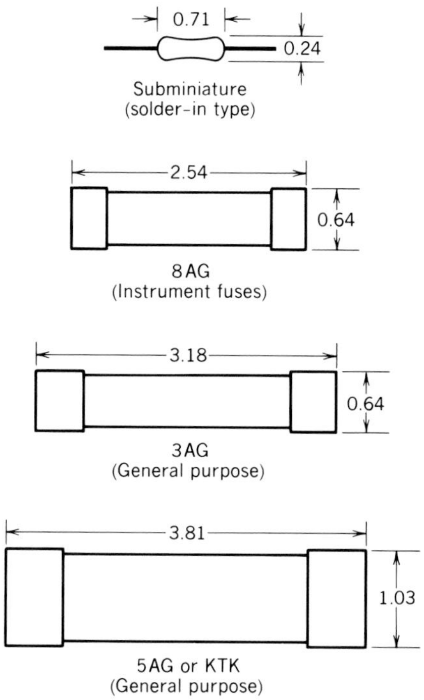

Figure 6.31 Some fuse sizes.

miliar with the fuses and circuit breakers used in home power distribution systems, automobiles, and in many electrical and electronic units. Fuses are components that serve as purposely weakened portions of a circuit. They have two principal functions: unit or circuit protection and unit or circuit isolation. The fuse is a current-sensitive device. It is designed to melt and produce an open circuit when the current exceeds some level. When used as a unit or circuit-protective device, the fuse must open the circuit before any other circuit components are damaged. In this sense, the fuse is the weakest link in the circuit and is designed to fail before any other component.

When used for isolation, the fuse is not the weakest link in the circuit. The fuse will act to open the circuit only after some component or branch of a circuit has failed. In this application, the fuse acts to protect the undamaged portion of the unit or circuit by creating an open circuit that isolates the faulty component or part of the circuit from the undamaged section.

Fuses are manufactured in a variety of sizes and shapes as shown in Figure 6.31. Those most generally used in electronic units are glass cylinders about 0.03 m long (1.25 in., to be exact), with tin-plated brass end caps. The fuse element, frequently in the form of a thin wire, connects the two end caps together as shown in Figure 6.32. When the fuse is placed in a circuit as seen in Figure 6.33, the fuse element is in

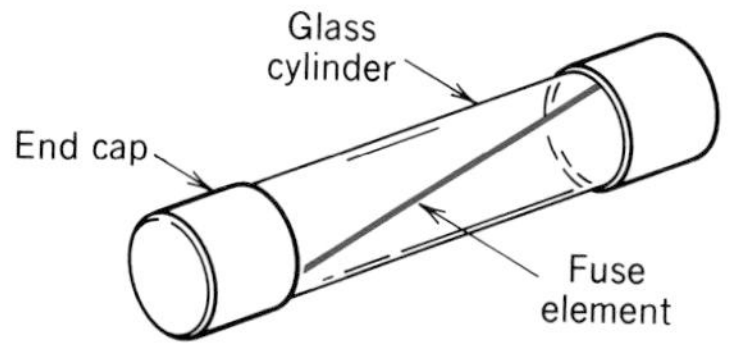

Figure 6.32 Type of fuse frequently used in electronic units.

series with the rest of the circuit. (Note the schematic symbol for a fuse.)

When the circuit current rises above the level for which the fuse was designed, the power dissipation of the fuse element will produce enough heat to vaporize it. When this happens, current is interrupted and the other components and connecting wires in the circuit are protected from damage due to overheating. Once a fuse has opened, it must be removed from the circuit and replaced by a new one of the same type in order to restore the circuit to operation. A fuse that has opened is referred to as a *blown* fuse.

In the case of glass-bodied fuses, it is generally obvious that the fuse has blown, either from the absence of the fuse element or because of noticeable darkening of the glass due to the vaporization of the fuse element and the deposit of a dark metal film on the glass. Such visual checks are not always reliable, however, and can not be made on fuses with ceramic or other bodies. It is always best to perform a continuity check with an ohmmeter, as in the case of lamps. A good fuse will have a resistance of less than 10 Ω, normally considerably less, while a blown fuse has a resistance of more than 10 kΩ.

A fuse is an important device because it often acts as a warning flag. When a fuse opens under normal operating conditions, it may be an indication that some component in the circuit has changed its characteristics or may be about to fail. You should never replace a

Figure 6.33 The fuse element is placed in series with the rest of the circuit.

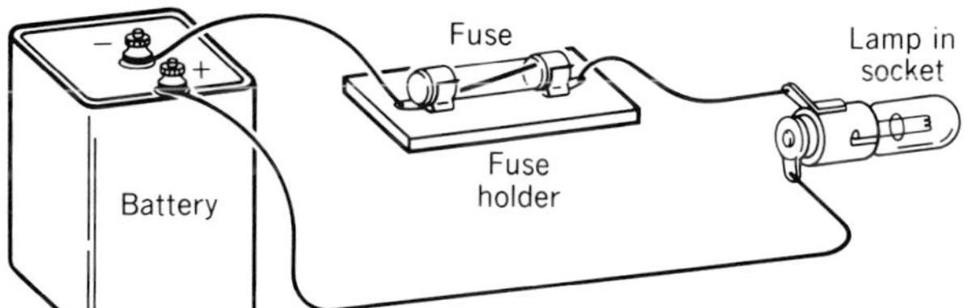

(a) Pictorial diagram

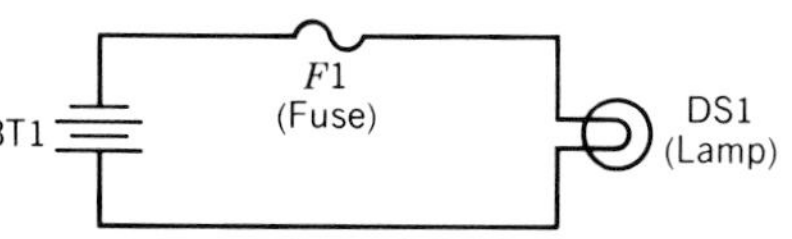

(b)

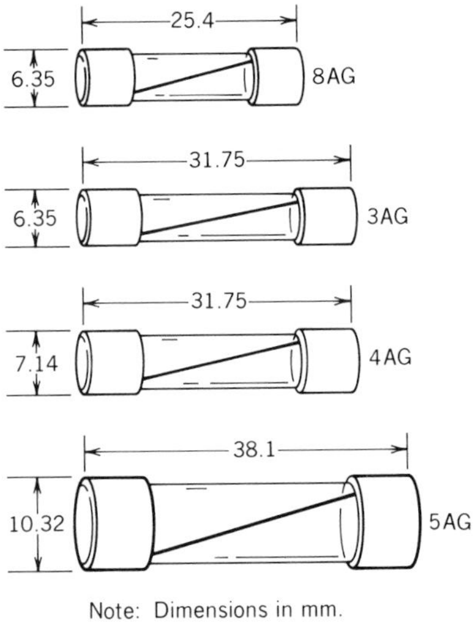

Figure 6.34 Common instrument fuse size designations formerly were 3AG, 5AG, and 8AG.

fuse without analyzing the causes for the previous failure. Inspection of the components for excessive discoloration due to heating and resistance measurements to detect a possible short circuit are highly recommended.

Unfortunately, fuses sometimes blow for no particular reason. Vibration or continued low-level current surges may weaken a fuse element to the point that it will fail or open even under normal operating conditions. This kind of fuse failure is called a *nuisance failure*. Just how great a nuisance this is can only be appreciated after you have spent time and energy looking for the nonexistent equipment failure that caused the fuse to open. Since fuses have to act quickly to protect sensitive circuit components, a certain amount of nuisance failure can be expected, particularly in fast-acting fuses with maximum current ratings below 2 A. This is because such fuses often have thin, easily broken elements.

Formerly, the most common instrument fuses and size designations were the 3AG, 5AG, and 8AG pictured in Figure 6.34. Some manufacturers have abandoned the older-type numbers, however, in favor of type numbers that give better indication of the speed of fuse action and the maximum potential difference permitted between the end caps of the fuse after it has blown.

There are three basic types of fuse designed for different applications. Fast-acting fuses are used to protect instruments such as meters and sensitive semiconductor circuits. A second category, general-purpose fuses, are used in most applications involving resistive circuits and medium-power semiconductors. Time-delay, or slow-blow fuses are used where surge currents are expected, as in lamp or motor circuits.

D.3.1 FAST-ACTING FUSES

Fast-acting fuses, sometimes called *fast-blow* fuses, are widely found in various sizes and in current ratings of $\frac{1}{500}$ to 5 A or more. They are designed to carry their full rated current indefinitely, but this depends on the kind of fuse holder used, on the temperature of the unit, and vibration. Very small current overloads, however, cause the fuse to open the circuit rapidly. For example, a size 8AG instrument fuse is supposed to carry 100 percent of its rated current for at least 4 hours, but it is also supposed to open at double its rated current in 5 s or less.

The sensitivity of this type of fuse is due to its construction. The fuse element is thin, so that it will vaporize quickly, and only a short length is used. In low-current fast-acting fuses, the element wire is supported by two heavier wire leads as shown in Figure 6.35*a*. The lead ends are held by a glass bead to minimize the effects of vibration, which could break the thin element. In the medium current-rating fast-blow

Figure 6.35*a* Cross section of a fast-acting fuse. Wire element is supported by two heavier wire leads; lead ends are held by glass beads.

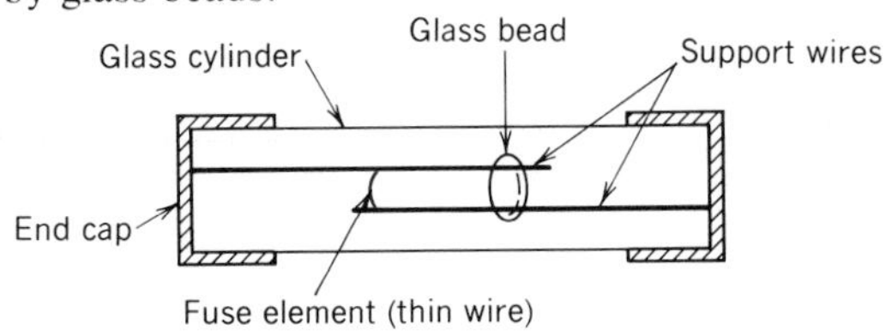

Figure 6.35*b* Cross section of medium lag (normal action) fuse. For some of the higher values, a single wire element connects the two end caps.

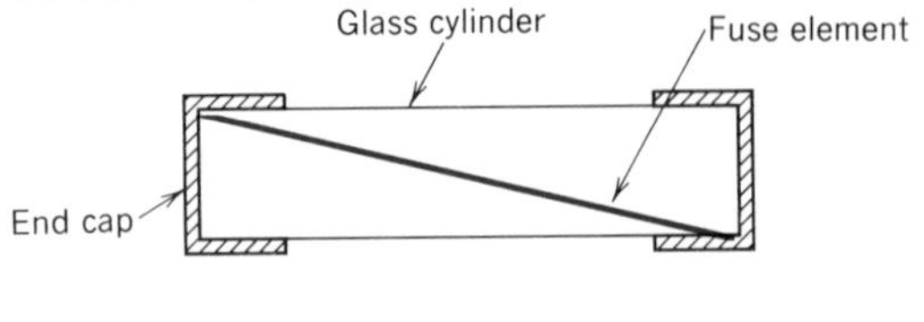

Figure 6.35*c* In the highest current-rating fast-blow fuses, an element strip may be used.

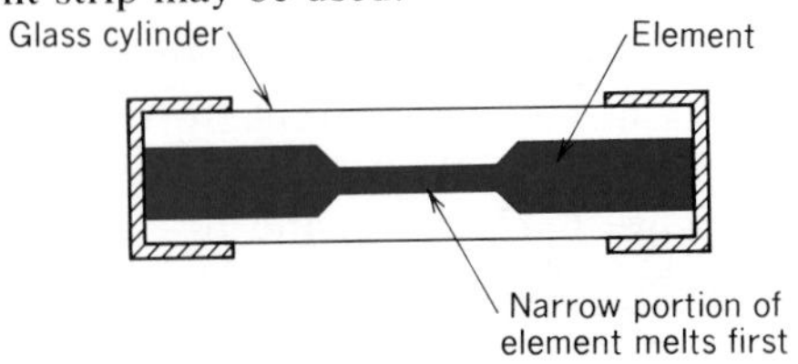

fuses, the diameter of the fuse element is larger. For some of the higher values, the element is sturdy enough to do away with the bead construction technique. A single wire element, as seen in Figure 6.35*b*, connects the two end caps. In the highest current rating fast-blow fuses, an element strip of the shape seen in Figure 6.35*c* is used. In all cases, the fast-acting fuse is designed so that the element is as light as possible and the heat generated by a higher-than-rated current will be confined to one area. This ensures rapid melting of the element.

D.3.2 GENERAL-PURPOSE FUSES

The general-purpose fuse is used where rapid action is not required. This is the case when the protected circuit tends to regulate itself or when it is relatively immune to short current surges. The general-purpose fuse is the most common and the cheapest. It will support a 110 percent current overload for a minimum of 4 hours, and a current 135 percent of its rated value for at least an hour. Higher currents, however, cause the fuse element to vaporize. Depending on the manufacturer, a current twice that of the fuse rating will cause it to blow in 10 to 30 s. The physical construction of general-purpose fuses is usually like that of the medium or higher rating fast-acting fuses shown in Figures 6.35*b* and 6.35*c*. Some typical current and voltage ratings are given in Table 6.5.

D.3.3 SLOW-BLOW (TIME-DELAY) FUSES

Circuits containing motors and lamps show a large current surge when a potential difference is first applied. In motor circuits this surge is often six or eight times the normal operating current. In lamp circuits, the current surge is even greater, and can be as much as 10 or 12 times the operating current. Although these surges last for only a short time, until the motor comes up to operating speed or the lamps begin to glow, the high surge currents make circuit protection difficult.

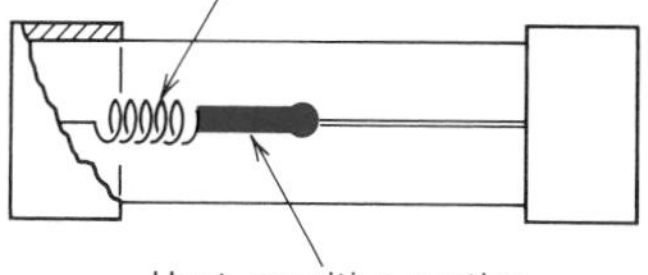

Figure 6.36 One way of obtaining a time delay in fuse operation is to separate the heat-producing and heat-sensitive parts of the fuse element.

One solution is to use a slow-blow or time-delay fuse. This kind of fuse has a massive element. The large amount of metal in the element dissipates the heat produced by the surge, so that the fuse does not open immediately. Another method for obtaining a time delay is to separate the heat-producing and heat-sensitive parts of the fuse element. This is done by manufacturing the element in two parts: a relatively massive spring or coil that produces heat when a current passes through it and a short wire of low-temperature melting metal as shown in Figure 6.36. Since the heat-sensitive part of the element has to be heated to the melting point by the relatively massive coil, a short-term surge occurring at turn-on will not cause it to melt. On the other hand, a serious overload lasting more than a second or two, or a current surge taking place *after* the heating coil temperature has been established during the first moments of operation, will produce enough heat to melt the temperature-sensitive metal.

Table 6.5 Typical Current and Voltage Ratings of General Purpose Fuses (For dimensions, see Figure 6.34)

Fuse Designation	*Current Range (A)*	*Voltage Ratings (V)*	*Body Material*
3AG	$\frac{1}{500}$ to 30	32	glass
(AGC)		125	
		250	
3AB	1 to 40	32	ceramic
		125	
		250	
4AG	10 to 40	32	glass
		125	
		250	
5AG	10 to 60	32	glass
		125	
		250	

Table 6.6 Slow-blow Fuse Current and Voltage Ratings (For dimensions, see Figure 6.34)

Fuse Designation	*Current Range (A)*	*Voltage Ratings (V)*	*Body Material*
3AB	1 to 30	32	ceramic
(MDA)		125	
		250	
3AG	$\frac{1}{100}$ to 20	32	glass
(MDL)		125	
(MDX)		250	
4AG	$\frac{1}{16}$ to 30	32	glass
		125	
		250	
5AG (FNQ)	$\frac{1}{2}$ to 30	32	glass
(FNM)		125	fiber
		250	

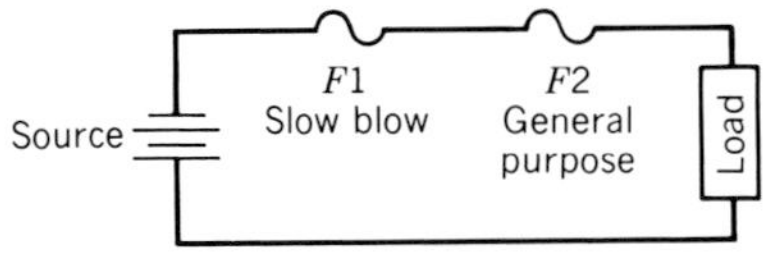

Figure 6.37 Using a general-purpose fuse in series with a slow-blow fuse. The general-purpose fuse opens quickly if the current reaches seven times normal.

Slow-blow fuses will generally permit a current 110 percent of their rating for at least 4 hours, and a current twice that of their rating for up to 2 min, depending on fuse construction and characteristics. Some typical slow-blow fuse current and voltage ratings are given in Table 6.6. In some circuits, as shown in Figure 6.37, a higher-current rating general-purpose fuse is used in series with a slow-blow fuse. The general-purpose fuse is selected to open quickly if the circuit current reaches seven times the normal rating. Some manufacturers of slow-blow fuses build this feature into all their slow-blow fuses.

D.3.4 FUSE MOUNTING

Many industrial fuse holders are little more than a pair of spring clips mounted on an insulating base (Figure 6.38). This kind of mounting is almost the only one used for large-sized, high-power, cartridge fuses with ratings of 30 A or more. It requires considerable force to remove these fuses from the clips. To prevent breakage or accidents, plier-type fuse pullers like those shown in Figure 6.39 are used.

In electronic units, which use smaller, glass-bodied fuses, holder blocks like that pictured in Figure 6.38 are sometimes mounted inside the unit case. When this is done, it is necessary to remove the unit cover before the fuse can be inspected or changed. The effect of this kind of mounting is to double the nuisance value of a nuisance failure. Not only do you have to replace the fuse but you may also have to partially disassemble the unit to do it.

Figure 6.38 An industrial fuse holder may be little more than a pair of clips mounted on an insulating base.

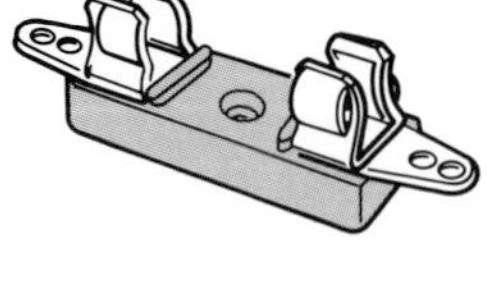

Figure 6.39 Plier-type fuse pullers.

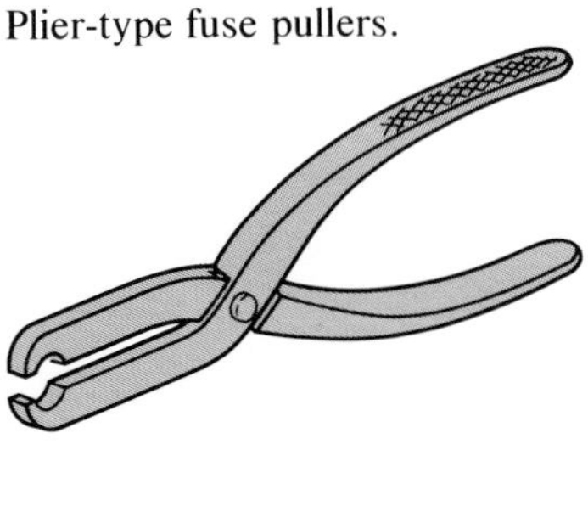

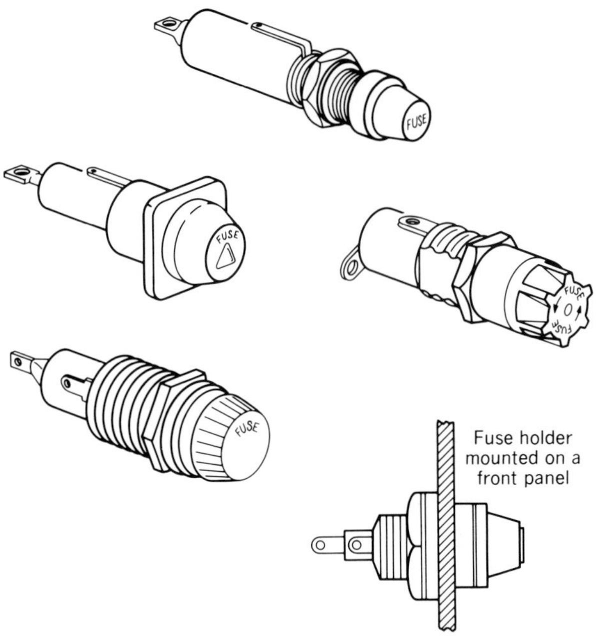

Figure 6.40 Panel-mounted fuse holders facilitate the changing of fuses.

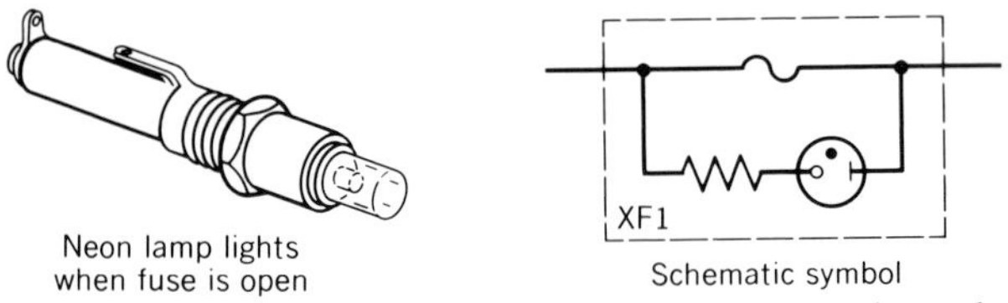

Figure 6.41 An indicating fuse holder lights to show that the fuse has blown.

In the interest of maintainability, industrial units frequently use standard design fuse holders, mounted on the front panel of the unit (Figure 6.40). It is easy to unscrew or remove the cap of these holders and inspect the mounted fuse, which comes out when the holder cap is removed. Some applications even use an indicating fuse holder as shown in Figure 6.41. This type of fuse holder cap contains a small neon lamp in parallel with the fuse. If the fuse opens, the full circuit potential difference is applied across the lamp, causing it to glow. This serves as a signal to maintenance personnel that the fuse is blown.

D.4 SWITCHES

Just as you probably have some experience with fuses, you have some knowledge of switches of various kinds. In a technological society, people are always flipping, pressing, or turning switches to control electrical energy. However, the technical details of switches are even less familiar to the general public than those of fuses. A large number of Americans can replace blown fuses, but few have the knowledge required to check and replace faulty switches.

Today, there are two broad categories of switches: mechanical switches and solid-state (semiconductor) switches. All switches are devices used to open or close conduction paths. Mechanical switches do this by moving a metallic contactor so that it touches or is moved away from one or more fixed contacts. Solid-state switches contain a piece of semiconductor material that becomes a good conductor when it is activated by a control current or signal. As in the case of LEDs, solid-state switches are best considered with semiconductor circuits.

Mechanical switches may be operated either automatically, when certain conditions of pressure or temperature are present, or manually, when actuated by an equipment operator. Since many automatic switches are actually based on manual switches, only manual switches will be discussed in this section.

Even with this limitation, there are so many types of switches, it is difficult to discuss more than just the most common kinds. The best method is to classify switches by their *action*, that is, the type of motion that operates the switch. Four basic switch actions are the most common: the push, slide, toggle, and rotary actions. Since switches are nonrepairable mechanical devices, which are frequently mishandled and occasionally wear out, you will be required to check switch operation and to replace faulty units.

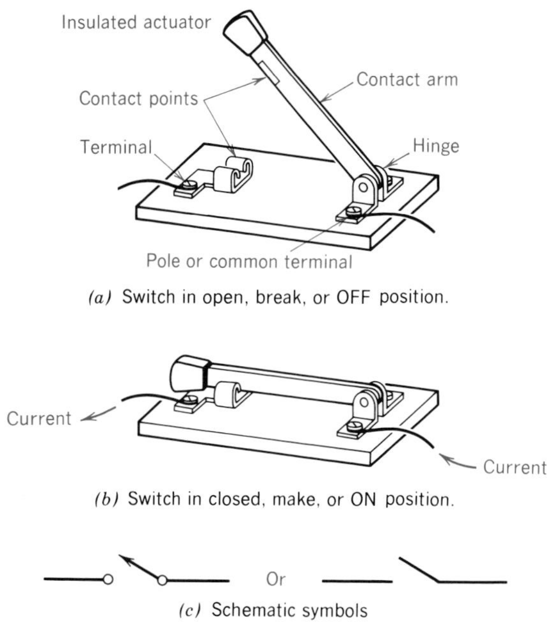

Figure 6.42 Switch operations can be seen in the knife switch.

D.4.1 AN INTRODUCTION TO SWITCH OPERATION

The basic operation of a switch can be seen from the old-fashioned knife switch shown in Figure 6.42. This switch consists of two terminals and a conductive bar. The bar is hinged to one of the terminals in such a way as to provide a conductive path between the terminals when the switch is in the ON position, see Figure 6.42*b*. The terminal to which the bar is attached is called the *common pole*, or more simply the *pole*. The common pole is connected to and disconnected from the other switch terminal by a mechanical action. Since there is only one terminal to which the common pole can be connected, this action is referred to as a *single throw*. The entire switch is therefore referred to as a *single-pole, single-throw switch*, abbreviated SPST. Figure 6.42*c* shows the schematic diagram of an SPST switch.

If another terminal is added, as in Figure 6.43, the switch becomes a single-pole, double-throw, or SPDT switch. There are two possible contacts to which the hinged bar may be connected, each one being considered a throw.

A double-pole, single-throw (DPST) switch is illustrated in Figure 6.44. In this switch a second hinged bar is connected to the first by an insulator so that both bars move at the same time. There is no electrical connection between the two bars. Adding another pair of terminals to the switch in Figure 6.44 produces the double-pole, double-throw (DPDT) switch illustrated in Figure 6.45. Note the dotted line in the schematic diagram. It is used to show that the two bars are mechanically connected.

Figure 6.43 In a single-pole double-throw switch there are two contacts to which the hinged bar can be moved.

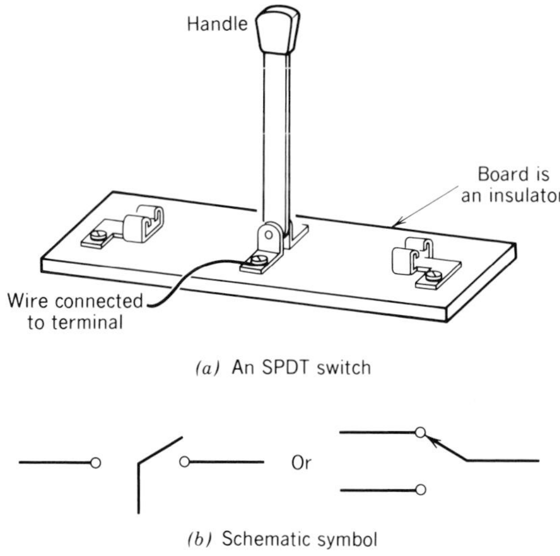

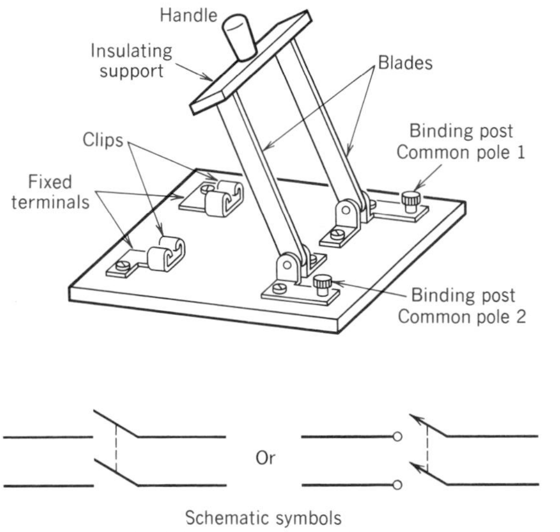

Figure 6.44 A double-pole switch adds a second hinged bar electrically insulated from but mechanically connected to the first.

In addition to the concepts of pole and throw, you will have to become familiar with a number of other basic terms and characteristics of switches. One of these is *contact resistance*. In the knife switch, you can see that two mechanial joints are involved when the switch is closed, one at the hinge and one at the contact point. Because of this, the resistance of the switch is frequently larger than that of the hook-up wires in the circuit. After a switch has been in service for a time, its contact resistance may increase. This is true even if the switch is a dust- and moisture-sealed unit. Contact pitting and corrosion over a period of time will reduce the contact area between the bar and the two terminals and increase the contact resistance. When switch contact resistance increases beyond a certain point, the switch will no longer function well in certain applications. Some manufacturers specify a contact resistance of 0.020 to 0.025 Ω as the maximum allowable for their products, although many switches in service today have contact resistances that are considerably higher.

Contact resistances of an ohm or so generally mean problems in the function of most equipment. This is true because circuit designers normally think of switches as having nearly the characteristics of an ideal switch. Ideal switch characteristics are:

a. Zero contact resistance in the closed position.

b. Infinite contact resistance in the open position, that is, no current leakage at all through the open switch.

c. The ability to go from the open to the closed position, or the other way around, in no time at all.

Naturally, no real switch has any of these ideal characteristics. On the other hand, mechanical switches can approximate the first two closely enough for most practical purposes.

In order to reduce the damage done to switch contacts by sparking and heating, switches are rated for a certain maximum continuous current and a certain maximum surge current. These maximum ratings should never be exceeded, either in the original design or in the choice of replacement parts. Switches are often given several ratings, depending on whether ac or dc is being switched and on the type of load involved. Resistances provide the least strain upon switches. Lamps, motors, and other components are capable of producing large surge currents and spikes, which are sudden short-term increases in the potential difference in various parts of a circuit. For example, a switch used in a lamp circuit must be able to withstand surge currents of 10 to 12 times normal.

Sparking, which takes place when switch contact is first made or opened, is responsible for most of the damage to switch contacts. This damage can be reduced by speeding up the making or breaking of contact. In the knife switch used to illustrate switch operation, the opening or closing of the switch is a rather slow process. If the open-circuit potential difference across the switch is great enough, the air between the switch contacts and the bar will ionize and create a conductive path along which an arc, a continuous spark, will form. If the opening and closing of the switch can be speeded up, the damage resulting from arcing can be reduced or even eliminated. One way to do this is by using a *sensitive switch*. A sensitive switch has an

Figure 6.45 A double-pole double-throw switch.

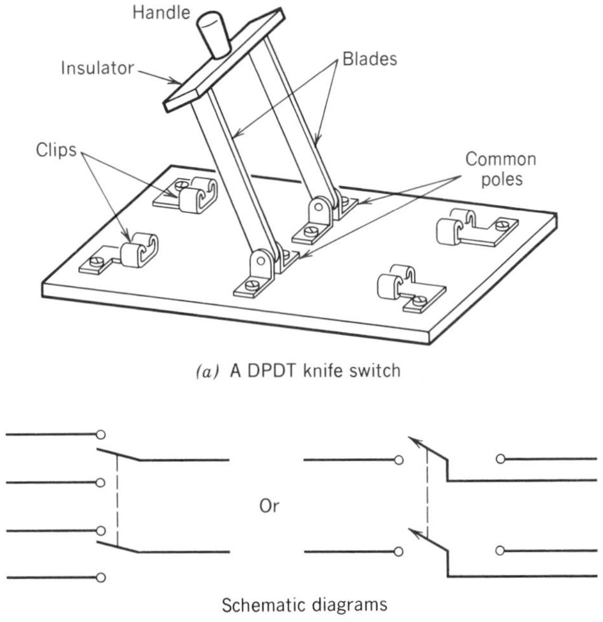

actuator that is not directly connected to the contacting bar but acts as a trigger. When the trigger is actuated, a spring brings the closely set contacts together or pulls them apart quickly. This shortens the time during which sparking or arcing can occur.

Two additional switch characteristics are important: voltage rating and insulation resistance. The *voltage rating* of a switch is the maximum potential difference across the switch in its open position. The voltage rating depends on the kind of insulating materials used and on the distance between the contacts when the switch is in the open position. In the case of the knife switch, a large air gap exists between the contacts and the bar when the switch is open, so it is the insulating material that determines the switch voltage rating. This will be high, on the order of a 1000 V, if good-quality materials are used. In pushbutton, slide, toggle, and rotary switches, however, contact separation becomes an important factor. The dc voltage ratings are lower than ac ratings because arcing is more common with dc.

The *insulation resistance* of a switch is the measured resistance between its open terminals. The insulation resistance of a new switch depends on the materials of which it is made, but the accumulation of dust, oil, and water droplets reduces the insulation resistance of most switches in service. Even sealed units suffer from the buildup of metal particles that result from the vaporization of contacts during sparking. The typical industry standard for switches is to consider them to have reached their end of life when the switch resistance drops below 1000 MΩ with an applied potential difference of 100 or 500 V dc.

Table 6.7 Current and Voltage Ratings for Standard Switches

	Current Rating		
Switch Type	*Resistance Load*	*Motor Load*	*Voltage Rating*
Pushbutton			
Small	0.5	—	30 V DC
	1.5	—	125 V AC
Toggle			
Small	1.5	—	30 V DC/125 V AC
Medium	15–20	12–15	(240 V AC) (30 V DC)
Rotary			
Small	1.5	—	30 V DC
	0.5	—	125 V AC
Medium	15.0	15	125 V AC
	11.0	—	30 V DC
Slide			
Small	1	—	125 V AC
	0.25	—	30 V DC
Medium	3	—	125 V AC

Some typical current and voltage ratings for standard switches are given in Table 6.7.

D.4.2 PUSHBUTTON SWITCHES

Although many of the basic characteristics of switches can be seen in the structure and function of the knife switch, this type is no longer frequently used in industry. Its fairly large size and the danger arising from the exposed terminals limits its use in most applications. One of the most familiar switches in use is the smaller pushbutton switch. Where the knife switch requires a relatively large movement of the actuating handle for opening and closing, the pushbutton switch is actuated by a short-distance thrust in line with the direction of button travel. A typical pushbutton switch is shown in Figure 6.46. It is composed of two parts: the actuator, which includes the pushbutton, and the switch itself. Sometimes, the switch and actuator are formed into a single, nonseparable unit, although more elaborate actuator–switch combinations have a two-part construction that makes it possible to replace either a faulty actuator or a faulty switch separately.

The switch portion of a standard pushbutton switch may be as simple as an SPST ON/OFF switch or as elaborate as a four-pole, double-throw unit for complex switching tasks. The actuator of the switch shown in Figure 6.46 is a relatively simple device. It consists of a plastic button, usually color coded or printed to provide information about the switch function, a spring, and in some cases, a detent assembly. Without the detent assembly, the switch is actuated only when the pushbutton is pressed. It returns to its initial position when the pushbutton is released. This type of switch is called a *momentary action switch*. Figure 6.47 shows the schematic symbols for two momentary action switches. In the first of these, the switch contacts are in the open position unless the switch is actuated. When the pushbutton is pressed, the contacts close and "make" or complete the circuit. This switch is referred to as a *pushbutton, normally open*, or PBNO switch. The switch in Figure 6.47*b* has its contacts in the closed position unless the pushbutton is pressed. It is there-

Figure 6.46 A typical pushbutton switch.

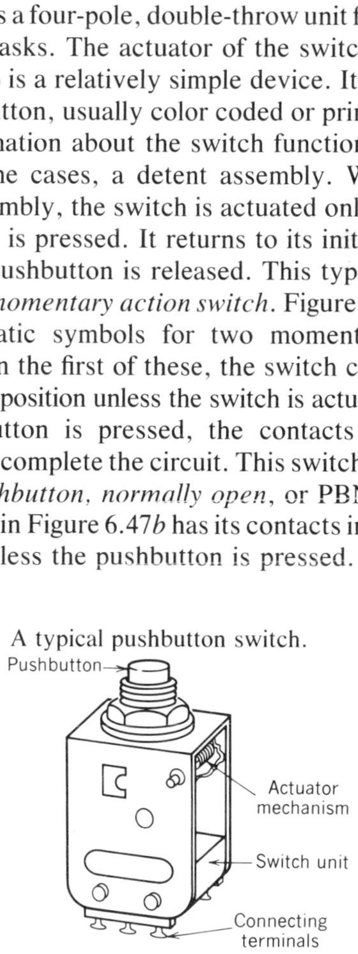

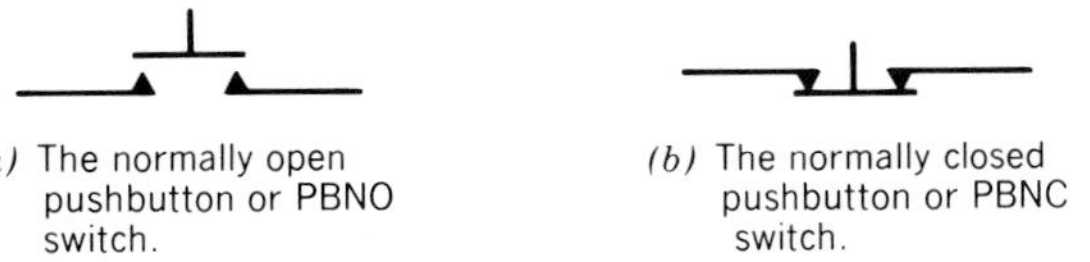

(a) The normally open pushbutton or PBNO switch.
(b) The normally closed pushbutton or PBNC switch.

Figure 6.47 The schematic symbols of two momentary action switches.

fore called a *pushbutton, normally closed*, or PBNC switch. In schematic diagrams, it is a general rule to show all switches (as well as other components) in their unactuated, unpowered positions.

The schematic of Figure 6.48 shows a more complex DPST switch. Notice that one pole of the switch is normally open, while the second is normally closed. Pressing the pushbutton makes, or completes, the normally open circuit and breaks the normally closed circuit. The order of these events is usually of no importance and depends upon the contact arrangement. In some cases, however, it is important that only one of the circuits is closed at a time. In these cases, a *break-before-make* switch is used. In this switch, the closed circuit is always broken before the open circuit is made. A short, but definite, period of time exists when both circuits are open.

In other cases, damage to components might occur if both circuits are open at the same time. An example of this is certain semiconductor circuits. This situation is prevented by using a *make-before-break* switch. In this kind of switch, the normally open circuit is closed before the normally closed circuit is opened. For a short time both circuits are closed.

The momentary action pushbutton switch is used to change circuits for a brief period or to initiate actions that complete themselves. For functions that require the switch to remain in the pressed position for more than a few seconds, an *alternate action* pushbutton switch is used. This type of switch has an actuator with a detent, that is, a spring-loaded assembly that holds the switch in the pressed position. To reset the switch

Figure 6.48 Two-pole pushbutton switch.

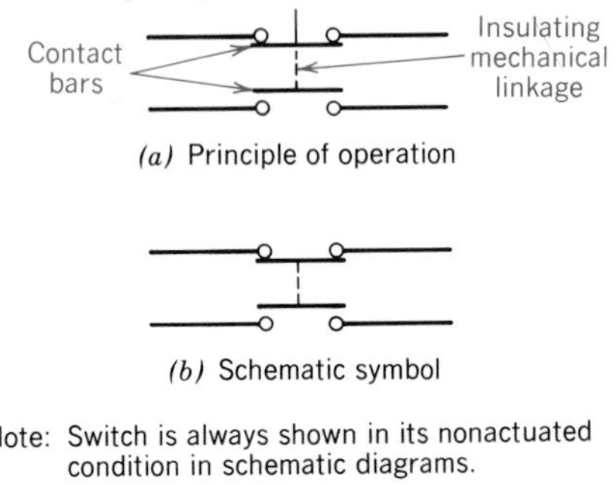

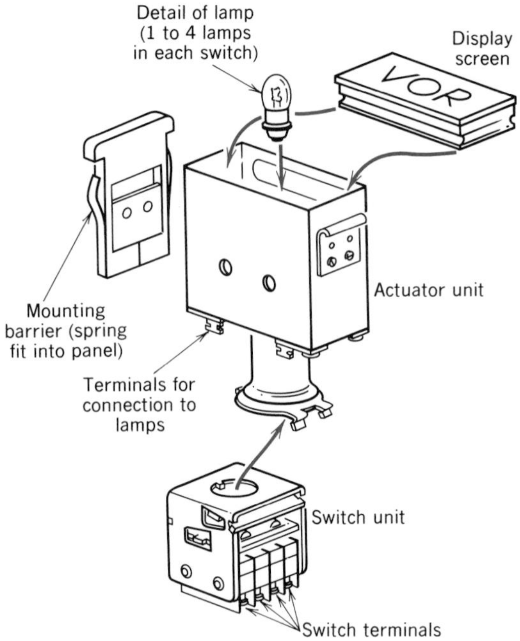

Figure 6.49 An illuminated pushbutton switch.

to its original position, it is necessary to press the pushbutton again. This releases the detent.

One problem of the alternate action pushbutton switch is that it is difficult to tell whether the switch is in its OFF or ON position. A number of mechanical solutions to this problem have been used, such as holding the pushbutton in a partially depressed position when the switch is ON. Another solution is causing a plate or tab with a distinctive marking to appear in the clear pushbutton when the switch is ON. In many modern assemblies a lighted pushbutton is used. The pushbutton is a large unit that contains one or more lamps that are lighted when the switch is in its ON position. Color-coded plastic inserts, engraved with the names of the functions controlled by the switches, are used with the lighted pushbuttons to produce sophisticated control assemblies. Such a switch is shown in Figure 6.49.

In lighted pushbutton switches, the switch and actuator portions are frequently separable units. If either fails, it can be replaced without replacing the entire assembly. Replacing burned out lamps, however, can be tricky. Often, the button cap is removed to provide access to the lamps. The lamps frequently have flanged bases and require special removal tools.

D.4.3 SLIDE AND TOGGLE SWITCHES

Although quite different in construction, slide and toggle switches are frequently found in the same applications. Both are actuated by means of a short handle. The handle is slid in the case of the slide switch and

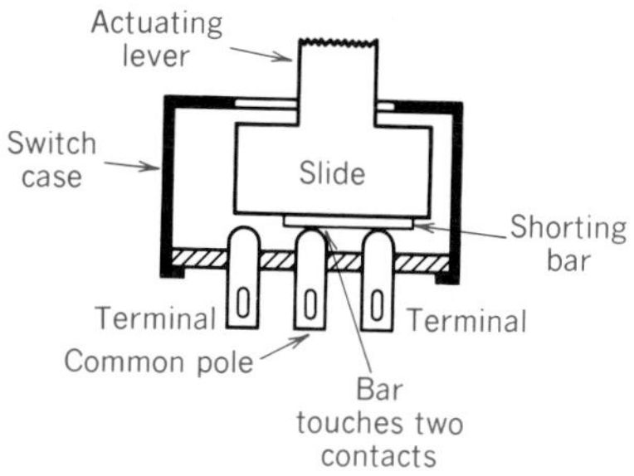

Figure 6.50 Cutaway view of a slide switch.

flipped in the case of the toggle switch. A cutaway view of the slide switch is shown in Figure 6.50. As you can see, the handle moves a slide that causes a moving contact to touch a fixed one, completing the circuit. The toggle switch, on the other hand, is a sensitive switch. Once the lever or bat shown in Figure 6.51 has been moved beyond a certain point, a small, powerful spring is released. This spring forces the moving and fixed contacts together or apart to make or break the circuit. As in the case of the pushbutton switch, slide and toggle switches are available in both momentary and detent models. Commonly found switches range from single-pole, single-throw (SPST) to four-pole, double-throw (4PDT) switches. On some double-throw units, there is a center OFF position. With the handle or bat in the center position, the common pole or poles are not connected to any of the fixed contacts. Lighting arrangements are usually not needed for slide and toggle switches since the position of the handle or bat shows which of the throws has been selected.

Slide switches are inexpensive and are generally not sealed units. This means that they are subject to corrosion and contamination by dust, water, and oil droplets in the air. On the other hand, it is relatively easy to clean these switches with an application of a special contact cleaner in aerosol form. Toggle switches are almost always sealed units and can not be cleaned easily, but since they are sealed, contamination is less frequent.

Figure 6.51 Cross section of a typical toggle switch.

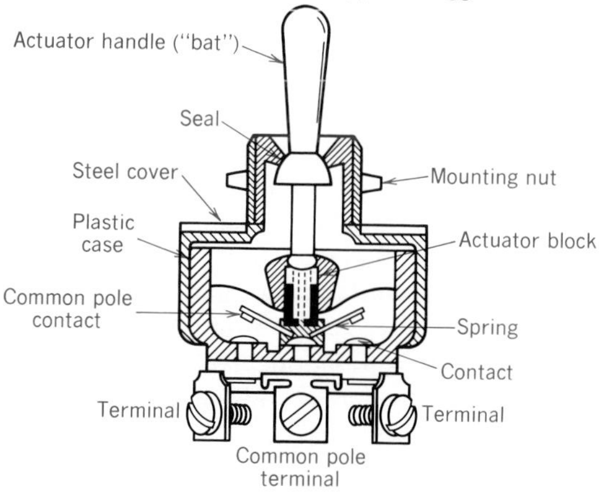

With the increased use of computer technology, one of the problems of switches in general and toggle switches in particular has become critical. This is the problem of bounce or chatter. This occurs when there is a certain amount of recoil or bouncing when the fixed and moving contacts are brought together. Since this recoil period lasts only a few milliseconds, it is relatively unimportant in most applications, except for the increased contact wear due to sparking when the contacts come together and separate several times. Computer circuitry, however, operates at such high speeds that even a very short period of contact bounce may upset normal operating sequences. To eliminate this problem, computer circuit switches are buffered. That is, they control the computer circuit through electronic switching devices, which are immune to contact bounce.

As in the case of pushbutton switches, faulty slide and toggle switches must be replaced with units capable of withstanding current surges when motors or lamps are part of the switched circuit. Slide and toggle switches in normal use have low to medium current ratings. These are marked on the switch itself or given in the unit parts list.

D.4.4 ROTARY SWITCHES

Switches actuated by a twisting motion are classified as rotary switches. A knob is attached to the switch shaft so that the rotation will select any one of a number of circuits or combinations of circuits. A typical rotary switch and its principal parts are shown in Figure 6.52. Figure 6.53 is a detailed view of one switch deck, also called a *section* or *gang*. Notice that the selector tab makes and then breaks the contact between the common terminal or pole and each of the other terminals as the switch shaft is rotated.

The index wheel shown in Figure 6.52 prevents the switch from stopping between positions, that is,

Figure 6.52 A typical rotary switch.

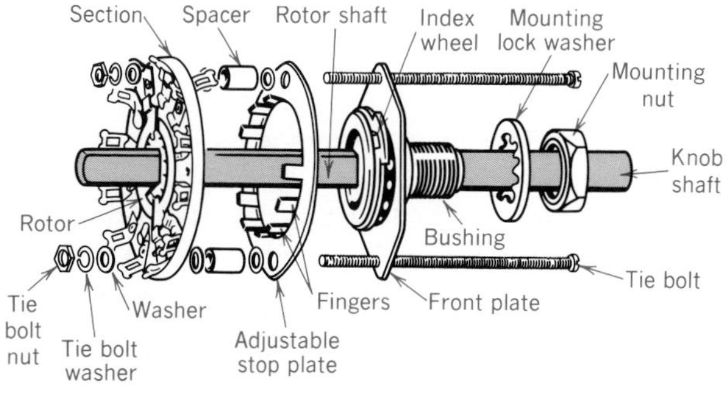

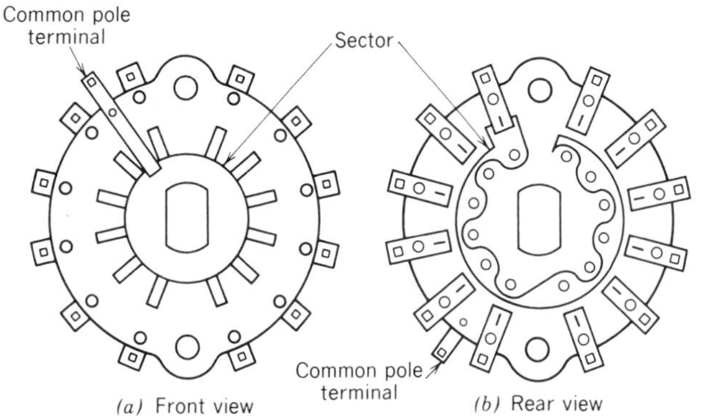

Figure 6.53 A switch deck, section, or gang. The selector tab makes and then breaks the contact between the common terminal and each of the other terminals as the switch shaft is rotated.

when the selector tab is between terminals. It is designed to provide an action very much like that of the spring-loaded toggle switch. The index wheel provides a resistance to the turning of the shaft, which drops suddenly when the twisting action reaches a certain force. At this point, the index wheel detent releases. The force applied to the shaft then carries it around quickly to the next detent position. At this point, the selector tab will touch the next contact. If the twisting force on the shaft is continued, this process will be repeated. If the switch has a stop plate, as shown in Figure 6.52, the rotation will be limited to the number of positions allowed by the stop plate. The plate can be set to permit the number of positions required for that particular switching function. When a metal tab attached to the index wheel strikes the stop plate, no further rotation in that direction is possible. The switch knob must then be turned in the opposite direction. Omitting or removing the stop plate or tab makes the switch an unlimited rotation switch. This means that the knob can be rotated through more than a complete circle.

The number of detent positions on a rotary switch is also determined by the index assembly, which may be designed to provide detents or holding positions every 30°, 45°, or 90° of rotation. A contact terminal is usually provided at each detent position. For a detent position every 30°, the common pole can be connected to one of up to 12 contact terminals. This switch is therefore called a *single-deck (or single-gang), single-pole, 12-position rotary switch*. It is a single-pole switch because there is only one common terminal, and there are 12 positions because $12 \times 30° = 360°$, a complete circle. An index assembly with a detent position every 45° would have a maximum of eight contact terminals to which the common pole might be connected ($8 \times 45° = 360°$). A 90°-index would have four positions. In industrial and test equipment, indexes with as many

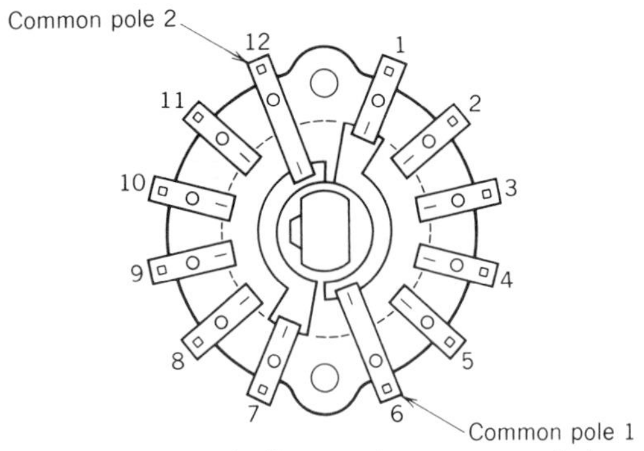

Figure 6.54 A two-pole five-section rotary switch section.

as 36 detent positions are found, but 12-, 8-, and 4-position indexes are the most common.

Adding a second identical switch section or gang to the switch of Figure 6.52 produces a two-deck, single-pole, 12-position switch. Multiple-deck switches, sometimes with six or more separate decks, are driven by a single shaft for complex switching tasks. Notice that although there are two poles present in the two-deck switch, the accepted name still is "single-pole." It is the number of common poles per deck that is given.

Some decks may have more than one common pole. Such a deck is shown in Figure 6.54. The differences between this section and that shown in Figure 6.53 are the presence of two common terminals and two selector tabs. In normal use, the stop plate is adjusted so that the shaft can be in one of six positions. A single gang switch using this switch section would be called a *single-deck, two-pole, six-position switch*. Schematic diagrams of rotary switches with more than two or so positions are often simplified views of the switch sections, as shown in Figure 6.55. Multiple-section switches operating off a single shaft are shown by connecting the individual symbols with a dashed line representing the mechanical linkage.

The selector tabs shown in the previous examples are of the break-before-make variety. Their switching function is like that of the break-before-make pushbutton switch. During the rotation of the selector, the contact between the common pole and the selected terminal is broken before contact is made between the selector tab and the next terminal. As in the case of the break-before-make pushbutton switch, this means that there is a period of time *after* the selector tab has broken its contact with one terminal and *before* contact has been made with the next terminal. During this time, the common pole is not connected to any of the circuit terminals. In cases where this situation can not be allowed, a make-before-break switch must be used. As shown in Figure 6.56*a*, this type of selector is made by widening the selector tab. If this is done, the tab

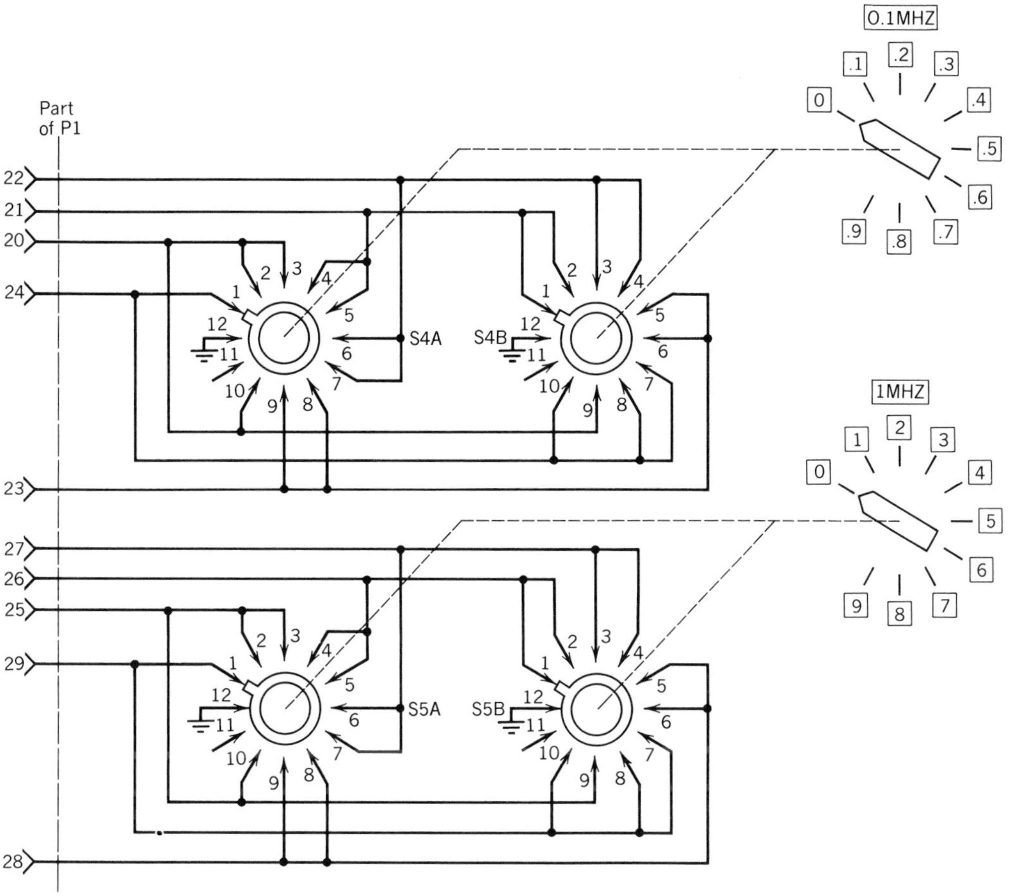

Figure 6.55 Schematic diagrams of rotary switches with more than two positions are often simplified views of the switch sections.

will make contact with the next terminal before contact with the previous terminal is broken, as shown in Figure 6.56*b*.

In addition to break-before-make and make-before-break selector tabs, a great variety of special types are found. Some of these correspond to special switching needs, while others are nothing more than variations of the standard switch designs. The progressive shorting switch section shown in Figure 6.57*a* is a common special unit. This type of switch is used when it is necessary to add circuits to a common line, for example, adding parallel loads to a single power source. In the progressive shorting switch, the selector tab is

Figure 6.56 Make-before-break rotary switch section.

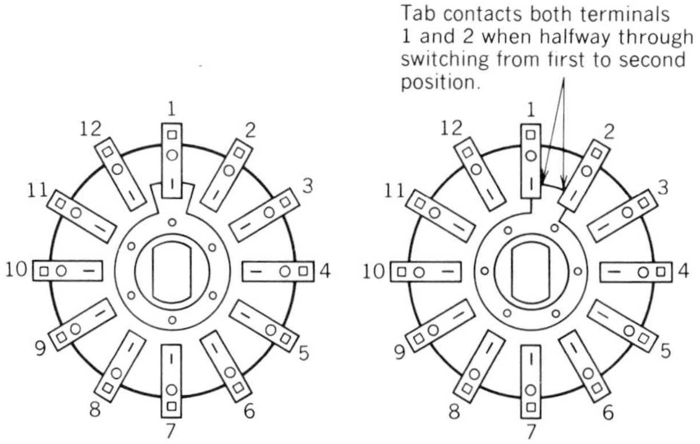

Tab contacts both terminals 1 and 2 when halfway through switching from first to second position.

(a) Notice the wide selector tab. *(b)* Switch midway between first and second positions.

Figure 6.57 A progressive shorting switch.

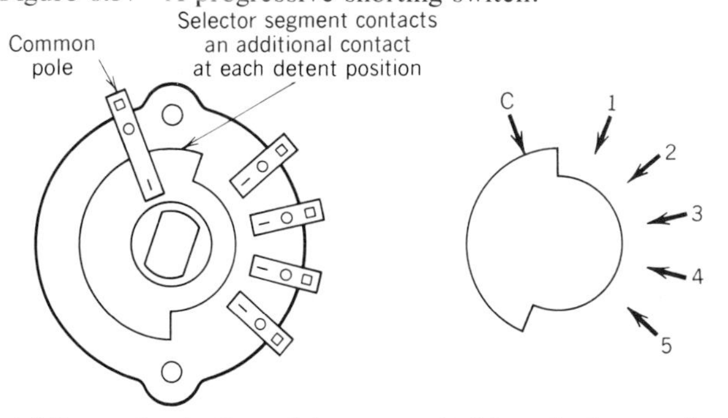

Common pole
Selector segment contacts an additional contact at each detent position
C

(a) Progressive shorting switch section *(b)* Schematic of progressive shorting switch

replaced by a segment so that the common pole makes contact with the additional terminals as the switch is rotated. This is fairly clear in the schematic of the deck in Figure 6.57*b*.

E. PROGRAMMED REVIEW

FRAME 1

Power is the __________ at which work is done. In the U.S. customary system, one unit for the measurement of power is the __________. In the metric system, mechanical power is measured in __________.

a. Rate; horsepower; joules per second. (2)
b. Any other answer, review Section B.2.

FRAME 2

The unit of electric power is the power used when the field caused by a potential difference of one volt moves an electric charge of one coulomb in one second. This unit is called the __________.

a. Watt. (3)
b. Any other answer, review Section B.2.

FRAME 3

When a load consisting of a resistance is connected to a source, the power supplied by the source is converted into __________ in the load.

a. Heat. (4)
b. Any other answer, review Section B.2.

FRAME 4

The formula $P = EI$ is a basic statement of the power law in electricity. In a resistive circuit, this formula can refer to two things, they are __________ and __________.

a. The power supplied by the source; the power dissipated as heat by the resistance. (5)
b. Any other answer, review Section B.2.

FRAME 5

A small incandescent lamp is rated at 0.5 W and is designed to operate at a potential difference of 6.3 V. What is the hot resistance of the lamp?

a. 79.38 Ω. (6)
b. Any other answer, review Section B.2.

FRAME 6

If the resistance of a load and the current through it are known, the easiest way to calculate the power dissipation is to use the formula $P =$ __________.

a. $P = I^2R$. (7)
b. Any other answer, review Section B.2.

FRAME 7

What is the power dissipation in $R1$ in Figure 6.58?

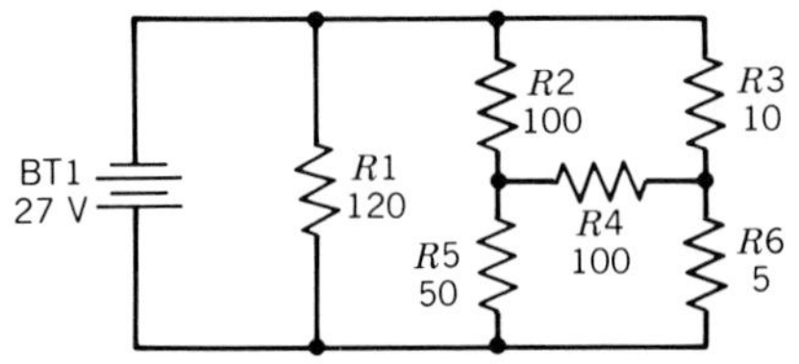

Figure 6.58 Circuit for Frame 7.

a. 6.075 W. (9)
b. Any other answer (8).

FRAME 8

Did you try to calculate the total resistance of the circuit, and find that you could not? Loads $R2$ through $R6$ have nothing to do with the power dissipated by $R1$. Review Section B5 and try Frame 7 again.

FRAME 9

What is the power dissipated by $R3$ in Figure 6.59? What is the potential difference across it?

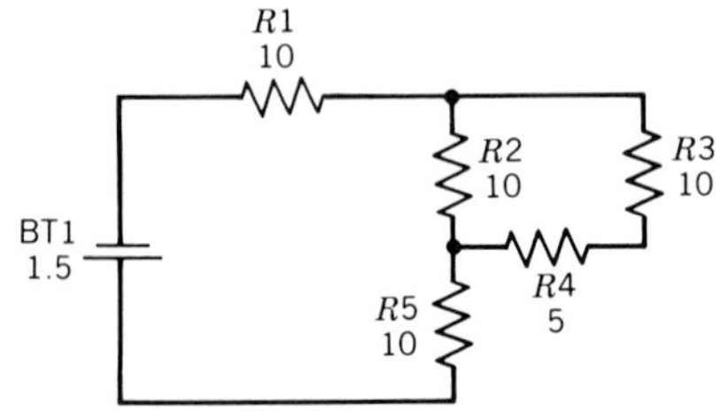

Figure 6.59 Circuit for Frame 9.

a. 5.92 mW; 0.231 V. (10)
b. Any other answer, review Sections B.6 and B.7.

FRAME 10

A negative exponent, such as $5^{-\frac{1}{2}}$, means $\frac{1}{5^{\frac{1}{2}}}$. Calculate $4^{-0.5}$.

a. $\frac{1}{2}$. (12)

b. $\frac{1}{4}$. (11)

c. Any other answer, review Section C.1.

FRAME 11

Your answer is not quite correct

$$4^{-0.5} = \frac{1}{4^{0.5}} \quad \text{or} \quad \frac{1}{\sqrt{4}} = \frac{1}{2}$$

Go on to Frame 12

FRAME 12

Adding another resistance to a parallel circuit ________ the total resistance of the circuit. The total resistance is always ________ than the resistance of the smallest parallel load.

a. Decreases; less. (13)
b. Any other answer, review Section C.4.

FRAME 13

A 10-W bulb is operating in a circuit with a source potential of 5 V. If the solid copper connecting wires, which are open to the air, have a resistance of 0.1 Ω, what is the thinnest wire that can be used in this circuit? Use Table 6.3.

a. AWG 17. (14)
b. Any other answer, review Section D.1.

FRAME 14

The three main categories of light-emitting indicators are ________ , ________ , and ________ .

a. Incandescent lamps; neon lamps; LEDs. (15)
b. Any answer not naming the three categories, review Section D.2.

FRAME 15

The glowing portion of an incandescent lamp is called the ________ . It is usually made of ________ , and is quite brittle when cold.

a. Filament; tungsten. (16)
b. Any other answer, review Section D.2.

FRAME 16

Neon lamps glow because a small amount of neon or other inert gas is ionized when the potential difference across the lamp reaches between ________ and ________ V.

a. 65; 135. (17)
b. Any other answer, review Section D.2.

FRAME 17

A T-3 bulb is ________ of an inch in diameter.

a. $\frac{3}{8}$ (18)
b. Any other answer, review Section D.2.

FRAME 18

Fuses are classified by size and by their speed of operation. The three common operating speeds are ________ , ________ , and ________ .

a. fast blow; general purpose (medium); slow blow. (19)
b. Any other answer, review Section D.3.

FRAME 19

The fuse pictured in Figure 6.60 is a ________ fuse.

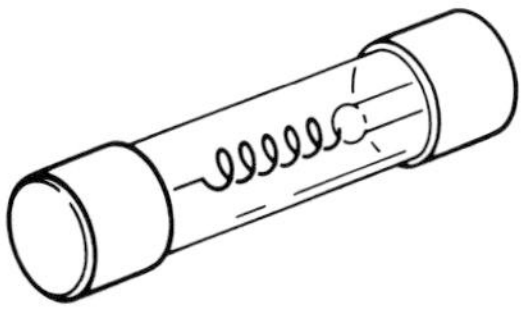

Figure 6.60 Figure for Frame 19.

a. Slow blow or delayed action. (20)
b. Any other answer, review Section D.3.3.

FRAME 20

SPDT refers to a ____________ ____________ ____________ switch.

a. Single-pole, double-throw. (21)
b. Any other element answer, review Section D.4.

FRAME 21

Damage to switch contacts from arcing can sometimes be prevented by using a ____________ switch in which spring action forces the contacts together or apart quickly.

a. Sensitive. (22)
b. Any other answer, review Section D.4.1.

FRAME 22

The insulation resistance of a switch is a measure of ____________ .

a. The resistance between its open terminals. (23)
b. Any other answer, review Section D.4.1.

FRAME 23

A switch without a detent returns to its original position when released. This kind of switch is called a "____________ ____________" switch.

a. Momentary action. (24)
b. Any other answer, review Section D.4.2.

FRAME 24

One type of sensitive switch frequently used in electronic units is the ____________ switch.

a. Toggle (END)
b. Any other answer, review section D.4.3.

E. PROBLEMS FOR SOLUTION OR RESEARCH

1. You have been hired to design and build a lighting system for a circular jogging path 1 km long and have been instructed to use one hundred 60-W light bulbs. The source supply is 120 V, and the bulbs have to be spaced every 10 m. Using Table 6.3, determine the AWG number wire to purchase if you allow a safety factor of 200 percent of the maximum expected load.

2. Calculate the following exponential expressions. Round off to three significant figures.

a. 3.5^3
b. $\sqrt{3.615}$
c. 14.5^2
d. $\frac{1}{\sqrt{3}}$
e. $2.567^{-0.5}$
f. $64^{\frac{1}{3}}$
g. $19^{-0.5}$
h. $(\sqrt{8}) \times (\sqrt{2})$
i. $19^{\frac{2}{3}}$
j. 6.04^5
k. $\sqrt{27}$
l. $(3.2 \times 10^2)^2$
m. $64^{\frac{3}{2}}$
n. $X^2 - 3X$, where $X = 6$
o. $5.225^{-0.5}$
p. $\sqrt{106}$
q. $84^{-1.5}$
r. $64^{.25}$
s. $\sqrt{144}$
t. $2^{-2.5}$

3. You have four 10 Ω resistances that can be put together in any combination. How many different resistant values can you obtain by various connections?

4. What is the smallest number of resistances you would need to construct all the whole number resistance values from 1 to 10? What are the values of the resistances you would need?

5. Your stairway is dark so you decide to put a small lamp in the middle of it. But you want to turn the light on or off using switches at the top and the bottom of the stairs. Draw the schematic of a circuit that will do this using a minimum number of parts.

6. The wires from the distribution panel to an outlet in a lab are AWG 16 wire. What is the maximum power dissipation of the load that can be attached to the outlet? Use Table 6.3.

7. Consult local and national electrical codes for recommended wire gauge sizes for residential and light industrial loads.

8. Prepare a list of the rated power consumption of some of the appliances in your home (power requirements are often marked on a label on the back of the appliance or in the instruction manual.)

CHAPTER 7

CIRCUIT ANALYSIS AND PRACTICAL RESISTORS

A. CHAPTER PREVIEW

1 This chapter will improve your ability to analyze circuits by introducing another method of mapping electric circuits and two extensions of Ohm's law. These two extensions are called Kirchhoff's laws. They are based on very simple principles, although they are capable of sophisticated applications.

2 The Examples and Computations section presents topics that will be of use in this and later chapters. These are graphs, angles, and the solution of equations with more than one unknown quantity.

3 This section also discusses tolerance, a subject required to work with the practical components discussed in the Applications section.

4 The Applications section is an introduction to the resistor, a very commonly used component. You will learn what a resistor is, and what its uses are. You will learn to recognize types of fixed and variable resistors and how to read the codes for resistance value, power rating, and other essential information.

B. PRINCIPLES

B.1 INTRODUCTION TO CIRCUIT ANALYSIS

The skills you have developed in calculating potential difference, current, resistance, and power in circuits are the basis for a subject called *circuit analysis*. Circuit analysis is important for both the design and troubleshooting of electrical and electronic circuits. When used in circuit design, circuit analysis techniques enable the engineer or design technician to calculate the component values that must be used to obtain the potential or current required at different points in a circuit. The maintenance technician uses circuit analysis techniques to determine the current or potential that should be present at various points. Comparing these calculated values with those actually measured can help the technician find faulty components quickly.

Circuit analysis has a point of view and a set of technical terms that concentrate on the way in which components are connected. Consider the schematic diagrams shown in Figure 7.1. Although these diagrams look quite different, electrically they are the same. Each schematic diagram, regardless of the way in which the symbols are placed, represents a *network* or arrangement of four resistances and one source. Circuit analysis views the components in the network as though they were connected at specific points, called either *nodes* or *junctions*. This may seem curious at first because real components are connected by wires or strips of copper on a printed circuit. But recall that there are no wires in a schematic diagram. The symbols for the various components such as resistances, switches, and sources are connected by lines of arbitrary length that show current paths. In short, the connecting lines between the graphic symbols on a schematic diagram can be thought of as elongated "points" of connection between the components or circuit elements. A point of this sort, at which two or more components are connected, is called a *node*. The term *junction* is generally used for a node at which three elements are connected. The electrical similarity of the schematics shown in Figure 7.1, as well as the concepts of node and junction, become clearer if a *network graph* is drawn.

Figure 7.1 Four schematic representations of the same circuit.

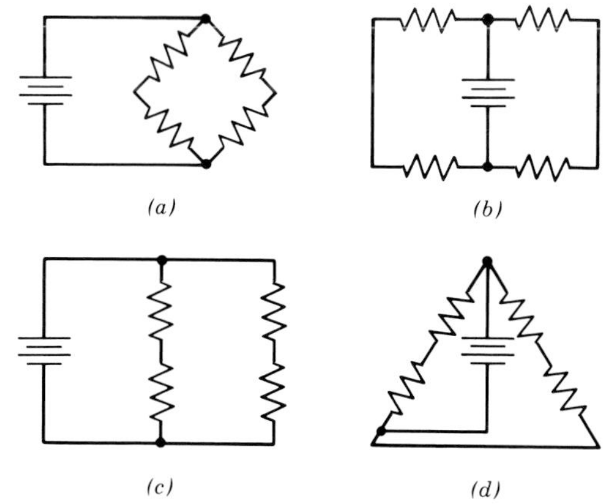

B.2 NETWORK GRAPHING

Figure 7.2*a* shows the pictorial diagram of a circuit composed of a number of different components. Some of the components, such as the resistors studied in Section D of this chapter, have lead wires for connection to other components. Others, like the lamp, require a socket and lengths of wire for connection. All these leads have some resistance, but in most circuits of this kind, the resistance is small and is ignored. In the schematic diagram of this circuit, Figure 7.2*b*, the components have been replaced by symbols connected by lines. The lines themselves may be of any shape or length and are representations of connections, not actually symbols for wires with actual resistance. In addition to the fact that the resistance of hook-up wires is small, it is also hard to show the resistance of a wire as a symbol. This is because there is no one place where the resistance exists, rather it is distributed along the length of the wire. When wire resistance is important, it is necessary to pretend that it is to be found at some point, and may be symbolized by a resistance symbol, as though it was a load. A load which is not really a component and does not have its resistance in

Figure 7.2 A circuit and its schematic diagram.

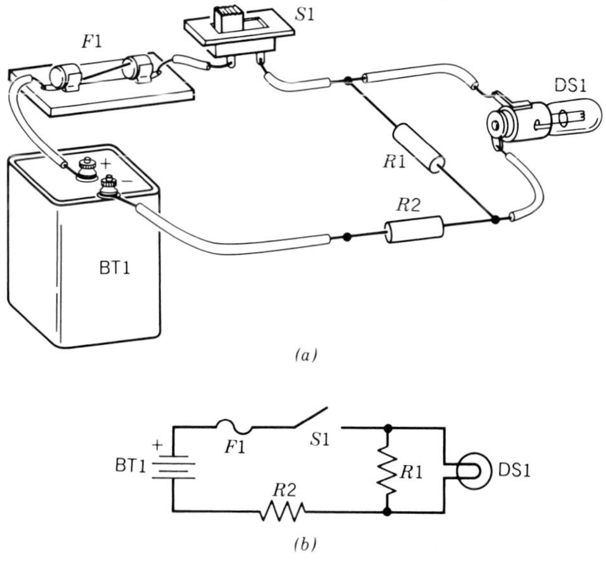

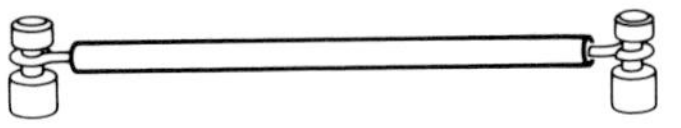

(a) Pictorial

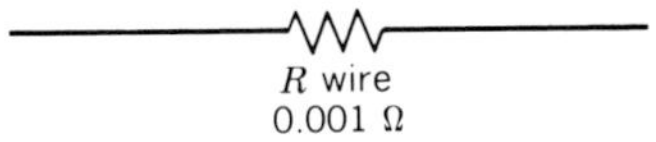

(b) Schematic showing wire as "lumped" load

(c) Schematic showing wire as distributed load

Figure 7.3 Ways of showing a distributed load on a schematic diagram.

a particular place in a circuit is called a *distributed load*. When it is drawn as a single symbol, however, it is frequently called a *lumped load,* that is, a distributed resistance which is considered to exist at a particular point, as shown in Figure 7.3*b*. The remaining lines on the schematic are then considered to be resistanceless current paths. In the few cases where it is especially important that the wire resistance is recognized as a distributed load, a series of resistance symbols can be shown, as in Figure 7.3*c*. From this you can see that the straight lines connecting the symbols in schematic diagrams are abstractions, that is, convenient constructions that only resemble reality.

It is possible to carry this kind of abstraction one step further and to produce a diagram like that shown in Figure 7.4. This type of diagram is called a *network graph*. It is particularly valuable in circuit analysis, and it is sometimes useful for making sense of a poorly arranged or overly complex schematic. In a network graph, all the schematic symbols are replaced by curved lines, labeled with their reference designators such as F1, R2, DS1, and the connecting lines of the schematic have been shrunk to single points.

Using the network graph, it is easy to recognize the nodes *A*, *B*, and *E* and junctions *C* and *D* in the network in Figure 7.4 since it emphasizes the interconnection of the components. Note also that tiny plus and minus signs are placed at the ends of the curve

Figure 7.4 Network graph of the circuit shown in Figure 7.2.

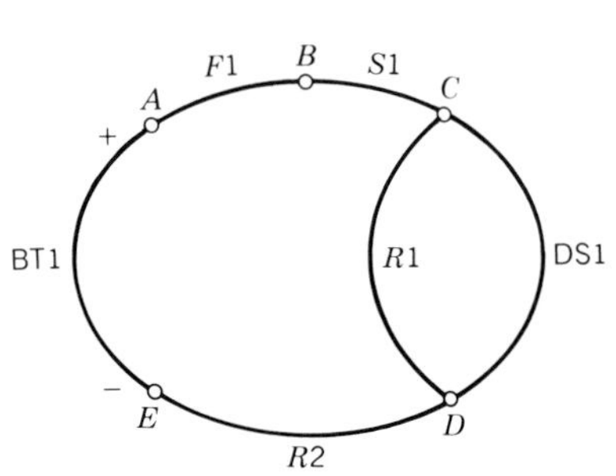

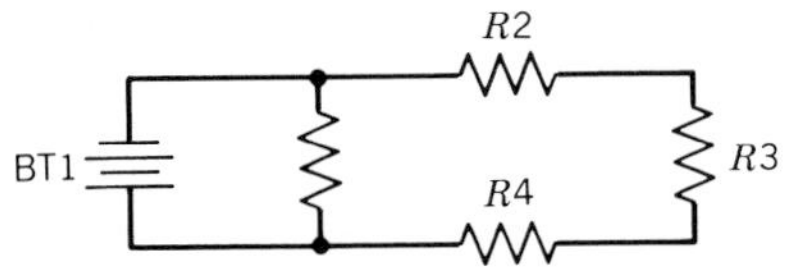

(a) Schematic diagram

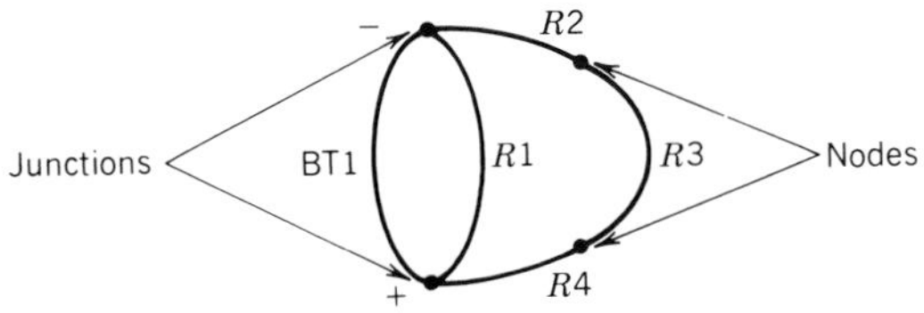

(b) Network graph

Figure 7.5 Recognizing branches in a network graph.

representing BT1, the source. This is done to facilitate the analysis of the network.

Network graphs also make it easier to define the branches and loops in a network. For the purposes of circuit analysis, a *branch* is defined as the portion of a network between two junctions. For example, there are three branches in the network graph shown in Figure 7.5*b*: (1) BT1, (2) *R*1, and (3) *R*2–*R*3–*R*4. A *loop,* which is also called a mesh, is defined as a complete path traced through a network without backtracking, back to its beginning point. Two loops or meshes are considered different if there is at least one element (a line in a network graph) that is found in only one of them. Beginning at point *A* in Figure 7.6, there are three different loops: (1) *R*1–*R*3–BT1, (2) *R*2–*R*4–BT1, and (3) *R*2–*R*4–*R*3–*R*1.

Another use for the network graph is the simplification of schematic diagrams. This is possible because the element lines used to represent components can be lengthened, shortened, or rearranged if the way in which these lines are interconnected is not changed. Figure 7.7*a–d* shows a number of possible ways in which the network graph can be redrawn. It is not difficult to see that all the element lines are connected at the same nodes or junctions in each graph. Drawing network graphs is frequently an easy way of comparing two schematic diagrams to see if they are the same.

EXAMPLE:
Do the schematic diagrams shown in Figure 7.8*a* and 7.8*b* represent the same network? ■

Figure 7.6 Recognizing loops in a network graph.

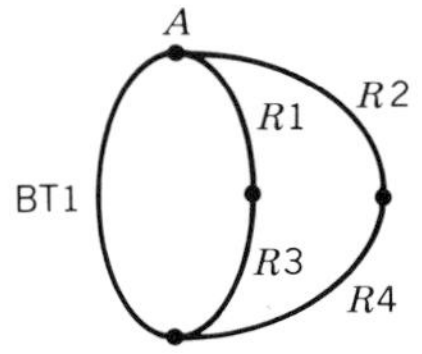

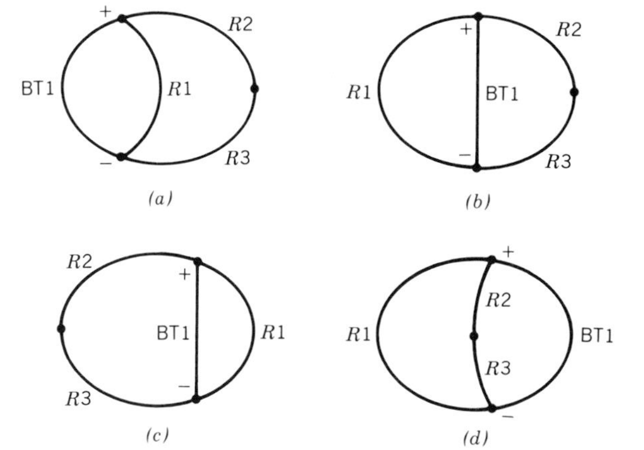

Figure 7.7 As long as the interconnection of the element lines in a network graph is not changed, it may be redrawn in any way.

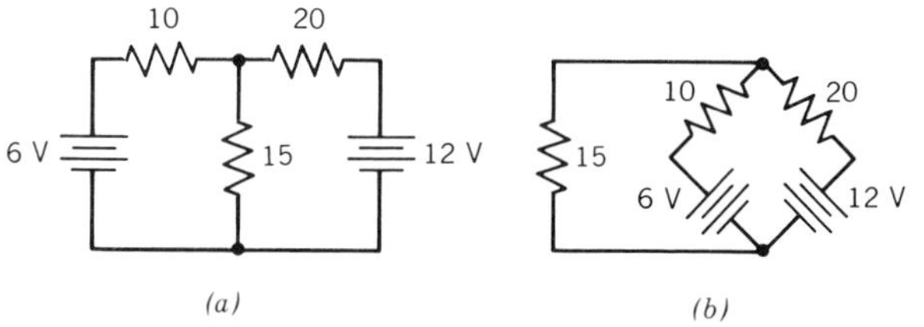

Figure 7.8 Do these two schematic diagrams represent the same network?

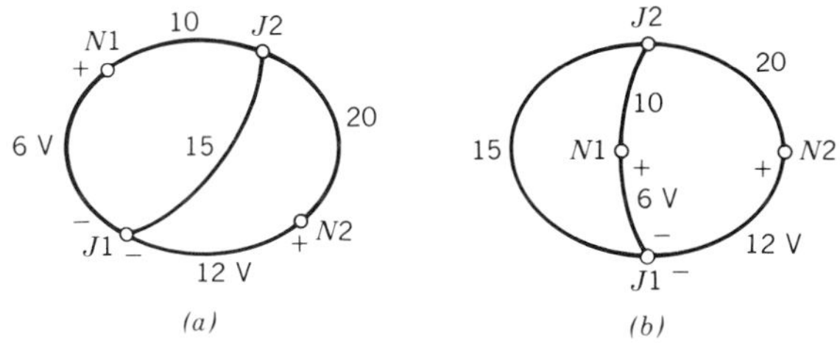

Figure 7.9 The network graphs of the schematics shown in Figure 7.8.

SOLUTION:
Draw the network graphs of both schematics by replacing the connecting lines with dots and the graphic symbols for the components with curved lines as shown in Figure 7.9*a* and 7.9*b*. Except for the location of the 15Ω resistance line, the two are identical; that is, the interconnection is exactly the same, as can be seen by comparing the connection of the element lines at the nodes and junctions. ■

B.3 VOLTAGE RISES AND VOLTAGE DROPS

The potential at the various nodes and junctions in a circuit is one of the key pieces of information about the circuit. The potential of an electron drifting through

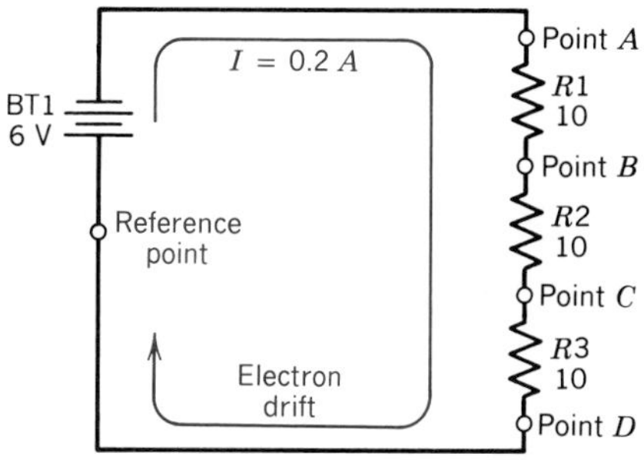

Figure 7.10 Voltage rises and voltage drops in a circuit.

circuit loads is described, as you know, by Ohm's law. Consider the circuit of Figure 7.10. Electrons leave the negative terminal of the battery with a certain potential. Taking the positive terminal of the battery as the point of reference, or zero potential point, the electrons possess a potential of 6 V at the negative pole. That is, the potential difference between the negative and positive poles of the battery is 6 V. While drifting through *R*1, the electrons lose some of this energy since the potential of an electron at point *B* is less (closer to zero) than that at point *A*. The amount of this potential loss, or voltage drop, can be calculated using Ohm's law:

$$E_{\text{potential drop}} = I_{\text{circuit}} \times R1$$
$$E = 0.2 \times 10$$
$$= 2 \text{ V}$$

The loss in potential across *R*1 is 2 V. In other words, the potential at point *B* is 2 V closer to zero, or more positive, than it is at point *A*. The potential difference between point *B* and the reference point, then, is 4 V. Similarly, the voltage drops across *R*2 and *R*3, according to Ohm's law, are also 2 V. The potential difference between point *C* and the reference point is 2 V. When the electrons have drifted through *R*3, they are at the same potential as the reference point (the resistance of wires being disregarded.) Therefore, the potential difference between point *D* and the reference is 0 V. Thus, an electron traveling from the negative terminal of the source to its positive terminal through *R*1, *R*2, and *R*3 has passed through a *potential drop* of 6 V, from −6 V to zero:

$$E_{\text{drop total}} = E_{\text{drop } R1} + E_{\text{drop } R2} + E_{\text{drop } R3}$$

From the positive terminal of the battery, these electrons are transferred back to the negative terminal by application of chemical energy. During this process, the electrons undergo a *potential rise* from 0 to −6 V.

It is important to remember that when you are using the electron drift convention, a potential drop is de-

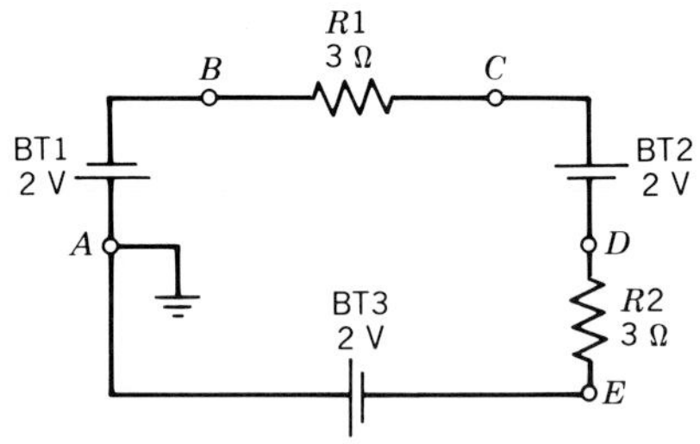

Figure 7.11 Calculating voltage rises and voltage drops around a closed loop.

fined as the loss of energy of an electron when it moves from a more negative point to a more positive point (that is, a point at which the potential is closer to zero).

EXAMPLE:
Show the potential drops and rises in the loop from point A through points B, C, D, E, and back to A in Figure 7.11. ■

SOLUTION:
In order to determine the potential or voltage drops using Ohm's law, it is necessary to calculate the circuit current. Since the circuit of Figure 7.11 is a series circuit, the two series resistances can be added directly to yield a total circuit resistance of 6 Ω. If careful notice is paid to the direction of the electric field of the three cells, these may be added also

$$\begin{aligned} E_{\text{total}} &= E_{\text{BT1}} + E_{\text{BT2}} - E_{\text{BT3}} \\ &= 2 + 2 - 2 \\ &= 2 \text{ V} \end{aligned}$$

The circuit current then is $\frac{2}{6}$ or 0.333 A, and the direction of the current is from A through B, C, D, and E. Tracing the circuit from point A to B, you enter the positive terminal of cell BT1 and leave it through the negative terminal. An electron moving this way would experience a potential *rise* of 2 V. Since this rise means that the electron will be at a more negative potential, a negative sign is given to the change in voltage

$$E_{A \text{ to } B} = -2 \text{ V}$$

In passing from point B to point C, an electron loses a potential equal to $I \times R1$ or $3.0 \times 0.333 = 0.999$ V (rounded off to 1 V). Since the electron is moving from a more negative to a more positive point, its potential at point C will be closer to zero

$$E_{B \text{ to } C} = +1 \text{ V}$$

From A to C, then, the potential is

$$E_{A \text{ to } B} + E_{B \text{ to } C} = -2 + 1 \quad \text{or} \quad -1 \text{ V}$$

From C to D, drifting electrons again enter the positive pole of a cell and leave the negative pole, experiencing a voltage rise of 2 V, or

$$E_{C \text{ to } D} = -2 \text{ V}$$

Therefore,

$$\begin{aligned} E_{A \text{ to } D} &= E_{A \text{ to } B} + E_{B \text{ to } C} + E_{C \text{ to } D} \\ &= -2 + 1 - 2 \\ &= -3 \text{ V} \end{aligned}$$

From D to E, resistance $R2$ provides a voltage drop of $E = IR$ volts, or

$$E_{D \text{ to } E} = 0.333 \times 3.0 = 0.999$$

Rounding off, $E_{D \text{ to } E} = +1$ V, and

$$\begin{aligned} E_{A \text{ to } E} &= E_{A \text{ to } B} + E_{B \text{ to } C} + E_{C \text{ to } D} + E_{D \text{ to } E} \\ &= -2 + 1 - 2 + 1 \\ &= -2 \text{ V} \end{aligned}$$

Between points E and A, the drifting electrons enter the *negative* terminal of a cell and leave through its positive terminal. Cell BT3 is in series opposing and its electric field impedes the drift of electrons, so a voltage *drop* exists between points E and A,

$$E_{E \text{ to } A} = +2 \text{ V}$$

The potential around the entire loop is then $E_{\text{loop}} = E_{A \text{ to } B} + E_{B \text{ to } C} + E_{C \text{ to } D} + E_{D \text{ to E}} + E_{E \text{ to } A}$

$$\begin{aligned} &= -2 + 1 - 2 + 1 + 2 \\ &= 0 \end{aligned}$$

The fact that the sum of the voltage rises and voltage drops around the loop is zero is not an accident, as will be shown in the next section. ■

B.4 KIRCHHOFF'S VOLTAGE LAW

In 1847, about 20 years after the discovery of Ohm's law, Gustav Kirchhoff (pronounced Keerk-hoff) published a statement of the two laws that are named after him. Kirchhoff's laws, like Ohm's law, are mathematical descriptions of the behavior of electric circuits.

Kirchhoff's first law, called the *voltage law,* was introduced in the last section. Stated simply, Kirchhoff's voltage law is: *Around a loop or mesh in a circuit, the sum of the voltage drops and voltage rises is zero*. This is actually a way of saying that the potential difference produced by the sources in a network is used up in producing a drift of electrons through the components in the circuit.

Compare the circuit shown in Figure 7.12 with that of 7.11. In spite of the fact that the circuit of Figure

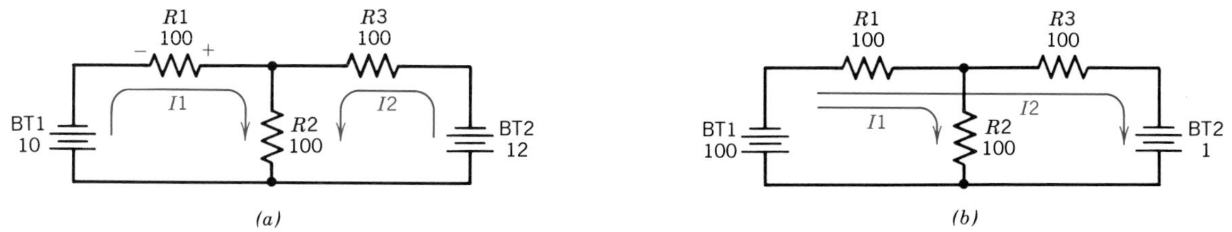

Figure 7.12 A circuit that can not be analyzed by Ohm's law alone.

7.11 had three sources, these were arranged to form a simple series circuit. This is not the case in the circuit of Figure 7.12. It is not possible to use Ohm's law alone in this circuit to calculate the current through each of the resistances. Kirchhoff's voltage law provides the additional information needed before Ohm's law can be used in this circuit. Each of the two sources shown produces an electric field that causes a drift of electrons, seemingly in the direction of the arrows. There is, however, no assurance that these directions are correct. In fact, if the potential difference supplied by BT1 was much greater than that of BT2, the electron drift directions would more likely resemble those of Figure 7.12*b*.

The first step in applying Kirchhoff's voltage law to the circuit of Figure 7.12*a* is to assign a direction and name to each of the currents in the circuit. The actual direction chosen is not important. For example, in Figure 7.12*a*, I_1 is assumed to be clockwise through *R*1 and I_2 to be counterclockwise through *R*3. With these directions selected, both I_1 and I_2 must pass through *R*2 in the same direction. It would *not* be correct to assign a clockwise direction to I_1 as it passes through *R*1 but a counterclockwise direction to the same current through *R*2. If you are consistent in the way the direction is chosen, the solution of the Kirchhoff's law statement will show whether or not your direction is correct. If you chose the correct direction, the solution will be a positive number. This means that the current does indeed flow in the selected direction. If, on the other hand, the solution is a negative number, the true direction of that current is the opposite of the one you chose. For example, if the solution for I_2 in Figure 7.12*a* came out to be −0.5 A, this would mean that the actual current in that part of the circuit was 0.5 A in a clockwise direction.

The first step in applying Kirchhoff's voltage law is to assign a direction and name to each of the currents in the circuit.

The next step in applying Kirchhoff's voltage law can be simplified by drawing a polarity diagram for the circuit. This can be done directly on the schematic diagram, as shown in Figure 7.13*a*, or on a network graph as shown in Figure 7.13*b*. Whichever method you choose, this should be done as soon as the directions for the various currents in the circuit have been chosen. The polarities of sources are usually shown in the schematic diagram, so there is no choice involved. The polarities of the other components can be determined from the direction taken by the electrons drifting through them. The end of the component or element that the electrons are assumed to enter is the negative end. The end the electrons leave is the positive end. If the selected current direction was not correct, the symbols can be reversed.

In cases where more than one current flows through a component or element, there are two possibilities. If all the currents through an element pass through in the same direction, there is no difficulty in determining the polarity of that element. All the electrons enter at the negative end and leave at the positive end. If the currents through an element do not all flow in the same direction, the polarity of that element is determined by what is assumed to be the direction of the larger current, as shown in Figure 7.14*b* and 7.14*c*. In this figure, it is assumed that the current caused by the electric field of BT2 and BT3, I_2, will be greater than I_1, the current caused by BT1, which flows through *R*3 and BT2 in the opposite direction.

The second step in applying Kirchhoff's voltage law is to mark the component polarities on either the schematic diagram or a network graph.

Figure 7.13 Polarity diagrams for the circuit of Figure 7.12*a*.

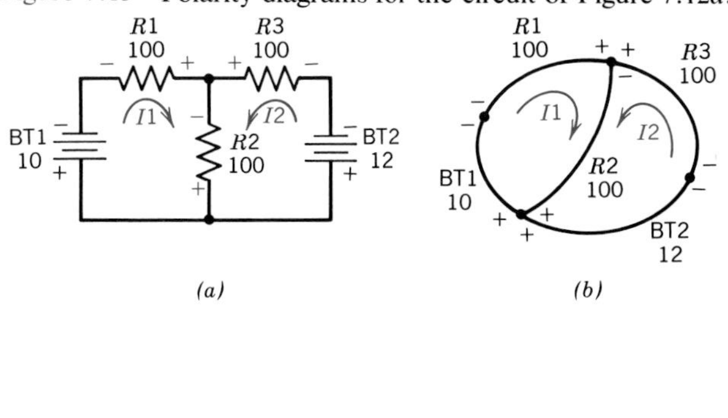

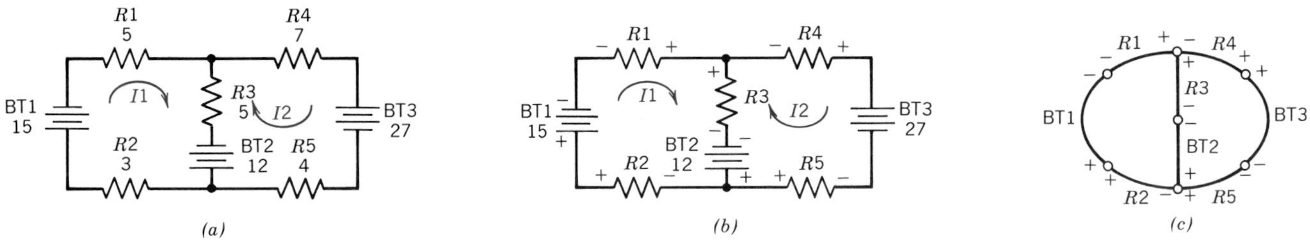

Figure 7.14 In an element or component in which the current flows are not in the same direction, the polarity is determined by the most current.

Returning to the circuit of Figure 7.12*a*, the third step in applying Kirchhoff's voltage law is to determine the number of mathematical statements or equations that you need to write. This number is equal to the number of independent unknown quantities in the circuit. There are two unknown quantities in the circuit of Figure 7.12*a*, I_1 and I_2. The current through *R*2 is also unknown, but it is not independent since it is the sum of I_1 and I_2. Three different closed loops can be traced through this circuit without backtracking:

a. BT1–*R*1–*R*2 and back to BT1.
b. BT2–*R*3–*R*2 and back to BT2.
c. BT1–*R*1–*R*3–BT2 and back to BT1.

The third step in a voltage law analysis is to determine the number of mathematical statements (equations) required to relate the unknown quantities. This number is equal to the number of independent unknown currents.

The last step in the process of applying Kirchhoff's voltage law to this circuit to determine I_1 and I_2 is to write the statement of what happens in two of the loops. It is possible to trace through a loop in any direction, so long as there is some consistency. Some books suggest tracing through each loop in a clockwise direction to prevent confusion. Actually, it is probably easier to trace in the assumed direction of the electron drift. Recall that the statement of the voltage law was that the sum of the voltage drops and the voltage rises around a closed loop is zero.

In the loop composed of BT1, *R*1, and *R*2, the only voltage rise is E_{BT1}. The voltage drop across *R*1 according to Ohm's law is

$$E_{R1} = I_1 R1$$

$$E_{R1} = 100 I_1$$

Calculating the voltage drop across *R*2 is not quite as simple since both I_1 and I_2 flow through *R*2. Still, Ohm's law applies, and since I_1 and I_2 flow through *R*2 in the same direction, that is, from its negative end to its positive end,

$$E_{R2} = I \times R$$

$$= 100(I_1 + I_2)$$

or

$$E_{R2} = 100 I_1 + 100 I_2$$

Since you now have expressions for all the voltage rises and drops in this loop, it is possible to write

$$-E_{\mathrm{BT1}} + E_{\mathrm{R1}} + E_{R2} = 0$$

Notice that the voltage rise is given a negative sign, while the voltage drops have positive signs. Substituting the expressions for the voltage rises and drops,

$$-10 + 100 I_1 + 100(I_1 + I_2) = 0$$

or

$$10 = 200 I_1 + 100 I_2 \quad \text{(loop 1 equation)}$$

For the loop composed of BT2, *R*3, and *R*2, tracing the loop in the assumed direction of the current, the path enters *R*3 at the negative end and leaves through the positive end. E_{R3} should then be written into the equation as a voltage drop, or $+E_{R3}$. The same is true of the path through R_2. It is only the source, BT2, that acts as a voltage rise if the path through the loop is traced in this direction. The loop equation is

$$-E_{\mathrm{BT2}} + E_{R3} + E_{R2} = 0$$

Substituting the values,

$$-12 + 100 I_2 + 100(I_1 + I_2) = 0$$

or,

$$-12 + 200 I_2 + 100 I_1 = 0$$

transposing

$$12 = 100 I_1 + 200 I_2 \quad \text{(loop 2 equation)}$$

You now have two equations, or mathematical descriptions, of this circuit that have two unknown quantities, I_1 and I_2, in them. In algebra, two or more equations with the same unknown quantities are called *simultaneous equations*. If you have as many equations as there are unknown quantities, and if the equations are truly different (that is, they are not just restatements of each other, such as multiplying both sides of one equation by 2), it is possible to solve them and find the values of the unknown quantities. There are various ways to do this. One of the most general, and least likely to get you more involved in mathematical computation than electrical circuit analysis, is presented in the Examples and Computations section of this chapter.

For now, a method of solving simultaneous equations called *the substitution method* will be used. Begin by writing the two voltage law equations:

1. $10 = 200I_1 + 100I_2$.

2. $12 = 100I_1 + 200I_2$.

Now, equation 2 can be transposed so that one of the unknowns, say I_1, appears alone on the left side of the equation:

$$12 = 100I_1 + 200I_2$$

Subtracting 12 from both sides yields

$$0 = 100I_1 + 200I_2 - 12$$

Subtracting $100I_1$ from both sides,

$$-100I_1 = 200I_2 - 12$$

Dividing both sides by 100,

$$-I_1 = 2I_2 - 0.12$$

And finally, multiplying both sides by -1,

$$I_1 = -2I_2 + 0.12$$

Now, you can take this statement of what I_1 is equal to and substitute the value $-2I_2 + 0.12$ for I_1 in equation 1.

$$10 = 200\,(-2I_2 + 0.12) + 100I_2$$

Notice that this gives you an equation with only *one* unknown quantity, I_2. Solving,

$$10 = -400I_2 + 24 + 100I_2$$

$$10 = -300I_2 + 24$$

$$300I_2 + 10 = 24$$

$$300I_2 = 14$$

$$I_2 = \frac{14}{300} = 0.0467 \text{ A}$$

Now you have a value for one of the unknown currents. This value can be substituted in either equation 1 or 2 to calculate I_1. Using equation 1

$$10 = 200I_1 + 100I_2$$

$$10 = 200I_1 + 100\,(0.0467)$$

$$10 = 200I_1 + 4.67$$

$$5.33 = 200I_1$$

$$0.0267 = I_1$$

Knowing the two currents, it is now possible to calculate the voltage drops across the resistances, or the power dissipations.

The last step in a Kirchhoff's law analysis is to write and solve the loop equations for the value of each unknown current.

If battery BT2 is connected in the opposite way, as shown in Figure 7.15, the electron drift called I_2 can also be assumed to have reversed. Now the two currents through $R2$ will be in opposite directions. In this case, the circuit currents will be different, but the way in which the Kirchhoff law statements are obtained is still the same. For loop 1, the voltage rise provided by BT1 is 10 V, and the voltage drop across $R1$ is $100 \times I_1$. Since the two currents flow through $R2$ in opposite directions, the voltage drop across $R2$ is $100(I_1 - I_2)$, although it would have been equally correct to write $100(I_2 - I_1)$.

Therefore, the first equation is

$$10 = 100I_1 + 100(I_1 - I_2) \quad \text{or} \quad 10 = 200I_1 - 100I_2$$

For the second equation, going around the loop in the assumed current direction, there is a 12-V voltage rise across BT2. There is also a voltage rise through $R2$ since the path enters the positive end of the component and leaves through the negative end. The potential difference across this component is therefore a voltage rise of $100(I_1 - I_2)$, written as $-100(I_1 - I_2)$ in the voltage law equation for loop 2. The potential difference E_{R3} across $R3$ is a voltage drop of $100I_2$. The

Figure 7.15 Reversing the connection of BT2 in Figure 7.12*a*.

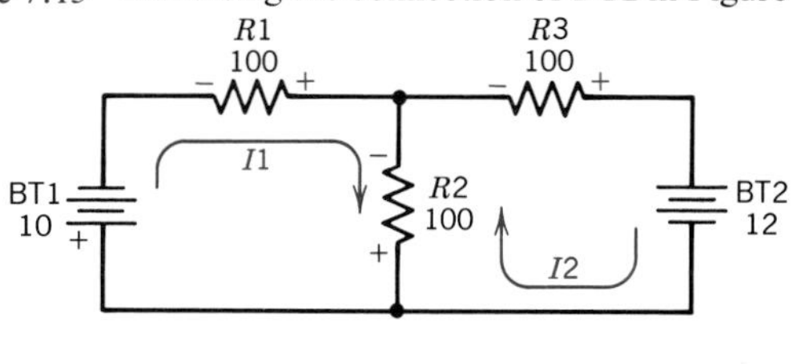

second equation then is

$$-E_{BT2} - E_{R2} + E_{R3} = 0$$

$$-12 - 100(I_1 - I_2) + 100I_2 = 0$$

or

$$12 = -100I_1 + 200I_2$$

The values of I_1 and I_2 can be calculated using the same method as the previous example. The second equation is transposed so that I_1 appears alone on the left side of the equation:

$$12 = -100I_1 + 200I_2$$

Adding $100I_1$ to both sides gives

$$12 + 100I_1 = 200I_2$$

Subtracting 12 from both sides,

$$100I_1 = 200I_2 - 12$$

Finally, dividing both sides by 100 gives

$$I_1 = 2I_2 - 0.12$$

Substituting this expression for I_1 in the first equation,

$$10 = 200I_1 - 100I_2$$

$$10 = 200(2I_2 - 0.12) - 100I_2$$

or

$$10 = 400I_2 - 24 - 100I_2$$

Simplifying,

$$34 = 300I_2, \quad \text{or} \quad I_2 = 0.113 \text{ A}$$

Since you now know the value of I_2, you can substitute it in either of the original equations

$$12 = -100I_1 + 200I_2$$

or

$$12 = -100I_1 + 200(0.113)$$

Solving,

$$I_1 = 0.106 \text{ A}.$$

Additional practice in applying Kirchhoff's voltage law equation will be given in the Examples and Computations section.

B.5 KIRCHHOFF'S CURRENT LAW

Although it is sometimes hard to apply, Kirchhoff's voltage law is based on a very simple principle: the sum of the voltage drops and voltage rises around any closed loop in a network is equal to zero. Kirchhoff's second rule, called *the current law,* is based on an

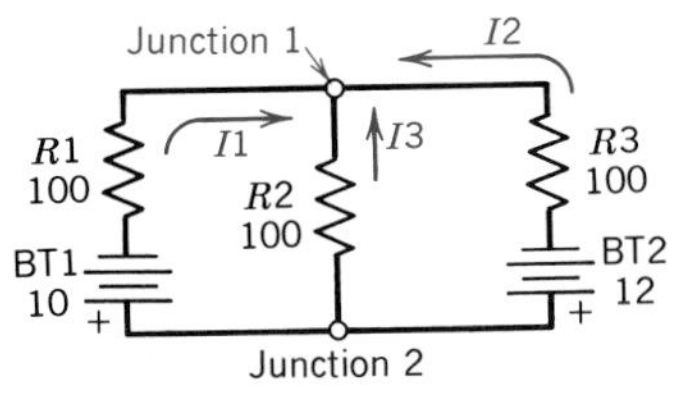

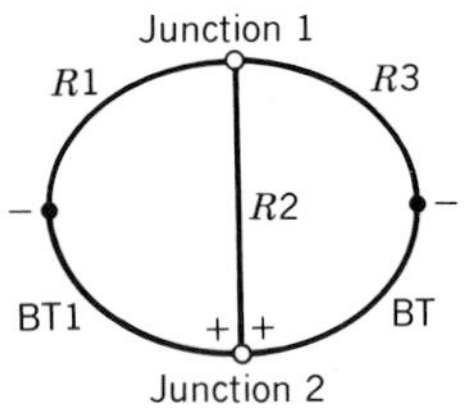

Figure 7.16 The circuit of Figure 7.12*a* arranged for Kirchhoff's current law analysis.

equally simple idea: *At any node or junction in a circuit, the sum of the currents entering a node or junction is equal to the sum of the currents leaving.* This can be stated in a very simple way mathematically:

$$I_{in} = I_{out} \quad \text{or} \quad I_{in} - I_{out} = 0 \qquad \text{FORMULA 7.1}$$

Because current law analysis considers the current into or out of junctions, it is frequently called *nodal analysis,* although *junction analysis* would be a better name.

Like the voltage law, Kirchhoff's current law can be used with series networks, but it is particularly helpful when used to determine potential difference and current in parallel networks. Figure 7.16 shows the identical schematic and network graph of the circuit of Figure 7.12*a*, but in this figure the parallel quality of the branches has been emphasized by the arrangement of the symbols. From the network graph, you can see that this circuit has three branches and two junctions. Any network will have one less current law equation than its network graph has junctions. Therefore, the circuit of Figure 7.16 can be described with a single equation with only one unknown quantity. This is true because the current law expresses currents in terms of junction voltages. One of the two junctions in Figure 7.16*b* is the reference junction, or ground junction, because the potential at the other junction is calculated in comparison with its potential. A circuit without junctions is a simple series circuit, and Ohm's law can be applied directly.

The reference junction in a nodal analysis is generally any junction that is grounded. Where no ground connection is present in the circuit, the junction with the most connections is chosen to be the reference junction. Since a current law equation is not written for the reference junction, choosing the one with the most connections as the reference can simplify matters considerably. Both junctions 1 and 2 in Figure 7.16*b* are formed by the connection of three elements. Therefore, there is no advantage in choosing one over the other as a reference. Junction 2 has been used as the reference because it is connected to the positive terminals of both sources.

The first step in a Kirchhoff's current law analysis is to choose a reference junction.

Once the reference junction has been chosen, it is possible to look at the currents at the remaining junction or junctions. As in the case of voltage law analysis, current directions can be assigned even if you are not sure of the actual direction. If the assigned direction is wrong, this will be shown by a negative sign in the solution for the value of the current.

The second step in a current law analysis is assigning directions to the current flowing into and out of each junction.

Figure 7.16*a* shows the directions arbitrarily assigned to the currents flowing into junction 1. Since the circuit in Figure 7.16 is a parallel circuit, the potential difference across all of its branches is the same. This means that the branch currents, I_1, I_2, and I_3, can all be expressed in terms of a single quantity, V_A, the potential at junction 1 with respect to junction 2, the reference junction. For branch 1, composed of BT1 and *R*1, the expression relating V_A to I_1 can be obtained by summing the potential drops and rises between junction 1 and the reference junction. Remember that a voltage rise is given a minus sign and a potential drop is given a positive value when you are using the electron drift convention. At junction 1, the potential is V_A. Working from the reference junction to junction 1 along branch 1, a voltage rise of 10 V and a voltage drop of $100I_1$ are encountered. Since the potential at the reference junction is zero, it is possible to write:

$$0 - 10 + 100I_1 = V_A$$

This expression is easy to solve for I_1:

$$100I_1 = V_A + 10 \quad \text{or} \quad I_1 = \frac{V_A + 10}{100} \qquad \text{(Expression 1)}$$

For branch 2, composed only of *R*2, V_A is equal to the voltage drop across *R*2, or

$$V_A = 100I_3, \text{ and } I_3 = \frac{V_A}{100} \qquad \text{(Expression 2)}$$

Finally, for branch 3, composed of BT2 and *R*3, V_A is equal to the sum of the potential difference supplied by BT2 and the voltage drop across *R*3:

$$V_A = -12 + 100I_2$$

Solving for I_2:

$$I_2 = \frac{V_A + 12}{100} \qquad \text{(Expression 3)}$$

The third step in performing a current law analysis is to substitute these values for the branch currents in Formula 7.1. This produces a single equation with only one unknown:

$$\frac{V_A + 10}{100} + \frac{V_A}{100} + \frac{V_A + 12}{100} = 0$$

Multiplying through by 100:

$$V_A + 10 + V_A + V_A + 12 = 0$$

Collecting terms and transposing:

$$3V_A = -22 \quad \text{or} \quad V_A = -7.33 \text{ V}$$

Using this value for V_A, Expressions 1, 2, and 3 can be solved to yield the branch currents.
Expression 1:

$$I_1 = \frac{V_A + 10}{100} = 0.0267 \text{ A}$$

Expression 2:

$$I_3 = \frac{V_A}{100} = -0.0733 \text{ A}$$

Expression 3:

$$I_2 = \frac{V_A + 12}{100} = 0.0467 \text{ A}$$

The negative value obtained for I_3 means that this current is flowing out of junction 1. These values are exactly those obtained for I_1 and I_2 using the voltage law in the analysis of the circuit of Figure 7.12*a*.

The final step in a current law analysis is to substitute the branch expressions into the basic statement of Kirchhoff's current law

$$I_{in} = I_{out} \quad \text{or} \quad I_{in} - I_{out} = 0$$

and then to solve for the junction potential and individual branch currents.

C. EXAMPLES AND COMPUTATIONS

C.1 GRAPHS

The section on network graphs may have been somewhat misleading because a network graph is actually not a graph. It is called that to distinguish it from sche-

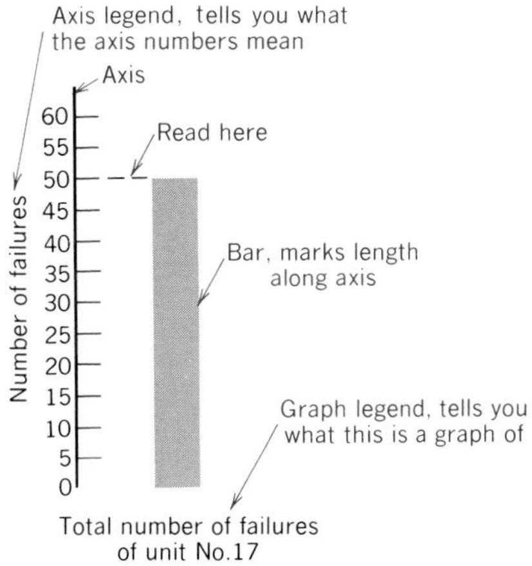

Figure 7.17 A simple form of graph.

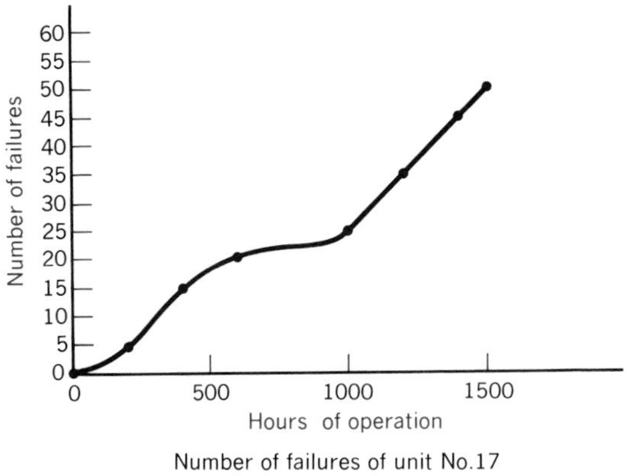

Figure 7.19 Connecting the points plotted on a graph can provide additional information.

matic and interconnect diagrams. A true graph is a drawing that represents the numerical value or values of a quantity. The simplest sort consists of a single line, called an *axis,* and a bar, line, or dot that marks the correct place on the axis, as shown in Figure 7.17. This graph shows the number of failures of an imaginary electronic unit. The bar, which marks a length along the numbered axis, shows that 50 failures have occurred. No information is given about the period of time over which the unit failed. To present information about two related quantities, another sort of graph is needed. This type is shown in Figure 7.18. Here, there are two axes, one for the number of failures and one for the time, that is, the number of hours of operation. Traditionally, the horizontal axis, here used to mark time, is called the *x axis,* and the vertical axis is called the *y axis*. A point is placed on a line drawn upward from the time as shown on the x axis at a distance showing the number of failures on the y axis. Taking

Figure 7.18 Graphing the number of failures during a particular number of hours of operation requires a graph with two axes.

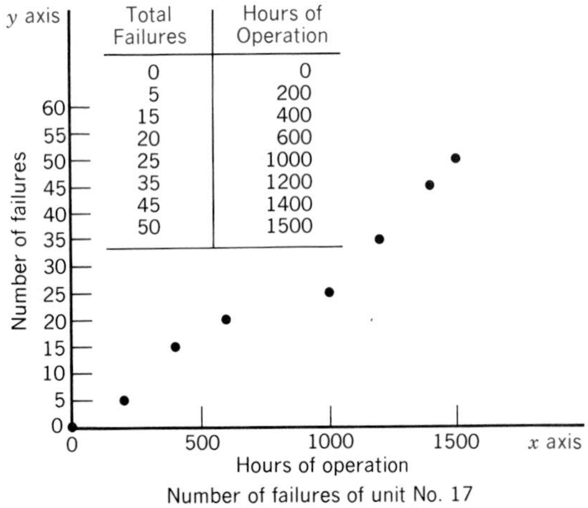

Total Failures	Hours of Operation
0	0
5	200
15	400
20	600
25	1000
35	1200
45	1400
50	1500

these numbers from a chart and marking them on the graph is called *plotting*. Notice that the numbers on the two axes are placed in a linear manner, that is, each interval between the numbers on the y axis represents five failures, and each interval on the x axis represents 500 hours of operation.

Once the points on the graph have been plotted, it is customary to connect them with either straight-line segments or with a smoothly curved line as in Figure 7.19. These lines can be quite useful, both for guessing at information you do not have and for analyzing and making use of the information presented by the graph.

For example, the graph of Figure 7.19 permits you to make a reasonable guess at the total number of failures that had occurred when the unit had been in operation for 300 hours, even though this is not recorded on the table from which the graph was drawn. Find the point on the x axis that corresponds to 300 hours and trace a line straight up. At the point at which this line crosses, or *intersects* the line connecting the plotted points, a horizontal line drawn to the y axis will permit reading the approximate number of failures

Figure 7.20 Estimating from a graph.

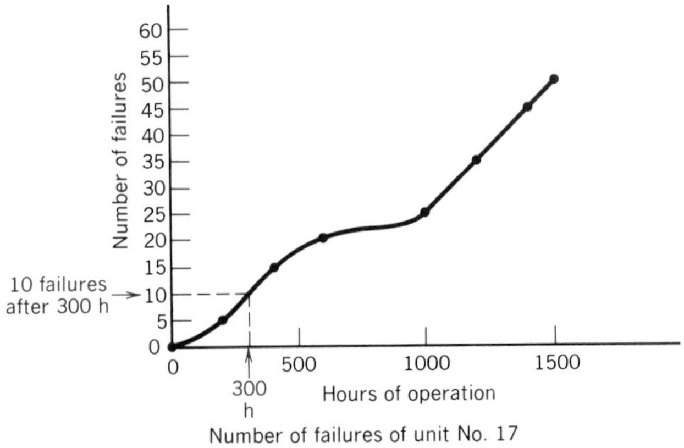

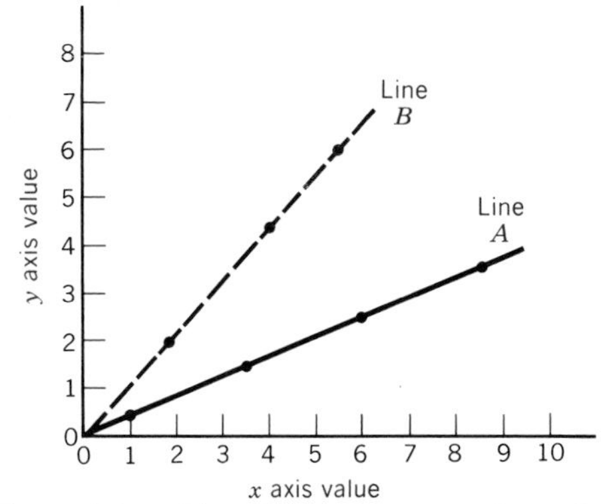

Figure 7.21 Line *B* has a greater slope than line *A*. Its *y* axis value changes more quickly than that of *A* for equal changes in the *x* axis value.

after 300 hours of operation (see Figure 7.20). The figure of 10 failures after 300 hours can be expected to be reasonably accurate, but since the line connecting the points has shown some other irregular bends, it is an approximation, and not as sure as an actually observed value.

The fact that the line connecting the plotted points is neither a straight line nor a smooth curve is another piece of important information. If this line were a straight

Figure 7.22 The slope depends on how the graph is drawn as well as on how the values change.

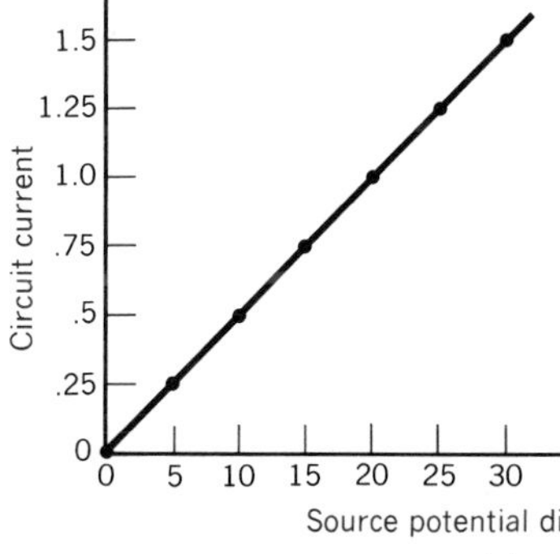

Source Potential Difference	Circuit Current
0	0
5	0.25
10	0.5
15	0.75
20	1.0
25	1.25
30	1.5

(a)

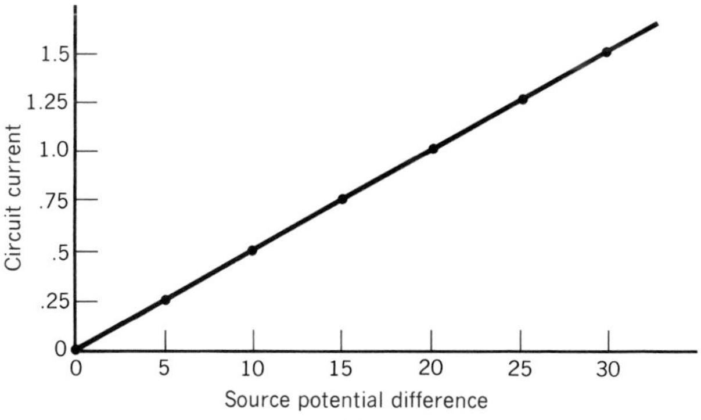

(b)

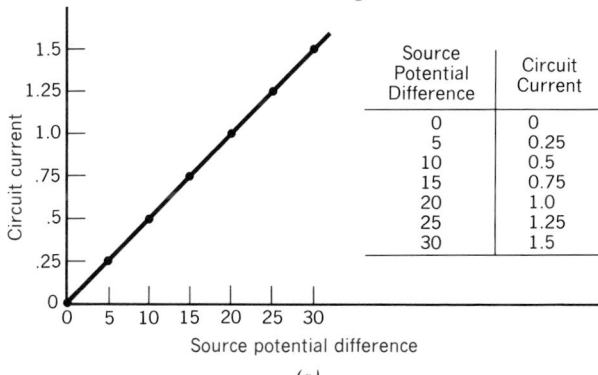

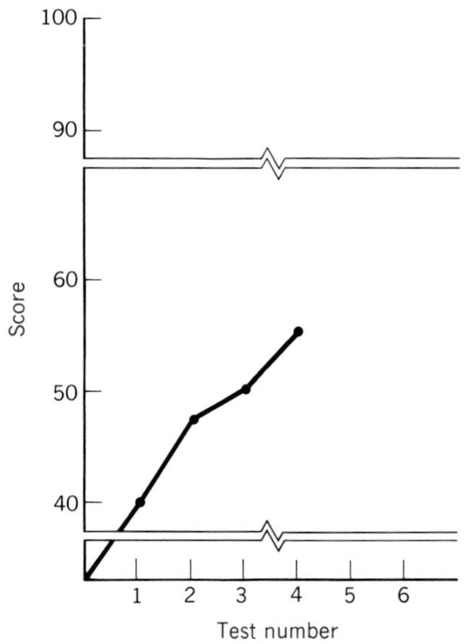

Figure 7.23 Dimwit makes rapid progress through the magic of graphs.

line, it would be possible to say that the number of failures increased in a steady and predictable manner. In Figure 7.20, you can see that the number of failures increased more rapidly between 1000 and 1500 hours of operation than it did between 500 and 1000 hours. This is shown by the "steepness" of the curve between the points. A steeper curve represents a greater change in the value of the quantity charted along the *y* axis with respect to a change in the quantity marked along the *x* axis.

This is more clearly shown in Figure 7.21, where it is evident that for equal changes in the *x*-axis value, the *y*-axis value of *B* increases much more quickly. The mathematical term used for the steepness of a line on a graph is the *slope*. The slope of line *B* is greater than that of *A*.

It is important not to be misled, however; the slope of a line or a curve on a graph depends on *two* things. These are how rapidly the value changes and on how the graph is drawn. In Figure 7.22, the same table of current and voltage values was used for both graphs, but because the *x*-axis values change more slowly in Figure 7.22*b*, the slope of the line in 7.22*a* appears greater. The intervals between two values on a graph axis are normally chosen so that the graph will fit into a page, but it is also possible to engage in a form of lying with graphs, as illustrated in the graph of Dimwit's grades in Figure 7.23. Judging from the slope of the line, student Dimwit appears to be making quick improvement; actually this is not so. All the grades were within 15 points of each other, and all were failing. The break lines, used to reduce the size of the graph, make it look as though this student's grades were getting much better. Pay close attention to the distances along the axes of a graph to avoid confusions of this sort.

The way to draw the graph of an equation or a formula is to substitute values and construct a table.

EXAMPLE:

Draw a graph relating the power dissipated in a 12 Ω resistance with a current flow ranging between 0.1 and 2.5 A. ■

SOLUTION:

The correct power law formula is $P = I^2R$. Using this formula construct a table with at least nine values for the current between 0.1 and 2.5 A.

Current	*Power*
0.1	0.12
0.5	3
0.75	6.75
1.0	12
1.25	18.75
1.5	27
1.75	36.75
2.0	48
2.25	60.75
2.5	75

Next calculate and fill in the value for the power at each of these current values. (Since the current values were chosen, the current is called *the independent variable*. The power, called *the dependent variable,* is then calculated from the current and the resistance.) Once the table has been filled in, the graph can be drawn. Choose values for the axis markings so that your graph will fit on a single sheet of paper. It is customary to measure the dependent variable along the vertical or y axis and the independent variable on the horizontal or x axis, although this is not always true. Your graph should look something like that in Figure 7.24. ■

Figure 7.24 Graph of power dissipated in a resistance with different circuit currents.

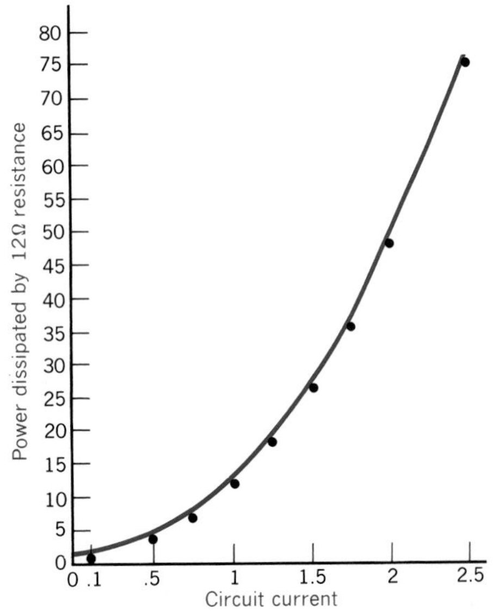

Compare the graph in Figure 7.24 with those relating potential difference and current in a circuit (Figure 7.22). Notice that the graph of Figure 7.22 is a straight line and is called a *linear* function, while that of Figure 7.24 is a changing curve and is called a *nonlinear function*.

Construct value tables where necessary and draw the following graphs. Which are linear?

a.

x	y
1	3
2	10
3	29
4	66
5	127
6	218

b.

x	y
0	5
1	7
2	9
3	11
4	13
5	15
7	17

c. $y = x - 0.5x$, where x ranges from 0 to 5.

d. $P = \dfrac{E^2}{20}$, where E ranges from 1 to 3.8.

e.

x	0	1	2	3	4	5	6	7
y	0	1	1	2	2	3	3	4

f. $y = x^2$, where x ranges from 0.1 to 6.

g. $y = 2^x$, where x ranges from 1 to 4. (Use at least 9 values, including 1.5, 1.75, 2.25, and 2.75.)

h. $P = I^2R$, where I ranges from 0.5 to 2.5 A and R is 10, 20, and 50 Ω. (This is a family of curves. First draw one for 10 Ω; then, on the same axis, curves for 20 and 50 Ω.)

i. $y^2 = 10 - x^2$, where x ranges from 0 to 3.

j.

x	y
0	0
1	1
2	2.83
3	5.2
4	8
5	11.2
6	14.7

k. Try reading your graphs for the following values of x.

a. 4.5 in j	e. 3.5 in c
b. 0.5 in b	f. 2.75 in j
c. 3.6 in d	g. 1.75 in g
d. 5.25 in a	h. 3.5 in f

C.2 ANGLES

Graphs such as those discussed in section C.1 are frequently used to present information and to solve problems in electricity and electronics. In order to use them to the extent of their capabilities, however, you must apply some of the knowledge you have derived from the everyday world of objects and shapes to the characteristics of lines and shapes drawn on paper. This field of study is called *geometry*, that is, the measurement of the Earth, because it grew out of the skills needed to measure land and define the boundaries of farms and fields. Given its history, you can understand that a great deal of geometry has to do with measuring things. Most of this is of very little use in electricity and electronics. The concept of angle, however, is of great importance. Angles are frequently referred to in the world of shapes and things, but in the flat world of geometry, an *angle* is defined as the shape formed when two lines are drawn to a common point. See Figure 7.25. The point at which the two lines meet is called the *vertex* of the angle.

Another way of looking at an angle is to picture a line segment OA as shown in Figure 7.26. If point O

Figure 7.25 An angle is formed when two lines meet at a point.

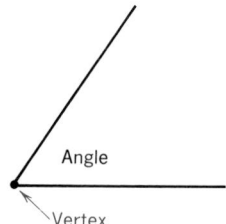

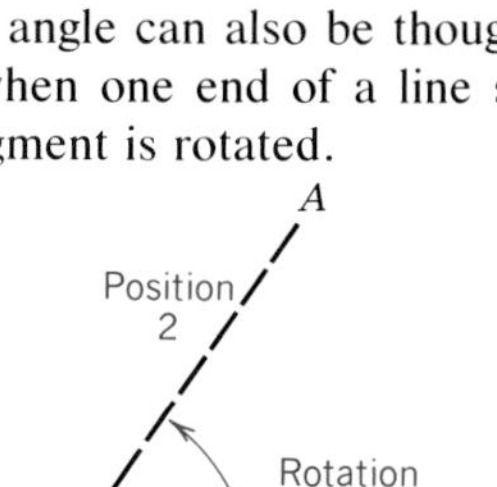

Figure 7.26 An angle can also be thought of as the figure that is formed when one end of a line segment is held in place and the segment is rotated.

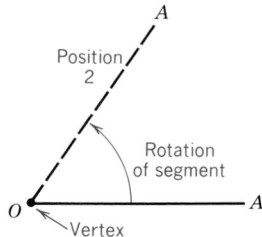

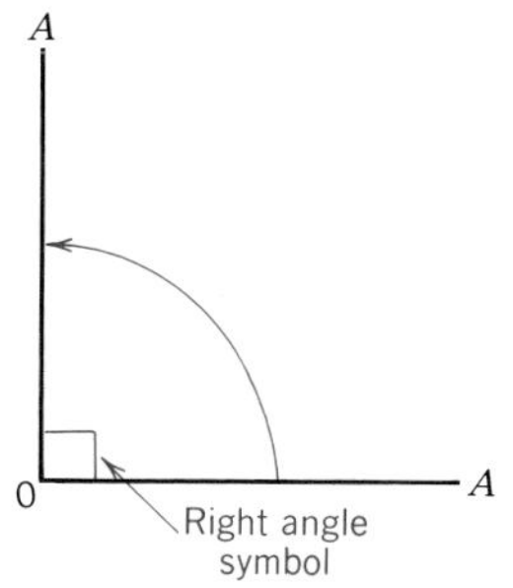

Figure 7.27 A right angle.

is held in place, and the line segment is rotated counterclockwise (positive rotation is always counterclockwise) to position 2, an angle is formed, with point O as its vertex. Rotating the line segment a quarter of the way around produces a familiar shape, the right angle shown in Figure 7.27. A right angle is frequently marked as shown.

Angles are most frequently measured in degrees. A degree is $\frac{1}{360}$ of a complete rotation of the line segment. This means that the right angle, which is one quarter of a complete rotation measures 90 degrees or 90°. Angles are often measured with a plastic semicircle called a protractor, pictured in Figure 7.28. In the machine shop and the science laboratory, there are more precise instruments for measuring angles, but the plastic protractor is generally sufficient for the majority of technical angle measurements.

An angle of less than 90° is called an *acute* angle, meaning that it comes to a "sharp point," as shown in Figure 7.29*a*, while an angle of more than 90° (Figure 7.29*b*) is called an *obtuse* angle. An angle of more than 180° is sometimes called a *reflex* angle, as shown in Figure 7.29*c*

Certain technical problems require that you calculate the size of an angle that will produce a right angle when added to an angle whose size is known. This is shown in Figure 7.30, where angle A, the known

Figure 7.28 A protractor is used for measuring angles. (Photo by M. Hermes.)

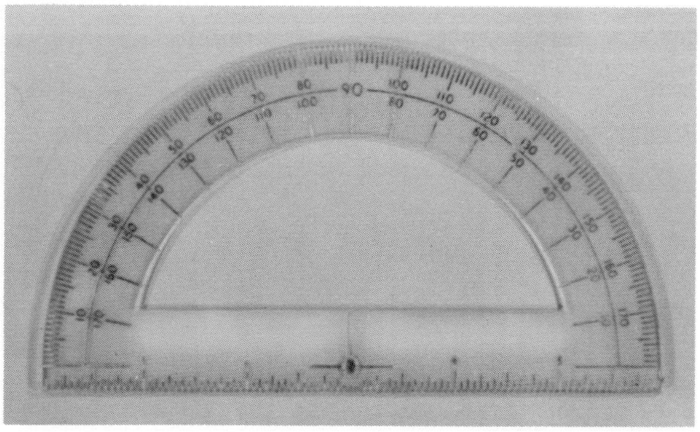

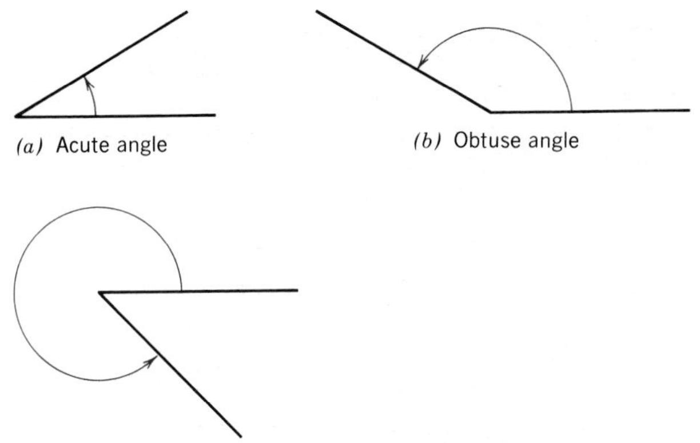

(a) Acute angle (b) Obtuse angle (c) Reflex angle

Figure 7.29 Acute, obtuse, and reflex angles.

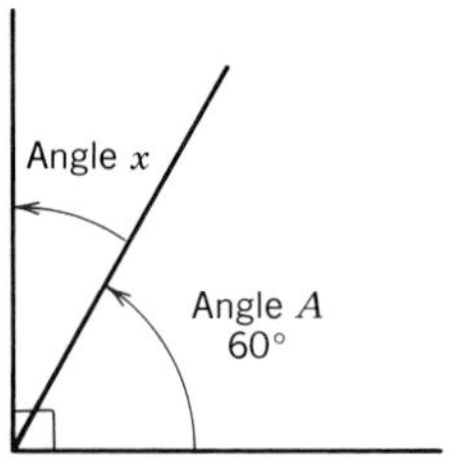

Figure 7.30 Two angles whose sum is a right angle (90°) are called complementary angles.

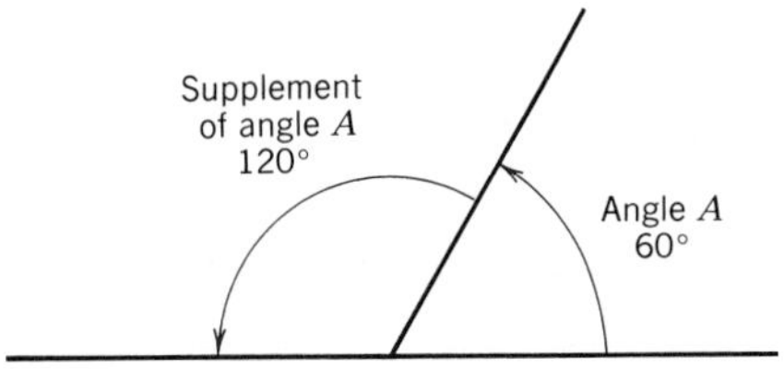

Figure 7.31 Two angles whose sum is 180° are called supplementary angles.

angle, measures 60°. Since a right angle represents a rotation of 90°, angle x must be $90° - 60° = 30°$. This is expressed by saying that a 30° angle is the *complement* of a 60° angle.

Two angles whose sum is exactly equal to 90 degrees, that is, a right angle, are complementary angles.

Supplementary angles are two angles whose sum adds up to 180°. As shown in Figure 7.31, the supplement of an angle of 60° is $180° - 60° = 120°$. When an angle and its supplement are placed together, the result is a straight line.

Two angles whose sum is exactly equal to 180 degrees are supplementary angles.

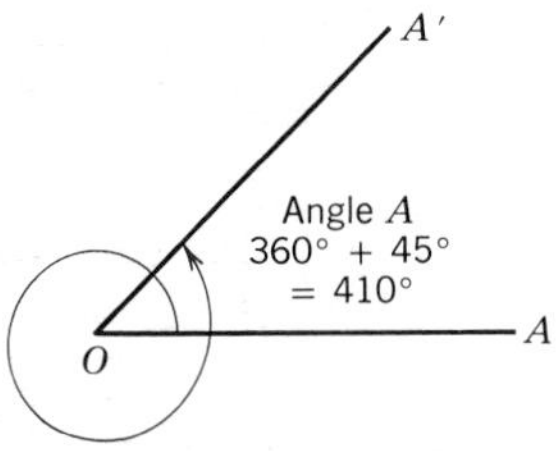

Figure 7.32 An angle obtained by rotating line segment OA through more than a complete circle.

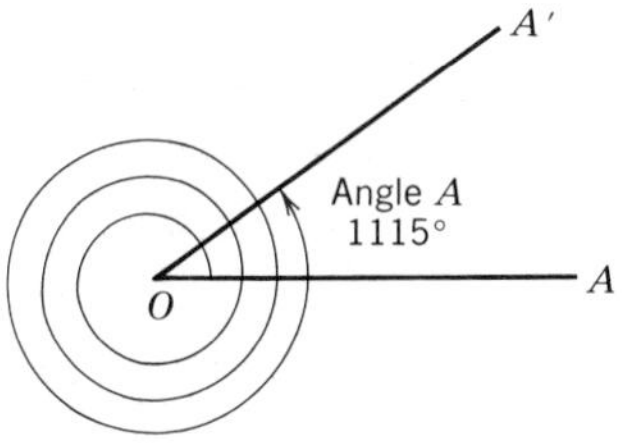

Figure 7.33 A line segment can be rotated through several complete circles to form an angle.

Up to this point, this section has considered only those angles formed when a line segment has been rotated around one of its end points for less than a full circle. There is no reason to stop at that point, however. In Figure 7.32 a line segment is shown which has been rotated through a complete circle, plus another 45°. The angular measurement of this angle then is $360° + 45° = 410°$. The characteristics of the angle formed are, however, the same as an angle of $410° - 360° = 45°$.

The line segment can be rotated through several complete circles, as shown in Figure 7.33. The characteristics of the angle formed will be identical to some angle of less than 360°. This angle can be found by dividing the number of degrees in the multirotation angle by 360. The whole-number quotient will be the number of complete rotations made by the line segment, while the remainder will be the angle whose characteristics are identical to the multirotation angle.

EXAMPLE:
A line segment has been rotated through 1115°. What angle do the characteristics of the angle formed resemble? ■

SOLUTION:
Divide 1115 by 360

$$\begin{array}{r} 3 \\ 360\overline{)1115} \\ \underline{1080} \\ 35 \end{array}$$

The remainder is 35. An angle of 1115° resembles an angle of 35°. ■

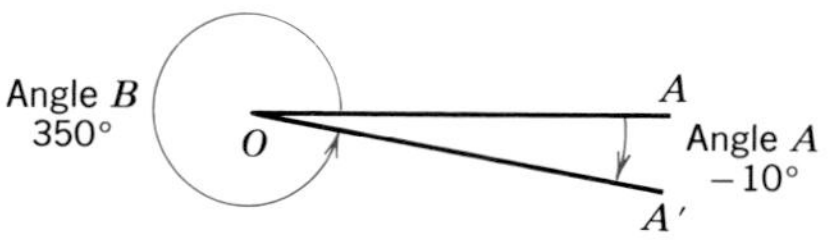

Figure 7.34 Line segment OA has been rotated 10° in a clockwise direction to produce an angle of −10°.

Rotation of the line segment in a counterclockwise direction is normally considered to produce a *positive* angle. There is no specific reason for this, it is a convention. Similarly, rotating the line segment in a clockwise direction is thought of as producing a *negative* angle. Figure 7.34 shows line segment OA rotated to produce a negative angle of −10°. The characteristics of angle A, which is a negative angle, are exactly those of positive angle B. From the figure you can see that the size of angle B can be calculated by adding the size of angle A to 360°. Angle B = 360 + angle A or

$$B = 360 - 10;$$
$$B = 350°.$$

Another way of measuring angles frequently found in electrical engineering and technology is called *radian* or π (pi) measure. A radian is an angle that, when placed with its vertex at the center of a circle, as shown in Figure 7.35, produces an arc equal in length to the radius of the circle. A radian has a value of 57.3° to three significant figures.

Radian measure is used in technology because it can make a number of calculations easier to do, since it can be expressed in terms of the Greek letter π. You will recall that π is a constant equal to 3.1416 to five significant figures, and that it is used to calculate the length around a circle or the area of the circle if the radius is known.

There are 360° in a complete circle, and this is exactly equal to 2π radians. An angle of π radians is equal to 180°, and $\frac{\pi}{2}$ radians are 90°. These angles, frequently expressed in radian measure, are common in electricity and electronics. Converting between radians and degrees is a fairly simple matter if you have a calculator equipped for angle measure in radians. Otherwise use the following formula and express radians in terms of π.

Figure 7.35 A radian is an angle that when placed with its vertex at the center of a circle, produces an arc equal in length to the radius of the circle.

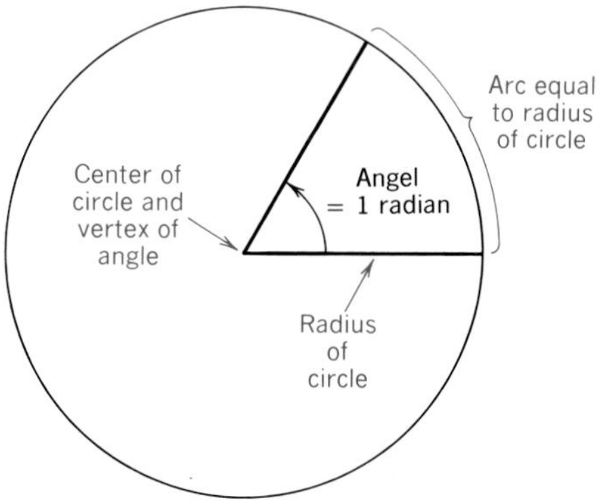

$$\frac{\text{No. of radians}}{\pi} = \frac{\text{No. of degrees}}{180} \qquad \text{FORMULA 7.2}$$

EXAMPLE:

Convert 45° to radians. ■

SOLUTION:

Using Formula 7.2 and substituting,

$$\frac{\text{No. of radians}}{\pi} = \frac{45}{180}$$
$$\frac{\text{No. of radians}}{\pi} = 0.25$$

Now, multiplying both sides of the equation by π yields the number of radians in terms of π

$$\frac{\text{No. of radians}}{\pi} \times \pi = 0.25 \times \pi$$
$$\text{No. of radians} = 0.25\pi \quad \text{or} \quad \frac{\pi}{4}$$ ■

Converting a number of radians expressed in terms of π into degrees is equally straightforward.

EXAMPLE:

Convert $\frac{\pi}{6}$ radians into degrees. ■

SOLUTION:

Using Formula 7.2 and substituting,

$$\frac{\text{No. of radians}}{\pi} = \frac{\text{No. of degrees}}{180}$$
$$\frac{\frac{\pi}{6}}{\pi} = \frac{\text{No. of degrees}}{180}$$

Simplifying gives

$$\frac{1}{6} = \frac{\text{No. of degrees}}{180}$$

When both sides are multiplied by 180, the result is

$$\frac{180}{6} = \frac{\text{No. of degrees}}{180} \times 180$$

or

$$\text{No. of degrees} = 30$$

$$\frac{\pi}{6} \text{ radians} = 30°$$

■

Test your understanding of this section by trying the following problems.

1. Place a point in the middle of a paper and draw a line segment *OA* 0.08 m long from that point in any direction. Using a protractor, draw line *AB* 0.06 m long at an angle of 150° from point *A*. Now draw line *BC* 0.055 m long at an angle of −90° from point *B*. Now draw a line *CD* at an angle of 30° degrees from point *C*. Which previously placed point will line *CD* pass through?

2. Convert the following from radians to degrees or degrees to radians. (Radians should be given in terms of π.)

a. 180° = ? R
b. 327° = ? R
c. $\frac{3}{2\pi}$ R = ?°
d. 2 π R = ?°
e. 60° = ? R
f. 600° = ? R
g. $\frac{4}{5}$ π R = ?°
h. 45° = ? R
i. 8 π R = ?°
j. 57.3° = ? R

C.3 SIMULTANEOUS EQUATIONS

In the Principles section of this chapter, you saw how the application of Kirchhoff's laws produced equations that described the relationship among a number of unknown circuit quantities. When the number of different equations was equal to (or greater than) the number of unknown quantities, it was shown that these simultaneous equations could be solved and the value of the unknown quantities could be determined. One method of solving simultaneous equations was shown. This involved solving one of the equations for one unknown quantity in terms of the other or others and then substituting this expression into the second equation, which then becomes an equation with one unknown. This method is generally useful, but the amount of arithmetic involved makes it difficult and clumsy to use if fractions or decimals with three or more significant figures are involved.

EXAMPLE:
As a result of applying Kirchhoff's voltage law, two equations were written

$$100.28 = 8I_1 + 27I_2$$

$$21.24 = 4I_1 + 5I_2$$

Solve for the unknown currents. ■

SOLUTION:
These equations can be solved by the method used in Section B.4 in spite of the fact that the arithmetic gets somewhat involved. The second equation can be solved for I_1:

$$21.24 = 4I_1 + 5I_2$$

Transposing $4I_1$ and 21.24,

$$-4I_1 = 5I_2 - 21.24$$

Multiplying both sides by $-\frac{1}{4}$

$$I_1 = -\frac{1}{4}(5I_2 - 21.24)$$

This value for I_1 can then be substituted in the first equation

$$100.28 = 8\left(-\frac{1}{4}\right)(5I_2 - 21.24) + 27I_2$$

Simplifying,

$$100.28 = -2(5I_2 - 21.24) + 27I_2$$

$$100.28 = -10I_2 + 42.48 + 27I_2$$

$$100.28 = 17I_2 + 42.48$$

Subtracting 42.48 from both sides,

$$57.8 = 17I_2$$

Dividing by 17,

$$I_2 = 3.4$$

This value for I_2 can then be substituted into the original second equation

$$21.24 = 4I_1 + (3.4)$$

$$21.24 = 4I_1 + 17$$

Subtracting 17 from both sides,

$$4.24 = 4I_1$$

Dividing by 4 gives the values for I_1

$$1.06 = I_1$$

■

Another way of solving these two equations is to write them both in column form and then find some way to add or subtract the two equations that will give an expression involving just one unknown.

EXAMPLE:
Solve the equations

$$100.28 = 8I_1 + 27I_2$$
$$21.24 = 4I_1 + 5I_2$$

by the above method. ■

SOLUTION:
If both sides of the second equation are multiplied by 2, the multiplier of the I_1 term will be 8 in both cases:

$$2 \times (21.24) = 2 \times (4I_1 + 5I_2)$$

Once this has been simplified, it can be subtracted from the first equation

$$\begin{aligned} 100.28 &= 8I_1 + 27I_2 \\ -\ (42.48 &= 8I_1 + 10I_2) \\ \hline 57.8 &= \qquad 17I_2 \end{aligned}$$

From this point, division by 17 yields $I_2 = 3.4$. This value can be substituted in either of the original equations to calculate I_1; $I_1 = 1.06$. ■

This method of solving simultaneous equations requires somewhat less arithmetic than does the method shown in Section B.4. Another weakness of both these methods, besides the amount of arithmetic involved, is that they can not be adapted for calculator or computer solution.

There is another method of solving simultaneous equations, called *the method of determinants,* that is seldom taught in school today. In some ways it is even more complicated than the other methods, but it is better to use in problems involving three equations; and best of all, the steps can be set up as a computer program in BASIC. This means that if you have a small computer, it is only necessary to key in the determinant program once, and you can then save it on tape or disk. With a small computer and the determinant program, solving Kirchhoff's law equations is about as easy as applying Ohm's law.

Although the determinant program will be given in the next chapter, it is good to familiarize yourself with determinants and their operation, so that you will be able to write the Kirchhoff's law equations in the correct form and avoid any of the difficulties that might occur.

The method of determinants is an easily applied and general way of solving two equations with two unknown quantities, or three equations with three unknown quantities. It is unlikely that you will have to deal with more than three simultaneous equations because alternate methods of circuit analysis can be used

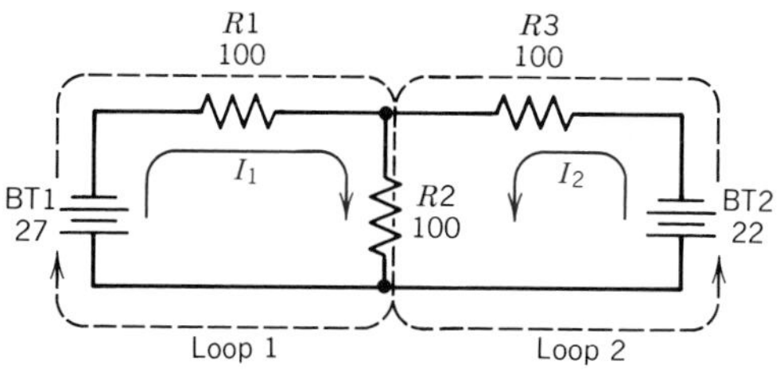

Figure 7.36 Circuit for solution by the method of determinants.

to reduce a given network to a three-mesh network. Determinants called *second-order* determinants are used to solve any two independent equations with two unknowns, which can be written in the form

$$\begin{aligned} E_1 &= a_1I_1 + b_1I_2 \\ E_2 &= a_2I_1 + b_2I_2 \end{aligned} \qquad \text{FORMULA 7.3}$$

Here a_1 and b_1 are the numerical coefficients, that is, the numbers by which the unknown currents I_1 and I_2 are multiplied. E_1 is the sum of the voltage rises in the first loop. Similarly, a_2, b_2, and E_2 are the coefficients of I_1 and I_2 and the sum of the voltage rises in the second circuit loop. When you write the voltage law equations for a two-loop circuit such as that shown in Figure 7.36, a_1, b_1, a_2, b_2, E_1, and E_2 are all known.

The equations for the circuit of Figure 7.36 are

$$27 = 100I_1 + 100(I_1 + I_2) \quad \text{(loop 1)}$$
$$22 = 100I_2 + 100(I_1 + I_2) \quad \text{(loop 2)}$$

These two equations can be simplified and transposed to resemble those of Formula 7.3:

$$27 = 200I_1 + 100I_2$$
$$22 = 100I_1 + 200I_2$$

The method of determinants for solving these equations consists of writing three *arrays,* or arrangements of numbers, which are called N_1, N_2, and D and using the following formulas:

$$I_1 = \frac{N_1}{D} \qquad \text{FORMULA 7.4}$$

$$I_2 = \frac{N_2}{D} \qquad \text{FORMULA 7.5}$$

D is an array denominator and N_1 and N_2 are the array numerators. The array denominator D is written in the form

$$\begin{vmatrix} a_1 & b_1 \\ a_2 & b_2 \end{vmatrix}$$

The lines on either side of the array show that this array is a determinant. Every 2-row, 2-column (2 ×

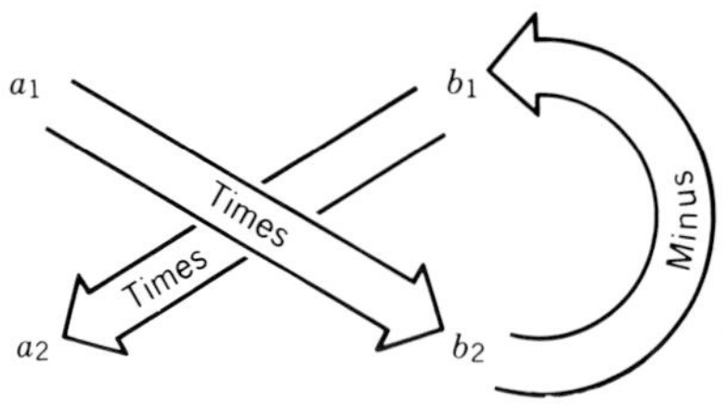

Figure 7.37 Evaluating a 2 × 2 determinant.

2) determinant of this sort has a numerical value that can be obtained by multiplying a_1 and b_2 together and subtracting from this product the product of b_1 and a_2. This is shown symbolically in Figure 7.37. The array denominator for both equations, then, is

$$D = \begin{vmatrix} 200 & 100 \\ 100 & 200 \end{vmatrix}$$

and its numerical value is $(200 \times 200) - (100 \times 100) = 30{,}000$.

The N_1 array is obtained by replacing a_1 and a_2, respectively, by E_1 and E_2 in array D

$$N_1 = \begin{vmatrix} E_1 & b_1 \\ E_2 & b_2 \end{vmatrix} = \begin{vmatrix} 27 & 100 \\ 22 & 200 \end{vmatrix}$$

The numerical value of this array is obtained in the same way as before:

$$N_1 = (E_1 b_2) - (b_1 E_2)$$
$$= (27 \times 200) - 22 \times 100 = 3200$$

After N_1 and D are known, I_1 can be calculated by substituting in Formula 7.4.

$$I_1 = \frac{N_1}{\text{D}} = \frac{3200}{30{,}000} = 0.107 \text{ A}$$

The N_2 array is obtained by replacing b_1 and b_2 by E_1 and E_2 in D.

$$N_2 = \begin{vmatrix} a_1 & E_1 \\ a_2 & E_2 \end{vmatrix} = \begin{vmatrix} 200 & 27 \\ 100 & 22 \end{vmatrix}$$

Evaluating $N_2 = (200 \times 22) - (27 \times 100) = 1700$. Substituting these values in Formula 7.5,

$$I_2 = \frac{N_2}{D} = \frac{1700}{30{,}000} = 0.0567 \text{ A}$$

The process of using determinants to solve simultaneous equations may seem a bit mystifying at first, but it quickly becomes more familiar, particularly when a computer is used to perform the arithmetic.

EXAMPLE:

Determine both loop currents in the circuit shown in Figure 7.38 using Kirchhoff's voltage law and the method of determinants. ■

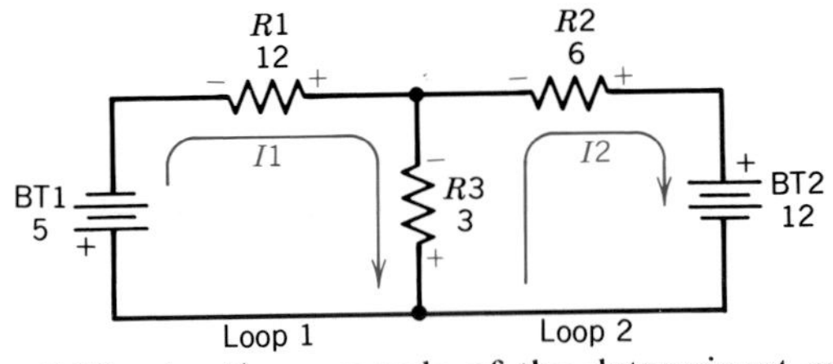

Figure 7.38 Another example of the determinant method used to solve Kirchhoff's law problems.

SOLUTION:

Begin by writing voltage law equations for the two loops in Figure 7.38 based on the assumed current directions and component polarities.

$$-5 + 12I_1 + 3(I_1 - I_2) = 0$$
$$5 = 15I_1 - 3I_2 \quad \text{(loop 1)}$$
$$-12 - 3\,(I_1 - I_2) + 6I_2 = 0$$
$$12 = -3I_1 + 9I_2 \quad \text{(loop 2)}$$

Write and evaluate D, N_1, and N_2

$$D = \begin{vmatrix} 15 & -3 \\ -3 & 9 \end{vmatrix} = 135 - 9 = 126$$

$$N_1 = \begin{vmatrix} 5 & -3 \\ 12 & 9 \end{vmatrix} = 45 - (-36) = 81$$

$$N_2 = \begin{vmatrix} 15 & 5 \\ -3 & 12 \end{vmatrix} = 180 - (-15) = 195$$

These values are then substituted in Formulas 7.4 and 7.5:

$$I_1 = \frac{N_1}{D} = \frac{81}{126} = 0.643 \text{ A}$$

$$I_2 = \frac{N_2}{D} = \frac{195}{126} = 1.55 \text{ A}$$ ■

Solve the following simultaneous equations using the method of determinants. Be careful, some of them may not permit the use of determinants, some may not have solutions.

a. $5I_1 + 17I_2 = 72.5$
 $-3I_1 + 2I_2 = 0.8$

b. $10I_1 - 2I_2 = 10.18$
 $-3I_1 - 1.4I_2 = -4.174$

c. $2.4I_1 + 8I_2 = 6.4$
 $-2(3.1I_1 - I_2) = 22$

d. $X - 2Y = 1$
 $Y - X = 0.5$

e. $\dfrac{X - Y}{3} - 4 = -6;\ 3Y = X + 14$

f. $2I_1 - 3I_2 = 2$
$-6I_2 + 4I_1 = 4$

g. $-2I_1 + 5I_2 = 4$
$2I_2 - 0.8 = I_1$

h. $2X^2 - Y = -1$
$\frac{Y - 9}{x^2} = 0.25$

i. $1.3I_1 - 0.3I_2 = 4$
$9.1I_1 - 2.1I_2 = 28$

j. $9I_1 + 3I_2 = 4.5$
$4I_1 + 2I_2 = 3$

The use of determinants makes the solution of simultaneous equations such as those obtained from voltage law or current law analysis an almost trivial job. Determinants are nothing more than a formalized way of multiplying two equations by common factors, eliminating one of the unknown quantities by subtraction, and then solving for the other unknown quantity. With some practice, the entire process, from charting the loops or mapping the junctions, assigning current directions and polarities, to solving by determinants, becomes fairly automatic. The method of determinants is particularly valuable in circuits that require the solution of three equations with three unknowns. This method *can* be used to solve four equations in four unknowns, but 4 × 4 arrays are clumsy and require many arithmetic manipulations for solution. Fortunately, three-equation networks appear to be about the most complicated you will have to face in practical circuit analysis.

Figure 7.39*a* illustrates a widely used electronic circuit called a *bridge*. It represents one of the more complex networks to which Kirchhoff's laws are directly applied. There are four junctions in the circuit. This means that three equations involving three unknowns will have to be solved, whether you use the voltage or current law. Since the loops involve resistances in series, the voltage law is most convenient, although your analysis will require reference to the current law as well. From Figure 7.39*b*, you can see that there are three unknown currents: I_1 which flows through $R1$, I_2 which flows through $R2$, and I_3, the current through the bridging resistance $R3$. The currents through $R4$ and $R5$ are derived from the other three currents according to the principle of the current law. That is, the current through $R4$ is the sum of I_1 and I_3, while the current through $R5$ is $I_2 - I_3$. Therefore, if I_1, I_2, and I_3 could be calculated, all the currents through the components in the circuit could be calculated.

Figure 7.39 A bridge circuit can be analyzed with Kirchhoff's laws.

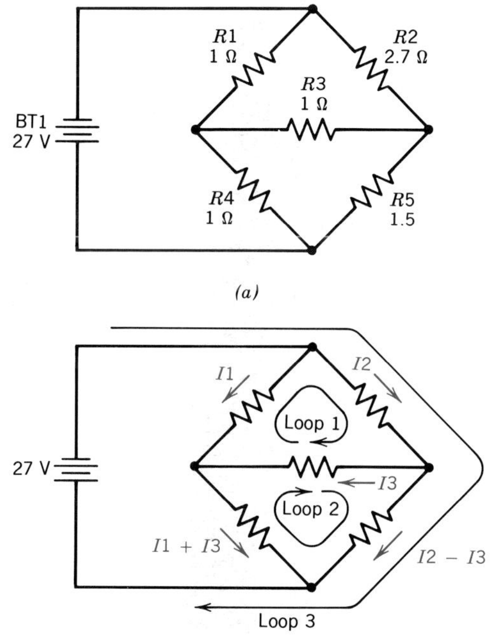

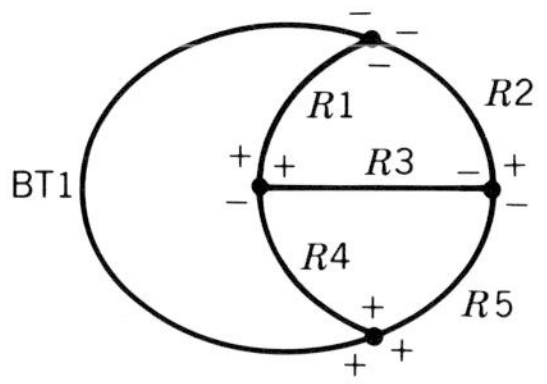

Figure 7.40 The network graph of the circuit shown in Figure 7.39.

Before writing the voltage law equations, it is a good idea to mark the assumed polarities of the various resistances either on the schematic or on a network graph as in Figure 7.40. As in the case of the two-loop circuits, the assumed currents enter the more negative end of a resistance and leave through the more positive end. Remember that this is true only if you are using the electron drift convention in your work. If you are using conventional current, the opposite is true.

There are a number of different ways in which the loops could have been traced in Figure 7.39*b*. Three independent loops are shown in the figure. Notice that only loop 3 contains a source. But, since Kirchhoff's voltage law applies to each of the loops, you can expect to find voltage rises and voltage drops in all three. Consider loop 1, starting at the junction of $R1$ and $R2$ and moving clockwise. Going through $R2$ there is a voltage drop of $2.7I_2$. Through $R3$, there is a voltage drop of I_3. The path through $R1$, on the other hand, enters $R1$ at its positive end and leaves through the negative end, so it is a voltage rise of I_1. The loop 1 equation then is

$$-I_1 + 2.7I_2 + I_3 = 0$$

Tracing loop 2, also in a clockwise direction beginning from the junction of $R3$ and $R5$, the path passes through $R5$, which is a voltage drop of $1.5(I_2 - I_3)$. The path goes through $R4$ from positive to negative, that is, a voltage rise of $1 \times (I_1 + I_3)$. Another voltage rise is encountered through $R3$, caused by I_3. The loop 2 equation is

$$1.5(I_2 - I_3) - (I_1 + I_3) - I_3 = 0$$

Simplifying,

$$-I_1 + 1.5I_2 - 3.5I_3 = 0$$

The third loop can be started at the negative terminal of the battery. Passing through $R2$, there is a voltage drop of $2.7I_2$, and through $R5$, a voltage drop of $1.5(I_2 - I_3)$. The source, BT1, provides a voltage rise of 27 V. Notice that there is no I_1 term in this loop, so the place keeper $0I_1$ is used. The loop 3 equation is

$$+2.7I_2 + 1.5(I_2 - I_3) - 27 = 0$$

or

$$0I_1 + 4.2I_2 - 1.5I_3 = 27$$

Once the three equations have been written, the next step is solving by determinants. Since there are three equations in three unknowns, you will have to evaluate a 3×3 determinant to obtain the denominator or D value, and another 3×3 determinant to obtain each of the three numerators N_1, N_2, and N_3. Once this is done, it is a simple matter to calculate

$$I_1 = \frac{N_1}{D} \qquad \text{FORMULA 7.6}$$

$$I_2 = \frac{N_2}{D} \qquad \text{FORMULA 7.7}$$

$$I_3 = \frac{N_3}{D} \qquad \text{FORMULA 7.8}$$

A 3×3 determinant is an extension of the 2×2 form. The 3×3 determinant is an array made up of the coefficients of the three unknown currents in the three equations

$$\mathrm{D} = \begin{vmatrix} a_1 & b_1 & c_1 \\ a_2 & b_2 & c_2 \\ a_3 & b_3 & c_3 \end{vmatrix}$$

where a_1 is the coefficient of the I_1 term in the first equation, and so on. Evaluating 3×3 determinants is more complex than evaluating 2×2 determinants. First, the determinant plus values are obtained by multiplying:

a. The numbers in the diagonal a_1, b_2, and c_3
b. The factors a_3, b_1, and c_2
c. The factors a_2, b_3, and c_1.

Adding these three products gives the total of the *plus* factors of the determinant $(a_1b_2c_3 + a_3b_1c_2 + a_2b_3c_1)$, see Figure 7.41*a*. The total of the minus factors is obtained by multiplying:

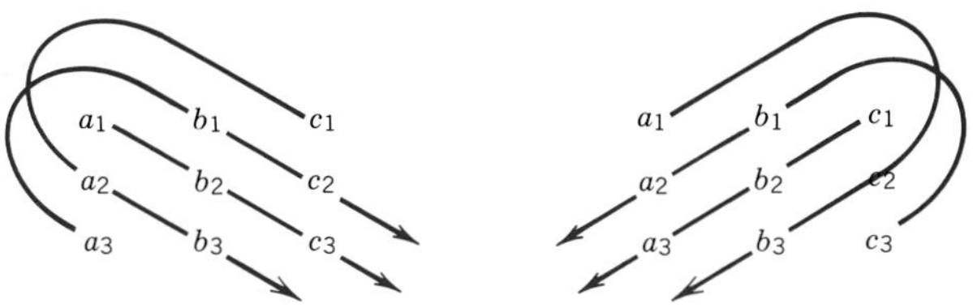

(a) Plus factors *(b)* Minus factors
Figure 7.41 Evaluating a 3×3 determinant. Multiply the numbers connected by the lines to obtain three *plus* and three *minus* factors. Then subtract the sum of the minus factors from the sum of the plus factors.

a. The factors in the diagonal c_1, b_2, and a_3
b. The factors a_1, c_2, and b_3
c. The factors c_3, b_1, and a_2.

Adding these three products gives the total of the *minus* factors of the determinant $(c_1b_2a_3 + a_1c_2b_3 + c_3b_1a_2)$, as shown in Figure 7.41*b*. The value of the determinant is obtained by subtracting the total of the minus factors from the total of the plus factors.

Using the coefficients of the three loop equations obtained from the circuit of Figure 7.39,

$$D = \begin{vmatrix} -1 & +2.7 & +1 \\ -1 & +1.5 & -3.5 \\ 0 & +4.2 & -1.5 \end{vmatrix}$$

The three plus values of this determinant are 2.25, 0, and −4.2. Their sum is −1.95. The three minus factors are 0, +14.7, and +4.05. Their sum is 18.75. Subtracting the minus factors from the plus factors,

$$D = -1.95 - 18.75 = -20.7$$

The N_1 determinant is obtained by substituting the loop equation constant terms 0, 0, and 27 for the first column in the D determinant:

$$N_1 = \begin{vmatrix} 0 & 2.7 & 1 \\ 0 & 1.5 & -3.5 \\ 27 & 4.2 & -1.5 \end{vmatrix}$$

Evaluating this determinant in the same way as D gives a value of $N_1 = -295.65$. Similarly,

$$N_2 = \begin{vmatrix} -1 & 0 & 1 \\ -1 & 0 & -3.5 \\ 0 & 27 & -1.5 \end{vmatrix} = -121.5$$

and

$$N_3 = \begin{vmatrix} -1 & 2.7 & 0 \\ -1 & 1.5 & 0 \\ 0 & 4.2 & 27 \end{vmatrix} = 32.4$$

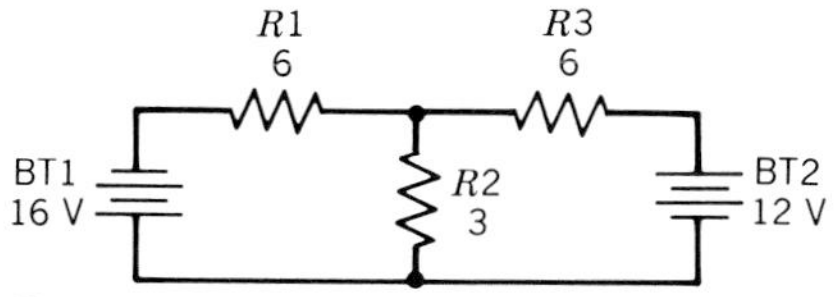

Figure 7.42

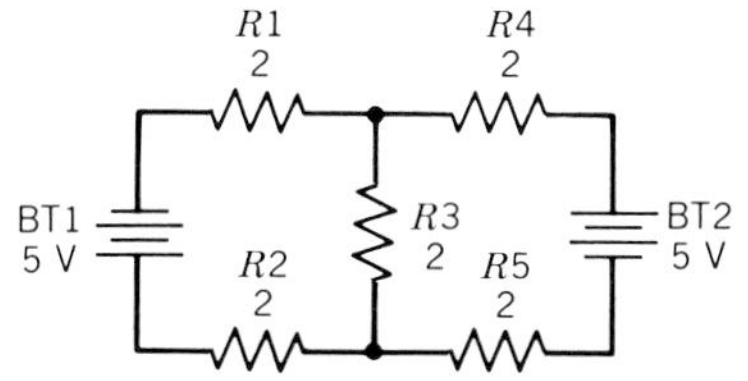

Figure 7.43

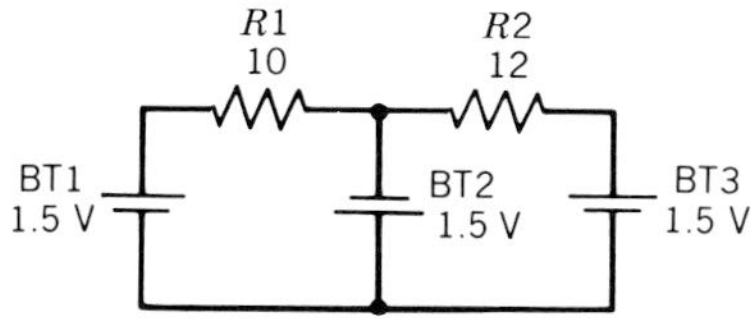

Figure 7.44

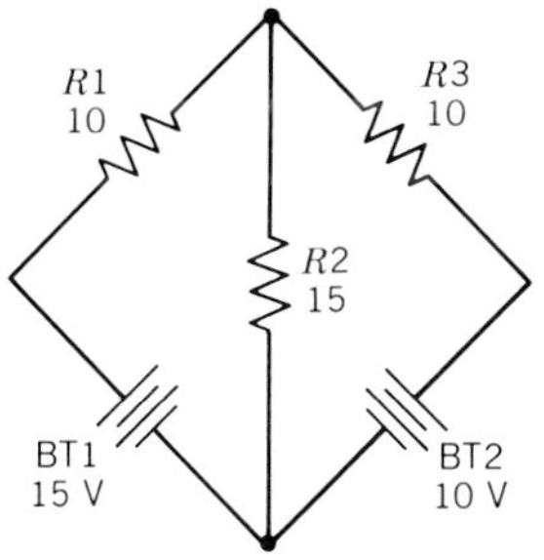

Figure 7.45

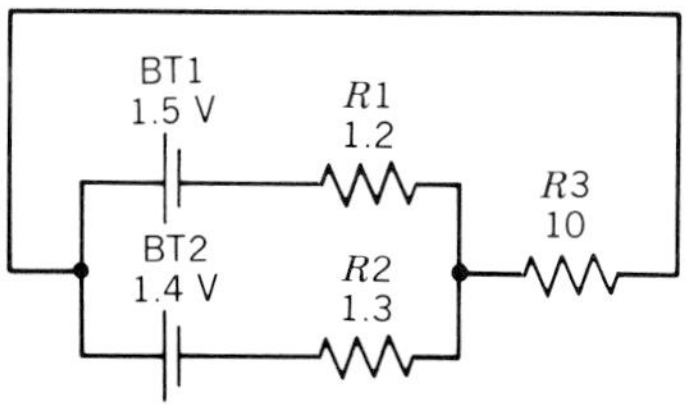

Figure 7.46

Substituting these values into the determinant formulas for I_1, I_2, and I_3 gives

$$I_1 = \frac{N_1}{D} = \frac{-295.65}{-20.7} = 14.3 \text{ A}$$

$$I_2 = \frac{N_2}{D} = \frac{-121.5}{-20.7} = 5.87 \text{ A}$$

$$I_3 = \frac{N_3}{D} = \frac{32.4}{-20.7} = -1.57 \text{ A}$$

The fact that I_3 is negative means only that the assumed direction of this current was incorrect.

Calculate the potential difference across each resistance in these circuits.

a. Figure 7.42.
b. Figure 7.43.
c. Figure 7.44.
d. Figure 7.45.
e. Figure 7.46.

C.4 TOLERANCE CALCULATIONS

Until now, this book has not distinguished between *nominal* values, that is, the ideal or marked values of components, and *actual* values, the values of resistance, voltage, or power dissipation actually possessed by the components. For example, the resistance of a particular component may be marked at 10 Ω, but it is rare that the accurately measured resistance will be exactly 10.000 Ω. In general, measured values like 10.13 or 9.965 are much more common. In most circuits and situations, a slightly higher or lower value will make no difference, but this is not always the case. In the drawings of mechanical parts, the fact that the dimensions of few manufactured items are ever exactly their nominal value is taken into account by specifying a range of values for a particular dimension. The drawing dimensions of Figure 7.47 are typical. The rod is shown to have a nominal length of 0.1 m, but the ± 0.001 means that the true length may be as much as 0.101 m (0.1 + 0.001) or as little as 0.099 m (0.1 − 0.001). Any value between these two limits is considered satisfactory for the part shown in the figure. The combination of the plus and minus signs shows that the real value is permitted to range above or below the nominal value by the same amount. Sometimes the allowed range above and below the nominal value is not the same. The width of the rod in Figure 7.47 may be as much as 0.002 less than the nominal value, but only 0.001 more. This is shown in the fraction form in the drawing. Since the nominal value of the width is 0.025 m, the maximum width then may be as large as 0.026, while the minimum is 0.023.

The permitted actual value range for electronic components is normally given as a percentage of the marked or nominal value. This percentage is called the *tolerance* of the component. For example, a 1-kΩ re-

Figure 7.47 A dimension drawing showing tolerances.

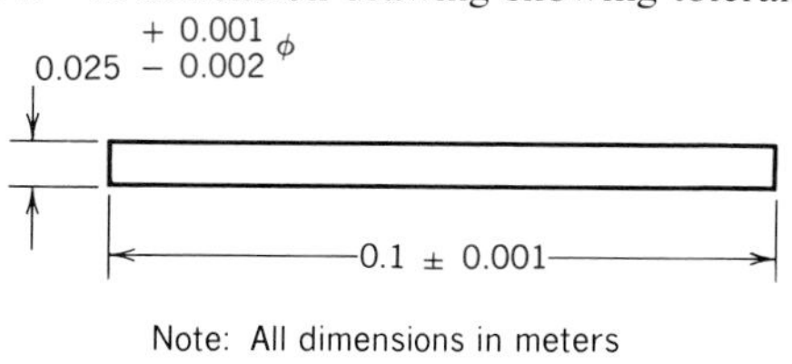

sistance may have a tolerance of 10 percent. This means that the actual measured resistance could range between 10 percent greater than 1000 Ω and 10 percent less. Often it is necessary to calculate the actual range of a component value when the nominal value and the tolerance are known. This is done by multiplying the nominal value by the tolerance and adding this product to the nominal value to obtain the maximum actual value. In formula form, this is

Maximum value = nominal value + (tolerance × nominal value) FORMULA 7.9

The minimum value can be obtained by multiplying the nominal value by the tolerance and then subtracting this product from the nominal value:

Minimum value = nominal value − (tolerance × nominal value) FORMULA 7.10

EXAMPLE:
A resistance is marked to show a nominal value of 2.2 kΩ and a tolerance of 5 percent. What is the range of actual resistances this component can have? ■

SOLUTION:
Since the nominal value and the tolerance are known, Formulas 7.9 and 7.10 can be used to calculate the maximum and minimum resistance values that this component may actually have.

$$\text{Maximum value} = \text{nominal value} + (\text{tolerance} \times \text{nominal value})$$

$$\text{Maximum value} = 2200 + (0.05 \times 2200)$$

$$\text{Maximum value} = 2310\ \Omega$$

For the minimum value,

$$\text{Minimum value} = \text{nominal value} - (\text{tolerance} \times \text{nominal value})$$

$$\text{Minimum value} = 2200 - (0.05 \times 2200)$$

$$\text{Minimum value} = 2090\ \Omega$$

In other words, the range of values that a 5 percent tolerance, 2.2-kΩ resistance may possess is from 2090 to 2310 Ω. ■

Sometimes, it is necessary to check the values of components to see if the marked tolerance is true. The same formulas can be used for this.

EXAMPLE:
A resistance with a nominal value of 620 Ω and a marked tolerance of 5 percent is found to have a resistance of 580 Ω. Is this resistance correctly marked? ■

SOLUTION:
Since 580 is less than 620, Formula 7.10 is used to calculate the actual tolerance.

$$\text{Minimum value} = \text{nominal value} - (\text{tolerance} \times \text{nominal value})$$

$$580 = 620 - (620 \times T)$$

$$-40 = -620\,T$$

dividing both sides by −620

$$0.0645 = T$$

T, the actual tolerance, is almost 6.5 percent. The resistance has been incorrectly marked or its value has changed. ■

Inexperienced circuit designers sometimes forget that component tolerances are important. In general, components with greater tolerance, that is, those whose values may fall into a larger range, are cheaper than components whose possible values are closer to the nominal value. For example, a 15-kΩ resistance with a 10 percent tolerance may possess a value between 13,500 and 16,500 Ω, while a 15-kΩ, 0.1 percent resistance has a range from 14,985 to 15,015Ω. On the other hand, the component with the lower tolerance will cost considerably more. This means that manufacturers will use components with greater tolerances whenever possible. This can lead to trouble if the circuit designer has not taken component tolerances into consideration in the design.

EXAMPLE:
Engineer Vardis has designed the series circuit shown in Figure 7.48, using three 100 Ω resistances in series with a 9-V source. Since the circuit current is

$$I = \frac{E}{R} = 30\text{ mA},$$

the power dissipated by each resistance should be

$$P = I^2R = 0.09\text{ W}.$$

Figure 7.48 Will resistors with a power dissipation rating of 0.1 W operate safely in this circuit?

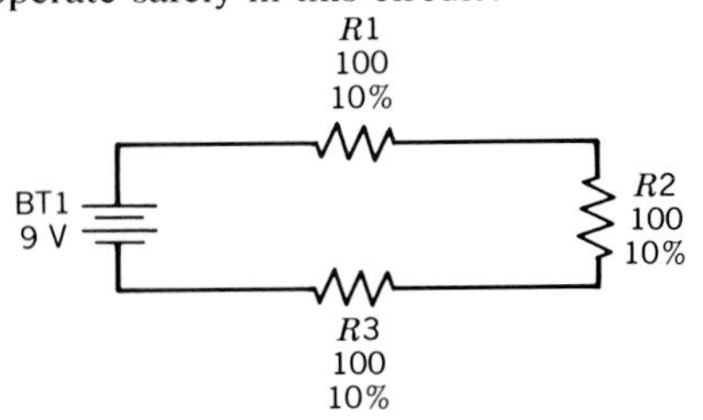

Vardis specifies using resistances with a power dissipation of 0.1 W. Will this be sufficient if the manufacturer of the circuit uses resistances with a 10 percent resistance tolerance? ■

SOLUTION:
Since the nominal resistance value is 100 Ω and the tolerance is 10 percent, the value range of each resistance is

$$\begin{aligned}\text{Minimum value} &= \text{nominal value} - (\text{tolerance} \times \text{nominal value})\\ &= 100 - (0.1 \times 100)\\ &= 90\ \Omega\end{aligned}$$

while the maximum value is

$$\begin{aligned}\text{Maximum value} &= \text{nominal value} + (\text{tolerance} \times \text{nominal value})\\ &= 100 + (0.1 \times 100)\\ &= 110\ \Omega\end{aligned}$$

The range of *each* resistance is from 90 to 110 Ω. If all three resistances exhibit their nominal value, the circuit current is

$$I = \frac{E}{R} = \frac{9}{300} = 0.03 \text{ A}$$

and the power dissipated by each resistance is $P = I^2R = 0.09$ W. This is within the 0.1-W rated value. If all three resistances have the maximum value allowed by the range, 110 Ω, things are better still. The circuit current is

$$I = \frac{E}{R} = \frac{9}{330} = 0.0273,$$

and the power dissipated in each resistance is

$$P = I^2R = 0.0819 \text{ W}.$$

Even if each resistance is at its minimum value of 90 Ω and the circuit current is

$$I = \frac{E}{R} = \frac{9}{270} = 0.0333,$$

the power I^2R is at its rated limit, with $P = 0.0999$, or 0.1. Stopping at this point, however, would be a mistake. If one resistance was at its maximum, 110 Ω, while the other two were at their minimum, the circuit current would be

$$I = \frac{E}{R} = \frac{9}{290} = 0.0310 \text{ A}.$$

The power dissipated in the 110 Ω resistance would be

$$P = I^2R = 0.106 \text{ W},$$

some 6 percent *higher* than permitted. ■

Although the computations are rather simple, try the following problems so that tolerance calculations become familiar.

1. Given the following nominal values and tolerances, calculate the range of actual values for each component.

a. 8.1 kΩ, 2 percent b. 1 MΩ, 10 percent
c. 1.55 V, 15 percent d. 0.33 nF, 20 percent
e. 1.066 Ω, 0.1 percent f. 51 kΩ, 2 percent
g. 10 H, 30 percent h. 1.36 k, 1 percent

2. A series circuit is composed of a source rated at 10 V, 1.5 percent, and three resistances, 12 Ω, 10 percent; 80 Ω, 5 percent; and 150 Ω, 2 percent (see Figure 7.49). What is the maximum current that might flow through the circuit? The minimum?

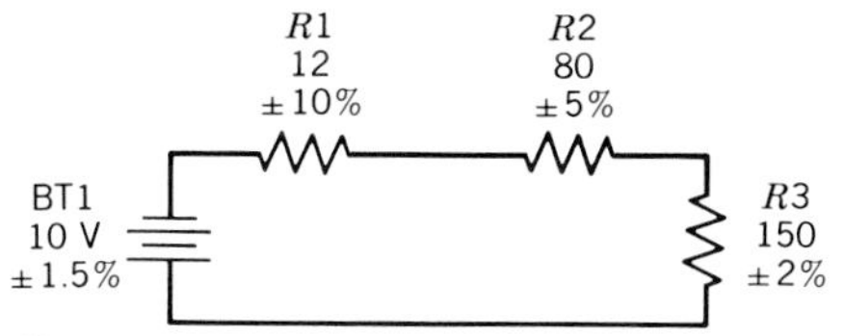

Figure 7.49 Circuit for problem 2.

3. The resistances in Problem 2 are now connected in parallel across the source. What are the maximum and minimum total currents provided by the source? What is the maximum power dissipated by the 150Ω resistance?

4. Complete the following table of resistance values and tolerances.

Nominal Value	*Measured Value*	*Marked Tolerance*	*Tolerance Based on Measured Value*
39 k	40,500	2%	?
15	16.5	5%	?
6.8 k	6.3 k	None	?
12.2 k	13 k	1%	?
180 k	168 k	None	?

5. Engineer Vardis is designing another circuit, shown in Figure 7.50. What would the greatest resistance tolerance be if the power dissipated by R_1 could never exceed 2.0 W? Both the resistances are to have the same tolerance, and this tolerance is a whole percent (not a fraction or decimal.)

Hint: Try 5 percent as a trial value.

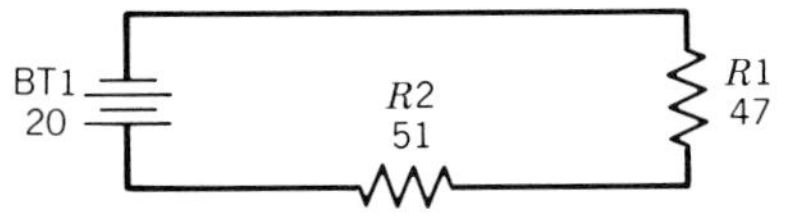

Figure 7.50 Circuit for problem 5.

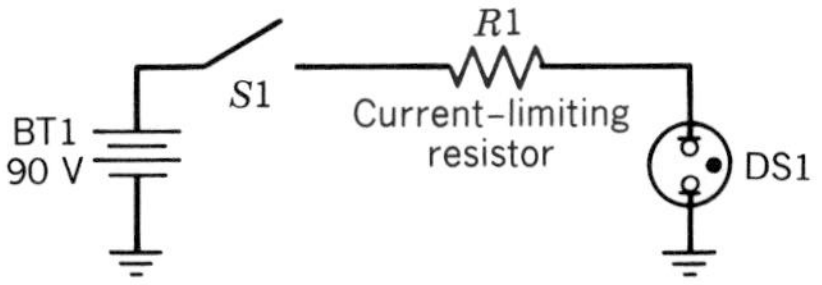

Figure 7.52 A resistor in series with a neon lamp limits the current through the lamp after the neon gas is ionized.

D. APPLICATIONS

D.1 WHAT IS A RESISTOR?

You have probably seen some small, cylindrical components painted with bright color stripes in photographs of electronic units. Most of these components, resembling those shown in Figure 7.51, are *resistors*. The resistor is the electrical or electronic component that provides resistance in a circuit. Of course, all of the components discussed in previous chapters, such as wires, lamps, and switches, possess resistance. All conductors operating at or near commonly encountered temperatures possess resistance. The difference is that the only function of the resistor is to provide a specific amount of resistance in a standard-sized, easy-to-connect package. Regardless of its shape or composition, the schematic diagram symbol for a resistor is exactly like that previously used for any resistance, -\/\/\/-, and its resistance is measured in ohms. The reference designator for a resistor is also R, so $R1$ may refer either to resistance 1 or resistor 1.

D.2 WHY RESISTORS ARE USED

Since any resistance in a circuit will dissipate electrical energy as heat, you may wonder why resistors are used at all. Except for wire, resistors are the most common electronic components. There must be a good reason. Actually, there are four general uses for resistors.

The first is to limit the amount of current flowing in a circuit. In many cases, the resistance of the connecting wires and other components in a circuit is so low that the circuit current would cause damage if a current-limiting resistor was not used. The resistor (R1) shown in series with the neon lamp (DS1) in Figure 7.52 is a good example of the series-connected current-limiting resistor. When the switch is first closed, the neon gas in the lamp is not yet ionized, and so there is no conducting path through the lamp. The lamp acts as an open circuit. Since there is no circuit current, the potential drop across the resistor is zero:

$$E = I \times R = 0 \times R = 0$$

This means that the full potential difference supplied by the source is applied across the lamp. This causes the gas in the lamp to ionize and creates a relatively low-resistance path through the glowing lamp. At this point, if the resistor was not in the circuit, a large current would flow through the lamp, quickly overheating and destroying it. Almost the whole circuit resistance is supplied by the resistor, which limits the circuit current to a couple of milliamperes, a safe level for this lamp.

A second use of a series-connected current-limiting resistor is shown in Figure 7.53*a* and 7.53*b*. In this circuit, the incandescent lamps have a low cold resistance. Since there are several in parallel, the effective circuit resistance is very low the moment that the switch is closed. The surge current produced in the circuit might be sufficient to damage the switch, the source, or even the connecting wires. To prevent this damage, a small series resistor can be included, as shown in Figure 7.53*b*. The moment the switch is closed, the surge resistor R_1 provides most of the circuit resistance. This limits the amount of current through the circuit. When the lamps have come up to operating temperature, their resistance is greater, and the presence of the surge resistor has little effect on the circuit.

These two are examples of the use of series resistors to reduce or control circuit current. A resistor can also be placed in parallel with a component to reduce the amount of current through it. The parallel resistor shown in Figure 7.54 is called a *shunt*. The shunt resistor frequently has a resistance that is lower than that of the components with which it is in parallel. This means that most of the current flows through the shunt. Shunt resistors may be used in parallel with any sort of component, and they are frequently found in parallel with current-measuring meters. Since the presence of the shunt controls the amount of circuit current that flows through the meter, this resistor can be used

Figure 7.51 Typical resistors. (Photo by M. Hermes.)

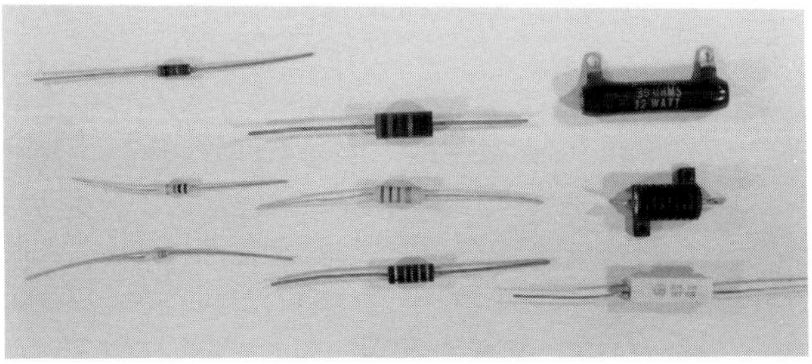

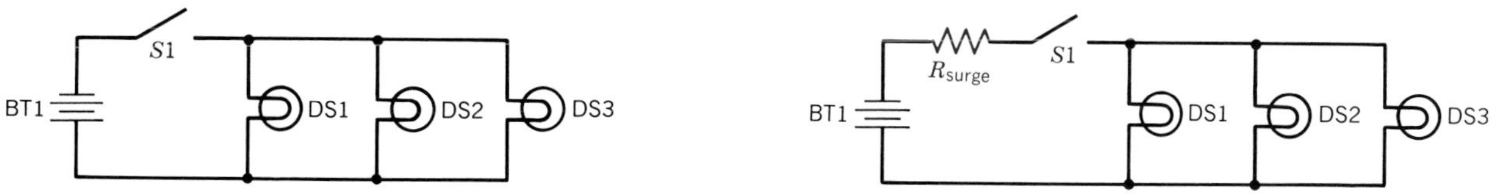

(a) Without a series resistance a very large current will flow when S1 is closed.

(b) Including R_{surge} limits the circuit current when S1 is closed.

Figure 7.53 A series resistor is used to prevent current surges in a circuit.

to increase the range of a meter. For example, the meter shown in Figure 7.54 normally indicates a full-scale reading when 1 mA flows through it. If it is necessary to use this meter to measure 0 to 10 mA instead of 0 to 1 mA, a shunt is used that will conduct 9 mA of the circuit current when this current is 10 mA. The actual value of the shunt resistor depends on the resistance of the meter itself. The calculation of meter shunt values is discussed in Chapter 8.

The second of the four major applications of resistors is to provide a load for a circuit. Some circuits, such as those used in transmitters and stereo amplifiers, require a load of some sort to prevent overheating and destruction of the semiconductors. Some power supply circuits also require loads in the form of resistors to function properly.

The potential dropping ability of resistors is a third useful characteristic. For example, Figure 7.55 shows how a 6-V, 150-mA lamp can be operated from a 12-V source by using a 40 Ω resistor in series with the lamp. The voltage drop across the resistor is $E = I \times R = 6$ V, so that the potential difference across the lamp is $12 - 6 = 6$ V, as required. Voltage-dropping resistors are among the most commonly used electronic components.

Another, and final common use for resistors resembles voltage dropping. It is the use of two or more

Figure 7.54 A shunt resistor used with a meter.

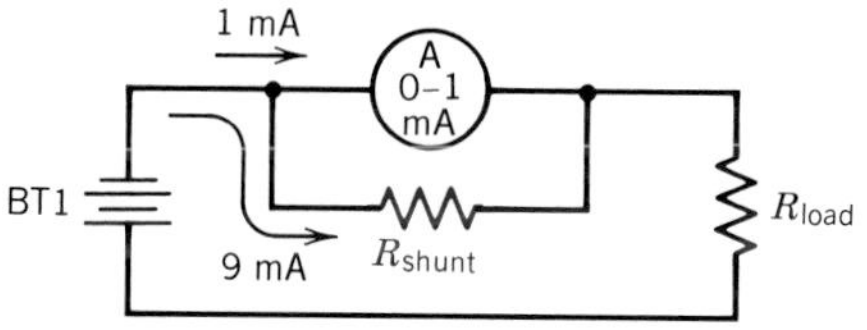

Figure 7.55 A resistor used to reduce the potential difference of a 12-V battery so that a 6-V lamp can be used.

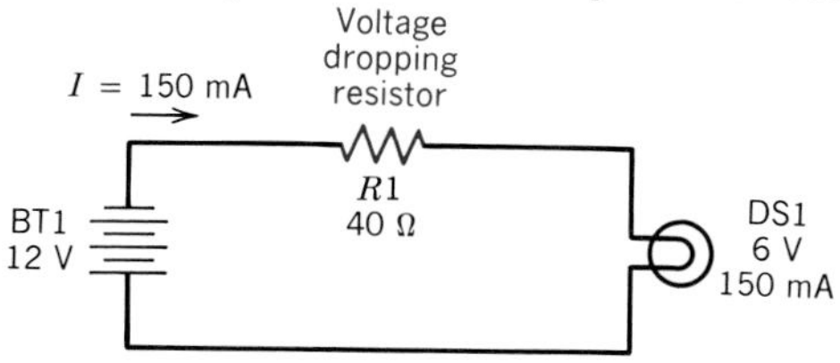

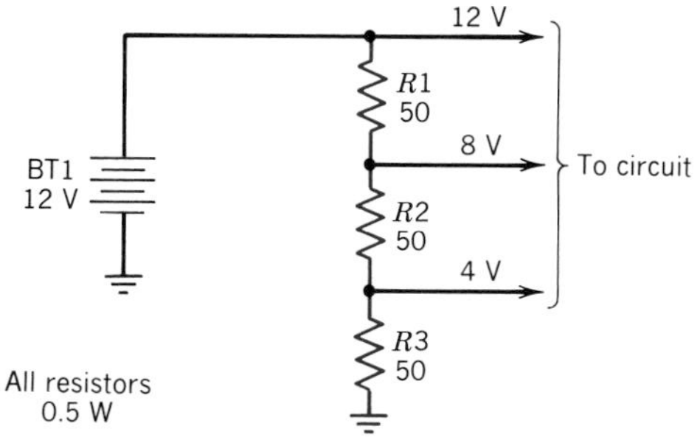

Figure 7.56 A voltage divider is used when several potential differences are required in different parts of the circuit.

resistors in series, as shown in Figure 7.56, to obtain specific potentials for use in other parts of the circuit. Such arrangements of resistors are called *voltage dividers*. Voltage dividers will be discussed more fully in the next chapter.

D.3 TYPES OF FIXED RESISTORS

There are two main kinds of resistors, *fixed* resistors, which have a certain nominal resistance value, and *variable* resistors, devices whose resistance can be changed by moving a contact point. Fixed resistors are the most common, and their various forms will be considered first.

D.3.1 WIRE-WOUND RESISTORS

The wire-wound resistor, shown in Figure 7.57*a*, is composed of a coil of wire wound around a cylindrical form made of ceramic or other heat-resistant, insulating material. Wire materials of various resistivities are used, depending on whether a high or low resistance is required. Size and lead or connection lug details vary with the manufacturer. Typical small units like that shown in Figure 7.57*a* rated at a power dissipation of 2 W, are 0.014 m in length and 0.0057 m in diameter. Large, commercially available units are wound with a heavy-gauge wire and are 0.26 m long and about 0.03 m in diameter. They are rated at a power dissipation of 225 or 250 W depending on the manufacturer. Depending on the power dissipation, wire-wound resis-

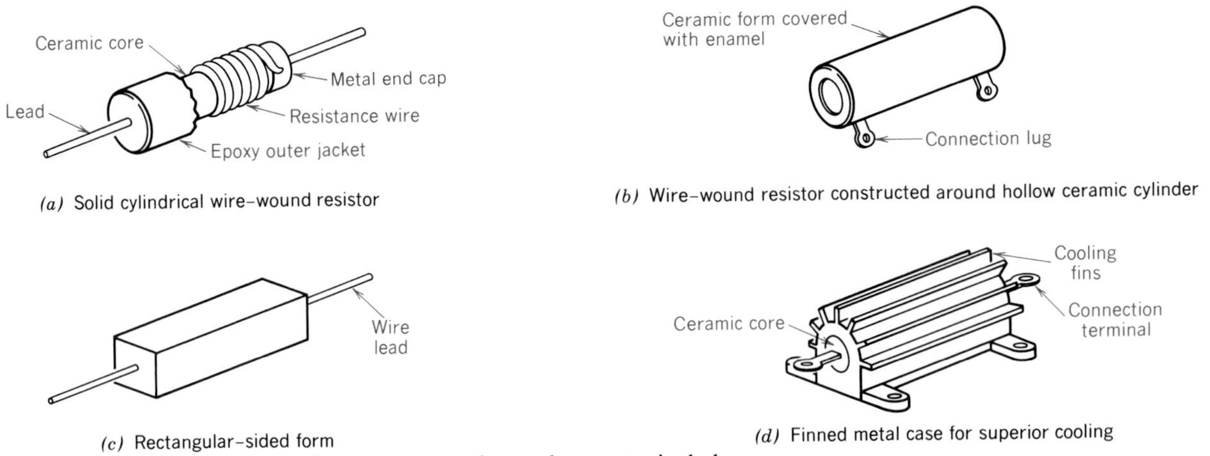

(a) Solid cylindrical wire-wound resistor

(b) Wire-wound resistor constructed around hollow ceramic cylinder

(c) Rectangular-sided form

(d) Finned metal case for superior cooling

Figure 7.57 Wire-wound resistors; construction and some typical shapes.

tors are easily available in resistances from less than 1 Ω to 270 kΩ. Tolerances range from 1 to 10 percent.

The shape and appearance of the wire-wound resistor has changed little during the last 50 years. The solid cylindrical form in Figure 7.57*a* and the hollow cylinder, which allows for better air circulation and improved cooling (Figure 7.57*b*) are still popular styles. Two newer case types are shown in Figure 7.57*c* and 7.57*d*. The rectangular sides of 7.57*c* permit the resistor to be placed against a metal chassis or plate to dissipate heat more effectively. The style shown in Figure 7.57*d* surrounds the ceramic resistor with a finned metal case, which can be attached to a plate or chassis with screws. This arrangement permits effective cooling of the resistor, which is insulated from the case.

In addition to these general-purpose units, special low-resistance wire-wound resistors are used as meter shunts and in other applications where high-accuracy, low-resistance components are required. Tolerances as low as 0.1 or 0.05 percent can be obtained in standard manufacture. Although nearly all the high power dissipation resistors in use today are wire wound, this type of resistor has two serious drawbacks: it provides problems when used in some ac circuits, and it is considerably more expensive than the carbon or film types.

D.3.2 CARBON COMPOSITION RESISTORS

Like wire-wound resistors, carbon resistors were among the first electronic components used. One form of carbon resistor consisted of a carbon rod of a specific length and thickness with connecting wires wrapped about either end. Later improvements were the use of a specifically formulated carbon composition core material in place of the pure carbon, and the encapsulation of the core in a moulded plastic or epoxy case, as shown in Figure 7.58. The component pictured here is called a *carbon composition resistor* and, except for wire, used to be the most commonly used electronic component. Even though they are being replaced by film resistors, composition resistors are so cheap that many millions of them are manufactured and used every year. Standard resistances from 1 Ω or less to 22 MΩ or more, in power dissipations ranging from $\frac{1}{10}$ to 2 W, and tolerances of 2, 5, and 10 percent are usually stocked by suppliers.

Carbon composition resistors have a number of disadvantages. First, they are surprisingly sensitive to damage by excessive heat, moisture, shock, and static discharge. For example, carbon composition resistor power ratings should never be exceeded. If a 0.5-W carbon composition resistor is forced to dissipate a full watt, even for brief periods of time, the heating effect will considerably shorten the effective life of the component and cause its resistance value to change.

Even if operated within its ratings, a carbon composition resistor will show a steady change in resistance throughout its life span. This gradual change can result in a change in resistance value of 15 percent or so, even in a 5 percent tolerance resistor. Because of this, a 100 Ω, 5 percent tolerance resistor, which originally had a resistance range of 100 ±5 percent, that is, 95 to 105 Ω, could end its life with a resistance range of 80.75 to 120.75 Ω, or a total tolerance of 20 percent. In certain circuits, changes of this sort could cause a deterioration of performance, faulty operation, or even damage to other components. Therefore, in critical cir-

Figure 7.58 Cutaway view of a typical carbon composition resistor.

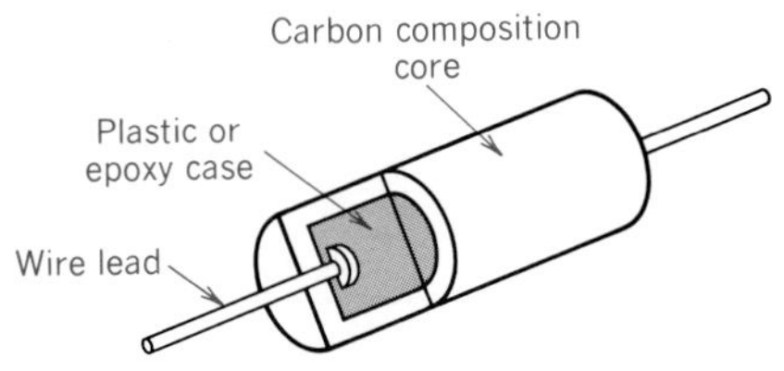

cuits where change in resistance value might be troublesome, either a wire-wound or film resistor is used.

Moisture, shock, and, as has been recently discovered, static discharge will also shorten the life expectancy of carbon composition resistors by increasing the rate of resistance change. The application of excessive heat during soldering has a dramatic effect on carbon composition resistors. The resistance value changes measurably and, if sufficient heat is applied, the case may blister or crack.

D.3.3 FILM RESISTORS

The film resistor differs from the carbon composition resistor in the form of its resistance element. In the film resistor, the resistance element is a thin film or coating of carbon or metallic film deposited on an insulating core of ceramic or glass. This film is frequently etched or cut in the form of a helix, as shown in Figure 7.59, to increase the length of the path between the resistor leads. The leads are attached to the core by means of metal caps and the whole assembly is covered with an epoxy or other insulating plastic jacket.

Film resistors are regularly manufactured in a greater range of power dissipation ratings than carbon composition resistors. Standard ratings are $\frac{1}{10}$, $\frac{1}{8}$, $\frac{1}{4}$, $\frac{1}{2}$, 1, and 2 W. Metal film resistors are more stable than carbon resistors. They have a smaller percent change in resistance value because of temperature change or operational life. Since the coating process can be very precisely controlled, film resistor tolerances better than those of carbon resistors are easily obtained. Standard film resistors are available in tolerances of 5, 2, 1, 0.5, and 0.1 percent.

Although even less expensive than carbon composition resistors, carbon film resistors tend to be less tolerant of overheating. Even with this limitation, the carbon film resistor, usually distinguishable from the carbon composition resistor by the end cap bulges shown in Figure 7.59, is replacing the more costly component in many applications.

Metal film resistors are used where precision resistors are required. It is relatively more difficult to produce low-resistance metallic films than wire-wound units, but for resistances greater than 10 Ω and power dissipations of less than 1 W, a metallic film resistor is often the choice.

Figure 7.59 Cross section of a typical film resistor.

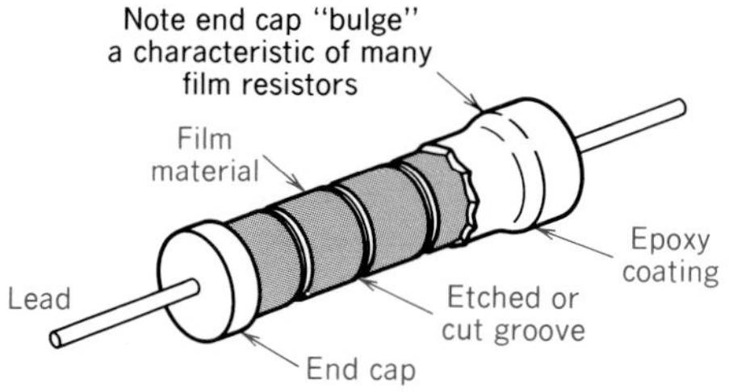

D.4 STANDARD RESISTOR VALUES

In the early days of electronics, industry-wide standard values were unheard of. Each manufacturer could sell components such as resistors without worrying about tolerances or final value checking. The range of actual resistance values in these early components must have been enormous, and early technicians must have been satisfied if a component worked, without worrying much about tolerances.

As the electronics industry grew, the standardization of component values came into being to reduce the number of different resistors manufacturers had to produce, as well as the number that had to be stocked for replacement. This was accomplished by carefully choosing values so that it would be possible to manufacture a set of 10 percent tolerance resistors whose nominal values would be within 10 percent of nearly any resistance that might be required, or a set of 5 percent tolerance resistors whose nominal values would be within 5 percent of any resistance that might be required. The process was to choose a set of base values. The resistors actually manufactured have resistances that are decimal multiples (×1, ×10, ×100, etc.) of the base values. The base values for 10 and 5 percent resistors are shown in the left-hand columns of Tables 7.1 and 7.2. Using these tables it is possible to find the nominal values of the 10 and 5 percent value resistors in standard manufacture. This is done by multiplying a base number by a decimal multiplier (10^{-1}, 10^0, 10^1, 10^2, 10^3, 10^4, 10^5, and 10^6 are standard multipliers). The resistance range values are listed next to each base number in the table. For example, the range

Table 7.1 Ten percent tolerance resistor base values

Base Value	*Maximum*	*Minimum*
1.0	1.1	0.9
1.2	1.32	1.08
1.5	1.65	1.35
1.8	1.98	1.62
2.2	2.42	1.98
2.7	2.97	2.43
3.3	3.63	2.97
3.9	4.29	3.51
4.7	5.17	4.23
5.6	6.16	5.04
6.8	7.48	6.12
8.2	9.02	7.38

Table 7.2 Five percent tolerance resistor values

Base Value	*Maximum*	*Minimum*
1.0	1.05	0.95
1.1	1.155	1.045
1.2	1.26	1.14
1.3	1.365	1.235
1.5	1.575	1.425
1.6	1.68	1.52
1.8	1.89	1.71
2.0	1.9	2.1
2.2	2.31	2.09
2.4	2.52	2.28
2.7	2.835	2.565
3.0	3.15	2.85
3.3	3.465	3.135
3.6	3.78	3.42
3.9	4.095	3.705
4.3	4.515	4.085
4.7	4.935	4.465
5.1	5.355	4.845
5.6	5.88	5.32
6.2	6.51	5.89
6.8	7.14	6.46
7.5	7.875	7.125
8.2	8.61	7.79
9.1	9.555	8.645

of a 12 × 10^3, or 12 kΩ, 10 percent resistor is 10.8 to 13.2 kΩ.

The range values listed in the tables are useful for choosing a standard value resistor for a particular circuit function.

EXAMPLE:
Select a 10 percent tolerance resistor that will provide a 7-V voltage drop in a circuit with a current of 40 mA. ■

SOLUTION:
The exact value of the resistance is found by using Ohm's law

$$R = \frac{E}{I} = \frac{7}{0.04} = 175\ \Omega$$

From Table 7.1 you can see that 175 Ω lies within the range of a standard 180 Ω, 10 percent resistor. ■

There are 12 base value numbers in Table 7.1. This means that each power of 10 multiplier from 10^{-1} to 10^6 contains 12 resistors, or a total of 96 standard values in common use. Notice that two significant digits plus an exponent are sufficient to specify any of the base values.

Because of the reduced range of 5 percent resistors, 24 values are required for each power of 10 multiplier as shown in Table 7.2. This means that a total of 192 different 5 percent tolerance standard resistors must be stocked for replacement purposes.

Most of the resistors used in consumer electronics equipment today are 10 percent tolerance, with some 5 percent components being used in critical circuits. Industrial equipment generally uses 5 percent resistors, with 2 and 1 percent units in critical circuits. Two percent tolerance resistors are frequently manufactured in the same values as 5 percent units. They are used when resistances closer to the nominal value than those provided by 5 percent resistors are needed.

D.5 THE COLOR CODE

One of the most obvious things about an electronic unit, once its covers have been removed, are the bright color bands that decorate resistors and some other components. Since resistors are rather small, it is difficult to print the resistance, tolerance, and power dissipation on the units themselves. Because of this, color bands are frequently used to code some of this information on the components.

The use of color bands to encode the resistance value and tolerance of resistors has become a widely followed practice among manufacturers. The most common form of color coding, used for 20, 10, 5, and 2 percent resistors is shown in Figure 7.60 and Table 7.3. This system uses from three to five color bands to represent the two significant figures of the resistance, the exponent or decimal multiplier, and, in most cases, the tolerance and either the reliability of the component or the percentage change in resistance expected per thousand hours of operation.

The numbers represented by these color bands are shown in Table 7.3. Notice that the meaning of a particular color band can be different in the third, fourth, or fifth positions. For example, a resistor is banded brown, black, red, gold, yellow. The two significant

Figure 7.60 Color-coding system commonly used for 20, 10, 5, and 2 percent tolerance resistors.

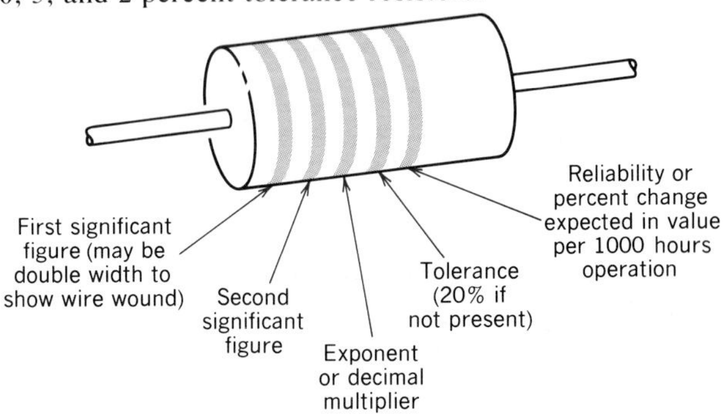

Table 7.3 Color code values for resistors

Color	*Value as First Significant Figure*	*Value as Second Significant Figure*	*Value as Multiplier*	*Value as Tolerance*	*Reliability or Percent Change Expected*
Black	Not used	0	10^0	Not Used	Not used
Brown	1	1	10^1	1%	1%
Red	2	2	10^2	2%	0.1%
Orange	3	3	10^3	Not used	0.01%
Yellow	4	4	10^4	Not used	0.001%
Green	5	5	10^5	Not used	Not used
Blue	6	6	10^6	Not used	Not used
Violet	7	7	10^7	Not used	Not used
Grey	8	8	Not used	Not used	Not used
White	9	9	Not used	Not used	Not used
None	—	—	—	20%	—
Silver	—	—	10^{-2}	10%	—
Gold	—	—	10^{-1}	5%	—

figures of its resistance value are 1 (brown) and 0 (black). The third band means that the two significant figures are multiplied by 10^2. The nominal resistance therefore is 10×10^2 or 1000 Ω. The fourth band sets the tolerance at 5 percent, while the fifth band most likely means that the failure rate of resistors of this sort is 0.001 percent per thousand hours of operation. That is, in tests of this type of resistor, one unit in 100,000 could be expected to fail after a thousand hours of operation.

Notice that gold or silver bands can also be used in the third position for resistance values of less than 10 Ω. For example, a resistor banded green, blue, gold, gold has 5 and 6 for its significant figures and 0.1 for its multiplier. Its nominal resistance is 5.6 Ω.

The resistor color coding system is the most common in use today, and must be learned thoroughly, both in terms of remembering the values of the various colors and being able to read them on resistors. Memorizing the color values is actually the easier task. Mnemonics and various memory helps have been devised, ranging from the obscene to the absurd, for example:

0	Black	Base
1	Brown	Balls
2	Red	Rip
3	Orange	Off
4	Yellow	Your
5	Green	Glove
6	Blue	But
7	Violet	Volleyballs
8	Gray	Generally
9	White	Won't

A more serious problem is reading the color code. Sometimes it is difficult to decide which is the first band, especially on small-sized resistors when all five bands are present. One way of determining which is the first band is to look for the tolerance band, which is most generally gold, silver, or red. Once the fourth tolerance band has been identified, it is easy to read the value of the two significant figures and the multiplier. Another problem arises from the colors themselves. Sometimes heat will discolor the coding bands so badly that it is difficult to distinguish them. In other cases, it is difficult to distinguish between violet and brown when these colors are too thinly painted over the standard dark brown case of a carbon composition resistor. In some cases, measuring the resistance is the only solution.

You will sometimes come across a resistor that has a double-width first band. Certain manufacturers use this to show a wire-wound resistor. Beware, however, of components that look like resistors but have a black or silver first band. These are not resistors. Remember, the color band coding is used for other components as well.

At first glance, there seem to be two problems with this system. First, nothing is said about power dissipation. Since the power dissipation depends greatly on the surface area of a component, the size of a resistor itself will convey this information. The second problem of this system is that it does not make provision for encoding more than two significant figures before the multiplier. Since the standard values for 10 and 5 percent resistors only possess two significant figures, there was no difficulty with this. Resistors with 1 percent or better tolerances were usually larger wire-wound units and had sufficient room to print the resistance value. The introduction of carbon and metallic film resistors may be bringing this happy state of affairs to an end. One percent tolerance resistors, which require three significant figures plus a multiplier, are be-

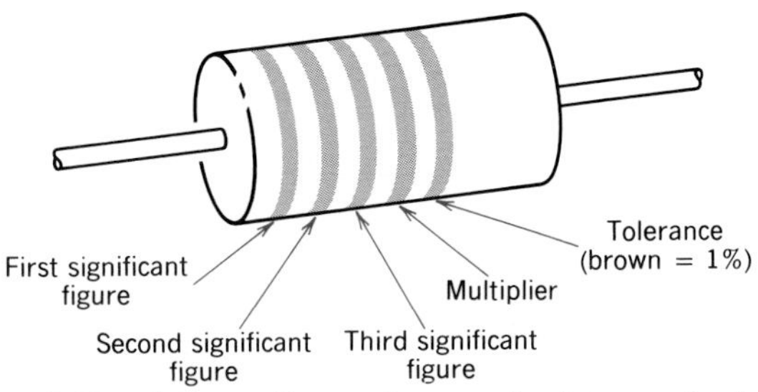

Figure 7.61 Color-coding system coming into use for 1 percent tolerance resistors.

coming more common. The color banding and band values for these units are shown in Figure 7.61. For example, a resistor banded blue, gray, orange, red, brown is a 1 percent tolerance, 68,300 Ω resistor.

In practice, there is not too much chance of confusion between the two- and three-significant-figure systems. The 20 percent tolerance resistors, which are rare today, only have three color bands. Ten and 5 percent resistors have distinctive silver or gold tolerance bands. One percent, three-significant-figure resistors all have a brown fifth tolerance band. Because of these distinctive features, there is much more danger of reading a three-significant-figure resistor backward than there is of confusing the two- and three-significant-figure coding systems.

D.6 RESISTOR SIZE AND POWER DISSIPATION

The size of a resistor is totally independent of its resistance value. By changing the composition of the materials used in resistor manufacture, a resistance of 100 MΩ can be placed in the same size component as a resistance of 0.1 Ω. The physical size of the resistor is chosen on the basis of the amount of heat the component will be required to dissipate while operating, which is the power dissipation of the resistor.

A large-size resistor will have a large surface area and will be better cooled by the air than a smaller component. This means that regardless of its resistance, a large-size resistor will dissipate more heat, operate at a cooler temperature, and have a higher power dissipation rating than a smaller resistor. A small resistor may char or actually burn if required to dissipate too much heat.

Because of the connection between size and power dissipation, it was not thought necessary to use a color code or any special marking to give the power dissipation of resistors with dissipations of 2 W or less.

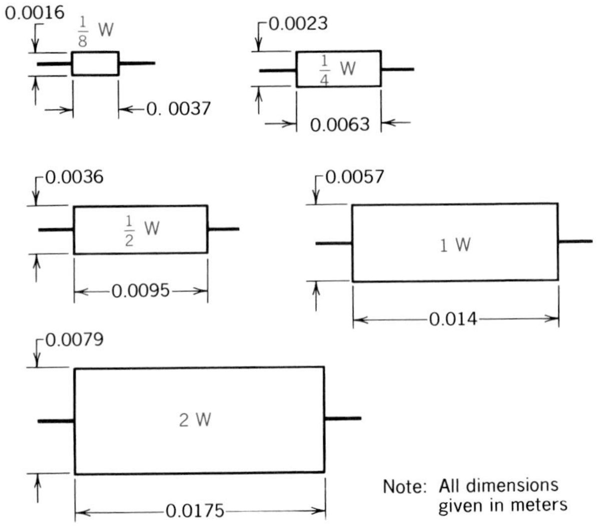

Figure 7.62 Power ratings of carbon composition resistors are shown by the case sizes.

Instead, a limited number of standard dissipations were selected and packaged in more or less standard sizes. These are shown in Figure 7.62. These standard sizes were based on carbon composition resistors that would produce temperatures of 70°C or less during operation. For larger resistors, with power dissipation ratings of 3 W or greater, size and shape are not standardized, and the power rating, like the resistance, is printed on the component.

The newer film resistors do not fit so well into the power and size categories of the carbon composition types. Some manufacturers have departed somewhat from the standard sizes, while others, quite truthfully, claim that their 1-W size products can dissipate 2 or even 3 W without exceeding the 70°C temperature level. In spite of this, the majority of the resistors produced today still approximate the dimensions shown in Figure 7.62.

Due to the trend toward smaller electronic equipment and the lower power requirements of modern circuits, the number of 1- and 2-W resistors in modern units is decreasing. Even the $\frac{1}{2}$ W resistor, which was the most common component in vacuum tube circuits, is now less common than the $\frac{1}{4}$ W size. The growth of computer technology is in the process of allowing further reduction of resistor power ratings. Soon the $\frac{1}{8}$ and $\frac{1}{10}$ W sizes may become more popular than the $\frac{1}{4}$ W.

D.7 OTHER ENCODING SYSTEMS

In addition to the color band systems described in section D.5, a number of other methods of using color to encode resistance values were used with now obsolete resistor designs. Since you will probably not see these except in museums, there is no point in detailing them. The codes used for printing resistance values on the components, however, are important. These range from plain language statements like "150 Ω, 5 percent, 5 W," to obscure comments such as "RCO8GF102J." Strings of letters and numbers of this type are sometimes found on resistors in consumer or industrial products. They are frequent in units built for or approved by the military or government agencies. These codes refer to specific military specifications, familiarly called "MIL SPECs," which describe the standard characteristics of components. There are a number of specifications pertaining to resistances, but the two most common are MIL-R-11 for carbon composition resistors and MIL-R-10509 for film resistors. As explained in the specification and shown in Figure 7.63, the code printed on the resistor consists of a number of parts. The first two letters establish the type of component: *R* for resistor, and either *C* for composition or *N* for film. This is followed by two numbers that give the power rating and maximum recommended potential difference. The characteristic letter or letters follow. These are used for a variety of purposes, particularly to explain the conditions of the other characteristics. A three- or four-digit number follows, which is made up of the significant figures of the resistance plus the exponent of the multiplier. For example, 823 means 82,000 Ω, or 82 kΩ, and 1001 means 1000 Ω or 1 kΩ. The letter *R* is sometimes used to represent a decimal point: 47R0 means 47.0 Ω, while R470 means 0.470 Ω. Finally, the tolerance is encoded by a single letter, *F*, *G*, *J*, or *K*.

You should be able to find and interpret the resistance value and tolerance codes for these systems, although the power dissipation and maximum values can be looked up as necessary.

D.8 VARIABLE RESISTORS

The values of the components used in modern circuits are not exactly the nominal values, but fall within a component tolerance range. This means that a practical circuit may not function as intended once it has been constructed. Of course, it is always possible to keep redesigning or changing components until exactly the desired function and circuit characteristics are obtained. But this would take a long time and would mean that electronic units would have to be built one at a time. Even after the desired circuit function had been obtained, the gradual change in component values during operation would mean that any circuit would have to be rebuilt or redesigned after a certain number of hours of use. Even more absurd would be the necessity

Figure 7.63 Military-style resistor markings.

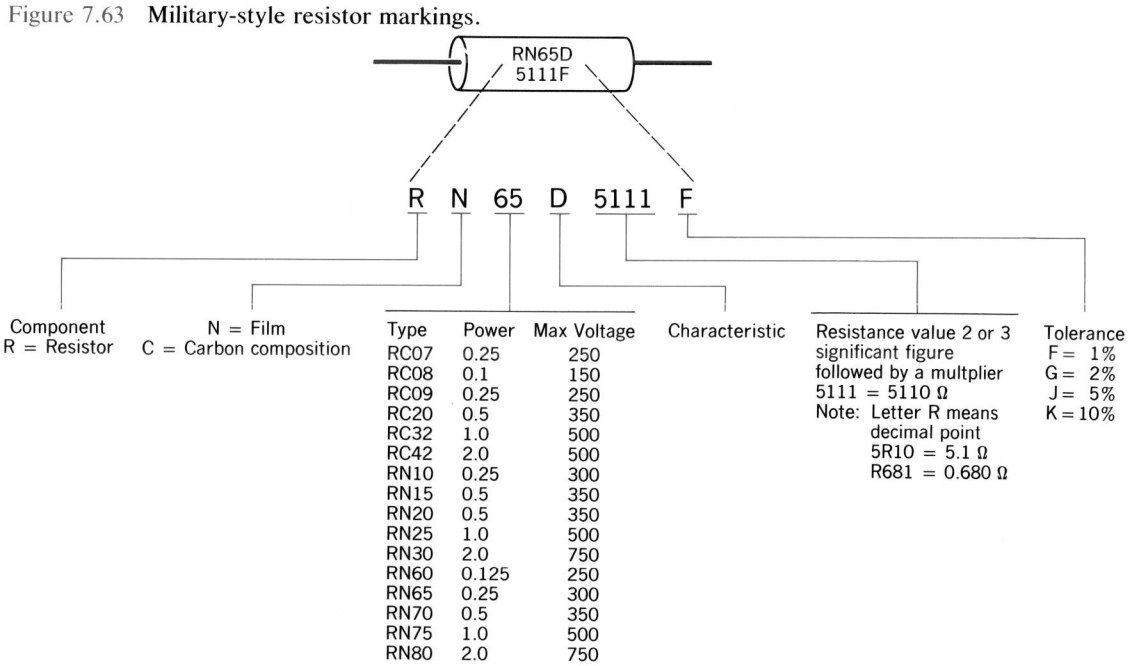

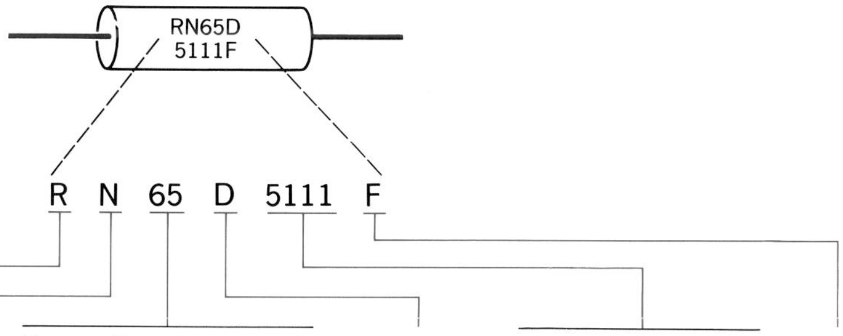

Component
R = Resistor

N = Film
C = Carbon composition

Type	Power	Max Voltage
RC07	0.25	250
RC08	0.1	150
RC09	0.25	250
RC20	0.5	350
RC32	1.0	500
RC42	2.0	500
RN10	0.25	300
RN15	0.5	350
RN20	0.5	350
RN25	1.0	500
RN30	2.0	750
RN60	0.125	250
RN65	0.25	300
RN70	0.5	350
RN75	1.0	500
RN80	2.0	750

Characteristic

Resistance value 2 or 3 significant figure followed by a multplier
5111 = 5110 Ω
Note: Letter R means decimal point
5R10 = 5.1 Ω
R681 = 0.680 Ω

Tolerance
F = 1%
G = 2%
J = 5%
K = 10%

of rebuilding or redesigning each circuit to fit similar, but slightly different needs. For example, you might have to own one stereo set for quiet listening and another for playing records at parties.

This absurd situation points out the need for variable components such as resistors whose resistance can be changed by a simple mechanical adjustment. Components of this type are frequently referred to as *variable resistors*, although there are a number of quite different types with specific characteristics and applications.

D.8.1 ADJUSTABLE RESISTORS

Figure 7.64 pictures a typical adjustable resistor. It is similar to a wire-wound resistor and consists of a length of resistance wire wound on a ceramic core. The wire ends are connected to the fixed terminals. The whole unit, except for the ends of the terminals and a contact area, is coated with an insulating glaze. Frequently, only one of the fixed terminals is actually used to provide electrical contact with the circuit. The second electrical contact with the resistance element is made through a contact point on a sliding ring. A tab, which is part of the sliding ring, provides the second electrical connection to the circuit. When the sliding ring is closest to one of the fixed terminals, the value of the resistance between that terminal and the ring is at a minimum. Moving the ring away from that terminal and toward the other fixed terminal increases the value of the resistance between the first terminal and the ring because there is a longer resistance path between them. Once the required amount of resistance has been obtained, a locking screw in the ring can be tightened to hold the ring in place.

Adjustable resistors of this sort are useful to adjust the circuit resistance when power is first applied after construction. They are easily readjusted from time to time as the values of other components vary. Although there are three electrical terminals on an adjustable resistor, if only two are used electrically, the schematic symbols shown in Figure 7.65*a* or 7.65*b* are used. When all three terminals are used electrically, the component

Figure 7.64 A typical adjustable resistor.

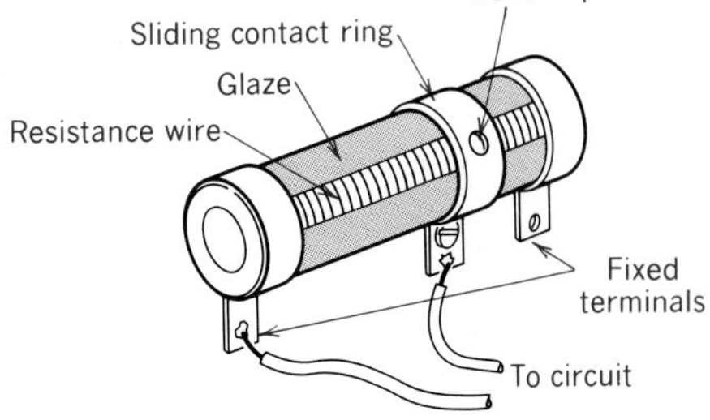

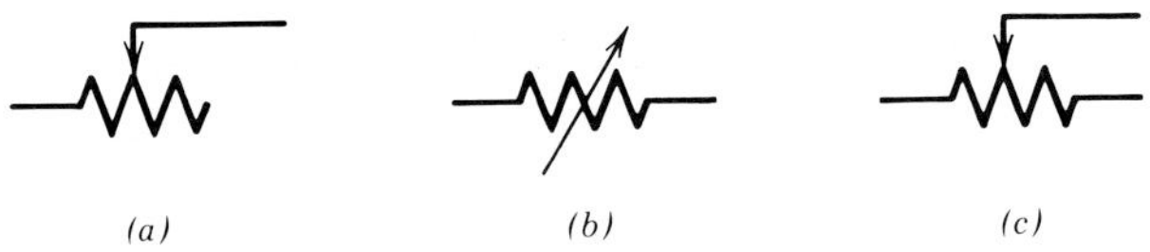

Figure 7.65 Adjustable resistor schematic symbols.

should be called a "potentiometer" and the schematic symbol shown in Figure 7.65*c* should be used.

D.8.2 THE RHEOSTAT

A *rheostat* is a two-terminal device of the sort pictured in Figure 7.66. It is similar to the adjustable resistor except that the resistance element has been wound around a ring-shaped form, and the movable contact point is fixed to a shaft that can be turned to change the point of contact with the resistance element. With this arrangement, the resistance between the terminal connected to the moving contact and the fixed terminal can be varied from nearly zero (when the movable contact touches the metal pad that connects the resistance element to the fixed terminal) to the resistance

Figure 7.66 A rheostat.

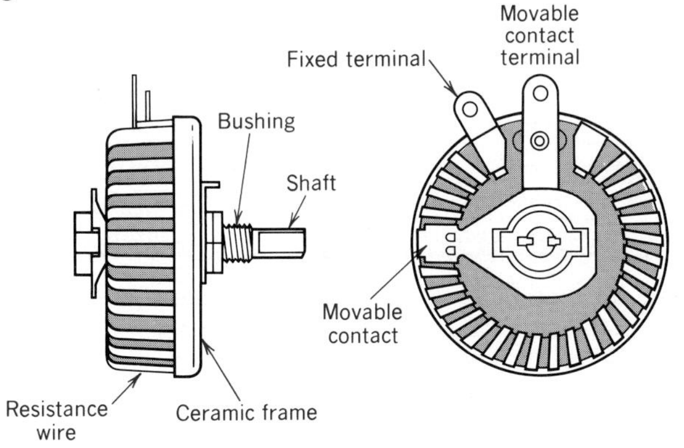

Figure 7.67 A potentiometer using a film resistance element.

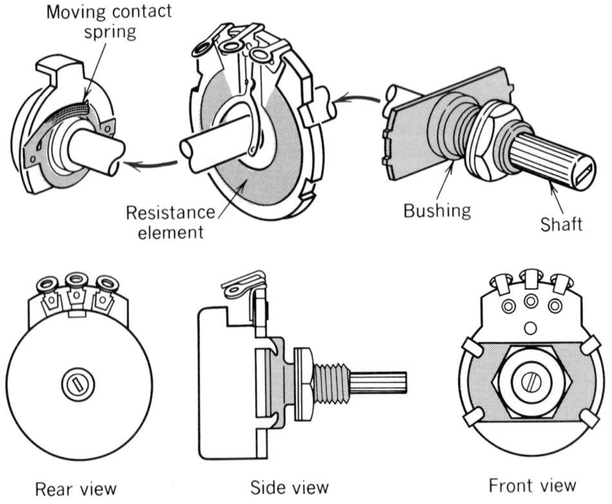

of the entire element (when the sliding contact is at the other end of the element.) Note that the terminal connected to the moving contact does not itself move.

In some models, the resistance element is not made of wire but is in the form of a carbon or metallic film deposited on the ring or horseshoe-shaped form (see Figure 7.67). A carbon or metallic film element cannot be used when it is necessary to dissipate large amounts of power. Carbon or film rheostats are, however, considerably less expensive than a wire-wound rheostat.

Two-terminal rheostats are regularly found in power distribution and industrial control equipment where high currents and therefore high power ratings are needed. Typically, the maximum resistance values of these larger units is low, from 1 to 100 Ω when the slider is at its farthest point from the fixed terminal and the power dissipation is from 5 to 50 W, although higher power rating components are available.

The rheostat is used when it is necessary to adjust circuit resistance frequently, so it is often placed on the front panel of a unit. The same schematic symbols used for the adjustable resistor are used for the rheostat.

D.8.3 THE POTENTIOMETER

If a second pad and fixed terminal are added to a rheostat as shown in Figure 7.67, the component is called a *potentiometer*, or *pot*, for short. Unlike the rheostat, the potentiometer is a three-terminal device, and all three terminals are connected to the circuit. Potentiometers get their rather long name from the fact that they are generally used to vary the potential applied at a point in a circuit. If, as in Figure 7.68, a potentiometer is connected across a source, the potential difference between its sliding contact represented by the arrow and the terminal connected to the positive terminal of the source can be adjusted from zero (when the sliding contact touches the terminal connected to the positive terminal of the source) to the full potential difference supplied by the source (when the slider touches the potentiometer terminal connected to the negative terminal of the source).

Figure 7.68 A potentiometer connected across a source.

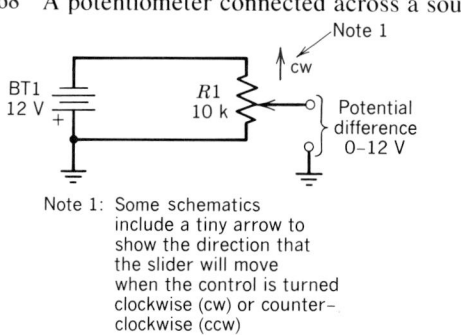

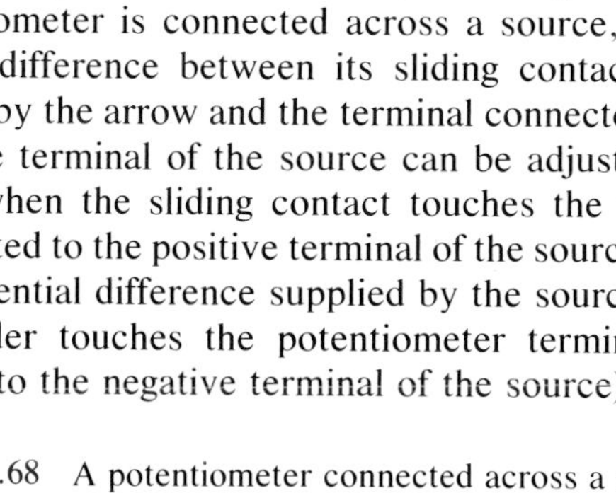
Note 1
cw
BT1
12 V
+
R1
10 k
Potential
difference
0–12 V
Note 1: Some schematics include a tiny arrow to show the direction that the slider will move when the control is turned clockwise (cw) or counter-clockwise (ccw)

Pots are generally not able to dissipate much power. Two watts is about the maximum for carbon or metallic film devices, and 4 W for wire-wound types. Potentiometer resistance elements are manufactured with much higher resistances than rheostat elements, and pots with carbon film resistance elements of 50 Ω up to 15 MΩ are available from distributors.

Most of the panel-mounting potentiometers used in industrial equipment today are manufactured so that their resistance varies linearly as the potentiometer shaft is turned. This means that the resistance between the moving contact and a fixed terminal will be half the element resistance when the shaft has been turned about 135° from counterclockwise to the clockwise stopping position. This is the halfway point since most panel potentiometer shafts only rotate 270° from their extreme clockwise to extreme counterclockwise stops. Rotating the shaft 10 percent of its total travel, or 27°, changes the resistance by 10 percent, and so on.

On the other hand, most of the front panel potentiometers used in entertainment equipment are *not* designed to be linear. This is because the human ear is not a linear device. Using a linear potentiometer to control the volume of a phonograph, radio receiver, alarm buzzer, or television set would result in too great a volume change for a given amount of control shaft rotation at low volume levels. Too little change would take place at the higher volume levels.

For this reason, special *audio taper* potentiometers are used in volume control circuits. The resistance of these components changes very slowly during the first third of the shaft rotation and then changes more quickly. Audio taper potentiometers should never be used in place of linear taper units or vice versa. If the wrong taper is used, it will be difficult to set the control properly.

D.8.4 TRIMMER POTENTIOMETERS

Another type of variable resistor is the *trimmer potentiometer*. "Trimmers," as they are frequently called, are actually a family of types. They are small, three-terminal devices used for the fine-tuning adjustment of electronic circuits. Trimmers used in consumer and in some industrial equipment resemble the resistance element and sliding contact of small panel potentiometers, but do not have a case or shaft. These components, pictured in Figure 7.69, are adjusted with a screw driver, or better yet, with a plastic alignment tool.

Because of the small size of the resistance element and the relatively large contact area between the sliding contact and the element, it is often difficult to set this type of trimmer exactly. The contact point can cover such a large area that even a minute rotation of the

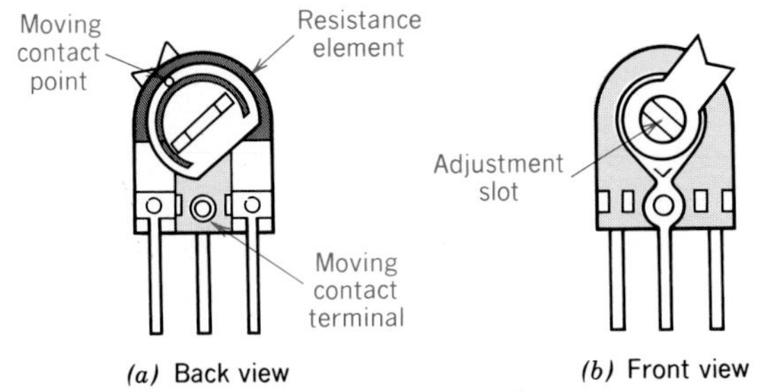

Figure 7.69 A typical trimmer potentiometer.

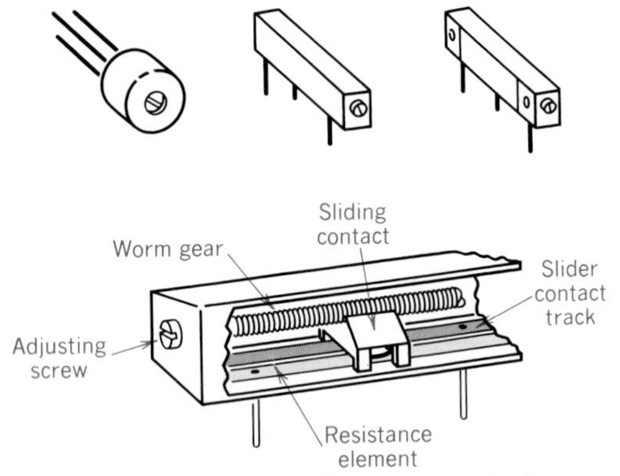

Figure 7.70 Multiturn potentiometers; typical case styles and construction.

adjustment tool causes a major change in the resistance between the sliding contact and fixed terminals. This is called a problem of poor *resolution*.

When poor resolution makes it difficult to adjust a circuit, the trimmers shown in Figure 7.69 are not used. Instead of devices that run through their entire resistance range with a single turn of the adjustment tool, *multiturn* potentiometers are used. Some typical multiturn pots are shown in Figure 7.70. In these units, a screw moves a contact along a resistance element. Better resolution is obtained since the contact area of the slide is smaller and the worm gear makes very slight movements possible. Anywhere from 4 to 25 complete turns of the adjustment screw, depending on the trimmer model, are required to move the slider from one end of the resistance element to the other.

The mechanical linkage between the adjustment screw and the slider is open to a certain amount of mechanical inaccuracy, particularly when the sliding contact has been moved to one end of its travel and the adjustment screw is turned further in the same direction. This makes it impossible to reset the trimmer to a particular position without making actual resistance or voltage measurements.

When extreme accuracy in setting a potentiometer, particularly a front-panel-mounted model, to an exact position is needed, a *multiturn control potentiometer* such as that pictured in Figure 7.71 is used.

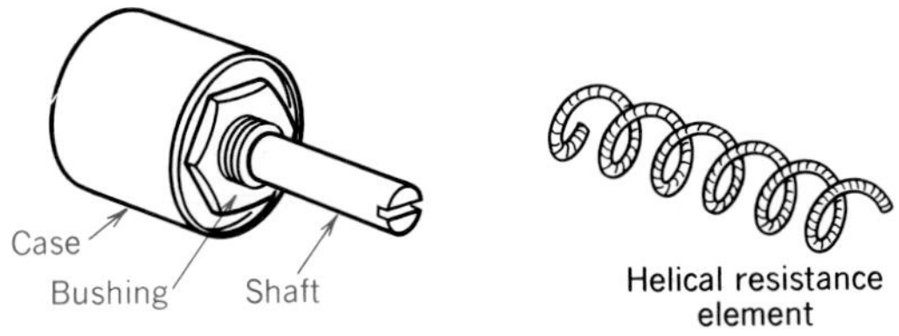

Figure 7.71 A multiturn control potentiometer.

Instead of a ring or horseshoe-shaped resistance element, multiturn control potentiometers use a helix-shaped element. It requires 10 or more full turns of the control shaft to move the sliding contact from one end of the resistance element helix to the other. When used with turn-counting dial plates and knobs, these potentiometers can be set to a predetermined position very precisely. In general, however, the high cost of a multiturn control pot and the associated turn counter limits the use of this system to test equipment or to extremely critical circuits.

E. PROGRAMMED REVIEW

FRAME 1

Circuit analysis can be defined as the subject that deals with the calculation of potential difference, current, resistance, and power in circuits. Circuit analysis techniques enable circuit designers to calculate the ______ ______ that must be used to obtain the potential or current required at different points in a circuit. The ____________ uses circuit analysis techniques to determine the current or potential that is supposed to be present at points in a circuit.

a. Component values; maintenance technician. (2)
b. Any other answer, review Section B.1.

FRAME 2

Select the correct definition for the technical terms listed below:

1. Network
2. Node
3. Junction
4. Network graph
5. Lumped load
6. Loop

a. A point at which three components are connected.
b. A diagram that replaces component symbols with lines.

c. An arrangement of electrically connected components.
d. A complete path traced through a circuit, without backtracking, to its beginning point.
e. A point at which two or more components are electrically connected.
f. A manner of treating a distributed resistance as though it were concentrated at one point in a circuit.

a. 1, c; 2, e; 3, a; 4, b; 5, f; 6, d. (3)
b. Any other arrangement, review Sections B.1, B.2, and B.4.

FRAME 3

Using network graphs, determine which two of the circuits in Figure 7.72 are electrically identical.

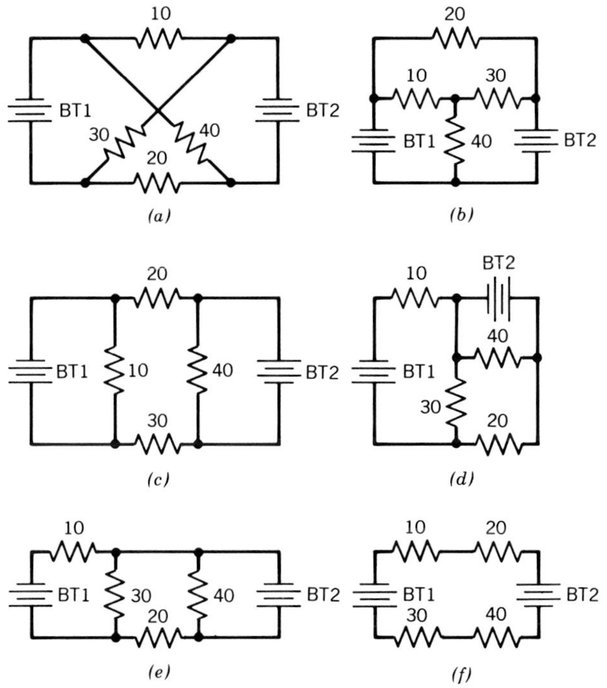

Figure 7.72 Circuits for Frame 3.

a. d and e. (4)
b. Any other answer, review Section B.2.

FRAME 4

A potential or voltage drop is defined as the ________ ____ .

a. Loss of energy of an electron when it moves from a more negative point to a more positive point. (5)
b. Any answer that did not include an electron moving from a negative to a positive point, review Section B.3.

FRAME 5

Kirchhoff's voltage law is: around a loop in a circuit, ____________ . In a Kirchhoff's voltage law equation, the voltage rises and drops are expressed in terms of ____________ .

a. The sum of the voltage drops and voltage rises is zero; current. (6)
b. Any other answer, review Section B.4.

FRAME 6

When using Kirchhoff's voltage law in circuit analysis, the number of equations that have to be written is equal to ____________ .

a. The number of independent unknown currents. (7)
b. Any other answer, review Section B.4.

FRAME 7

Write two different voltage law equations for the circuit shown in Figure 7.73. Use the current directions and polarities shown in the figure.

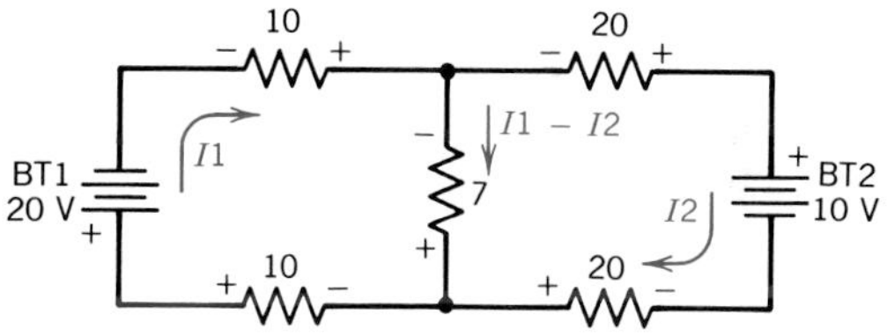

Figure 7.73 Circuit for Frame 7.

a. You should have two of the following, or transpositions of them:

$$27I_1 - 7I_2 - 20 = 0$$

$$-7I_1 + 47I_2 - 10 = 0$$

$$20I_1 + 40I_2 - 30 = 0. \quad (8)$$

b. Any other answers, review Section B.4.

FRAME 8

Kirchhoff's current law states that at any junction or node in a circuit, ____________ .

a. The sum of the currents entering a node or junction is equal to the sum of the currents leaving. (9)
b. Any other answer, review Section B.5.

FRAME 9

The number of current law equations required to analyze a network is one less than __________ .

a. The number of junctions in the network. (10)
b. Any other answer, review Section B.5.

FRAME 10

The first step in a current law analysis is to choose __________ .

a. A reference junction. (11)
b. Any other answer, review Section B.5.

FRAME 11

Solve for the unknown currents in the circuit of Figure 7.74 using current law analysis.

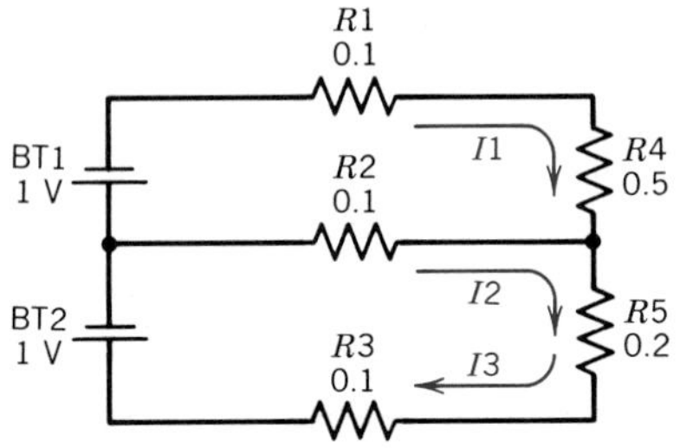

Figure 7.74 Circuit for Frame 11.

a. $I_1 = 1.85$ A, $I_2 = 1.11$ A, $I_3 = 2.96$ A. (12)
b. Any other answers, review Section B.5.

FRAME 12

A graph used to relate two different values has two __________ . These are generally called the ______ and the __________ .

a. Axes; x axis; y axis. (13)
b. Any other answer, review Section C.1.

FRAME 13

Convert 120° into radian measure.

a. $\frac{2}{3}\pi$. (14)
b. Any other answer, review Section C.2.

FRAME 14

Two angles whose sum is 180° are called __________ angles. If their sum is 90°, they are called __________ angles.

a. Supplementary; complementary. (15)
b. Any other answer, review Section C.2.

FRAME 15

Solve for each of the unknown quantities using the method of determinants:

$$0 = I_1 + 2I_2 + I_3$$
$$2 = 2I_1 + 4I_2 + 6I_3$$
$$-2.5 = I_1 + I_2 - 4I_3$$

a. $I_1 = -0.5$; $I_2 = 0$; $I_3 = 0.5$. (16)
b. Any other answer, review Section C.3.

FRAME 16

Complete the following table of nominal values and tolerances

Nominal Value	*Tolerance*	*Minimum Value*	*Maximum Value*
180 Ω	10%	?	?
12 Ω	?	11.76 Ω	12.24 Ω
5.1 kΩ	5%	?	?
680 Ω	?	646 Ω	714 Ω
9.1 kΩ	2%	?	?

a.

180 Ω	10%	162 Ω	198 Ω
12 Ω	2%	11.76 Ω	12.24 Ω
5.1 kΩ	5%	4848 Ω	5355 Ω
680 Ω	5%	646 Ω	714 Ω
9.1 kΩ	2%	8918 Ω	9282 Ω (17)

b. Any other answers, review Section C.4.

FRAME 17

The four general uses for resistors in a circuit are:

1. To limit the __________ in the circuit.
2. To provide a __________ for a circuit.
3. To reduce the potential difference across a circuit component. A resistor that performs this function is called a __________ resistor.

4. Two or more resistors may be used in series to ________ .

a. Current; load; voltage dropping; obtain specific potential differences. (18)
b. Any answer not containing these points, review Section D.2.

FRAME 18

The major types of fixed resistors, that is, resistors which possess a certain nominal resistance value are ________ , ________ , and ________ resistors.

a. Wire-wound; carbon composition; carbon or metal film (order is not important). (19)
b. Any other answer, review Section D.3.

FRAME 19

For power dissipations greater than 2 W, ________ resistors are generally used.

a. Wire wound. (20)
b. Any other answer, review Section D.3.1.

FRAME 20

Although they were once the most widely used of all electronic components, carbon composition resistors are now being replaced by ________ . This is because the carbon composition types are more sensitive to damage and are more ________ .

a. Carbon or metallic film resistors; expensive. (21)
b. Any other answer, review Sections D.3.2 and D.3.3.

FRAME 21

Carbon composition resistors are easily obtainable in resistances from less than ________ to more than ________ ; power dissipations of ________ W; in tolerances of ________ percent.

a. 1 Ω; 22 mΩ; $\frac{1}{8}, \frac{1}{4}, \frac{1}{2}$, 1, 2; 2; 5; 10. (22)
b. Any other answers, review Section D.3.2.

FRAME 22

List the base numbers for 5 percent resistors.

a. 1.0, 1.1, 1.2, 1.3, 1.5, 1.6, 1.8, 2.0, 2.2, 2.4, 2.7, 3.0, 3.3, 3.6, 3.9, 4.3, 4.7, 5.1, 5.6, 6.2, 6.8, 7.5, 8.2, 9.1. (23)
b. Any other answer, review Section D.4.

FRAME 23

Fill in the following table:

Nominal Value	*Tolerance*	*Band 1*	*Band 2*	*Band 3*	*Band 4*	*Band 5*
1000 Ω	5	?	?	?	?	XXX
1430 Ω	1	?	?	?	?	?
200 kΩ	10	?	?	?	?	XXX
?	?	Green	Blue	Orange	Gold	XXX
?	10	Yellow	Violet	Silver	Silver	XXX
?	?	Brown	Black	Brown	Red	XXX
?	?	Orange	Black	Black	Red	XXX
?	?	Violet	Brown	Green	Brown	Brown

a.

1000	5	Brown	Black	Red	Gold	XXX
1430	1	Brown	Yellow	Orange	Brown	Brown
200 K	10	Red	Black	Yellow	Silver	XXX
56 K	5	Green	Blue	Orange	Gold	XXX
0.47	10	Yellow	Violet	Silver	Silver	XXX
100	2	Brown	Black	Brown	Red	XXX
30	2	Orange	Black	Black	Red	XXX
7150	1	Violet	Brown	Green	Brown	Brown (24)

b. Any other answers, review Section D.5.

FRAME 24

A component has the following identification printed on it: RN80X151G. Interpret the symbols using Figure 7.63.

a. RN: film resistor

80: 2 W, 750 V
X: characteristic
151: 150 Ω
G: 2 percent tolerance (25)

b. Any other answer, review Section D.7.

FRAME 25

An __________ resistor and a __________ are considered two-terminal devices, a __________ is a three-terminal device.

a. Adjustable; rheostat; potentiometer or pot. (END)
b. Any other answer, review Section D.8.

E. PROBLEMS FOR SOLUTION OR RESEARCH

1. The circuit shown in Figure 7.75 represents a paralleled combination of sources, each of which has an internal resistance. What is the potential difference across and the current through the load?

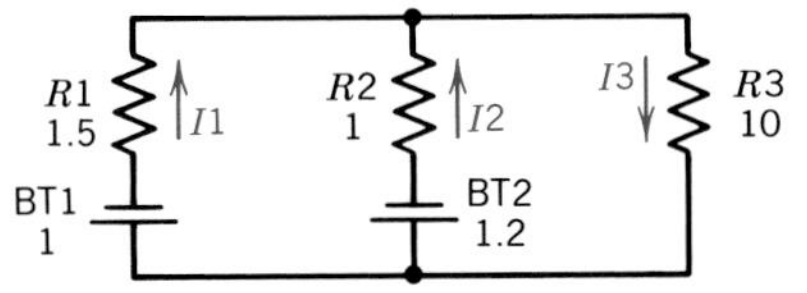

Figure 7.75 Circuit for Problem 1.

2. Solve for the unknown currents in Figures 7.76 through 7.80 using either Kirchhoff's current law or the voltage law.

3. Does the current law or the voltage law prove easier to use in each of the circuits given in Problem 2?

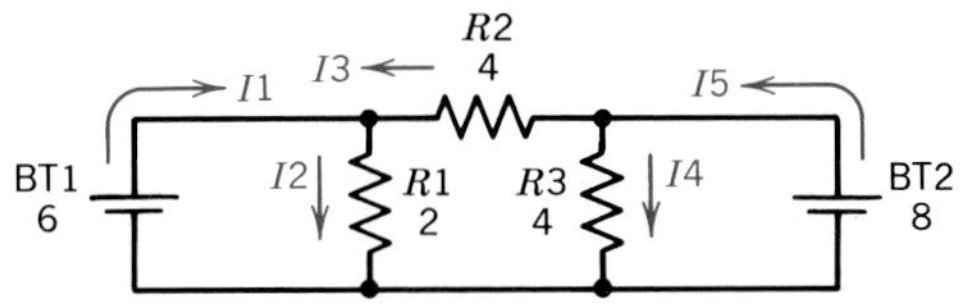

Figure 7.76 Circuit for Problem 2.

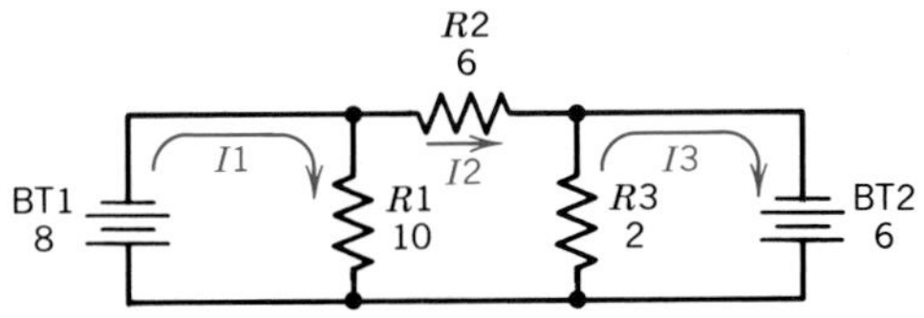

Figure 7.77 Circuit for Problem 2.

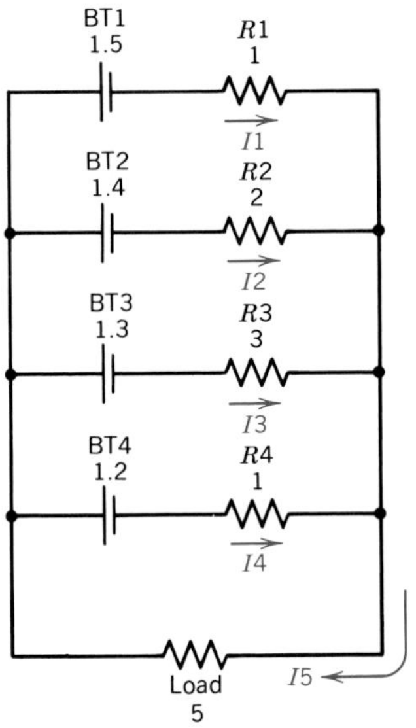

Figure 7.78 Circuit for Problem 2.

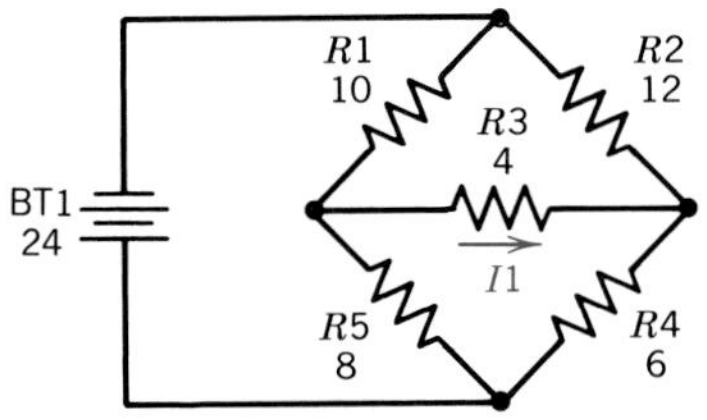

Figure 7.79 Circuit for Problem 2.

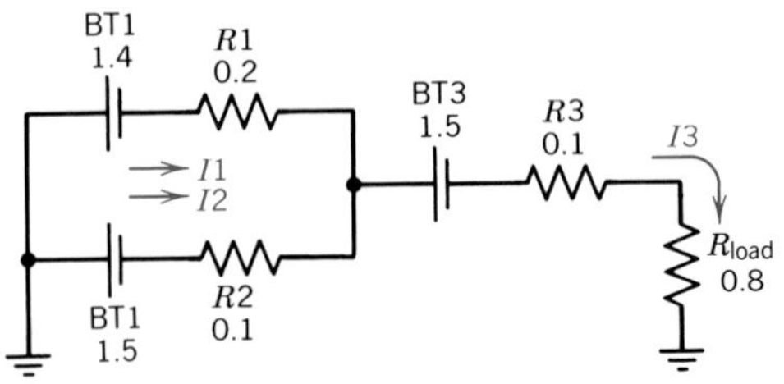

Figure 7.80 Circuit for Problem 2.

CHAPTER 8

NETWORK THEOREMS AND PRACTICAL RESISTOR CIRCUITS

A. CHAPTER PREVIEW

1 In previous chapters you learned to apply the two most general methods of circuit analysis, Ohm's and Kirchhoff's laws. This chapter introduces a number of network theorems that can be used to simplify the work of calculating current and potential in complex networks.

2 You will learn about ideal voltage and ideal current sources and the way in which these concepts were used in circuit analysis.

3 Three additional methods that can be used to simplify complex networks are discussed. You will learn to apply Thevenin's, Norton's, and Millman's theorems to practical circuits.

4 The Examples and Computations section contains BASIC programs that can be used for solving Kirchhoff's law equations and Δ–Y (delta–wye) equivalency calculations.

5 The Applications Section explains the function of some common resistor circuits and shows you how to use and troubleshoot them.

B. PRINCIPLES

B.1 NETWORK THEOREMS: THE Δ–Y EQUIVALENCY THEOREM

Network theorems are special methods for analyzing circuits. Unlike Ohm's and Kirchhoff's laws, which are mathematical descriptions of what happens in an electrical circuit, network theorems are ways of redrawing complex circuits so that Ohm's and Kirchhoff's laws may be applied more easily. Laws are true for almost any circuit, but network theorems may be applied only in special cases or to a particular kind of circuit. The principle of equivalency that you used to simplify series and parallel circuits is an example of a network theorem.

The Δ–Y equivalency theorem is a network theorem similar to the principle of equivalency. Its basic statement is that a delta-, or π-shaped arrangement of elements in a circuit such as those shown in Figure 8.1*a* and 8.1*b* can be replaced by a particular wye- or T-shaped arrangement such as those in Figure 8.2*a* and 8.2*b*, without changing any of the circuit characteristics. The opposite is also true. Any Y- or T-shaped arrangement can be replaced by a particular Δ- or π-shaped arrangement.

The Δ–Y equivalency theorem has many practical applications in electricity and electronics. One is the analysis of resistance bridge circuits like that shown in Figure 8.3*a*. If the Δ arrangement composed of *R*1, *R*2, and *R*3 is replaced by the Y arrangement shown in Figure 8.3*b*, the potentials at junction points 1 and 2 can be calculated directly by Ohm's law. Alternately, resistors *R*3, *R*4, and *R*5 in Figure 8.3*a* can be replaced by a Y arrangement. In either case, the resulting circuit is a series–parallel network of the sort analyzed in Chapter 5.

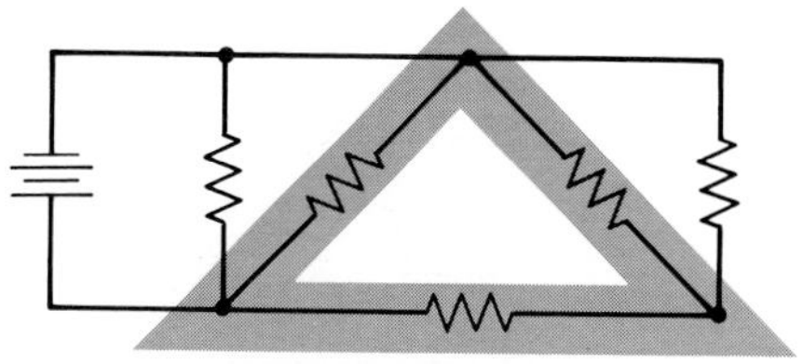

(a) Delta shape

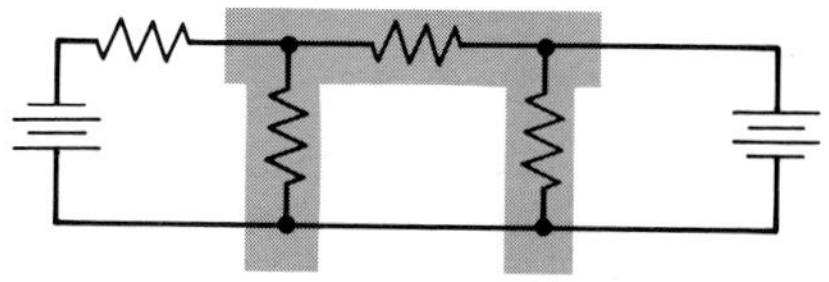

(b) Pi shape

Figure 8.1 A delta or π-shaped arrangement of components.

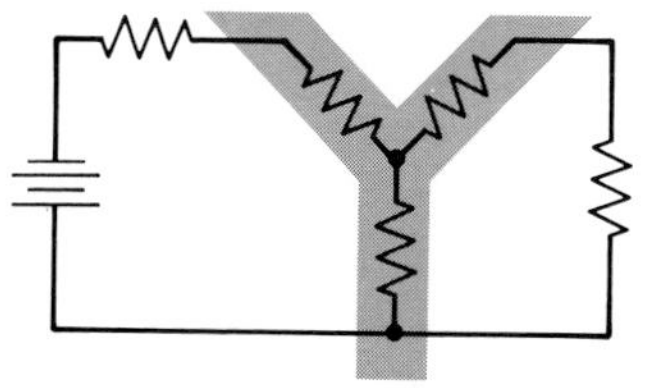

(a) Wye or y shape

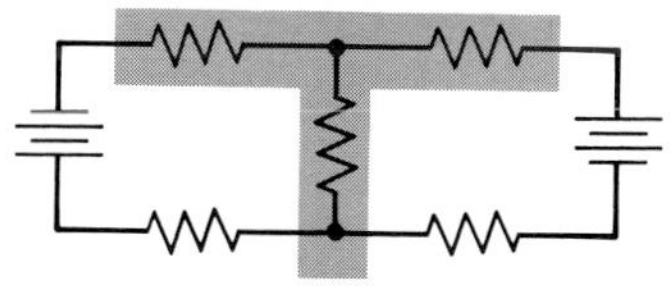

(b) T shape

Figure 8.2 A wye- or T-shaped arrangement of components.

The most difficult part of applying the Δ–Y equivalency theorem is calculating the values of the three resistors in the arms of the Y, which will be substituted for the Δ arrangement in the original circuit. The first step is to place a dot in the center of the Δ arrangement, as shown in Figure 8.4*a*. This will serve as the common connection point for the three resistors in the Y ar-

Figure 8.3 Using Δ–Y equivalency to analyze a bridge circuit.

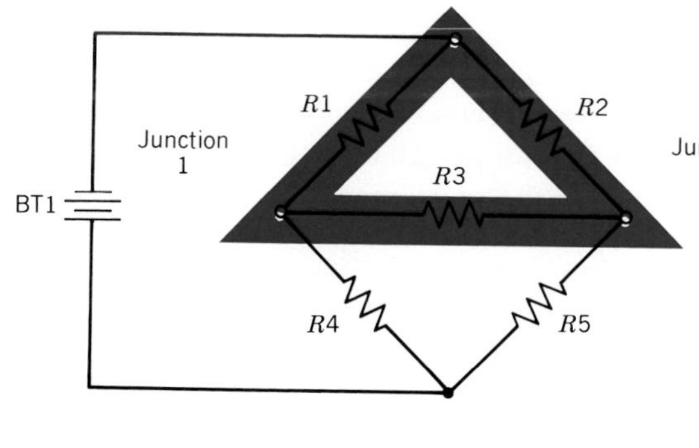

(a) A bridge circuit

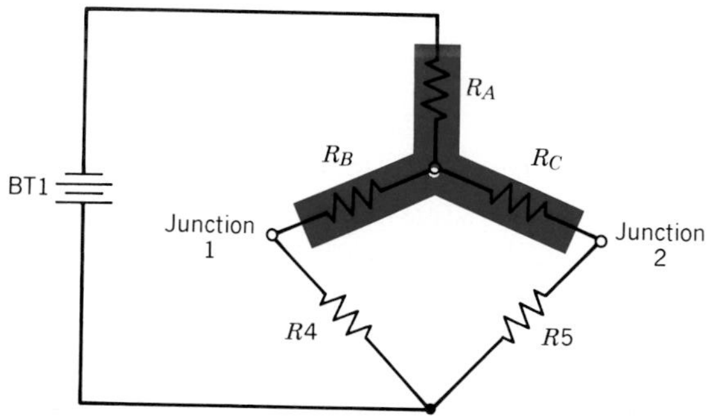

(b) The same circuit after replacing the Δ arrangement with a Y

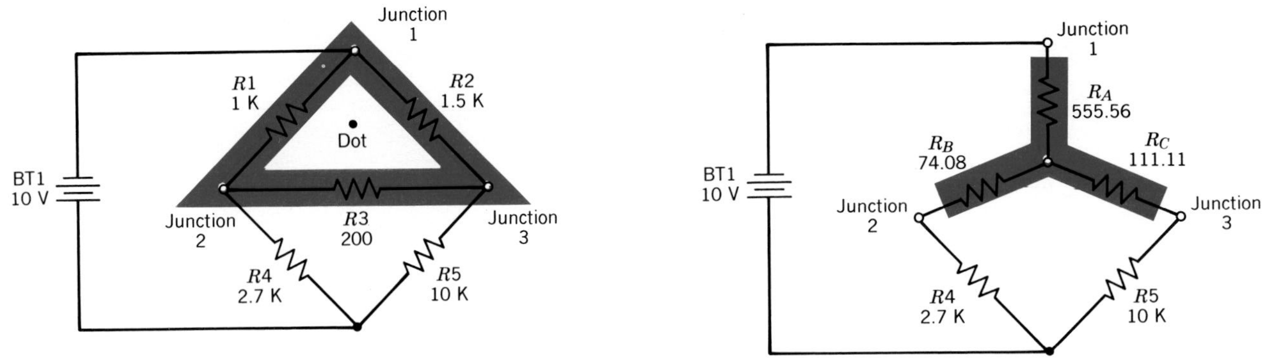

(a) Place a dot in the center of the Δ network to serve as the connection point for the Y network.
(b) Replace the Δ with a Y network

Figure 8.4 Steps in using the Δ–Y equivalency theorem to analyze a bridge circuit.

rangement. Next, start at any one of the three Δ network junctions. Each of these junctions is a connection point between two of the Δ network elements. Multiply the value of the two Δ resistors that meet at this junction and divide the product by the sum of the resistances of all three Δ resistors. This will give the resistance of the Y network resistor connected between the junction and the central point. For example, begin with junction 1 in Figure 8.4*a*. This junction is the connection point of Δ resistors *R*1 and *R*2. The value of R_A, the Y network equivalent resistor connected between junction 1 and the central point is

$$R_A = \frac{R1R2}{R1 + R2 + R3} \qquad \text{FORMULA 8.1a}$$

Junction 2 is the point of connection of Δ resistors *R*1 and *R*3. To obtain the value of the Y network resistor, R_B, connected between junction 2 and the central point, divide the produce of *R*1 and *R*3 by the sum of *R*1, *R*2, and *R*3:

$$R_B = \frac{R1R3}{R1 + R2 + R3} \qquad \text{FORMULA 8.1b}$$

The value of the third Y resistor, R_C, is

$$R_C = \frac{R2R3}{R1 + R2 + R3} \qquad \text{FORMULA 8.1c}$$

Substituting the values of *R*1, *R*2, and *R*3 in Formulas 8.1a to 8.1c, the values of the three Y resistors are $R_A = 555.56\ \Omega$, $R_B = 74.08\ \Omega$, and $R_C = 111.11\ \Omega$. These three resistors can then be drawn in, and the original Δ resistors erased. This produces the circuit shown in Figure 8.4b, a series–parallel circuit.

The resistance of the branch composed of R_B and *R*4 is 2774.08 Ω, and that of the branch composed of R_C and *R*5 is 10111.11 Ω. Combining the R_BR4 and R_CR5 parallel branches with R_A, the series resistance, the equivalent resistance is 2732.4 Ω. According to the Δ–Y equivalency theorem, this is also the resistance of the original bridge circuit as seen by the source. This is true because the substitution of the Y equivalent for the Δ arrangement is entirely unnoticed by the circuit outside the boundaries of the original Δ network.

In Chapter 7 you learned how to use Kirchhoff's laws to calculate the current through or voltage drop across a resistor in a bridge circuit. Using the Δ–Y equivalency theorem and Ohm's law, the same results can be obtained, often with less calculation. The current provided by BT1 in Figure 8.4*a* or 8.4*b* is

$$I = \frac{E}{R} = \frac{10}{2732.4} = 3.66\ \text{mA}$$

regardless of whether the original Δ network or its Y equivalent is found between junctions 1, 2, and 3. Using this information, it is not difficult to determine the potential at junctions 2 and 3 in Figure 8.4*b*. All the circuit current passes through R_A, so the voltage drop across the resistor must be $I \times R$, or 2.03 V, and the potential drop across each parallel branch ($R_B + R4$ and $R_C + R5$) must be 10 − 2.03, or 7.97 V. Since the potential drop across each branch is known, as well as its resistance, the branch current is

$$I_{\text{branch}} = \frac{E_{\text{branch}}}{R_{\text{branch}}}$$

or 2.87 mA for the branch composed of R_B and *R*4 and 0.788 mA for the branch composed of R_C and *R*5. After calculating the two branch currents, the voltage drops across *R*4 and *R*5 can be obtained by multiplying the branch current by the resistance:

$$\begin{aligned} E_{R4} &= I_{\text{branch}} \times R4 \\ &= 0.00287 \times 2700 \\ &= 7.749\ \text{V} \end{aligned}$$

$$\begin{aligned} E_{R5} &= I_{\text{branch}} \times R5 \\ &= 0.000788 \times 10000 \\ &= 7.88\ \text{V} \end{aligned}$$

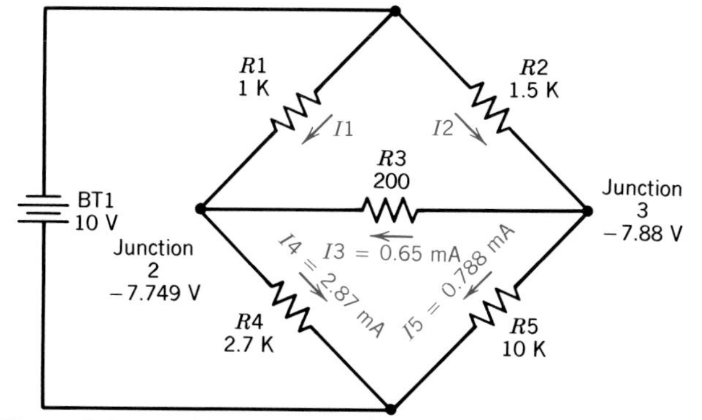

Figure 8.5 Marking the potentials at junctions 2 and 3 and the currents through $R4$ and $R5$ on the schematic of Figure 8.4a.

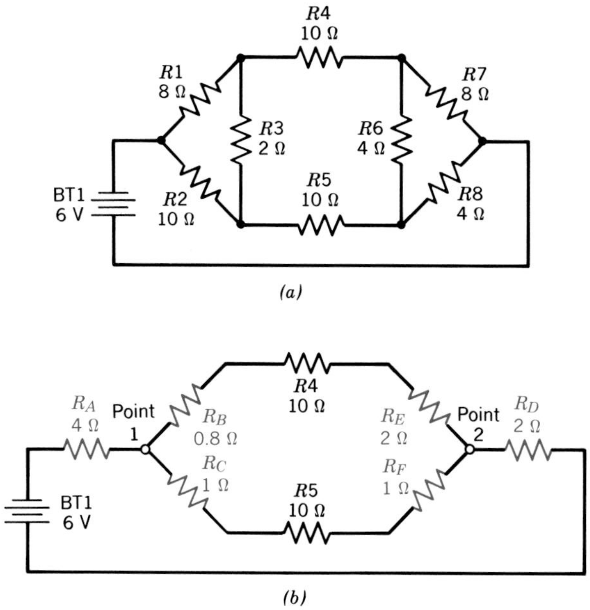

Figure 8.6 Using the Δ–Y equivalency theorem to simplify a circuit.

Since the potential drops across $R4$ and $R5$ are the same in both Figure 8.4a and 8.4b, the potentials at junctions 2 and 3 must be 7.749 and 7.88 V, respectively, in both circuits.

Once the potentials of nodes 2 and 3 and the currents through $R4$ and $R5$ are calculated from the Y-equivalent circuit, these quantities can be marked on a schematic diagram of the original bridge circuit, as shown in Figure 8.5. Using the information in this figure, it is possible to calculate the currents through $R1$, $R2$, and $R3$, the original Δ of resistors. The current through $R3$ is equal to the potential difference between nodes 2 and 3 divided by the resistance of $R3$:

$$I_3 = \frac{0.13}{200} = 0.65 \text{ mA}$$

Now, it is easy to see that

$$I_1 = I_4 - I_3 = 2.22 \text{ mA} \quad \text{and} \quad I_2 = I_5 + I_3 = 1.44 \text{ mA}$$

Once the current through each resistor in the bridge is known, the remaining voltage drops or power dissipations can be calculated as necessary.

In addition to its usefulness in analyzing bridge circuits, Δ-to-Y conversion can be used to simplify a number of other networks.

EXAMPLE:

Calculate the current supplied by the source in Figure 8.6a and the power dissipated in $R4$. ■

SOLUTION:

Ohm's law can not be applied directly to this circuit unless either a Kirchhoff's law analysis or two Δ–Y substitutions are performed first. Since the network is fairly complex, the Δ–Y substitutions will probably be easier. Using Formulas 8.1a to 8.1c in the first Δ composed of $R1$, $R2$, and $R3$:

$$R_A = \frac{R1R2}{R1 + R2 + R_3} = \frac{80}{20} = 4\ \Omega$$

$$R_B = \frac{R1R3}{R1 + R2 + R3} = \frac{16}{20} = 0.8\ \Omega$$

$$R_C = \frac{R2R3}{R1 + R2 + R3} = \frac{20}{20} = 1\ \Omega$$

The second Δ is composed of resistors $R6$, $R7$, and $R8$. Its equivalent Y circuit is also obtained by using Formula 8.1.

$$R_D = \frac{R7R8}{R6 + R7 + R8} = \frac{32}{16} = 2\ \Omega$$

$$R_E = \frac{R6R7}{R6 + R7 + R8} = \frac{32}{16} = 2\ \Omega$$

$$R_F = \frac{R6R8}{R6 + R7 + R8} = \frac{16}{16} = 1\ \Omega$$

Substituting the two Y arrangements for the Δ networks produces the circuit shown in Figure 8.6b. Since this is a series–parallel circuit, Ohm's law can be used directly.

The total resistance of the circuit is found by combining the two parallel branches composed of R_B–$R4$–R_E and R_C–$R5$–R_F, then adding the values of R_A and R_D.

$$R_{\text{total}} = \frac{12.8 \times 12}{24.8} + 4 + 2 = 12.19\ \Omega$$

The circuit current is $I = \dfrac{E}{R} = \dfrac{6}{12.19} = 0.492$ A. The problem requires the power dissipated by $R4$. Since this resistor was part of the original circuit and was not involved in the change from Δ to Y networks, it is not necessary to refer back to the original circuit at all. Calculating the current through the circuit branch composed of R_B–$R4$–R_E will give the current through $R4$ in the original circuit. One way of doing this is to find the potential difference between points 1 and 2 and divide by the resistance of the branch. The potential at point 1 is $E_{\text{BT1}} - (I \times R_A)$ or $6 - 1.968 = 4.032$ V. The potential at point 2 is 0 (the potential of the positive terminal of BT1) + $(I \times R_D)$, or 0.984 V. The potential difference between points 1 and 2, therefore, is $4.032 - 0.984 = 3.048$ V. The current through the branch containing R_B, $R4$, and R_E is

$$I_{\text{branch}} = \frac{E}{R_{\text{branch}}} = \frac{3.048}{12.8} = 0.238 \text{ A}$$

The power dissipated in $R4$ is $I^2 \times R$, or 0.567 W. ■

Sometimes, a complex circuit can be simplified by converting a portion of it from a Y to a Δ arrangement. A circuit of this sort is shown in Figure 8.7*a*. If the Y network is replaced by an equivalent Δ composed of resistances R_A, R_B, and R_C, as shown in Figure 8.7*b*, the circuit is reduced to three pairs of parallel resistors connected in a Δ arrangement. Each pair can then be replaced by a single equivalent resistor to produce the easily analyzed circuit shown in Figure 8.7*c*.

Finding the equivalent Δ network that can be substituted for a Y arrangement is simplified if the conductance values of the Y network resistors are used. The equivalent Δ network for the Y shown in Figure 8.7*a* consists of three resistors connected between the three junctions of the original Y network. Beginning with the resistor that will be connected between junctions 1 and 2, R_A, the *conductance* of R_A is equal to the product of the conductances connected to junctions 1 and 2 divided by the sum of the three conductances in the Y network.

$$G_{RA} = \frac{G_{R1}G_{R2}}{G_{R1} + G_{R2} + G_{R3}} \qquad \text{FORMULA 8.2a}$$

Notice that this formula closely resembles Formula 8.1, which was used to find the values of the resistors in the Y network equivalent of a Δ network. The difference is that in going from a Y network to a Δ, the formula uses conductance, which is the reciprocal of resistance.

The conductance of Δ network resistor G_{RB} that will be connected between junctions 2 and 3 is

$$G_{RB} = \frac{G_{R2}G_{R3}}{G_{R1} + G_{R2} + G_{R3}} \qquad \text{FORMULA 8.2b}$$

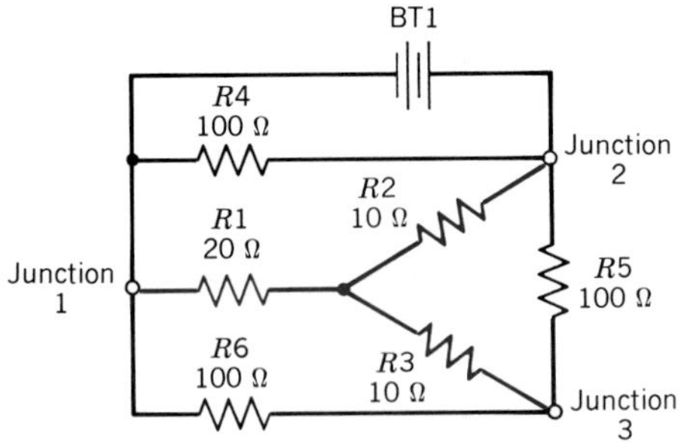

(a) Basic circuit containing a Y arrangement

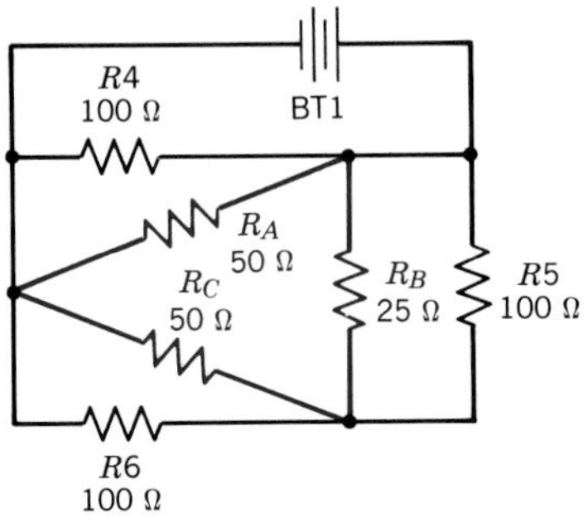

(b) The Y arrangement replaced by a Δ

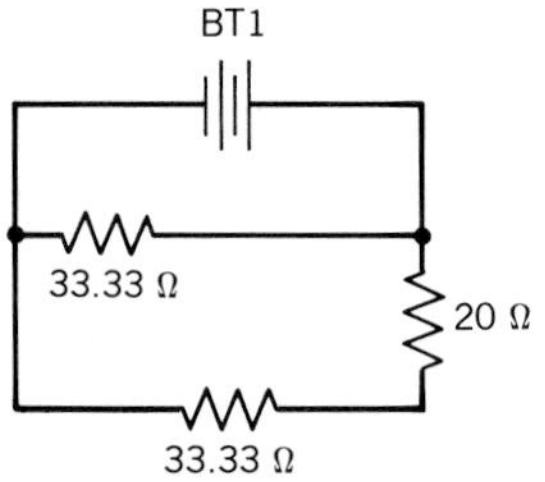

(c) Further simplifying the circuit by substituting equivalent resistances for the parallel pairs

Figure 8.7 Some circuits can be simplified by converting from Y to Δ arrangements.

The conductance of the final Δ resistor, G_{RC} is

$$G_{RC} = \frac{G_{R3}G_{R1}}{G_{R1} + G_{R2} + G_{R3}} \qquad \text{FORMULA 8.2c}$$

Substituting the conductance values $G_{R1} = \frac{1}{R1} = 0.05$ S, $G_{R2} = \frac{1}{R2} = 0.1$ S, and $G_{R3} = \frac{1}{R3} = 0.1$ S, in Formula 8.2 provides the conductance of the three Δ network resistors:

$$G_{RA} = \frac{0.05 \times 0.1}{0.05 + 0.1 + 0.1} = 0.02 \text{ S}$$

$$G_{RB} = \frac{0.1 \times 0.1}{0.05 + 0.1 + 0.1} = 0.04 \text{ S}$$

$$G_{RC} = \frac{0.05 \times 0.1}{0.05 + 0.1 + 0.1} = 0.02 \text{ S}$$

The resistance values of the three resistors are the reciprocals of their conductances: $R_A = 50\ \Omega$, $R_B = 25\ \Omega$, $R_C = 50\ \Omega$.

Using these values, the Y network can be replaced by the Δ as shown in Figure 8.7*b*, and then this circuit is easily reduced to the basic series–parallel arrangement shown in Figure 8.7*c*

When calculating the resistance values of a Y network to replace a given Δ network, divide the product of the two resistances connected to each Δ junction by the sum of the three Δ resistances. When calculating the conductance values of a Δ network to replace a given Y network, divide the product of the conductances connected to each pair of Y junctions by the sum of the conductances of all three Y resistors.

B.2 IDEAL VOLTAGE AND IDEAL CURRENT SOURCES

The principal current analysis techniques that you have studied, Ohm's and Kirchhoff's laws, treat all circuit sources as if they were *ideal* sources. More specifically, as though they were *ideal voltage sources*. Such a source has no resistance and keeps the same potential difference across its output terminals no matter how much current is drawn from it. In reality, no source is an ideal source. Whether it operates on chemical energy, like a cell, or uses mechanical energy, like a generator, there is some opposition to the movement of electrons in every source. This is illustrated in Figure 8.8, where a practical source of potential difference is shown as a battery in series with a resistance R_i. This resistance is the internal resistance of the source. When an external load is connected to the terminals of the practical source, the circuit current flows through the internal resistance as well as through the load. The potential drop across the internal resistance will be

Figure 8.8 A practical source of potential difference is composed of an ideal voltage source in series with an internal resistance.

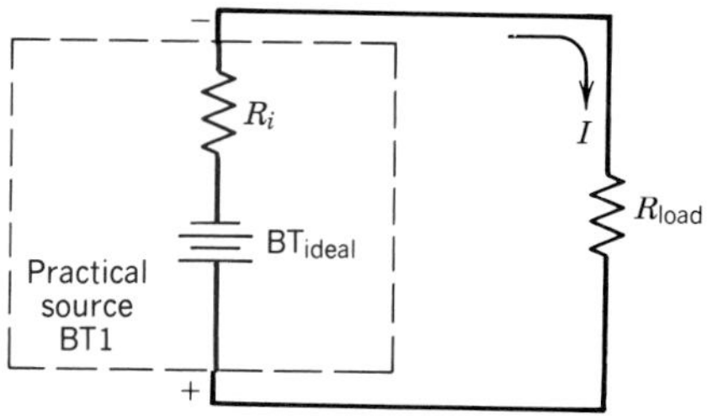

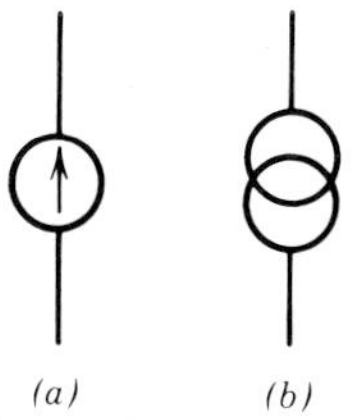

Figure 8.9 Schematic symbols for an ideal current source.

proportional to the circuit current:

$$E_{Ri} = I \times R_i$$

The potential difference between the terminals of the practical source is

$$E = E_{\text{ideal}} - (I \times R_i)$$

Only if the source resistance is zero will the potential difference supplied by the source be independent of the circuit current.

The network theorems discussed in this chapter generally assume that all voltage sources are ideal voltage sources. This permits consideration of each source separately and results in the simplification of the calculations involved. This assumption is actually not far from the truth in the case of chemical cells operated within allowed current ranges. Since the internal resistance of a chemical cell is low, it tends to approximate the function of an ideal voltage source and the internal voltage drop is small.

Another kind of source, often found in the analysis of semiconductor circuits, is the *ideal current source*. Figures 8.9*a* and 8.9*b* show two symbols commonly used to represent an ideal current source in schematic diagrams. The arrow in Figure 8.9*a* usually indicates current direction. An ideal current source is a source that will maintain a constant current through a circuit regardless of the circuit resistance.

An ideal current source must have a very high internal resistance in order to furnish the same current to any circuit connected to it. This can be better understood if you refer to Figure 8.10. The current source is shown by the battery symbol and its internal resist-

Figure 8.10 An ideal current source must have a high internal resistance to provide a constant current regardless of its load resistance.

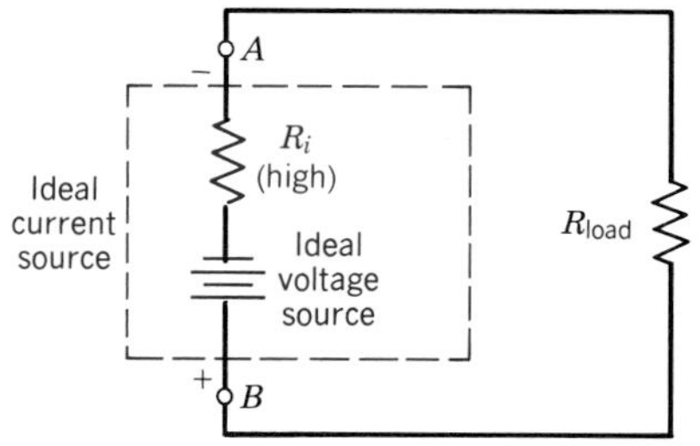

ance, R_i. If the potential difference produced by the source is 100 V and the internal resistance is 10 kΩ, the short-circuit current supplied when the output terminals A and B are connected together would be

$$I = \frac{E}{R} = \frac{100}{10{,}000} = 0.01 \text{ A}$$

If a 100 Ω load is connected across the terminals in place of the short circuit, the current through the load is

$$I = \frac{E}{R} = \frac{100}{10{,}000 + 100} = 0.009900 \text{ A}$$

Increasing the load resistance by a factor of 10 to 1000 Ω reduces the circuit current somewhat to

$$I = \frac{E}{R} = \frac{100}{11{,}000} = 0.00909 \text{ A}$$

But if the load resistance is close to or greater than the internal resistance of the current source, the circuit current is significantly reduced. For example, a load resistance of 47 kΩ reduces the circuit current to

$$I = \frac{E}{R} = \frac{100}{47{,}000 + 10{,}000} = 0.00175 \text{ A}$$

If the internal resistance of the source is much greater than the load resistance, the characteristics of the source approach those of an ideal current source more closely.

If the internal resistance is 10 MΩ, the short-circuit current will be 0.01 mA, the current with a 1-kΩ load will be 0.009999 mA, and the current with a 47-kΩ load 0.009953 mA. A number of semiconductor circuits approximate the behavior of ideal current sources for a limited range of loads. Analysis of circuits, particularly with the aid of network theorems, is simplified if all sources are considered to be either ideal voltage sources or ideal current sources.

Remember: An ideal voltage source has no internal resistance; an ideal current source has an infinite resistance.

B.3 THE SUPERPOSITION THEOREM

The network theorem most frequently used in circuits containing more than one source is the *superposition theorem*. In a multisource circuit with relatively simple element interconnections, this theorem can provide a full circuit analysis in much less time than Kirchhoff's laws.

There are two important conditions that a circuit must meet before the superposition theorem can be applied to it. First, the components in the circuit must be bilateral. In other words, current must be able to flow through them in either direction and they must have the same resistance to currents in either direction. Although resistors meet this condition, semiconductor components do not. For this reason, more complex Kirchhoff law analyses have to be used in transistor current analysis, rather than the simpler superposition theorem.

The second characteristic that the components in a circuit must possess before it can be analyzed is linearity. A linear component is one in which the resistance to current flow remains constant, regardless of the amount of current flowing through the component or the potential difference across it. Within their power dissipation and voltage ratings, most resistors are linear components. Semiconductors and some special-purpose resistors, on the other hand, are not linear.

In simple terms, the superposition theorem states that the current through any component or element in a linear, bilateral circuit is equal to the sum of the currents through that component or element due to each of the sources in the circuit considered individually. In the circuit shown in Figure 8.11, the current through any of the resistors is the sum of the currents that would be caused by BT1 and BT2 acting separately. As you have already learned, it is necessary to take the direction of the currents into consideration. Batteries BT1 and BT2 are assumed to be ideal voltage sources for the purposes of a superposition theorem analysis, and their internal resistance is considered to be zero. This means that the circuit current due to BT1 operating alone can be calculated by redrawing the circuit with a short circuit substituted for BT2, as shown in Figure 8.12*a*. The total circuit resistance in this series–parallel circuit is 133.33 Ω, and the current supplied by BT1 is 0.2025 A. The entire circuit current flows through $R1$ in the direction shown and currents of 0.135 A and 0.0675 A flow through $R2$ and $R3$, respectively.

The circuit current due to BT2 is calculated by redrawing the circuit with a short circuit substituted

Figure 8.11 The superposition theorem states that the current through a component in a circuit is equal to the sum of the currents caused by each source acting separately.

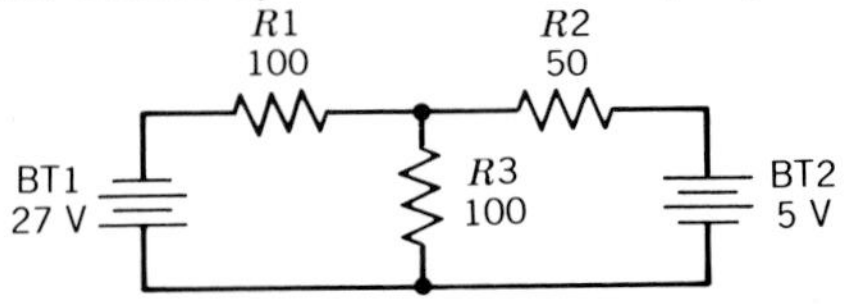

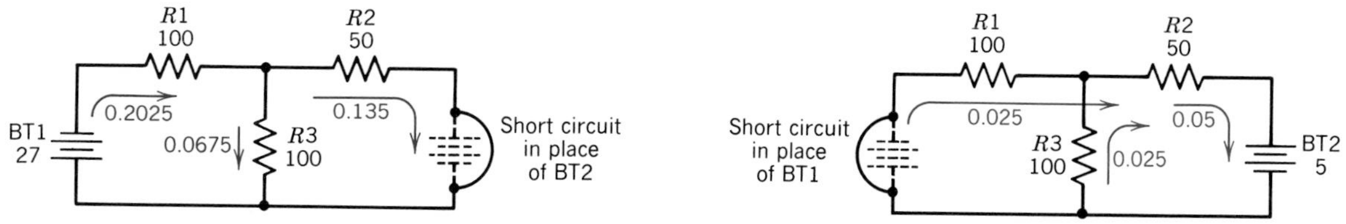

(a) (b)

Figure 8.12 Redrawing the schematic of Figure 8.11 to consider the currents produced by BT1 and BT2 acting separately.

for BT1, as in Figure 8.12*b*. The total resistance of the series–parallel circuit of Figure 8.12*b* is 100 Ω. Using Ohm's law, the total current supplied by the 5-V source is 0.05 A. This is the current that flows through *R*2 in the direction shown, while exactly half the total current, or 0.025 A, flows through *R*1 and *R*3.

According to the superposition theorem, the current through any component or element in the circuit is the sum of the currents due to each of the sources considered separately. The currents through *R*1 due to BT1 and BT2 both flow in the same direction, as shown in Figures 8.12*a* and 8.12*b*. The total current through this component is therefore obtained by adding the current due to BT1, 0.2025 A, and that due to BT2, 0.025 A, or 0.2275 A in all. Similarly, the currents due to both sources flow through *R*2 in the same direction. The sum of the currents through *R*2 is therefore

$$0.135 + 0.05 = 0.185 \text{ A}$$

Through *R*3, however, the currents due to BT1 and BT2 flow in opposite directions. In order to "add" these together, one of the currents must be assigned a negative sign to indicate the difference in direction. The largest of the current flows defines the "positive" direction, and the other currents are referenced to this direction. In the case of *R*3, the largest current is 0.0675 A, and the flow due to BT2 is −0.025. The sum is

$$0.0675 + (-0.025) = 0.0425 \text{ A}$$

These calculations can be checked by either a voltage law or current law analysis.

Using the superposition theorem in circuits containing current sources requires a slightly different method. Recall that the internal resistance of an ideal current source is infinite. For this reason, an open circuit is substituted for the current source of the circuit, rather than a short circuit as in the case of an ideal voltage source.

EXAMPLE:

Use the superposition theorem to calculate the current through *R*2 in Figure 8.13. ■

SOLUTION:

In order to use the superposition theorem, it is first necessary to establish the fact that all the components in the circuit are bilateral and linear. Since the circuit is made up only of ideal resistors and ideal sources, both these conditions are met. The first step is to determine the current through *R*2 due to the ideal voltage source alone. This is done, as shown in Figure 8.14*a* by substituting an open circuit for the current source. This also removes *R*4 from the circuit, leaving a series chain of resistors *R*1, *R*2, and *R*3, with a total resistance of 18 Ω. The circuit current, and also the current through *R*2 due to BT1, is

$$I = \frac{E}{R} = \frac{10}{18} = 0.556 \text{ A}$$

The current through *R*2 due to the current source alone is obtained by substituting a short circuit for the voltage

Figure 8.13 Using the superposition theorem in circuits with current sources.

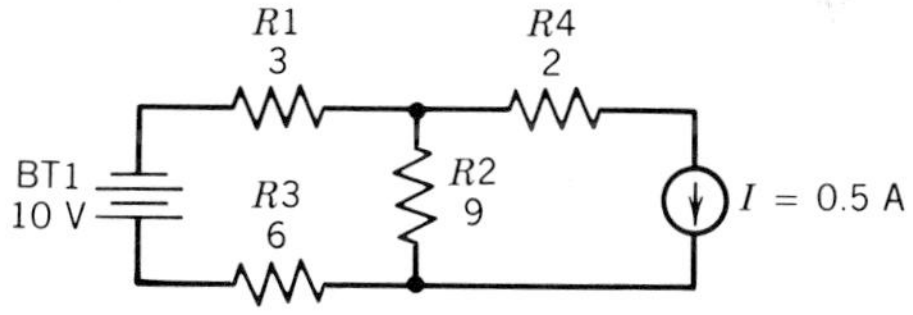

Figure 8.14 A current source is replaced by an open circuit, a voltage source by a short circuit, when using the superposition theorem.

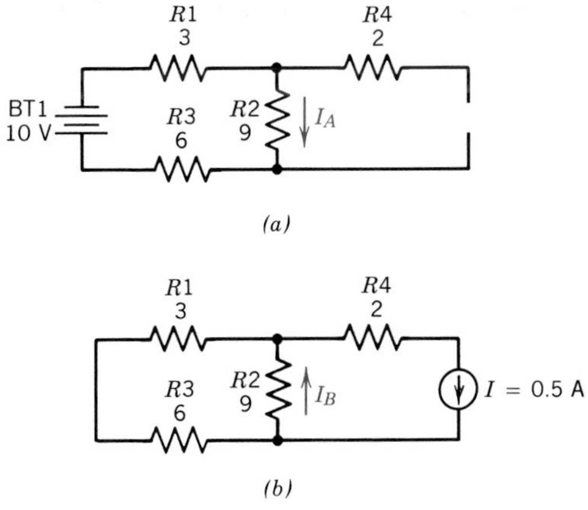

source. This produces the series–parallel circuit shown in Figure 8.14*b*. Here, the circuit current, 0.5 A, is equally divided between the *R*2 branch and the branch composed of *R*1 and *R*3. The current through *R*2 is 0.25 A. Notice that the currents through *R*2 due to the two sources considered separately would flow in opposite directions, so the actual current through *R*2 is

$$I_{R2} = I_A - I_B = 0.556 - 0.25 = 0.306 \text{ A}$$

in the direction shown in Figure 8.14*a*. ■

In addition to circuit analyses of the sort shown here, you will also use the superposition theorem in circuits containing both direct and alternating current.

B.4 THEVENIN'S THEOREM

Thevenin's theorem (pronounced Táy-ven-in) is another network theorem that is widely used for simplifying circuit analysis. Like the superposition theorem, Thevenin's theorem can only be used if the components are linear and bilateral. But these limiting conditions do not exclude Thevenin's theorem from use in circuits containing semiconductor components. This is because Thevenin's theorem, unlike the superposition theorem, is applied only to a part of a circuit.

Thevenin's theorem is a method for substituting an equivalent circuit, composed of a single ideal voltage source and a series resistor, for a network of sources and resistors, no matter how they are interconnected. For example, Figure 8.15*a* is the schematic of a power supply with a voltage source, voltage-dropping resistors, and loads. A typical problem in the troubleshooting of this circuit would be comparing the measured potential difference across *R*4 with the calculated value. Although either Kirchhoff's laws or the Δ–Y equivalency theorem could be used here, both these methods require calculation of several currents, potential differences, and resistances before the potential difference across *R*4 is obtained. Use of Thevenin's theorem often reduces the number of such calculations.

Since the basic function of Thevenin's theorem is to replace a two-terminal network composed of sources and resistors with a simple equivalent, the problem in Figure 8.15 can be solved by dividing the circuit of Figure 8.15*a* in such a way as to isolate *R*4. In Figure 8.15*b* terminals have been inserted into the circuit, dividing it into a load network consisting of *R*4, and a source network, consisting of the rest of the circuit. By replacing the complex source network with its simple Thevenin equivalent, the task of calculating either the potential difference across the load network or the current through it is simplified.

The method of calculating the potential difference produced by the ideal voltage source and the resistance of the series resistor in a Thevenin equivalent network requires the schematic to be redrawn. This is done as in Figure 8.15*c*, omitting the load network entirely. From this diagram, the potential difference between the terminals is calculated. This will be the potential difference supplied by the voltage source in the Thevenin equivalent circuit. In the example of Figure 8.15*c*, the total network current supplied by the source is

$$I = \frac{27}{R_{\text{total}}} = \frac{27}{52.857} = 0.51 \text{ A}$$

Figure 8.15 Steps in using Thevenin's theorem.

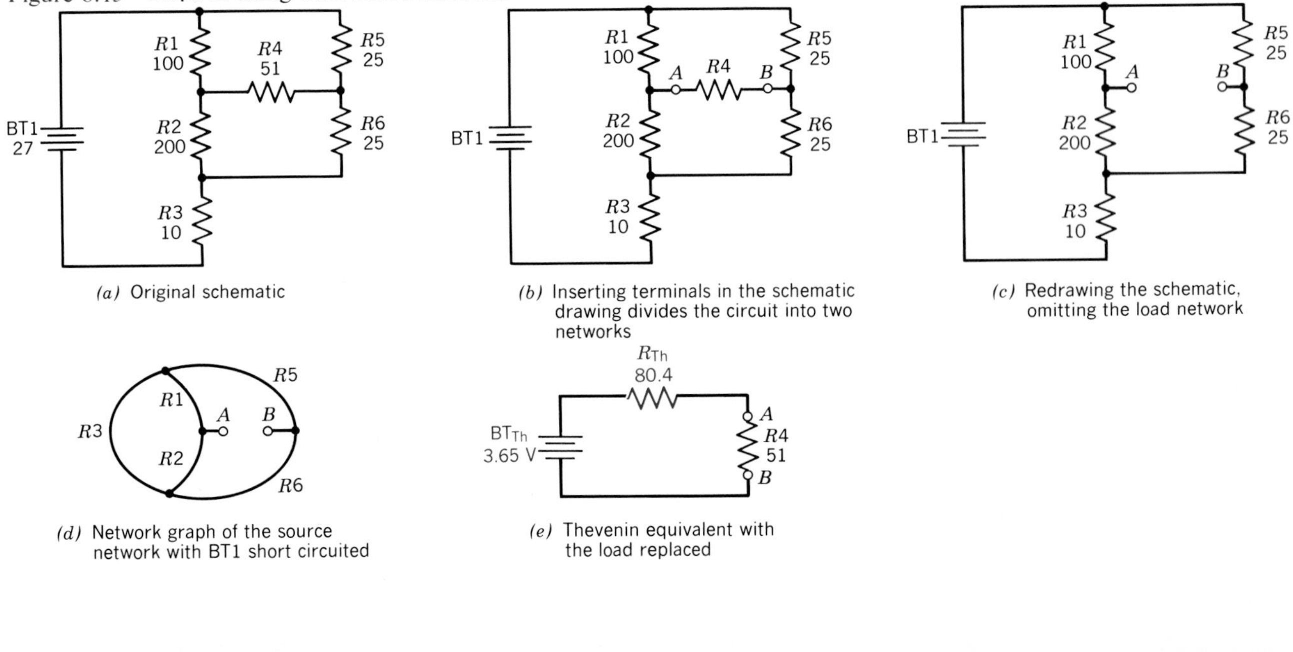

(*a*) Original schematic

(*b*) Inserting terminals in the schematic drawing divides the circuit into two networks

(*c*) Redrawing the schematic, omitting the load network

(*d*) Network graph of the source network with BT1 short circuited

(*e*) Thevenin equivalent with the load replaced

The voltage drop across $R3$ is 5.1 V, so that the potential difference across the two branches $R1R2$ and $R5R6$ is 27 − 5.1 or 21.9 V. From this it is an easy matter to calculate the two branch currents and the potential difference between the terminals.

The current through the $R1R2$ branch is

$$I_{R1R2} = \frac{21.9}{300} = 0.073 \text{ A}$$

The current through the $R5R6$ branch is

$$I_{R5R6} = \frac{21.9}{50} = 0.438 \text{ A}$$

and the potentials at points A and B are

$$E_A = 21.9 - I_{R5R6}R6 = 10.95 \text{ V}$$

$$E_B = 21.9 - I_{R1R2}R2 = 7.3 \text{ V}$$

The potential difference between the two points is

$$E_A - E_B = 10.95 - 7.3 = 3.65 \text{ V}$$

This is the potential difference of the ideal voltage source in the Thevenin equivalent.

The resistance of the series resistor in the Thevenin equivalent is calculated by short circuiting all the voltage sources and open circuiting all the current sources in the schematic diagram of the source network and then calculating the resistance between the source network terminals, points A and B. Drawing the network graph, as shown in Figure 8.15*d* is often helpful. In this case, a Δ–Y equivalency can be used to calculate a resistance of 80.4 Ω between the terminals. This, then, is the value of the Thevenin series resistance. Replacing the source circuit with its Thevenin equivalent, as shown in Figure 8.15*e*, permits calculation of either the voltage drop or current through the load network. In this example, the potential difference across $R4$ is 1.42 V.

Note that the Thevenin equivalent can *only* be used for the calculation of current, voltage, and power in the load network. The Thevenin equivalent is only indirectly related to the structure of the original source network, so it should not be used for any analysis of the source network itself.

To summarize, Thevenin's theorem permits the substitution of an equivalent circuit composed of an ideal voltage source and a series resistor for any network made up of sources and linear, bilateral components. The steps in using Thevenin's theorem are:

1. Divide the circuit into a source network and a load network by placing two terminals in the circuit schematic.

2. Check to make sure that the components in the part of the circuit to be replaced by the Thevenin equivalent are linear and bilateral.

3. Redraw the circuit, omitting the load network.

4. Determine the potential difference between the terminals of the source network, with the load network removed. This is the potential difference of the equivalent Thevenin source.

5. Calculate the resistance between the terminals of the source network with all voltage sources short circuited and all current sources open circuited. This is the resistance of the Thevenin equivalent series resistor R_{Th}.

6. Redraw the original schematic diagram replacing the source network with its Thevenin equivalent.

B.5 NORTON'S THEOREM

In the last section you saw that it is possible to substitute a Thevenin equivalent, that is, an ideal voltage source and series resistor for a source network made up of sources and linear, bilateral components. Norton's theorem shows how a Norton equivalent network consisting of an ideal current source and a parallel resistor may be substituted for a source network. Figure 8.16*a* is the schematic of a circuit that has been divided into source and load networks by terminals A and B. Notice that it is the same as Figure 8.15*b*. In Figure 8.16*b* the circuit is shown with the source network replaced by a Norton equivalent. The resistor in

Figure 8.16 Norton's theorem applied to the circuit of Figure 8.15.

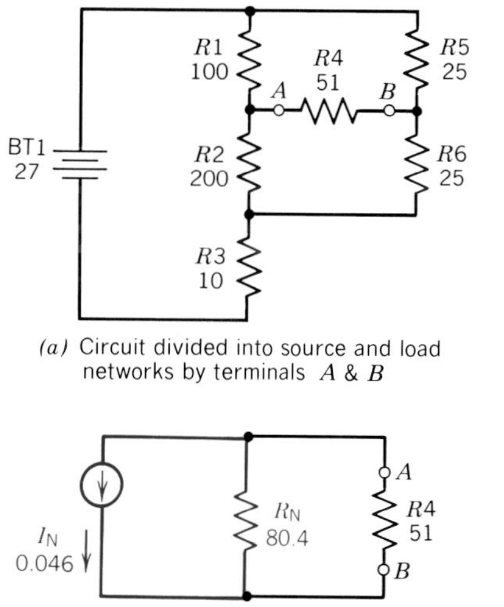

(*a*) Circuit divided into source and load networks by terminals *A* & *B*

(*b*) Same circuit with the source network replaced by a Norton equivalent

the Norton equivalent circuit, R_N, is in parallel with the current source.

The methods used to calculate the current supplied by the ideal current source and parallel resistor in a Norton equivalent are somewhat like those used to calculate the values of the components in a Thevenin equivalent. The similarity is based on the fact that as far as a load network is concerned, there is no difference between an ideal voltage source with a series resistor and an ideal current source with a parallel resistor.

Once the circuit has been divided into source and load networks by the placement of terminals, and it has been checked to ensure that the components involved are linear and bilateral, the source network can be redrawn, omitting the load network. Since the Norton equivalent source is a current source, the short-circuit current between the load terminals is determined. This is done by drawing a short-circuiting connection between the source terminals and calculating the current through it. This is the current supplied by the ideal current source in the Norton equivalent. The value of the resistor placed in parallel with the ideal current source is calculated by erasing the short circuit drawn between the terminals, short circuiting all the voltage sources and open circuiting all the current sources in the source network. The resistance between the terminals is then calculated. This is the resistance of the parallel resistor in the Norton equivalent.

EXAMPLE:
Use Norton's theorem to calculate the potential difference across R in Figure 8.16*a* and the current through it. ■

SOLUTION:
As in the case of using Thevenin's theorem, it is necessary to divide the circuit into source and load networks and to check that the source network is composed of ideal sources and linear, bilateral components. The next step is to calculate the current produced by the Norton equivalent current source. This is done by redrawing the circuit and substituting a short circuit for the load, $R4$. The total current provided by BT1 can be calculated by finding the equivalent resistance of $R1$ in parallel with $R5$, $R2$ in parallel with $R6$, and $R3$. Summing these resistances, $R_{\text{total}} = 52.22\ \Omega$. The circuit current is

$$I = \frac{E}{R} = \frac{27}{52.22} = 0.517 \text{ A}$$

This aids in calculating the short-circuit current I_3. The current through $R2$ is

$$I_{R2} = \frac{25}{225} \times I_{\text{total}} \quad \text{or} \quad 0.057 \text{ A}$$

and through $R6$ is

$$I_{R6} = \frac{200}{225} \times I_{\text{total}} \quad \text{or} \quad 0.46 \text{ A}$$

Notice that the voltage drops across $R1$ and $R5$ must be the same since the ends are connected. Therefore, it is possible to write

$$100(I_1 - I_3) = 25(I_2 + I_3)$$

or

$$100(0.057 - I_3) = 25(0.46 + I_3)$$
$$5.7 - 100I_3 = 11.5 + 25I_3$$

transposing

$$125I_3 = 5.8$$
$$I_3 = 0.046$$

This is the current produced by the equivalent Norton source. The parallel resistance is found by removing the short circuit between terminals A and B, short circuiting the voltage source BT1, and calculating the resistance of the source network between A and B. This is 80.4 Ω, the same result obtained in Section B.4. The source network can then be replaced by a 0.046-A ideal current source in parallel with an 80.4-Ω resistor as in Figure 8.16*b*.

Calculation of the current through the load network is simpler if you use the formula

$$I_{\text{load}} = I_N \times \frac{R_N}{R_N + R_L} \qquad \text{FORMULA 8.3}$$

Substituting the values from Figure 8.16*b*,

$$I_{R4} = \frac{80.4}{80.4 \times 51} \times 0.046 = 0.028 \text{ A}$$

and

$$E_{R1} = 0.028 \times 51 = 1.42 \text{ V}$$

Notice that the solutions to this circuit by Thevenin's and Norton's theorems agree. ■

As in the case of the Thevenin equivalent, the Norton equivalent can only be used to aid in the calculation of current and potential difference in the load network since the current supplied by the Norton source and the parallel resistance are only indirectly related to the components in the original source network.

In summary, the steps in using Norton's theorem to simplify a circuit are:

1. Divide the circuit into a source network and a load network by placing two terminals in the circuit schematic.

2. Check to make sure that the components in the part of the circuit to be replaced by the Norton equivalent are linear and bilateral.

3. Redraw the circuit schematic, replacing the load network with a short circuit.

4. Calculate the current through the short circuit. This is the current produced by the ideal current source of the Norton equivalent.

5. Erase the short circuit drawn between the terminals and calculate the resistance between them with all voltage sources short circuited and all current sources open circuited. This is the resistance of the Norton equivalent parallel resistor R_N.

6. Redraw the original schematic diagram replacing the source network with its Norton equivalent.

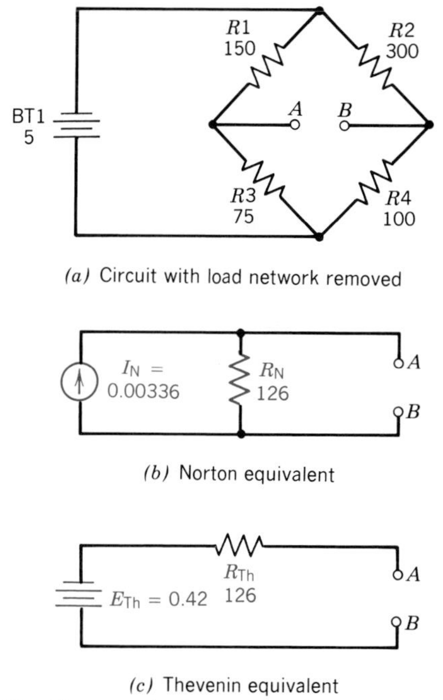

Figure 8.17 The equivalence of Thevenin and Norton equivalents.

B.6 THE RELATIONSHIP BETWEEN THEVENIN AND NORTON EQUIVALENTS

Figures 8.15 and 8.16 show more than the fact that both Thevenin and Norton equivalents can be substituted for the same source network. Since there is only one Thevenin equivalent and only one Norton equivalent for any source network composed of linear, bilateral components and sources, it is easy to understand that there must be some relationship between them. In fact, the Thevenin equivalent of a source network is also the Thevenin equivalent of the Norton equivalent of that network. For example, Figure 8.17*a* shows the schematic of a circuit, while its Norton equivalent is shown in 8.17*b*. The Thevenin equivalent shown in 8.17*c* could have been obtained from either 8.17*a* or 8.17*b*.

The equivalence of Thevenin and Norton equivalents is particularly useful in analyzing some circuits because it makes it possible to replace a current source with a voltage source for voltage law analyses, or a voltage source with a current source for current law analyses.

Converting from a Thevenin voltage source and series resistor to a Norton current source and parallel resistor requires hardly any calculation. Starting with a Thevenin equivalent such as that shown in Figure 8.17*c*, assume that a short circuit is connected between the terminals of the voltage source. The current through the short circuit will be the rated current of the Norton current source. The value of the Norton resistor R_N will be the same as the Thevenin series resistor. To sum it up mathematically:

$$I_N = \frac{E_{Th}}{R_{Th}}$$

and FORMULA 8.4

$$R_N = R_{Th}$$

The Norton equivalent for the Thevenin source is shown in Figure 8.17*b*.

To convert from a Norton equivalent to a Thevenin equivalent use a similar process. In the circuit shown in Figure 8.17*b*, a Norton ideal current source and parallel resistor form the source network. The potential difference produced by the Thevenin equivalent of the Norton source is found by calculating the potential difference across the parallel resistor with the load network omitted, that is, open circuited. The value of the resistance of the series resistor in the Thevenin equivalent is the same as that of the parallel Norton resistor. Writing this in the form of two equations,

$$E_{Th} = I_N \times R_N \qquad \text{FORMULA 8.5}$$
$$R_{Th} = R_N$$

Figure 8.17*c* shows the Thevenin equivalent of the Norton source seen in 8.17*b*.

An example of the use of the Thevenin–Norton equivalence is shown in Figure 8.18*a*. Here a circuit

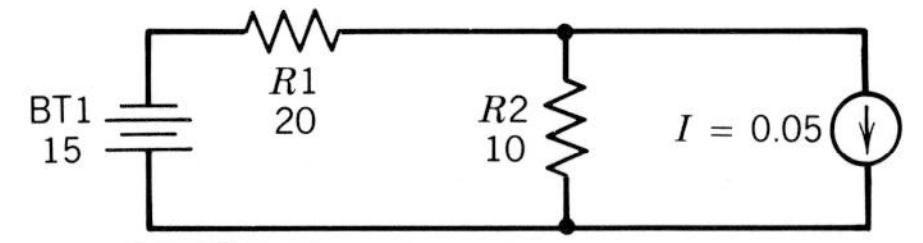

(a) Circuit containing voltage and current sources

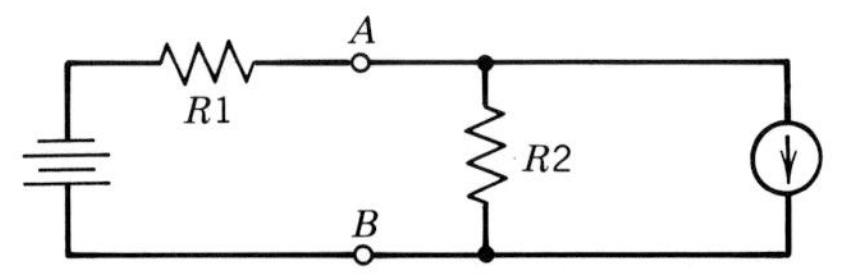

(b) Dividing the circuit into two networks

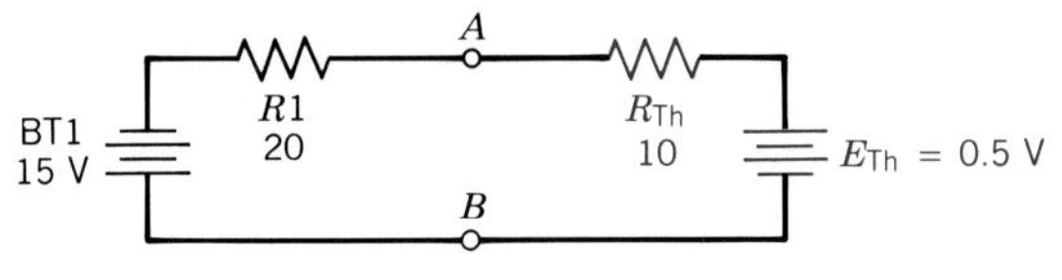

(c) Replacing the current source with its Thevenin equivalent

Figure 8.18 Using Thevenin–Norton equivalence.

contains both a voltage and a current source, making the task of calculating the potential difference across and the current through $R1$ more complicated. If, however, the circuit is redrawn so that both sources are voltage sources, as shown in Figure 8.18*c*, the result is a simple series circuit, and the current and potential across $R1$ can be calculated directly. The replacement of the current source and parallel resistor can be accomplished easily if it is recognized as a Norton equivalent. First, two terminals are drawn on the schematic as shown in Figure 8.18*b*. This divides the circuit into two networks. Applying Formula 8.5 to the current source and $R2$:

$$R_{\text{Th}} = R_{\text{N}} = 10\ \Omega$$

$$E_{\text{Th}} = I_{\text{N}} \times R_{\text{N}} = 0.05 \times 10 = 0.5\ \text{V}$$

The calculated Thevenin equivalent is substituted for $R2$ and the current source in Figure 8.18*c*. The current through $R1$ is

$$I = \frac{15 + 0.5}{20 + 10} = 0.517 \quad \text{and}$$

$$E_{R2} = I \times 20 = 10.33\ \text{V}$$

B.7 MILLMAN'S THEOREM

The final network theorem to be covered in this chapter is based on the relationship between Thevenin and Norton source networks. Called *Millman's theorem*, it is of use in simplifying circuits that contain parallel branches involving resistances and either current or voltage sources. The circuit shown in Figure 8.19 is a

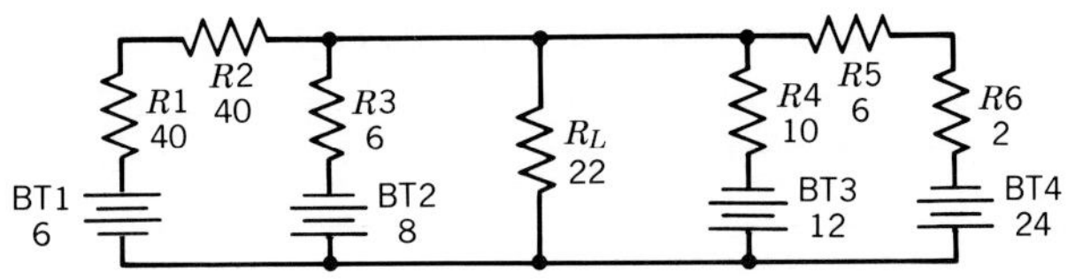

(a) Example of a circuit application for Millman's theorem

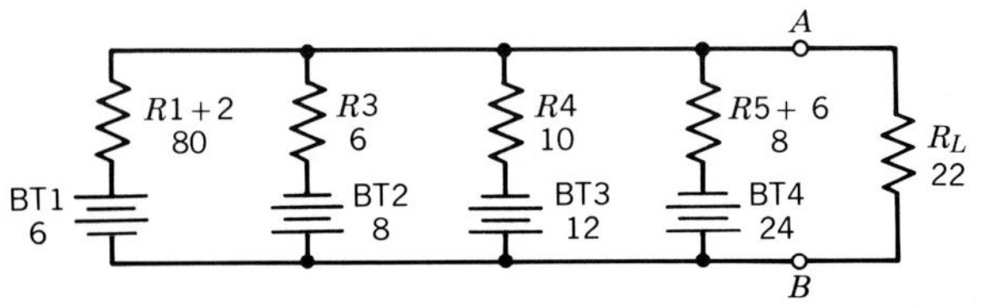

(b) Circuit redrawn to emphasize parallel branches; terminals *A* and *B* inserted to separate load and source networks

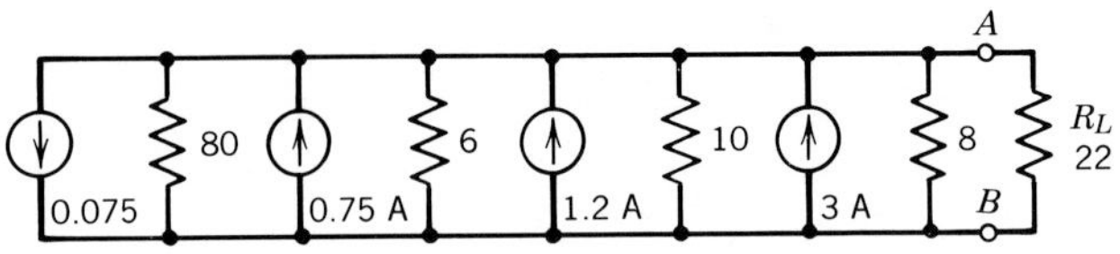

(c) Replacing each branch with a current source and parallel resistance

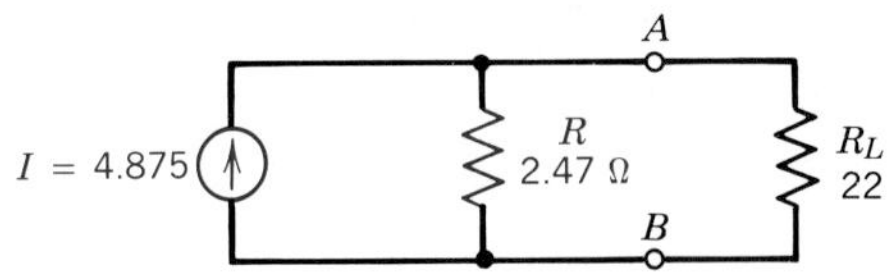

(d) Combining the current sources and parallel resistance according to Millman's theorem

Figure 8.19 An illustration of Millman's theorem.

typical example of a circuit in which Millman's theorem can be of great help. If the current through the load R_{L} is required, the presence of four distinct meshes means that a Kirchhoff's voltage law analysis is going to be a difficult process. Even the superposition theorem will result in complicated calculations because of the fact that four sources are involved. On the other hand, if the circuit is redrawn as in Figure 8.19*b*, you can see that except for the load, each parallel branch contains a voltage source and a series resistor. If each branch is treated as if it were a Thevenin source, the corresponding Norton equivalent could easily be substituted. For example, the Norton equivalent for the branch composed of the 24-V source and 8 Ω resistor produces a current of 3 A and has an 8 Ω parallel resistor. In Figure 8.19*c* each branch has been replaced by a current source and parallel resistance using the equivalence of Thevenin and Norton equivalents.

Millman's theorem states that a network composed of any number of ideal current sources connected in parallel and parallel resistors can be replaced by an equivalent composed of a single ideal current source and parallel resistor. The current supplied by the Millman equivalent source is equal to the sum of the currents of the ideal sources replaced, with attention paid to the current direction. The Millman equivalent resistance is the result of combining the parallel resistances.

In the example of Figure 8.19, the resulting current is

$$I_1 + I_2 + I_3 + I_4 = -0.075 + 0.75 + 1.2 + 3$$
$$= 4.875 \text{ A}$$

The parallel combination of the four resistors is a resistance of 2.47 Ω. The Millman equivalent is shown in Figure 8.19*d*.

Although Millman's theorem refers to ideal current sources, the fact that the potential difference across any branch of a parallel circuit is equal to the potential difference across any other, makes this theorem useful for quickly and easily analyzing voltage source circuits of the type shown in Figure 8.20*a*. If the potential difference between points *A* and *B* is known, it requires very little calculation to find the current through any branch or the potential drop across any resistor. Redrawing the circuit to emphasize the parallel branches as is done in Figure 8.20*b* permits using a single formula derived from Millman's theorem to calculate the potential difference between *A* and *B*. This formula is

$$E_{AB} = \frac{I_{\text{total}}}{R_{\text{total}}} = \frac{I_{\text{branch 1}} + I_{\text{branch 2}}}{R_{\text{total}}} = \frac{\dfrac{E_{BT1}}{R1} + \dfrac{E_{BT2}}{R2}}{\dfrac{1}{R1} + \dfrac{1}{R2} + \dfrac{1}{R3}} \qquad \text{FORMULA 8.6}$$

Although this formula may look a bit complex at first glance, it is actually quite simple. I_{total} is equal to the sum of each voltage source potential divided by its series resistor, and the denominator R_{total} is the equivalent resistance of all the resistors in the parallel branches, including the load.

EXAMPLE:
Use Millman's theorem to calculate the power dissipated by each of the resistors in Figure 8.20*a*. ■

Figure 8.20 Using Millman's theorem permits quick analysis of this circuit type.

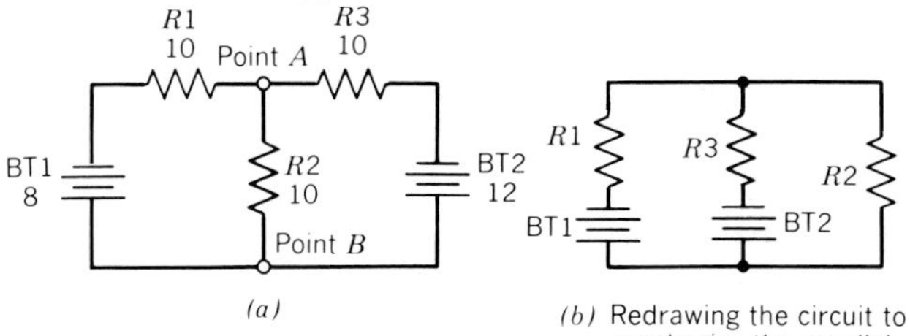

(*b*) Redrawing the circuit to emphasize the parallel branches

SOLUTION:
Redraw the circuit to emphasize the parallel branches as shown in Figure 8.20*b*. The easiest method for solution of this problem is to calculate the potential difference between points *A* and *B*, using Millman's theorem and Formula 8.6. Once this has been done, the potential difference across each resistor in the circuit can be noted and the power dissipation $P = \dfrac{E^2}{R}$ calculated. The potential difference between points *A* and *B* is

$$E_{AB} = \frac{\dfrac{8}{10} + \dfrac{12}{10}}{\dfrac{1}{10} + \dfrac{1}{10} + \dfrac{1}{10}} = 6.667$$

Then,

$$P_{R1} = \frac{(E_{R1})^2}{R1} = \frac{(8 - 6.667)^2}{10}$$
$$= 0.178 \text{ W}$$
$$P_{R2} = \frac{(E_{R2})^2}{R2} = \frac{(6.667)^2}{10} = 4.44 \text{ W}$$

and

$$P_{R3} = \frac{(E_{R3})^2}{R3} = \frac{(12 - 6.667)^2}{10} = 2.84 \text{ W}$$ ■

C. EXAMPLES AND COMPUTATIONS

C.1 SIMULTANEOUS EQUATIONS ON A SMALL COMPUTER USING BASIC

In the last chapter the method of determinants was used to solve the equations produced by Kirchhoff's voltage law analyses. Frequently, it is much easier to write the equations than to solve them, and even the method of determinants requires lengthy arithmetic computations that can result in errors. Because of these difficulties, many technicians tend either to avoid circuit analysis when troubleshooting or, when possible, to use one of the network theorems presented in this chapter. Since there is no better method for isolating a faulty component in a circuit than calculating the operating potential at various points in the circuit and then comparing the actual measured voltages, it is fortunate that the invention of small computers and programmable calculators has made the solution of Kirchhoff's law equations an automatic and essentially error-free process.

Program 8.1 is used to solve two simultaneous equations, Program 8.2 is for solving three simulta-

PROGRAM 8.1

```
10   REM PROGRAM FOR SOLVING
20   REM TWO SIMULTANEOUS EQUATIONS
30   REM COPYRIGHT 1984, S.L. ROSEN
40   PRINT “THIS PROGRAM SOLVES TWO”
50   PRINT “INDEPENDENT EQUATIONS”
60   PRINT “OF THE FORM”
70   PRINT: PRINT “A1X + B1Y = C”
80   PRINT “A2X + B2Y = D, OR”
90   PRINT “A1I1 + B1I2 = E1, AND”
100  PRINT “A1I1 + B2I2 = E2”
110  PRINT “ARE YOUR EQUATIONS IN”
120  INPUT “THIS FORM? ( TYPE Y OR N)”,
       A$
130  REM THE NEXT SECTION DISPLAYS
       ADDITIONAL
140  REM INSTRUCTIONS ONLY IF NEEDED
150  IF A$ = “Y” GOTO 300
160  IF A$ = “N” GOTO 180
170  GOTO 110
180  PRINT “A1, B1, AND E1 ARE THE”
190  PRINT “COEFFICIENTS OF THE X”
200  PRINT “AND Y OR I1 and I2 UN-”
210  PRINT “KNOWNS AND E1 IS THE CON-”
220  PRINT “STANT TERM IN THE FIRST”
230  PRINT “EQUATION. A2, B2, AND E2”
240  PRINT “ARE THE COEFFICIENTS”
250  PRINT “AND THE CONSTANT TERM”
260  PRINT “OF THE SECOND. THESE”
270  PRINT “CAN BE WHOLE NUMBERS,”
280  PRINT “DECIMALS, OR FRACTIONS”
290  PRINT “IN THE FORM 3/2.”
300  REM PUTTING THE INPUTS ON
       SEPARATE
310  REM LINES MAKES IT EASIER TO
       CHECK
320  INPUT “A1 = ”, A1
330  INPUT “B1 = ”, B1
340  INPUT “E1 = ”, E1
350  INPUT “A2 = ”, A2
360  INPUT “B2 = ”, B2
370  INPUT “E2 = ”, E2
380  PRINT “ARE YOUR INPUTS CORRECT?”
390  INPUT “TYPE Y OR N”, A$
400  IF A$ = “Y” GOTO 420
410  GOTO 300
420  REM COMPUTE D, N1, AND N2
430  D= A1*B2 - B1*A2
440  IF D = 0 GOTO 500
450  N1 = E1*B2 - B1*E2
460  N2 = A1*E2 - A2*E1
470  PRINT: PRINT “I1 or X = ”;N1/D
480  PRINT “I2 OR Y = ”;N2/D
490  END
500  PRINT:PRINT:PRINT “ SOLUTION NOT
       POSSIBLE”
510  PRINT “CHECK TO SEE IF ONE”
520  PRINT “ EQUATION IS A MULTIPLE”
530  PRINT “OF THE OTHER, OR TRY”
540  PRINT “INPUTTING THE
       INFORMATION”
550  PRINT “AGAIN”: PRINT: PRINT: GOTO
       300
```

PROGRAM 8.2

```
10   REM PROGRAM FOR SOLVING
20   REM THREE SIMULTANEOUS
       EQUATIONS
30   REM COPYRIGHT 1984, S.L. ROSEN
40   PRINT “THIS PROGRAM SOLVES
       THREE”
50   PRINT “INDEPENDENT EQUATIONS”
60   PRINT “OF THE FORM”
70   PRINT: PRINT “A1X + B2Y + C1Z = M”
80   PRINT “ A2X + B2Y + C2Z = N”
85   PRINT “A3X + B3Y + C3Z = P, OR”
90   PRINT “A1I1 + B1I2 + C1I3 = E1”
100  PRINT “ A2I1 + B2I2 + C2I3 = E2”
105  PRINT “A3I1 + B3I2 + C3I3 = E3”
110  PRINT “ARE YOUR EQUATIONS IN”
120  INPUT “THIS FORM? (TYPE Y OR N)”, A$
125  REM THE NEXT SECTION DISPLAYS
       ADDITIONAL
126  REM INSTRUCTIONS ONLY IF NEEDED
130  IF A$ = “Y” GOTO 265
135  IF A$ = “N” GOTO 150
140  GOTO 110
150  PRINT “A1, B1, C1, AND E1 ARE THE”
160  PRINT “COEFFICIENTS OF THE X,”
170  PRINT “Y, AND Z OR I1, I2, AND I3 UN-”
180  PRINT “KNOWNS AND E1 IS THE CON-”
190  PRINT “STANT TERM IN THE FIRST”
200  PRINT “EQUATION. A2, B2, AND E2”
205  PRINT “AND A3, B3, C3, AND E3”
210  PRINT “ARE THE COEFFICIENTS”
220  PRINT “AND THE CONSTANT TERM”
230  PRINT “OF THE SECOND, AND THE
       THIRD”
231  PRINT “RESPECTIVELY. THESE”
240  PRINT “CAN BE WHOLE NUMBERS,”
250  PRINT “DECIMALS, OR FRACTIONS”
260  PRINT “IN THE FORM 3/2.”
265  REM PUTTING THE INPUTS ON
       SEPARATE
```

```
266   REM LINES MAKES IT EASIER TO
        CHECK
270   INPUT "A1 = ", A1
280   INPUT "B1 = ", B1
285   INPUT "C1 = ", C1
290   INPUT "E1 = ", E1
300   INPUT "A2 = ", A2
310   INPUT "B2 = ", B2
315   INPUT "C2 = ", C2
320   INPUT "E2 = ", E2
321   INPUT "A3 = ", A3
322   INPUT "B3 = ", B3
323   INPUT "C3 = ", C3
324   INPUT "E3 = ", E3
330   PRINT "ARE YOUR INPUTS CORRECT?"
340   INPUT "TYPE Y OR N",A$
350   IF A$ = "Y" GOTO 370
360   GOTO 265
370   REM COMPUTE D, N1, N2, and N3
379   J = (C1*B2*A3 + A1*C2*B3 + C3*B1*A2)
380   D = (A1*B2*C3 + C1*A2*B3 + A3*B1*C2)
        - J
390   IF D = 0 GOTO 440
399   J = (C1*B2*E3 + E1*C2*B3 + C3*B1*E2)
400   N1 = (E1*B2*C3 + C1*E2*B3 + E3*B1*C2)
        - J
409   J = (C1*E2*A3 + A1*C2*E3 + C3*E1*A2)
410   N2 = (A1*E2*C3 + C1*A2*E3 + A3*E1*C2)
        - J
411   J = (E1*B2*A3 + A1*E2*B3 + E3*B1*A2)
412   N3 = (A1*B2*E3 + E1*A2*B3 + A3*B1*E2)
        - J
420   PRINT: PRINT "I1 OR X = "; N1/D
430   PRINT "I2 OR Y = "; N2/D
433   PRINT "I3 OR Z = "; N3/D
435   END
440   PRINT:PRINT:PRINT " SOLUTION NOT
        POSSIBLE"
450   PRINT "CHECK TO SEE IF ONE"
460   PRINT "EQUATION IS A MULTIPLE"
470   PRINT "OF THE OTHER, OR TRY"
480   PRINT "INPUTTING THE
        INFORMATION"
490   PRINT "AGAIN": PRINT: PRINT: GOTO
        265
```

neous equations. It would be possible to combine them into one program, but that has not been done here because it is easier to follow the logic of the programs when they are separated. Extensive "on-screen" instructions have been incorporated into both programs.

Notice that an effort has been made to keep the logical order of this program similar to the steps followed in working out the method of determinants with pencil and paper. This makes it easier to correct programming or entry errors. Test your program by solving for x and y in the following pair of equations:

$$16x - 8y = -8$$
$$6x + 9y = 69$$

If you get $x = 2.5$ and $y = 6$, your program is running properly.

Solving for three unknown quantities requires a somewhat longer program, but the steps followed are much the same as in Program 8.1.

Again, after entering the program check it carefully and use it to solve for x, y, and z in the three following equations:

$$3x - 2y - 2z = 7$$
$$x - 2y - 3z = 1.5$$
$$2x + 2y + 8z = 5$$

If your result was $x = 3$, $y = 1.5$, and $z = -0.5$ your program is operating properly.

Saving your programs on floppy disk or magnetic tape will permit you to use them for solving Kirchhoff's law equations.

Try using your programs to solve the following problems:

1. Solve for the unknown quantities, if possible.

a. $3x + 4y = 1$
$x + y = -2$

b. $2(x + y) = 0.06$
$3x + 2y = -1.31$

c. $-1.193 + 3(I_1 - I_2) = 0$
$-12.87x + 10(I_1 + I_2) = 0$

d. $\frac{3x}{y} = 2$
$x - 4 = \frac{y}{3}$

e. $2.667x + 4y = 3$
$8x + 12y = 9$

f. $-21.62 + 6(I_1 - I_2) + 2I_1 = 0$
$-9.12 + 4I_2 - 6(I_1 - I_2) = 0$

g. $2x - y = 1$
$3x - 6y = 0$

h. $-70.695 + 51(I_1 - I_3) + 27I_2 = 0$
$-36.54 + 6(I_3 - I_2) + 22(I_2 + I_3) = 0$

i. $x + 6y - 3z = -13.5$
$2x + 2y + z = 2$
$4x + 2y - 2z = 1$

j. $1.3I_1 + 2I_2 - 4I_3 = 0$
$7I_1 - 2I_2 + 3I_1 = 5$
$5.2(I_1 - I_3) + 8I_2 = 0$

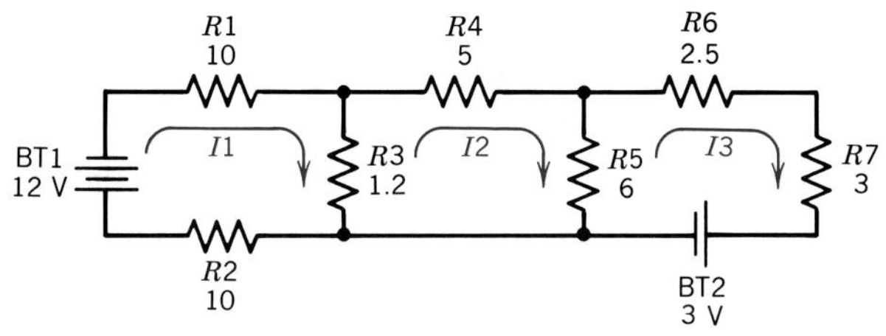

Figure 8.21 Schematic diagram for problem 2.

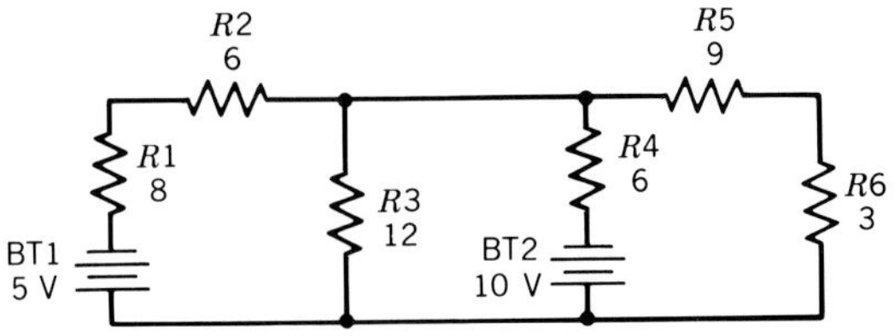

Figure 8.22 Schematic diagram for problem 3.

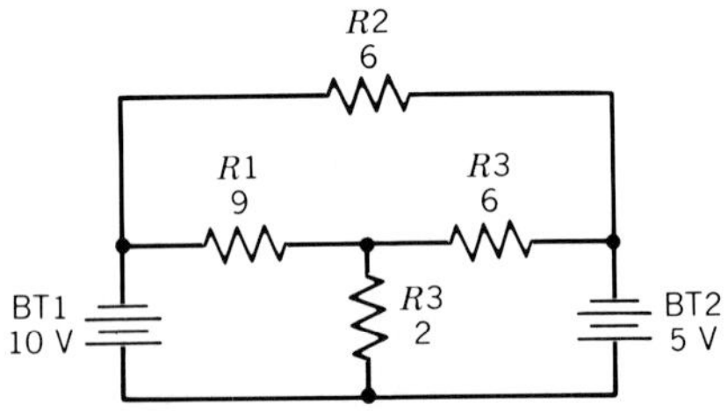

Figure 8.23 Schematic for problem 4.

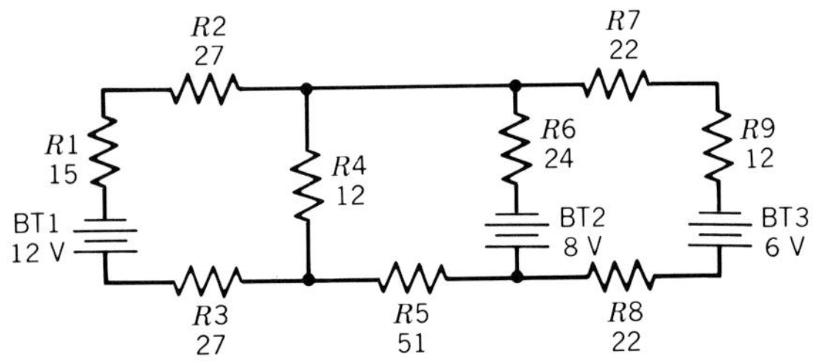

Figure 8.24 Schematic for problem 5.

2. Use Kirchhoff's voltage law to calculate the potential drops across *R*1, *R*3, and *R*5 in Figure 8.21.

3. Solve for the voltage drop across each resistor in Figure 8.22 using a Kirchhoff's current law analysis. Check your answer by performing a voltage law analysis. Which method took less time?

4. You do not need to write any equations to determine the current through *R*2 in Figure 8.23. Check your answer by performing a voltage law analysis.

5. You are troubleshooting the circuit whose schematic is shown in Figure 8.24. The batteries have been checked and are operating correctly. Resistor *R*5 is slightly charred and you suspect that its value has changed. What should the voltage drop across *R*5 be? Will a measurement more than 50 percent higher than that calculated prove that *R*5 is faulty?

C.2 Δ–Y AND Y–Δ EQUIVALENCY USING A SMALL COMPUTER

Of the various network theorems you have studied in this chapter, the Δ–Y and Y–Δ equivalency theorems involve enough calculation to offer good examples for the use of BASIC programs. As in the case of the previous programs, the logic of Programs 8.3 and 8.4 follow the paper-and-pencil methods of solution for ease in analysis.

PROGRAM 8.3

```
10   PRINT "THIS PROGRAM CALCULATES"
20   PRINT "THE RESISTANCE VALUES"
30   PRINT "OF A WYE NETWORK"
40   PRINT "EQUIVALENT TO A"
50   PRINT "GIVEN DELTA NETWORK."
60   PRINT "COPYRIGHT S.L. ROSEN, 1984"
70   PRINT: PRINT "STEP 1: PLACE A DOT"
80   PRINT "IN THE CENTER OF THE
90   PRINT "SCHEMATIC OF THE DELTA"
100  PRINT "NETWORK"
110  PRINT "TYPE Y AND RETURN"
120  INPUT "TO CONTINUE"; A$: PRINT
130  IF A$ = "Y" THEN GOTO 140
140  PRINT "LABEL THE JUNCTIONS"
150  PRINT "OF THE DELTA 1, 2, AND 3"
160  PRINT: PRINT "WHAT IS THE VALUE"
170  PRINT "OF THE RESISTOR"
180  INPUT "BETWEEN JUNCTIONS 1 AND
       2"; R1
190  INPUT "BETWEEN JUNCTIONS 1 AND
       3"; R3
200  INPUT "BETWEEN JUNCTIONS 3 AND
       1"; R2
210  RA = R1*R2/(R1 + R2 + R3)
220  RB = R1*R3/(R1 + R2 + R3)
230  RC = R2*R3/(R1 + R2 + R3)
240  PRINT: PRINT "FROM JUNCTION 1 TO
       THE"
250  PRINT "CENTER DOT, DRAW"
260  PRINT "A "; RA "OHM RESISTOR,"
270  PRINT: PRINT "FROM JUNCTION 2, A ";
       RB "OHM"
280  PRINT: PRINT "AND FROM 3, A "; RC
       "OHM."
290  END
```

PROGRAM 8.4

```
10   PRINT "THIS PROGRAM CALCULATES"
20   PRINT "THE RESISTANCE VALUES"
```

```
30  PRINT "OF A DELTA NETWORK"
40  PRINT "EQUIVALENT TO A"
50  PRINT "GIVEN WYE NETWORK"
60  PRINT "COPYRIGHT S.L. ROSEN, 1984"
70  PRINT: PRINT "LABEL THE THREE
      OUTER"
80  PRINT "JUNCTIONS OF THE WYE"
90  PRINT "NETWORK 1, 2, AND 3. DO NOT"
100 PRINT "LABEL THE CENTRAL
      JUNCTION."
110 PRINT "TYPE Y AND RETURN"
120 INPUT "TO CONTINUE"; A$: PRINT
130 IF A$ = "Y" THEN GOTO 140
140 PRINT "WHAT IS THE VALUE"
150 PRINT "OF THE RESISTOR"
160 INPUT "CONNECTED TO JUNCTION 1";
      R1
170 INPUT "CONNECTED TO JUNCTION 2";
      R2
180 INPUT "CONNECTED TO JUNCTION 3";
      R3
190 J = 1/R1 + 1/R2 + 1/R3
200 GA = 1/R1*1/R2/J
210 GB = 1/R2*1/R3/J
220 GC = 1/R3*1/R1/J
230 J = 1/GA: K = 1: L= 2
240 GOSUB 300
250 J = 1/GB: K = 2: L= 3
260 GOSUB 300
270 J = 1/GC: K = 3: L = 1
280 GOSUB 300
290 PRINT: PRINT "AND ERASE THE WYE
      NETWORK": END
300 PRINT: PRINT "DRAW A "; J "OHM
      RESISTOR"
310 PRINT "BETWEEN "; K "AND "; L:
      PRINT
320 RETURN
```

Test your entry of Program 8.3 by determining the Y equivalent of the Δ network shown in Figure 8.25*a*. If you came up with the network shown in Figure 8.25*b*, your program is functioning correctly.

Test Program 8.4 by entering the values shown in Figure 8.25*b*. Your solution should be the values for the Δ network of Figure 8.25*a*.

Use Programs 8.3 and 8.4 to solve the following problems.

1. What is the current furnished by the source in Figure 8.26? Convert *R*1, *R*2, and *R*3 to a Y network to find the answer.

2. Convert *R*1, *R*3, and *R*4 in Figure 8.26 to a Δ network and recompute the current furnished by BT1. Did your answer agree with the previous problem?

3. Calculate the potential difference across *R*3 in Figure 8.27 using the Δ-to-Y conversion program.

4. Figure 8.28 consists of a complex network formed of 10 Ω resistors. What is the resistance between the terminals? If the terminals are connected to a 12-V source, what will be the current through *R*2?

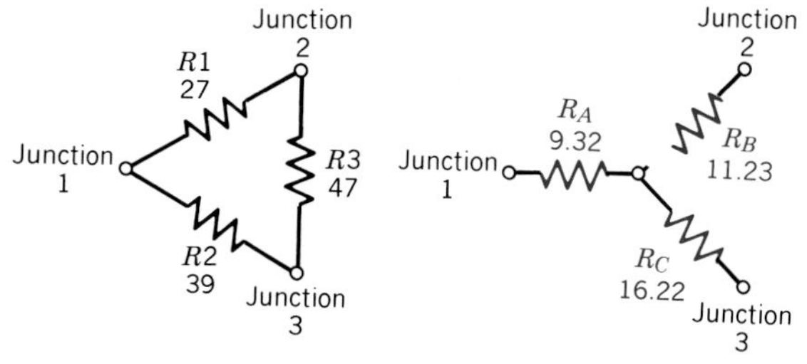

(*a*) Δ network (*b*) Equivalent y network

Figure 8.25 Test your entry of Program 8.3 by calculating the Y equivalent of (*a*).

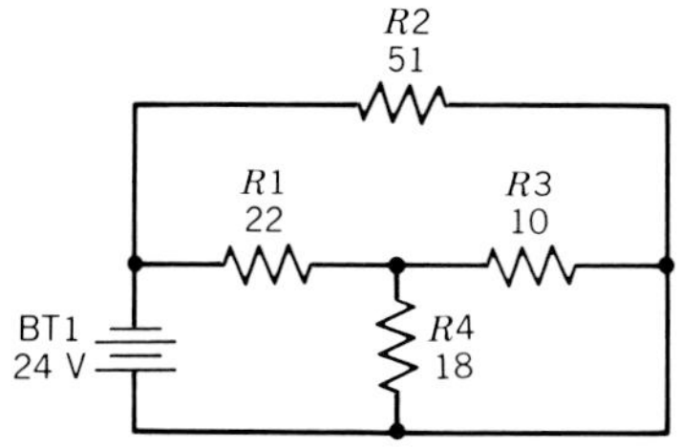

Figure 8.26 Schematic for C.2 problems 1 and 2.

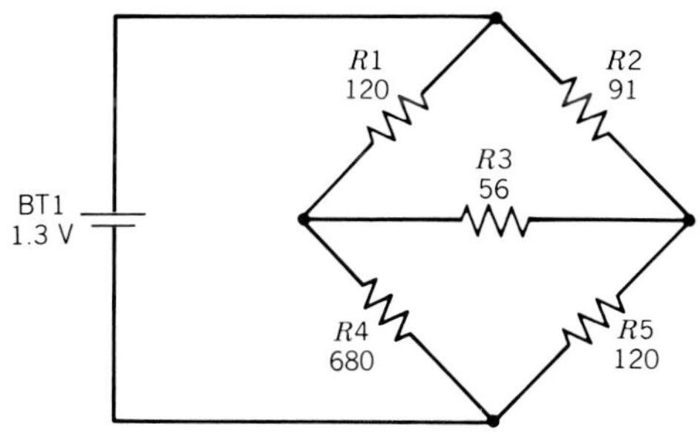

Figure 8.27 Schematic for 8.C.2 problem 3.

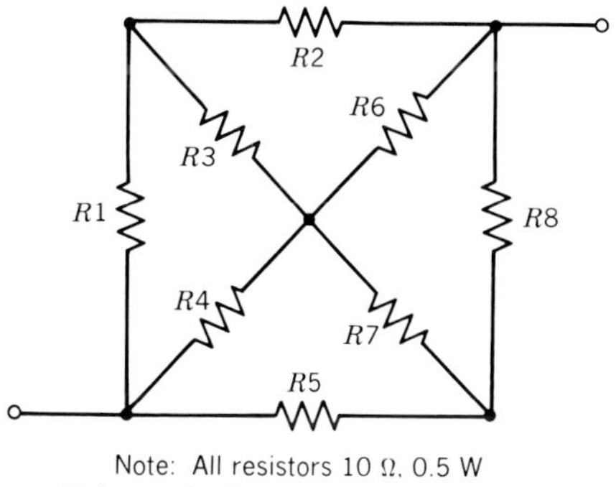

Figure 8.28 Schematic for resistor network for 8.C.2 problem 4.

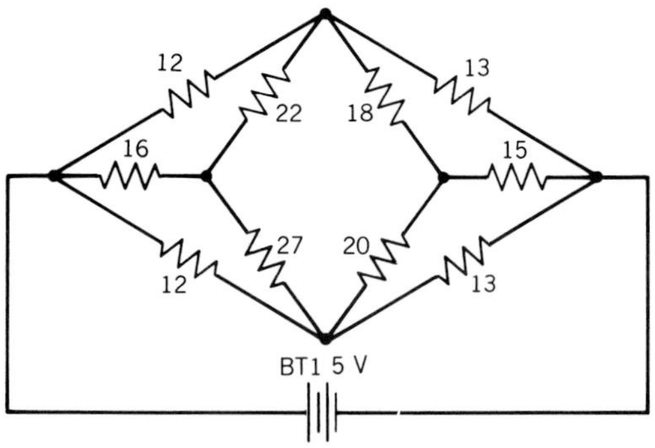

Figure 8.29 Schematic for 8.C.2 problem 5.

5. What is the current supplied by BT1 in Figure 8.29?

C.3 COMPARISON OF KIRCHHOFF'S LAW ANALYSES AND NETWORK THEOREMS

In order to see how network theorems are used to escape the tedious arithmetic or a Kirchhoff law analysis, solve the following problems using the suggested methods. Keep careful track of the amount of time required by each method. Were any of the network theorems easier to use than Kirchhoff's laws when combined with your computer program?

1. Solve for the current through and voltage drop across each resistor in Figure 8.30:

a. Using Kirchhoff's current law
b. Using Millman's theorem

2. Calculate the current through and potential difference across *R*3 in Figure 8.31:

a. Using the Δ–Y equivalency theorem
b. Using Kirchhoff's voltage law
c. Using Thevenin's theorem.

Figure 8.30 Schematic for 8.C.3 problem 1.

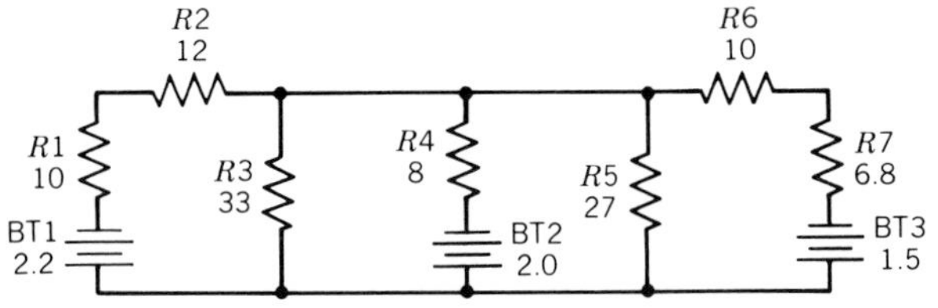

Figure 8.31 Schematic for 8.C.3 problem 2.

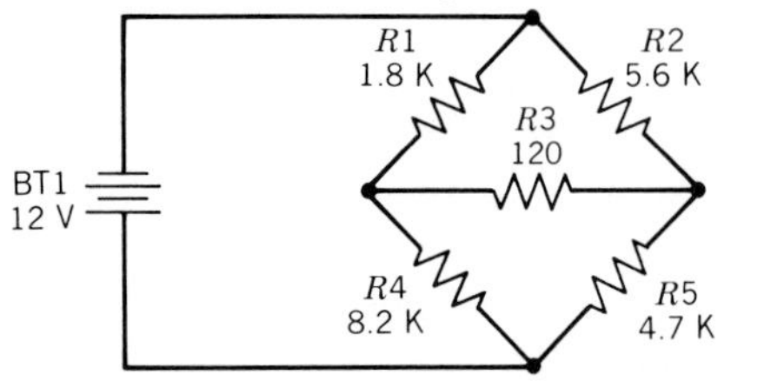

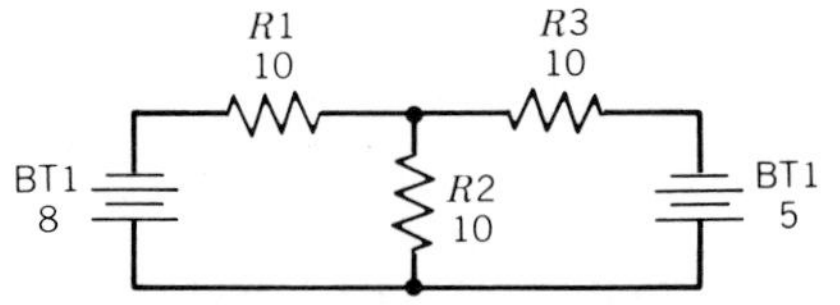

Figure 8.32 Schematic for 8.C.3 problem 3.

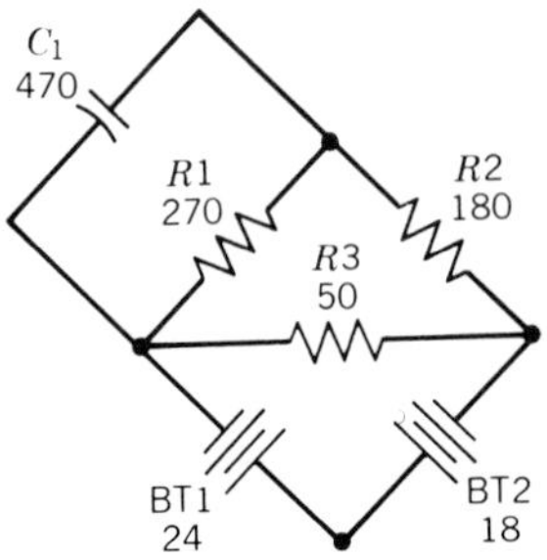

Figure 8.33 Schematic for 8.C.3 problem 4.

3. Calculate the current through and potential difference across *R*2 in Figure 8.32:

a. Using Norton's theorem
b. Using the superposition theorem
c. Using Kirchhoff's voltage law
d. Using Kirchhoff's current law
e. Using Millman's Theorem

4. Figure 8.33 contains a schematic symbol that has not yet been introduced. Component *C*1 is a capacitor. Calculate the potential difference across it using two different network theorems.

D. APPLICATIONS

D.1 SHUNTS

One of the most common circuits involving fixed resistors is the shunt circuit. The shunt resistor is placed in parallel with the load, as shown in Figure 8.34, and acts to reduce the current through the load. A typical application of this resistor circuit is shown in Figure 8.35*a*. Here a 27-V source is used to power a load with a resistance of 60 Ω. In order to observe the circuit

Figure 8.34 A shunt is placed in parallel with a load.

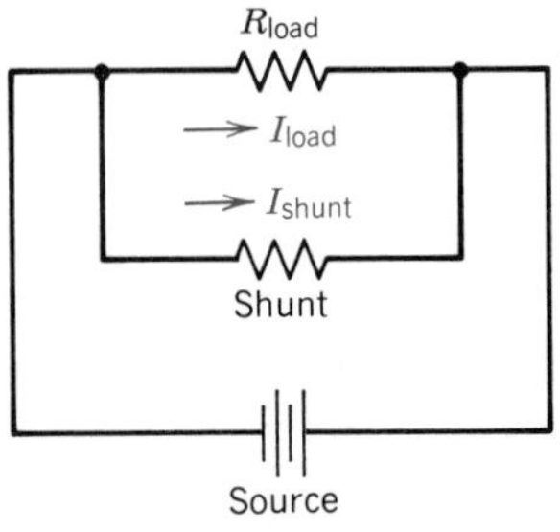

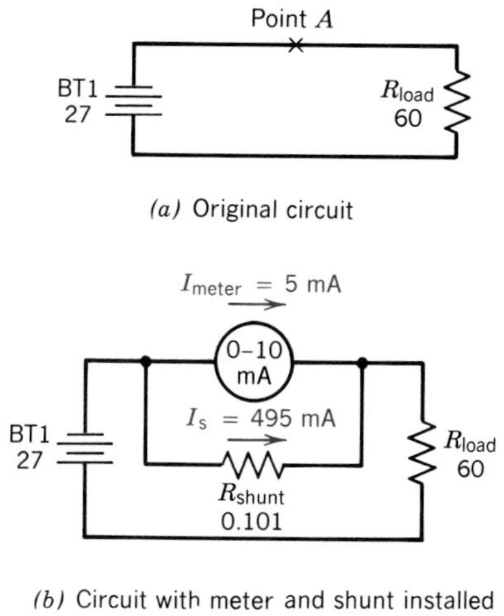

Figure 8.35 A meter shunt is used to extend the range of an ammeter.

current during operation, a service technician wishes to place a small milliammeter into the circuit at point A. The meter available for this is a 0 to 10 mA meter, that is, a meter which indicates a full-scale reading when the current through it is 10 mA. The resistance of the meter is 10 Ω. In order to use this meter in the circuit of Figure 8.35*a* a shunt resistance will have to be placed across it so that the meter indicates half scale when the circuit current is 500 mA, as shown in Figure 8.35*b*. How would the service technician go about calculating the value of the shunt resistor?

If the meter current is to be 5 mA when the circuit current is 500 mA, the current through the shunt will be 500 − 5 = 495 mA. Since the meter and the shunt resistor are in parallel, the potential difference, that is, the voltage drop across both, must be the same:

$$I_{shunt} \times R_{shunt} = I_{meter} \times R_{meter} \qquad \text{FORMULA 8.7}$$

The value of the shunt resistor can then be obtained by substituting the known values:

$$0.495R_{shunt} = 0.005 \times 10 \quad \text{or} \quad R_{shunt} = 0.101\ \Omega$$

Since the shunt current is equal to the total circuit current minus the meter current, Formula 8.7 can also be written as

$$R_{shunt} = \frac{I_{meter} \times R_{meter}}{I_{total} - I_{meter}} \qquad \text{FORMULA 8.8}$$

Substituting the values of the previous example in this formula provides the same results as Formula 8.7:

$$R_{shunt} = \frac{0.005 \times 10}{0.500 - 0.005} = 0.101\ \Omega$$

This second formula is generally easier to use because it does not require you to calclate the current through the shunt resistor.

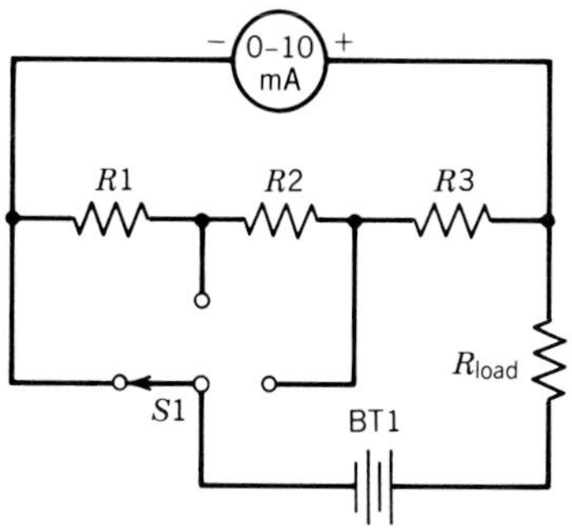

Figure 8.36 An Ayrton shunt provides several meter ranges.

If the service technician could not purchase a 0.101 Ω resistor from a local supplier, either a length of wire with the proper resistance could be used, or a 0.1 Ω resistor could be made up by connecting ten 1 Ω resistors in parallel. The difference between 0.1 Ω and the calculated value of 0.101 Ω is only 1 percent and would not result in a great difference in the meter reading.

Calculating the value of a simple shunt is a fairly common task in electronics. Using this information you can adjust the current range of a meter upward to fit circuit requirements. You can not, of course, increase the meter sensitivity. There is no shunt resistor that will turn a 0 to 10 mA meter into a 0 to 1 mA device. Complex shunt circuits, such as the Ayrton or "universal" shunt shown in Figure 8.36, are frequently used, but it is rarely necessary to calculate their resistance values.

The advantage of the Ayrton shunt over the three separate switched shunts shown in Figure 8.37 is that the portion of the shunt that is not in parallel with the meter is placed in series with it. This increases the resistance of the branch containing the meter and enables larger value resistors to be used in the shunt. Further, through careful choice of the meter and ranges, standard value components can be used.

Any shunt resistor, particularly a meter shunt, which provides an alternate path for circuit current, is liable to burn out if forced to dissipate too much current. In cases where the shunt conducts the major por-

Figure 8.37 An example of switching to provide several meter ranges.

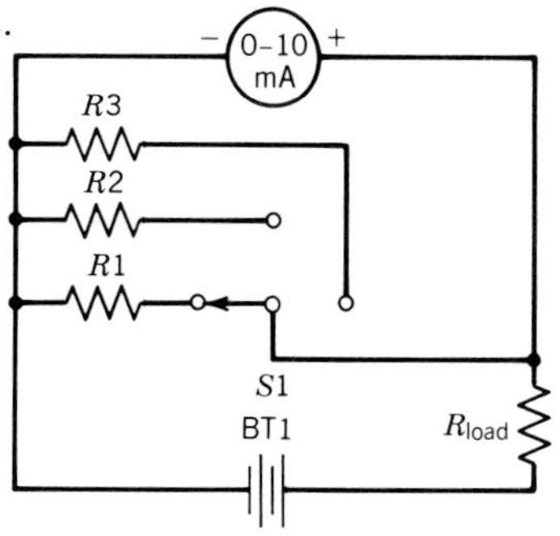

tion of the circuit current, burnout of the shunt is usually followed almost immediately by damage to the meter or other components with which the shunt is in parallel. For this reason, shunt resistors need a wide margin of power dissipation. If you are designing a shunt circuit, allow for surge currents when specifying the power dissipation of shunt resistors. Allowing free circulation of air around the shunt will also keep it from heating and tend to keep its resistance constant. When maintaining units containing shunt resistors, make sure that they are clean and free of dust so they are cooled by the air.

D.2 RANGE MULTIPLIERS

Another common resistor circuit associated with meters is the range multiplier. As was stated earlier, there is no real difference between the electromechanical ammeter and the voltmeter. For example, Figure 8.38*a* shows the 0 to 10 mA meter discussed in the previous section connected as a voltmeter to measure the potential difference produced by source BT1. Since the resistance of the meter is 10 Ω, it indicates full scale when the current through it is 10 mA. This means the meter itself will be a useful voltmeter for measuring potential differences from 0 to 0.1 V:

$$E = I \times R = 0.01 \times 10 = 0.1 \text{ V}$$

If the potential difference produced by BT1 is greater than 0.1 V, serious damage may be done to the meter. On the other hand, connecting a fairly high value of resistance *in series* with the meter, as shown in Figure

Figure 8.38 Using a meter to measure potential difference.

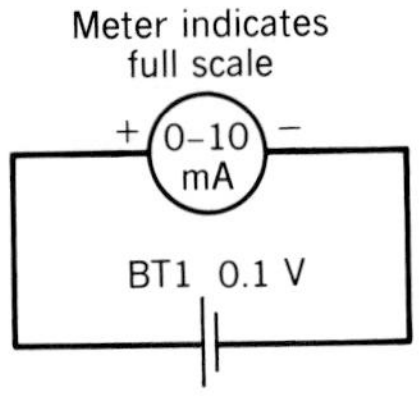

(a) Connected across a source, the meter can measure small potential differences

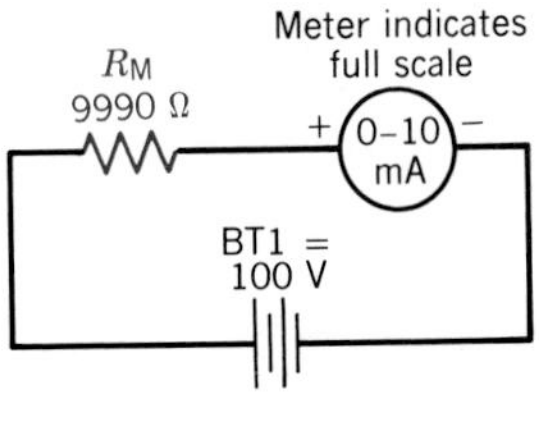

(b) In series with a multiplier, the meter can measure larger potential differences

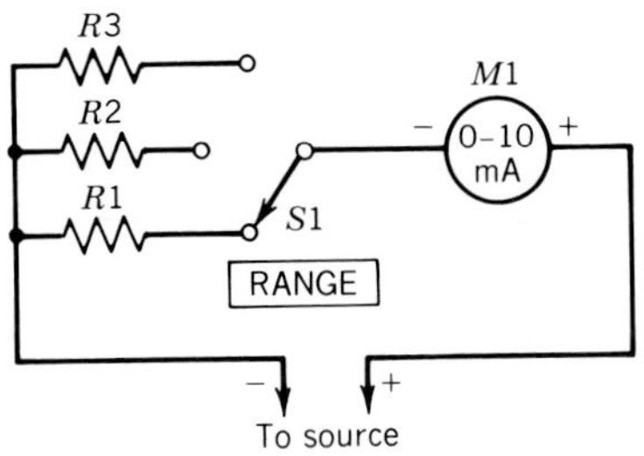

Figure 8.39 Switching multipliers to produce a multirange voltmeter.

8.38*b*, will limit the circuit current. This resistance is called a *range multiplier*, or *multiplier*.

When the full-scale meter current and the meter resistance are known, it is easy to produce a formula for calculating the correct value of the multiplier needed for any full-scale voltage measurement. Consider Figure 8.38*b* again. Since it is a series circuit, the current through the meter and the multiplier resistor will be the same, and the total resistance of the circuit is $R_{\text{multiplier}} + R_{\text{meter}}$. Therefore, with a circuit potential difference equal to the desired full scale of the voltmeter,

$$E_{\text{full-scale}} = I_{\text{meter at full scale}} \times (R_{\text{meter}} + R_{\text{multiplier}})$$

or, solving for $R_{\text{multiplier}}$,

$$R_{\text{multiplier}} = \frac{E_{\text{full-scale}}}{I_{\text{meter}}} - R_{\text{meter}} \qquad \text{FORMULA 8.9}$$

Using this formula, it is possible to calculate the resistance of a multiplier that will provide a full-scale reading for any potential difference greater than that which will produce a full-scale current through the basic meter resistance (0.1 V in the case of the meter used here).

For multirange meters, a circuit like that shown in Figure 8.39 is used so that one of several ranges can be selected. In the shunt circuit, special precautions have to be taken to ensure that there is always some resistor connected. Otherwise, it is easy to overload the meter. On the other hand, if a series resistor burns out or is switched out, the series circuit is cut, and there is no further danger to the meter. Since open circuiting is a primary failure mode of resistors, this circuit is, in a sense, self-protecting.

D.3 THE BRIDGE CIRCUIT

Another frequently used resistor circuit is the bridge circuit shown in Figure 8.40*a*. In many cases *R*3 is actually a meter, and one of the resistances is replaced

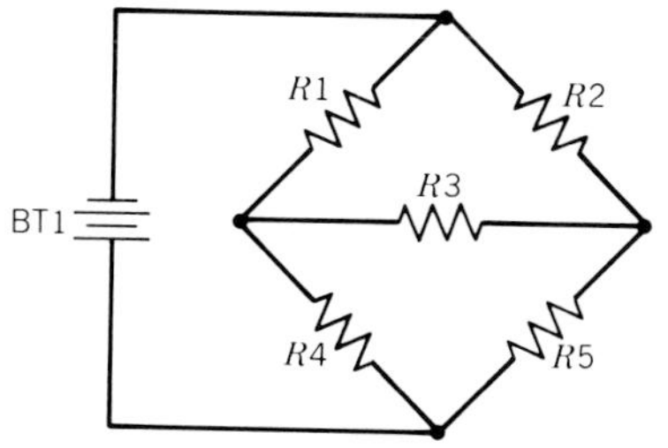

(a) Basic bridge

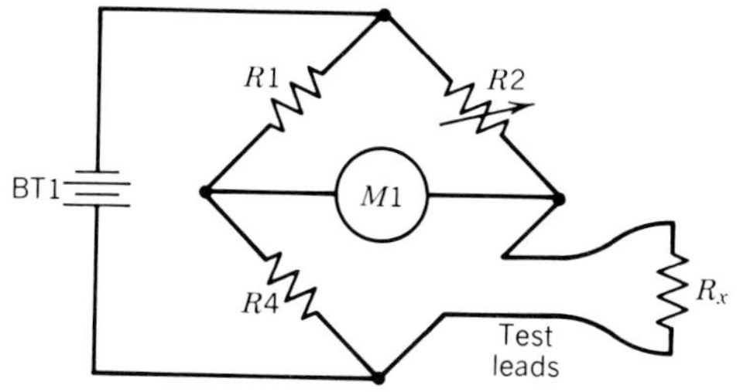

(b) Bridge modified to measure resistance

Figure 8.40 One application of the bridge circuit.

by a variable resistor or potentiometer, as shown in Figure 8.40*b*. This circuit is frequently called a *Wheatstone bridge*. In this form, the bridge circuit can serve as a device for measuring unknown resistances, R_x in the schematic. The operation of the bridge circuit is clearer if it is redrawn in a simplified form, eliminating the meter and replacing the variable resistor, as in Figure 8.41. In this simplified circuit, it is evident that the voltage drop across $R1$ is the same as that across $R2$. Similarly the drop across $R4$ is the same as that across $R5$. This means that points A and B are at the same potential and that there would be no drift of electrons through a wire connecting them. If the meter is inserted between points A and B, it would indicate zero. When this condition exists, the bridge is referred to as a *balanced bridge*.

It is not always necessary to use equal value resistors in a balanced bridge. In the bridge shown in Figure 8.42, four different value resistors are used, but the bridge is still balanced. Redrawing the circuit of Figure 8.42*a* as if for calculating a Thevenin equivalent,

Figure 8.41 A simplified form of Figure 8.40*b*.

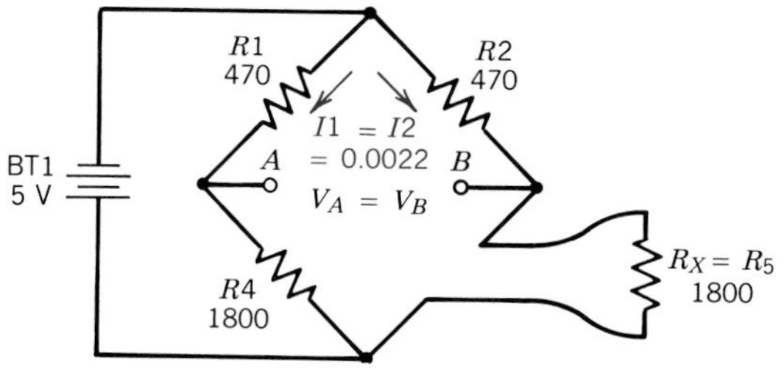

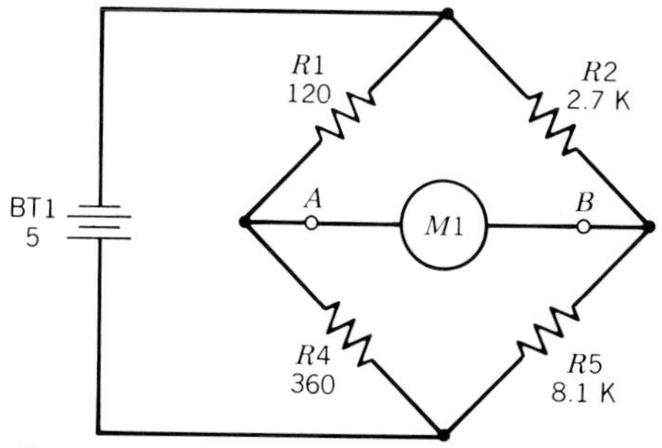

Figure 8.42 A balanced bridge may be constructed with four resistors of different values, provided $\frac{R1}{R4} = \frac{R2}{R5}$.

and calculating the voltage drops across $R1$ and $R2$:

$$I_{R1\text{-}R4} = \frac{E}{R} = 0.0104$$

$$E_{R1} = I_{R1\text{-}R4} \times R1 = 1.25 \text{ V}$$

$$I_{R2\text{-}R5} = \frac{E}{R} = 0.000463$$

$$E_{R2} = I_{R2\text{-}R5} \times R2 = 1.25 \text{ V}$$

Since both A and B are at the same potential, the bridge is balanced.

The balanced condition of the bridge depends on the fact that the resistances of $R1$ and $R2$ are in the same proportion to the resistances of $R4$ and $R5$, respectively. That is, the 120 Ω resistance of $R1$ is one-third of the 360 Ω resistance of $R4$, just as $R2$ is one-third of the resistance of $R4$. Mathematically expressed, the bridge will be balanced when

$$\frac{R1}{R4} = \frac{R2}{R5} \qquad \text{FORMULA 8.10}$$

Looking back at Figure 8.40*b*, you can see how this circuit can be used to measure resistance. If the potentiometer has a calibrated scale, it can be adjusted so that the meter indication will be zero. When this happens, the ratio between the resistance of the potentiometer and the unknown resistance R_x is the same as the ratio between $R1$ and $R4$. The value of R_x can then be calculated using Formula 8.10. Meters with the zero position at mid-scale, called *null detectors*, are used in bridges of this sort since current flow in either direction is possible. Bridge devices are frequently used for laboratory resistance measurements and calibration of other measurement devices.

Since many bridge circuits are of the balanced type and contain a meter or other type of null indicator, a component failure or even a change in component value is generally easy to spot. Laboratory and test equipment bridge circuits often include a variable resistor or potentiometer for nulling the indicator. If the bridge can not be balanced by the adjustment of this control, it is a sure sign of either a faulty component or connection. Generally, measuring the potential difference across each resistance will reveal a burned-out component. A Kirchhoff's law or network theorem analysis will provide the theoretical value of the potential difference across each resistor. Comparing the calculated and measured values with the null indicator removed from the circuit will show which branch is faulty.

D.4 VOLTAGE DIVIDERS

One common application of resistors is to provide a particular potential difference or a number of potential differences from one voltage source. Figure 8.43 shows two resistors connected to a 12-V source in such a way as to provide a potential difference of 9 V between an output terminal and ground. The potential difference across a section of a voltage divider can be calculated by forming a ratio:

$$\frac{E_{\text{across a section}}}{E_{\text{across divider}}} = \frac{R_{\text{section}}}{R_{\text{divider}}} \qquad \text{FORMULA 8.11}$$

Solving for $E_{\text{across a section}}$ provides an easy-to-use expression:

$$E_{\text{across a section}} = E_{\text{across divider}} \times \frac{R_{\text{section}}}{R_{\text{divider}}}$$

FORMULA 8.12

EXAMPLE:
Calculate the potential difference between each of the output terminals and ground in the voltage divider shown in Figure 8.44. ■

SOLUTION:
Since the circuit shown is a series string, the same current flows through each resistor in the divider. Ground is taken as the reference potential, so the potential of terminal 1 with respect to ground is the full potential difference produced by BT1, or +48 V. The potential difference between ground and terminal 2 will be 48 V $- E_{R1}$. Using Formula 8.12,

$$E_{R1} = 48 \times \frac{10}{960} = 0.5$$

Figure 8.43 A simple voltage divider provides a 9-V potential difference from a 12-V source.

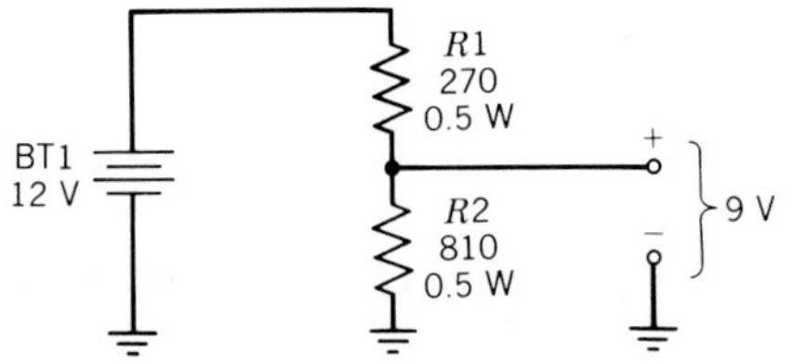

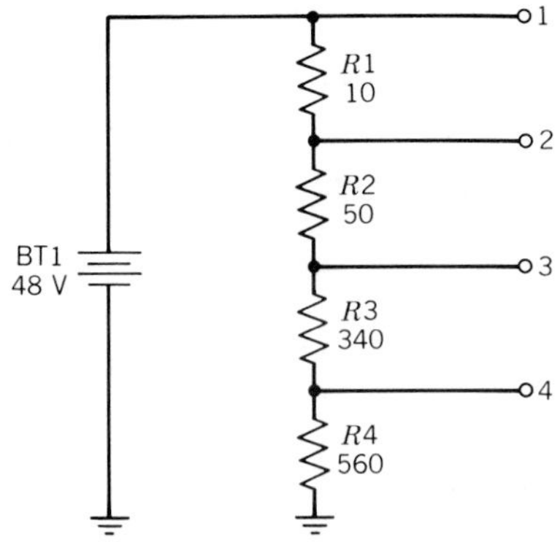

Figure 8.44 Example of a multisection voltage divider. Note that no loads are taken into consideration.

so $E_2 = 47.5$. The potential difference between terminal 3 and ground will be 48 V $- E_{R1} - E_{R2}$. Again using Formula 8.12,

$$E_{R1+2} = 48 \times \frac{60}{960} = 3$$

and $E_3 = 45$ V. At terminal 4, the potential will be $48 - E_{R1} - E_{R2} - E_{R3}$.

$$E_{R1\,+\,R2\,+\,R3} = 48 \times \frac{400}{960} = 20$$

$$E_4 = 28 \text{ V}$$ ■

The voltage divider circuits shown so far in this section will work as long as no current is drawn from the divider. Since no allowance has been made for branch currents, the divider resistance values will not be correct when the divider is required to supply current to a load. To illustrate this, assume that current of 1 A is required for loads connected to the output terminals of the divider shown in Figure 8.45. These loads are shown in the schematic of Figure 8.45. Notice that in this case the same current does not pass through

Figure 8.45 Formulas 8.11 and 8.12 can not be used when a voltage divider is required to furnish current to loads.

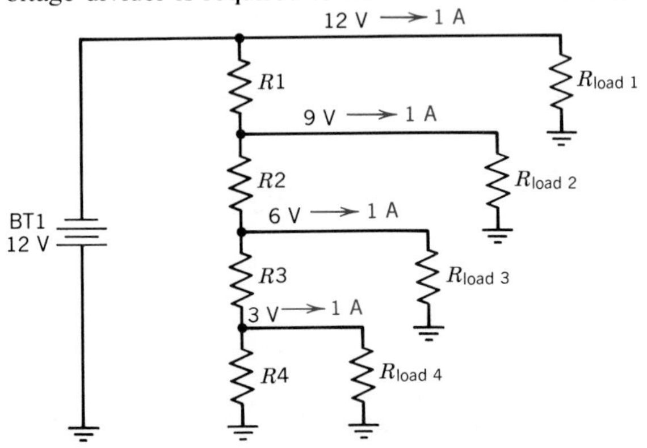

each resistor making up the divider. For example, the current through $R1$ is 1 A greater than the current through $R2$, and Formula 8.12 can not be applied to this circuit.

In order to make the voltage drop across each resistor in this divider equal to 3 V, it is necessary to change the resistance of each divider resistor to adjust for the differences in the current through the divider resistors. A standard way to do this is to begin by assigning a value to the resistor through which the least current flows, $R4$ in the case of Figure 8.45. This resistor is called the *bleeder resistor*, and if a convenient value is assigned to it, the other divider resistors can be calculated. There are two limits on the value assigned to the bleeder resistor:

a. Its resistance can not be so low as to cause a current flow that would place a strain on the source or require the use of resistors of too high wattage.

b. The resistance chosen must not be so large that a divider chain can not be calculated.

In most divider networks that are required to deliver currents to loads, the bleeder resistor is chosen so that the current through it is about 10 percent of the sum of the currents supplied to the loads. Since the voltage drop across the bleeder resistor is known (it is the potential difference between the ground or reference potential and the smallest voltage supplied by the divider), and its current has been estimated, the resistance of the bleeder can be calculated.

In the example of Figure 8.45, the sum of the currents supplied to the loads is 4 A. Therefore, the current through the bleeder resistor should be about 0.4 A, and the voltage drop across it is 3 V. The resistance of the bleeder can then be calculated using Ohm's law:

$$R = \frac{E}{I} = \frac{3}{0.4} = 7.5\ \Omega$$

The power dissipated by the bleeder resistor is $P = EI$, or 1.2 W, so a 2-W resistor should be sufficient to dissipate the heat produced.

It is now a relatively easy matter to calculate the resistance and power dissipation of the next divider resistor $R3$. The current through $R3$ is made up of the bleeder resistor current 0.4 A, plus the current through load 4, 1 A, for a total of 1.4 A. The voltage drop across $R3$, that is, the potential difference between its two ends, is 3 V. The resistance of $R3$ is therefore

$$R = \frac{E}{I} = \frac{3}{1.4} = 2.14\ \Omega$$

The power dissipation of $R3$, $P = E \times I = 4.2$ W. Since this is not a standard value, it would have to be made up, for example, either by using a 2 Ω and a 0.15 Ω 5-W resistor in series, or a 10 Ω and a 2.7 Ω 3-W resistor in parallel. Both these combinations produce resistance close enough to the calculated 2.14 Ω for practical purposes.

The third resistor, $R2$, carries a current composed of the 0.4-A bleeder current, the 1-A current through load 4 and the 1-A current through load 3, for a total of 2.4 A. Its resistance is

$$R = \frac{E}{I} = \frac{3}{2.4} = 1.25\ \Omega$$

Its power dissipation is 7.2 W. Again, either a variable resistor, or a series or parallel combination could be used, or even a 1.2 Ω, 10-W unit, if extreme accuracy is not required.

The final divider resistor, $R1$, has a resistance of $\frac{3}{3.4} = 0.88\ \Omega$ and a power dissipation of 10.2 W. A 0.91 Ω, 15-W unit would be the closest standard value available.

In order to calculate the resistance values for a voltage divider, you must know the potential difference and current required by each of the loads and the potential difference supplied by the source. The calculation of the resistances of the series divider string begins with the bleeder resistor (the resistor through which the smallest current passes). A current of about 10 percent of the sum of the currents supplied to the loads is assumed to flow through the bleeder resistor. Each of the resistances can then be calculated in turn.

Troubleshooting a faulty voltage divider is generally not a difficult job. This is true because the most common failure mode is a burned or charred resistor. Sometimes this occurs because of poor original design. For example, in the divider shown in Figure 8.46, the load consisting of four lamps will draw heavy surge

Figure 8.46 Damage to components can occur if the power ratings of divider resistors are not high enough.

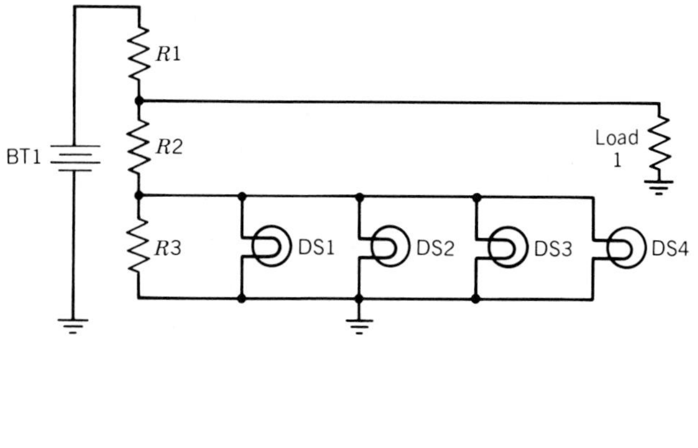

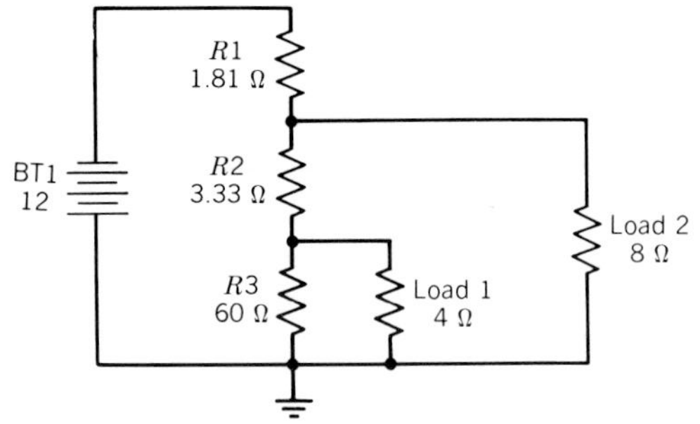

Figure 8.47 A voltage divider for troubleshooting analysis.

currents, placing greater strains on $R1$ and $R2$ than might have been allowed for in initial design. Most frequently, however, damage to a voltage divider is caused by a malfunction of one of the loads. For example, consider the voltage divider shown in Figure 8.47. Resistor $R1$, which has a calculated power dissipation of 8.8 W, would probably be a 10- or 15-W resistor in a practical circuit. A momentary short circuit in load 2 or the power leads to it would, however, put the source potential difference of 12 V across $R1$, resulting in a power dissipation of

$$P = \frac{E^2}{R} = \frac{144}{1.81} = 79.56 \text{ W}$$

This would burn up $R1$ in a short time.

A short circuit in load 1 or in the power leads to it would change the electrical characteristics of this circuit to those shown in the schematic of Figure 8.48. This is a simple series–parallel circuit, and the circuit resistance is equal to $R1$ plus the value of the parallel combination of $R2$ and load 2:

$$R = R1 + \frac{R2 \times \text{load 2}}{R2 + \text{load 2}} = 1.81 + 2.35 = 4.16\ \Omega$$

The circuit current, then, is $\frac{12}{4.16}$, or 2.88 A, and the voltage drop across $R1$ is $I \times R1$ or 5.21 V, instead of 4 V in normal divider operation. This means that the potential difference supplied to load 2 is $12 - 5.21 = 6.79$ V instead of the 8 V supplied by the normally

Figure 8.48 The result of a short circuit in load 1 in Figure 8.47.

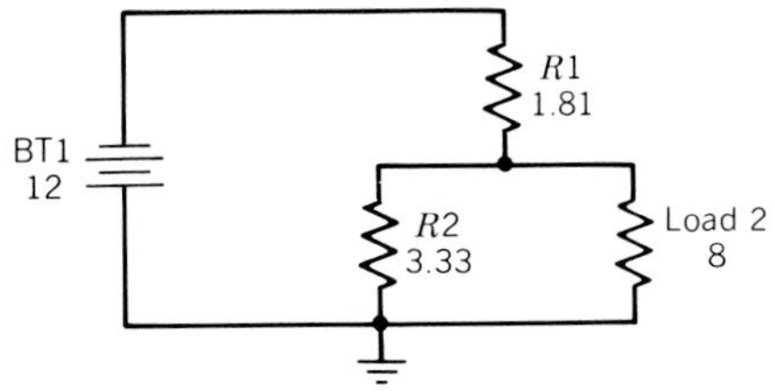

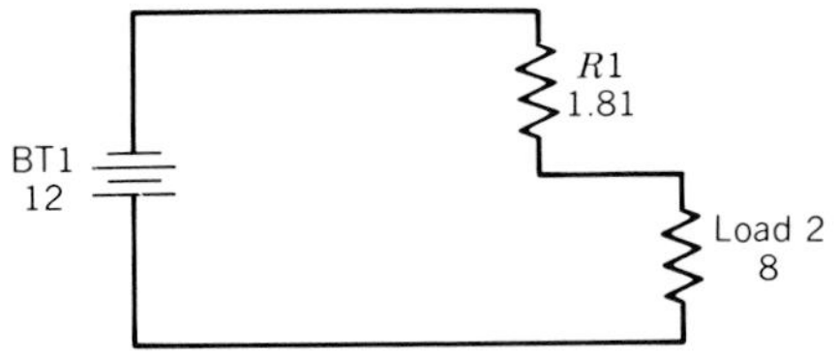

Figure 8.49 A short circuit in load 1 in Figure 8.47 could also result in the destruction of $R2$; the remaining circuit would look like this.

functioning divider. The power dissipated in $R1$ is

$$P = E \times I = 5.21 \times 2.88 = 15 \text{ W}$$

This is nearly twice the calculated power dissipation of 8.8 W, and could result in serious overheating if a 10- or 12-W resistor had been chosen for this component. The potential difference across $R2$, calculated above, is 6.79 V, therefore, its power dissipation is

$$P = \frac{E^2}{R} = 13.84 \text{ W}$$

This is considerably higher than the 3.96 W calculated in the normally functioning divider.

Notice that in both these examples, it is the divider resistor immediately before the shorted load that is most likely to show greatest signs of overheating. Unfortunately, the burnout of one resistor in a voltage divider can also destroy the loads connected to it. For example, a short circuit in the power leads to load 1, as shown in the previous example, will result in a power dissipation of 13.84 W by $R2$. If $R2$ burns up, the resulting circuit will be that shown in Figure 8.49. Here, the voltage drop across $R1$ will be 2.21 V instead of the 4 V in the normally functioning divider. Instead of the required 8 V, the potential difference supplied to load 2 will be 9.79 V, which might be enough to damage it. Chain reaction failures of this sort with voltage divider circuits occur frequently enough to justify the inclusion of protective devices such as fuses in these circuits. When troubleshooting a defective voltage divider, it is also wise to check the condition of the loads attached to it. Sometimes large-scale parts replacement is necessary to repair all the damage.

D.5 MAXIMUM POWER TRANSFER AND RESISTIVE NETWORKS

On the surface, it seems that nothing could be easier than connecting a load to a source of electric power. Low-resistance leads of sufficient diameter to handle the power used by the load should be enough to ensure maximum power transfer from the source to the load,

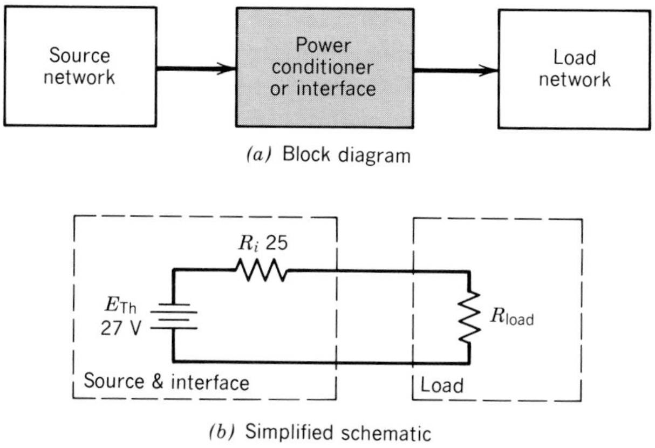

Figure 8.50 Power transfer from source to load.

right? No, is the surprising answer. In fact, sometimes the transfer of power to the load can be improved if resistance is added to the circuit. Since connecting units to different sources is a common task in electronics, it would be a good idea to explore this notion carefully. Consider the block diagram and simplified schematic in Figures 8.50*a* and 8.50*b*. The simplified schematic shows the source and power conditioner as a Thevenin equivalent source and the load as a single resistor. If the intention is to produce the largest possible power dissipation in the load, what should the resistance of the load be? This question is best answered by filling in a table of the sort shown in Table 8.1 and then graphing the results as in Figure 8.51. Notice that the maximum amount of power is used in the load when the value of the load resistance is equal to the value of the series resistor in the Thevenin source. Even though the fraction of the power used by the load to the total power supplied by the source continues to increase as the load resistance increases, the maximum power in the load is obtained when the load resistance is equal to the source resistance.

Table 8.1 Load resistance and load power in Figure 8.50

Load Resistance (Ω)	*Circuit Current* (*A*)	*Source Resistor Power* (*W*)	*Load Power* (*W*)	*Load Power / Source Power Supplied* ($E \times I$)
5	0.9	20.25	4.05	0.1667
10	0.77	14.82	5.93	0.29
15	0.675	11.39	6.83	0.375
20	0.6	9.0	7.2	0.44
25	0.54	7.29	7.29	0.5
30	0.49	6.02	7.20	0.54
35	0.45	5.06	7.09	0.58
40	0.42	4.41	7.06	0.62
45	0.39	3.80	6.84	0.65

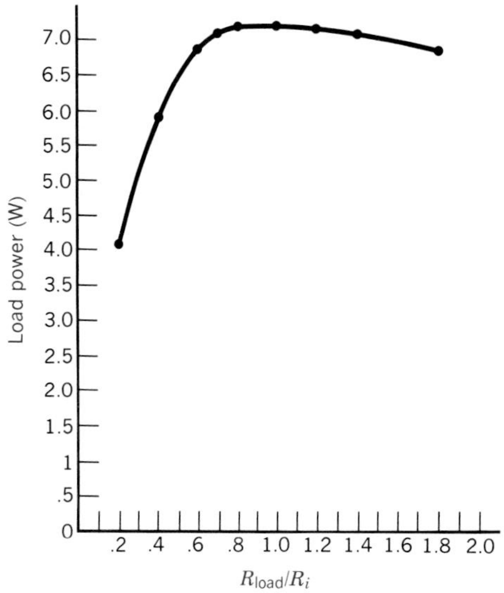

Figure 8.51 Graph of the load power in Figure 8.50.

The result of this graphical demonstration is called the *maximum power transfer theorem*. It states that *the maximum power is transferred to a load when the resistance of the load is equal to the internal resistance of the source network*. Because of this, one of a number of resistive networks is frequently used to match the resistance of a source with the resistance of a load, as well as to modify either the potential difference of the source or its current output. These networks are called *interfacing* or *resistance matching* networks.

The simplest form of interface network is shown in Figure 8.52. It consists of a single resistance and is generally used to limit the current to the load or lower the potential difference applied across the load. Troubleshooting this sort of interface generally involves measuring the potential difference between point *B* and point *A* and ground. Finding either no potential difference or too large a potential difference, on the order of the source voltage, can indicate a faulty resistor or some other problem in the source or load network. Remove all power, unsolder one of the resistor leads from the circuit, and measure the resistance of the resistor with an ohmmeter to check for an open circuit or short circuit, as shown in Figure 8.53.

A single parallel resistor is another common interface between two electronic units or circuits. See Figure 8.54*a*. The output potential difference of the source unit or circuit is developed across the resistor,

Figure 8.52 Series resistor interface.

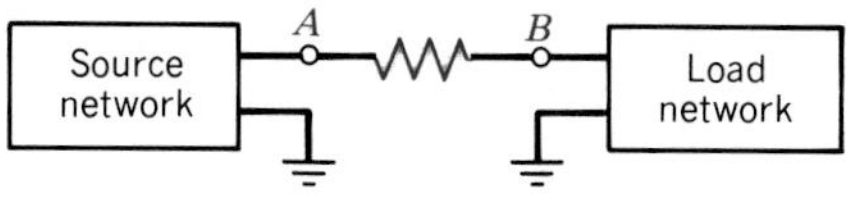

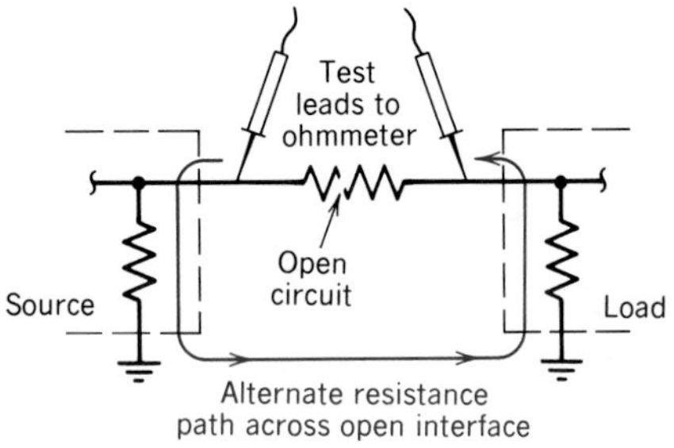

(a) With the interface resistor connected, an open resistor could be overlooked

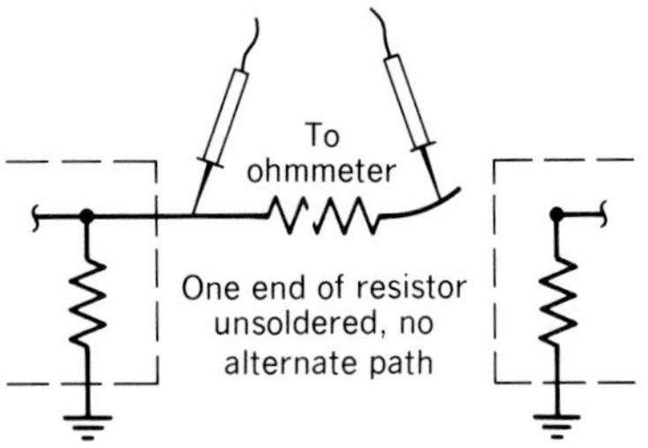

(b) Measurement reveals open resistor

Figure 8.53 Why it is necessary to unsolder one end of a series resistor interface before making a resistance measurement.

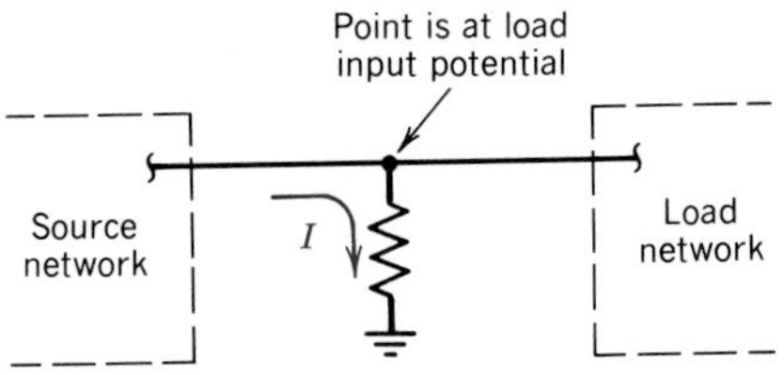

(a) Parallel resistor is used to link two networks

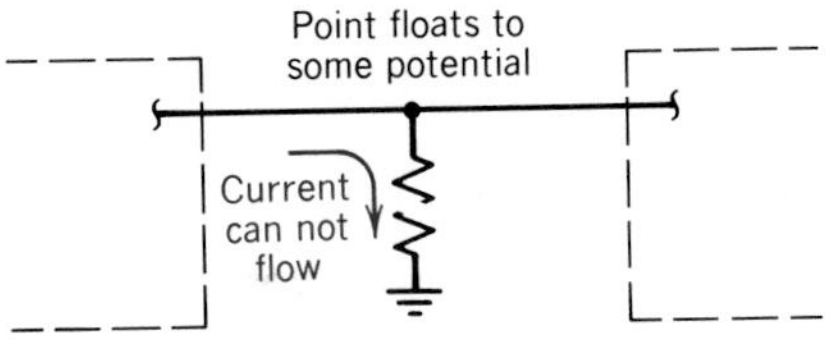

(b) A burned-out parallel resistor causes the junction to "float"

Figure 8.54 Parallel resistor interface.

and this is the potential difference that serves as the input for the second unit or circuit. The failure of this resistor can produce problems in a unit or system. An open circuiting of *R*1 as in Figure 8.54*b* can result in a condition called *floating*, if other paths to ground are not present. A point that is electrically floating will assume some potential level and behave rather like an object with an electrostatic charge. The transfer of power or signals between the two units or circuits will

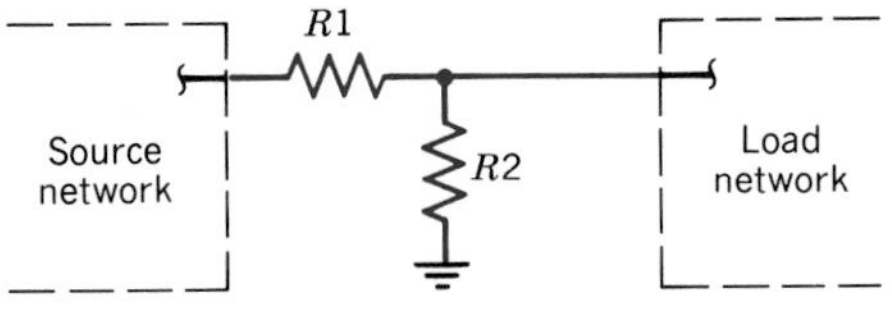

(a)

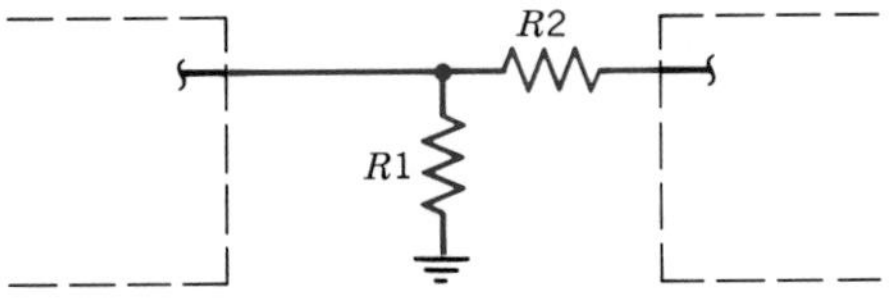

(b)

Figure 8.55 L-network interfaces.

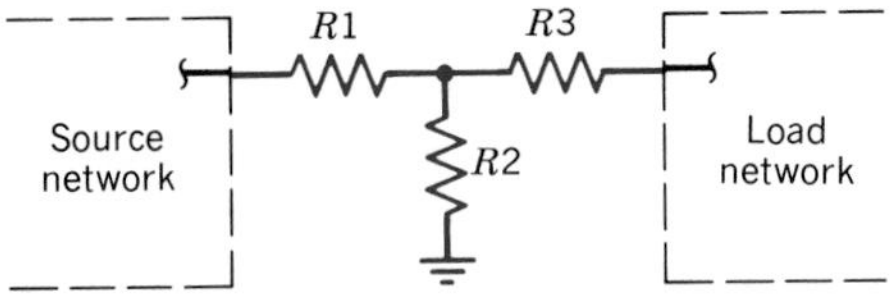

(a) A T or Y interface

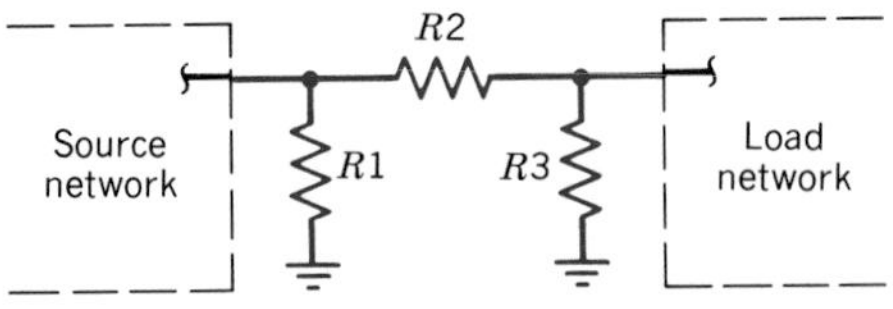

(b) A π or Δ interface

Figure 8.56 T and π interface networks.

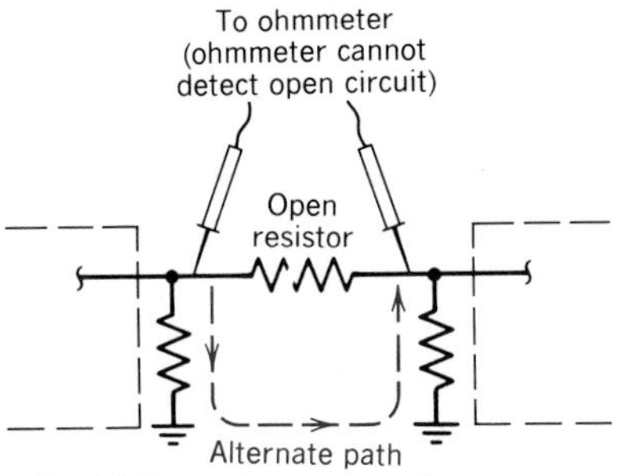

Figure 8.57 Multiple resistance paths to ground make the checking of resistance matching networks complicated.

be prevented or impaired, leading to improper function.

A combination of the two previously illustrated interface networks is called an L network. If connected in the manner shown in Figure 8.55*a*, it functions as a voltage divider to reduce the potential difference of the input to the second unit or circuit. Connecting it as shown in 8.55*b* provides a load for the first circuit (*R*1) and a coupling to the second circuit (*R*2).

Figures 8.56*a* and 8.56*b* are, respectively, a T network and a π (pi) network. These more complex networks are sometimes used to control the potential difference, current, or power transferred from one circuit to another, and are frequently composed of components other than resistors. Troubleshooting or checking interface and resistance matching networks is complicated by the fact that there are usually several resistance paths to ground, as shown in Figure 8.57.

E. PROGRAMMED REVIEW

FRAME 1

The principal difference between a law like Ohm's law and a network theorem is that laws are ________, while a theorem can be applied only in special cases or to a particular kind of circuit.

a. True for (almost) any circuit. (2)
b. Any other answer, review Section B.1 and go on to Frame 2.

FRAME 2

Determine the total circuit current in Figure 8.58 by using the Δ–Y equivalency theorem to convert the bridge circuit into a series–parallel circuit.

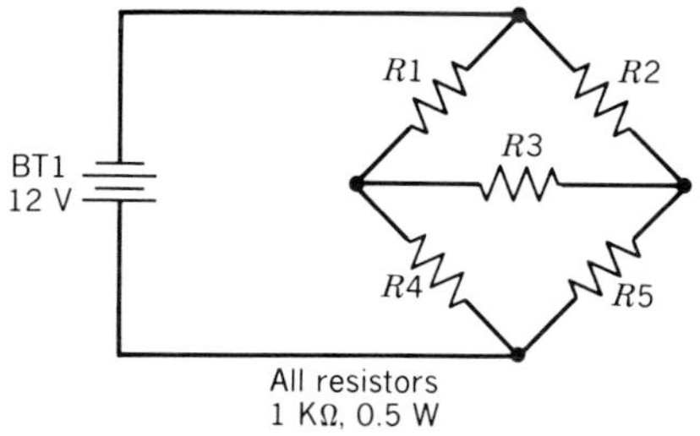

Figure 8.58 Schematic for FRAME 2.

a. 12 mA. (3)
b. Any other answer, review Section B.1.

FRAME 3

Which of the Δ or π networks in Figure 8.59 is the equivalent of the Y or T network in Figure 8.59(*a*).

a. 3 (4)
b. Any other answer, review Section B.1.

Figure 8.59 Diagram for FRAME 3.

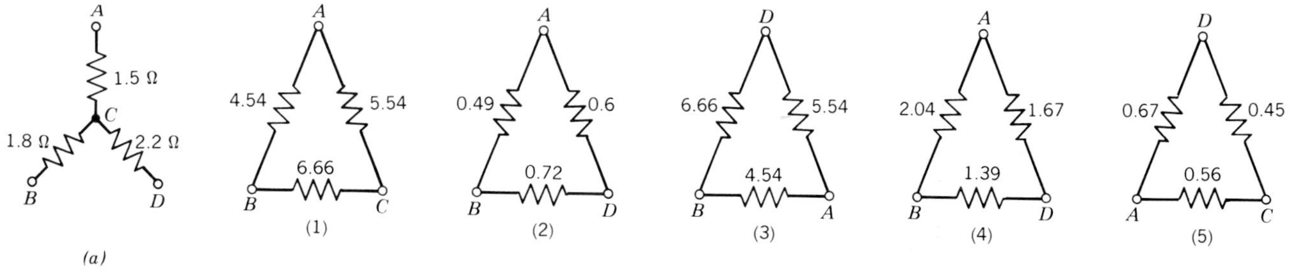

FRAME 4

State the characteristics of an ideal voltage source.

a. 1. An ideal voltage source has no internal resistance.
   2. An ideal voltage source is capable of maintaining the same potential difference across its output terminals no matter how much current it is required to supply. (5)
b. Any answer that does not contain both these ideas, review Section B.2 and go on to Frame 5.

FRAME 5

Identify the type of source shown in Figure 8.60. The value of the resistance R_{int} is *very high/low/zero*.

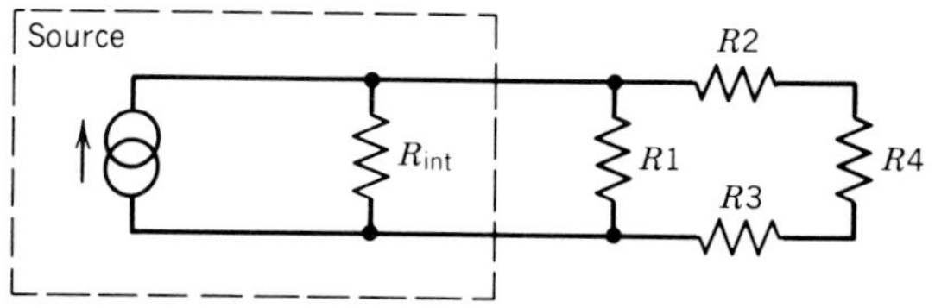

Figure 8.60 Diagram for FRAME 5.

a. Ideal current source; very high. (6)
b. Any other answers, review Section B.2 and go on to Frame 6.

FRAME 6

Before using the superposition theorem to analyze a circuit, two conditions must be checked. The circuit components must be ________ and ________.

a. bilateral; linear (7)
b. Any answer that does not include both, review Section B.3.

FRAME 7

In applying the superposition theorem to the circuit shown in Figure 8.61, the currents through *R*2 are ________, flowing from point ________ to point

__________ and __________, flowing from point __________ to point __________. The total current through $R2$ is __________, flowing from point __________ to point __________.

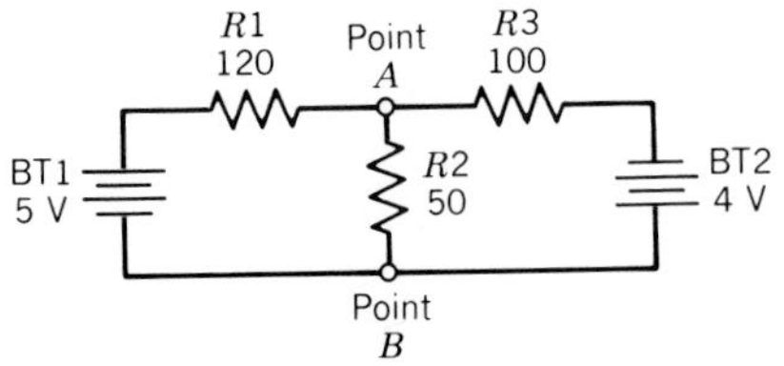

Figure 8.61 Diagram for FRAME 7.

a. 0.033 A; B; A; 0.021 A; A; B; about 0.012 A; B; A (8)
b. Any other answer, check you arithmetic; if the arithmetic is correct, but your answers are wrong, review Section B.3.

FRAME 8

Thevenin's theorem states that there is an equivalent circuit consisting of an __________ and a __________, which can be substituted for a network made up of sources and resistors, regardless of how they are interconnected.

a. Ideal voltage source; series resistance (or series resistor). (9)
b. The answer must specify *ideal voltage* source and *series* resistor; for any other answer review Section B.4 and go on to Frame 9.

FRAME 9

The Thevenin equivalent of the network shown in Figure 8.62 is composed of a source that provides a potential difference of __________ V and a series resistor of __________ Ω.

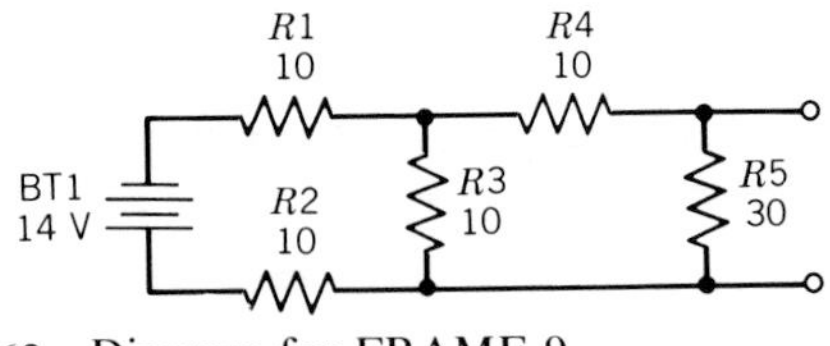

Figure 8.62 Diagram for FRAME 9.

a. 3; 10.72 (10)
b. Any answer not approximately the same, review Section B.4.

FRAME 10

The Norton equivalent of the network shown in Figure 8.63 is composed of an ideal current source supplying __________ A and a parallel resistance of __________ Ω.

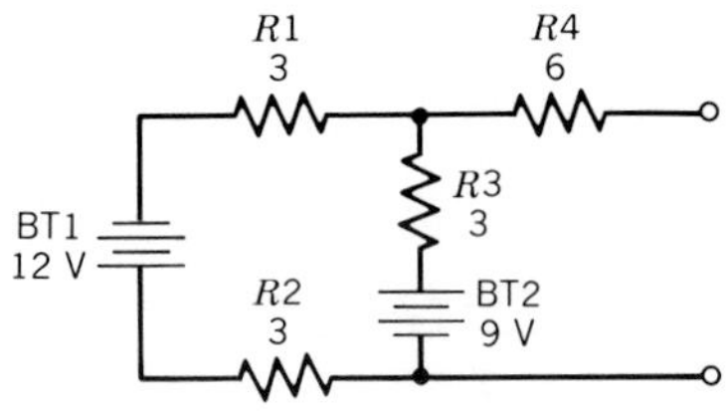

Figure 8.63 Diagram for FRAME 10.

a. 0.25; 8 (11)
b. Any other answer, review Section B.5.

FRAME 11

To convert from a Thevenin equivalent circuit to a Norton equivalent, the following formulas are used:

$I_N =$ __________ and $R_N =$ __________.

a. $I_N = \dfrac{E_{Th}}{R_{Th}}$
$R_N = R_{Th}$ (12)
b. Any other answer, review Section B.6 and go on to Frame 12.

FRAME 12

Millman's theorem states that a network composed of any number of ideal current sources connected in parallel and parallel resistors can be replaced by an equivalent composed of __________.

a. A single ideal current source and parallel resistor. (13)
b. Any answer not including these points, review Section B.7 and go on to Frame 13.

FRAME 13

A 0 to 20 mA meter with an internal resistance of 100 Ω is to be used to measure currents ranging up to 1 A. Calculate the value of the shunt resistance needed.

a. 2.04 Ω (14)
b. Any other answer, review Section D.1.

FRAME 14

It is necessary to produce a voltmeter that will measure 100 V full scale using a 0 to 10 mA meter with an internal resistance of 100 Ω and a range multiplier. What is the value of the multiplier?

a. 9900 Ω (END)
b. Any other answer, review Section D.2.

F. PROBLEMS FOR SOLUTION OR RESEARCH

1. Convert the T or Y interface between the two circuits in Figure 8.64 into a π or Δ interface.

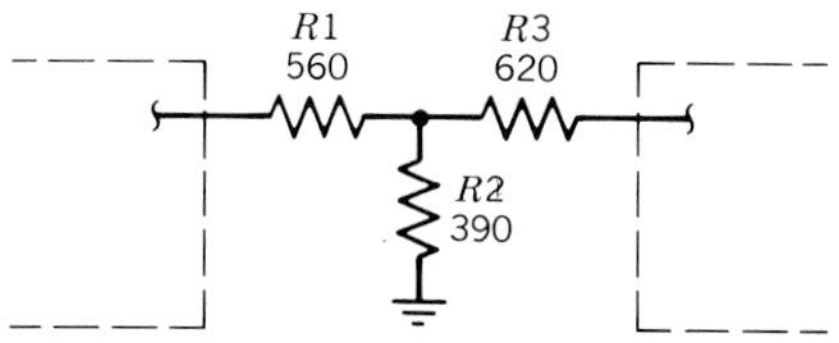

Figure 8.64 Schematic for problem 1.

2. Use the Δ-to-Y equivalency theorem to calculate the current through each of the resistors in Figure 8.65.

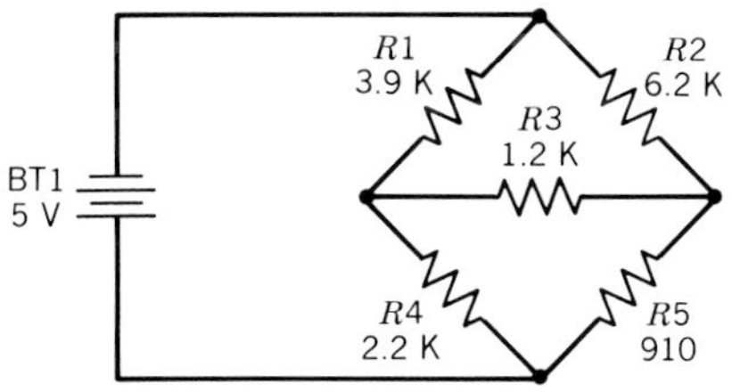

Figure 8.65 Schematic for problem 2.

3. Use Thevenin's theorem to calculate the current through $R2$ in Figure 8.66.

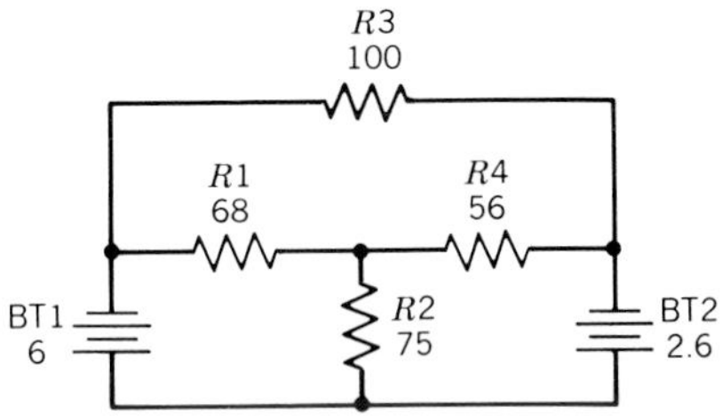

Figure 8.66 Schematic for problems 3 and 4.

4. If all the resistors in Figure 8.66 have a tolerance of 5 percent, what is the largest power dissipation expected in $R2$ in normal operation. (The sources are presumed to be at the given potential.)

5. Use Norton's theorem to convert all the sources and resistances in Figure 8.67 to current sources and parallel resistors. Use Millman's theorem to combine these into a single current source and parallel resistance.

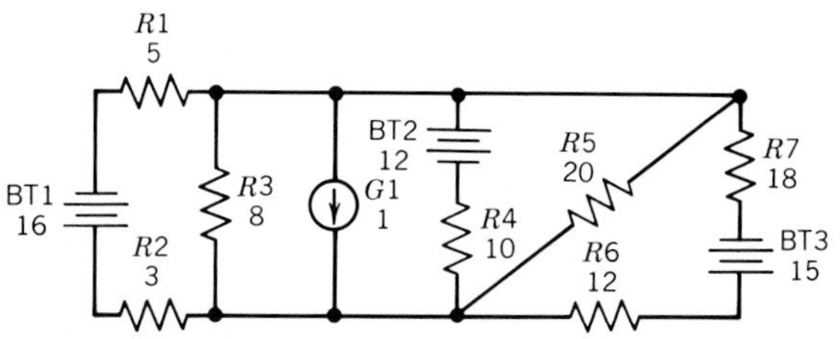

Figure 8.67 Schematic diagram for problem 5.

6. Use the method of determinants to solve for the unknown currents in the following simultaneous equations:

a. $-60 + 120I_1 + 100(I_2 - I_1) = 0$
$-17.5 + 220I_1 - 100(I_2 - I_1) = 0$

b. $-16.75 + 5I_1 + 1.8I_2 + I_3 = 0$
$-8 - 4.267I_1 + 4I_2 - 4I_3 = 0$
$-2 + 0I_1 + 9I_2 - I_3 = 0$

c. $3X + 2Y - 2Z = 30$
$9(X + 3Y) - Z = -1$
$\frac{X}{3} + 2Y + 8Z = 0$

d. $3.2j + 4K + 1.2L = 0$
$4j + 5K + 1.5L = 0$
$10.67j + 13.33K + 4L = 0$

e. $-28.25 - 3I_1 + 5.6(I_2 - I_3) = 0$
$-30.36 - 5.6(I_2 - I_3) + 6.8I_3 = 0$
$3.83 + 2I_1 + I_2 - 3I_3 = 0$

f. $2X + 4Y - 8Z = -5.5$
$6X - 8(Z - Y) = 17.5$
$X + 2Y + 4Z = 6.25$

g. $-2.93 + 9I_1 + 10(I_2 + I_3) = 0$
$-20.29 + I_1 + 8I_2 - 10(I_2 + I_3)$
$5.125 + 1.5I_1 - 8I_2 + 5I_3 = 0$

h. $-36.3 + 12I_1 + 18(I_1 - I_2) = 0$
$28.08 - 18(I_1 - I_2) + 9(I_2 - I_3) = 0$
$-0.66 - 9(I_2 + I_3) + 12I_3 = 0$

7. You have to power a unit that requires 9 V at 1.2 A and a unit that requires 6 V at 3 A from a single 12-V source. Draw the schematic of a practical voltage divider to do this job.

8. Engineer Vardis was promoted to field engineer. During a job, a chipmunk ran off with the digital multimeter. The job requires dc current measurements ranging from about 7 mA to 2 A, and dc voltage measurements from 1 to 150 V. Vardis has a 0 to 1 mA dc meter with an internal resistance of 100 Ω, switches, soldering equipment, resistors, and wire in gauge sizes from AWG 10 to AWG 30. Draw the schematic of an emergency multimeter that can be built in the field.

9. Vardis has found a couple of new Leclanché cells and a multiturn control potentiometer in the tool box. Add resistance measuring capability to the emergency multimeter. How would you calibrate the ohmmeter?

CHAPTER 9

MAGNETISM AND ELECTROMAGNETIC COMPONENTS

A. CHAPTER PREVIEW

1 This chapter introduces the effects that are referred to under the name *magnetism* and classifies materials according to their magnetic properties.

2 You will study a widely accepted theory that explains the existence of magnetic effects in terms of the movement of electrical charge. The concept of domains also relates the magnetic effects of electric current with those of magnetized materials.

3 You will learn that magnetic effects, like electrical effects, are caused by a field, and how a magnetic field is mapped. The quantities describing the strength of a magnetic field are defined and related to the electrical quantities that cause the field.

4 The Computations section of this chapter expands upon the earlier discussion of angles to show some of the relationships between the sides and angles of all right triangles. This material is essential for understanding the introduction to alternating current in the following chapter.

5 The Applications section of this chapter explains the operation and troubleshooting of two components that make use of magnetic effects. These are circuit breakers and relays.

B. PRINCIPLES

B.1 WHAT IS MAGNETISM?

Just as the early Greeks were familiar with the effects of static electricity, they were also familiar with magnetism in the form of the curious ability of certain stones to attract bits of iron. Like the word *electricity*, the word *magnetism* is of Greek origin. It comes from the name of an ancient city, Magnesia, where natural magnets were found. These natural magnets, called *lodestones* during the Middle Ages, were valued for their imagined magical powers.

As in the case of electrical effects, the ability of a magnet to exert a force on a bit of iron can best be understood by referring to a magnetic field. In Chapter 1 a field was defined as a change or modification of the space around the body that generates the field. The gravitational field around the earth and the electric field around a charged sphere are examples of fields surrounding the bodies that generate them.

In Chapter 1, you learned that an electric field could be mapped with lines of force that show the direction of the force on a small, positively charged object placed in the field. Since it is a painstaking job to measure the force on small, charged objects, the diagrams in Chapter 1 have to be accepted on faith. In the case of a lodestone or an artificial magnet, however, it is easy to show evidence of the magnetic field and to map it. This is done by placing the magnet under a sheet of rough-surfaced drawing paper and sprinkling the paper with powdered iron. When the paper is tapped gently, the powdered iron forms curved line patterns as shown in Figure 9.1. The lines of powder form because the iron particles tend to attract each other in the magnetic field, and rough-surfaced paper is used since it produces a sharper image. The direction and spacing of the lines show the general form and strength of the magnetic field, and are referred to as *magnetic lines of force*.

As in the case of the lines of force used to map electric fields, magnetic lines of force DO NOT exist.

Figure 9.1 Pattern formed by iron filings in the field of a magnet. (From *Basic Electric Circuits*, 3rd Ed. by Donald P. Leach. Copyright © 1984 by John Wiley & Sons, Inc. Reprinted by permission of John Wiley & Sons, Inc.)

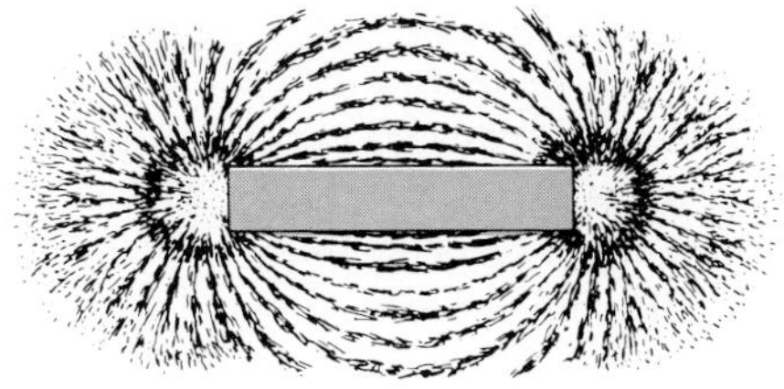

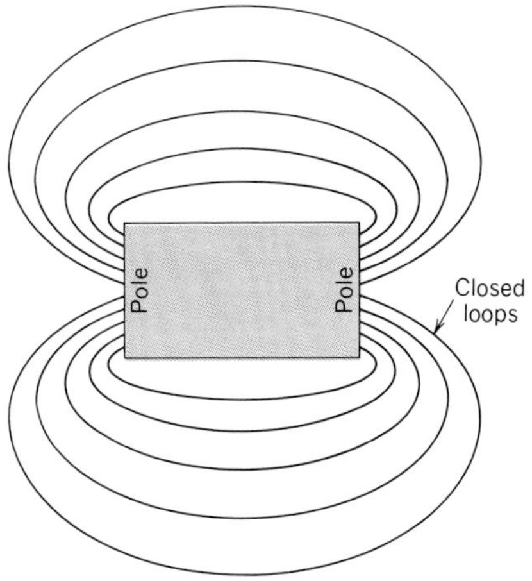

Figure 9.2 Magnetic lines of force form closed loops between the two poles of a magnet.

They are a map of a fairly uniform field surrounding a piece of lodestone or other form of magnet. Many textbooks refer to "the cutting of magnetic lines of force," which can result in confusion on the part of students. It is possible to move an object through a magnetic field, but magnetic lines of force are not "cut." This would be rather like expecting to feel a bump in an aircraft passing over a meridian of longitude or a national border.

Note that the powdered iron clusters around two areas on the magnet in Figure 9.1. These are points at which the field is strongest and are referred to as *magnetic poles*. The lines of powdered iron all come together at the poles, showing that these are the points of greatest magnetic activity. No such points or areas of activity were noted in the maps of the electric field shown in Chapter 1. Thus, although there are similarities between magnetic and electric fields, there are also significant differences.

Another of these differences is that the magnetic lines of force form closed loops between the two poles of a magnet, unlike the lines of force surrounding an isolated, charged object (see Figure 9.2). A third difference is that on the surface of a charged object, such as a sphere, there is no point where the electric field is strongest, since the charge distributes itself evenly over the entire area. The poles of a magnet are points of much stronger magnetic activity and the magnetic field is strongest at the poles.

The two poles of a magnet are different. This is clearly illustrated by placing a second magnet or lodestone a short distance from the first and observing the field between them with drawing paper and powdered iron. The powdered iron may form a pattern of lines like that shown in Figure 9.3*a*. Here, the magnetic field is strongest between the two magnets and the shape

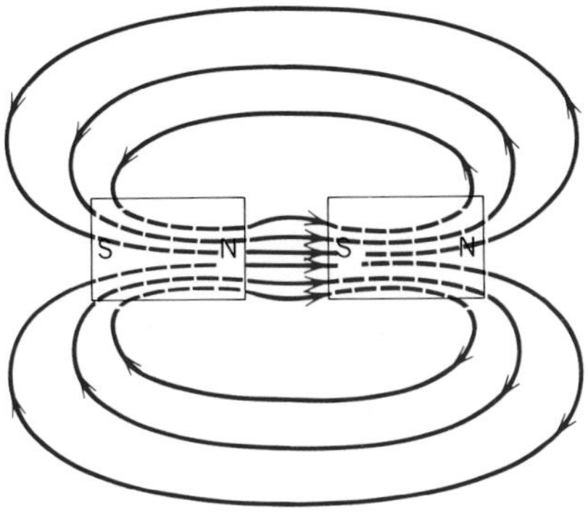

(*a*) Attraction of unlike poles

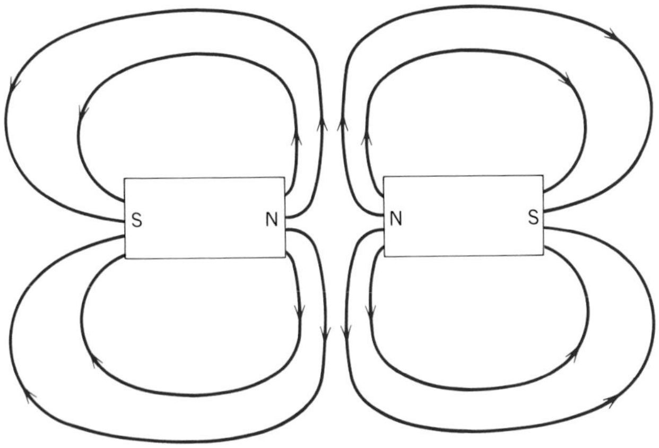

(*b*) Repulsion of like poles

Figure 9.3 The magnetic field between two magnetic poles. (From *Introduction to Electricity and Electronics*, 2nd Ed. by Allen Mottershead. Copyright © 1986 by John Wiley & Sons, Inc. Reprinted by permission of John Wiley & Sons, Inc.)

of the lines that map the magnetic field resemble those used to map the electric field between opposite charges in Figure 2.7. As in the case of the objects with opposite charges, a strong force of attraction exists between the two magnets. The field exerts a force that tends to pull them together.

If one of the magnets is turned so that its other pole is now close to the pole of the first magnet, the field takes the form shown in Figure 9.3*b*. Here the field between the poles is weak, and the lines resemble those used to map the electric field between similar charges, as in Figure 2.8. The force due to the field tends to push the two magnets apart.

These demonstrations illustrate the effects connected with a magnetic field and magnetic poles. They also show that the two poles of a magnet are different, and that one magnet can attract or repel a second magnet, depending on which poles are brought together.

Artificial magnets can be made by rubbing iron with a lodestone or simply by placing the iron near a

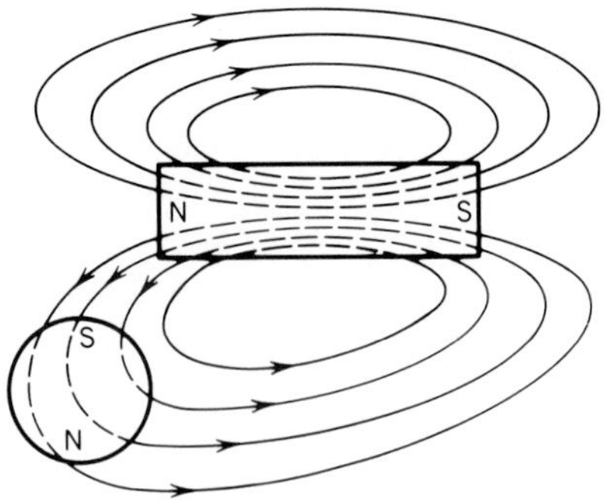

Figure 9.4 An unmagnetized iron disk placed in the field of a small magnet. (From *Introduction to Electricity and Electronics*, 2nd Ed. by Allen Mottershead. Copyright © 1986 by John Wiley & Sons, Inc. Reprinted by permission of John Wiley & Sons, Inc.)

lodestone for a length of time. This is understandable if the magnetic field around a magnet and a piece of unmagnetized iron is mapped. The field will resemble that shown in Figure 9.4. Notice that many of the magnetic lines of force enter and leave the unmagnetized iron disk, showing that the field is strong near and in it: The unmagnetized iron behaves as if it were a magnet. This is known as *magnetizing by induction*. If the magnet and piece of iron are allowed to remain together for a time, depending on the strength of the magnet and the nature of the unmagnetized material, the piece of iron will still produce a weak magnetic field after the magnet has been removed. The ability to magnetize a piece of iron with another magnet is most easily seen if the magnet is rubbed along the piece of unmagnetized iron several times in the same direction. Regardless of the method used, some materials will easily take and retain magnetizing, while others will quickly lose the ability to produce a magnetic field. A magnet that retains its magnetism is called a *permanent magnet*. A magnet that quickly loses its ability to produce a magnetic field is called a *temporary magnet*.

B.2 THEORY OF MAGNETISM

In spite of the fact that a magnetic device, the compass, had played an important part in the history of the world, real knowledge of magnetism did not increase greatly until the beginning of the seventeenth century. In its earliest form, the compass was nothing more than a bit of lodestone hung from a thread. If a piece of lodestone or a magnet is free to turn, it will set itself with the same pole pointing in a northerly direction. In 1600, the English scientist William Gilbert tried to explain why this happened. Even as famous a sailor as Columbus thought that the compass aligned itself with a magnetic star in the sky. Gilbert showed that the earth itself possesses a weak magnetic field and exerts a force on all the lodestones and magnets on its surface.

Gilbert called the pole that turned toward the north when a magnet is free to turn, the *north pole*, although *north-seeking pole* would have been a better name. As in the case of electrical charges, similar poles repel each other, while a force of attraction exists between opposite poles. Therefore, the north poles of the earth and the small magnet would repel each other. The magnetic field between them would resemble the field mapped in Figure 9.3*b*. Because of this, the pole of a freely suspended magnet that is attracted to the north magnetic pole of the earth should actually be called the *south* pole of the magnet. Since this might result in needless confusion, it is best to name the north-seeking pole (the pole that points to the north when the magnet is free to turn) the *north pole*, as Gilbert did. The other pole (the one that swings toward the south magnetic pole of the earth) is called the *south pole* of the magnet.

As in the case of the electric field, serious mapping of the force due to a magnetic field had to wait until the invention of the Coulomb balance (Figure 2.2). Force measurements showed that the force due to a magnetic field was found to vary inversely with the square of the distance from the magnet. If a certain force is exerted on a bit of iron one unit of distance from a magnet, moving the iron two units away from the magnet will reduce the force on it to one quarter of its previous value.

An important advance in the explanation of magnetic effects was made when Hans Oersted (pronounced *Ér-sted*) discovered that electricity and magnetism are related. In 1819, while working with a battery, he found that a compass needle moved when it was near a current-carrying wire. Since this effect was not seen when a compass was placed near an electrostatically charged object, Oersted concluded that there was a magnetic field associated with the movement of electricity. This discovery provided clues to the nature of magnetism and also taught experimenters how to make artificial magnets many times more powerful than the lodestones previously used.

In 1845, using electromagnets made of many turns of current-carrying wire wrapped around iron bars, the British physicist Michael Faraday observed that a bit of the metallic element bismuth was repelled by both poles of his device. Faraday's electromagnets enabled him to show that almost all elements and compounds are either attracted or repelled by a magnetic field. Before the invention of the electromagnet, it was thought that only iron, steel, nickel, and cobalt reacted to a magnetic field. Faraday found that substances could be divided into two classes: paramagnetic materials, those attracted by either pole of a magnet, and diamagnetic materials, those always repelled by a magnetic field. Iron, nickel, cobalt, and various combinations of these elements, such as steel, showed a much greater reaction to a magnetic field than any other elements or compounds, and are called *strongly paramagnetic*, or *ferromagnetic*, substances. Air and aluminum are only slightly attracted by even the powerful field of a large electromagnet and are called *weakly paramagnetic* materials. There appear to be no substances that are strongly diamagnetic. Such materials as bismuth, quartz, water, and copper are weakly repelled by a field.

Another important result of Faraday's experiments was to show that compounds made of paramagnetic or diamagnetic materials could be either paramagnetic or diamagnetic. Clearly, the magnetic activity of a compound depended on the molecular structure of the material and not only on the elements of which the compound was made.

Further advances in the explanation of magnetic effects had to wait for the development of modern atomic theory. Once it was known that an atom is composed of moving charged particles, Oersted's discovery of the relationship between electric current and magnetism could be extended to explain the existence of lodestones. Briefly stated, modern theories find the root of magnetic behavior of all types in the movement of electrons, whether this movement is in the form of an electric current in a wire or in a quality called *spin*. Note that the notion of a *spinning* electron should be thought of as a model intended to simplify an idea rather than an actual description of what happens at the subatomic level.

There are two possible spins assigned to atomic electrons, as shown in Figure 9.5. These are called *up-spin* and *down-spin*, to show that they are opposite. In the molecules of diamagnetic materials, the number of

Figure 9.5 A physical model of the electron characteristic known as "spin."

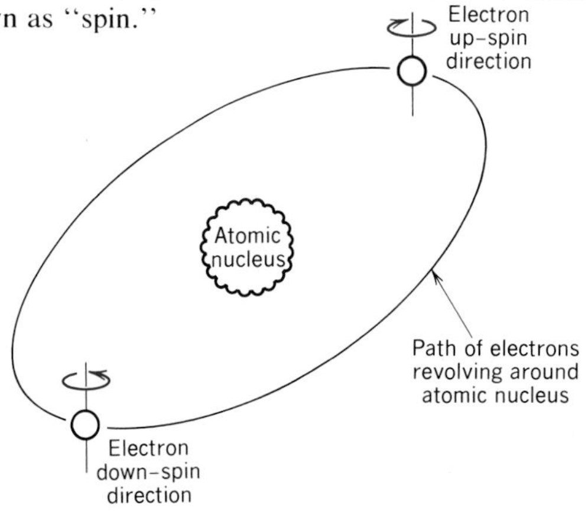

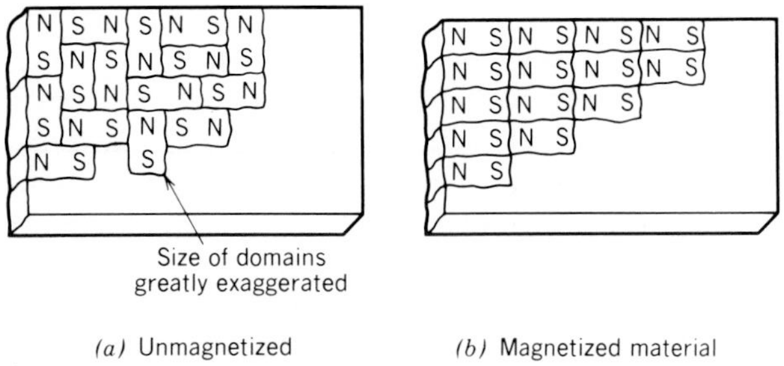

Figure 9.6 Many magnetic effects are explained by the alignment of magnetic domains.

up-spin electrons tends to equal the number of down-spin electrons, and the magnetic effects of the electrons cancel. In paramagnetic molecules, however, this cancellation does not happen, and the molecule is left with a weak magnetic field.

After this trip to the world of subatomic particles, it will probably come as a relief to learn that the difference between paramagnetic and ferromagnetic materials is explained by referring to structures that are actually visible through powerful microscopes. This explanation shows why it is possible to magnetize a piece of iron but not a piece of chromium, which is paramagnetic.

Although it is true that the two valence electrons in the ferromagnetic elements iron, nickel, and cobalt have the same direction of spin, such elements as chromium and wolfram should be as magnetically active as iron since the same or a greater spin imbalance exists. The difference between the weakly paramagnetic chromium and the ferromagnetic iron is that the ferromagnetic materials possess groups of atoms whose electron spins are aligned in the same direction. These groups are called *domains* and are large enough to be seen with a microscope. Although they are much larger than an individual atom, domains are still very small things. There are approximately 1×10^9 of them in a single cubic centimeter of iron.

In all unmagnetized materials, whether paramagnetic or ferromagnetic, the domains are oriented in a haphazard way, as shown in Figure 9.6*a*, and the magnetic fields tend to cancel each other. In a lodestone or magnet, however, the magnetic fields of the domains are aligned in the same direction (Figure 9.6*b*) so that an overall magnetic field is produced.

To a greater or lesser degree, the alignment of the domains in materials can be changed by putting them in a magnetic field. If the magnetic field is strong enough, it aligns the domains so that their magnetic fields tend to point in the same direction. The physical realignment of the domains is a complicated process, but this is basically what happens when you place a bar of unmagnetized iron in a coil of current-carrying wire, or otherwise place the bar in a strong magnetic field. The strength of the magnetic field required to align magnetic domains depends on the composition and past history of the material, as well as the direction of the applied field. Weakly paramagnetic materials require strong magnetic fields before they show any sign of domain alignment, and this alignment quickly disappears once the magnetic field has been removed. Ferromagnetic materials show domain alignment even in a relatively weak field, and this alignment tends to be retained for some time. Temporary magnets lose their domain alignment, while permanent magnets can retain it for many years. For certain materials there are "directions of easy magnetization," which do not require as strong an external field to cause domain alignment. An attempt to align the domains in any other direction will require a stronger field.

The concept of magnetic domain explains a number of things about magnets that are hard to explain otherwise. For example, if a magnet is heated, or is pounded repeatedly, its magnetic field weakens and eventually disappears. Since neither heating nor pounding will affect the spin of electrons, the loss of the magnetic field must be due to something else. The domain theory provides a solution: Heat or shock is sufficient to disturb the alignment of domains.

B.3 THE MAGNETIC FIELD AROUND A CURRENT-CARRYING WIRE

The magnetic field around a current-carrying conductor can be observed using the same paper and powdered iron method used to show the shape of the field around a bar magnet. A small hole is made in the paper and the wire is passed through it at a right angle to the paper, as shown in Figure 9.7*a*. If a high current is then passed through the wire, the powdered iron will form circles around the wire as shown in Figure 9.7*b*. This demonstration can be done at any point along the wire, showing that a current-carrying conductor is completely surrounded by a magnetic field of the shape shown by these patterns.

The direction of the magnetic lines of force, that

Figure 9.7 Method of mapping the magnetic field around a current-carrying wire.

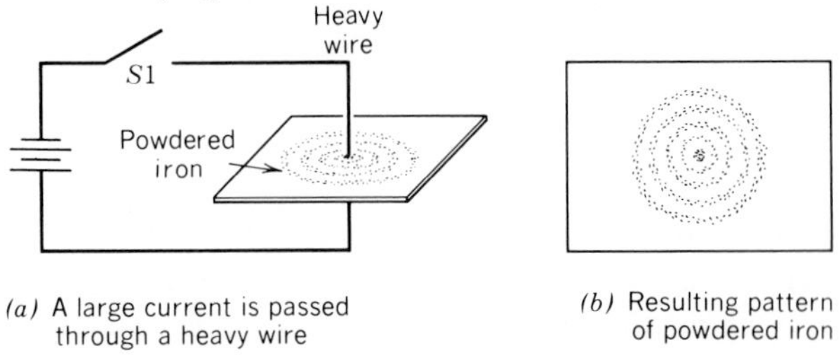

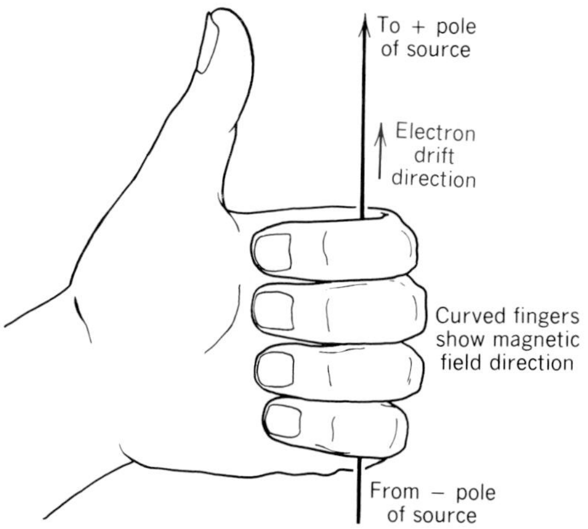

Figure 9.8 The left-hand rule for determining field direction around a conductor.

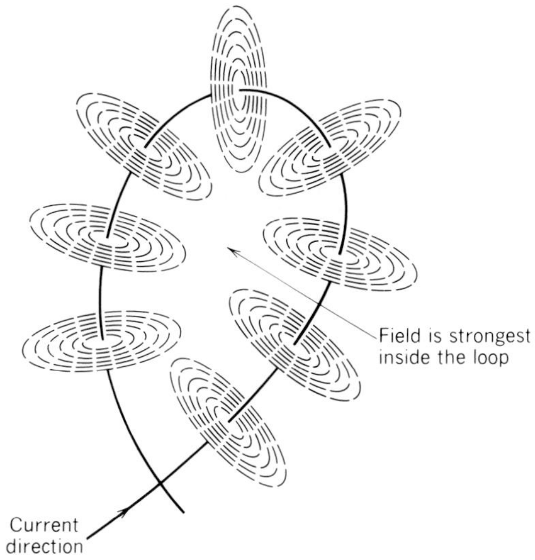

Figure 9.10 The magnetic field around a loop of wire.

is, the direction of the force on the north pole of a magnet placed in the field at that point, is determined by a conventional method called "the left-hand rule for determining field direction around a conductor." This is a long name for a simple rule, but there are so many left- and right-hand rules, that it is best to avoid confusion by using a long, descriptive name. Figure 9.8 shows this rule used to determine the field direction around a single current-carrying wire. The left thumb is pointed in the direction of the electron drift from the negative pole of the source to its positive pole, and the curved fingers show the direction of the field.

Figure 9.9 shows the shape of the magnetic field around two closely spaced wires carrying current in the same direction. Notice that most of the magnetic lines of force surround both wires, and that the field between them is relatively weak. The strength of the magnetic field at a point at some distance from the two wires is therefore nearly equal to the sum of the fields from each wire. It is this principle that permits the building of powerful electromagnets and coils in which the magnetic effects of a single current-carrying wire are multiplied many times.

If a single current-carrying wire is bent into a loop, the result is a large increase in the strength of the magnetic field at a point inside the loop. This is because the magnetic field from the entire length of wire passes through the center of the loop, as shown in Figure 9.10. Combining your knowledge of the shape of the magnetic field around single loops and parallel wires, it is possible to predict the result of winding a length of wire into a series of closely spaced loops called a *coil* or *solenoid*. Notice that the lines in Figure 9.11 all pass through the center of the solenoid and that the lines are most closely spaced inside it. This means that the magnetic field strength will be at its maximum along a line passing through the center of the coil. By adding additional layers of wire, the strength of the field can be increased to very high levels.

If you compare Figures 9.2 and 9.11 you will see that the magnetic lines of force form nearly identical patterns. That is, the magnetic field produced outside a current-carrying solenoid is the same as that produced outside a powerful bar magnet. Like a bar magnet, the

Figure 9.9 The shape of the magnetic field around a pair of closely spaced wires carrying current in the same direction.

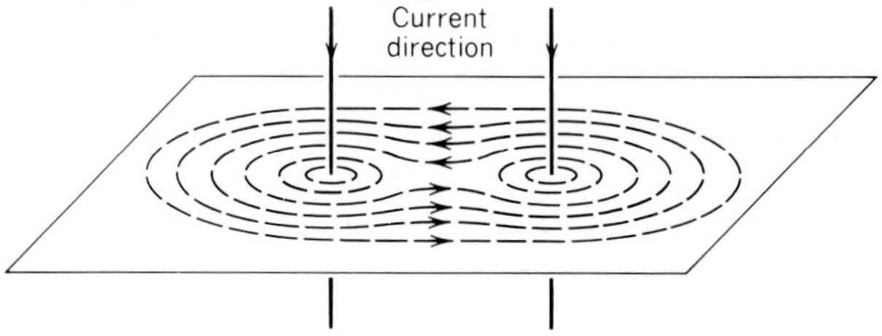

Figure 9.11 The magnetic field around a coil or solenoid.

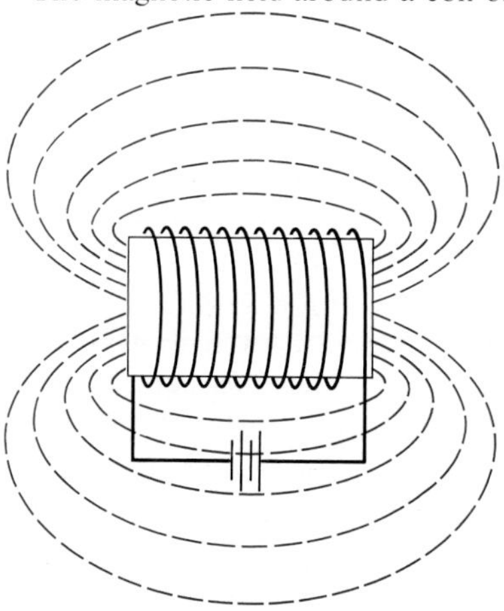

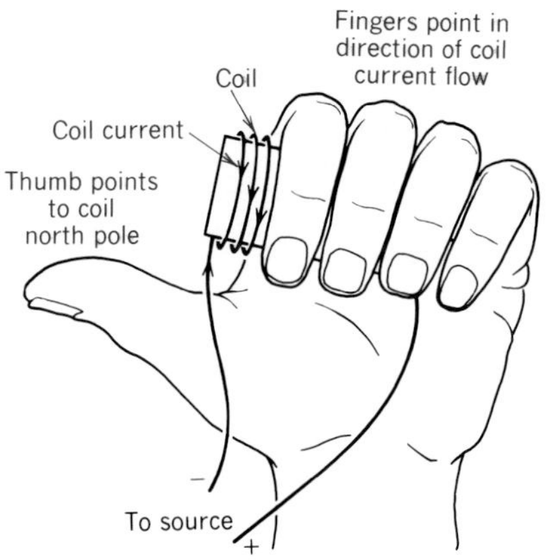

Figure 9.12 The left-hand rule for determining the north pole of a coil.

solenoid is able to attract iron or other ferromagnetic materials. A solenoid also has a north and south pole.

Another left-hand rule, called "the rule for determining the north pole of a coil" is shown in Figure 9.12. If the fingers of the left hand are curved in the direction of the electron drift through the coil, as shown in the figure, the thumb points to the north pole of the coil.

The measurable quantities of any magnetic field, whether it is produced by a permanent magnet or a current-carrying wire or solenoid, are based on the force produced by the field. Early experimenters used the force exerted by the field on moving charges to define a quantity B, called the *magnetic induction*. B represents the "strength" of the field at a point or through a small area at a right angle to the direction of the field. Since the strength of a magnetic field is illustrated by the spacing of the magnetic lines of force used to map the field, B is more commonly referred to as the *magnetic flux density* or more simply, the *flux density*. The unit of flux density is the tesla, abbreviated T.

To emphasize the role of B as a measure of flux density, it is also measured in units of webers per square meter, abbreviated Wb/m^2. In a field whose magnetic induction or flux density B is one tesla, that is, one weber per square meter, an electric charge of one coulomb moving at right angles to the field at a rate of one meter per second experiences a force of one newton due to the magnetic field.

Because considerable reality has been attributed to the magnetic lines of force used to map fields, an actual "number" of lines has been assigned to a flux density of one weber per square meter. That is, in order to map a flux density of one weber per square meter, 10^8 magnetic lines of force would be shown through an area of one square meter. Unfortunately, the tesla or weber/m^2 is too large a unit for measuring the flux densities found in electronics, so the microtesla (μT $= 10^{-6}$ T) or microweber per square meter (μWb/m$^2 = 10^{-6}$ Wb/m^2) is more common. When mapping a field whose flux density is 1 μT, an area of 1 m^2 will have $10^{-6} \times 10^8$, or 100 lines through it.

The total flux surrounding a magnet or a current-carrying conductor is called the *total magnetic flux*, or more simply the *flux*, and is related to the flux density through an area in a magnetic field. Flux is represented by the Greek letter Φ (phi), and is measured in webers. The mathematical relationship between flux (Φ) and the flux density (B) through an area is given by

$$B = \frac{\Phi}{A} \qquad \text{FORMULA 9.1}$$

where B is the flux density in webers/square meter, Φ is the flux in webers, and A the area in square meters.

EXAMPLE:
What is the flux density through an area of 1 cm^2 near the pole of a magnet if the total flux through this area is 25 μW. How many magnetic lines of force would have to be drawn through this area to represent the flux density? ■

SOLUTION:
Using Formula 9.1

$$B = \frac{25 \times 10^{-6}}{1 \times 10^{-4}}$$
$$= 0.025 = \mu\text{T} \quad \text{or} \quad \mu\text{Wb/m}^2$$

Since 10^8 lines must be drawn through an area of 1 m^2 to represent a flux density of 1 W/m^2, there would have to be 0.00025 lines drawn to represent a flux density of 0.025 μWb through an area of 1 cm^2. ■

The flux or flux density produced by a current-carrying coil or a magnet is rather easy to measure. Fluxmeters similar to those shown in the sketches in Figures 9.13*a* and 9.13*b* are relatively simple devices. Even simpler is the device shown in 9.13*c*, which consists of a small magnet that pivots when placed in a magnetic field, moving a pointer along a scale. A fourth type of device consists of a semiconductor, called a *Hall-effect device*, which produces a potential difference proportional to the flux density through it. Directions for building and using a simple Hall-effect meter are included in the laboratory manual that accompanies this book.

Since most of the magnetic fields used in electronics are produced by current-carrying conductors rather than permanent magnets, equal in importance to measurement of flux and flux density are measure-

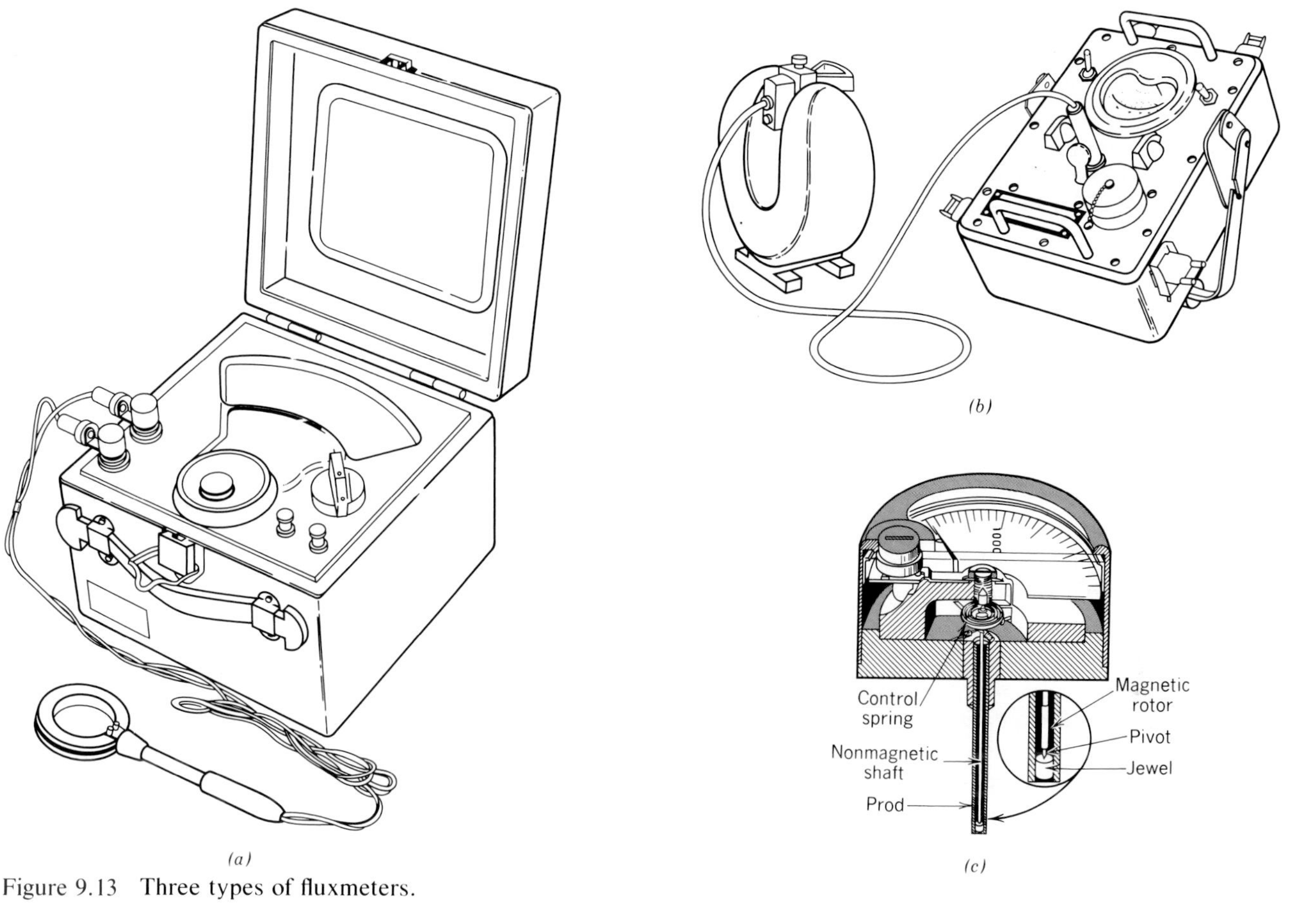

Figure 9.13 Three types of fluxmeters.

ments that relate flux density to the conductor current, length, and shape, and to the material in the neighborhood of the conductor. French experimenters including Ampère, the man whose name is used for the basic unit of current, discovered that the flux density at a point near a current-carrying conductor is directly proportional to the current in the wire. In addition, it was discovered that if the wire was wound into a coil composed of a series of loops, as shown in Figure 9.14, at a point not too near the end of the coil, the flux density B was also proportional to the number of turns in the coil and inversely proportional to its length. In other words, increasing the current through the coil or

Figure 9.14 At a point not too near the end of a coil, the flux density is proportional to the coil current and number of turns, but inversely proportional to the length of the coil.

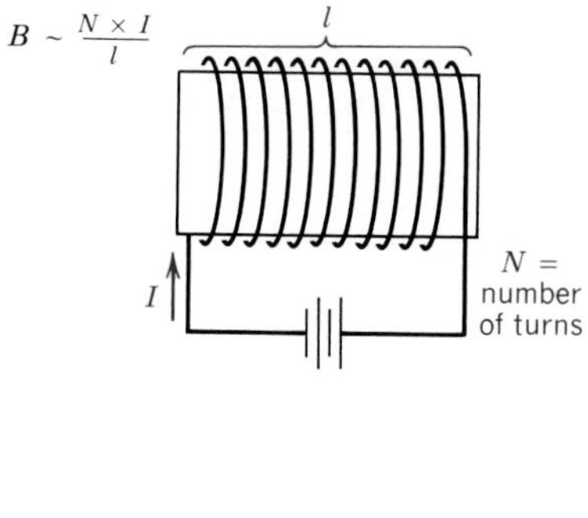

the number of turns in it would increase the flux density. Increasing the length of the coil alone, without adding to the number of turns, would reduce the flux density at a point in the field. This can be demonstrated by the experiment shown in Figure 9.15. In the illustration, a small piece of iron is suspended close to a coil. If the coil is connected to a source, there will be a force on the iron due to the magnetic field around

Figure 9.15 Experiment to show the factors governing the strength of a magnetic field from a coil.

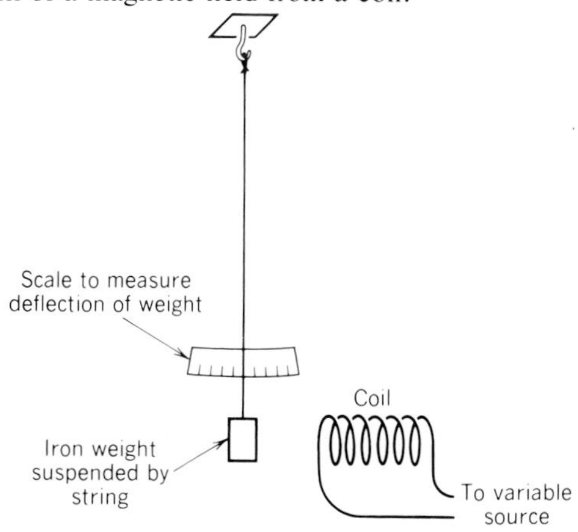

the coil and the iron will be attracted to the coil. The force on the piece of iron can be increased by increasing either the number of turns of wire or increasing the current through it. Decreasing the number of turns of wire in the coil or decreasing the coil current will decrease the force on the piece of iron.

The product of the number of turns or loops in a coil and the current through it is called the *magnetomotive force*. Magnetomotive force (mmf) was invented as an analog of the electric field quantity, electromotive force, or potential difference. It is symbolized by the script letter $\mathcal{F}$ and is measured in ampere-turns, abbreviated At. As a formula, this is

$$\mathcal{F} = NI \qquad \text{FORMULA 9.2}$$

Note that according to this formula, there is no difference in the magnetomotive force produced by a 100-turn coil with a current of 1 A and that produced by a 10-turn coil with a current of 10 A. In either case, the mmf is 100 ampere turns.

If the coil in Figure 9.15 is stretched to make it longer, without increasing the number of turns, the force on the piece of iron will decrease. On the other hand, changing the diameter of the coil, without changing the number of turns, will have no effect on the force produced if the changes in the coil diameter are kept within reason. The mathematical analyses that led to this discovery suggested another magnetic field quantity called the magnetic *field intensity*. Magnetic field intensity, symbolized by the letter H, is the magnetomotive force per unit length of a coil or solenoid:

$$H = \frac{\mathcal{F}}{l} = \frac{NI}{l} \qquad \text{FORMULA 9.3}$$

where l is the length of the coil or solenoid in meters. It is measured in ampere-turns per meter (At/m).

EXAMPLE:
A certain coil is composed of 100 turns of fine wire, is 0.1 m long, and has a diameter of 0.01 m. If the wire has a resistance of 2.5 Ω and is connected to a 6-V source, what is the magnetomotive force produced? What is the magnetic field intensity? ■

SOLUTION:
According to Formula 9.2, the magnetomotive force $\mathcal{F}$ is equal to the product of the number of turns in the coil and the current through it. Although not stated, the current is easily calculated using Ohm's law:

$$I = \frac{E}{R} = \frac{6}{2.5} = 2.4 \text{ A}$$

$$\mathcal{F} = N \times I = 100 \times 2.4 = 240 \text{ At}$$

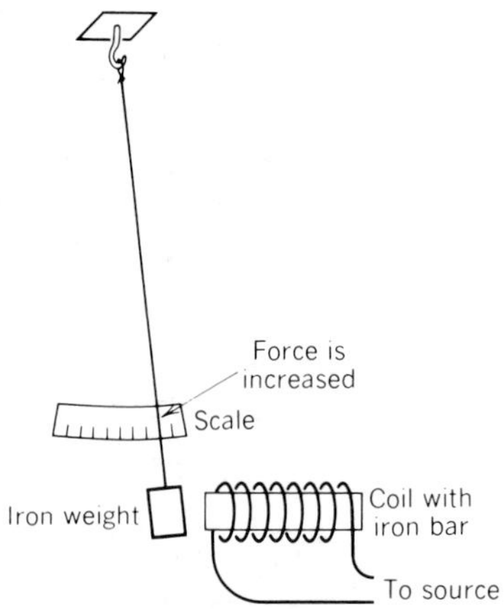

Figure 9.16 Winding a coil around an iron form greatly increases the strength of the magnetic field produced.

The magnetic field intensity H is obtained from Formula 9.3.

$$H = \frac{\mathcal{F}}{l} = \frac{240}{0.1} = 2400 \text{ At/m}$$ ■

If the coil used in the experiment pictured in Figure 9.15 is wound on an iron form or if an iron bar is inserted into it, as shown in Figure 9.16, the force on the suspended piece of iron will be much greater. One reason for this is that the magnetic field from the coil aligns the magnetic domains in the iron core in the direction of the coil field. This means that the magnetic flux of each of the many tiny domains in the iron core aids the magnetic field of the coil.

This does not, however, explain certain of the effects observed when an electromagnet is provided with a ferromagnetic core. For example, mapping the field with powdered iron will show that the magnetic lines of force are concentrated by the core. If the core is a closed loop or torus shape as shown in Figure 9.17, the magnetic field is almost totally within the core. Another effect that cannot be explained by referring to domains is seen in Figure 9.18. Here a sheet of

Figure 9.17 If the core of a coil is a closed loop or torus, the magnetic field is contained almost totally in the core.

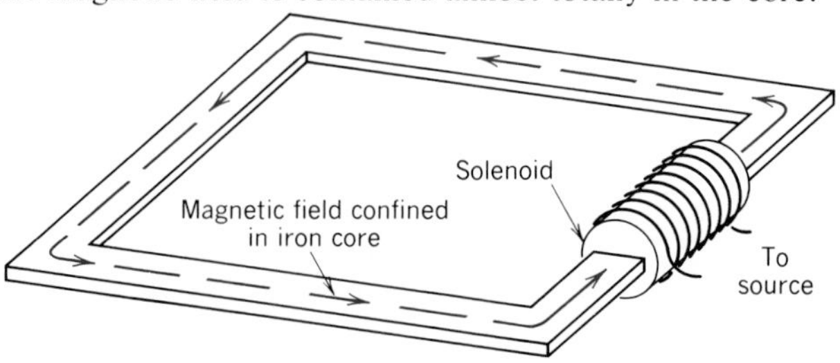

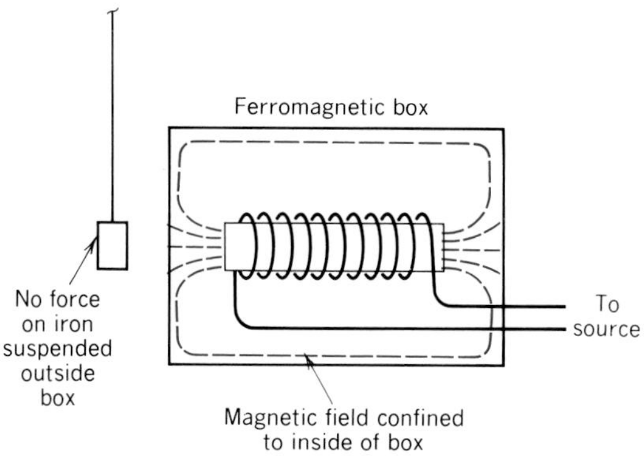

Figure 9.18 A solenoid is shielded by a closed ferromagnetic box.

ferromagnetic material acts as a shield, preventing the field from the coil inside the shield from acting on the piece of iron outside the shield. These effects suggest that the field "prefers" to travel within a ferromagnetic material.

The closed path followed by the magnetic field around a coil can be considered a magnetic *circuit*, and a new unit can be defined as the amount of magnetomotive force necessary to produce a unit of magnetic flux through the magnetic circuit. This new unit is called the *reluctance* of the magnetic circuit, and is symbolized by a script $\mathcal{R}$. From the mathematical statement of the definition of $\mathcal{R}$,

$$\mathcal{R} = \frac{\mathcal{F}}{\Phi} \qquad \text{FORMULA 9.4}$$

You can see that reluctance is measured in ampere-turns per weber, or At/Wb.

Because it defines the *resistance* to the passage of a magnetic field through a magnetic circuit, Formula 9.4 is sometimes called *Ohm's law for magnetic circuits*. One of the uses of this formula is to explain why a magnetic circuit tends to follow ferromagnetic material. Since the reluctance of ferromagnetic materials is much less than that of air, these materials provide a better path for the magnetic field than air. A comparison between resistance and reluctance is shown in Figure 9.19. In 9.19*a*, the conduction electrons drift from point *A* through point *B* to point *C* even though a direct path from *A* to *C* would be "shorter." This is true because the resistance of the wire between *A* and *C* is low when compared to the resistance of the air gap between *A* and *C*. In Figure 9.19*b* the reluctance of the ferromagnetic circuit path from *A* through *B* to *C* is also low when compared to the reluctance of the air gap between *A* and *C*. The reluctances of all nonferromagnetic materials are about the same as that of air.

The final magnetic field quantity to be discussed in this section is permeability. It is a measure of the amount of magnetic field intensity required to produce a particular flux density in some material. Permeability, like resistivity, is a characteristic of a material and is independent of the size or shape. Permeability is symbolized by the Greek letter μ (mu) and is measured in webers per ampere-turn meter. The mathematical definition for μ is

$$\mu = \frac{B}{H} \qquad \text{FORMULA 9.5}$$

The letter μ is frequently found with a subscript, for example, μ_0, read "mu sub zero." This particular quantity is the permeability of empty space and is equal to $4\pi \times 10^{-7}$ or 12.57×10^{-7} Wb/At·m. This means that a field intensity H of 1 At/m will produce a flux density B of

$$\mu_0 = \frac{B}{4} \quad \text{or} \quad B = \mu_0 H = 12.57 \times 10^{-7}\ \text{Wb/m}^2$$

A high permeability means that a small magnetizing force or magnetic field intensity will create a relatively large flux density in the material, while a low permeability means that a much greater magnetizing force will have to be used.

The permeability of air is about that of empty space, while that of weakly paramagnetic materials is higher. Diamagnetic materials have permeabilities somewhat

Figure 9.19 A comparison of resistance and reluctance.

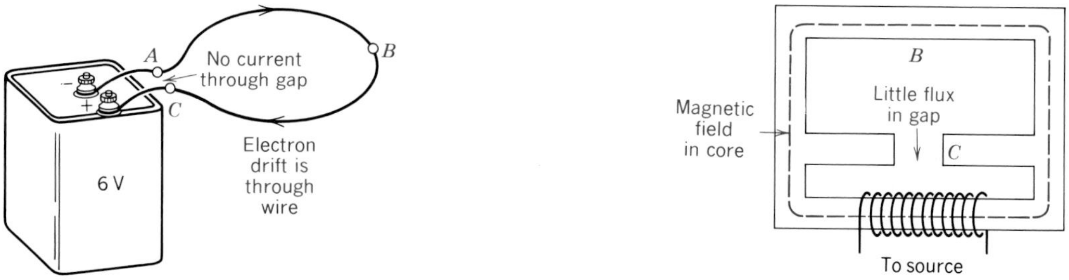

(a) Conduction electrons drift through low resistance

(b) Flux is through low reluctance

lower than that of air. In order to simplify calculations, another quantity, called *relative permeability*, is frequently used in technology. This quantity is used to specify the permeability of the core materials frequently used for coils in electrical or electronic units. Relative permeability is symbolized by μ_r or just μ and is

$$\mu_r = \frac{\mu_{\text{material}}}{\mu_{\text{space}}} \qquad \text{FORMULA 9.6}$$

There are no units attached to relative permeability; a μ_r of 550 merely means that the permeability of that material is 550 times that of empty space. Materials with relative permeabilities as high as 10^5, or 100,000 times greater than that of empty space are currently in use. Many coil cores have their relative permeability printed on them or this information can be obtained from manufacturers' catalogs. Just as the resistivity of a material is related to the resistance and conductance of an electric circuit formed of that material, the permeability of a magnetic material μ is related to the reluctance of a magnetic circuit. Putting together the formulas that are the definitions of the magnetic quantities, a simple and usable expression for the reluctance of a magnetic circuit can be found. The definition of reluctance is given by Formula 9.4:

$$\mathcal{R} = \frac{\mathcal{F}}{\Phi}$$

Φ, the magnetomotive force, is equal to the number of turns of wire in a coil or solenoid times the current as shown in Formula 9.2, so,

$$\mathcal{R} = \frac{NI}{\Phi}$$

An expression for the flux Φ can be obtained from Formula 9.1, $\Phi = BA$. Substituting,

$$\mathcal{R} = \frac{NI}{BA}$$

Solving Formula 9.3 for N produces

$$N = \frac{Hl}{I}$$

Substituting this in

$$\mathcal{R} = \frac{NI}{BA} = \frac{\frac{Hl}{I} \times I}{BA}$$

This can be reduced to

$$\mathcal{R} = \frac{Hl}{BA} \text{ or } \frac{H}{B} \times \frac{l}{A}$$

But

$$\frac{H}{B} = \frac{l}{\mu},$$

so

$$\mathcal{R} = \frac{l}{\mu A} \qquad \text{FORMULA 9.7}$$

This formula is quite useful since it provides information about the magnetic circuit, which is independent of the number of turns, current, or flux.

EXAMPLE:
Two closed magnetic cores are available. One is 0.1 m long, 0.025 m^2 in cross-sectional area, and has a relative permeability of 550. The other is 0.125 m long, has a cross-sectional area, of 0.018 m^2, and a relative permeability of 440. Which core would provide the greatest flux with a coil of 480 turns and a current of 100 mA? ■

SOLUTION:
The largest flux for a given magnetomotive force would be provided by the core with the smaller reluctance since, according to Formula 9.4, the flux is inversely proportional to the reluctance:

$$\mathcal{R} = \frac{\mathcal{F}}{\Phi}$$

The formula for the reluctance of a core is

$$\mathcal{R} = \frac{l}{\mu \text{A}}$$

The permeability of the two cores is given in relative units that can be converted to absolute units using Formula 9.6,

$$\mu_r = \frac{\mu_{\text{material}}}{\mu_{\text{space}}}$$

$$550 \times 4\pi \times 10^{-7} = 6.91 \times 10^{-4} \quad \text{and}$$
$$440 \times 4\pi \times 10^{-7} = 5.53 \times 10^{-4}$$

This step isn't actually necessary since it is only necessary to determine which core has the smaller reluctance. The actual value of the reluctance is not required.

Substitute the dimensions and value for μ for both cores in Formula 9.7. For core 1,

$$\mathcal{R}_1 = \frac{0.1}{6.91 \times 10-4 \times 0.025} = 5.788 \times 10^3 \text{ At/Wb}$$

For core 2,

$$\mathcal{R}_2 = \frac{0.125}{5.53 \times 10-4 \times .018} = 1.256 \times 10^4 \text{ At/Wb}$$

The first coil will provide almost twice the flux for the same magnetomotive force. ■

C. EXAMPLES AND COMPUTATIONS

C.1 FUNCTIONS USED IN ELECTRONIC TECHNOLOGY

Up to this point, the formulas used for defining quantities or the relationship between quantities have been of a fairly simple sort. In the following chapters, however, mathematical relationships assume more importance. In some cases, for example, the only "explanation" of what happens in a particular circuit is a mathematical description of some change to an input signal. In order to understand explanations of this kind and the new ideas that are presented in the next chapter, it is important to formalize your knowledge of algebraic terms and graphing.

You have been using formulas such as $E = IR$ for some time now, without any formal definition of the equation or its parts, and should have come to view algebra as an aid and powerful tool in technology. The principal way in which algebra differs from arithmetic is evident in the two following statements:

a. $3 + 2 = 5$
b. $x + 3 = y$

Both (a) and (b) are *expressions* (also called *algebraic expressions*) since both are meaningful collections of numbers, symbols, and signs for mathematical operations. But (a) is composed only of numbers and signs for mathematical operations, while (b) contains two symbols (x and y) that represent one or more members of a set of numbers or values. For this reason, x and y are called *variables* to distinguish them from numbers, which are called *constants*. It is easy to see that 3, 2, and 5 in (a) and 3 in (b) are constants. But not all constants are represented by number symbols. For example,

$$\mu_0 + 2\pi l = 64$$

In this expression, there is only one variable, l. Although μ_0 and π are letter symbols, they are in effect constants since there is only one value associated with the symbol:

$$\mu_0 = 12.57 \times 10^{-7} \quad \text{and} \quad \pi = 3.1416$$

There is actually no difference between a symbolized constant μ_0 or π and a number constant such as 2 or 64.

In a mathematical expression, constants and variables are arranged to form *terms*. A term is any constant, variable, or combination of constants and variables separated from other terms by plus signs or minus signs. In the expression

$$19XYZ + Y - 13\,Z^2 + 14$$

there are four terms: $19XYZ$, Y, $-13Z^2$, and 14. Generally, any arrangement contained within parentheses is considered a single term.

EXAMPLE:
How many terms are present in the expression

$$2\pi fL + 6A(r^2 + Z^2) + 19$$ ■

SOLUTION:
There are three terms $2\pi fL$, $6A(r^2 + Z^2)$, and 19. $6A$ and $(r^2 + Z^2)$ are considered a single term. ■

A fraction bar can also serve to tie a combination of constants, variables, and symbols for mathematical operations together into a single term. For instance, the expression

$$13XY + 8(X + Y) + \frac{X^2 + 2XY + Y^2}{d^2}$$

contains only three terms: $13XY$, $8(X + Y)$, and

$$\frac{X^2 + 2XY + Y^2}{d^2}$$

When you used the method of determinants for solving two or three equations involving two or three unknown quantities, you ran across the word *coefficient*. The coefficient of a variable, more properly called the *numerical coefficient*, is the number by which a variable is multiplied in a term.

EXAMPLES:
In $3.5X$ the coefficient is 3.5 and the variable is X:

In $-2Z$ the coefficient is -2 and the variable is Z.

In j the coefficient is 1 and the variable is j. ■

In some cases, the coefficient, although it is a constant and not a variable, is not specified, and the first letters of the alphabet, usually in lowercase form, are used. For example, in $ax + by$, a and b are the coefficients of x and y, respectively. Another notation frequently found is the use of subscript numbers to distinguish coefficients: $a_1 + a_2x + a_3x^2 + a_4x^3$. In this expression, a_1, a_2, a_3, and a_4 are the coefficients of the terms, and x, x^2, and x^3 are forms of the variable. Although a_1, a_2, a_3, and a_4 could all be different, x, x^2, and x^3 are a number, its square, and its cube.

Review your command of the language of algebra by performing the following exercises:

1. Identify the terms in the following expressions:

a. $14x + 3$
b. $3x + b(x - 2)$
c. $a_0 + a_1x_1 - a_2x_2$
d. $\dfrac{x^2 - 3x - 3}{g}$
e. $\dfrac{x}{5} + \dfrac{x - y}{7}$
f. $15z + 3(x + y) + \dfrac{(z + 1)}{2}$
g. $(x + y + 7)$
h. $\sqrt{x + y}$

2. Identify the coefficients in the following expressions:

a. $7q + 3m$
b. $\dfrac{1}{9}x + \dfrac{1}{3}z + 15$
c. $8x^2 - x + 8y$
d. $2x - y + 8\sqrt{3}\, z$
e. $\dfrac{d + e}{3} + \dfrac{x}{7} + 9dx$
f. $-b + \sqrt{b^2 - 4ac}$
g. $-a_0 + a_1x - a_2x^2 + a_3x^3$
h. $\dfrac{x}{a_1} + \dfrac{y}{b_1} + a_1b_1xy$

3. Using the letters x and y for the variables, write the algebraic expressions for the following statements:

a. The sum of one unknown quantity and twice a second unknown.
b. Seven more than the square of a quantity.
c. Twice the difference between two unknowns.
d. An unknown quantity times the difference between a second unknown and 7.
e. A quantity decreased by 2 and multiplied by 8.
f. An unknown current x is divided into two equal portions.
g. Four times a quantity subtracted from another unknown quantity.
h. An unknown quantity is equal to three times the sum of another quantity and one.
i. One-third the sum of two quantities, multiplied by 16.
j. Twice the product of a quantity squared and a second unknown quantity is added to 2 divided by the second unknown quantity.

C.2 GRAPHING THE FUNCTIONS USED IN ELECTRONIC TECHNOLOGY

Many formulas, that is, mathematical statements of the relationships among electrical quantities, provide useful information about the nature of these relationships when corresponding quantity values are presented in the form of a graph. This method was invented by the French philosopher Descartes (pronounced *day-kárt*), and has become so much a part of modern electronic technology that what it actually represents is sometimes forgotten. The application of Descartes' method, called the *Cartesian coordinate* method, is begun by isolating one of the variables in a two-variable equation on one side of the equals sign. For example, suppose that the equation is $8 = 3x - 2y$. Adding $2y$ to both sides of the equation and dividing by 2 produces:

$$4 + y = \frac{3}{2}x$$

Subtracting 4 from both sides of this equation isolates y on the left side of the equals sign

$$y = \frac{3}{2}x - 4$$

You will recall that this is referred to as "solving for y." Now, if a number of values are chosen for x, corresponding values for y can easily be calculated. The isolated variable, y in this case, is called the *dependent variable*, because its value depends on the value chosen for x. The nonisolated variable, x, is called the *independent variable* because its value is chosen rather than calculated.

Another way of putting this is to say that y is a *function* of x since the value or values of y are obtained by performing some sort of mathematic operation on the independent variable x. The Cartesian graphing method consists of creating a table of corresponding values for x and y and plotting these points on a pair of axes of the type shown in Figure 9.20. It is usual to plot the independent variable values along the horizontal axis, commonly called the *x axis*, and the dependent variable values along the vertical axis, called the *y axis*. Notice that the $x = 0$, $y = 0$ point is at the center, as a convention. The two axes make it possible to assign an x and y value to every point on the paper on which they are drawn. These values are conventionally enclosed in parentheses and separated by a comma. The x value, or independent variable, is given first, so $(3.5, -2)$ specifies the point at which $x = 3.5$ and $y = -2$.

The two axes also divide the paper into four portions, called *quadrants*, and numbered counterclock-

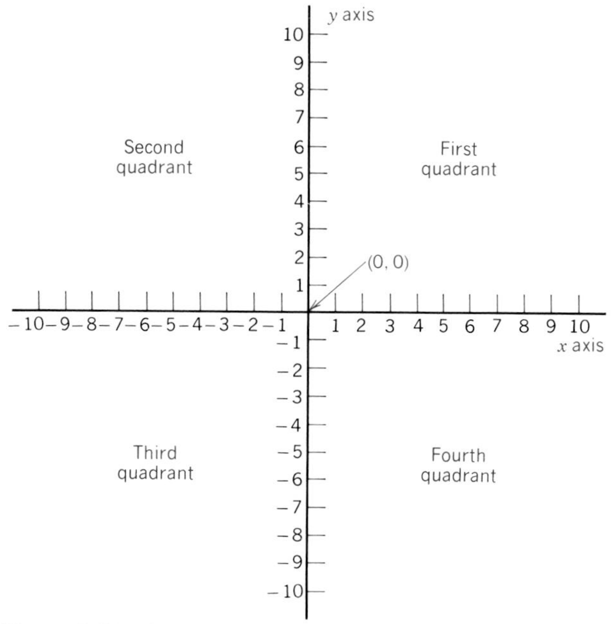

Figure 9.20 Coordinate axes and the Cartesian graphing method.

wise as shown in Figure 9.20. It is worth remembering that:

In the first quadrant both x and y are positive numbers
In the second quadrant x is negative and y is positive
In the third quadrant both x and y are negative
In the fourth quadrant x is positive and y is negative

This makes it easier to locate points on the graph.

EXAMPLE:
Locate the following points on a Cartesian coordinate graph.

a. (3, 4)
b. (−1, −3)
c. (4, −4) ■

SOLUTION:
Refer to Figure 9.21. ■

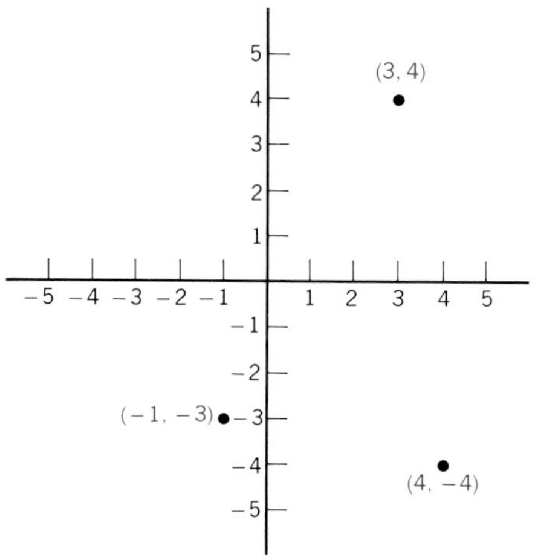

Figure 9.21 Solution to point plotting example.

Once you have mastered the skill of plotting points on a Cartesian coordinate graph, you can begin to use this method for analysis.

EXAMPLE:
A bilateral network has a resistance of 2 Ω. Plot the potential drop across the network as a function of the current through it. ■

SOLUTION:
A good place to start is to draw a diagram of the problem, as shown in Figure 9.22*a*. The network is bilateral, meaning that current can pass through it in either direction. Consider an electron drift and voltage drop from left to right to be positive, and a drift and drop from right to left to be negative. With this information, it is possible to begin filling out the table shown in Figure 9.22*b* and plotting the points on the axes. Connecting the points, you can see that the result is a straight line. ■

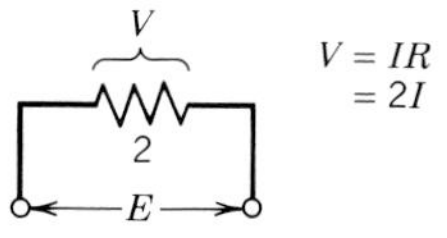

(a) Network

I	V
−4	−8
−2	−4
0	0
1	2
2	4
4	8

(b) Table

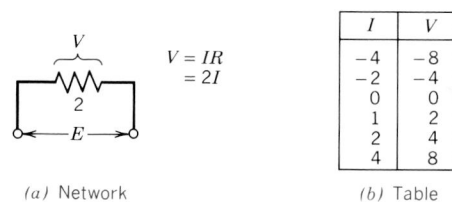

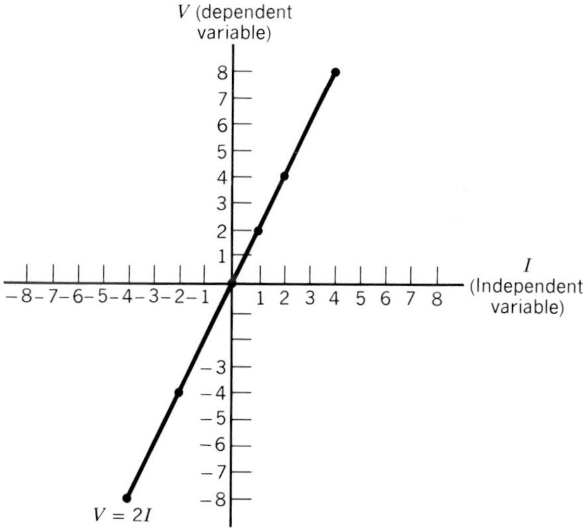

(c) Graph

Figure 9.22 Plotting a function.

Try graphing the following functions:

a. $2x + 3y = 6$
b. $13x + y = 5$
c. $x + 20y = 3$
d. $y + \frac{y}{x} = 3$
e. $y = \frac{1}{x}$
f. $6I_1I_2 = 24$
g. $x^2 + 2y^2 = 9$
h. $x^2y + yx = 12$

Because the graph of the equation $y = x + 3$ is a straight line, it is called a *linear function*. Another way of describing the relationship between x and y in this equation is to say that y is a linear function of x. Not all the relationships found in electronics are linear. Some have very curious graphs, as shown in Figures 9.23*a* and *b*.

Many of the graphs used in electronics chart the variation of some dependent variable such as current or voltage as a function of time. The figures on these graphs, particularly when they are complex and repetetive, are called *waveforms*. They are still waveforms even when they are simple, but no one feels the need to call them that. Consider the circuit of Figure 9.24*a*. At a certain time, call it $t = 0$ for convenience, switch *S*1 is closed. If the potential difference across *R*1 is plotted as a function of time, a graph like that shown in Figure 9.24*b* results. The function shown is linear. A graph of the current through *R*1 would show the same form. In the next chapter, you will learn that these graphs constitute a definition of pure direct current (dc).

The function whose graph is shown in Figure 9.23*b* is a common function describing the relationship between voltage or current and time in an electronic circuit. It is called a *logarithmic function* and will be discussed in the chapters on inductance and capacitance. Even more familiar than the logarithmic function is that shown in Figure 9.23*a*. Here the potential difference between two points in a circuit is shown as a function of time. Notice that this function has voltage values ranging from +1 to −1 and back again. It is called a *sine function* and is one of the most important concepts in electronics. In order to understand the mathematical expression that results in a sine function, you will have to learn a little about a branch of mathematics called trigonometry.

Figure 9.23 Some functions used in electronics. Many of these are not linear.

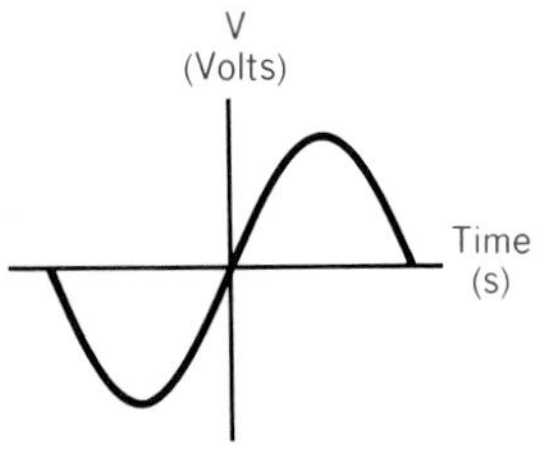

(a) Sine function

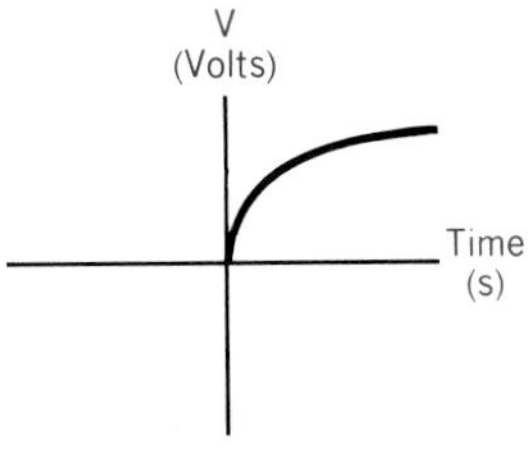

(b) Logarithmic function

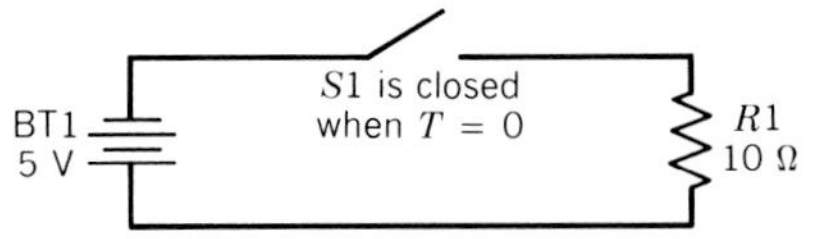

(a) Circuit S1 is open until T = 0 and then remains closed

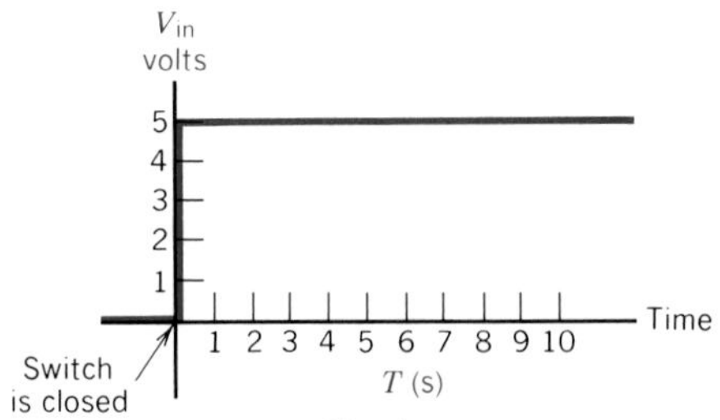

(b) Waveform graph

Figure 9.24 A circuit and its waveform graph.

C.3 TRIGONOMETRIC FUNCTIONS

The subject of trigonometry is the peculiar properties of triangles that contain a right angle. Figure 9.25*a* shows two such triangles, both composed of the same angles. Triangles whose corresponding angles are the same are called *similar triangles*. Placing the two tri-

Figure 9.25 Relationship between a side and the hypotenuse: the sine of an angle.

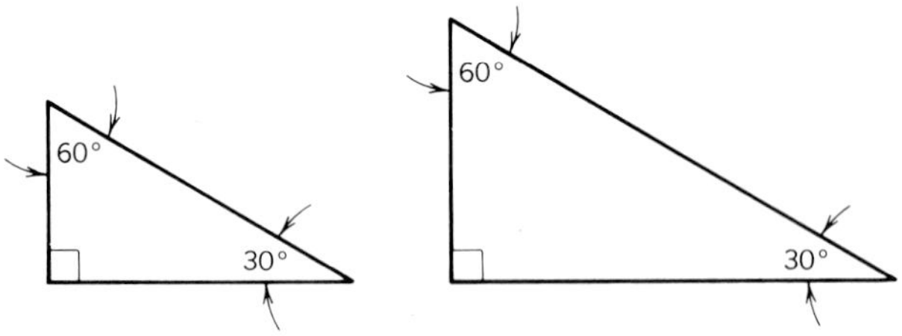

(a) Two similar triangles

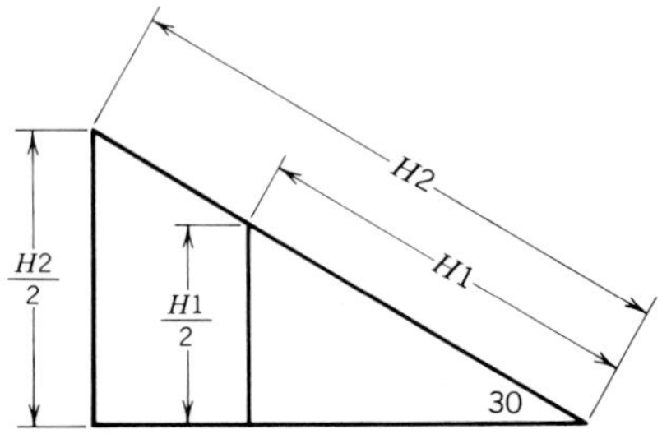

(b) Two triangles placed together

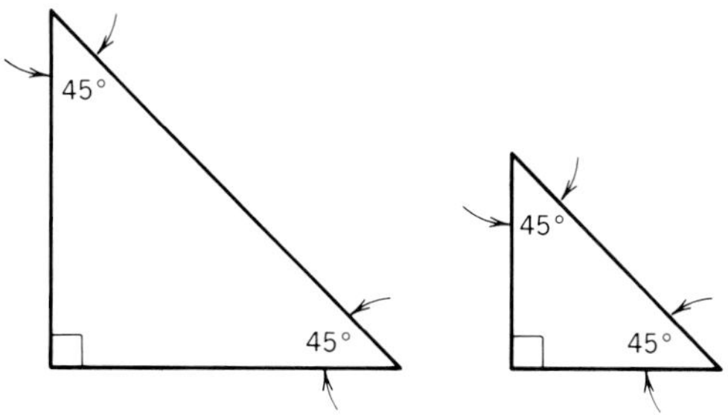

(a) A pair of 90°-45°-45° similar triangles

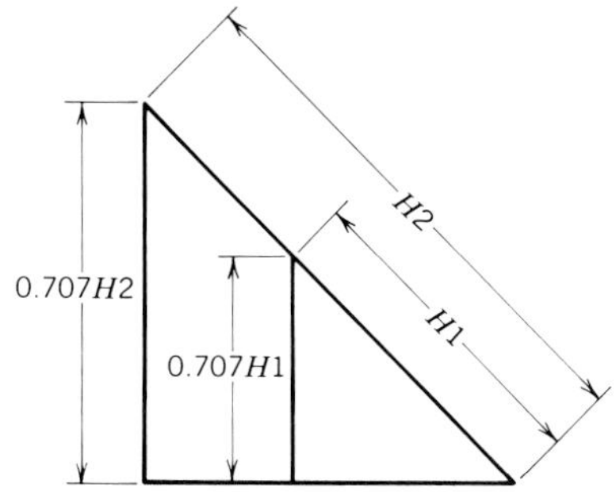

(b) Placing the triangles together illustrates the ratio of the opposite side to the longest side

Figure 9.26 With a different pair of similar triangles, the ratio between length of a side opposite an angle and the longest side is different.

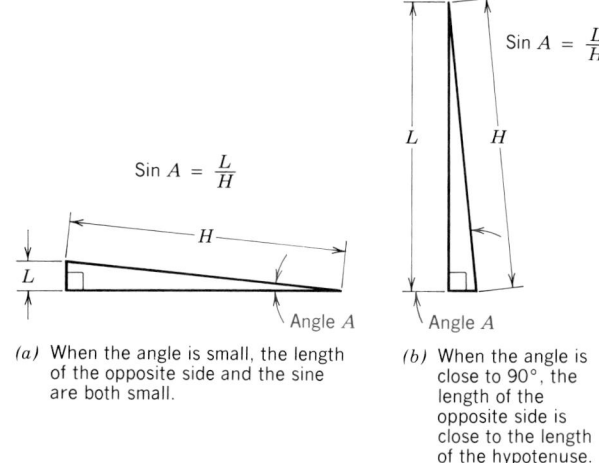

angles together so that the vertices of an angle coincide as in Figure 9.25*b* reveals an important relationship. Notice that the longest side (the side opposite the right angle) of the largest triangle is exactly twice as long as the side opposite the 30° angle. If a different pair of triangles is chosen, as in Figure 9.26, there is still a distinct ratio. The side opposite the right angle is still the longest side, although the actual length of this longest side, called the *hypotenuse*, and the length of the side opposite angle *A* are now different. The ratio of the length of the side opposite angle *A* to the length of the hypotenuse of the triangle is called the "sine of angle *A*." In mathematical form,

$$\text{sine } A = \frac{\text{length of opposite side}}{\text{length of hypotenuse}} \qquad \text{FORMULA 9.8}$$

When angle *A* is made quite small, the opposite side is also small, as shown in Figure 9.27*a*. As the angle increases, the length of the opposite side becomes closer to the length of the hypotenuse as in 9.27*b*. This means that the value of sin *A* varies from almost zero to almost 1 as the size of angle *A* varies from almost 0° to almost 90°. Note that there is no way of calculating the sine of a particular angle without either measuring, using a table, performing a calculation, or solving a complex approximation formula.

For angles between 90° and 180°, the sine of angle

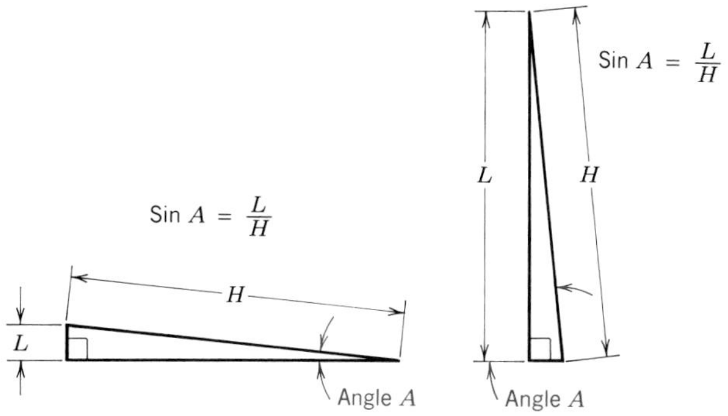

(a) When the angle is small, the length of the opposite side and the sine are both small.

(b) When the angle is close to 90°, the length of the opposite side is close to the length of the hypotenuse.

Figure 9.27 The value of the sine varies from almost 0 for a small angle to almost 1 for an angle near 90°.

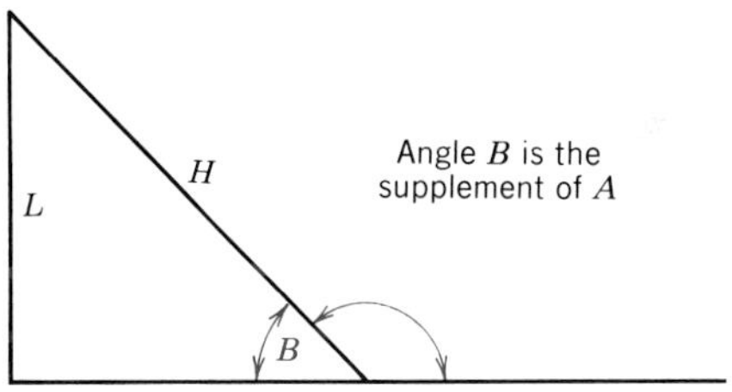

For angles greater than 90° but less than or equal to 180°, sin *A* = sin(180 − *A*)

Figure 9.28 The definition of the sine of an angle greater than 90° and less than or equal to 180°.

A is defined as the sine of its supplementary angle *B*, as shown in Figure 9.28. Since the size of an angle in degrees plus the size of its supplement is equal to 180°, it is possible to determine the sine of angles between 90° and 180°.

$$\sin A \text{ (greater than 90 but less than or equal to 180)} = \sin(180 - A) \qquad \text{FORMULA 9.9}$$

EXAMPLE:
Using the table of sine values in the Appendix, determine the value of the sine of an angle of 130° (abbreviated sin 130). ■

SOLUTION:
Since an angle of 130° is between 90° and 180°, the sine is defined as the sine of 180 − 130 or sine 50°. The value is 0.7660. ■

For angles greater than 180° and equal to or less than 270°, as shown in Figure 9.29, the sine of the angle is defined as the negative of the sine of the angle minus

Angle B = Angle A − 180°

For angles greater than 180° but less than
or equal to 270°, sin A = −sin(A − 180)

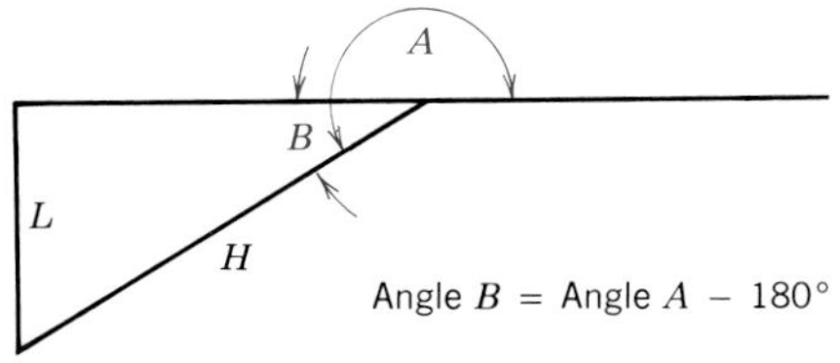

Figure 9.29 The definition of the sine of an angle greater than 180° and less than or equal to 270°.

180°, or

$$\text{sin } A \text{ (greater than 180 but less than or equal to 270)} = -\sin(A - 180) \qquad \text{FORMULA 9.10}$$

EXAMPLE:
Determine the sine of 250°. ∎

SOLUTION:
Since 250° is between 180° and 270°, the sine of 250 = −sin(250 − 180) = −sin 70. Since sin 70 = 0.9397, sin 250 = −0.9397. ∎

For angles greater than 270° but less than or equal to 360°, as shown in Figure 9.30 the sin of an angle A is defined as the negative of sin(360 − A). As a formula, this is written

$$\text{sin } A \text{ (greater than 270 but less than or equal to 360)} = -\sin(360 - A) \qquad \text{FORMULA 9.11}$$

EXAMPLE:
Determine the sine of angle A when A = 300°. ∎

SOLUTION:
Since 300° is between 270° and 360°, sin 300 = −sin (360 − 300) = −sin 60. According to a table of sine values, sin 60 is 0.8660, so sin 300 = −0.8660. ∎

Figure 9.30 The definition of the sine of an angle greater than 270° and less than or equal to 360°.

Angle B = 360° − Angle A

For angles greater than 270° but less than
or equal to 360°, sin A = −sin(360 − A)

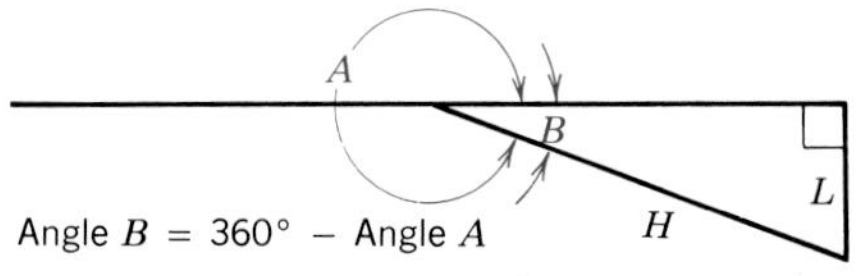

Sine calculations are not difficult if you remember the following facts.

a. The sine of an angle is the length of the opposite side divided by the length of the hypotenuse, or

$$\sin A = \frac{\text{opposite}}{\text{hypotenuse}}$$

b. For angles greater than 90° but less than or equal to 180°, sin A = sin(180 − A).

c. For angles greater than 180° but less than or equal to 270°, sin A = −sin(A − 180).

d. For angles greater than 270° but less than or equal to 360°, sin A = −sin(360 − A).

e. sin 0° = 0
sin 90° = 1
sin 180° = 0
sin 270° = −1
sin 360° = sin 0° = 0

For angles greater than 360°, reduce the angle to one between 0° and 360° as discussed in Chapter 7. Although a sine table is useful, it is not nearly as handy or easy to use as the sine function on a small scientific calculator.

EXAMPLE:
Calculate sin 243 using a calculator. ∎

SOLUTION:

Enter angle ② ④ ③
Select sin function (sin)
Read answer −0.8910065.

Notice that the minus sign has been supplied by the calculator. The graph of $y = \sin x$ where x varies from −360° to +360° degrees is shown in Figure 9.31. ∎

Figure 9.31 The graph of $y = \sin x$ for x = −360° to +360°.

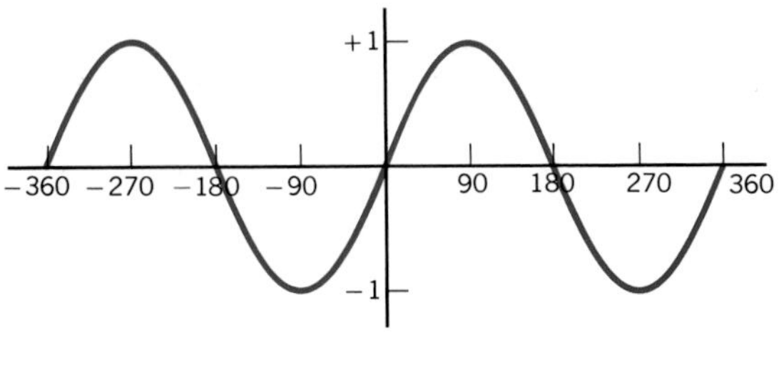

Calculate the following sine functions using a calculator:

a. sin 36°	b. sin 45°
c. sin 160°	d. sin 189°
e. sin 220°	f. sin 90°
g. sin −13°	h. sin 270°
i. sin 345°	j. sin 390°
k. sin 180°	l. sin 0°
m. sin −723°	n. sin −7°

o. $\sin\left(\dfrac{\pi}{2}R\right)$

Hint: either convert $\dfrac{\pi}{2}R$ to degrees or use the RADIAN setting of your calculator.

Another trignometric function found in electronics is the cosine function. The cosine of an angle in a right triangle is defined as the length of the adjacent side divided by the length of the hypotenuse, as shown in Figure 9.32. In contrast to the sine of an angle of 0°, which is equal to 0, the adjacent side of an angle is almost equal to the hypotenuse when the angle is nearly 0°, as shown in Figure 9.33a. At 0° the cosine of the

Figure 9.32 The cosine of an angle.

$$\text{Cosine } A \text{ or } \cos A = \frac{\text{Adjacent side}}{H}$$

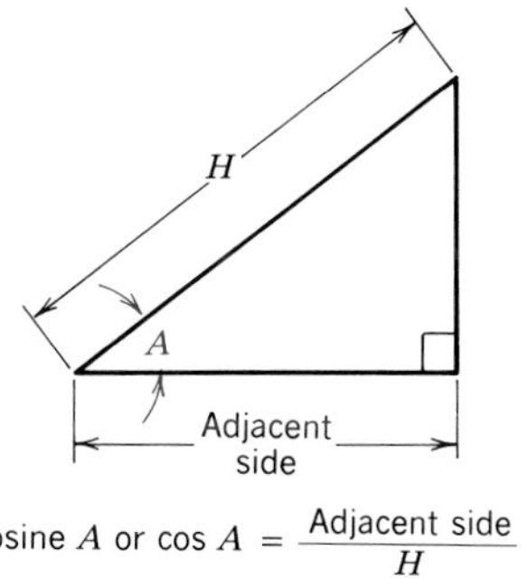

Figure 9.33 The value of the cosine varies from almost 1 for a small angle to almost 0 for an angle near 90°.

$$\text{Cos } A = \frac{L}{H}$$

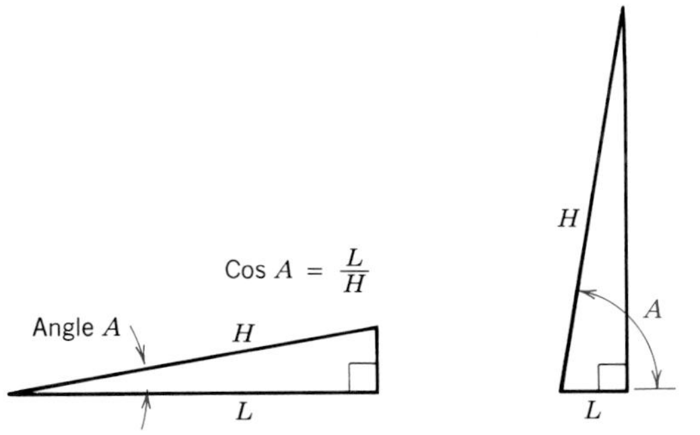

(a) When the angle is small, the length of the adjacent side is nearly the length of the hypotenuse.

(b) When the angle is close to 90°, the length of the adjacent side and the cosine are both small.

Angle B is the supplement of A
For angles greater than 90° but less than or equal to 180°, cos A = −cos(180 − A)

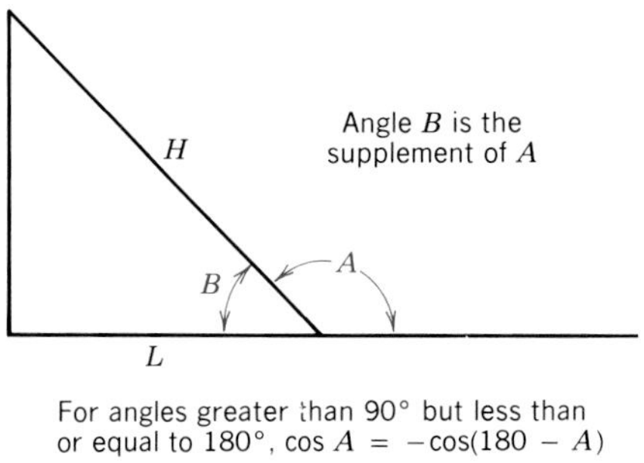

Figure 9.34 The definition of the cosine of an angle greater than 90° and less than or equal to 180°.

For angles greater than 180° but less than or equal to 270°, cos A = −cos(A − 180)

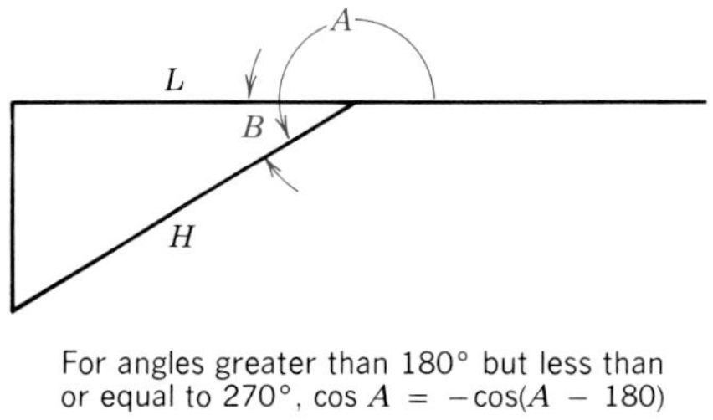

Figure 9.35 The definition of the cosine of an angle greater than 180° and less than or equal to 270°.

For angles greater than 270° but less than or equal to 360° cos A = cos(360 − A)

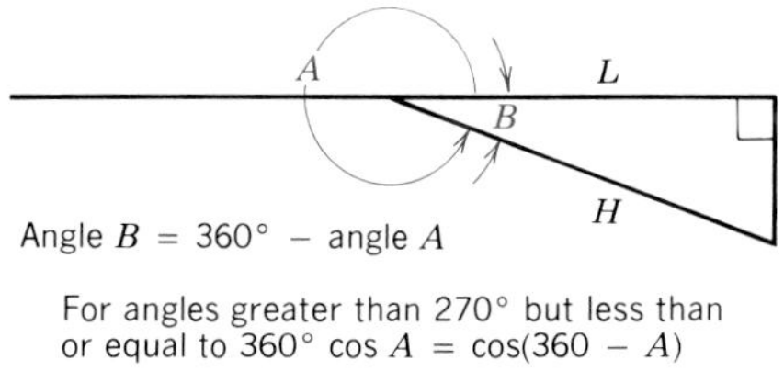

Figure 9.36 The definition of the cosine of an angle greater than 270° and less than or equal to 360°.

angle, then, is 1. As the angle increases, as seen in Figure 9.33b, the length of the adjacent side decreases, and the value of the cosine function is zero when the angle is 90°. For angles greater than 90° and less than or equal to 180°, as shown in Figure 9.34, the cosine of angle A is equal to −cosine (180 − A). For example, cos 120° = −cos(180 − 120), or −cos 60. As a formula this is

cos A (greater than 90 but
　　less than or equal to 180)　　FORMULA 9.12
　　= −cos(180 − A)

As can be seen from the formula, cos 180 = −1. Between 180° and 270°, as shown in Figure 9.35, the correct formula is

cos A (greater than 180 but
　　less than or equal to 270)　　FORMULA 9.13
　　= −cos(A − 180)

At 270°, the cosine of the angle is zero. Between 270° and 360°, as shown in Figure 9.36, the value of the

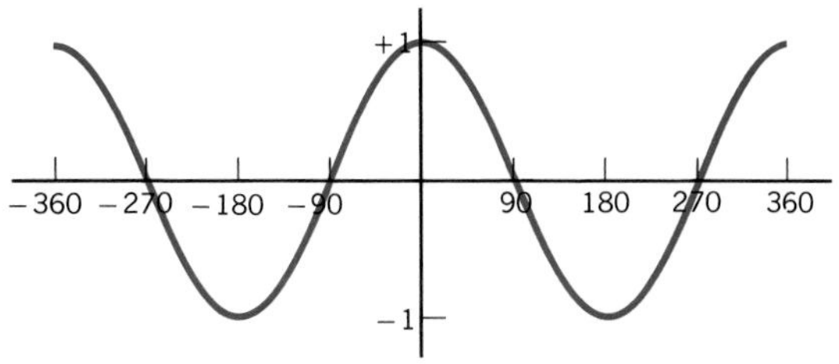

Figure 9.37 The graph of $y = \cos x$ for $x = -360°$ to $+360°$.

cosine is positive:

$\cos A$ (greater than 270 but less than or equal to 360) $= \cos(360 - A)$ FORMULA 9.14

The graph of a cosine function, $y = \cos x$ where x varies from $-360°$ to $+360°$ is shown in Figure 9.37.

In summary, the important facts to remember about the cosine function are:

a. The cosine of an angle A in a right triangle is equal to the length of the side adjacent to the angle divided by the length of the hypotenuse, or,

$$\cos A = \frac{\text{adjacent}}{\text{hypotenuse}}$$

b. For angles greater than 90° but less than or equal to 180°, $\cos A = -\cos(180 - A)$.

c. For angles greater than 180° but less than or equal to 270°, $\cos A = -\cos(A - 180)$.

d. For angles greater than 270° but less than or equal to 360°, $\cos A = \cos(360 - A)$.

e. $\cos 0° = 1$

$\cos 90° = 0$

$\cos 180° = -1$

$\cos 360° = \cos 0° = 1$

EXAMPLE:

Calculate the cosine of 119° using a calculator. ■

SOLUTION:

Enter the angle	[1] [1] [9]
Select cos function	[cos]
Read answer on display	−0.4848096.

As in the case of sine values, the calculator supplies the negative for the cosine of an angle between 180° and 270°. ■

Compute the following cosine values using a calculator

a. cos 30°
b. sin 60°
c. cos 60°
d. sin 30°
e. cos 0
f. cos 115°
g. cos 181.9°
h. cos 226°
i. cos 270°
j. cos 282 − cos 60
k. cos 45/sin 45
l. cos 30/sin 30
m. cos(−680)
n. cos(−37)
o. $\cos\left(\frac{3\pi}{2}\text{R}\right)$

Hint: either convert $\frac{3\pi}{2}$R to degrees or use the RADIAN setting of your calculator.

If you know the value of the sine or the cosine of an angle, it is an easy task to calculate the angle on a scientific calculator. The angle whose sine is 0.5 is called "arcsin 0.5." This is frequently also written as $\sin^{-1} 0.5$, and is read as "the angle whose sine is 0.5." The angle whose cosine is 0.5 is called "arccos 0.5," or $\cos^{-1} 0.5$. Some calculators have separate keys for arcsin and arccos, while others require the pressing of an arc or inv key before the sin or cos key.

EXAMPLE:

In a right triangle, the length of the side adjacent to an angle is 0.06 m long. The hypotenuse is 0.08 m long. What is the angle formed? ■

SOLUTION:

If this subject is rather new to you, it may help to draw a diagram, as is done in Figure 9.38. The cosine of angle A is adjacent/hypotenuse $= 0.75$, so,

Enter cosine	[0] [.] [7] [5]
Select arccos	[INV] or [ARC] [cos]
Read angle on the display	41.409622° ■

There are four additional trigonometric functions, but they are less frequently used in electronics and

Figure 9.38 Example of an arccos calculation.

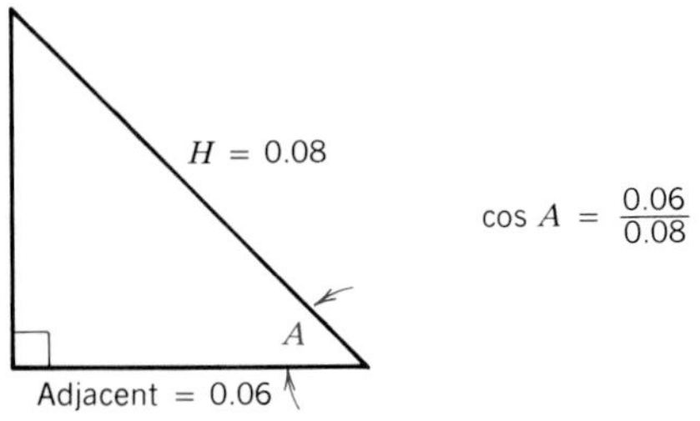

need not be studied at this point. Use your calculator to find the following angles. Round off the answers to three significant figures.

a. arccos 0 b. arccos 0.7071
c. $\sin^{-1} 0.866$ d. $\cos^{-1} - 0.03489$
e. arcsin 354 f. $\dfrac{\cos 272}{\text{arccos } 0.3489}$
g. $\sin^{-1} 0$
i. arcsin -0.1218 h. $\cos^{-1} - 0.45$
k. arcsin 0 j. $\cos^{-1} - 0.866$
m. arccos -0.3256 l. $\cos^{-1} - 1$

Provide the following angles in radians:

n. $\cos^{-1} 0.5253$ o. $\cos^{-1} 0.8910$
p. arcsin 0.3090 q. $\sin^{-1} 0.45$

D. APPLICATIONS

D.1 ELECTROMAGNETIC COMPONENTS

Some of the "electronic" components in use today are actually electromagnetic in nature. The most important of these will be discussed in this and following chapters. In fact, as you will learn in later chapters, it is almost impossible to consider electrical effects without dealing with magnetism also. In this section two common electromagnetic components will be studied: electromagnetic circuit breakers which are used like fuses for component protection, and electromagnetic relays, which are electrically operated switches.

D.2 CIRCUIT BREAKERS

Although the fuse is a simple way to protect circuits and components, the use of a fuse is not suitable in certain applications. Where power surges are common, nuisance failure of fuses is frequent. In addition to the expense of purchasing and keeping fuses in stock, the time wasted in fuse replacement is sometimes a problem.

Another solution to the problem of circuit protection has been the development of the circuit breaker, which combines the functions of a fuse and an off–on switch. There are three principal kinds of circuit breakers: the magnetic breaker, which is a fast-acting device; the thermal breaker, which is operated by a buildup of heat; and a third type, which combines both the magnetic and thermal types. All types of circuit breakers operate by changing from closed-circuit to open-circuit devices when tripped by the passage of a current greater than their rated current. Most have no automatic reset ability: Once they have been tripped by a greater-than-rated current, they have to be manually reset. Some breakers, however, particularly the thermally operated type, may be of the automatic reset type. Once set and then tripped by excessive current, automatic reset breakers will attempt to reset themselves and restore the circuit they have opened. Sometimes, the condition that caused the breaker to trip will no longer exist. In this case, the breaker will reset and the power connection will be restored to the circuit. If, however, the condition that caused the excessive current flow is still present, the breaker will again trip, opening the electric power connection to the protected unit or circuit.

Still another characteristic that distinguishes some circuit breakers from others is the fact that some breakers are *trip free*. This means that the tripping mechanism in the breaker is always free to operate and to open the circuit. Even if the actuating pushbutton or lever is held in the ON position, an overload will still open the circuit.

D.2.1 THERMAL CIRCUIT BREAKERS

A fuse, you will recall, burns out and opens a circuit when the current passing through it causes a certain amount of heat to be produced. A thermal, or heat-operated, circuit breaker also opens a circuit when too high a current produces a certain amount of heat. The difference between the two is that the circuit breaker can be reset. Nothing burns out. Instead, a bi-metallic element bends and releases a trigger, which allows switch contacts to be pulled apart. A simplified, cutaway view of a typical thermal breaker is shown in Figure 9.39. When a current passes through the ele-

Figure 9.39 Cutaway view of a push-type thermal circuit breaker.

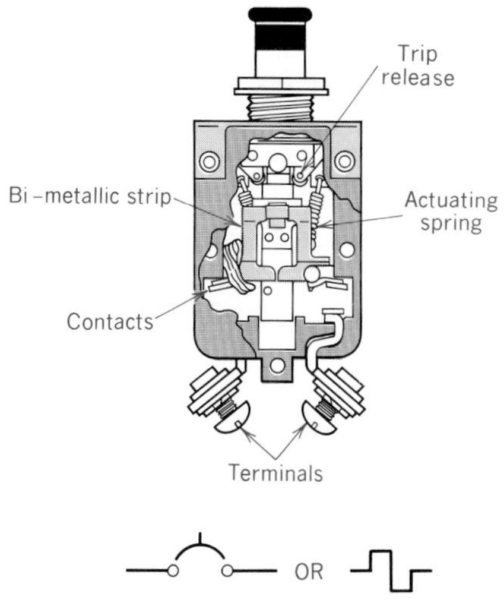

Schematic symbols

ment, a certain amount of heat is produced. This heat causes the two metal strips that make up the bi-metallic strip to expand. Since it is made up of two different metals, one of which expands more than the other, the bi-metallic strip bends as it is heated. The bending of the strip releases the trigger when a certain temperature is reached. Thus, if the current through the breaker is greater than the breaker rating, the bending of the bi-metallic strip will trip the breaker. If the current is not higher than the breaker rating, the heat loss through the breaker body will serve to keep the bi-metallic strip below its trip temperature.

Once the thermal breaker has tripped, the element and bi-metallic strip begin to cool. In an automatically resetting breaker, the cooling of the bi-metallic element and the return to its original shape releases the trigger, which is then reset by a second spring mechanism. In the non-self-resetting, trip-free breaker, the cooling of the element will make it possible to manually reset the breaker.

Thermal circuit breakers are not quick-acting devices. The buildup of heat in the relatively massive breaker mechanism takes a certain amount of time. Naturally, it will also take a certain amount of time to cool the system. This means that there will always be a delay between the beginning of an overload condition and the time that the breaker trips. The reverse is also true. It is necessary for the bi-metallic strip to cool sufficiently before the breaker can be reset. These two delay times are called the *trip delay* and *reset delay*, respectively.

The trip-delay time of a thermal breaker, like that associated with the opening of a fuse, depends on the percentage of the overload and on the starting temperature of the element. A standard trip thermal breaker will typically trip within 30 s with an overload of double its rated current, within 2.5 s with an overload of 5 times its rated current, and within 0.6 s with an overload of 10 times its rated current. If the circuit element is at a high temperature due to high air temperatures, the trip delay will be shorter, while the reset delay will be longer. At ambient temperatures approaching 54°C, nuisance tripping becomes a problem. On the other hand, extreme cold can increase the breaker rating and the trip delay. Sensitivity to ambient temperatures is the principal reason thermal breakers are not as widely used as they might be.

Although their sensitivity to temperature and relatively long delay time make thermal circuit breakers less desirable for protecting solid-state circuits, they are ideal for use with motors, lamps, and wiring. The way in which wiring reacts to current overloads is exactly the way in which a thermal breaker reacts, both in terms of ability to resist very short-term current surges and sensitivity to ambient temperature. Using a thermal circuit breaker that has a rating of about 80 percent of the safe current capacity of the wiring will provide good protection.

D.2.2 MAGNETIC CIRCUIT BREAKERS AND THERMAL-MAGNETIC CIRCUIT BREAKERS

The reason for not including circuit breakers in the discussion of fuses in Chapter 6 is that a large percentage of the circuit breakers in service today are magnetically operated. In principle, a magnetic circuit breaker is a coil of wire and switch contact in series with the protected circuit. When a magnetic circuit breaker is set, the breaker contacts are closed as shown in Figure 9.40. The flow of current through the breaker coil produces a magnetic field that exerts a force on a metal tab. Since the amount of force on the tab is proportional to the current in the coil, the tab will only trip the breaker when its current rating is exceeded. Unlike the fuse or thermal circuit breakers, which require a buildup of heat in order to actuate a mechanism or melt a fuse element, the force in a magnetic circuit breaker is produced almost instantaneously, and the trip-delay time can be very short. The typical trip time for a magnetic breaker carrying a current six times its normal rating can be as low as 20 milliseconds. On the other hand, the trip time for a commercially available magnetic breaker carrying twice its rated current sometimes closely approaches that of a thermal breaker with the same rating. This is true because many magnetic circuit breakers used in industry include a mechanism that reduces the possibility of nuisance tripping when the equipment is first turned on. This mechanism generally uses a principle called *hydraulic damping*. In simplified form, the breaker tripping mechanism is required to overcome the resistance of a fluid before it

Figure 9.40 Cutaway view of a magnetic circuit breaker.

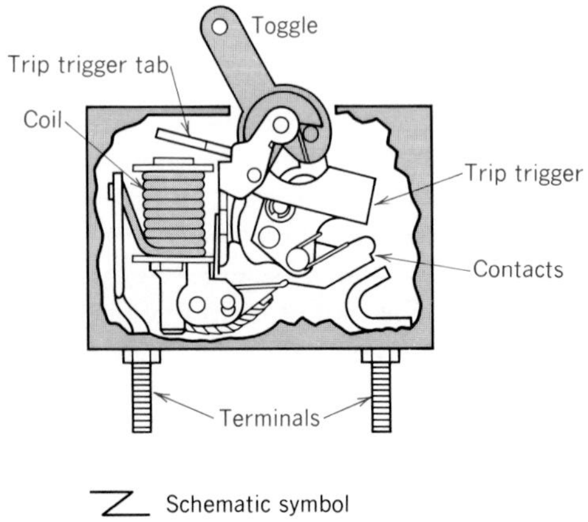

reaches the trip point. Magnetic and hydraulically damped magnetic circuit breakers are manufactured in ratings from 0.1 A to hundreds of amperes, and with built-in time delays to fit many applications.

A thermal-magnetic circuit breaker combines a thermal breaker and a magnetic breaker in a single package. In this type of breaker, the thermal breaker mechanism has a lower rating than the magnetic breaker with which it is connected in series. The thermal breaker is more resistant to nuisance tripping since it takes a certain amount of time for the bi-metallic strip to heat up and deform sufficiently to trip the breaker. On the other hand, a massive overload on the order of five or six times the rated current of the magnetic breaker portion will cause this quick-acting device to trip.

D.3 RELAYS

D.3.1 RELAYS IN GENERAL

A relay is actually a special kind of switch. Although certain other kinds of components are called relays, for the purposes of this chapter, a relay is a component with the following characteristics:

a. It is operated by an electric current, which produces a magnetic field.

b. A mechanical action caused by the magnetic field opens or closes pairs of electrical switch contacts that make or break one or more circuits.

The first of these characteristics eliminates a large number of automatic, mechanically-operated switches, such as air-pressure-operated switches. This characteristic eliminates the *thermal relay*, previously used as a time-delay device, and also eliminates the modern *solid-state relay*. The solid-state relay is a semiconductor device that has no moving parts and does not make use of a magnetic field.

The second characteristic eliminates certain electromechanical devices such as solenoids and hydraulic valves. In certain respects, these devices resemble the armature relay, but are not used for electrical switching purposes.

There are two major kinds of electromagnetic relays in use today: the armature relay and the reed relay. They are similar in that they both contain a coil of wire, usually in the shape of a solenoid. Electric current is supplied to the coil to activate the relay.

D.3.2 ARMATURE RELAYS

The armature relay was one of the earliest electronic components to be developed and has not changed much over time. In this type of relay, as shown in Figure

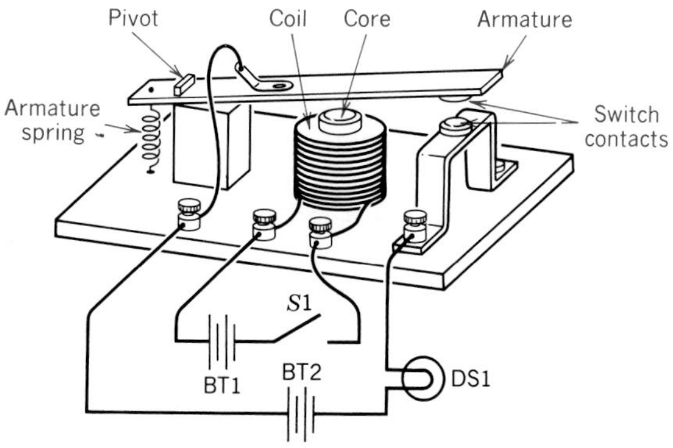

Figure 9.41 An armature relay and circuit.

9.41, the coil is wound in the shape of a solenoid and has a ferromagnetic core. When an electric current passes through the coil, a strong magnetic field is produced that attracts a hinged or pivoted metal bar called the *armature*. This mechanical action brings the switch contacts together and completes the circuit composed of source BT2 and lamp DS1. When the coil current is cut off, the armature spring pulls the armature back to its rest or unenergized position. This separates the two switch contacts and breaks the circuit between BT2 and DS1.

Another form of armature relay is shown in Figure 9.42. Here the armature is pivoted near the electromagnetic core. When a high enough current passes through the coil, the force produced overcomes the force of the spring and the twisting motion of the armature pushes a small lever that brings the contacts together, completing the external circuit. When the current through the coil is interrupted, the spring quickly brings the armature back to the rest or unenergized position.

In all forms of the armature relay, the essential characteristic is that one or more sets of electrical con-

Figure 9.42 Exploded view of a pivoted armature relay.

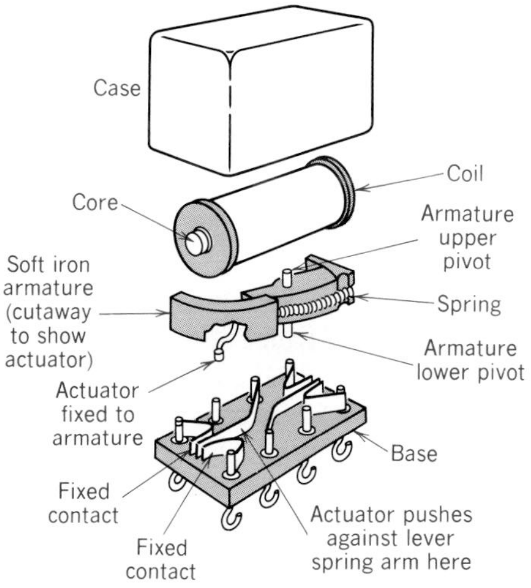

tacts are opened or closed by mechanical action when a ferromagnetic armature is attracted by the field of an electromagnet. Since the armature relay contains moving parts, it is more subject to breakdown than a purely electronic circuit. A technician must understand the operating characteristics of an armature relay and its failure modes in order to maintain units containing such relays. Each major class of armature relays has certain special operating characteristics and failure modes. The four major classes of armature relays are general-purpose relays, sensitive relays, low-level relays, and power relays.

a. General-Purpose Relays. Most of these relays are operated by direct current, although relays with coils operated by alternating current are fairly common. (It is not too hard to spot a relay designed for ac operation, even if it is not marked—most have a copper ring around the core near the armature. General-purpose relays have a wide variety of contact types and are used to switch currents of up to 10 A.

b. Sensitive Relays. These relays are called *sensitive* because they require very little power for operation. The coil power is on the order of 100 mW or less.

c. Low-Level Relays. Low-level relays are designed with switch contacts for switching very low power circuits. These circuits are also called *dry circuits* and have circuit currents of a few microamperes. Small currents provide special problems for the switching contacts. Do not confuse the low-level relay with the sensitive relay. The sensitive relay requires very little coil power to operate, although its contacts may switch a fair amount of current. The coil of a low-level relay may require quite a bit of power, but the switch contacts are designed to provide reliable switching of very small currents.

d. Power Relays. These are relays designed to switch circuit currents greater than 10 A. Power relays, particularly those with heavy-duty switching contacts, are sometimes called *contactors*. They are frequently used in industrial equipment.

Relay manufacturers vary the design and materials used in the coil, contacts, armature, and frame to produce relays that fall into one of these major classes.

The relay coil consists of turns of insulated copper wire wound on a form called a *bobbin*. Depending on the total length of wire used and on the wire diameter, the coil will have a resistance ranging between several tens of ohms to several thousands. Generally, a relay is designed to operate when some standard potential difference is placed across the coil. Common operating voltages are 3, 5, 6, 12, 24, and 48 V dc, and 6, 12, 24, 120, and 240 V ac. Five-volt dc relay coils are becoming more popular in modern digital equipment.

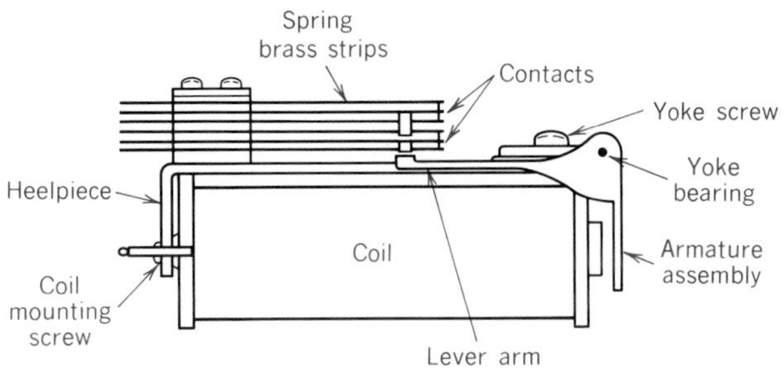

Figure 9.43 A telephone-type, general-purpose, armature relay.

In Section B, you learned that the magnetomotive force produced by a coil is equal to the number of turns times the coil current. Since the force on the armature must overcome the force of a spring, and hold the switch contacts together, the strength of the magnetomotive force produced by the coil is a critical factor in the operation of the relay. Where a coil current on the order of 1 A is used, sufficient force may be produced by a moderate number of turns of heavy wire. The coil resistance will be low. On the other hand, if the circuit supplying current to the relay coil can provide only a few milliamperes, the relay coil will have to be made up of a larger number of turns of wire in order to produce enough force to hold the armature against the spring tension.

In the simplified relay drawing, Figure 9.41, the simplest form of relay contact is shown. A moving contact attached to the relay armature is held in its open position by a spring. When the coil is magnetized, the armature pivots on its hinge and the moving and stationary contacts are brought together. A more practical arrangement is shown in Figure 9.43. In this type, the contacts are attached to strips of spring brass. When the relay coil is energized, the armature assembly pivots about the yoke bearing and the lever arm forces the common contacts away from the normally closed contacts and into contact with the normally open con-

Figure 9.44 Schematic diagram of the relay shown in Figure 9.43.

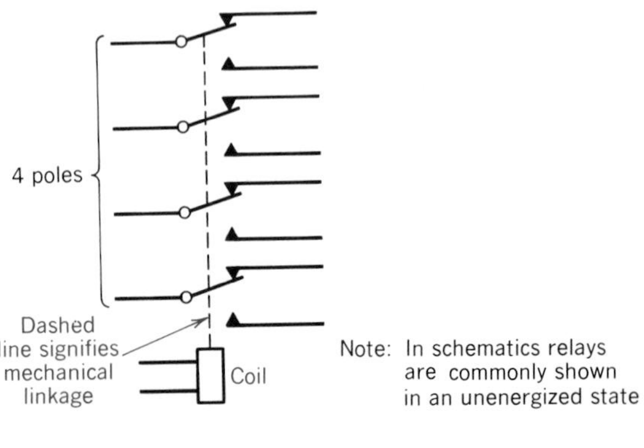

tacts. When the relay current is cut off, the spring brass strips to which the common contacts are fastened force the armature back into its rest or unenergized position.

As you can see from Figure 9.43, a fairly complex collection of contacts can be operated by a single coil and armature. The schematic diagram of the relay pictured in Figure 9.43 is shown in Figure 9.44. As in the case of the toggle switch, each movable contact and its associated normally open and normally closed contacts are referred to as a *pole*. (Using the same word for a switch pole and a magnetic pole is unfortunate, but no confusion should occur.)

A single switch pole may be composed of a stationary contact and a movable contact that are brought together when the coil is energized. This type of pole is called a *single-throw, normally open (NO) contact*, or a *FORM A contact*. Figure 9.45 shows the schematic symbol for a FORM A contact. Notice that the switch contacts are normally shown in the position they are in when the coil is de-energized. A second sort of pole consists of a combination of a stationary contact and a movable contact that are touching when the relay coil is de-energized and are separated when there is current through the coil. This type of pole is called a *single-throw, normally closed (NC) contact*, or a *FORM B contact*. The schematic symbol for a FORM B contact is given in Figure 9.46. A double-throw transfer pole is a combination of two stationary contacts and a common or movable contact, which touches one of the stationary contacts when the coil is deenergized but switches to touch the other stationary contact when there is current through the relay. A transfer pole is called a *FORM C contact*; its schematic symbol is shown in Figure 9.47.

Another kind of relay switch pole is the double-make contact. In this kind of pole, a movable contact or pair of connected contacts simultaneously makes the connection between two stationary contacts. An example of this type is shown in Figure 9.48*a*. It is common to combine a pair of double-make and double-break poles together, producing the arrangement shown in Figure 9.48*b*. This type of switch contact is frequently used for the higher current models of the general-purpose relay and for many power relays.

Figure 9.45 Schematic symbol for a FORM A contact.

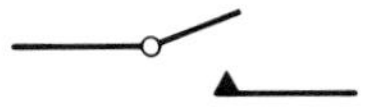

Figure 9.46 Schematic symbol for a FORM B contact.

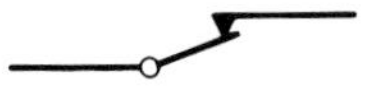

Figure 9.47 Schematic symbol for a FORM C or TRANSFER contact.

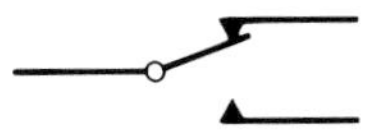

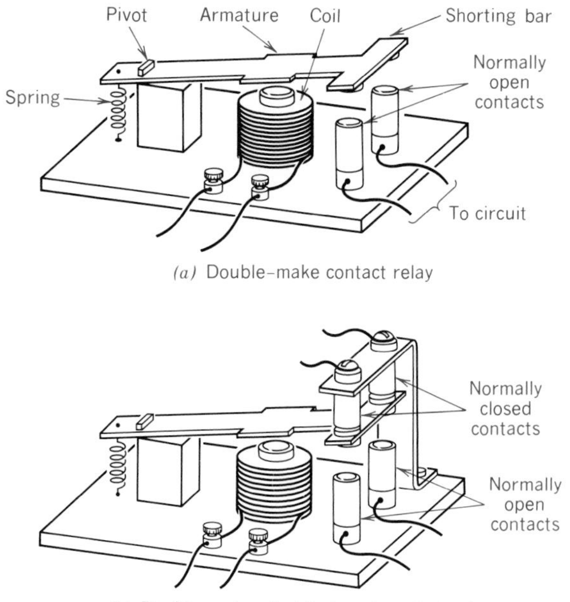

(a) Double-make contact relay

(b) Double-make, double-break contact relay

Figure 9.48 Double-make contacts.

Regardless of the type of switching arrangement used in a relay, it takes some time for the mechanical operation to take place. This time is called the *response time*, or *response speed*, of the relay. For armature relays with a small gap between the contacts or an armature with a small mass, the time necessary for the relay to go from its unenergized to its energized state is about 2 to 3 milliseconds. This is the *pull-in time* of the relay. The *release time*, that is, the time it takes the relay to go back to its unenergized position once the current has been cut off, is somewhat less than the pull-in time. For large-sized, general-purpose relays, the pull-in time is on the order of 15 to 25 milliseconds. Since modern digital circuits operate at a speed of a *microsecond* (10^{-6} s) or less, a millisecond is a long time.

D.3.3 REED RELAYS

A solution to the difficulties found in using relays in modern, high-speed equipment is the reed relay. The central part of a reed relay is a magnetically-operated reed switch. The switch takes the place of the armature, armature spring, pivot, core, and contacts used in the armature relay. A typical reed switch is shown in Figure 9.49. It consists of two flat reeds made of a springy ferromagnetic material. The reeds are sealed in a glass tube filled with nitrogen gas to prevent oxidation of the contact areas. The reed switch is then used as the core of a solenoid, as shown in Figure 9.50. When an electric current passes through the coil, the

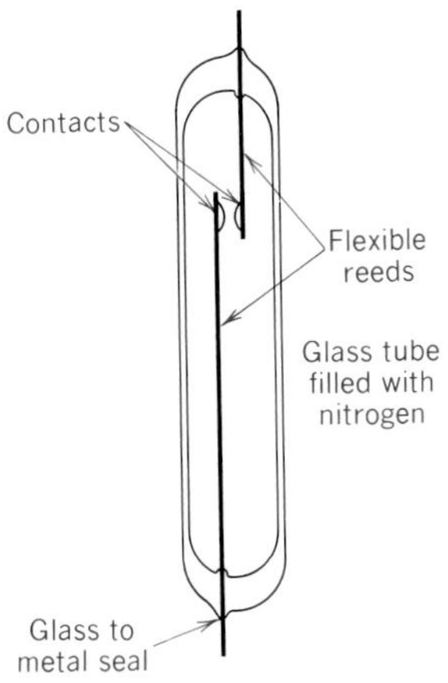

Figure 9.49 Typical reed switch.

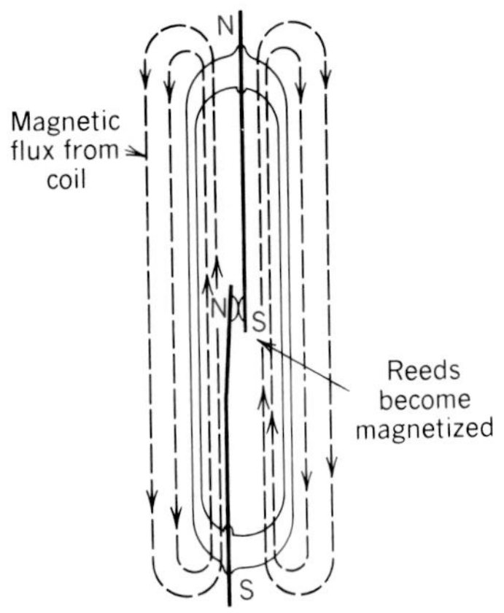

Figure 9.51 The flux produced by the coil causes the overlapping ends of the reeds to become opposite magnetic poles and to attract each other.

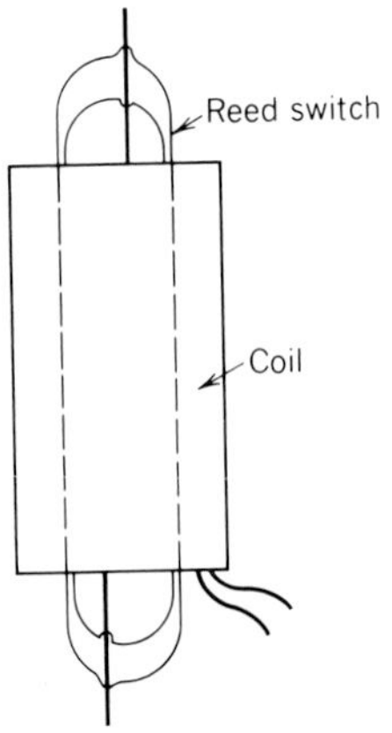

Figure 9.50 The reed switch is used as the core of the relay coil.

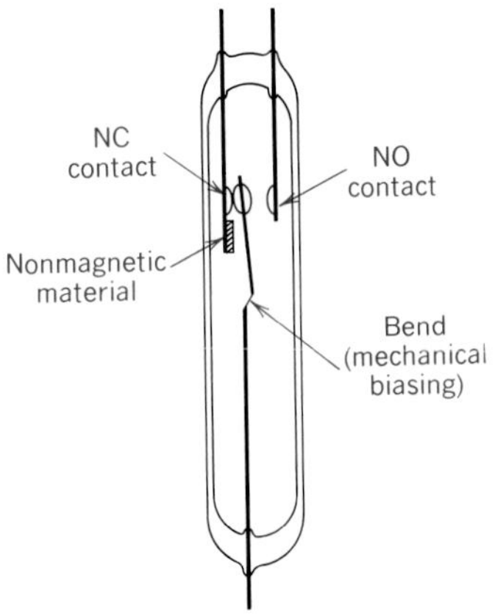

Figure 9.52 A FORM C reed switch.

magnetic field produced around the solenoid passes through the reed switch and the overlapping ends of the two reeds become opposite magnetic poles. If the force of attraction between the two reeds is strong enough to overcome the force of the spring, the reeds move together and touch. This brings the two contact areas together and completes the external circuit, as seen in Figure 9.51. When the current through the coil is cut off, the magnetic field no longer produces a force of attraction between the contact ends of the two reeds. The reeds then spring back to the position of Figure 9.49.

A number of contact types exist in addition to the single-pole, single-throw or FORM A type switch shown in Figure 9.49. The next most widely used form is the single-pole, double-throw or FORM C contact shown in Figure 9.52. In this switch type, only one of the reeds actually moves. The longer reed is bent so that it will touch the normally closed contact when there is no magnetic field present. The use of such a bend is called *mechanical biasing*. In the unenergized condition, the movable reed is held against the normally closed contact by its spring action. Notice that a small block of nonmagnetic metal has been added. This block is welded or brazed to the normally closed terminal. When the coil surrounding this type of switch is energized, the resulting magnetic field causes the contact end of the movable reed and the normally open reed to develop opposite magnetic polarities. This moves the movable reed toward the normally open contact. The block of nonmagnetic material prevents the normally closed reed from attracting the movable reed. When the current to the relay coil stops, the magnetic flux disappears and the mechanical biasing of the spring action returns the movable reed to the position of Figure 9.52.

In addition to the mechanical biasing method described above, *magnetic biasing* is also used. This method uses a small permanent magnet placed so that its magnetic field holds the movable reed contact tightly against the normally closed contact. When the solenoid coil is energized, the magnetic field of the coil overcomes the weaker field of the biasing magnet, and the movable reed is forced against the normally open contact.

Because the reed switch is sealed in a pressurized glass tube that has been filled with an inert gas, the distance between the fixed and moving contacts of the switch can be separated by a smaller space than is required in an armature relay. The inert gas prevents oxidizing or contamination of the reed switch contacts and the gas pressure in the glass tube minimizes arcing. The reduced spacing in the reed switch means that the actual distance traveled by the moving switch contact is smaller, and the switching time required is less than that required for an armature relay. The fact that the movable reed and contact are less massive than an armature also contributes to the faster operation of the reed relay. Reed relay operation times of 1 millisecond or less are common.

Because of the close spacing of the reed switch contacts, special alloys that resist surface pitting are required. The most widely used in low-to-medium power applications is an alloy of gold and rhodium. Contacts made of this material often have a life expectancy of 20 million operations or more. For medium or higher power ratings, tungsten contacts may be used, although reed relays are rarely found in power circuits that require switching of more than 1 to 2 A.

Another type of switch contact is the mercury-wetted contact, in which a thin film of liquid mercury coats the relay contacts. This type of contact has an extremely long life since the liquid mercury, which is a conductor, is not subject to pitting. In addition, the mercury film reduces or entirely eliminates contact bounce. Because the mercury is liquid, this type of relay must be kept in an upright position at all times.

D.3.4 RELAY CASES

In contrast to resistors, which are manufactured in standard sizes and markings, relay manufacturers have gone to great lengths to vary the physical shape and size of their products. Choosing a relay for use in a new circuit or replacing a failed relay that is no longer available is therefore a matter not only of finding a unit with the proper operating characteristics but also of finding a unit that fits in the space available.

An example of a widely used relay shape is that based on the old-fashioned crystal can shown in Figure 9.53. Used for early airborne armature-type relays, this case style is well suited for mounting on a metal chassis. Although the base size has remained fairly constant, the height of this type of relay varied. Thus more room could be provided for more complex or heavier-duty switch contacts.

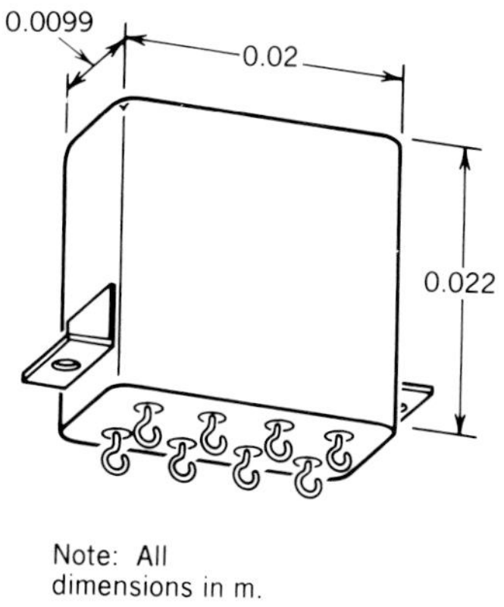

Figure 9.53 A crystal can relay package.

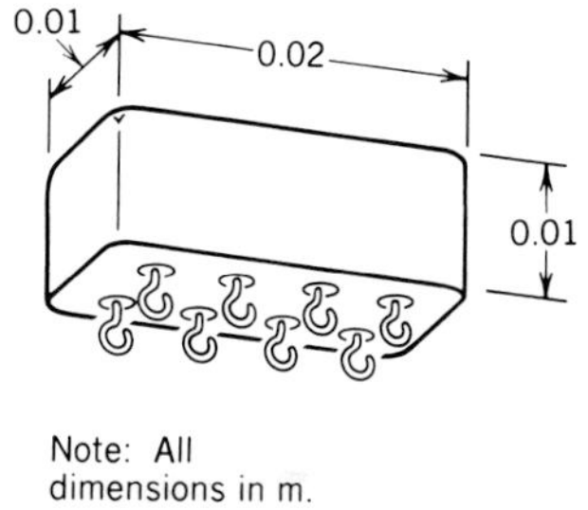

Figure 9.54 The 1/2-sized crystal can relay.

The most popular relay size in this series is the $\frac{1}{2}$ crystal can relay illustrated in Figure 9.54. This case style is frequently sealed under nitrogen gas pressure, which keeps the relay free from dust contamination and considerably increases the life of the switch contacts. Because of the convenient shape, a large number of $\frac{1}{2}$ crystal can relays can be mounted in a small space, and the all-metal cover provides a good degree of shielding to prevent interference with low-level signals caused by sparking relay contacts.

Other sizes used are the full crystal can, which provides a great deal of room for the switching contacts or for a large-sized, high-sensitivity coil, and the stubby $\frac{1}{6}$ crystal can relay. The latter size is particularly useful for mounting on slide-out assemblies.

With the necessity for increased miniaturization, reliability, and speed of operation, the relay lost ground to the transistor. Relay manufacturers began to put their products in cases that would rival transistors in size or be suitable for mounting on printed circuit boards. One method was to place a tiny relay into a standard-sized transistor package, as shown in Figure 9.55. Another solution was the use of the low-profile case style for reed relays illustrated in Figure 9.56.

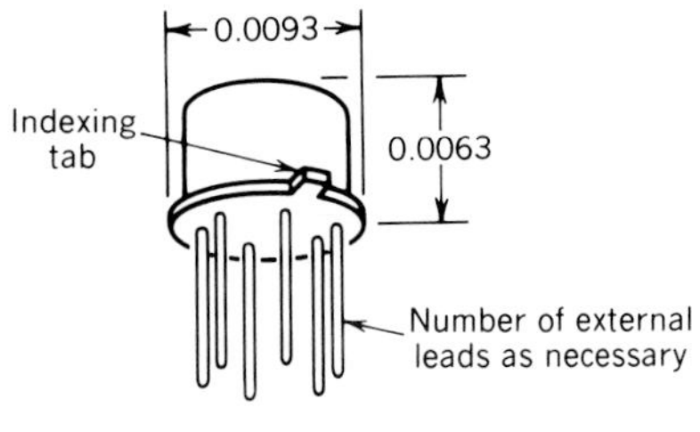

Figure 9.55 Transistor-sized relay package.

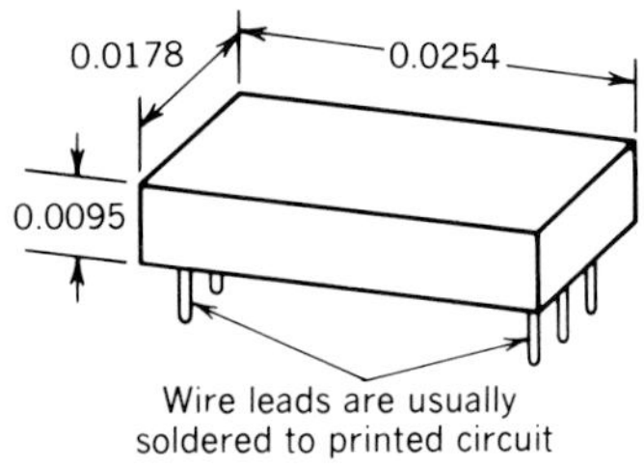

Figure 9.56 Low-profile case style.

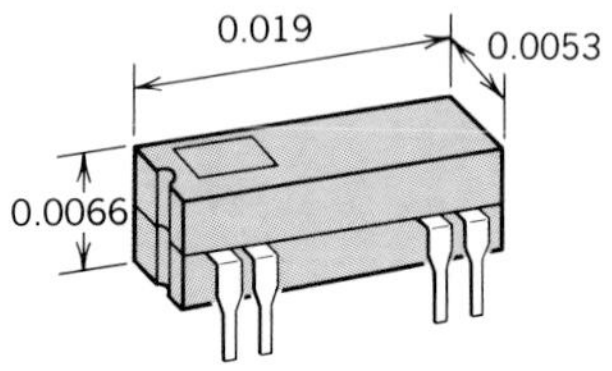

Figure 9.57 The dual in-line pin, or dip relay case.

With the invention and use of integrated circuits, the dual in-line pin, or *dip* relay, has been introduced. This small reed relay is enclosed in a case that is the same size and shape as an integrated circuit (see Figure 9.57). Because it is the same size and shape as an integrated circuit and has the same mounting requirements, this type of relay is suitable for many applications.

Looking to the future, the trend points to a survival of the electromechanical relay in special applications, particularly where medium to high power handling capacity is required.

D.3.5 CAUSES OF FAILURE IN RELAY CIRCUITS

Relays are electromechanical components and are subject to both electrical and mechanical failure. Temperature extremes and vibration can shorten the useful life of a relay considerably. Manufacturers' specification sheets often list lifetimes of 1 million switching operations for an armature relay and as many as 10 million operations for a reed relay. High vibration may reduce these figures to one-tenth of their normal values.

In addition to vibration, some causes of relay failure are: poor contact alignment; contaminated, welded, or pitted contacts; loss of resiliency in springs; and open-circuited or burned-out coils. When a relay has failed, it is important to determine the reason for failure. If the failure was due to simple wearing out of the mechanical parts (and this is *not* the most common failure mode), substitution of an identical relay provides the solution. On the other hand, if it appears that the current switching limits of the relay have been exceeded because of some change to the circuit, the use of a higher-capacity relay should be considered.

A common cause of relay failure is damage to the contact points. The size of the contact points, what they are made of, and the size of the gap between them in the open position are important characteristics. The current that flows through the contact area between the stationary and movable contacts of the relay can create enough heat to weld the contacts together, particularly if the contact area is small and the resistance at the point of contact is high. For this reason, contacts that are intended for circuits with high currents are large and made of materials that provide a compromise between hardness, ability to withstand high temperatures, and low resistance.

As in the case of switches, special attention must be paid to circuits that contain lamps. Lamps, you will recall, have very low resistance when they are cold. As the filament of the lamp heats, however, its resistance increases to the point at which the lamp draws its rated current. This means that relay contacts that switch lamp loads of about 2 A must be able to withstand an initial surge current of 10 times this figure, or 20 A. In order to keep these contacts from being welded together, massive contacts must be used in order to provide a large contact area and to channel away the heat produced at the point of contact.

In cases where the switched circuit consists of a number of lamps and relay failure occurs because of contact welding, a widely used "fix" is to insert a low-value resistor in series with the lamp, as shown in Figure 9.58. It is important that the resistor power dissipation be sufficient for the job since the resistor acts as the only load during the first few instants after the relay closes. Since nearly the entire potential difference supplied by the source, BT1, is applied across the load resistor, the power dissipated in the series resistor is given by $P = \dfrac{E^2}{R}$. For a 12-V line and a 5 Ω load resistor, this is just below 30 W. Using a 10 Ω resistor would lower the required dissipation to under

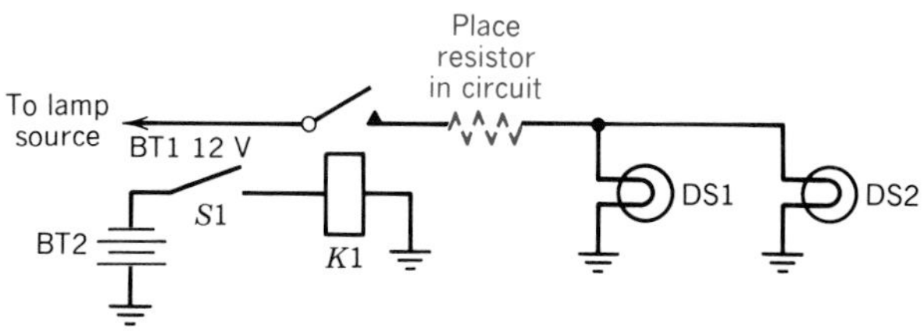

Figure 9.58 Placing a low resistance in series with a lamp circuit to protect relay contacts.

15 W. When the series resistor is inserted in the line to the lamps, the relay contact resistance does not act as the only line load during the initial moments of relay closing. It is the resistor and not the relay contact that heats up. This method of protecting relay contacts that are used to switch lamps is very effective and can result in an appreciable lengthening of the relay life. Because there is always a voltage drop across the resistor, this method can not be used in high-current circuits since the voltage drop across the resistor will cause the lamps to dim.

Certain loads, such as coils and motors, also produce large surge currents through relay contacts. Unlike lamps, however, they also produce voltage spikes that cause sparking when the contacts separate again after having been closed. This sparking, or *arcing* as it is generally called, may result in pitting, burning, and oxidation of the contact surfaces. Some contact sparking is desired if the contact material is hard enough to resist pitting. A reasonable amount of spark activity actually serves to clean the contacts by puncturing or knocking off the oxide coating that forms on the contacts.

Some sparking between relay contacts is necessary if the current through the relay contacts is just sufficient to cause surface contamination of the contacts, but is not sufficient to penetrate this surface layer or to provide a low-resistance current path. This is frequently the cause of failure in low-level relays. In operation, low-current, low-voltage contacts will sometimes operate properly, but at other times will not make electrical contact at all, or will provide a high-resistance contact, even though the relay is energized and the contacts are touching. A contact failure of this sort is called a *miss*. Intermittant failures of this sort are very hard to detect. This is especially true when the relay is removed from the circuit and is tested with higher currents or higher voltage applied to the switch contacts. The testing current will clean the contacts and the relay will operate properly. If the relay is then reinstalled in the circuit, it will continue to operate well, until the contact contamination layer is built up again.

Related to the miss due to the buildup of an oxide layer is the increase in the resistance between the relay contacts. This is called the *contact resistance* of the relay. Increase in contact resistance is one of the more common reasons for relay failure. The normal resistance between new relay contacts is generally on the order of only a few thousandths of an ohm. Pitting and the building up of irregular spikes in the contact area can raise the resistance to several hundred ohms or higher. The switch contacts of larger armature relays can sometimes be cleaned and polished using special cleaning tools and products. If this is not possible, as in the case of sealed case or reed relays, a large increase in the contact resistance means that a relay must be replaced.

Another problem associated with relay contacts is the problem of contact bounce. This is exactly what the name implies: When the moving and stationary contacts of the relay come into contact, the springiness of the armature or contact support permits the contacts to recoil and touch several times before the bouncing stops. This is a serious problem in many modern circuits. Special techniques are used to minimize contact bounce or to prevent its effects on computer-type circuits.

One problem of operation shared by both the armature-type and reed-type relay is the dependence of coil resistance upon temperature. In Chapter 5 the effect of temperature upon the resistance of a length of conducting wire was described. Since a relay coil is made up of many turns of thin copper wire, we may expect that the coil resistance will vary over an appreciable range as the temperature changes. Figure 9.59 is a graph showing how the resistance of a relay coil varies with its temperature. The x axis of the graph shows the temperature in degrees centigrade, while the

Figure 9.59 Graph showing how the resistance of a relay coil varies with its temperature.

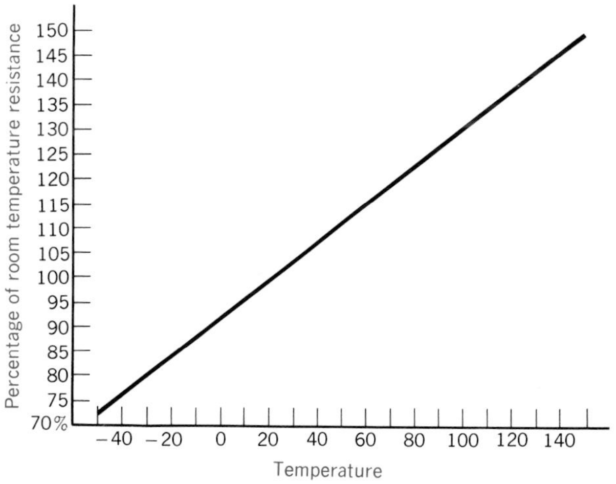

y axis shows the resistance of the coil as a percentage of its resistance at a normal room temperature of 20°C. For example, if a relay coil is marked as having a resistance of 1500 Ω, what is its resistance at −20°C and at 50°C?

This question is easy to answer using the graph of Figure 9.59 or Formula 5.2. The coil resistance marked on the relay, according to manufacturer's practice, is the room temperature resistance, called R_{20}. Tracing upward from the −20°C mark on the graph, we see that the coil resistance at this temperature will be only about 84.3 percent of the room temperature resistance,

$$1500 \times 0.843 = 1264.5\ \Omega$$

At a temperature of 50°C, the coil resistance can be seen to be about 110 percent of the R_{20} value. At 50°C, then, the resistance of the coil is 1650 Ω. In certain cases, this variation of the coil resistance may cause a relay to operate inconsistently, especially if other problems, such as worn switch contacts, are also present.

E. PROGRAMMED REVIEW

FRAME 1

The ability of a magnet to exert a force on a bit of iron can best be understood by referring to a ________ .

a. Magnetic field. (2)
b. Any other answer, review Section B1 and go on to Frame 2.

FRAME 2

Cite two important differences between an electric field and a magnetic field.

a. Your answer should include two of the following:
   i. The existence of magnetic poles.
   ii. The magnetic lines of force form closed loops between magnetic poles.
   iii. Magnetic poles are points of strongest magnetic activity in contrast to the distribution of electric charge over the surface of a charged object. (3)
b. Any answer that does not include two of these points, review Section B.1 and go on to Frame 3.

FRAME 3

A magnet which retains its ability to produce a magnetic field for a long time is referred to as a _______ .

a. Permanent magnet. (4)
b. Any other answer, review Section B.1 and go on to Frame 4.

FRAME 4

The pole of a magnet that turns toward the north is called the __________ , although __________ would be a better name.

a. North pole; north-seeking pole. (5)
b. Any other answer, review Section B.2.

FRAME 5

The force due to a magnetic field varies _________ .

a. Inversely with the square of the distance from the magnet. (6)
b. Any answer that does not specify inverse square, review Section B.2 and go on to Frame 6.

FRAME 6

There is a __________ near a current-carrying wire but not near an electrostatically charged object that is at rest.

a. Magnetic field. (7)
b. Any other answer, review Section B.2.

FRAME 7

Substances can be divided into three groups: those that are strongly attracted by either pole of a magnet, which are called __________ or __________ substances; those weakly attracted, which are called ________ ; and those that are repelled by either pole of a magnet, which are called __________ substances.

a. Strongly paramagnetic or ferromagnetic; paramagnetic, or weakly paramagnetic; diamagnetic. (8)
b. Any other answer, review Section B.2.

FRAME 8

Magnetic effects are explained by reference to two theories. These are __________ and __________ .

a. Electron spin; domains. (9)
b. Any answer that does not include both theories, review Section B.2 and go on to Frame 9.

FRAME 9

The direction of the magnetic field around a current-carrying conductor can be determined by using the __________. This rule states that if the __________ is pointed in the direction of the __________, the curved fingers will point in the direction of the force on a __________ placed at that point.

a. Left-hand rule for determining field direction around a conductor; thumb; current or electron drift; north magnetic pole or north pole. (10)
b. Any answer that does not include these points, review Section B.3.

FRAME 10

A __________ or __________ is produced by winding a length of wire into a series of closely spaced loops.

a. Coil; solenoid. (11)
b. Any other answer, review Section B.3.

FRAME 11

To determine the north pole of a current-carrying coil or solenoid, use the __________. This rule states that __________.

a. Left-hand rule for determining the north pole of a coil; if the fingers are curved in the direction of the current or electron drift through the coil, the thumb points to the north pole of the coil. (12)
b. Any answer that does not incorporate these ideas, review Section B.3.

FRAME 12

Magnetic induction, or flux density, is the name given to the quantity __________. It is defined as the strength of a magnetic field at a point or __________. It is measured in __________ or __________ /m^2.

a. B; through a small area at a right angle to the direction of the field; teslas; webers or Wb. (13)
b. Any other answer, review Section B.3.

FRAME 13

__________ magnetic lines of force per square meter represents a flux density of 1 tesla.

a. 10^8 (14)
b. Any other answer, review Section B.3 and go on to Frame 14.

FRAME 14

What does the quantity Φ represent in the formula $B = \Phi/A$? What unit is it measured in?

a. Flux or total magnetic flux; webers. (15)
b. Any other answer, review Section B.3 and go on to Frame 15.

FRAME 15

A hollow solenoid consisting of 1500 turns of fine wire is 0.1 m. long and has a resistance of 3 Ω. If it is connected to a 12-V battery, what will be the magnetic field intensity H produced?

a. 6×10^4 At/m (17)
b. Any other answer (16)

FRAME 16

The magnetic field intensity H is

$$H = \mathcal{F}/l = NI/l$$

The current will be $I = E/R$, or $12/3 = 4$ A, so

$$H = \frac{1500 \times 4}{0.1} = 60000 \text{ At/m}$$

Go on to Frame 17.

FRAME 17

When a closed metal core is placed in the solenoid of Frame 15, the flux density in the core is 0.24 T. What is the permeability of the material?

a. 4×10^{-6} Wb/At·m (18)
b. Any other answer, review Section B.3.

FRAME 18

The permeability of free space, μ, is __________.

a. $4\pi \times 10^{-7}$ or 12.57×10^{-7} Wb/At·m. (19)
b. Since many calculations involve μ_0, it is necessary to "memorize" this number. (19)

FRAME 19

How many terms are there in the equation $-6I_2 + 100(I_1 - I_3) + 48I_2 = 96$?

a. 4 (20)
b. Any other answer, review Section C.1 and go on to Frame 20.

FRAME 20

Match the terms in columns A and B.

Column A	*Column B*
1. cos *A*	a. $-\sin 9°$
2. arcsin *A*	b. cos 180°
3. sin 189°	c. adjacent/hypoteneuse
4. cos 320°	d. $\sin^{-1} A$
5 −1	e. $+\cos 40°$
6. cos −7°	f. + cos 7°
	g. opposite/hypoteneuse

a. 1–c, 2–d, 3–a, 4–e, 5–b, 6–f (21)
b. Any mismatches, review Section C.3.

FRAME 21

There are three types of circuit breakers; the ________, ________, and ________. The ________ type is often very fast-acting, while the ________ type combines the ability to tolerate surge currents with fast action in case of short circuit.

a. Thermal; magnetic; thermal-magnetic; magnetic; thermal-magnetic. (22)
b. Any other answer, review Section D.2.

FRAME 22

In a ________ circuit breaker, the breaker is able to open the circuit even if the lever is held in the ON position.

a. Trip free. (23)
b. Any other answer, review Section D.2 and go on to Frame 23.

FRAME 23

The major classes of armature relays are ________, ________, ________, and ________.

a. General purpose; sensitive; low level; and power (order not important). (24)
b. Any other answer, review Section D.3.2.

FRAME 24

A FORM B pole is normally ________.

a. Closed. (25)
b. Any other answer, review Figures 9.45, 9.46, and 9.47. Go on to Frame 25.

FRAME 25

The ________ relay makes use of the flux produced by a coil wound around the relay switch.

a. Reed. (26)
b. Any other answer, review Section D.3.3 and go on to Frame 26.

FRAME 26

The component pictured in Figure 9.60 is probably a ________. The package is called a ________.

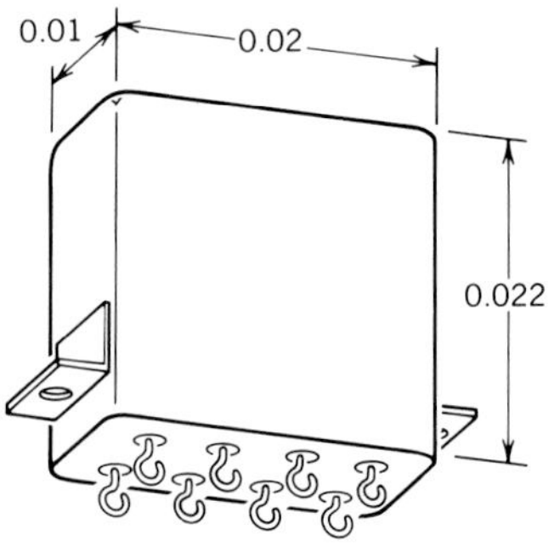

Figure 9.60 Figure for Frame 26.

a. Relay; crystal can package. (27)
b. Any other answer, review Section D.3.4 and go to Frame 27.

FRAME 27

True or False:

1. One million switching operations is not an unusual lifetime for an armature relay.

2. Arcing between relay switch contacts must always be eliminated.

3. Most relays just wear out.

4. Mercury-wetted relays can be used in any position.

5. Putting a low resistance in parallel with the load can protect relay switch contacts in lamp circuits.

6. A miss occurs when relay switch contacts touch but a built-up oxide layer provides only a high-resistance path between them.

7. The normal resistance between new relay contacts when they are closed is only a few tens of ohms.

8. Vibration is the principal cause of relay misses.

9. Contact bounce is desirable because it helps clean oxides off relay contacts.

10. Relays are sensitive to temperature extremes.

a. 1, T; 2–5, F; 6, T; 7–9 F; 10, T (END)
b. Any other answer, review Section D.3.5.

F. PROBLEMS FOR SOLUTION OR RESEARCH

1. A solenoid 50 mm long produces a magnetic field intensity of 45 At/m, the circuit current is 0.25 A. How many turns are in the solenoid?

2. Look up the permeabilities of commonly available *ferrite cores* in a manufacturer's catalog. How do these compare with iron?

3. A torus-shaped core is marked $\mu = 220$, and has a radius of 0.05 m. It is necessary to produce a flux density of 0.001 T in the core. How many turns of wire should be spaced evenly around the core, and what should the coil current be?

4. If the cross-sectional area of the torus in Problem 3 is 1 cm^2, what is the reluctance of the torus?

5. The reluctance of a magnetic circuit 0.25 m long is 2000 At/Wb and its cross-sectional area is 0.01 m. What is the permeability of the core material? What is its relative permeability?

6. What flux will be produced in the core described in Problem 5 if a 90-turn coil carrying a current of 200 mA is wound on it?

7. Using your calculator to obtain the values, plot the following functions between $-360°$ and $+360°$. Calculate the values for every 15°.

a. $y = \sin A \times \cos A$

b. $y = \sin A + \frac{1}{2}\sin 2A + \frac{1}{3}\sin 3A$

c. $y = \sin A - \frac{1}{2}\cos 2A + \frac{1}{3}\sin 3A$

d. $y^2 = 1 - (\sin A)^2$

CHAPTER 10

WAVEFORMS AND THE OSCILLOSCOPE

A. CHAPTER PREVIEW

1 This chapter builds your understanding of magnetism and presents the relationship among the magnetic field, the electric field, and motion.

2 Motor and generator effects are introduced. You will learn how a generator operates and the type of output obtained from generators. The difference between dc and ac will be discussed.

3 As an extension of the discussion of dc and ac, various repetitive waveforms will be introduced. You will learn the characteristics of sine waves (sinusoids), and square waves, triangle, and ramp functions.

4 The Examples and Computations section introduces several concepts necessary for the study of waveforms. You will learn to use such concepts as frequency, period, peak-to-peak, average, and effective value in conjunction with waveforms.

5 The applications section of this chapter is a tutorial in the function and use of a modern oscilloscope, a device which makes it possible to view waveforms.

B. PRINCIPLES

B.1 RELATIONSHIP BETWEEN A MAGNETIC FIELD AND AN ELECTRIC FIELD

In Chapter 9 you learned that an electric current produces a magnetic field around current-carrying conductors. If two such conductors are placed close together, the magnetic fields interact and a force is produced that tends to push the wires apart or draw them closer together, if they are not held in place. The direction of the force between the wires depends on whether the currents through the wires are in the same or in opposite directions. Figure 10.1*a* shows the fields and the resulting force when the current flow is in the same direction through both wires. Notice that the force tends to move the wires in the direction of the lower flux density. This is also true in the case of parallel wires with current flow in opposite directions as shown in Figure 10.1*b*. In this case, the region of greatest flux density is between the two wires and the force tends to push the wires apart.

The same effect occurs, and a force is also produced on a single current-carrying conductor placed in the magnetic field of a permanent magnet (Figure 10.2). Notice that the three lines representing the direction of the current through the wire, the direction of the magnetic field from the permanent magnet, and the direction of the force on the conductor are at right angles to each other. Such a configuration is called an *orthogonal system*. In precise terms, an orthogonal system is a set of three vector quantities, such as force, magnetic field direction, and current, that are always at right angles to each other. A number of the vector quantities studied in physics, particularly those related to electricity, form orthogonal systems.

Figure 10.1 The magnetic field around current-carrying parallel wires.

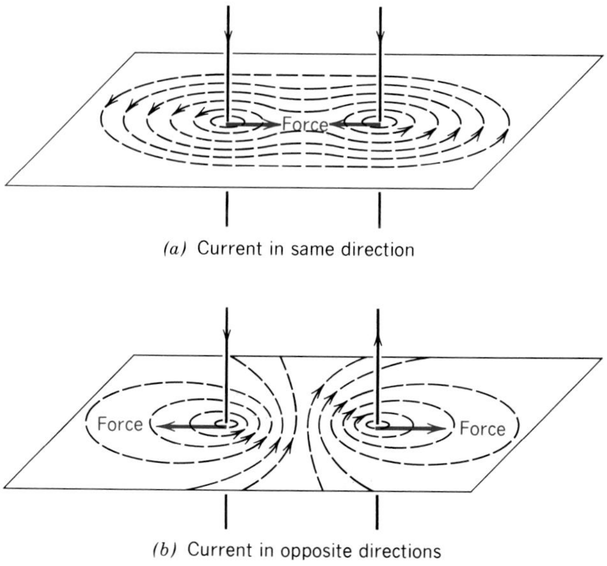

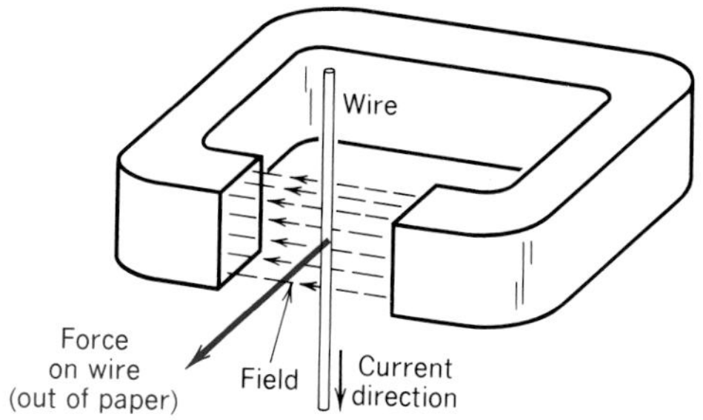

Figure 10.2 A current-carrying wire in a magnetic field. The current, field, and force form an orthogonal system.

Another hand rule, called *the right-hand rule for motors,* is a convenient way of remembering the relationship among force or motion, the magnetic field, and current direction. This rule is illustrated in Figure 10.3. It is called the "rule for motors" because it only applies when a combination of an electric current and a magnetic field *causes* a force on or motion of the current-carrying conductor. To use this rule, point the first finger in the direction of the magnetic field or magnetic flux and the middle finger, bent to form a right angle with the first finger, in the direction of the current. The thumb, held at right angles to both the first and middle fingers, then points in the direction of the force on the conductor, or its direction of motion, if the conductor is free to move. Some instructors use the following device to help remember this:

Current	= Center finger
Flux	= First finger
THrust or Motion	= THuMb

Figure 10.3 The right-hand rule for motors.

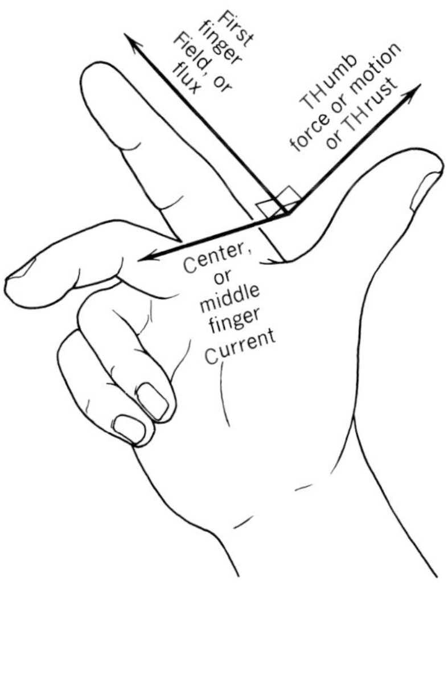

The motor effect described in these paragraphs is the basic principle of operation of all the electric motors in use today. No attempt has been made in this book to cover the operation of a practical electric motor because this material is best treated in a specialized textbook.

B.2 CONDUCTORS, FORCES, AND MAGNETIC FIELDS: THE GENERATOR EFFECT

The fact that an electric current through a conductor placed in a magnetic field produces a force on or motion of the conductor is a demonstration of the relationship of these three quantities. Another demonstration of this relationship is the fact that moving a conductor in a magnetic field actually generates an electric current in the conductor. This is known as the *generator effect,* and the current produced is called an *induced* current. The generator effect is illustrated in Figure 10.4. In this figure, a conducting wire loop is shown, with one segment of the loop moving through an area of high magnetic flux density between the poles of a magnet. As the wire is moved in the direction shown by the arrow, a movement of conduction electrons is set up in the loop. This occurs because of the orthogonal relationship of motion, the magnetic field, and an electric current or electric field. It is customary to talk about a conductor "cutting magnetic lines of force," but this is a simplification. Recall that these lines are not real; they are a way of mapping the magnetic field between the poles.

The direction of the current induced in the moving loop can be determined by using another left-hand rule, called *Fleming's rule,* or *the left-hand rule for generators.* This rule states that if the thumb, first, and middle fingers of the left hand are held at right angles to each other, and if the thumb is pointed in the direction of conductor motion, while the first finger points in the

Figure 10.4 The generator effect.

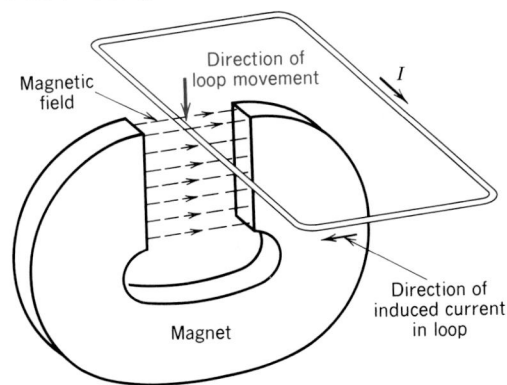

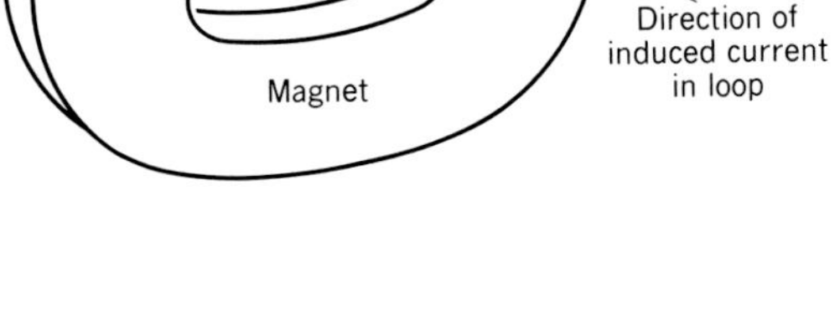

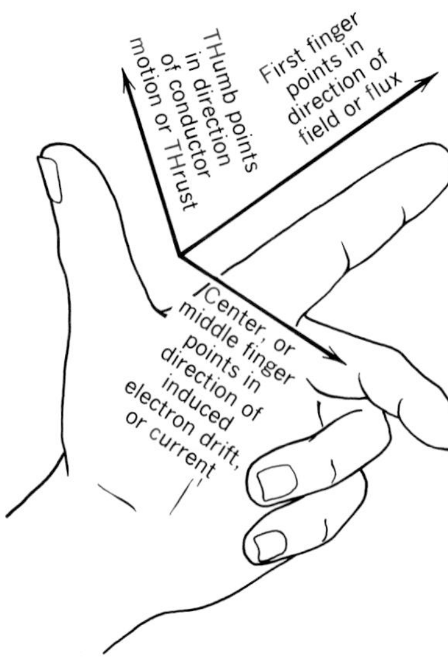

Figure 10.5 Fleming's rule, the left-hand rule for generators.

direction of the magnetic field, then the middle finger will point in the direction of the electron drift through the conductor. The left-hand rule for generators is illustrated in Figure 10.5. You can also use the memory aid:

Current	=	Center finger
Flux	=	First finger
THrust or Motion	=	THuMb

As in the case of motors, no attempt will be made to deal with practical generators in this book. The generator principle is, however, the basis for the discussion of inductance in the following chapters.

Taken together with the previous discussion of electromagnets and the motor principle, the generator effect underlines the relationship among the three orthogonal quantities motion, electric current, and the magnetic field. You can see that if two of these are present, the third is produced. Furthermore, any one of the three quantities is directly proportional to the other two. For example, if the strength of the magnetic field or the speed at which a conductor moves through the field is increased, the current produced by the generator effect will also increase.

In mathematical terms, the potential difference between the ends of a conductor that is moving through a magnetic field is given by

$$E = Blv \qquad \text{FORMULA 10.1}$$

where E is the potential difference in volts, B the magnetic field intensity in webers per square meter, or teslas, l the length of the conductor in meters, and v the speed of the conductor passing at a right angle through the field in meters per second. For example, if a conductor 1 m long is moving at a right angle through a magnetic field with a uniform intensity of 2 T at a speed of 5 m/s, the potential difference between the ends of the conductor will be 10 V.

When the path of the conductor is not at right angles to the direction of the magnetic field, the conductor speed value will have to be changed to reflect only the movement of the conductor that is at a right angle to the field. This is done by "resolving" the velocity of the conductor into two vectors, one at a right angle to the field and a second parallel to the field. This method will be treated in detail in Section C. Since only the component of the velocity that is at a right angle to the field has any effect upon the potential difference produced between the ends of the conductor, Formula 10.1 can be modified to take this into account:

$$E = Blv \sin\theta \qquad \text{FORMULA 10.2}$$

where θ is the angle between the conductor speed or velocity vector and the direction of the magnetic field (see Figure 10.6). The term $v \sin\theta$ is the portion of the conductor velocity that is at a right angle to the direction of the field. Notice that when the conductor motion is parallel to the field as in Figure 10.7, $\theta = 0°$ and the term $v \sin\theta$ is equal to zero. In this case, there is no component of the velocity vector that is at a right angle to the magnetic field. Therefore, there will be no potential difference produced between the ends of the conductor, regardless of how fast it is moving.

Formula 10.2 is called *Faraday's law*. It states that the voltage induced between the ends of a conductor being moved through a magnetic field is directly proportional to the product of the flux density of the field, the length of the conductor, and the rate at which the length of conductor moves through the field at a right angle to the field direction.

The principle stated by Faraday's law explains the operation of electromechanical current sources such

Figure 10.6 The movement of the conductor can be broken up into two components.

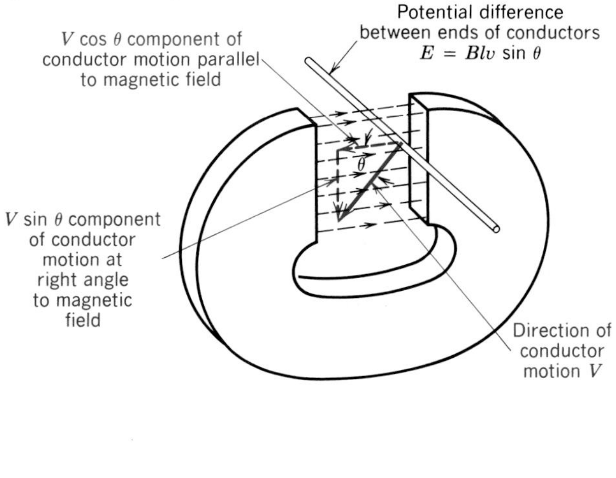

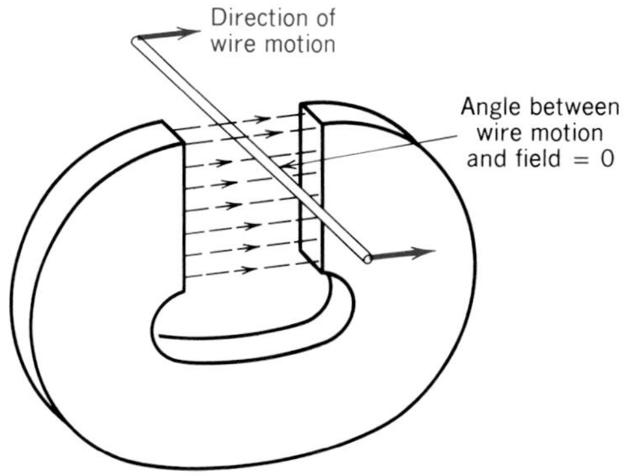

Figure 10.7 When the direction of the conductor movement is parallel to the field, $E = Blv \sin\theta = 0$.

as generators, alternators, and magnetos. It must be understood that the source of the electrical energy produced by these devices is the work required to move the conductor through the magnetic field. The amount of mechanical energy needed to move the conductor depends in part on the amount of electrical energy that the system is furnishing to the load. Early experimenters had observed that it took more force to push a conductor through a magnetic field when it was formed into a closed circuit, as in Figure 10.4, than when no current path existed between the ends of the conductor, as in Figure 10.7. This is because in Figure 10.4 there is an electric current that is dissipating power (converting electrical energy into heat) in the conductive loop. In the case shown in Figure 10.7, a potential difference is produced between the ends of the conductor, but since this potential difference does not sustain a current, less energy is being removed from the system.

The difference between Figures 10.4 and 10.7 is shown in Figures 10.8*a* and 10.8*b*. In Figure 10.8*a*, there is no complete circuit, so the induced potential difference causes only a momentary flow of conduction electrons along the length of the conductor. Using the left-hand rule for generators, you can see that the end of the conductor labeled *A* receives a negative charge due to the drift of electrons. As long as the conductor is kept moving through the magnetic field at a constant speed, there will be no further change. The only work done on the system composed of the field and the conductor, in addition to what it takes to move the conductor, is the small amount necessary to maintain the potential difference between the ends of the conductor.

In the situation shown in Figure 10.8*b*, the ends of the conductor are connected to a lumped load that represents the resistance of the conductor loop. Since this is a closed circuit, there will be a continuing drift of conduction electrons through the loop in the direction shown. Recall, however, that a current-carrying conductor in a magnetic field will experience a force

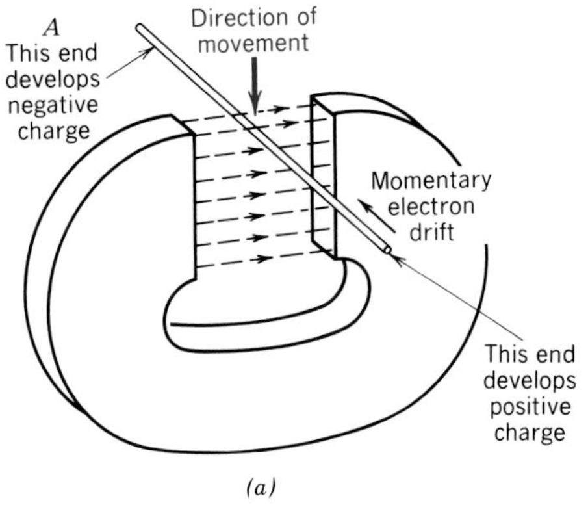

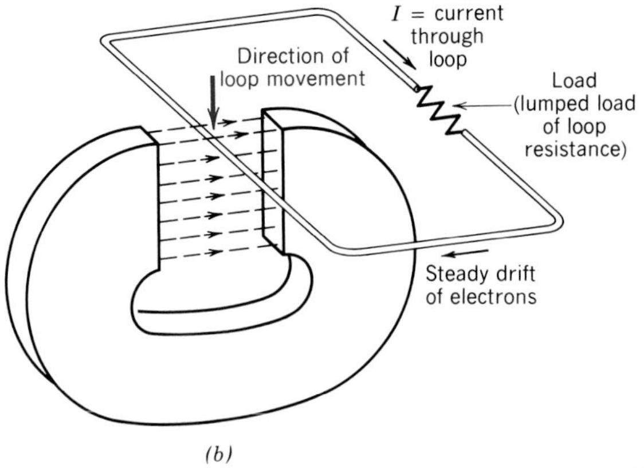

Figure 10.8 Additional work is done when the potential difference induced by the generator effect causes a current to flow through a load.

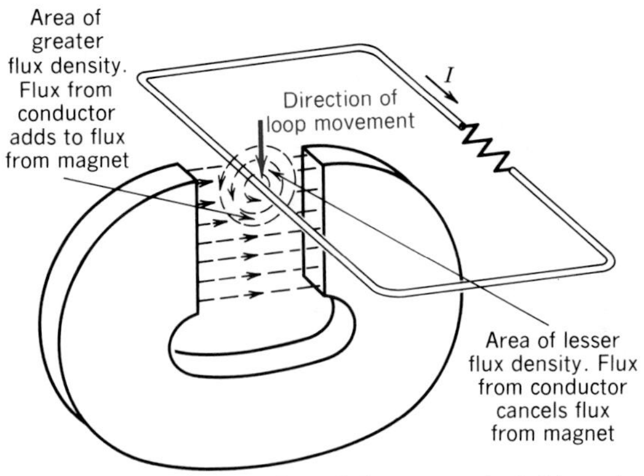

Figure 10.10 The interaction of the magnetic field produced by the current in the loop and the field from the magnet.

due to the motor effect. The direction of this force, not to be confused with the force that is pushing the conductor through the field, can be determined from the right-hand rule for motors, and is shown in Figure 10.9. Notice that this force *opposes* the force used to push the conductor through the field. Thus, the work involved in moving the conductor shown in Figure 10.8*b* through the field must include overcoming the force produced on a current-carrying conductor moving in a magnetic field.

Figure 10.9 The force on the current-carrying conductor due to the motor effect.

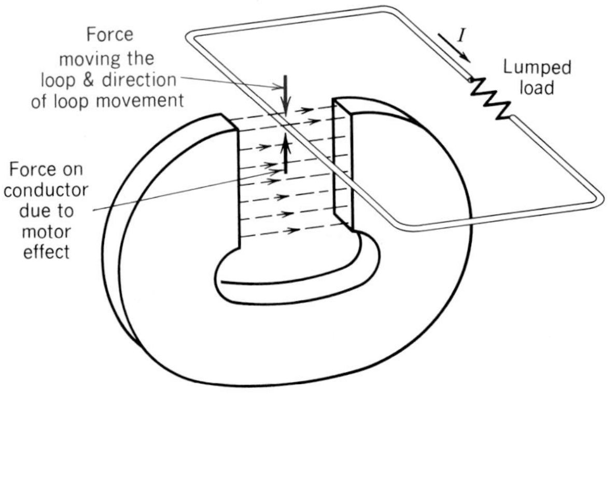

The operation of this opposing force is summarized by a general statement called *Lenz's law*. This law states that an induced current is accompanied by a magnetic field that acts to oppose the action that produces the current. Figure 10.10 is the same as that of Figure 10.8*b*, except that the magnetic field around the moving conductor due to the current is shown. Notice how this field opposes the field of the magnet above the conductor and aids it below the conductor. This results in a net force that opposes the force causing the loop movement. If this were not the case, there would be no opposing force on the moving conductor, and the work needed to move the conductors in Figures 10.8*a* and 10.8*b* would be the same. But this must be impossible since the energy dissipated as heat in the resistance of Figure 10.8*b* must come from the work needed to move the conductor. Otherwise, it would be possible to obtain an unlimited amount of energy from a moving conductor by reducing the resistance of the loop. In reality, reducing the resistance *would*, according to Ohm's law, produce a greater current. However, the increased current would also mean that the magnetic field produced by this current would be stronger. This would provide greater opposition to the movement of the conductor through the field of the magnet and require more work to keep the velocity of the conductor the same.

B.3 GENERATOR OUTPUT

Although the chemical cell is a common source of electrical energy, modern technology is based on electrical energy derived from mechanical energy and the generator principle. The basic operation of a power line generator is illustrated in Figures 10.11*a* through 10.11*f*. Here a single loop of wire is rotated in a magnetic field. The rings attached to the ends of the loop are contacted

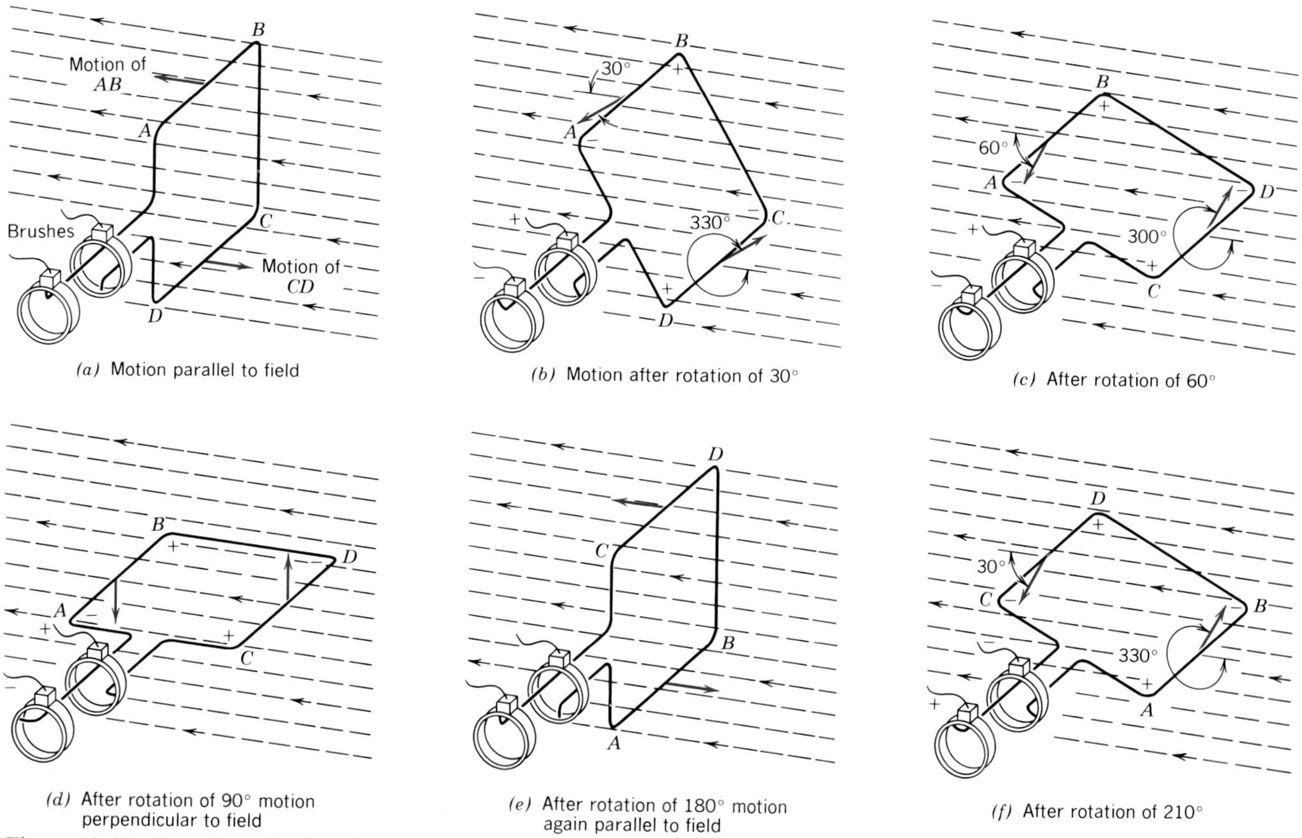

Figure 10.11 Rotation of a loop in a magnetic field.

by carbon bars called *brushes*, which provide a sliding contact with the rings and enable the current produced in the turning loop to be brought to a load. At the moment shown in Figure 10.11*a*, the direction of the motion of loop segments *ab* and *cd* is, as shown by the arrows, parallel to the direction of the magnetic field. At this moment, there is no potential difference produced between the ends of the loop segments, since θ in Formula 10.2, $E = Blv \sin \theta$, is zero and $\sin 0 = 0$. In Figure 10.11*b*, however, the loop has rotated through an angle of 30° from its original position. At this moment, loop segments *ab* and *cd* are moving in the directions shown, and the angle between the velocity vector of segment *ab* and the magnetic field direction is 30°. The potential difference across segment *ab* is

$$E = Blv \sin 30$$

Since $\sin 30 = 0.5$, $E_{ab} = 0.5\,Blv$. The polarity of this potential difference, obtained by using the left-hand rule for generators, is shown in the figure. Loop segment *cd* is moving at an angle of 330° to the direction of the field, so the potential difference across it is

$$E_{cd} = Blv \sin 330 \quad \text{or} \quad -0.5\,Blv$$

In this case, the negative sign shows that the polarity of the potential difference across this segment has a direction opposite to that of segment *ab*. In other words, as shown in Figure 10.11*b*, the two potential differences are in series aiding. Table 10.1 relates the angle through which the loop has rotated to the potential difference across each segment and the total potential difference as it would be measured between the two carbon brushes. The polarity of the potential difference between the carbon brushes reverses after it has dropped to zero at a rotation of 180°. A graph of the potential difference produced by the entire loop as it completes two full rotations is shown in Figure 10.12. Notice that the amount of rotation is given both in degree and in radian measure. As you might guess from the presence of the term $v \sin \theta$ in Formula 10.2, the line produced is the same as the shape of a graph of the sine function. If a load is connected between the brushes in Figure 10.11, the graph of the current through the load will be of the same shape as that shown in Figure 10.12. Although the machines used to produce the electrical energy for mains distribution are considerably more complicated than the single loop shown in Figure 10.11, the graph of the potential difference at a receptacle will closely resemble that shown in Figure 10.12. Because

Table 10.1 Loop Rotation in Figure 10.11

Angle through which Loop Has Rotated	*Angle Made with Magnetic Field* by AB	*by CD*	*Potential across Segment E = Blv sin θ* AB	*CD*	*Potential between Brushes*
0	0	0	0	0	0
30	30	330	0.5 *Blv*	−0.5 *Blv*	*Blv*
60	60	300	0.866 *Blv*	−0.866 *Blv*	1.73 *Blv*
90	90	270	+ *Blv*	− *Blv*	2 *Blv*
120	120	240	0.866 *Blv*	−0.866 *Blv*	1.73 *Blv*
150	150	210	0.5 *Blv*	−0.5 *Blv*	*Blv*
180	180	180	0	0	0
210	210	150	−0.5 *Blv*	0.5 *Blv*	− *Blv*
240	240	120	−0.866 *Blv*	0.866 *Blv*	−1.73 *Blv*
270	270	90	− *Blv*	+ *Blv*	−2 *Blv*
300	300	60	−0.866 *Blv*	+0.866 *Blv*	−1.73 *Blv*
330	330	30	−0.5 *Blv*	+0.5 *Blv*	− *Blv*
360		0	0	0	0

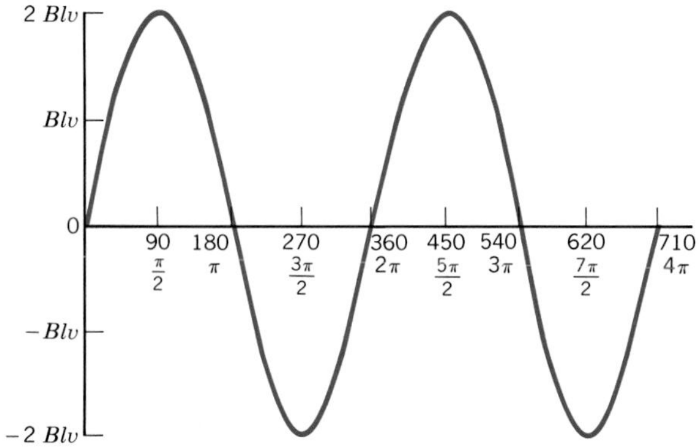

Figure 10.12 Graph of the potential difference between the brushes as a loop rotates through 360°.

the direction of the potential difference and the current through the load change, this type of current is called *alternating current.*

B.4 WAVEFORMS

Graphs like that of Figure 10.12, which relate potential difference or current to time, are called *waveforms,* or *waveshapes,* (because the loop is turning at a constant rate, the number of degrees it has turned through is actually a measure of time.) Since it follows the values of the sine function, the waveform in Figure 10.12 is referred to as a *sine wave.* Notice that the x axis in this figure could be extended to the right; the result would be a continuation of the basic shape. Waveforms that are composed of one basic shape that is repeated without change are called *recurrent,* or *periodic,* waveforms. Figures 10.13*a* through 10.13*f* are examples of recurrent waveforms frequently met in electronics. Figures 10.13*c*, square waves, and 11.13*d*, rectangular pulses, are frequently encountered in computer-type circuits. Figure 10.13*f*, the amplitude-modulated sine

Figure 10.13 Waveforms frequently encountered in electronics.

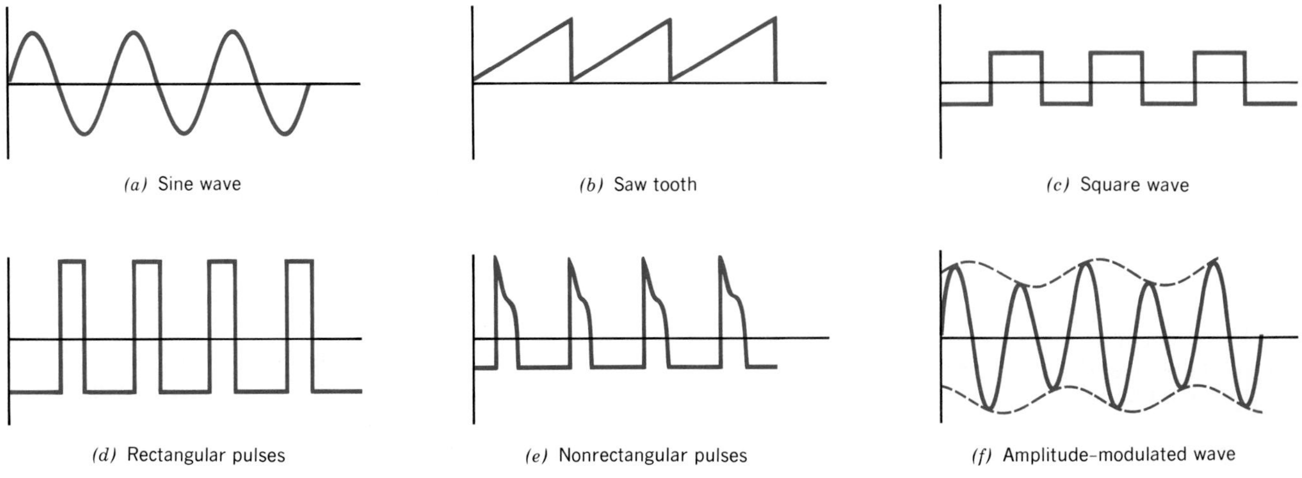

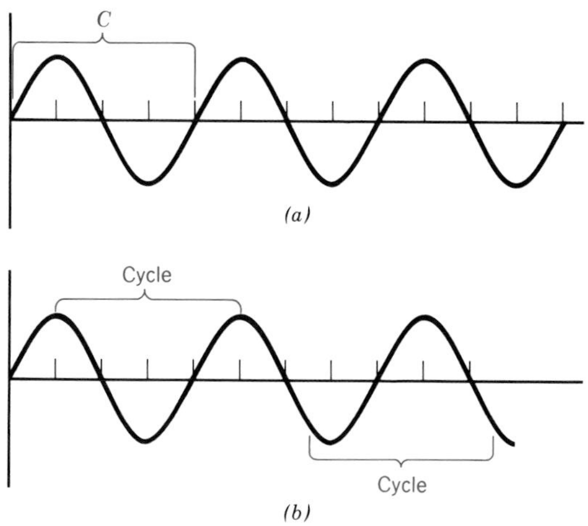

Figure 10.14 A complete, single unit of a recurrent waveform is called a cycle.

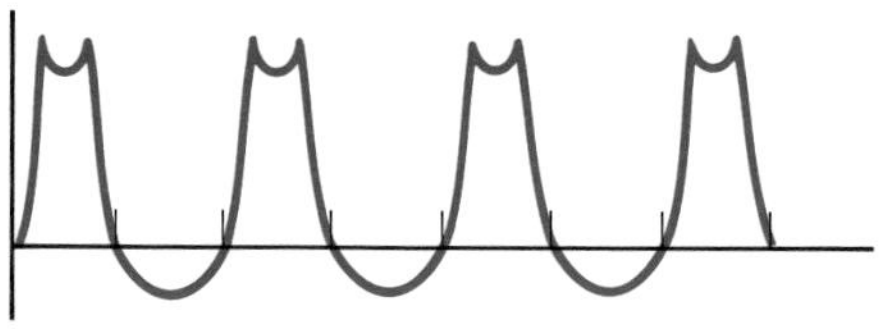

Figure 10.15 Complex waveform for example.

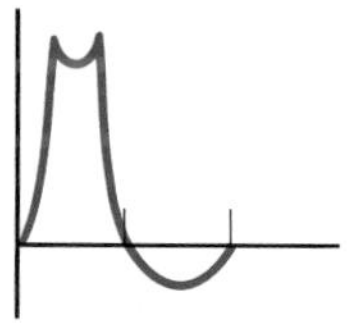

Figure 10.16 A single cycle of the complex waveform shown in Figure 10.15.

wave, is an example of two sine waves combined in a special way.

A complete, single unit of a recurrent waveform such as the portion of the sine wave labeled *C* in Figure 10.14 is called a *cycle*. The entire graph in Figure 10.14*a* shows three complete cycles. Note that any point could be selected as the beginning point for the cycle, as shown in Figure 10.14*b*.

EXAMPLE:
How many cycles are shown of the complex waveform in Figure 10.15? ■

SOLUTION:
To answer this question, it is necessary to determine the basic waveshape of a single cycle, as illustrated in Figure 10.16. Three and a half cycles are shown in Figure 10.15. ■

The *y*-axis dimension of a waveform is called its *amplitude*. The amplitudes of the square waves shown in Figures 10.17*a* and 10.17*b* are 5 V and 100 mA, respectively. When a waveform has both positive and

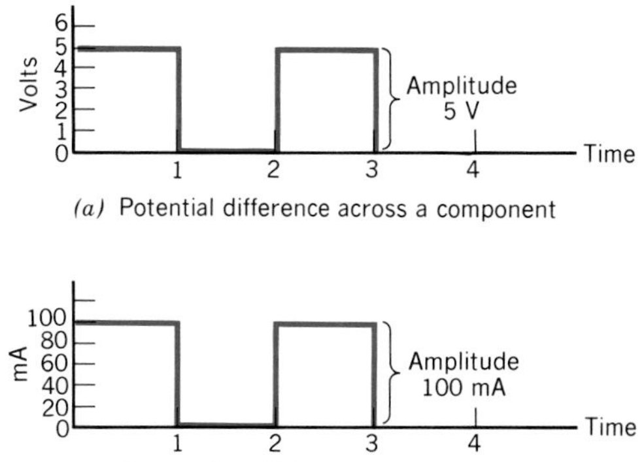

Figure 10.17 Potential difference across and current through a component.

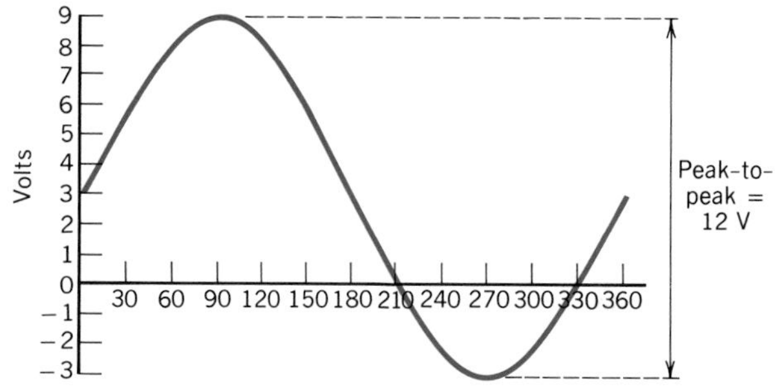

Figure 10.18 The peak-to-peak value of a waveform.

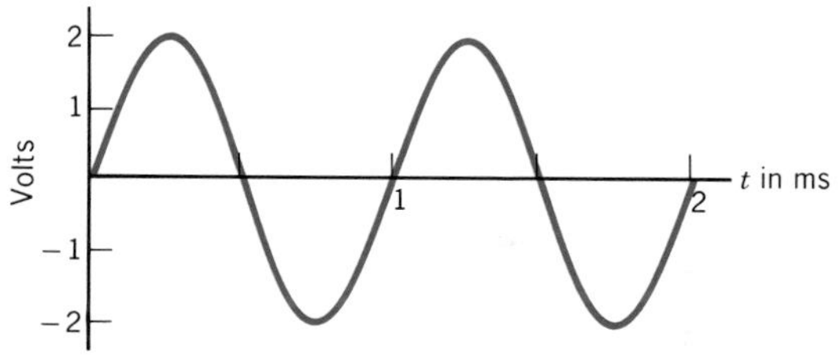

Figure 10.19 Sine wave with a period of 1 mS.

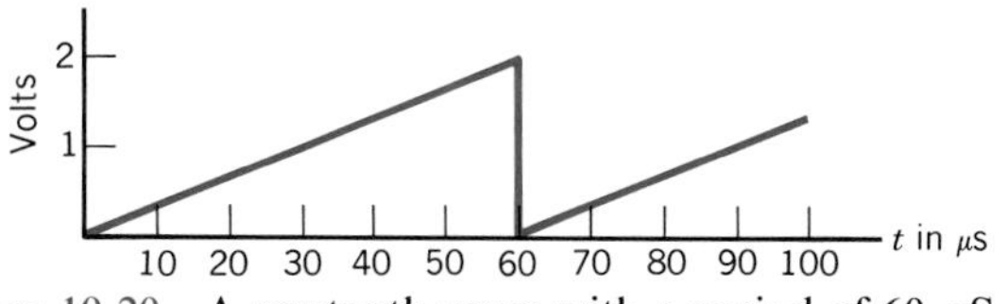

Figure 10.20 A sawtooth wave with a period of 60 μS.

negative values, like that in Figure 10.18, it is common to refer to the peak-to-peak amplitude of the waveform. This is the distance, as measured in *y*-axis units, between the positive peak and the negative peak of the waveform.

When the *x* axis of a recurrent waveform graph is divided into time units, it is possible to determine the amount of time necessary for a complete cycle. This is called the *period* of the waveform and is symbolized by the letter *t*. The sine wave illustrated in Figure 10.19 has a period of 1 ms, while the sawtooth in Figure 10.20 has a period of 60 μs.

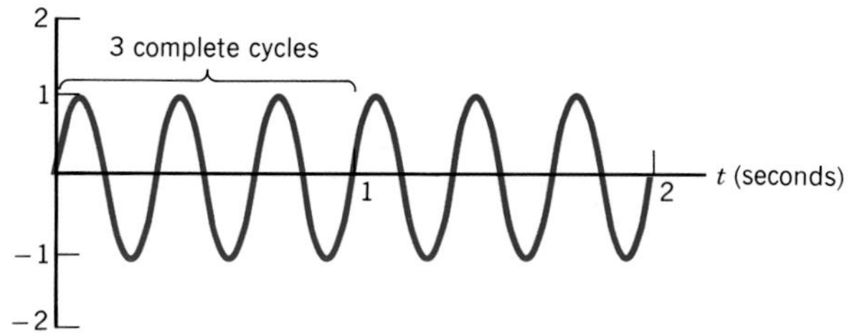

Figure 10.21 Sine wave with a frequency of 3 cycles per second, or 3 Hz.

The number of cycles that a waveform goes through in one second is called the *frequency* of the waveform. Frequency is symbolized by the lowercase letter f. The sine wave in Figure 10.21 forms three complete cycles in one second, so it has a frequency of three cycles per second, abbreviated cps. The unit "cycles per second" was renamed the hertz, abbreviated Hz, in honor of one of the early pioneers of radio, so a waveform with a frequency of 3 cps is usually referred to as a 3-Hz waveform. The most common waveform you will run into is the 60-Hz sine wave of the potential difference and the current supplied by commercial power lines. Waveforms of various kinds ranging from a few hertz to several gigahertz (10^9 Hz) are used for certain applications. Table 10.2 lists some of the applications of waveforms from dc (0 Hz) to extremely high frequency (EHF).

Since the frequency (f) of a waveform is the number of cycles the waveform goes through in one second, and the period is the amount of time required for one cycle, then

$$f \times t = 1 \qquad \text{FORMULA 10.3}$$

This relationship becomes obvious if you consider the units used to measure frequency and period:

$$\frac{\text{cycles}}{\text{second}} \times \frac{\text{seconds}}{\text{cycle}} = 1$$

Because frequency and period are reciprocal quantities, it is also possible to write:

$$f = \frac{1}{t} \quad \text{and} \quad t = \frac{1}{f} \qquad \text{FORMULA 10.4}$$

Table 10.2 Waveform Applications

Frequency	*Nomenclature*	*Band*	*Applications (typical)*
0 to 400 Hz		Audio frequency	Power distribution Commercial 60 Hz Aircraft 400 Hz
400 Hz to 30 kHz	Very low frequency (VLF)	↓ Radio frequency	VLF submarine navigation and communications
30 kHz to 300 kHz	Low frequency (LF)		Marine navigation
300 kHz to 3 MHz	Medium frequency (MF)		Communications 535 to 1605 kHz Commercial radio Navigation
3 MHz to 30 MHz	High frequency (HF)		Long distance communications Mobile radio 27.0 to 27.265 MHz CB radio
30 MHz to 300 MHz	Very high frequency (VHF)		Mobile radio TV 50 to 88 MHz 88 to 108 MHz commercial FM 174 to 216 MHz TV
300 MHz to 3 GHz	Ultra high frequency (UHF)	↓ Microwave	470 to 890 MHz UHF TV Aviation
3 GHz to 30 GHz	Super high frequency (SHF)		Radar and microwave communications
30 GHz to 300 GHz	Extremely high frequency (EHF)	↓	Satellite communications

EXAMPLE:
How much time does a 60-Hz power line signal require to complete one cycle? ■

SOLUTION:

Using Formula 10.4, $t = \frac{1}{f} = \frac{1}{60} = 0.01667$ seconds per cycle. ■

Additional information and definitions of waveform characteristics that require certain calculations have been included in the Examples and Computations section of this chapter.

C. EXAMPLES AND COMPUTATIONS

C.1 RESOLVING VECTOR QUANTITIES

A vector, you will remember, was defined as a quantity that has both a magnitude and a direction. This definition is a simplified form of the definition of a vector used in mathematics, but makes such quantities easier to visualize. Any quantity that possesses both magnitude and direction, such as force, or velocity, can be represented by a vector. Quantities that have only magnitude, such as heat, or mass, are referred to as *scalar quantities,* or *scalars,* and can not be represented as vectors. A vector quantity is usually represented as an arrow whose length gives the magnitude of the quantity and whose direction with respect to some reference line gives the direction of the vector. There are two ways to define a vector drawn on a flat surface like that in Figure 10.22. One way, 10.22*a*, is to give the length of the vector and the angle it forms with an x axis. In this figure, the vector length is 5, and it forms an angle of about 36.87° with the x axis shown. A second way, 10.22*b*, is to give the x- and y-axis values of the end of the vector when its beginning is placed at the origin, the (0,0) point of a pair of coordinate axes. Since it is customary to give the x value first, vector A in Figure 10.22*b* can be completely described as the vector from the origin to point (4,3). In addition to specifying vector A, the x and y values, or *coordinates,* as they are sometimes called, each describe another vector, which begins at the origin and

Figure 10.22 Ways of defining vector quantities.

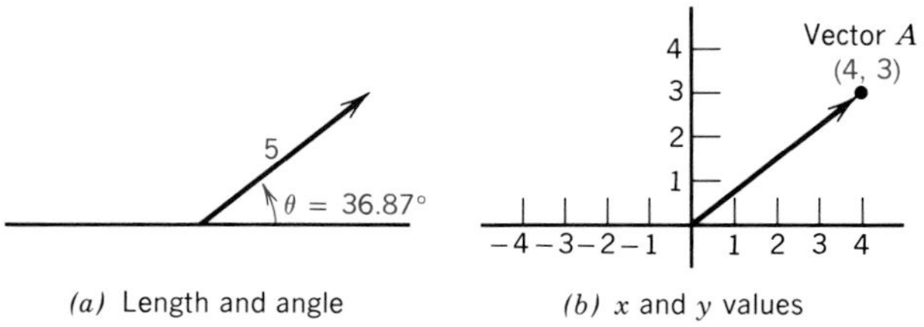

(a) Length and angle

(b) x and y values

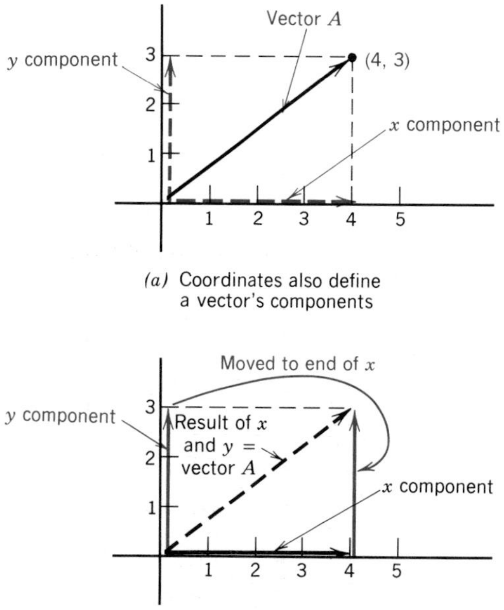

(a) Coordinates also define a vector's components

(b) Vector A is the result of the x and y components

Figure 10.23 A vector is the sum of its x and y components.

lies along the x or y axis. This is shown in Figure 10.23*a*. These two vectors are called the *x and y components* of vector A. You can see from Figure 10.23*b* that if the beginning of the y component is placed at the end of the x component, the result is vector A.

Calculating the x and y components of a vector is an easy and frequently necessary job. For example, in Section B you learned that only a conductor motion perpendicular to the direction of a magnetic field contributed to the production of a potential difference between the ends of the conductor. If the conductor motion or velocity vector is resolved into two components, one parallel to and one perpendicular to the magnetic field, the component of the velocity that contributes to the production of the potential difference will be known. The way in which this is done is shown in Figure 10.24. A pair of coordinate axes is drawn so

Figure 10.24 Resolving the motion or velocity vector into its components.

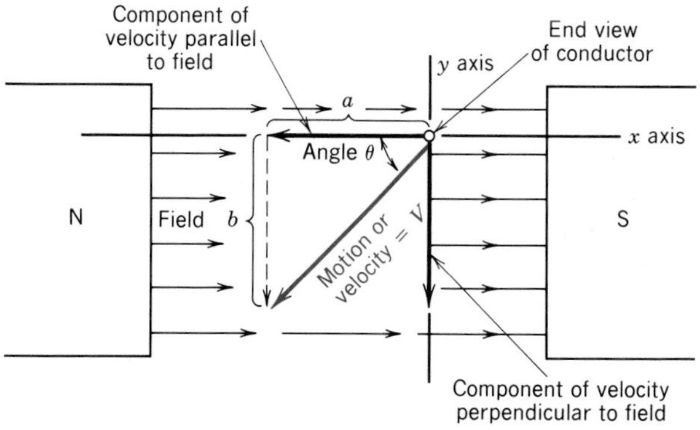

that the x axis is in the direction of the magnetic field and the origin is at the beginning of the velocity vector. The sine of angle θ is equal to the length of the opposite side divided by the length of the hypotenuse (in this case the length of the velocity vector). In mathematical terms,

$$\sin\theta = \frac{\text{length of line } b}{\text{length of velocity vector}}$$

But the length of line b is the same as the y component of the velocity vector; so substituting and multiplying both sides of the equation by the length of the velocity vector,

Length of vector times $\sin\theta$
= the y component of velocity

This is why Formula 10.2 had a sin θ term in it, since this is the component of the velocity vector y that is perpendicular to the field.

To summarize, if θ is the angle between the x axis and a vector whose length is v, as in Figure 10.24, the y component of vector v is $v \sin\theta$. Similarly, you can see that the x component of vector v is $v \cos\theta$ since

$$\cos\theta = \frac{\text{length of line } a}{\text{length of hypotenuse}}$$

or

$$v \cos\theta = \text{length of line } a$$

The components of a vector that makes an angle of more than 90° with the x axis can be calculated using the formulas given in Chapter 9, but it is necessary to make sure that the proper sign, plus or minus, is used. Remember that all x measurements to the left of the origin and all y measurements below the origin are negative, as shown in Figure 10.25.

EXAMPLE:
Find the x and y components of a vector with a length of 13 that makes an angle of 202.62° with the x axis. ■

SOLUTION:
The solution is easier to understand if a diagram is drawn, as shown in Figure 10.26. The sine and cosine functions of an angle of 202.62° are the same as the sine and cosine functions of 202.62 − 180 or 22.62°. Since the 202.62° angle lies between 180° and 270°, both components of the vector will be negative.

x component = −13(cos 22.62) = −11.999 = 12

y component = −13(sin 22.62) = −5.000 = 5 ■

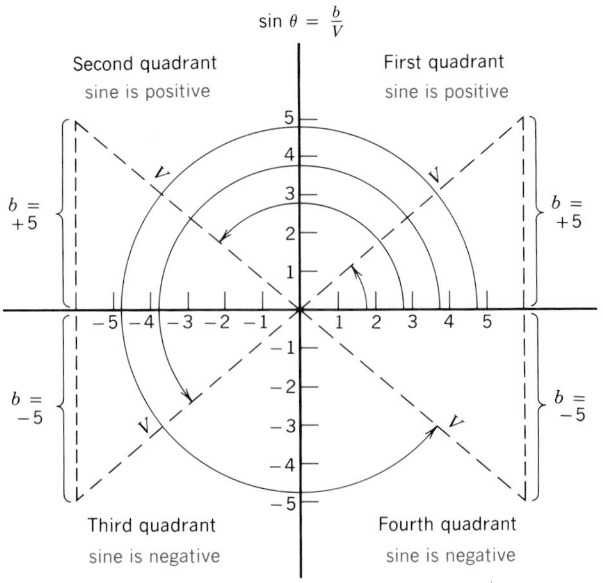

Figure 10.25 The sine function is positive in the first and second quadrants, negative in the third and fourth.

When a calculator is used to find vector components, it is not necessary to keep track of the quadrant of the vector since this is done automatically. Using a calculator, find the x and y components of the following vectors:

a. $V = 5$ at 30°
b. $R = 17$ at 45°
c. $V = 4$ at 156°
d. $R = 7$ at 180°
e. $V = 9$ at $1R$
f. $M = 24$ at 212°
g. $P = 83$ at −74°
h. $F = 5$ at $\frac{3\pi}{2}R$
i. $R = 9$ at 240°
j. $V = 12$ at −16°
k. $F = 1.27$ at $\frac{\pi}{8}R$
l. $J = 16A$ at 30°
m. $F = 2.5q_1$ at 105°

The opposite of resolving a vector, that is, specifying the length and angle of a vector whose components are known, involves two more facts about right triangles. The first was discovered by the Greek mathematician and philosopher Pythagoras (pronounced *Pi-thá-gor-as*) (580–500 B.C.) and is called the *Pythagorean theorem*. This theorem states that *if any triangle is drawn*

Figure 10.26 Diagram for example.

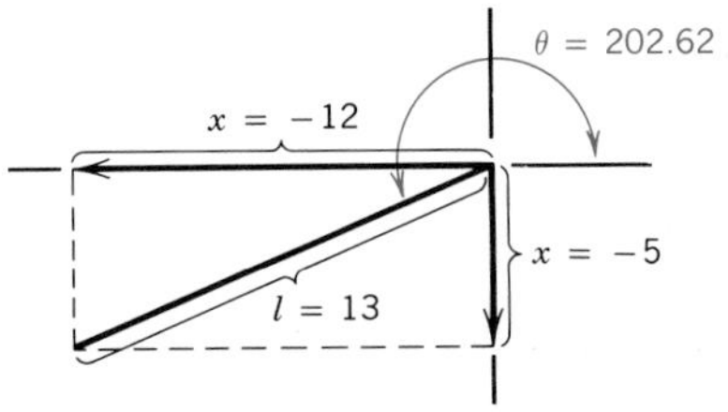

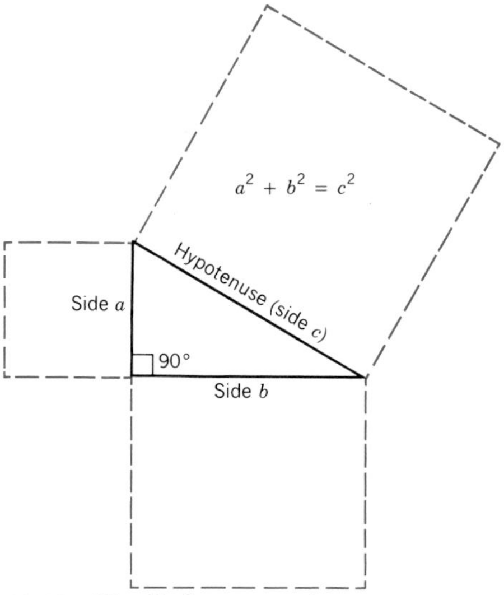

Figure 10.27 The Pythagorean theorem.

on a flat surface, and if that triangle contains a right angle, the square of the length of one side plus the square of the length of the other side is equal to the square of the length of the hypotenuse (the side opposite the right angle). This theorem is illustrated in Figure 10.27. Mathematically, the Phythagorean theorem is written

$$a^2 + b^2 = c^2 \quad \text{FORMULA 10.5}$$

Another useful form of the same formula is obtained by taking the square root of both sides. (Remember the square root of $a^2 + b^2$ is $\sqrt{a^2 + b^2}$ and NOT $a + b$.

$$\sqrt{a^2 + b^2} = c \quad \text{FORMULA 10.6}$$

Practice your recall of the Phythagorean theorem by calculating the length of the unknown side in Figures 10.28*a* through 10.28*l*.

Another trigonometric function is needed in order to specify the magnitude and angle of a vector when its x and y components are known. This function is related to the sine and cosine functions and is called the *tangent*, or *tan*. For an angle in a right triangle, the tangent is equal to the length of the opposite side divided by the length of the adjacent side. In Figure 10.29,

$$\tan \theta = \frac{\text{length of side } b}{\text{length of side } a} \quad \text{or} \quad \frac{\text{opposite}}{\text{adjacent}}$$

Unlike the sine and cosine functions, which vary between +1 and −1 as the angle changes, the tangent function assumes a strange form when graphed as in Figure 10.30. The value of the tangent can be obtained in three ways. If you know the length of the opposite

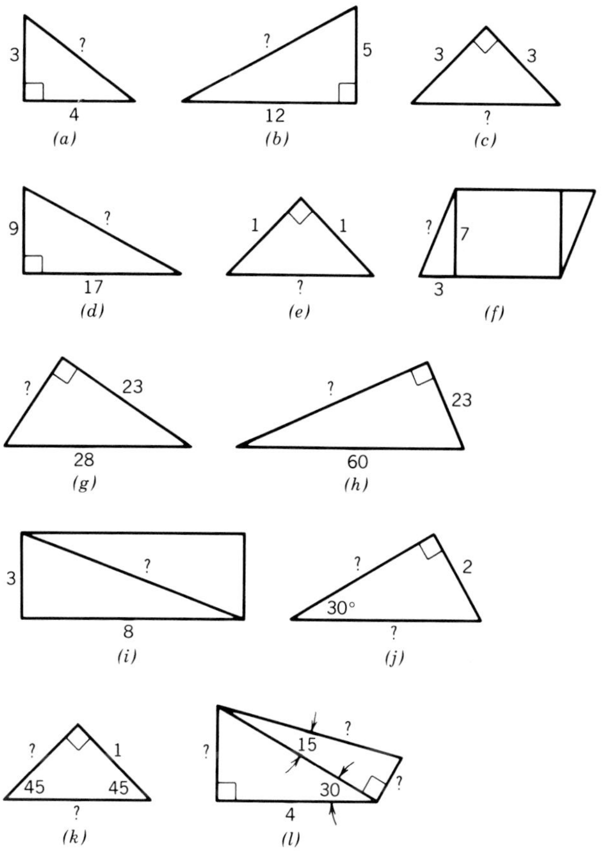

Figure 10.28 Pythagorean theorem problems.

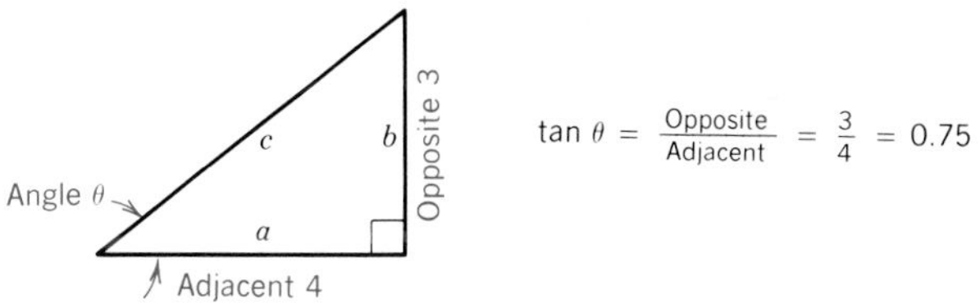

Figure 10.29 The tangent of an angle in a right triangle is the length of the opposite side divided by the length of the adjacent side.

Figure 10.30 Graph of the tangent function.

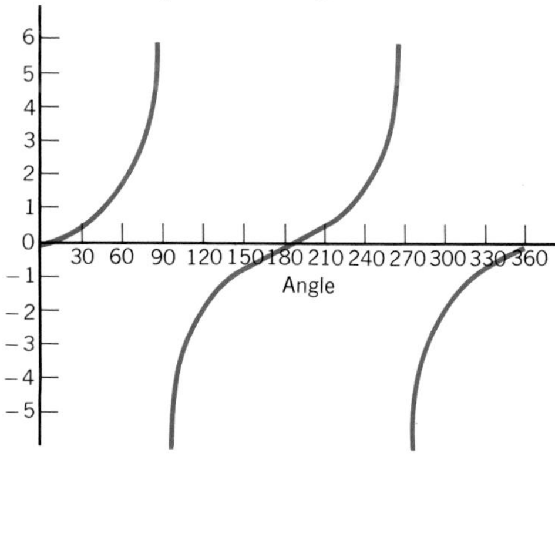

and adjacent sides, as is the case when you know the x and y components of a vector, the value of the tangent can be obtained by dividing:

$$\tan\theta = \frac{\text{opposite}}{\text{adjacent}} \qquad \text{FORMULA 10.7}$$

If the angle is known, the value of the tangent can be obtained from tables or a scientific calculator. Finally, the value of the tangent of an angle is equal to the value of the sine of that angle divided by the value of its cosine:

$$\tan\theta = \frac{\sin\theta}{\cos\theta} \qquad \text{FORMULA 10.8}$$

If you remember what the sine and cosine of an angle actually mean, it is easy to show that Formula 10.8 is correct:

$$\frac{\sin\theta}{\cos\theta} = \frac{\dfrac{\text{opposite}}{\text{hypotenuse}}}{\dfrac{\text{adjacent}}{\text{hypotenuse}}} = \frac{\text{opposite}}{\text{hypotenuse}} \times \frac{\text{hypotenuse}}{\text{adjacent}} = \frac{\text{opposite}}{\text{adjacent}} = \tan\theta$$

With these two facts about triangles, it is not difficult to reconstruct a vector from its components, as shown in Figure 10.31. The length of the vector is the square root of the sum of the squares of the components

$$v = \sqrt{x^2 + y^2} \qquad \text{FORMULA 10.9}$$

The value of the tangent of the angle that the vector forms with the x axis is the value of the y component divided by the value of the x component.

$$\tan\theta = \frac{\text{opposite}}{\text{adjacent}} = \frac{y}{x} \qquad \text{FORMULA 10.10}$$

Figure 10.31 Determining the length and angle of a vector when its x and y components are known.

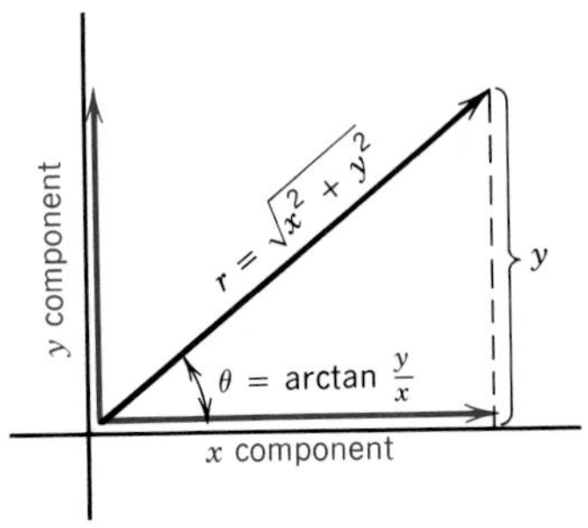

Formula 10.10 gives the *value* of the tangent of the angle. The angle itself can be determined by using either the trigonometric tables in the Appendix or a calculator. In either case, it is necessary to check the signs (+ or −) of the components to determine which quadrant the vector will be in. A negative value for the x component and positive y component, for example, mean that the angle is in the second quadrant, that is, an angle between 90° and 180°. Once the proper quadrant has been determined, the tangent value can be calculated and the size of an angle obtained. This angle is subtracted from 180° for an angle in the second quadrant, added to 180° for an angle in the third quadrant, or subtracted from 360° for an angle in the fourth quadrant.

If you are using a calculator rather than tables, it is easy to find the size of the angle when the value of the tangent is known. This is usually done with a second or inverse function key followed by the tan key, an arc key followed by the tan key, or a $\tan^{-1}$ key. The angle in degrees of a known tangent value is called the *arctangent* of that value, and is written as arctan (value), or $\tan^{-1}$ (value). Check your calculator instruction manual, if necessary, to determine the correct key names for this function.

EXAMPLE:

Determine the length and angle of a vector whose x and y components are −7 and −3, respectively. ■

SOLUTION:

The length of the vector is given by Formula 10.9 as

$$c = \sqrt{(-7)^2 + (-3)^2} = \sqrt{49 + 9} = \sqrt{58} = 7.62$$

Since both the x and y components are negative, the angle of the vector is between 180° and 270°. Using Formula 10.7,

$$\tan\theta = \frac{-3}{-7} = 0.4286 \quad \text{so} \quad \tan^{-1}(0.4286) = 23.2°$$

and the angle is 180 + 23.2, or 203.2°. ■

A number of scientific calculators have a special procedure for converting from vector length and angle directly to x and y components or the opposite. In these calculators the vector length and angle are called *polar coordinates* and the x and y components are called *rectangular coordinates*. Additional information about coordinate systems will be included later in this book.

Try the following problems in converting from vector to components or components to vector.

a. $x = 4, y = 3; r = ?, \theta = ?$
b. $x = 7, y = 5; r = ?, \theta = ?$

c. $x = 5, y = 19; r = ?, \theta = ?$
d. $x = -8, y = 5; r = ?, \theta = ?$
e. $x = -3, y = -4; r = ?, \theta = ?$
f. $x = -12, y = 12; r = ?, \theta = ?$
g. $x = \sqrt{2}, y = -2\sqrt{2}; r = ?, \theta = ?$
h. $x = -9, y = ?; r = 10, \theta = 244.16°$
i. $x = 7, y = ?; r = 8.6, \theta = 35.54°$
j. $x = ?, y = -4; r = 8.94, \theta = 333.42$

C.2 COMPUTATIONS WITH SINE WAVES

You have previously learned some of the terms, such as *amplitude, period,* and *frequency,* that are associated with waveforms. In this section, certain additional ideas and mathematical methods for working with sine waves will be covered. Sine waves are important for a number of reasons. Power distribution system potential differences and currents are in the form of sine waves. Many circuits produce sine-wave output even though they are supplied by dc sources. Finally, by means of some rather complicated mathematics, any waveform can be viewed as a collection of sine waves of different frequency and amplitude added together.

One of the most striking things about a potential difference or current whose graph is a sine function is that over a period of one or more complete cycles, the strict mathematical average of the potential difference or current is zero! This is evident if you examine a sine graph. For every point on the positive side of the *y* axis, there is a corresponding point on the negative side. This bit of information, however, is deceptive. Light bulbs connected across the ac power distribution mains still light. Heating elements glow and dissipate heat. Therefore, a sine-wave ac potential difference and the current caused by it are still able to do work, even though both the potential difference and current are changing and both reverse their direction many times each second. In many cases, it is the fact that electrons are drifting under the influence of an electric field that causes useful work to be done in a circuit. The direction of the drift and the continual change in the value of the potential difference and current do not prevent the operation of electrical machines or some electronic components.

It is, however, necessary to determine what the useful or effective values of a sine voltage or current are. One way to do this is to take the average of the sine-wave values over each half of the complete cycle separately. This provides a convenient numerical value for some kinds of calculations since it permits the sine-wave voltage or current to be viewed as a square wave that changes from a positive to negative value as shown in Figure 10.32. If a large number of sine values over a series of half sine cycles are averaged, the average turns out to be 0.637. This means that the average value of a sine-wave potential difference or current is 0.637 or 63.7 percent of the peak or maximum value:

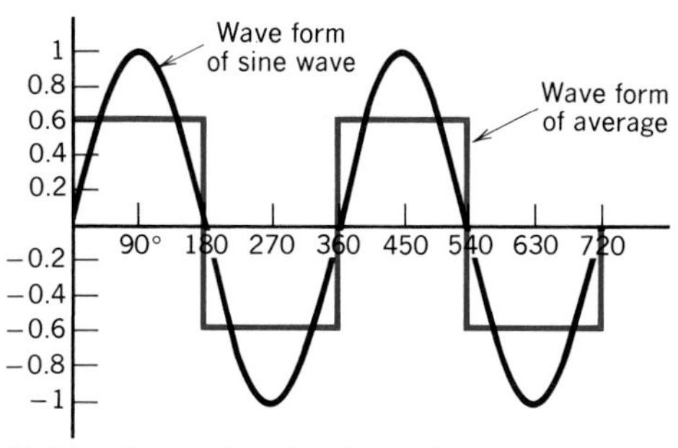

Figure 10.32 Averaging the sine values over each of several half-cycles produces the AVERAGE value of a sine wave.

$$E_{\text{average}} = 0.637E_{\text{peak}} \quad \text{or} \quad 63.7\% \; E_{\text{peak}}$$

FORMULA 10.11

$$I_{\text{average}} = 0.637I_{\text{peak}} \quad \text{or} \quad 63.7\% I_{\text{peak}}$$

The average value is normally given as a positive value, even though both the potential and current change direction.

EXAMPLE:
Determine the peak-to-peak and average value of a sine-wave potential difference with a peak amplitude of 5 V. ■

SOLUTION:
Since the peak amplitude of the sine-wave graph is +5 V. The negative peak is −5 V, and the peak-to-peak value is 5 + 5 = 10 V. Using Formula 10.11, the average value is

$$E_{\text{average}} = 0.637E_{\text{peak}} = 3.185 \text{ V}$$ ■

If the average value of a sine waveform is known, the positive peak value can be found by an easily derived formula. Starting with Formula 10.11, $E_{\text{average}} = 0.637E_{\text{peak}}$, multiplying both sides by $\frac{1}{0.637}$, produces

$$1.57E_{\text{average}} = E_{\text{peak}} \quad \text{and} \quad 1.57I_{\text{average}} = I_{\text{peak}}$$

FORMULA 10.12

EXAMPLE:
A certain circuit requires an ac supply with an average current of 100 mA for reliable operation. The power supply is required to produce at least twice the peak current. Disregarding surges and transients, what is the current rating of the supply? ■

SOLUTION:
If the average current of the circuit is 100 mA, using Formula 10.12, the peak current is

$$I_{peak} = 1.57 \times 100 \text{ mA} = 157 \text{ mA}$$

Twice this would be 314 mA. ■

Although the average value of a sine wave is useful in a few applications, in most cases it is necessary to determine the ac potential difference or current that will have the same effect as a dc potential difference or current. This value is known as the *effective value* and is based on the power dissipation of direct an alternating current in resistive loads. Since the powe. dissipated in a resistive load is proportional to the square of the current through the resistor or to the square of the potential difference across it, the effective value of a sine wave is the square root of the average of the values of the potential difference or current squared. This value is called the *root mean square,* or *rms,* value and is equal to 0.707 times the peak potential or current:

$$E_{rms} = 0.707E_{peak} \quad \text{and} \quad I_{rms} = 0.707I_{peak}$$
FORMULA 10.13

NOTE: Formula 10.13 is true *only* for sine waves. The rms value is the most frequently used value for an ac waveform, and the subscript rms is frequently omitted. For example, a statement like "6.3 VAC" on an electronic component actually means "6.3 V rms."

EXAMPLE:
A certain electrical heating unit is supplied by an ac line with an E_{peak} of 18 V. What dc potential difference would be required to provide the same power dissipation in the heater? ■

SOLUTION:
The amount of heat produced by an ac power source depends on the rms potential or current provided by the source. According to Formula 10.13, for a supply with an 18-V peak this is

$$E_{rms} = 0.707E_{peak} = 12.726 \text{ V}$$

Therefore, a dc supply that produces a potential difference of 12.726 V would produce the same heating as an ac supply with a peak amplitude of 18 V. ■

Since it is the rms value of an ac voltage or current that is usually given, it is frequently necessary to calculate the peak or peak-to-peak amplitude. A formula for this calculation is easily obtained from Formula 10.13:

$$E_{rms} = 0.707E_{peak}$$

Multiplying both sides by $\frac{1}{0.707}$,

$$\frac{1}{0.707}E_{rms} = E_{peak} \quad \text{or}$$

$$E_{peak} = 1.41E_{rms}$$ FORMULA 10.14

$$\text{and} \quad I_{peak} = 1.41I_{rms}$$

EXAMPLE:
A power supply delivers 12 VAC and 2 A to an electronic unit. Some of the components in this unit are rated at 30 $V_{peak\text{-}to\text{-}peak}$ and the unit wiring is rated at 5 A_{peak} ac. Are any of these ratings exceeded in the normal operation of the unit? ■

SOLUTION:
Without subscripts, the 12 V and 2 A of the power supply are rms values. The peak voltage delivered by the supply is given by Formula 10.14,

$$E_{peak} = 1.41E_{rms} = 16.92 \text{ V}_{peak}$$

The peak-to-peak value is twice this, or 33.84 V. The component ratings *are* exceeded. In the case of the current, the peak current is

$$I_{peak} = 1.41I_{rms} = 2.82 \text{ A}_{peak}$$

Since the ratings are in terms of the peak amplitude and *not* the peak-to-peak, the current is well within the accepted ratings. ■

The ability to perform calculations using frequency, period, peak values, and rms values are of great importance in electronics. Solve the following problems for practice.

1. The potential difference across a 15 Ω resistance is a sine wave that completes 120 cycles in 3 s. The peak value of the waveform is 8.883 V. What are the frequency, period, peak-to-peak, average, and rms values of the current through this resistance?

2. The rms value of the potential difference supplied by the power mains is 120 V, the frequency is 60 Hz. What is the peak-to-peak value? What is the period?

3. Engineer Vardis has learned that light bulbs last longer when operating from an ac source. In order to extend the operating time of a set of 5-V dc bulbs, an ac power source producing what peak voltage is needed? What is the rms voltage of this source?

4. A small electric train transformer is marked 8 V AC OUT. What is the average potential difference across its output terminals?

5. What is the peak-to-peak potential difference produced by a current of 1.6 A ac through a resistance of 82 Ω?

6. Aircraft and some industrial applications use 400 Hz power instead of 60 Hz. What is the period of the 400 Hz sine wave?

7. Fill in the blanks.

a. 180 V_{rms} = ________ V_{peak}
b. 10 $A_{average}$ = ________ A_{rms}
c. 10 $V_{peak\text{-}to\text{-}peak}$ = $V_{average}$
d. V_{peak} = ________ × $V_{average}$
e. If $t = 8.63 \times 10^{-4}$ S, f = ________ .
f. If 150 waveforms take 2.6 s, f = ________ ,
t = ________ .
g. $E_{peak\text{-}to\text{-}peak} = 120$, $E_{average}$ = ________ .
h. $V_{peak\text{-}to\text{-}peak}$ = ________ × E_{rms}
i. $E_{average}$ = ________ × E_{rms}
j. E_{peak} = ________ × $E_{average}$

C.3 COMPUTATIONS WITH SQUARE WAVES AND PULSES

At one time, mathematical work with square-wave and pulse waveforms was the private property of radar engineers and technicians, but this is no longer true. Those working with computers, communications, or control equipment are expected to know the technical definitions and mathematical relationships required to describe square waves and pulses. From Figure 10.33 you can see that the concepts of period, frequency, amplitude, and peak-to-peak amplitude apply equally to square waves and pulses as well as to sine waves. As in the case of the sine wave, it is customary to consider the beginning of a square wave or pulse period at a zero crossing that occurs when the value of the graph is increasing, as shown in Figure 10.33. For regular square waves and pulses, the period is the time between two such zero crossings. The period of the square wave shown in Figure 10.33 is 0.2 s and the frequency is 5 Hz.

Another pair of related terms necessary for understanding square waves and pulses are *pulse width* and *duty factor*. These terms are particularly important when the sides of the square waves or pulses are not exactly perpendicular to the x axis, as shown in Figure 10.34. The pulse width is usually defined as the time between two successive points at which the amplitude

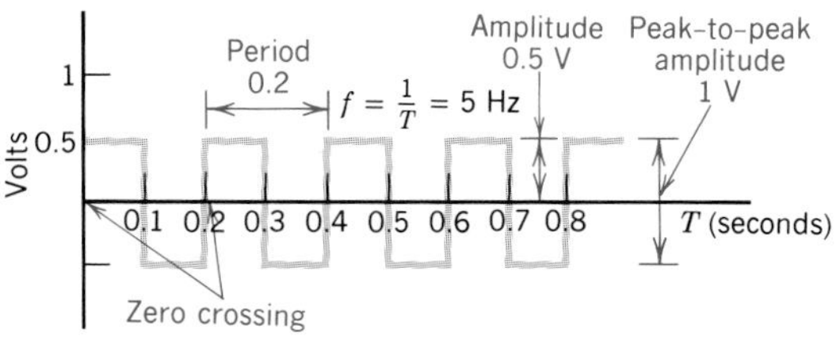

(a) Square wave

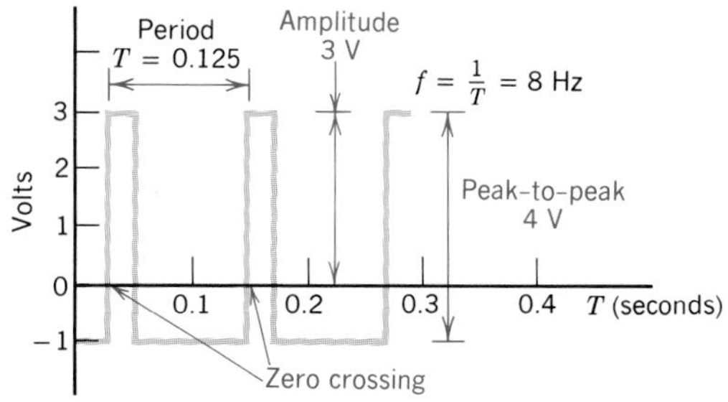

(b) Pulses

Figure 10.33 Terms such as frequency, period, and amplitude apply both to square waves and pulses.

reaches 50 percent of its peak amplitude. The duty factor is the comparison of the pulse width to the period:

$$\text{Duty factor} = \frac{\text{pulse width}}{\text{period}} \qquad \text{FORMULA 10.15}$$

Sometimes, the duty factor is expressed not as a decimal or fraction but as a percentage. In this case it is called the *duty cycle*.

$$\text{Duty cycle (in \%)} = \text{duty factor} \times 100 \qquad \text{FORMULA 10.16}$$

For a straight-sided square wave, the time between two successive 50 percent points is exactly one-half of the period, so the duty factor is 0.5 and the duty cycle is 50 percent.

Figure 10.34 Illustration of pulse width.

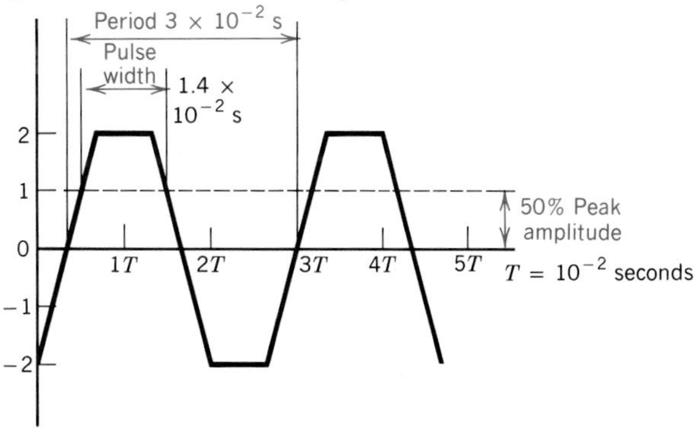

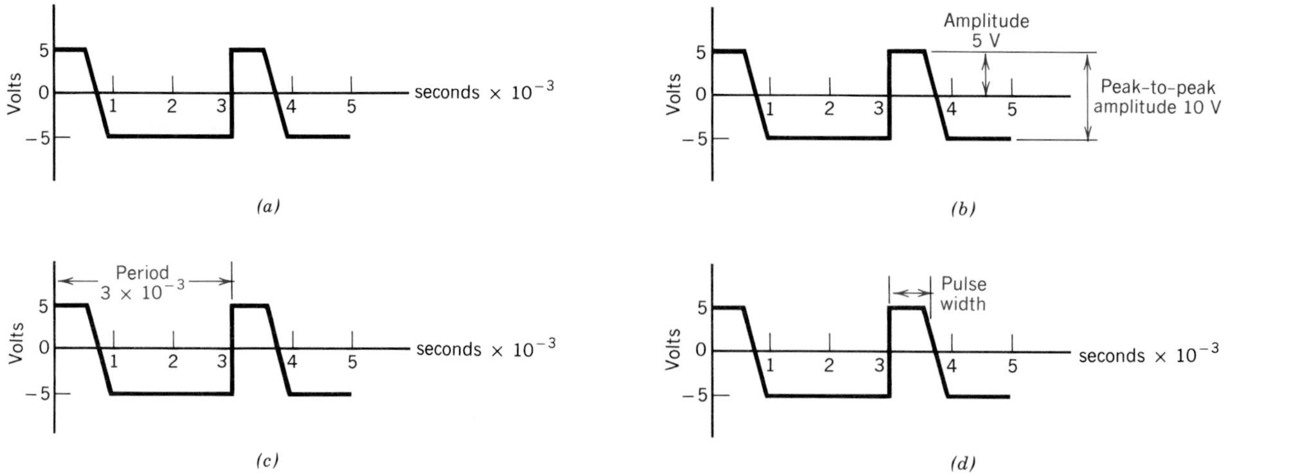

Figure 10.35 Example of the analysis of a pulse waveform.

EXAMPLE:
Determine the amplitude, peak-to-peak amplitude, period frequency, and duty cycle of the pulse waveform shown in Figure 10.35*a*. ■

SOLUTION:
Using the y-axis scale, it is easy to see from Figure 10.35*b* that the amplitude is 5 V and the peak-to-peak amplitude is 10 V. The period of the waveform is defined as the time between two zero crossings when the value of the waveform is increasing. The time interval markings on the x axis, Figure 10.35*c*, show this to be 3×10^{-3} s. To find the frequency of the waveform, the number of cycles in 1 s can be counted, otherwise, Formula 10.3 can be used

$$f = \frac{1}{t} = \frac{1}{3 \times 10^{-3}} = 333.33 \text{ Hz}$$

Since the pulses are not straight sided, there is a difference between the pulse width and the time between two successive zero crossings. In Figure 10.35*d*, you can see that the pulse width is about 6×10^{-4} s. The duty factor is

$$\text{Duty factor} = \frac{\text{pulse width}}{\text{period}} = \frac{6 \times 10^{-4}}{3 \times 10^{-3}} = 0.2$$

and the duty cycle is:

$$\text{Duty cycle} = \text{duty factor} \times 100 = 20\%$$ ■

Practice your understanding of these definitions by providing the period, frequency, peak, peak-to-peak,

Figure 10.36 Waveforms for analysis.

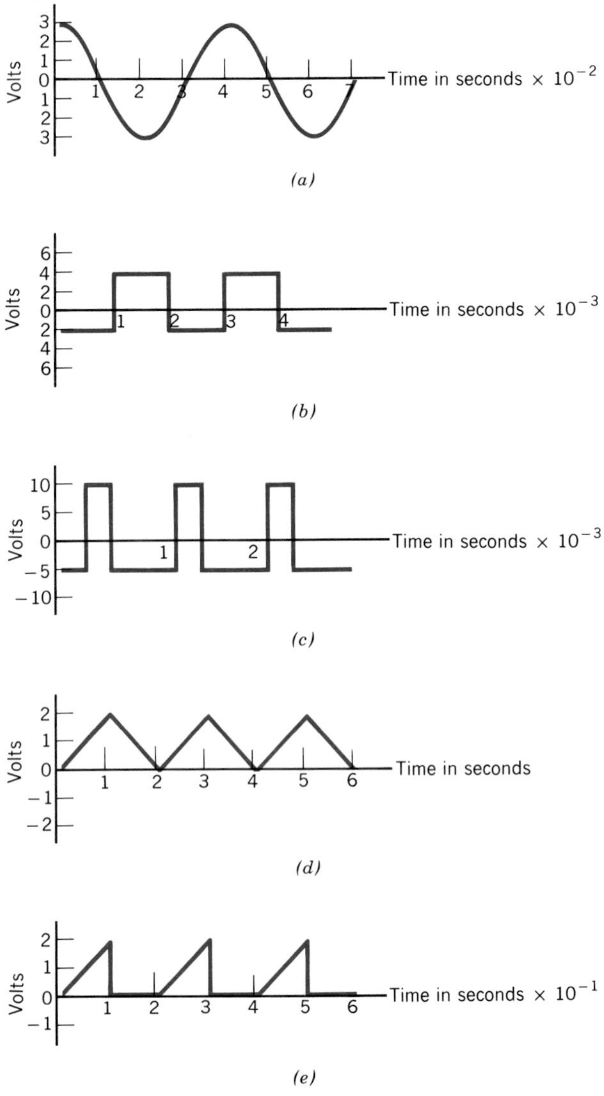

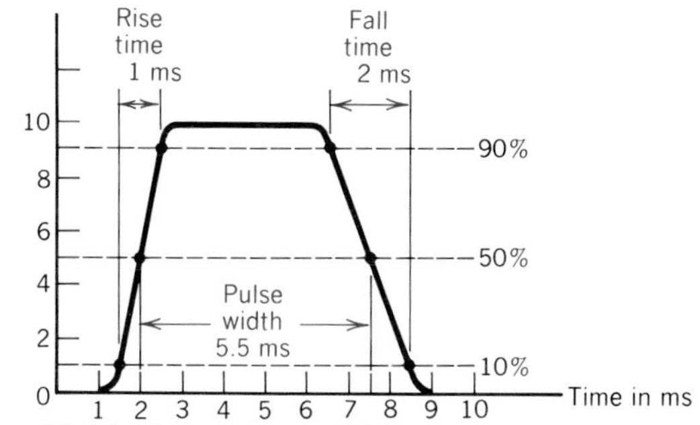

Figure 10.37 Pulse rise and fall terms.

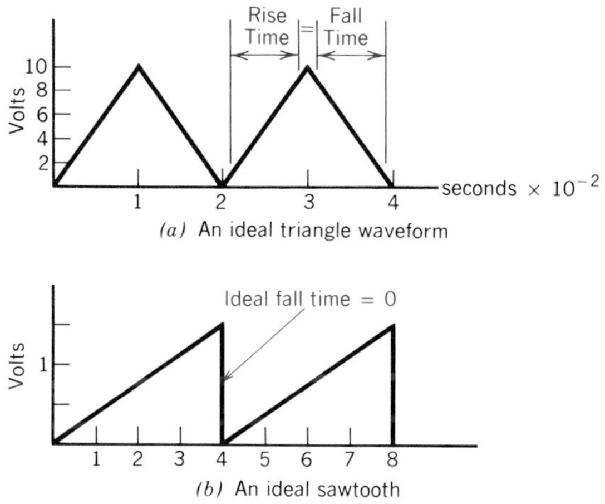

Figure 10.38 Rise and fall times in ideal triangle and sawtooth waveforms.

average, and rms values for the sine waveforms in Figure 10.36 and the period, frequency, peak-to-peak, duty factor, and duty cycle values for the other waveforms.

Real electronic equipment can only get close to producing straight-sided waveforms. In general, the graph of a pulse looks more like that shown in Figure 10.37. The slope of both the leading and trailing edges of the pulse are due to the fact that it takes a current or potential difference a certain amount of time to change from one value to another. When the amplitude of a waveform is increasing, the amount of time it takes to go from 10 percent of its peak value to 90 percent of its peak is called its *rise time*. Similarly, the amount of time needed to drop from 90 percent of peak value to 10 percent is called the *fall time*. These two terms apply to triangle and sawtooth waveforms as well as square-wave and rectangular pulses. In the ideal triangle waveform, the rise time is equal to the fall time. In the ideal sawtooth, the fall time should be zero. These ideal conditions are shown in Figures 10.38*a* and 10.38*b*.

D. APPLICATIONS

D.1 THE OSCILLOSCOPE

This section is devoted to the discussion of the modern oscilloscope, the second most important piece of test and analysis equipment used to analyze, troubleshoot, or adjust electronic circuits. Ranking second only to the multimeter among the tools of the trade in electronics, use of the oscilloscope is important for engineers and technicians. In order to use it effectively, you must understand how the oscilloscope works, how to operate its many controls and switches, and how to take readings and interpret the information displayed on its screen.

Although an oscilloscope can be adapted to function in many ways, it is usually used to draw a graph showing how the potential at one or more points in a circuit changes over a short time, generally hundredths or thousandths of a second. In effect, the oscilloscope displays the waveform of the potential at a point in a circuit. Since it displays not only potential difference, but potential difference changes, the oscilloscope presents much more information than a meter. Figure 10.39 is the simplified block diagram of an oscilloscope, identifying some of the principal circuits required to detect and trace potential differences. Notice that the TRIGGER block is enclosed in dashes rather than solid lines. This is because older oscilloscopes as well as some more modern "hobby" units do not make use of complex trigger circuitry. Such oscilloscopes are referred to as *synchronized* in contrast to *triggered* oscilloscopes. If the horizontal section is allowed to operate without any trigger or synchronizing signal from the vertical section, the oscilloscope is referred to as a *free-running scope*. Free-running scopes are not generally used.

By means of a probe, the potential difference between a point in a circuit and the ground reference is applied to the VERTICAL AMPLIFIER section of the oscilloscope. This potential difference is referred to as the *input signal*, or simply *input*. In triggered scopes,

Figure 10.39 Simplified block diagram of an oscilloscope.

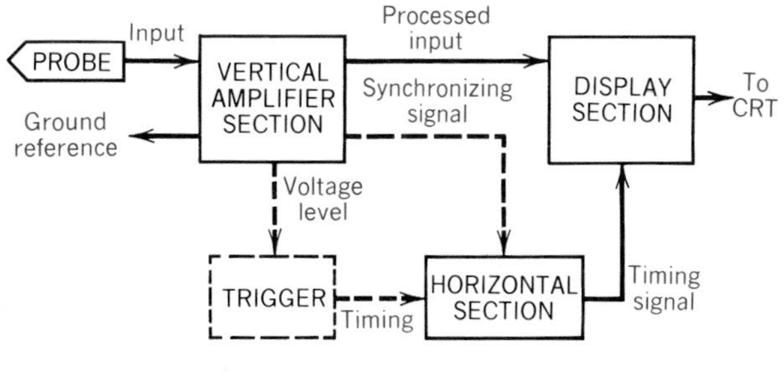

the voltage level of the input signal is compared to a set value by the TRIGGER circuits. When the potential of the input is equal to or greater than the set trigger level, a timing signal is sent to the HORIZONTAL circuitry. Timing signals from the HORIZONTAL circuitry and the input signal processed by the VERTICAL AMPLIFIER are sent to the DISPLAY circuits for display on the cathode-ray tube (CRT).

D.2 THE DISPLAY SECTION

Figure 10.40 is a detailed block diagram of the power and DISPLAY circuits of a modern oscilloscope, showing typical front panel controls that must be adjusted for a correct display. Most of the circuits and controls in this section provide operating power for the CRT, which displays the waveform of the input signal. A few years ago, only one waveform at a time could be displayed. Now, the majority of the scopes used in industry can show two waveforms at once. The scope shown in Figure 10.41 is of this type, called a *dual-trace* oscilloscope.

Troubleshooting computer circuitry often requires the comparison of several waveforms, and oscilloscopes that can display four and even eight different waveforms at once are becoming common. Regardless of the number of waveforms displayed, the display is obtained by producing a narrow beam of electrons in the CRT and electrostatically focusing this beam at a point on the phosphor-coated face of the tube. This point of focus will then glow brightly. The point of focus can be moved horizontally across the screen by adjusting the potential difference between the horizontal deflection plates in the tube. Similarly, by setting the potential difference between the vertical deflection plates, the focus point can be moved vertically.

Refer to the detailed block diagram of a typical oscilloscope display section shown in Figure 10.40. Power is obtained from commercial power service and is applied to the POWER INPUT circuits through an ON/OFF switch. When the switch is in its ON position, the POWER INPUT circuits provide power for the CRT heater and to a REGULATOR circuit that protects the unit from surges, spikes, and power line voltage changes. REGULATOR power output is then fed to the LOW-VOLTAGE SUPPLY to provide the operating power for the solid-state circuits of the oscilloscope and to the HIGH-VOLTAGE SUPPLY that provides a high voltage, low current for the operation of the CRT. The high voltage is applied across the CRT to direct the electrons, which are emitted from the heated cathode toward the phosphor-coated area at the front of the tube. The FOCUS CIRCUIT also receives high voltage, which is used to place a potential on the

Figure 10.40 Detailed block diagram of an oscilloscope display section.

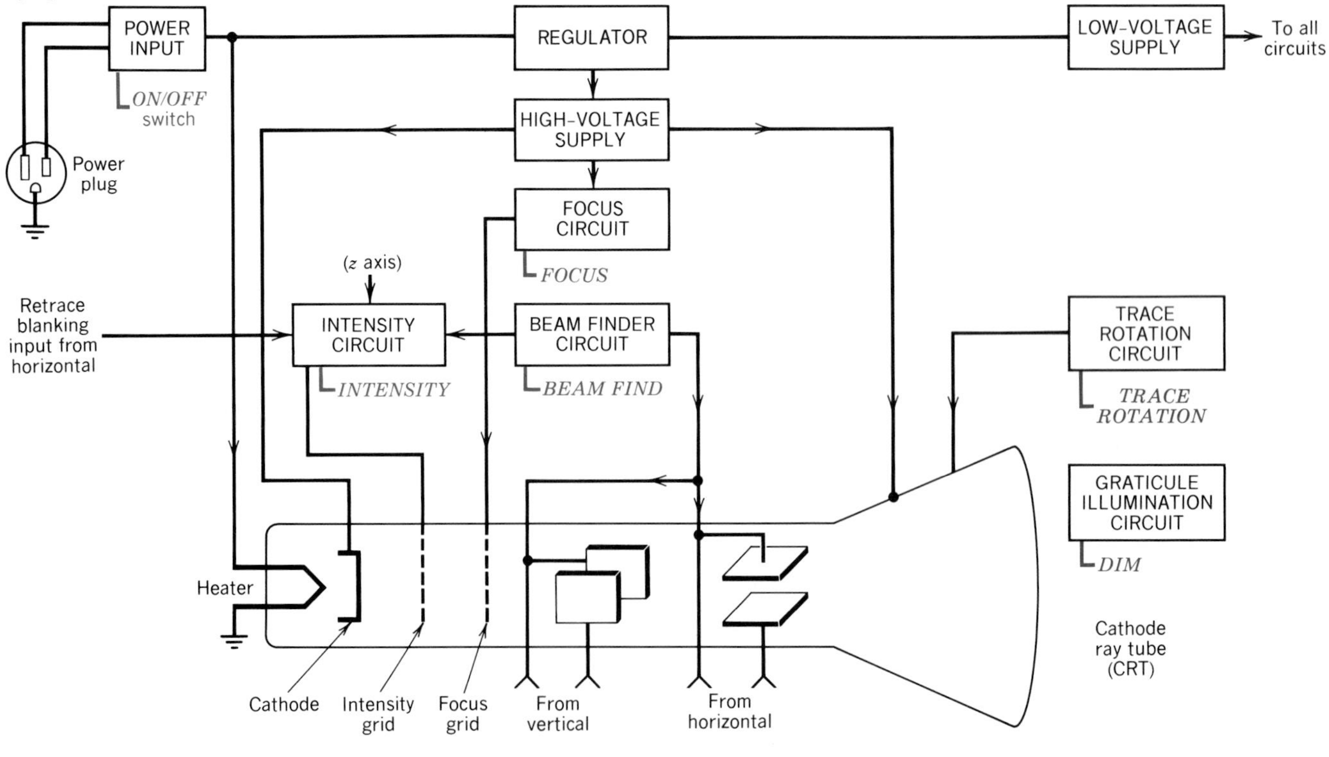

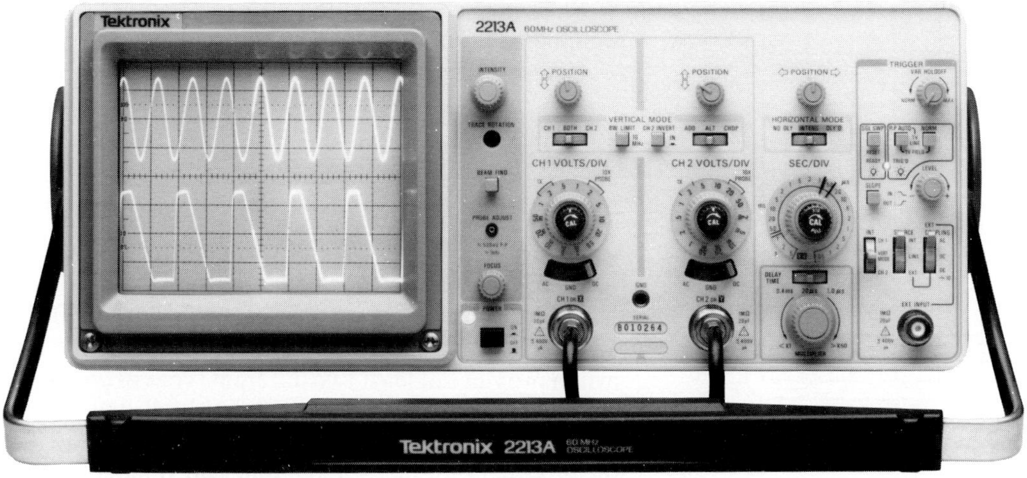

Figure 10.41 Typical dual-trace, triggered oscilloscope. (Photo courtesy of Tektronix, Inc.)

focus grid of the CRT. The *FOCUS* control makes it possible to adjust the thickness of the CRT electron beam. This controls the size of the glowing spot on the face of the CRT.

The INTENSITY CIRCUIT and *INTENSITY* control provide the potential for the intensity grid of the CRT. This tube element controls the brightness of the glowing spot on the tube face. The *INTENSITY* control is frequently used because the more quickly the electron beam is moved across the face of the CRT, the dimmer the glowing spot will be. The spot is being moved very quickly when high-frequency waveforms are being observed, so it may be necessary to increase the intensity to make the graph traced by the display brighter. On the other hand, when the electron beam is moving slowly, or is held in one place, the intensity of the glowing spot should be decreased. If it is not, the phosphor can be burned or the tube damaged. Notice that there are a number of inputs to the INTENSITY CIRCUIT in addition to the *INTENSITY* control. These will be discussed in later sections. Many modern, industrial-quality oscilloscopes have automatic as well as manual intensity control. This reduces the amount of control resetting that the oscilloscope operator has to do when switching from one kind of input to another.

The INTENSITY CIRCUIT receives an input from the BEAM FINDER CIRCUIT. This circuit is found on most better oscilloscopes and provides a convenient way of determining where the electron beam is aimed. Sometimes the vertical movement of the beam is so large that it is no longer aimed at the phosphor-coated area of the CRT. When this is the case, pressing the front panel *BEAM FIND* pushbutton will cause a very bright spot to appear. The position of this spot will indicate whether the beam is too high, too low, or off the screen to one side.

Another circuit considered as a part of the display section is the TRACE ROTATION CIRCUIT. Sometimes, perhaps because of a slight movement of the CRT, the path assumed by the graph of a straight line (i.e., a dc input to the scope) will be slightly slanted, as shown in Figure 10.42*a*. Adjusting the *TRACE ROTATION* control will correct this problem as shown in

Figure 10.42 Function of the TRACE ROTATION control.

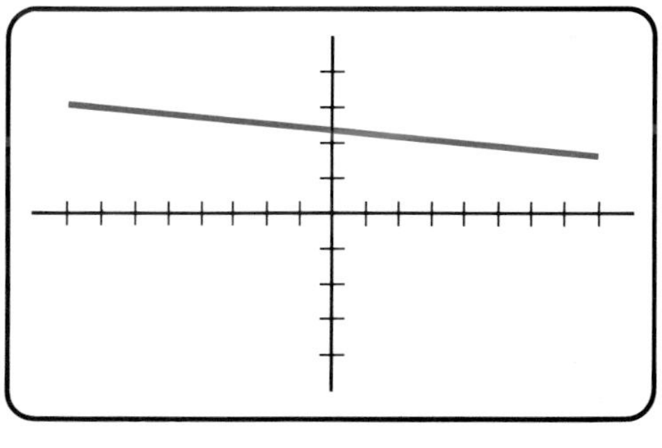

(a) Improperly adjusted trace rotation (input signal is dc)

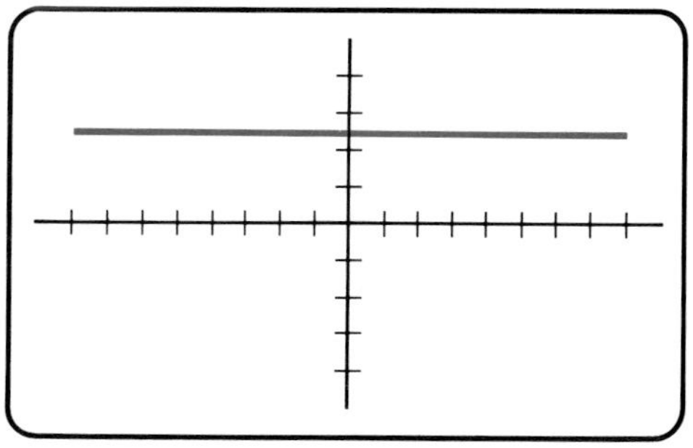

(b) Properly adjusted trace rotation

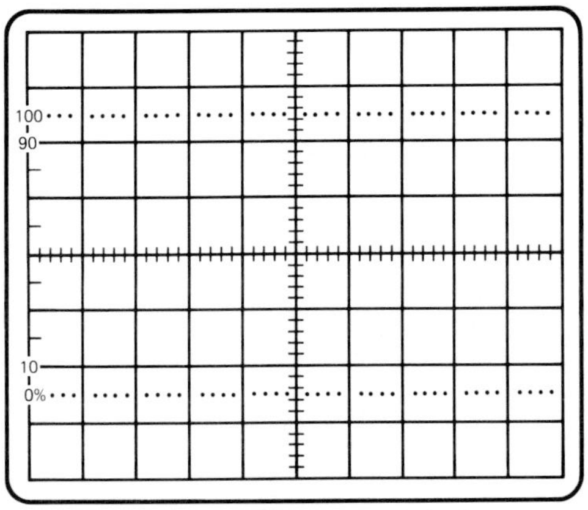

Figure 10.43 Popular oscilloscope graticule.

Figure 10.42*b*. This control does not need frequent adjustment.

Although it is not an electronic circuit, the CRT graticule is an important part of the oscilloscope. The graticule is the grid of lines that appears on the front of the CRT. Previously, the graticule was painted or etched on a protective glass that covered the face of the CRT, but the modern practice is to paint or etch these lines directly on the inside of the tube. Many scopes, particularly those used for photographing waveforms, provide a means by which the graticule lines can be illuminated by small lamps mounted around the front of the CRT. There is sometimes a *SCALE* or *GRATICULE BRIGHTNESS* control, which is used to vary the illumination of the graticule.

A variety of graticule types have been used by different manufacturers, but that shown in Figure 10.43 appears to be the most popular. It closely resembles the axes used in graphs.

Figure 10.44 Typical grouping of display section controls. (Photo courtesy of Tektronix, Inc.)

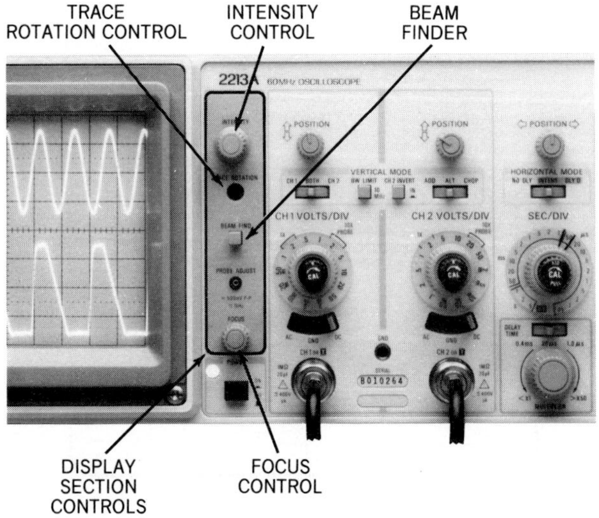

The various display section controls are usually grouped to permit easy setup by the operator. Figure 10.44 shows the grouping on a typical oscilloscope.

D.3 THE VERTICAL SECTION

The vertical system of an oscilloscope produces the vertical or *y*-axis information of the graph presented on the CRT. An input signal, as shown in the simplified block diagram of Figure 10.45 is coupled to the INPUT ATTENUATOR CIRCUIT. The *COUPLING* selector switch provides at least two different types of coupling, *AC* and *DC*. Selecting *DC* coupling will display nearly the exact waveform of the input signal, while the *AC* position incorporates a filter that will remove the dc component from a complete waveform. Often a third position, *GND*, is also provided. In this position, the input signal is disconnected from the INPUT ATTENUATOR. The ATTENUATOR is grounded. (*NOTE:* Only the scope ATTENUATOR is grounded, the input signal is *not* grounded.) The ATTENUATOR contains a voltage divider string used to divide the potential of the input signal. The *VOLTS/DIV* or volts per division control, which controls this divider, therefore determines the graph scale of the *y*-axis or vertical display. If the 5 VOLTS/DIV position is selected, each major division on the graticule *y* axis represents 5 V of input potential. As in the case of the axes of a graph, the *x* axis represents points at which $y = 0$. Point *A* in Figure 10.46, with the *VOLTS/DIV* control set at 2, represents input signals of 4 V; point *B* represents input signals of -5 V. The attenuated input signal is then amplified by a PREAMPLIFIER. In this circuit, a dc component is added to the input signal to position the waveform on the screen. Usually, it is desirable that the horizontal axis coincides with an input of 0 V, but this is not always the case. Consider the complex waveform shown in Figure 10.47*a*. Here, all the "action" is at the top of the waveform, and some of it can not

Figure 10.45 Simplified oscilloscope vertical amplifier section.

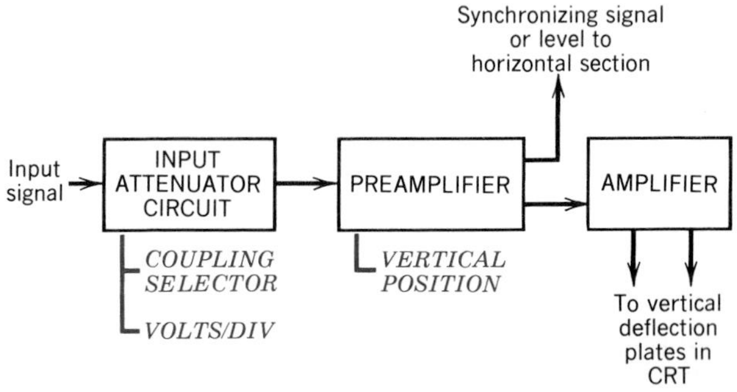

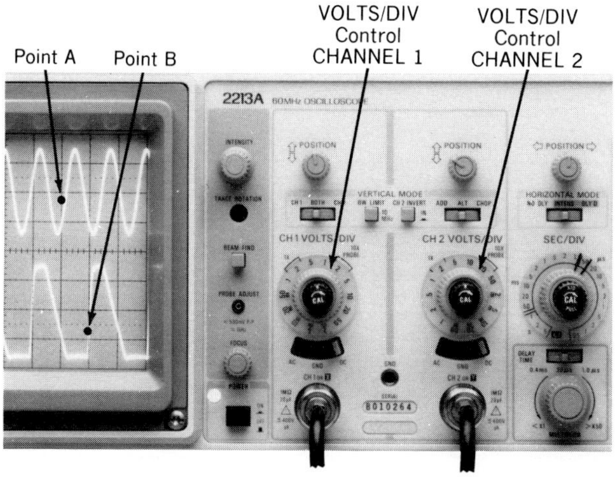

Figure 10.46 VOLTS/DIV control sets the graph scale. (Photo courtesy of Tektronix, Inc.)

Figure 10.47 One use of the vertical position control.

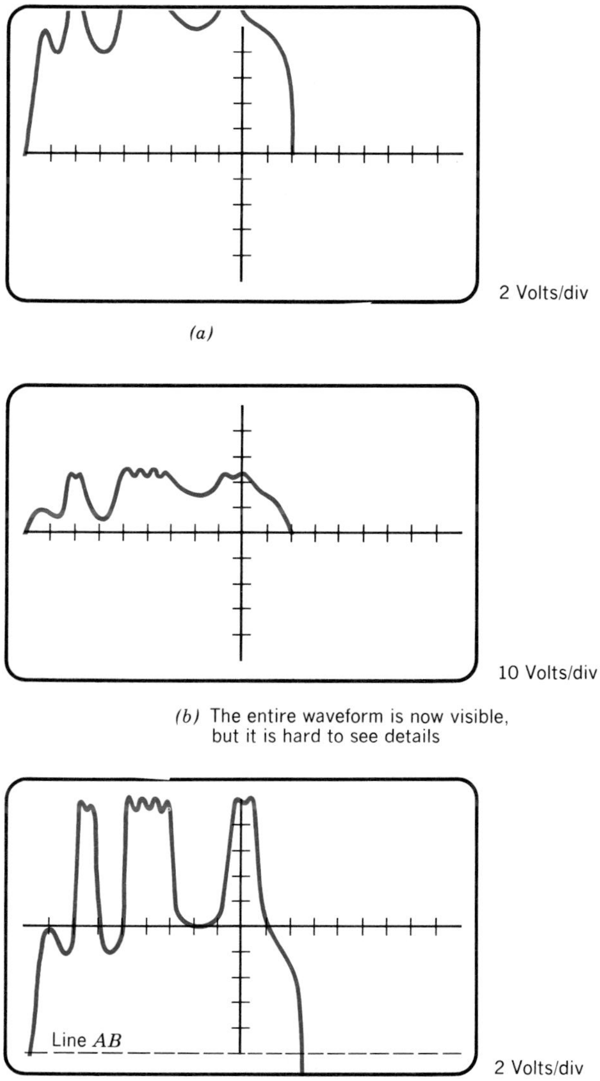

(a)

(b) The entire waveform is now visible, but it is hard to see details

(c) Detail is preserved and whole waveform is visible

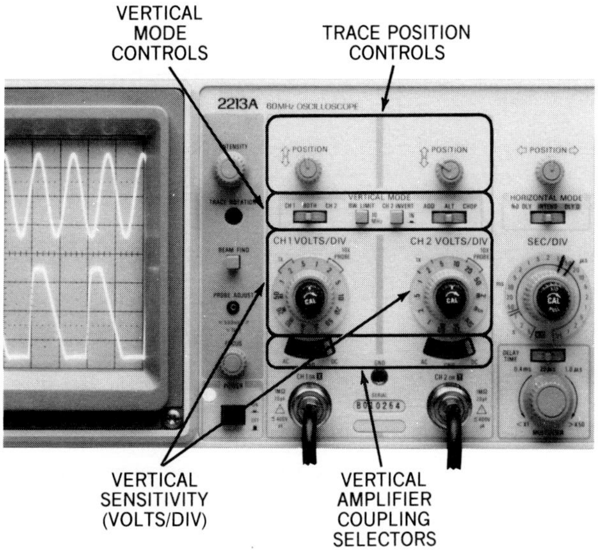

Figure 10.48 Typical grouping of vertical section controls. (Photo courtesy of Tektronix, Inc.)

be seen. Increasing the scale to 10 VOLTS/DIV, as in Figure 10.47*b* does bring the entire waveform into the screen area, but some of the detail is lost. On the whole, it is better to adjust the *VERTICAL POSITION* control to bring the waveform to the position shown in Figure 10.47*c*. Of course, you will have to remember that the *x* axis of the graph is now graticule line *AB*, and not the original axis. The *VERTICAL POSITION* control has a number of uses, and, as you will see in a later section, is particularly important when two or more waveforms are being observed together. The output of the PREAMPLIFIER is raised to the voltage level necessary to deflect the electron beam by the AMPLIFIER stage, and the deflection voltage is routed to the CRT deflection plates. The vertical section controls of an oscilloscope are shown in Figure 10.48. Note that the *VOLTS/DIV* control is actually a complex control. The center section operates a potentiometer used for "fine tuning" the *VOLTS/DIV* setting when necessary. The potentiometer is generally kept in its *CAL* or calibrated position so that the switch setting will be the actual voltage setting on the screen.

D.4 THE HORIZONTAL SECTION

Figure 10.49 is the simplified block diagram of an oscilloscope horizontal section. Although it is much simpler than the horizontal sections used in modern industrial scopes, an understanding of its operation will prepare you for the discussion of the operation of the triggered dual-trace oscilloscope. The horizontal section of the oscilloscope produces the deflection voltage

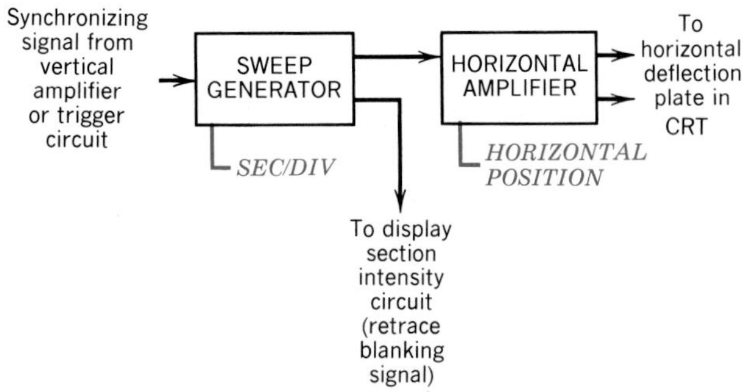

Figure 10.49 Simplified block diagram of an oscilloscope horizontal section.

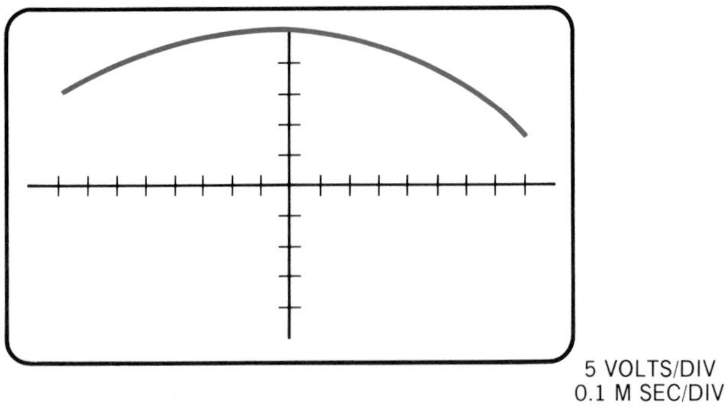

Figure 10.51 Selecting too fast a trace speed makes it impossible to determine the shape of the waveform.

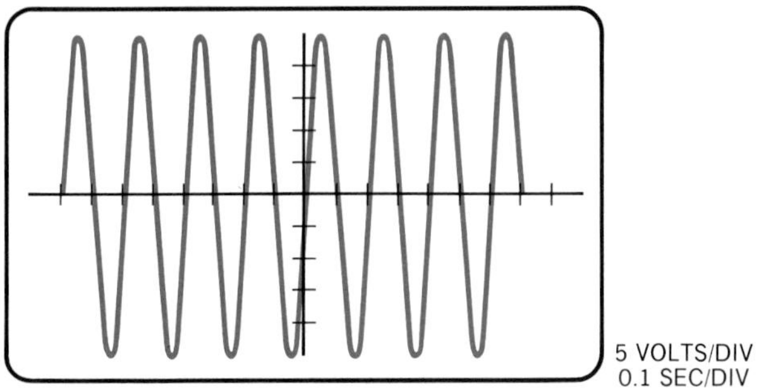

Figure 10.52 Selecting too slow a trace speed causes too many cycles to be displayed. Waveform shape is difficult to distinguish.

for the horizontal deflection plates of the CRT. In usual operation, it is necessary to move the electron beam across the CRT screen in a steady manner so that each x-axis graticule division represents an equal interval of time. The rate at which the beam is moved from left to right across the screen is controlled by the SWEEP GENERATOR. The waveform of the simple, synchronized SWEEP GENERATOR is shown in Figure 10.50. When the generator output is at its negative peak, as at point A, the beam is aimed at the left-most point on the x axis. The sweep output then begins to rise. When this voltage reaches its positive peak, the electron beam is at the right-hand edge of the x axis. The output of the SWEEP GENERATOR then drops rapidly to its negative peak again. During this time, called the *retrace,* the beam moves back to the left-hand side of the screen. Since the line drawn by the retrace might confuse the graph drawn on the screen, a signal is sent to the display section intensity circuit, which reduces the spot intensity to below the visible level during the retrace period. This is called *retrace blanking*. The rate at which the beam is moved across the screen is controlled by the seconds per division or *SEC/DIV* selector switch. This control has a number of settings that make it possible to adjust the time it takes to move the beam across the screen from several seconds to 100 ns (100×10^{-9} s). The number of settings and their range depends on the scope type. When observing regular, periodic waveforms, it is usual to

Figure 10.50 Waveform shape of a sweep generator output.

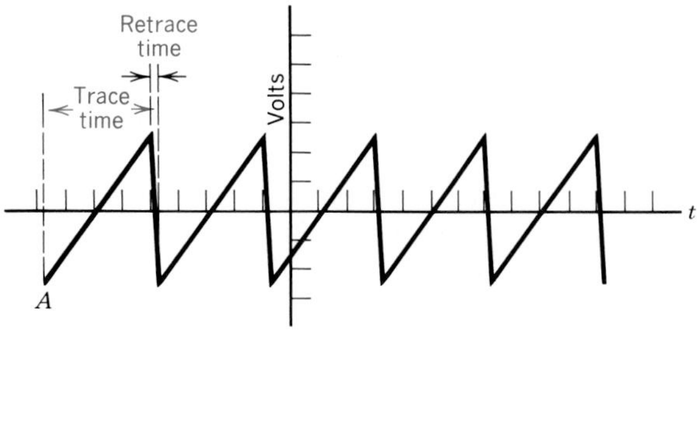

select a sweep speed that will permit anywhere from 1 to 10 complete cycles to be displayed. If too fast a speed is selected, as in Figure 10.51, it is impossible to determine the true shape of the waveform. Too low a sweep speed means that too many cycles are displayed, and significant detail may be lost as in Figure 10.52. As in the case of the *VOLTS/DIV* control, the *SEC/DIV* control central portion is a potentiometer used for "fine tuning." This portion of the control is generally left in its calibrated (*CAL*) position so that the sweep speed will be as indicated on the switch portion of the control.

The fact that the oscilloscope graph appears to be a line even though the electron beam is causing only one small area at a time to glow is due to the tendency of the screen phosphor material to continue to glow for a time after the beam has continued on. This tendency is called the *persistance* of phosphor. At very slow sweep speeds, the phosphor of a standard CRT does not have enough persistance to continue to glow until the next time the beam sweeps over it. At slow sweep speeds, the left-hand half of the trace will disappear while the right-hand half is being traced. At the slowest speeds, the glowing dot can be seen to move across the screen. Care must be taken to reduce the intensity at these speeds, or the phosphor will be burned.

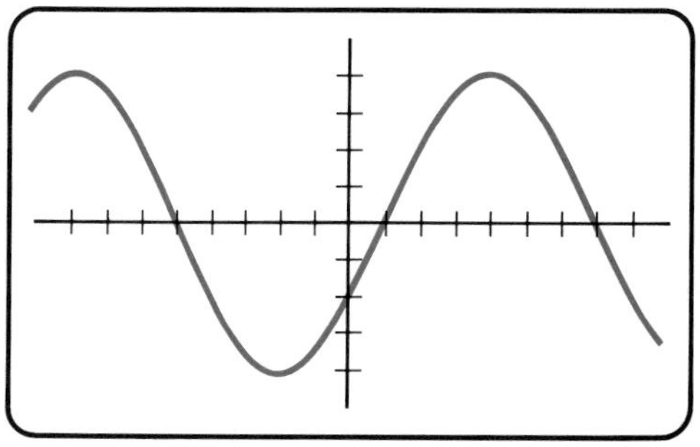

(a)

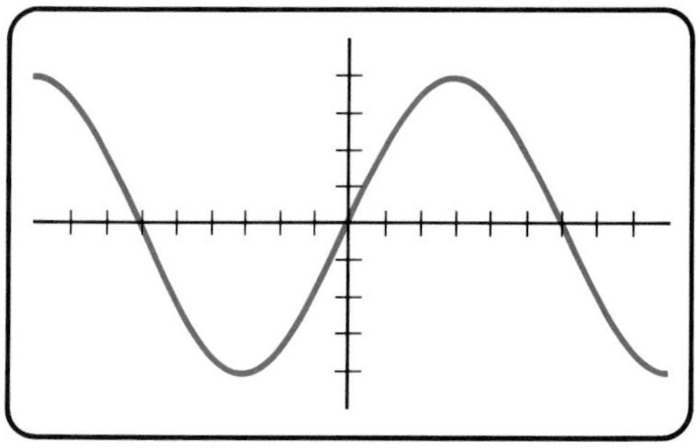

(b)

Figure 10.53 A waveform viewed on a free-running (*a*) and a triggered (*b*) oscilloscope.

In Figure 10.53*a*, you can see that the waveform begins with a *y*-axis or voltage value other than zero. Also the origin, that is, the intersection of the *x* and *y* axes, does not coincide with a zero value for *y*, or voltage. For some oscilloscope measurements, one or both of these conditions is desired. Use of a triggered oscilloscope, which begins its trace when the input reaches a set voltage, permits the trace to be set as shown in Figure 10.53*b*. Therefore, the free-running or synchronized type of oscilloscope horizontal section is rarely found in industrial applications. The differences between this simpler oscilloscope and the popular dual-trace, triggered oscilloscope are described in Section D.6.

D.5 OSCILLOSCOPE PROBES

A variety of devices are used to connect the input jack or terminal of an oscilloscope to points in a circuit or electronic unit. These devices are called *probes* and are composed of a length of coaxial cable with a plug at one end and some sort of instrument for making electrical contact or holding a contact point on the other. Figure 10.54 shows some of the probe types currently in use.

Figure 10.54 Some of the probe types and accessory tips currently in use. (Photograph courtesy of Tektronix, Inc.)

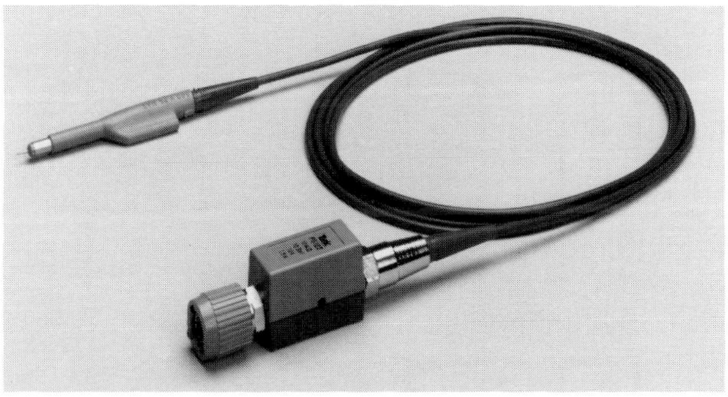

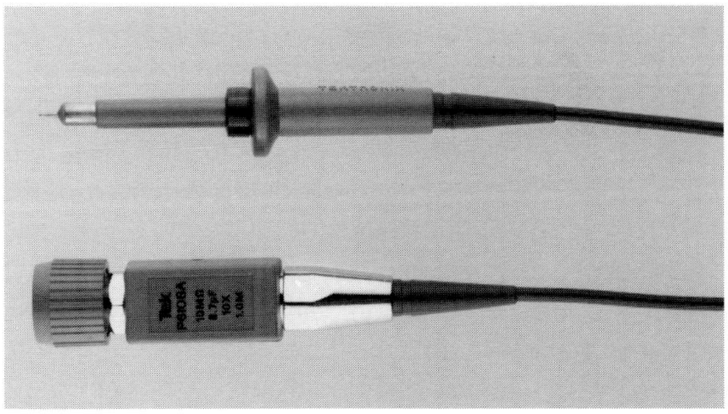

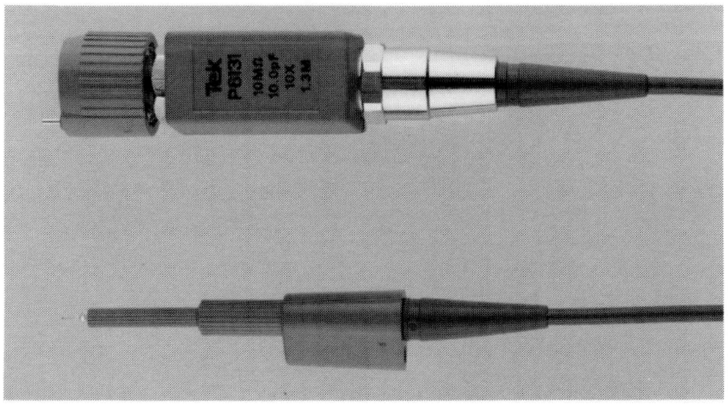

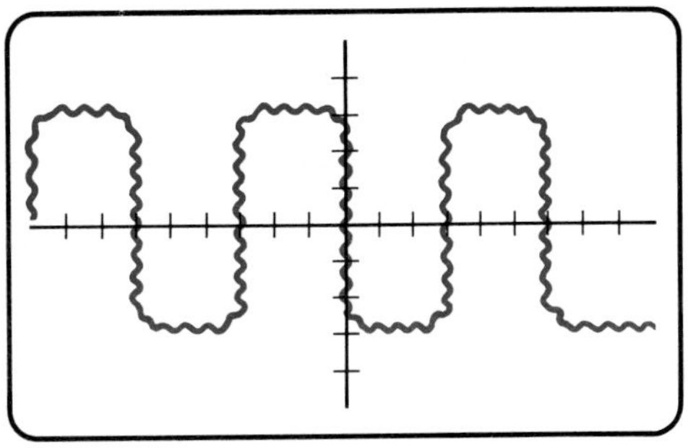

(a) Square wave coupled to scope with unshielded wire

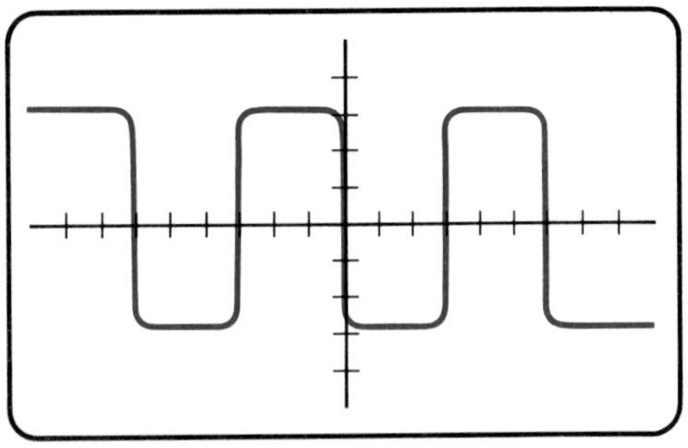

(b) Signal coupled with coaxial cable

Figure 10.55 It is important to eliminate interference when connecting the oscilloscope to the circuit being tested.

Notice that the connections between the probe and oscilloscope are made by coaxial cable. Figure 10.55*a* shows a square-wave signal coupled to the oscilloscope input with a length of unshielded wire. Distortion and changes to the waveform from a number of causes are evident. The rounding of the corners is probably due to excessive power being drawn from the signal generator, while the wavy quality (exaggerated in the figure) is due to the pick up from 60-Hz ac power lines in the area. Television and CB radios can also distort the waveform image. If the signal is coupled to the scope with a length of coaxial cable, and the shield braid of the cable is grounded, the amount of interference from power lines, nearby radio transmitters, and such electrical devices as motors is reduced, as shown in Figure 10.55*b*. This is why probes are connected to the scope input with coax. The distortion due to the excessive power drawn from the signal generator by the low-resistance input of the oscilloscope is still present.

The accuracy of the waveform observations made with an oscilloscope can also be affected if too much power is drawn from the source of the input signal. For this reason, it is common to use high-resistance probes called *attenuator probes*. Although an attenuator probe reduces the potential of the input signal at

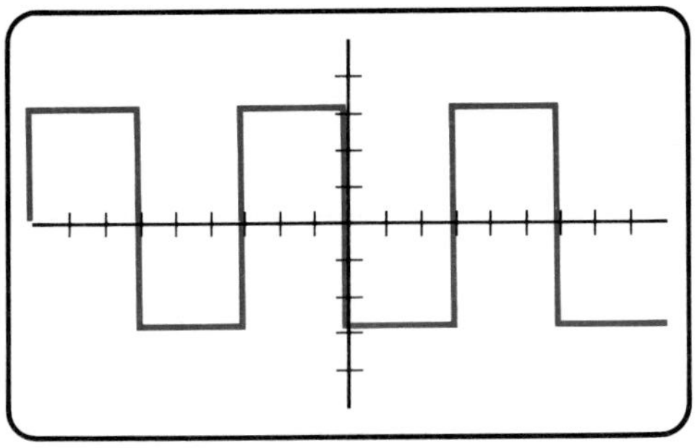

Figure 10.56 Using a $\times 10$ attenuator probe eliminates the rounding shown in Figure 10.55*b*.

the oscilloscope input connector, this is easily restored by changing the setting of the *VOLTS/DIV* control.

If a high-resistance 10X probe connected to the scope input by a coaxial cable is used, almost all this distortion disappears, as shown in Figure 10.56. However, since the resistance of this probe multiplies the input resistance of the oscilloscope by a factor of 10, the *VOLTS/DIV* control must be reset to restore the vertical deflection of the waveform. Although nonattenuating ($\times$ 1) probes and high-voltage ($\times$ 100) probes are sometimes used, the $\times$ 10 attenuator probe is the most common.

Most attenuator probes contain a control called

Figure 10.57 (*a*) or (*c*) means that the probe compensation must be adjusted.

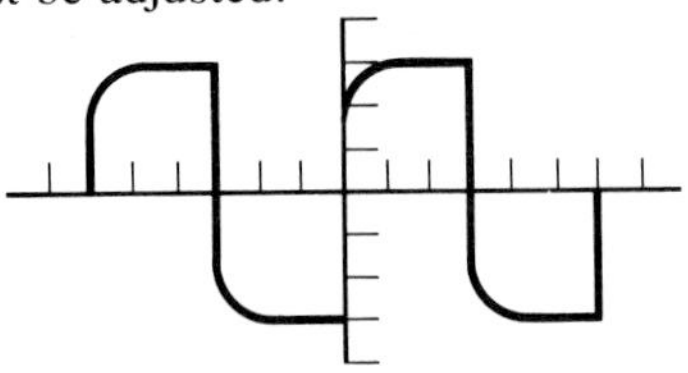

(a) Probe is undercompensated

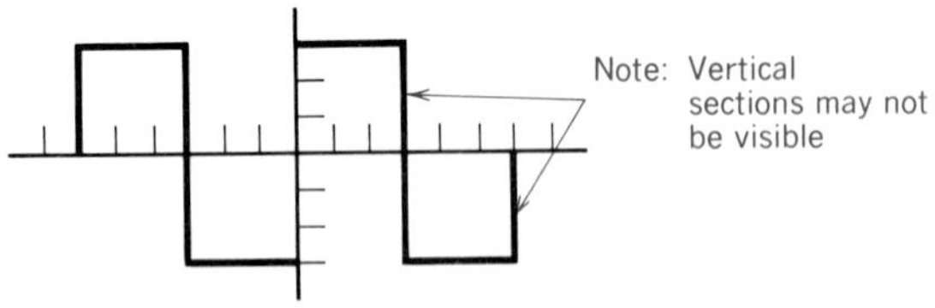
Note: Vertical sections may not be visible

(b) Correct compensation

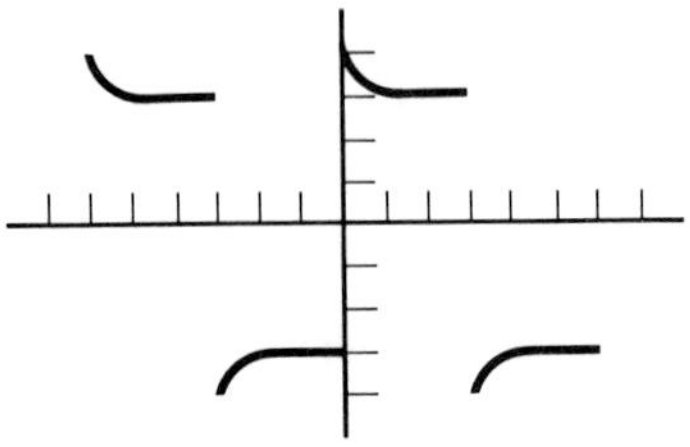

(c) Probe is overcompensated

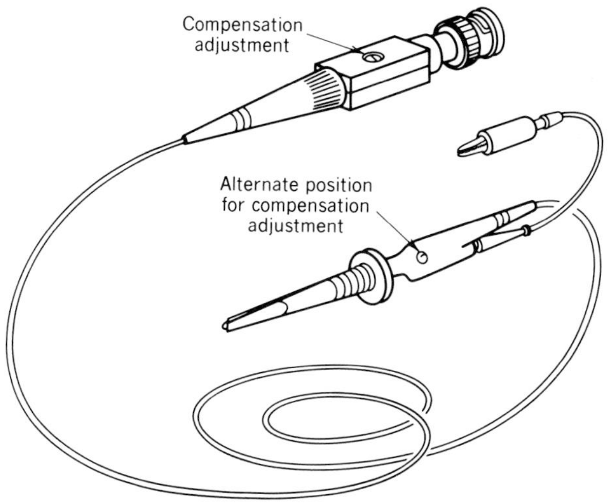

Figure 10.58 A screwdriver-adjusted probe.

the *probe compensation* control used to match the electrical characteristics of the probe to those of the oscilloscope. Since these characteristics are dependent on temperature, humidity, and the frequency of the input signal, the setting of the probe compensation control should be checked regularly before making measurements or each time you change accessory tips. Adjusting the compensation on some scopes is made easier by the presence of a calibration signal generated by a circuit in the scope itself. The calibration signal is a square wave. When the probe is connected to the calibration signal terminal, a waveform similar to one of the three shown in Figure 10.57 should be seen. If the pattern resembles either 10.57*a* or 10.57*c*, adjustment is necessary. The adjustment generally requires either a screwdriver (Figure 10.58) or is accomplished by turning a portion of the probe itself (Figure 10.59). If the probe is not properly compensated, the waveform observations you make will be misleading and will tend to hide rather than reveal circuit malfunctions.

Figure 10.59 The compensation of some probes can be adjusted by turning a portion of the probe itself.

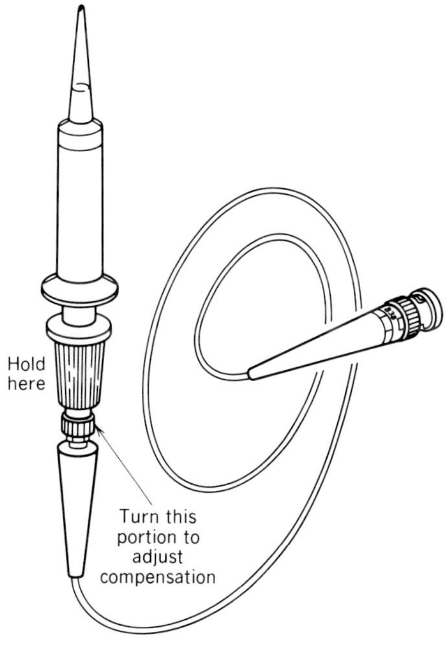

D.6 THE DUAL-TRACE, TRIGGERED OSCILLOSCOPE

The typical oscilloscope shown in Figure 10.41 possesses a number of features not discussed in the previous sections. The most striking of these is the fact that two waveforms can be examined at the same time. This is generally done, as shown in Figure 10.60, by providing two inputs, called CHANNEL 1 and CHANNEL 2, which are coupled to separate INPUT ATTENUATORS and separate PREAMPLIFIERS. A *MODE* control, which is actually a part of the HORIZONTAL SECTION of the oscilloscope, permits you to select either the *ALTERNATE* or the *CHOPPED* mode of operation. In the *ALTERNATE* mode of operation, the CHANNEL 1 PREAMPLIFIER is connected to the AMPLIFIER by the SWITCHING CIRCUIT while the CHANNEL 2 PREAMPLIFIER is disconnected. One whole trace, that is, one horizontal movement of the beam is completed, and then the SWITCHING CIRCUIT disconnects the CHANNEL 1 PREAMPLIFIER and connects the CHANNEL 2 PREAMPLIFIER. Because the persistance of the CRT phosphor is longer at most sweep settings than the time required for two complete horizontal sweeps of the electron beam, two separate waveform graphs are drawn even though only one electron beam is used. These two waveform graphs can be separated on the screen as seen in Figure 10.61*a* through the use of two independent *VERTICAL POSITION* controls. Or, if desired, the two traces can be superimposed for purposes of comparison as in Figure 10.61*b*.

When using slow sweep speeds, the *ALTERNATE* mode cannot be used since one trace will fade before the second is completed. Another mode of operation, the *CHOPPED* mode, is used in this situation. Instead of completing a whole trace before switching the channels, the SWITCHING CIRCUIT changes rapidly between the two preamplifiers. If the sweep speed is too fast, and if you look closely, you can actually see the tiny gaps in the trace patterns, as shown in Figure 10.62.

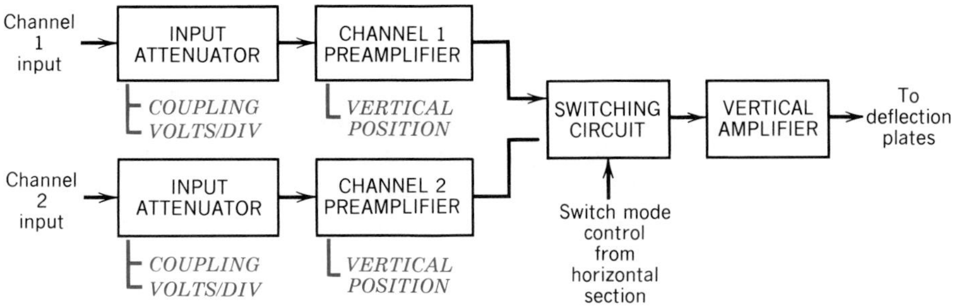

Figure 10.60 Block diagram of the vertical amplifier section of a dual-trace oscilloscope.

Figure 10.61 A principal function of the vertical position controls on a dual-trace scope is the comparison of input signals.

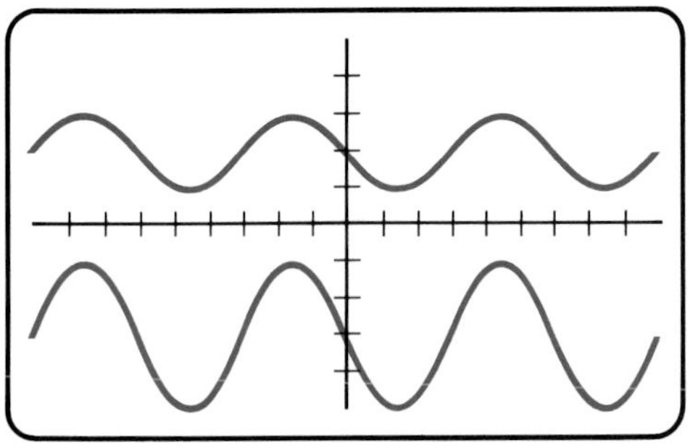

(a) Input signals viewed separately

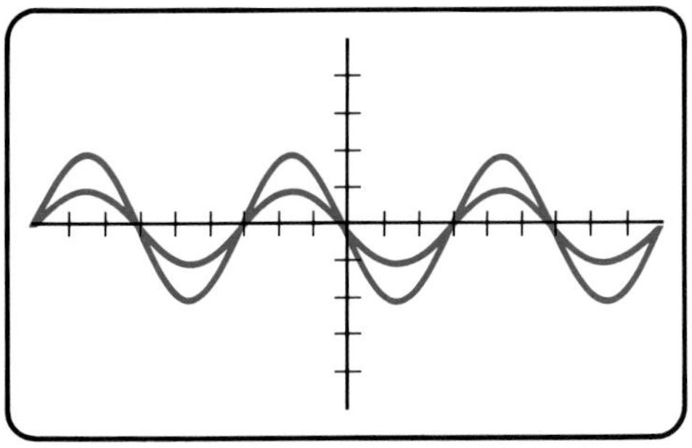

(b) Input signals superimposed for purposes of comparison

Figure 10.62 The chopped mode as seen when the sweep speed is set too high.

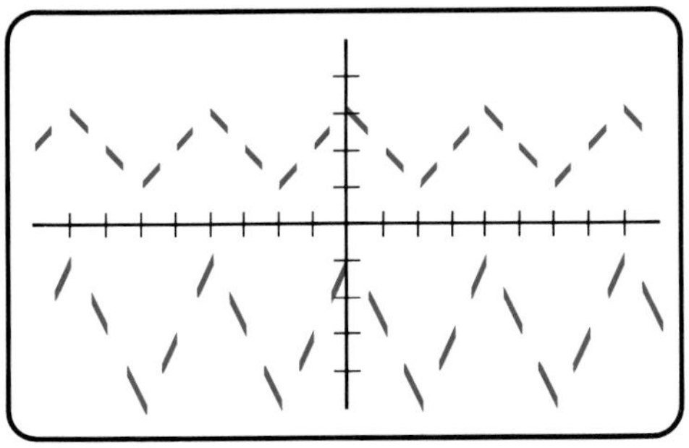

Figure 10.63 *MODE* and *VOLTS/DIV* controls on a dual-trace oscilloscope. (Photo courtesy of Tektronix, Inc.)

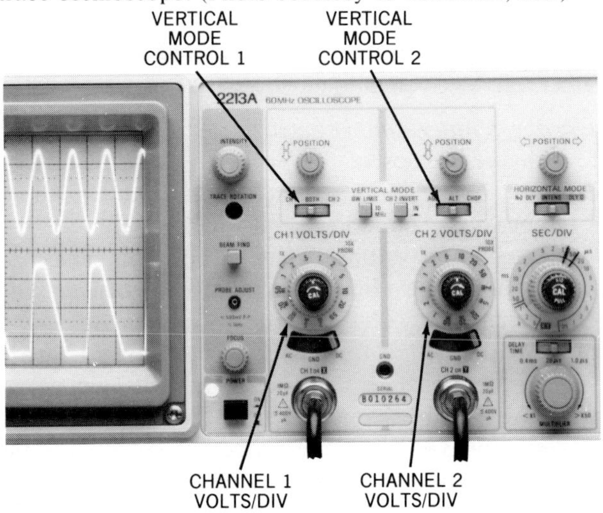

The *MODE* control switch, which selects either the alternate or chopped mode of operation, will generally also provide several other choices. In some cases, as in the oscilloscope shown in Figure 10.63, several mode controls are included. In this figure, there are two *VERTICAL MODE* switches. One switch permits either *CHANNEL 1* or *CHANNEL 2* to be observed alone, or *BOTH* to be observed together. The second switch selects either *ALT* or *CHOP*, and provides a third mode *ADD*. In this mode, the internal switching circuit is disabled, and a single trace is produced on the screen, which represents the sum of the two input signals. Some oscilloscopes also provide a *MODE* control setting that inverts the input signal to one channel. This makes it possible to display only the difference of the signals to the two channels. Notice that there are two separate sets of vertical system controls, including *VOLTS/DIV* and *COUPLING*.

The horizontal section of this scope (see Figures 10.49 and 10.64) is considerably more complex than

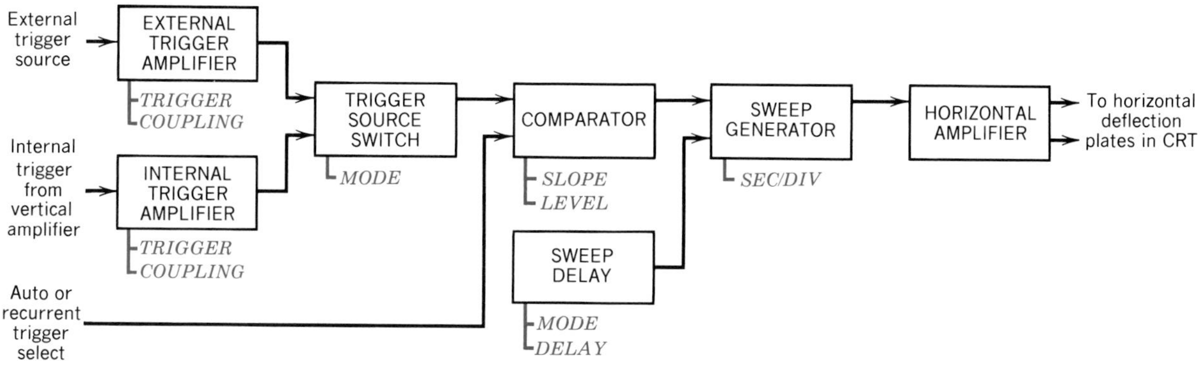

Figure 10.64 Block diagram of the horizontal section of a dual-trace oscilloscope.

that of the simple, synchronized oscilloscope. The principal difference is the presence of the trigger circuits, which determine the moment at which the SWEEP GENERATOR begins its operation. The *TRIGGER SOURCE* switch, through the setting of its *MODE* control switch, permits the choice of one of a number of conditions to begin the horizontal movement of the electron beam in the CRT. In its *RECURRENT* position, the system operates exactly as a free-running scope, that is, the sawtooth output of the SWEEP GENERATOR repeats at regular intervals. In its *NORMAL* mode, however, it requires a signal input of a particular voltage level and direction of change to start or "trigger" the SWEEP GENERATOR. This voltage level and the direction or sense of the level change (that is, whether the potential of the input is increasing or decreasing) are set by the position of the *SLOPE* switch and *LEVEL* control shown in Figure 10.64.

The reason it is necessary to select either a positive or negative slope is shown in Figure 10.65. Suppose that a trigger potential of 1 V is chosen. The waveform is at this level twice during each cycle, once when the potential of the input signal is increasing, and again when it is decreasing. If the positive slope is selected, the sweep generator will trigger at the point shown in Figure 10.66*a*, resulting in an oscilloscope trace as in 10.66*b*. If the negative slope is selected, the sweep generator will trigger at the point shown in Figure 10.67*a*, and the displayed waveform will resemble that shown in 10.67*b*. Some oscilloscopes use the symbol ⟋ to indicate a positive slope or ascending voltage level and ⟍ to indicate a negative slope or descending voltage level.

Finally, some oscilloscopes contain two independent sweep generators so that different sweep speeds

Figure 10.65 The trigger level control selects the input potential at which the trigger circuit starts the sweep generator.

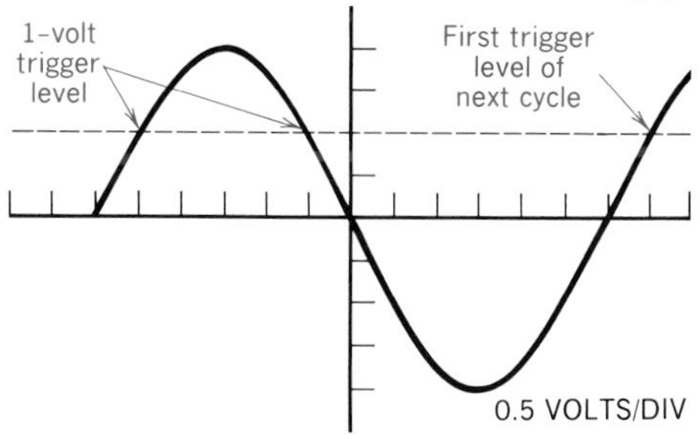

Figure 10.66 A trigger level of 1 V and positive slope seen on waveform (*a*) and the resulting trace (*b*).

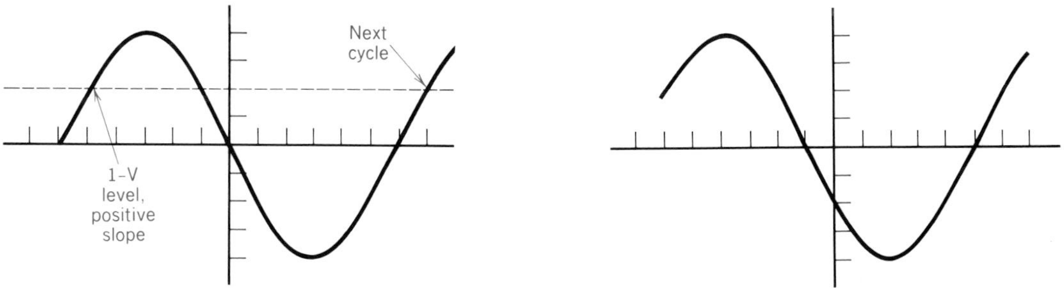

(*a*) 1-V level, positive slope selected

(*b*) Oscilloscope trace

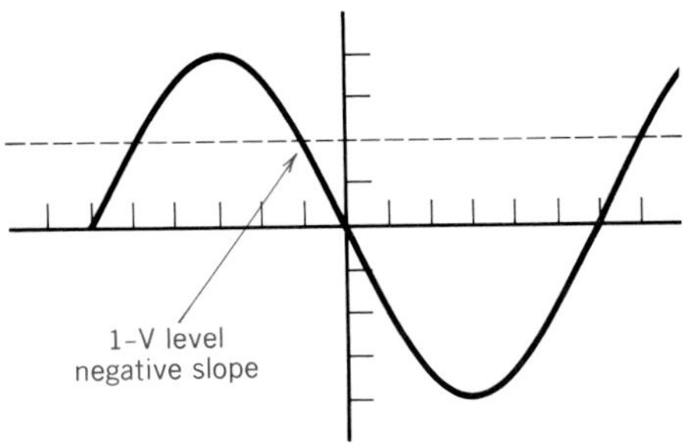

(a) 1-V level, negative slope selected

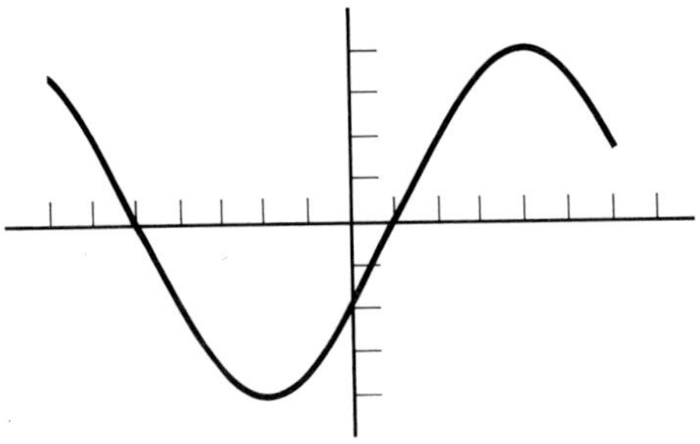

(b) Oscilloscope trace

Figure 10.67 A trigger level of 1 V and negative slope seen on waveform (*a*) and the resulting trace (*b*).

can be used for the *CHANNEL 1* and *CHANNEL 2* sweeps. Another feature not covered at this point is the delayed sweep, which permits the start of the sweep generator to be delayed for a time set by the operator.

D.7 OBSERVING WAVEFORMS AND MAKING MEASUREMENTS WITH AN OSCILLOSCOPE

Properly used, an oscilloscope is close to being a complete troubleshooting laboratory. The following instructions and flow diagrams represent step-by-step instructions for setting up, compensating the probes, and observing waveforms with a typical oscilloscope. Since control names, locations, and operating procedures differ, these instructions should be compared to those given in the operating instructions of your equipment. For more sophisticated procedures such as using the oscilloscope for frequency, period, and phase measurements, also refer to the Laboratory Manual that accompanies this book.

D.7.1 START-UP

The first step in any scope use should be checking the present position of the controls, resetting them, if necessary, to some initial position *before* turning on scope power.

a. Check that the vertical and horizontal sweep *VARIABLE* controls are in their *CALIBRATED* (fully clockwise) position.

b. Check that the *INTENSITY* control has not been set too high. If you are not familiar with this model scope, set the control fully counterclockwise to minimum intensity. You will have to turn the control clockwise to see the trace after turning on the power.

c. Set the controls to obtain a free-running trace on *CHANNEL 1*.

CH 1 VOLTS/DIV	5 V
VERTICAL MODE	CH 1
HORIZONTAL MODE	NO DELAY AUTO
CH 1 SEC/DIV	1 ms
POWER	ON

d. After a minute, press the *BEAM FIND* pushbutton. A bright spot should appear at the left of the screen. If this does not occur, adjust the horizontal position control until the spot appears.

e. Slowly turn the *INTENSITY* and *HORIZONTAL POSITION* controls until a straight-line trace is obtained. If necessary, adjust the *INTENSITY* and FOCUS controls to obtain a thin line of medium brightness.

f. If your scope is a dual-trace model, bring the second or *CHANNEL 2* trace on to the screen.

CH 2 VOLTS/DIV	5 V
VERTICAL MODE	BOTH
CH 2 SEC/DIV	1 ms

g. If necessary, adjust the *CH 2 VERTICAL POSITION* control so that the screen resembles Figure 10.68.

h. Calibrate your test probes by connecting the CH 1 probe between the CH 1 INPUT jack and the

Figure 10.68 Using the *VERTICAL POSITION* controls, adjust the two traces to allow sufficient space for both waveforms.

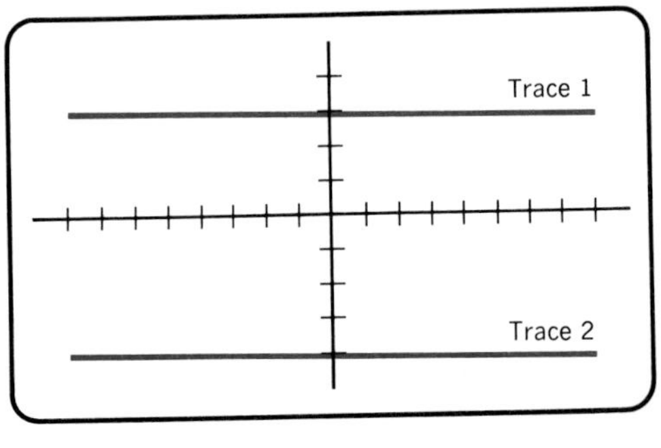

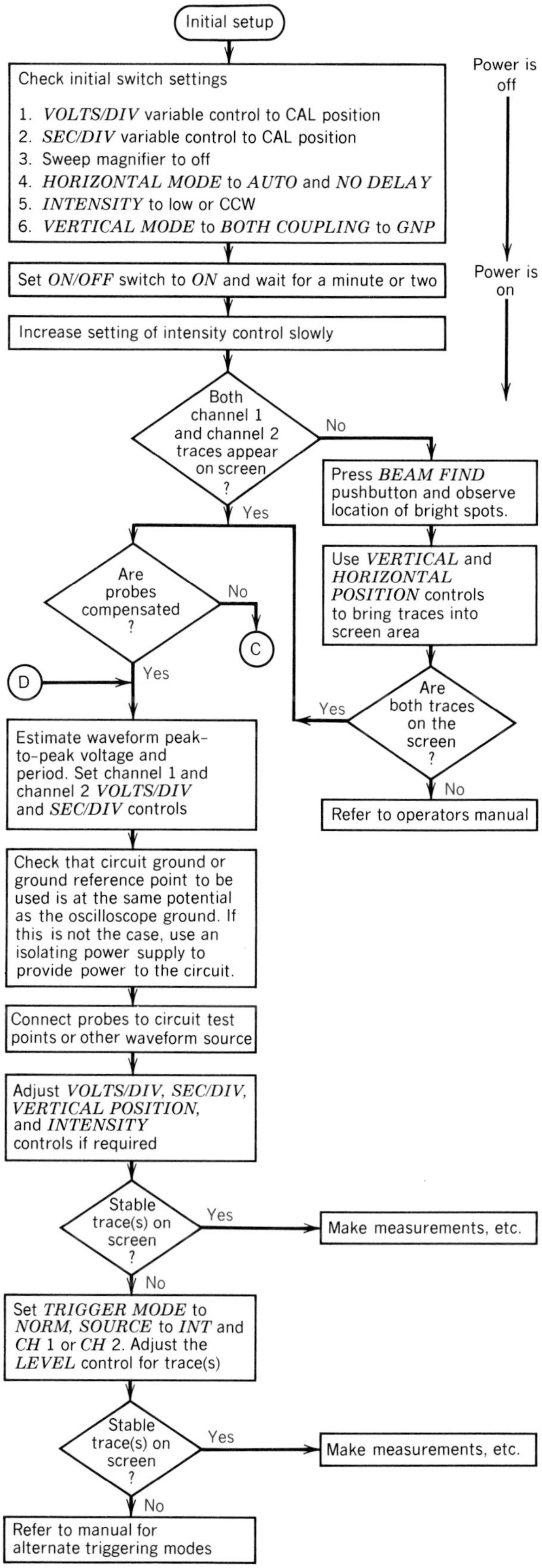

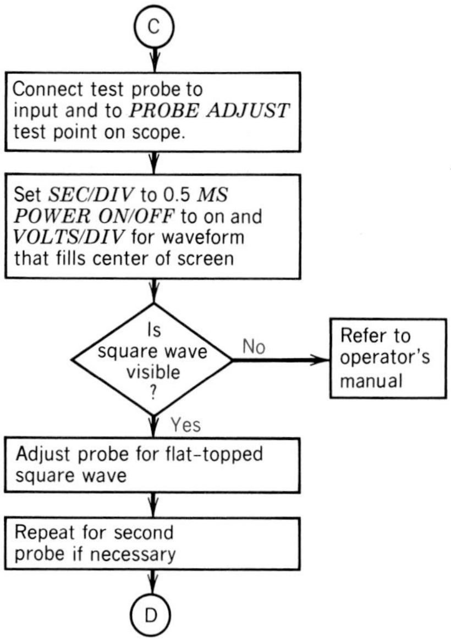

Figure 10.69 Flow diagram for viewing a waveform.

built-in calibrator point. Set the *CH 1 VOLTS/DIV* and *CH 1 SEC/DIV* controls so that at least two complete square waves are shown on the screen. Adjust the probe COMPENSATION control so that the waveform resembles that shown in Figure 10.57*b*. Repeat this procedure for the CH 2 probe. Note that compensating a particular probe for CH 1 does not mean that it is calibrated for CH 2.

D.7.2 OBSERVING WAVEFORMS AND MAKING VOLTAGE MEASUREMENTS

After adjusting your oscilloscope to obtain a free-running trace and compensating your oscilloscope probes, it is a matter of simple control adjustment to observe the shape of a waveform and use the etched graticule lines to measure voltages. The flow diagram in Figure 10.69 shows the steps that should be followed when using a typical oscilloscope to observe waveforms.

CAUTION

MOST OSCILLOSCOPE INPUT JACKS ARE INTENDED FOR A MAXIMUM VOLTAGE OF 500 V. DIRECT CONNECTION OF POTENTIALS HIGHER THAN +500 OR −500 VOLTS WITH RESPECT TO GROUND CAN RESULT IN EQUIPMENT DAMAGE.

A ×10 or higher voltage probe must be used if waveforms with peak voltages in excess of +500 or −500 V are to be observed. With the TRIGGER MODE switch in the AUTO position, connect the probe or probes to test points at which the signals to be observed

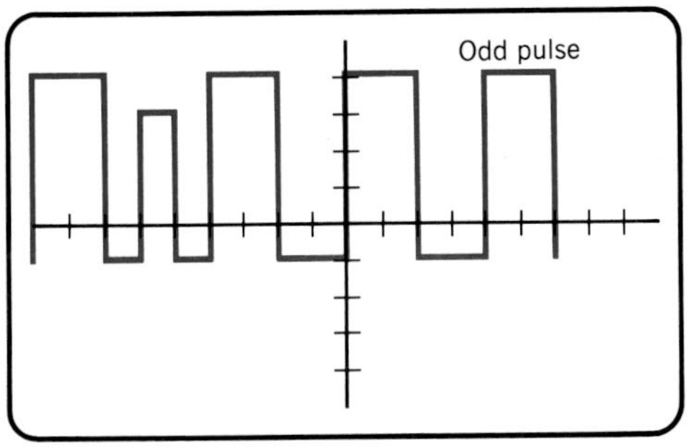

(a) Waveform showing odd pulse

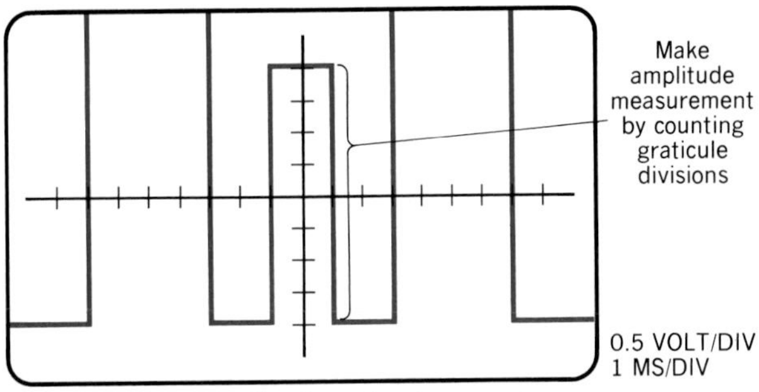

Figure 10.70 Amplitude and voltage measurements are most accurate when the waveform covers the center of the display.

are present. If two signals are to be observed at the same time, the *VERTICAL MODE* switches must be in the *BOTH* and *ALT* or *CHOP* positions.

Voltage or amplitude measurements are most accurate when the waveform to be measured covers the whole center of the screen. For example, if you wish to measure the peak-to-peak amplitude of the odd pulse shown in Figure 10.70*a*, use the *VOLTS/DIV, VERTICAL POSITION,* and *HORIZONTAL POSITION* controls to center the pulse against the vertical graticule line and increase its height as in Figure 10.70*b*. The pulse peak-to-peak amplitude is 4 V (be sure to multiply by 10 if a ×10 probe is used.)

Sometimes a waveform will not "lock in" on your oscilloscope. The effect is something like that shown in Figure 10.71*a*. This means that either the frequency of the waveform being observed is changing or that the automatic trigger cannot find a trigger point on the waveform. This frequently occurs with signals with low amplitudes. When this occurs, it is generally sufficient to set the *TRIGGER MODE* control to *NORMAL* and adjust the *TRIGGER LEVEL* control for a stable trace. Some older oscilloscopes had a *STABILITY* control for this purpose. Another frequently used technique is to set the input *VOLTS/DIV* control to a more sensitive setting. Many oscilloscopes trigger more easily if the vertical height of the displayed waveform is increased.

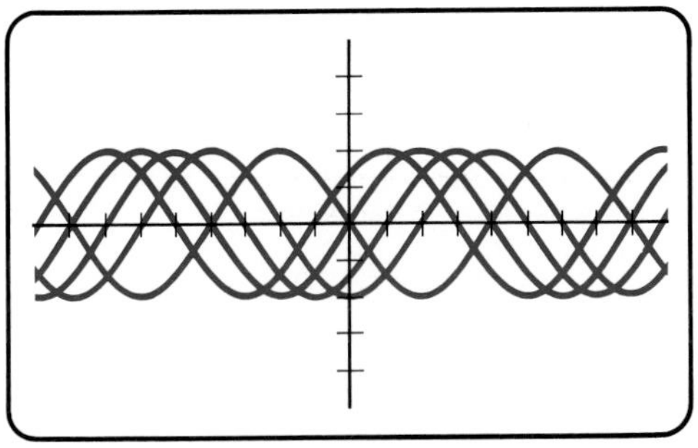

(a) Waveform not triggering properly

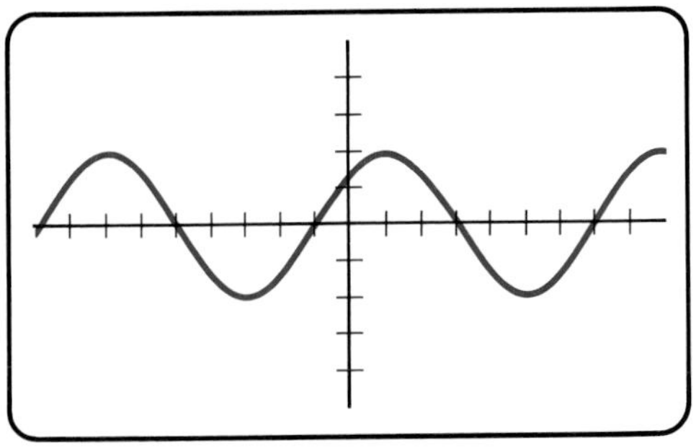

(b) Single trace is obtained when trigger mode control is set to normal and trigger level control is adjusted

Figure 10.71 When the waveform of an input signal will not "lock in," the *TRIGGER LEVEL* control can be used to provide a stable trace.

D.7.3 MAKING TIME AND PERIOD MEASUREMENTS

As in the case of voltage and amplitude measurements, time and waveform period measurements will be most accurate when made in the center of the oscilloscope display. The flow diagram in Figure 10.72 details the steps required to determine the period of a waveform or to measure the pulse width of a pulse. Once a stable trace has been obtained, as shown in Figure 10.73*a*, the *VOLTS/DIV, VERTICAL POSITION,* and *SEC/DIV* controls should be set to make your time measurement on the graticule center line as shown in Figure 10.73*b*. Check to see that the variable sweep control, *CAL*, is in its calibrated position (fully clockwise) and is pushed in, turning off the magnifier. Counting the number of graticule divisions on the horizontal graticule line and multiplying by the setting of the *SEC/DIV* control shows that the pulse width is 0.6 ms. (Recall that pulse width is measured at 50 percent of pulse amplitude.)

Sometimes time or period measurements must be made on extremely high frequency waveforms or very narrow pulses. In cases of this sort, it is sometimes hard to obtain a trace with sufficient width in the center of the display to count graticule lines, as shown in Figure 10.74*a*. The pulse width of one of these wave-

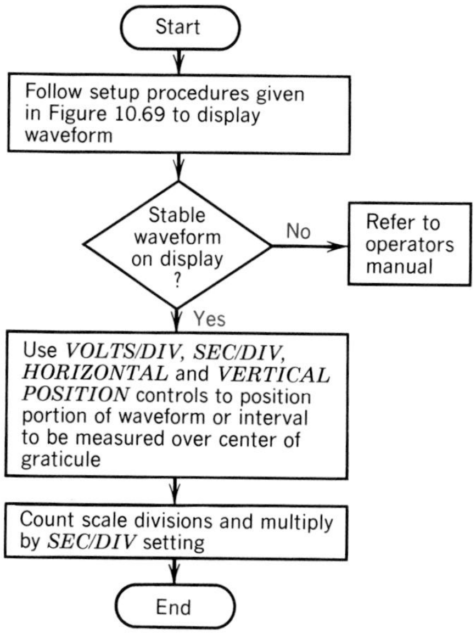

Figure 10.72 Flow diagram for making time or period measurements.

form pulses could not be estimated at the highest sweep speed of 0.05 μs/div, so it is necessary to provide sweep magnification by pulling out the $\times 10$ ($\times 5$ on some oscilloscopes) sweep control. This results in a sweep of 0.005 μs per division. The sweep speed is *increased*

Figure 10.73 Time and period measurements are most accurate when made against the horizontal graticule line in the center of the display.

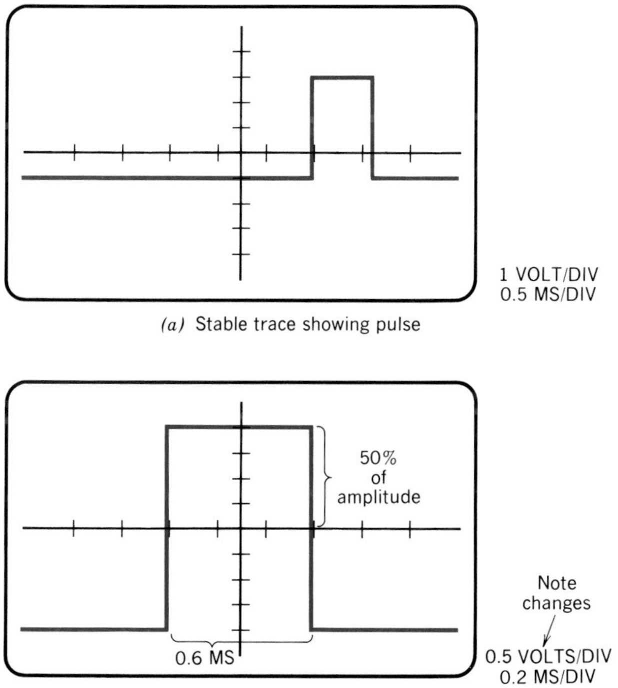

(a) Stable trace showing pulse

(b) Make measurements in center

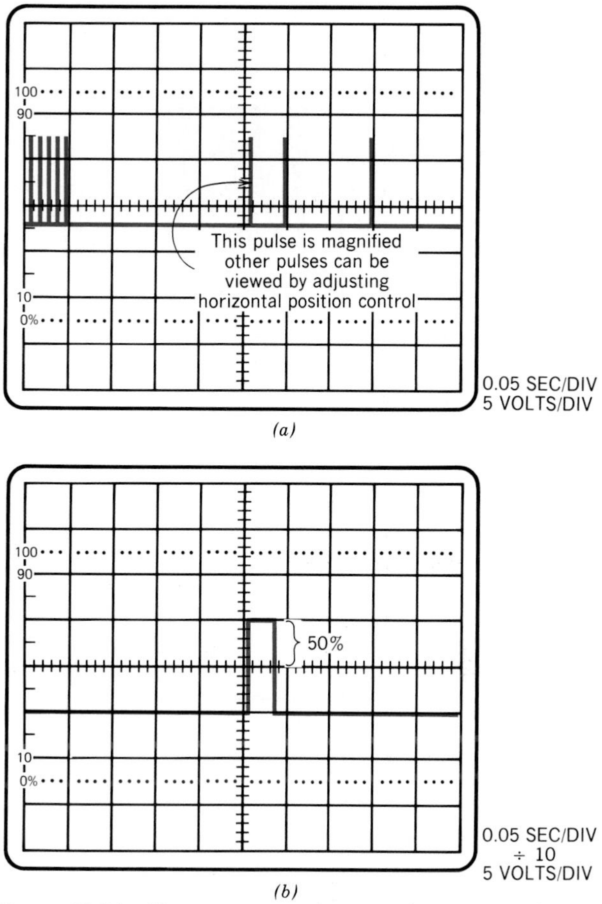

(a)

(b)

Figure 10.74 Very narrow pulses can be measured using the sweep magnifier, which increases the sweep speed by a factor of 10.

by a factor of 10, which *divides* the time taken to sweep through each horizontal division by 10. It is a relatively easy matter to count the number of minor divisions to determine that the pulse width is 0.003 μs, or 3 nS (3×10^{-9} s).

D.7.4 MAKING SINE-WAVE FREQUENCY MEASUREMENTS USING LISSAJOUS PATTERNS

Although the frequency of an input signal can be calculated from its period measurement, most oscilloscopes provide an X–Y MODE of operation that can be used for comparing the frequency of a sine-wave input with that of a signal generator, which produces an output of a known frequency. In the oscilloscope shown in Figure 10.41, the *X–Y MODE* is selected by the *SEC/DIV* sweep speed control. When this mode is selected, the vertical movement of the beam is produced by the input of CHANNEL 2 (*Y*), while the horizontal movement is produced by the input to CHANNEL 1. With the two input signals connected and the *X–Y MODE* selected, you will probably see a figure some-

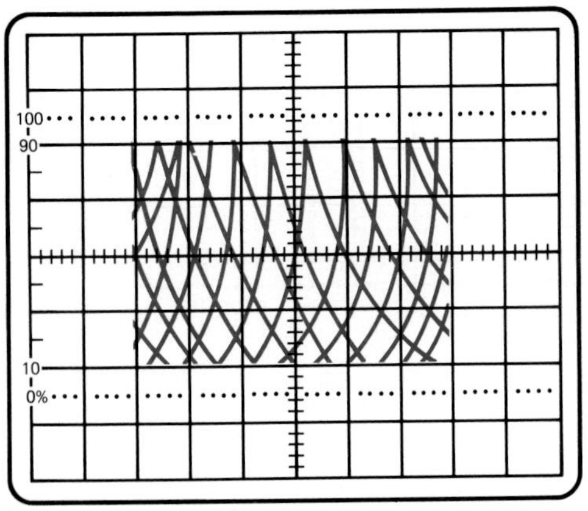

(a) x input signal level higher than y and frequencies not in whole-number ratio

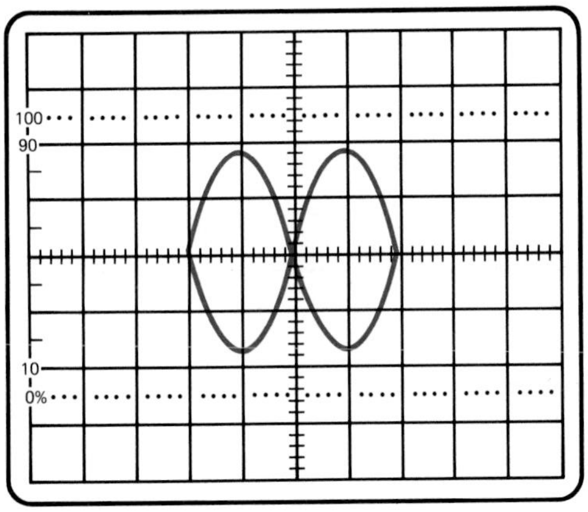

(b) x input signal frequency is twice that of y

Figure 10.75 Lissajous figures.

thing like that of Figure 10.75*a*. Adjust the *X* and *Y* input VOLTS/DIV controls until the figure is square and center it with the *VERTICAL POSITION* controls.

Now, slowly adjust the frequency of the signal generator until a sharply defined figure appears. This figure will probably take the form of a slowly rotating pattern, of which Figure 10.75*b* is an example. These figures are called *Lissajous figures,* (pronounced *lee-sa-shu*). The shape of the Lissajous figure depends on the relationship between the x and y input signal frequencies as shown in Figure 10.76. When the two frequencies are equal, the figure is a circle, a straight line, or an ellipse, depending on the relationship between the zero-crossing points of the two signals. If the two input signals are not derived from the same source, the figure produced will seem to rotate. Notice that the speed of the rotation of a Lissajous figure decreases as the two frequencies approach a whole number ratio, for example 2 to 1, or 5 to 3. Frequency measurements using Lissajous figures were more common before the

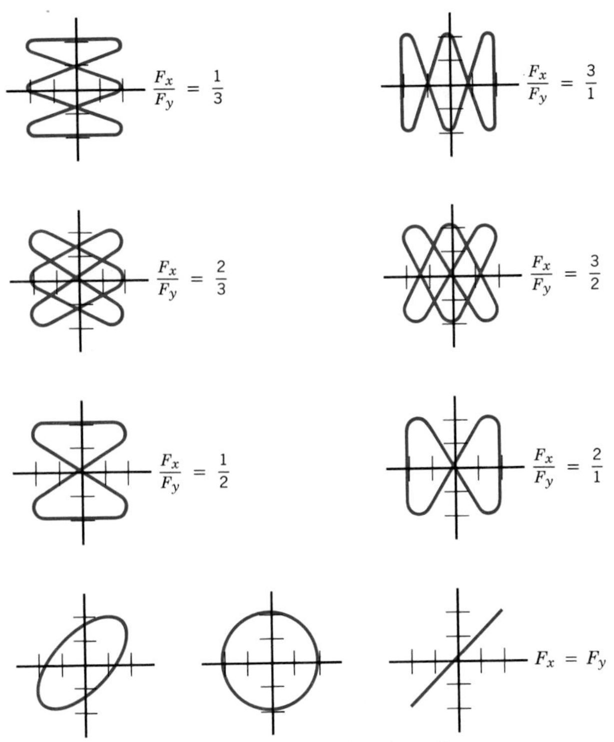

Figure 10.76 Interpretation of Lissajous figures.

Figure 10.77 Flow diagram for making frequency measurements using Lissajous figures.

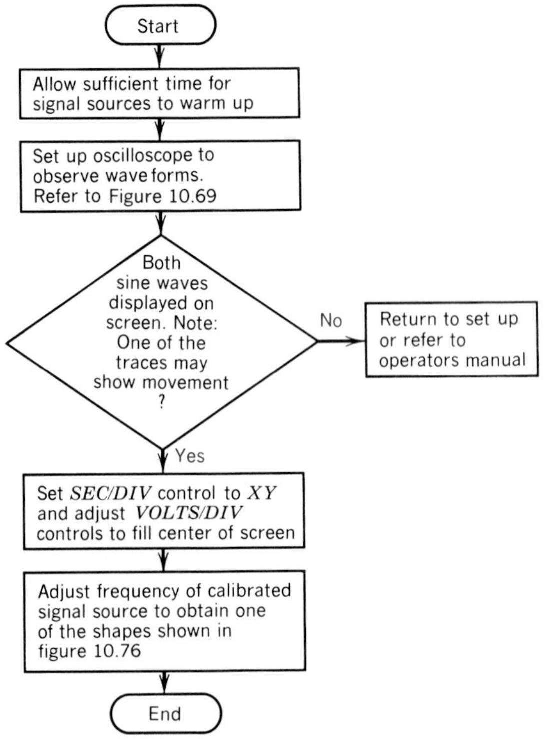

introduction of small, relatively inexpensive frequency counters, when the average technician's bench could be expected to hold an oscilloscope, but not a frequency counter. The method is quite precise and still useful, particularly when used to compare one sine-wave signal with another that has been derived by shifting the axis crossing points. This is called *phase shift* and will be discussed at great length in following chapters. Figure 10.77 provides a flow diagram for making frequency comparisons using Lissajous patterns.

E. PROGRAMMED REVIEW

FRAME 1

The direction of the current through a conductor, an external magnetic field, and the direction of the force on the conductor are at right angles to each other, forming an __________ system.

a. Orthogonal. (2)
b. Any other answer, review Section B.1.

FRAME 2

The direction of the force on a current-carrying conductor in a magnetic field can be determined by using the __________, which states that if the first finger is pointed in the direction of the __________ and the middle finger is pointed in the direction of the __________, the thumb, held at right angles to the two fingers will point in the direction of the ______.

a. Right-hand rule for motors; magnetic field; current; motion or force on the conductor. (3)
b. Any other answer, review Section B.1.

FRAME 3

The direction of the current produced when a wire loop is moved at right angles to a magnetic field can be determined by using the __________ -hand rule for __________. Also called __________ rule, it states that if the thumb is pointed in the direction of the __________ and the first finger is pointed in the direction of the __________, the thumb, held at right angles to the fingers, will point in the direction of the __________.

a. Left; generators; Fleming's; motion of the conductor; magnetic field; current through the conductor. (4)
b. Any other answer, review Section B.2.

FRAME 4

A potential difference of 4 V is induced between the ends of a conductor 1 m long moving at right angles through a magnetic field with a velocity of 0.8 m/s. What is the flux density of the field?

a. 5 teslas. (6)
b. Any other answer, (5).

FRAME 5

The formula relating potential difference to the length (l) and velocity (v) of a conductor moving through a magnetic field with a flux density of B is $E = Blv \sin \theta$, where θ is the angle between the conductor motion and the direction of the magnetic field. Since the conductor in Frame 4 is moving at a right angle to the magnetic field, $\sin \theta = \sin 90° = 1$. So,

$$E = Blv \quad \text{or} \quad 4 = B \times 1 \times 0.8 \quad \text{and} \quad B = 5\ \text{T}$$

Go on to Frame 6.

FRAME 6

A wire 0.1 m long moving at a velocity of 10 m/s parallel to a magnetic field of 3×10^{-7} Wb/m^2 produces a potential difference of __________ Volts between its ends.

a. 0 (7)
b. Any other answer, go to Frame 5.

FRAME 7

Graphs that relate potential difference or current to time are called __________. If a basic shape is repeated, they are called __________.

a. Waveforms (or wave shapes); recurrent or periodic waveforms. (8)
b. Any other answer, review Section B.4 and go on to Frame 8.

FRAME 8

What is a complete, single unit of a recurrent waveform called?

a. Cycle. (9)
b. Any other answer, review Section B.4.

FRAME 9

Identify the portions of the waveform shown in Figure 7.78. *A* is the ____________, *B* is the ____________, *C* is the ____________.

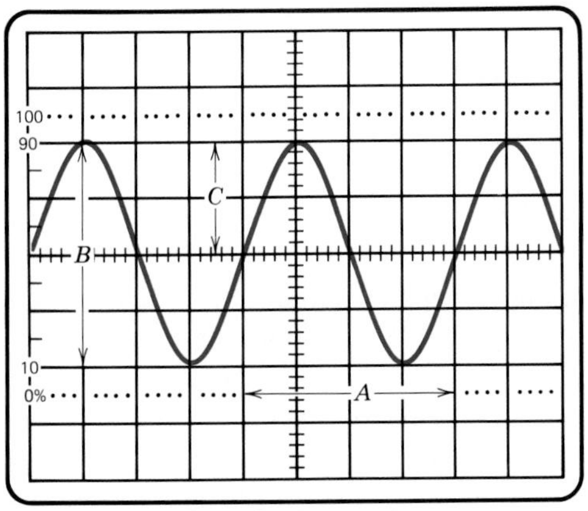

Figure 10.78 Waveform for Frame 9.

a. Period; peak-to-peak amplitude; peak amplitude. (10)
b. Any other answer, review Section B.4 carefully.

FRAME 10

The number of cycles that a waveform goes through in 1 s is called the ____________. For a waveform with a period of 0.0025 s, this would be ____________.

a. Frequency; 400 Hz. (11)
b. Any other answer, review Section B.4.

FRAME 11

Commercial power line frequency is ____________.

a. 60 Hz (12)
b. Review Section B.4 and Table 10.2. Go on to Frame 12.

FRAME 12

What does each of the following abbreviations stand for? What frequency range is included in it?

a. HF
b. VHF
c. UHF
d. VLF

a. High frequency, 3 to 30 MHz; Very High Frequency, 30 to 300 MHz; Ultra High Frequency, 300 MHz to 3 GHz; Very Low Frequency, 400 Hz to 30 kHz. Only approximate frequencies are required. (13)
b. Any abbreviation or more than two frequency ranges incorrect, review Table 10.2.

FRAME 13

A certain vector 27 units long makes an angle of 143° with the x axis. What are its x and y components?

a. -21.56, 16.25 (14)
b. Any other answer, check your arithmetic or review Section C.1.

FRAME 14

The components of the velocity vector of a conductor are $x = -6$ and $y = -9$. What is the length of the vector and what is the angle formed with the x axis?

a. $r = 10.82$; $\theta = 236.31°$ (15)
b. Any other answer, check your arithmetic or review Section C.1.

FRAME 15

The coordinate system that defines a vector by its length and the angle it makes with an axis is called the ____________ system. A vector is specified by its x and y components in the ____________ system.

a. Polar; rectangular. (16)
b. Any other answer, review Section C.1.

FRAME 16

Provide the following characteristics of the sine wave shown in Figure 10.79. (A ×1 probe is used)

a. Period
b. Frequency
c. Average value
d. Peak value
e. Peak-to-peak value
f. rms value

a. 8 ms; 125 Hz; 9.55 V; 15 V; 30 V; 10.6 V (17)
b. Any other answer, review Section C.2.

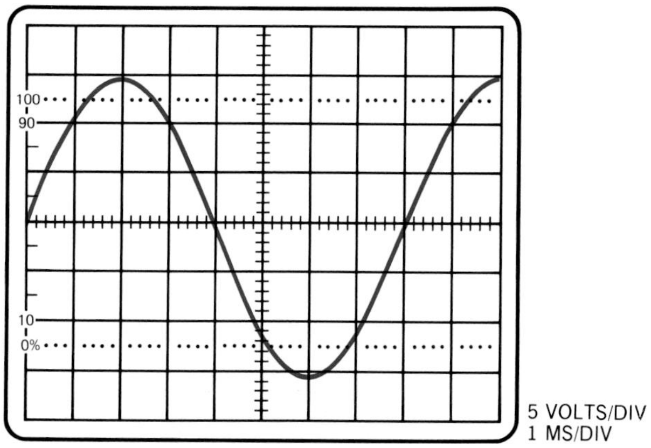

Figure 10.79 Sine wave for Frame 16.

FRAME 17

It would require an ac source providing a potential difference of __________ V to produce the same heating effect in a 10 Ω resistor as a new Leclanché cell.

a. 2.1 or 2.2 V (18)
b. Any other answer except 2.1 or 2.2 V, review Section C.2.

FRAME 18

An averaging circuit produces an output of 12 V dc. What is the amplitude of the ac sine-wave input?

a. 18.84 V (19)
b. Any other answer, review Section C.2.

FRAME 19

Figure 10.80 represents the oscilloscope trace of a pulse train, using a ×1 probe. Provide the following information:

a. Frequency	b. Period
c. Amplitude	d. Peak-to-peak amplitude
e. Pulse width	f. Duty cycle

a. 2000 Hz (or 2 kHz); 0.5 ms; 1.5 V; 2 V; 0.14 ms; 28 percent (20)
b. Any other answer, review Section C.3.

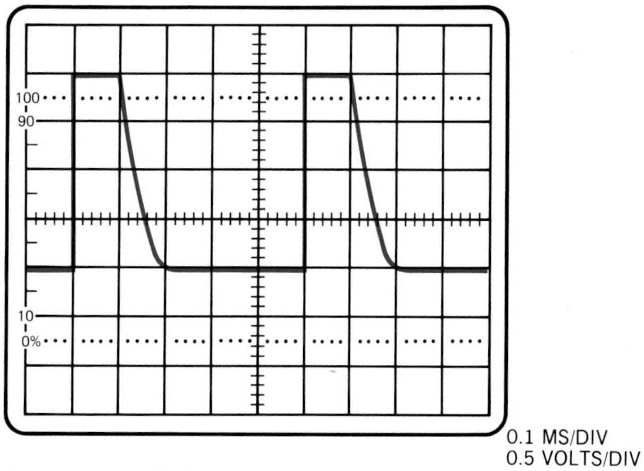

Figure 10.80 Pulse train for Frame 19.

FRAME 20

The principal sections of an oscilloscope are the __________, __________, and __________ sections. Almost all the scopes used in industry also contain a __________ section.

a. Horizontal; vertical; display; trigger (order of the first three does not matter). (21)
b. Any other answer, review Section D.1.

FRAME 21

The oscilloscope section that contains the sweep generator and that determines the sweep speed is the __________ section. The front panel control that sets the sweep speed is the __________ control.

a. Horizontal; *SEC/DIV* (22)
b. Any other answer, review Sections D.1 and D.4.

FRAME 22

Match the following oscilloscope control or control panel position names with their functions:

a. *VERTICAL POSITION*	1. Selects either the leading or trailing edge of the waveform for location of the trigger point
b. *SLOPE*	2. Adjusts the sharpness of the trace
c. *X–Y*	3. Adjusts the amplitude of the waveform on the screen
d. *TRIGGER LEVEL*	4. Permits a small portion of the trace to be spread across the entire screen

e. *BEAM FIND*	5. The *SEC/DIV* control setting used for Lissajous figures
f. *FOCUS*	6. Provides an aid in the location of an off-screen trace
g. *VOLTS/DIV*	7. Selects the amplitude at which the sweep is started
h. *×10 MAG*	8. Determines the *y* axis location of a sweep

a. a, 8; b, 1; c, 5; d, 7; e, 6; f, 2; g, 3; h, 4 (23)
b. Any other answer, review Sections D.2 through D.7.

FRAME 23

An oscilloscope sweep generator that operates without any triggering or synchronizing signal from the vertical section is referred to as a ___________. An oscilloscope in which the sweep is started each time the input signal reaches a certain amplitude is called a ___________.

a. Free-running scope; triggered scope. (24)
b. Any other answer, review Sections D.1 and D.4.

FRAME 24

Too high a setting of the *INTENSITY* control can result in ___________.

a. Burning of the phosphor or damage to the CRT. (25)
b. Any answer that does not include one of these, refer to Section D.2 and go on to Frame 25.

FRAME 25

Oscilloscope probes have to be ___________ at least once per day.

a. Compensated. (26)
b. Any other answer, review Section D.5 and go on to Frame 26.

FRAME 26

Match the terms in the two columns:

a. Slow sweep speeds	1. Very low amplitude waveform
b. *NORMAL* mode	2. Chopped mode
c. Fast sweep speeds	3. An ac waveform with a dc component
d. dc coupling	4. Alternate mode

a. a, 2; b, 1; c, 4; d, 3 (27)
b. Any other answer, review Sections D.6 and D.7.

FRAME 27

If the waveform shown in Figure 10.81 is seen, the relationship between the two input frequencies is ___________.

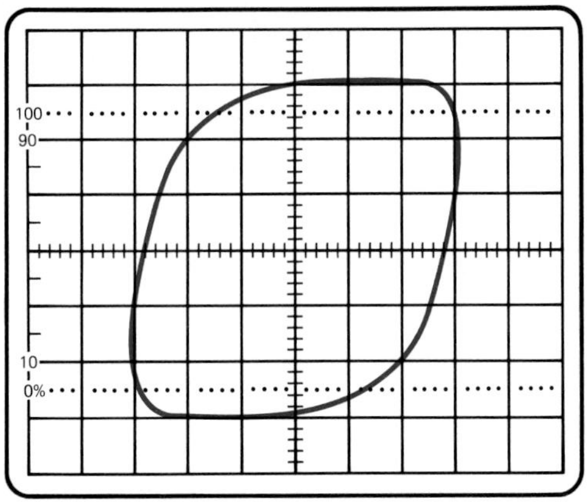

Figure 10.81 Pattern for Frame 27.

a. 1:1 (END)
b. Any other answer, review Figure 10.76.

E. PROBLEMS FOR SOLUTION OR RESEARCH

1. The 120-V, 60-Hz commercial power distribution system is familiar to all, but are you aware of the peak amplitude of the potential? What is it? Sketch the waveform of three cycles on a simulated oscilloscope screen, giving the *VOLTS/DIV* and *SEC/DIV* settings.

2. The frequency spectrum shown in Table 10.2 is only intended to give a rough idea of the various applications and frequency allotments assigned by the Federal Communications Commission. An interesting research project would be to produce a detailed spectrum chart, listing all the various assignments, including local radio and television stations, amateur radio, and mobile radio bands.

3. Sketch each of the following oscilloscope patterns on a simulated graticule. Be sure to give the *VOLTS/DIV* and *SEC/DIV* for each.

a. A 500-kHz sine wave with a peak-to-peak amplitude of 17 V, trigger *MODE NORM, SLOPE* _/‾, *LEVEL* 8 V.
b. A square wave with a frequency of 1.6 kHz and an amplitude of 1 V, with trigger *MODE* set to *AUTO*

c. A pulse train with a duty cycle of 25 percent, a frequency of 30 Hz, an amplitude of 24 V, and rise and fall times too short to be measured
d. The Lissajous figure produced when scope *CHANNEL 1* is connected to a 26-Hz sine signal and *CHANNEL 2* is connected to a 39-Hz source
e. The waveform produced by a 26-V, 60-Hz, ac generator in series with a 12-V dc source when ac coupling is used; when dc is used.

4. Engineer Vardis is trying to observe the waveform of the commercial 60-Hz power distribution system. The display of the scope looks like that shown in Figure 10.82. Explain at least two reasons for this curious trace.

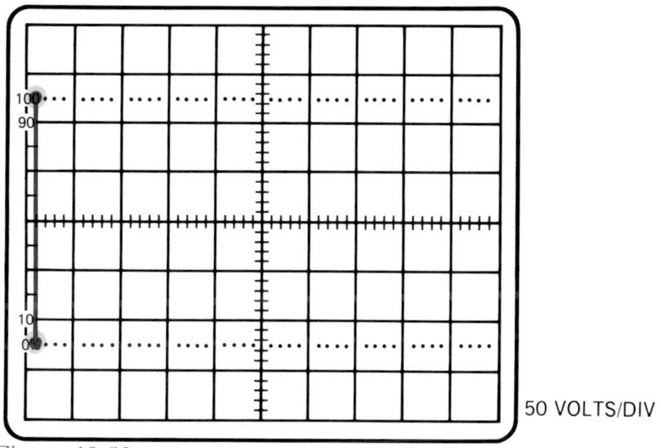

Figure 10.82 Scope pattern in Problem 4.

5. Engineer Vardis, hastily dismantles the oscilloscope and, borrowing another scope from a co-worker, observes the waveform of the sweep generator of the first scope. What does this look like? Does this observation help pinpoint the problem?

6. At one time technicians would sometimes remove the power line grounding connector from their oscilloscopes. This was a dangerous practice that resulted in injuries. From Figure 10.83 can you see why they did this?

Hint: What would happen if the oscilloscope was grounded?

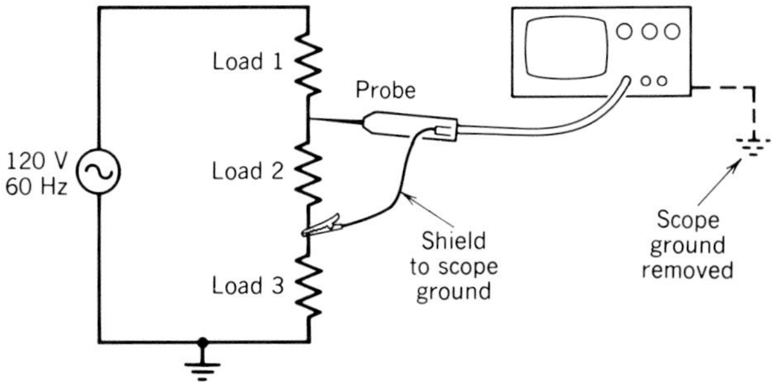

Figure 10.83 Diagram for Problem 6.

7. The method for measuring the rise and fall times of a pulse was not given in this chapter, although most of the information is present. If you recall that the *VOLTS/DIV* control is actually double (the knob center is a continuously variable potentiometer and the outer part a switch), can you discover a method for making these measurements?

Hint: Look closely at the left side of the graticule in Figure 10.43.

CHAPTER 11

AC MEASUREMENTS AND WAVEFORM GENERATION

A. CHAPTER PREVIEW

1 All the laws and theorems you have previously learned, such as Ohm's law, Kirchhoff's laws, and the power law are true for ac as well as dc. In this chapter you will learn how these laws and theorems are applied.

2 You will also learn how to make ac and other non-dc measurements, including frequency measurements, using meters and frequency counters.

3 The operation of signal sources used to produce sine waves as well as other waveforms for test and troubleshooting are discussed.

4 The Examples and Computations section of this chapter provides additional information about phase angles and practice in phase angle calculation.

5 The Applications section deals with the types, principles of operation, and general maintenance of analog meter movements.

B. PRINCIPLES

B.1 MEASUREMENT OF CURRENT AND POTENTIAL DIFFERENCE IN AC, SQUARE WAVE, AND PULSE CIRCUITS

Although the value of the current and the potential at a point in an ac circuit is changing, the effective, or rms value of both quantities can be measured with the same multimeter used to measure dc currents and potential differences. Almost all multimeters, both analog and digital, have an *AC/DC* selector that can be set to either position, as shown in Figure 11.1.

CAUTION

SOME METERS SET TO MEASURE DIRECT CURRENT CAN BE DAMAGED OR DESTROYED IF CONNECTED TO AN AC SOURCE.

If the proper range has been selected, there is no danger in connecting a meter set to measure ac to a dc source. The reading will not be correct, however. For these reasons, it is a good idea to observe the waveform of the potential at a point in an unfamiliar circuit with an oscilloscope before trying to measure it with a meter. Some of the possible waveforms you might see are shown in Figures 11.2*a* through 11.2*d*. Figure 11.2*a* is a pure dc potential and should be measured using the *DC* setting of the meter. Figure 11.2*b* is a pure sine wave ac waveform, and the *AC* setting of the multimeter should be used. All but the most elaborate (and expensive) meters measure the *average* value of the waveform and convert the measured average value to an rms value that is displayed. This rather confusing process is detailed in Figure 11.3. An electronic circuit converts the ac input signal into a dc signal proportional to the average ac input regardless of the polarity of the input. The ac scales in an analog meter are designed so that this average value is multiplied by a constant and the meter pointer is actually displaying the rms value. In a digital meter, this correction is performed electronically.

Figure 11.1 The AC/DC selector on two typical multimeters. (Reproduced with permission of John Fluke Mfg. Co., Inc.)

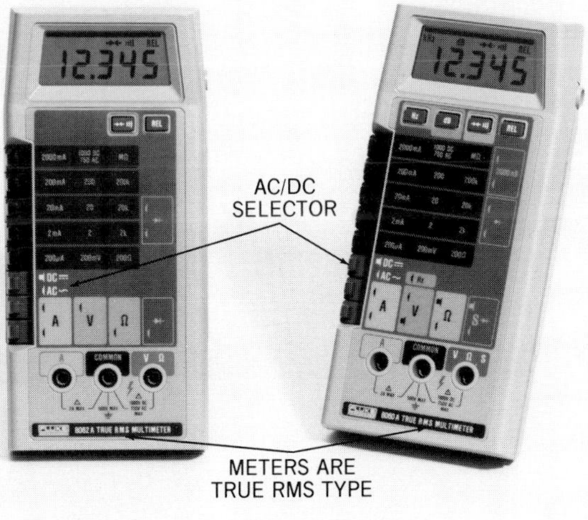

This system has a number of problems that you must keep in mind. First, the correction is only accurate for sine waves, or *sinusoids,* as they are frequently called. For nonsinusoids such as square waves, pulses, and irregular waveforms like that of Figure 11.2*c*, the correction factor will introduce an error in the measurement. Furthermore, most multimeters are designed for ac potential and current measurements at low ac frequencies centering around 60 Hz. In many meters the accuracy becomes poor as the frequency increases, although better-quality meters will still be accurate to within 5 percent of the reading at frequencies of 10 kHz or more. To accurately measure potential or current with an irregular waveform such as that shown in Figure 11.2*c*, a *true rms* meter should be used. Comparing the measuring process that goes on in the true rms meter shown in Figure 11.4 with that of the averaging meter shown in Figure 11.3 illustrates the difference between the two meter types. The true rms meter actually measures the rms value of the waveform at a large number of instants and then combines these samples to obtain a true rms value for display. If enough samples are taken, this kind of meter can measure the rms potential or current of any irregular waveform.

When high-frequency waveforms or very complex nonsinusoidal waveforms are involved, even a true rms multimeter cannot provide accurate measurements. Special, high-frequency meters must be used. In these meters, the high-frequency current heats a small resistance, and the temperature change is converted into a dc potential difference by a device called a *thermocouple,* as shown in Figure 11.5. The thermocouple is nothing more than a junction of wires made of different metals. As you learned in Chapter 1, there is always a potential difference across such a junction because of the differing energy levels of conduction electrons in the two metals. Since temperature changes at the junction will affect the potential difference in a predictable way, the thermocouple will produce a potential difference that is proportional to the power being

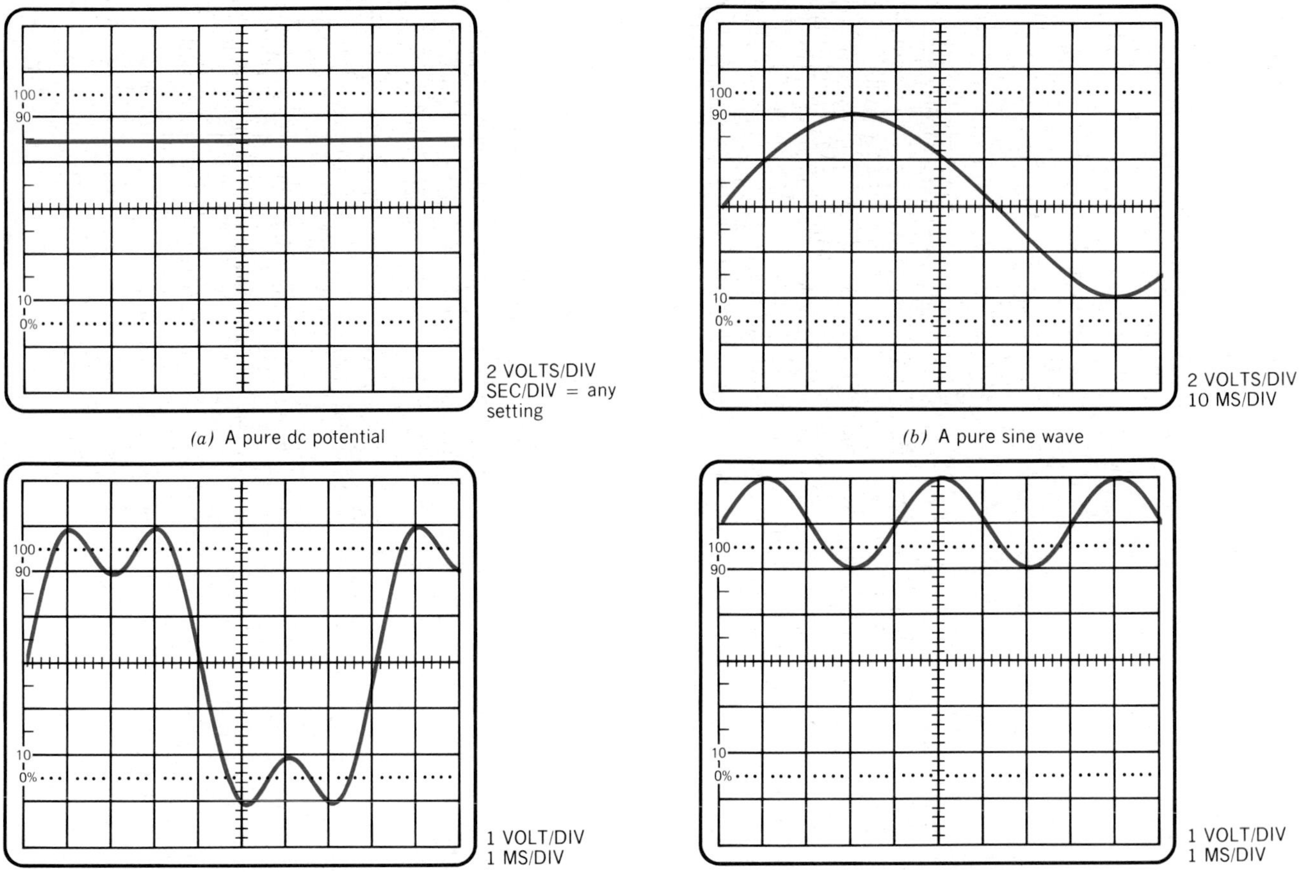

(a) A pure dc potential

(b) A pure sine wave

(c) Irregular waveform

(d) A 1-Volt peak-to-peak ac component riding on a 3-Volt dc level

Figure 11.2 Commonly observed waveforms.

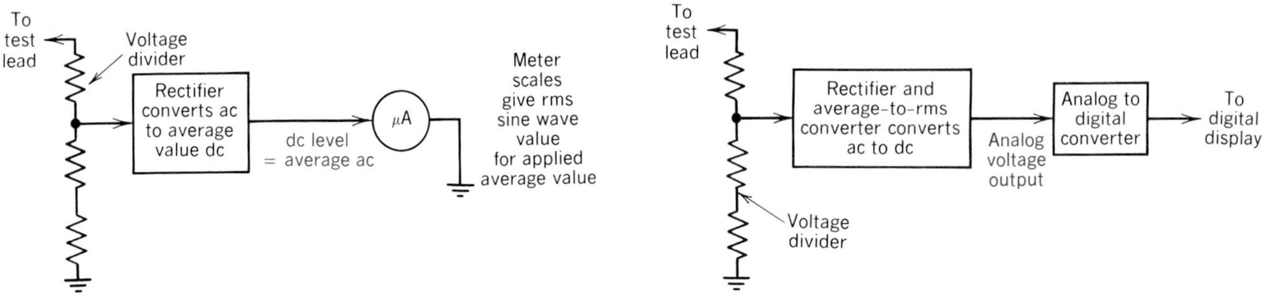

(a) Analog meter

(b) Digital meter

Figure 11.3 Most multimeters measure the average value of an ac waveform and convert this to an rms value for display.

Figure 11.4 The true rms meter contains a circuit that measures the instantaneous value of the input and sums these values to obtain rms.

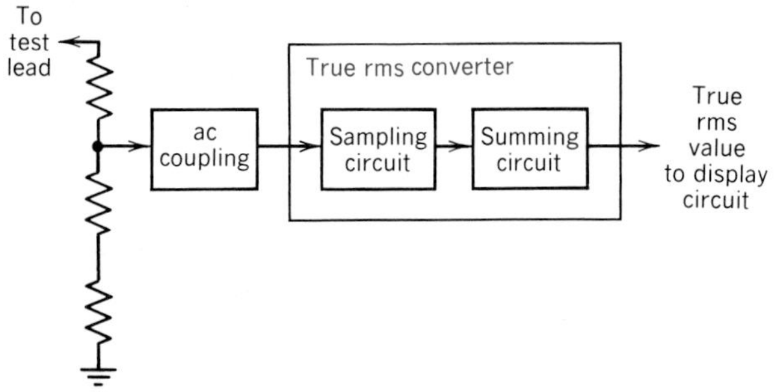

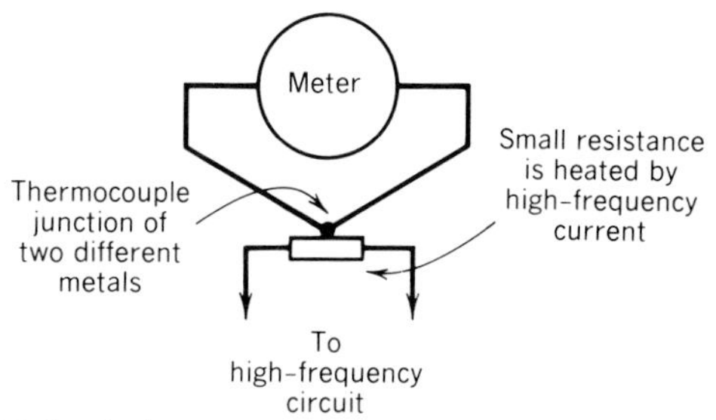

Figure 11.5 A thermocouple meter depends on the potential difference produced at the junction of two different metals.

dissipated in the load resistance. Since the definition of rms is based on the heating power of an ac current, the thermocouple meter provides a true rms measurement.

The waveform shown in Figure 11.2*d* is common in electronic circuits and is capable of providing difficulties for even good-quality multimeters. It is composed of two parts or components that are added together. There is a 3-V dc component and an ac component with a 2-V peak-to-peak waveform. This sort of waveform is referred to as an ac waveform or signal "superimposed" on or "riding on" a dc signal or dc level. It is rather difficult to obtain accurate potential or current measurements of waveforms of this type with a meter because of the inaccuracies in the measurement of the dc component when the meter is set for ac measurements. If the multimeter is an analog type set for dc measurement, the ac component of the waveform may cause the pointer to vibrate and can result in damage. Even if there is no damage, the ac component will not be measured. Certain meters, such as the true rms meter shown in Figure 11.6, provide a method for obtaining true rms values for waveforms of this sort. The method is based on the input circuit of the meter. When in the dc mode, *only* the dc component of the waveform is measured, and the ac component is blocked by the multimeter input circuit. For the waveform of Figure 11.2*d*, the multimeter dc component reading is then 3 V. When the multimeter is set to measure ac, only the true rms value of the ac component is displayed. The dc component is blocked out and the reading will be the rms value of the 2-V peak-to-peak or 1-V peak signal. This is $0.707 \times 1 = 0.707$ V. The rms potential difference of the combination can then be obtained by using a simple formula:

Figure 11.6 A true rms multimeter, which is capable of measuring a potential consisting of both an ac and dc component. (Reproduced with permission from the John Fluke Mfg. Co., Inc.)

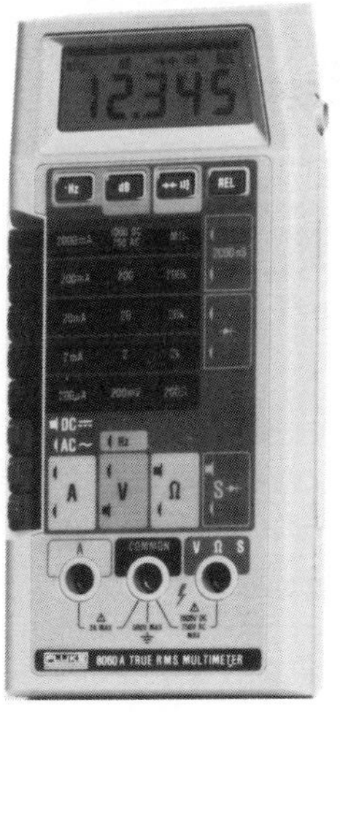

$$E_{rms} = \sqrt{(\text{dc component})^2 + (\text{ac component})^2}$$

FORMULA 11.1

In this case,

$$E_{rms} = \sqrt{(3)^2 + (0.707)^2} = 3.08 \text{ V}$$

In addition to the meters with the capability of separating components, a thermocouple meter can also be used to measure composite waveforms with dc and ac components.

B.2 OHM'S AND KIRCHHOFF'S LAWS IN AC CIRCUITS

Ohm's and Kirchhoff's laws can be used for ac circuits if all the electronic components in the circuits are either sources or resistances. If some of the components are not resistances, the laws are still true, but the mathematical statement of these laws is more complex. The basic statements of Ohm's law can be extended to include the rms values of current and potential difference.

$$I_{rms} = \frac{E_{rms}}{R} \qquad E_{rms} = I_{rms} R \qquad R = \frac{E_{rms}}{I_{rms}}$$

FORMULA 11.2

Capital or uppercase letters are used in this formula to show that the rms value of the current and voltage is intended. Remember the rms value is not the constantly changing instantaneous value. The instantaneous value is the precise value of the current or voltage at a particular instant in time.

EXAMPLE:

In the circuit shown in Figure 11.7, an ac sine-wave generator produces a potential difference waveform with a peak-to-peak value of 24 V. Determine the rms value of the current through and potential difference

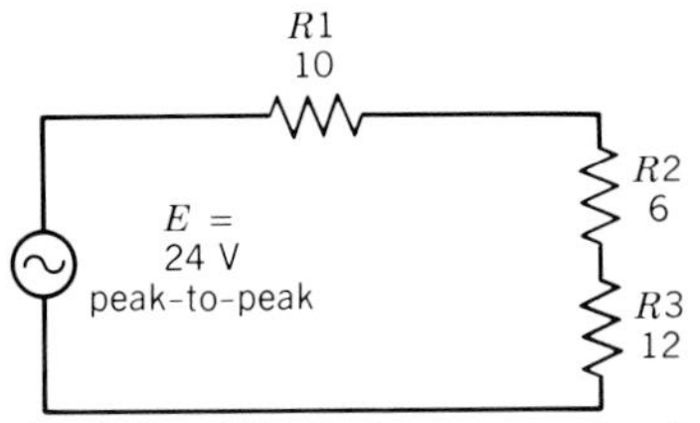

Figure 11.7 Applying Ohm's law to ac circuits.

across $R2$. (Note the schematic symbol for an ac generator.) ■

SOLUTION:
The total resistance of this series circuit is $R1 + R2 + R3$, or 28 Ω. The rms value of the potential difference is $0.707 \times E_{\text{peak}}$. Since $E_{\text{peak}} = \frac{1}{2}E_{\text{peak-to-peak}}$,

$$E_{\text{rms}} = 0.707 \times 12 = 8.484 \text{ V}.$$

The circuit current $I_{\text{rms}} = \frac{E_{\text{rms}}}{R} = 0.303$ A. This is also the current through $R2$. The potential difference across $R2$ is $E_{\text{rms}} = I_{\text{rms}} \times R$, or 1.818 V. ■

When referring to current or potential difference in ac circuits with sinusoidal waveforms, the rms value is almost always the value given, so that it is usual to drop the rms subscript. In other words, in ac circuits, E means E_{rms} and I means I_{rms}. Since peak, average, and peak-to-peak values are less frequently referred to, their subscripts are given to prevent confusion with rms values, for example, I_{peak}, E_{average}, $E_{\text{peak-to-peak}}$.

Ohm's and Kirchhoff's laws are also true for the instantaneous values of current and potential difference in a resistive ac circuit. These are the values at a particular instant of time. Lowercase letters, you will recall, are used to identify instantaneous values of changing quantities. In other words,

$$i = \frac{e}{R} \qquad e = iR \quad \text{and} \quad R = \frac{e}{i}$$

Notice that when the instantaneous potential difference e and current i in a circuit are zero, the value of the resistance is 0/0. This value is called *indeterminate* and is impossible to calculate. Although it appears rather strange, this is in agreement with reality. If the potential difference and current in a circuit are zero, the circuit resistance can be any value.

You will recall from Chapter 10 that $E_{\text{peak}} = 1.414\ E_{\text{rms}}$ and $I_{\text{peak}} = 1.414\ I_{\text{rms}}$. Thus, for a specific time or point on a graph of a sine wave corresponding to an angle θ, the rms and instantaneous values are related by:

$$e_\theta = E_{\text{peak}}\sin\theta = 1.414E_{\text{rms}}\sin\theta$$

and FORMULA 11.3

$$i_\theta = I_{\text{peak}}\sin\theta = 1.414I_{\text{rms}}\sin\theta$$

EXAMPLE:
A certain generator produces a sine-wave potential with an effective or rms value of 120 V. What is the instantaneous value of its potential when the sinusoid is at 220°? ■

SOLUTION:
Since $E = 120$ V, according to formula (11.3),

$$e_\theta = 1.414E_{\text{rms}}\sin\theta$$

or

$$e_\theta = 1.414 \times 120 \sin 220$$
$$= -109.068 \text{ V} \quad \text{or} \quad -109 \text{ V}$$

rounding off to three significant digits. ■

For ease in solving formulas, engineers and technicians frequently use radian rather than angle measurements. You will recall that there are 2π radians in 360°. If f represents the frequency of a sine waveform or sinusoid, the expression $2\pi f$ represents the number of radians that the graph waveform will contain during the x-axis interval of one second. This expression is also referred to by the lowercase Greek letter ω (omega) and is called the *angle velocity*, or *angular velocity*, of a sinusoid. Multiplying $2\pi f$ or ω by t, the time in seconds from the 0 radian or 0 time point of the sinusoid, gives a value in radians for the angle of the sinusoid at time t. Therefore, it is possible to write the two forms of equation 11.3 as

$$e_t = 1.414E_{\text{rms}}\sin 2\pi ft$$
$$e_t = 1.414E_{\text{rms}}\sin \omega t$$
$$i_t = 1.414I_{\text{rms}}\sin 2\pi ft$$
$$i_t = 1.414I_{\text{rms}}\sin \omega t$$

FORMULA 11.4

Notice that for a sine waveform with a particular frequency, these equations relate the instantaneous value to the time elapsed since the angle and value of the sine were both zero when $t = 0$ at the x-axis origin (see Figure 11.8).

EXAMPLE:
A sine wave has an rms value of 36 V and a frequency of 0.1 Hz. What is the instantaneous value of the voltage when $t = 2.5$ s if its value is 0 at $t = 0$. ■

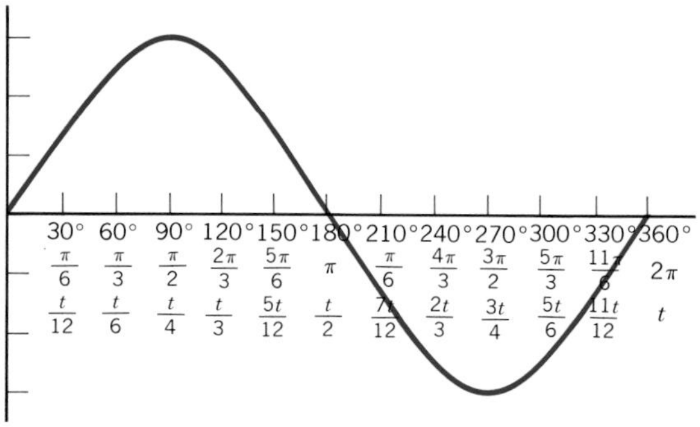

Figure 11.8 The relationship between angle and time for a sine wave, where $t = 1/f =$ the period in seconds.

SOLUTION:
Since the beginning of the waveform is at the origin, Formula 11.4 can be used directly:

$$e_{(2.5)} = 1.414E_{\text{rms}}\sin 2\pi ft$$
$$= 1.414 \times 36 \times \sin(2\pi \times 0.1 \times 2.5)$$

Remember that the factor in parentheses represents an angle expressed in radians. This can be converted to degrees using Formula 7.2 or may be calculated directly if your calculator is equipped for radian calculations:

$$e_{(2.5)} = 50.9 \text{ V}$$

(The angle $2\pi \times 0.1 \times 2.5$ radians $= 1.571$ rad $= 90°$.) ■

This may seem somewhat confusing at first glance, but the advantages of converting from a measurement of angle to one of time are numerous. For example, a time expression is easier to relate to the horizontal sweep of an oscilloscope trace, which is given in seconds, milliseconds, or microseconds per division.

B.3 POWER IN AC CIRCUITS

Recall that for a dc circuit, power is related to current, potential difference, and resistance by three formulas:

$$P = EI$$
$$P = I^2R$$
$$P = \frac{E^2}{R}$$

Since rms values of ac current and potential difference provide the same heating or power dissipation as a dc current and potential difference, then for an ac circuit

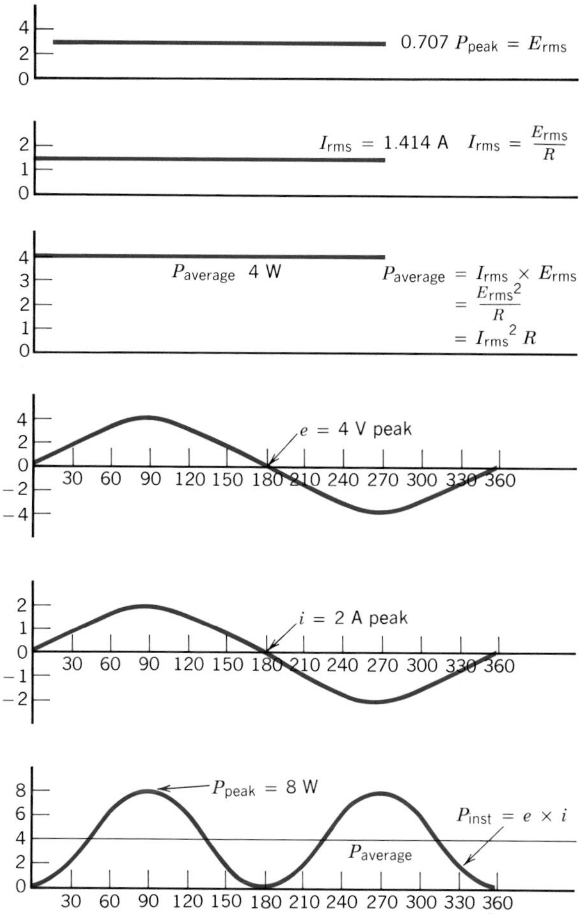

Figure 11.9 Graphs of the average power and instantaneous power dissipated in a 2 Ω resistor connected across a 4-V rms source.

composed of resistances,

$$P = E_{\text{rms}} \times I_{\text{rms}}$$
$$P = E_{\text{rms}}^2 R \qquad \text{FORMULA 11.5}$$
$$P = \frac{E_{\text{rms}}^2}{R}$$

Notice that P in this formula DOES NOT have the subscript rms. That is because the power given by this formula is the arithmetic average of the instantaneous power values in the circuit. This can be shown by the graph of the power in an ac circuit. Figure 11.9 shows the power in a 2 Ω resistor when the potential difference across it is a sine waveform with a 4-V peak value. According to Ohm's law, then, the current through the resistor is also a sine function, with a peak value of 2 A. The graph of the instantaneous power is also shown in this figure. The power graph is a waveform that drops to zero when the current and potential difference are zero.

Now, the peak power, P_{peak}, is equal to the peak instantaneous current, i_{peak}, times the peak instantaneous voltage, e_{peak}, or

$$P_{peak} = i_{peak}\, e_{peak} \quad \text{FORMULA 11.6}$$

From Formula 10.14 you know that $E_{peak} = 1.414E_{rms}$ and $I_{peak} = 1.414I_{rms}$. Substituting these two values in Formula 11.6 produces

$$P_{peak} = 1.414E_{rms} \times 1.414I_{rms}$$

$$P_{peak} = 2E_{rms}\, I_{rms}$$

$$\frac{P_{peak}}{2} = E_{rms}\, I_{rms}$$

But $\frac{P_{peak}}{2}$ is the *average* power dissipated by the resistor during a period of time. This average power level is shown by the line drawn parallel to the time, or x-axis, midway through the power waveform. If this line, which represents the average power level, is thought of as an axis, the graph of the instantaneous power in the circuit has a frequency that is twice that of the sinusoids representing the current and the potential difference.

EXAMPLE:
The potential difference across a 5 Ω load resistor is described by the function

$$e_t = 10 \sin 0.06283t$$

Draw a graph of the power and state the peak and average power dissipated by the resistor. ■

SOLUTION:
The power dissipated in the resistance at an instant of time, in other words, the instantaneous power, is equal to $\frac{e^2}{R}$, so a graph can be drawn by charting a number of values of $\frac{e^2}{R}$ for different values of t, as has been done in Figure 11.10. Notice that the angle is in radians rather than degrees. The peak power dissipated in the resistor occurs when e_t is at its maximum. This occurs when sin $0.06283t$ is equal to one, so $E_{peak} = 10 \times 1$. Since this is a resistive circuit,

$$P_{peak} = \frac{E_{peak}{}^2}{R} = \frac{100}{5} = 20 \text{ W}$$

The dissipated power varies between 20 W and zero, so the average power is $\frac{20 + 0}{2} = 10$ W. ■

Remember that these simplified calculations can only be made in resistive circuits. This is because the

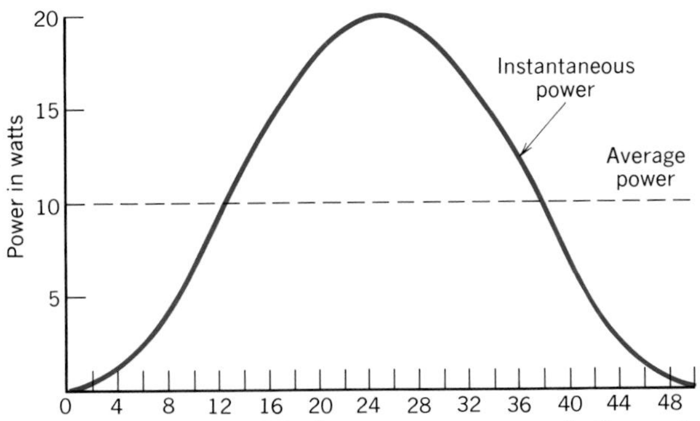

Figure 11.10 Graph of the instantaneous power in Example.

peak potential difference and peak current are reached at the same time. In the next chapter, you will learn about components that cause the peak potential difference and peak current to occur at different times.

B.4 MEASURING FREQUENCY

Frequency measurement using the Lissajous figures shown in Chapter 10 is a usable method if you are dealing with sine waves and have an accurate sine-wave source whose frequency can be varied. In cases where the waveform of unknown frequency is not a pure sinusoid or no suitable waveform generator is available, either a calculation based on the waveform period observed on an oscilloscope or a frequency meter/counter can be used.

A variety of devices have been used for frequency measurement, ranging from an electromechanical display composed of vibrating metal reeds to complex circuits that produce a potential difference that is proportional to the frequency of an input signal. The modern frequency meter, like the example shown in Figure 11.11, is really a product of the technology associated with the computer. These devices determine frequency by counting the number of cycles or pulses that occur in a waveform during a given time. They can also determine the amount of time that has elapsed during one cycle or between the time that a "start" pulse has been received at the input and the time a "stop" pulse is sent. An additional function is to count the number of pulses in a random pulse train like that shown in Figure 11.12.

The block diagram of a typical frequency meter/counter, or as the device is usually called *frequency counter,* or just *counter,* is shown in Figure 11.13. It is composed of four major sections: the INPUT, the CONTROL LOGIC AND GATE, a TIME BASE, and a DISPLAY. The INPUT section of the frequency counter makes it possible for a wide variety of signals of different amplitude, different frequency, and with

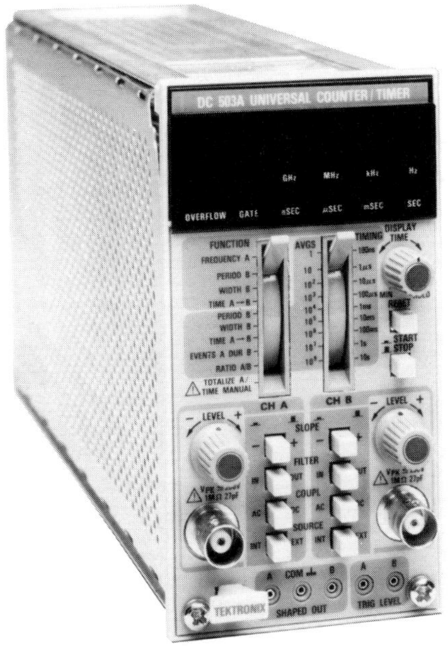

Figure 11.11 Typical frequency meter/counter (Photograph courtesy of Tektronix, Inc.)

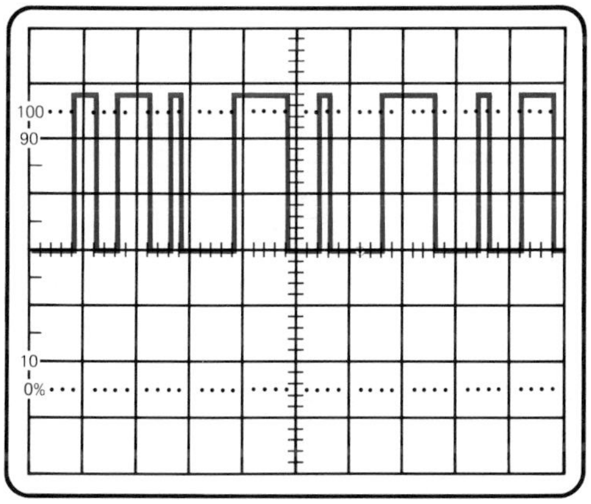

Figure 11.12 A random pulse train. A counter is capable of counting the total number of pulses.

or without a dc component to be applied to the counter input. The ATTENUATOR CIRCUIT and *ATTENUATION* selector switch adjust the amplitude of the signal applied to the INPUT connector to a level that can be safely handled by the GATE section. The actual operation of the GATE is determined by the front panel *MODE* selector switches and CONTROL LOGIC. In the *FREQUENCY* mode, the GATE permits the input signal to pass through to a group of counting circuits for a fixed amount of time. In the *PERIOD* mode, the GATE is turned on by a start pulse from the INPUT and turned off again by a second pulse. During the time when the GATE is on, or open, pulses of an accurately known frequency and period from the TIME BASE are passed through the GATE and counted by the counting circuits. The total count is then processed to obtain the time between the start and stop pulses. In the *TOTAL COUNT* mode, all pulses placed on the input are passed through the GATE and counted, and this is the number displayed.

Similar in operation to oscilloscope controls, the TRIGGER *LEVEL* and *SLOPE* controls found on many counters permit the setting of the point on a waveform at which the GATE and COUNTER circuits respond. When measuring the frequency of complex waveforms, such as that shown in Figure 11.14, setting the TRIGGER *LEVEL* point at *B* rather than *A* and the *SLOPE* on either the + (rising) or − (falling) setting will prevent false counts at points *C*, *D*, *E*, and *F*.

The heart of the counter is the TIME BASE (Figure 11.13), which produces an accurate square-wave signal used to control all the timing functions in the counter. Since the accuracy of the measurements depend on the ability of the TIME BASE to produce square waves that do not change either their frequency or duty cycle, great care is taken in the design of this

Figure 11.13 Block diagram of a typical frequency meter/counter.

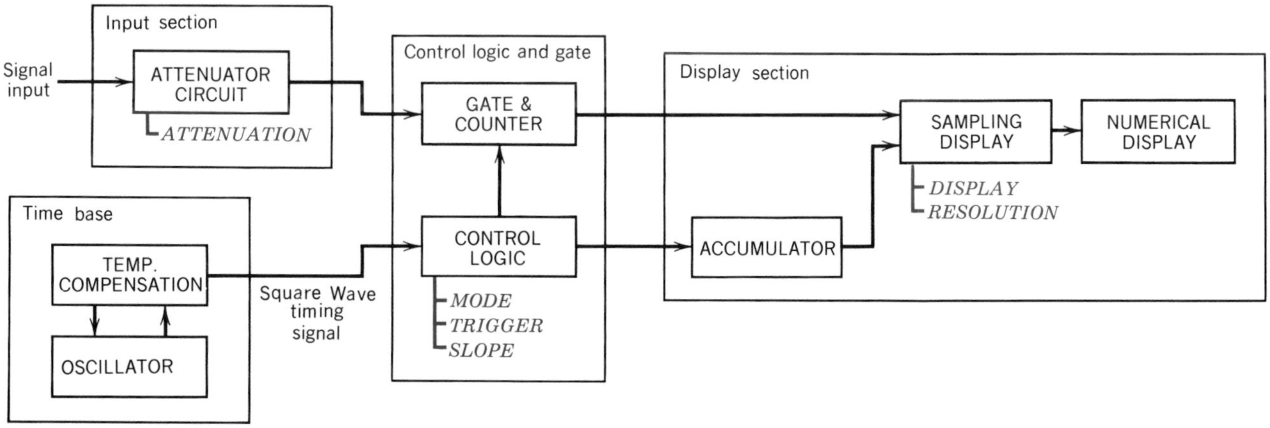

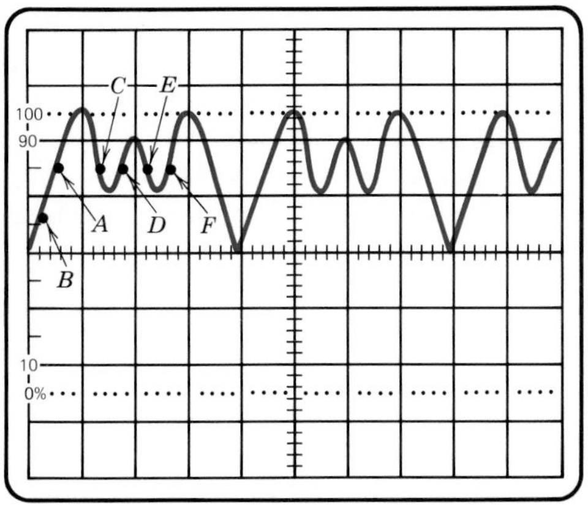

Figure 11.14 Frequency meter/counter TRIGGER LEVEL and SLOPE.

circuit. Some meters also provide a connector that permits the TIME BASE output to be connected to an external circuit for checking other equipment or for periodic checking of the time base signal itself. Very high quality counters will use a temperature-compensated time base to keep the output frequency and duty cycle constant regardless of changes in instrument temperature, and may also enclose part or all of the circuit in a small oven to keep its temperature constant.

If the counter uses manual ranging, it is necessary to set the front panel *RANGE* switches to the range suitable for the measurement being made. If too low a range is selected on a manually-ranged counter, an overrange indication will be displayed. When an overrange is indicated, switch to the next higher range. No damage will be caused by an overrange condition. The majority of the newer counters are autoranging, that is, they automatically select the correct display range in the frequency mode. When the pulse counting, or *TOTAL COUNT,* mode is selected, however, it is necessary to select the time during which incoming pulses are to be counted.

The DISPLAY section of the counter (Figure 11.13) is composed of two major circuits: an ACCUMULATOR, where the count obtained by the COUNTER section is totaled and stored, and a SAMPLING/DISPLAY section, which periodically reads the count stored in the ACCUMULATOR and displays it on the NUMERICAL DISPLAY. The CONTROL LOGIC circuit is also responsible for the correct placement of the decimal point. In order to avoid rapid changes of the display, a *DISPLAY,* or *RESOLUTION,* control is frequently included. The *DISPLAY* control determines the sampling rate so that the display can be held constant for periods of time ranging up to several seconds or "frozen" completely. This prevents small, annoying changes in the right-most display digits. The *RESOLUTION* control performs the same function by rounding off the displayed value so that only significant changes in the input signal will affect the display.

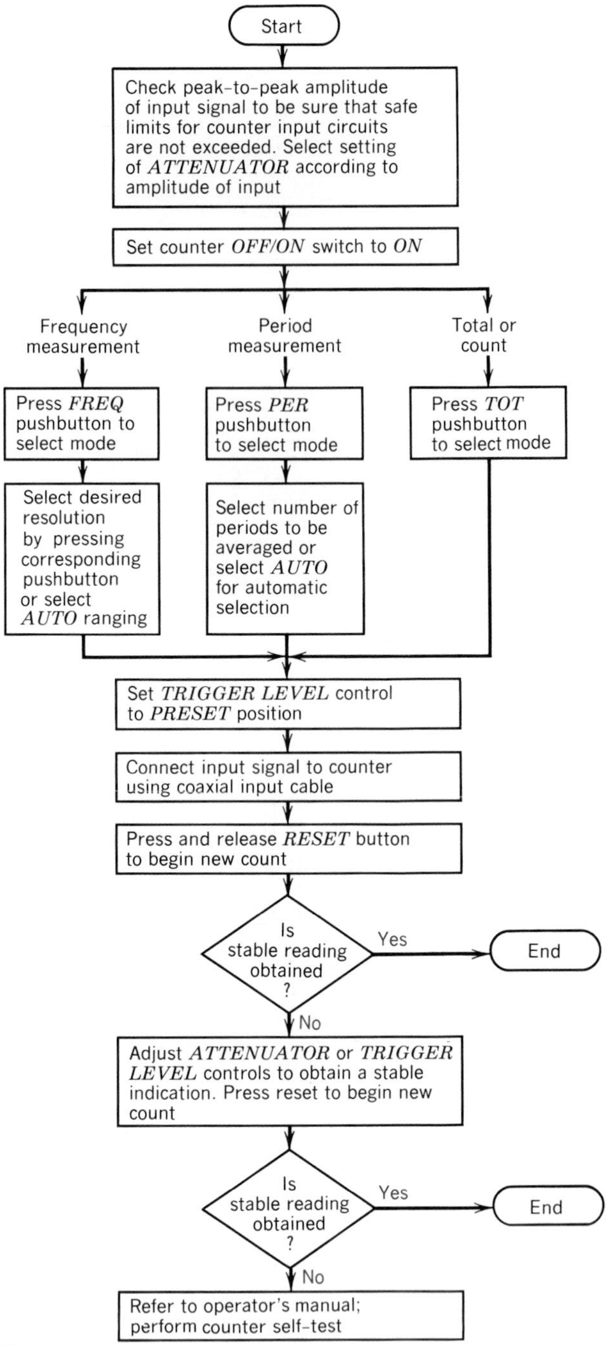

Figure 11.15 Flowchart for making frequency, period, and count measurements with a counter.

Figure 11.15 is a flowchart showing the method of making frequency, period, and total count measurements using a typical counter. The most important point to remember when making measurements with a frequency counter is to check the peak potential of the input signal to prevent overloading or damaging the counter input circuits. At frequencies above 1 kHz, the maximum allowable input potential of your counter may be less than 50 V peak. Be sure to read your counter instruction manual carefully.

B.5 SIGNAL SOURCES

All of the complex waveforms shown in this chapter and Chapter 10 are produced in common electronic units. In addition to those shown, a large number of additional waveforms are used to transmit information or control electromechanical devices. In order to test, adjust, and troubleshoot systems and circuits, it is important to understand the function and operation of signal sources.

Most of the signal sources in common use belong to one of four types: signal generators, function generators, pulse generators, and signal synthesizers. These divisions are not sharply defined, so that a function generator, for example, may be capable of doing some of the work of a signal generator or a pulse generator.

B.5.1 SIGNAL GENERATORS

The signal generator, or oscillator, is the most popular signal source. It produces a sine-wave output whose frequency and amplitude can be varied continuously over a specific range. Figure 11.16 shows a typical signal generator. Signal generators capable of producing sine-wave outputs with frequencies ranging from

Figure 11.16 Typical signal generator. (Photograph courtesy of Tektronix, Inc.)

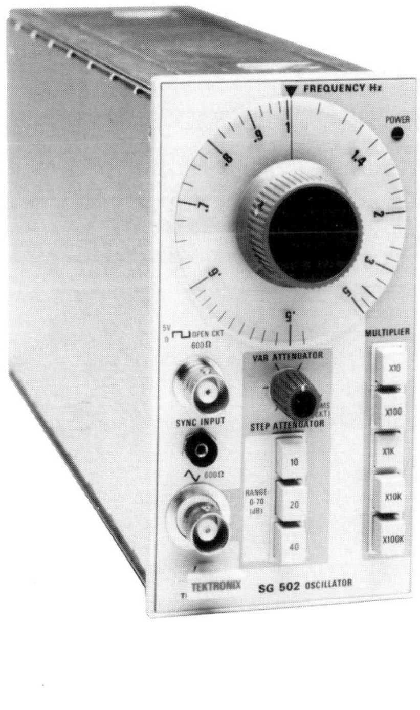

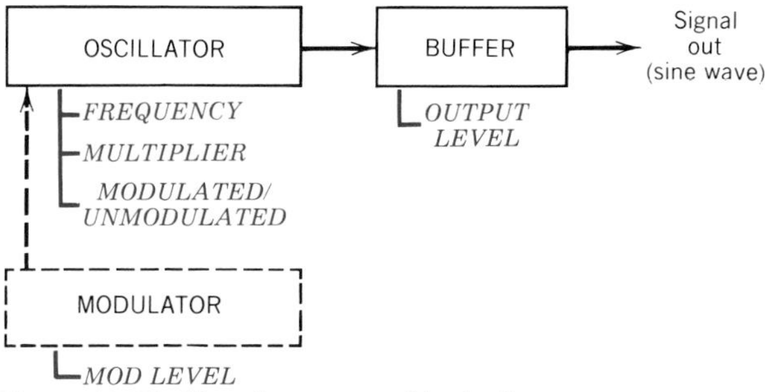

Figure 11.17 Signal generator block diagram.

about 10 Hz up to about 100 kHz are called *audio-frequency*, or af, generators since the lower portion of this range would be detectable by the human ear if the signal generator is connected to a device capable of converting electrical signals into sound waves. One such device is the electromagnetic loudspeaker or "speaker," as it is usually called. A signal generator capable of producing sine waves with frequencies from about 100 kHz up to as high as 500 MHz is referred to as a radio-frequency, or rf, generator. Some commercial units provide both af and limited rf signals to 10 MHz or so, but these wide-range units tend to be either less accurate or greatly more expensive than separate af and rf generators.

The function of most low- and medium-cost signal generators is explained by the block diagram in Figure 11.17. The sine-wave frequency of an OSCILLATOR circuit is controlled by a continuously variable control and a MULTIPLIER, which may be composed of one multiposition switch or a set of push buttons. The amplitude of the sine wave is controlled by one or more OUTPUT *LEVEL* controls that permit peak-to-peak amplitudes from a few microvolts to 10 V or so. The BUFFER section serves to keep the frequency and amplitude output constant even under varying load conditions. The MODULATOR section, enclosed in dashed rather than solid lines, is present in certain rf signal generators, particularly those intended for radio receiver troubleshooting. The purpose of the MODULATOR is to add a 400-Hz or 1-kHz signal to the output of the OSCILLATOR in order to modify the amplitude of the OSCILLATOR in accordance with the amplitude of the 400-Hz or 1-kHz sine waveform. This facilitates certain troubleshooting procedures, and is referred to as *amplitude modulation,* or AM. Figure 11.18 shows the waveform of an AM signal.

B.5.2 SWEEP GENERATORS

An important variety of signal generator is referred to as a *sweep generator.* A sweep generator should not be confused with a frequency modulated or FM generator. An FM generator is similar to the AM signal

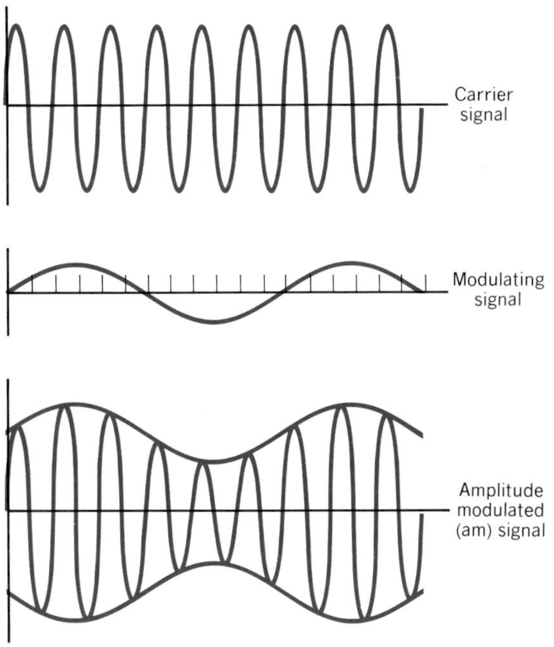

Figure 11.18 An AM signal is produced when the amplitude of a sine wave (the carrier) is modified in accordance with another signal.

generator except that the modulator signal modifies the frequency of the oscillator output rather than its amplitude. Like AM generators, FM generators are very important for the test, adjustment, and troubleshooting of radio receivers of various kinds. Sweep generators produce an output signal whose frequency varies, that is, sweeps back and forth between an upper and lower limit. These limits are generally much further apart than the upper and lower limits of an FM generator. In addition, the sweep rate of the sweep generator can be set to a variety of speeds independent of the base frequency or sweep range. Some sweep generators provide a continuous sweep rate control, while others have a number of switch settings. Nor is it necessary for the output frequency to change at a linear rate. For determining or checking the behavior of certain circuits with input signals of various frequencies, a sweep generator with a nonlinear rate of frequency change is preferable. Sweep generators are usually used with an oscilloscope. For this reason, a modification of the output signal is made when the output is at certain frequencies. These modifications, generally consisting of pulses or spikes that are easy to spot on an oscilloscope screen, are called *markers*. The marker pulses make it possible to determine the exact frequency produced by the sweep generator when a change in the characteristics of the oscilloscope trace is noted.

Figure 11.19 is the block diagram of a sweep generator. It resembles that of a standard signal generator except that the master oscillator is a VCO, or voltage-

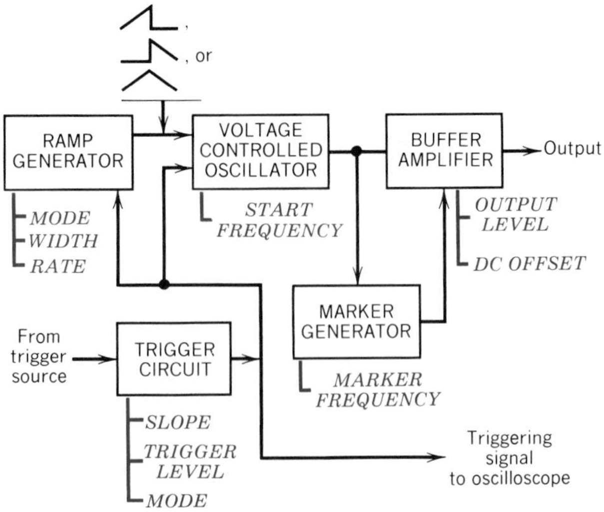

Figure 11.19 The block diagram of a sweep generator.

controlled oscillator. The output frequency of the VCO can be varied over a large range when differing potentials are applied to its control input. The input to the VCO is produced by a RAMP GENERATOR, which is capable of producing either a positive ramp as in Figure 11.20*a*, a triangle wave (11.20*b*), or a negative ramp as in (11.20*c*), depending on the setting of a front panel switch. Since the amplitude of the RAMP GENERATOR controls the output frequency of the VCO, selection of a positive ramp as shown in Figure 11.20*a* would produce a sweep generator output that would begin at its lower frequency limit and then increase in a linear manner as the potential of the ramp increased. When the ramp reached its maximum potential, the sweep generator output would be at the maximum frequency for that sweep. Since the ramp function drops off quickly after its maximum is reached, the sweep generator would quickly return to its lower frequency limit, ready to repeat the process during the next sweep.

Figure 11.20 Ramp generator waveforms.

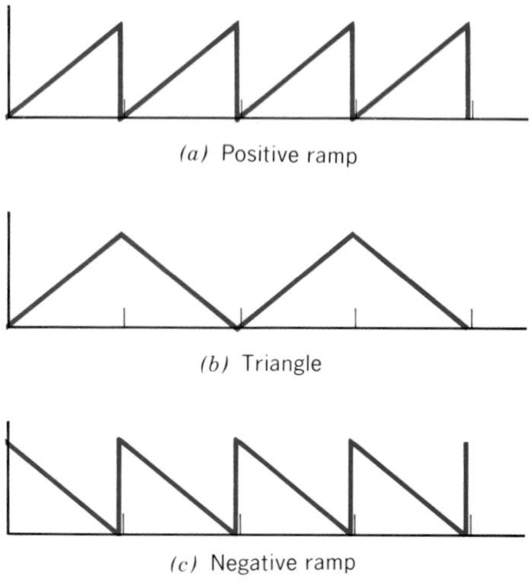

Selecting a triangle-wave output, instead of a positive ramp, for the RAMP GENERATOR means that the VCO output frequency will increase to its maximum at the rate set by the *SWEEP RATE* control and then decrease to its minimum at the same rate. Selecting a negative ramp causes the output of the sweep generator to start at its maximum frequency limit and then drop to its minimum at the rate determined by the RAMP GENERATOR output.

B.5.3 FUNCTION GENERATORS

The various kinds of signal generators in common use are principally sine-wave signal sources. Where it is necessary to use square, sine, and triangle waveforms

Figure 11.21 A function generator. (Photograph courtesy of Tektronix, Inc.)

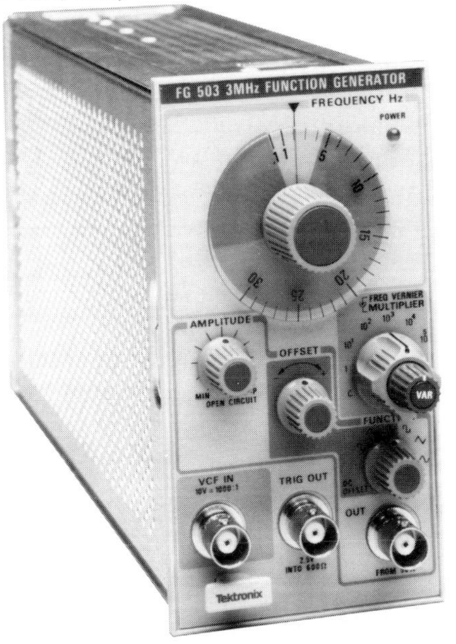

for test purposes, a device called a *function generator* is used. Although they vary greatly in their features, accuracy, frequency range, and cost, function generators like the typical model shown in Figure 11.21 are designed to be extremely versatile. The tuned frequency range of the function generator usually covers af and some rf frequencies or a large range of the rf. The output signal can be amplitude or frequency modulated by the connection of a signal generator or be swept between limits as in a sweep generator. A dc offset feature permits the addition of a dc component to the output signal.

The accuracy of the typical function generator is obtained by means of a process called *feedback,* as shown in the block diagram of Figure 11.22. Unlike the signal generator in which an OSCILLATOR produces a sine wave, the basic waveform-generating circuit in the function generator is a voltage-controlled generator (VCG), which produces triangle waves whose frequency depends on the potential present at the voltage input of the VCG. This is set by the front panel tuning control. Often a second input is provided for a front panel connector that permits the output to be swept through a frequency range by a ramp signal from an external generator. The triangle-wave output of the VCG is routed to three WAVE SHAPERS. The TRIANGLE WAVE SHAPER buffers the signal and prevents varying load conditions at the function generator output from affecting the frequency or amplitude of the output. This WAVE SHAPER also contains circuits for increasing or decreasing the rate of change of either the leading or trailing edge of the triangle. Adjustment of these controls can produce the waveforms shown in Figures 11.23*a* through 11.23*d*.

A second output of the VCG goes to the SINE WAVE SHAPER. This circuit produces smooth si-

Figure 11.22 The block diagram of a function generator.

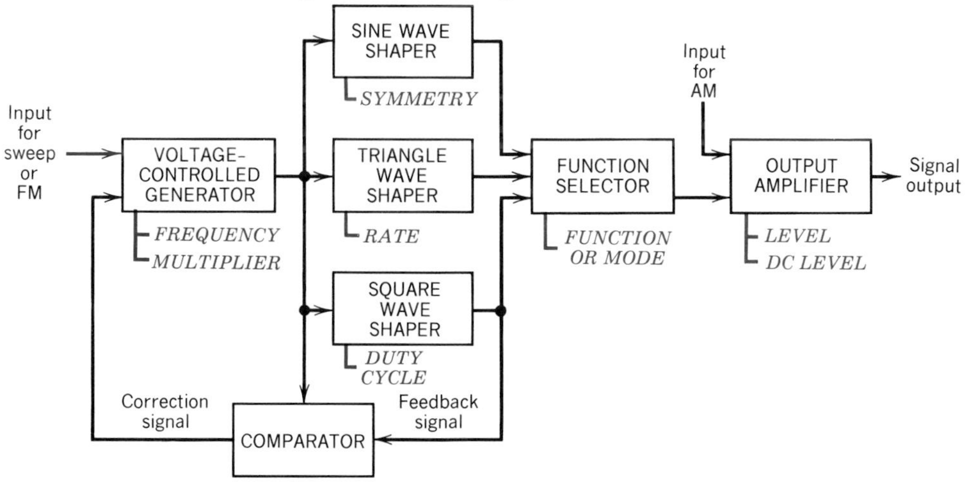

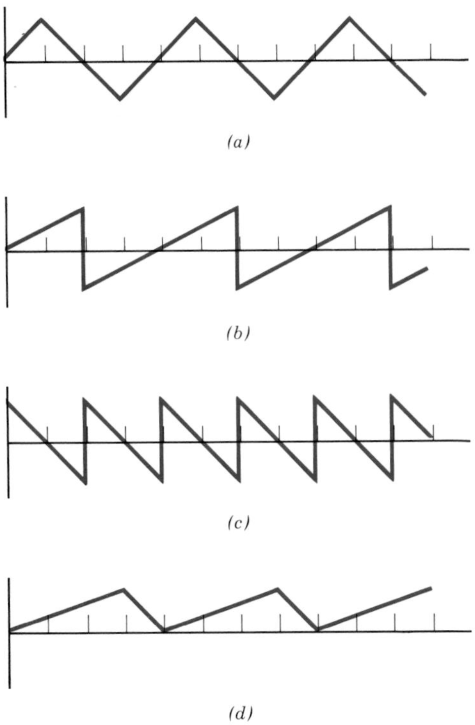

Figure 11.23 Adjustment of function generator TRIANGLE WAVESHAPER *RATE* controls produces a variety of waveforms.

nusoidal waveforms over the entire frequency range covered by the generator. In some generators, front panel controls provide the ability to modify the rise or fall time of the sine waves, producing the nonsinusoids shown in Figure 11.24. These waveforms produce the same effects as distorted sine waves on circuits and are useful for checking distortion correction features in equipment.

The third wave shaper converts the incoming triangle waveforms into square waves. Some of the square-wave output is routed back to be compared with the output of the VCG by a COMPARATOR. The COMPARATOR produces a correction signal that is used to correct frequency or waveform errors in the VCO. Using a reference signal obtained from the output of a circuit for control purposes is an example of feedback. You will learn a great deal about feedback techniques in your study of transistor circuits.

Figure 11.24 In some function generators, front panel *SYMMETRY* controls permit changing the rise and fall times of sine waves.

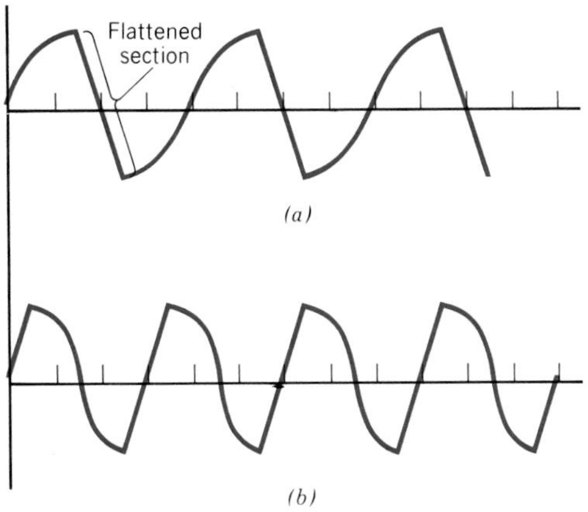

A front panel *MODE* or *FUNCTION* switch selects which of the wave shapers is connected to the OUTPUT AMPLIFIER stage. The *LEVEL* control associated with this circuit controls the amplitude of the generator output. Additional inputs to the OUTPUT AMPLIFIER make possible amplitude or frequency modulation or the addition of a dc component, controlled by the *DC LEVEL* control.

Reasonably priced function generators are available that tune a frequency range of 1 Hz to 10 or 20 MHz and are accurate to better than 5 percent of the FREQUENCY control setting. For very high frequencies from 10 to 500 MHz or higher, special, costly, function generators are available. The output amplitude of most function generators is on the order of 10 or 20 V peak-to-peak.

B.5.4 PULSE GENERATORS

The third major type of signal source is the pulse generator. Although there is a trend toward including the features of pulse generators in commercial function generators, a good-quality pulse generator is a handy

Figure 11.25 The block diagram of a typical pulse generator.

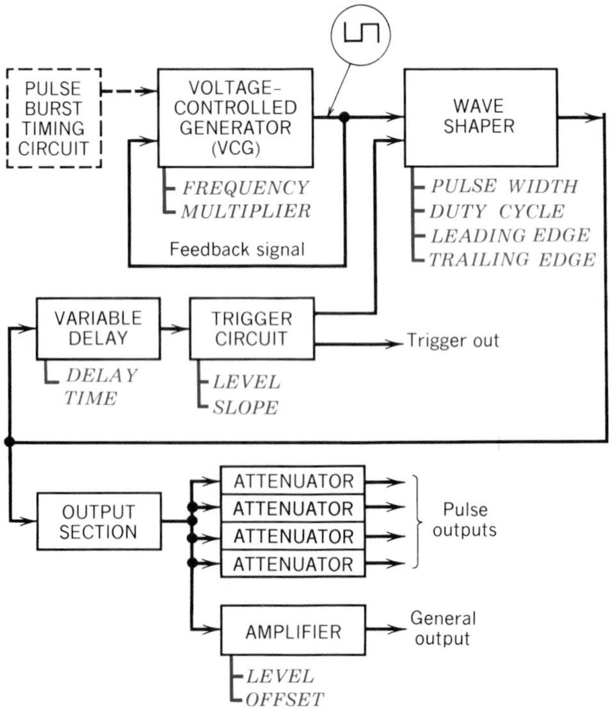

device to have for oscilloscope adjustment and for testing computer-type circuits. The functional block diagram of a typical pulse generator is shown in Figure 11.25. A VOLTAGE-CONTROLLED GENERATOR (VCG) produces square waves at the frequency set by the front panel *FREQUENCY* and *MULTIPLIER* switches. Feedback of some of the square-wave frequency provides control of the VCG. An additional control input, on some pulse generators, is derived from a PULSE BURST TIMING CIRCUIT. This circuit is used to provide bursts of pulses from the pulse generator output by turning the VCG on and off at specific times. This feature is not found on all pulse generators, but is particularly useful for adjusting or troubleshooting data communications equipment.

The output of the VCG is routed to a WAVE SHAPER, which converts the square-wave VCG signal to pulses. The WAVE SHAPER provides *PULSE WIDTH, DUTY CYCLE, LEADING EDGE,* and *TRAILING EDGE* controls that can be set to produce pulses of varying duty cycle and shape. A special circuit connected to the WAVE SHAPER provides the output of a trigger pulse from a front panel *TRIGGER* connector. The trigger pulse is produced when either the leading or trailing edge of each pulse reaches a preset potential. Front panel controls select triggering on the leading or trailing edge of the pulse and set the potential at which the trigger pulse is produced. This is shown in Figure 11.26. Trigger pulses from the pulse generator are used to turn on or enable circuits being adjusted with the pulse generator. Or, more commonly, the trigger pulses are used to trigger the sweep of an oscilloscope so that the effect of the pulse generator output on a circuit under test can be observed.

Some pulse generators provide a variable DELAY circuit that enables control over the amount of time between the trigger pulse and the pulse generator output. The effect of this control is shown in Figure 11.27.

The OUTPUT section of the typical pulse generator is more complicated than that of other signal sources because this device is intended to provide pulses with amplitude and polarities suitable for different families of semiconductor components. Each of these outputs is fed via a fixed value ATTENUATOR that reduces the pulse amplitude to the level required by that particular output. A GENERAL OUTPUT is derived by passing the signal through a controlled AMPLIFIER. This circuit is adjusted to provide any pulse amplitude up to about 10 V peak in most typical pulse generators. A variable *OFFSET* control permits the addition of a positive or negative dc component to the GENERAL OUTPUT pulse.

Pulse generators providing pulse outputs from less than 10 Hz to 50 MHz or more with output amplitude of up to 10 to 20 V are common. More expensive and elaborate units provide extremely high frequency pulses to 500 MHz or several GHz.

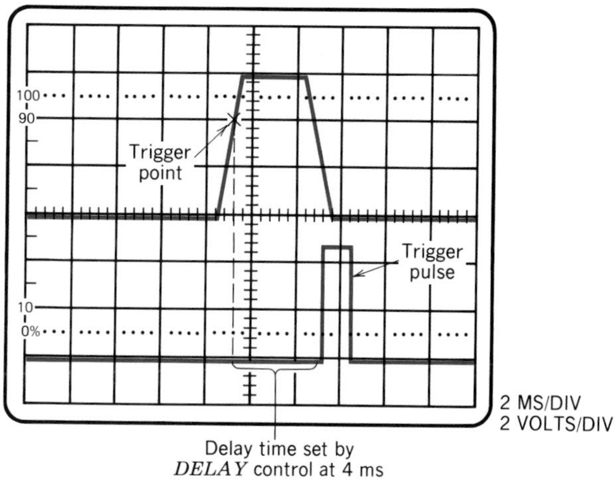

Figure 11.27 The effect of the trigger pulse *DELAY* control.

Figure 11.26 Pulse generator front panel controls determine the amplitude and slope point at which the trigger pulse is produced.

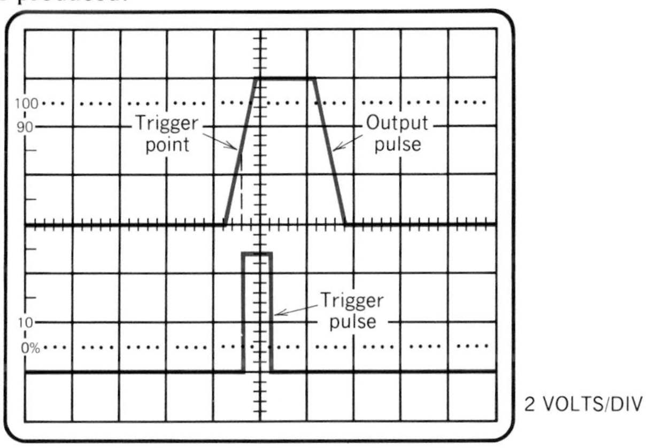

(a) Pulse generator trigger settings: *LEVEL* 4 VOLTS, *SLOPE* positive

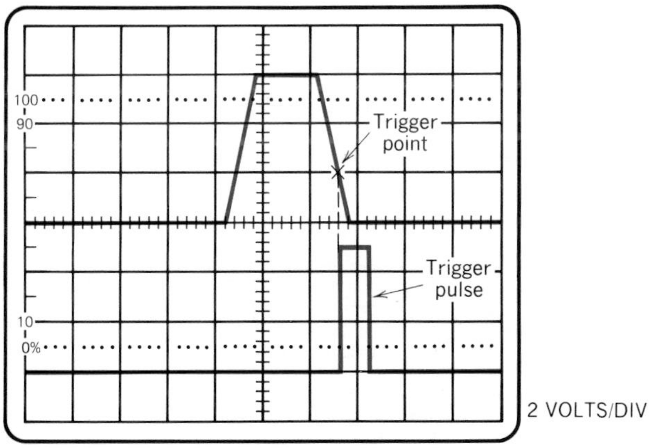

(b) Pulse generator trigger settings: *LEVEL* 2 VOLTS, *SLOPE* negative

B.5.5 SYNTHESIZERS

The fourth type of signal source, called *synthesizers*, or *arbitrary waveform synthesizers*, depending upon the way in which they produce their basic signals, are complicated instruments and much less frequently encountered than the signal, function, and pulse generators discussed in the previous sections. For this reason, a discussion of this instrument type is not included here.

B.5.6 OPERATING SIGNAL SOURCES

Exercises in the operation of typical signal sources have been included in the Laboratory Manual that accompanies this book, and the general flow diagrams given in Figures 11.28 to 11.31 can be used as guides for signal source operation. Because they are required to produce outputs of high frequency and precise waveshape, most signal source outputs are not protected from damage due to faulty connection. Two common

Figure 11.28 Flowchart for signal generator operation.

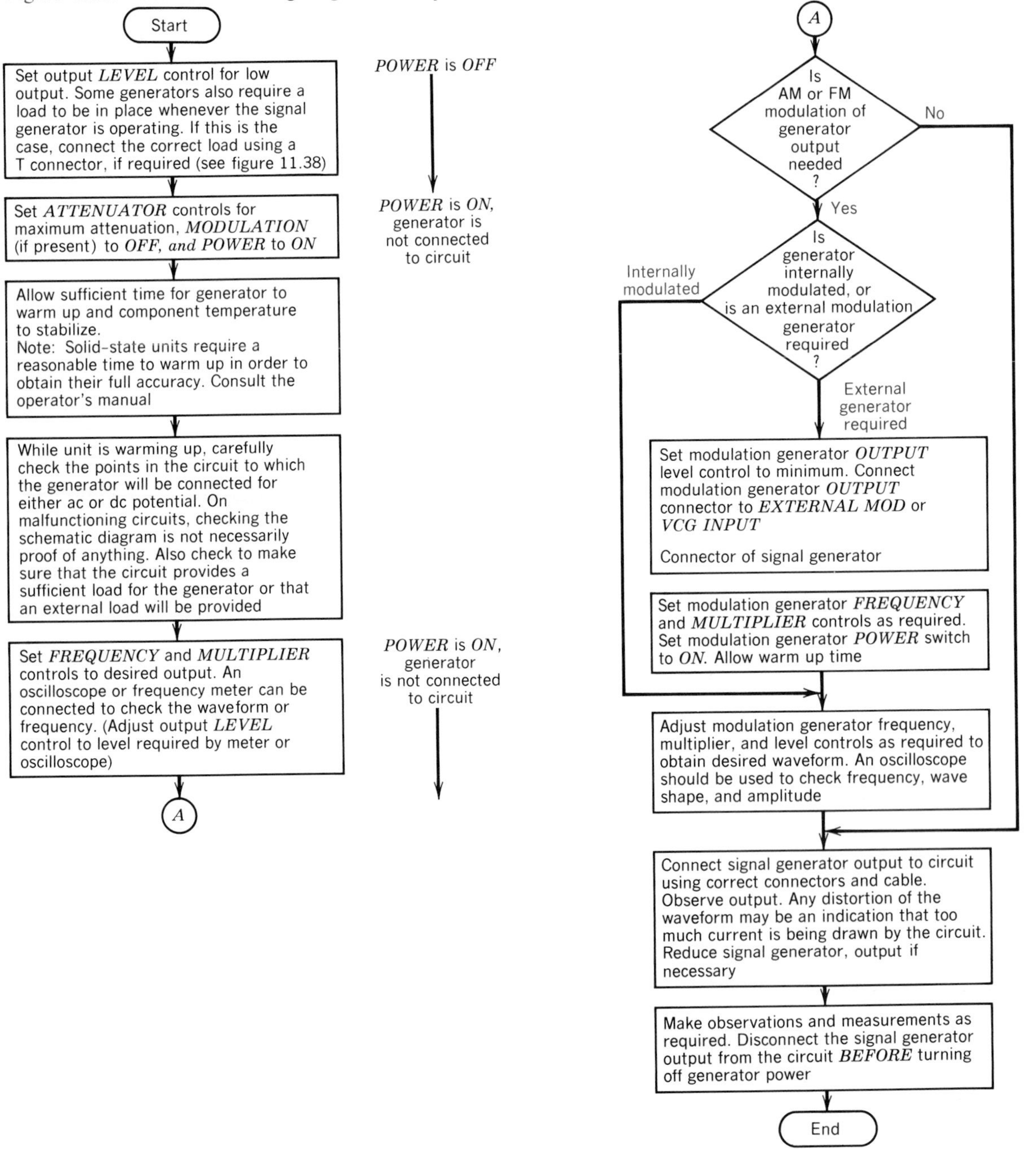

reasons for signal source failure are short circuiting the output and connecting the source output to points at high potential (either dc or ac).

Except for certain units specifically designed to deliver large amounts of power, signal sources are NOT intended to produce much current or power output. Even a small power drain will often distort the output waveform and change the frequency. Continued power drain can also destroy the accuracy of the source. For this reason, it is important not to connect a low-resistance load and to prevent the short circuiting of the generator output. Considerations of waveform accuracy also make it necessary to have fairly direct connections between output stage semiconductor components and the output connector in most signal sources. Output stage components can be easily damaged by potentials or signals present in the unit or circuit to which the signal source is connected. Following these simple precautions will help prevent damage to test equipment:

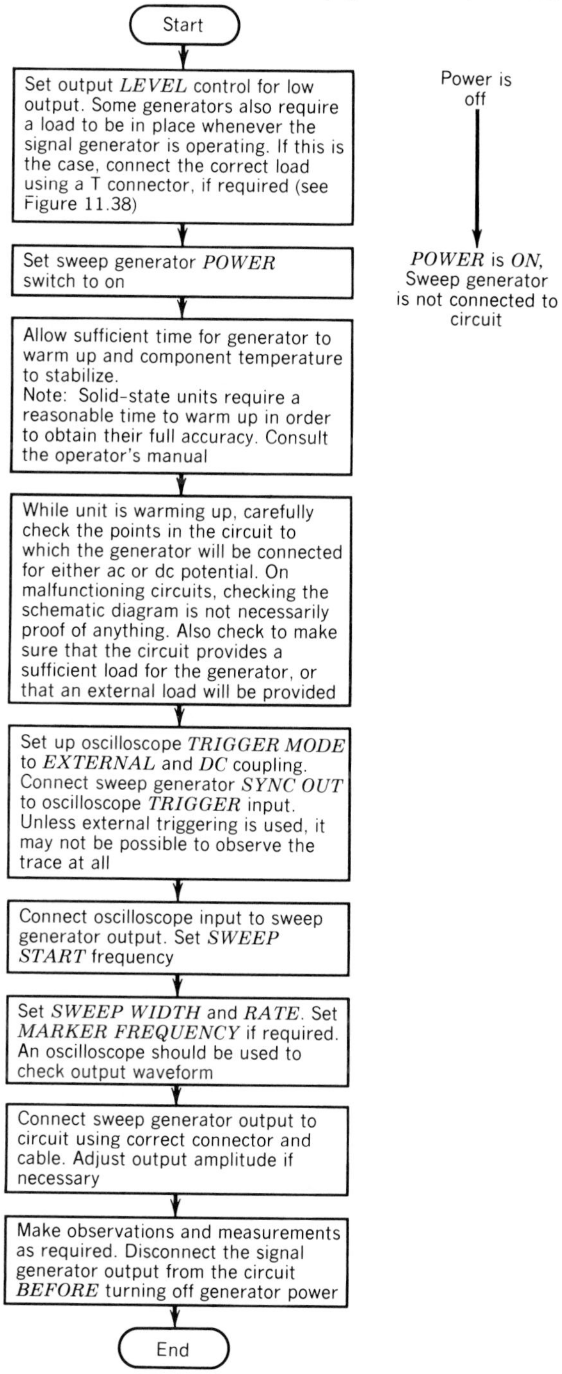

Figure 11.29 Flowchart for sweep generator operation.

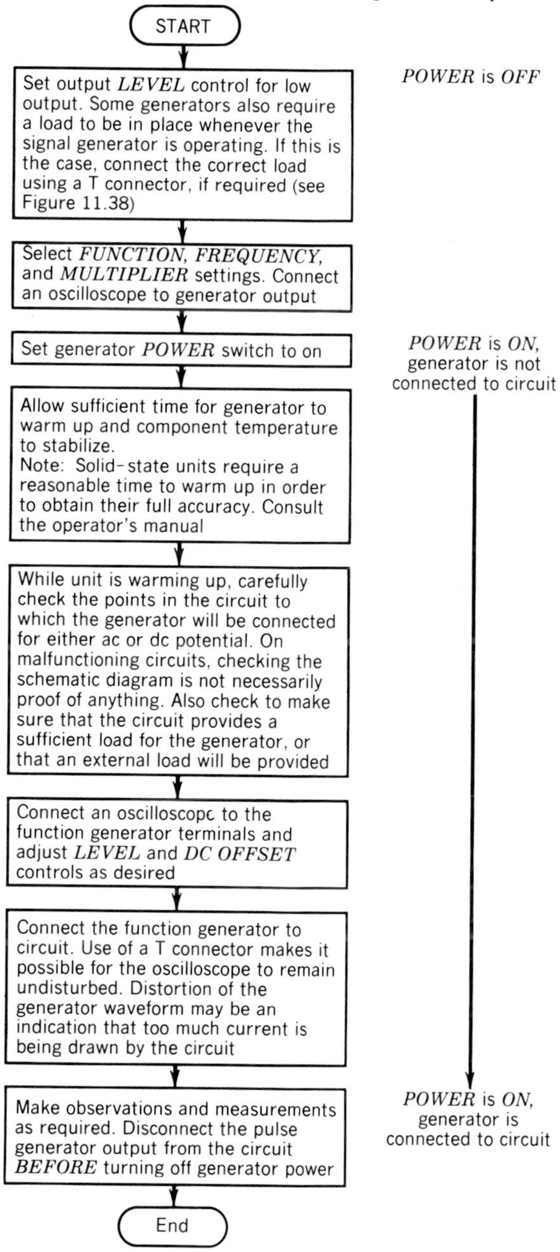

Figure 11.30 Flowchart for function generator operation.

a. Never connect a signal source to a unit or circuit without verifying that the circuit provides an adequate load for the signal source.

b. Never connect a signal source to a unit or a circuit, particularly a malfunctioning unit or circuit, without verifying that the dc and ac potential differences between the points of connection are within those specified by the signal source manufacturer in the operation manual that accompanies the signal source. Use a voltmeter or oscilloscope for this purpose.

c. In some cases it is a good idea to set the *OUTPUT AMPLITUDE* or *LEVEL* and *DC OFFSET* (if present) controls to zero before connecting the signal source or turning on signal source power. In all cases, proceed carefully and follow manufacturer's test procedures whenever possible.

Figure 11.31 Flowchart for pulse generator operation.

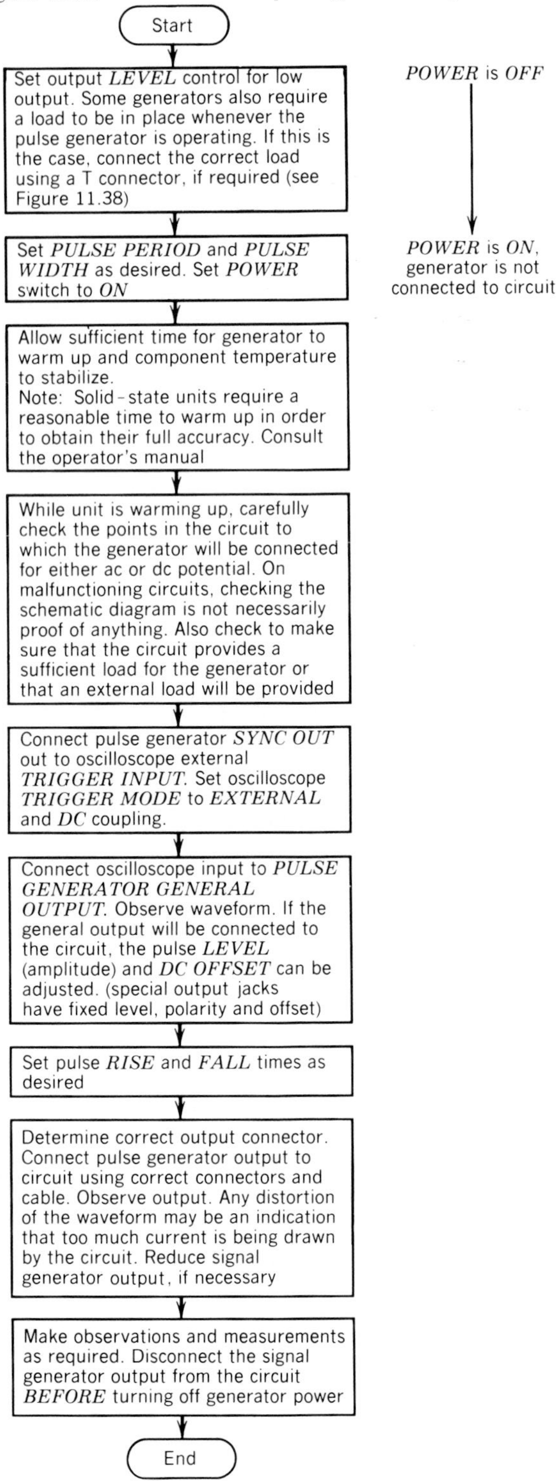

B.6 SIGNAL SOURCE CONNECTORS AND CABLES

One of the best examples of how much change has taken place in the electronics industry in recent years is the way in which signal source and oscilloscope connectors and cables have changed. Low-frequency, high-power signal sources and oscilloscopes were at one time connected to circuits by means of two wires twisted together to reduce some of the interference that the signal source might pick up from or cause in nearby

Figure 11.32 Pin or banana plugs and jacks were once the principal type of front panel connectors.

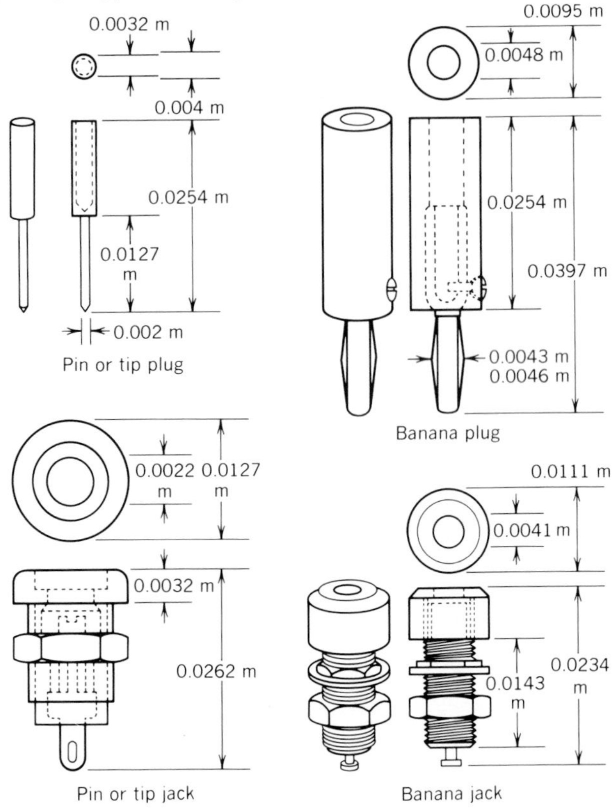

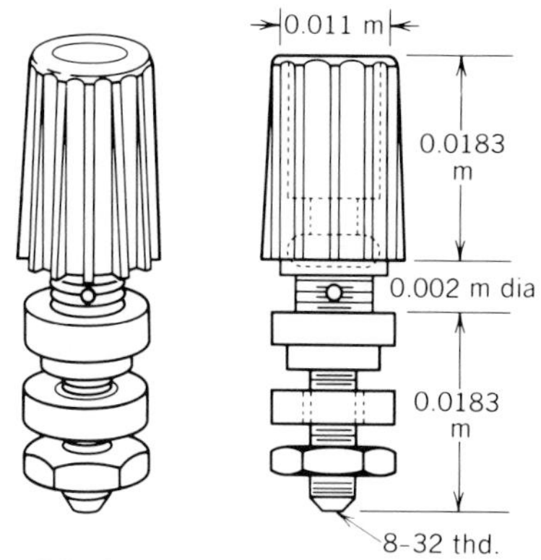

Figure 11.33 Binding posts provide connection for bare wire, lugs, and banana plugs.

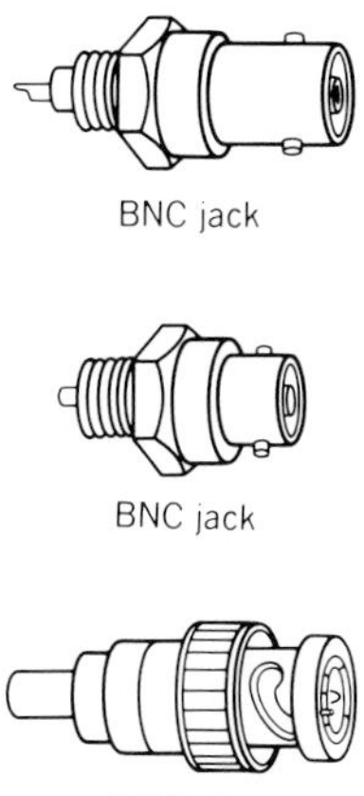

Figure 11.35 BNC plug and jacks.

circuits. The connectors mounted on the test equipment consisted, for the most part, of pin or banana jacks (Figure 11.32) much like those found in modern multimeters. Binding post terminals (Figure 11.33) were also frequently used. These terminals were particularly versatile since they could provide connection for bare wire, lugs, or banana plugs. Often, test equipment using connectors of this sort was designed to operate with twisted pair cables and a load of 600 Ω. A 620 Ω carbon composition or film resistor will provide a load for equipment of this type.

Twisted pair connections result in a great deal of power loss and are sensitive to noise from nearby motors or other circuits. One way to reduce interference was to produce shielded twisted pairs by enclosing the pair of twisted wires in a flexible metal braid shield. The same 620 Ω carbon composition or film resistor will provide an adequate load for signal sources using this type of cable.

The best sort of cabling for the connection of oscilloscopes and signal sources is coaxial cable, particularly the thinner, more flexible sizes. For the most part, the industry seems to have settled on the RG-58 cable types as the standard, although even thinner coaxial cables, possessing the same electrical characteristics as RG-58, are becoming popular. For a while, relatively massive cable connectors like the UHF series shown in Figure 11.34 were used. They are still seen where high-potential or high-power UHF connections have to be made.

Figure 11.34 UHF connector system.

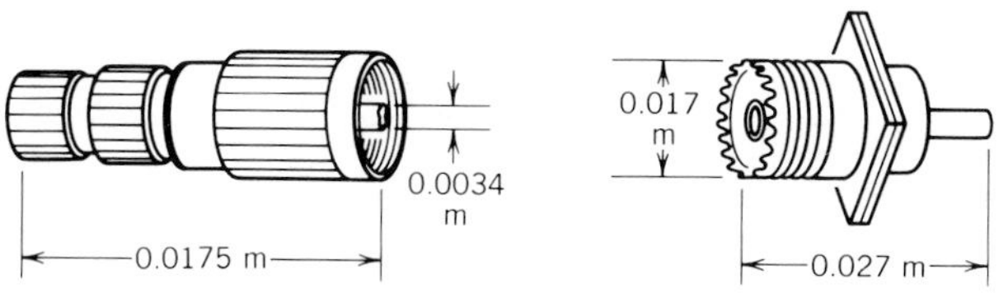

In recent years, however, the BNC series connectors shown in Figure 11.35 have become nearly universal where signal sources produce frequencies of less than 30 MHz. The BNC connector locking action resembles that of the bayonet base lamp. The connection is secure, moisture-proof, and quick to open or close. In some of the early models, however, the two bayonet pins permitted some movement of the plug. The result in radio transmitters subject to vibration was an intolerable level of noise. For this reason, a threaded connector system of the same size and form was designed called the *TNC* series, see Figure 11.36. TNC connectors are used for higher-frequency signals and in mobile or airborne units, but are not nearly as common as the BNC series.

Although some electronic devices are designed to provide 75 Ω loads, the majority of oscilloscopes and signal sources operate best with 50 Ω loads. A BNC or TNC connector on the panel of a source can be considered an indication of this. Most 83 or UHF series connectors are also evidence of 50 Ω units.

The use of BNC connectors and coaxial cables does make it easier to conduct signals from one unit to another with less loss, but it also complicates the wiring of test setups. The task of interconnecting an oscilloscope, the unit or circuit under test, and a variety of signal sources is made easier through the use of specialized connector hardware. The right-angle

Figure 11.36 The TNC connector system is a threaded version of the BNC type.

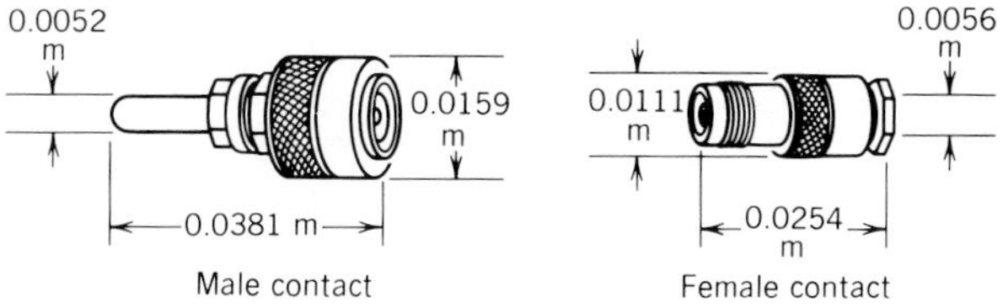

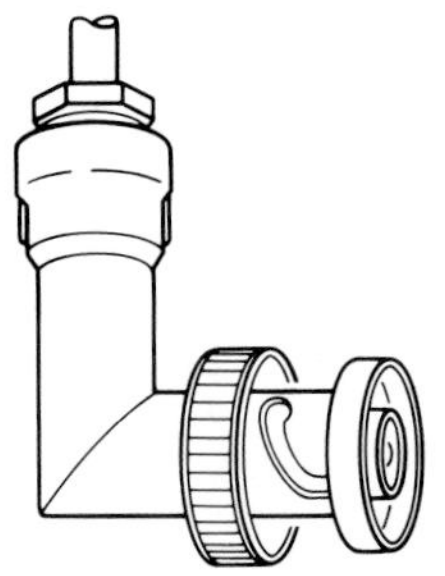

Figure 11.37 Right-angle connectors can help reduce the clutter by directing cables away from the center of the panel.

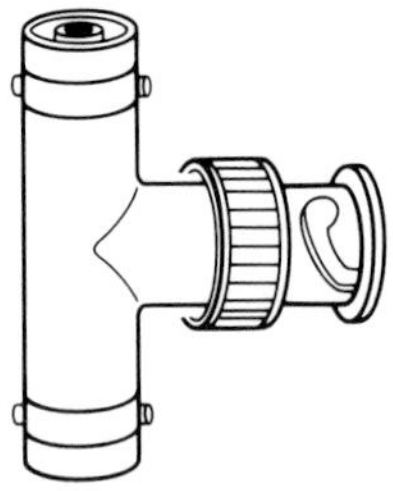

Figure 11.38 The BNC T-connector is very useful when branching connections must be made.

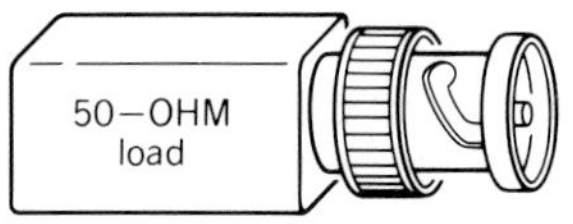

Figure 11.39 A "dummy" load for BNC connector system.

Figure 11.40 Examples of adapters that permit the interconnection of units using different connector systems.

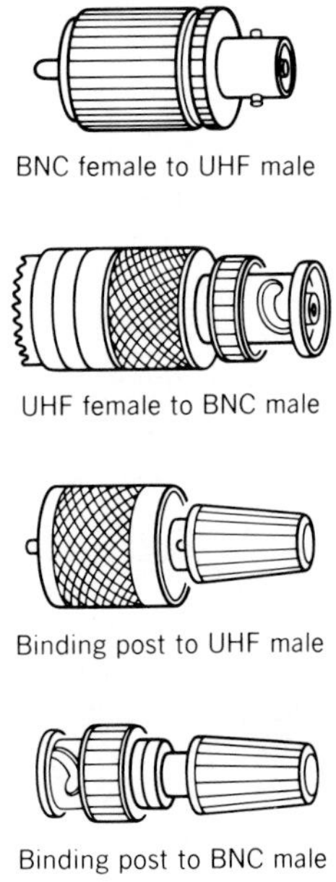

connectors shown in Figure 11.37, for example, reduce the clutter in front of an oscilloscope or signal source front panel. T-connectors, shown in Figure 11.38, are the only way of producing connection branches, and should be a part of a signal source accessory kit. A T-connector can be used, for example, to connect both a unit under test and an oscilloscope to the output of a signal source. Another handy item that should be a part of the signal source accessory kit is a 50 Ω resistor soldered into a BNC male connector. This device can be used as a load for terminating a cable or ensuring that a load is available for a signal source. Examples of commercial BNC connector loads are shown in Figure 11.39.

If you expect to work with older equipment, you should be aware of the existence of adapters, which make it possible to interconnect units using different connector systems. Some of these are shown in Figure 11.40.

C. EXAMPLES AND COMPUTATIONS

C.1 PHASE AND PHASORS

In the circuit shown in Figure 11.41*a*, two ac generators producing different potential differences but operating at the same frequency are connected in series. If the load is a resistance, and the two generators start op-

Figure 11.41 Two generators in series produce potential differences with the same zero crossings if both rotate at the same speed and start at the same instant.

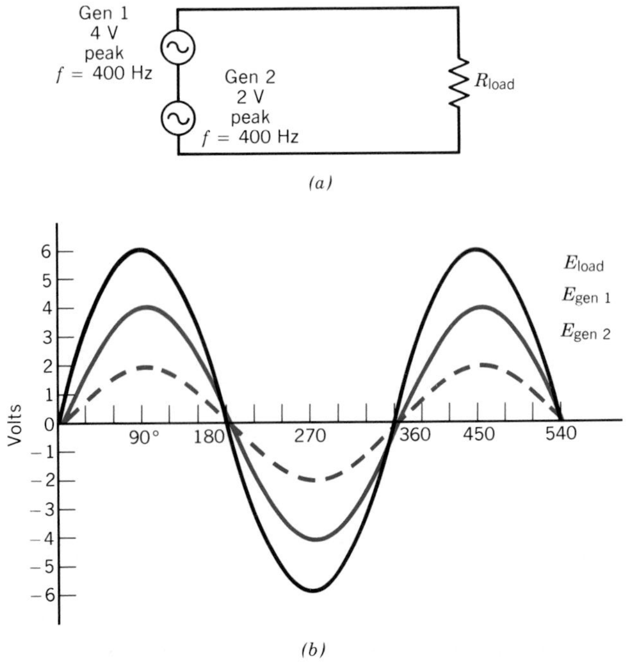

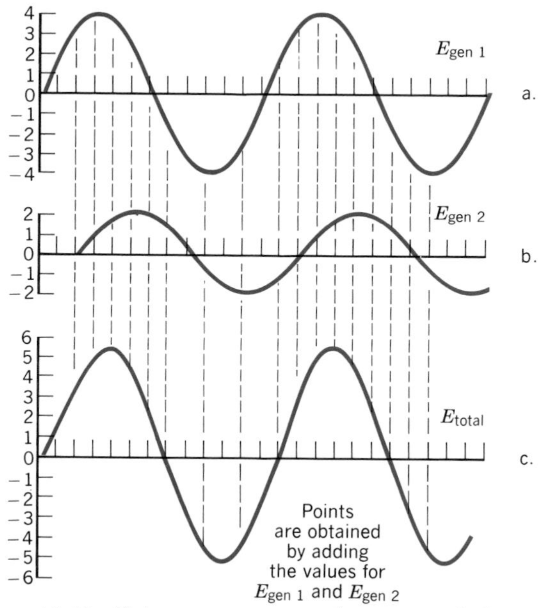

Figure 11.42 If the two generators do not start their rotation at the same moment, the result is an out-of-phase condition.

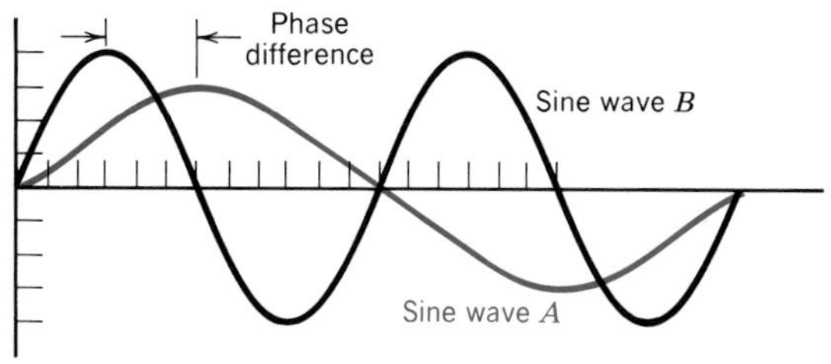

Figure 11.43 Only sine waves of the same frequency can be in phase.

erating at the same moment, the instantaneous potential difference across the load will be the sum of the instantaneous potential differences produced by the two generators, as shown in Figure 11.41*b*. The peak and rms values of the resulting potential difference across the load can be obtained by adding the peak or rms potentials produced by both generators.

But what will happen if generator 2 starts moving a short time after generator 1 does? Generator 1 will have started to produce its waveform, and its output will have reached a certain instantaneous potential when 2 begins. The two resulting waveforms are shown in Figures 11.42*a* and 11.42*b*. The graph of the sum of the instantaneous values of the potentials in 11.42*a* and 11.42*b* is shown in 11.42*c*. Notice that in contrast to the waveforms in Figure 11.41*b*, in Figure 11.42 the peak value of the total potential across the load does not come at the same point on the x axis as the peak value of Gen 1 or Gen 2. The two waveforms produced by the generators in Figures 11.42*a* and 11.42*b* are said to be *out of phase*. On the other hand, the two generator waveforms shown in Figure 11.41*b* reach their positive and negative peaks and have their zero crossings at the same point on the x axis. These two sine waves are said to be *in phase*.

The amplitude of two sine waves has no effect on whether they are in phase or not. Only sine waves of the same frequency can be in phase. As shown in Figure 11.43, even if two sine waves of different frequency begin their cycle at the same time, either their peak values or zero crossings or both will occur at different times. Sine waves whose frequencies are exact multiples of the frequency of another sine wave are said to be *harmonics* of that frequency, which is called the *fundamental*. A large part of the study of electronic circuits is devoted to the production, control, or elimination of harmonics.

EXAMPLE:
A certain signal source produces a 60-Hz sine-wave fundamental with an rms amplitude of 8.484 V. In addition, it also produces the second harmonic with an rms amplitude of 2.828 V. Graph these two functions, showing the resulting peak potential difference that this generator would produce across a resistive load. ■

SOLUTION:
Since $E_{peak} = 1.414E_{rms}$, for the fundamental,

$$E_{peak} = 1.414 \times 8.484 = 11.996$$

or rounding off, 12 V, and

$$e_1 = 12 \sin 2\pi ft = 12 \sin 377t$$

For the second harmonic, $f = 2 \times 60 = 120$ Hz, and

$$E_{peak} = 1.414 \times 2.828 = \text{about } 4$$

so

$$e_2 = 4 \sin 2\pi ft = 4 \sin 754t$$

Once these expressions for e_1 and e_2 have been calculated, plotting the points for both functions, graphing them, and adding their values is a tedious job, even with the help of a calculator. A computer program, however, makes short work of calculating the values for e_1, e_2, and $e_1 + e_2$. In fact, you might even program the computer to draw the graphs for you! Since the program for printing out a graph depends on the type of printer you are using, Program 11.1 is limited to providing four sets of values: the first column is t, the second is e_1, the third is e_2, and the fourth is $e_1 + e_2$. This program will print out 100 values. Plotting a number of these points produces the graph shown in Figure 11.44. ■

Use a calculator to add the following sinusoids:

a. $\sin \theta$ and $\sin 2\theta$
b. $12 \sin A + (-3 \sin 1.5A)$
c. A 400-Hz sine wave with a peak value of 8 and a 1000-Hz sine wave with a peak value of 3, both beginning at $t = 0$
d. $4 \sin \theta + 4 \cos \theta$
e. A sine wave with a peak value of 4 beginning at 0° and a sine wave with a peak value of 4 beginning at $t = 60°$
f. $\sin \frac{1}{3} \theta + \sin (\frac{1}{5} \theta + 30°)$

Two sinusoids of the same frequency that are out of phase can be described by arbitrarily choosing one of them to be the reference sinusoid. Generally, the reference sinusoid, as shown in Figure 11.45, is one which begins its positive half-cycle at the graph origin. The sinusoid that is being compared to the reference can then be said either to "lead" the reference by so many degrees or radians or to "lag" the reference. The angle by which the sinusoid leads or lags the reference is called the *phase difference*. Sinusoid *B* in Figure 11.45 leads the reference by $\frac{\pi}{6}$ radians (30°). Sinusoid *C* in Figure 11.45 lags the reference sinusoid by 270° $\left(\frac{3\pi}{2}\text{ radians.}\right)$ Mathematically, a sinusoid with a peak value of 5 that leads a reference sinusoid by 20° can be expressed as $e = 5 \sin(\theta + 20)$; a sinusoid with a peak value of 6.3 that lags the reference by 75° can be expressed as $e = 6.3 \sin(\theta - 75°)$. Radian angle measure rather than degrees could have been used in these expressions.

Program 11.1 Program for calculating sine wave values in Example.

```
10  FOR T = 0 TO 0.0173613 STEP 0.0006945
20  J1 = 12 * SIN (377 * T): LPRINT T,:
    LPRINT J1,
30  J2 = 4 * SIN (754 * T): LPRINT J2,
40  LPRINT J1 + J2: LPRINT
50  NEXT T
60  END
```

Figure 11.44 Graph of fundamental and second harmonic.

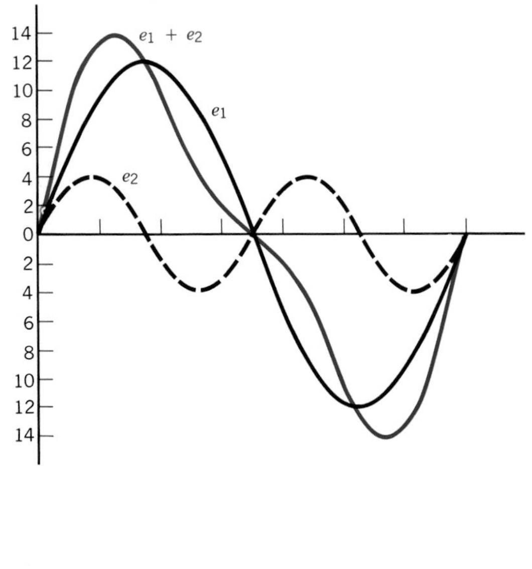

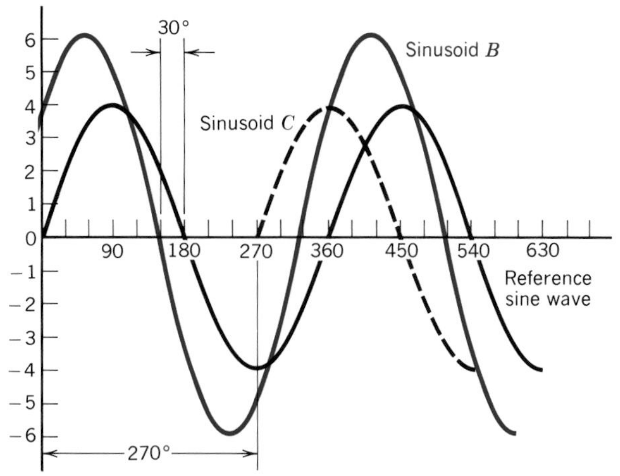

Figure 11.45 Phase relationship of sine waves.

Drawing sine waves is a time-consuming and often inaccurate process, but fortunately there is an easier method to represent out-of-phase sine waves *of the same frequency*. Not only can the out-of-phase signals be represented, but they can be added or subtracted with a minimum of calculation. This method involves using graphical representations called *phasors*. Phasors are related to vectors. A vector, you will recall, is a graphical method for representing a quantity that possesses both a magnitude and a direction. A sinusoid has a maximum or peak value and a zero crossing at the beginning of its positive half-cycle, which occurs at some angle with respect to the origin. If the reference sinusoid is represented as a line with a length the same number of units as its magnitude lying along a positive *x* axis, a sinusoid described by $e = 3 \sin(\theta + 30°)$ could be represented as shown in Figure 11.46. This sinusoid leads the reference by 30°. A sinusoid with a length of 2 that lags the reference by 90° would be represented along the negative *y* axis as in Figure 11.47.

Figure 11.46 Phasor representations of a reference sine wave and a sine wave with the formula $e = \sin(\theta + 30°)$.

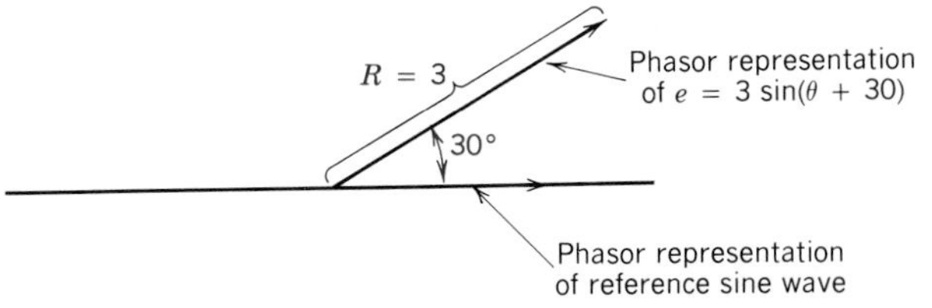

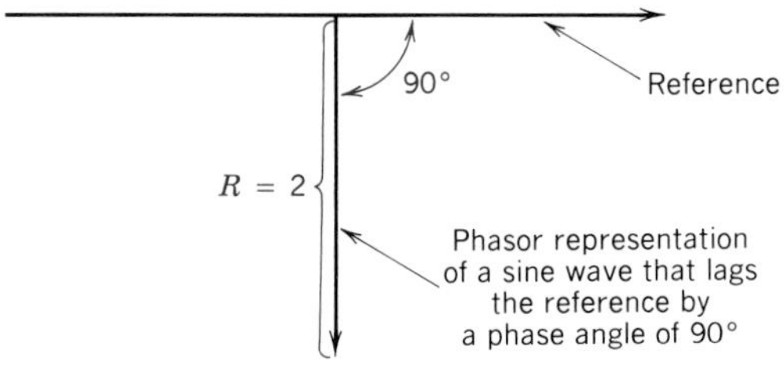

Phasor representation of a sine wave that lags the reference by 90° and has a peak amplitude of 2.

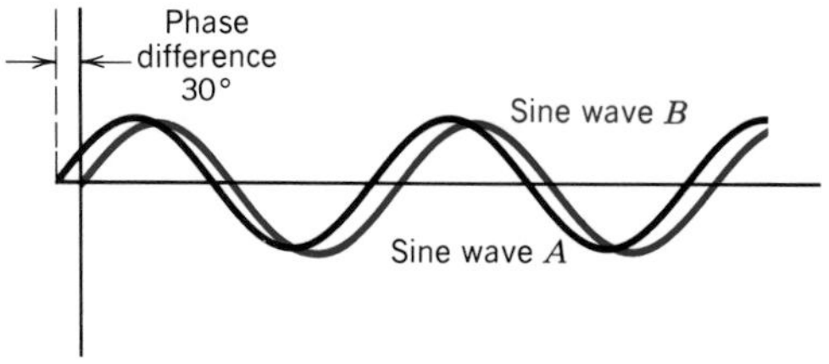

(a) Two sine waves separated by a phase angle of 30°

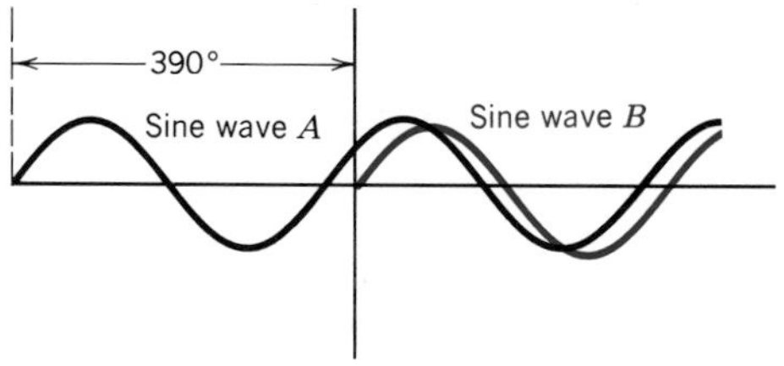

(b) Two sine waves separated by a phase angle of 390°

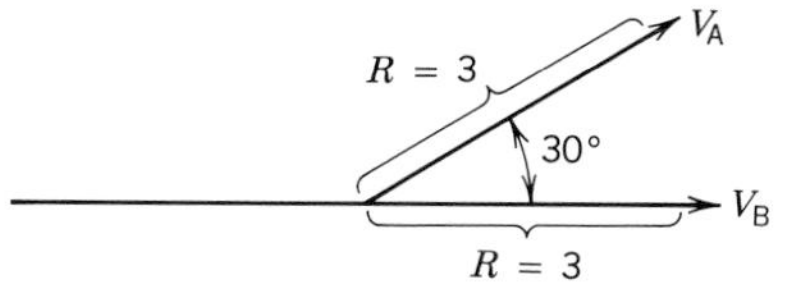

(c) Phasor representation of A and B

Figure 11.48 Phasor diagram cannot represent a lag of one or more complete cycles.

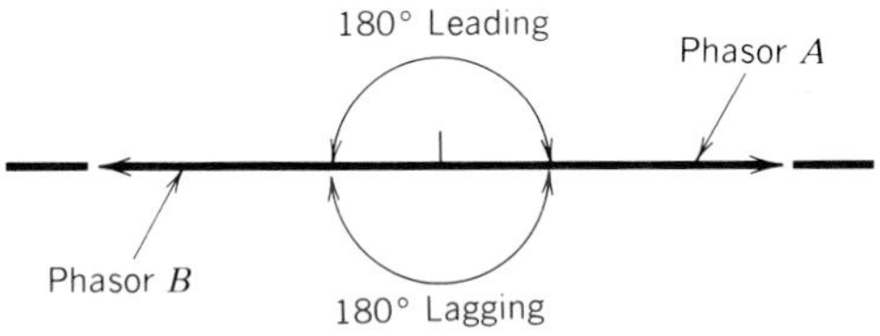

Figure 11.49 A waveform that leads another by 180° is represented in the same way as one that is lagging by 180°.

Phasor notation is useful, but there are a number of problems associated with it. First, there is no way of determining the frequency of the sine wave represented by a phasor, unless it is written as a part of the representation. It is easy, therefore, to assume that several phasor diagrams representing phase angles in a particular unit or circuit all have the same frequency, even though this is not necessarily the case. In most cases, however, phasors and phase angle notation are used to describe changes in phase angle as a signal passes through a circuit, and the frequency does not change. The second point to keep in mind is that the phasor diagram showing two phasors does not take into account the fact that one of the waveforms might have begun several cycles before or after the other. For example, both Figures 11.48*a* and 11.48*b* are represented by the phasor diagram shown in 11.48*c*. Finally, it is necessary to be aware that a waveform that leads its reference by 180° can also be thought of as lagging by 180°, as shown in Figure 11.49.

In addition to being easier to draw than sine waves, phasors, like the vectors they resemble, can be added by resolving them into components, adding the components, and then determining the magnitude and phase angle of the resulting phasor. Two phasors representing sine waves of the same frequency are shown in Figure 11.50*a*. The process of calculating the phase angle and magnitude of the waveform produced by the sum of these is not at all complicated. Since the reference phasor lies along the x axis, it has no y component, and its x component is the same as its length, 2. The x and y components of phasor B, as shown in Figure 11.50*b* can be obtained using the methods introduced in Chapter 10:

$$x = E_{\text{peak}} \cos \theta \quad \text{and} \quad y = E_{\text{peak}} \sin \theta$$

The x component is 1.3 and the y component 0.5. As shown in Figure 11.50*c*, the two x components are added and recombined with the single y component using Formula 10.9,

$$r = \sqrt{x^2 + y^2} \quad \text{and} \quad \theta = \arctan \frac{y}{x}$$

Figure 11.50 Two phasors can be added by resolving them into components.

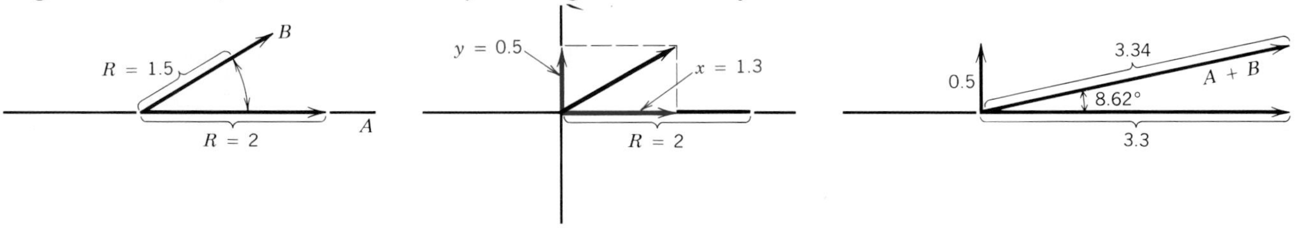

(a) *(b)* *(c)*

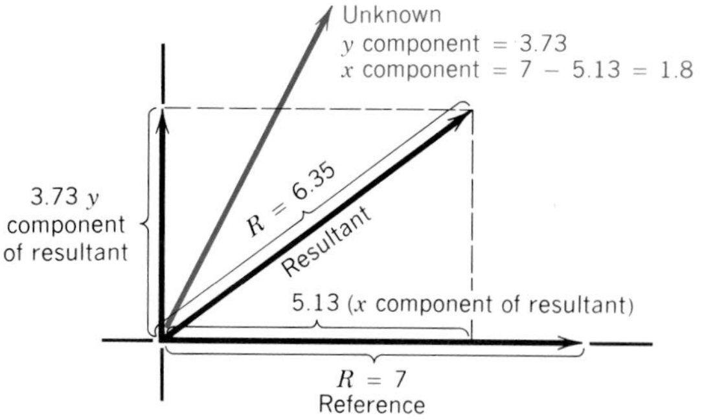

Figure 11.51 Example: Using phasor subtraction.

Similarly, the phasor produced by the difference between two phasors can be determined by subtracting the components.

EXAMPLE:
A 60-Hz sine function with a peak value of 6.35 and a phase angle of 36° is produced by the addition of a reference phasor with a peak value of 7.00 and a second phasor. Calculate the peak value and phase angle of this second phasor. ■

SOLUTION:
The unknown phasor is the difference between the resultant 6.35 at an angle of 36° and the reference 7.00 at 0° as shown in Figure 11.51. The x and y components of the unknown phasor are

$$x = 7.00 - 5.13 = 1.87$$
$$y = 3.73$$

The length of the unknown phasor is

$$r = \sqrt{x^2 + y^2} = \sqrt{17.4098} = 4.1725 \quad \text{or} \quad 4.17$$

and its angle is

$$\theta = \arctan \frac{y}{x} = 63.37°$$ ■

Use the method of phasors to represent and perform the following operations on sine functions:

a. $2 \sin \theta + 1.75 \sin(\theta + 30°)$
b. $\sin (A + 175°) + \sin(A - 60°)$
c. $\sin B + \sin (B - 180°)$
d. $8 \sin B - 4 \sin(B - 180°)$
e. A phasor that produces a resultant of 9.35 at an angle of 45° when added to a reference phasor of length 3
f. The reference phasor that when added to a phasor of length 10 at 60° produces a resultant of length 8 at 45°
g. A pair of phasors whose sum is 2 at 0°

Hint: How many answers are possible?

D. APPLICATIONS

D.1 TYPES OF ELECTROMAGNETIC METERS AND THEIR APPLICATIONS

Although the digital display is rapidly becoming an industry standard in many applications, the typical electromagnetic meter shown in Figure 11.52 is still a popular display for numerical values. With the exception of the comparatively rare electrostatic meter, all analog electromagnetic meters make use of the motor principle for their operation. That is, they use the force developed between a current-carrying conductor and a magnetic field to move a pointer or indicator across a scale. There are four common electromagnetic meter types or movements in use today: the D'Arsonval, the electrodynamic, the moving iron, and the moving magnet.

D.1.1 THE MOVING-MAGNET METER

The moving-magnet meter is probably the simplest to understand since it operates very much like the conductor and compass with which Oersted discovered the relationship between electric current and magnetism. The moving-magnet mechanism is also called the *polarized iron* movement, which makes it easy to confuse inexpensive and usually inaccurate meters using this system with the superior moving-iron type. Like a compass, the moving-magnet mechanism contains a small magnet that is pivoted so that it can turn as shown in Figure 11.53. A light-weight pointer is connected to

Figure 11.52 Typical electromagnetic meter (Photo by M. Hermes).

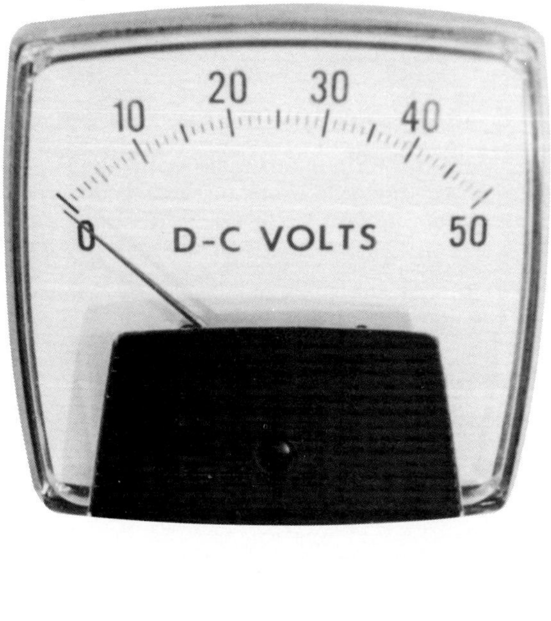

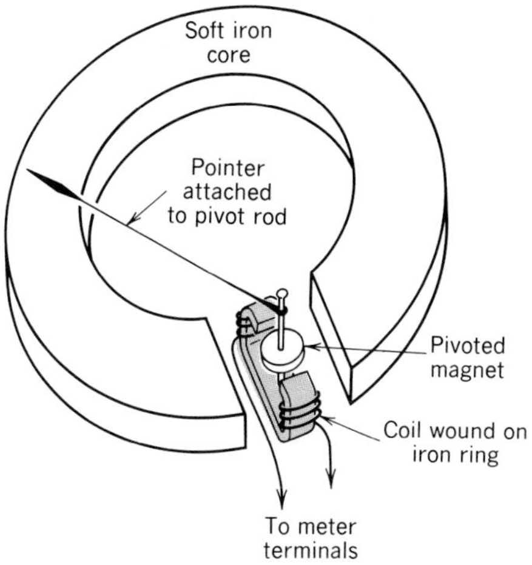

Figure 11.53 A moving-magnet meter contains a small, pivoting magnet.

the magnet. A coil of wire connected to the meter terminals completes the essential parts of this movement. When a direct current passes through the coil, the magnet turns, moving the pointer. A soft iron coil core and split iron ring are included to direct the field produced by the coil. This makes it possible to use a coil with fewer turns.

The moving-magnet mechanism is a dc device since an alternating current applied to the coil would produce a rapidly reversing magnetic field. This would cause the magnet to vibrate rather than turn. Applying ac would also demagnetize the magnet over a period of time. Even if used properly, the magnetic field intensity of the tiny magnet will change under use, so high accuracy is not generally expected of meters using this mechanism. Automobile ammeters are frequently of this type since great accuracy is not necessary.

D.1.2 THE MOVING-IRON METER

The moving-iron mechanism should not be confused with the moving-magnet type. There is no permanent

Figure 11.54 Simplified diagram to explain the operation of an attraction-type moving-iron meter mechanism.

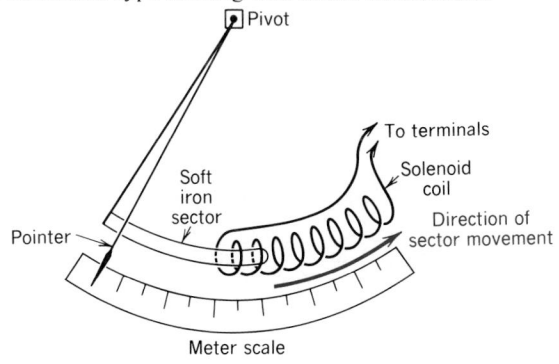

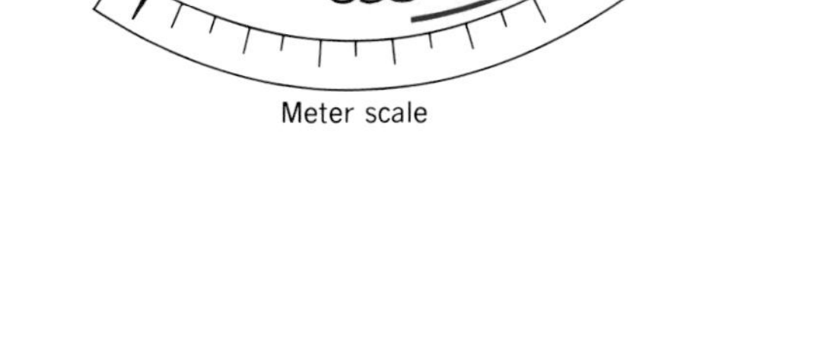

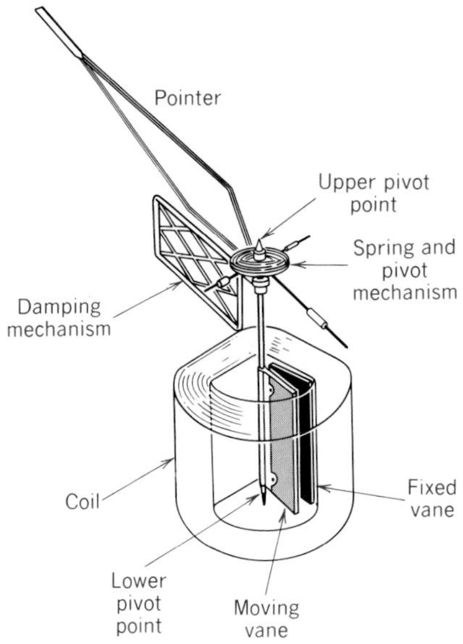

Figure 11.55 Typical form of a repulsion-type moving-iron meter mechanism.

magnet in the moving-iron mechanism: The magnetic field is produced by a coil, so that the force on the moving piece of iron, which carries the pointer, depends on the amount of current through the coil. There are two basic kinds of moving-iron mechanism: the attraction type and the repulsion type. A third type combines the principles of the attraction and repulsion types.

Figure 11.54 shows a simplified diagram of an attraction-type movement. A solenoid coil attracts a soft iron core when there is a current through the coil. The core is attached to a pivoting rod on which the indicator is mounted. The repulsion-type movement shown in Figure 11.55 represents a typical design. A relatively large coil surrounds two rectangular iron plates called *vanes*. One of the plates is attached to the frame of the instrument, while the other is free to pivot. The indicator or pointer is linked to the pivoting vane. When current flows through the coil, the magnetic flux through the center of the coil magnetizes both vanes. Since they are both magnetized by the same field, the two vanes are magnetized with their north and south poles adjacent as shown in Figure 11.56. This causes a force of repulsion between the vanes, and the movable vane pivots, causing a displacement of the indicator across the scale. Note that the direction of the field does not matter. Reversing the field direction would just reverse the north and south poles produced on *each* vane. The two vanes would still be forced apart. If the coil were supplied with an alternating current, the vanes would be forced apart as the current rose from zero to its maximum; then the force would lessen as the current

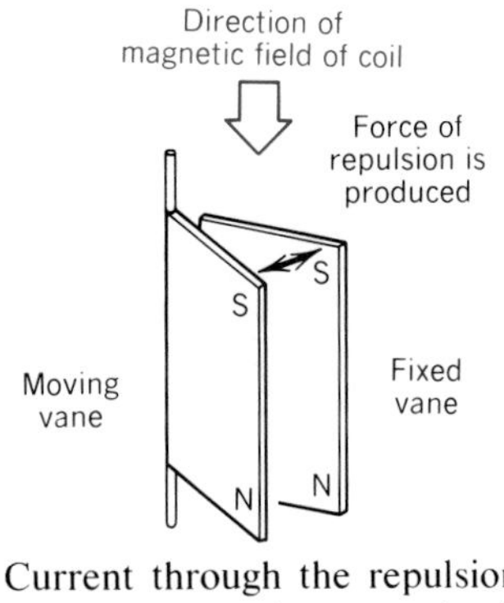

Figure 11.56 Current through the repulsion-type moving-iron meter causes the vanes to be magnetized with like poles adjacent.

dropped to zero. At the beginning of the negative half-cycle, the magnetic polarities of both vanes would be reversed and the force pushing the vanes apart would begin to increase again. The result of this, for frequencies above a few hertz, would be a vibrating indicator that would make it difficult to read the meter. This vibration is eliminated by means of a damping mechanism, either a paddle-shaped piece that provides enough resistance to movement or a segment whose movement is damped by a magnetic field. Therefore, the moving-iron mechanism is a meter movement that works on ac. Since the force on the moving-iron vane is the result of the magnetic field caused by the coil current *and* the force of repulsion from the fixed vane, which is also proportional to the coil current, the force on the moving vane at any instant is proportional to the *square* of current through the meter coil. The averaging effect produced by the mechanical friction of the pivot and the damping mechanism averages this force, so that the meter indication is related to the rms value of the meter current.

Moving-iron meters can be used to measure alternating currents to around 1 kHz, but the amount of power necessary to cause vane motion limits the lowest practical range to 10 mA full scale. Commercially available units are found with accuracies up to 0.5 percent, maximum current ranges of 50 A, and maximum voltage ranges of 750 V. Shunts and multipliers can be used to extend these ranges. The accuracy of moving-iron meters in dc measurements is not as good as for ac measurements. In fact, it is necessary to make two measurements to get accurate results. This is called the *reverse-reading technique*. Reverse reading consists of making a reading and noting the value, reversing the meter leads, and taking a second reading. Averaging the two readings provides a fairly accurate measurement.

D.1.3 THE ELECTRODYNAMOMETER

The electrodynamometer (pronounced *eléktro-dina-mámetr*) also called the *dynamometer* or *electrodynamic meter*, is the most versatile of all the meter movements. That is, it can be used to construct a wide variety of measuring devices through modifications of its structure. In Figure 11.57, you can see that there is no permanent magnet or magnetic material involved in this meter movement. Instead, a pivoted coil or coils moves in the magnetic field produced by current through a stationary coil or coils. Since this movement is based on the interaction of magnetic fields caused by electric currents, and there are no magnetic materials or magnets whose field strength or magnetic characteristics change over a period of time, the electrodynamic meter is the most accurate of those discussed in this section. The movement shown in Figure 11.57 is called a *single-element* dynamometer, even though three coils are shown. The two fixed coils are connected in series to form a single large coil. This arrangement keeps the force on the smaller, pivoted coil directly proportional to the current, in spite of the angle through which it has been rotated. The single-element dynamometer can be used for measurement of current, voltage, or power, depending on the arrangement of electrical connection between the fixed and moving coils. Since the interaction of the coils does not depend on the polarity, these meters are usable for both ac and dc, without using the reverse-reading technique.

Some dynamometers have two moving coils at a right angle, as shown in Figure 11.58. This is called a *crossed-coil movement*. Crossed-coil dynamometers are frequently used in industrial applications where certain kinds of components or devices in ac circuits cause a difference in phase between the potential dif-

Figure 11.57 The electrodynamometer or dynamometer.

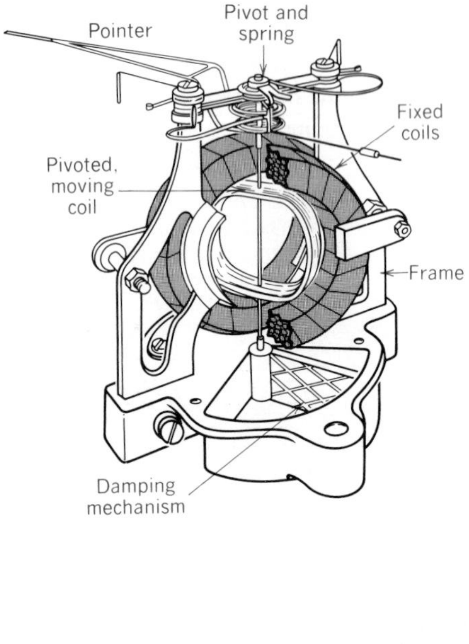

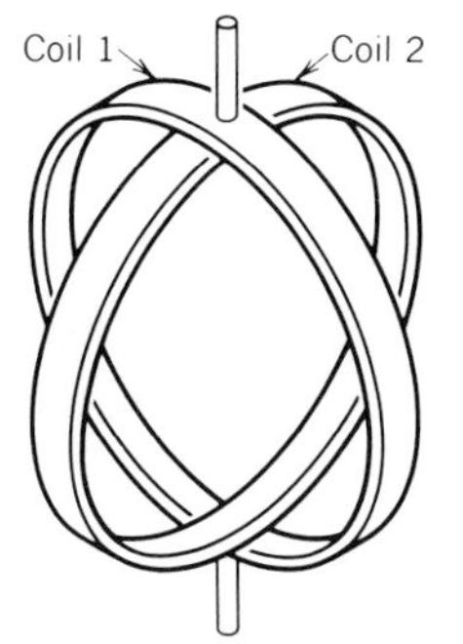

Figure 11.58 Some dynamometers have two moving coils mounted at right angles on a common pivot.

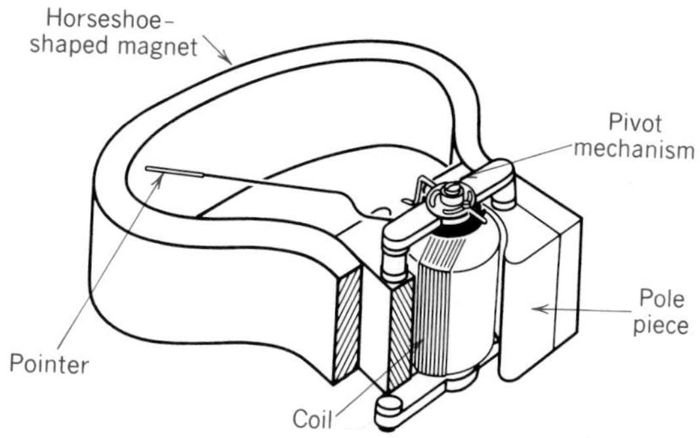

Figure 11.59 One form of the D'Arsonval or PM/MC meter movement. One pole piece has been cut away to show the coil.

ference across a circuit and the current through it. The cosine of the phase difference angle, as you will see in greater detail in a later chapter, is called the *power factor*. A crossed-coil dynamometer can be used to measure power factor. Other instruments can be constructed by using two separate fixed coils or using a common moving-coil support shaft to link two separate units.

Dynamometers are used to measure current, voltage, and power in dc and ac circuits with frequencies below a few hundred Hz. The accuracy is comparable with that of a typical digital meter, 0.1 percent; but, as in the case of the moving-iron meter, a certain amount of current is needed to overcome the friction of the moving-coil pivots or suspension, so it is not possible to produce very low current dynamometers. Other measurements, such as frequency and power factor are possible directly with special meters of this type.

D.1.4 THE D'ARSONVAL MOVEMENT

The most common type of meter movement in use in test equipment today is the permanent-magnet moving-coil or PM/MC movement, also called the D'Arsonval movement, after its inventor. Shown in Figure 11.59, the PM/MC movement consists of a pivoting coil supported in the field of a permanent magnet. An indicator attached to the moving coil is displaced across a scale when a current passes through the coil. The D'Arsonval movement is an accurate, fairly inexpensive, and versatile component. There are two coil arrangements. The first, shown in Figure 11.59, places the pivot in the center of the coil. A second form, shown in Figure 11.60, has the coil pivoted off center. This permits the construction of a flat meter for use where front panel space is limited.

Another important mode in the basic design of the D'Arsonval movement has been the elimination of the large, horseshoe magnet shown in Figure 11.59. Permanent-magnet materials with extremely high permeabilities like Alnico™, and certain indium alloys, have resulted in the reduction of the size of the magnet to a small cylinder or arc-shaped segment. This permits the magnet and moving coil to be enclosed in a soft iron shield, which eliminates the need for the shielding required to protect older model meters from stray magnetic fields caused by nearby wiring.

The PM/MC is a dc meter movement since reversal of the current direction in the moving coil would cause it to pivot in the opposite direction. Connecting alternating current directly to this type of movement will result in vibration of the pointer without meaningful deflection. For measuring ac voltages or currents, the PM/MC can be fitted with a component called a *rectifier*. This converts an ac input into dc, which is measureable by the meter. Moreover, the design of most D'Arsonval movements requires the coil to be connected so that the current passes through in a specific direction. If connected so that the polarity is reversed, the pointer could be bent against a stop pin. Some meters, however, have a center zero position and can deflect either clockwise or counterclockwise,

Figure 11.60 Another form of the D'Arsonval movement has the coil pivoted at a point not on its center.

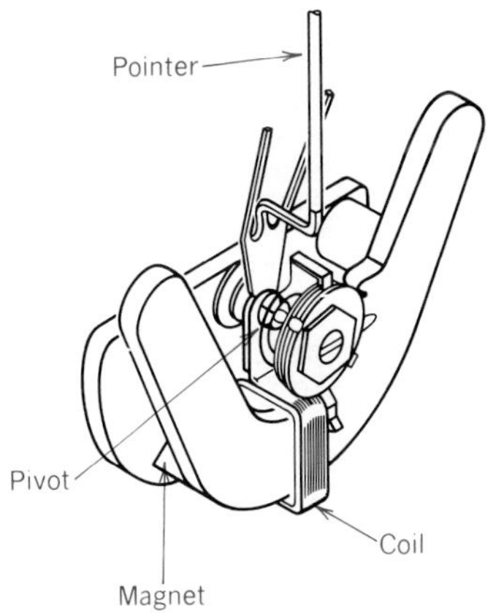

depending on the polarity of the current through the coil.

The D'Arsonval movement is the most sensitive of all electromagnetic meter movements. This permits the construction of high-resistance meters that will register full scale with currents of 1 microampere. Accuracy is also excellent, comparable with that of an electrodynamic movement (0.1 percent). The principle disadvantages of the PM/MC movement are its inability to measure ac directly and its limited versatility. In contrast to the electrodynamic movement, the PM/MC cannot measure frequency or power directly.

D.2 ELECTROMAGNETIC METER MOVEMENT SUSPENSIONS AND MAINTENANCE

Although many texts stop after describing the coil and magnet of a meter movement, the manner in which the pivoting device is held in place and returned to its original position is of importance. There are only two widely used methods for supporting the pivoting coil or vane. The first is shown in Figure 11.61. Here the two pivot points are connected to the coil and friction is reduced by the use of jewel bearing points. The pointer is returned to its initial position by one or two hair springs connected between the coil support and the frame of the meter movement. The hair springs are fragile and can be damaged if the meter is dropped or subjected to vibration.

The second method used for supporting the moving coil is called the *taut-band suspension* and is shown in Figure 11.62. Here, the moving coil or vane is suspended by two ribbonlike bands that are anchored to the moving coil and kept under tension by a pair of springs. This type of suspension eliminates friction almost completely and makes the use of hair springs unnecessary. Generally more expensive than pivot suspensions, the taut-band movement is more accurate and more rugged.

Figure 11.61 One method for supporting the moving coil in the D'Arsonval or PM/MC movement.

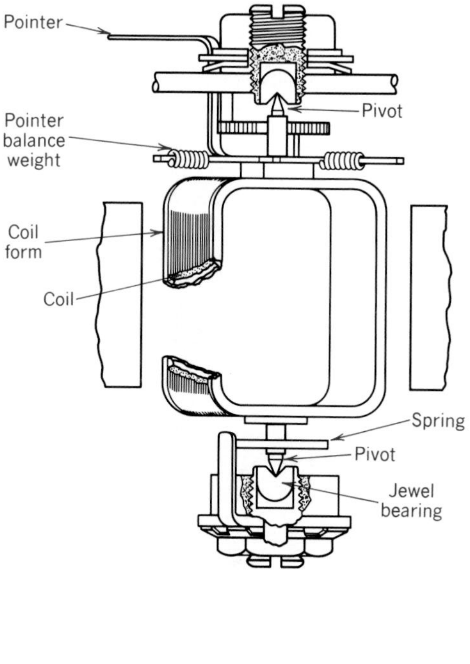

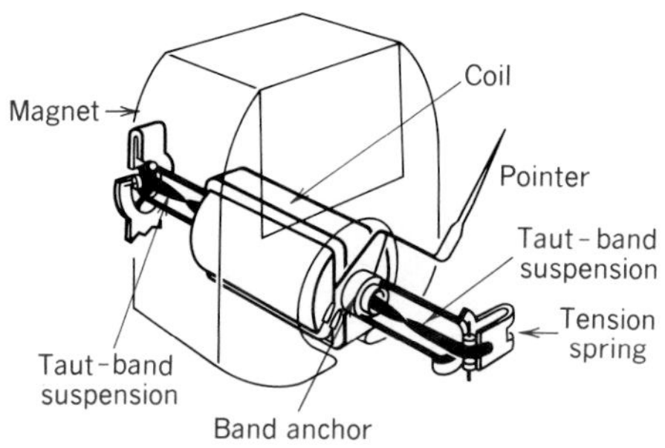

Figure 11.62 A second method for supporting the coil is the taut-band suspension.

Both the pivot and taut-band suspension mechanisms have a small adjusting screw for touching up the setting of the meter initial or zero position. This screw, shown in Figure 11.63, can easily be adjusted without opening the meter or disturbing the sensitive pivot or band tension settings. This is one of the few meter adjustments or repairs than can be made without special tools.

One of the critical meter adjustments that you should be aware of but *not* try to do without special tools is the adjustment of the pointer balance weights. A good-quality meter cancels the weight of the pointer with two or three tiny counterweights, as shown in Figure 11.64. These weights resemble coils of fine wire and have been adjusted to properly balance the weight of the long pointer. These weights can be moved with a special tool if it is necessary to rebalance the pointer, for example, after a bent pointer has been straightened or repainted. One way to tell if the pointer counter-

Figure 11.63 The zero position adjustment can be made without special tools.

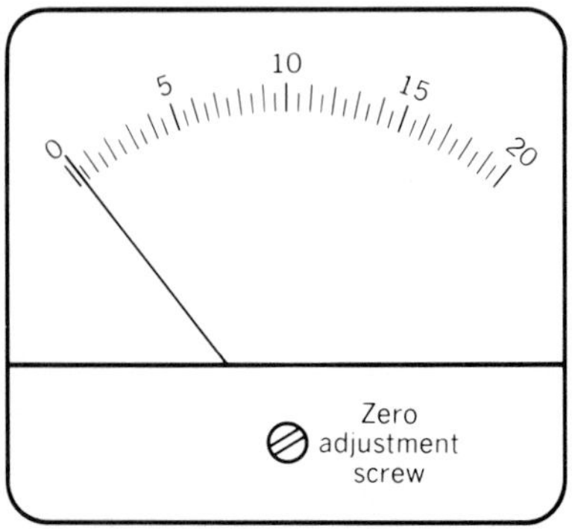

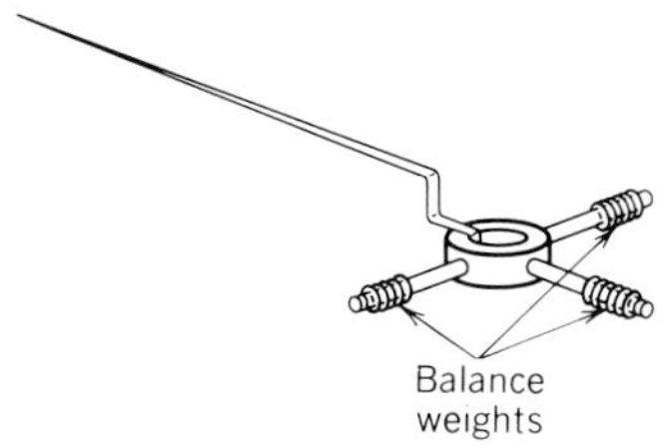

Figure 11.64 Pointer balance weights.

weights need adjustment is to zero the meter accurately using the zero adjust screw while the meter is in an upright position. Then, if the indication shifts more than a millimeter or two when the meter is placed on its back, the counterweights may need adjustment.

Unless you intend to become a specialist in the field, you should limit your meter repairs to zero adjustment and replacing scratched or broken glass or plastic faces. If the pivot and pointer have not been bent or damaged, the replacement of a meter face is not too complex a job. Replacement faces can generally be obtained from the meter manufacturer and come in one of a few standard sizes and shapes. Clear plastic meter cases are usually molded in two pieces. Plastic tabs hold the meter face in place as shown in Figure 11.65, and the face can be carefully popped off using a thin-bladed screwdriver. Glass faces are glued in place, and it is necessary to disassemble the meter case in order to scrape out the broken face and replace it. Carefully remove the screws holding the meter front to the case. Temporarily store the case and meter mechanism in a dust-proof container and scrape off the remaining glass and glue. A new glass can be glued into place with model airplane glue. Allow the glue to dry thoroughly before reassembly. When reassembling the meter, be sure that the zero adjust screw fits into the yoke on the meter mechanism.

Sensitive meters, particularly those with plastic cases, frequently develop a static charge that causes the pointer to deflect. This can be distinguished from poor zero adjustment by the fact that the zero adjust screw cannot correct the deflection. Although commercial liquid and spray products are available to correct this, a solution of several tablespoons of an antistatic liquid fabric softener in a quart of water can be used to moisten a clean cloth. Wiping the meter case with the damp (not wet) cloth will neutralize the static charge and keep the meter face free of the dust usually attracted to charged surfaces.

Figure 11.65 All-plastic meter face is held by two tabs.

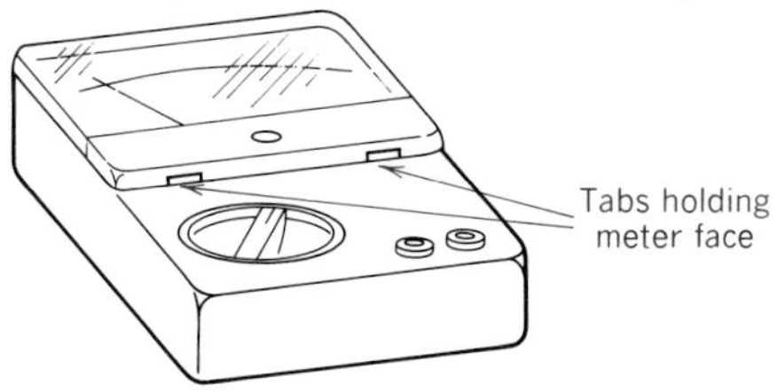

D.3 ELECTROMAGNETIC METER SENSITIVITY, ACCURACY, AND EFFECT ON A CIRCUIT

Through reading earlier chapters and the practice you have gained in making measurements of electrical quantities in the Laboratory Manual exercises, you have probably become quite good at using a digital or analog multimeter. For example, you have probably learned that most analog meters are slightly more accurate if the meter is kept in the same position during a series of measurements. On the other hand, you may not have thought of the effect that connecting a meter has on a circuit or about the changes in the magnitude of the circuit quantities caused by different meters.

All electromagnetic meters have a certain amount of resistance. When built into a multimeter circuit, the resistance of the meter, along with any shunt or multiplier resistors, must be taken into consideration. When current measurements are made, as shown in Figure 11.66, the meter and the parallel shunt resistors, which may be used to extend the range of the meter, are placed in series with the load. The resistance of the circuit is increased by the addition of the meter, and therefore the circuit current is reduced. It should be clear that the lower the resistance of the ammeter, when compared to the load resistance, the more accurate the reading of the ammeter will be. For example, if the circuit load resistor in Figure 11.66 is 50 Ω, and the resistance of the meter is also 50 Ω, the measured current will be 0.1 A. Using Ohm's law, you can see that the load current before the meter was connected was 0.2 A. The greater the resistance of the ammeter, when compared to the load, the less accurate the measurement. A 150 Ω ammeter would provide a reading of 0.05 A, one-quarter of the actual current.

One way around this problem is to use a meter with a very low full-scale current range and a series of

Figure 11.66 The meter, in parallel with any shunt resistances, is in series with the load.

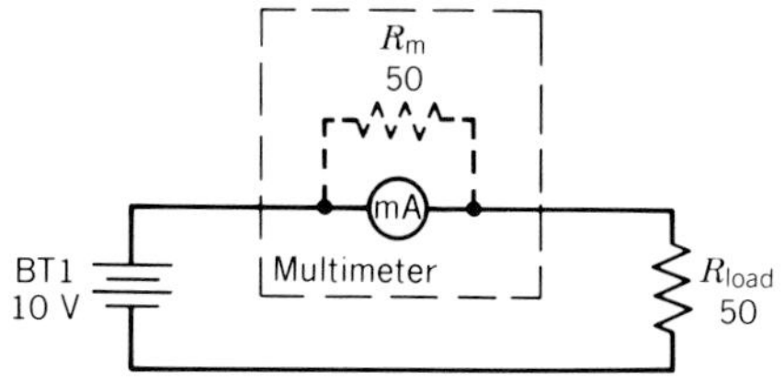

shunt resistors. If the 50 Ω meter in Figure 11.66 is a unit that measures full scale when a current of 50 microamperes flows through it, a shunt resistor of 0.0005 Ω can be connected in parallel with the meter to produce a full-scale indication of 0.5 A. Notice that the total resistance of the 50 Ω meter and its parallel 0.0005 Ω shunt is

$$R_{\text{total}} = \frac{R_{\text{meter}} R_{\text{shunt}}}{R_{\text{meter}} + R_{\text{shunt}}} = \frac{0.025}{50.0005} = 0.000499$$

or about 0.0005 Ω, the resistance of the shunt. This is a very low figure compared to the value of the load, and the total circuit current will be 0.19998 A. This value would be indistinguishable from the calculated circuit current of 0.2 A. Since most digital voltmeters use low-value current shunts, the resistance of these meters is comparable to that of a sensitive electromagnetic meter.

The accuracy of voltage measurements made with an electromagnetic meter also depends on the relationship between the circuit load resistance and the total of the meter resistance and its multiplier resistor. This can be seen from Figure 11.67, which shows how the connection of a voltmeter across a circuit load $R1$ changes the characteristics of the circuit. In this illustration, the resistance of the two load resistors and the voltmeter (the meter plus its multiplier) are the same. Before the connection of the meter and its multiplier, the circuit current is $I = \frac{E}{R} = \frac{24}{20000} = 1.2$ mA, and the voltage drop across each load resistor is 12 V. When the meter and its multiplier are connected, it is in parallel with load resistor $R1$. The total resistance of the circuit is now $R2 + \frac{R_1 R_m}{R1 + R_m}$, or 15,000 Ω, and the circuit current increases to 1.6 mA. The voltage drop across $R2$ is 1.6 × $R2$, or 16 V, and the potential difference across both $R1$ and the meter and its multiplier is 8 V. The meter will indicate a potential difference of 8 V across $R1$ instead of the original 12 V. This change in the circuit characteristics because of the connection of a meter is called *meter loading.*

The effects of meter loading can be reduced by increasing the resistance of the meter plus the multiplier resistor. A "perfect" voltmeter would have an enormously high resistance and would draw no current from the circuit.

Figure 11.67 The effect of connecting a voltmeter to a circuit.

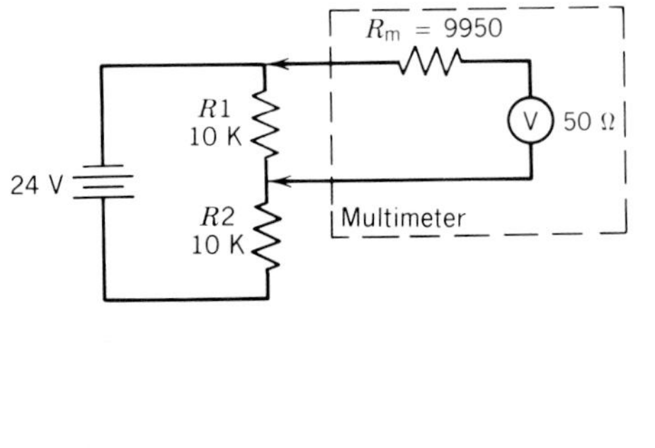

Fortunately, the need for low resistance in an ammeter and high resistance in a voltmeter can both be met if a sensitive meter is used. When used to measure current, the sensitive meter is used with low-resistance shunts and so possesses a low resistance. When it is used as a voltmeter, high-resistance multipliers minimize the effect on the circuit.

There are two ways to express the sensitivity of a meter movement. The first is to state the amount of current necessary to produce a full-scale indication. The designations "50 microamperes" or "0 to 50 μA" mean that this meter indicates a full-scale value when a current of 50 μA flows through the coil. The second way of specifying meter sensitivity is referred to as the *ohms-per-volt rating*. This rating specifies the amount of resistance that must be connected in series with the meter to produce full-scale indication when a potential difference of 1 V is applied across the meter and multiplier. For example, a 20,000 ohms-per-volt meter indicates a meter that will show a full-scale indication when a 1-V potential difference is applied to the meter and a 20,000 Ω multiplier.

Notice that Ohm's law relates the sensitivity of a meter expressed in ohms per volt and the current required for full-scale indication. For example, a 20,000 ohms-per-volt meter indicates full scale when the current through it is

$$I = \frac{E}{R} = \frac{1}{20{,}000} = 5 \times 10^{-5} \quad \text{or} \quad 50\ \mu\text{A}$$

Ohm's law can also be used to calculate the ohms-per-volt sensitivity when the full-scale indication of the meter movement is known. The sensitivity of a 1-mA meter movement is

$$I = \frac{E}{R}, \qquad 0.001 = \frac{1}{R}$$

$$R = 1000 \text{ ohms-per-volt}$$

The ohms-per-volt sensitivity rating is useful for predicting the effect that a VOM will have when connected to a circuit to perform voltage measurement. Simply multiply the ohms-per-volt sensitivity of the meter movement by the VOM range setting to determine the resistance of the VOM. For example, a VOM with sensitivity of 10,000 ohms-per-volt is being used on its 5-V range. The resistance of the VOM, that is, of its meter movement and multiplier resistor, will be sensitivity × range setting = 10,000 × 5 = 50,000 Ω. If used to measure the potential difference across a 5-

kilohm resistor, this meter would reduce the total resistance to

$$R_{\text{total}} = \frac{R_{\text{resistor}} R_{\text{meter}}}{R_{\text{resistor}} + R_{\text{meter}}} = \frac{250{,}000{,}000}{55{,}000} = 4545.45\ \Omega$$

This would result in a substantial voltage reading error.

On high-range settings, a 100-V range for example, the VOM has a high enough resistance for most practical measurements. But the fact that the resistance of the VOM changes with its range setting is an annoyance. Electronic multimeters and digital multimeters usually have a fixed resistance of 10 or 11 MΩ, regardless of the range setting. This makes it easier to calculate possible loading effects.

E. PROGRAMMED REVIEW

FRAME 1

Connecting a multimeter set to measure dc to an ac source could damage the meter; connecting a meter set to measure ac to a dc source will ________.

a. Not result in damage to the meter, but the indication will not be correct. (2)
b. Your answer must include the ideas that no damage will be done and that the reading will have no meaning. If it does not, review Section B.1 and go on to Frame 2.

FRAME 2

When used to measure ac current or potential difference, most multimeters actually measure the ________ value of the current or potential difference and then convert this to the ________ value.

a. Average; rms. (3)
b. Any other answer, review Section B.1.

FRAME 3

To accurately measure the effective potential difference or current of an irregular waveform a ________ should be used.

a. True rms meter; or, a thermocouple meter. (4)
b. Any other answer, review Section B.1.

FRAME 4

The rms value of the waveform shown in Figure 11.68 is ________ volts.

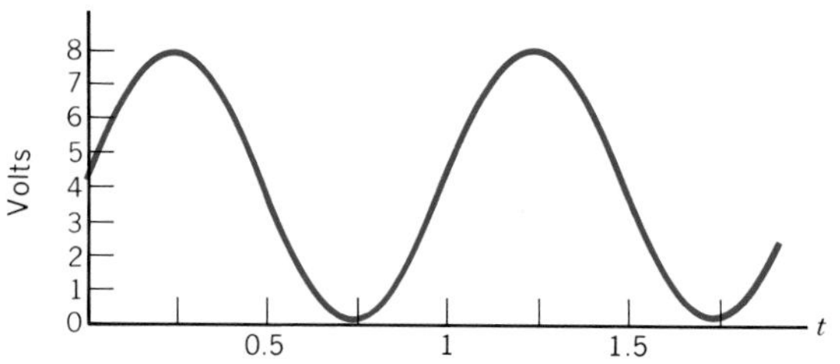

Figure 11.68 Waveform for Frame 4.

a. 4.89 or 4.9 V. (5)
b. 5.65 or 5.7 V; this answer is not correct. You have to use the rms, not the peak value of the ac component.
c. Any other answer, review Section B.1.

FRAME 5

The waveform shown in Figure 11.68 is filtered to remove the dc component, and the resulting signal is applied across a 10 Ω load. The effective current I = ________.

a. 0.2828 A (6)
b. Any other answer, review Section B.2.

FRAME 6

An ac potential difference whose value is given by $e = 120 \sin 377t$ is applied to a load. At $t = 16.667 \times 10^{-3}$ s, the current through the load is ________ A.

a. 0 (7)
b. Any other answer, draw a graph of the waveform from $t = 0$ to $t = 20 \times 10^{-3}$. Go on to Frame 7.

FRAME 7

The angular velocity of a sine wave is 188.5. What is the frequency (to the nearest Hz)?

a. 30 Hz (8)
b. Any other answer, review Section B.2.

FRAME 8

A low-frequency (3-Hz) sine wave with an effective value of 18 V is combined with a dc level of 118 V. What is the value of the potential 1.3 s after the instant when t and v are zero?

a. 103.04 V (9)
b. 133 Volts; you have incorrectly added the instantaneous value of the ac sine-wave component. At $t = 1.3$, the sine is negative. Go on to Frame 9.
c. Any other answer, review Formula 11.4.

FRAME 9

$E_{rms} \times I_{rms}$ is equal to the __________ dissipated in a resistive circuit during a period of time.

a. Average power. (10)
b. Any other answer, review Section B.3 and go on to Frame 10.

FRAME 10

Give three methods for measuring the frequency of a sine-wave signal.

a. __________
b. __________
c. __________

a. Comparison with a sine wave of known frequency using Lissajous figures; a calculation based on measuring the period using an oscilloscope; and measuring the frequency with a frequency meter/counter. (11)
b. Any answer that does not include these three, review Section B.4.

FRAME 11

The TRIGGER LEVEL and SLOPE controls found on many counters function to __________.

a. Set the points on a waveform at which the GATE and COUNTER circuits respond. (12)
b. Any other answer, review Section B.4. Go on to Frame 12.

FRAME 12

The four major sections of a frequency meter/counter are the __________, the __________, the __________, and the __________.

a. Input section; control logic and gate; time base; display. (13)
b. If any of the four are incorrect, review Section B.4.

FRAME 13

Signal sources that produce only sine waves are generally referred to as __________. Those with outputs ranging from about 10 Hz to about 100 kHz are more specifically called __________, while those capable of ranges from about 100 kHz to as high as 500 mHz are called __________.

a. Signal generators; audio frequency or af generators; radio frequency or rf generators. (14)
b. Any other answer, review Section B.5.1.

FRAME 14

The purpose of a modulator section in a signal generator is to __________.

a. Add a 400-Hz or 1-kHz signal to the output of the generator oscillator; or, to amplitude modulate the oscillator output. (15)
b. Any other answer, review Section B.5.1 and go on to Frame 15.

FRAME 15

The output signal of a sweep generator __________. The oscillator in a sweep generator is a __________.

a. Varies in frequency between an upper and lower limit; voltage-controlled oscillator. (16)
b. Any other answer, review Section B.5.2 and go on to Frame 16.

FRAME 16

In addition to the pulses that can be produced by some models, a function generator can produce __________, __________, and __________ over a range of frequencies.

a. Sine waves; square waves, triangle waves. (7)
b. Any other answer, review Section B.5.3.

FRAME 17

The __________ section of most pulse generators is more complex than that of other signal sources.

a. Output. (18)
b. Any other answer, review Section 3.5.4 and go on to Frame 18.

FRAME 18

Two common reasons for signal-source failure are __________ and __________.

a. Short circuiting the output; connecting the source output to points at high potential. (19)
b. Any other answer, review Section B.5.6.

FRAME 19

Older signal sources frequently used banana plugs and jacks for connection to units under test. __________ was frequently used for cable. This form of cable was usually designed for a load of __________ Ω. Modern signal generators use __________ -type connectors and __________ cable. This is generally designed to work with loads of __________ Ω.

a. Twisted pair; 600; BNC; coaxial; 50. (20)
b. Any incorrect, review Section B.6.

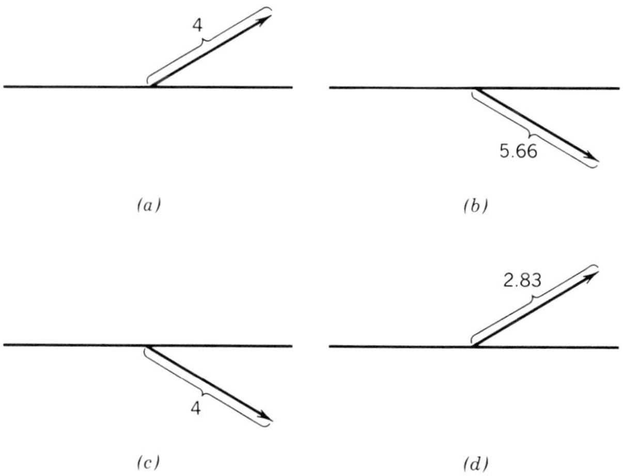

Figure 11.69 Phasor diagrams for Frame 20.

FRAME 20

Which of the phasors shown in Figure 11.69 correctly represents a sine wave whose rms value is 4 V and which begins its first positive half-cycle 30° after a reference sine wave?

a. *B* (21)
b. Any other answer, review Section C.1.

FRAME 21

Two names for the most popular type of meter movement used in test equipment are __________ and __________.

a. D'Arsonval; PM/MC, or permanent magnet moving coil. (22)
b. Any other answer, review Section D.1.4 and go on to Frame 22.

FRAME 22

The __________ and __________ electromechanical meter movements can be used to measure ac or dc potentials directly.

a. Electrodynamometer; moving iron. (23)
b. Any other answer, review Section D.1.

FRAME 23

The __________ coil suspension used on better-grade D'Arsonval meter movements significantly reduces friction.

a. Taut band (END)
b. Any other answer, review Section D.2.

F. PROBLEMS FOR SOLUTION OR RESEARCH

1. Using test equipment manufacturers' catalogs, determine the difference in cost for true rms meters and meters of similar type and accuracy that are not true rms meters.

2. Using manufacturers' catalogs, look up the cost of various multimeters ranging from 20 to 200 K ohms-per-volt. How many dollars per ohms-per-volt will it cost to replace a 20 K ohms-per-volt meter with a 200 K ohms-per-volt model?

3. Meter cost is also a function of meter accuracy. Draw a graph showing how meter cost increases as the percent full-scale accuracy improves for the product lines of several manufacturers.

4. You have determined that a 4-V rms sine signal should pass through a complex portion of an electronic unit without change except for the dc level at various points. Using a true rms voltmeter with ac and dc modes that operate in the manner described in Section B.1 (the ac setting measures only the ac component, while the dc setting gives only the dc component), the following readings have been obtained:

Point	*ac Component (volts)*	*dc Component (volts)*
A	4	4.5
B	3	16
C	8	1.5
D	4	0
E	2	−6

Trace the oscilloscope waveform that would be seen at each test point and give the rms value of the total potential difference at that point.

5. Draw phasor diagrams of the following sine waves:

a. $\sqrt{2} \sin A$
b. $16 \sin(A + 30°)$
c. $12 \sin(A - 75°)$
d. $9.8 \sin(B - 180°)$
e. $12 \sin(A + 435°)$
f. $12.75 \sin(A - 90°)$

6. Use the phasor diagrams drawn in Problem 5 to perform the following additions or subtractions:

a. $b + a$
b. $b - a$
c. $c - e$
d. $d + f$
e. $c + e$
f. $a + e$

7. Using your knowledge of signal sources and manufacturers' catalogs, what signal sources would you expect to find on electronics benches at the following:

a. A small radio and TV repair shop
b. A large firm specializing in custom design of hi-fi music systems
c. A mobile microwave communications maintenance lab
d. A large computer repair facility
e. A medium-sized aircraft electronics equipment manufacturer
f. A one-person, arcade game repair shop

8. Try to visit the facilities or shops named in Problem 7 and make careful note of the types and numbers of signal sources. How well were you able to guess the signal source requirements when you answered Problem 7?

9. It is not too early to start a file on operating test equipment. Carefully consult the manufacturer's manual for the oscilloscopes, meters, power supplies, counters, and signal sources in your lab. Draw a sketch of the front panel, identifying each control and describing its function. Note any peculiarities of operation. Keep your file up-to-date by adding notes on new units as you learn to operate them.

CHAPTER 12

INDUCTION AND PRACTICAL INDUCTORS

A. CHAPTER PREVIEW

1 In this chapter you will learn how the generator principle explains the effects of inductance. Inductance is the second of three basic electrical qualities possessed by components. You have already studied the first of the three, resistance.

2 You will learn the effects of inductance in circuits and how these effects are measured. Since inductance appears to produce different effects in dc and ac circuits, you will also study the reasons for these differences.

3 You will learn about the voltage spikes generated in inductive circuits when equipment is turned off. These spikes are a frequent cause of component malfunction in some circuits.

4 The Examples and Computations section of this chapter introduces a new mathematical function, the logarithm, which is necessary for calculating the current through an inductance in a circuit.

5 In the Applications section you will learn to identify some of the components used to provide inductance in modern electronic circuits and the characteristics of the different types.

B. PRINCIPLES

B.1 MUTUAL INDUCTION

In Chapter 10 you saw that a potential difference is induced between the ends of a conductor moving through a magnetic field when there is a component of the conductor velocity at right angles to the magnetic field. It was assumed that the conductor was pushed through the field. In Chapter 10, however, you learned that the potential difference is produced by motion and not by the force applied to the conductor. This means that it makes no difference whether the conductor is moved through the field, as shown in Figure 12.1*a*, or the field is moved with respect to the conductor, as in Figure 12.1*b*. As long as there is a relative motion between the field and the conductor, a potential difference will be induced between the ends of the conductor.

Adding this information to the fact that a current through a conductor produces a magnetic field leads to the concept of mutual induction, illustrated in Figure 12.2. With switch *S*1 open, the voltmeter connected across the ends of conductor *B* will show no potential difference. When *S*1 is closed, however, a current is produced in conductor *A*. This produces a magnetic field around *A*, which quickly expands outward from the conductor as shown in Figures 12.3*a* through 12.3*c*. This field expands until it reaches its *steady-state condition,* that is, the field shape and intensity that will exist when the changes due to the initial closing of the switch have ceased. The expansion of this magnetic field produces a relative motion between the field and conductor *B*. Because of this, a potential difference is produced between the ends of the conductor, as indicated by the voltmeter. As soon as the magnetic field around conductor *A* reaches its steady-state condition, and is no longer expanding, this relative motion between the field and the conductor ceases. The potential difference between the ends of conductor *B* again falls to zero. To distinguish it from the steady-state condition, the period of time during which the field is expanding is called the *transient state*.

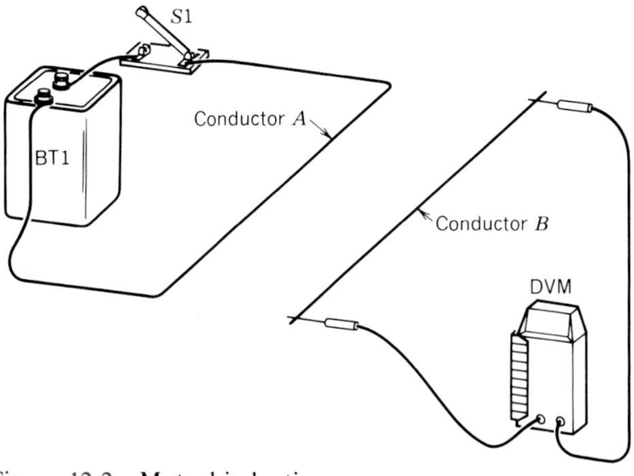

Figure 12.2 Mutual induction.

Figure 12.1 As long as there is a relative motion between the magnetic field and the conductor, a potential difference will be induced.

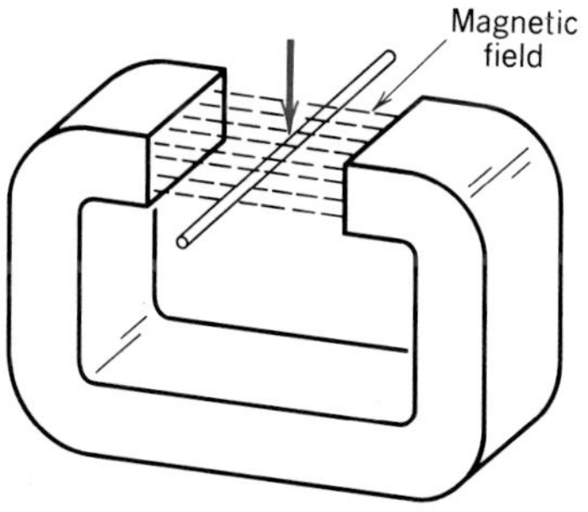

(a) A conductor is moved through a stationary magnetic field

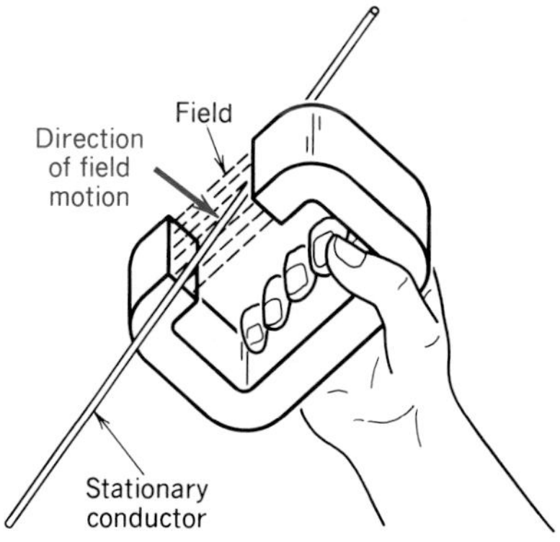

(b) A magnetic field is moved past a stationary conductor

Another transient-state condition occurs if switch *S*1 is again opened to cut off the current in *A*. The magnetic field around conductor *A* begins to collapse back toward *A*, producing a relative motion between the conductor and the field, as shown in Figure 12.4. Note that the polarity of the potential differences induced in Figures 12.3 and 12.4 are different. This is because of the difference in the direction of the relative motion between the conductor and the field in the two cases. The ability of a current in one conductor to induce a potential difference or current in a second conductor is referred to as *mutual induction*.

In cases involving straight conductors, except where extreme lengths are involved, as with telephone or telegraph wires, the effects of mutual induction are too weak and too quickly over to be noticed. When the wires are wound into solenoids, however, the effects of mutual inductance are more easily noticed. As shown in Figure 12.5, the use of two solenoids results in a substantial increase in the flux densities of the magnetic

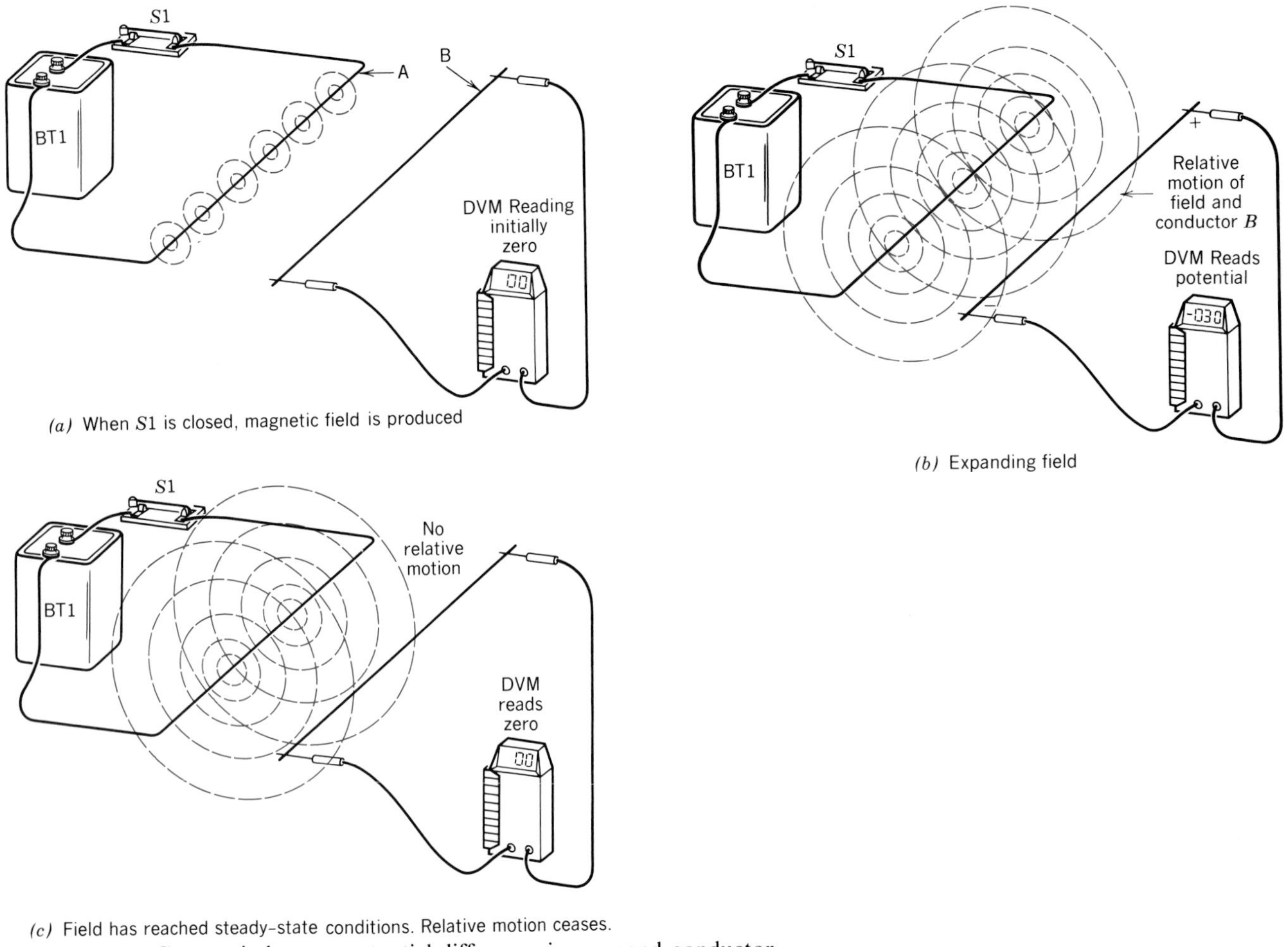

(a) When S1 is closed, magnetic field is produced

(b) Expanding field

(c) Field has reached steady-state conditions. Relative motion ceases.

Figure 12.3 Current induces a potential difference in a second conductor.

fields linking the two conductors. This linkage is referred to as *coupling* and will be treated in greater detail in the discussion of the transformer effect in Chapter 13.

In 1831, Michael Faraday discovered that an arrangement like that of Figure 12.5 could produce a very high potential difference across the ends of solenoid *B* each time the switch was opened or closed. By winding both solenoids on an iron core, Faraday was able to greatly increase the effects of mutual inductance since

Figure 12.4 A second transient state occurs when the switch is opened again.

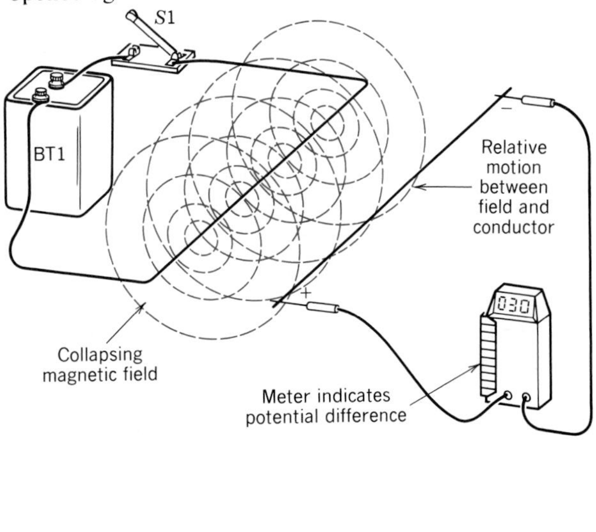

Figure 12.5 Winding the two conductors into solenoids results in an increase in flux densities in the fields linking the coils.

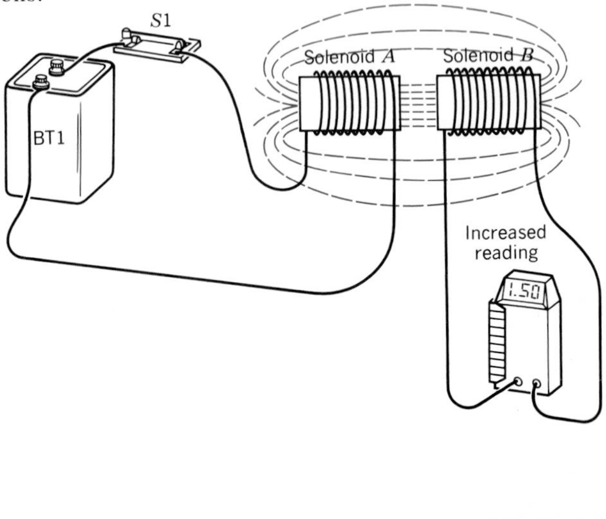

the high relative permeability of the core material produces a substantial increase in the flux density near the second coil.

EXAMPLE:
Two solenoids, shown in Figure 12.6, are wound on a torus-shaped core with a relative permeability of 400 that has a total length of 0.3 m. Each coil has a length of 0.05 m and consists of 100 turns of fine wire with a total resistance of 0.5 Ω. If a 6-V battery is connected across coil *A*, what will be the magnetic flux density in the neighborhood of coil *B* when steady-state conditions are reached? What if the relative permeability of the core is 1? ■

SOLUTION:
When connected to a 6-V battery, the steady-state current in the coil is

$$I = \frac{E}{R} = \frac{6}{0.5} = 12 \text{ A}$$

Since $\mathcal{R} = \dfrac{l}{\mu A}$ and $\mathcal{R} = \dfrac{NI}{BA}$, as you learned in Chapter 9, it is possible to write

$$\frac{l}{\mu A} = \frac{NI}{BA}.$$

Multiplying both sides of the equation by μA and solving for *B* produces

$$B = \frac{\mu NI}{l},$$

where l is the length of the magnetic path and μ is $4\pi \times 10^{-7}$. Substituting,

$$B = \frac{4\pi \times 10^{-7} \times 400 \times 100 \times 12}{0.3} = 2.01 \text{ Wb/m}^2$$

With a core material with a relative μ of 1, the flux density would be

$$B = \frac{2.01}{400} = 0.005 \text{ Wb/m}^2$$ ■

Figure 12.6 Example of two solenoids wound on a toroidal core.

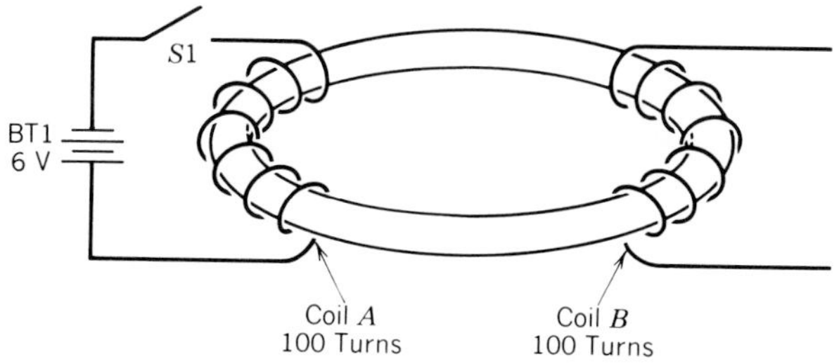

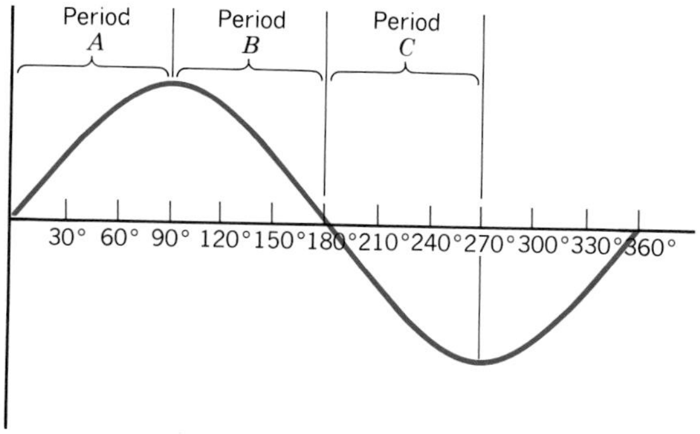

Figure 12.7 Waveform of the potential difference supplied by an ac source substituted for BT1 across coil *A* in Figure 12.5.

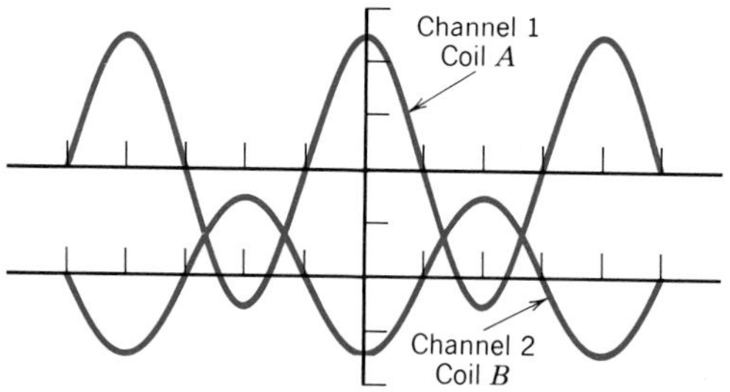

Figure 12.8 Waveforms produced by connecting one channel of a dual-trace oscilloscope to each of the coils.

As you can see, the flux density near coil *B* depends on the current through coil *A*, the number of turns in *A*, and the permeability of the core. Increasing any of these quantities will increase the transfer of energy from coil *A* to coil *B*. That is, the coupling between the two coils will increase. If coil *B* is wound of many turns of fine wire, the device pictured in Figure 12.5 resembles the induction or spark coil used to provide high potential differences for operating the spark plugs in many automobile ignition systems.

When an ac source is substituted for BT1 in Figure 12.6, the switch opening and closing operation is performed by the changing potential of the source, as shown in Figure 12.7. During time period *A*, the field around coil *A* is expanding. During time period *B*, the field around coil *A* is collapsing since the current that causes it is decreasing. During time period *C* the coil current begins to increase, and the magnetic field is again expanding, but the direction of the field has been reversed. If a channel of a dual-trace oscilloscope is connected across each of the coils, the waveforms will resemble those shown in Figure 12.8. When one of its coils is connected to an ac source, this device is called a *transformer* and is capable of converting power at one potential difference and current into power at a different potential difference and current. Transformers will be discussed in detail in Chapter 13.

B.2 SELF-INDUCTION

You have just seen how starting or stopping the current in a coil will induce a potential difference across a nearby coil because the expansion or collapse of the magnetic field causes a relative motion between the nearby coil and the field. But it is also true that the expansion or collapse of the magnetic field produces a relative motion between the first coil and the field, as shown in Figure 12.9. This relative motion induces a potential difference in the coil which acts like a second source in the circuit during the transient state when the field is expanding or collapsing. The technical name for this effect is *self-induction,* although this is usually shortened to *induction.*

Because of self-induction, closing the switch in the circuit of Figure 12.9 produces an effect like that shown in Figure 12.10, where there are two sources of potential difference in series. One of these sources is the battery, which will provide a potential difference while the switch is closed and the electrochemical action inside the cells continues. The second source is an equivalent source, which represents the potential difference produced by the relative motion of the expanding magnetic field and the coil. According to Lenz's law, the potential difference induced in the coil by the expanding magnetic field should possess a polarity that opposes that of the effect that causes it. This can be seen in Figure 12.11, where a detailed view of a short segment of the coil is shown, along with the direction of the relative movement of the field and conductor. The polarity of the potential difference induced by the field can be determined using Fleming's rule. Notice that this opposes the potential difference produced by the battery, as predicted by Lenz's law. The induced potential difference due to the magnetic field is called the *counter electromotive force,* or *counter emf* (cemf). The effect of the counter emf is to impede the flow of current through the coil.

When the switch is opened and the circuit is broken as shown in Figure 12.12, the potential difference supplied by the battery is removed. This causes the magnetic field around the coil to collapse, producing a relative motion between the field and the coil. A potential difference is again induced in the coil, but in this case, the polarity of the induced potential difference is the same as that provided by the source. There-

Figure 12.9 The expansion or collapse of a magnetic field around a coil produces a relative motion between the field and the coil.

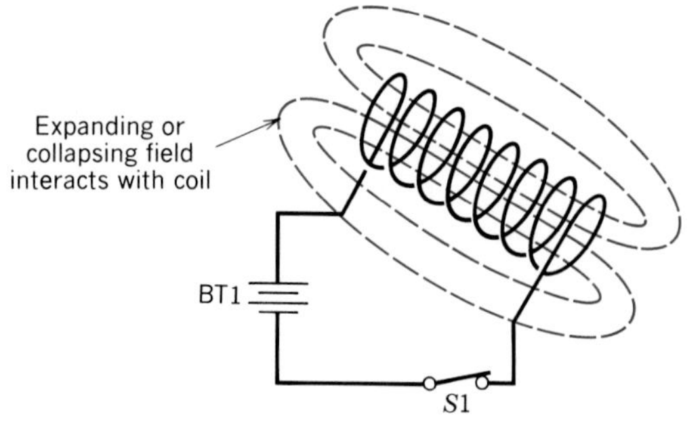

Figure 12.10 Closing the switch in the circuit of Figure 12.9 produces an effect similar to a circuit with two sources.

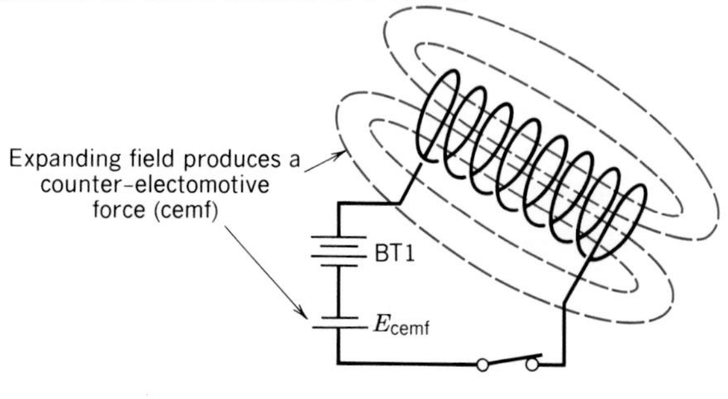

Figure 12.11 Isolating one turn of the coil of Figure 12.10 shows that the expanding field produces a force on the drifting electrons that is opposite to that produced by the potential difference of BT1.

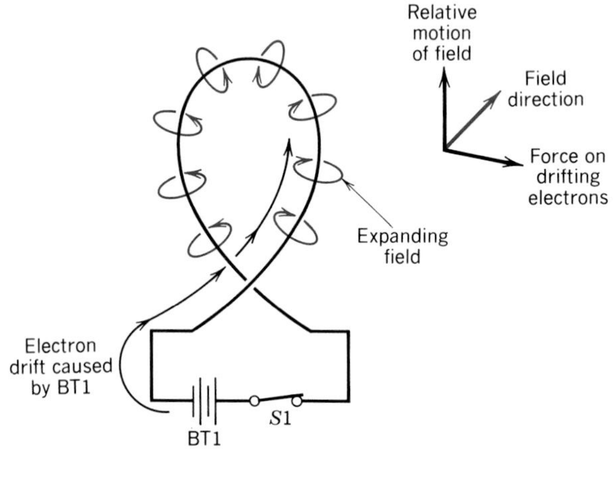

Figure 12.12 When the switch is again opened, the collapsing magnetic field produces a potential difference in the same sense as the potential difference of BT1.

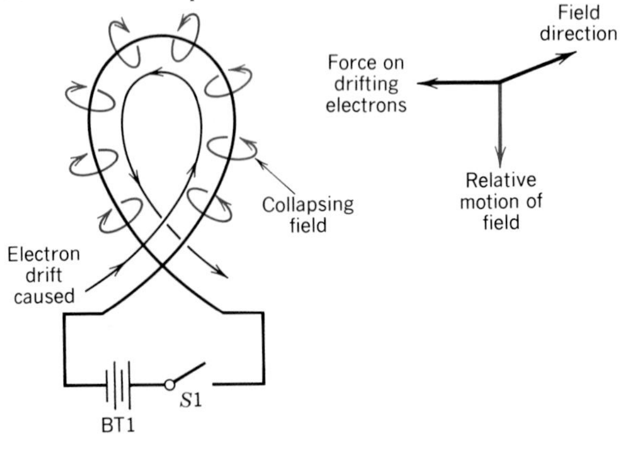

fore, the effect of the induced emf when the switch is opened is to continue the action of the battery after it has been removed from the circuit.

In other words, the polarity of the counter emf *opposes any change in the current* through the circuit. Before the switch is closed, the circuit current is zero, and so the counter emf attempts to keep the current at zero. When the transient state is over, and the magnetic field has for all practical purposes completed its expansion, the current through the coil becomes very close to the value predicted by Ohm's law. From the point of view of the energy delivered by the source, part of this energy is used to produce the magnetic field around the coil during the transient state, and the remainder of the power furnished is dissipated by the resistance of the coil. Once the magnetic field has expanded to nearly its steady-state value, almost all the power provided by the source is dissipated by the coil resistance. If, at this point, the switch is opened and the source is removed from the circuit, the magnetic field collapses. The energy that was used to produce the magnetic field is now returned to the circuit and is dissipated by the coil resistance.

B.3 THE UNIT OF INDUCTANCE

The opposition to the change in current through a component or a circuit is called *inductive reactance*. Inductive reactance depends on the rate of change of the current through the component or circuit. It is frequently thought of as a quantity associated with the response of a component or circuit to alternating current. Inductance, on the other hand, is a characteristic of a component or circuit. The letter L is used to symbolize an inductance or a component designed to provide inductance in a circuit, that is, an *inductor*. The unit of inductance is the *henry,* named after the American physicist Joseph Henry (1797–1878). By definition, a component or circuit has an inductance of one henry (abbreviated H) when a uniform rate of change in the circuit current or current through the component of one ampere per second causes a counter emf of one volt to be induced across the component or circuit. If the symbol $\frac{\Delta i}{\Delta t}$ (read as "delta i divided by delta t") is used for the rate of change in the current, the definition of inductance can be expressed mathematically as

$$L = \frac{-e}{\frac{\Delta i}{\Delta t}} \qquad \text{FORMULA 12.1}$$

This formula contains a minus sign because the induced emf opposes the potential difference produced by the source of the current. The use of the symbol $\frac{\Delta i}{\Delta t}$ to represent the rate of change of the current is a way of avoiding complex mathematics. As long as the changes in time and current are small and linear, this formula is accurate enough for practical purposes.

EXAMPLE:

There is a uniformly changing current through a component. At $t = 0$, the current is 0.15 A; 0.1 s later, the current is 0.18 A. A cemf of -0.03 V is produced across the component. What is its inductance? ■

SOLUTION:

The schematic of this circuit is shown in Figure 12.13. Notice the general symbol used for the inductive component. In order to use Formula 12.1 to determine the inductance of $L1$, it is necessary to first calculate the quantity $\frac{\Delta i}{\Delta t}$. The change in the current is

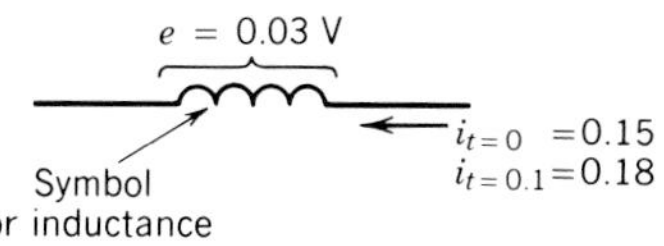

Figure 12.13 The relationship between current, cemf, and inductance is given by the formula

$$L = \frac{-e}{\frac{\Delta i}{\Delta t}}$$

$$\Delta i = i_2 - i_1 \quad \text{or} \quad 0.18 - 0.15 = 0.03 \text{ A}$$

and the change in time is

$$\Delta t = t_2 - t_1 \quad \text{or} \quad 0.1 - 0 = 0.1$$

so

$$\frac{\Delta i}{\Delta t} = \frac{0.03}{0.1} = 0.3 \text{ A/s}$$

and the inductance is

$$L = \frac{e}{\frac{\Delta i}{\Delta t}} = -\frac{-0.03}{0.3} = 0.1 \text{ H}$$

Since the cemf is in the direction *opposite* to that of the current, it is assigned a minus sign. ■

The inductance of a conductor depends on its length, shape, the number of turns if it is wound into the shape of a coil, and the permeability of the materials in its vicinity. The inductance of a conductor is increased by:

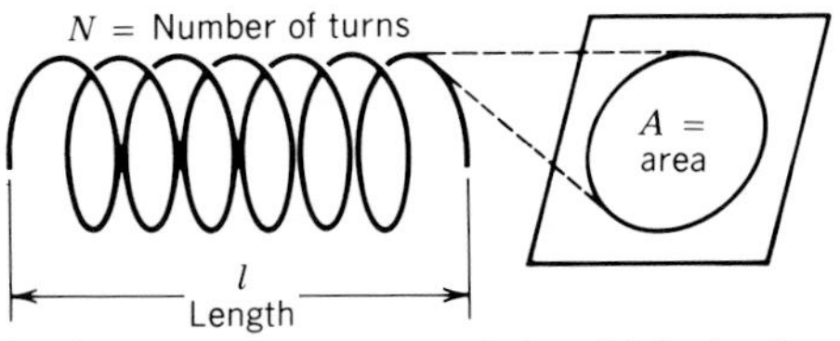

Figure 12.14 A solenoid is a coil in which the length is at least several times the diameter of the coil.

1. Increasing the length of the conductor. For a straight conductor, the inductance is proportional to the length.

2. Winding the conductor into a coil. The formula for the inductance of a solenoid-shaped coil (see Figure 12.14) is

$$L = \frac{\mu N^2 A}{l} \qquad \text{FORMULA 12.2}$$

where μ is the permeability is the material around which the solenoid is wound, $4\pi \times 10^{-7}$ in the case of air, N is the number of turns in the solenoid, A is the cross-sectional area of the solenoid in square meter, and l is the solenoid length in meters.

3. Increasing the number of turns, increasing the diameter of a coil, or decreasing the spacing of the turns. From Formula 12.2, you can see that the inductance is directly proportional to the cross-sectional area of the coil and to the number of turns squared, and inversely proportional to the length of the coil. The formulas for the calculation of the inductance of different-shaped coils are given in Figure 12.15. The formulas given in this figure are the products of experimentation rather than calculation and have been rounded off for dimensions in *inches* rather than the mks units used throughout this book. Since conversion to mks units would introduce cumbersome decimals, these formulas have been left in their original form. From time to time, you may find it necessary to construct a coil of known inductance, either for troubleshooting or for experimentation. Although most suppliers, electronics industry employers, and technicians generally have a supply of resistors available, particular inductors are harder to find. Cardboard tubes or acrylic plastic rods are frequently used as coil cores. The formulas given in Figure 12.15 can be used for calculating and constructing small inductances.

Figure 12.15 Formulas for various air core coil shapes.

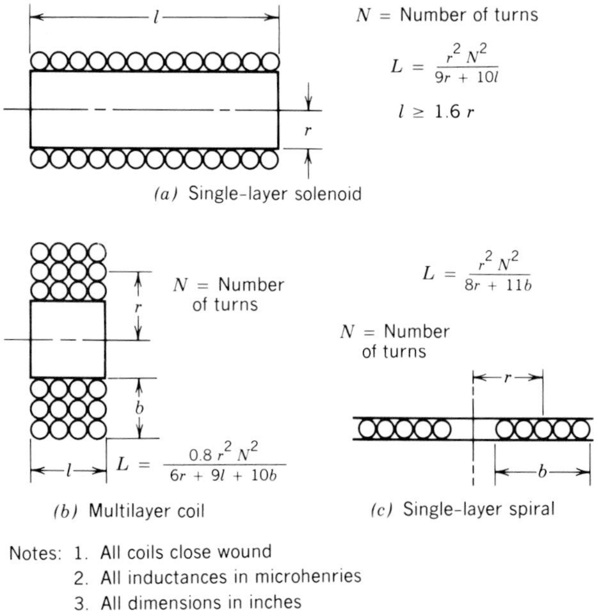

4. Using a ferromagnetic core. Notice the μ term in Formula 12.2. Use of a core material with a relative permeability greater than that of air (μ_0 is about $4\pi \times 10^{-7}$) will increase the inductance of the coil. Cores of paramagnetic material (μ is greater than μ_0) will increase the inductance of the coil. Cores of diamagnetic material (μ is less than μ_0) can be used to reduce it.

B.4 POTENTIAL DIFFERENCE ACROSS AND CURRENT THROUGH AN INDUCTOR

In the schematic diagram shown in Figure 12.16, a source is connected to a coil. The resistance of the wire that forms the coil is 100 Ω and is shown as a lumped load by resistor R_{eq}. Once steady-state conditions are reached, the current in this circuit will be determined by Ohm's law

$$I = \frac{E}{R} \quad \text{or} \quad \frac{5}{100} = 50 \text{ mA}$$

During the transient state, however, the instantaneous current i will be equal to the steady-state current minus some quantity that represents the opposition to the change in current of the inductance. In mathematical terms,

i = steady-state current − the current that would be produced by the cemf

$$i = \frac{E}{R} - \frac{e_{cemf}}{R} \qquad \text{FORMULA 12.3}$$

Figure 12.16 Calculating the current in a circuit containing an inductance.

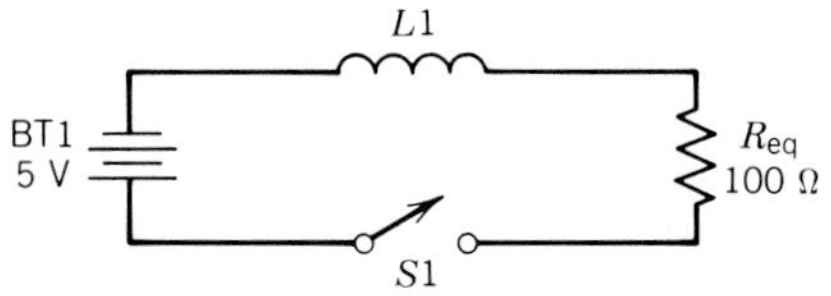

The quantity e_{cemf} turns out to be a function that depends on the steady-state potential difference, the resistance of the circuit, the inductance, the amount of time that has elapsed, and on a mathematical constant symbolized by the lower case Greek letter epsilon, printed as ϵ. ϵ is a repeating decimal equal to 2.7182818.

$$e_{\text{cemf}} = E\epsilon^{\frac{-Rt}{L}} \qquad \text{FORMULA 12.4}$$

Substituting this statement of the value of e_{cemf} into Formula 12.3 produces a formula for the current through an inductor at any moment during the transient state:

$$i = \frac{E}{R} - \frac{E\epsilon^{\frac{-Rt}{L}}}{R}$$

This expression can be written as:

$$i = \frac{E}{R}\left(1 - \epsilon^{\frac{-Rt}{L}}\right) \qquad \text{FORMULA 12.5}$$

When the inductance is first connected to the source, t is equal to zero, and the expression $\epsilon^{\frac{-Rt}{L}}$ is equal to 1 since $\frac{-Rt}{L}$ is zero and any number to the zero power is equal to 1. As t increases, the expression $\epsilon^{\frac{-Rt}{L}}$ becomes smaller and smaller, so that the circuit current approaches $\frac{E}{R}$.

If the circuit of Figure 12.16 is changed as shown in Figure 12.17, it is possible to examine the potential difference across $L1$ and the current through it when the magnetic field around the coil is collapsing. If switch $S1$ is moved to position 2 after the steady state has been reached, a second transient state occurs. In this case, however, the potential difference across the coil is due only to the cemf produced by the collapsing magnetic field. Since BT1 is no longer in the circuit, the first term of Formula 12.3 is not present and the polarity of the potential difference (cemf) and current are reversed. The formula for the current through $L1$ after the switch has been placed in position 2 is there-

Figure 12.17 The circuit of Figure 12.16 is changed so that the potential difference and current due to the collapsing magnetic field of an inductor can be calculated.

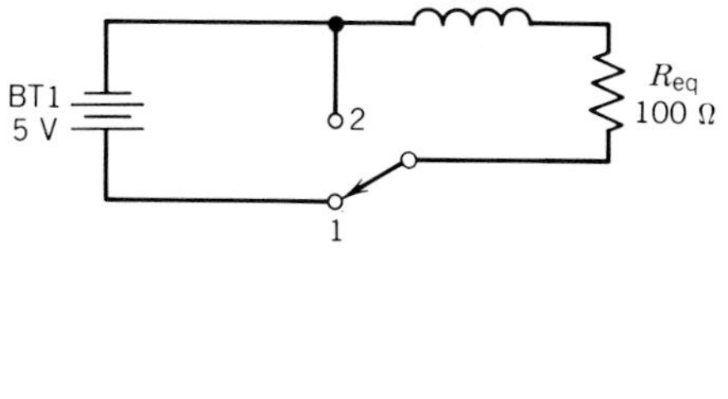

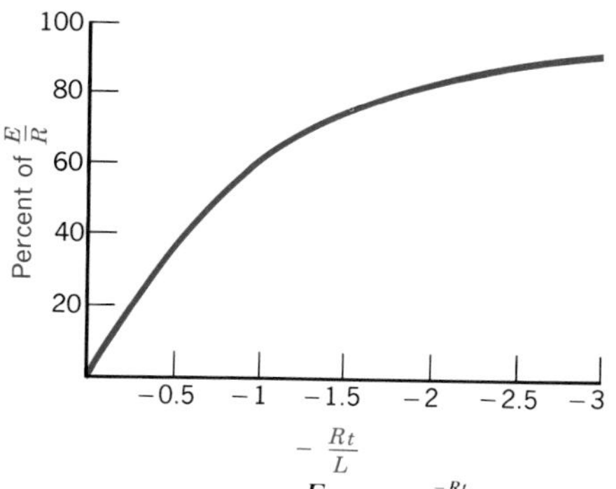

Figure 12.18 Graph of $L = \frac{E}{R}(1 - \epsilon^{\frac{-Rt}{L}})$

fore

$$i = \frac{e_{\text{cemf}}}{R} \text{ or } \frac{E}{R} \times \epsilon^{\frac{-Rt}{L}} \qquad \text{FORMULA 12.6}$$

At the moment that $S1$ is placed in position 2, and t is equal to zero, $\epsilon^{\frac{-Rt}{L}}$ is equal to 1, so the current through the inductor is $\frac{E}{R}$. As time passes, and t increases, the exponent $\frac{-Rt}{L}$ becomes larger, and $\epsilon^{\frac{-Rt}{L}}$ becomes smaller. Formulas 12.5 and 12.6 have been graphed in Figures 12.18 and 12.19. The two curves shown in these figures are called *logarithmic curves*. Notice that the curve in Figure 12.18 never actually reaches the value $\frac{E}{R}$, although the difference between the value of the curve and $\frac{E}{R}$ decreases steadily as the value of t increases. In mathematical terms, the value of the curve is said to approach $\frac{E}{R}$ as a *limit*. The value is never actually *equal* to $\frac{E}{R}$, although for all practical purposes it can be thought of as equal to $\frac{E}{R}$ after a certain amount of time has elapsed.

Figure 12.19 Graph of $i = \frac{E}{R}\epsilon^{\frac{-Rt}{L}}$

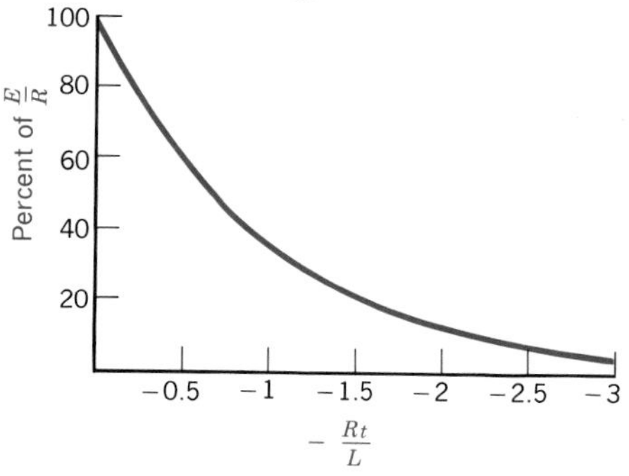

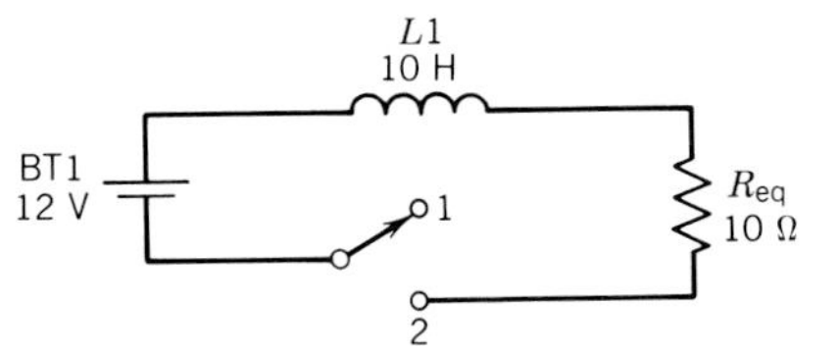

Figure 12.20 Calculating current in an inductive circuit using the graph of Figure 12.18.

EXAMPLE:
In the circuit shown in Figure 12.20, switch $S1$ is set to position 2 at time $t = 0$. What is the current through $L1$ at $t = 0.6$ s? At $t = 1.6$ s? ■

SOLUTION:
Using the curve in Figure 12.18, you can see that the current at $t = 0.6$ s is about 45 percent of $\frac{E}{R}$, or about 0.54 A, and at $t = 1.6$ s it is about 80 percent of $\frac{E}{R}$, or about 0.96 A. ■

When the source is removed from the circuit and the coil is short circuited, the circuit current approaches zero as a limit, as shown in Figure 12.21. The fact that the circuit current in an inductive circuit is always either slightly less than $\frac{E}{R}$ or slightly more than zero means only that some additional energy is being stored in or taken from the magnetic field, even though only an infinitesimally small amount is being added to or removed from the amount in the field.

A convenient way of calculating the value of the cemf across an inductor or the current through it is to refer to the *time constant* of the circuit. When the time t in the term $\epsilon^{\frac{-Rt}{L}}$ is equal to $\frac{L}{R}$, the term becomes ϵ^{-1}, or 1/2.718. Rounded off, this is 0.368. Using Formula 12.4, one time constant, or $\frac{L}{R}$ seconds after a coil has been connected across a dc source producing a potential difference of E, the E_{cemf} across the coil is $0.368E$,

Figure 12.21 When the source is removed and the coil is short circuited, the circuit current approaches 0 as a limit.

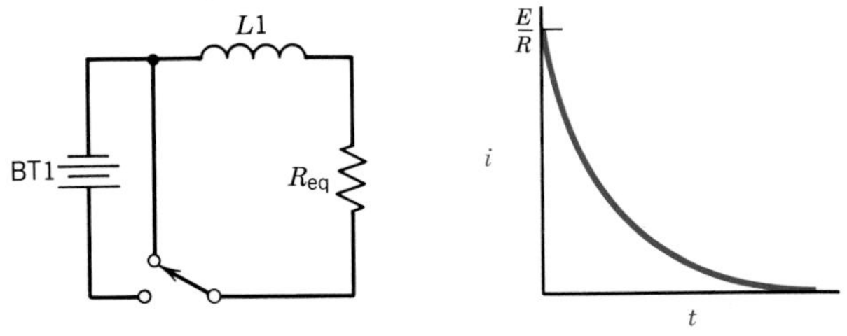

or 36.8 percent of the source potential. Recall that L is the inductance in the circuit in henries and R is the resistance of the entire circuit, including the resistance of the coil, the source, and any other resistors that might be in series. At this point the current through the circuit will be equal to

$$i = \frac{E}{R}(1 - 0.368) \quad \text{or} \quad 0.632\,\frac{E}{R}.$$

In other words, the current will be 63.2 percent of its steady-state value. As shown in the graph of Figure 12.18, the cemf decreases rapidly and the current increases to nearly its full $\frac{E}{R}$ value. At a point when $t = 5 \times \frac{L}{R}$, the current has reached more than 99 percent of the $\frac{E}{R}$ value. Although the current will continue to increase, its value after five time constants is conventionally accepted as the final steady-state value in practical applications.

$$TC = \frac{L}{R} \qquad \text{FORMULA 12.7}$$

The time constant, $\frac{L}{R}$, provides a convenient and easily calculated way to predict the behavior of dc circuits containing inductors and resistors. With the switch S1 in Figure 12.22 in position 1, neither the source nor $R2$ is connected to the inductor. If the switch is placed in position 2, the source and resistor $R1$ are placed in series with the coil. The time constant of this combination is

$$\frac{20}{5 + 150 + 30} = \frac{20}{185} = 0.108 \text{ s}$$

If the switch is kept in position 2 for 5×0.108, or 0.54 s or longer, the current and cemf of the circuit can be assumed to have reached their steady-state values. If the switch is then set to position 3, removing the source and $R1$ from the circuit, a new circuit time constant is established. The only resistances in this circuit are $R2$ and the resistance of $L1$ itself. The time

Figure 12.22 The $\frac{L}{R}$ time constant of a circuit containing inductance and resistance.

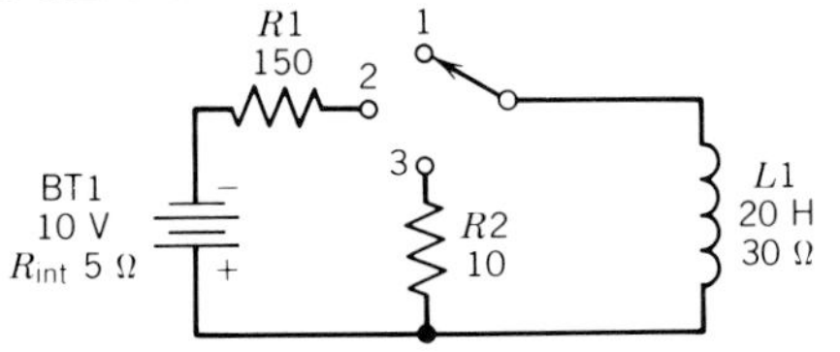

constant of this circuit is

$$\frac{L}{R} = \frac{20}{40} = 0.5 \text{ s.}$$

With the switch in position 2 in Figure 12.22, the circuit current after one time constant, or slightly more than 0.1 s, will be 63.2 percent of $\frac{E}{R}$, or 34.2 mA rounded off to three significant figures. After 0.54 s, or longer, the circuit current will be about 54.1 mA, the steady-state value. At this time, the potential difference across $L1$ is equal to the current times the resistance of the coil, or 1.62 V. Switching to position 3 changes the total resistance of the circuit from 185 Ω to 40 Ω, so the current through the circuit at the moment that the switch is placed in position 3 is that produced in the 40 Ω circuit by the cemf produced by the collapsing magnetic field. Since the time constant of the circuit is now $\frac{L}{R}$ = 0.5 s, according to Figure 12.19, the circuit current will have dropped (or "decayed" since the change involved is a gradual one) to 36.8 percent of its steady-state value, that is, 19.9 mA.

B.5 INDUCTIVE VOLTAGE SURGES

The circuit shown in Figure 12.23 illustrates a curious event that occurs when an inductive circuit is broken. When the switch is set from position 1 to position 2, the time constant of the circuit $\frac{L}{R}$ becomes extremely small since the resistance of the circuit now includes the high resistance of an open circuit. This means that the magnetic field collapses almost immediately, producing a very high cemf across the coil. This is evident from a consideration of Formula 12.1, which can be written in the form

$$-e = L\frac{\Delta i}{\Delta t}. \qquad \text{FORMULA 12.8}$$

Since the time required to go from the steady-state coil current to nearly zero, about five time constants, has become small, $\frac{\Delta i}{\Delta t}$ will be a large number, even for a relatively modest change in current. Because of this, cemf values of hundreds of volts can be briefly reached in circuits that have source potentials of 5 V or less. The effect of this high cemf is to produce a spark across the switch contacts, which can result in switch or component damage. Frequently called *inductive kick*, this is a common problem in switching components such as relays or motors that have relatively high inductances. In later chapters, you will see how certain components can be used to cancel the effects of inductive kick.

Another way of looking at inductive kick is in terms of the tendency of the inductance to oppose changes of the current through it. When the switch in Figure 12.23 is set to position 2 after steady-state conditions have been reached, the energy stored in the magnetic field is now converted into a potential difference which attempts to continue the current flow. Since only a limited amount of energy, proportional to the inductance of the coil, is stored in the field, it is quickly used up in the production of an intense spark.

Figure 12.23 Setting switch $S1$ from position 1 to 2 causes the time constant of the circuit to become very short since it includes the high resistance of the open circuit. The magnetic field around $L1$ collapses very quickly.

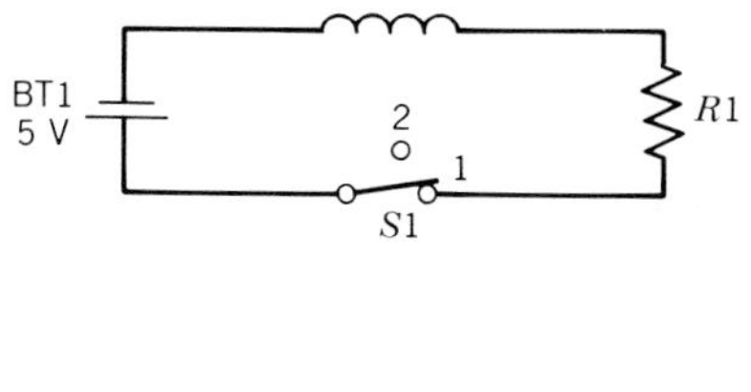

B.6 INDUCTORS AND RESISTORS IN AC CIRCUITS

In Figure 12.24, a sine-wave source providing a peak potential difference of 5 V at a frequency of 60 Hz is connected to a 100 Ω resistor and a 1 H coil. Unlike the case in which a dc source is connected to a coil, the potential difference produced by the ac source is continually changing, so that the current through the coil will also be a changing value. The exact relationship between the potential difference supplied by the source and the circuit current in a circuit containing a resistor and a coil has been the subject of a great many curious attempts at explanation. The reason for this is that although it is easy enough to visualize and use this relationship, its explanation and the way in which it is connected to the principles you have previously learned is based on some rather complex mathematics. Attempts to explain the way in which the potential and current are related can be confusing if the mathematical relationships are not presented, but the actual steps in deriving the final set of formulas requires a working

Figure 12.24 A circuit that shows the effect of inductance in an ac circuit.

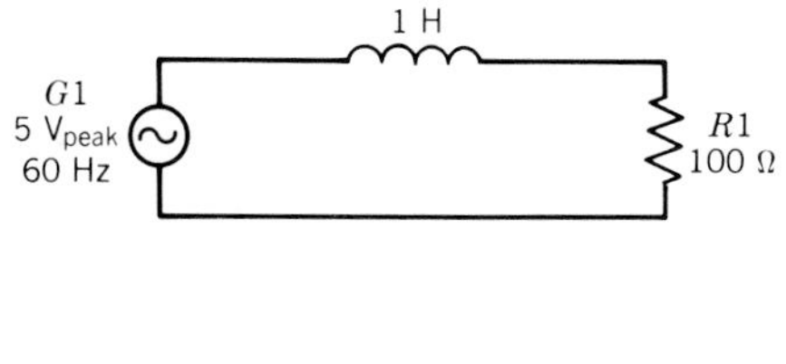

knowledge of that branch of mathematics known as calculus. Rather than attempt to proceed without explanation, some of the more difficult steps in the following discussion have been summarized.

In a Kirchhoff's voltage law analysis of the circuit shown in Figure 12.24, writing the voltage law equation provides a little extra difficulty since the polarities of the potential differences and current directions change. In Figure 12.24, the generator produces a potential difference given by $E_{peak} \sin 2\pi ft$, which is assigned a minus sign since it is a voltage rise. The resistance, which can be either an actual resistance, a lumped load representing the resistance of the coil, or both, produces a potential drop of $i \times R$. Finally, the cemf produced by the current through the coil is given by Formula 12.1, $e = -L\frac{\Delta i}{\Delta t}$. Since this potential difference opposes the direction of the source, it is recorded as $-(-L\frac{\Delta i}{\Delta t})$ or $L\frac{\Delta i}{\Delta t}$. The voltage law equation can then be written as

$$0 = L\frac{\Delta i}{\Delta t} + Ri - E_{peak}\sin 2\pi ft$$

FORMULA 12.9

This formula is a form of a general formula describing the behavior of circuits containing nonlinear components such as inductors and linear components like resistors when the circuit source provides a sinusoidal potential difference. If the change in current, Δi, for a Δt approaching zero is considered, Formula 12.9 becomes what is called a *differential equation* and can be rewritten as

$$0 = L\frac{di}{dt} + Ri - E_{peak}\sin 2\pi ft$$

Equations of this type can be solved for i, the independent variable. In this case, the steady-state value of the current is

$$i = \frac{E_{peak}}{\sqrt{R^2 + (2\pi fL)^2}} \times \sin(2\pi ft - \theta)$$

where FORMULA 12.10

$$\theta = \tan^{-1}\frac{2\pi fL}{R}.$$

Don't become alarmed, this formula is not as complicated as it appears. There is a great deal of information here that is simpler if it is examined one piece at a time.

Notice that the term $\frac{E_{peak}}{\sqrt{R^2 + (2\pi fL)^2}}$ is actually a constant for any given circuit and source frequency,

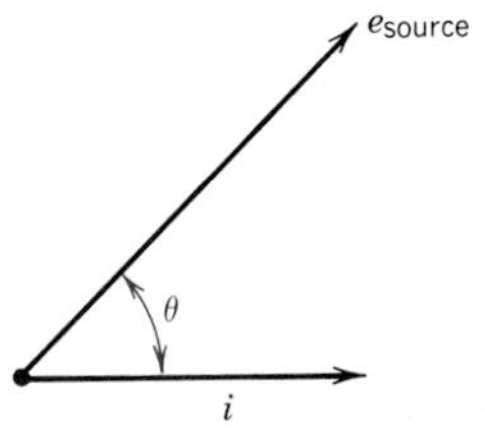

Figure 12.25 Phasor diagram of the source potential difference and current in the circuit of Figure 12.24 (circuit current used as reference phasor).

and its denominator, $\sqrt{R^2 + (2\pi fL)^2}$ resembles the form used to add the magnitudes of two vectors. The second term, $\sin(2\pi ft - \theta)$ is the formula of a sine wave with the same frequency as the potential difference of the source, except for the phase difference of θ degrees between the two waveforms. The phase difference or phase angle is given by the second part of the formula, that is, θ is that angle whose tangent is $\frac{2\pi fL}{R}$. Note that the two terms in this expression for the phase angle are the same as those under the square root sign. Taken together, these two expressions give the magnitude and angle of the vector sum of two components.

Substituting the symbol K for the constant expression $\frac{E_{peak}}{\sqrt{R^2 + (2\pi fL)^2}}$ in Formula 12.10 produces

$$i = K\sin(2\pi ft - \theta)$$

From this you can see that the current through the circuit of Figure 12.24 is a sinusoid with the same frequency as the source potential $E_{peak} \sin 2\pi ft$. If both waveforms are graphed, the current waveform will lag that of the voltage by an angle of θ, as shown in the phasor diagram in Figure 12.25.

Inductance in an ac circuit causes the circuit current to lag the potential difference of the source by a phase angle $\theta = \tan^{-1}\frac{2\pi fL}{R}$ *where* f *is the frequency of the source,* L *is the total inductance in the circuit, and* R *is the total resistance. The relationship between the peak voltage and the current is given by*

$$i = \frac{E_{peak}}{\sqrt{R^2 + (2\pi fL)^2}}\sin(2\pi ft + \theta)$$

In a purely resistive ac circuit ($L = 0$)*, the circuit current is in phase with the source potential difference. In a purely inductive ac circuit* ($R = 0$)*, the circuit current lags the source potential difference by 90°.*

B.7 INDUCTIVE REACTANCE

You will recall from the previous section that a purely inductive circuit ($R = 0$), Formula 12.10 assumes the form

$$i = \frac{E_{\text{peak}}}{2\pi fL} \sin(2\pi ft - 90°)$$

while in a purely resistive circuit,

$$i = \frac{E_{\text{peak}}}{R} \sin(2\pi ft)$$

Other than the phase shift of the current waveform in the first of these formulas, the difference between the two is the appearance of the term $2\pi fL$ in place of R. Since both formulas are otherwise the same, the units for the quantity $2\pi fL$ and R must be the same, and the quantity $2\pi fL$ must play the same role in an inductive circuit that R does in a resistive circuit.

In these equations, $2\pi fL$ represents the magnitude of the opposition to alternating current in an inductive circuit. As stated before, this opposition is called inductive reactance. It is measured in ohms and is symbolized by X_L. Expressed as a formula:

$$X_L = 2\pi fL \qquad \text{FORMULA 12.11}$$

Note that unlike resistance, which is not thought of as depending on frequency (although the resistance of some materials and components does increase as the frequency of an applied signal increases) the inductive reactance of an inductor is directly proportional to its frequency and inductance.

EXAMPLE:
What is the inductive reactance of a 150 mH inductor if the applied potential difference has a frequency of 12 kHz? ■

SOLUTION:
Using Formula 12.11,

$$\begin{aligned} X_L &= 2\pi fL \\ &= 71{,}061.152 \quad \text{or} \quad \text{rounded off, } 71{,}100\ \Omega \end{aligned}$$ ■

Formula 12.11 is often used to calculate the amount of inductance necessary to provide a particular amount of inductive reactance at a given frequency.

EXAMPLE:
What inductance would be chosen to provide an inductive reactance of 2.7 kΩ at a frequency of 400 Hz? ■

SOLUTION:
Transposing Formula 12.11 produces

$$L = \frac{X_L}{2\pi f} = \frac{2700}{2513.274} = 1.07\text{ H} \quad \text{or} \quad 1\text{ H}$$ ■

Sometimes, the inductive reactance and inductance are known, and the frequency must be calculated from Formula 12.11. This type of calculation occurs, for example, in the design or adjustment of filter circuits. The inductive reactance of a coil, even at the 60-Hz power line frequency is often considerably higher than the coil resistance. In cases of this sort, the *magnitude* of the circuit potential difference or circuit current is simple to calculate, but it is necessary to remember that the circuit current will lag the source potential difference by nearly 90°. The following formulas, resembling the basic Ohm's law formulas for alternating current, can be used for approximate answers with the peak, rms, or average values of current and potential difference in circuits where the inductive reactance is more than about 10 times the total resistance.

$$I = \frac{E}{X_L} \qquad \text{FORMULA 12.12}$$

$$E = IX_L \qquad \text{FORMULA 12.13}$$

$$X_L = \frac{E}{I} \qquad \text{FORMULA 12.14}$$

Remember, however, if the inductive reactance is less than 10 times the resistance, using Formulas 12.12 through 12.14 will result in errors greater than 1 percent.

EXAMPLE:
A 455-kHz signal generator with a 10-V peak output is to be connected to a 5 mH coil that has a resistance of 120 Ω. What will be the rms value of the current? ■

SOLUTION:
A quick calculation of the reactance of a 5-mH coil at a frequency of 455 kHz gives

$$\begin{aligned} X_L = 2\pi fL &= 2 \times \pi \times 455{,}000 \times 0.005 \\ &= 14{,}294.25\ \Omega \end{aligned}$$

Since this is greater than 10 times the resistance (the signal generator resistance being ignored), Formula 12.12 can be used with an error of no more than 1 percent. Since $E_{\text{rms}} = E_{\text{peak}} \times 0.707$,

$$I_{\text{rms}} = \frac{10 \times 0.707}{14{,}294.25} = 494.6\ \mu\text{A}$$ ■

If the frequency in the above example had been the power line frequency, Formula 12.12 could not have been used since

$$X_L = 2\pi f L = 2 \times \pi \times 60 \times 0.005 = 1.88\ \Omega$$

In this case, the resistive element is considerably greater than the inductive portion, and the familiar forms of Ohm's law for resistive ac circuits should be used.

EXAMPLE:
What would the current be when the signal generator of the previous example is tuned to a peak output of 10 V and a frequency of 300 Hz? ■

SOLUTION:
The inductive reactance at 300 Hz is

$$X_L = 2\pi f L = 2 \times \pi \times 300 \times 0.005 = 9.42\ \Omega$$

The reactance at 300 Hz is five times higher than the reactance at 60 Hz because 300 Hz is five times 60 Hz. However, the resistance is still more than 10 times the reactance, so Formula 12.12 can not be used. ■

B.8 INDUCTANCES IN SERIES AND PARALLEL

When there is no interaction between the magnetic fields of several inductances, the result of connecting them in series or in parallel resembles the series or parallel connection of resistances. In Figure 12.26, two coils are shown in a series connection. The total inductance in the circuit is

$$L_{\text{total}} = L1 + L2 \qquad \text{FORMULA 12.15}$$

and the inductive reactance is

$$X_L = X_{L1} + X_{L2} \qquad \text{FORMULA 12.16}$$

In the schematic diagram shown in Figure 12.27, two coils are connected in parallel. In this instance, the inductance is

$$L_{\text{total}} = \frac{1}{\dfrac{1}{L1} + \dfrac{1}{L2}} \quad \text{or} \quad \frac{L1L2}{L1 + L2}$$

FORMULA 12.17

Figure 12.26 If two series inductances are not magnetically coupled, the total inductance is $L1 + L2$.

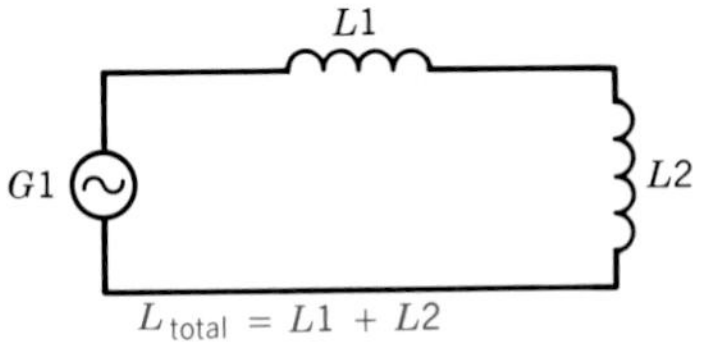

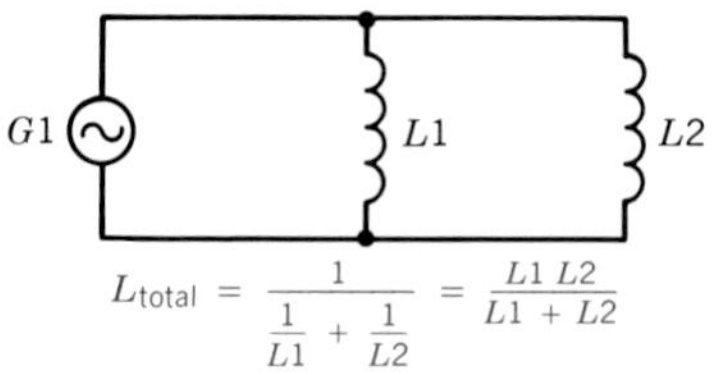

Figure 12.27 If two parallel inductances are not magnetically coupled, the total inductance is $\dfrac{L1L2}{L1 + L2}$

As might be expected, the inductive reactance is given by

$$X_{L\ \text{total}} = \frac{1}{\dfrac{1}{X_{L1}} + \dfrac{1}{X_{L2}}} \quad \text{or} \quad \frac{X_{L1}X_{L2}}{X_{L1} + X_{L2}}$$

FORMULA 12.18

EXAMPLE:
Given a 6.3-V, 60 Hz ac source, and two inductors (one with an inductance of 1 H and a resistance of 100 Ω and the other with an inductance of 1.5 H and a resistance of 150 Ω), how many different circuits can be constructed? Give the inductance, resistance, and inductive reactance of each circuit. Assume that there is no possibility of magnetic interaction. ■

SOLUTION:
Two circuits can be produced by connecting each of the inductors separately, as shown in Figures 12.28*a* and 12.28*b*. A third circuit shown in 12.28*c* is produced by connecting the two inductors in series. In this case the total inductance is

$$L_{\text{total}} = L1 + L2 = 1 + 1.5 = 2.5\ \text{H}$$

the resistance is

$$R_{\text{total}} = R_{L1} + R_{L2} = 100 + 150 = 250\ \Omega$$

and the inductive reactance of the combination is

$$X_{L\ \text{total}} = X_{L1} + X_{L2} = 2\pi f L_1 + 2\pi f L_2 = 942.5\ \Omega$$

Alternately, the inductive reactance can be calculated from the total inductance:

$$X_L = 2\pi f L_{1+2} = 2 \times \pi \times 60 \times 2.5 = 942.5\ \Omega$$

Finally, a fourth circuit can be constructed as shown in 12.28*d* by connecting both inductors in parallel across the source. The total inductance in this circuit is:

$$L_{\text{total}} = \frac{L1 \times L2}{L1 + L2} = \frac{1.5}{2.5} = 0.6\ \text{H}$$

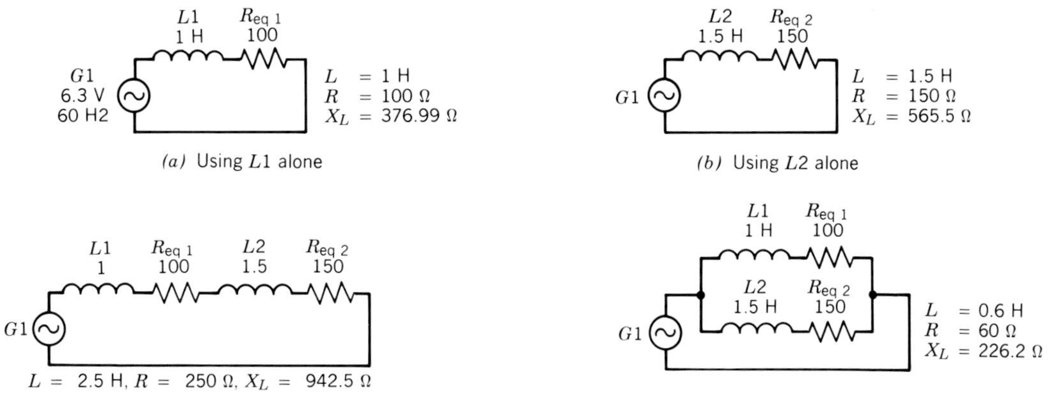

(a) Using *L*1 alone

(b) Using *L*2 alone

(c) Using *L*1 and *L*2 in series

(d) Using *L*1 and *L*2 in parallel

Figure 12.28 Four different circuits can be constructed with two inductors.

the total resistance of the combination is

$$R = \frac{R1R2}{R1 + R2} = \frac{100 \times 150}{250} = 60\ \Omega$$

and the inductive reactance is

$$X_L = 2 \times \pi \times 60 \times 0.6 = 226.2\ \Omega$$

The total inductance is known, so it is easier to use Formula 12.11 than 12.18 to calculate the reactance. ■

For series or parallel connections of more than two inductances, the following general formulas can be used:

For series connections

$$L_{total} = L1 + L2 + \cdots + = L_n \qquad \text{FORMULA 12.19}$$

$$R_{total} = R_{L1} + R_{L2} + \cdots + R_{Ln} \qquad \text{FORMULA 12.20}$$

$$X_{L\ total} = 2\pi f(L1 + L2 + \cdots + L_n) \qquad \text{FORMULA 12.21}$$

For parallel connections

$$L_{total} = \frac{1}{\frac{1}{L1} + \frac{1}{L2} + \cdots + \frac{1}{L_n}} \qquad \text{FORMULA 12.22}$$

$$R_{total} = \frac{1}{\frac{1}{R_{L1}} + \frac{1}{R_{L2}} + \cdots + \frac{1}{R_{L_n}}} \qquad \text{FORMULA 12.23}$$

$$X_{L\ total} = \frac{1}{\frac{1}{X_{L1}} + \frac{1}{X_{L2}} + \cdots + \frac{1}{X_{L_n}}} \qquad \text{FORMULA 12.24}$$

EXAMPLE:

Calculate the total inductance, resistance, and inductive reactance of the network shown in Figure 12.29. ■

SOLUTION:

As in the case of a resistive network, the resistances of coils can be combined into a single equivalent resistance. The resistance of *L*2, *L*3, and *L*4 combined is

$$R_{L2,3,4} = \frac{1}{\frac{1}{R_{L2}} + \frac{1}{R_{L3}} + \frac{1}{R_{L4}}} = \frac{1}{\frac{1}{10} + \frac{1}{15} + \frac{1}{36}}$$

$$= 5.14\ \Omega$$

Adding R_{L1} and R_{L5} = 18 + 5.14 + 52 = 75.14 Ω. The inductance of the parallel network composed of *L*2, *L*3, and *L*4 is

$$L2{,}3{,}4 = \frac{1}{\frac{1}{L2} + \frac{1}{L3} + \frac{1}{L4}}$$

$$= \frac{1}{\frac{1}{15 \times 10^{-3}} + \frac{1}{22 \times 10^{-3}} + \frac{1}{56 \times 10^{-3}}}$$

$$= 7.7\ \text{mH}$$

Figure 12.29 Calculating the inductance in a series–parallel combination of inductors.

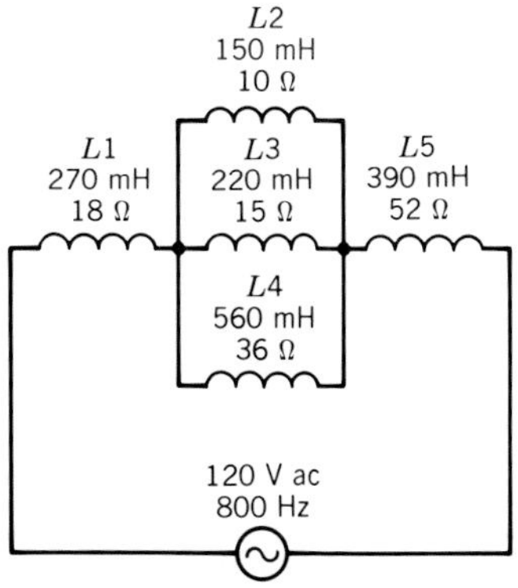

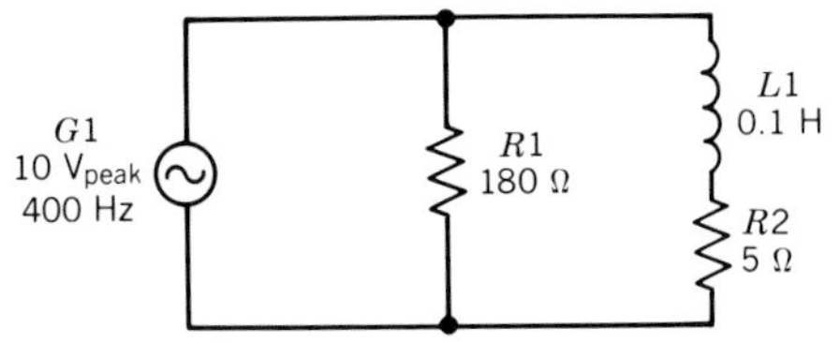

Figure 12.30 A parallel circuit containing an inductance. $R2$ is the internal resistance of $L1$.

This inductance is in series with $L1$ and $L5$, so the total circuit inductance is

$$L1 + L2{,}3{,}4 + L5 = 0.27 + 0.0077 + 0.39 = 667.7 \text{ mH}$$

At a frequency of 800 Hz, the total inductive reactance of this network is

$$X_L = 2\pi f L = 2 \times \pi \times 800 \times 0.6677 = 3356.23\ \Omega \quad \text{or} \quad 3360\ \Omega$$ ■

A different example is shown in Figure 12.30. Here, $R1$ is a circuit resistor, while $R2$ represents the resistance of coil $L1$. Since the resistance of the inductor is low compared to the inductive reactance, it can be ignored for the purposes of current calculation. The same potential difference is supplied across both branches, but there will be a difference in the phase angle between the potential difference and current in the branch containing $L1$. In the branch containing only $R1$, the current is in phase with the applied potential; that is, the phase angle is 0°. In the branch containing $L1$ and its resistance $R2$, the phase angle between the applied potential and the current is

$$\theta = \tan^{-1}\frac{X_L}{R} = \frac{251.3}{5} = 89.8° \quad \text{or} \quad 90°$$

In a series circuit, the phase angle between the potential difference and the series current is determined by the relationship between the sum of the inductances in series and the sum of the series resistances. In a parallel circuit of the sort shown in Figure 12.30, there are two distinct current paths, and the phase angle will be the result of the effects produced by the two branches. This is easiest to visualize by considering the phasor diagram of Figure 12.31. In a series circuit, the current through all parts of the circuit is the same, so that it is the current that is the reference phasor. As shown in Figure 12.31a, the current through the $R1$ branch of the circuit is in phase with the source potential difference. In the $L1$ branch, however, the potential difference leads the branch current by 90°, as shown in Figure 12.31b. Remember, the phase angle is 90° because the inductive reactance of $L1$ is more than 10 times its resistance. In order to add the two currents, the ref-

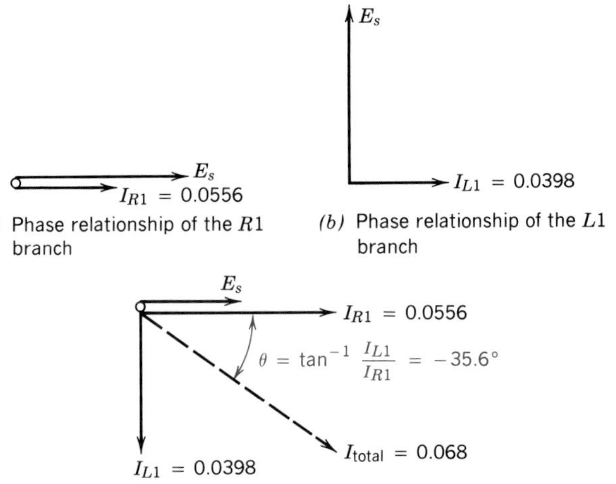

Figure 12.31 Phasor diagrams of the circuit shown in Figure 12.30.

erence phasor used is the source potential difference, as shown in Figure 12.31c. The peak current through the resistive branch of the circuit is

$$I1 = \frac{E_{\text{peak}}}{R} = \frac{10}{180} = 0.0556$$

Notice that the current through the resistive branch is shown as the reference phasor since it is in phase with the potential difference. The inductive branch peak current, given by Formula 12.12, is

$$I2 = \frac{E_{\text{peak}}}{\sqrt{R^2 + X_L^2}} = \frac{10}{251.3} = 0.0398 \text{ A}$$

at a phase angle of 90°, that is,

$$\theta = \tan^{-1}\frac{X_L}{R2} = 90°$$

The peak circuit current, then, is the sum of these currents, shown on the phasor diagram as the sum of the two branch phasors.

B.9 IMPEDANCE

The square root of the sum of the squares of the resistance and the inductive reactance in a series circuit or in a branch of a parallel circuit, that is, $\sqrt{R^2 + X_L^2}$ is the magnitude of the *impedance* of the circuit or branch. The impedance of a circuit, a branch of a circuit, or of a single component is the phasor sum of the resistance and the reactance. It is symbolized by Z and is measured in ohms. Therefore, for a circuit or part of a circuit containing only resistance and inductance,

$$Z = \sqrt{R^2 + X_L^2} \qquad \text{FORMULA 12.25}$$

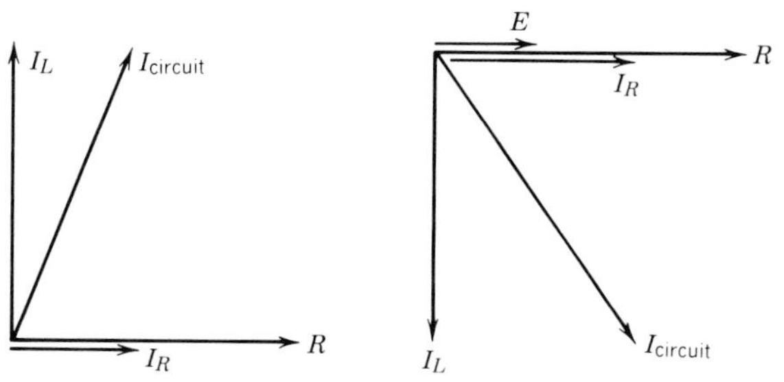

(a) Series circuit *(b)* Parallel circuit

Figure 12.32 Inductive reactance phasors in series and parallel circuits.

The concept of impedance is one of the most important and most frequently referred to in electronics.

Impedance is a phasor quantity, and the student new to this subject is sometimes confused by the fact that the current in an inductive circuit, as shown in Figure 12.32, is drawn 90° ahead of the current through the resistive element in a series circuit, but is 90° behind the reference phasor in a parallel circuit. The reason for this is that the circuit potential difference, rather than the circuit current, is the reference phasor in a parallel circuit. The topic of impedance will be covered in greater detail in the following chapters.

C. EXAMPLES AND COMPUTATIONS

C.1 INTRODUCTION TO LOGARITHMS

By the time you have reached this point in your studies, the importance of the exponential method of writing very large and very small numbers should be clear. The method of logarithms is nothing more than an extension of the method of exponents. Before the popularization of pocket calculators, logarithms were used extensively to simplify computations that involved multiplication or division. Although less frequently used today, a number of formulas in the field of electronics require the use of logarithms. Logarithms are also useful to solve equations in which an unknown appears as an exponent.

The method of logarithms is based on the fact that for every positive number N, regardless of whether it is an integer or a decimal, there is some number x such that

$$N = b^x$$

where b is any positive number or fraction greater than 1. The number represented by b is called the *base,* while the power to which the base is raised, x, is called the *logarithm* of N. In other words,

$$x = \log_b N,$$

or x is the logarithm of N in the base b. In the exponential system you have been using, the base is 10. For example,

$$100 = 10^2, \text{ so}$$

$$2 = \log_{10} 100.$$

Logarithms to the base 10 are called *common,* or *Briggsian,* logarithms. The common or Briggsian logarithm is generally referred to by the symbol *log* in mathematical terms.

EXAMPLE:

What is log 100,000? ■

SOLUTION:

The logarithm of a number is the value of the exponent or power to which 10 must be raised to produce that number. Since there are five places after the 1 in 100,000, you know that it is equal to 10^5. Therefore log 100,000 = 5. ■

Although the common logarithm of 100,000 can be determined without calculation, the definition of the logarithm states that any positive number such as 365.12 or 3.14159 has a logarithm. There are two practical ways of obtaining the logarithm of any number. One is to use a logarithm table, which takes time, and frequently involves some calculation to get the value required. Of course, in the days before pocket calculators, looking up numbers in logarithm tables could actually save time, by permitting long multiplications or divisions to be performed quickly. Today, the use of logarithms in electronics tends to be limited to a number of special applications, and the most practical manner of using these functions is to calculate their value with a scientific calculator.

EXAMPLE:

Calculate $\log_{10} 5130.65$. ■

SOLUTION:

Enter number	[5] [1] [3] [0] [.] [6] [5]
Select log function	[log]

Read displayed answer 3.7101724

Therefore, $10^{3.7101724} = 5130.65$. ■

Briggsian, or base 10, logarithms are necessary for comparison of voltage and power levels in electronic units. For inductance calculations, however, the so-called *natural* or *Naperian* logarithms are used. The base for these logarithms is the mathematical constant ϵ (epsilon). This constant is equal to 2.7182828 . . . , and is symbolized by the lower case letter *e* in most mathematics texts. In order to prevent confusion with *e* used as the symbol for the instantaneous value of a potential difference, almost all electronics texts use the Greek letter ϵ. For example, in Section B you learned that the cemf in an inductive circuit is

$$e_{\text{cemf}} = \epsilon^{\frac{-Rt}{L}}.$$

Expressing this in another way,

$$-\frac{Rt}{L} = \ln e_{\text{cemf}}$$

Note that the symbol *ln* is used for logarithms to the base ϵ to eliminate confusion with the *log* used in logarithms to the base 10.

Although tables of natural logarithms are available, the scientific calculator provides the most practical way of calculating these functions.

EXAMPLE:
Calculate ln 5130.65. ■

SOLUTION:

Enter number [5] [1] [3] [0] [.] [6] [5]

Select natural logarithm [LNX]

Read displayed answer 8.5429876
Therefore, $\epsilon^{8.5429876} = 5130.65$. ■

If you know the logarithm of a number, either to the base 10 or base ϵ, calculating the number itself is called *obtaining the antilogarithm*. This process is symbolized by $\log^{-1}$ for common logarithms and $\ln^{-1}$ for natural logarithms in printed formulas, although the calculator key markings tend to differ a great deal from model to model. Some calculators use [10^x] and [e^x] for $\log^{-1}$ and $\ln^{-1}$, respectively, while others use an inverse key [INV] followed by [LOG] or [LNX].

EXAMPLE:
Calculate $\epsilon^{-3.75}$. ■

SOLUTION:

Enter exponent [3] [.] [7] [5]

Change sign [+/−]

Select antilogarithm to base ϵ [INV] [LNX]

Read answer on display 0.0235177 ■

Before attempting to use logarithmic functions in actual applications, practice calculating the logarithms and antilogarithms in the following exercise.

Use your calculator to obtain the following logarithms or numbers.

a. log 3.6
b. ln 15.87
c. log 140,000
d. ln 3960.75
e. $\log^{-1}3.8$
f. $\ln^{-1}3.8$
g. $\ln^{-1}-6$
h. $\log^{-1}-4.8$
i. ln 38.68
j. $\epsilon^{-3.2}$
k. $10^{-0.46}$
l. $\epsilon^{-1.5}$
m. ϵ^{2}
n. ϵ^{0}

C.2 USING LOGARITHMS IN INDUCTANCE CALCULATIONS

The solution of problems involving inductance requires you either to calculate the cemf developed by an inductor, that is, to calculate $\epsilon^{\frac{-Rt}{L}}$ when *R*, *t*, and *L* are known, or to solve for one of these quantities when two of them and the cemf are known or can be calculated. When *R*, *t*, and *L* are known and the cemf must be calculated, the antilogarithm function is used.

EXAMPLE:
A certain circuit has a total resistance of 15 Ω and an inductance of 150 mH. What is the value of the cemf produced by the inductance 0.001 s after a 12-V dc source is connected. ■

SOLUTION 1:
As an aid to visualizing, the schematic has been drawn in Figure 12.33. The cemf is given by Formula 12.4:

$$e_{\text{cemf}} = E\epsilon^{\frac{-Rt}{L}}$$

Using your calculator, multiply the resistance by the time in order to calculate $R \times t$

[1] [5] [×] [.] [0] [0] [1]

Divide by *L* to obtain $\frac{Rt}{L}$

[÷] [1] [5] [=]

Change sign to get $\frac{-Rt}{L}$

[+/−]

Now calculate the antilogarithm

[INV] [LNX]

Figure 12.33 Using logarithms to calculate e_{cemf} in an *RL* circuit.

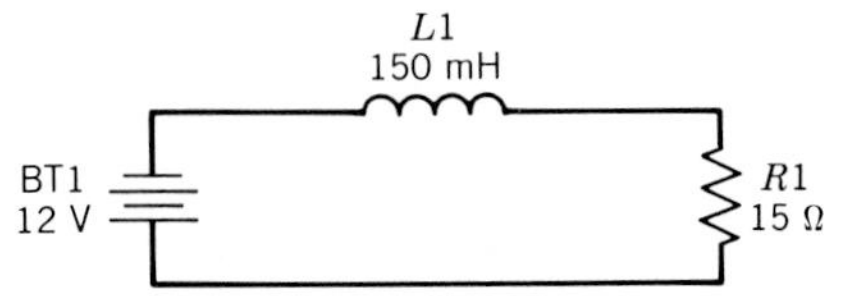

(This solves $\epsilon^{\frac{-Rt}{L}}$) and now you can obtain the e_{cemf} by multiplying by E.

[×] [1] [2]

Read answer in display 10.858049

Rounded off to three significant figures, the answer is $e_{cemf} = 10.9$ V. Notice that the equals sign key was pressed to display $\frac{-Rt}{L}$ before the antilogarithm is computed. If this is not done, only the antilogarithm of the number displayed at that moment is calculated. Alternately, parentheses could be used to make sure that the antilogarithm of the entire expression $\frac{-Rt}{L}$ is computed: ■

SOLUTION 2:

[(] [1] [5] [×] [.] [0] [0] [1]
[÷] [1] [5] [)]
[+/−]
[INV] [LNX]
[×] [1] [2] [=]

The answer displayed is 10.858049 ■

The second type of problem consists of solving for one of the factors in the exponent when the cemf is known. To do this, the [LNX] function is used to calculate $\frac{-Rt}{L}$.

EXAMPLE:
How long after the source is connected to the circuit in Figure 12.33 does the cemf drop to 0.707 V? ■

SOLUTION:
Begin by writing the mathematical statement of the problem using Formula 12.4 and substitute the known quantities:

$$0.707 = 12\ \epsilon^{\frac{-15t}{0.15}}$$

Simplifying the exponent,

$$0.707 = 12\ \epsilon^{-100t}$$

and dividing both sides by 12,

$$0.0589167 = \epsilon^{-100t}$$

but

$$\ln 0.0589167 = -2.8316307$$

so

$$-100t = -2.8316307$$

and

$$t = 0.028316307 \quad \text{or} \quad 28.3 \times 10^{-3}\ \text{s}$$

Although it is possible to perform these calculations without writing down the separate steps, the method shown makes it easier to follow the reasoning involved and to correct any errors in entering numbers. ■

The calculation of the current through an inductive circuit with a dc source is based on the use of Formulas 12.5 and 12.6.

EXAMPLE:
What is the current through the circuit in Figure 12.33, 2 ms after the source is connected? ■

SOLUTION:
Using Formula 12.5, $i = \frac{E}{R}(1 - \epsilon^{\frac{-Rt}{L}})$, and substituting the known quantities produces

$$i = 0.8(1 - \epsilon^{-0.2})$$

The antilogarithm of -0.2 is 0.8187308, so

$$i = 0.8(1 - 0.8187307) \quad \text{or} \quad 0.8 \times 0.1812693 = 0.1450154$$

This rounds to 145 mA. ■

Calculations with R, t, or L as the unknown quantity are equally straightforward if you analyze the problem carefully.

Provide the unknown quantity in each of the following cases:

a. A 15-V source is connected in series with a 1-H inductor and a 10 Ω resistance. What is the amount of time that has elapsed after the source was connected if the cemf is 5.52 V?

b. In the circuit of problem (a), the current is now 1.125 A. How much time has passed since the source was connected?

c. A 12-V dc source is connected to a coil that has a resistance of 50 Ω. 0.4 seconds after the source is connected, the cemf is 6 V. What is the inductance of the coil?

d. A certain inductor is connected in series with a 15 Ω resistance across a 27-V source. After 1.066 s the circuit current is 1.56 A. What is the inductance? (Ignore the resistance of the inductor.)

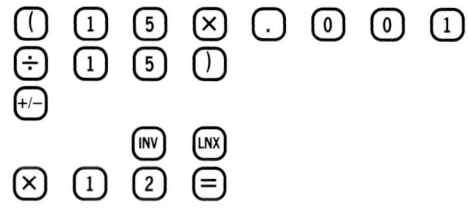

e. What is the current in a series circuit consisting of a 5-V dc source, a 27 Ω resistor, and a 150-mH inductor with an internal resistance of 33 Ω exactly 7.5 ms after the source is connected?

D. APPLICATIONS

D.1 PRACTICAL INDUCTORS

Inductors or coils are components designed to provide a specific amount of inductance in a circuit. The units designed to operate at power or audio frequencies are referred to as *inductors* in military specifications, while units intended for higher-frequency operation are referred to as *radio-frequency coils*. Unfortunately, this useful difference in terms is rarely used elsewhere, even though it underlines some important differences in package and construction. Throughout this book, as in the electronics industry in general, the terms *inductor* and *coil* refer to any component that supplies inductance. Another term that is sometimes seen is *choke*.

D.1.1 POWER- AND AUDIO-FREQUENCY INDUCTORS

Inductors intended for use at frequencies below 20 kHz tend to be rather bulky, are composed of many turns of wire, and possess a ferromagnetic core. This is the case because it takes a substantial number of coil turns to provide an inductance of 100 mH or greater at low frequencies. At power frequencies of 60 Hz, an inductance of 100 mH only has an inductive reactance of $X_L = 2\pi fL = 37.7\ \Omega$, so that if the circuit also contains resistors totalling 400 Ω or so, the effect of the inductor will be minimal. Audio-frequency inductors generally have inductances ranging from 0.1 to 10 H or higher and are constructed in the manner shown in Figure 12.34. In this illustration, a large number of turns of enamel-coated, solid copper wire are wound around a form that is then placed inside a framework of thin iron plates. These plates, shown in Figure 12.35 are E and I shaped and are usually interleaved to provide a closed magnetic circuit for the field produced

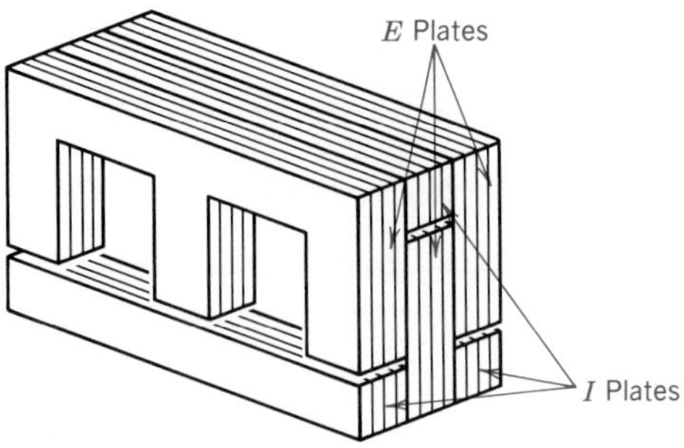

Figure 12.35 E- and I-shaped plates are generally interleaved to form the core of an audio-frequency inductor.

by the coil. This stack of plates is generally referred to as the *core* of the inductor. Thin plates are used rather than a solid bar to minimize the currents induced in the core by the changing magnetic field of the coil. These currents are called *eddy currents* and account for some of the loss of energy when a current flows through an inductor. After the inductor core has been assembled around the coil and coil form, the whole unit is coated with a lacquer or plastic compound, which provides some protection against moisture. The core plates may be bolted or clamped in place by an external frame as shown in Figure 12.34. This results in the so-called *open-frame* inductor. For applications where the magnetic field of the coil must not interact with other circuits, or where the coil itself must be protected from moisture, the coil and core are sealed inside a steel case, which is then filled with resin, oil, or more recently, epoxy compounds. This produces a unit referred to as a *metal-encased* inductor. Figure 12.36 shows such an inductor. This case is intended for mounting on a metal chassis, and connections are made to the coil through solder terminals on the bottom of the inductor. Figure 12.37 provides the dimensions for selected cases. The case symbol given in the table is part of the MIL SPEC type designation marked on the cases of inductors used in U.S. military and government equipment. The type designation for standard

Figure 12.34 Basic construction of an audio-frequency inductor.

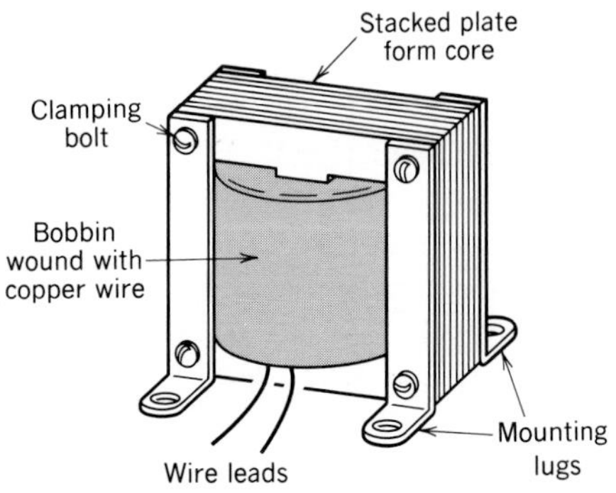

Figure 12.36 A metal-encased inductor.

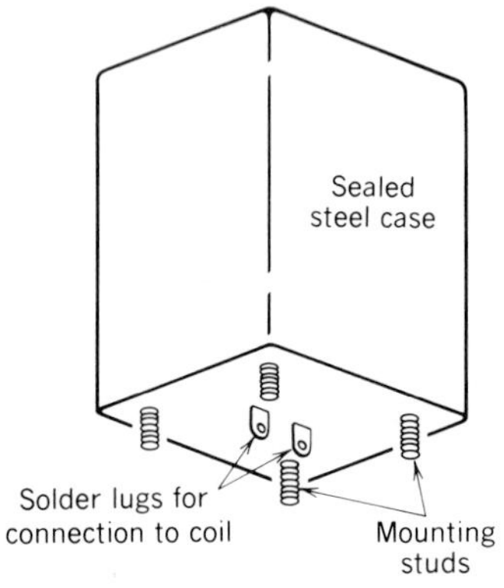

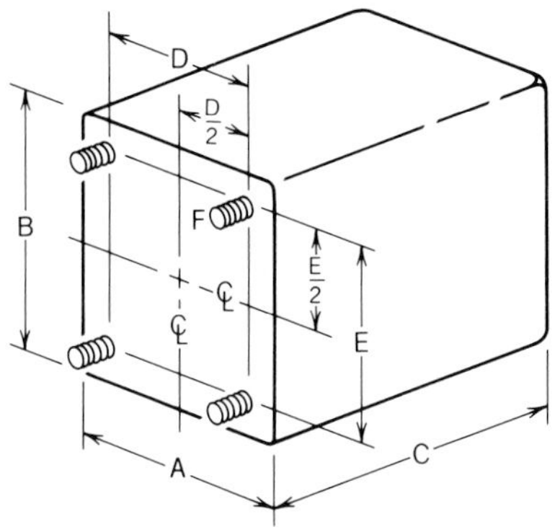

Case Symbol	A	B	C	D	E	F
AF	1.00	1.00	2.86	—	—	4–40
AG	2.54	2.54	3.49	—	—	4–40
AH	3.33	3.33	4.44	—	—	6–32
AJ	4.13	4.13	6.03	3.01	3.01	6–32
EA	4.92	4.60	6.98	3.49	2.86	6–32
EB	4.92	4.60	6.19	3.49	2.86	6–32
FA	5.87	5.23	7.94	4.29	3.65	6–32
FB	5.87	5.23	6.35	4.29	3.65	6–32
GA	6.98	6.03	9.68	5.39	4.44	6–32
GB	6.98	6.03	7.14	5.39	4.44	6–32
HA	7.77	6.66	10.79	5.83	4.72	8–32
HB	7.77	6.66	8.1	5.83	4.72	8–32
JA	9.05	7.77	12.38	6.66	5.40	8–32
JB	9.05	7.77	9.84	6.66	5.40	8–32
KA	10.00	8.57	13.33	7.62	6.19	10–32
KB	10.00	8.57	10.95	7.62	6.19	10–32
LA	10.95	9.37	14.13	8.41	6.83	10–32
LB	10.95	9.37	11.48	8.41	6.83	10–32
MA	11.9	10.16	15.24	9.37	7.62	$\frac{1}{4}$–20
MB	11.9	10.16	12.54	9.37	7.62	$\frac{1}{4}$–20

All dimensions in centimeters. Except F (inches)

Figure 12.37 Case dimensions for metal-encased inductors.

Figure 12.38 MIL SPEC inductor and transformer markings.

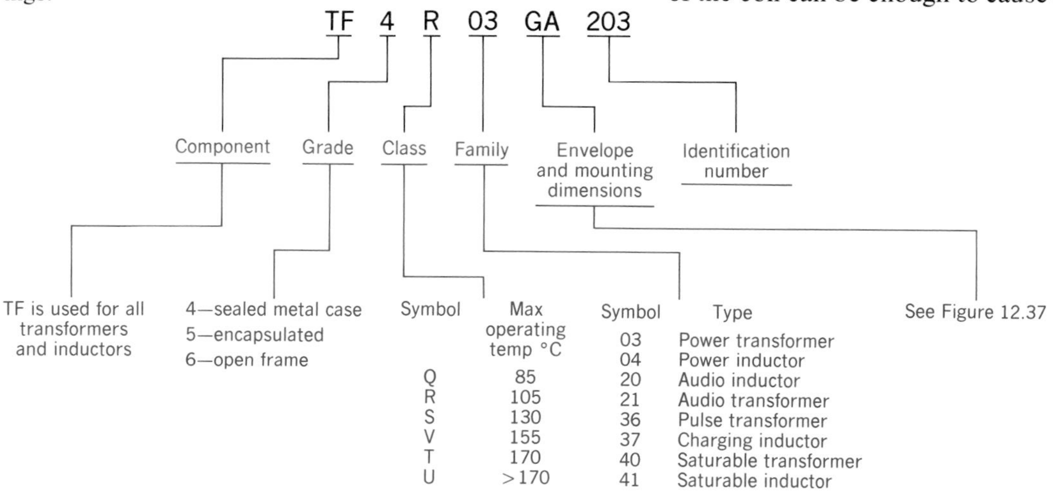

audio-frequency inductors is explained in Figure 12.38. MIL SPEC inductors almost always have the unit inductance and frequently the coil resistance and maximum safe current clearly marked on the case. Commercial products, on the other hand, frequently give only the manufacturer's name and a model number. If it is not given in the unit schematic, the best way to obtain the inductance of such a component without actually removing it from the circuit and measuring it is to look up the model number in the manufacturer's catalog. Small, open-frame inductors used in consumer products frequently provide no information at all.

Audio-frequency inductors fail in one of two ways: either through an open circuit or through a short circuit, which can occur between the turns or between the coil and the inductor core. Since an audio-frequency inductor is a relatively large component, manufacturers generally try to reduce the package size as much as possible. One way to do this is to use the smallest diameter wire that can safely carry the rated inductor current. If the current through the inductor is much greater than its rated capacity, the heat produced cannot escape. The result is the overheating of the wire insulation and the coil form materials, or the fusing or melting of the coil itself. In most cases, a hot spot forms at one point in the interior of the coil and an open circuit is produced.

When the inductor current is slightly less than that necessary to melt the copper wire, charring of the lacquer or enamel insulation can occur. This can cause a short circuit between a coil turn near the beginning of the coil and one near its end. The effect is the same as short circuiting the coil, and produces a drastic change in circuit behavior. In some cases, short circuits form between a number of adjacent turns or between the coil and the inductor core. If this happens, the effect on the circuit is less drastic, but is frequently harder to find. A 20 or 30 percent reduction in the inductance of the coil can be enough to cause improper operation,

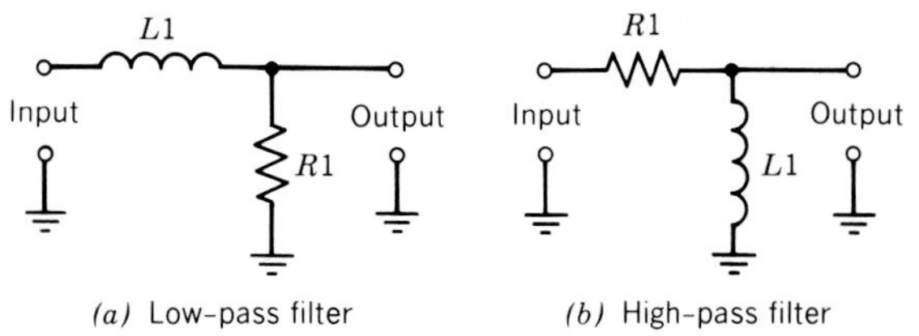

Figure 12.39 Filter circuits using inductors.

but checking the coil resistance with a multimeter might not reveal the shorted condition. This is due in part to the fact that the coil resistance is quite low, and only a meter specifically designed for very low resistance measurement will detect the change. Another problem arises from the fact that the low potential difference used by an ohmmeter might not be enough to produce a short-circuit current through the charred insulation. The inductor resistance will appear to be normal. When used in a circuit at a higher potential difference, however, current paths through the charred insulation are produced. The existance of a leakage path to the inductor frame will usually result in losses of signal power or noisy operation of the circuit.

The principal applications of audio-frequency inductors are based on the ability of an inductance to resist changes in circuit current. In dc power circuits, inductors are used for reducing an ac component or for eliminating current surges. This function is referred to as *smoothing*. In audio-frequency circuits, inductors are used to block or reduce the amplitude of high-frequency signals, while providing a low-impedance path for low-frequency signals. The circuit shown in Figure 12.39*a*, for example, will tend to pass low-frequency signals to its output terminal. High-frequency signals will be severely reduced in amplitude across the output terminals because the impedance of $L1$ will be greater for high frequencies. The circuit shown in Figure 12.39*b*, on the other hand, will pass high-frequency signals through to its output terminal, while reducing the amplitude of the low-frequency signals. In both cases, the combination of $L1$ and $R1$ acts as a voltage divider. Because of the low reactance of $L1$ at low frequencies, the potential difference of the low-frequency signals is greater across $R1$ in both cases. Circuits of this type are called *filters* and in more elaborate forms are among the most common electronic circuits.

One frequently encountered circuit, which uses audio-frequency inductors, is the cross-over network illustrated in Figure 12.40. The purpose of this circuit is to separate the high- and low-frequency audio signals. The low-frequency signals are directed to large, massive speakers capable of turning these variations in potential difference into sound. The higher audio frequencies are sent to smaller speakers or driver units, which are better able to vibrate at a faster rate and produce high-frequency sound waves.

Figure 12.40 An *RL* cross-over network.

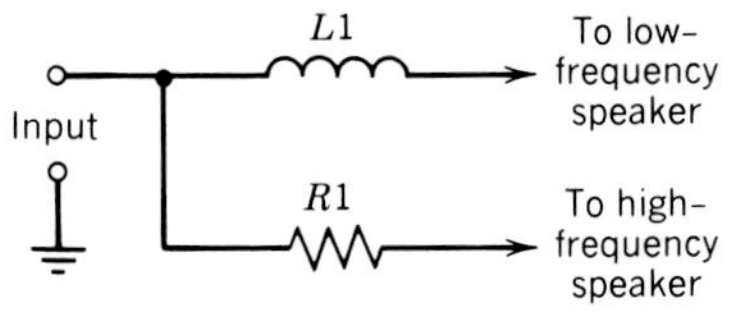

D.1.2 RF CHOKES

A second type of inductor, generally possessing a lower inductance than the audio-frequency inductor, is pictured in Figure 12.41. The purpose of this component is to prevent high-frequency ac signals from distributing themselves throughout an electronic unit via the power wiring. These components, called *radio-frequency chokes,* or RFCs, provide the means of connecting one dc power supply to several circuits while isolating them for high-frequency ac. The size, shape, and inductance of the RFC depends on the frequencies that require blocking. The type shown in Figure 12.41*a* has an inductance of 10 mH and a resistance of less than 10 Ω. This means that it has an impedance of 28,588 Ω if the frequency is a 455-kHz radio signal, and an impedance of almost 63 kΩ for a 1 mHz signal, while providing very little resistance to dc. For higher frequencies, physically smaller coils, with or without ferromagnetic cores, such as those pictured in Figure 12.41*b*, are used. For isolating UHF circuits, a few turns taken in the power leads or slipping a bead of an

Figure 12.41 Radio-frequency chokes.

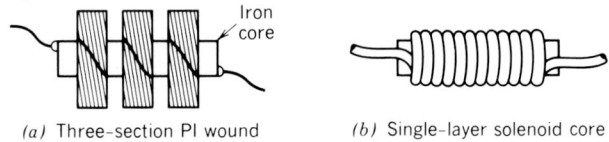

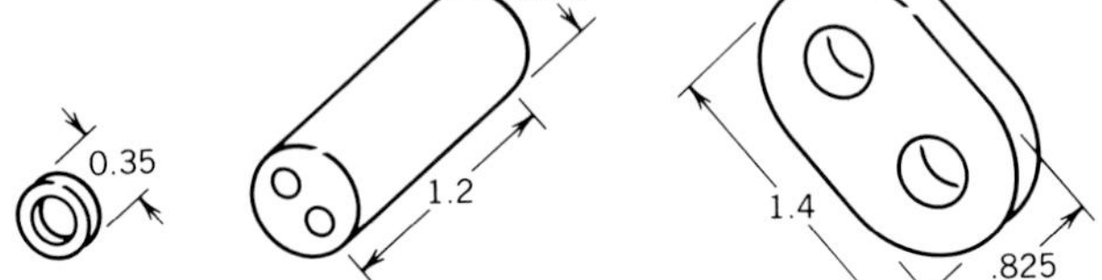

Figure 12.42 Ferrite beads used as high-frequency chokes.

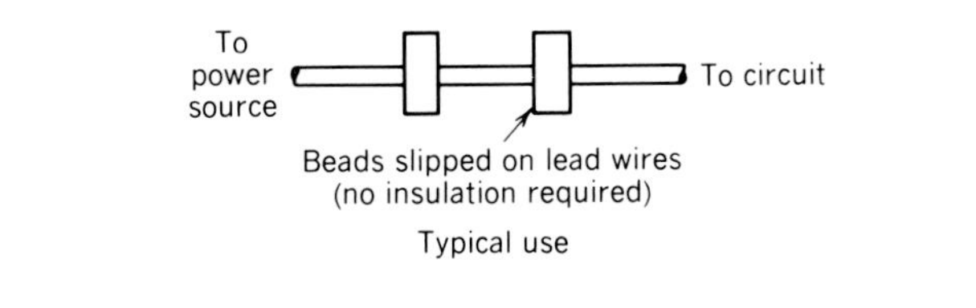

iron-ceramic material called *ferrite* on the power lead is sufficient. A number of typical ferrite beads are shown in Figure 12.42, and the subject of ferrite and pressed iron cores is covered in greater detail in Section D.3.

Except for certain high current models, RFCs are made of thin wire, AWG 30 or finer being common. Since these components are also required to pass appreciable currents, burning out and open circuiting are the most common failure modes. Charred insulation and short-circuiting between turns is less frequent than it is in audio-frequency inductors.

D.1.3 RADIO-FREQUENCY COILS

Any inductor that is neither an audio-frequency inductor nor an RFC is probably a radio-frequency coil. These components come in a bewildering variety of shapes and sizes. The principal application of radio-frequency coils is in tuned circuits, that is, circuits that select or block signals of a particular frequency or band of frequencies. During the early days of the electronics industry, radio-frequency coils tended to be fairly large because suitable core materials capable of functioning at high frequencies were unknown, and coils had to be made up of many turns of wire. Today, the use of special core materials has significantly reduced radio-frequency coil size. One common package type, shown in Figure 12.43, resembles that of a carbon composition resistor. To carry the resemblance still further, the inductance value is frequently marked on the inductor case using a color band system which can be confused with resistor markings. Figure 12.44 illustrates the identification, significant figure, and decimal point bands on a typical color-coded inductor. Remember that if the first color-coded band is double width and is silver, the component is an inductor and not a resistor. The inductance value given by the code is in microhenries (μH). When no decimal point is present, the fourth band represents a multiplier.

Radio-frequency coils of the encapsulated type shown in Figure 12.43 are commercially available in a large range of inductances. A typical range of products is from 0.1 μH to 100 mH. In addition to the encapsulated types, form-wound radio-frequency coils like those shown in Figure 12.41 are also commercially available in inductances from 0.1 μH to 100 mH.

Radio-frequency coils are not generally required to carry appreciable direct currents, and except in

Figure 12.43 Encapsulated radio-frequency coils.

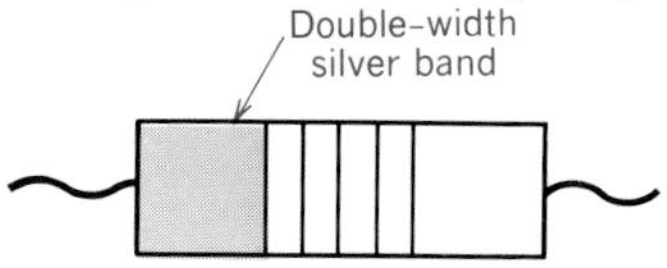

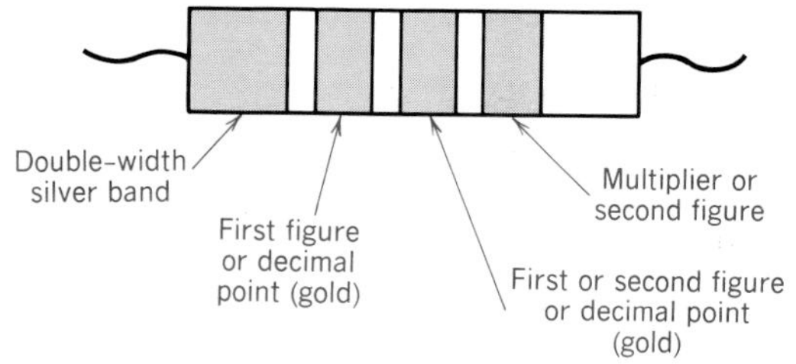

Examples: Silver, Gold, Red, Violet .27 μH
Silver, Green, Blue, Brown 560 μH
Silver, Yellow, Gold, Violet 4.7 μH

Figure 12.44 Reading encapsulated radio-frequency coil color codes.

transmitter or high-power, high-frequency applications, the current-carrying capacity of these coils is low. The principal failure mode of radio-frequency coils is a change in the inductance or increase of leakage of high-frequency energy caused by moisture or the breakdown of the insulating coatings and materials used in the packaging. However, failure of other components in a circuit will sometimes place a dc potential difference across an rf coil, and the resulting current will cause the coil to burn out.

D.2 COIL CHARACTERISTICS: *Q*

In addition to its inductance, there are a number of additional characteristics that must be considered when an inductor or coil is selected for a new design or as a replacement for a failed component. One of the most important of these is current-carrying ability. In most cases, although this is not always true, the manufacturer's specifications will provide an indication of the maximum safe current which a particular product can take. Besides the very real danger of having an inductor burn up, in the case of audio-frequency inductors, there are potential problems due to the magnetic field caused by a direct current through the inductor. With any sort of ferromagnetic core, a field due to a direct current can result in a condition known as *saturation*. Saturation occurs when the magnetizing force produced by the coil current is so great that a change in this current cannot significantly increase or decrease the flux density in the core. The result of this is the absence of any inductive reaction to small changes in coil current. In other words, the coil acts only like a small resistance. Except for certain components, which are called *saturable reactors*, or *swinging chokes*, the cores of audio-frequency inductors include an air gap to prevent saturation within certain limits of coil current. The presence of an air gap, which has a much higher reluctance than a closed iron magnetic circuit, reduces the magnetic flux density in the core below the saturation level. Of course, having a lower flux density in the core makes it necessary to have more coil turns and a larger inductor for a given inductance. For this reason, manufacturers will generally design the core air gap for a specific range of dc values. Selecting an inductor with an air gap or dc rating too low for a particular application could therefore result in poor operation, in addition to overheating.

Another characteristic of inductors and coils is the maximum allowable signal frequency. Particularly in the case of coils with ferromagnetic cores, using a unit designed for low-frequency operation at higher frequencies will probably result in overheating, poor operation, and equipment failure. Most iron plate inductor cores are designed for frequencies under 20 kHz. In power circuits, frequencies of 50, 60, or 400 Hz are specified. Core materials and designs are formulated for specific frequency ranges, and should not be used at frequencies outside this range.

Operating potential differences are also important since the wire insulation and breakdown potentials of the coil form and other insulating materials used in the inductor or coil determine the package size. Because electronic unit manufacturers lose profits when space inside their products is wasted, component manufacturers try to design inductors to take up as little space as possible. This means that wire insulation and insulating materials between layers of windings will be as thin as possible for a particular maximum safe working voltage. Since the core of an inductor is connected to or supported by the coil mounting hardware in certain designs, this would effectively ground the high-frequency signals.

In addition to these characteristics, the ability of a coil to provide inductance in a circuit without excessive losses due to coil resistance is referred to as the *quality factor,* or more commonly the Q of the coil at a particular frequency. Q is the ratio of the inductive reactance to the coil resistance, in other words,

$$Q = \frac{X_L}{R} = \frac{2\pi f L}{R} \qquad \text{FORMULA 12.26}$$

Radio-frequency coil manufacturers frequently list the inductance and the minimum Q for each of their products as well as the frequency at which Q was measured. Using these parameters, it is possible to calculate the coil resistance from Formula 12.26.

EXAMPLE:
A certain manufacturer produces a 24 μH coil with a minimum Q of 65 at 2.5 MHz. What is the resistance of this coil and what will be the phase shift of a 2.5 MHz sine wave? ■

Condition	X_L	Q
Inductance is increased	↑	↑
Inductance is decreased	↓	↓
Resistance of circuit or inductor is increased	=	↓
Resistance of circuit or inductor is decreased	=	↑
Frequency of source is increased	↑	↑
Frequency of source is decreased	↓	↓
Source potential difference is changed	=	=

Figure 12.45 Variational analysis chart relating circuit conditions to Q.

SOLUTION:
Substituting the known values for f, L, and Q in Formula 12.26,

$$Q = \frac{2\pi f L}{R} \quad \text{or} \quad 65 = \frac{2\pi \times 2.5 \times 10^6 \times 24 \times 10^{-6}}{R},$$

$$R = 5.79 \quad \text{or} \quad 5.8\,\Omega$$

The phase shift produced by the inductor at this frequency is

$$\theta = \tan^{-1}\frac{X_L}{R} = \tan^{-1} Q = 89.10$$

Note that once you have calculated the resistance of a certain coil, it is an easy matter to calculate the phase shift caused by it at any frequency. ■

The ratio of the reactance to the coil resistance at a particular frequency will be greater with a coil possessing a high Q than with a low Q coil. Figure 12.45 is a variational analysis chart relating Q to other inductor characteristics.

In this chapter, only the Q of a coil has been discussed. In a later part of this book you will see that the Q of a circuit or a part of a circuit is an important concept.

D.3 COIL CORE MATERIALS: POWDERED IRON AND FERRITES

The reduction of component and equipment size remains one of the most important research projects in the electronics industry. Comparing electronic communications units of today with those used 30 or more years ago reveals a great change in the appearance and size of the inductors and rf coils. Part of this is due to the fact that two types of coil core materials have been

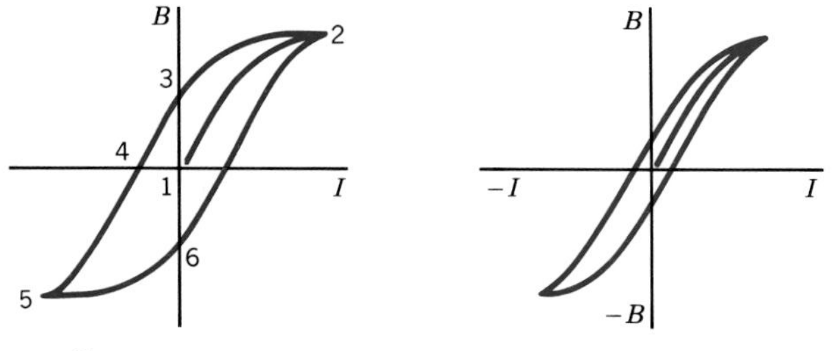

Figure 12.46 Hysteresis effect in different core materials.

perfected that make it possible to obtain greater inductance from smaller units. Previously mentioned, these core materials are referred to as *powdered iron* and *ferrite*. Both contain finely powdered iron or other ferromagnetic alloys bound together in a matrix of insulating material. Unlike the hard iron plates used in audio-frequency inductors, ferrites and powdered iron cores are composed of soft iron. This means that the materials will not exhibit the hysteresis losses found in cores composed of hard iron plates.

Hysteresis effects are illustrated in the graph of Figure 12.46*a* and 12.46*b*. In 12.46*a*, the curve shows the relationship between the magnetic flux density in a core composed of hard iron and the magnetomotive force produced by an alternating current in the coil. Curve segment 1–2 represents the period of time following the first application of an alternating potential difference to the coil. As the coil current increases, so does the flux density in the core. The result of the field in the core is to align the magnetic domains in the core material. Notice that the curve "flattens out" in the area of point 2 because of saturation, that is, the alignment of all the domains in the core. The curve segment from 2 to 3 represents the period of time during which the coil current is dropping. Notice that the flux density in the coil core remains fairly constant. This happens because the magnetic domains in the hard iron core tend to remain aligned until the reversing of the coil current causes them to be aligned in the opposite direction. This begins to occur at point 3. From point 3 to 4 along the curve, the reversed current through the coil forces the flux density in the core to zero, when the field of the core domains is exactly balanced by the field due to the reversed current through the coil. The increasing coil current and its magnetic field then aligns the core domains in the direction opposite to that of their original alignment. Saturation also occurs here, as shown by the flattening of the curve. Portion 5–6 of the curve represents the period of time during which the coil current is again approaching zero, after having reached its negative peak value. At point 6, the positive current half-cycle again begins, and the direction of the alignment of the core domains again begins to change. The figure produced by the graph is called a *hysteresis loop*.

Comparing the hysteresis loop for a soft iron core drawn in Figure 12.46*b* shows that there is little retention of alignment direction of magnetic domain alignment in soft iron. When the current and therefore the magnetizing force reach zero, the flux density within the core also drops to nearly zero. The area within the hysteresis curve is proportional to the amount of electrical power used in moving the magnetic domains in the core. This ac power is called the *hysteresis loss*, and like the power dissipated as heat in the coil and core, it is power that is lost. These losses are in contrast to the ac power used to produce the magnetic field around a coil, which is returned to the circuit when the coil current drops from its maximum to zero during every ac half-cycle.

The use of powdered iron and ferrite cores reduces the amount of power loss through hysteresis since relatively soft iron is used in their composition. Core heat losses due to eddy current are also minimized since the small bits of ferromagnetic material in the core are insulated from each other and large eddy currents cannot develop.

Well, you will ask, if powdered iron and ferrite cores are so effective at minimizing power losses, why are laminated cores used at all? The answer lies in the fact that properly designed laminated cores can easily have relative permeabilities of several thousand times that of air, while pressed iron cores normally possess permeabilities of less than 500 and usually less than 100 for commercially manufactured ferrites. When large inductances are needed for low-frequency applications, laminated cores will provide the smallest package size.

Powdered iron and ferrite cores come in a variety of sizes and materials, and in the five basic shapes shown in Figures 12.47*a* through 12.47*e*. The coil cores shown in 12.47*e* that resemble set screws are used with plastic or ceramic coil forms and permit *tuning*, that is, adjusting the inductance of the coil by positioning the core within the coil form. Cores of this type are usually made of pressed iron alloys for different operating frequencies, although ferrite cores are also sometimes produced in this form. Standard core sizes are $\frac{3}{16}$ (inch) with a 6–32 screw thread, $\frac{5}{16}$ (inch) with a 10–32 screw thread, and $\frac{3}{8}$ (inch) with a $\frac{1}{4}$–28 screw thread. The recommended frequencies for each core material type are encoded by a colored dot on the core. These codes are listed for reference purposes in Table 12.1.

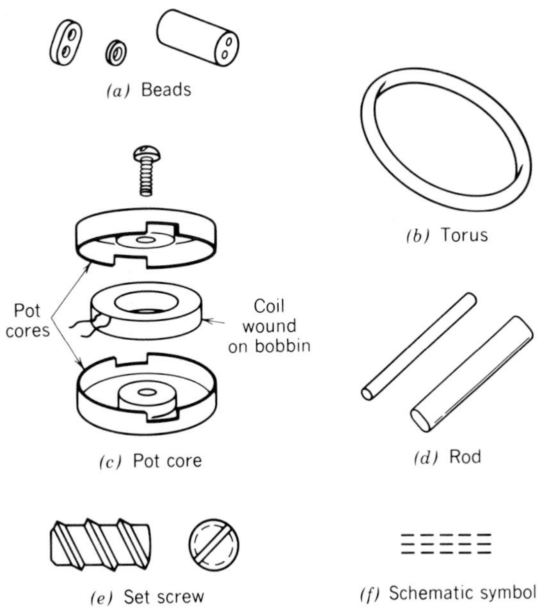

Figure 12.47 Ferrite and powdered iron core shapes.

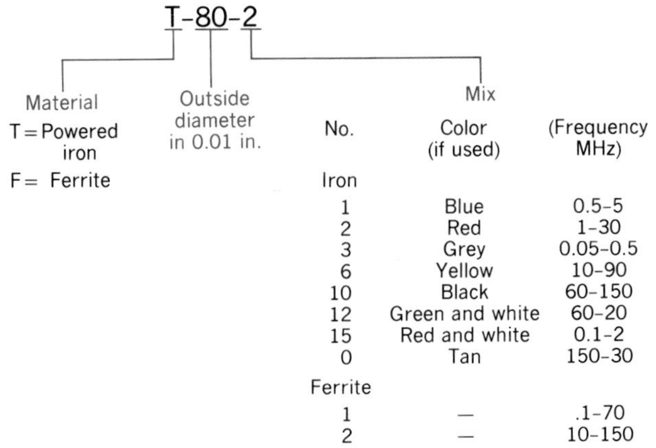

Figure 12.48 Ferrite and powdered iron toroidal core identification.

The ferrite rods shown in Figure 12.47*d* are most frequently used in small transistor radios. They do not provide the closed magnetic circuit for the field obtained in the toroid (12.47*b*) or pot cores (12.47*c*), but are considerably less expensive and are easy to use. The recommended frequency range for commercial ferrite rods covers the radio portion of the frequency spectrum from 100 kHz to 70 MHz.

The pot cores shown in Figure 12.47*c* are designed to fit around a multilayer coil wound on a plastic bobbin. If the circuit power is moderate or low, audio-frequency coils of this type can be used, as is the case in telephone circuits. Pot cores, also called *cup cores,* are available in either ferrite or powdered iron. The relative permeability of the core is frequently marked, although it is wise to check the manufacturer's specifications to determine the conditions under which the permeability was measured. Since it is an easy matter to change cores or coils, inductors composed of bobbin wound coils and pot cores are favored by engineers and technicians for prototype constructions.

Table 12.1 Set Screw Core Color Codes

Material	*Color*	*Frequency Range (MHz)*
Powdered iron		
	Yellow	0.2–1.5
	Red	0.5–20
	Green	4.5–20
		20–50[a]
	Purple	20–40
	White	20 and up[a]
		50–200
Ferrite		
	Dark blue	Under 25
	Light blue	Over 25

[a]Depending on material.

Inductors and coils wound on the toroidal or torus-shaped cores shown in Figure 12.47*b* are becoming very popular components in electronics. These cores are available in a wide variety of sizes, either ferrite or powdered iron, and can be used for operating frequencies of 100 kHz to over 400 MHz depending on the materials used. Ferrite cores normally have a dull grey appearance, while the powdered iron toroids appear to be glazed. Some manufacturers add coloring material to this glaze to indicate the type of alloy used in the powdered iron forms. Figure 12.48 explains the core identification numbers, which encode the diameter of the toroid in hundredths of an inch. The prefix letter T represents powdered iron; F refers to ferrite. The dash number following the size code designates a particular code material. For example, a ferrite toroidal core $\frac{1}{2}$ inch in outside diameter composed of type 2 material would be specified as an F-50-2 core in a standard catalog. The figure also lists some of the core materials and the color codings used to identify them.

The ferrite beads shown in Figures 12.47*a* and 12.42 are useful devices that can serve as small rf chokes at high frequency. When high-frequency signals from one part of an electronic unit cause interference with other circuits because of coupling through a common power supply, one or more of these beads can be slipped on the power leads to provide additional impedance to the high-frequency signals, preventing them from entering other portions of the unit. Since the beads do not conduct electricity, they can be slipped over both insulated or bare wire leads. Figure 12.49 illustrates one manufacturer's type specification. The initial letters FB stand for ferrite bead, the following two num-

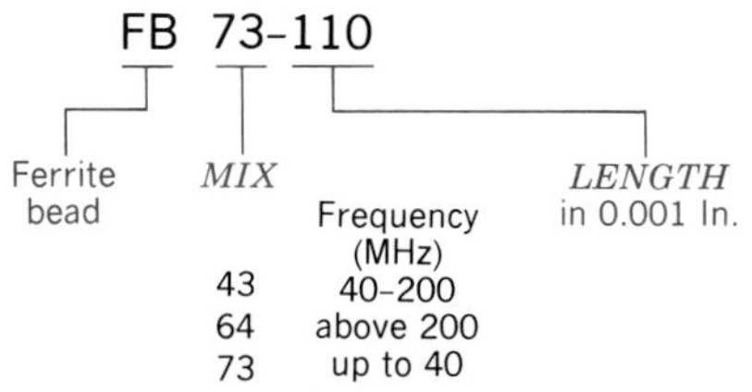

Figure 12.49 Ferrite bead nomenclature.

bers specify the material used and therefore the recommended frequency range, while the final three numbers give the minimum length of the bead in thousandths of an inch.

E. PROGRAMMED REVIEW

FRAME 1

As long as there is a __________ between a magnetic field and a conductor, a potential difference will be induced between the ends of the conductor.

a. Relative motion. (2)
b. Any other answer, review Section B.1.

FRAME 2

The period of time during which the magnetic field around a dc-carrying conductor is either expanding or collapsing is referred to as the __________ to distinguish it from the __________ condition when the field is stationary.

a. Transient state; steady state. (3)
b. Any other answer, review Section B.1.

FRAME 3

According to __________ law, the potential difference induced across a current-carrying conductor by the relative movement of the field and the conductor acts in such a way as to oppose any __________ in the __________.

a. Lenz's; change; current through the conductor. (5)
b. Any other answer go to Frame 4.

FRAME 4

According to Lenz's law the potential difference induced in a coil or conductor opposes the effect that produced the potential difference. For this reason, the induced potential difference is called a counter electromagnetic force, or cemf. If this concept is not clear to you, review Section B.2 and go on to Frame 5.

FRAME 5

The letter symbol for inductance is __________; it is measured in __________, abbreviated __________. The letter symbol for inductive reactance is __________; it is measured in __________.

a. L; henries; H; X_L; ohms. (6)
b. Any other answer, review Sections B.3 and B.7.

FRAME 6

An inductor of 6 H has a current through it that changes uniformly from 0 to 650 mA in 0.5 s. What is the cemf induced across the inductor during this time?

a. 7.8 V (7)
b. Any other answer; review Formula 12.1 and the first example in Section B.3.

FRAME 7

Complete the variational analysis in Figure 12.50.

Figure 12.50 Figure for Frame 7.

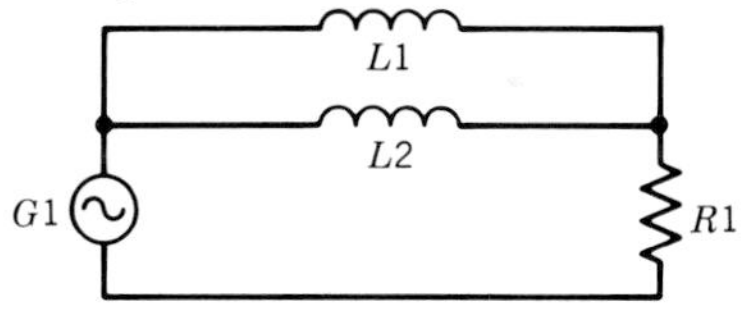

(a) Circuit

Condition	X_{L1}	X_{L2}	I_{R1}
Frequency of *G*1 is decreased	? (a)	? (b)	? (c)
Value of *L*2 is increased	=	? (d)	? (e)
Voltage of *G*1 is increased	? (f)	? (g)	? (h)

a. (a) decreases
   (b) decreases
   (c) increases
   (d) increases
   (e) decreases
   (f) remains the same
   (g) remains the same
   (h) increases (9)
b. More than one incorrect, review Section B.3 and go to Frame 8.

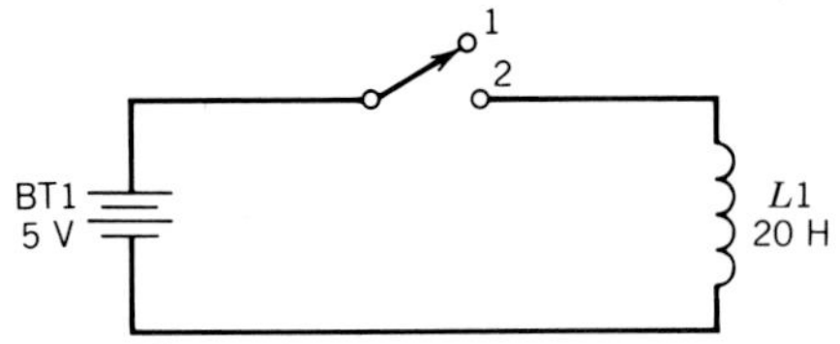

Figure 12.51 Circuit for Frame 9.

FRAME 8

Use the formula $L = \dfrac{\mu_r \mu_0 N^2 A}{l}$ to solve the following problem.

An inductor of 80 μH is required. Wire and a ferrite rod 0.0254 m long with a cross-sectional area of 0.05 m^2 and a μ_r of 75 are available. Ignoring the diameter of the wire, how many turns of wire are necessary?

a. 23.2 turns. (9)
b. Any other answer, review the final part of Section B.3.

FRAME 9

In the circuit of Figure 12.51, switch $S1$ is set to position 2 at $t = 0$. What is the current through the coil at $t = 0.1$ s, if the coil has a resistance of 120 Ω?

a. 0.019 A (10)
b. Any other answer, review Section B.4 and go on to Frame 10.

FRAME 10

One time constant after the inductor shown in Figure 12.51 is connected to the dc source, the current through the coil will be __________ percent of its maximum value. After __________ time constants or longer, the coil current is assumed to have reached its maximum value. If the source is removed and the coil is then short circuited, after one time constant the current through the short circuit will be about __________ percent of its maximum value.

a. 63.2; 5; 36.8 (11)
b. Any other answers, review Section B.4.

FRAME 11

The sparking that can occur when an inductive circuit is quickly disconnected from its source is due to __________ .

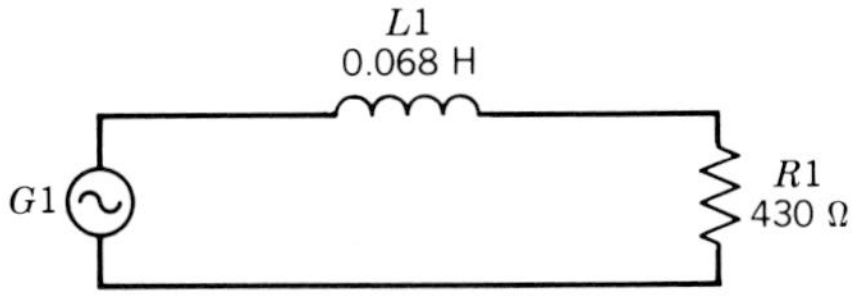

Figure 12.52 Circuit for Frame 13.

a. Inductive kick; or, self-induction. (12)
b. Any other answer, review Section B.5 and go on to Frame 12.

FRAME 12

An ac potential difference with a peak value of 5 V and a frequency of 150 Hz is applied to a circuit composed of a resistor of 1500 Ω and a 3-H inductor with a resistance of 100 Ω. Write an expression for the current through the circuit as a function of time. What is the phase angle of the current with respect to the potential difference?

a. $i = 1.53 \sin(942.48t + \theta)$ mA; $\theta = 60.5°$. (13)
b. Any other answer, review Section B.6.

FRAME 13

The phase angle of the current in the series circuit shown in Figure 12.52 is 45°. What is the frequency of the source?

a. 1006 Hz or about 1 kHz. (14)
b. Any other answer, review Section B.7 and go on to Frame 14.

FRAME 14

Figure 12.53 shows an arrangement of three 3-H inductors. Draw in a set of connecting wires so that the equivalent inductance obtained is 2 H.

Figure 12.53 Figure for Frame 14.

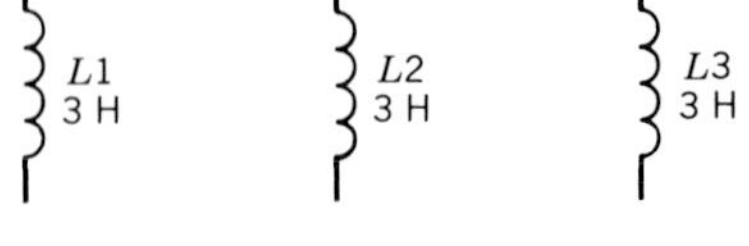

a. Any arrangement that connects two of the inductors in series and the third in parallel with the series connection. (15)
b. Any other answer, review Section B.7 and go on to Frame 15.

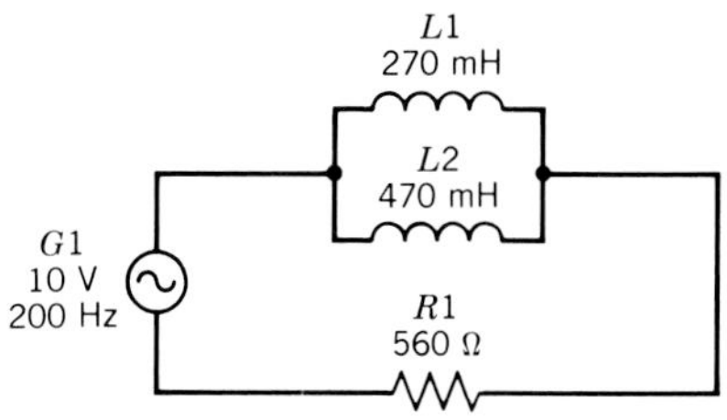

Figure 12.54 Circuit for Frame 15.

FRAME 15

What is the total impedance of the network in Figure 12.54?

a. 599.36 Ω (16)
b. Any other answer, review Section B.9.

FRAME 16

The letter b in the expression $\log_b N$ specifies the __________ of the logarithm.

a. Base. (17)
b. Any other answer, review Section C.1.

FRAME 17

Natural, or Naperian, logarithms are logarithms to the base __________, a constant equal to 2.718281 . . . and are indicated by the abbreviation __________.

a. ϵ; ln. (18)
b. Any other answer, review Section C.1.

FRAME 18

Audio and power frequency inductors generally have inductances ranging from __________ to __________ H, and a ferromagnetic core composed of __________.

a. 0.1; 10; plates or laminations. (19)
b. Any other answer, review Section D.1.1 and go on to Frame 19.

FRAME 19

List three failure modes of audio and power frequency inductors.

a. Open circuit, short circuit between turns, and short circuit between turns and core. (20)
b. Any answer that does not include all three concepts, review Section D.1.1.

FRAME 20

The component used to prevent high-frequency signals from being distributed throughout an electronic unit via the power wiring is called a __________ __________ __________ or __________. Ferrite beads are sometimes used for this.

a. Radio-frequency choke or rf choke; RFC. (21)
b. Any other answer, review Section D.1.2 and go on to Frame 21.

FRAME 21

What are the inductances of the coils shown in Figures 12.55*a* and 12.55*b*?

Figure 12.55 Figure for Frame 21.

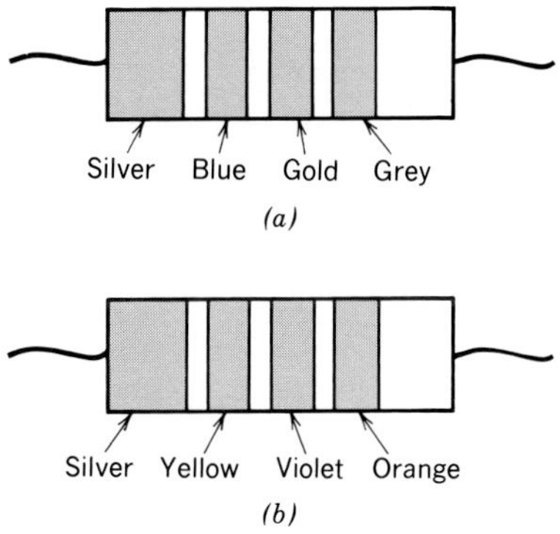

a. 6.8 μH, 47,000 μH (or 47 mH) (22)
b. Any other answer, review Figure 12.44.

FRAME 22

The effect that occurs when a direct current through an inductor causes all the magnetic domains in the inductor core to remain aligned in one direction regardless of the polarity of the alternating current through the coil is referred to as __________.

a. Saturation. (23)
b. Any other answer, review Section D.2.

FRAME 23

The ratio of the inductive reactance of a coil at a particular frequency to its resistance is called __________.

a. Q (25)
b. Any other answer, review Section D.2 and go on to Frame 24.

FRAME 24

A 270-mH inductor with a resistance of 80 Ω is operating in a 120-Hz circuit. What is the Q of the inductor?

a. 2.54 (25)
b. Any other answer, review Section D.2.

FRAME 25

Hard iron inductor cores tend to remain magnetized even when the magnetizing current in an ac circuit has dropped to zero. This causes power losses called ___________ losses.

a. Hysteresis. (26)
b. Any other answer, review Section D.3.

FRAME 26

An F 68–2 toroidal core has an outside diameter of ___________ and is composed of a type ___________ material.

a. 0.68 in.; 2 ferrite. (27)
b. Any other answer, review Section D.3 and go on to Frame 27.

FRAME 27

Ferrite toroids normally have a ___________ appearance, while powdered iron toroids appear to be ___________.

a. Dull grey; glazed. (END)
b. Any other answer, review Section D.3.

E. PROBLEMS FOR SOLUTION OR RESEARCH

1. Calculate the following quantities:

a. log 268	g. log 55.8
b. $\log^{-1}(3 \times 10^{-7})$	h. $\log^{-1} -1$
c. $\log^{-1} 0$	i. log 3459
d. log 2.767	j. log 0.07
e. $\log^{-1} 1$	k. $\log^{-1} 0.0038$
f. $\log(8.76 \times 10^{3})$	l. log −4

2. Calculate:

a. ln 268	b. $\log_{\epsilon} 3 \times 10^{-7}$	c. $\ln^{-1} 0$
d. ln 2.767	e. $\ln^{-1} 1$	f. $\ln^{-1} 0.3$
g. $\log_{\epsilon} 55.8$	h. $\ln^{-1} -1$	i. ln 3459
j. $\log_{\epsilon} 0.07$	k. $\ln^{-1} 0.0038$	l. ln −4

3. Calculate log ϵ and divide your answer to Problem 1a by this number. Is the result similar to the answer obtained from Problem 2a? Verify the principle involved here by dividing the answers to Problems 1b, 1c, and 1d by log ϵ.

4. Calculate ln 10 and divide your answer to problem 2a by this number. Is the result similar to the answer to Problem 1a? Can you formulate the results of Problems 3 and 4 into a general rule?

Hint: Try to write a formula relating the logarithm of a number to one base with the logarithm of that same number to another base.

5. How many turns of wire would be necessary to produce a 470-mH inductor if the wire is wound on a 0.0127-m diameter form 0.0254 m long without a core. Disregard the diameter of the wire.

6. What is the time constant of the network shown in Figure 12.56. If a 3.58-kHz, 5-V peak ac potential difference is supplied, what will the circuit current be? Draw a phasor diagram of the source potential and the circuit current.

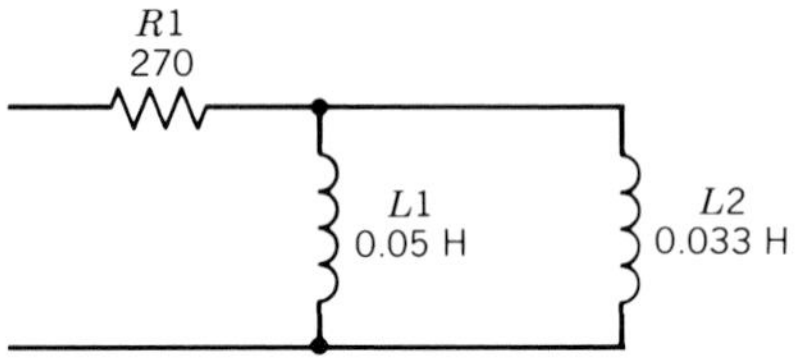

Figure 12.56 Circuit for Problem 6.

7. In the circuit shown in Figure 12.57, an ac source is connected to a network that causes the current to *lead* the potential difference by an angle of 30°. Networks of this type are called *capacitive networks,* and will be studied in Chapter 14. An inductor with a 100 Ω resistance is added in series with the circuit, and the source potential difference and circuit current are then found to be in phase. What is the value of the inductance added? What is the Q of the inductor?

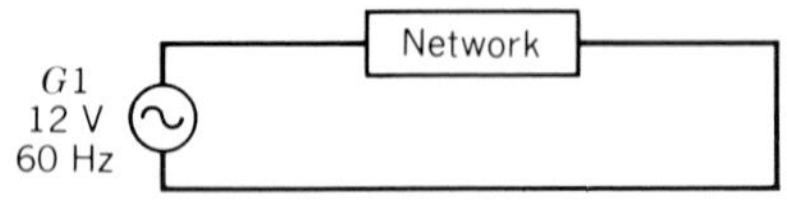

Figure 12.57 Circuit for Problem 7.

8. Engineer Vardis suspects that one of the coils in the schematic of Figure 12.58 is not operating properly although none of them appears burned out or completely short circuited. Describe a method that Vardis can use to determine whether this is true without disassembling the network.

Hint: Lengths of wire can be used to short circuit some of the components for the time necessary to make observations. Disregard the resistance of the coils.

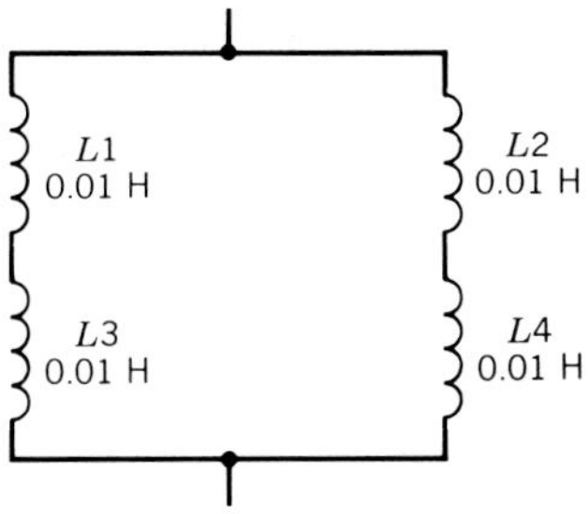

Figure 12.58 Network for Problem 8.

9. Calculate the current and the phase angle in the circuit shown in Figure 12.59. Draw a phasor diagram for the circuit.

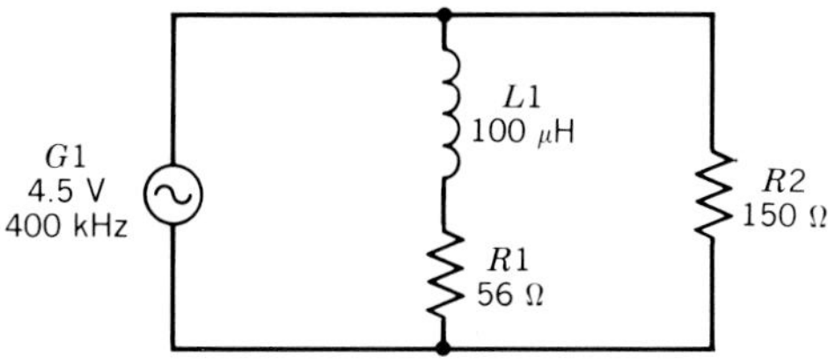

Figure 12.59 Circuit for Problem 9.

10. Try to write an expression for the instantaneous current through $R2$ in Figure 12.60.

Hint: Consider each source independently.

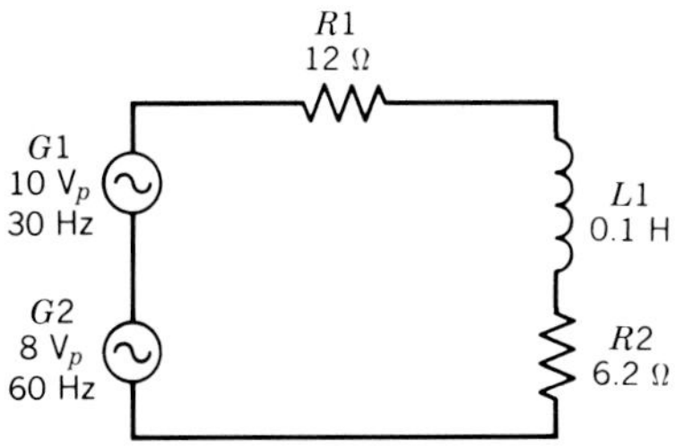

Figure 12.60 Circuit for Problem 10.

CHAPTER 13 INDUCTIVE CIRCUITS AND TRANSFORMERS

A. CHAPTER PREVIEW

1 In this chapter, you will continue your study of the effects of inductors in both series and parallel circuits with a variety of sources, including square-wave and pulse generators.

2 The concept of Q, which you learned about in regard to components, will be extended to both parallel and series circuits.

3 The interaction of two magnetically coupled inductances will be studied, both as a preparation for the study of transformers, and as a practical requirement for the troubleshooting of inductive circuits.

4 The transformer effect will be presented from the points of view of energy transfer and the principles underlying the operation of practical transformers. Output variation under varying load conditions and impedance matching will be considered.

5 The Examples and Computations section of this chapter introduces the concept of the *j* operator, which simplifies the mathematical work of calculating potential differences and currents in complex circuits. The applications of mathematical analysis to complex waveforms and practice with transformer calculations are also included.

6 The Applications section of this chapter covers the types, characteristics, and failure modes of power-, audio-frequency, and radio-frequency transformers.

B. PRINCIPLES

B.1 COMPOSITE AC AND DC SOURCES IN *RL* CIRCUITS

In Chapter 12 the effects of dc and ac sources on inductive circuits were considered separately. In many electronic circuits, however, the potential and current waveforms consist of a combination of a complex ac signal and a dc power source. The ac signal may be the product of a microphone responding to a human voice, as shown in Figure 13.1*a*, or a changing potential level caused by the variations in the speed of a tachometer coupled to a motor shaft as in Figure 13.1*b*. These signals are waveforms whose amplitude, frequency, or phase is proportional to a factor such as the vibrations due to speech or the speed of the motor. Signals of this sort can assume any value between some maximum and some minimum, and are called *analog* signals. Earlier in this book, it was mentioned that any complex, nonsinusoidal waveform could be thought of as a combination of dc level and a variety of sine waves. For this reason, it is useful to be able to calculate current, phase angles, and potential drops in circuits with sources that provide ac signals combined with some dc level.

The method of doing this involves using the separation of the dc and ac components of the source signal. Figure 13.2 shows how a complex source *G* can be redrawn as a combination of a dc source and one or more sine-wave ac sources of differing frequency, amplitude, and phase.

After the transient state has passed, as you will recall, an inductor provides only resistance to a dc

Figure 13.1 Examples of analog signal generation.

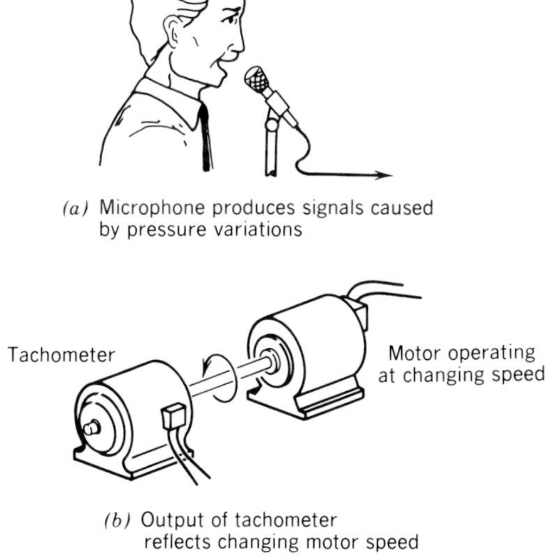

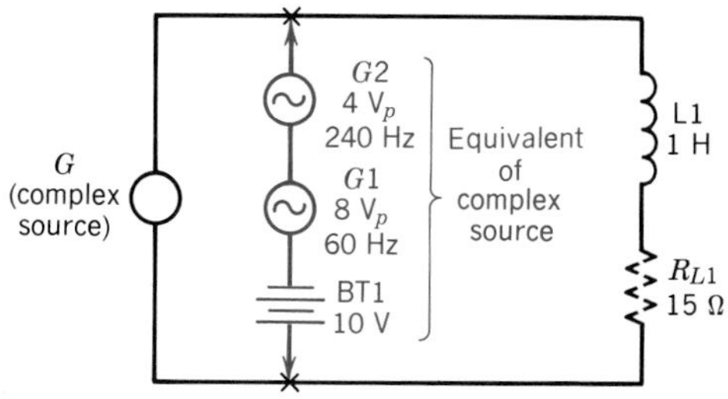

Figure 13.2 A source with a complex waveform is replaced by an equivalent source consisting of a dc source and several sine-wave sources of different frequency and phase.

source. The equivalent dc circuit of Figure 13.2 with sources *G*1 and *G*2 short circuited is shown in Figure 13.3. The circuit with BT1 and *G*2 short circuited is shown in Figure 13.4. In the circuit of Figure 13.4, the *RL* network can not be thought of as a resistor, as it was in the previous case. On the other hand, when the *impedance* is considered, an analysis of this circuit becomes possible. The impedance of this circuit is equal to the phasor sum of the reactance of *L*1 and the resistance of its coil, R_{L1}, as shown in the phasor diagram in Figure 13.4. From Formula 12.10,

$$X_L = 2\pi f L = 376.99\ \Omega$$

so that the magnitude of the impedance is

$$Z = \sqrt{R^2 + X_L^2} = 377.3\ \Omega$$

as you can see from the phasor diagram in Figure 13.4, the phase angle θ between the reference phasor and the impedance phasor is

$$\theta = \tan^{-1}\frac{X_L}{R} = 87.7°$$

This is also the angle between the circuit current and source potential difference. Therefore, it is possible to write

$$i_p = \frac{E_p}{z}\sin(2\pi f t - \theta)$$

Figure 13.3 The equivalent source and circuit of Figure 13.2 with *G*1 and *G*2 shorted.

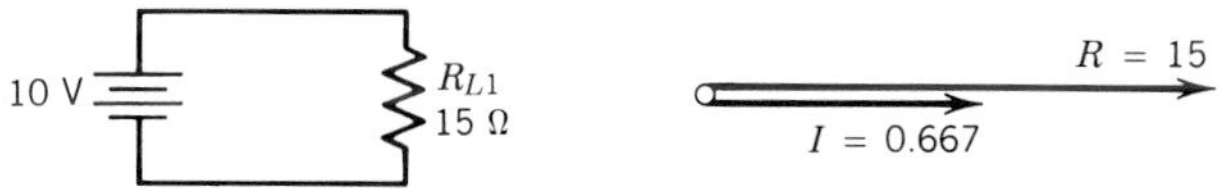

Figure 13.4 The equivalent source and circuit of Figure 13.2 with BT1 and *G*2 shorted.

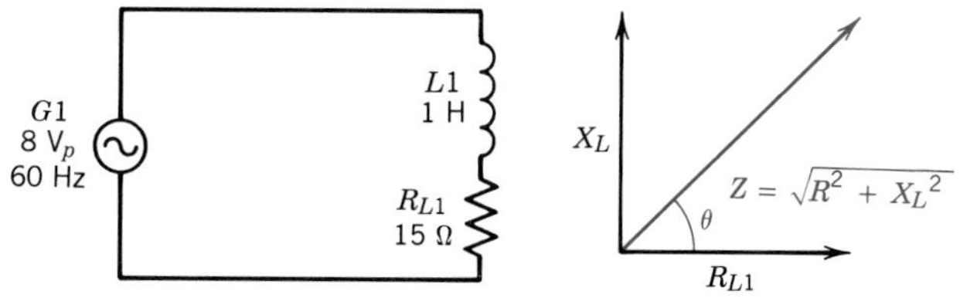

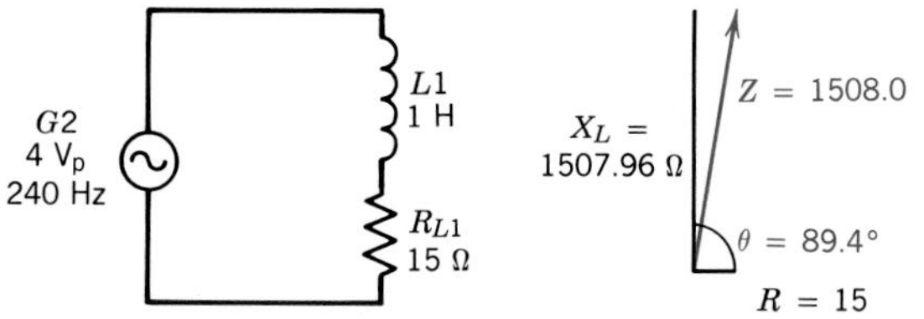

Figure 13.5 The equivalent source and circuit of Figure 13.2 with BT1 and $G1$ shorted.

Substituting values,

$$i_p = \frac{8}{377.3} \sin (377t - 87.7°)$$
$$= 0.021 \sin(377t - 87.7°)$$

When only $G2$ is considered as in Figure 13.5, the inductive reactance is $X_L = 2\pi fL = 1507.96\ \Omega$. The impedance is

$$Z = \sqrt{(15)^2 + (1507.96)^2} = 1508.0\ \Omega$$

and the phase angle is

$$\theta = \tan^{-1} \frac{X_L}{R} = 89.4°$$

Therefore, considering $G2$ only, the circuit current is

$$i_p = \frac{E_p}{Z} \sin(2\pi ft - \theta)$$
$$= 0.0027 \sin(1507.96t - 89.4°)$$

The circuit current with the complex source is then the phasor sum of the three currents:

$$i_{\text{total}} = 0.667 + 0.021 \sin (377t - 87.7°)$$
$$+ 0.0027 \sin (1507.96t - 89.4°)$$

There is no convenient way in which these expressions can be simplified, since the two sine terms are at different frequencies. An alternate method of analyzing circuits using the mathematical operator j is introduced in Section C.3.

The currents due to the dc and ac components of a complex source can be calculated separately, and the results can then be combined to produce a mathematical expression for the circuit current. It is quite common to find a sinusoid of some frequency combined with another sinusoid at a frequency that is a whole-number multiple of the first. Often, there is also a dc component.

The previous example involved a complex condition where the generator provided a dc component and ac components of different frequencies. In cases where there are only ac components of the same frequency, these can be added by phasor methods to reduce the source waveform to a simpler equivalent source.

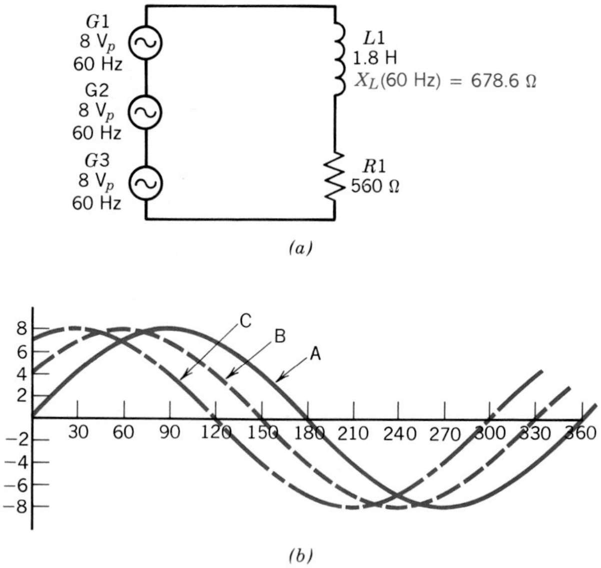

Figure 13.6 A circuit with three sources with the same frequency but different phase angles.

EXAMPLE:

The input to the circuit shown in Figure 13.6*a* consists of three 60-Hz potential differences having a peak value of 8 V. The second leads the first by 30°, while the third leads the first by 60°, as shown in Figure 13.6*b*. Determine the total circuit current and draw a phasor diagram showing the relationship of the applied potential differences and the current through $L1$. ■

SOLUTION:

A convenient way to start work on this problem is to draw a phasor diagram of the input potential difference. This is done in Figure 13.7. Since all three potential differences are sine waves of the same frequency, they can be added together using the methods introduced in Section 10.C.1. The resultant phasor, as shown, has a length of 21.86-V and a phase angle of 30°. The total

Figure 13.7 Phasor diagram of the sources in Figure 13.6.

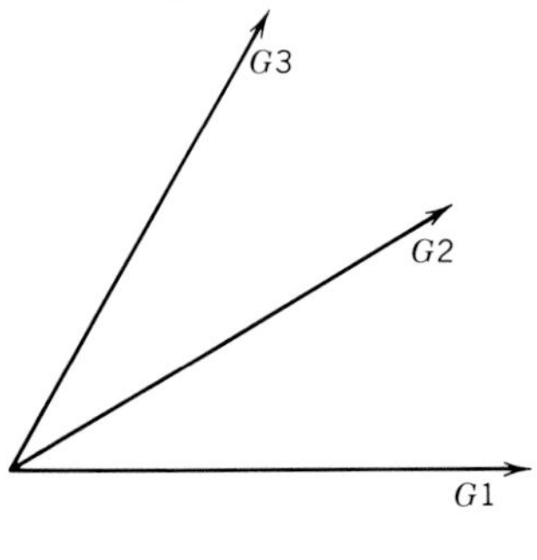

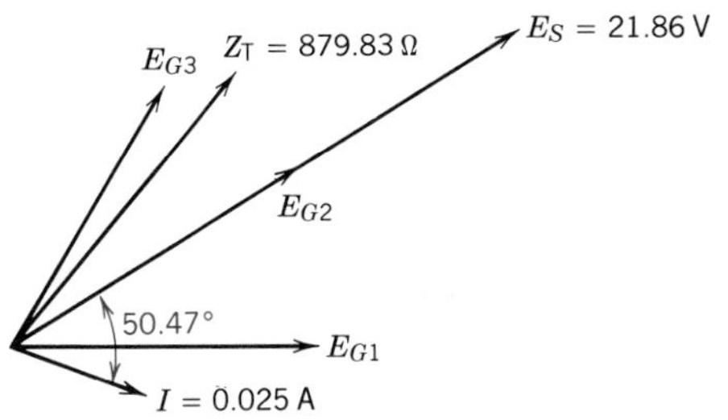

Figure 13.8 Phasor relationships of the applied potential differences and current in the circuit of Figure 13.7.

impedance of this circuit is

$$Z = \sqrt{560^2 + 678.6^2} = 879.83\ \Omega$$

at a phase angle of

$$\theta = \tan^{-1}\frac{678.6}{560} = 50.47^\circ$$

This is also the phase angle by which the equivalent source potential difference leads the current. The magnitude of the current is

$$I_p = \frac{21.86}{879.83} = 0.025\ \text{A}$$

The phasor diagram is shown in Figure 13.8. In most phasor diagrams involving series circuits, the circuit current is taken as the reference. To use the current as the reference in this case would require the E and I phasors to be rotated in a counterclockwise direction. (Remember, that although it is customary and convenient to use the circuit current as the reference phasor in series circuit analysis, there is no reason why some other phasor could not be used. As long as the phase angles are preserved, the phasor diagrams are equivalent. Figure 13.8 uses the potential difference of $G1$ as its reference.) ■

B.2 SQUARE WAVES AND PULSES IN INDUCTIVE CIRCUITS

In contrast to the complex analog signals discussed in the previous section, the waveforms found in computer logic circuits are called *digital signals*. Waveforms of this type do not freely assume any value between an upper and lower limit, as do analog waveforms. In general, digital signals are at one of two values, either maximum or minimum, and change from one value to the other quickly. The square waves, pulses, and complex pulse train shown in Figure 13.9 are examples of digital signals.

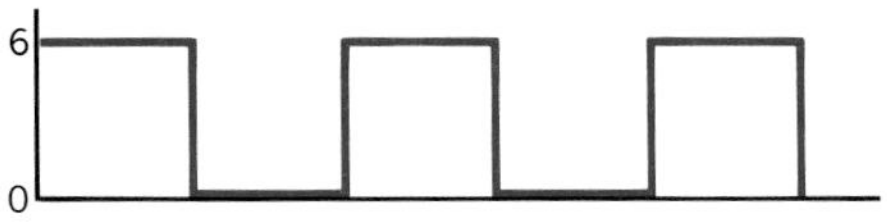

(a) Square wave

(b) Pulses

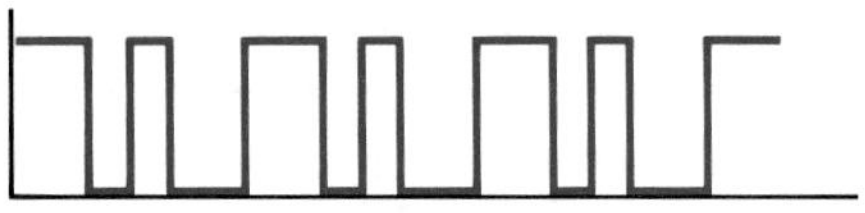

(c) Pulse train

Figure 13.9 Examples of digital signals.

When a potential difference whose waveform resembles those in Figure 13.9 is applied to a circuit containing an inductance, the waveform of the current through the inductor will not resemble the waveform of the potential difference, as it does when the applied potential difference is a sinusoid. You can readily understand that this will be the case because the waveforms shown in Figure 13.9 are marked by rapid changes in potential differences, as shown in Figure 13.10. Since it is the property of inductance to resist rapid changes in circuit current, the waveform of the current through the series circuit shown in Figure 13.11*a* will resemble that shown in Figure 13.11*b* when the applied potential has a waveform like that shown in Figure 13.9*a*.

A better understanding can be obtained by considering a square wave or any repetitive series of pulses as made up of a combination of sinusoidal functions of different amplitude and frequency. First mentioned in Chapter 9, this method is known as *Fourier analysis* (pronounced *Fáu-re-ay*). Using Fourier analysis, any periodic wave can be thought of as the sum of a dc component and a number of sinusoids with frequencies that are multiples of the frequency of the waveform being analyzed. Since it is based on a branch of ad-

Figure 13.10 Magnified view of the square wave of Figure 13.9a showing rapid changes in potential difference.

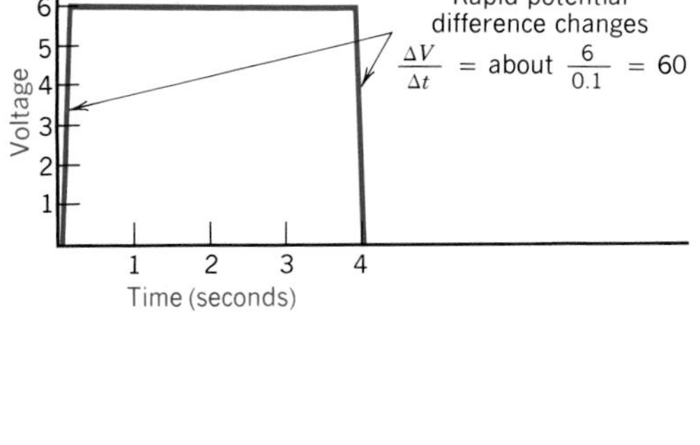

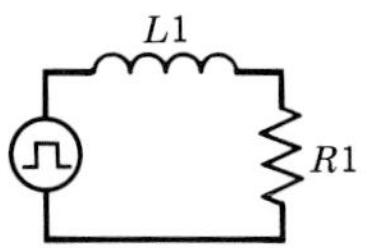

(a) Circuit with square-wave source

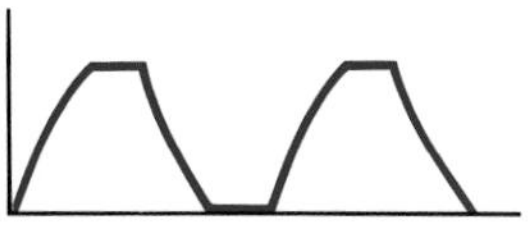

(b) Circuit current (long time constant)

Figure 13.11 Response of an *RL* circuit to square-wave input.

vanced mathematics called *integral calculus*, a complete explanation of Fourier analysis is beyond the scope of this book, though this analytic tool is frequently used in the design and analysis of electronic equipment. Even the use of a small computer is not sufficient to make it possible for the beginning student to determine the frequencies and amplitudes of the sinusoids that make up complex waveforms. On the other hand, it is an easy matter to learn the formulas for amplitudes and frequencies of the sinusoids that compose the most common digital waveforms or nonsinusoidal waveforms.

For the square wave, the formula is

$$E_n = \frac{2E_p}{n\pi} \qquad \text{FORMULA 13.1}$$

where E_p is the peak-to-peak amplitude of the component whose frequency is n times the frequency of the square wave, and n is an odd integer.

For example, a square wave with a peak amplitude of 6 V and a frequency of 30 Hz can be thought of as the combination of a dc level and 30, 90, 150, and 180 Hz sine waves of different amplitude. Using Formula 13.1,

$$E_1 = \frac{2 \times 6}{1 \times \pi} = 3.82 \ \ (30\text{ Hz})$$

$$E_3 = \frac{2 \times 6}{3 \times \pi} = 1.27 \ \ (90\text{ Hz})$$

$$E_5 = \frac{2 \times 6}{5 \times \pi} = 0.76 \ \ (150\text{ Hz})$$

$$E_7 = \frac{2 \times 6}{7 \times \pi} = 0.55 \ \ (210\text{ Hz})$$

$$\vdots$$

Putting this into the form of an equation:

$$e = \text{dc value} + 3.82 \sin(188.5t) + 1.27 \sin(565.5t) + 0.76 \sin(942.5t) + 0.55 \sin(1319.5t) + \cdots$$

The dc component of the Fourier series is obtained by obtaining a mathematical quantity called "the integral of the waveform over a complete cycle." In spite of this complex name, the process involved is fairly simple for most waveforms. First, one cycle of the waveform of the potential difference is drawn, as shown in Figure 13.12. Then, the area between the negative portion of the waveform and the axis is calculated. This quantity is subtracted from the area between the positive portion of the waveform and the axis. This difference is divided by the period of one complete cycle. In mathematical terms, this is summarized as

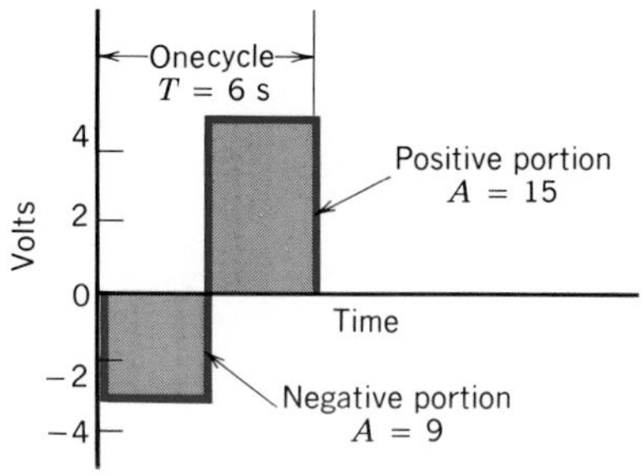

Figure 13.12 Calculating the dc component of a waveform.

$$E_{dc} = \frac{A_{plus} - A_{minus}}{T} \qquad \text{FORMULA 13.2}$$

EXAMPLE:
Determine the value of the dc component of the square wave shown in Figure 13.12. ■

SOLUTION:
Using Formula 13.2, the area between the negative portion of the waveform and axis is 9 volt·seconds. The area between the positive portion of the waveform and the axis is 15 volt·seconds. Substituting these values and the period in Formula 13.2 produces

$$E_{dc} = \frac{15 - 9}{6} = 1 \text{ V}$$

The dc component in the Fourier analysis of this waveform is 1 V. ■

In cases where the waveform lies wholly above the x axis or wholly below it, it is convenient to move the axis itself before using Formula 13.2, as shown in Figures 13.13*a* and 13.13*b*. Simply record the number of volts of *offset*, that is, the distance and direction in which the axis was moved, and add this value to the calculated E_{dc}. Moving the axis upward is a positive offset; moving it downward is a negative offset.

Combining the methods used to perform Fourier analyses shown in Formulas 13.1 and 13.2, it is possible to calculate the dc and ac components of any square-wave signal. For example, the square wave shown in

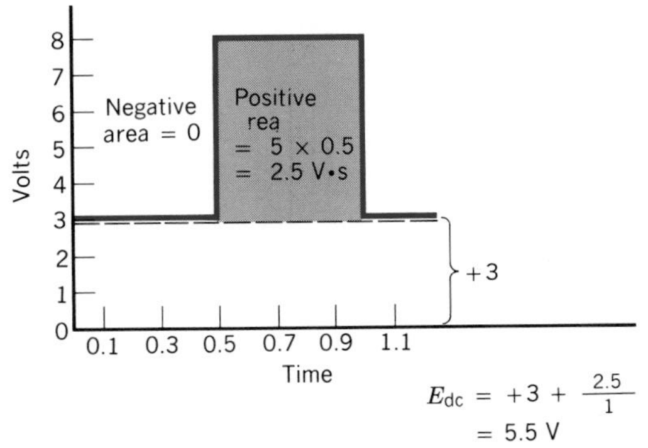

(a) When the waveform is always above the axis

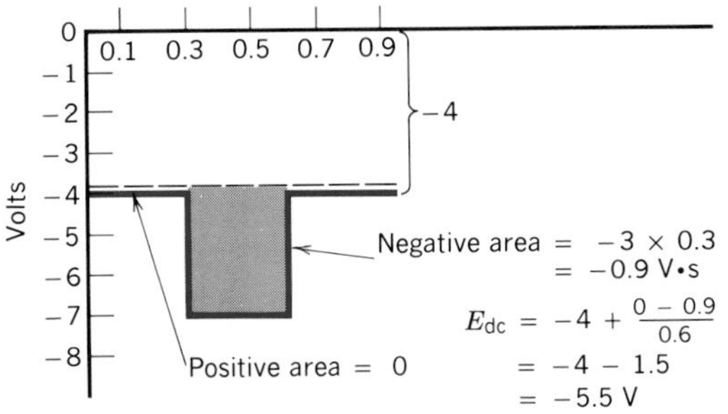

(b) When the waveform is always below the axis

Figure 13.13 The dc component when the waveform is wholly above or below the axis.

Figure 13.14 can be thought of as a combination of a dc component of

$$E_{dc} = \frac{2.4 - 1.2}{1.2} = 1 \text{ V}$$

and a *fundamental*, or lowest frequency, sine wave with a peak value of

$$E_1 = \frac{2 \times 6}{\pi} = 3.82 \sin(5.24t)$$

The next sine-wave component in the series has a frequency three times that of the fundamental, called the *third harmonic*. Its peak amplitude is

$$E_3 = \frac{2 \times 6}{3\pi} = 1.27 \sin(15.71t)$$

Calculating a number of higher-frequency odd harmonics,

$$E_5 = 0.76 \sin(26.2t)$$

$$E_7 = 0.55 \sin(36.7t)$$

$$E_9 = 0.42 \sin(47.2t)$$

Although this process could be extended to calculate higher and higher frequency harmonics, it is generally sufficient to calculate the dc component and five or six of the ac terms. The analysis of the waveform in Figure 13.14 is

$$e = E_{dc} + E_1\sin(2\pi ft) + E_3\sin(2\pi ft) + E_5\sin(2\pi ft) + E_7\sin(2\pi ft) + E_9\sin(2\pi ft)$$

or

$$e = 1 + 3.82 \sin(5.24t) + 1.27 \sin(15.71t) + 0.76 \sin(26.2t) + 0.55 \sin(36.7t) + 0.42 \sin(47.2t)$$

Adding the instantaneous values of these sine functions and the dc component graphically produces a waveform *similar* to the square wave in Figure 13.14. Calculating and adding the instantaneous values of additional sine terms would produce a waveform closer to that of the original square wave. In order to produce a waveform exactly like the original, a large number of ac harmonics would have to be calculated and added. For most practical purposes, however, it is possible to ignore any terms with peak amplitudes less than 5 percent of the peak amplitude of the original waveform.

Once you have performed a Fourier analysis on a given waveform, it is possible to accurately calculate the response of an inductive circuit to a source signal with this waveform. For example, if the waveform in Figure 13.14 represents the potential difference produced by the source in Figure 13.15, you can calculate the current through $L1$ due to each of the source components separately. Adding these currents by graphical means would then make it possible to draw the waveform of the current through $L1$.

EXAMPLE:
Draw a graph of the current through $L1$ in Figure 13.15 when the source potential difference is a square wave whose waveform is shown in Figure 13.14. ■

Figure 13.14 One cycle of a square wave for analysis.

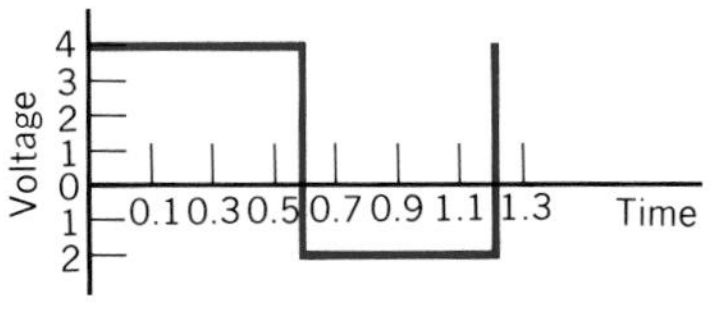

Figure 13.15 The square wave of Figure 13.14 applied to an RL circuit.

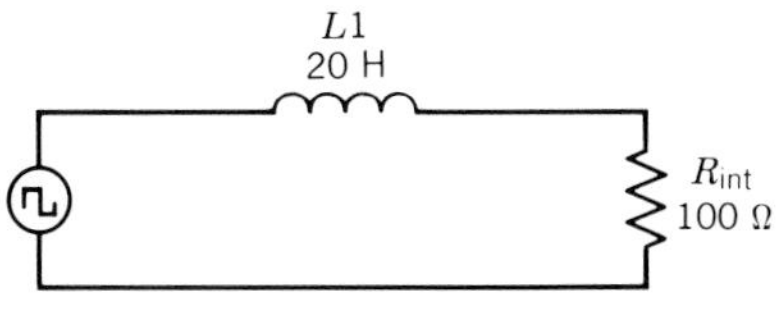

SOLUTION:
The waveform of the current through $L1$ is the sum of the currents through $L1$ due to each of the components, which can be thought of as separate voltage sources connected in series. First, consider the dc component. The dc component of the waveform is +1 V.

Again looking at the diagram of the waveform, you can see that the peak-to-peak amplitude is 6 V and the period is 1.2 s. Using Formula 13.1 and calculating the first four odd harmonics,

$$E_1 = 3.82 \sin(5.24t)$$

$$E_3 = 1.27 \sin(15.71t)$$

$$E_5 = 0.76 \sin(26.2t)$$

$$E_7 = 0.55 \sin(36.7t)$$

As in the examples in the previous section, each of these components can be though of as an ac generator. Now it is quite an easy matter to determine the current and phase angle due to the potential difference of each source component. After the transient state following the connection of the source has passed, the current through R_{int} and $L1$ is

$$I_{\text{dc}} = \frac{E}{R} = \frac{1}{100} = 0.01 \text{ A}$$

Because the circuit contains inductive reactance as well as the internal resistance of the inductor, each of the ac components of the potential difference will find a different circuit impedance. The circuit impedance for the fundamental, that is, the sine wave whose frequency is the same as the input square wave, is

$$Z_{f_1} = \sqrt{(R_{\text{int}})^2 + (2\pi f_1 L)^2} = 144.8\ \Omega$$

The instantaneous current through the circuit due to this component of the source potential is

$$i_{f_1} = \frac{e_{f_1}}{Z_{f_1}} = 0.026 \sin(2\pi f t + \theta)$$
$$= 0.026 \sin(5.24\text{t} + \theta)$$

The phase angle is

$$\theta = \tan^{-1}\frac{2\pi f_1 L}{R} = \tan^{-1}\frac{104.7}{100} = 46.3°$$

Repeating the same calculations for two of the higher-frequency components produces:

$$i_{f_3} = 0.0039 \sin(15.7t + \theta) \qquad \theta = 72.34°$$

$$i_{f_5} = 0.0014 \sin(26.2t + \theta) \qquad \theta = 79.19°$$

You now have an expression for the circuit current and phase angle due to each of the components of the square wave. It is then possible to draw each component of the circuit current on a graph and add the values at a number of points to produce the current waveform. ■

The waveform of the solution to this example used only the dc, ac fundmental, and two of the higher harmonics, so it will not be as accurate a representation of the actual waveform as an oscilloscope trace. Note that in working out this example, the impedances and phase shifts of the currents are considerably greater for the higher-frequency harmonics than for the ac fundamental. Because of this, the circuit current due to the higher-frequency components is small, and this effect is called *high-frequency attenuation*. Practical applications of this effect will be covered in detail in Chapter 17.

In the past this method of calculating circuit currents or potential differences, like many of the circuit analyses techniques covered in Chapters 7 and 8, were avoided by technicians because of fear of the mathematics involved. Where quite complicated waveforms are involved, this method does present difficulties. However, modern electronic units make frequent use of square-wave, ramp, and triangle signals that can be easily resolved into dc and ac components, as shown in Figure 13.16. In each case the formula for the ac harmonics is given beneath the waveform. The value of the dc component is calculated in the same way as

Figure 13.16 Common waveforms and formulas for calculating component coefficients.

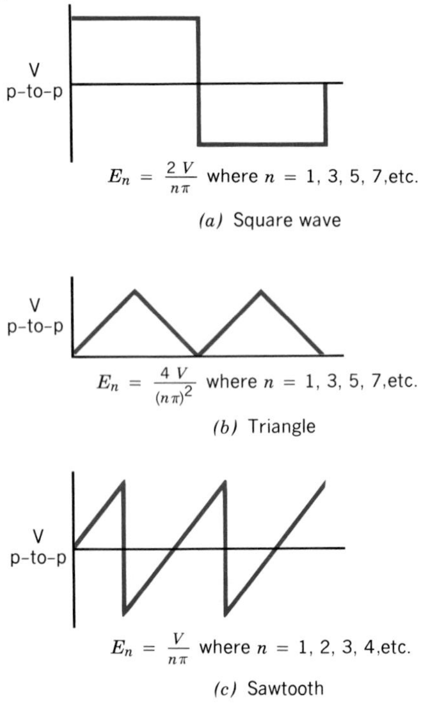

for the square wave in the previous example. When you are required to deal with a waveform unlike those pictured in Figure 13.16, a device called a *spectrum analyzer* can be used to provide a CRT display of the amplitudes and frequencies that comprise the waveform.

B.3 Q IN CIRCUITS AND CIRCUIT BRANCHES

In Chapter 12, the concept of the *quality* or Q of inductive components was introduced. As a final topic in the discussion of self-induction, it is necessary to extend this concept to parts of circuits or to entire circuits. Recall that the formula for the Q of an inductor was given as

$$Q = \frac{2\pi f L}{R_L}$$

where R_L is the resistance of the coil itself. If a resistor is placed in series with the coil, as shown in Figure 13.17, it is possible to refer to the Q of the entire circuit composed of the resistor, the coil, and the internal resistance of the coil. As far as the circuit is concerned, there is no difference between the resistance of the resistor and that of the coil. Therefore, the Q of the series circuit is

$$Q = \frac{2\pi f L}{R_L + R_S} = 1.57$$

In general terms, the Q of a series circuit is

$$Q = \frac{2\pi f L_{\text{circuit}}}{R_{\text{circuit}}} \qquad \text{FORMULA 13.3}$$

EXAMPLE:
When the source frequency in a circuit containing only an inductor is 400 kHz, the Q of a 5-mH coil is found to be 83.78. For certain purposes, this is found to be too high. What value resistor can be inserted in series with the coil to reduce the circuit Q to 50.27? ■

Figure 13.17 An *RL* circuit, a circuit with an inductor and resistor.

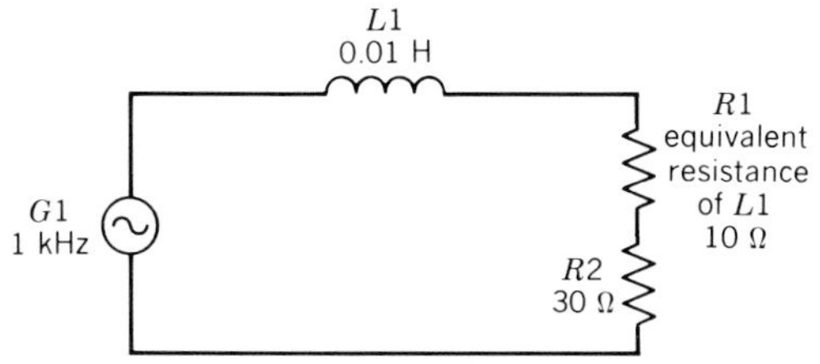

SOLUTION:
This problem can be solved in two steps. First, the resistance of the coil itself must be calculated. This is done by substituting the known values into Formula 13.3.

$$Q = \frac{2\pi f L}{R_{\text{coil}}} \quad \text{or} \quad 2\pi f L = QR_{\text{coil}}$$

Therefore,

$$12566.37 = 83.78R_{\text{coil}} \quad \text{and}$$
$$R_{\text{coil}} = 149.99 \quad \text{or} \quad 150\ \Omega$$

Once the internal resistance is known, the value of the series resistor can be calculated using Formula 13.3 and the fact the the circuit resistance is the sum of the resistance of the coil and the series resistor. In other words,

$$Q_{\text{circuit}} = \frac{2\pi f L}{R_{\text{coil}} + R} \quad \text{or} \quad \frac{12566.37}{150 + R} = 50.27$$

Solving for R,

$$R = 12566.37 = 7540.5 + 50.27R$$
$$R = 99.98\ \Omega$$

A resistance of about 100 Ω will have to be placed in series with the coil to reduce the Q of the combination to 50.27. ■

To find the Q of a series *circuit containing inductances and resistances, divide the inductive reactance of the series circuit by the sum of the circuit resistances.*

As pointed out in Chapter 12, the resistance of high-frequency coils tends to be rather low. Because of this, circuits resembling that shown in Figure 13.18 are common. This figure shows a parallel network composed of a coil and a resistor connected across an rf source. Because the resistance of the coil is low, and its inductive reactance is high at radio frequencies, the Q of the coil itself will be quite high (62.8 in the component shown). In contrast to the series circuit, where increasing the value of the series resistance reduces the current through the coil, in a parallel circuit, increasing the value of the parallel resistor increases the current through the coil.

Since the Q of an *RL* circuit is a comparison of the resistance and inductive reactance effects in the circuit, you can see that this comparison in a parallel circuit will be different from that in a series circuit.

In fact, in the circuit shown in Figure 13.18, where the resistance of the coil is less than one-tenth of the

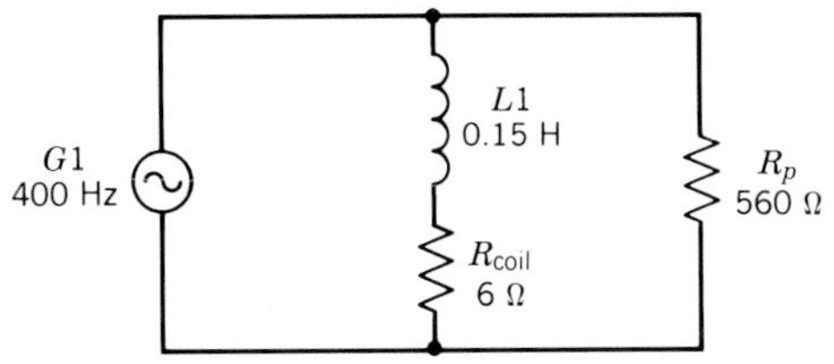

Figure 13.18 A parallel *RL* circuit.

inductive reactance, and the parallel resistance is less than 10 times the inductive reactance, the circuit Q is approximately

$$Q = \frac{R_{\text{parallel}}}{2\pi f L} \qquad \text{FORMULA 13.4}$$

In other words, in this parallel circuit, the circuit Q is equal to the resistance of the parallel branch containing R_P divided by the inductive reactance of $L1$, or

$$Q = \frac{R_P}{2\pi f L} = 1.49$$

EXAMPLE:
An *RL* circuit with a Q of 45 is required for operation in a 50-kHz circuit. The coil to be used has an inductance of 1 mH and an internal resistance of 1.8 Ω. What is the value of the resistor that would have to be placed in parallel with this coil to produce the required *RL* circuit? ■

SOLUTION:
The first step in solving this problem is to calculate the inductive reactance of the 1-mH coil at a frequency of 50 kHz. This will be $X_L = 2\pi f L = 314.16\ \Omega$. Clearly, a coil resistance of 1.8 Ω is less than one-tenth of the inductive reactance at this frequency. The coil resistance can therefore be ignored, and Formula 13.4 can be used. Substituting the known values,

$$Q = \frac{R_p}{2\pi f L} \quad \text{or} \quad 45 = \frac{R_p}{314.16} \quad R_p = 14137.2\ \Omega$$

Using standard values, $R_p = 15\ \text{k}\Omega$. ■

Remember, different formulas are used to calculate Q in series and parallel RL circuits. In a parallel circuit, where the internal resistance of the coil can be ignored and the parallel resistance is less than 10 times the inductive reactance, circuit Q *is given by*

$$Q = \frac{R_p}{2\pi f L}$$

Note that this formula is the reciprocal of the formula used to calculate the Q of a series circuit.

From Formula 13.4, it appears that the Q of a parallel circuit could be made any value desired by choosing the value of the parallel resistance accordingly. Actually, this is not the case, although many textbooks forget to mention this point. The reason for this is that the Q of a *RL* circuit containing both parallel and series resistance such as that shown in Figure 13.18 is given by the formula

$$Q = \frac{X_L}{R_s + \dfrac{(2\pi f L)^2}{R_P}} \qquad \text{FORMULA 13.5}$$

An easier to remember form of this is

$$Q = \frac{X_L}{R_s + \dfrac{X_L^2}{R_P}} \qquad \text{FORMULA 13.6}$$

Looking at Formula 13.6, you can see that if R_P is a very large number compared to X_L, the term $\dfrac{X_L^2}{R_P}$ will be a very small number, approaching zero as R_P is made larger and larger. In this case, the formula is reduced to

$$Q = \frac{X_L}{R_s + 0} \quad \text{or} \quad \frac{X_L}{R_s}$$

which is exactly the formula for the Q of an *RL* series circuit. In other words, when the resistance of the parallel resistor in an *RL* circuit is made much larger than X_L^2, the circuit Q approaches that of a series *RL* circuit.

EXAMPLE:
Calculate the Q of the circuit shown in Figure 13.19 when the parallel resistor R_P is 100 ohms and when it is 100 kΩ. ■

SOLUTION:
The first step in solving a problem of this type is to calculate the inductive reactance of the coil at its operating frequency. This is $X_L = 2\pi f L = 138.23$

Figure 13.19 When the parallel resistance is much greater than X_L^2, the Q of the circuit approaches $\dfrac{X_L}{R_s}$, the Q of the coil itself.

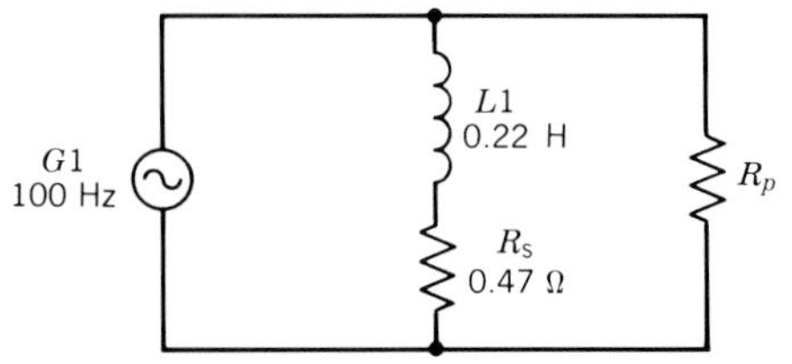

Ω. The coil resistance is less than one-tenth of the reactance, so it should be possible to ignore it, using either Formula 13.4 or 13.6. Both formulas should provide nearly the same value for Q. Using Formula 13.4,

$$Q = \frac{R_P}{X_L} = \frac{100}{138.23} = 0.723$$

With Formula 13.6,

$$Q = \frac{X_L}{R_s + \frac{X_L{}^2}{R_p}} = \frac{138.23}{0.47 + \frac{(138.23)^2}{100}} = 0.722$$

With a parallel resistance of 100 kΩ, on the other hand, the two formulas produce different values. Using Formula 13.4,

$$Q = \frac{R_P}{X_L} = \frac{100{,}000}{138.23} = 723.4$$

Using Formula 13.6,

$$Q = \frac{138.23}{0.47 + \frac{(138.23)^2}{1 \times 10^5}} = 209.1$$

In this case, Formula 13.4 provides a wrong value for Q. ■

Note that the circuit Q in the above example with a parallel resistance of 100 kΩ as calculated by Formula 13.6 is closer to the value $\frac{2\pi fL}{R_L} = 294.1$ when the value of the parallel resistor is much greater than $X_L{}^2$. Regardless of the value of the parallel resistor, however, if you look at the denominator of Formula 13.6, you will see that there is no positive value of R_P that will make the value of the denominator less than R_s. This means that $R_s + \frac{(X_L)^2}{R_P}$ will always be greater than R_s and the Q of an RL circuit will always be *less* than the Q of the inductor itself. This is an important point to keep in mind during later discussions of tuned circuits.

Table 13.1 provides a variational analysis of Formula 13.6. Notice that in the third line of the table the Q of the circuit approaches zero as R_p is made smaller and smaller. In line 4 you can see that if R_s (the resistance of the coil and any resistors that might be in series with the coil) approaches zero, the circuit Q approaches $\frac{R_P}{2\pi fL}$.

Table 13.1 A Variational Analysis of Formula 13.6

Condition	*Q*
1. Inductance $L1$ is increased	Decreases in most cases
2. Inductance $L1$ is decreased	Increases in most cases
3. R_p is decreased	Decreases to zero
4. R_p is increased	Increases to $\frac{X_L}{R_s}$
5. R_s is decreased	Increases to $\frac{R_p}{X_L}$
6. R_s is increased	Decreases to zero

B.4 COUPLING AND MUTUAL INDUCTANCE

Although the concepts of both mutual and self-inductance were introduced at the beginning of Chapter 12, the methods shown for determining the equivalents of inductors in series and in parallel have assumed that there was no magnetic linkage between the coils in the series or parallel network. In many circuits, extreme care is taken to prevent such linkage, by putting the coils at right angles to each other. If this is done, any expansion or collapse of the magnetic field around one would be, as far as the other coil is concerned, a relative motion parallel to the field. Recall that a parallel relative motion of the field would not induce a potential difference across the second coil. Grounded metal shields surrounding coils were formerly much used to prevent linkage, but today, winding the coils on toroidal cores or placing bobbin-wound coils in pot cores provides a better containment of the magnetic field without taking up as much space as shielding.

In rare cases, the linkage of flux between two series-connected coils is purposely used to produce a variable inductor. However, the use of such coils is limited to special applications, and the explanation of their function will not be stressed. The inductance of a pair of series-connected, mangetically linked coils such as those shown in Figure 13.20 is

$$L_{\text{total}} = L1 + L2 \pm 2k\sqrt{L1L2} \qquad \text{FORMULA 13.7}$$

Compare this formula with Formula 12.15, which is used for calculating the inductance of two series-connected coils that are not magnetically linked. The difference between the two formulas is the expression $\pm\, 2k\sqrt{L1L2}$, which accounts for the additional inductance due to the magnetic linking of the two coils in Formula 13.7. The constant k, called the *coefficient of coupling*, is some number less than one that represents the percentage of the flux from one coil that links with the other. A coefficient of coupling of 1 means that all the flux produced by each coil also links

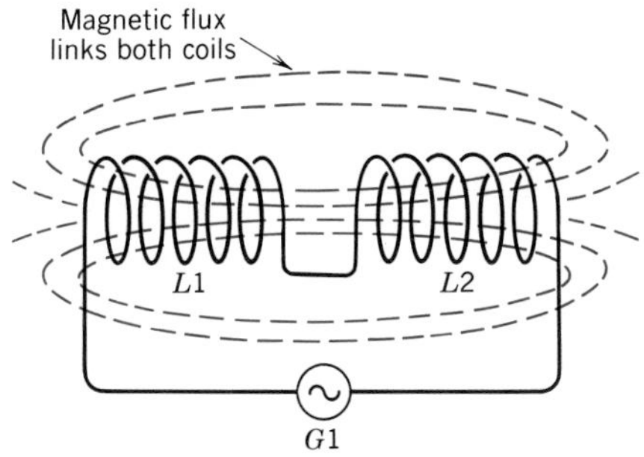

Figure 13.20 Magnetically linked, series-connected inductors.

with the second, while a coefficient of 0.5 means that only 50 percent of the flux produced by either coil is linked to the other. When the two coils are not linked magnetically, and k is zero, Formula 13.7 becomes $L_{total} = L1 + L2$, the formula for the total inductance of two series-connected coils. Notice that the plus or minus sign is used. This is because there are two ways of connecting a pair of coils, as shown in Figures 13.21*a* and 13.21*b*. In Figure 13.21*a* the coils are connected so that the winding directions are the same and the magnetic fields reinforce each other. In this case, the plus sign is used in Formula 13.7. The coils are said to be in *series aiding*. In Figure 13.21*b*, the winding direction of the second coil is the opposite of the first. This means that the fields produced by the two coils will cancel, and so the inductance of the two will be *less* than the sum of their individual inductances. This connection of the coils is referred to as *series opposing*. When coils are in series opposing, the minus sign in Formula 13.7 applies. Some schematics use dots or small squares, called *phasing marks*, to show whether a pair of magnetically linked coils is connected in series aiding or series opposing.

EXAMPLE:
Given a pair of coils of 10 mH and 5 mH, respectively, wound on the same toroidal core (coefficient of coupling is about equal to 1), what inductances can be obtained through different series connections of the coils? ■

Figure 13.21 Magnetically linked coils connected in series aiding and series opposing.

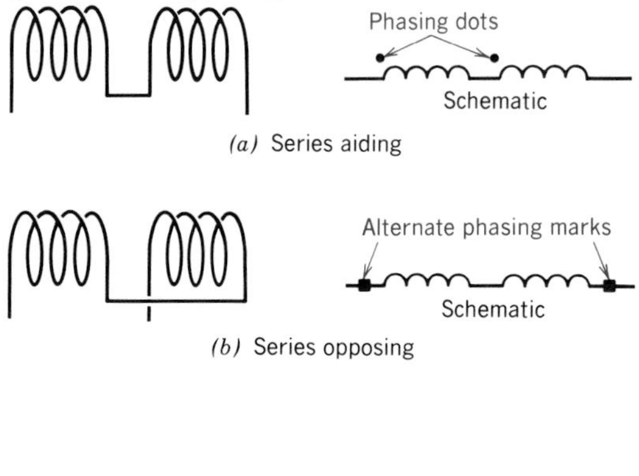

SOLUTION:
Since both coils are wound on the same toroidal core, the flux produced by both coils is largely confined to the core. This means that k is about equal to 1. If both coils are connected in series aiding, the inductance of the combination is

$$\begin{aligned} L_{total} &= L1 + L2 + 2k\sqrt{L1L2} \\ &= 0.010 + 0.005 + 2\sqrt{0.00005} \\ &= 0.029 \text{ H} \quad \text{or} \quad 29 \text{ mH} \end{aligned}$$

Connecting the two coils in series opposing produces a total inductance of

$$\begin{aligned} L_{total} &= L1 + L2 - 2k\sqrt{L1L2} \\ &= 0.010 + 0.005 - 2\sqrt{0.00005} \\ &= 0.000857 \\ &= 0.86 \text{ mH} \end{aligned}$$

Note that in the above example, with a coupling coefficient of 1, an inductance considerably higher than that of either coil is produced in series aiding. ■

B.5 THE TRANSFORMER EFFECT

The magnetic coupling of two unconnected coils, first discussed in Chapter 12, is the principle of operation of the transformer, a component found in many electronic units. In that chapter, you will remember, it was shown that a *changing* magnetic field in one conductor or coil would produce a potential difference in a nearby conductor or coil because of an effect called *mutual inductance*. Figure 13.22 shows a schematic representation of two coils wound on the same iron core. One of these coils is connected to an ac source providing a peak potential difference of 12 V. If the coefficient of coupling between the two coils is 1, and other losses are disregarded, the potential difference induced across the ends of coil 2 is in ratio with the potential difference of the source:

$$\frac{e_{coil\ 1}}{e_{coil\ 2}} = \frac{N_{coil\ 1}}{N_{coil\ 2}} \qquad \text{FORMULA 13.8}$$

where N represents the number of turns in a coil.

Figure 13.22 A schematic representation of two coils wound on the same iron core: *A* transformer.

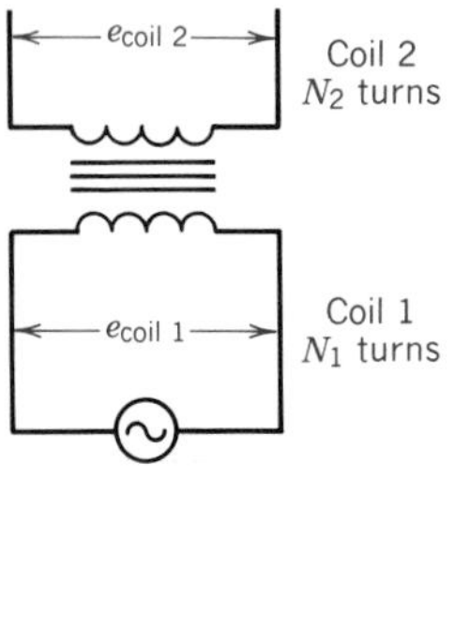

The potential difference across coils 1 and 2 can be expressed in any of the measurements used for the potential difference of an ac waveform, that is, peak, peak-to-peak, average, or rms values. As long as both are the same, the formula is correct. Another useful form is obtained by multiplying both sides of the equation by $e_{\text{coil 2}}$, giving

$$e_{\text{coil 1}} = \frac{N_{\text{coil 1}}}{N_{\text{coil 2}}} \times e_{\text{coil 2}} \qquad \text{FORMULA 13.9}$$

When the turns ratio and the potential difference provided by the source is known, a third form of the basic formula can be used. This third form is obtained from Formula 13.9 by transposing the left and right sides of the equation and multiplying both by $\frac{N_{\text{coil 2}}}{N_{\text{coil 1}}}$:

$$\frac{N_{\text{coil 2}}}{N_{\text{coil 1}}} \times \frac{N_{\text{coil 1}}}{N_{\text{coil 2}}} \times e_{\text{coil 2}} = \frac{N_{\text{coil 2}}}{N_{\text{coil 1}}} \times e_{\text{coil 1}}$$

or

$$e_{\text{coil 2}} = \frac{N_{\text{coil 2}}}{N_{\text{coil 1}}} \times e_{\text{coil 1}} \qquad \text{FORMULA 13.10}$$

EXAMPLE:
You are given an arrangement of two coils, coil 1 with 1250 turns and coil 2 with 750 turns, respectively, wound on the same ferrite core (coefficient of coupling = 1). If the source potential across coil 1 is 13.5 V_{peak}, what is the potential difference produced across the second coil? ■

SOLUTION:
Since the number of turns and the source potential difference are known, Formula 13.10 is the most convenient:

$$e_2 = \frac{N_2}{N_1} \times e_1 \quad \text{or} \quad e_2 = \frac{750}{1250} \times 13.5 = 8.1\ V_{\text{peak}}$$

■

A component consisting of two or more coils linked magnetically is called a *transformer*. The coil to which the ac source is connected, coil 1 in Figure 13.22, is referred to as the *primary winding*, or simply the *primary*. All other coils, usually not connected to the ac source, are referred to as *secondaries*. Figure 13.23 shows a transformer with one primary winding and three secondaries. In cases where there are several secondaries, Formulas 13.8 to 13.10 will be true for the primary and each secondary.

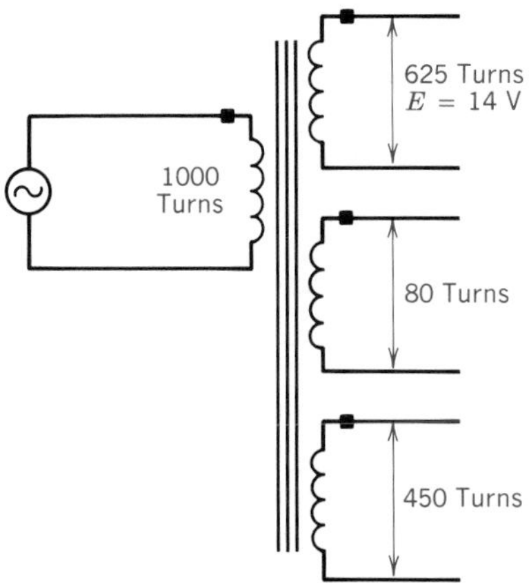

Figure 13.23 A transformer with three secondaries.

EXAMPLE:
In the transformer diagram in Figure 13.23, only the potential difference across one secondary winding is known. Assuming a coefficient of coupling of 1, what is the potential difference produced by the source, and what are the potential differences across the two other secondaries? ■

SOLUTION:
Notice that the potential difference across secondary 1 has no subscript, so the measurement should be assumed to be volts rms. Since the number of turns in the coils and one secondary potential are known, Formula 13.9 can be used to calculate the potential difference of the source. Capital rather than lowercase letters are used to represent potential difference since the rms rather than instantaneous values will be used in the calculation. Rewriting Formula 13.9,

$$E_{\text{primary}} = \frac{N_1}{N_2} \times E_2$$

Substituting,

$$E_{\text{primary}} = \frac{1000}{625} \times 14 = 22.4 \text{ V rms}$$

Substituting the number of turns and the primary potential in Formula 13.10 gives the potential difference produced across the other two primary coils:

$$E_3 = \frac{N_3}{N_1} \times E_1 = \frac{80}{1000} \times 22.4 = 1.792 \text{ V rms},$$

and

$$E_4 = \frac{N_4}{N_1} \times E_1 = \frac{450}{1000} \times 22.4 = 10.08 \text{ V rms}$$

■

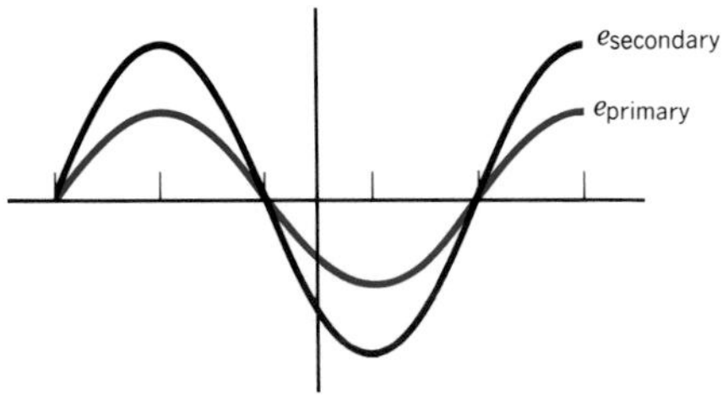

(a) In-phase connection

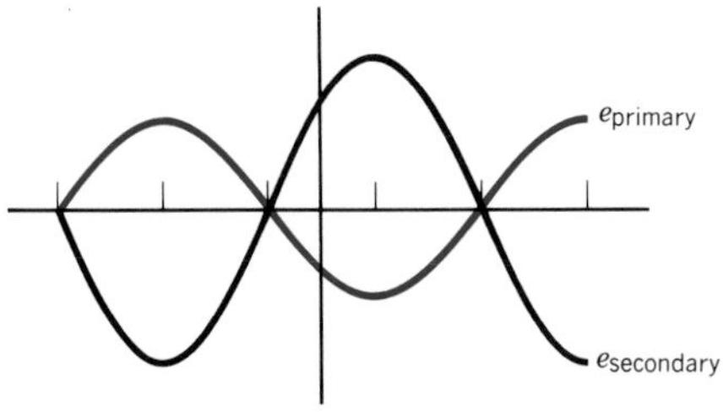

(b) Out-of-phase connection

Figure 13.24 Oscilloscope traces of in-phase and out-of-phase transformer connections (phase shifts due to inductance effects ignored).

Notice the phasing symbols used in Figure 13.23. These symbols on the secondary windings show those points at which the induced potential difference is in phase with the similarly marked point on the primary coil. Figure 13.24 shows oscilloscope traces of the primary and secondary coil waveforms at the in-phase and out-of-phase transformer connections.

So far, the transformer sounds like a wonderous component: If a transformer with a 1-turn primary and a 100-turn secondary is connected to a 1-V ac source, the secondary potential difference will be 100 V (disregarding losses from coil resistance or a coefficient or coupling of less than 1.) Since a transformer is not a source of energy itself, it should be clear to you that the amount of energy taken out of this component is going to be less than the amount put in. Clearly, something has been left out of the discussion. This is the current in both the transformer primary and in the secondary when it is part of a closed circuit. In the transformer circuit shown in Figure 13.25, a resistive load has been placed across the secondary winding. Because of the potential difference induced across the secondary, an alternating current will exist in the circuit composed of the secondary coil and the resistance. The current in the transformer primary produces a magnetomotive force (mmf) of $N_p i_p$ in the transformer core, where N_p is the number of turns in the primary and i_p is the primary current. The primary current depends on the potential difference across the primary and the primary impedance. You will recall that the impedance of a coil is

$$Z = \sqrt{R^2 + (X_L)^2}$$

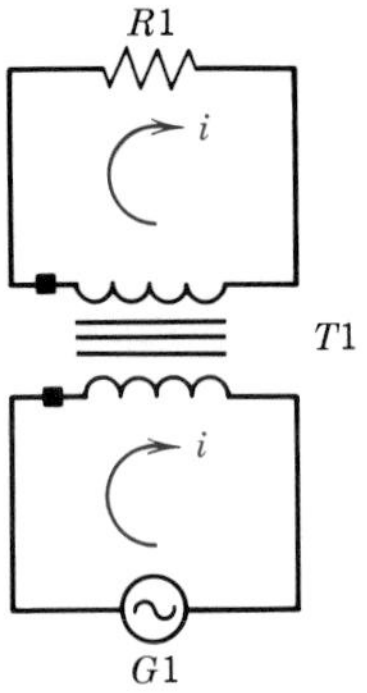

Figure 13.25 Current in transformer circuits.

Although the resistance of the primary winding of a transformer remains constant, the inductive reactance X_L depends on, among other things, the inductance of the coil. When there is a current through the secondary winding, as shown in Figure 13.25, the flux produced by the magnetomotive force opposes the flux produced by the primary current. The effect of this opposition is to reduce the flux in the transformer core. Because the inductance of the primary coil depends in part on the flux in the core, the primary inductance and its inductive reactance will also be lower. What this means is that the current in the transformer primary will increase when an electric current is produced by the potential difference induced by the secondary.

Disregarding losses in the core and in the wires forming the coils and connections, a short circuit across a transformer secondary would mean that the mmf produced by the secondary would completely cancel mmf produced by the primary. In other words, *all* the mmf produced by the current in the primary would be used to produce a current through the secondary circuit. Expressing this mathematically,

$$N_p i_p = N_s i_s \qquad \text{FORMULA 13.11}$$

Remember that this represents a situation in which all losses have been ignored. In the form

$$i_p = \frac{N_s}{N_p} i_s \qquad \text{FORMULA 13.12}$$

this formula can be used to calculate the minimum primary current for an ideal, or lossless transformer when the secondary supplies a current of i_s to a given load. As in the case of Formula 13.11, the currents can be expressed as peak, peak-to-peak, rms, or instantaneous values.

EXAMPLE:

A certain transformer has a primary consisting of 120 turns and a secondary composed of 50 turns. Disregarding losses of any sort, if the secondary delivers an rms current of 100 mA to an external circuit, what is the minimum rms current in the primary circuit? ■

SOLUTION:
Notice that this problem involves an ideal, that is, lossless transformer. Therefore, Formula 13.12 can be used (capital letters are used for symbolizing current since rms rather than instantaneous values are involved)

$$I_p = \frac{N_s}{N_p} I_s \quad \text{or} \quad I_p = \frac{50}{120} I_s = 0.042 \text{ A}$$ ■

Multiplying both sides of Formula 13.12 by $\frac{N_p}{N_s}$ provides a formula for calculating the current in an ideal transformer secondary when the primary current is known:

$$i_p \times \frac{N_p}{N_s} = \frac{N_s}{N_p} \times \frac{N_p}{N_s} \times i_s$$

Transposing,

$$i_s = \frac{N_p}{N_s} i_p \qquad \text{FORMULA 13.13}$$

Combining Formulas 13.10 and 13.13, you can see that even in an ideal transformer, an increase in potential difference is paid for with a *decrease* in maximum current. Consider the transformer circuit shown in Figure 13.26*a*. Here, according to Formula 13.10, a potential difference of 12 V ac rms applied to the pri-

Figure 13.26 Potential difference and current in a step-up transformer.

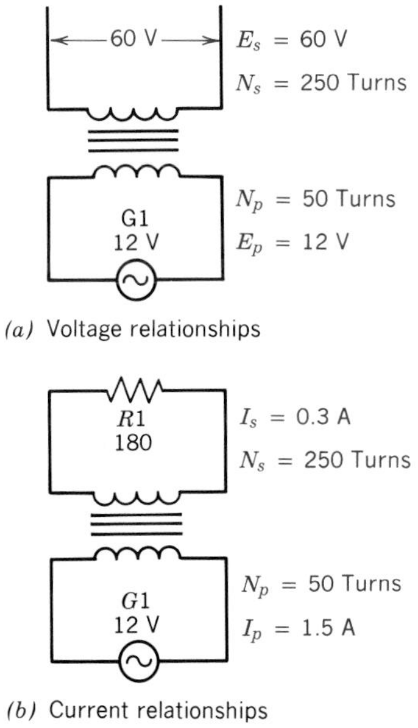

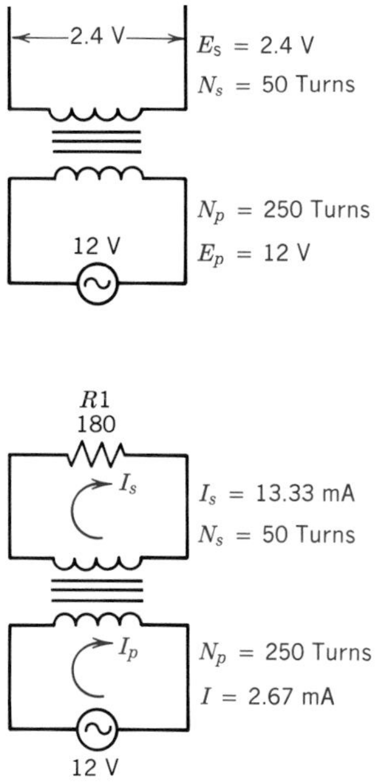

Figure 13.27 Potential difference and current in a step-down transformer.

mary winding produces a 60-V rms potential difference across the open secondary. since this transformer increases the potential difference, it is called a *step-up transformer*. When the primary and secondary currents are considered, however, as shown in Figure 13.26*b*, when a 180 Ω load is connected across the secondary and the secondary current is 0.3 A, the primary current will be

$$I_p = \frac{N_s}{N_p} I_s = 1.5 \text{ A}$$

If the 250-turn coil of this transformer is used as the primary and the 50-turn coil as the secondary, the result is the circuit shown in Figure 13.27. (In the next section you will see that the primary and secondary of many transformers can be interchanged without any problem, although this is not always true.) With the 12-V ac rms source connected to the 250-turn coil, the potential difference across the 180 Ω load will be 2.4 V rms. In other words, the source potential has been reduced by the transformer. A transformer whose secondary potential difference is less than that applied to its primary is called a *step-down transformer*. Although the potential difference supplied to the load is less, the current through the 180 Ω load,

$$I = \frac{E}{R} = 13.33 \text{ mA}$$

will be considerably greater than the primary current in this ideal transformer. Using Formula 13.12 to calculate the current,

$$I_p = \frac{N_s}{N_p} I_s = 2.67 \text{ mA}$$

In short, the step-down transformer provides a smaller potential difference at its secondary than that produced by the source connected to its primary, but the current in the secondary circuit is larger than that in the primary circuit.

Remember, a step-up transformer has more turns in its secondary winding than in its primary. It produces a larger potential difference across its secondary than the potential across its primary, but the primary current is larger than the secondary current.

A step-down transformer has more turns in its primary than in its secondary. It produces a secondary potential difference that is less than the potential across the primary, but the current that can be drawn from the secondary is greater than the current in the primary circuit.

$$e_s = \frac{N_s}{N_p} e_p \quad \text{and} \quad i_s = \frac{N_p}{N_s} i_p$$

B.6 REAL TRANSFORMERS

Although the previous section showed that the transformer is a component that receives an ac input at one potential difference and current and *transforms* this input into an output at a different potential difference and current, the formulas and explanations were based on ideal, lossless components with coefficients of coupling of 1. Clearly, transformer windings must have some resistance, and not all the magnetic flux produced by a transformer primary is linked to the secondary. This is not to say that Formulas 13.8 through 13.13 can not be used. Rather, it is necessary to understand how these formulas predict the behavior of real transformers in operating electronic units. For example, one commercial step-down transformer has the following characteristics:

Primary voltage	120 V 60 Hz
Secondary voltage	6 V
Secondary current	1.2 A

Applying Formula 13.10 to this transformer, the primary-to-secondary turns ratio $\frac{N_p}{N_s}$ is calculated to be $\frac{20}{1}$. This would mean that a 100 Ω resistive load connected to the secondary would result in a secondary circuit current of 60 mA. In these conditions, the primary current should be 3 mA. Actual measurements show that these characteristics do not necessarily reflect measured values. If the transformer primary is connected directly to the 120-V ac mains, the open-circuit potential difference measured across the secondary with a digital multimeter is 8.5 V. Table 13.2 shows the primary and secondary potential differences and currents for a variety of secondary loads. Note that the secondary potential difference decreases rapidly as the current in the secondary circuit increases. For load resistor values between 10 and 5 Ω, the rms value of the secondary voltage times the secondary current is greater than 60 percent of the product of the rms value of the primary voltage and primary current. Since the product of the rms values of current and potential difference is the power in either the primary or secondary winding, this percentage can be considered as a measure of the *efficiency* of the transformer as a component for transforming power at one potential difference and current into power at a second potential and current. Summarizing this in the form of an equation,

$$P_{\text{secondary}} = \% \text{ efficiency} \times P_{\text{primary}}$$

FORMULA 13.14

EXAMPLE:
Figure 13.28 provides the primary and secondary current and the secondary potential for a transformer with different loads operating from a 120-V ac line. Calculate the transformer efficiency for each load condition. ■

SOLUTION:
In the first set of values given, there is no secondary current. This is the condition that exists when no load is connected across the secondary transformer. For the second case, the primary potential difference is 120 V and the primary current is 0.045 A. The primary power is 5.4 VA (the unit volt amperes is used instead of watts in reactive circuits as you will see in Chapter 16). The secondary power is $E_s \times I_s = 1.996$ VA. Using Formula 13.14, the efficiency is

$$\text{eff} = \frac{P_s}{P_p} = 0.37, \text{ or } 37 \text{ percent.}$$

Use the same method to verify that the efficiencies in the following cases are 45, 62, 68, and 73 percent. ■

There are several things worth noting in this example. First, the transformer efficiencies are all less than 90 percent. This is typical of small transformers operating at power frequencies. Second, the efficiency of a transformer is not constant. As the load draws

Table 13.2 Primary Current and Secondary Voltage and Current for a Variety of Load Conditions

R_L	E_s	I_s	I_p	E_p	$P_s = E_s \times I_s$	$P_p = E_p \times I_p$	eff %
Open ckt	8.51	0	0.05	120	—	—	—
100 Ω	8.39	0.084	0.052	120	.705	6.24	11.0
50 Ω	8.28	0.16 A	0.054	120	1.32	6.48	20.3
25 Ω	8.06	0.32 A	0.059	120	2.58	7.08	36.4
10 Ω	7.50	0.75 A	0.075	120	5.625	9	62.5
7.5 Ω	7.27	0.97 A	0.085	120	7.06	10.2	69.2
5 Ω	6.66	1.33 A	0.104	120	8.86	12.48	70.9
1 Ω	3.47	3.47 A	0.233	120	12.04	26.76	44.9

more power from the transformer secondary, the secondary potential difference drops. The transformer efficiency rises but will then begin to drop. This is due to the increase in the power losses in the transformer as the secondary current increases beyond some value.

There are three major kinds of power loss in real transformers. You have already learned about all of them, but it will help if they are considered again in relation to transformers.

The first of these is inefficient coupling between the primary and secondary windings of a transformer. In Section B.4., it was assumed that the coefficient of coupling between primary and secondary coils was unity, or 1. In other words, it was assumed that all the magnetic flux produced by the primary coil is linked to the secondary. Although this is very nearly true, there is frequently some flux that does not pass through the secondary coil if the primary and secondary are not wound one on top of the other.

Another source of power loss related to the coefficient of coupling is the power loss caused by flux linkage to a metal transformer case, shield, or shell. The case surrounds the primary and acts like a single-turn, short-circuited secondary winding. The expansion and collapse of the magnetic field around the primary coil induces a current in the case. Transformer manufacturers minimize this loss by using case materials with fairly high resistance and by placing the case in such a way as to reduce the linkage between the case and the field. In most applications, a power loss of a few percent is better than allowing the flux from an unshielded transformer to induce currents in nearby circuit wiring.

Similar to the power losses due to coupling are those commonly referred to as *core losses*. Small current flows induced in the ferromagnetic core of a transformer are commonly called *eddy currents*. As in the case of iron core inductors, eddy current loss is minimized by using cores made of thin, insulated laminations shown in Chapter 12. The hysteresis effect discussed in Chapter 12 also contributes to the power losses classiffied as core losses. The additional energy required to realign the magnetic domains in the core when the polarity of the source reverses must be supplied by the power in the primary circuit. The amount of primary power lost due to hysteresis is found to be proportional to the area contained within the hysteresis curve for the core material. For example, the curve shown in Figure 13.29*a* represents a greater loss than

Figure 13.28 Calculating transformer efficiency.

E_p (V)	I_p (A)	E_s (V)	I_s (A)
120	0.02	29.59	—
120	0.045	27.38	0.0729
120	0.055	26.85	0.111
120	0.068	25.2	0.2
120	0.073	24.9	0.24
120	0.078	24.0	0.285

Figure 13.29 The core losses in a transformer core are proportional to the area inside the hysteresis loop.

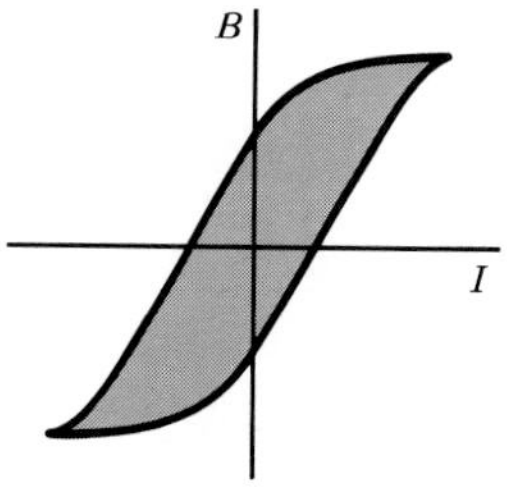

(*a*) Large area hysteresis loop

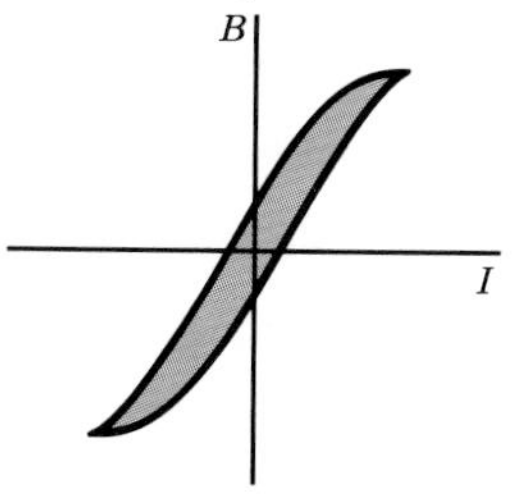

(*b*) Small area hysteresis loop

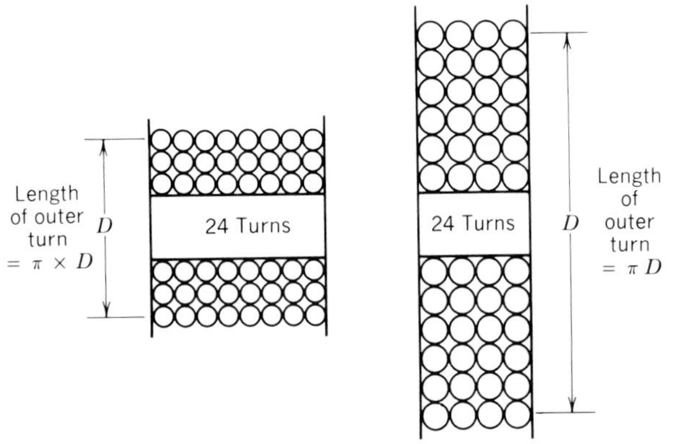

Figure 13.30 Use of larger-diameter wire in multilayer coils also means that the total length of wire is increased.

that shown in 13.29*b*. Transformer core materials are selected to minimize losses due to hysteresis.

The power losses due to the resistance of the transformer windings are called *copper losses* and are the easiest to understand. The power dissipated by even the low resistance of heavy copper wire causes transformer heating and is one of the most important factors reducing transformer efficiency. Using heavier gauge wire with a lower resistance does reduce the copper losses, but this solution is not quite so simple. Larger-diameter wire takes up more space than thinner wire. This means that the total length of the thicker wire will be greater, as shown in Figure 13.30, and that the length of the magnetic circuit will also be greater, thereby canceling some of the gains in efficiency obtained through the use of the larger-diameter wire.

As you can see, the design of a modern transformer is based on compromises among such characteristics as length of magnetic circuit, resistance of windings, and coefficient of coupling. These characteristics, in addition to the turns ratio of the primary to the secondary, determine the efficiency of the transformer and its suitability for a particular application.

B.7 TRANSFORMERS FOR IMPEDANCE MATCHING

The previous sections of this chapter have concentrated on the transformer as a device that transforms electric power from one potential difference and current to a different potential and current. Another important function of the transformer in electronic circuits is based on the fact that the primary and secondary coils of a transformer are inductors, each possessing a particular impedance. You have learned that, according to the power transfer theorem, maximum power could be transferred from a dc source to a load when the resistance of the load circuit is equal to the resistance of the source circuit. By way of review, this principle is shown in Figure 13.31. In the circuit of Figure 13.31*a*, a real dc source with an internal resistance is connected to a load. Figure 13.31*b* provides a table of the amount of power transferred to the load at different load resistances. Note that the power transferred is highest when the source and load resistances are matched.

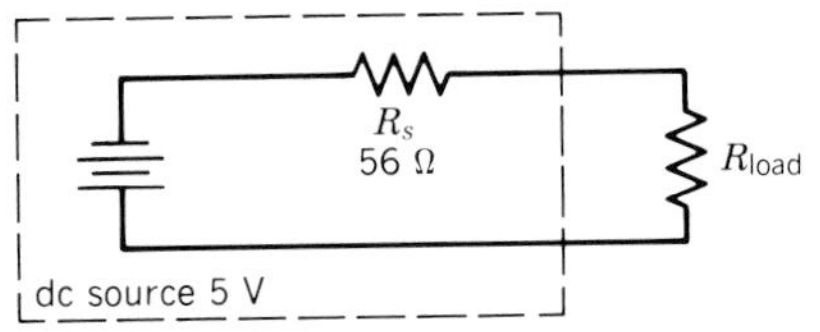

(*a*) Circuit for observing power transfer theorem

R_L	$I_{CIRCUIT}$ (A)	$P_{RS} = I^2R_s$ (W)	$P_L = I^2R_L$ (W)
15	0.0704	0.2775	0.0743
27	0.0602	0.2029	0.0978
39	0.0526	0.1549	0.1079
47	0.0485	0.1317	0.1106
56	0.0446	0.1114	0.1114 ← MAXIMUM
75	0.0382	0.0817	0.1094
82	0.0362	0.0734	0.1075
91	0.0340	0.0647	0.1052

(*b*) Table of P_L for values of R_L

Figure 13.31 Review of power transfer theorem.

As you might expect, the maximum power transfer theorem applies to ac as well as dc circuits. In dealing with ac circuits, however, it is the *impedance* and not the resistance of the source and load networks that must be considered. Figure 13.32 is the schematic diagram of a real ac source connected to a resistive load. As you can see from the diagram, the impedance of the load circuit is greater than that of the source circuit. Figure 13.33 shows the same source and load networks connected by means of an *impedance-matching transformer*. This component is able to transfer power from a source to a load with much less loss than a resistive network since there is little power dissipation in the transformer.

The impedance of the transformer primary in Figure 13.32*b* is the same as that of the source, while the impedance of the secondary matches that of the load. You will recall that, if rms values are used, the impedance of a circuit is given by $Z = \frac{E}{I}$. Using this relationship and Formulas 13.10 and 13.13, it is possible to obtain a formula that relates the ratio of the turns in a transformer primary and secondary to the primary and secondary circuit impedances that the transformer will match. For the primary circuit composed of the source and its internal resistance, $Z_p = \frac{E_p}{I_p}$. For the secondary circuit composed of the load, $Z_s = \frac{E_s}{I_s}$.

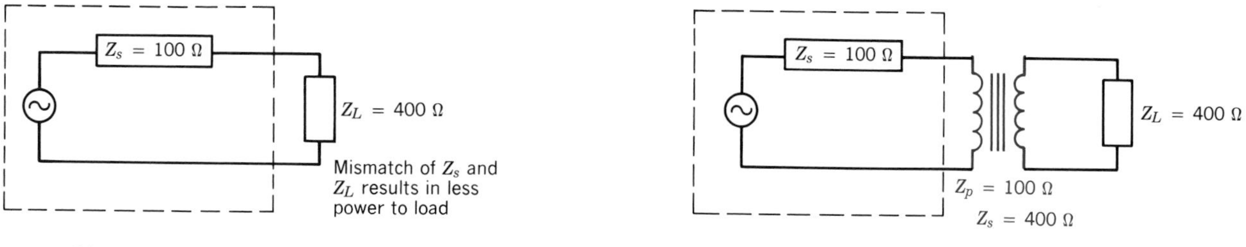

(a) Direct connection of source and load

(b) Using a transformer to match the load and source impedances results in maximum power in load.

Figure 13.32 Using a transformer as an impedance-matching device.

Therefore,

$$\frac{Z_p}{Z_s} = \frac{\dfrac{E_p}{I_p}}{\dfrac{E_s}{I_s}}$$

Simplifying this by inverting the denominator $\dfrac{E_s}{I_s}$ and multiplying $\dfrac{Z_p}{Z_s} = \dfrac{E_pI_s}{E_sI_p}$. Now E_s and I_s can be expressed in terms of E_p, I_p, N_p, and N_s using Formulas 13.10 and 13.13:

$$E_s = \frac{N_s}{N_p} E_p \quad \text{and} \quad I_s = \frac{N_p}{N_s} I_p$$

If these two expressions are substituted for E_s and I_s in $\dfrac{Z_p}{Z_s} = \dfrac{E_pI_s}{E_sI_p}$, a simple formula results:

$$\frac{Z_p}{Z_s} = \frac{N_p^2}{N_s^2} \qquad \text{FORMULA 13.15}$$

In other words, the ratio of the primary circuit impedance to the secondary circuit impedance that an ideal transformer will match is the same as the ratio of the square of the number of turns in the primary to the square of the number of turns in the secondary. You will probably find that the mathematical expression of this relationship is both clearer and easier to remember.

Although Formula 13.15 is sometimes neglected in beginning courses, it is every bit as important as Formulas 13.8 and 13.13, especially since many small transformers are marked with the impedances their primaries and secondaries will match, rather than a turns ratio.

Figure 13.33 Calculation of turns ratio when primary and secondary impedances are known.

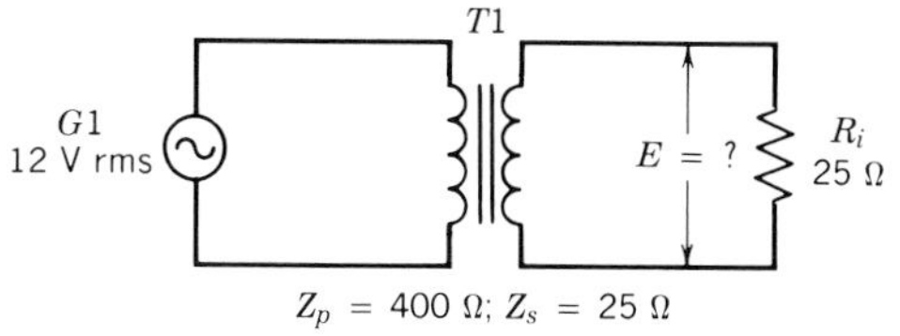

EXAMPLE:
The circuit whose schematic is shown in Figure 13.33 consists of an ideal impedance-matching transformer connected between an ac source producing 12 V ac rms and a resistive load. The transformer primary winding is marked "400 Ω" and its secondary "25 Ω." What is the potential difference across the load? ■

SOLUTION:
The required secondary potential difference could easily be calculated from Formula 13.10 if the primary to secondary turns ratio was known. This ratio can be calculated using Formula 13.15. Substituting the known values,

$$\frac{400}{25} = \frac{N_p^2}{N_s^2} \quad \text{or} \quad 16 = \frac{N_p^2}{N_s^2}$$

Taking the square root of both sides,

$$16 = \frac{N_p^2}{N_s^2} \quad \text{or} \quad 4 = \frac{N_p}{N_s}$$

Since $\dfrac{N_p}{N_s} = 4$, $\dfrac{N_s}{N_p} = 0.25$, and this value can be substituted in Formula 13.10:

$$E_s = \frac{N_s}{N_p} \times E_p \quad \text{or} \quad E_s = 0.25 \times 12$$

$$E_s = 3 \text{ V ac rms}$$ ■

Another way of looking at the function of an impedance-matching transformer is to think of it as a device that transforms a secondary circuit impedance into an equivalent primary circuit impedance. In the circuit shown in Figure 13.34*a*, a real 12-V ac rms source is matched to a 270 Ω resistive load by a transformer with a primary consisting of 100 turns and a secondary with 300. From the point of view of the source, the 270 Ω load appears the same as an equiv-

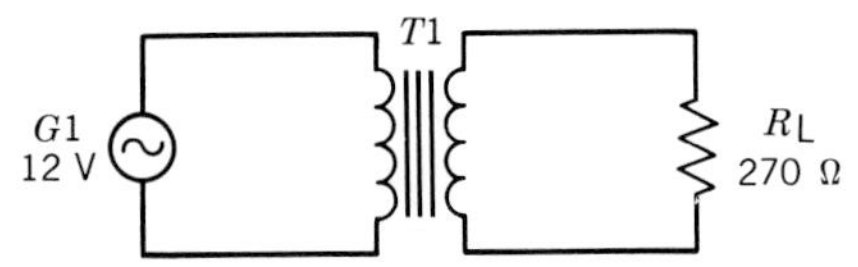

(a) Circuit with a transformer matching a load to a source

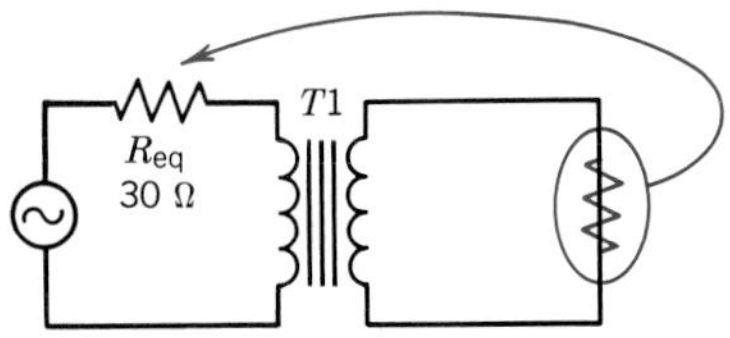

(b) The effect of *T*1 is to "reflect" the load into the primary circuit.

Figure 13.34 Another way of looking at impedance matching.

alent load placed in the source circuit, as shown in Figure 13.34*b*. The impedance of this equivalent load can be calculated using Formula 13.15:

$$\frac{Z_p}{Z_s} = \frac{N_p^2}{N_s^2}$$

$$\frac{Z_p}{270} = \frac{10000}{90000}$$

$$Z_p = \frac{1}{9} \times 270 = 30\ \Omega$$

In effect, the 270 Ω impedance in the load circuit is the equivalent of a 30 Ω impedance in the source circuit. This 30 Ω equivalent impedance is referred to as the value of the 270 Ω load impedance "reflected into the primary circuit."

This way of considering impedance matching is useful when it is necessary to specify the turns ratio of the transformer needed to couple two circuits.

EXAMPLE:
A certain stereo amplifier has been designed to operate with a speaker system that has an impedance of 16 Ω. The only speakers available are those having an impedance of 4 Ω. What is the turns ratio of the transformers needed to couple the amplifier to these speakers? ■

SOLUTION:
Using Formula 13.15,

$$\frac{Z_p}{Z_s} = \frac{N_p^2}{N_s^2} \quad \text{or} \quad \frac{16}{4} = \frac{N_p^2}{N_s^2}$$

Taking the square root of both sides,

$$\frac{4}{1} = \frac{N_p^2}{N_s^2} \quad \text{or} \quad 2 = \frac{N_p}{N_s}$$

The required transformers have twice as many turns in their primaries as in their secondaries. ■

C. EXAMPLES AND COMPUTATIONS

C.1 WHY USE SINE-WAVE ANALYSIS?

The methods of sine-wave analysis presented in this chapter, like the network analysis theorems discussed in Chapter 8, should be considered tools. Multimeters and oscilloscopes are electronic devices that enable the engineer or technician to determine what is actually going on in a circuit, while analysis methods are tools for determining what *should* be going on. Used together, diagnostic test equipment and diagnostic analysis techniques remove much of the guesswork from equipment maintenance. In the circuit shown in Figure 13.35, for example, using no calculation and without breaking the circuit, a multimeter could be used to determine if the following faults existed:

a. *R*1 burned out
b. *R*1 short circuited
c. *L*1 burned out
d. *L*2 short circuited
e. *R*2 or *L*2 short circuited
d. Generator *G*1 producing no potential difference or *R*1, *L*1, *and* either *R*2 or *L*2 short circuited.

Notice, however, that without calculation of the expected potential differences and phase shifts across the components in the circuit, it is impossible to check for component value changes, which are as likely to occur in properly designed circuits as short- or open-circuit failures. Such common troubles as the short-circuiting of a large percentage of the turns in *L*1 would go unnoticed until increased circuit current caused *L*1 itself or some other component to fail.

The ability to predict the potential waveform in any part of a circuit or to calculate it with some degree of accuracy will uncover component value changes when these theoretical quantities are compared to observed values. Comparing these observed values with those calculated using sine-wave analysis can frequently identify a faulty component.

Figure 13.35 Sine-wave analysis can be used to detect component value change in complex reactive circuits.

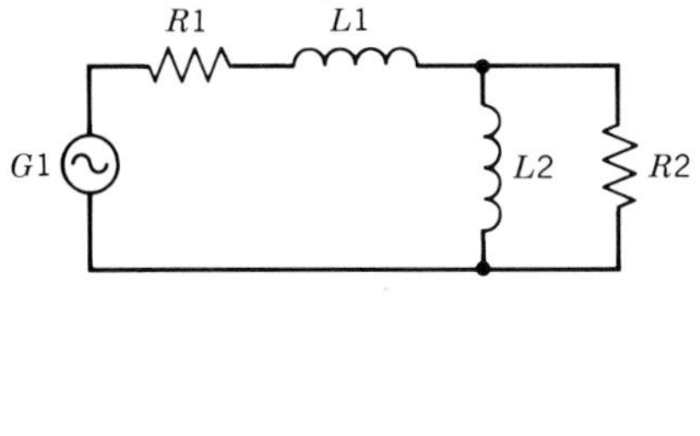

C.2 MUTUAL INDUCTANCE AND TRANSFORMER CALCULATIONS

Although calculations involving the coefficient of coupling between coils are rare in most electronics jobs, transformer calculations are frequent enough to justify a number of review and practice problems. The following exercises are intended to suggest how the theoretical principles and formulas presented in Section B can be applied to real equipment situations.

1. A transformer has a primary consisting of 800 turns of fine wire. If the source provides 60 Hz, 120 V rms, what would the open-circuit potential difference be across the 400-turn secondary, assuming ideal transformer characteristics?

2. A 10 Ω resistor is placed across the secondary of the transformer described in Problem 1. Assuming an ideal transformer, calculate the primary current.

3. A certain transformer primary consists of 170 turns and is connected to a 5-V ac source. If the potential difference across the secondary is 19.5 V, how many turns are in the secondary?

4. A transformer draws a primary current of 100 mA when connected to a 120-V ac source. The secondary furnishes 24 V to a 96 Ω load. What is the efficiency of the transformer?

5. It is necessary to reduce the mains potential difference to 5 V. What should be the turns ratio of the ideal transformer required? If the transformer has to deliver a maximum current of no more than 6 A, what would be the value of a protective fuse placed in the primary circuit?

6. A certain transformer has a 400-turn primary and a 100-turn secondary. If a 4 Ω load is placed across the secondary, what input impedance will be matched?

7. A transformer has a primary composed of 800 turns and is connected to an impedance of 1200 Ω. The impedance matched to the secondary is 300 Ω. How many turns are in the secondary?

8. Two transformers are connected back-to-back, as shown in Figure 13.36. What is the source impedance if the power in the 12 Ω load is at its maximum?

Figure 13.36 Circuit for Problem 8.

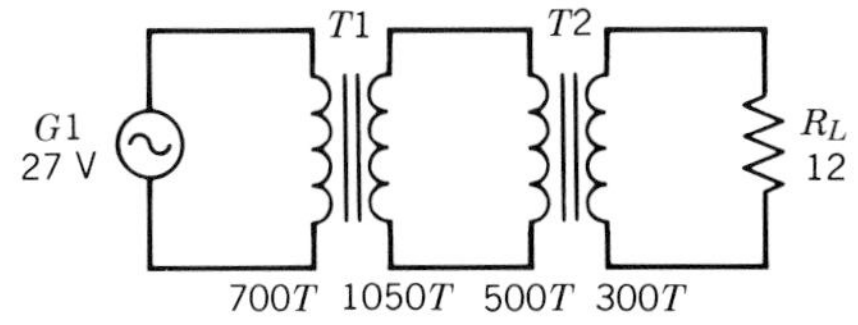

C.3 RECTANGULAR COORDINATES, POLAR COORDINATES, AND THE j OPERATOR

By this time you should have begun to realize the importance of dealing with phasor quantities like ac voltages, currents, and impedances. In many calculations in electronics it is necessary to add, subtract, multiply, and divide phasor quantities. The methods for performing these calculations are complex, but you must master them in order to do the kind of troubleshooting and circuit analysis required in many jobs.

In order to simplify phasor calculations, a number of different ways of expressing phasor quantities are used. You are already fairly familiar with two of these. The method of representing a phasor as a line segment of a particular length drawn from an origin point and forming a particular angle with a reference axis is shown in Figure 13.37. In mathematics, when this method is used for locating a point on a plane, it is called the *method of polar coordinates*. In electronics, the phasor itself is of importance, rather than its end point, but the name *polar coordinate system* and the mathematical method of notation are still retained. For example, an impedance of 5 Ω with a phase angle of 45° to the reference phasor is written as $5 \angle 45^\circ$ in the polar coordinate system. Note that the length of the phasor is always a positive number.

EXAMPLE:
Sketch the following phasors given in the polar coordinate system:

a. $7 \angle 30^\circ$
b. $4 \angle 90^\circ$
c. $7 \angle 170^\circ$
d. $3 \angle -15^\circ$
e. $9 \angle -120^\circ$
f. $8 \angle 260^\circ$ ■

SOLUTION:
The phasors are shown in Figure 13.38. Note that although the length of the phasor is always positive, the angle can be given either as a positive (counterclockwise) or negative (clockwise) rotation. ■

Figure 13.37 The polar coordinate method of defining a phasor.

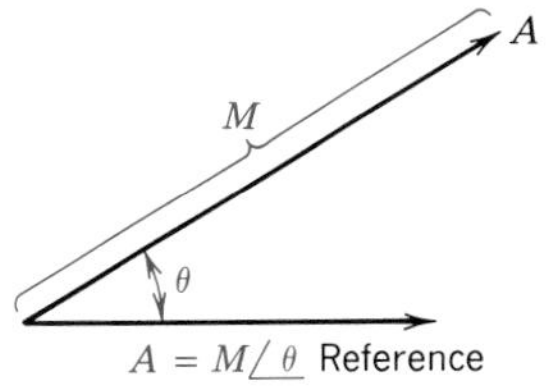

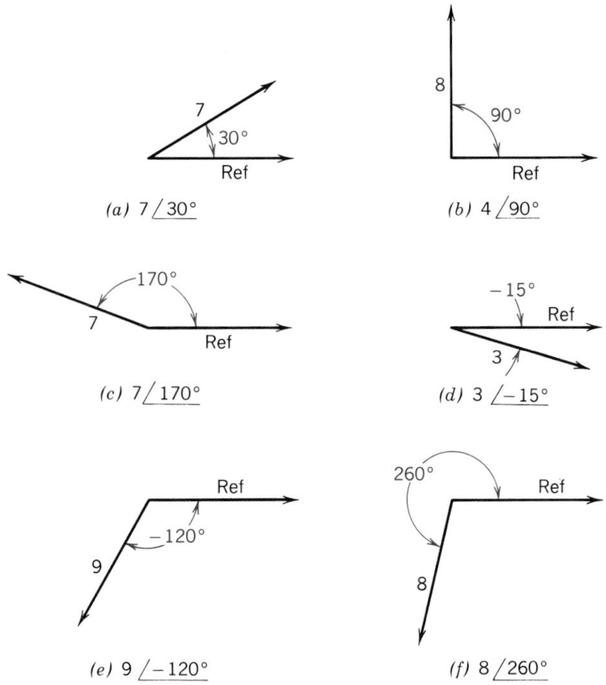

Figure 13.38 Phasors defined in polar coordinate system: Some examples.

Using the polar form makes it easy to represent phasor quantities without bothering to draw a phasor diagram.

EXAMPLE:
An inductor of 150 mH and an internal resistance of 30 Ω is connected to a 100 Hz source. Represent the component impedance as a phasor quantity using polar form. ■

SOLUTION:
The magnitude of the impedance is

$$Z = \sqrt{R^2 + (2\pi f L)^2} = \sqrt{900 + 8882.64} = 98.9\ \Omega$$

The phase angle is $\tan^{-1} \dfrac{X_L}{R} = 72.3°$. In polar form, $98.9\ \underline{/72.3°}\ \Omega$. ■

Express the following electrical quantities in polar form:

a. A current with a peak value of 3.75 A that leads the reference voltage phasor by 30°.

b. A potential difference of 6 V ac that lags the current reference by 12°.

c. A reference phasor of 10 A.

d. An inductive reactance of 56 Ω in a series circuit.

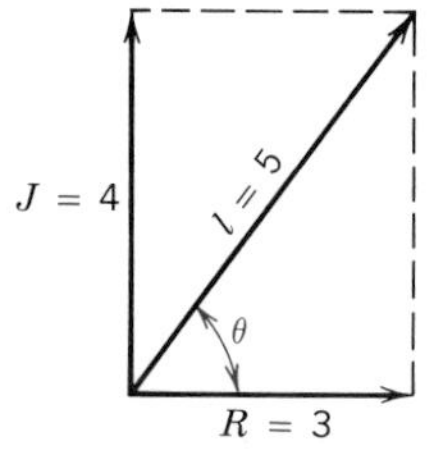

Figure 13.39 A phasor resolved into R and J components.

e. A 68 mA current in one branch of a parallel circuit that lags the source by 45°.

f. An inductive reactance of 1.5 kΩ at an angle of 84° in a series circuit.

g. A current making a phase angle of −34° with the reference.

h. Two phasors of 18 making +90 and −90 degree angles with the reference.

i. An inductive reactance of 65 Ω in a series circuit.

In addition to the polar form of expressing a phasor quantity, you will also have to use a form called the *rectangular form*, or *complex rectangular form*, which is based on expressing the phasor as the vector sum of two components that lie along two axes at right angles to each other. Figure 13.39 shows a phasor resolved into two components, R and J. You will recall from your work with vectors in Chapter 10 that the magnitudes of the two components can be obtained from the length of the phasor by trigonometry:

$$R = I \cos \theta \quad \text{and} \quad J = I \sin \theta$$

EXAMPLE:
A certain sine wave is represented by a phasor of length 12 at an angle of 63° to the reference R axis. What are the R and J components of this phasor? ■

SOLUTION:
Using the two relationships for R and J, $R = +5.45$, $J = +10.69$. ■

From this example you can see that the phasor $12\ \underline{/63°}$ can be defined by the rectangular coordinates $R = +5.45$ and $J = +10.69$. An easy way to write this is $5.45 + j10.69$. Notice that the horizontal axis value is always given first, and the vertical axis value is given *after* the letter j, to avoid confusion with j as a variable. In this case the letter j is called an *operator*, to distinguish it from a variable. In a moment you will see that the operator j represents more than just the name of an axis, but first it is wise to become familiar with rectangular coordinate notation.

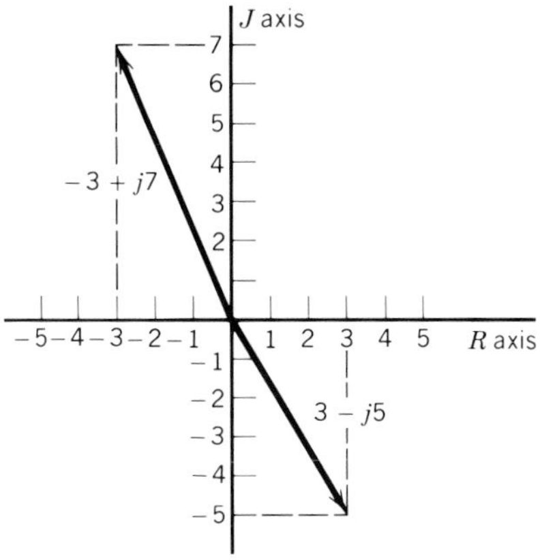

Figure 13.40 Drawing phasors when their R and J components are known.

Just as the values of the horizontal axis are considered positive to the right of the origin ($0 + j0$) and negative to the left, the j values above the origin are $+j$ values, while those below are $-j$.

EXAMPLE:
Draw the phasors $3 - j5$ and $-3 + j7$. ■

SOLUTION:
The phasor components are laid out on the coordinate axes and the phasors drawn in Figure 13.40. ■

An immediate practical use for rectangular coordinates is to represent impedances easily. Measuring the internal resistance of a coil along the horizontal axis and the inductive reactance along the positive j axis defines the impedance phasor in a series circuit.

EXAMPLE:
Draw the impedance phasor of an inductor of 0.001 H with a resistance of 8 Ω when connected to a 455 Hz source. ■

SOLUTION:
As shown in Figure 13.41, the internal resistance of the coil is measured on the positive R axis. The inductive reactance

$$X_L = 2\pi f L = 2.86\ \Omega$$

is measured on the positive j axis, and the resulting phasor is drawn. ■

Figure 13.41 Phasor representation of the impedance of a 0.001-H inductor across a 455-Hz source.

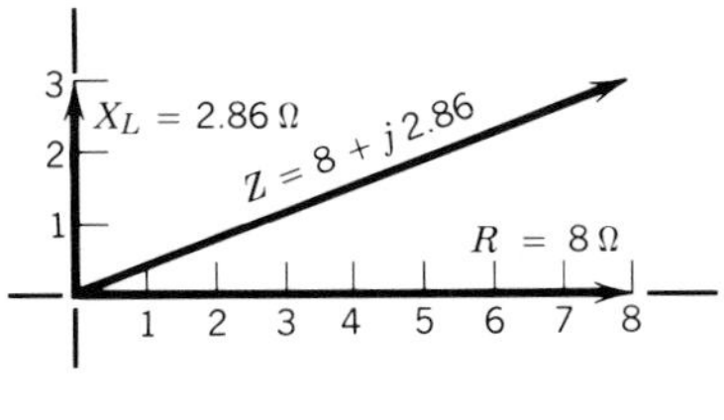

Practice your ability to define phasors from their rectangular coordinates by drawing the following:

a. $6.5 + j0$	f. $8.25 - j4.5$
b. $3.4 + j3.4$	g. $-53 - j40$
c. $0 - j5.7$	h. $10.5 + j8.4$
d. $4.25 - j3.8$	i. $-6.2 + j4$
e. $-6 - j4$	j. $-19 - j4.9$

Recalling a few trigonometric formulas that will be familiar to you makes it easy to convert between the polar and rectangular systems. This switching is desirable because it is easier to perform certain calculations on phasors represented in their polar form, while other calculations are only possible in rectangular form.

Given a phasor in polar form, such as $M \angle \theta$ the R and j components can be calculated using the formulas discussed earlier.

$$R = M \cos \theta \quad \text{FORMULA 13.16}$$

$$\text{and} \quad j = M \sin \theta \quad \text{FORMULA 13.17}$$

EXAMPLE:
Express $39.3 \angle 30°$ in the rectangular system. ■

SOLUTION:
Using Formulas 13.16 and 13.17,

$$\begin{aligned} R &= M \cos \theta \\ &= 39.3 \cos 30 \\ &= 34.03 \\ J &= M \sin \theta \\ &= 39.3 \sin 30 \\ &= 19.65 \end{aligned}$$

Therefore, $39.3 \angle 30° = 34.03 + j19.65$. ■

You can prevent difficulties when the angle of a phasor expressed in polar coordinates is greater than 90° or is negative if you draw a diagram. This will enable you to check the sign of the R and j components. For example, Figure 13.42 shows that the R and j components of $19.6 \angle 240°$ or $19.6 \angle -120°$ both have negative signs.

Converting from a rectangular coordinate system to the polar system also requires the use of two formulas, although a number of choices are possible when calculating the angle involved. M, the length of the

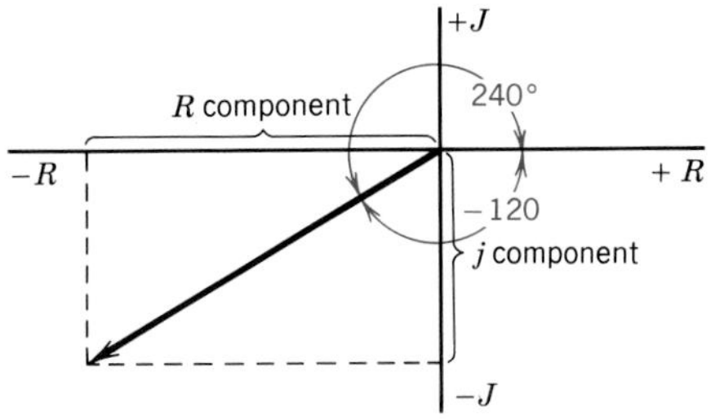

Figure 13.42 A quick sketch will show that both components of 19.6 −120° will have negative signs.

phasor in the polar system, is given by

$$M = \sqrt{R^2 + J^2} \quad \text{FORMULA 13.18}$$

For the angle between the phasor and the reference either the arctangent, arcsin, or arccos functions can be used. Since you will probably be using a calculator to do this, there is no real difference. The three formulas are

$$\theta = \tan^{-1}\frac{J}{R}$$

$$\theta = \sin^{-1}\frac{J}{M}$$

$$\theta = \cos^{-1}\frac{R}{M} \quad \text{FORMULA 13.19}$$

Each of these forms provides a value for θ.

EXAMPLE:
Convert $1.7 + j3.2$ to polar form. ■

SOLUTION:
Using Formula 13.18,

$$M = \sqrt{R^2 + J^2} = \sqrt{1.7^2 + 3.2^2} = 3.62$$

For calculating the angle θ, the first formula, resembling the formula for the phase angle in an RL circuit, is easiest:

$$\theta = \tan^{-1}\frac{J}{R} = 62.02°$$

So,

$$1.7 + j3.2 = 3.62 \underline{/62.02°}$$ ■

Many calculators have special function keys that permit easy conversion between polar and rectangular coordinates. However, there is not much standardization in either the key markings or the order in which the keys are pressed. If your calculator has such a feature, practice its use with the following problems. Otherwise, use Formulas 13.16 through 13.19.

1. Convert the following to rectangular form:

a. $12 \underline{/30°}$
b. $1.414 \underline{/45°}$
c. $2.38 \underline{/-60°}$
d. $4.5 \underline{/90°}$
e. $6.75 \underline{/-40°}$
f. $5.5 \underline{/-110°}$
g. $36 \underline{/270°}$
h. $4.25 \underline{/-16.5°}$
i. $8.25 \underline{/110°}$
j. $3.2 \underline{/-60°}$

2. Convert the following to polar form:

a. $18 + j0$
b. $1.5 + j1.5$
c. $16 - j12$
d. $0 - j4.5$
e. $3.0 + j4.0$
f. $-6.27 + j5.3$
g. $-6.8 - j4.5$
h. $18 - j30$
i. $2.7 + j10$
j. $17 - j1.5$

Comparing the polar and rectangular systems of phasor notation, you can see that in the polar form the concept of an angle of rotation is clearly involved. In the rectangular coordinate system, this is implied by the operator j. This operator therefore serves two functions: one to show that the R and J components represent different sorts of quantities and that these quantities can be represented on a pair of orthogonal axes, that is, two axes at right angles to each other.

The ability of the operator j to function in this manner comes from the fact that the squares of both positive and negative numbers are positive, that is,

$$(+2)^2 = +2 \times +2 = +4 \quad \text{and} \quad (-2)^2 = -2 \times -2 = +4$$

Because of this, the expression $\sqrt{4}$ is equal to $+2$ *or* to -2. On the other hand, the expression $\sqrt{-4}$ would seem to have no meaning at all. Expressions like $\sqrt{-4}$, $\sqrt{-1}$, or $\sqrt{-N}$, are called *imaginary numbers* in mathematics because there is no number that produces a negative product when multiplied by itself. The term *imaginary number* is used to distinguish numbers like $\sqrt{-4}$ and $\sqrt{-1}$ from numbers like $\sqrt{4}$, 2, or -2, which are called *real numbers*. All imaginary numbers can be expressed as multiples of $\sqrt{-1}$. For example:

$$\sqrt{-4} = \sqrt{(4) \times (-1)} = \sqrt{4} \times \sqrt{-1} = 2\sqrt{-1}.$$

In the general case, where a is any positive number,

$$\sqrt{-a} = \sqrt{a \times -1} = \sqrt{a} \times \sqrt{-1}.$$

In mathematics texts, -1 is symbolized by the letter i. Since this would lead to confusion in the study of electronics, the letter j is used. This means that it is possible to express any imaginary number as the product of a real number and the operator j, or $\sqrt{-1}$. For example, $\sqrt{-36} = \sqrt{-1 \times 36} = \sqrt{-1} \times \sqrt{36} = j6$. Recall that the j is written first to avoid confusion between the operator j and the letter used to represent a variable.

Exercise your understanding of imaginary numbers by expressing the following in terms of j. Simplify your answers as much as possible.

a. $\sqrt{-9}$
b. $\sqrt{-3}$
c. $\sqrt{-6} + \sqrt{-9}$
d. $-b\sqrt{-6}$
e. $\sqrt{-10a^2b}$
f. $\dfrac{2}{\sqrt{-4ab}}$
g. $\sqrt{-6c} + \sqrt{6d^2}$
h. $\sqrt{-56b^2}$
i. $\dfrac{1}{\sqrt{-3M}}$
j. $-E\sqrt{-2E^2}$
k. $\sqrt{3} \cdot \sqrt{-3}$
l. $\sqrt{(3)(-a)}$

Like the number infinity, imaginary numbers are sometimes written about in rather confusing and mystical terms. For purposes of the study of electronics, imaginary numbers and the operator j are practical tools for analysis. This begins to make sense if you realize that imaginary numbers are not comensurate with real numbers. This is a fancy way of saying that if all the real numbers are laid out on a line, as shown in Figure 13.43*a*, the imaginary numbers have no place on that line. All the real numbers, including decimals, do have places on the real number line. For example, 1.5 would be halfway between 1 and 2. But where would you place $\sqrt{-1}$ on that line? The problem is even worse than it appears. Since any number can be multiplied by j, there appear to be *two* number lines, a real one and an imaginary one, as shown in Figure 13.43*b*. And this is all the word *imaginary* means in this instance, that 6 and $j6$ can not be symbolized on the same number line.

In fact, there is one number that is common to both the number lines in Figure 13.43*b*, and that is zero. By definition, $a \times 0 = 0$, so $j0 = 0$. Since this is true, it would be more accurate to draw the two number lines as shown in Figure 13.44. But this is exactly the form of the R and J axes shown in Figure 13.40. The two axes in the rectangular coordinate system represent two magnitudes that are not comensurate, like resistance and inductive reactance.

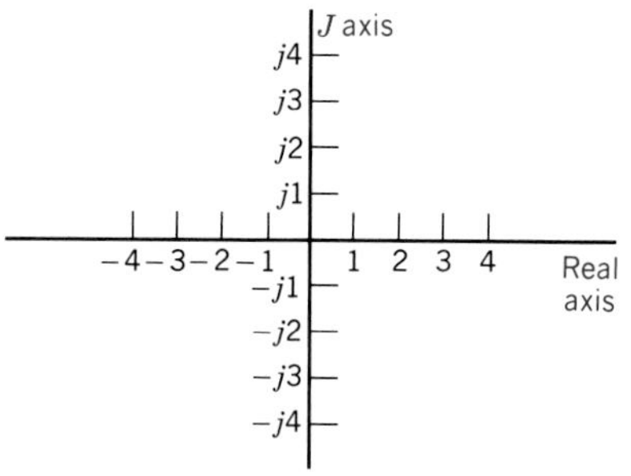

Figure 13.44 Since 0 is shared by both the real and imaginary number lines, it is more meaningful to draw the number lines so that they intersect.

Now, note the function of the j operator. If a number, like 4, on the $+R$ or positive side of the real number line is multiplied by j, the result is an imaginary number $j4$, which is located on the positive imaginary axis. In other words, multiplication by j is interpreted as the rotation of a phasor four units long that lies on the R axis through an angle of 90°. After rotation, the phasor lies along the J, or imaginary, axis and has a value of $j4$. The operator j therefore provides the ability to indicate the rotation of a phasor quantity from the real, or reference, axis in a phasor diagram.

Using the j operator, it then becomes possible to express the components of an impedance or phase-shifted current or potential difference using its two components.

EXAMPLE:
Using rectangular coordinates, express the impedance of a 0.68 mH coil with an internal resistance of 100 Ω when it is connected to a 60 Hz source. ■

SOLUTION:
Since the phasor for the inductive reactance of a component or circuit is represented as having a 90° phase shift from the reference or resistance, use of the j operator makes this an easy process. The resistance of the inductor is 100 Ω, and its inductive reactance is $2\pi fL = 256.35\ \Omega$. Figure 13.45 shows a phasor diagram of the two components. The impedance phasor Z can be expressed as $Z = 100 + j256.35$. ■

The impedance in the above example is written in what is called *complex number notation*. A complex number is any expression that has both a real axis and imaginary axis portion. In other words, the rectangular

Figure 13.43 Number lines to show the meaning of "imaginary" when referring to numbers.

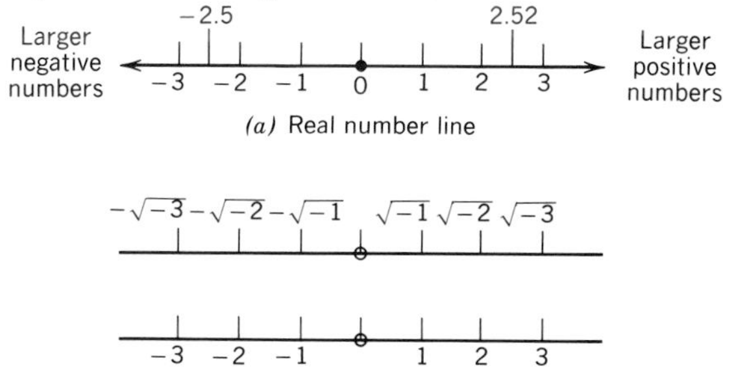

(b) One possibility: A separate number line for imaginary numbers

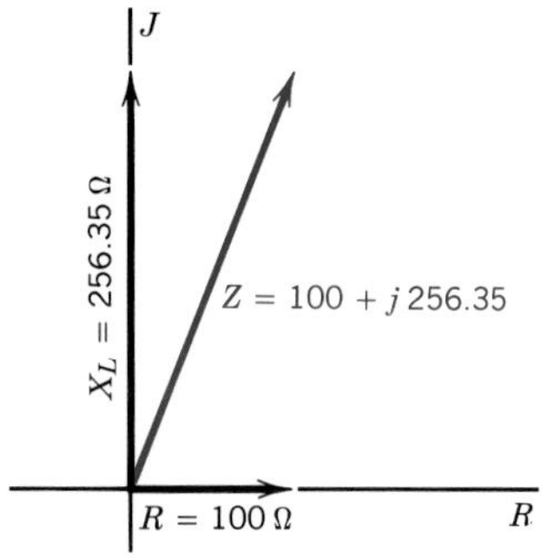

Figure 13.45 Using the complex rectangular coordinate system to express impedances.

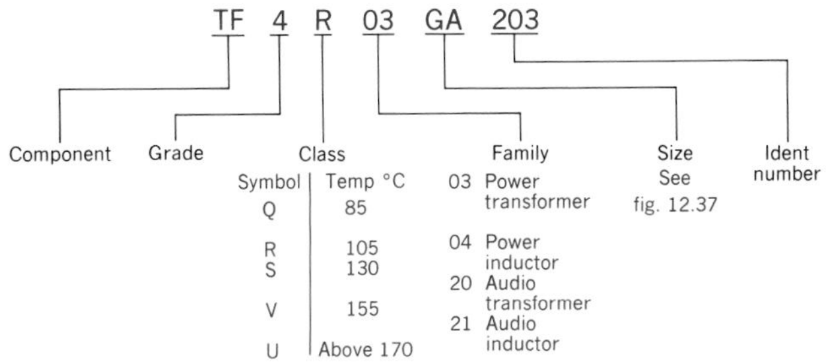

Figure 13.46 MIL-T-27D transformer type designation.

coordinate system and j operator can be used to express impedances, potential differences, and currents as complex numbers.

Develop your familiarity with complex number notation by expressing the following phasor quantities as complex numbers in the complex rectangular system.

a. $X_L = 180\ \Omega$, $R = 56\ \Omega$, $Z = ?$
b. $X_L = 19.75\ \Omega$, $R = 12.38\ \Omega$, $Z = ?$
c. $Z = 5.3\ \angle 30^\circ$, $X_L = ?$, $R = ?$
d. $Z = 19\ \angle 90^\circ$, $X_L = ?$, $R = ?$
e. $X_L = 45.53\ \Omega$, $R = 37.2\ \Omega$, $Z = ?$
f. In a series circuit, $X_{L1} = 43.3\ \Omega$, $X_{L2} = 56\ \Omega$, $R1 = 27\ \Omega$, $Z = ?$

D. APPLICATIONS

D.1 TRANSFORMER TYPES: CHARACTERISTICS AND FAILURE MODES

The existence of many commercial types of transformers is in part due to the fact that the transformer is one of the most costly of electronic components. Size considerations aside, it would cost an equipment manufacturer only a few additional pennies to use a 2-W resistor in a circuit where a $\frac{1}{4}$-W resistor would be adequate. On the other hand, the difference in the list prices for a transformer capable of delivering 1 A at 24 V from the 120-V mains and one that will provide 4 A is on the order of twice the cost of the lower capacity transformer in single unit quantities. Thus, although the extra cost of ordering and stocking several sizes of resistors might offset any saving realized by using the less costly, smaller dissipation units, the large price differential in transformers will tend to make each manufacturer use exactly the transformer needed for a particular application. For this reason, in addition to series of more or less standardized inductors and transformers, consumer and industrial electronic units tend to contain nonstandard, specially designed components.

The most widely used classification method for transformers is the military scheme defined in military specification MIL-T-27. Designed to cover power transformers and inductors weighing less than 300 pounds (136 kg), audio-frequency transformers and inductors, as well as a number of miniature and special-function types, transformers produced according to this specification are marked with a type designation of the sort seen in Figure 13.46. The first two letters of this designation are always TF, whether the component is an inductor or a transformer. The following single number is called the *grade* of the component and specifies the type of case involved. A grade 4 component is completely enclosed in a metal case, while a grade 5 unit is encapsulated. An encapsulated transformer is either completely surrounded by some epoxy or other compound or placed in an open metal shell that is then filled with the encapsulating compound. Class 6 components are open type.

Following the grade number is the class letter. This letter identifies the maximum operating temperature of the component. The two-digit number following the class symbol is the family code. The family code identifies the function of the transformer or inductor. The next piece of information is a two-letter code that provides the case and mounting dimensions. These codes are identical to those given in Chapter 12. Finally, the primary and secondary coil characteristics may be specified by a three-digit number that refers to a particular transformer. This number is the identification number. If the transformer is not identical to one listed in the specification supplement, there is no identification number, and the required information will usually be printed on the component case.

D.1.1 TYPES AND CHARACTERISTICS

Military specifications do not include radio-frequency transformers in the same classification as power and audio transformers since the construction techniques and characteristics are different. With the increased use of ferrite and powered iron cores, however, the operational similarities of power, audio, and radio-frequency transformers outweigh their differences and can be discussed in this section.

One type of transformer that has not been considered here is the pulse transformer. These components are still less common than power, audio, or rf transformers but are found in power supplies of computers and the high-voltage power sections of television receivers.

In addition to these transformer types, three additional transformer families with specific functions will be considered in this section. These are isolation transformers, dc blocking transformers, and autotransformers.

D.1.2 POWER TRANSFORMERS

The replacement of the vacuum tube by transistors and other solid-state devices has brought about a change in the design of power transformers. With few exceptions, vacuum tubes required a high-voltage, low-current dc supply *and* a separate low-voltage, medium to high current ac or dc supply for operation. A typical six-tube radio receiver of the 1940s might need 250 V dc at 100 mA and 12.6 V ac at 3.5 A. These operating potentials were obtained from the 120-V ac mains service via a step-up transformer and a rectifier (a circuit that converted the stepped-up ac potential to dc). Additional secondaries on the transformer provided low-voltage, high-current ac potentials at 6.3 or 12.6 V, and, in some designs, 5.0 V ac for operating the rectifier. Figure 13.47*a* shows a typical power transformer of this type. Connections were usually made via color-coded wire leads welded directly to the copper windings of the transformer. A schematic representation of this transformer, including the color coding of the wire leads is given in Figure 13.47*b*. Note that several of the secondary windings have an additional lead called a *center tap*. This is rather common and is necessary in some applications. Center tap leads are commonly distinguished by combining the solid color with a yellow stripe. Note that the primary lead also has an additional tap.

Although modern electronic unit power transformers physically resemble the component shown in Figure 13.47*a*, they generally possess fewer secondary windings and are usually step-down transformers. Since solid-state circuits require a low-voltage, high-current dc source and no ac filament power, a single secondary is the most common configuration. The definition of a power supply transformer has become a unit that transforms the mains supply to low-voltage ac, generally

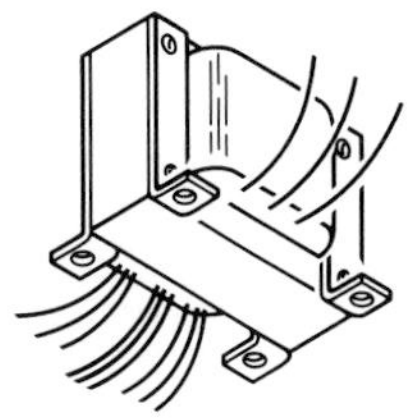

(a) Chassis-mounted power transformer

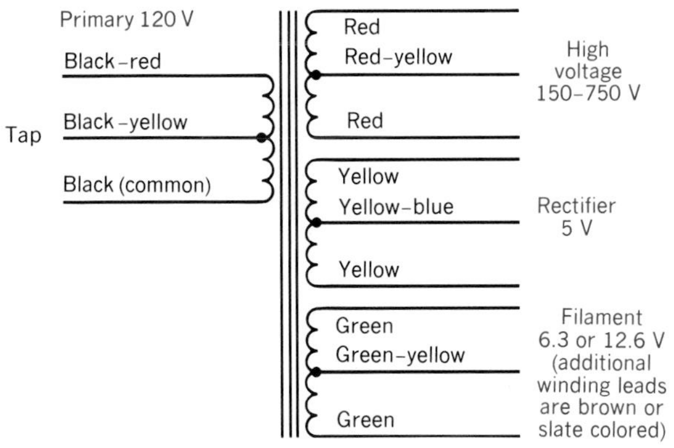

(b) Schematic diagram showing lead color coding

Figure 13.47 A typical transformer widely used in tube-type equipment.

less than 50 V ac rms for conversion to dc by a solid-state rectifier.

In the United States, power transformers intended for smaller electronic units usually possess primaries rated at 120 V ac, although larger units such as transmitters and big computer systems frequently use transformers with 220/240 or even 440-V ac primaries. Except for aircraft and certain special shipboard and industrial installations, which operate at a power frequency of 400 Hz, all commercial power distribution in the United States operates at a frequency of 60 Hz. For the most part, 50 Hz and 220 or 240 V ac is standard in Europe. Many manufacturers have designed their power transformers for operation at both 50 and 60 Hz, although this is not always the case. You must consult the manufacturer's specifications before using a 60-Hz transformer on a 50-Hz power line. In transformers intended for use on both 120 and 240 V ac service, a single primary coil with taps at different points as in Figure 13.48*a* or two separate primaries are provided as shown in Figure 13.48*b*. When there are two primary windings, they are connected in parallel for 120 V ac service and in series for 240 V ac. This arrangement is quite popular since it permits the manufacturer to use thinner wire for the primaries, without increasing the copper losses. In Figure 13.49*a*, the two primary windings are connected in parallel and they act as a single coil of 1000 turns. Each coil carries half the total primary current. In Figure 13.49*b*, the two primaries are connected in series and will act as a single coil of

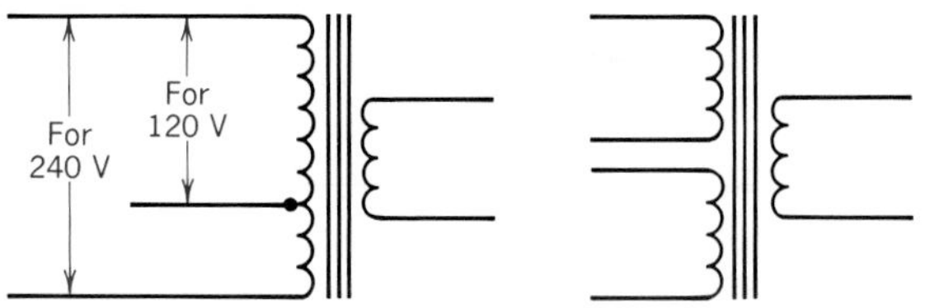

Figure 13.48 Some modern transformers are designed for operation at 120/240 V 50/60 Hz.

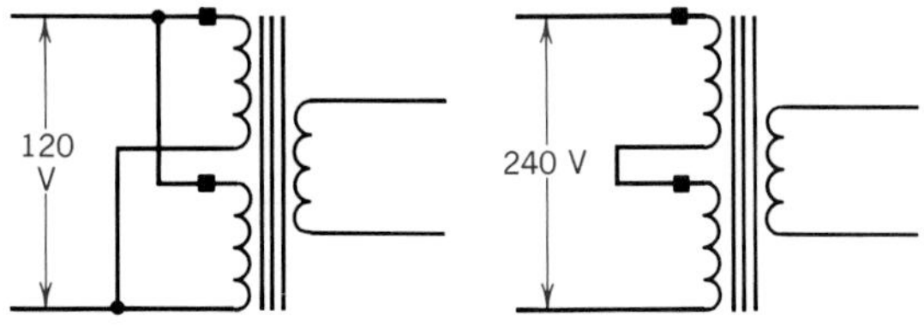

Figure 13.49 Connecting dual-primary transformers for 120- and 240-V operation. Phasing must be as shown.

2000 turns. Since the primary potential difference is twice that of 13.49*a*, the secondary potential difference will remain the same even though the turns ratio of the primary to the secondary has been halved. The primary current is still the same as that in one of the primary coils shown in Figure 13.49*a*. When connecting the primaries of a dual primary transformer, care must be taken to phase the coils properly, as shown in the figure.

It is very important to remember, however, that even though many 50 Hz, 240-V ac transformers have provisions for operation at 60 Hz, 120 V ac, operation at 400 Hz is an entirely different matter. Power transformers designed for operation at 400 Hz are usually considerably smaller than 50/60 Hz units and a primary winding will have much less impedance at 60 Hz than it does at 400 Hz. The few power transformers that can be used at both 60 and 400 Hz are almost always marked with their operating frequency range or this ability is noted in the specifications. Any transformer that is not so marked should never be used at a different power frequency.

In addition to physical size, primary voltage and current, and turns ratio of a power transformer, there are a number of characteristics that affect component operation. If you are selecting a replacement for a burned out transformer or selecting a component for a design, you should be aware of these characteristics:

1. Rated primary voltage(s) and range. A transformer has been designed to operate most efficiently and without overheating at a certain nominal primary potential (potentials in the case of a transformer with primary taps or more than one primary winding). Better quality power transformers can operate efficiently with typical variations of 10 percent in their primary voltage without overheating. Some components, called *constant voltage transformers*, are even designed to keep their secondary voltage constant in spite of variations in the primary potential.

2. Frequency range. Most power transformers commercially available in the United States have been designed for 60 Hz operation. Some of these, slightly oversized for better dissipation of heat, are also capable of efficient operation at 50 Hz. The operating frequency range for a particular transformer is either printed on the case or is included in the manufacturer's specifications. The operating frequency tolerance is not often given for power transformers, but ± 10 percent is a typical figure.

3. Secondary rms voltages under rated load at nominal primary voltage. When a manufacturer specifies the potential difference of a power transformer secondary, it is understood that this value represents the potential difference across a secondary resistive load drawing the rated current.

4. Insulation resistance. The transformer manufacturer's terms *insulation resistance* or *insulation test voltage* refer to the maximum potential difference permitted between any winding and the core or between any two windings. Both the peak ac potentials and the windings as well as any dc produced by sources must be considered. If the insulation resistance rating of the transformer is exceeded, a continuous arcing can occur. This would destroy the enamel insulating coating on the copper wire or the thin layers of insulation used to separate the turn layers. Another problem caused by exceeding the allowed potential difference of a transformer is called *corona*. This is the ionization of the air between transformer windings or between windings and the core. This problem can be detected by the production of a buzzing sound in the transformer. Most commercially available power transformers have an insulation resistance of about 1500 V, although units with a rated insulation of 2500 or 7500 V are available.

5. Regulation factor. You have already learned that the potential difference measured across the secondary terminals of a real transformer is not necessarily equal to the theoretical value obtained by multiplying the primary voltage by the primary to secondary turns ratio. Since manufacturers define a transformer's secondary potential difference at what is considered rated full load, the measured potential difference across the secondary terminals will be higher than this when there is no load. A load that draws more than the rated secondary current will cause the measured secondary potential difference to drop below the nominal potential difference. Since the load on a power transformer can vary considerably in some electronic units, a characteristic called the *percent regulation,* or *regulation %,* is used to give some indication of how much the secondary potential difference will change under varying load conditions.

$$\text{Regulation } \% = \frac{V_{\text{no load}} - V_{\text{full load}}}{V_{\text{full load}}}$$

FORMULA 13.20

The regulation percent of a transformer depends on both core and copper losses and on the number of winding turns per volt in the primary and secondary. It is, therefore, a good indication of the quality and efficiency of a transformer. Substituting a transformer with poor regulation in a circuit designed for a higher regulation percentage can cause power supply failure.

6. Shielding. Many transformers provide a shield to prevent an electric field linkage between the primary and secondary. In the next chapter, you will learn that this effect is referred to as *capacitance*. The existence of an electrostatic shield is important in some units and must not be omitted. Magnetic shielding of the entire transformer is another concern. Never replace a transformer enclosed in a ferromagnetic case with one of the unshielded variety unless it is certain that the flux leakage from the unshielded unit will have no effect on nearby components.

7. Surge conditions and application. The final group of power transformer characteristics are all related to the ability of the unit to resist damage due to transient conditions caused by line voltage changes or transient state conditions in the circuits powered by the transformer secondary. Formerly, a distinction was made between power transformers intended for vacuum tube rectifiers that used filters with inductors as their first element and filters that used capacitors. The difference in this case refers to the fact that capacitors cause current surges in the transformer secondary. Although some manufacturers still make this distinction, the use of inductors in rectifier filter circuits has become less common. Instead, capacitors and solid-state voltage regulators are used in most new unit power supplies.

D.1.3 AUDIO TRANSFORMER CHARACTERISTICS

Audio-frequency transformers are used either to transfer an audio-frequency signal from one circuit or unit to another or to link an electromechanical device such as a microphone or speaker to an electronic unit. They are frequently also called *interstage transformers,* or *impedance-matching transformers,* although these terms could also include radio-frequency components and are therefore misleading. Audio-frequency transformers often resemble small power transformers, but their important electrical characteristics differ greatly from those of power transformers.

1. Source and load impedances. Taking the place of the primary and secondary potential differences of the power transformer are the required primary and secondary impedances in the audio transformer. These impedances are often printed on the transformer itself, sometimes along with a schematic of the unit where multiple or tapped windings are involved. These are the impedances when the frequency of the source is at the middle of the marked operating range.

2. Frequency range. Power transformers are generally used at a single source frequency, while audio-frequency transformers are expected to operate over a range of frequencies. Depending on the application for which the transformer is designed, the operating frequency range can cover any frequency spread between about 30 Hz and 50 kHz or higher. The actual recommended range for any transformer is usually printed on the case and is always given in the manufacturers' specifications. A typical range for audio transformers is 30 Hz to 20 kHz.

3. DC Ratings. Unlike power transformers, audio transformers are designed for operation with dc components in both their primary and secondary windings. Since these dc components could cause the saturation of the transformer core, maximum dc levels must be observed.

4. Frequency response. This characteristic is related to the recommended frequency range but provides additional information. Frequently presented in terms of a graph called a *frequency response curve,* this characteristic shows how the transfer of energy from the transformer primary to secondary is affected by the frequency. There will generally be a drop off in power transfer at both the high- and low-frequency ends of the curve. This drop off in the amount of energy transferred is more marked than manufacturers' graphs would seem to show because the *y*-axis scale, as is traditional in the frequency response curve, is logarithmic. The results of using a transformer with the poor frequency response are an overall loss of signal power and distortion of the waveform of a complex signal. When the frequency response graph is essentially flat over the operating frequency range, less power is lost, and the waveform of the secondary circuit more closely resembles that of the primary circuit. Manufacturers will

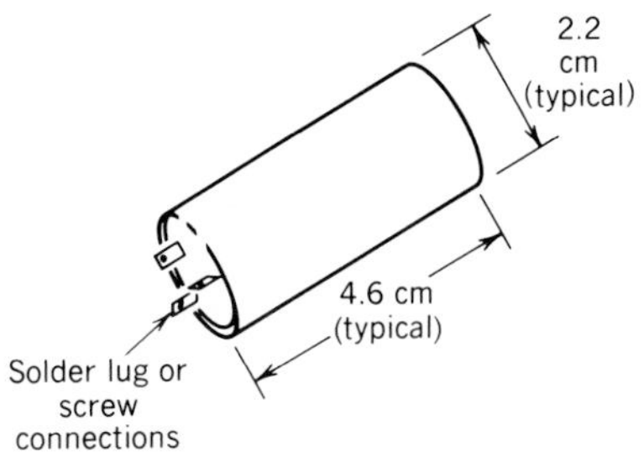

Figure 13.50 In addition to the smaller case sizes shown in Figure 12.37, audio transformers are also found in cylindrical cases.

generally specify the input power level at which the frequency response curve measurements are made since low power tends to mask poor frequency response. Also related to the frequency range of an audio transformer is the characteristic known as *harmonic distortion,* which results from the fact that some of the sine-wave harmonics that compose any waveform may be above or below the "flat" area in the transformer's frequency response curve.

5. Insertion loss. This characteristic, composed of the copper and core losses of the transformer, is a measure of the power lost in the transformer itself. Like the *y*-axis in a frequency response curve, insertion loss is measured in logarithmic units called *decibels,* which will be treated in Chapter 16.

6. Shielding. The presence of magnetic shielding around an audio transformer and an electrostatic shield between its primary and secondary is of greater importance than in the case of power transformers. This is true because the secondary potential difference of most electronic unit power transformers is converted into dc, thereby eliminating the resulting problems caused by stray magnetic or electric fields. On the other hand, any noise produced by a stray field in the audio transformer becomes a part of the signal in the transformer secondary circuit. For example, replacing a burned-out audio transformer that had adequate shielding with one that has no shielding in a stereo system would probably result in an unacceptable level of hum and noise in the output to the speakers.

7. Case styles. The final characteristic of audio transformers that you must consider when selecting a component for a new design or as a replacement is case size and style. In addition to the smaller sizes and case styles used for power transformers, audio transformers of cylindrical shape with powdered iron or ferrite cores are common. These shapes and small sizes (Figure 13.50) are possible because many audio transformers carry currents on the order of a few milliamperes. This means that copper losses will be low, and fine wire can be used in the windings.

D.1.4 DC BLOCKING TRANSFORMERS

Transformers of this category are used when it is necessary to pass low-frequency ac signals from one unit or circuit to another while keeping the two units or circuits isolated from each other with respect to dc. A typical example would be coupling an ac signal from a solid-state audio-frequency signal generator to a transmitter with a fairly high power supply potential. As you can see, except for the fact that either or both windings of the blocking transformer might be required to pass a larger dc component than a typical audio transformer, there is no difference in overall function. Thus, although the term *dc blocking transformer* is used, the component can be considered an audio transformer.

D.1.5 RF TRANSFORMERS

Transformers designed for use at frequencies higher than 50 kHz are often called *radio frequency,* or *rf transformers.* There are many different component types and functions represented in this classification. The most common transformers in this category are the units designed to couple certain of the circuits of a radio or television receiver. Like the typical units pictured in Figure 13.51, these components are of two types: *antenna transformers,* or *antenna coils,* and *intermediate frequency,* or *if transformers.* Regardless of their differing shapes, these transformers are designed to form parts of tuned circuits, which are covered in Chapter 17.

Figure 13.51 IF and antenna transformers.

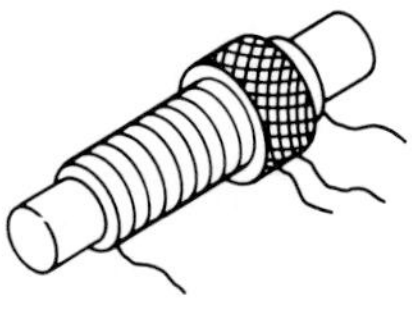

(a) Antenna coil wound on ferrite rod

(b) Coils wound on hollow plastic form

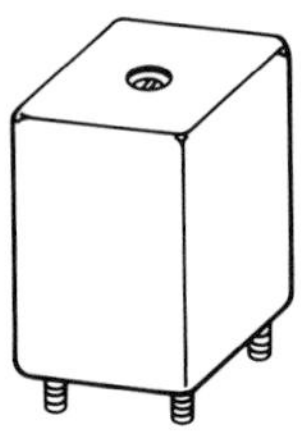

(c) Typical if transformer enclosed in aluminum shield. A small opening provides access for adjustment of the core.

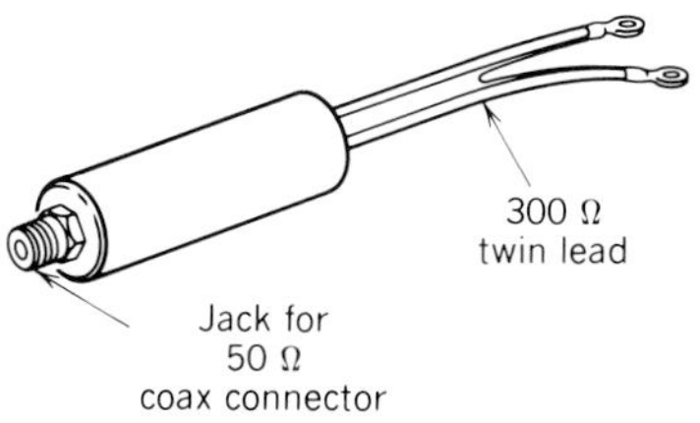

Figure 13.52 A transformer intended for matching a 300 Ω antenna to a 50 Ω impedance.

Another common type of rf transformer is the impedance-matching transformer. Frequently used to match an antenna with a characteristic impedance of 300 Ω to a length of coax cable with a 50 Ω impedance, these transformers take the form shown in Figure 13.52. Since they are intended for VHF or UHF operation, these components use ferrite or air cores. Their most important characteristics are:

a. Frequency range
b. Primary and secondary impedance
c. Insertion loss

The power-handling capacity of these impedance-matching devices only becomes important in the case of transmitters.

The wide-band transformers wound on toroidal or elongated ferrite cores are becoming popular in radio transmitter and other applications. The ability of modest-sized ferrite cores to provide low-loss, high-power transformers has enabled major reductions in size over the air core transformers that were once used.

D.1.6 AUTOTRANSFORMERS

One curious type of transformer that you should know about is the single-winding autotransformer illustrated in the schematics of Figure 13.53. Instead of the separate primary and secondary windings found in a standard transformer, the autotransformer consists of a single winding with three terminals. Depending on the connection of the three terminals, the autotransformer can act as a step-up transformer, as in Figure 13.53*a*,

Figure 13.53 Autotransformer connections.

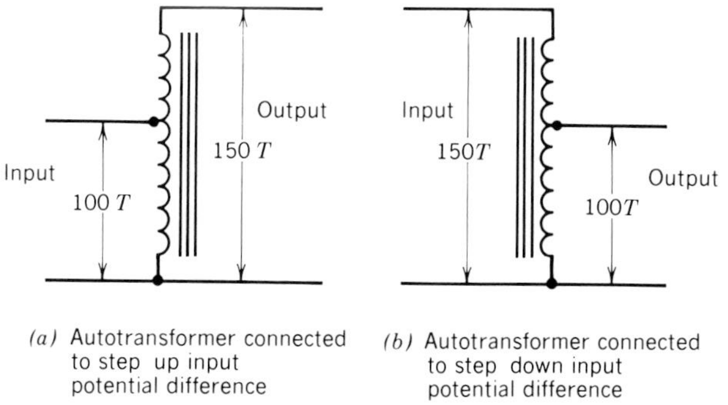

(*a*) Autotransformer connected to step up input potential difference

(*b*) Autotransformer connected to step down input potential difference

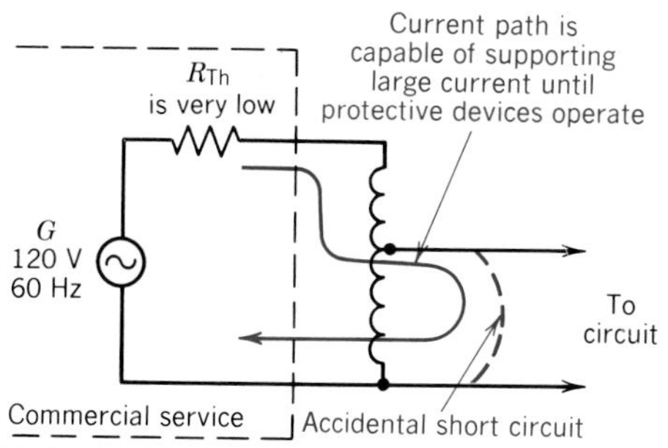

Figure 13.54 An autotransformer provides no isolation from the power mains.

or a step-down transformer, as in 13.53*b*. Note that Formulas 13.8 through 13.15 can be used to calculate voltages or currents if it is kept in mind that a part of the coil is shared by both the input and output of the autotransformer. In Figure 13.53*b*, for example, N_p = 150 and N_s = 100, so the output voltage is

$$E_s = \frac{N_s}{N_p}E_p = \frac{2}{3}E_p$$

Since both the input and output current flow in the shared part of the coil, manufacturers frequently wind this part of the coil using a heavy-gauge wire, while a thinner, higher-gauge wire is used for the remainder of the coil. Because only one winding is used, the autotransformer can be considerably smaller than a standard transformer that produces the same potential difference and current. On the other hand, the output tap of the autotransformer is not isolated from the AC source. In the case of an autotransformer connected to the power mains, this means that the output tap is linked to an almost ideal voltage source with a very low Thevenin equivalent resistance, as shown in Figure 13.54. An accidental short circuit between the output tap and ground could, therefore, result in a very large current flow. For this reason, the autotransformer is considered unsafe for certain applications where it is important that the unit is isolated from the power mains.

Autotransformers are commonly used in two applications. The first is to change 220/240-V European service power to 120 V power for the operation of American appliances in Europe, or the reverse, that is, to raise the 120-V potential of American service power to 240 V to operate European appliances. Since tourists and travelers do not wish to be burdened with bulky transformers, the smaller, lighter autotransformer is used. A second application is the voltage-adjusting autotransformer. Appearing under a variety of trade names, this component consists of a single coil wound on a toroidal core. A movable contactor takes the place of the fixed tap, as shown in Figure 13.55*a*.

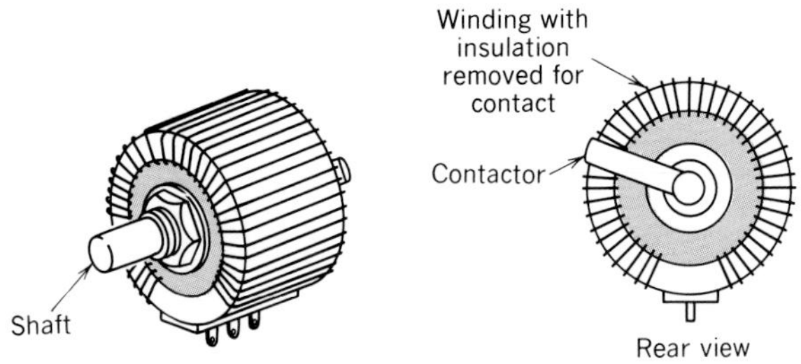

(a) Variable autotransformer

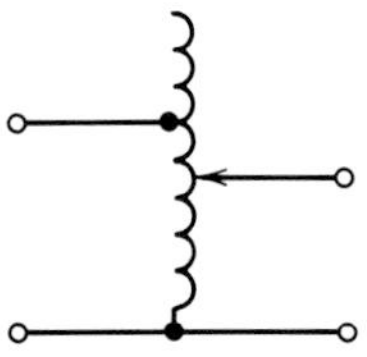
(b) Schematic symbol

Figure 13.55 The variable autotransformer.

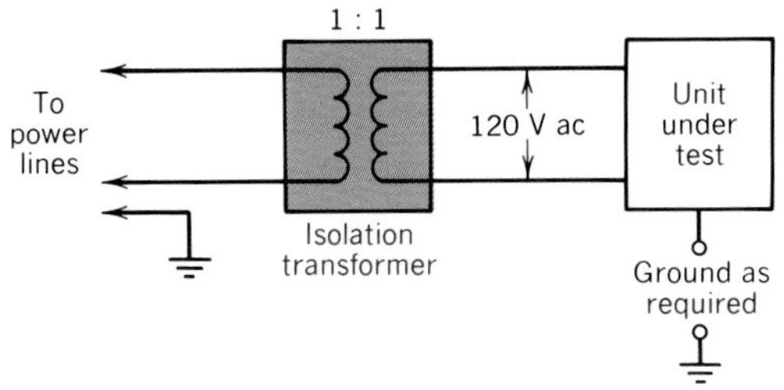

Figure 13.56 Using an isolation transformer in troubleshooting.

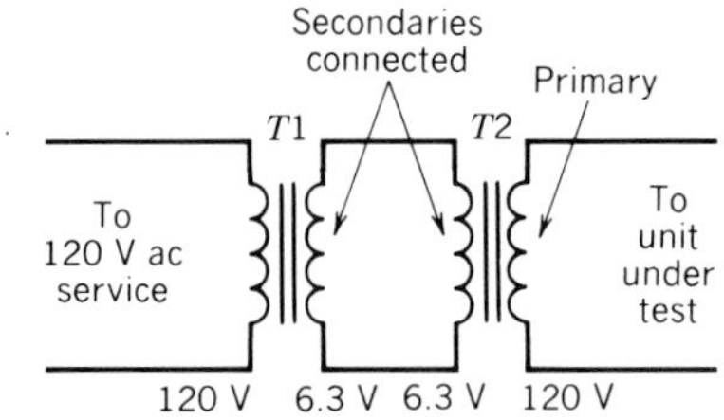

Figure 13.57 Two identical step-down transformers can be used in place of an isolation transformer.

Turning the shaft to which the contactor is fixed permits the selection of the primary to secondary turns ratio and provides an adjustable output potential. Variable autotransformers are used in instruments to compensate for slightly low or slightly high service potentials. In large cities, for example, the service line voltage can dip to 105 V ac rms during periods of heavy use. Larger variable autotransformers are used for control purposes in industry. The schematic symbol for a variable autotransformer is shown in Figure 13.55*b*.

D.1.7 ISOLATION TRANSFORMERS

The final type of transformer to be considered in this section is the isolation transformer. As mentioned in the previous section, the major drawback of the autotransformer is the lack of isolation between the source and the output tap. In effect, the output of the autotransformer is connected to the service line. Now, any standard power transformer will provide isolation between the circuits connected to its secondary and the service line or other source connected to its primary. Because of this, a special isolation transformer, having the same number of turns in both its primary and secondary is often used by maintenance technicians when servicing malfunctioning equipment. The isolation transformer prevents some types of electrical shock due to faulty circuits in the unit under test, and eliminates problems that might arise from the use of grounded test equipment. Figure 13.56 shows the block diagram of an isolation transformer used in troubleshooting.

If you need to isolate a unit from the power line, but do not have an isolation transformer, a simple solution is to use a pair of identical step-down transformers, as shown in Figure 13.57. If the current required by the circuit connected to *T*2 and the copper and core losses are below the maximum operating current of the transformers, this combination provides excellent isolation.

D.2 TRANSFORMER FAILURE MODES AND TROUBLESHOOTING

The problem of transformer reliability is marked by a curious contradiction. According to reliability reports, the military-type electronic transformer is one of the most reliable components used in electronic equipment. The transformer is a massive unit and is generally able to withstand the heat produced by surge currents as well as other stress conditions. On the other hand, practical experience shows that transformers fail more frequently than would be expected. The reason for this is that many component failures or abnormal operating conditions place stress on the unit power transformer or audio transformers. The graph shown in Figure 13.58 charts typical transformer failures as a function of operating time. Notice that this graph falls into three distinct areas, two with a larger number of failures, and a long period of few failures. During the initial period of operation, manufacturing defects in the transformer and in the components connected to the transformer, as well as errors in assembling the unit, result in what are called *infant failures*. After this initial *burn-in* period is over, the number of failures drops sharply. A number of failures still occur, however,

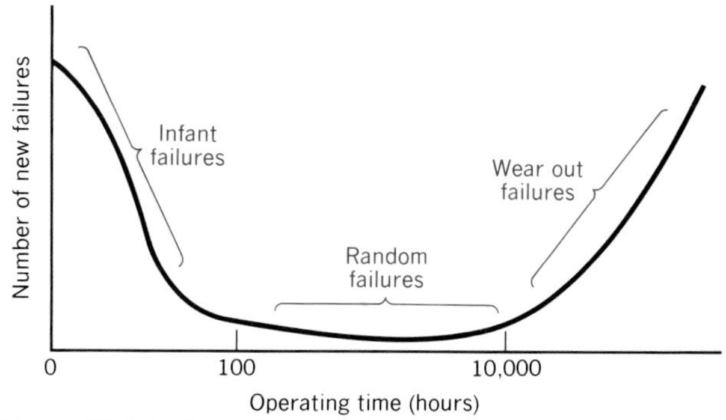

Figure 13.58 Transformer failure categories.

when the electrical or mechanical stresses on the transformer exceed the ability of the component to withstand them. These failures are referred to as *random failures*. For the most part, the transformer does not respond to stresses during the random failure period by failing. Instead, points of weakness accumulate until the third, or *wear-out,* phase. During this period, the number of unit failures will again increase because of accumulated damage.

There are five principal causes of stress on transformers that result in either immediate or eventual failure:

1. Temperature stress. Over a period of time, high temperature will cause the deterioration of the insulating materials used to separate the layers of windings from each other and from the transformer core. Temperature stress also weakens the soldered or welded joints between windings and lead-in wires or connection terminals and chars or deteriorates the enamel insulation on the wire used to wind the coils.

2. Dielectric stress. High potential differences between adjacent conductors alone usually have little effect unless the insulation rating is exceeded and arcing or corona occurs. On the other hand, ac dielectric stress below the insulation rating can result in transformer failure when mechanical faults exist, for example, the wear-out of wire insulation at certain points.

3. Vibration and shock stress. Vibration and shock produce failure by abrading insulation and causing wear in the mechanical parts of a transformer.

4. Thermal shock stress. Thermal shock, which should not be confused with high-temperature stress, is a sudden change in temperature. Repeated thermal shock stresses can cause wire fatigue and breaking, as well as the erosion of insulation.

5. Humidity stress. Exceeding the recommended humidity range of a transformer acts to cause failures in insulation previously weakened by temperature and thermal shock.

To summarize the effects of stress, temperature, vibration, mechanical shock, and thermal shock act to deteriorate a transformer over time. These stresses operate together and are the principal causes of transformer failure other than the failure of other components powered by the transformer. Humidity and dielectric stress act together with other stresses to increase the chance of failure of transformer insulation.

There are three modes of transformer failure that can result from the stresses discussed above. The first of these is short circuiting due to a failure of insulation, a short circuit between two turns or two windings which is referred to as a *dielectric failure* by component engineers. A failure of this type will usually change the electrical characteristics of the transformer and can often be detected by disconnecting the transformer secondary circuit and substituting a rated load. Measuring the potential difference produced across the rated load will reveal dielectric failures.

Turn-to-turn and turn-to-core dielectric failures are sometimes harder to detect than winding-to-winding shorts, particularly when the failure takes the form of a medium resistance current path that develops only when the transformer is operating under full power. One way of checking the isolation of primary and secondary windings or the isolation between a winding and the transformer core is to use a megohmmeter. This device, commonly called a *Megger,*® is a popular piece of equipment among industrial electricians and is used to judge the quality of ground connections, the insulation of electrical machines, and to detect medium to high resistance current leakage paths. Since the Megger® consists of a sensitive current meter and a source that produces potential differences of anywhere from several hundred to several thousand volts, its use around solid-state electronic units is dangerous. If you wish to use a megohmmeter to measure, for example, the leakage between a transformer winding and the core, the transformer should be completely disconnected and removed from the unit. A hand-cranked Megger® that produces from 100 to 1000 V dc by means of a hand-operated generator is shown in Figure 13.59.

Whether it is fortunate or not is hard to decide, but many hard-to-detect dielectric failures tend (because of heat buildup) to transform themselves into an easier to spot failure mode, the conductive failure. This is the name given to a failure due to an open circuit in a transformer winding or in the connection between the winding and a terminal inside the transformer. Unlike the dielectric failure, the conductive failure usually

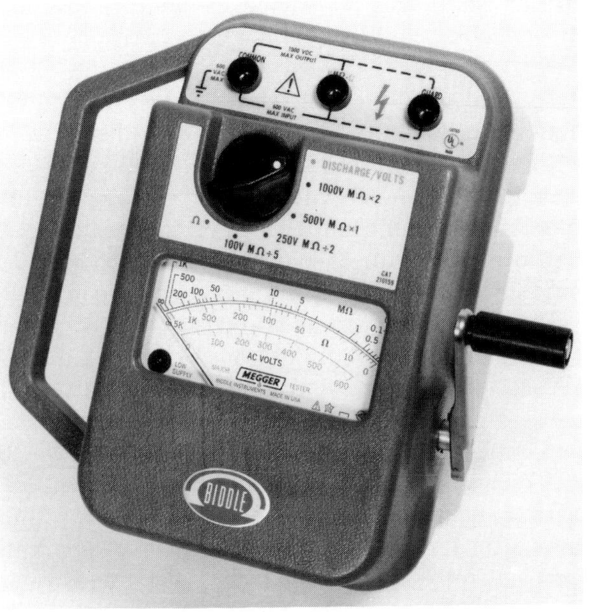

Figure 13.59 A megohmmeter. (Megger® is a trademark of Biddle Instruments, Blue Bell, PA 19422.)

causes the transformer to become completely inoperative. If you have a schematic diagram of the transformer circuit, you can usually use the ohmmeter function of your multimeter to detect a conductive failure in a transformer.

WARNING

BE SURE TO DISCONNECT ALL POWER SOURCES FROM THE UNIT CONTAINING THE TRANSFORMER TO BE TESTED. THEN, DISCHARGE ANY STORED POTENTIAL DIFFERENCES.

When a low-resistance load is connected across a transformer secondary winding, it is necessary to make potential difference measurements with the unit under power rather than resistance measurements, unless you want to go to the trouble of temporarily disconnecting the transformer winding from the load. The smell of burned insulation around an open case-type transformer is often an indication of a conductive failure, which is frequently the result of a heat buildup in the transformer windings.

The hardest form of transformer failure to spot is the magnetic failure. This failure mode results when the transformer core changes its magnetic properties. In addition to a change in the percentage of regulation, this type of failure is marked by increased primary current in power transformers and a reduced frequency range or saturation in audio transformers. The destruction of the insulation layer between iron core laminations by excessive heat is one cause of magnetic failure. Fortunately, this failure mode is considerably less common than dielectric or conductive failure; it is extremely difficult to spot magnetic failures in troubleshooting.

E. PROGRAMMED REVIEW

FRAME 1

A complex source can be redrawn as the combination of a __________ and one or more __________ of differing __________, __________, and __________.

a. dc source; ac sources; frequency; amplitude; phase. (2)
b. Any other answer, review Section B.1 and go on to Frame 2.

FRAME 2

The source circuit in Figure 13.60*a* produces the waveform shown in 13.60*b*. The complex source can be resolved into a dc source with a potential of __________ V and a series of ac sine-wave sources. The lowest frequency of the equivalent sine-wave sources is __________ Hz.

Figure 13.60 Diagram of Frame 2.

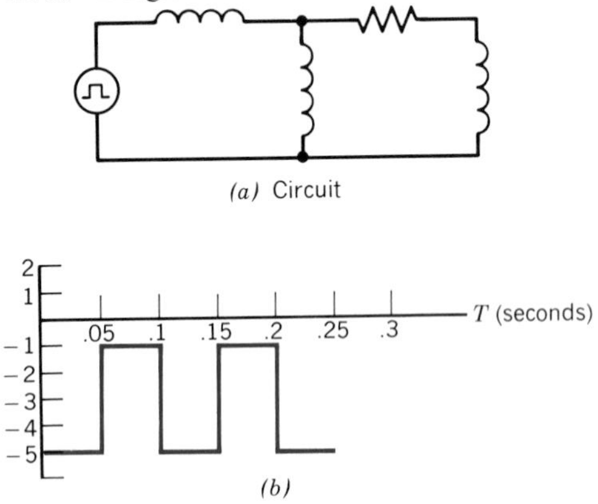

a. −3; 10 (3)
b. Any other answer, review Sections B.1 and B.2.

FRAME 3

The currents or voltage drops due to the dc and ac components of a complex source can be __________ and then combined.

a. Calculated separately. (4)
b. Any other answer, review Section B.1 and go on to Frame 4.

FRAME 4

Waveforms that are free to assume any value between an upper and lower limit are generally referred to as ___________.

a. Analog signals. (6)
b. Any other answer, review definitions at the beginning of Sections B.1 and B.2 and go on to Frame 5.

FRAME 5

A counter that produces a pulse every time an automobile passes through an intersection is an example of a ___________ circuit. On the other hand, a circuit that produces a signal proportional to the speed of the auto as it passes is an example of a ___________ circuit.

a. Digital; analog. (6)
b. Any other answer, review the definitions at the beginning of Sections B.1 and B.2 again.

FRAME 6

A ___________ is a piece of test equipment that displays the frequencies and amplitudes of the sine-wave components that make up a complex waveform.

a. Spectrum analyzer. (7)
b. Any other answer, review Section B.2 and go on to Frame 7.

FRAME 7

The Q of the component shown in Figure 13.61 is ___________ when it is connected to a 1 kHz source. If a 51 Ω resistor is placed in series with the coil and the source, the circuit Q will be ___________. If the resistor is in parallel with the source, the circuit Q will be ___________.

Figure 13.61 Figure for Frame 7.

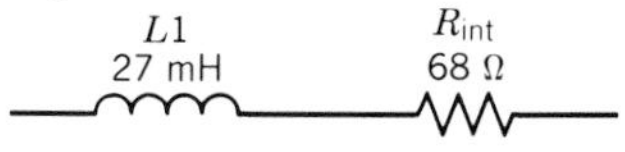

a. 2.49; 1.426; 0.27 (8)
b. Any other answers, review Section B.3.

FRAME 8

To find the Q of a ___________ circuit containing inductances and resistances, divide the inductive reactance of the circuit by the sum of the circuit resistances. The Q of a circuit composed of an inductor and series and parallel resistances can be calculated by using the formula ___________.

a. Series; $Q = \dfrac{X_L}{R_s + \dfrac{X_L^2}{R_p}}$
b. Any other answer, review Section B.3.

FRAME 9

The linkage of the flux produced by two series-connected coils produces a combined inductance that is different from the sum of the inductances of the two coils. The combined inductance depends on the inductances of the two coils, their phasing, and the ___________.

a. Coefficient of coupling. (10)
b. Any other answer, review Section B.4.

FRAME 10

The transformer effect is based on the fact that a ___________ magnetic field in one coil will induce a potential difference across the ends of a nearby coil.

a. Changing. (11)
b. Any other answer, review the first paragraph of Section B.5.

FRAME 11

If the coefficient of coupling between the two coils in Figure 13.62 is assumed to be unity, and all losses are ignored, the potential difference produced by the source is ___________ V rms.

Figure 13.62 Figure for Frame 11.

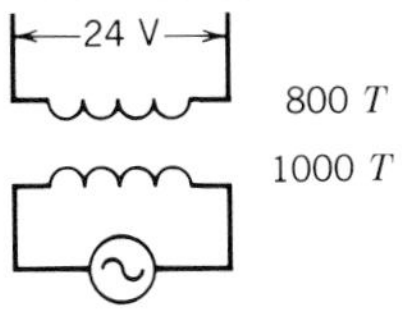

a. 30 (13)
b. Any other answer, review Section B.5.

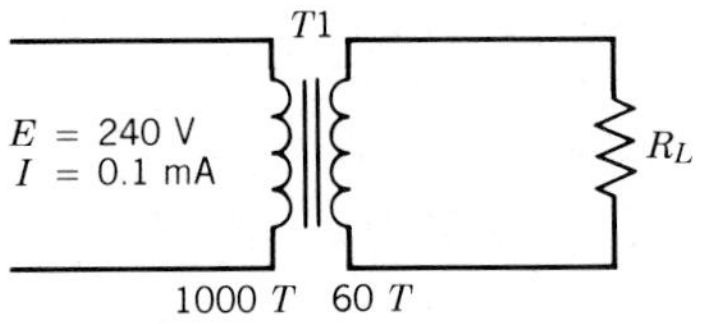

Figure 13.63 Figure for Frame 13.

FRAME 12

To calculate the potential difference and current in one of the windings of a transformer with a coefficient of coupling equal to 1, without losses, the relationships

$$e_{\text{primary}} = \_\_\_\_ \times e_{\text{secondary}}$$

and

$$i_{\text{primary}} = \_\_\_\_ \times i_{\text{secondary}}$$

can be used.

a. $\dfrac{N_{\text{primary}}}{N_{\text{secondary}}}; \dfrac{N_{\text{secondary}}}{N_{\text{primary}}}$ (13)
b. Any other answer, review Section B.5.

FRAME 13

Assuming a transformer efficiency of 100 percent, what is the current that transformer T1 in Figure 13.63 is supplying to the load?

a. 1.6 mA (14)
b. Any other answer, review Section B.4 and go back to Frame 12.

FRAME 14

An ideal transformer is connected to a 120-V ac power source; the secondary potential difference is 8 V. What is the primary to secondary turns ratio?

a. 15:1 or $\dfrac{15}{1}$ (15)
b. Any other answer, return to Frame 12.

FRAME 15

The primary of a real transformer is marked 120 V ac and its secondary is marked 24 V ac at 1 A. What load would have to be connected across the transformer secondary to assure that the secondary potential difference is as marked?

a. a 24 Ω resistive load. (16)
b. Any other answer, review Section B.5.

FRAME 16

A real transformer primary is connected to the 120-V ac mains service. The measured primary current is 15 mA. If the transformer secondary supplies 12 V at 0.1 A to a resistive load, what is the efficiency of the transformer?

a. 66.7 percent (17)
b. Any other answer, review Section B.5.

FRAME 17

Core losses in a transformer are due to ________ or ________.

a. Eddy currents; hysteresis. (19)
b. Any other answer, review Section B.5 and go to Frame 18.

FRAME 18

Losses due to the resistance of transformer windings are called ________.

a. Copper losses. (19)
b. Any other answer, review Section B.5.

FRAME 19

In addition to transforming ac power from one potential difference and current to a different potential or current, transformers are frequently used for ________. A transformer used to match an ac source with an impedance of 450 Ω to an impedance of 50 Ω will have a turns ratio of ________.

a. Impedance matching; 3:1 or $\dfrac{3}{1}$. (20)
b. Any other answer, review Section B.7.

FRAME 20

An ac potential difference of 10 V rms is applied to the primary of a transformer designed to match a 400 Ω primary circuit to an 8 Ω secondary. What is the potential difference across the secondary if the transformer operates at 100 percent efficiency?

a. 70.7 V (21)
b. Any other answer, review Section B.7.

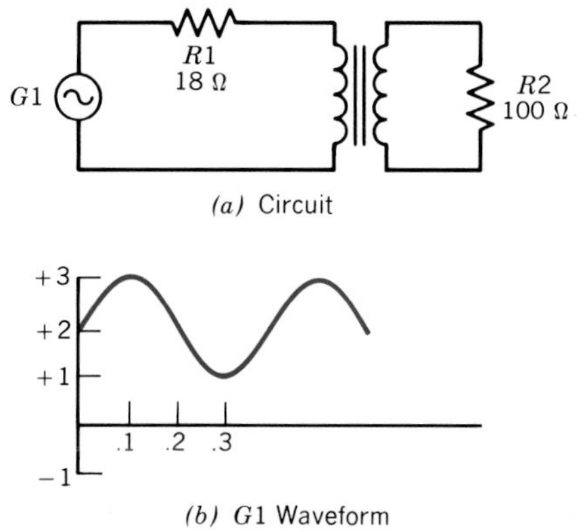

Figure 13.64 Circuit and waveform for Frame 21.

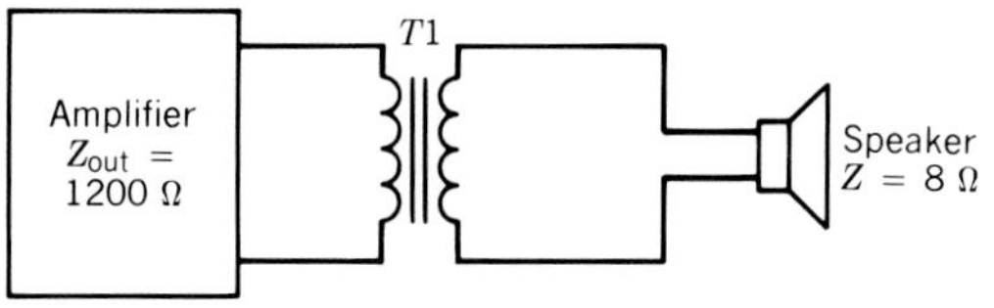

Figure 13.65 Diagram for Frame 22.

FRAME 21

A sine-wave potential difference as shown in Figure 13.64 is applied to the *RL* circuit. What is the magnitude of the dc component through the transformer primary?

a. 2 V (22)
b. Any other answer, review Sections B.2 and C1.

FRAME 22

In the circuit shown in Figure 13.65, the impedance of the output circuit is 1200 Ω; the impedance of the speaker is 8 Ω. If the potential difference across the matching transformer primary is 40 V, what will be the maximum potential across the speaker? (Assume an ideal transformer)

a. 3.27 V (23)
b. Any other answer, review the solved problems in Section C.2.

FRAME 23

Two coordinate systems which can be used to describe phasor quantities are the ____________ and the ____________ coordinate systems.

a. Polar; complex rectangular. (24)
b. Any other answer, review Section C.3 and go on to Frame 24.

FRAME 24

A sine wave has a peak value of 12 V and lags the reference phasor by 17°. Specify this phasor in polar form.

a. $12 \angle -17^\circ$ (25)
b. Any other answer, review Section C.3.

FRAME 25

Write the impedance of a 10 H, 1 kΩ inductor operating at 25 Hz in complex rectangular form and in polar form.

a. $1000 + j1570.8$; $1862.1 \angle 57.5^\circ$ (26)
b. Any other answers, review Section C.3.

FRAME 26

The primary of a power transformer is usually connected to ____________. Older transformers of this type generally had one ____________ secondary and several ____________ secondaries.

a. 120-V ac power line; step-up; step-down. (27)
b. Any answer that does not contain these points, review Section D.1.2.

FRAME 27

The insulation resistance of a transformer refers to ____________. Most commercial units have insulation resistances of ____________.

a. The maximum potential difference permitted between any winding and the core or between any two windings; 1500. (28)
b. Any other answer, review Section D.1.2.

FRAME 28

A certain power transformer provides a secondary potential difference of 13.6 V without a load connected, and a potential difference of 12.4 V when operating into a load of its rated current. What is its regulation percentage?

a. 9.68 percent (29)
b. Any other answer, review Section D.1.2.

FRAME 29

Among the differences between the essential characteristics of power transformers and audio transformers is the recommended frequency range of the audio transformer. This information is frequently given in the specifications by a ________.

a. Frequency response curve. (30)
b. Any other answer, review Section D.1.3.

FRAME 30

A transformer that uses the same winding for both the primary and the secondary is called ________.

a. An autotransformer. (31)
b. Any other answer, review Section D.1.6 and go on to Frame 31.

FRAME 31

The five types of stress that act to deteriorate a transformer over time are: ________; ________; ________; ________; and ________.

a. Temperature stress; dielectric stress; vibration and shock stress; thermal shock stress; humidity stress. (32)
b. Any other answers, review Section D.2.

FRAME 32

The three major types of transformer failures are ________, ________, and ________.

a. Dielectric; conductive; magnetic (in any order). (END)
b. Any other answer, review Section D.2.

E. PROBLEMS FOR SOLUTION OR RESEARCH

1. Draw the following phasors:

a. $5.6\angle 0^\circ$	g. $6.75 - j4$
b. $23\angle 19^\circ$	h. $0 - j3.2$
c. $5 + j7$	i. $9.2 + j3.6$
d. $8.86\angle -63^\circ$	j. $-8.7 - j4.5$
e. $9.75 - j6.3$	k. $9.6\angle -90^\circ$
f. $27\angle -350^\circ$	l. $0 - j2.3$

2. Convert the following to complex rectangular form:

a. $5.6\angle 0^\circ$	f. $32.5\angle 16^\circ$
b. $3.9\angle 45^\circ$	g. $12\angle -90^\circ$
c. $185\angle -30^\circ$	h. $5.8\angle 36^\circ$
d. $7.75\angle 23^\circ$	i. $1.2\angle 190^\circ$
e. $5.56\angle -48^\circ$	j. $3.7\angle -345^\circ$

3. Convert the following to polar form:

a. $3 + j4$	e. $9.75 + j18$
b. $12 - j23$	f. $0 + j6.3$
c. $-9.2 + j6$	g. $3.75 - j7.25$
d. $5 - j11$	h. $-5 - j8$

4. Give the complex rectangular and polar coordinate expressions for the impedance of the following series circuits:

a. $X_L = 156.19\ \Omega$, $R1 = 180\ \Omega$
b. $X_L = 5614.3\ \Omega$, $R_{int} = 86\ \Omega$, $R1 = 15\ \text{k}\Omega$
c. $L1 = 0.15$ H, $f_s = 1$ kHz, $R1 = 1200\ \Omega$
d. $L1 = 1$ mH, $L2 = 1.5$ mH, $f_s = 12$ kHz, $R1 = 100\ \Omega$
e. $L1 = 680\ \mu\text{H}$, $f_s = 450$ kHz, $R1 = 2.7\ \text{k}\Omega$
f. $L1 = 80$ mH, $f_s = 65$ kHz, $R1 = 56\ \text{k}\Omega$, $R2 = 18\ \text{k}\Omega$

5. You have an inductor of 0.039 H with an internal resistance of 5 Ω and a 27 Ω resistor. Can you provide three different values of circuit Q using a 100 Hz source? Draw schematic diagrams of the connections and calculate the Q in each case.

6. Calculate the turns ratio required to match an amplifier with an output impedance of 3600 Ω to a 16 Ω speaker.

7. The square wave shown in Figure 13.66 is applied to a 1 H inductor with an internal resistance of 6 Ω.

a. What is the dc current in the coil?
b. Give the frequency of the fundamental and the first eight harmonics present in the waveform.
c. What is the peak current caused by each component in part (b)?

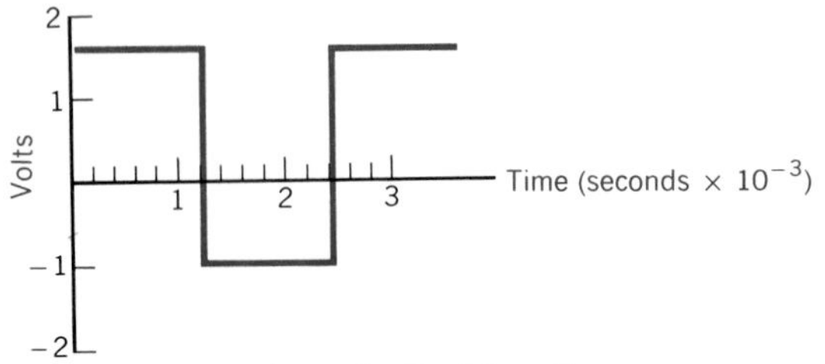

Figure 13.66 Waveform for Problem 7.

8. Obtain a number of power transformers marked to show full-load secondary current and potential difference. Measure the input power at full-load conditions and calculate the efficiency for each.

9. Determine the percent regulation for the transformers used in Problem 8. Does the size of a transformer appear to have anything to do with its regulation?

CHAPTER 14 CAPACITANCE IN DC CIRCUITS AND CAPACITORS

A. CHAPTER PREVIEW

1 In this chapter, you will learn about capacitance, which is the third of the major electrical effects. The other two are resistance and inductance.

2 You will learn about the effects of capacitance both in steady-state and transient-state dc circuits and how the effects of capacitance contrast with those of inductance.

3 The methods for calculating the total capacitance of parallel and series capacitor networks are presented.

4 The Principles section concludes with a detailed discussion of how energy from the electric field is stored in the dielectric of a capacitor. This energy storage is compared to the energy stored in the magnetic field around a current-carrying wire.

5 The Examples and Computations section of this chapter begins with a section of practice examples involving capacitor calculations and then continues the presentation of polar and rectangular coordinate systems begun in Chapter 13.

6 In the Applications section you will learn the characteristics and failure modes of the most commonly used types of nonpolarized, fixed capacitors. A detailed presentation of the ways in which information is coded on capacitor cases concludes this section.

B. PRINCIPLES

B.1 WHAT IS CAPACITANCE?

In the previous chapters, you have seen that electrical energy is stored in the magnetic field around a current-carrying conductor. At the beginning of your studies in this book, it was shown that a potential difference between two points produced an electric field between the points. In addition to producing a uniform drift of charge carriers called an *electric current,* an electric field is also capable of storing appreciable amounts of energy. As in the case of the magnetic field, it would be possible to use the energy stored in an electric field to operate devices equivalent to the motors, relays, and loudspeakers, which use the energy stored in a magnetic field to transform electrical into mechanical energy and vice versa. However, electric field machines are less popular and tend to be rather specialized. Therefore, it is not profitable for the technician to devote as much time to the study of the electric field as was devoted to the magnetic field. On the other hand, the operation of a very widely used electronic component, the capacitor, is based on the electric field.

Figure 14.1 illustrates the operation of a capacitor. In this figure, two conductive metal plates are connected to a source of potential difference. Before the two wires were connected to the source, the wires and metal plates were electrically neutral, that is, the number of protons and electrons in each plate was about the same. Once the two plates are connected to the terminals of the source, a transient-state movement of electrons takes place, even though there is no closed circuit between the terminals of the source. The fact that there is a drift of electrons means that there is an electric field, as shown in Figure 14.2. A number of conduction electrons will enter the positive terminal of the source from the left-hand plate, while a number enter the right-hand plate from the negative terminal of the source. This process will continue until each plate and the source terminal to which it is attached become an equipotential surface, as shown in Figure 14.3*a*. You will remember that the potential difference between any point on an equipotential surface and a reference point, such as ground, is the same.

Note that there is an electric field between the two plates at this time because of the potential difference between them. If the wire leads are now removed from the source, the result will be as shown in Figure 14.3*b*. There will be a positive charge of $+Q$ coulombs on the plate that was connected to the positive terminal and a negative charge of $-Q$ on the plate that was connected to the negative terminal. A potential difference V, equal to the potential difference that had been supplied by the source, now exists between the plates. The capacitance of the two plates is defined as the ratio of the charge Q on either of the plates to the potential

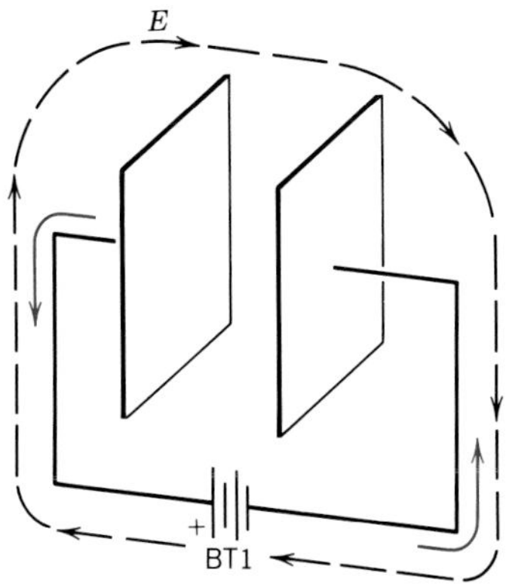

Figure 14.2 The transient drift of electrons as described in the text implies the existence of an electric field.

Figure 14.1 Two conductive metal plates connected to a source of potential.

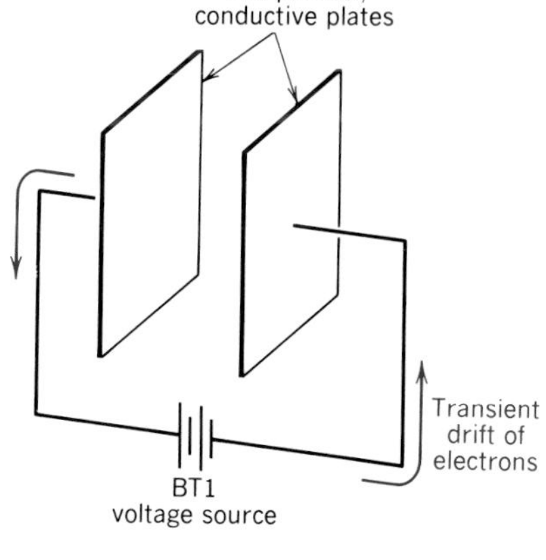

Figure 14.3 After the parallel plates have received a charge, it will remain even though the source is removed.

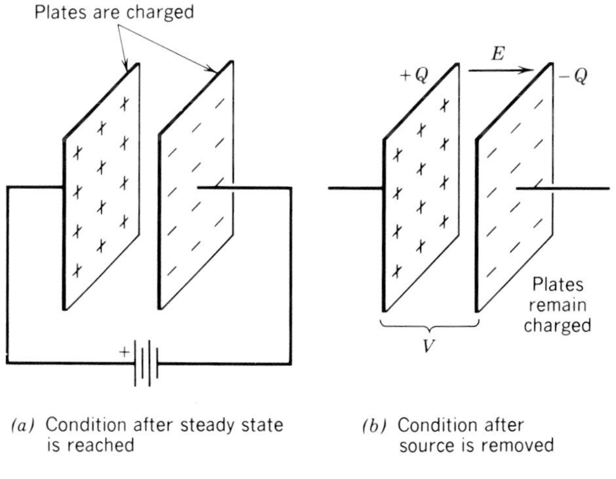

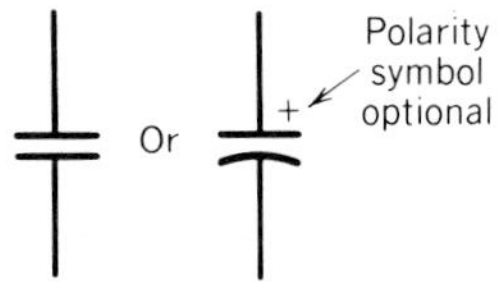

Figure 14.4 Standard schematic symbols for a general capacitor.

difference between the plates. In terms of a formula,

$$C = \frac{Q}{V} \qquad \text{FORMULA 14.1}$$

The unit of capacitance is the Farad, named after Michael Faraday, whose method of mapping the electric field was studied in Chapter 2. The Farad, abbreviated F, is a very large unit and practical capacitors generally have capacitances in the microfarad (10^{-6} F, or μF), nanofarad (10^{-9} F, or nF), or picofarad (10^{-12} F, or pF) range. The general schematic symbol for a capacitor is shown in Figure 14.4.

The capacitance of a particular pair of plates as defined by Formula 14.1 is found to be reasonably constant over a range of different applied potential differences. This means that when a particular pair of plates is connected to different sources, the amount of charge on either plate will be proportional to the potential difference provided by the source. Any change in the physical size or arrangement of the plates, however, will cause a change in the amount of charge stored, even though the source potential difference is kept constant. The reason for this lies in the fact that the movement of charge carriers that occurs when the plates are first connected to a dc source depends on the existence of an electric field between the two source terminals through the two wire leads, the plates, and the space separating the plates. In Chapter 5, you saw that the opposition to the passage of an electric field through a conductor was relatively small. In fact, a field will tend to follow a longer path through a conductor rather than a somewhat shorter path through an insulator or air. Since part of the path in Figure 14.1 passes through an area that does not contain a conductor, the field will have more difficulty passing through this region than it will in other parts of the circuit. The ease with which an electric field can pass through a region is referred to as the *permittivity* of the region. Permittivity is an electric field characteristic similar to permeability for magnetic fields. A detailed discussion of permittivity is not necessary to see that any change in the physical arrangement of the capacitor plates in Figure 14.1 that increases the permittivity of the system formed by the two plates will increase the strength of the electric field between the terminals of the source when the wire leads are first connected. A stronger electric field will raise more electrons in the plates into the conduction energy levels, and the amount of charge Q that is moved to the positive terminal of the source from the positive capacitor plate and to the negative plate from the negative source terminal will be greater. Again considering Formula 14.1, it is possible to say that any change in the capacitor circuit that provides a greater permittivity between the terminals of the source will increase the capacitance C of the parallel plate arrangement since the amount of charge on either plate will be greater, even though the source potential has remained the same.

There are two principal ways of increasing the permittivity of the path between two parallel plates separated by air. One of these is to decrease the distance between the plates. This reduces the length of the low-permittivity portion of the path between the two source terminals. Decreasing the length of the low-permittivity portion of the path will result in a stronger electric field. This in turn will mean that more energy is available to raise electrons to conduction energy levels in the plates and to cause them to drift into or out of the source. The second way of increasing the permittivity of the space between the two parallel plates is to place a material with a greater permittivity than air between them. Of course, this material has to be an insulator. If the material is a conductor, the electric field produced by the potential difference between the two source terminals will just move conduction electrons from the negative terminal to the positive terminal until the source ceases to provide the potential difference. There will be no storage of charge on the capacitor plates, nor will the plates and the respective source terminals to which they are connected become equipotential surfaces. Instead, a potential gradient and an electric current will exist between the two terminals of the source, as shown in Figure 14.5*a*. When an insulating material with a permittivity greater than that of air is placed between the plates, the result is as shown in Figure 14.5*b*. As in the case of moving the plates closer together, the electric field moves more charge carriers from the source toward the negative capacitor plate and away from the positive plate, even though the source potential difference remains the same. The effect of both these changes in the physical arrangement of the two plates, that is, decreasing the spacing and placing an insulator between the plates, is therefore to increase the capacitance of the system.

An insulating material placed between a pair of plates to form a capacitor, as shown in Figure 14.5*b*, is called a *dielectric*. You have already met this term as it is used to refer to the insulating materials used in inductor and transformer construction, in terms such as *dielectric breakdown*. In fact, there is good reason to use the same term in both places because it is the

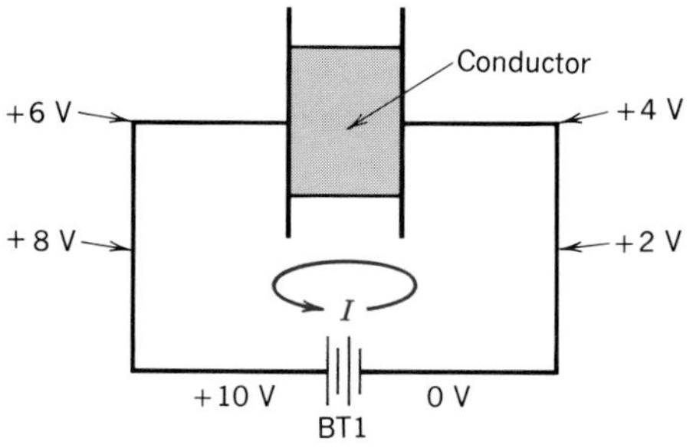

(a) With a conductor between the plates, there is a current and potential gradient

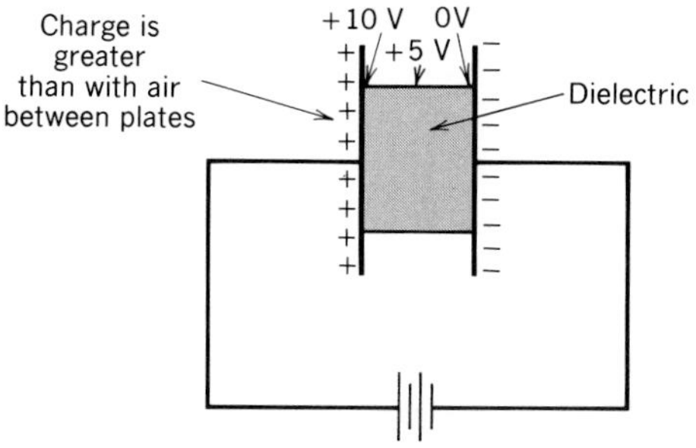

(b) With an insulator (dielectric) between the plates, there is no current and the potential gradient exists only in the dielectric

Figure 14.5 The difference between a conductor and dielectric placed between the plates of a parallel-plate capacitor.

nonconductive quality of the material that is of importance. There are important differences, however. In the case of the insulating materials used in inductors and transformers, the only function of these materials is to maintain a distance between conductors and to prevent arcing between adjacent conductors. In capacitors, solid dielectrics also serve to support the capacitor plates and to maintain the spacing between them, but equally important are the facts that the permittivity of capacitor dielectrics are high in comparison with air, and the effect of the electric field on the dielectric is to store a certain amount of energy in the dielectric. Thus, the choice of capacitor dielectrics depends on more factors than those used for the selection of insulating materials in inductors and transformers.

The capacitance of a parallel-plate capacitor can also be increased by increasing the area of its plates, although why this is so requires some further explanation. Mathematically, and by the use of a coulomb balance and test charge, it is found that E, the intensity of the field between a pair of electrically charged plates, is equal to a constant times the charge per unit area of one of the plates. This can be written as a formula:

$$E = \frac{1}{\epsilon_0} \times \frac{Q}{A} \qquad \text{FORMULA 14.2}$$

The factor ϵ_0 in this formula is a constant in physics, associated with the permittivity of free space, and is equal to 8.85×10^{-12}, Q is the charge in coulombs on the plate, and A is the plate area in square meters. In the first chapters of this book, you also learned that the potential difference between two points, such as a pair of points directly opposite each other on the parallel plates of a capacitor, is determined by the amount of work necessary to move a positive unit charge from the more negative plate to the more positive plate. By a mathematical process, it is possible to relate the electric field intensity between a pair of parallel plates in space and the potential difference between the plates. This relationship is

$$V = E \times d \qquad \text{FORMULA 14.3}$$

where V is the potential difference between the plates, E is the intensity of the electric field, and d is the distance between them. Solving Formula 14.3 for E produces $E = \frac{V}{d}$. Now, this can be substituted for the left-hand term of Formula 14.2 to produce

$$\frac{V}{d} = \frac{1}{\epsilon_0} \times \frac{Q}{A}$$

If Formula 14.1 is solved for Q, that is, $Q = C \times V$, and this expression is substituted, the result is

$$\frac{V}{d} = \frac{1}{\epsilon_0} \times \frac{C \times V}{A}$$

Simplifying this equation will provide a useful formula relating the capacitance of a parallel-plate capacitor and its dimensions. First, multiply both sides of the equation by d:

$$\frac{V}{d} \times d = \frac{1}{\epsilon_0} \times \frac{C \times V}{A} \times d$$

Next, multiply both sides by $\frac{1}{V}$.

$$V \times \frac{1}{V} = \frac{1}{\epsilon_0} \times \frac{C \times V}{A} \times d \times \frac{1}{V}$$

or

$$1 = \frac{Cd}{\epsilon_0 \times A}$$

Solving for C,

$$C = \epsilon_0 \frac{A}{d} \qquad \text{FORMULA 14.4}$$

This is a simple formula relating the area of one plate of a parallel-plate capacitor and the distance between the plates to the capacitance when the dielectric between the two plates is empty space or air, which has about the same permittivity.

From Formula 14.4, you can see that the capacitance of a parallel-plate capacitor is proportional to the area of the plates and inversely proportional to the distance between them. You can also use this formula to see how really large a unit the Farad is.

EXAMPLE:
If a 1 F capacitor were constructed of two square plates 1mm apart, how big would the plates be? ■

SOLUTION:

Using Formula 14.4, $C = \epsilon_0 \frac{A}{d}$, and solving for A,

$$A = \frac{Cd}{\epsilon_0}$$

$$A = \frac{1 \times 0.001}{8.85 \times 10^{-12}} = 1.13 \times 10^{8} \text{ m}^2$$

The length of one side would then be $\sqrt{A}$, or about 10,630.15 m. ■

From this example, you can see that it is rather impractical to think in terms of a 1 F parallel-plate capacitor. Even a 1 μF parallel-plate unit with a 1-mm spacing would measure slightly more than ten and a half meters on one side! Fortunately, there are methods for constructing capacitors that are physically smaller than parallel-plate capacitors. From Formula 14.4, you can see that one of these methods is to reduce the distance between the capacitor plates. One type of practical capacitor, discussed at length in the next chapter, uses a thin film of gas or an oxide coating as the dielectric. This makes very close spacing possible. Another physical solution is to stack a number of plates as shown in Figure 14.6. This makes it possible to have both sides of the interior plates count as part of the plate area, reducing the capacitor size considerably. This method is often combined with the use of dielectrics that provide much greater permittivity than air, resulting in the convenient-sized units found in modern electronic equipment.

Figure 14.6 One way to produce a high capacitance in a limited space is to stack a number of alternately connected plates.

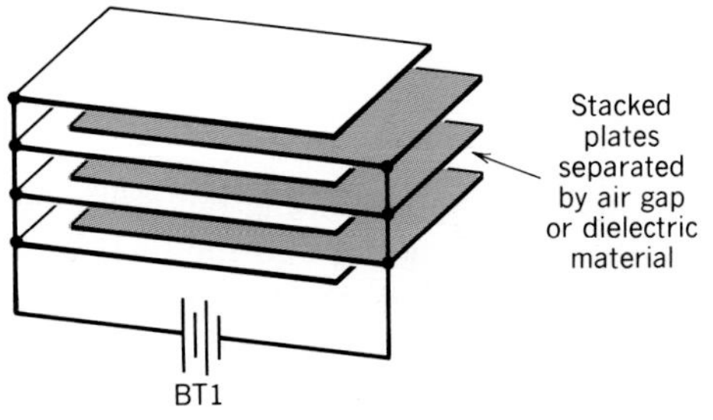

The methods for producing capacitors with high capacitance are subject to a number of limitations. The first of these is size. Banks of giant capacitors might be possible at industrial sites, but the size of components must be related to the practical size of the units of which they are a part. The use of high-permittivity dielectrics provides a better solution than such physical means as stacking parallel plates, but there is a limit to the permittivities of modern dielectrics. Finally, decreasing the distance between the capacitor plates to increase capacitance also has its limits. When the potential difference between the plates is high enough to ionize the molecules in the narrow gap, arcing will occur, and the capacitor will act as a short circuit. If a solid dielectric material is used between the capacitor plates, reducing the thickness of the dielectric can result in spark discharges that will pierce the dielectric. This effect is called *dielectric rupture,* or *dielectric breakdown*.The potential difference between the capacitor plates at which dielectric breakdown occurs for a given separation between the capacitor plates is called the *dielectric breakdown voltage.*

In general, all three techniques are used to reduce the size of practical capacitors to meet the space requirements of modern electronic equipment.

When a parallel-plate capacitor is removed from the source as in Figure 14.3*b*, the attraction of the electrons on the negatively charged plate by the excess positive charge on the other plate will tend to keep the charge carriers in place. Although some leakage of charge occurs across the dielectric and there is also some loss of charge through the wire leads, if the dielectric medium between the plates has a fairly high resistance, the capacitor will retain its "charged" condition for a long time. If, however, a conductive path is provided between the plates, either by a short circuit or the connection of a resistance lower than that of the dielectric between the leads, a second, much stronger electric field will be produced, as shown in Figure 14.7.

Figure 14.7 When a high-permittivity, low-resistance path is provided between the capacitor plates, the opposite charges cancel.

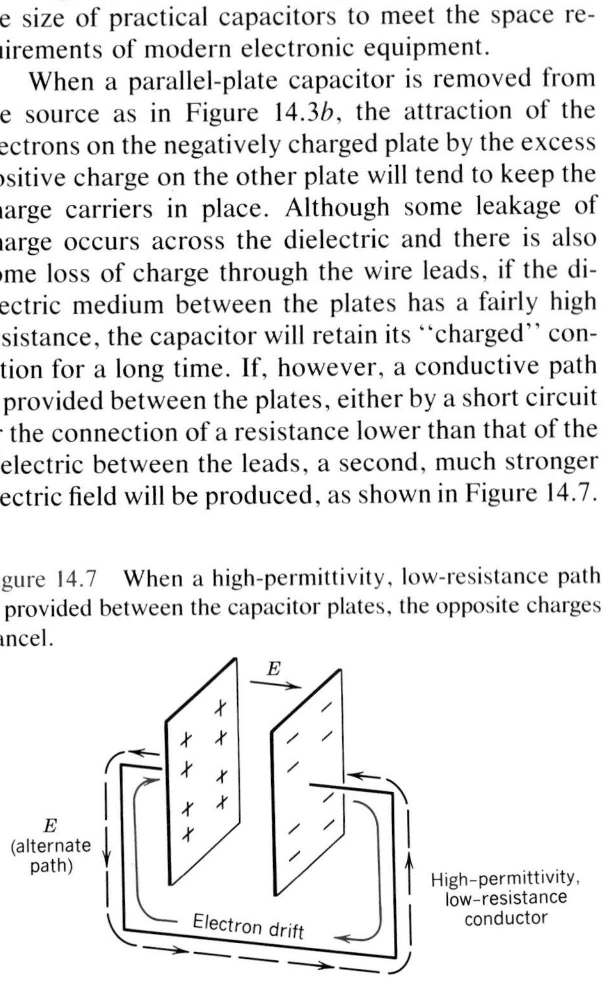

This field is stronger because of the greater permittivity of the shorting conductor. Due to the influence of this second field, electrons will drift from the negatively charged plate, through the shorting conductor, to the positive plate. This effectively neutralizes the charge on both plates of the capacitor, and is referred to as *discharging*. Although most of the discussion of capacitor operation has been in terms of the charging of a capacitor from a dc source, in practical operation, the ability of a capacitor to retain electrical charge or to return it to a circuit is of equal importance. Unlike a resistor, in which electrical energy is converted into heat and dissipated into the air, in a capacitor, electrical energy is converted into the potential energy of the charged plates and the electric field in the dielectric. This potential energy can be, for the most part, returned to a circuit.

The amount of energy that can be returned to a circuit by a capacitor of even modest size is surprising. This is why the notion of discharging a capacitor through a resistive path rather than short circuiting the lead wires is stressed in this book. With its leads short circuited, a 100 μF capacitor charged from a 25-V source will produce a fair-sized spark. When it is charged from a 150-V source, it is capable of producing a painful shock if both leads are grasped at the same time.

During the day of vacuum tube electronic units, power supplies produced potential differences anywhere from several hundred to several thousand volts. Capacitors charged to such high voltages can easily cause death if they discharge through a human body. A device called a *shorting stick,* an insulated rod with a grounded conductive cable attached to one end, was a standard part of the maintenance technician's tool kit. Using the insulated rod, the various large capacitors in a circuit could be touched with the grounded cable, quickly discharging them. This practice is still found in television servicing. Because of the danger of working around charged capacitors, the stresses placed on the capacitors themselves by such rapid discharging were ignored. In modern semiconductor circuits, where power supply potential differences are rarely higher than 40 V, discharging such low-voltage power supply capacitors can be accomplished with a 1 kΩ, 2- to 10-W resistor. This takes a bit longer but is considerably gentler on the capacitors.

B.2 CAPACITORS IN DC CIRCUITS

When an inductor is first connected across a dc source, the production of a counter emf by the expanding magnetic field around the coil limits the initial circuit current. As you learned in Chapter 12, the current increases exponentially, approaching its Ohm's law value of $\frac{E}{R}$ as a limit. The period of time during which the current in an inductive circuit is increasing rapidly is referred to as the *transient state* of the circuit. After five time constants ($TC = \frac{L}{R}$), the current has reached a level close to what would be its level if the inductor was replaced by a resistance. At this time, the circuit is said to have reached its *steady-state* conditions.

When a capacitor is connected across a dc source, there is also a period of time during which transient-state conditions exist. At the moment of connection, the electric field produces a large current out of the negative source terminal and into the positive terminal. In fact, the amount of current is limited only by the resistance of the capacitor leads. This initial surge current is very nearly the current that would exist in the circuit if the capacitor was replaced by two resistors whose values were those of the capacitor leads. Notice that there is no voltage drop across the capacitor at this time, nor is there actually a current through the capacitor, although the circuit behaves as though a short circuit existed between the capacitor plates. As the electric field produced by the source moves electrons from the source to the negative plate of the capacitor and from the positive plate back to the source, the circuit current begins to drop. Notice also that the addition or removal of electrons from the capacitor plates gives both of them an electrical charge. The charge on the capacitor plates can be related to Formula 14.1.

At a certain time $t = t_1$, the charge on one of the capacitor plates will be

$$Q_1 = CV_1$$

where V_1 is the potential difference across the plates at t_1. At a later time, $t = t_2$, both the charge and the potential difference will be greater:

$$Q_2 = CV_2$$

The equation for t_1 can be subtracted from the equation for t_2 to obtain an expression for the difference in capacitor charge and voltage:

$$\begin{array}{rl} Q_2 &= CV_2 \\ -\ Q_1 &= CV_1 \\ \hline Q_2 - Q_1 &= CV_2 - CV_1 \quad \text{or} \\ Q_2 - Q_1 &= C(V_2 - V_1) \end{array}$$

But $Q_2 - Q_1$ is the change in Q, or ΔQ, and $V_2 - V_1$ is the change in V, or ΔV. So $\Delta Q = C\,\Delta V$. But it is the change over the period of time $t_2 - t_1 = \Delta t$ that is of interest. Dividing both sides of this by Δt produces

$$\frac{\Delta Q}{\Delta t} = C\frac{\Delta V}{\Delta t}$$

Recall that i, the current in a circuit, is defined as $\frac{\Delta Q}{\Delta t}$, so it is possible to write

$$i = C\frac{\Delta V}{\Delta t} \qquad \text{FORMULA 14.5}$$

This is a useful mathematical expression that relates the transient-state current in a capacitive circuit to the potential difference measured across the capacitor plates of a capacitor during a short period of time.

EXAMPLE:
An uncharged 10 μF capacitor is connected to a dc source. The potential difference across the capacitor is 150 V 0.001 s after the source is connected. What was the average circuit current during this period of time? ■

SOLUTION:
The circuit of this example is shown in Figure 14.8. Recall that when the capacitor is first connected to the source, the potential difference across it is zero. Since there is no actual current flow through the capacitor, there is no potential difference across it. As the charge carriers are moved by the electric field, however, a potential difference is developed between the two capacitor plates. There *is* a circuit current from the negative source terminal to the negative plate and from the positive plate to the source terminal. The average value of this current between $t = 0$ and $t = 1$ ms can be calculated using Formula 14.5 since $V = 0$ at $t = 0$.

$$i = C\frac{\Delta V}{\Delta t} = 10 \times 10^{-6} \times \frac{150 - 0}{1 \times 10^{-3} - 0} = 1.5 \text{ A}$$

■

Determining the instantaneous potential difference across a capacitor during the transient state or the instantaneous circuit current is a problem rather like that of determining these values in an inductive circuit. You can visualize the solution to this better if you begin with an application of Kirchhoff's voltage law to the circuit in Figure 14.9. Here, the resistance of the capacitor leads and of the plates themselves is represented by a single resistor, called the *equivalent series resistance* in capacitor specifications. To avoid confusion between the constant potential difference supplied by the source BT1 and the changing potential difference produced by the charge on the capacitor, the source potential is referred to as E, that across the capacitor as e. Note that the potential difference e across the capacitor is in series opposing with the potential difference produced by the source. At any given moment, then, the Kirchhoff's voltage law equation for this circuit would be

Figure 14.8 The current in a circuit containing a capacitor connected across a dc source is $i = C\frac{\Delta V}{\Delta t}$

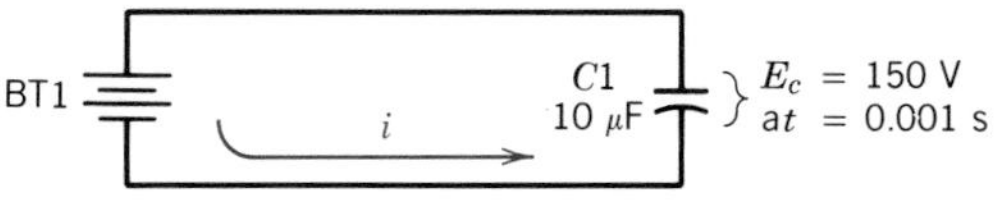

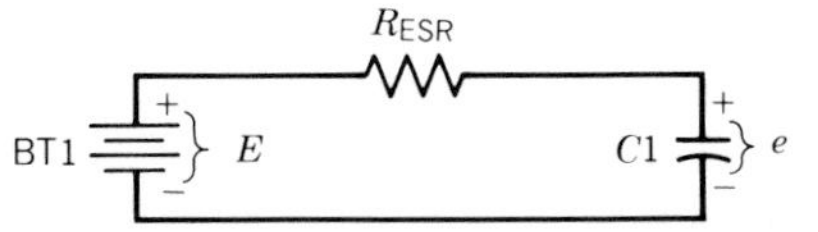

Figure 14.9 Applying Kirchhoff's voltage law to a circuit containing a capacitor. The resistance R_{ESR} represents the resistance of the leads and the capacitor plates.

$$-E + iR_{\text{ESR}} + e = 0$$

It is possible to write such an equation even though there is no real current path through the capacitor. There are actual potential rises and potential drops, and Kirchhoff's law is a statement about the potential energy of a charge carrier. Transposing terms to isolate the iR term,

$$-iR_{\text{ESR}} = E - e$$

But the current in the circuit I has been shown to be

$$i = C\frac{\Delta e}{\Delta t}$$

Substituting this in the transposed Kirchhoff law equation produces

$$R_{\text{ESR}}\,C\frac{\Delta e}{\Delta t} = E - e \quad \text{or} \quad \frac{\Delta e}{\Delta t} = \frac{E - e}{R_{\text{ESR}}C}$$

Now this equation can be solved for a Δt that is made to approach zero by the methods of integral calculus. This provides an expression for the potential difference across the capacitor in terms of time, capacitance, the potential difference provided by the source, and the circuit resistance:

$$e = E(1 - \epsilon^{\frac{-t}{RC}}) \qquad \text{FORMULA 14.6}$$

The exponential term $\epsilon^{\frac{-t}{RC}}$ closely resembles the $\epsilon^{\frac{-Rt}{L}}$ term found in calculating the current through an inductive circuit. In fact, graphing the two functions $\epsilon^{\frac{-t}{RC}}$ and $1 - \epsilon^{\frac{-t}{RC}}$ for an arbitrary value of $R \times C$, as

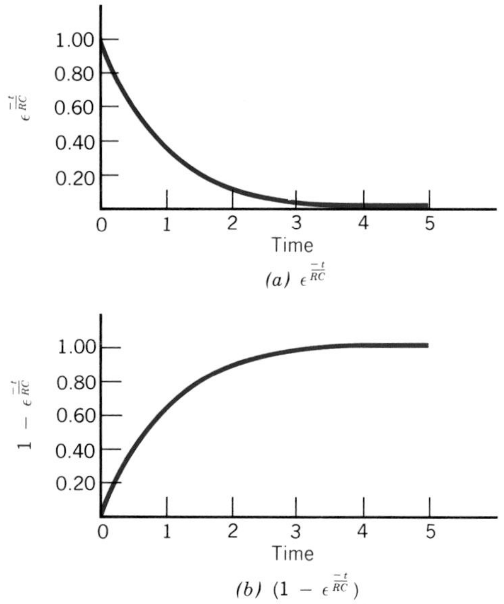

Figure 14.10 Graphs of $\epsilon^{\frac{-t}{RC}}$ and $(1 - \epsilon^{\frac{-t}{RC}})$ for arbitrary values of R and C.

shown in Figures 14.10*a* and 14.10*b*, results in the charge and discharge curves shown in Chapter 12. Note that the potential difference across the capacitor given by Formula 14.6 shows that initially the potential difference across the capacitor is zero, since $\epsilon^{\frac{-t}{RC}}$ is equal to 1 when $t = 0$. Formula 14.6 becomes

$$\begin{aligned} e &= E(1 - \epsilon^{\frac{-0}{RC}}) \\ &= E(1 - \epsilon^{-0}) \\ &= E(1 - 1) \end{aligned}$$

As time passes and t becomes larger, $\epsilon^{\frac{-t}{RC}}$ actually becomes smaller. Formula 14.6 shows that the potential difference across the capacitor becomes nearly as large as the potential difference across the source.

As in the case of the formulas relating time to the current through an inductor during the transient state, Formula 14.6 is not difficult to use if you have a calculator with the $\ln^{-1} X$ or INV LNX function.

EXAMPLE:
A 1 μF capacitor with an equivalent series resistance (ESR) of 6 Ω is connected across a 12-V dc source. What will be the potential difference across the capacitor after 3 μs? ■

SOLUTION:
Using a calculator, it is an easy matter to substitute the known values in Formula 14.6:

Calculate $-\frac{t}{RC}$	3 EE +/− 6 ÷ (6 × 1 EE +/− 6) = +/−
The display reads	−5 −01 or −0.5
Which is $-\frac{t}{RC}$.	
Calculate $\epsilon^{-0.5}$	INV LNX
The answer displayed should be	0.6065307 or 0653066 −01
Calculate $1 - \epsilon^{\frac{-t}{RC}}$	+/− + 1 =
Display reads	0.3934693
Multiply by 12	× 1 2 =
Read potential difference	4.7216321
Rounding off, $e = 4.72$ V	■

Formula 14.6 provides an expression for e, the instantaneous potential difference across the capacitor. This can be substituted into the Kirchhoff's voltage law equation for Figure 14.9 so that the equation can be solved for i as a function of t, E, C, and R_{ESR}:

Kirchhoff's law equation for Figure 14.9:

$$-E + iR_{ESR} + e = 0$$

Kirchhoff's law equation with Formula 14.6 substituted for e:

$$-E + iR_{ESR} + E(1 - \epsilon^{\frac{-t}{RC}}) = 0$$

or,

$$-E + iR_{ESR} + E - E\,\epsilon^{\frac{-t}{RC}} = 0$$

multiplying and simplifying,

$$iR_{ESR} = E\,\epsilon^{\frac{-t}{RC}} \quad \text{and} \quad i = \frac{E\,\epsilon^{\frac{-t}{RC}}}{R_{ESR}} \qquad \text{FORMULA 14.7}$$

This formula provides a great deal of information about the current in a capacitive circuit. Initially, at $t = 0$, $\epsilon^{\frac{-t}{RC}}$ is equal to 1, so that the current in the circuit is $i = \frac{E}{R_{ESR}}$, the same value it would have if the capacitor was replaced by a resistance equal to its equivalent series resistance. As time passes and t becomes larger, the term $\epsilon^{\frac{-t}{RC}}$ becomes smaller. The circuit current falls to nearly zero, similar to the way in which the cemf developed by an inductor falls to zero in a dc circuit.

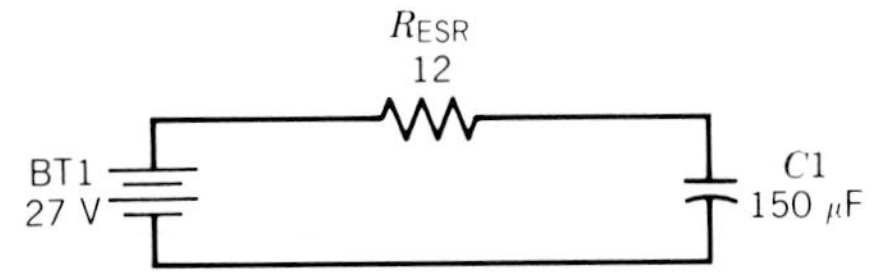

Figure 14.11 Circuit for the calculation of current in a capacitive circuit.

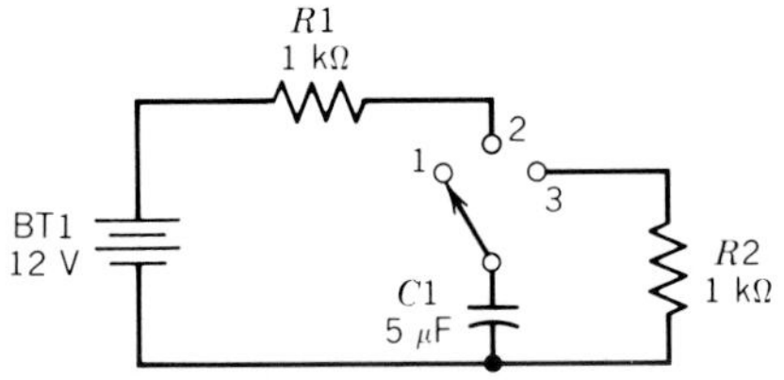

Figure 14.12 A switching circuit to illustrate capacitor charging and discharging.

EXAMPLE:
A 150 μF capacitor with an ESR of 12 Ω is connected across a 27-V dc source. What is the circuit current after 0.001 s? What is the potential difference across the capacitor? ■

SOLUTION:
The schematic diagram of this circuit is shown in Figure 14.11. Using Formula 14.7 and a calculator, the circuit current can be determined by simple substitution:

Calculate $-\frac{t}{RC}$	[.] [0] [0] [1] [÷] [(] [1] [2] [×] [0] [EE] [+/-] [6] [)] [=] [+/-]
The display should read	$-$ 5.5555556 $-$ 01 or $-$ 0.555556
which is $-\frac{t}{RC}$.	
Calculate $\ln^{-1}$	[INV] [LNX]
The display now shows $\epsilon^{\frac{-t}{RC}}$, or	5.7375342 $-$01
Multiply the result by E and divide by R_{ESR}	[×] [2] [7] [÷] [1] [2] [=]
The display should now read the current	1.2909452 00 or 1.29 A

There are two ways to find the potential difference across the capacitor at $t = 0.001$. One way is to use Formula 14.6:

$$e = E\,(1 - \epsilon^{\frac{-t}{RC}})$$

$$e = 27(1 - \epsilon^{\frac{-0.001}{1.8 \times 10^{-3}}})$$

$$e = 27(1 - 0.574)$$

$$e = 11.5 \text{ V}$$

The second method, which should produce about the same answer, involves the value obtained for the current and Kirchhoff's voltage law. Because of the rounding off, the two values will not be exactly the same, but they will be close enough to provide a check.

The Kirchhoff's law equation can be written from the information shown in Figure 14.11:

$$-E + Ri + e = 0$$

Substituting,

$$-27 + (12 \times 1.29) + e = 0$$

$$e = 11.52 \text{ V}$$

This answer compares well with that obtained using Formula 14.6. ■

When a fully charged capacitor is discharged, both the potential difference across the capacitor and the discharging circuit current follow the discharge curve shown in Figure 14.10*a*, as does the circuit current during changing. Consider the circuit shown in Figure 14.12*a*. Here, the switch is moved from position 1 to position 2 at $t = 0$, and the capacitor begins to charge to the 12-V source potential through the 1000 Ω equivalent series resistor. (This rather high value has been chosen to simplify the arithmetic.) Just after the switch has been placed in position 2, the charge on the capacitor is still nearly zero, and the circuit current is

$$i = \frac{E}{R}\epsilon^{\frac{-t}{RC}}$$

$$= \frac{12}{1 \times 10^3} \times 1 \quad \text{or} \quad 0.012 \text{ A}$$

After 0.005 s, the potential difference across the capacitor is

$$e = E(1 - \epsilon^{\frac{-t}{RC}})$$

$$= 12(1 - 0.368)$$

$$= 7.58 \text{ V}$$

The current at this point is

$$i = \frac{E}{R}\epsilon^{\frac{-t}{RC}}$$

$$= \frac{12}{1 \times 10^3} \times 0.368$$

$$= 0.0044 \text{ A}$$

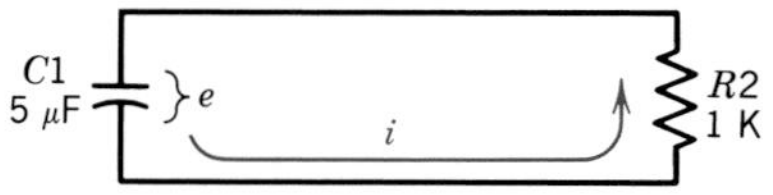

Figure 14.13 With the switch of Figure 14.12 in position 3, the resulting circuit contains only a capacitor and resistor.

If at this time, the switch is set to position 3, the capacitor, which has charged to a potential difference of 7.58 V, will begin to discharge through the 1 kΩ equivalent series resistor. Just after the switch is placed in position 3, the charge on the capacitor is 7.58 V, the level to which it had previously charged before the source was switched out of the circuit. The circuit now resembles that shown in Figure 14.13, with the charged capacitor as the only potential source in the circuit. Applying Kirchhoff's voltage law to this circuit produces the equation

$$-e + iR = 0 \quad \text{or} \quad e = i \times R$$

which is nothing more than a statement of Ohm's law. From Formula 14.7, the current i in a capacitive circuit is $i = \frac{E}{R} \epsilon^{\frac{-t}{RC}}$. Substituting this value for i in the Kirchhoff's voltage law equation above produces

$$e = \frac{E}{R} \epsilon^{\frac{-t}{RC}} \times R \quad \text{or} \quad e = E\,\epsilon^{\frac{-t}{RC}} \qquad \text{FORMULA 14.8}$$

where e is the potential difference across the discharging capacitor at time t and E is the potential difference that existed across the capacitor when it began to discharge. Thus, different formulas must be used to calculate the instantaneous potential difference across the charging and discharging capacitors, although only one formula is needed for the current in a capacitive circuit during the transient state.

In the discharging circuit shown in Figure 14.13, the initial potential difference across the capacitor is 7.58 V, and the circuit current is

$$i = \frac{E}{R} \epsilon^{\frac{-t}{RC}}$$

$$= \frac{7.58}{1000} \epsilon^{0}$$

$$= 0.00758 \text{ A}$$

After the passage of 0.005 s, the potential difference across the discharging capacitor is

$$e = E\epsilon^{\frac{-t}{RC}}$$

$$e = 7.58\ (0.368)$$

$$e = 2.79 \text{ V}$$

The circuit current at $t = 0.005$ is

$$i = \frac{E}{R} \epsilon^{\frac{-t}{RC}}$$

$$= \frac{7.58}{1000} \epsilon^{-1}$$

$$= 0.0028 \text{ A}$$

Remember the following formulas for the current in a capacitive circuit during the transient state and the potential differences across charging and discharging capacitors

$$i = \frac{E}{R} \epsilon^{\frac{-t}{RC}}$$

For a charging capacitor:

$$e = E(1 - \epsilon^{\frac{-t}{RC}})$$

where E is the potential difference of the dc source. For a discharging capacitor:

$$e = E\,\epsilon^{\frac{-t}{RC}}$$

where E is the potential difference across the capacitor when discharging starts.

B.3 THE TIME CONSTANT IN *RC* CIRCUITS

From the examples in Section B.2 you have seen that Formulas 14.7 and 14.8 can be used to calculate the circuit current and the capacitor potential difference when a capacitor with a certain equivalent series resistance is connected directly across a dc source. In the examples used, the value of the term $\epsilon^{\frac{-t}{RC}}$ has generally been quite small. This is because practical capacitors generally have capacitances measured in microfarads, nanofarads, or even picofarads, and because the equivalent series resistance of most properly functioning capacitors is on the order of a few ohms. If a resistor is placed in series with the capacitor, the effect is to raise the series resistance of the circuit to a much higher value. As far as the Kirchhoff's voltage law equation and Formulas 14.7 and 14.8 are concerned, there is no difference between a capacitor with a very large equivalent series resistance and a capacitor with a normal ESR connected in series with a resistor. The effect of adding a series resistance to a capacitor connected across a dc source is best seen by considering the time constant of the circuit. The time constant, you should remember from your study of *RL* circuits, is that value of *t* that makes the exponent part of the term $\epsilon^{\frac{-Rt}{L}}$ equal to -1. For the *RL* circuit, this occurs when $t = \frac{L}{R}$. At this time, in an *RL* circuit that has just been connected to a dc source, the circuit current reaches about 63.2 percent of its steady-state value and the cemf produced across the coil has fallen to 36.8 percent of its initial value, which was the same as the source potential when the coil was first connected.

In an *RC* circuit, the exponent of the ϵ term takes the form $\frac{-t}{RC}$, so that it will be -1 when

$$TC = RC \qquad \text{FORMULA 14.9}$$

This formula should be considered the definition of the time constant of an *RC* circuit. Setting $t = RC$ in Formula 14.6,

$$e = E(1 - \epsilon^{-1})$$

or about 36.8 percent of $\frac{E}{R}$, you can see that when $t = RC$, e will be $0.632E$, or about 63.2 percent of the source potential. At this time, the current will be

$$i = \frac{E}{R}\,\epsilon^{\frac{-t}{RC}}$$

where *R* is the sum of all the series resistances in the circuit. In most *RC* circuits, the ESR of the capacitor itself is quite small when compared to the resistance of the resistor connected in series with the capacitor, and is frequently not considered in the calculation at all.

EXAMPLE:

A 1.8 μF capacitor with an ESR of 4 Ω is connected in series with a 10 kΩ resistor across a 13.75-V dc source as shown in Figure 14.14. What is the time constant of the *RC* circuit? What is the potential difference across the capacitor one time constant after the switch is moved from position 1 to position 2? ■

Figure 14.14 A series *RC* circuit.

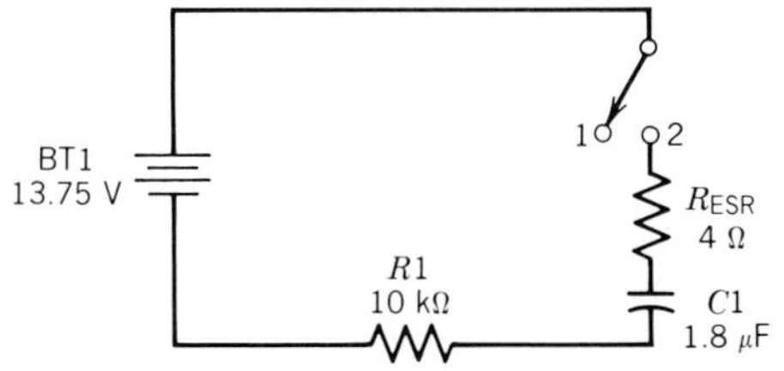

SOLUTION:

Notice that the ESR of the capacitor can be ignored since the resistance of the series resistor is considerably larger. From Formula 14.9, the time constant of the series circuit is

$$TC = R \times C = 1 \times 10^4 \times 1.8 \times 10^{-6}$$
$$= 1.8 \times 10^{-2} \quad \text{or} \quad 0.018 \text{ s}$$

One time constant after the capacitor has begun to charge, the potential difference across it will be 63.2 percent of the source potential:

$$e = 0.632 \times 13.75 = 8.69 \text{ V}$$

After one time constant, the circuit current will be 36.8 percent of its maximum value, $\frac{E}{R}$:

$$i = 0.368 \times \frac{E}{R} = 0.51 \text{ mA}$$

■

When a capacitor is discharging through a resistance, the potential difference across it and the circuit current follow the discharge curve. In other words, after one time constant, the potential difference across a capacitor discharging through a resistor will be 36.8 percent of the initial potential difference across the capacitor. The discharge circuit current after one time constant will also be 36.8 percent of the initial discharge current, or $0.368 \times \frac{E}{R}$, where *E* is the potential difference to which the capacitor was originally charged.

As in the case of *RL* circuits, an *RC* circuit is assumed to have reached steady-state conditions after five time constants. This means that for a charging capacitor, the potential difference across the capacitor will be assumed to be the same as the potential difference supplied by the dc source after five time constants, and the circuit current is assumed to have reached zero. Five time constants after a charged capacitor has begun to discharge through a resistance, both the potential difference across the capacitor and the circuit current can be assumed to be zero. Although these steady-state values are not actually reached after five time constants, the difference is too small to be considered.

This fact is important if you use a resistance to discharge capacitors before servicing a power supply. The total capacitance of the capacitors in certain types of power supplies are frequently 10,000 μF or greater. It will take almost a minute for such a power supply to discharge through a 1 kΩ resistor. Be sure to allow sufficient time for large capacitors to discharge fully before attempting to make any resistance measurements or other power-off maintenance checks. Take the extra time required to discharge large capacitors fully through a resistor after turning off the unit power rather than short circuiting them or starting to work on a unit without discharging. This will prevent unnecessary strain on the capacitors and can prevent equipment damage or possible technician injury. Although most well-designed power supplies have resistors called *bleeder resistors,* which are supposed to discharge the unit capacitors once the power has been turned off, it is not wise to trust their operation, particularly in malfunctioning equipment.

It is interesting to contrast the time constant of an *RL* circuit with that of an *RC* circuit. Recall that the time constant of an inductive circuit is $\frac{L}{R}$. In order to obtain an inductive circuit with a time constant on the order of several seconds, it would be necessary to make the circuit resistance very low, while still retaining a fairly high inductance. Another method would be to use a very large inductor that had a low resistance. Both of these methods require fairly large, expensive inductors. On the other hand, the time constant of an *RC* circuit is $R \times C$. Since the resistance value of a resistor is independent of its package size, fairly long time constants, on the order of tenths of a second or even several seconds, can be obtained using fairly small, relatively inexpensive components. One such circuit is shown in Figure 14.15. The purpose of the capacitor in this circuit is to provide a time delay of about 0.1 s in the pull-in of the relay, an application that is commonly found in many industrial control units. When switch *S*1 is first closed, the potential difference across the capacitor and across the relay coil is near zero. As the capacitor begins to charge through *R*1, the potential difference across it increases, reaching the 5 V required to operate the relay after a time determined by the value of the capacitor and *R*1. As long as the source is connected to the circuit, the charge will be maintained on the capacitor. When *S*1 is again opened, the capacitor will begin to discharge through the relay coil, and the potential will decrease below the relay coil drop-out level.

Figure 14.15 Using an *RC* circuit to delay the pull-in of a relay by about 0.1 s.

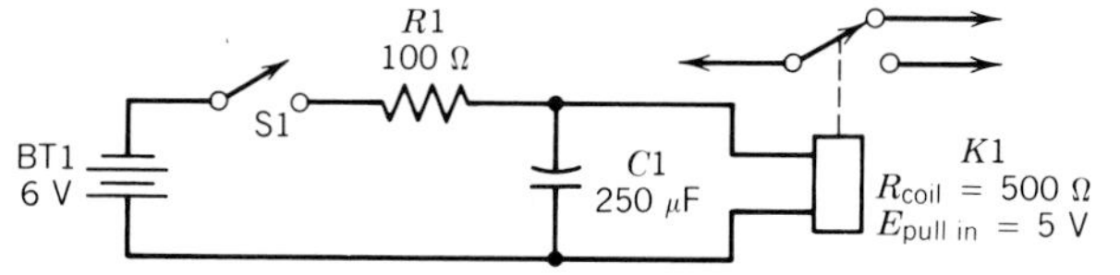

B.4 PARALLEL AND SERIES–PARALLEL *RC* CIRCUITS

Although the series connection of a resistor and capacitor is the most common arrangement when the source is a dc source, parallel and series–parallel *RC* circuits are found. The parallel *RC* circuit shown in Figure 14.16 is used when it is necessary to prevent momentary loss of dc power to a load due to a very short-term interruption of the dc power supply. Frequently used in computer applications, a capacitor connected in parallel with a load is capable of maintaining the potential difference across the load and compensating for short-term power outages of a few milliseconds. Since the equivalent series resistance of most capacitors is quite low, the capacitor charges quickly and then has no further effect on the potential difference supplied by the source, so long as the source output voltage is constant. Notice that unlike the series *RC* circuit, there is always a current in a parallel *RC* circuit, as long as the source is connected.

The series–parallel *RC* circuit with a dc source is less common. As shown in Figure 14.15, it is sometimes used to delay the pull-in of a relay or to provide a gradual change in the potential difference across a load. Figure 14.17 shows a series–parallel *RC* circuit of this type. The difficulty in calculating the circuit current and potential differences across the components in Figure 14.17 is that the voltage drops across *R*1 and *R*2 depend on the circuit current, which is determined by the charge on *C*1. The use of Thevenin's theorem, however, can replace the series–parallel network with an *RC* series network, as shown in Figure 14.18. The first step is to isolate the capacitor as the Thevenin load network as in Figure 14.18*a*. In 14.18*b*, the potential difference is calculated across the terminals with *C*1 disconnected. In 14.18*c*, the source is short circuited, and the value of the Thevenin series

Figure 14.16 A parallel *RC* circuit used to maintain the power to the load represented by R_L.

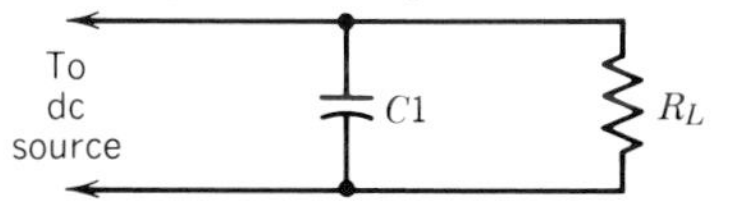

Figure 14.17 The dc series–parallel *RC* circuit can be used to provide a gradual change in the potential difference across a load, even when the source is switched on and off quickly.

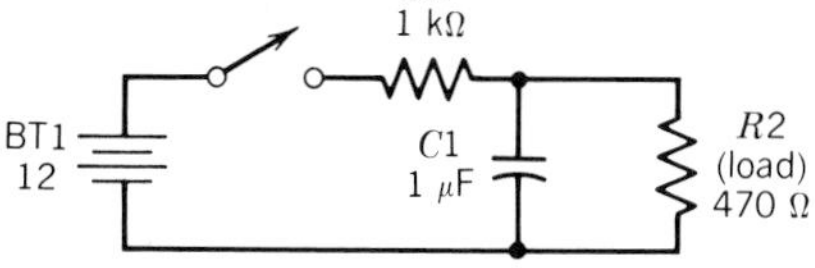

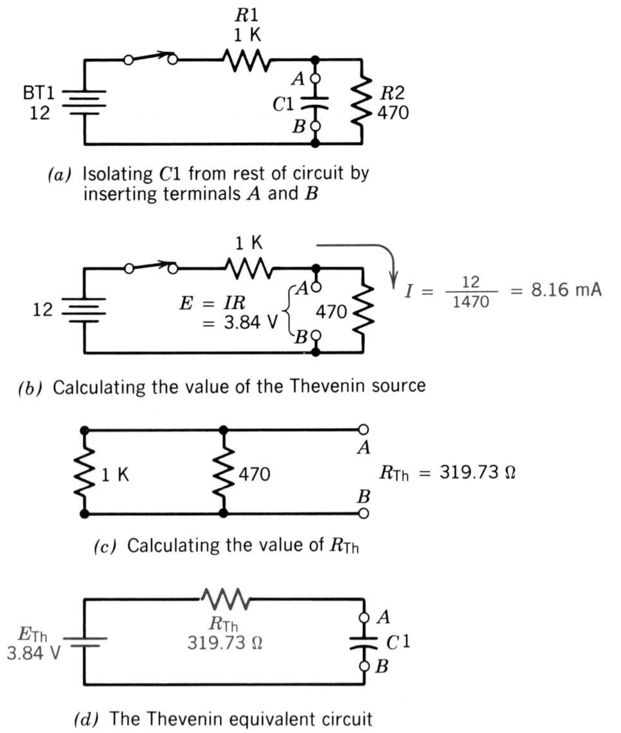

Figure 14.18 The potential difference across $C1$ and, therefore, across the load in Figure 14.17, can be calculated as a function of time if Thevenin's theorem is used.

resistor is calculated. Figure 14.18*d* shows the Thevenin source with the load network consisting of $C1$ reconnected. The potential difference across the capacitor during the transient state is then

$$e_{C1} = E_{\mathrm{Th}}\left(1 - \epsilon^{\frac{-t}{R_{\mathrm{Th}}C}}\right)$$

and the current is

$$i = \frac{E_{\mathrm{Th}}}{R_{\mathrm{Th}}}\,\epsilon^{\frac{-t}{R_{\mathrm{Th}}C}}$$

It is important to remember the statement made when Thevenin's theorem was first introduced: The results obtained by transforming a source network into a Thevenin equivalent can only be used to calculate potential differences or currents in the load network. There is no direct relationship between the voltage drop across $R1$ in Figure 14.17 and R_{Th} in 14.18*d*.

In order to understand what is going on in the series–parallel circuit of Figure 14.17, it is necessary to use the computed current into and out of the capacitor to derive expressions for the current through $R1$ and $R2$ and the potential difference across $R2$. Initially, when the circuit is first connected and the capacitor is uncharged, the potential difference across $C1$ is zero. Since $C1$ is in parallel with $R2$, the potential difference across $R2$ must also be zero. In other words, the combination of $C1$ and $R2$ initially acts like a short circuit. The entire source potential difference is applied across $R1$, and so the voltage drop across it is equal to E_s. The circuit current is $\frac{E_s}{R1}$ or 12 mA. As the capacitor begins to charge up, the parallel combination of $R2$ and $C1$ no longer acts as a short circuit, but since $R2$ and $C1$ are in parallel, the potential difference across the resistor is always the same as that across the capacitor. Using Kirchhoff's voltage law, it is possible to write the equation for this circuit:

$$E_s = e_{R1} + e_{C1} \quad (\text{remember } e_{C1} = e_{R2})$$

Solving for $e_{R1} = E_s - e_{C1}$. It is now possible to use the expression for e_{C1} obtained from the Thevenin circuit to calculate e_{R1}, the voltage drop across $R1$ at any moment of time.

$$e_{R1} = E_s - E_{\mathrm{Th}}\left(1 - \epsilon^{\frac{-t}{R_{\mathrm{Th}}C}}\right)$$

or

$$e_{R1} = 12 - 3.84\left(1 - \epsilon^{\frac{-t}{3.2 \times 10^{-4}}}\right)$$

Notice that there is a difference between the potential difference of the source E_s and the Thevenin potential difference E_{Th}.

EXAMPLE:
What is the transient-state potential difference across $C1$ in Figure 14.19 exactly 2.2 ms after the source is connected? What is the peak potential difference across $C1$. ■

SOLUTION:
The first step in solving this problem is to obtain the Thevenin equivalent for the source circuit shown in Figure 14.20*a*. The potential difference supplied by the Thevenin source is the potential between the two terminals after the capacitor is removed. It is 8 V. The value of the Thevenin series resistance is obtained by replacing the source with a short circuit and calculating

Figure 14.19 Example: Calculating the potential difference across a load in a series–parallel RC circuit.

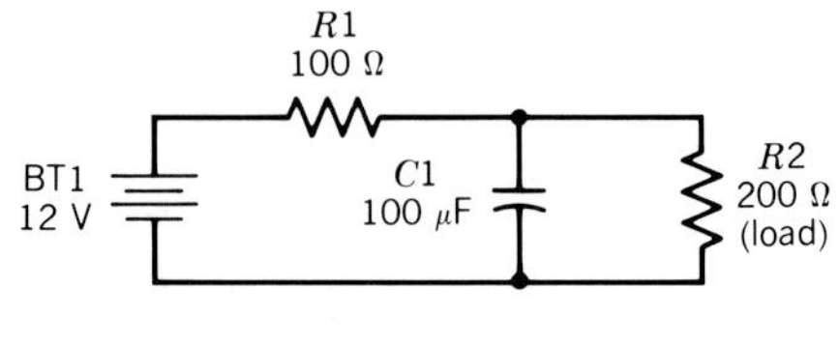

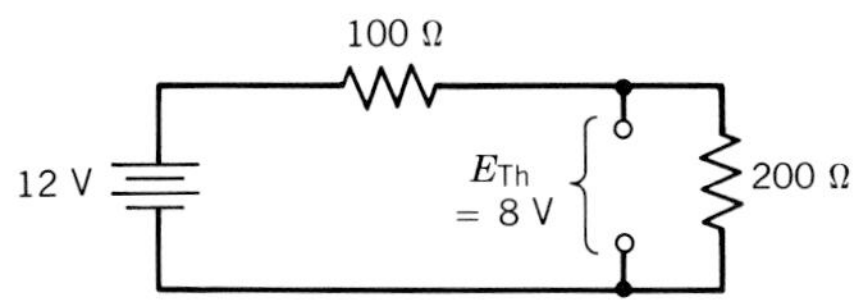

(a) Obtaining the value of the Thevenin source

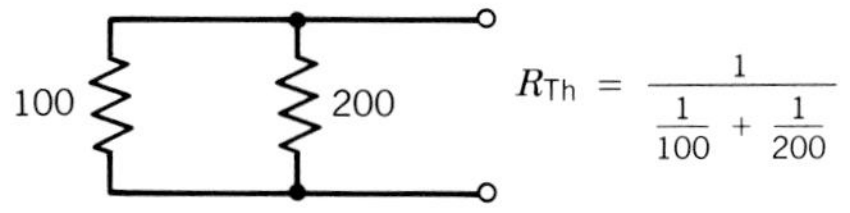

(b) Obtaining the value of R_{Th}

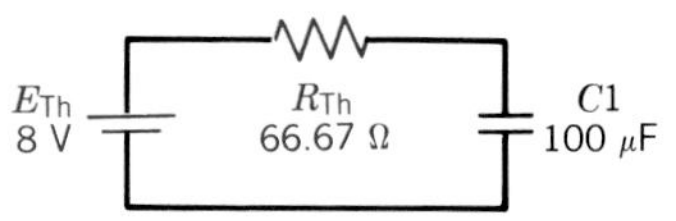

(c) The Thevenin equivalent circuit

Figure 14.20 Applying Thevenin's theorem to the circuit of Figure 14.19.

the resistance between the terminals. Since $R1$ and $R2$ are in parallel when BT1 is replaced by a short,

$$R_{\mathrm{Th}} = \frac{1}{\frac{1}{100} + \frac{1}{200}} = 66.67\ \Omega$$

The Thevenin equivalent with the capacitor reconnected is shown in Figure 14.20*b*. Using the Thevenin equivalent to calculate the potential difference across $C1$ 2.2 ms after the capacitor has begun to charge,

$$\begin{aligned} e_{C1} &= E_{\mathrm{Th}}\,(1 - \epsilon^{\frac{-t}{R_{\mathrm{Th}}C1}}) \\ &= 8\,(1 - 0.72) \\ &= 2.25\ \mathrm{V} \end{aligned}$$

The peak potential difference across the capacitor will be reached when the time is equal to or greater than five time constants. At this time,

$$\epsilon^{\frac{-t}{RC}}$$

will be close to zero, so $e_{C1} = E_{\mathrm{Th}} = 8$ V. ■

Using Kirchhoff's voltage law and the above calculations, you can compute the potential difference across or current through $R1$ or $R2$ at any time during the transient state.

EXAMPLE:
What is the current through $R2$ at 3 ms after the capacitor in Figure 14.19 begins charging? ■

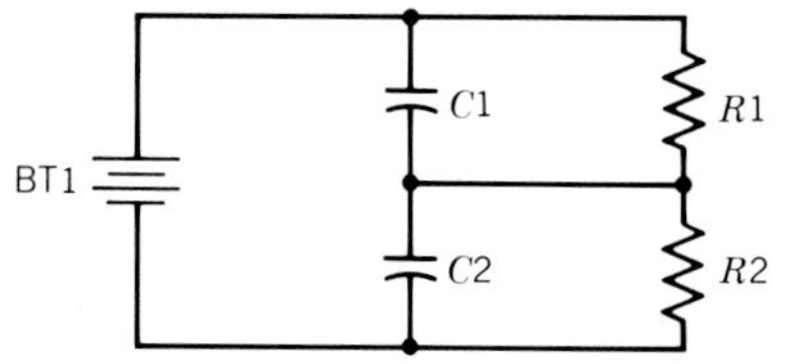

Figure 14.21 Series–parallel RC circuit used when two capacitors are connected in series to provide a higher working voltage.

SOLUTION:
Since $R2$ and $C1$ are in parallel, the potential difference across resistor $R2$ will be the same as the potential difference across $C1$. According to Ohm's law, the current through the resistor will be the potential difference across it divided by the resistance:

$$e_{R2} = e_{C1} = E_{\mathrm{Th}}(1 - \epsilon^{\frac{-t}{R_{\mathrm{Th}}C1}}) \quad \text{and} \quad i_{R2} = \frac{e_{C1}}{R2}$$

$$\begin{aligned} i_{R2} &= \frac{E_{\mathrm{Th}}(1 - \epsilon^{\frac{-t}{R_{\mathrm{Th}}C1}})}{R2} \\ &= \frac{8}{200}\,(1 - \epsilon^{\frac{-3 \times 10^{-3}}{66.67 \times 100 \times 10^{-6}}}) \\ &= 14.5\ \mathrm{mA} \end{aligned}$$

■

Comparing the series–parallel network with the series RC circuit illustrates two very important differences. When the capacitor in the series circuit is fully charged, the circuit current falls to a value that is practically zero, and the potential difference is the same as the source potential difference. In the series–parallel circuit, there will always be a current through the resistors after the moment of circuit connection, and the steady-state potential difference across the capacitor is the *Thevenin equivalent source potential*, which is less than that of the source. This means that a capacitor with a working voltage of less than the source potential but greater than the Thevenin equivalent source potential can be used.

Series–parallel circuit analysis can also be used to explain the function of the balancing resistors that are often used when capacitors are connected in series to operate across a source potential difference that is higher than the working voltage of either of the capacitors. Such a network is shown in Figure 14.21. The resistances are chosen so that the potential difference across either capacitor will be limited to a safe value in spite of either increased leakage current through one of the capacitors or a capacitance much higher than the nominal value in one of the components. Either of these conditions would place the larger potential difference across the other capacitor, if the resistors were not present.

B.5 CAPACITORS IN PARALLEL AND IN SERIES

In Chapters 6 and 12 you learned how to calculate the equivalent resistances and inductances of series, parallel, and series–parallel networks. Capacitors are also frequently connected in networks to provide a specific, nonstandard capacitance value, or a working voltage higher than that of a single unit.

Figure 14.22*a* shows a parallel connection of two parallel-plate capacitors, *C*1 and *C*2. Since plates 1 and 3 are connected together, as are plates 2 and 4, the same source potential difference is applied across both capacitors. In order to determine the total capacitance of the parallel arrangement, consider the characteristics of an equivalent capacitor, C_{eq}, which can be substituted for the two capacitors as shown in Figure 14.22*b*. Now the charge on C_{eq}, according to Formula 14.1, is $Q_{eq} = C_{eq} \times E$, where E is the potential difference of the source. Similarly, the charge $Q1$ on $C1$ is $Q1 = C1 \times E$ and that on $C2$ is $Q2 = C2 \times E$. Since the equivalent capacitor is to be substituted for *C*1 and *C*2, it must store the same charge as these two capacitors, in other words:

$$Q_{C_{eq}} = Q_{C1} + Q_{C2}$$

Substituting the previously obtained expressions for these charges,

$$C_{eq} \times E = C1 \times E + C2 \times E$$

When this expression is divided by *E*, it gives a simple formula for the equivalent of two capacitors connected in parallel:

$$C_{eq} = C1 + C2 \qquad \text{FORMULA 14.10}$$

That is, the equivalent capacitance of two capacitors in parallel is the sum of the capacitances. Similarly, it can be shown that the equivalent capacitance of any number of capacitors connected in parallel is the sum of the individual capacitances.

$$C_{eq} = C1 + C2 + \cdots + C_n \qquad \text{FORMULA 14.11}$$

Figure 14.22 Calculating the equivalent capacitance of two capacitors connected in parallel.

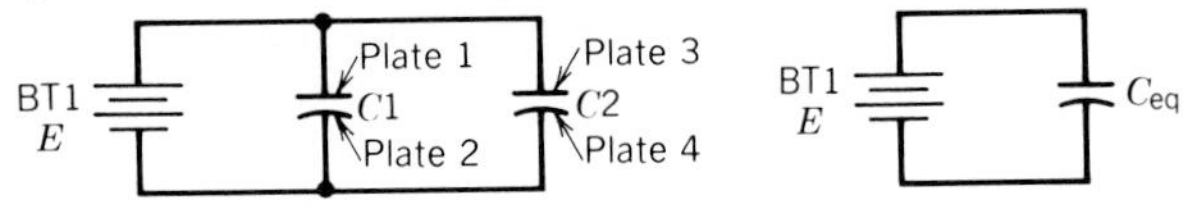

(*a*) Two parallel-plate capacitors connected in parallel across a source

(*b*) The equivalent circuit of (*a*)

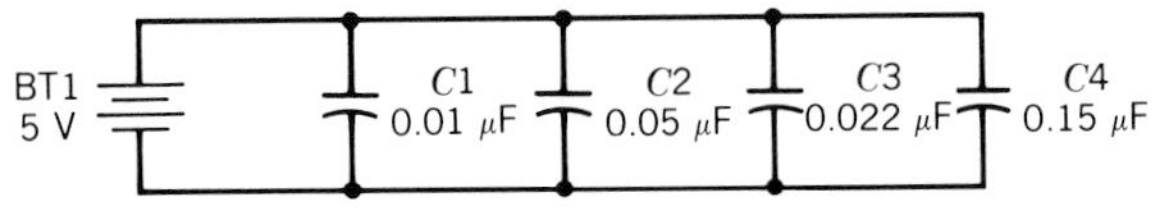

Figure 14.23 The equivalent capacitance of a number of capacitors connected in parallel.

where $C1$ is the first and C_n is the last of the capacitors in the parallel network.

EXAMPLE:
What is the equivalent capacitance of the network shown in Figure 14.23? ■

SOLUTION:
According to Formula 14.11, the equivalent capacitance can be obtained by adding the four individual capacitances:

$$\begin{aligned} C_{eq} &= C1 + C2 + C3 + C4 \\ &= 0.01 \times 10^{-6} + 0.05 \times 10^{-6} \\ &+ 0.022 \times 10^{-6} + 0.15 \times 10^{-6} \\ &= 0.232\ \mu\text{F} \end{aligned}$$

Notice that the same potential difference exists across each of the capacitors. ■

Networks consisting of a number of capacitors connected in parallel are often used to obtain high capacitances in power supplies. For example, five 1000 μF units could be connected in parallel to produce 5000 μF. In critical tuned circuits, two or more capacitors can be connected in parallel to provide a special, nonstandard value. For example, a capacitance of 1377 pF could be produced by connecting a 1000 pF, a 330 pF, and a 47 pF unit in parallel. Naturally, 1 percent or better tolerance capacitors would be used in critical circuits.

The calculation of the equivalent capacitance of two or more capacitors connected in series is more difficult than a parallel capacitor calculation. Figure 14.24 shows two parallel-plate capacitors connected in series across a source. Notice that plate 2 of *C*1 and plate 3 of *C*2 are joined together. When steady-state conditions are reached, plate 4 of *C*2 and the negative terminal of the source will become an equipotential

Figure 14.24 Two parallel-plate capacitors connected in series across a source.

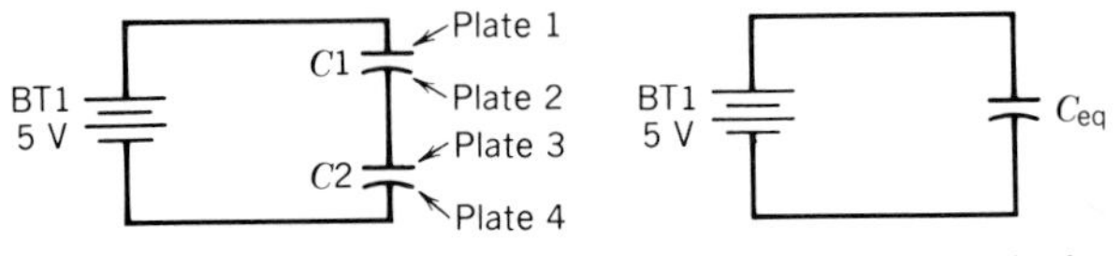

(*a*) Circuit

(*b*) The equivalent circuit of (*a*)

surface. Similarly, plate 1 of $C1$ and the positive terminal of the source also become an equipotential surface. The electric field produced by the electrical charges on plates 1 and 4 also causes a certain number of conduction electrons to drift from plate 3 of $C2$ to plate 2 of $C1$. Because there is no other source of conduction electrons, all the excess electrons on plate 2 have come from plate 3. In other words, the charge on plate 3 is $+Q$, and the charge on plate 2 is $-Q$. But the charge on both plates of the same capacitor must have the same magnitude, although the signs are opposite. Therefore, both $C1$ and $C2$ have the same charge Q Using Formula 14.1, it is possible to write

$$E_{C1} = \frac{Q}{C1} \quad \text{and} \quad E_{C2} = \frac{Q}{C2}$$

Also, the source potential E_s is equal to the charge on one of the plates of the equivalent capacitor C_{eq}. The charge on a plate of this equivalent capacitor is the same as the charge of $C1$ or $C2$ since the equivalent capacitor will have the same effect on the circuit as the series combination of $C1$ and $C2$. So,

$$E_s = \frac{Q}{C_{eq}}$$

Substituting these relationships in the Kirchhoff voltage law equation for the current, $E_s = E_{C1} + E_{C2}$, produces

$$\frac{Q}{C_{eq}} = \frac{Q}{C1} + \frac{Q}{C2}$$

Dividing by Q,

$$\frac{1}{C_{eq}} = \frac{1}{C1} + \frac{1}{C2}$$

Taking the reciprocal of both sides produces a formula similar to that used for calculating the equivalent of two parallel resistors,

$$C_{eq} = \frac{1}{\dfrac{1}{C1} + \dfrac{1}{C2}} \qquad \text{FORMULA 14.12}$$

By repeating the process, it is possible to show that the general formula for calculating the equivalent of any number of resistors in series is

$$C_{eq} = \frac{1}{\dfrac{1}{C1} + \dfrac{1}{C2} + \cdots + \dfrac{1}{C_n}} \qquad \text{FORMULA 14.13}$$

As in the case of parallel resistors, the easiest way to calculate the equivalent of a number of series capacitors is to use the product over the sum form of Formula 5.12 until all the capacitors have been combined:

$$C_{eq} = \frac{C1 \times C2}{C1 + C2} \qquad \text{FORMULA 14.14}$$

EXAMPLE:
In order not to exceed the 15-V working voltage of the 1000 μF capacitors in stock, it is necessary to connect three of them in series across the 35-V source. What will be the total capacitance across the source? ■

CAUTION

WHEN CONNECTING CAPACITORS IN SERIES ACROSS A POTENTIAL DIFFERENCE GREATER THAN THE RECOMMENDED WORKING VOLTAGE OF ONE OR MORE OF THE CAPACITORS IN THE STRING, IT IS IMPORTANT TO CALCULATE THE POTENTIAL DIFFERENCE THAT WILL APPEAR ACROSS EACH OF THE CAPACITORS. THIS WILL ENSURE THAT THE RECOMMENDED WORKING VOLTAGE IS NOT EXCEEDED. FREQUENTLY, BALANCING RESISTORS WILL BE REQUIRED, AS SHOWN IN FIGURE 14.21.

SOLUTION:
Using Formula 14.13,

$$C_{eq} = \frac{1}{\dfrac{1}{1000 \times 10^{-6}} + \dfrac{1}{1000 \times 10^{-6}} + \dfrac{1}{1000 \times 10^{-6}}} = 333.3\ \mu\text{F}$$

Similarly, Formula 14.14 could be used twice:

$$\frac{1000 \times 10^{-6} \times 1000 \times 10^{-6}}{2000 \times 10^{-6}} = 5 \times 10^{-4}$$

and

$$\frac{1000 \times 10^{-6} \times 5 \times 10^{-4}}{1000 \times 10^{-6} + 5 \times 10^{-4}} = 3.333 \times 10^{-4} \quad \text{or} \quad 333.3\ \mu\text{F}$$ ■

Since the values of the three series capacitors are the same in the previous example, you can also use the trick used with a number of parallel resistors with the same resistance: A number N of identical capacitors connected in series produces a total capacitance of $\dfrac{C}{N}$.

EXAMPLE:
Four 18-pF capacitors are connected in series. What is the equivalent capacitance of the network? ■

SOLUTION:

$$C_{eq} = \frac{C}{N} = \frac{18}{4} = 4.5 \text{ pF}$$ ■

It is a relatively simple matter to show how to derive the formula for the potential difference across one of two series capacitors. In the series circuit shown in Figure 14.25, the total circuit capacitance, according to Formula 14.14 is

$$C_{eq} = \frac{C1C2}{C1 + C2}$$

From Formula 14.1, you know that charge on one plate of the equivalent capacitor is

$$Q = CV = \frac{C1C2}{C1 + C2} E_s$$

But this is the same charge found on one of the plates of $C1$ or $C2$. Because of this, it is possible to write

$$Q_{C1} = C1E_{C1} = \frac{C1C2}{C1 + C2} E_s$$

Therefore,

$$E_{C1} = \frac{C2}{C1 + C2} E_s \qquad \text{FORMULA 14.15}$$

In the same way, it is possible to show that E_{C2}, the potential difference across $C2$, is

$$E_{C2} = \frac{C1}{C1 + C2} E_s \qquad \text{FORMULA 14.16}$$

EXAMPLE

Figure 14.26 shows the output filter section of a power supply. Determine if the working voltage recommendations are exceeded for any of the capacitors. ■

Figure 14.25 Calculating the potential difference across one of two series-connected capacitors.

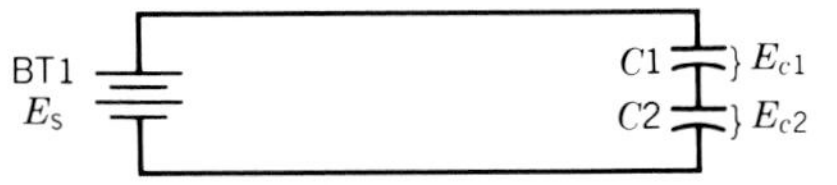

Figure 14.26 A practical example of the calculation of the potential difference across capacitors connected in series: a power supply filter.

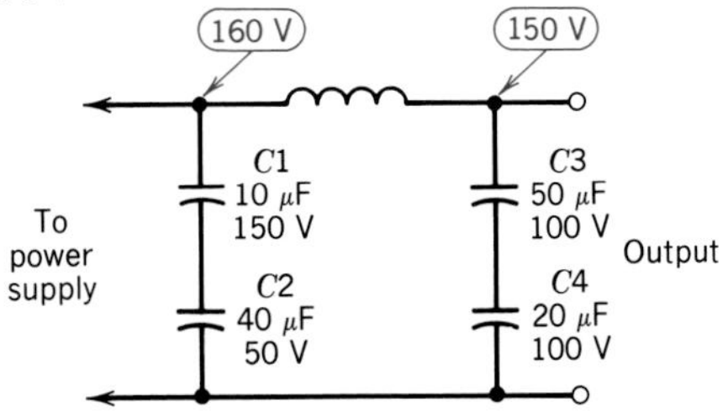

SOLUTION:

Notice that the potential differences between test points 1 and 2 and ground are different. The source potential across the series network of $C1$ and $C2$ is 160 V, while 150 V appears across the combination of $C3$ and $C4$. The potential difference across $C1$ is

$$E_{C1} = \frac{C2}{C1 + C2} E_{s1} = 128 \text{ V}$$

across $C2$,

$$E_{C2} = \frac{C1}{C1 + C2} E_{s1} = 32 \text{ V}$$

across $C3$,

$$E_{C3} = \frac{C4}{C1 + C2} E_{s2} = 42.86 \text{ V}$$

across $C4$

$$E_{C4} = \frac{C3}{C1 + C2} e_{s2} = 107.2 \text{ V}$$

Only the working voltage of $C4$ is exceeded by the potential difference across it. ■

C. EXAMPLES AND COMPUTATIONS

C.1 EXERCISES IN CAPACITOR CALCULATIONS

Due to the number and complexity of the formulas introduced in this section, it is worthwhile to practice using them to solve the sorts of problems that occur in troubleshooting electronic units. Such basic tasks as calculating the capacitance of two capacitors in series, the time constant of an *RC* circuit, or the potential difference across series, parallel, and series–parallel circuits are important steps in the understanding of complex circuits.

The most frequently used formulas introduced in this section are those for calculating the equivalent capacitance of a number of capacitors connected in series or parallel. For parallel connections, use

$$C_{total} = C1 + C2 + \cdots + C_n$$

For capacitors connected in series, either the reciprocal form:

$$C_{total} = \frac{1}{\frac{1}{C1} + \frac{1}{C2} + \cdots + \frac{1}{C_n}}$$

or the product over the sum

$$C_{\text{total}} = \frac{C1 \times C2}{C1 + C2}$$

can be used.

Solve the following problems using these formulas.

1. Solve for C_{total}:

a. A 1 μF capacitor in parallel with 3.7 μF capacitor.

b. A 0.027 μF capacitor in parallel with a 39 nF capacitor.

c. A 0.02 μF capacitor in series with a 0.1 μF capacitor.

d. A 470 pF capacitor in series with a 1.2 nF capacitor.

e. A 370 nF capacitor in series with a 1.2 μF capacitor.

f. A 22 nF capacitor in parallel with two 0.01 μF units.

g. A series combination of 0.022 μF, a 1 μF, and a 56 nF capacitor.

h. Three 39 μF capacitors in parallel.

i. A series–parallel combination formed by two 0.15 μF capacitors in parallel; this in series with a 0.2 μF capacitor.

j. A 100 pF and 27 nF capacitor in parallel, with a 0.0033 μF capacitor in series with them.

2. Calculate the total capacitance of the network shown in Figure 14.27.

3. Calculate the equivalent capacitance across the source in Figure 14.28.

4. What is the total capacitance between the + and − leads in Figure 14.29?

5. Fill in the missing capacitance.

a. 0.1 μF in parallel with ?, C_T = 320 nF.

b. 1200 pF in parallel with ?, C_T = 4.7 nF.

Figure 14.27 Capacitor network for Problem 2.

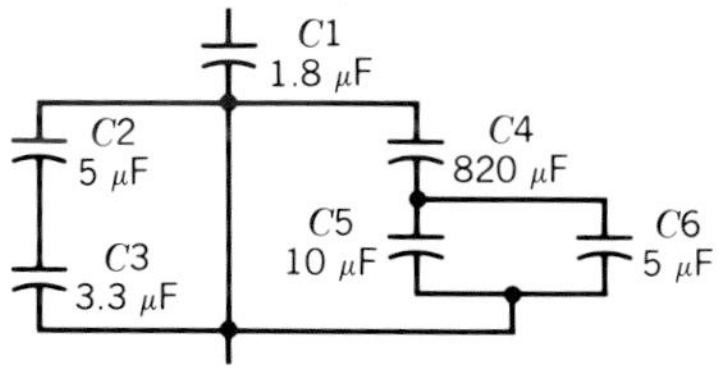

Figure 14.28 Circuit for Problem 3.

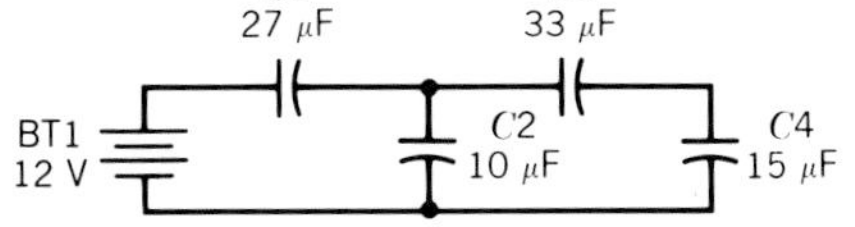

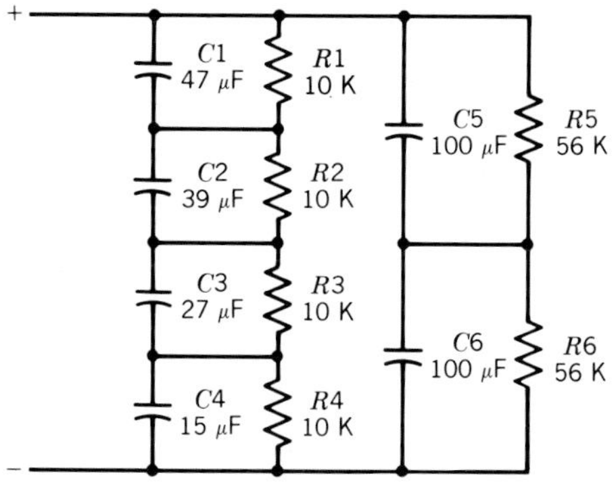

Figure 14.29 Circuit for Problem 4.

c. 8.2 nF in series with ?, C_T = 1.48 nF.

d. ? in series with 100 μF, C_T = 60 μF.

e. 120 pF in series with 82 pF, C_T = ?

f. 47 μF in parallel with ?, C_T = 86 μF.

g. 1.03 μF in series with ?, C_T = 0.51 μF.

h. 0.0033 in series with 0.0015, C_T = ?

The formula given for the time constant of an *RC* circuit, $TC = RC$, is also frequently used in timing and other circuits. Calculate the time constants in the following series networks.

a. $R1$ = 180 Ω, $C1$ = 10 μF

b. $R1$ = 10 kΩ, $C1$ = 4.7 nF

c. $R1$ = 1 MΩ, $C1$ = 1500 pF

d. $R1$ = 180, $R2$ = 150, $C1$ = 39 μF

e. $R1$ = 10 kΩ, $C1$ = 150 μF, $C2$ = 100 μF

f. $R1$ = 6.2 MΩ, $C1$ = 180 nF, $C2$ = 0.065 μF

The equations for calculating the potential difference across a charging or discharging capacitor in a series *RC* circuit, or the circuit current, are less frequently used but are valuable in certain types of timing problems or when trying to predict the length of time during which a capacitor connected across the dc supply leads of a circuit will provide a sufficient potential difference to maintain the circuit function in spite of a temporary loss of power. Use the equation

$$e = E_s(1 - \epsilon^{\frac{-t}{RC}})$$

to calculate the potential difference *e* across a capacitor that is charging, and

$$e = E\epsilon^{\frac{-t}{RC}}$$

to find the value of the potential difference at a time *t* when the capacitor is discharging. The current in a series *RC* circuit can be found by using the formula

$$i = \frac{E\,\epsilon^{\frac{-t}{RC}}}{R}$$

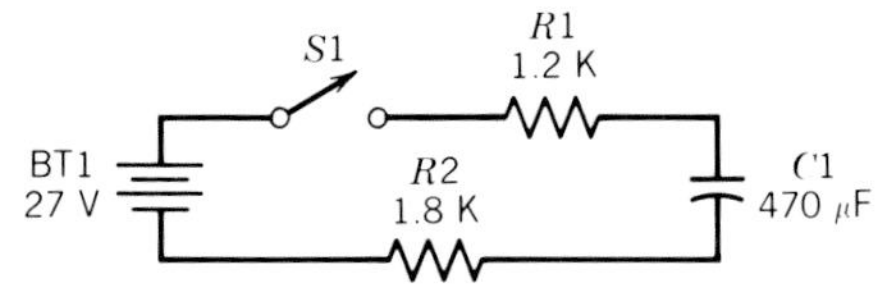

Figure 14.30 Circuit for Problem 4.

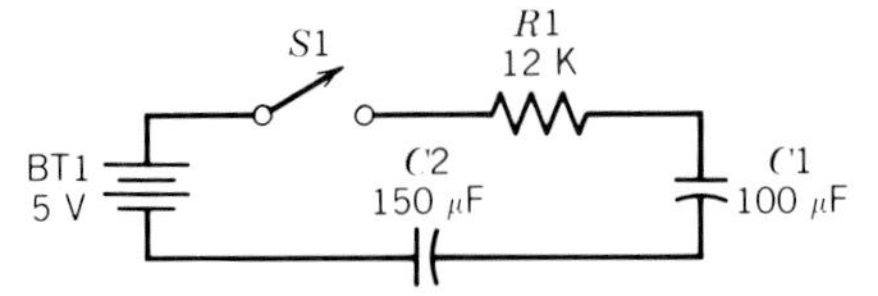

Figure 14.31 Circuit for Problem 5.

Use these formulas to solve the following problems.

1. A series circuit consisting of a 1 MΩ resistor and a 1 μF capacitor is connected across a 10-V dc source. What is the potential difference across the capacitor 0.5 s after the source is connected? What is the circuit current at this time?

2. After the capacitor in Problem 1 is allowed to charge for 1.5 s, it is removed from the circuit and allowed to discharge through a 180 kΩ resistor. What is the potential difference 300 ms after the discharge begins?

3. A 100 μF capacitor has been charged to 10 V and is being discharged through a 330 Ω relay coil. As long as the coil current is greater than 5 mA, the relay will be energized. How long will the capacitor hold the relay in its energized state?

4. At $t = 0$, switch $S1$ in Figure 14.30 is closed. How long will it be until the potential difference across the capacitor rises to 12 V? What will the power dissipation of $R1$ be when the potential difference across the capacitor is 12 V?

5. Calculate the circuit current in Figure 14.31 1.4 s after switch $S1$ is closed.

The two formulas used to find the potential difference across each of two series-connected capacitors are

$$E_{C1} = \frac{C2}{C1 + C2} E_s \quad \text{and} \quad E_{C2} = \frac{C1}{C1 + C2} E_s$$

Use these formulas to calculate the steady-state potential differences across $C1$ and $C2$ in Figure 14.31.

C.2 COMPUTATIONS WITH RECTANGULAR AND POLAR COORDINATES

The Examples and Computations section of Chapter 13 introduced two ways of defining quantities that possess both a magnitude and a phase angle. These are the rectangular coordinate or complex number system and the polar coordinate system. There are two additional notations, called the *trigonometric form* and the *exponential form*, that are less frequently used than the other two. The trigonometric form can be thought of as another way of expressing rectangular coordinates, while the exponential form serves as a variation of polar notation.

C.2.1 ADDITION AND SUBTRACTION WITH RECTANGULAR COORDINATES

Figure 14.32 shows a series network composed of two inductors and a source. In order to compute the total impedance of the circuit using the methods you have previously learned, several different computations are required. However, if the inductive and resistive components of the impedences of $L1$ and $L2$ are written in rectangular form, the problem becomes considerably simpler. The inductive reactance of $L1$ is $2\pi fL1 = 37.70\ \Omega$, that of $L2$ is $2\pi fL2 = 188.5\ \Omega$. Writing these in rectangular form,

$$Z = R + jX_L$$

$$Z_{L1} = 56 + j37.70 \quad \text{and} \quad Z_{L2} = 82 + j188.5$$

As in the case of the addition of two vector quantities when the components of the vectors are known, the two R components can be directly added to give the total resistive component of the circuit impedance, and the two components of the inductive reactance can also be added to give the total inductive reactance of the circuit. The total impedance of the circuit, then, is

$$\begin{aligned} Z_{\text{total}} &= Z_{L1} + Z_{L2} \\ &= (56 + j37.70) + (82 + j188.5) \\ &= (56 + 82) + j(37.69 + 188.5) \\ &= 138 + j226.2 \end{aligned}$$

In general, the sum of any two phasors expressed in rectangular form is

$$(a + jb) + (c + jd) = (a + c) + j(b + d)$$

FORMULA 14.17

where a, b, c, and d are any numbers, including zero.

Figure 14.32 Using rectangular coordinates to add two impedances.

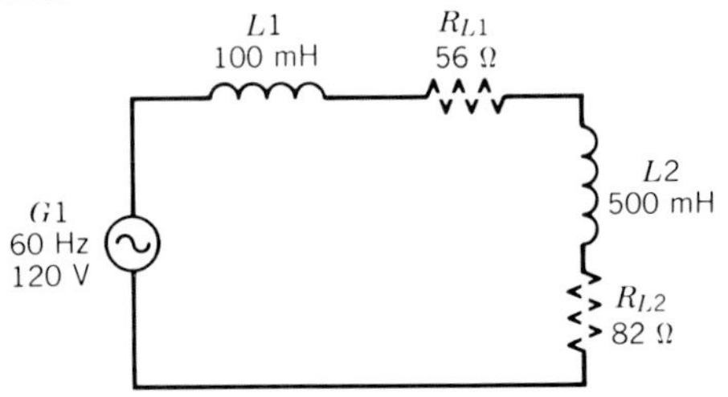

EXAMPLE:
Two ac generators producing potential differences of the same frequency are connected in series. Generator $G1$ produces a peak amplitude of 12.6 V and has a phase angle of 45°. Generator $G2$ produces a peak amplitude of 4.5 V at a phase angle of 60°. Express the instantaneous potential difference across the series combination as a phasor quantity. ■

SOLUTION:
The two voltage phasors are given in a form that can easily be converted into polar form:

$$G1 = 12.6 \angle 45°$$
$$G2 = 4.5 \angle 60°$$

Since it is necessary to use rectangular form to add the two voltages, Formulas 13.16 and 13.17 must be used:

$$R = M \cos \theta \quad \text{and} \quad J = M \sin \theta$$
$$G1 = 12.6 \angle 45° = 8.9 + j8.9 \quad \text{and}$$
$$G2 = 4.5 \angle 60° = 2.25 + j3.9$$

It is now easy to express the sum of the two phasors:

$$\begin{aligned} G_{\text{total}} &= G1 + G2 \\ &= (8.9 + j8.9) + (2.25 + j3.9) \\ &= (8.9 + 2.25) + j(8.9 + 3.9) \\ &= 11.15 + j12.8 \end{aligned}$$

If the polar form of the phasor is required, this can be obtained by using Formula 13.18:

$$\begin{aligned} M &= \sqrt{R^2 + J^2} \\ &= \sqrt{(11.15)^2 + (12.8)^2} \\ &= 16.98 \end{aligned}$$

and

$$\begin{aligned} \theta &= \tan^{-1} \frac{12.8}{11.15} \\ &= 48.94° \end{aligned}$$

or

$$E = 16.98 \angle 48.94°$$ ■

Subtracting one phasor quantity from another is performed in almost the same manner. The signs of the two terms of the subtrahend (the phasor to be subtracted) are changed, and then the two rectangular notations are added.

EXAMPLE:
Subtract the phasor $8 + j4$ from $5 - j3$. ■

SOLUTION:
$8 + j4$ is the subtrahend since it is subtracted from $5 - j3$. Changing the signs of the terms of the subtrahend produces $-8 - j4$. Adding the two phasors,

$$\begin{aligned} (5 - j3) + (-8 - j4) &= (5 - 8) + j[-3 + (-4)] \\ &= -3 + j(-7) = -3 - j7 \end{aligned}$$ ■

In general terms,

$$\begin{aligned} &(a + jb) - (c + jd) \\ &\quad = (a + jb) + (-c - jd) \qquad \text{FORMULA 14.18} \\ &\quad = (a - c) + j(b - d) \end{aligned}$$

As in the case of addition, phasors must be in rectangular form to be subtracted, and careful attention has to be paid to the signs of both the R and J components.

EXAMPLE:
Figure 14.33 illustrates the currents flowing into and out of a node in a Kirchhoff's current law problem. Express current I_4 as a phasor quantity. ■

SOLUTION:
The figure shows two currents into the node, and two flowing out, one of which, I_4, is unknown. Assuming that I_1 and I_2 are sine waves of the same frequency,

$$I_4 = I_1 + I_2 - I_3$$

The first step is to express I_1, I_2, and I_3 as complex numbers:

$$\begin{aligned} I_1 &= 24.2 \angle 30° \\ &= 24.2 \cos 30 + j \times 24.2 \sin 30 \\ &= 20.96 + j\,12.1 \\ I_2 &= 8.75 + j\,0 \\ I_3 &= 2.5 \cos 60 + j \times 2.5 \sin 60 \\ &= 1.25 + j\,2.17 \end{aligned}$$

Notice that I_2 lies along the reference phasor, that is, it forms an angle of 0° with the R axis. This means that its R component is the full length 8.75, while its J component is zero. Still, it can be expressed in complex form as $8.75 + j0$. (If the phasor had been $8.75 \angle 90°$, the R component would have been zero and the J com-

Figure 14.33 A node in a Kirchhoff's current law analysis illustrates the subtraction of phasor quantities.

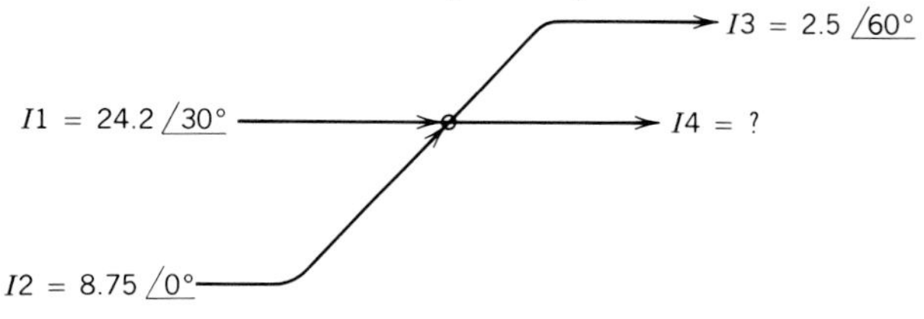

ponent 8.75.) Now that all the phasors are in rectangular form, the two can be added

$$\begin{array}{rl} I_1 = & 20.96 + j12.1 \\ + I_2 = & 8.75 + j0 \\ \hline I_1 + I_2 = & 29.71 + j12.1 \end{array}$$

and I_3 subtracted from the total. To subtract, change the sign of *both* components and add:

$$I_2 + I_2 - I_3 = 29.71 + j12.1 + (-1.25 - j2.17)$$
$$= (29.71 - 1.25) + j(12.1 - 2.17)$$
$$I_4 = 28.46 + j9.93$$ ■

Addition and subtraction can be carried out both in column form or horizontally, as shown in this example. To develop your familiarity with these calculations, try the following exercises. Express your answers in both complex rectangular form and polar coordinates.

a. $\begin{array}{r} 19.73 + j8.2 \\ \underline{+.84 + j3} \end{array}$ b. $\begin{array}{r} 1.24 - j3.7 \\ \underline{+2.16 + j2.5} \end{array}$

c. $\begin{array}{r} 6.72 - j8.3 \\ \underline{+3.9 + j4.7} \end{array}$ d. $\begin{array}{r} 0.07 + j0.4 \\ \underline{+0.96 + j1.2} \end{array}$

e. $\begin{array}{r} 18.32 - j6.7 \\ \underline{-(3.7 + j8)} \end{array}$

f. $-9.34 + j6.2 - (3.7 + j0)$

g. Subtract $9.73 + j4.8$ from $3.31 - j5.6$

h. Add $16 \angle -43^\circ$ and $12 \angle 16^\circ$

i. Subtract $19.4 \angle 57^\circ$ from $37.6 \angle -19^\circ$

j. Subtract $8 \angle -90^\circ$ from $27 \angle 45^\circ$

C.2.2 MULTIPLICATION AND DIVISION OF PHASOR QUANTITIES USING POLAR COORDINATES

If addition and subtraction of phasor quantities requires them to be in complex rectangular form, multiplication and division are much simplified if polar coordinate notation is used. Multiplication and division can be performed using complex rectangular coordinates, as will be shown in the next part of this section. On the other hand, it is much easier to use the polar coordinates for this.

To multiply two phasors expressed in polar form, multiply the two magnitudes together and add the phase angles. In terms of a formula,

$$(M_1 \angle \theta_1) \times (M_2 \angle \theta_2 = M_1M_2 \angle \theta_1 + \theta_2$$

FORMULA 14.19

It is again necessary to pay close attention to the signs of the magnitudes and the phase angles.

EXAMPLE:

Multiply the phasor $14.8 + j3.6$ by $3.2 - j5.1$. ■

SOLUTION:

Place both phasors in their polar form, noting that the J term of the second phasor is negative. For $14.8 + j3.6$,

$$M = \sqrt{R^2 + J^2} = \sqrt{(14.8)^2 + (3.6)^2} = 15.23$$

$$\theta = \tan^{-1}\frac{J}{R} = 13.67^\circ \quad \text{or} \quad 15.23 \angle 13.67^\circ$$

and for $3.2 - j5.1$,

$$M = \sqrt{(3.2)^2 + (-5.1)^2} = 6.02$$

$$\theta = \tan^{-1}\frac{J}{R} = \tan^{-1}\frac{-5.1}{3.2}$$
$$= -57.89 \quad \text{or} \quad 6.02 \angle -57.89^\circ$$

The product of the two phasors is

$$M_1M_2 \angle \theta_1 + \theta_2 = 91.68 \angle 13.67^\circ + (-57.89)^\circ$$
$$= 91.68 \angle -44.22^\circ$$ ■

To divide a phasor $M_1 \angle \theta_1$ by a second phasor $M_2 \angle \theta_2$, divide M_1 by M_2 and subtract θ_2 from θ_1:

$$M_1 \angle \theta_1 \div M_2 \angle \theta_2 = \frac{M_1}{M_2} \angle \theta_1 - \theta_2$$

FORMULA 14.20

The only trick in performing such division is to be sure which of the phasors is the divisor and to avoid errors when θ_2 is a negative angle.

EXAMPLE:

The peak potential difference across a particular circuit is given by the phasor quantity $6.2 \angle 20^\circ$. The impedance of the circuit is $390 \angle -45^\circ$. What is the current through the circuit in phasor form? ■

SOLUTION:

Now that you can perform multiplication and division on phasor quantities, it is possible to apply Ohm's law to problems of this type:

$$I = \frac{E}{Z} = \frac{6.2 \angle 20^\circ}{390 \angle -45^\circ}$$
$$= \frac{6.2}{390} \angle 20 - (-45)$$
$$= 0.016 \angle 65^\circ \text{ A}$$ ■

1. Perform the following calculations with phasor quantities.

a. $12.7\angle 60^\circ \times 4.9\angle 18^\circ =$
b. $9.38\angle -37^\circ \times 12.7\angle 64^\circ =$
c. $18.7\angle -90^\circ \times 4.8\angle 0^\circ =$
d. $(6.3 - j5) \times (1.2 + j8) =$
e. $27\angle 0^\circ \div 4.5\angle 16^\circ$
f. $8.38\angle -43^\circ \div 2.17\angle -20^\circ$
g. $(3.45 - j6.8) \div (2.4 - j3.9)$
h. $(2.8 + j0) \div (2.4 - j1.7)$
i. $120\angle -30^\circ \div 9.4\angle 30^\circ$
j. $(6.28 - j4.75) \times (8.3 + j1.2)$

2. A source produces a potential difference of 120 V at a phase angle of 60° across a circuit with an impedance of 5.6 kΩ at a phase angle of −60°. What is the circuit current?

3. The impedance of a circuit is $749.2\angle 40^\circ$ Ω and the circuit current is $22\angle 0^\circ$ mA. What is the potential difference of the source?

4. Two networks are connected in parallel. One has an impedance of $620\angle 48^\circ$ Ω, the other has an impedance of $480\angle 36^\circ$ Ω. If both impedances are referenced to the source potential, what is the total impedance of the circuit?

(*Hint:* use the product-over-the-sum formula.)

C.2.3 MULTIPLICATION AND DIVISION OF PHASOR QUANTITIES USING COMPLEX RECTANGULAR COORDINATES

Although it almost always means less work to convert phasors from rectangular to polar form to multiply and divide them, it is possible to perform these computations when the phasors are in complex rectangular form. All that is necessary is knowing the numerical value of j raised to some power n, that is, j^n, and a bit of algebra. (On the other hand, there is no way to add phasor quantities expressed in polar form, except graphically.)

The value of j raised to a power n is not difficult to memorize.

$j^0 = (\sqrt{-1})^0 = 1$ (any number to the zero power is 1)

$j^1 = \sqrt{-1} = j$

$j^2 = \sqrt{-1} \times \sqrt{-1} = -1$

$j^3 = \sqrt{-1} \times \sqrt{-1} \times \sqrt{-1} = -1 \times j = -j$

$j^4 = \sqrt{-1} \times \sqrt{-1} \times \sqrt{-1} \times \sqrt{-1} = -1 \times -1 = 1$

Notice that $j^4 = j^0$. As you might expect, $j^5 = \sqrt{-1}$. You can see that raising j to a power n that is one higher results in the rotation of a phasor through an

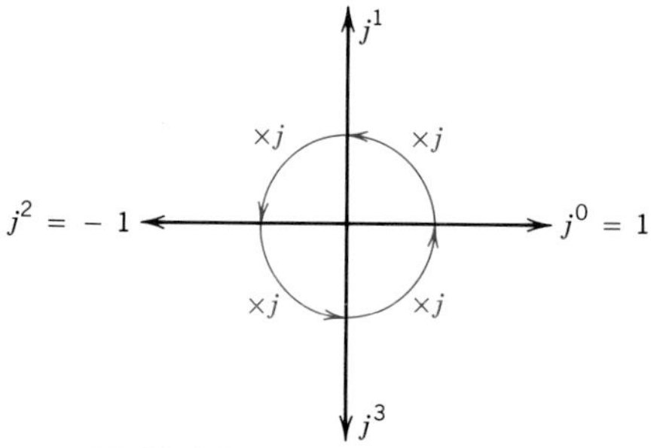

Figure 14.34 Multiplying by j has the same effect as rotating a phasor 90° in a counterclockwise direction.

angle of 90°: j^0 lies along the positive real axis, j^1, along the positive imaginary axis, and so on, as shown in Figure 14.34.

With this in mind, it is possible to multiply $4 + j3$ by $5 + j2$. Notice that each complex number is composed of two terms: 4 and $j3$, and 5 and $j2$. First multiply the two real components:

$$(4 + j3) \times (5 + j2) = 20 + \cdots$$

Next find the product of the two imaginary components:

$$(4 + j3) \times (5 + j2) = 20 + j^2 6 + \cdots$$

But $j^2 = -1$, so

$$(4 + j3) \times (5 + j2) = 20 + (-1 \times 6) + \cdots = 14 + \cdots$$

Now the two cross products $j3 \times 5$ and $4 \times j2$ are added:

$$(4 + j3) \times (5 + j2) = 14 + j8 + j15$$

Summing,

$$(4 + j3) \times (5 + j2) = 14 + j23$$

This might be a little difficult to follow if you are not familar with this process. It is, however, easy to reduce to a step-by-step process.

1. Multiply the two real factors and write down this partial product.

2. Multiply the two imaginary terms.

3. Simplify, using the fact that $j^2 = -1$.

4. Multiply the first real term by the second imaginary term and the first imaginary term by the second real term (the two cross products).

5. Obtain the sum of all the factors.

EXAMPLE:
Multiply $Z_1 = 1.5 + j3$ by $Z_2 = 2 + j4$. ■

SOLUTION:

$$(1.5 + j3) \times (2 + j4)$$

Step 1 $(1.5 + j3) \times (2 + j4) = 3 + \cdots$
Step 2 $(1.5 + j3) \times (2 + j4) = 3 + j^2\,12 + \cdots$
Step 3 $(1.5 + j3) \times (2 + j4) = 3 + (-1 \times 12) + \cdots$
Step 4 $(1.5 + j3) \times (2 + j4) = -9 + j6 + j6$
Step 5 $(1.5 + j3) \times (2 + j4) = -9 + j12$

A quick way to check this multiplication is to convert Z_1, Z_2, and their product into polar form and see if $Z_1 \times Z_2$ still equals the answer:

$$Z_1 = 1.5 + j3 = 3.35 \underline{/63.43^\circ}$$

$$Z_2 = 2 + j4 = 4.47 \underline{/63.43^\circ}$$

The product in polar form

$$M_1 \times M_2 \underline{/\theta_1 + \theta_2} = 14.97 \underline{/126.86^\circ}$$

The polar form of the answer $-9 + j12$ is $15 \underline{/126.87^\circ}$, which is practically the same as that obtained through the multiplication of Z_1 and Z_2 in polar form. The small difference is due to rounding off. ■

Sometimes it is easier to follow the steps of a complex number multiplication if the work is done in a column form.

EXAMPLE:
Multiply $3 + j2$ by $2 - j4$. ■

SOLUTION:
Before beginning, you should notice that the imaginary term of the second phasor is negative. This will not cause any problem in the calculation, if the signed number multiplication is carried out properly.

$$\begin{array}{r} 3 + j2 \\ \times \quad 2 - j4 \\ \hline \end{array}$$

Step 1 6
Step 2 $-j^2\,8$
Step 3
$$\begin{array}{r} 3 + j2 \\ \times \quad 2 - j4 \\ \hline 6 \\ +8 \end{array}$$

Step 4
$$\begin{array}{r} 3 + j2 \\ \times \quad 2 - j4 \\ \hline 14 + j4 - j12 \end{array}$$

Step 5
$$\begin{array}{r} 3 + j2 \\ \times \quad 2 - j4 \\ \hline 14 - j8 \end{array}$$
■

Perform the following multiplications in the rectangular system. Check your answers by converting to polar coordinates.

a. $(2 + j4) \times (4 + j6)$
b. $(6.2 - j2) \times (3.7 + j4.8)$
c. $(4.2 + j3) \times (4.2 - j3)$
d. $(9.37 - j4.8) \times (6.25 - j0.27)$
e. $(9.2 + j0) \times (1.24 + j3.1)$
f. $(0.065 - j0.03) \times (-2.21 - j0.047)$
g. $(0 + j37.2) \times (0 - j14.7)$
h. $(2.86 - j14.3) \times (3.14 - j21)$
i. $(-6.1 + j3.2) \times (6.1 - j3.2)$

Dividing one phasor quantity by another is also possible when both are expressed in complex rectangular coordinates. The method used is to change the process of division into multiplication. This is done by writing the division computation in the form of a fraction and then multiplying both the numerator and denominator of the fraction by a complex number, referred to as the *complex conjugate* of the denominator. The complex conjugate of a complex number is formed by changing the sign of the j term. For example, the complex conjugate of $7 + j4$ is $7 - j4$. In general terms, the complex conjugate of $(a + jb)$ is $(a - jb)$, while the complex conjugate of $(a - jb)$ is $(a + jb)$.

EXAMPLE:
Divide $8 - j6$ by $4 - j7$. ■

SOLUTION:
First write the problem as a fraction:

$$\frac{8 - j6}{4 - j7}$$

Then determine the complex conjugate of the denominator, which is $4 + j7$. Multiplying both the numerator and denominator of a fraction by one does not change the value of the fraction, so

$$\frac{8 - j6}{4 - j7} = \frac{(8 - j6) \times (4 + j7)}{(4 - j7) \times (4 + j7)}$$

Performing the multiplication of the denominator first,

$$\begin{aligned}(4 - j7) \times (4 + j7) &= 16 - j^2 49 + 28j - 28j \\ &= 16 + 49 \quad \text{or} \quad 65\end{aligned}$$

Notice that the effect of multiplying a complex number by its complex conjugate is to eliminate the imaginary factor completely. The result of the multiplication of the numerator is

$$\begin{aligned}(8 - j6) \times (4 + j7) &= 32 - j^2\,42 + j56 - j24 \\ &= 32 + 42 + j32 = 74 + j32\end{aligned}$$

The fraction after the multiplication is completed is

$$\frac{74 + j32}{65} \quad \text{or} \quad \frac{74}{65} + j\frac{32}{65}$$

Dividing,

$$\frac{8 - j6}{4 - j7} = 1.14 + j0.49$$

As in the case of multiplication, the division of phasors in rectangular form can be checked by converting to polar coordinates. In this example, the polar forms of the two phasors are $8 - 6j = 10 \angle -36.87°$ and $4 - j7 = 8.1 \angle -60.26°$. The quotient of the two is $\frac{10}{8.1} \angle -36.87° - (-60.26)°$, or $1.23 \angle 23.39°$. Converting this into rectangular form yields $1.13 + j0.49$, which is within the round-off value of the quotient obtained by division of the complex rectangular coordinates. ■

The ability to perform computations with phasor quantities makes it possible to use many of the laws, such as Ohm's and Kirchhoff's laws, and some of the methods of network analysis in ac circuits containing resistance, inductance, and capacitance. Ohm's law, for example, is utilized by replacing resistance with impedance.

EXAMPLE:
A 500-mH choke with an internal resistance of 15 Ω is connected in series with a 180 Ω resistor and an 80 Hz ac source that produces a potential with a peak value of $12 \angle 15°$. What is the circuit current? ■

SOLUTION:
The total impedance of the circuit shown in Figure 14.35 is the phasor sum of the impedance of the resistor and that of the inductor and its internal resistance. These impedances are easily written and added in rectangular coordinates. The inductive reactance of the coil is $2\pi fL = 251.3$ Ω, so the impedance of the coil is $Z = 15 + j251.3$, and the impedance of the resistor is $Z = 180 + j0$. The sum of the two is $(15 + j251.3) + (180 - j0) = 195 + j251.3$. Using Ohm's law in its ac form to determine the current,

$$I = \frac{E}{Z} = \frac{12\angle 15°}{195 + j251.3}$$

Putting the denominator in polar form for easier computation,

$$I = \frac{12 \angle 15°}{318.1 \angle 52.19°} = 0.038 \angle -37.19°$$ ■

Use the three forms of Ohm's law as rewritten for ac circuits: $I = \frac{E}{Z}$, $E = IZ$, and $Z = \frac{E}{I}$ to solve the following problems.

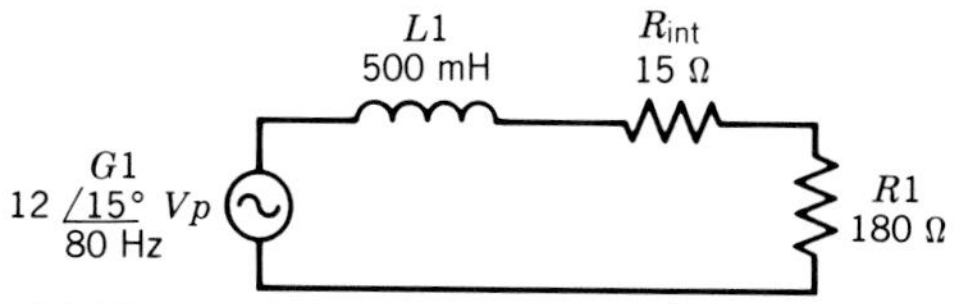

Figure 14.35 Adding impedances to calculate circuit current.

1. A certain circuit consists of a 1.7 mH inductor in series with a 470 Ω resistor. Both are across a 10-V peak ac source operating at a frequency of 40 kHz and a phase angle of 37°. Calculate the current and its phase angle.

2. A 1 H inductor with an internal resistance of 120 Ω is connected in parallel across a 6.8 kΩ resistor. What is the impedance of the resulting network if the source frequency is 200 Hz?

3. If the network of Problem 2 is connected across a 400 Hz, 27-V source operating at a phase angle of 0°, what will be the current in the branch containing the inductor? Give your answer in both complex rectangular and polar form.

4. Generator *G*1 produces a 10 kHz sine wave current of $1 \angle -16°$ A through a series circuit consisting of a 10 μF capacitor and a 5.6 Ω resistor. What are the potential difference and phase of the source?

5. What is the polar form of the potential difference developed across an impedance of $6 - j18$ Ω when a current of $0.012 + j0.035$ A flows through it?

6. At a source frequency of 500 kHz, a 1 mH inductor has a potential difference of $18 \angle 60°$ V across it. What is the current through the inductor?

7. At an applied potential difference of $4.48 \angle -21°$ V, a certain network has a current of $12.0 \angle 5°$ mA in it. What is the impedance of the network?

8. A generator produces a sine-wave potential difference at a frequency of 4 kHz. If the current through a 0.01 H inductor with an internal resistance of 80 Ω is 10 mA at a phase angle of 0°, what is the source potential difference in polar form?

D. APPLICATIONS

D.1 CAPACITOR TYPES AND CHARACTERISTICS

The parallel-plate capacitor used as an example in Section B is useful for illustrating the operating principles of capacitors but does not provide much information about the many different types of capacitors commonly used. Since there are many applications for capacitors in different circuits, it is no wonder that capacitors appear in many different forms. In the early days of electronics, typical units would contain almost as many coils and transformers as capacitors, and the number of resistors was usually greater than the number of all other components. In recent years, however, it has been possible to combine a large number of resistors and semiconductors into tiny integrated circuit chips. In many units, therefore, the most common component appears to be the capacitor since it is not possible to produce capacitors of relatively large value on integrated circuits. Moreover, there are more different varieties of capacitors than of any other components.

There are two main classes of capacitors currently used in electronic units. These are referred to as *fixed capacitors* and *variable capacitors*. Fixed capacitors are designed to provide a single value of capacitance in a circuit. This value is referred to as the *nominal capacitance* of the component. Variable capacitors provide a capacitance value that can be varied within a specific range. Fixed capacitors are often divided into groups depending on the dielectric material used because this determines the physical size of the capacitor and many of its electrical characteristics. Variable capacitors are generally divided into classes depending on their function or construction details. Only the fixed capacitors using solid dielectric materials will be considered in this chapter. Electrolytic capacitors, which use a thin film of gas or an oxide layer as the dielectric material, and the various types of variable capacitors are considered in Chapter 15.

When working with fixed capacitors, you must be aware of a number of distinguishing characteristics in addition to the capacitance. These characteristics are not really independent of one another. For example, a practical 1000 μF capacitor can not be placed in a tiny square case or use glass as the dielectric. For the purposes of introducing these characteristics, however, they will be discussed separately.

Since the typical electronic unit contains a number of capacitors, and the space within the unit is usually considered to be one of the factors determining capacitor size and shape, the characteristics of physical size and shape are important. Figure 14.36 shows some of the case shapes which have been used. Capacitors whose terminals are in the form of screw terminals or solder lugs are most commonly found as cylindrical aluminum cans (14.36*a*) or, less frequently, metal boxes (14.36*b*). The tub-shaped units (14.36*c*), once a standard in military and other high-reliability applications, are now considerably less common than they were 10 or 15 years ago. Bulky cylindrical cans about 0.1 m high containing two or three separate capacitors have long been popular in the dc power supplies of industrial and consumer electronics units, and are still used in many applications. A newer form of leadless capacitor

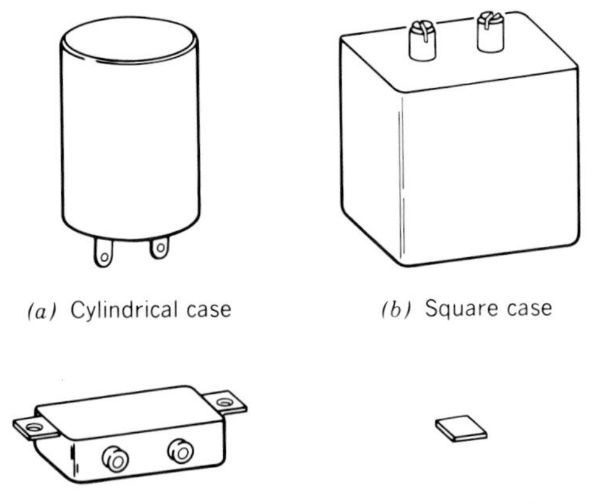

Figure 14.36 Some of the capacitor case shapes that have been used. Only the cylindrical can (*a*) and chip (*d*) are still used in modern electronic units.

is the chip capacitor, Figure 14.36*d*, which is becoming popular in UHF circuits. At ultra-high frequencies even short lead lengths possess high inductive reactance, so the chip capacitor, which is soldered directly to a circuit board, is used.

Capacitor leads fall into three categories, as shown in Figure 14.37. It is common for a manufacturer to produce families of capacitors that are identical in all respects except for lead style. Frequently, these units have similar manufacturer's part numbers and confusion can result if careful attention is not paid to the descriptions in the parts catalog. There is nothing more tempting than trying to bend the leads of an axial lead type so that it can be used to substitute for a single-ended unit or vice versa because the wrong component has been ordered. This is really not a good idea and should be avoided since any vibration is likely to break the long, bent leads. The single-ended case style is most common for capacitance values above 1 μF. Below this value, all three styles seem to be equally common.

For the most part, capacitor size, particularly in larger cylindrical units, is not entirely standard. Square case units of low capacitance, however, are fairly uniform. These case styles and their dimensions are illustrated in Figure 14.38. In spite of their resemblance to the single-ended lead type, these capacitors are considered radial lead. The square design and standard lead spacing makes this package suitable for automatic assembly machines. For this reason, the radial lead,

Figure 14.37 The three types of capacitor leads.

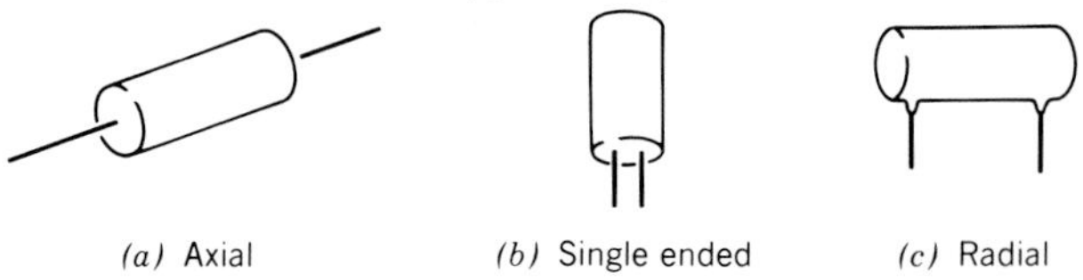

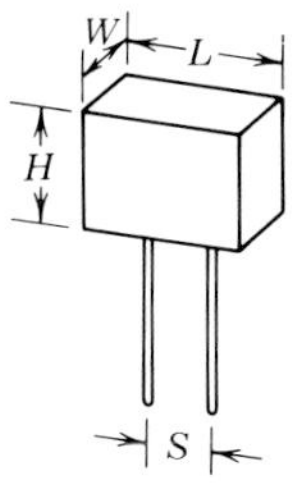

MIL SPEC TYPE	H	L	W	S
CC05	4.83 ± 0.25	4.83 ± 0.25	2.29 ± 0.25	5.08 ± 0.38
CC06	7.37 ± 0.25	7.37 ± 0.25	2.29 ± 0.25	5.08 ± 0.38
CC07	12.19 ± 0.51	12.19 ± 0.51	3.56 ± 0.25	10.16 ± 0.51
CC08	12.19 ± 0.51	12.19 ± 0.51	6.1 ± 0.25	10.16 ± 0.51

All dimensions in millimeters. S = lead spacing

Figure 14.38 Standardized miniature square case styles.

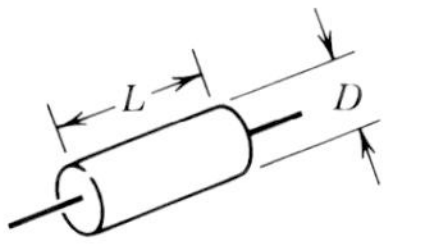

MIL SPEC TYPE	L	D
CC75	4.06 ± 0.25	2.29 ± 0.25
CC76	6.35 ± 0.25	2.29 ± 0.25
CC77	9.91 ± 0.25	3.56 ± 0.25
CC78	12.7 ± 0.25	6.35 ± 0.38
CC79	17.53 ± 0.76	8.89 ± 0.51

All dimensions in millimeters

Figure 14.39 Standardized miniature cylindrical styles.

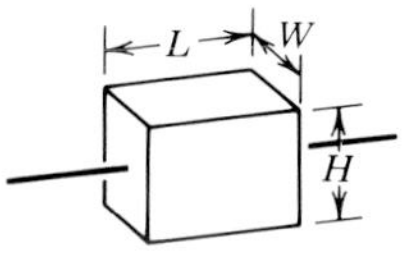

MIL SPEC TYPE	L	H	W
CM15	13.1	7.54	4.76
CM20	18.65	11.1	4.76
CM25	27.0	11.1	4.76
CM30	20.24	20.24	6.35
CM35	20.24	20.24	7.94
CM40	25.8	15.9	7.94

All dimensions in millimeters, typical sizes listed

Figure 14.40 Sizes of the "postage stamp" cases formerly the most widely used for mica capacitors.

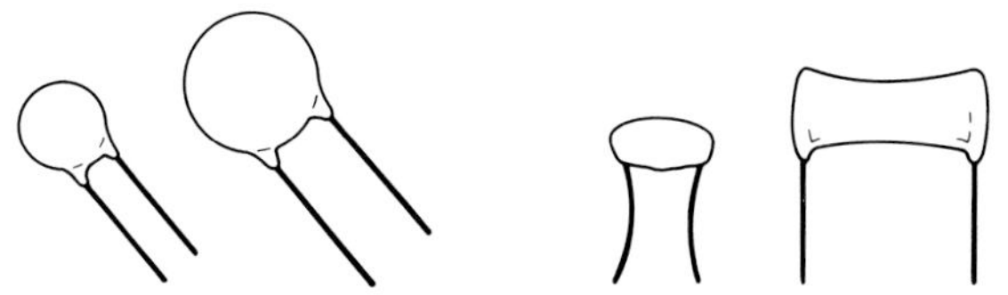

(a) Disk style capacitors (b) "Dog bone" case styles

Figure 14.41 Popular disk and "dog bone" shapes.

square capacitor has become somewhat more popular in smaller sizes than the axial lead, cylindrical style shown in Figure 14.39. In some applications, ceramic capacitors in this square shape have also begun to replace the very popular "postage stamp" mica dielectric capacitors. The standard "postage stamp" mica capacitor sizes are shown in Figure 14.40.

The disk ceramic capacitors shown in Figure 14.41 and radial lead "dog bone" mica capacitors are still very popular case styles, although their irregular shapes make automatic assembly more difficult. For working voltages over 250 V, the axial lead tubular shape appears to be the most common, particularly in the capacitance range of 0.001 to 1.0 μF.

The two most critical characteristic electrical values of a capacitor are its capacitance and the potential difference at which the dielectric layer between the capacitor plates begins to break down. This potential difference depends on the type of material and the thickness of the dielectric used and often upon the physical construction of the capacitor. In general, the manufacturer will specify a suggested maximum voltage or recommended working voltage for a particular component. This can be as low as 3 V for the tiny units used in portable radio receivers or as high as 15,000 V for special high-voltage disk ceramics. A working voltage value represents the suggested peak potential difference that should ever be applied to the capacitor. Although lower than the dielectric breakdown value, regularly exceeding the working voltage can lead to eventual failure of the capacitor.

Another characteristic of a capacitor is its tolerance. In the past, it was very difficult to manufacture capacitors to the same close tolerances possible with resistors. This was due in part to the fact that early dielectrics were such natural materials as mica and oil, and were not uniform. In more recent times, however, the most popular dielectrics can be controlled to more uniform standards, and better tolerance values are possible. As might be expected, however, capacitors with a very narrow tolerance range are frequently more expensive than wider-range components because of the additional effort required in manufacturing and testing. Fortunately, capacitors do not often need tolerances better than 5 or 10 percent. In some sensitive tuned circuits, special capacitor types with tolerances of 1 or 2 percent or better are used, but this is usually limited to signal source circuits such as oscillators.

In many cases, particularly where capacitance values are greater than 10 μF, a small tolerance range is not important. High-capacitance electrolytic capacitors can have tolerances in the range of -80 to $+150$ percent. This means that a capacitor marked 100 μF might have an actual capacitance as low as 20 μF or as high as 250 μF. This large range is not a problem in power supply circuits, for example. Capacitor tolerance is generally marked on the component case, along with the capacitance value and the working voltage.

Another capacitor characteristic is the temperature coefficient. In Chapter 5 you learned that changes in temperature will produce changes in the resistance of a length of wire. It should therefore not be surprising to learn that temperature changes will affect capacitance. Other than the changes in the characteristics of the dielectric, the expansion or contraction of the metal parts of a capacitor due to temperature changes will produce temporary changes in the characteristics and sizes of these parts. In circuits where capacitor value must be very nearly constant in spite of changed temperature, an ultrastable dielectric material is used. In military specifications, capacitors of this type are referred to as "NPO," "CG," or "BP" capacitors and as "COG" capacitors in the industrial and consumer EIA specifications. The temperature coefficient for NPO units is usually given in parts per million per degree centigrade (ppm/degree). To calculate the actual change in capacitance for a particular temperature change, use the formula:

$$\text{Change in capacitance} = \frac{\text{nominal}}{\text{capacitance}} \times \frac{\text{temperature}}{\text{coefficient}} \times \frac{\text{change in}}{\text{temperature}}$$

FORMULA 14.21

Note that the coefficient is expressed as some number times 10^{-6}, and that it may be positive or negative, depending on whether an increase in temperature produces an increase or decrease in the capacitance. A positive temperature coefficient means that an increase in temperature will cause an increase in the capacitance of the component.

EXAMPLE:
A certain capacitor has a nominal value of 750 pF at a temperature of 20°C and a temperature coefficient of +500 ppm/degree C. What is its capacitance at 40°C? ■

SOLUTION:
The change in capacitance for a 20°C temperature rise can be calculated using Formula 14.21.

$$\text{Change in capacitance} = 750 \times 10^{-12} \times 500 \times 10^{-6} \times 20 = 7.5 \times 10^{-12}$$

Since the temperature coefficient and the change in temperature both have a positive sign, the capacitance will be 7.5 pF greater, or 750 + 7.5 = 757.5 pF. In other words, an increase of 1 percent. ■

NPO or COG capacitors are defined as those having a temperature coefficient of between -30 ppm/degree and $+30$ ppm/degree C whether a pure ac or ac + dc potential is placed across them. EIA types X7F and X7R are rated as "stable" rather than "ultrastable." They show capacitance ranges of 7.5 and 15 percent, respectively, over their stable operating range, which varies from -55 to $+125$°C. These figures are specified for ac operation only and will be considerably poorer if a dc potential close to the recommended maximum working voltage is applied across the capacitor. EIA general-purpose capacitors are marked "Z5U" and possess tolerances between $+22$ and -56 percent over their operating range of $+10$ to $+85$ °C.

Finally, one capacitor characteristic that has become more important in recent years is the equivalent series resistance. Abbreviated as "ESR," it represents the sum of all the resistance effects present in a capacitor and is comparable to the internal resistance of a coil. In most capacitor circuits, the ac component of the source potential tends to be small. It is particularly small when compared to the dc potential difference that exists across the capacitor. In these circuits the ESR, being rather low, on the order of 10 Ω or less, has little effect on the circuit or on the capacitor itself. In some modern power supply circuits, there is a large alternating current component that would result in high power dissipation and heating in the circuit capacitors if the ESR is higher than a few ohms. Special low ESR capacitors must be used in these circuits to avoid dangerous overheating conditions.

D.1.1 CERAMIC CAPACITORS

The ceramic capacitor is one of the most common electronic components in use today. Although not as common as the film resistor, most electronic units will use at least a few of these small components. Regardless of the shape of its case, a ceramic capacitor is defined as a capacitive component whose dielectric material is an inorganic material that has been formed into a solid by a high-temperature sintering process, to distinguish

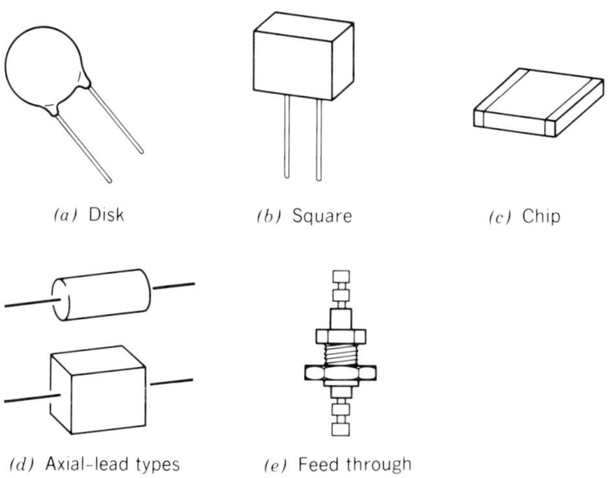

Figure 14.42 Case styles used for ceramic capacitors.

it from the high-temperature fusing process used to manufacture glass parts. The dielectric in modern ceramic capacitors generally incorporates titanium. Ceramic capacitors are low cost and provide a good deal of capacitance in a small package. Ceramics also perform well in both dc and high-frequency ac circuits.

There are five principal styles of ceramic capacitor shown in Figures 14.42*a* through 14.42*e*. The capacitor shown in 14.42*a* is the popular disk type. It is composed of a ceramic disk with a metal electrode plated onto each face. Metal leads are connected to the electrodes, and the whole is then covered with an insulating coating. The square style ceramic capacitor shown in Figure 14.42*b* is produced in the same manner.

In ultra-high-frequency circuits, where the inductance of a wire lead would introduce excessive inductive reactance, the leadless, chip style is used. In this form the capacitor is made of a stack of ceramic blanks. Each blank is partially coated with a silver film, and a tab on each end of the stack makes contact with alternate layers of film. The unit is then covered with an insulating coating and external contact surfaces are bonded to the tabs. The contact surfaces are soldered directly to conducting surfaces on a printed circuit board, as shown in Figure 14.43.

A fourth style of ceramic capacitor is the axial-lead cylindrical unit shown in Figure 14.42*d*, along with an alternate rectangular style. These are somewhat less common than the disk and square packages. The cylindrical models are frequently color coded like resistors and small rf coils and are sometimes hard to distinguish from 0.5-W resistors.

Finally, a form of ceramic capacitor used when high-frequency signals must be prevented from leaving or entering a metal enclosure is shown in Figure 14.42*e*. Called *feed-through* capacitor, it is frequently composed of a ceramic tube with conductive films on both its inside and outside, as shown in Figure 14.44*a*. Figure 14.44*b* shows how the feed-through capacitor operates to provide a low-impedance path for high-frequency signals, separating them from the low-frequency or dc power being "fed through" the shielding enclosure.

Ceramic capacitors fall into two classes, usually referred to as Class I and Class II. Class II ceramic capacitors are general-purpose components. They are not meant for applications requiring great precision but are used in circuits where relatively large changes in capacitance due to temperature change, changes in applied potential difference, or the aging of the component are permitted. The ceramic dielectrics used in Class II capacitors have a nonlinear reaction to temperature changes. In other words, there is no simple way to calculate the change in capacitance for a given change in temperature. Class II ceramic materials are also sensitive to voltage changes. This means that the capacitance of a particular unit will be different with

Figure 14.43 Soldering a chip capacitor directly to a printed circuit.

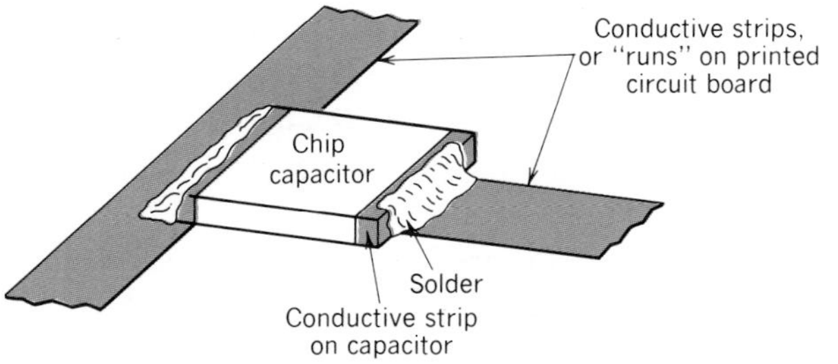

Figure 14.44 Construction and use of a feed-through capacitor.

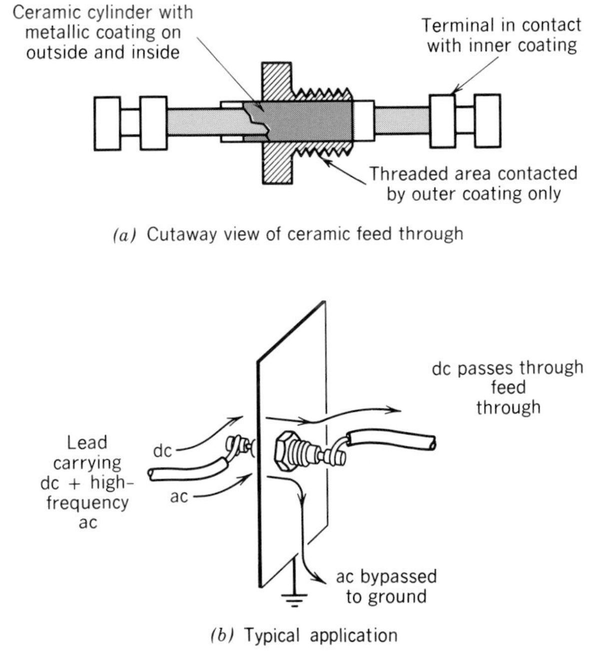

different dc potentials across the capacitor plates. The principal advantages of Class II ceramic capacitors are low cost and a very high dielectric constant, which can be between 200 and 16,000, depending on the materials used. The high dielectric constant means that high capacitance can be obtained from a physically small unit. In some applications, this offsets the problems of unpredictable capacitance changes with temperature, voltage, and component aging.

Class II general-purpose ceramic capacitors are widely available in capacitances ranging from a few picofarads to 0.1 μF, and with working voltages ranging from 3 to 1500 V dc or higher. Tolerances of 10 and 20 percent are available in most standard value components.

Where precise control of capacitance under varying conditions of temperature, voltage, and component age is required, Class I ceramic capacitors can be used. Using a dielectric based on titanium ceramic materials, these capacitors show very little change in capacitance with respect to time or changes in applied voltage. Their change in capacitance with respect to temperature change is linear and predictable. This linearity of capacitance change under conditions of changing temperature is the most important feature of Class I ceramics. The temperature coefficient can be adjusted from about +100 to −5600 parts per million per degree C (ppm/°C) by the manufacturer. NPO Class I ceramics, for example, are relatively independent of temperature variation through the operating temperature range of most electronic units. *P*-type ceramics have a positive temperature coefficient and *N*-type ceramics show a negative change in capacitance as their temperature increases. For example, a 1-nF capacitor marked N 1800 has a nominal capacitance of 1 nF at 20°C. At 40°C its change in capacitance, according to Formula 14.1, will be

$$\begin{aligned}\text{Change in capacitance} &\\ &= \text{nominal capacitance} \times \text{temperature coefficient} \times \text{change in temperature} \\ &= 1 \times 10^{-9} \times -1800 \times 10^{-6} \times 20 \\ &= -3.6 \times 10^{-11} \quad \text{or} \quad -36 \text{ pF}\end{aligned}$$

At 40°C, therefore, the capacitance will be 964 pF. If the capacitor in this example had been marked P 1800, the capacitance at 40°C would be 1000 pF + 36 pF = 1036 pF.

Because the temperature coefficient of Class I ceramic capacitors can be accurately controlled in the manufacturing process, these components are frequently used in circuits to cancel out the effects of temperature changes on other circuit components. Class I ceramic capacitors are normally marked with their nominal capacitance, working voltage, and their temperature coefficients.

Both Class I and Class II ceramic capacitors have a normal life expectancy of several thousand hours in properly designed circuits. The principal ways in which failure can occur are:

1. An open circuit. One lead of the capacitor becomes separated from the conductive film that serves as a capacitor plate

2. A short circuit. Any low-resistance current path between the capacitor leads. Frequently, this is the result of puncture of the dielectric when too high a potential difference is applied across it. Short circuiting is also caused by moisture or other contamination seeping under the outer covering of the capacitor.

3. A change in electrical characteristics. This failure can take the form of either a decrease in the breakdown voltage or an excessive change in capacitance when the operating temperature changes. Both of these problems are the result of a number of causes.

During the first thousand or so hours of operation, Class I ceramics will usually show less than a 1 percent change in capacitance. Class II capacitors, on the other hand, tend to show a capacitance decrease of 10 to 15 percent during the first thousand hours of operation. This is due to changes in the dielectric material itself and is called *aging*. It is interesting and useful to know that this aging process can be reversed. If the capacitor is heated to a temperature of about 150°C, it returns to its original manufactured value.

D.1.2 MICA AND GLASS DIELECTRIC CAPACITORS

Before the introduction of ceramic dielectrics, the mineral mica was generally used for low-capacitance components. Mica is a transparent material that is easily separated into thin sheets and is well fitted for use as a capacitor dielectric. Sheets as thin as 2.54×10^{-6} m can be obtained from the raw mineral by mechanical methods, and mica does not expand or contract much because of temperature changes. The dielectric constant of mica is rather low, between 6.5 and 8.5, depending on the variety used, but it tends to remain constant over a wide range of applied voltages. For these reasons, capacitors using mica as the dielectric have very small temperature coefficients and show little change in capacitance over time.

Mica capacitors are found in the case styles shown in Figures 14.45*a* and 14.45*b*, although the older, post-

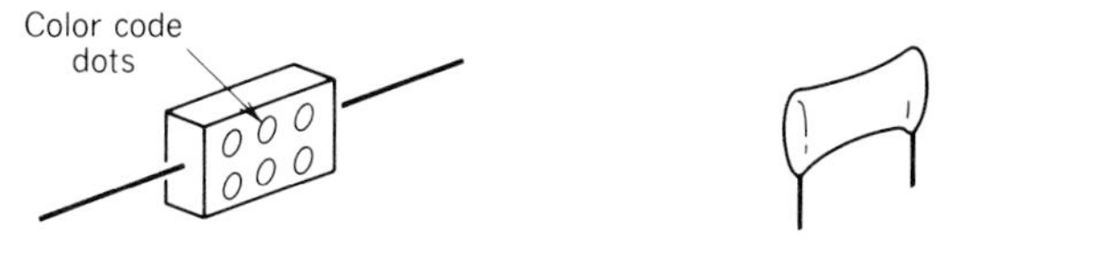

(a) The older, rectangular or postage stamp style (b) Epoxy-dipped, "dog bone" style

Figure 14.45 Mica capacitor case styles.

age stamp style 14.45*a* has been replaced by the maroon epoxy-dippled, radial lead type shown in 14.45*b*, even though the size classifications of the postage stamp style are still used.

Two varieties of mica capacitor are available, the standard unit and the silver mica. Silver mica capacitors differ from the standard variety in that the capacitor plates are formed by thin layers of silver deposited directly on the mica dielectric. In contrast with the metallic conductor films used in the standard units, silver mica capacitors can be produced to more exacting standards and tend to be more stable under temperature changes. One, 2 and 5 percent tolerance silver mica capacitors and 5 and 10 percent tolerance standard units are widely available in capacitance values from 1 pF to 10 nF. Typical recommended working voltages are 100, 300, and 500 V, although units possessing working voltages as high as 2500 V are available. The principle drawbacks of mica capacitors are their relatively high cost and greater size than equivalent ceramic units.

Large-scale use of glass dielectric capacitors started during World War II when it became difficult to obtain large shipments of mica from Europe. Recently, new manufacturing processes have lowered the cost of glass dielectric capacitors, and these units are becoming popular, particularly in computer-type circuits where large numbers of capacitors are needed. The characteristics of glass dielectric capacitors are similar to those of mica capacitors. They possess excellent long-term stability, small temperature coefficients, and good reliability. Since the dielectric constant of glass is relatively low, glass capacitors tend to be larger than equivalent ceramic types. Further problems found with the small, axial-lead, glass case and dielectric capacitors shown in Figure 14.46 are their ease of confusion with other glass-cased components such as diodes and the possibility of damage to the glass-to-metal lead seal or cracking of the case when the component leads are bent or soldered. Both forms of damage can be avoided by care in handling and the use of needle-nose pliers to prevent strain during bending and to absorb excess heat during soldering. One of the reasons that some glass capacitors are sensitive to heat damage is that the glass-to-metal seal on the leads undergoes a great deal of strain when the lead wire is heated and expands. Epoxy or plastic-cased glass dielectric capacitors do not suffer from these problems.

Like mica units, glass case, glass dielectric capacitors are widely available in working voltages up to 300 or 500 V, while moulded case units with working voltages up to 2500 V are found. Capacitances range from 1 pF to 0.05 μF or higher. Because of the stability of glass as a dielectric material, tolerances of 1 percent are fairly easy to obtain, although 2 or 5 percent are somewhat more common. Glass dielectric capacitor failure modes are most often related to physical damage of the case or the seal between the lead and the case. Moisture entering the case can change the electrical characteristics of the unit or lead to short circuiting.

D.1.3 PAPER AND PLASTIC CAPACITORS

Ceramic and mica or glass capacitors make up the majority of the capacitors of less than 0.01 μF, but for capacitance values between 0.01 and 1 μF, capacitors using plastic or some paperlike material are probably the most common. This group of capacitors includes a variety of dielectrics with different electrical characteristics, a number of case styles, and the voltage ratings and temperature coefficients suitable for nearly every application. Regardless of the actual dielectric used, all capacitors in this group are produced in the same manner. The capacitor core is formed by winding two metal foils, usually aluminum separated by two or more sheets of dielectric into a compact roll, as shown in Figure 14.47. After the roll is wound, the units are dipped in a sealing material such as resin, wax, or an epoxy compound. Contacts to the metal foils can be

Figure 14.46 Glass dielectric capacitor construction.

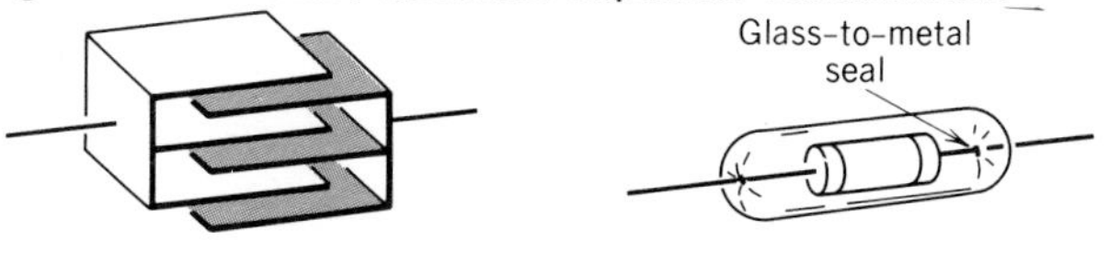

(a) Interleaved stack of plates (b) Whole unit is sealed in glass, which serves as case and dielectric

Figure 14.47 Paper and plastic dielectric capacitors are often composed of strips of foil and dielectric that are rolled.

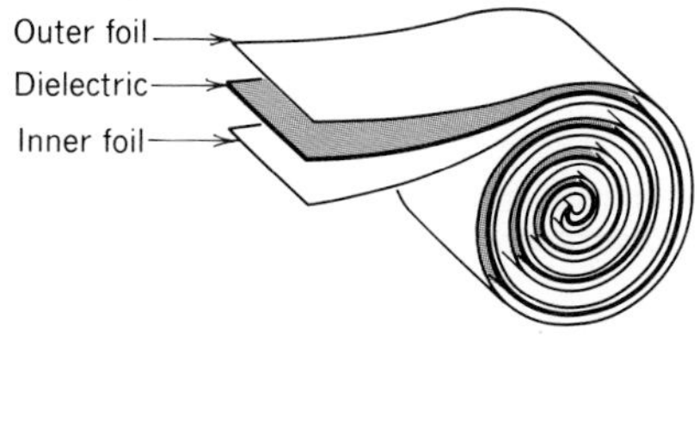

made by short, metallic strips inserted in the roll during the winding process or by extending the foils on opposite sides of the roll. After wrapping and dipping, the roll is inserted in a case and sealed.

Paper and plastic capacitors are available in capacitance values from about 1000 pF up to several microfarads and in working voltage ratings from 50 V up to several thousand volts. The highest capacitance and voltage ratings are restricted to dielectrics made of paper soaked in special oils. Paper and plastic dielectrics provide components from about 1 nF to 1 μF in voltage ratings from 100 to 600 V dc.

Paper dielectric capacitors are usually manufactured with tolerances of 20, 10, and 5 percent. Although it is possible to wind paper dielectric units to lower tolerances, the variation of capacitance with temperature and the gradual change during operation make it impractical to do so. Polycarbonate and polystyrene plastic dielectric components, in contrast to paper, have good temperature coefficient characteristics. Most manufacturers' products show capacitance changes of less than 2 percent of the nominal value over their operating temperature range. This makes it practical to produce polycarbonate and polystyrene dielectric capacitors to lower tolerances than paper dielectric units. These plastic dielectric capacitors are commercially available in tolerances as low as 1 percent.

Paper and plastic dielectric capacitors fail primarily because of short circuits caused by the breakdown of the dielectric material or because of an open circuit between a component lead and foil. Open circuits are sometimes the result of twisting a component that has been soldered into a circuit. In order to prevent this type of failure, make sure that the component is turned so that its value marking is easily visible when it is soldered to a circuit board. This eliminates the necessity of turning the component to read the value. In addition to failure due to short or open circuiting, low insulation resistance, large changes in capacitance value, and the unstable operation with temperature change make replacement of paper and plastic dielectric capacitors necessary.

D.2 CODING OF CAPACITOR CHARACTERISTICS

As in the case of small resistors, capacitor cases do not always provide enough space to print all the necessary information about a particular unit. For larger electrolytic capacitors, whose operation is covered in the next chapter, as well as for the larger sizes of paper and plastic dielectric units, there is sufficient room for the capacitance, the working voltage, and frequently the tolerance to be marked. When sufficient room is available, any coding other than a military specification number is avoided. The essential information is clearly printed. Not too many years ago, when components were larger, manufacturers sometimes took advantage of the empty space available on capacitor cases to engage in a bit of advertising. The company name or symbol and a snappy name for that particular capacitor model filled any vacant space.

One additional piece of information regularly included on paper and plastic dielectric capacitors is an indication of which lead is connected to the outermost foil layer. By connecting this lead to the electrical ground of the electronic unit, a result rather like a coaxial cable could be obtained. That is, the inner foil would be shielded and less likely to pick up noise from nearby conductors. Figure 14.48 shows a typical band marking the outer foil lead.

Postage stamp style, low-value mica capacitors and paper capacitors in these case styles were once marked with color dot codes. At one time, these color codes were widely used, and many textbooks still insist on including them, although capacitors with these codings are rarely seen today. The most common coding in use today is the MIL SPEC designation shown in

Figure 14.48 A single, black line or band is used to mark the capacitor lead connected to the outer foil of a rolled capacitor.

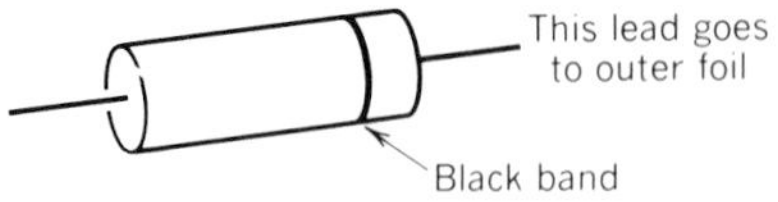

Figure 14.49 MIL SPEC capacitor markings.

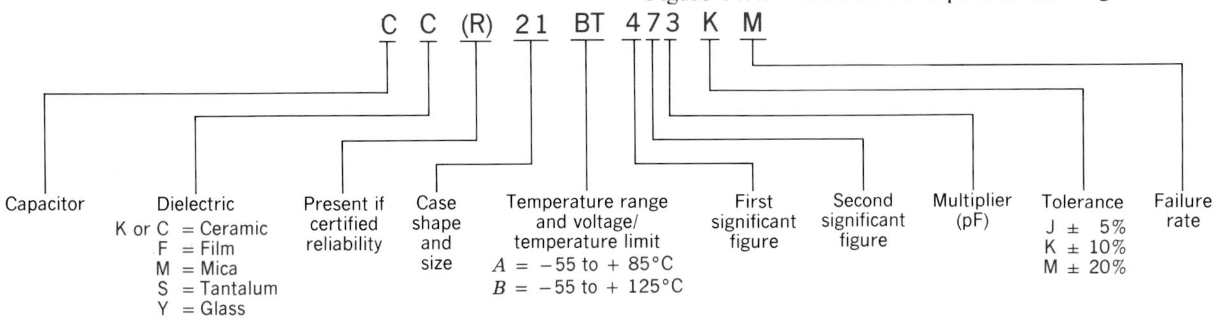

Figure 14.49. In the system shown, the first two letters indicate the type of component, *C* for capacitor in this case, and the dielectric material. The letter in the third position is an *R* if this description refers to a class of capacitors with certified reliability. If the capacitor does not belong to a certified reliability group, this letter is omitted. The next two numbers give the shape and size of the case. The recommended temperature range and working voltage are encoded in the following two letters. The capacitance is given in picofarads by two significant figures and a decimal multiplier. For example, the figure 104 means 1 0 0000, that is, 100,000 pF or 100 nF. The final letter, following the capacitor tolerance indicator, represents the rate of failure for units with certified reliability.

Sometimes a shortened form of this designation system is used, giving only the capacitance, the tolerance, and the recommended working voltage. For example, a unit marked

102 J
50

has a capacitance of 1000 pF, a tolerance of 5 percent, and a recommended maximum working voltage of 50 V.

E. PROGRAMMED REVIEW

FRAME 1

The capacitance of a parallel-plate capacitor is defined as the ratio of ________. Expressed as a formula, this is written $C =$ ________.

a. The charge on one of the plates to the potential difference between the plates; Q/V. (2)
b. Any answer not including these points, review Section B.1.

FRAME 2

Perform the following capacitance unit conversions:

$0.01\ \mu F =$ ________ nF
$10\ nF =$ ________ pF
$0.0022\ \mu F =$ ________ pF
$1800\ pF =$ ________ nF
$56\ nF =$ ________ μF
$0.0068\ \mu F =$ ________ pF
$51\ pF =$ ________ nF
$390\ nF =$ ________ μF

a. 10; 10,000; 2200; 1.8; 0.056; 6800; 0.051; 0.39 (4)
b. Any other answers, go to Frame 3.

FRAME 3

The metric system prefixes are used with the unit of capacitance, the farad, because this unit is too large for general purposes. These prefixes are

name	*symbol*	*value*
micro-	μ	10^{-6}
nano-	n	10^{-9}
pico-	p	10^{-12}

In other words,

$$1\ \mu F = 1000\ nF = 1{,}000{,}000\ pF$$
$$1\ nF = 0.001\ \mu F = 1000\ pF.$$

Try the unit conversions in Frame 2 again.

FRAME 4

Describe three ways of increasing the capacitance of a parallel-plate capacitor.

a. (i) Decrease the distance between the plates; (ii) place a dielectric with a higher permittivity than air between the plates; and (iii) increase the area of both capacitor plates. (Answers can be in any order.) (5)
b. Any answer not identifying all three, review Section B.1.

FRAME 5

The quantity ________ is a measure of the ease with which an electric field passes through a material?

a. Permittivity. (6)
b. Any other answer, review Section B.1 and go on to Frame 6.

FRAME 6

A 180 μF capacitor is fully charged from a 24-V dc source. What is the charge is coulombs on one of the capacitor plates?

a. 0.00432 C (8)
b. 4320 C; (you have forgotten the 10^{-6} term in your calculation, read Frame 3 and then go on to Frame 8.
c. Any other answer, go to Frame 7.

FRAME 7

It is useful to remember the relationship between capacitance and the charge that a capacitor will store when fully charged by a source. This relationship is $C = \frac{V}{Q}$. Go back to Frame 6.

FRAME 8

In addition to supporting the plates of a capacitor and maintaining the distance between them, the dielectric in a capacitor serves to __________.

a. Store electrical energy or increase the capacitance. (9)
b. Any answer other than one of the above, review Section B.1 and go on to Frame 9.

FRAME 9

The lowest potential difference at which the dielectric of a capacitor will be destroyed by a spark discharge is called the __________.

a. Dielectric breakdown voltage. (10)
b. Any other answer, review Section B.1.

FRAME 10

Creating a short circuit or low-resistance path between the plates of a charged capacitor is known as __________.

a. Discharging. (11)
b. Any other answer, review the final part of Section B.1 and go on to Frame 11.

FRAME 11

Although a short-circuiting cable can be used to discharge low-voltage power supply capacitors, it is less of a strain on the capacitors to use a __________. A suitable value is __________.

a. Resistor; 1 K, 2 to 10 W (12)
b. Any other answer, review the last paragraph of Section B.1.

FRAME 12

The period of time just after a capacitor is connected to a dc source is referred to as the __________. After a time, circuit conditions stop changing; this period is known as the __________.

a. Transient state; steady state. (13)
b. Any other answers, review Section B.2.

FRAME 13

At the instant that an uncharged capacitor is connected across a dc source, the potential difference between the plates of the capacitor is __________ and the current through it is __________, although the circuit behaves as though a __________ existed between the capacitor plates.

a. Zero; zero; short circuit. (14)
b. Any other answer, review Section B.2.

FRAME 14

A 5 μF capacitor in series with a 10 kΩ resistor is charged from a 12-V source. What is the potential difference across the capacitor after 0.075 s?

a. 9.32 V (16)
b. Any other answer, go on to Frame 15.

FRAME 15

The formula for the potential difference across a capacitor that is charging is $e = E(1 - \epsilon^{\frac{-t}{RC}})$ Using this in Frame 14,

$$\begin{aligned} e &= 12(1 - \epsilon^{\frac{0.075}{0.05}}) \\ &= 12(1 - \epsilon^{-1.5}) \\ &= 12(1 - 0.223) \\ &= 9.32 \text{ V} \end{aligned}$$

Check your arithmetic to determine the source of your error. Go on to Frame 16.

FRAME 16

If the equivalent series resistance of the capacitor of Frame 14 is 100 Ω, what will the circuit current be 0.05 s after the capacitor begins charging?

a. About 0.44 mA. (18)
b. Any answer not within a few percent of 0.44 mA, go to Frame 17.

FRAME 17

There are two ways to solve this problem. Regardless of the way you chose, you should have noticed that, in comparison with the 10K resistor, the equivalent series resistance of the capacitor is extremely small and could be ignored. The easiest way to solve the problem is to notice that 0.05 s is one time constant. This means that the circuit current, starting at its maximum value, $i = \frac{E}{R}$, will have decayed to 36.8 percent of this value, or $\frac{12}{10{,}000} \times 0.368 = 0.00044$ A. Alternatively, the formula for the current in a capacitive circuit could be used:

$$i = \frac{E}{R} \epsilon^{\frac{-t}{RC}}$$

Go on to Frame 18.

FRAME 18

The capacitance value marked on a fixed capacitor is referred to as its ________.

a. Nominal value (19)
b. Any other answer, review, Section D.1.

FRAME 19

A 100 μF capacitor is charged to a potential difference of 12 V and then discharged through a 1 Ω resistor. How long after the discharging has begun will the potential difference across the capacitor drop to 36.8 percent of its initial value?

a. 0.1 s (20)
b. Any other answer, review Section B.3.

FRAME 20

What is the impedance of the network shown in Figure 14.50 if the source has a frequency of 1 kHz?

a. 8637 $\angle 46.8°$ Ω (21)
b. Any other answer review Section C.2.

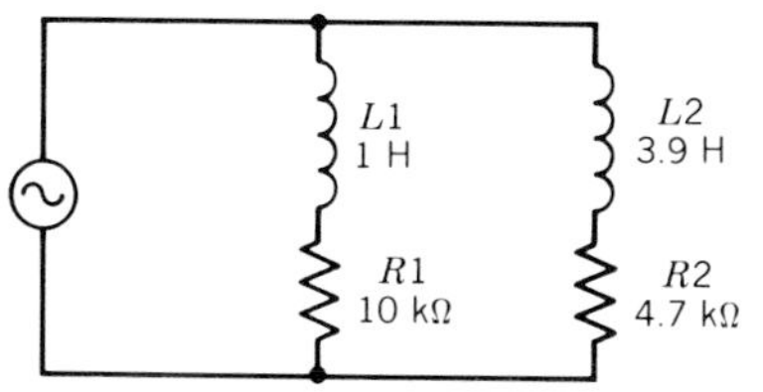

Figure 14.50 Circuit for Frame 20.

FRAME 21

A 6.8 μF capacitor is connected in parallel with a 3.9 μF capacitor, the total capacitance is ________ μF. If the two were connected in series, the total capacitance would be ________ μF.

a. 10.7; 2.48 (22)
b. Any other answers, review Section B.5.

FRAME 22

Identify the capacitor shapes and lead types shown in Figure 14.51.

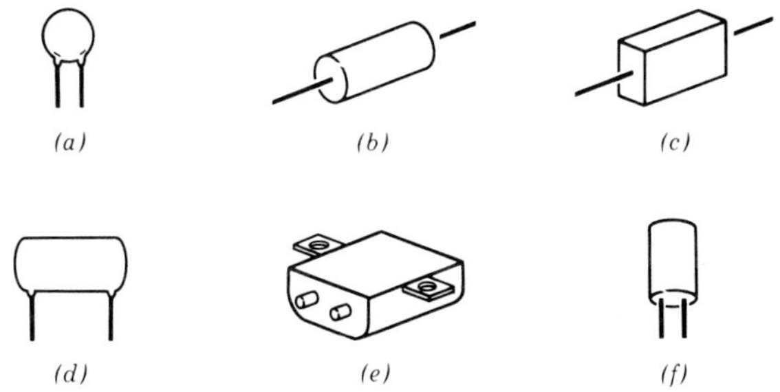

Figure 14.51 Figure for Frame 22.

a. (*a*) radial-lead disk
   (*b*) axial-lead cylindrical
   (*c*) axial-lead postage stamp
   (*d*) radial-lead dogbone
   (*e*) tub
   (*f*) single-ended cylindrical. (23)
b. More than one wrong, review Section D.1.

FRAME 23

The recommended working voltage of a capacitor represents the suggested ________ that should ever be applied to it.

a. Peak potential difference. (24)
b. Any other answer, review Section D.1.

FRAME 24

Capacitors that show nearly constant capacitance values are usually marked __________, __________, __________, or __________. Capacitors with these markings should be replaced by similar types to prevent changes in operating temperature from causing circuit malfunction.

a. NPO; CG; BP; COG. (26)
b. Any other answer (25).

FRAME 25

In military specifications, NPO, CG, and BP are the markings for capacitors with temperature coefficients close to zero. The EIA marking for consumer and industrial units is COG. Go on to Frame 26.

FRAME 26

The abbreviation ESR stands for __________. It is the sum of all the __________ effects in a capacitor.

a. Equivalent series resistance; resistance. (27)
b. Any other answer, review the last paragraph of Section D.1 and go on to Frame 27.

FRAME 27

The component shown in Figure 14.52 is most likely a __________. If it is a small, inexpensive, general-purpose component, it is said to belong to Class __________.

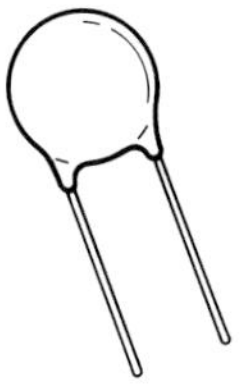

Figure 14.52 Figure for Frame 27.

a. Disk ceramic capacitor; II. (28)
b. Any other answer, review Section D.1.1.

FRAME 28

A Class I ceramic capacitor has a nominal capacitance of 1800 pF and is marked N4500. What is its capacitance at 60°C?

a. 1476 pF (29)
b. Any other answer, review Section D.1.1.

FRAME 29

Class II ceramic capacitors tend to show a 10 to 15 percent decrease in capacitance during the first thousand hours of operation. This is known as __________, but can be reversed by __________.

a. Aging; heating the capacitor. (30)
b. Any other answer, review the last paragraph of Section D.1.1 and go on to Frame 30.

FRAME 30

The component shown in Figure 14.53 is probably a __________.
The __________ variety is manufactured in tolerances of 1 percent.

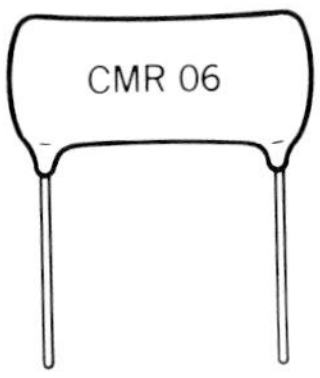

Figure 14.53 Figure for Frame 30.

a. mica capacitor; silver mica. (31)
b. Any other answer, review Section D.1.2.

FRAME 31

For capacitances between __________ and __________, particularly at working voltages greater than 100 V, paper or plastic capacitors are most commonly used.

a. 0.01 μF; 1 μF (32)
b. Any other answer, review Section D.1.3.

FRAME 32

The principal failure mode of paper or plastic capacitors is a short circuit caused by __________.

a. Breakdown of the dielectric material. (33)
b. Any other answer, review Section D.1.3.

FRAME 33

A mica capacitor is marked 153 K. Its capacitance and tolerance are __________ and __________.

a. 15 nF; $\pm$ 10 percent (END)
b. Any other answer, review Section D.2.

F. PROBLEMS FOR SOLUTION OR RESEARCH

1. Perform the following calculations. Give your answers in polar coordinate form.

a. $9.03 \angle 16° + 5.38 \angle 40°$
b. $17.67 \angle -37° - (2.83 \angle -24°)$
c. $(12 - j14.6) \times (3.35 + j19)$
d. $(6.93 - j12) \div (2.84 + j7.75)$
e. $5.65 \angle -90° \div (17.4 - j13.8)$
f. $(6.35 + j5.1) - (2.3 - j1.37)$
g. $84 \angle 30° + 13 \angle -60°$
h. $2.98 \angle 85° - 3.08 \angle -17°$
i. $(1.2 + j6.8) \times (2.7 - j6.8)$
j. $43.7 \angle 55° - 28 \angle -16°$

2. A 100 μF capacitor is connected across a 10-V dc source for several minutes. What is the charge on the capacitor in coulombs? What is the potential difference across the capacitor?

a. Once the capacitor is charged, it will be removed from the source and allowed to discharge through a resistor. After 0.05 s the voltage across the capacitor is 1.11 V. What is the value of the resistor?

3. You have three different capacitors; $C1 = 1\ \mu$F, $C2 = 1.5\ \mu$F, and $C3 = 3\ \mu$F. How many different networks can you produce using some or all of these capacitors? What is the capacitance of each network?

4. Calculate the time constant of the circuit shown in Figure 14.54?

a. What will the potential difference across $R2$ be 0.1 time constant after the source is first connected?

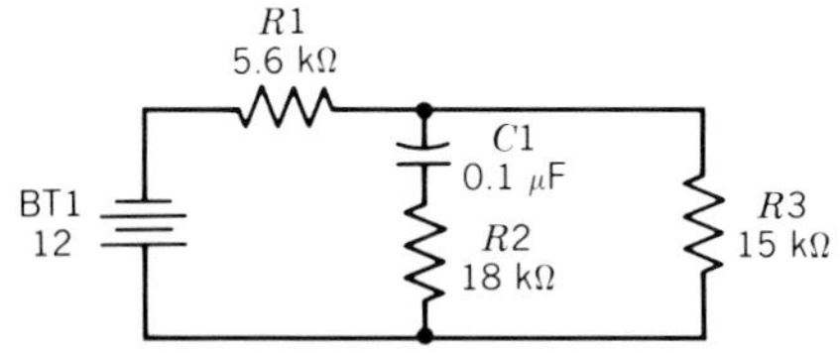

Figure 14.54 Circuit for Problem 4.

5. Find the current produced by a 10-V, 400 Hz source in a circuit consisting of 0.1 H inductor in series with a 100 Ω resistor. Assume that the potential difference is the reference.

6. A certain relay has a coil resistance of 1 kΩ and will close when the current through it is 1.5 mA. Design an *RC* timing circuit that will cause the relay to close about 0.2 s after a power switch is closed.

7. Carefully remove the outer case of a 100-pF polystyrene capacitor and measure the area of one of the aluminum foils and the thickness of the dielectric. Try to calculate the dielectric constant of polystyrene.

(*Hint:* Remember that *both* sides of each aluminum foil must be counted into the area.)

8. Switch $S1$ in Figure 14.55 is set to position 2 at $t = 0$.

a. What is the circuit current at the moment $S1$ is set to position 2?
b. At what time will the capacitor be charged to 18 V? What is the circuit current at this time?
c. If the switch is set to position 3 when the potential difference across the capacitor is 18 V, what will be the circuit current? ($C1$ is uncharged at $t = 0$.)

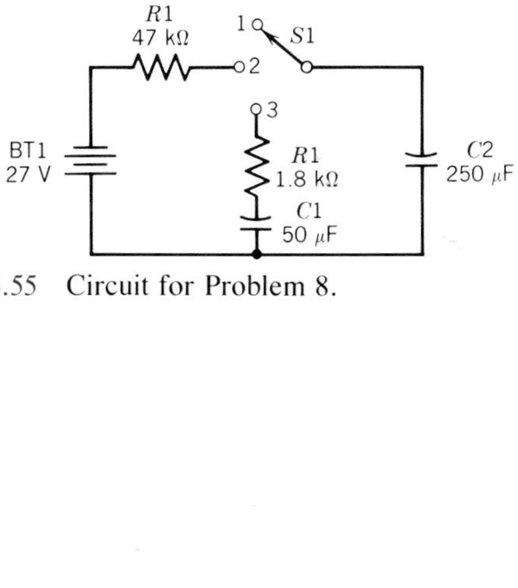

Figure 14.55 Circuit for Problem 8.

CHAPTER 15

CAPACITANCE IN AC CIRCUITS: ELECTROLYTIC AND VARIABLE CAPACITORS

A. CHAPTER PREVIEW

1 Completing this chapter will enable you to understand and to predict the effects of capacitors in ac circuits.

2 You will learn to calculate capacitive reactance, the impedance of an *RC* circuit, and the phase difference between circuit current and the potential difference across a capacitor in an ac circuit.

3 The methods used for predicting the wwaveforms in *RL* circuits when square-wave, pulse, and other nonsinusoidal sources are involved will be applied to *RC* circuits.

4 The Examples and Computations section of this chapter continues your study of polar and rectangular coordinate systems. You will learn to use these systems in the analysis of ac circuits.

5 The Applications section of this chapter will complete your introduction to practical capacitor types with discussions of electrolytic and variable capacitors.

B. PRINCIPLES

B.1 THE CAPACITOR IN CIRCUITS WITH CHANGING POTENTIAL DIFFERENCES

In Chapter 14, capacitors were considered only in circuits with pure dc sources and were viewed primarily as timing devices. Emphasis was placed on calculating the potential difference to which a capacitor charged or discharged in a given time. Although many circuits are based on this aspect of capacitor operation, there are also many circuits in which the function of a capacitor is to keep the potential difference across a part of the circuit constant. In Chapter 12, you learned that an inductor acts to keep the current in a circuit constant, and is therefore called a *constant-current device*. By similar reasoning, a capacitor could be called a *constant-voltage device*.

The constant-voltage aspect of a capacitor in a dc circuit where there are potential difference changes can be illustrated by the circuit in Figure 15.1. In its initial condition, the switch is in position 1, and the capacitor is uncharged. If the switch is set to position 2 for a period of more than 5 s, or five time constants, the capacitor will charge to nearly the source potential difference. The waveforms of the circuit current and the potential difference across the capacitor for this initial charging period are shown in Figures 15.2*a* and 15.2*b*. If at this point in time, the switch is set to position 3, an additional source is connected to the circuit. Since BT2 is in series opposing, the potential difference supplied to the circuit will be less when BT2 is included in the circuit. The capacitor, charged to a higher potential difference, will begin to discharge through the circuit. Eventually, the potential difference across the capacitor will be

$$e_C = E_{BT1} - E_{BT2}$$

Before the discharging is completed, however, the potential difference across the capacitor will be E_{BT1} minus a quantity that will be less than E_{BT2}. Since the

Figure 15.1 Circuit used to illustrate the constant-voltage characteristic of a capacitor.

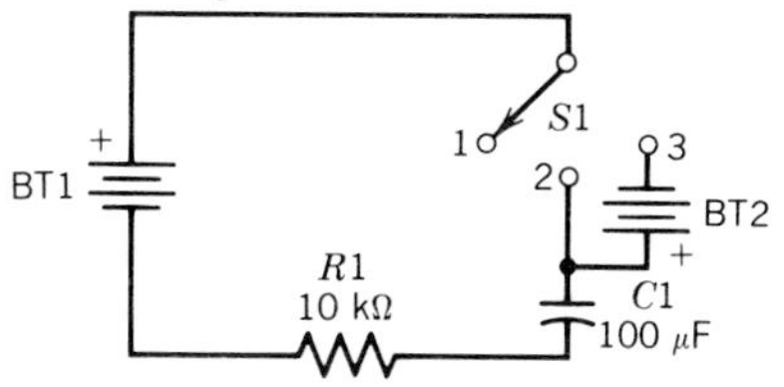

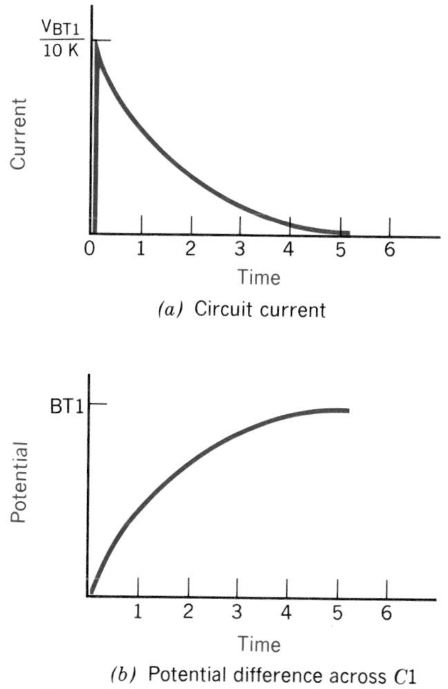

Figure 15.2 Waveforms for the circuit current and potential difference across *C*1 after switch *S*1 has been set to 2.

capacitor is discharging, the change in its potential difference in seconds will be

$$E_{BT2} - E_{BT2}\,\epsilon^{\frac{-t}{RC}} \quad \text{or} \quad E_{BT2}(1 - \epsilon^{\frac{-t}{RC}})$$

and the potential difference across the capacitor at time *t* will be

$$e_C = E_{BT1} - E_{BT2}\,(1 - \epsilon^{\frac{-t}{RC}})$$

or

$$e_C = E_{BT1} - E_{BT2} + E_{BT2}\,\epsilon^{\frac{-t}{RC}} \qquad \text{FORMULA 15.1}$$

When the switch is first set to position 3, the Kirchhoff's voltage law equation for the circuit is

$$-E_{BT1} + E_{BT2} + e_C + e_R = 0$$

Since $E_{BT1} = e_C$ at this moment, it is possible to write

$$E_{BT2} + e_R = 0 \quad \text{or} \quad E_{BT2} = -e_R$$

In other words, the potential difference across the resistor is equal to the potential difference of BT2 and opposite in polarity. The potential drop across the resistor is the product of the circuit current and the resistance, so $E_{BT2} = -I \times R$ at the instant that the switch is placed in position 3. As the potential difference across the capacitor drops toward $E_{BT1} - E_{BT2}$, the circuit current decays, as you learned in Chapter

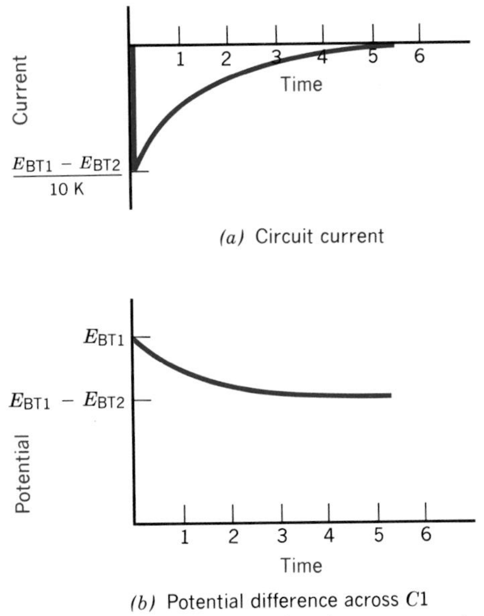

Figure 15.3 Waveforms for the circuit current and potential difference across $C1$ after switch $S1$ has been set to 3.

14. The formula for the current at a time t is therefore

$$i = \frac{E_{BT2}}{R}\epsilon^{\frac{-t}{RC}} \qquad \text{FORMULA 15.2}$$

The waveforms for the potential difference across the capacitor and the circuit current from the time that the switch is set to position 3 until steady-state conditions have been reached are shown in Figure 15.3. The current graph is drawn below the axis to show that the current will be in the direction opposite that of Figure 15.2*a*.

If switch $S1$ is allowed to remain in position 3 until the charge on the capacitor falls to $E_{BT1} - E_{BT2}$ volts and the circuit current returns to zero, and the switch is then set again to position 2, the effect is the opposite of that just noted. Now the capacitor is charging up to a potential difference of E_{BT1} volts from a level of $E_{BT1} - E_{BT2}$ volts. The potential difference across the capacitor as a function of time will be

$$e_C = (E_{BT1} - E_{BT2}) + E_{BT2}\,(1 - \epsilon^{\frac{-t}{RC}}) \qquad \text{FORMULA 15.3}$$

Figure 15.4 Conditions of e_c and e_r at the moment that the switch is reset to position 2.

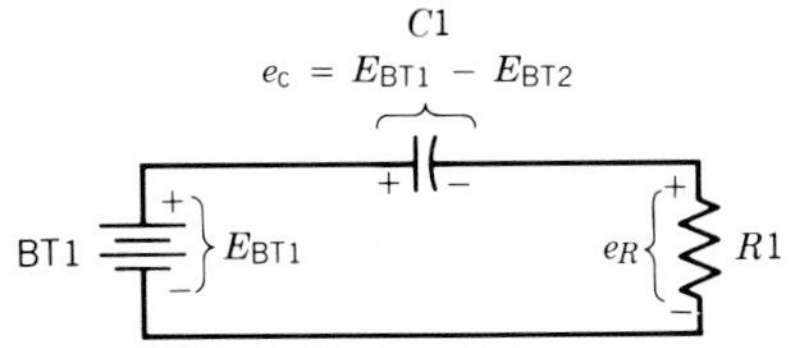

When the switch is first returned to position 2, the potential difference across the capacitor is $E_{BT1} - E_{BT2}$ volts, and the Kirchhoff's voltage law equation, illustrated in Figure 15.4, is

$$-E_{BT1} + e_C + e_R = 0 \quad \text{or}$$
$$-E_{BT1} + (E_{BT1} - E_{BT2}) + e_R = 0$$

Simplifying,

$$E_{BT2} = e_R$$

Since the potential drop across $R1$ is equal to the current through it times the resistance, $e_R = iR$, for the moment when the switch is returned to position 2, it is possible to write

$$E_{BT2} = iR \quad \text{or} \quad i = \frac{E_{BT2}}{R}$$

As the capacitor recharges to E_{BT1}, the circuit current decays to zero, following the discharge curve, so the actual expression for the circuit current at a particular time during the transient state is

$$i = \frac{E_{BT2}}{R}\epsilon^{\frac{-t}{RC}}$$

Circuit current and potential difference waveforms are shown in Figure 15.5.

With these formulas for the circuit current and the potential difference across the capacitor, it is possible to show how a capacitor acts to keep circuit potential

Figure 15.5 Waveforms for the circuit after the switch has been reset to position 2.

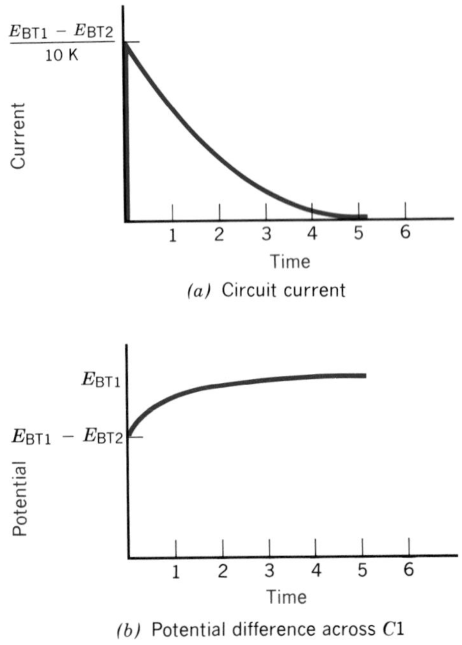

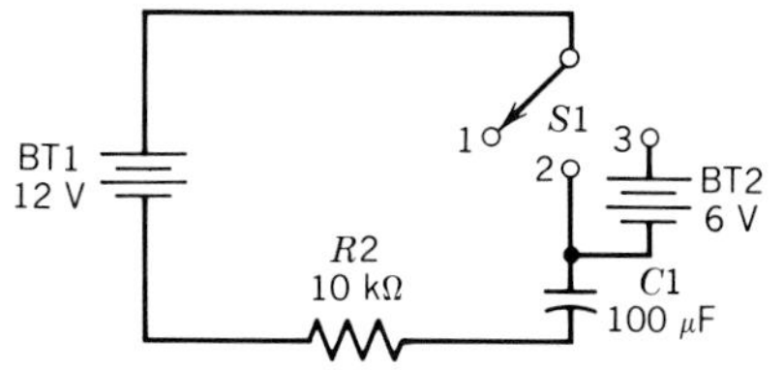

Figure 15.6 Assigning values to the potential differences of BT1 and BT2 makes it possible to see how the capacitor acts to keep the potential difference constant.

difference constant. Giving values to the various components makes the effect clearer. As shown in Figure 15.6, BT1 and BT2 supply potential differences of 12 and 6 V, respectively, $C1$ is a 100 μF capacitor, and $R1$ is 10 kΩ. The time constant of the RC combination is 1 s. Switch $S1$ is moved from position 1 to position 2, where it is allowed to remain for 5 s. After this time has elapsed, the capacitor is fully charged. Now, a source disturbance is created by setting $S1$ to position 3 for 0.5 s, and then back to position 2. Notice the seriousness of the disturbance: The source potential drops from 12 to 6 V, a 50 percent decrease, and then returns to 12 V after what is a fairly long time in an electrical circuit. The potential difference change across the capacitor, however, is considerably less. At the moment that the switch is set to position 3, the potential difference across the capacitor is 12 V. After 0.5 s, its potential difference is given by Formula 15.1.

$$
\begin{aligned}
e_C &= E_{BT1} - E_{BT2}\,(1 - \epsilon^{\frac{-t}{RC}}) \\
&= 12 - 6 + 6\,\epsilon^{\frac{-t}{RC}} \\
&= 12 - 2.36 \\
&= 9.64 \text{ V}
\end{aligned}
$$

The capacitor potential difference has lost less than 20 percent of its original value during the 0.5 s that the potential difference supplied by the source has dropped to 50 percent of its original value. On the other hand, a measurable amount of time is required for the potential difference across the capacitor to return to near 12 V after the switch has been set from position 3 back to position 2. The actual time needed is, as in the case of any RC circuit, roughly five time constants. In other words, it will be approximately 5 s before steady-state conditions are again reached. Figure 15.7 combines the waveforms of the total source potential difference and the potential difference across the capacitor. From this graph, you can see what is actually meant by saying that a capacitor is a constant-voltage device. The graph shows that the potential difference across the capacitor is maintained even when the circuit source potential drops suddenly. Notice that the capacitor also tends

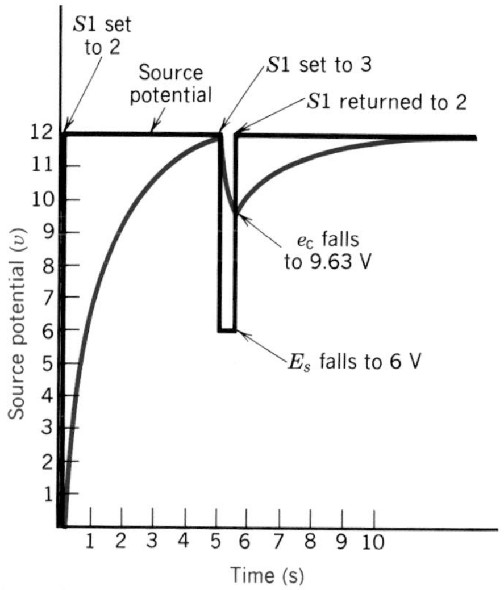

Figure 15.7 Graph of the source potential difference and the potential difference across the capacitor.

to resist sudden increases in potential difference. This means that although the source potential difference is restored to 12 V by switching BT2 out of the circuit, a period of time equal to five time constants is required before the potential difference across the capacitor increases from 9.63 V to nearly its previous level of 12 V.

B.1.1 EFFECT OF DIFFERENT SOURCE POTENTIAL DIFFERENCE CHANGES

By repeating the calculations for the potential difference across the capacitor, it is possible to observe the effects of changing the voltage of BT2, increasing or decreasing the length of time that the switch is allowed to remain in position 3, and changing the time constant of the RC circuit by changing the value of either $R1$ or $C1$.

Increasing the potential difference of BT2 to 10 V as shown in Figure 15.8*a*, for example, means that the potential difference across the capacitor 0.5 s after the switch is set to position 3 will be 8.1 V. After the switch is returned to position 2, the potential difference across the capacitor increases to nearly 12 V, and the circuit reaches steady-state conditions after $5RC$, or 5 s. The waveform of the potential difference across the capacitor with BT2 = 10 V is shown in Figure 15.8*b*. This figure should be compared to Figure 15.7.

B.1.2 EFFECT OF SOURCE POTENTIAL DIFFERENCES OF DIFFERING DURATION

The length of time that BT2 is in the circuit is the length of time during which the capacitor potential difference will decrease. The result of changing this time, while keeping the RC time constant of the circuit constant,

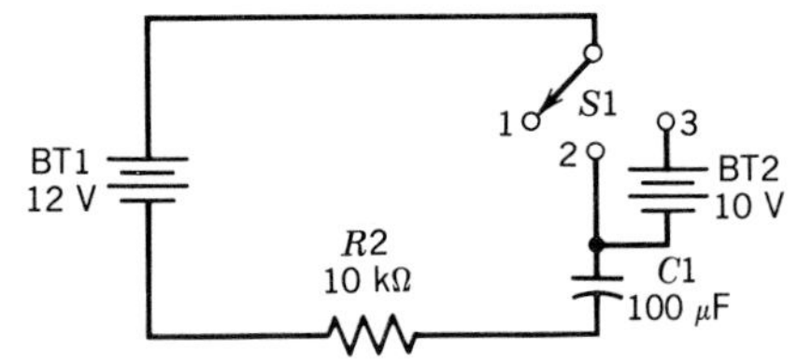

(a) Circuit with the value of BT2 increased

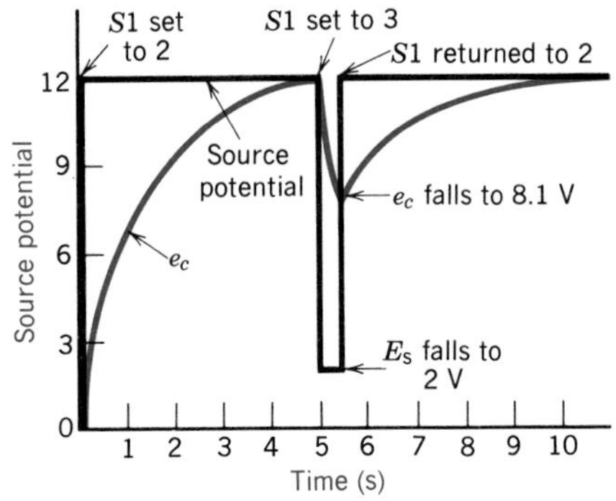

(b) Graph of the source potential difference and potential difference across *C*1

Figure 15.8 The effect of increasing the potential difference of BT2 to 10 V.

will affect the voltage level to which the capacitor discharges. Figure 15.9 shows the source and capacitor potential difference waveforms obtained by allowing *S*1 to remain in position 3 for 0.25 and 1.0 s. Comparing this figure to Figure 15.7 illustrates the effect of the duration of the change in source potential difference on the potential difference across the capacitor. When the switch is in position 3 for 0.25 s, the potential difference across the capacitor falls to

$$\begin{aligned} e_C &= E_{BT1} - E_{BT2}(1 - \epsilon^{\frac{-t}{RC}}) \\ &= 12 - 6\,(1 - \epsilon{-0.25}) \\ &= 12 - 6\,(1 - 0.7788) \\ &= 10.7 \text{ V} \end{aligned}$$

When the switch is left in position 3 for 1 s, the capacitor potential difference is

$$\begin{aligned} e_C &= E_{BT1} - E_{BT2}(1 - \epsilon^{-1}) \\ &= 12 - 6(1 - 0.368) \\ &= 8.2 \text{ V} \end{aligned}$$

From these waveforms you can see that a partial loss of source potential for a longer period means that the potential difference across the capacitor falls to a value closer to that of the lowered source potential.

When the switch is returned to position 2, the capacitor potential difference begins to increase. This increase follows the charging curve, and since the time constant of the circuit is 1 s, the potential difference across the capacitor will be nearly 12 V after 5 × *RC*, or 5 s, regardless of the voltage to which the capacitor has discharged. The conclusion of this is that the potential difference across the capacitor at the end of the reduction in the source potential depends on the time during which the reduction lasts, but that the time necessary for the capacitor to return to nearly its original potential difference does not.

B.1.3 EFFECT OF DIFFERENT TIME CONSTANTS

If the values of *R*1 or *C*1 in Figure 15.6 are changed, the time constant of the *RC* circuit will also change. For example, if *C*1 is increased to 200 μF, the time constant of the circuit will be increased to 10,000 × 200 × 10^{-6}, or 2 s. With BT1 = 12 V and BT2 = 6 V, if the switch is moved to position 3 after having remained in position 2 for 10 s or more, the potential difference across the capacitor after 0.5 s will be

$$\begin{aligned} e_C &= E_{BT1} - e_{BT2}(1 - \epsilon^{\frac{-t}{RC}}) \\ &= 12 - 6(1 - \epsilon^{\frac{-0.50}{2}}) \\ &= 12 - 6(0.22) \\ e_C &= 10.7 \text{ V} \end{aligned}$$

Figure 15.9 The effect of varying the duration of the source potential disturbance (the time during which BT2 is in the circuit).

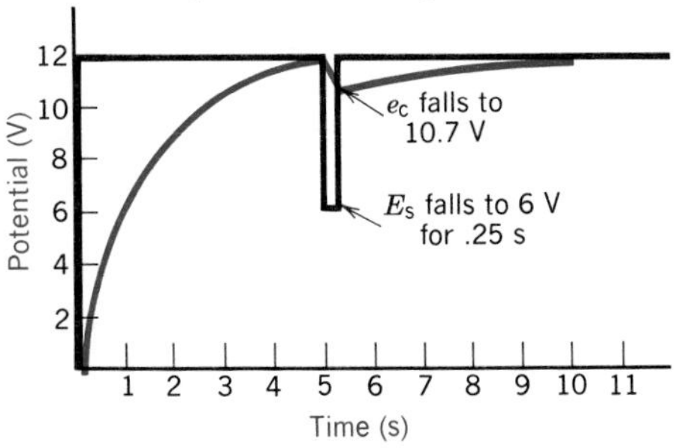

(a) Short duration: *S*1 in position 2 for 0.25 s

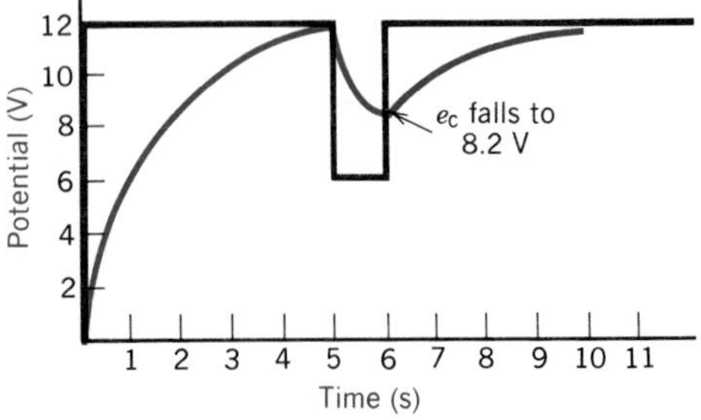

(b) Longer duration change in E_S: *S*1 in position 3 for 1 s

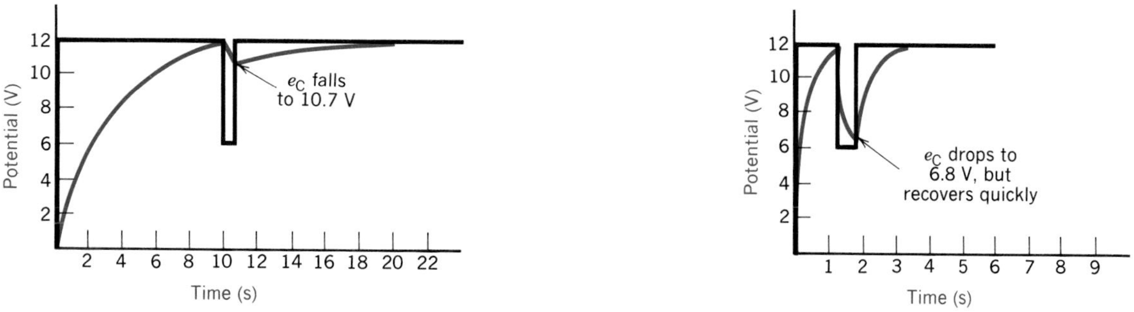

(a) With $C1 = 200\ \mu F$, the time constant is 2 s

(b) With $C1 = 25\ \mu F$, T is 0.25 s

Figure 15.10 Effect of changing the RC time constant.

If, on the other hand, the time constant of the circuit is reduced by lowering the capacitance of $C1$ to 25 μF, the potential difference across the capacitor 0.5 s after the switch is set to position is

$$e_C = E_{BT1} - E_{BT2}\left(1 - \epsilon^{\frac{-0.5}{1 \times 10^4 \times 25 \times 10^{-6}}}\right)$$
$$= 12 - 6\,(1 - \epsilon^{-2})$$
$$= 6.8 \text{ V}$$

Notice that when the time of the change in the source potential is greater than the time constant of the circuit, the capacitor potential difference drops considerably. In the first example in this section, the time constant of the circuit was made longer by increasing the value of the capacitor. With an RC time constant of 2 s, the circuit capacitor lost only 10.8 percent of its potential difference during a 50 percent loss of source lasting 0.5 s. On the other hand, when the circuit time constant was reduced to 0.25 s by lowering the value of $C1$ to 25 μF, the capacitor po tential difference dropped to 6.8 V, losing 43 percent of its initial value after 0.5 s.

After the switch is returned to position 2, the RC circuit with the shorter time constant returns the capacitor to a potential difference of 12 V more quickly. For the 25 μF capacitor, it takes five time constants, or 1.25 s, for the charge on the capacitor to return to nearly 12 V, while the time required for the circuit containing a 200 μF capacitor is 10 s. These time-to-recharge relationships are shown in Figure 15.10.

Figure 15.11 contains a variational analysis chart that summarizes the effects of changing the potential difference of BT2, the length of time that switch $S1$ is kept in position 3, and the values of $R1$ and $C1$. The chart also permits another way of thinking about the time constant of an RC circuit. This way considers the time constant as a measure of how rapidly circuit current and potential difference across the capacitor can respond to changes in the source potential. Looking at things in this way, you can see that a small time constant means that a circuit will respond to source potential changes quickly.

B.2 CAPACITORS IN AC CIRCUITS: CAPACITIVE REACTANCE

In Chapter 14, you saw that when a capacitor and a resistor are connected in series across a dc source, the resulting circuit reacts in two different ways. During the transient state, the period of time when the capacitor is charging, a current exists in the circuit, as shown in Figure 15.12*a*. Once the circuit has reached steady-

Figure 15.11 A variational analysis of the circuit of Figure 15.6.

Condition of Variation	*Time Constant of Circuit*	*Time for E_c to Reach E_{BT1} Initially*	*Level to which E_c Drops when BT2 in ckt.*	*Time for E_c to Return to E_{BT1}*
E_{BT2} increased	=		↓	=
E_{BT2} decreased	=	=	↑	=
Time that BT2 is in circuit increased	=	=	↓	=
Time that BT2 is in circuit decreased	=	=	↑	=
Value of $C1$ increased	↑	↑	↓	↑
Value of $C1$ decreased	↓	↓	↑	↓
Value of $R1$ increased	↑	↑	↓	↑
Value of $R1$ decreased	↓	↓	↑	↓

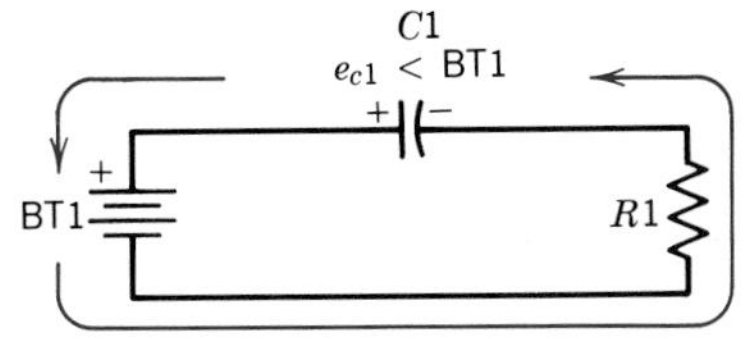

(a) Current is maintained until e_C reaches a value that can be considered equal to E_{BT1}

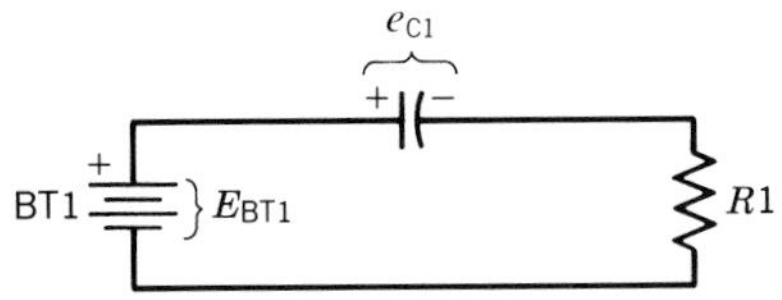

(b) When e_{C1} is equal to E_{BT1} for practical purposes, circuit current drops to a level that cannot be measured.

Figure 15.12 Once the capacitor in a dc series circuit reaches full charge, the circuit current drops to zero.

state conditions, however, there is no longer a measurable current in the circuit. This is shown in Figure 15.12*b*. The current ceases because the potential difference supplied by the source is balanced by the potential difference across the charged capacitor. This is clear if you perform a Kirchhoff's voltage law analysis on the circuit shown in 15.12*b*. If the potential difference across the capacitor is equal to the potential difference of the source, the equation is

$$-E_{BT1} + e_{C1} + iR = 0$$

The only way that this can be true is if the circuit current is zero since $E_{BT1} = e_{C1}$.

In a circuit with an ac source, however, the source potential difference and polarity are constantly changing. The result of this, momentarily ignoring the effect of circuit resistance and other complications, can be seen from Figure 15.13. The pure capacitive circuit and ac source are shown in Figure 15.13*a*, while the source potential difference and the potential difference across the capacitor are graphed in 15.13*b*. If a clockwise potential difference is considered positive, then the potential difference across the capacitor is initially negative, as shown in the graph. Since the resistance in the circuit is assumed to be zero for the purposes of this explanation, the potential difference across the capacitor is always equal to the source potential difference but opposite in polarity. This condition is exactly like the counter electromotive force, or cemf, discussed in connection with a resistanceless circuit containing an inductor.

Figure 15.13 Applying Kirchhoff's voltage law to this circuit, you can see that the potential difference across the capacitor will always have the opposite polarity of the source potential.

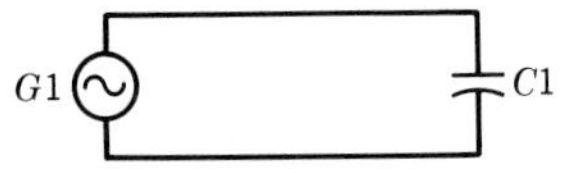

(a) Circuit consisting of a capacitor connected across an ac sine-wave source

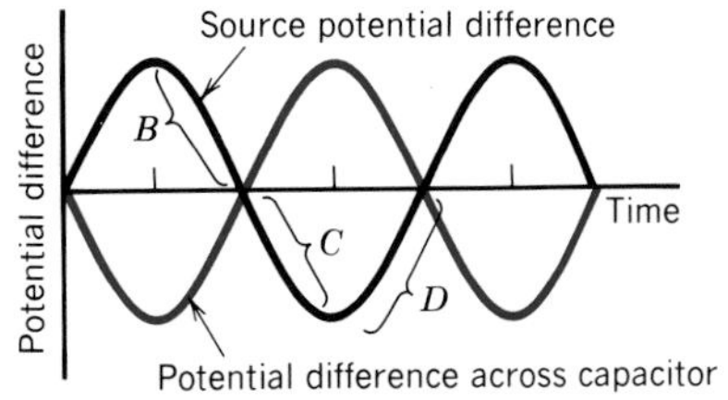

The current in a circuit like that shown in Figure 15.13 would vary according to the rate of change of the potential difference across the capacitor. Initially, with the source and capacitor potential differences at zero, the rate of change of the potential difference is highest, and the circuit current is at its clockwise maximum. As the source and capacitor potential differences increase, the rate of change decreases. The circuit current, too, decreases. Expressed in mathematical terms, this relationship can be written

$$i = C\frac{\Delta v}{\Delta t} \qquad \text{FORMULA 15.4}$$

where the term $\frac{\Delta v}{\Delta t}$ represents the change in potential difference over a very brief difference in time. Notice that this formula resembles the expression that relates the cemf developed across a coil

$$e = -L\frac{\Delta i}{\Delta t}$$

which you learned in Chapter 12. When the potential differences shown in Figure 15.13 reach their maximum values, the rate of change reaches zero, and the circuit current has decayed to zero as well. At this point, the potential difference supplied by the source begins to decrease. The capacitor, previously charged to the peak source potential, is now discharging through the source, and the circuit current direction is reversed. As the source potential difference again approaches zero, in the part of the cycle labeled *B* in Figure 15.13, the rate of change increases, as does the rate at which the capacitor is discharging. The circuit current therefore increases, reaching its peak value in a counterclockwise direction when the source and capacitor potentials are both zero. In the segment of the ac cycle marked *C*, the capacitor begins to charge with its polarity opposite to that of its first charge cycle. As the reversed source potential and the potential differ-

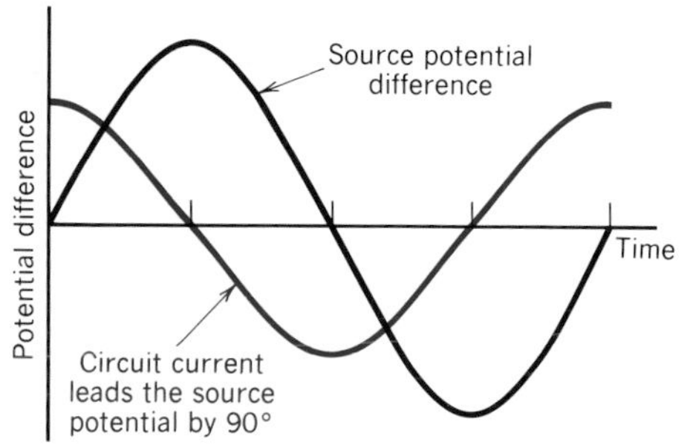

Figure 15.14 Source potential difference and circuit current in the circuit shown in Figure 15.13.

ence across the capacitor increase, their rate of change decreases. The circuit current decays to zero. During the part of the cycle labeled D, the potential difference supplied by the source is decreasing and the capacitor is discharging. The rate of potential difference change, however, is increasing, as is the circuit current.

The potential difference and circuit current graphs shown in Figure 15.14 show that the circuit current is a sinusoid with the same frequency as the source potential difference. The current sine wave *leads* the potential difference of the source by a phase angle of 90°. Recall that in a pure inductive circuit, the circuit current *lags* behind the source potential by a phase angle of 90°. These phase relationships are shown in the phasor diagram shown in Figure 15.15. In this diagram, the circuit current is assumed to be the reference, as is standard for a series circuit. It is somewhat easier to remember these phase relationships if mnemonics are used: Remember *eLi*—in an inductive circuit (L), the potential difference (e) comes before (leads) the current (i), and *iCe*—in a capacitive circuit (C), the current (i) comes before (leads) the potential difference (e).

Just as there is no circuit component that is a pure inductance, there is no circuit component that has only capacitance. The equivalent circuit of a capacitor connected directly across an ac source is shown in Figure 15.16. To be completely accurate, there is a small inductance L_{eq} in series with the resistor and capacitor, representing the inductance of the wire leads, and a

Figure 15.15 A phasor diagram of the source potential difference and circuit current in Figure 15.13. The current is shown as the reference phasor as is customary in series circuits.

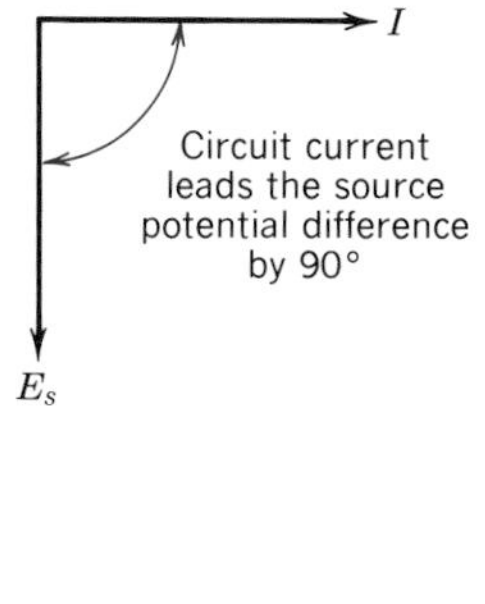

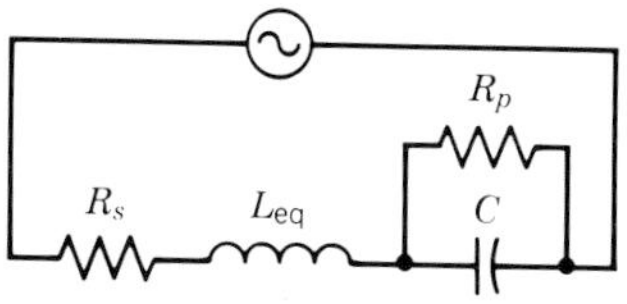

Figure 15.16 The equivalent circuit of a capacitor connected across an ac source.

large value resistor, R_p in parallel with the capacitor to represent the dielectric faults, which permit small leakage currents to flow between the capacitor plates. In most cases, the equivalent series resistance, R_s, and inductance, L_{eq}, are small, while the parallel resistance is high. This means that the equivalent circuit of Figure 15.16 operates very nearly like the theoretical, resistanceless capacitor discussed previously.

In many practical circuits, however, there is an actual resistor placed in series with the capacitor, as shown in Figure 15.17. In this circuit, the relationship of the source potential difference and the circuit current are different from that in a purely capacitive circuit. Applying Kirchhoff's voltage law to this circuit, you can see that the source potential difference is equal to the sum of the potential differences across the resistor and the capacitor; in mathematical terms,

$$-e_{source} + e_r + e_{capacitor} = 0$$
$$\text{or} \quad e_{source} = e_r + e_{capacitor}$$

The instantaneous potential drop across the resistor is iR, where i is the circuit current. Using the circuit current or resistor potential drop as the reference, the phasor diagram shown in Figure 15.18 can be drawn. The source potential difference, e_{source}, is then the phasor sum of e_r and $e_{capacitor}$, as shown by the dotted line in Figure 15.18. Notice that the angle θ between the source phasor and reference phasor is less than 90°.

Its actual value is $\tan^{-1} \frac{e_{capacitor}}{e_r}$.

Figure 15.17 In many practical circuits, a resistor is connected in series with a capacitor across an ac source.

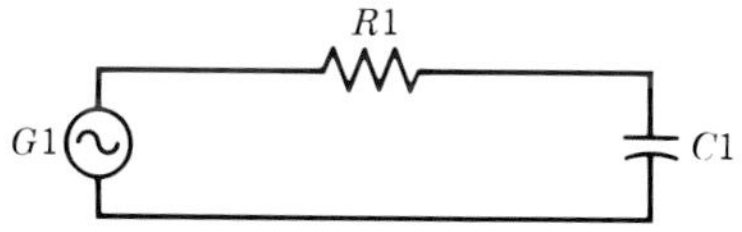

Figure 15.18 Phasor diagram of the potential differences across the components of Figure 15.17.

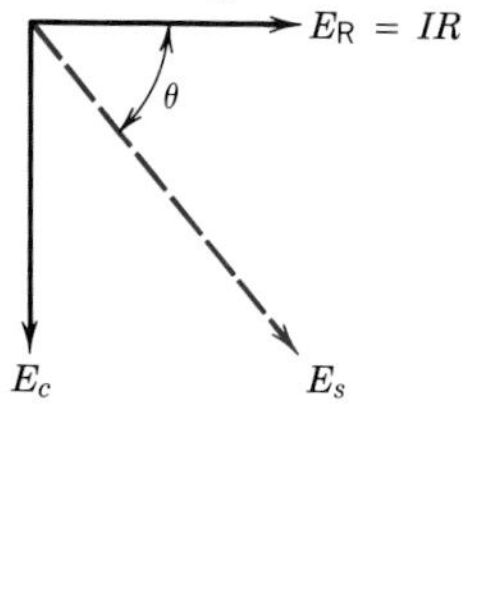

B.3 CAPACITIVE REACTANCE AND IMPEDANCE

Although the discussion in the previous section should have given you a sense of the phase relationships of current and potential difference in a circuit containing both capacitance and resistance, there was no method given for calculating either the circuit current or the phase angle between the current and source potential difference. In order to obtain the formulas necessary for these calculations, a method similar to that used to relate instantaneous potential difference and current in an *RL* circuit must be used. The method used in Chapter 12, you will recall, was a compromise between a bare statement of Formula 12.10 and a lengthy explanation involving the solution of a differential equation.

As in the case of the *RL* circuit, the relationship between the current and potential difference in an *RC* circuit with an ac source is obtained from Kirchhoff's voltage law. In the circuit shown in Figure 15.17, the voltage law equation is

$$e_s = iR + e_C$$

But the instantaneous value of the source potential is $E_{\text{peak}}\sin(2\pi ft)$, so it is possible to write

$$E_{\text{peak}}\sin(2\pi ft) = IR + e_C$$

From Formula 14.1, you know that $e_C = \frac{q}{C}$, where q is the charge on the capacitor at a particular time. Substituting this expression for e_C produces the relationship

$$E_{\text{peak}}\sin(2\pi ft) = iR + \frac{1}{C}q$$

Now if the rate of change of these quantities is obtained for a very short time by means of the mathematical process known as *differentiation*, the result is the equation

$$2\pi fE_{\text{peak}}\cos(2\pi ft) = R\frac{di}{dt} + \frac{1}{C}i$$

Notice that the q term is no longer present. This occurs because the change in the capacitor charge with respect to time is the circuit current. The resulting expression is a differential equation similar to that obtained in Chapter 12. Solved for i, the steady-state solution for the circuit current is

$$i = \frac{E_{\text{peak}}\sin(2\pi ft - \theta)}{\sqrt{R^2 + \left(-\frac{1}{2\pi fC}\right)^2}} \qquad \text{FORMULA 15.5}$$

where

$$\theta = \tan^{-1}\frac{-\frac{1}{2\pi fC}}{R}$$

Comparing this formula with Formula 12.10, you can see that the most significant differences are the form of the reactance term in the denominator and the sign of θ in the numerator. In an *RL* circuit, the inductive reactance is equal to $2\pi fL$. In a capacitive circuit, the capacitive reactance, that is, the opposition to current flow in the circuit, is $\frac{1}{2\pi fC}$. This quantity is symbolized by X_C, just as inductive reactance is symbolized by X_L. In other words,

$$X_C = \frac{1}{2\pi fC} \qquad \text{FORMULA 15.6}$$

Notice also that the sign of θ is negative, as is the sign of the X_C term in

$$\theta = \tan^{-1}\frac{-\frac{1}{2\pi fC}}{R}$$

These negative signs occur because the voltage lags the current in a capacitive circuit, and the current is considered as the reference phasor in a series circuit. Therefore, when the circuit current is used as the reference phasor, the phase angle between the reference and the resultant voltage or impedance will be negative, as shown in Figure 15.18.

The circuit current in Figure 15.19 can be calculated with respect to time using Formula 15.5.

$$i = \frac{12\sin(377t - \theta)}{\sqrt{100^2 + (176.84)^2}} = \frac{12\sin(377t - \theta)}{203.16}$$

The phase angle between the current and the source potential is

$$\theta = \tan^{-1}\frac{-\frac{1}{2\pi fC}}{R} = 60.5°$$

In drawing a phasor diagram, it is usual to use the

Figure 15.19 Calculating the circuit current in a series *RC* circuit.

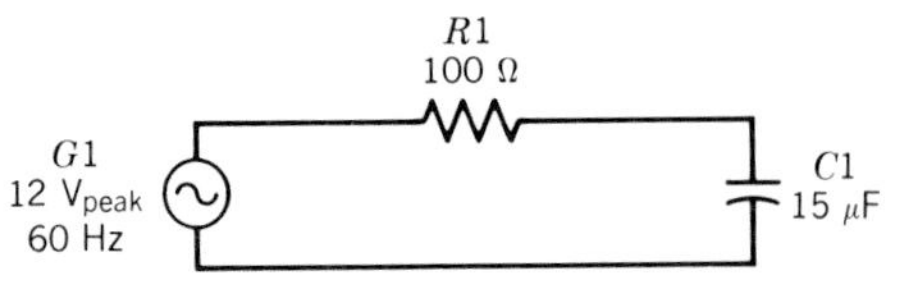

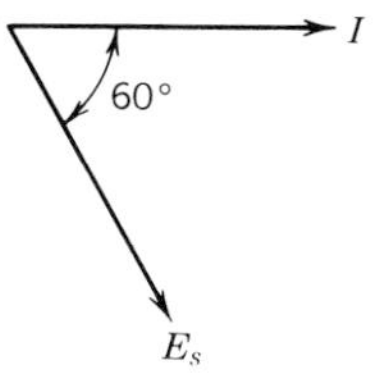

Figure 15.20 Phasor diagram of the source potential difference and circuit current in the circuit of Figure 15.19.

current as the reference phasor, as shown in Figure 15.20.

Examining Formula 15.5 again, it is possible to interpret the electrical quantities expressed by the numerator and denominator. The numerator $E_{peak}\sin(2\pi ft - \theta)$ represents the instantaneous value of the source potential difference. The denominator $\sqrt{R^2 + X_C^2}$ is the phasor sum of the circuit resistance and the capacitive reactance. In Chapter 12, you learned that the phasor sum of circuit resistance and reactance is called the *impedance* of the circuit and is symbolized by Z. With these two facts in mind, you can see that Formula 15.5 is nothing more than a statement of Ohm's law for the instantaneous values in ac circuits: $i = \dfrac{e}{Z}$.

Once a formula relating circuit current to time has been obtained, it is relatively easy to calculate the potential differences across the resistor and capacitor. The potential difference across the resistor is $I \times R$. This potential difference, or voltage drop, is in phase with the circuit current. The potential difference across the capacitor is $i \times X_C$, and, as explained in the earlier part of this section, lags the circuit current by 90°. Drawing a phasor diagram of the resistive and capacitive potential differences, as in Figure 15.21, you can see that the sum of these two components is a phasor representing the potential difference of the source, with a length of $\sqrt{e_r^2 + e_C^2}$ and making a phase angle of $\tan^{-1}\dfrac{-e_c}{e_r}$ with the reference phasor. Notice that this is in agreement with the Kirchhoff's voltage law equation originally written.

Figure 15.21 Phasor diagram of the potential differences across the resistor and capacitor in Figure 15.19.

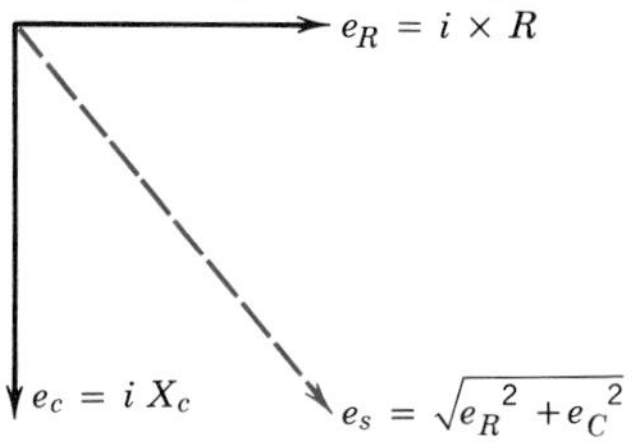

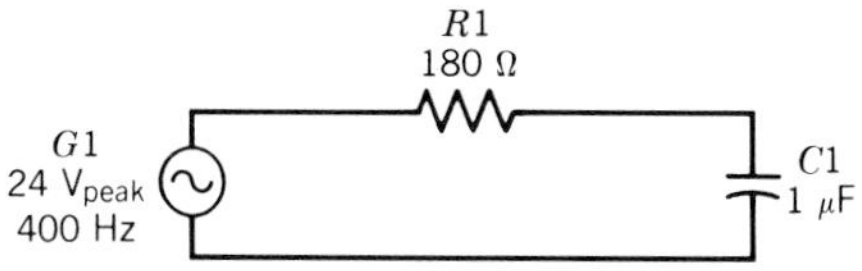

Figure 15.22 An example of the calculation of circuit current and phase angle in a series *RC* circuit.

Although the use of polar and rectangular coordinates and the j operator make it easier to perform current and potential difference calculations in capacitive circuits, the use of Formula 15.5 and the method followed above will also provide the current value.

EXAMPLE:

An ac source with a peak potential difference of 24 V and a frequency of 400 Hz is connected in series with a 180 Ω resistor and a 1 μF capacitor as shown in Figure 15.22. Calculate the circuit current, the phase angle between the current and the source potential difference, and the potential differences across the resistor and the capacitor. Check your answers using Kirchhoff's voltage law. ■

SOLUTION:

This is a rather lengthy problem that has to be solved step by step. In order to use Formula 15.5, the capacitive reactance of the circuit is needed. This is

$$X_C = \frac{1}{2\pi fC} = \frac{1}{2 \times \pi \times 400 \times 1 \times 10^{-6}} = 397.9\ \Omega$$

Since the circuit resistance is 180 Ω, you can now calculate the phase angle θ between the source potential and the circuit current using the second part of Formula 15.5. This angle is

$$\theta = \tan^{-1}\frac{-X_C}{R} = -65.7°$$

In other words, the source potential in this capacitive circuit *lags* the circuit current by 65.7°. Using these values, the circuit current can be calculated as a function of t using the first part of Formula 15.2:

$$i = \frac{E_{peak}\sin(2\pi ft - \theta)}{\sqrt{R^2 + X_C^2}} = \frac{24\sin(2513.3t - 65.7°)}{436.7}$$

or

$$i = \frac{24}{436.7}\sin(2513.3t - 65.7°)$$

The potential difference across the resistor is $i \times R$ or $9.9\sin(2513t - 65.7°)$.

To check these answers, the Kirchhoff's voltage

law equation for the circuit could be written: $e_s = e_r + e_C$, and the resistive and capacitive potential differences drawn on a phasor diagram, as in Figure 15.21. The sum of these two potential differences is

$$e_{\text{total}} = \sqrt{e_r^2 + e_C^2} = 24 \text{ V}$$

and the angle between the reference phasor and e_{total} is

$$\theta = \tan^{-1}\frac{-e_C}{e_r} = -65.7°$$

Since the source potential is a 24-V peak sine wave that lags the circuit current by 65.7°, the answers check. ■

Remember, in order to determine the current in a series RC circuit, use the relationship

$$i = \frac{E_{\text{peak}}\sin(2\pi f t - \theta)}{\sqrt{R^2 + X_C^2}}$$

to calculate the value of the current and the relationship $\tan^{-1}\frac{-X_C}{R}$ *to determine the phase difference between the circuit current and the source potential difference. The current will always lead the source potential difference in a series capacitive circuit. The potential difference across the resistor will be in phase with the circuit current and is equal to iR. The potential difference across the capacitor lags the circuit current by 90° and is equal to* iX_C.

Expressing circuit current in terms of t and θ can be useful for certain kinds of calculations, but for the purposes of troubleshooting and other practical applications, it is desirable to use specific potential difference and current values. As will be shown in Section B.4, either the peak or rms values of potential difference or current can be used to provide circuit values that do not include the variable t in the formula.

The methods of complex rectangular and polar notation can also be used in expressing the magnitudes and phase relationships in circuits containing resistance and capacitance. Consider the circuit shown in Figure 15.23*a*. Since the equivalent series resistance of the capacitor is small, less than 10 percent of the resistance or of the capacitive reactance of R_1, the capacitor can be considered to be a pure reactance. Drawing the phasor diagram of the potential differences across the capacitor and resistor provides the graph shown in Figure 15.23*b*. As is conventional in

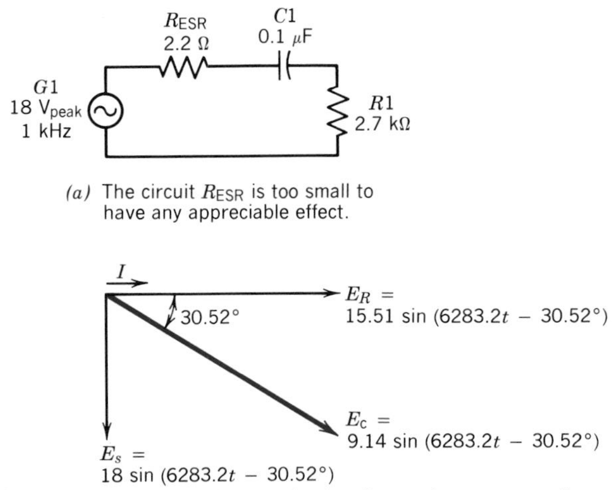

(*a*) The circuit RESR is too small to have any appreciable effect.

Figure 15.23 Using the methods of complex rectangular and polar coordinates to simplify *RC* circuit calculations.

phasor diagrams of series circuits, the circuit current is taken as the reference phasor, so the potential drop across the resistor is shown along the reference phasor. The potential difference across the capacitor *lags* the current or voltage drop across the resistor by 90° as shown. These two potential difference phasors form a pair of coordinate axes, with the potential difference across the capacitor lying along the $-j$ axis. The two phasors can then be expressed in rectangular complex terms as $e_R - je_C$. Since the source potential difference provided by the source, according to Kirchhoff's law, is the phasor sum of e_R and $-je_C$, it is possible to write

$$e_{\text{source}} = e_R - je_C \qquad \text{FORMULA 15.7}$$

The magnitude of e_{source}, as shown in Figure 15.23, is obtained by changing the complex rectangular notation $e_R - je_C$ into polar form, or,

$$m = \sqrt{e_r^2 + e_C^2} \quad \text{and} \quad \theta = \tan^{-1}\frac{-e_C}{e_R}$$

or

$$\sqrt{e_R^2 + e_C^2} \;\angle \tan^{-1}\frac{-e_C}{e_R}$$

Using a calculator, it is easy to find the source potential difference if the peak resistive and capacitive components are known.

EXAMPLE:
When an ac potential difference is applied across the circuit shown in Figure 15.24, the peak voltage drop across the resistor is 12 V and the peak potential difference across the capacitor is 21 V. Write a phasor expression for the source potential difference and its phase relationship with the circuit current. ■

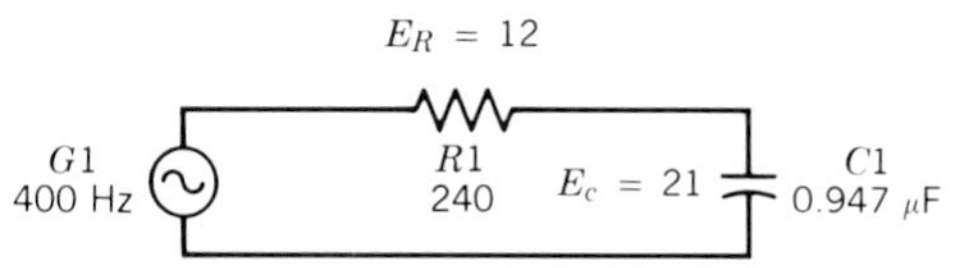

Figure 15.24 Calculating source potential difference when the potential difference across the series components is known.

SOLUTION:
From Formula 15.7, it is possible to write

$$e_{\text{source}} = 12 - j21$$

The peak source potential difference and phase are then easily obtained by converting to polar coordinates:

$$m = \sqrt{12^2 + 21^2} \angle \tan^{-1} \frac{-21}{12}$$

or

$$e_{\text{source}} = 24.2 \angle -60.26° = 24.2 \angle 299.74°$$ ■

If the magnitude and the phase angle between the source potential and the reference phasor are known, the potential differences across the capacitor and resistor can also be calculated.

EXAMPLE:
A series circuit is composed of a capacitor and a resistor and has a source potential of 6.3 V. The potential difference supplied the source lags the current in the circuit by 30°, as shown in Figure 15.25. What are the voltage drops across the resistor and capacitor? ■

SOLUTION:
Drawing the phasor diagram helps visualize what is going on, but to solve for the potential differences, all that is necessary is to convert the polar coordinate expression for the source potential difference $6.3\angle -30°$, or $6.3 \angle 330°$, into complex rectangular form. Using a calculator,

$$6.3 \angle -30° = 5.46 - j3.15$$

Since $e_{\text{source}} = e_r - je_C$, the potential drop across the

Figure 15.25 Calculating E_R and E_C in a series RC circuit when E_s and the phase angle between E_s and i are known.

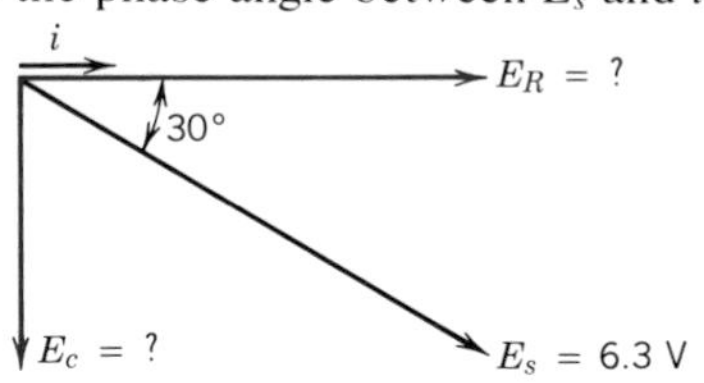

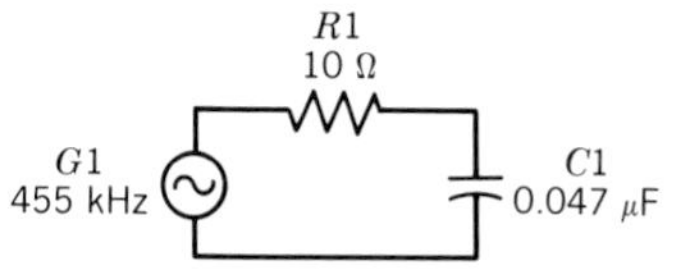

(a) Series RC circuit for example

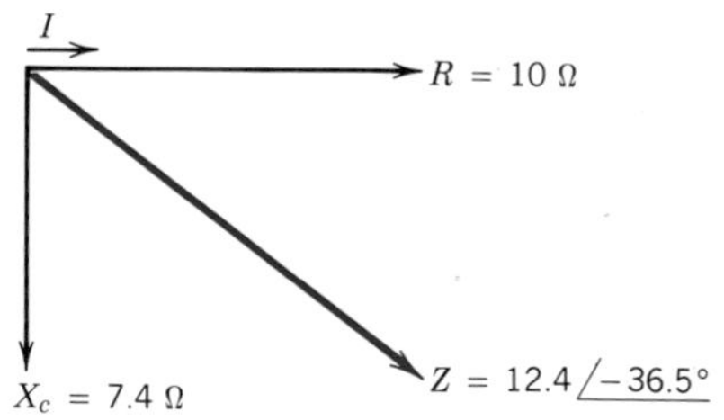

Figure 15.26 Calculating the impedance of a series RC circuit.

resistor is 5.46 V and the potential difference across the capacitor is 3.15 V. ■

The method of coordinate systems can also be used for calculating the impedance of a capacitive circuit if the resistance and capacitive reactance are known.

EXAMPLE:
Figure 15.26*a* shows a series RC circuit. What is its impedance if the source frequency is 455 kHz? ■

SOLUTION:
The impedance is the phasor sum of the resistance and capacitive reactance, as seen in Figure 15.26*b*. The reactance of a 0.047 μF capacitor at 455 kHz is

$$X_C = \frac{1}{2\pi f C}$$

$$= \frac{1}{2\pi \times 455 \times 10^3 \times 0.047 \times 10^{-6}} = 7.4\ \Omega$$

Therefore, the complex rectangular expression for the impedance is $Z = 10 - j7.4$. Converting this to polar form with a calculator gives $Z = 12.4 \angle -36.5°$. ■

It is also possible to determine the resistive and capacitive components of a known impedance if the phase angle between the impedance and the reference phasor is known or can be calculated. All that is necessary is to convert the polar form of the impedance into a complex rectangular expression.

In the next chapter, which deals with parallel and series–parallel as well as series RC and RL circuits, you will see that use of the polar and complex rectangular coordinate systems provides a means of rapidly calculating currents, potential differences, and phase angles in complex networks.

B.4 ANOTHER WAY OF LOOKING AT CAPACITIVE REACTANCE

Previous sections on the effects of capacitors in dc and ac circuits have viewed these components in terms of the time necessary to charge or discharge them, as constant-voltage devices, and as components that produce a phase shift between a source potential difference and the resulting circuit current. Another important way of looking at a capacitor is as a component that opposes an alternating current in a circuit. Even though there is only a very small drift of electrons, the leakage current, *through* a capacitor, there can be a large current *in* an ac circuit in which there is a capacitor. There is no disagreement between these two ideas, unless you insist on comparing circuit current to a physical model like golf balls pushing each other through a pipe. The constant change in the strength and direction of the electric field through an ac circuit keeps the conduction electrons in a constant state of drift, even though only a very few of them actually cross the dielectric by means of leakage paths.

In order to stress the relationship among the values of potential difference, current, capacitance, and frequency in a capacitive circuit, it is possible to eliminate time considerations from the formulas by working with the peak or rms (effective) values of potential difference and current. Although this method is simpler and provides values that can be compared to those actually measured in circuits, you must understand what these formulas represent. The values of potential difference and current used in Formula 15.5 are *instantaneous* values, that is, they relate the potential difference and the current at any instant of time t. Since the potential difference and the current in an ac circuit are constantly changing, these relationships are valuable. On the other hand, many practical applications of this theoretical material involve the comparison of calculated values with measured values. For this reason, it is convenient to have a set of formulas that define the relationships among such quantities as potential difference, current, resistance, and reactance at a particular moment of time. Because most measuring devices used in ac circuits measure either peak values or rms values, the formulas used are those derived from Formula 15.5 for the time when one of the quantities involved is at its peak, or is at its rms value, that is, $0.707 \times$ peak.

It is quite all right to do this, if you bear in mind that the relationships derived are true for the circuit at a particular instant of time only. Notice that phasor diagrams that are based on these relationships differ from those previously used in that the lines drawn represent the value of a sine function at a particular instant.

The formulas based on peak or rms values are simpler and generally easier to use, if you remember to take phase angle considerations into account.

Remembering that $\sqrt{R^2 + X_C^2}$ is the impedance of an RC circuit, Formula 15.5 can be rewritten as

$$I = \frac{E}{Z} \qquad \text{FORMULA 15.8}$$

Now, all three of these quantities are phasor quantities because they are related to particular angles. For a series RC circuit, therefore, Formula 15.8 assumes the form

$$I \angle 0^\circ = \frac{E \angle -\theta}{Z \angle -\theta} \qquad \text{FORMULA 15.9}$$

EXAMPLE:
Calculate the circuit current in the circuit of Figure 15.24. ■

SOLUTION:
In order to use Formula 15.8 both the source potential difference and the impedance have to be known. The source potential difference was calculated to be $24.2 \angle -60.26^\circ$ V. The impedance of the circuit is $Z = R - jX_C$,

$$240 - j\frac{1}{2\pi fC}$$

In complex rectangular form, the impedance is $240 - j420.16$. Converting this to polar form produces $Z = 483.87 \angle -60.26^\circ$. Notice that the phase angle of the source potential difference is the same as the phase angle of the total circuit impedance. If you look at Formula 15.9 again, you will see that this is just another way of saying that the reference phasor in a series circuit is the circuit current. Dividing, the current is

$$I = \frac{E}{Z} = \frac{24.2 \angle -60.26^\circ}{483.87 \angle -60.26^\circ} = 0.05 \angle 0^\circ \text{ A}$$ ■

When the circuit resistance is small compared to the capacitive reactance that it can be ignored, Formula 15.9 becomes

$$I \angle 0^\circ = \frac{E \angle -90^\circ}{X_C \angle -90^\circ} \qquad \text{FORMULA 15.10}$$

since the phase angle between the current and potential difference is 90° in a purely capacitive circuit.

EXAMPLE:
Calculate the circuit current in the circuit of Figure 15.27*a*. ■

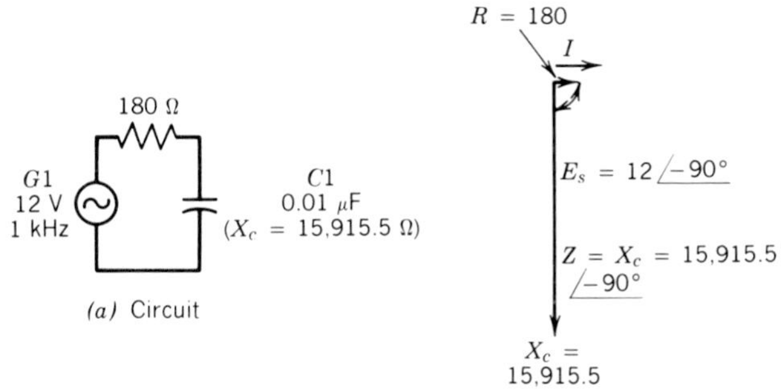

(a) Circuit

(b) Phasor diagram

Figure 15.27 When the resistance in a series *RC* circuit is small enough to be ignored, the phase angle between the current and source potential difference is 90°.

SOLUTION:
Since the capacitive reactance of the circuit is considerably more than 10 times the circuit resistance, the resistance can be ignored, and the current can be calculated as if the circuit consisted only of a 0.01 μF capacitor connected across the load. Using Formula 15.10,

$$I \angle 0° = \frac{E \angle -90°}{X_C \angle -90°} = \frac{12 \angle -90°}{15{,}915.5 \angle -90°}$$

$$= 0.754 \angle 0° \text{ mA}$$

Figure 15.27*b* shows a phasor diagram of the phase relationships in the circuit. As a check, the current can be calculated using Formula 15.9, without ignoring the resistance. The impedance is $Z = 180 - j15{,}915.5 = 15{,}916.5 \angle -89.35°$. Since this is a series circuit, the phase angle of the source potential is the same as that of the impedance, or,

$$E_s = 12 \angle -89.35°$$

The circuit current is

$$I = \frac{12 \angle -89.35°}{15{,}916.5 \angle -89.35°} = 0.754 \angle 0° \text{ mA}$$

That is, the value of the current is the same. ■

From Formula 15.10 it also follows that the potential difference across a capacitor in an ac circuit is

$$E_C = IX_C \qquad \text{FORMULA 15.11}$$

or, to keep track of the phase angle, in a series circuit,

$$E_C \angle -90° = I \angle 0° \times X_C \angle -90°$$
FORMULA 15.12

This very handy formula is used for calculating the potential difference across capacitors in any circuit where the current is known or can be calculated.

EXAMPLE:
When the network composed of *C*1, a 0.001 μF capacitor, and *C*2, a 0.0022 μF capacitor connected in series, is connected across a 455 kHz source, the network current is 1.8 ∠0° mA. What are the potential differences across *C*1 and *C*2? ■

SOLUTION:
At a frequency of 455 kHz, the reactance of *C*1 is $\frac{1}{2\pi fC} = 349.8\ \Omega$, and that of *C*2 is 159.0 Ω. Therefore,

$$E_{C1} = IX_{C1} = 0.0018 \angle 0° \times 349.8 \angle -90°$$
$$= 0.63 \angle -90° \text{V}$$

and

$$E_{C2} = IX_{C2} = 0.0018 \angle 0° \times 159 \angle -90°$$
$$= 0.29 \angle -90° \text{ V}$$ ■

Formula 15.11 can also be used in *RC* circuits to calculate the potential difference across the capacitor when the current is known or to calculate the current if the potential difference is measured.

If it is remembered that $I_{peak} = 1.414I$, and $E_{peak} = 1.414E$, the peak rather than the rms values can be used in calculations. Formulas 15.8 through 15.12 can then be rewritten using peak values, for example:

$$I_{peak} = \frac{E_{peak}}{Z} \quad \text{and} \quad E_{C\ peak} = I_{peak} X_C$$
FORMULA 15.13

In general, calculations using rms values are more common in practical work than those using peak values.

EXAMPLE:
Calculate the peak value of the current in Figure 15.28, and the peak value of the potential difference across the capacitor. ■

SOLUTION:
At a source frequency of 80 kHz, the capacitive reactance of C_1 is 35.53 ∠−90° Ω. The circuit current,

Figure 15.28 Using peak source potential difference value to calculate circuit current.

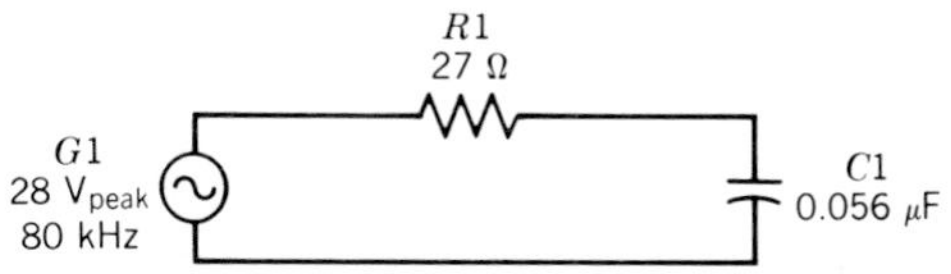

Condition	*Capacitive Reactance*	*Circuit Current*	*Phase Angle between E_s and I*	*Potential Difference Across Capacitor*	*Potential Difference Across Resistor*
E_s is increased	=	↑	=	↑	↑
E_s is decreased	=	↓	=	↓	↓
Source frequency is increased	↓	↑	↓	↓	↑
Source frequency is decreased	↑	↓	↑	↑	↓
Capacitance is increased	↓	↑	↓	↓	↑
Capacitance is decreased	↑	↓	↑	↑	↓
Resistance is increased	=	↓	↓	↓	↑
Resistance is decreased	=	↑	↑	↑	↓

Figure 15.29 Variational analysis chart of a series *RC* circuit.

using the peak source potential difference form of Formula 15.8 is

$$I_{\text{peak}}\ \angle 0^\circ = \frac{E_{\text{peak}}\theta}{Z\ \theta}$$

The impedance of the circuit is then $27 - j35.53$, or $44.62\ \angle -52.77^\circ$. The phase angle between the source potential and the circuit current is the same as the phase angle between the impedance and the circuit resistance, or $\angle -52.77^\circ$.

$$I_{\text{peak}} = \frac{28\ \angle -52.77^\circ}{44.62\ \angle -52.77^\circ} = 0.63\ \angle 0^\circ \text{ A}$$

$$E_{C\text{ peak}} = I_{\text{peak}}X_C = 0.63\ \angle 0 \times 35.53\ \angle -90$$
$$= 22.38\ \angle -90^\circ \text{ V}$$

■

Using the formulas given in this section, it is possible to produce a variational analysis chart for a series *RC* circuit as shown in Figure 15.29. Notice that the capacitive reactance of a circuit decreases as either the capacitance or the frequency increase. This is the opposite of the situation in an *RL* circuit, where increasing either the inductance or the source frequency serves to decrease the circuit current and to increase the inductive reactance.

B.5 PARALLEL *RC* CIRCUITS

The parallel *RC* circuit shown in Figure 15.30 requires some change of the analysis methods used for the series *RC* circuit. The change is necessary because the current is no longer the same in every part of the circuit.

Figure 15.30 A parallel *RC* circuit. The reference phasor for phasor diagrams is the source potential difference.

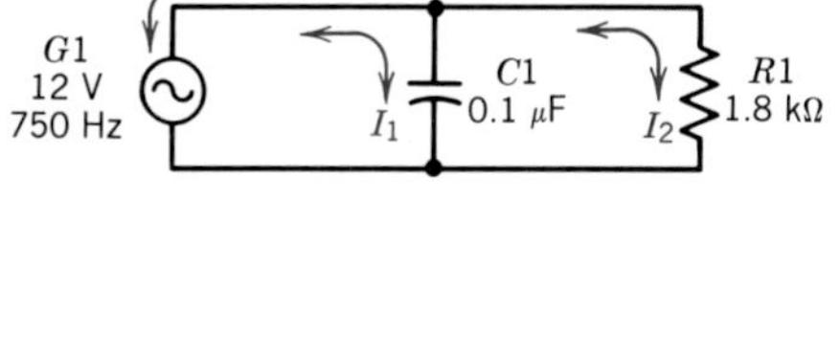

From Figure 15.30, you can see that the total current supplied by the source divides into I_1 and I_2 in the *C*1 and *R*1 branches, respectively. The potential difference across both branches, however, is the same. For this reason, the source potential difference is used as the reference phasor. Since the current leads the source potential difference in a capacitive circuit, a phasor diagram of the source potential difference and circuit current in Figure 15.30 will resemble that shown in Figure 15.31. Comparing this diagram to that drawn for a series *RC* circuit in Figure 15.20 illustrates a basic difference between the series and parallel *RC* circuits. Since the circuit current in any parallel circuit is made up of the sum of the branch currents, in Figure 15.30, the total current is the sum of the current through the *R*1 branch and the current in the *C*1 branch. The current through the *R*1 branch is

$$I_{R1} = \frac{E\ \angle 0^\circ}{R\ \angle 0^\circ} = \frac{12\ \angle 0^\circ}{1800\ \angle 0^\circ} = 6.67\ \angle 0^\circ \text{ mA}$$

The current in the C_1 branch is

$$I_{C1} = \frac{E\angle 0^\circ}{X_{C1}\ \angle -90^\circ} = \frac{12}{2122.1\ \angle -90^\circ}$$
$$= 5.65\ \angle 90^\circ \text{ mA}$$

Notice that the phase angle of the current in the *C*1 branch *leads* the source potential difference by 90°. The two current phasors, along with their sum, are shown in Figure 15.32. An interesting fact is seen if Figure 15.32 and Figure 15.21 are compared. This fact is that in a parallel *RC* circuit, the current phasor is situated above the reference phasor. In contrast, the

Figure 15.31 A phasor diagram of the source potential difference and circuit current in the circuit of Figure 15.30 showing the phase angle.

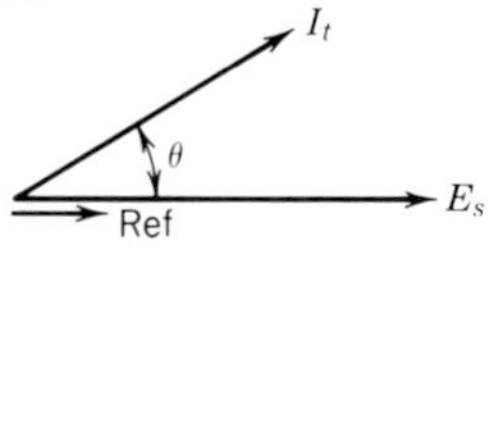

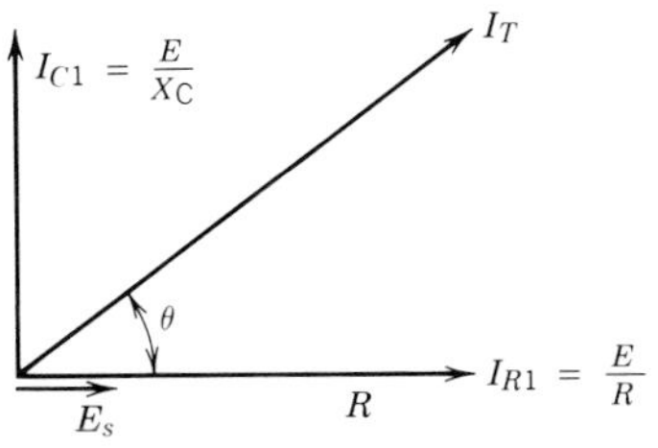

Figure 15.32 Phasor diagram of the branch currents and total circuit current in the circuit of Figure 15.30.

current phasor associated with the series *RC* circuit is situated below the reference phasor. In both cases there is a phase angle θ between the circuit current and the source potential difference.

In mathematical terms,

$$\theta = \tan^{-1}\frac{I_{C1}}{I_{R1}} = \frac{-X_C}{R}$$

Although it is possible to determine the circuit current in a parallel circuit by means of phasor addition of the branch currents, it is also possible to calculate the total impedance of the parallel network and to use Formula 15.8 to obtain the circuit current.

EXAMPLE:

Calculate the current provided by the 8-V source in Figure 15.33. ■

SOLUTION:

The capacitive reactance of $C1$ at a frequency of 1 MHz is $\frac{1}{2\pi fC} = 1061 \angle -90^\circ\ \Omega$. This, then, is the impedance of the $C1$ branch. In complex rectangular coordinates this is $0 - j1061$. The total impedance of the $C1$ and $R1$ branches can be found by using the product-over-the-sum formula:

$$Z_r = \frac{Z_{C1}\, R_{R1}}{Z_{C1} + Z_{R1}} = \frac{1061 \angle -90^\circ \times 1000 \angle 0^\circ}{(0 - j1061) + (1000 + j0)}$$

$$= \frac{1061000 \angle -90^\circ}{1000 - j1061}$$

To perform the division, it is necessary to convert the denominator to polar form:

$$Z_T = \frac{1061000 \angle -90^\circ}{1458 \angle -46.7^\circ} = 727.71 \angle -43.3^\circ\ \Omega$$

Figure 15.33 Calculating circuit current by the total impedance method.

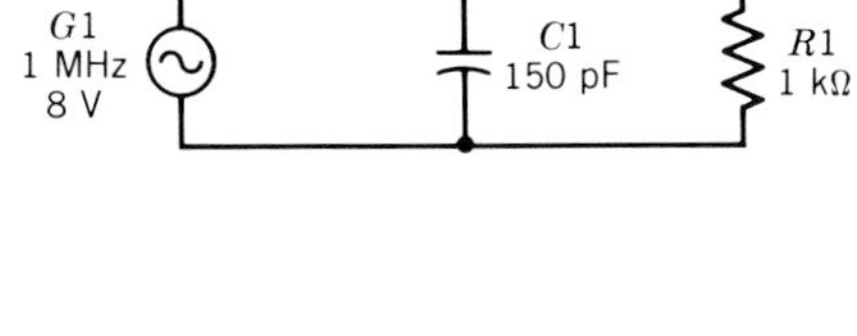

The total circuit current can then be calculated using Formula 15.8. Before this is done, however, it is important to notice that this total impedance is in series with the source. In other words, Z_T is the equivalent impedance of $C1$ and $R1$ at a source frequency of 1 MHz. In order that calculations using this equivalent impedance produce the correct phase angle results, it is necessary to pay close attention to the sign of the impedance phase angle.

In this example, the series expression for the impedance is $727.71 \angle -43.34^\circ\ \Omega$. When this is substituted in Formula 15.8, the result is

$$I = \frac{E}{Z} = \frac{8 \angle 0^\circ}{727.71 \angle -43.3^\circ}$$
$$= 0.011 \angle 43.3^\circ \text{ A} \quad \text{or} \quad 11 \angle 43.3^\circ \text{ mA}$$

The solution obtained by using the total impedance method can be checked by using the branch current method to find the total current. The current in the $R1$ branch of the circuit is

$$I_{R1} = \frac{E \angle 0^\circ}{R \angle 0^\circ} = \frac{8}{1000} = 0.008 \angle 0^\circ \text{ A}$$

The current in the $C1$ branch is

$$I_{C1} = \frac{E \angle 0^\circ}{X_C \angle -90^\circ} = \frac{8 \angle 0^\circ}{1061 \angle -90^\circ} = 0.00754 \angle 90^\circ \text{ A}$$

The sum of these two currents is $I = 0.008 + j0.00754$ A, or, in polar form, $0.011 \angle 43.3^\circ$ A. ■

B.6 OPERATION OF THE DIELECTRIC IN A CAPACITOR

In the discussion of magnetism in Chapter 9, you learned that magnetic effects were explained by referring to electron spin and to the concept of domains. These explanations are supported by experimental evidence, and it has been shown that other atomic particles, including neutrons and protons, also exhibit spin. Attempts made to explain the function of capacitor dielectrics on the basis of electron orbits and the behavior of molecules are less successful. Although it is known that an electric field will produce a force on a free or conduction electron, there is no certainty that a field has this effect on an electron bound to an atomic nucleus. A number of textbooks attempt to mirror the explanation of magnetism as a product of electron spin by explaining the effects of a capacitor dielectric in terms of *warped,* or distorted, electron orbits caused by an electric field. Although it is popular, this explanation fails to explain some of the effects observed in electronics, such as the *aging* effect in certain ceramic dielectric materials. Since an explanation of dielectric effects based on the molecular structure of the dielectric can serve to clarify some of the effects observed when using capacitors, it is worthwhile to address the subject briefly. For example, with certain dielectrics, discharging the capacitor completely and then checking the potential difference after a while will show a renewed potential difference across it. This phenomenon, which can cause trouble in capacitive timing circuits, is called *dielectric charge absorption*.

Another effect that supports the molecular explanation of the dielectric effect is the *electret effect*. Electrets are made of certain waxes, plastics, or resins and are capable of producing an electric field in the same way that a permanent magnet produces a magnetic field. An electret can be manufactured by pouring liquid wax between a pair of parallel plates that have a high potential difference between them. If the wax is allowed to harden and then removed, and a new set of plates is placed against the hardened wax, this new pair of plates will be found to have a measurable potential difference between them. In other words, the result is like the "freezing" of an electric field in the electret in the same way that producing a permanent magnet is like "freezing" a magnetic field in an iron bar.

The best available explanation for the electret effect is that the wax molecules are polarized. Although each molecule is electrically neutral, made up of the same number of electrons and protons, there are certain areas of the molecule that are negative while others are positive. When the wax or resin is liquid, the molecules of the electret are able to move freely. Because of the forces produced on them, they align themselves with the electric field between the two charged plates. As shown in Figure 15.34, the more negative portions of the molecules align so that they point toward the positive plate. The more positive molecule portions align so that they are closer to the negative plate. When the electret material hardens, it forms a crystalline structure that tends to retain this arrangement of the molecules. In this respect, the materials that can be used to manufacture electrets differ from the insulators used in capacitor dielectrics. In capacitor dielectrics, the mobility of the molecules in the solid material is greater.

Once the electret is solid and metal plates have been placed on the opposite faces, a brief current will flow through a conductor between the plates, as shown in Figure 15.35. This current will cease as soon as the electric field of the electret is canceled by the field from the charged plates. In this way, the electret is different from a chemical cell. Electrons from the negatively charged plate do not move through the insulating electret back to the other plate. There is no steady-state current.

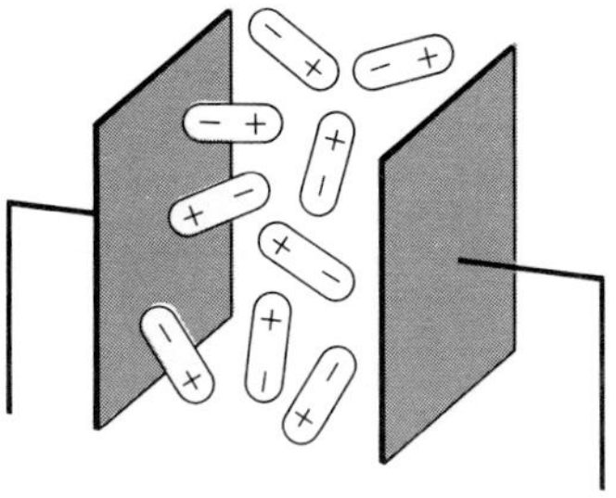

With electret material in liquid state and no potential difference between plates, the polar molecules line up in a random fashion

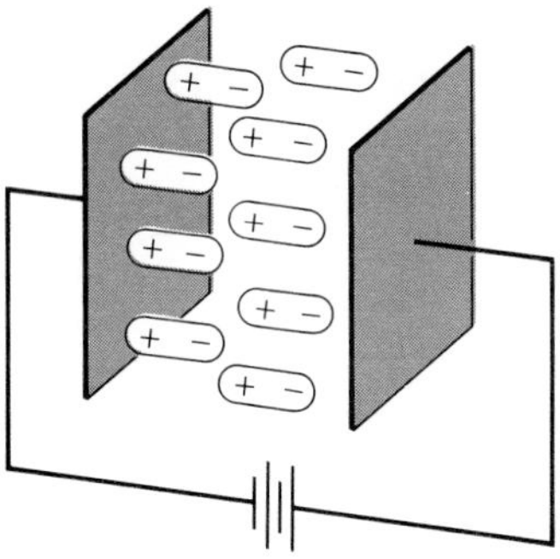

With material in liquid state, the polar molecules line up when a potential difference is applied across the plates

Figure 15.34 Formation of electrets.

In the materials used as capacitor dielectrics, the molecules are either polar or can be made polar by the electric field of the capacitor plates. The result of this is to increase the charge stored on the plates at a given source potential difference. This mechanism is shown in Figure 15.36. In 15.36*a*, a parallel-plate capacitor is connected to a source and is charged. In 15.36*b*, a slab of dielectric material has been inserted between the plates, and the molecules of the material have aligned along the electric field between the plates. Notice how this creates a surface layer of negative charge on the dielectric next to the positive capacitor plate and a surface layer positive charge next to the negative plate. The effect of these surface layer charges is to attract

Figure 15.35 The electric field of a formed electret can cause a brief current to flow in a wire between its plates.

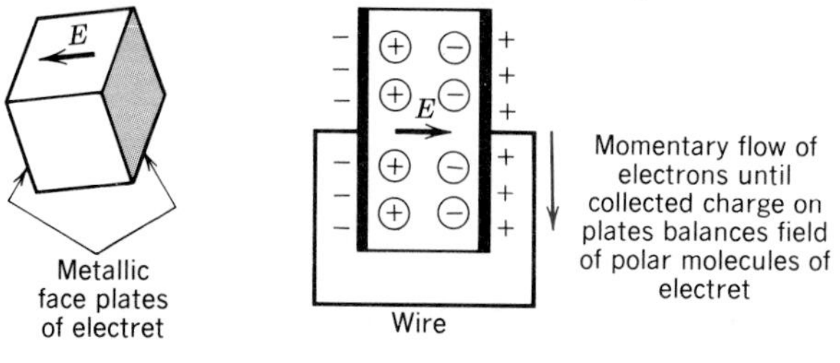

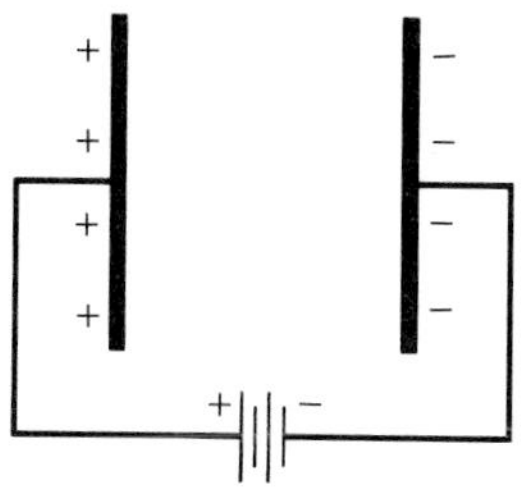

(a) Parallel-plate capacitor is fully charged

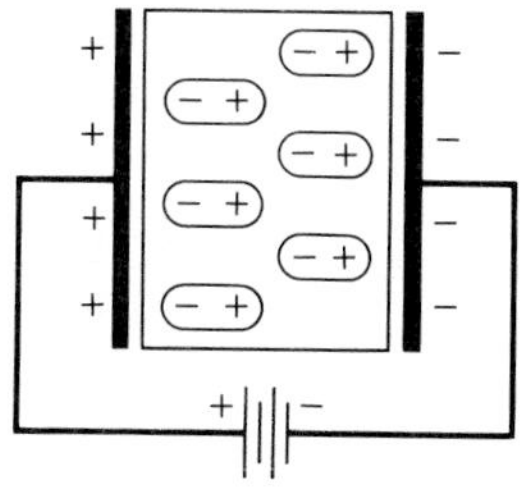

(b) A slab of dielectric material is placed between plates. Polar molecules in dielectric line up due to field between plates

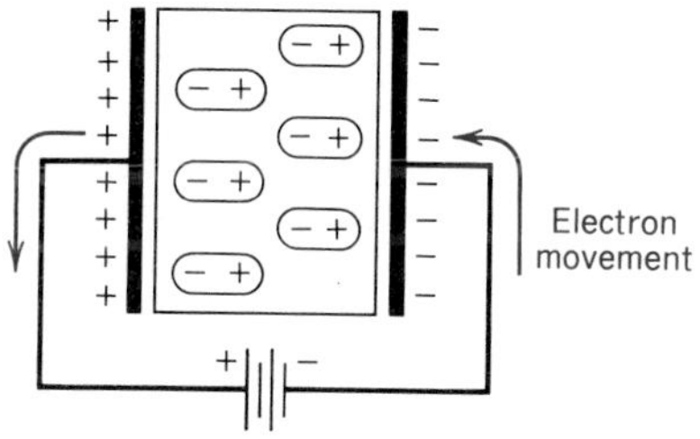

(c) Additional charge is deposited on the plates of the capacitor

Figure 15.36 Placing a slab of dielectric material between the plates of a parallel-plate capacitor permits additional charge to be stored.

additional electrons from the negative terminal of the source into the negative capacitor plate, and to repell additional electrons from the positively charged plate into the source, as shown in Figure 15.36*c*. The net result is to increase the charge on the capacitor plates. Since by Formula 14.1 $Q = CV$, if the charge on Q increases while the source potential is kept the same, the capacitance C of the capacitor must have been increased also. Therefore, the result of placing a dielectric between the plates of a capacitor is to increase its capacitance.

If the capacitance of a parallel plate capacitor in a vacuum is C_{vacuum}, and the capacitance of the same capacitor with a dielectric of a particular material is $C_{\text{dielectric}}$, a new quantity K can be defined so that

$$K = \frac{C_{\text{dielectric}}}{C_{\text{vacuum}}} \qquad \text{FORMULA 15.14}$$

K is called the *dielectric coefficient*, or *dielectric constant*, of the dielectric material and is always greater than 1.

EXAMPLE:

A parallel-plate capacitor is made of two rectangular plates, each 1.25 m long and 0.5 m wide. The spacing between the plates is 0.0015 m. When a slab of ceramic A is placed between the plates, the capacitance of the unit is 18 nF. What is the dielectric coefficient of the ceramic slab? (For practical problems, the dielectric coefficient of air and of a vacuum are considered to be the same. ■

SOLUTION:

Using Formula 14.4, the capacitance of the parallel-plate capacitor can be calculated. It is

$$C = \epsilon_0 \frac{A}{d} = 8.85 \times 10^{-12} \times \frac{1.25 \times 0.5}{0.0015}$$

$$C = 3.69 \times 10^{-9} \quad \text{or} \quad 3.69 \text{ nF}$$

Then, from Formula 15.14, the dielectric coefficient of ceramic A is

$$K = \frac{18 \times 10^{-9}}{3.69 \times 10^{-9}} = 4.88$$

■

If the dielectric coefficient of the dielectric is known, Formula 14.4 can be modified to calculate the capacitance of a parallel-plate capacitor with any dielectric:

$$C = K \epsilon_0 \frac{A}{d} \qquad \text{FORMULA 15.15}$$

The term $K\epsilon_0$ then can be considered as an expression for the permittivity of the dielectric.

Table 15.1 lists the dielectric coefficients of some commonly used capacitor dielectrics.

Table 15.1 Dielectric coefficients of some commonly used capacitor dielectrics

Material	*K*
Vacuum	1
Air	1
Paraffined paper	2.2
Polystyrene	2.5
Teflon®	2–3
Rubber	3
Glass	4–6
Mica	4–6
Oil (castor)	4–5
Ceramics	
Class I	Up to 200
Class II	Up to 10,000

C. EXAMPLES AND COMPUTATIONS

C.1 REVIEW OF SERIES AND PARALLEL *RL* CIRCUITS

It is important not to become confused over the sign of the j term in a series or parallel RL or RC circuit. The following exercises are included to provide practice in using polar and complex rectangular coordinates in RL circuits and have been designed for solution with the aid of a calculator.

1. Give the polar coordinates of the following terms in complex rectangular notation:

a. $1.7 + j0.6$ b. $120 + j49.5$
c. $83 + j0$ d. $16 - j12$
e. $0 - j13.35$ f. $4.7K + j5.6K$
g. $19 - j27$ h. $0.043 - j0.019$
i. $180K - j5.6K$ j. $9.1 + j0.019$
k. $91K - j0$ l. $1000 + j234.2$

2. Give the complex rectangular coordinates for the following terms in polar form:

a. $12 \angle 45°$ b. $63.7 \angle 37.2°$
c. $243.5 \angle 90°$ d. $5600 \angle -14°$
e. $32 \angle 30°$ f. $9.1K \angle 0°$
g. $68K \angle -90°$ h. $2.4 \angle -75.3°$
i. $3.14 \angle 0°$ j. $6.28 \angle 16°$

3. Express the total impedance of the following series RL networks in complex rectangular and polar coordinates. Draw an impedance phasor diagram of each.

a. $L1 = 10$ H, $R1 = 270\ \Omega$, $f = 60$ Hz
b. $L1 = 500\ \mu$H, $R1 = 270\ \Omega$, $f = 180$ kHz
c. $L1 = 4.7$ mH, $R1 = 10$ k Ω, $f = 455$ kHz
d. $L1 = 0.01$ mH, $R1 = 0\ \Omega$, $f = 50$ kHz
e. $L1 = 150$ mH with an internal resistance of $0.6\ \Omega$, $f = 2$ kHz.

4. The following are the source potential differences of the generators in Problem 3. Calculate the circuit current and the phase angle in each. Use the source potential differences as the reference.

a. $E_s = 120$ V
b. $E_s = 30$ V
c. $E_s = 15$ V
d. $E_s = 0.01$ V
e. $E_s = 2$ mV

5. Express the total impedance of the following parallel RL circuits in complex rectangular and polar coordinates. Draw an impedance phasor diagram of each.

a. $L1 = 8$ H, $R1 = 1.2$ kΩ, $f = 60$ Hz
b. $L1 = 150$ mH, $R1 = 56\ \Omega$, $f = 100$ Hz
c. $L1 = 180\ \mu$H, $R1 = 27$ kΩ, $f = 230$ kHz
d. $L1 = 5.6$ mH, $R1 = 100$ kΩ, $f = 627$ kHz
e. $L1 = 0.01$ mH, $R1 = 0.5\ \Omega$, $f = 10$ kHz
f. $L1 = 1$ H with an internal resistance of $10\ \Omega$, $R1 = 10\ \Omega$, $f = 60$ Hz.

6. The following are the source potential differences of the generators in Problem 5. Using the total impedance method, calculate the current supplied by the source in each and draw a phasor diagram showing the relationship between the current and source potential difference. Use the source potential difference as the reference.

a. $E_s = 120$ V b. $E_s = 12$ V
c. $E_s = 8.7$ V d. $E_s = 18$ mV
e. $E_s = 3\ \mu$V f. $E_s = 0.1$ V

7. A parallel circuit with three branches is formed by $L1$, an inductor of 10 mH with an internal resistance of $6\ \Omega$, $L2$, an inductor of 22 mH with an internal resistance of $8\ \Omega$, and $R1$, a $12\ \Omega$ resistor. The source is an ac source with a peak potential difference of 5.6 V and a frequency of 1 kHz.

a. Draw a schematic diagram of the circuit.
b. Calculate the current and phase angle in each branch and draw a phasor diagram of the circuit currents.
c. Calculate the current supplied by the source by adding the branch currents.
d. Check your answer to part (c) by calculating the current using the circuit impedance method.

8. Check your answers to Problem 6 by using the branch current method for calculating the current supplied by the source.

C.2 SOLVING SERIES AND PARALLEL *RC* CIRCUIT PROBLEMS

The ability to calculate phase angle, potential difference, current, and impedance in series and parallel RC circuits is important for understanding their function and for troubleshooting them. The key to correct calculations is to remember that the capacitive reactance in a series RC circuit is referenced to the circuit current and is expressed as a quantity on the $-j$ axis. In a parallel RC circuit, on the other hand, the current in the capacitive branch is referenced to the source potential difference, and is expressed as a quantity on the $+j$ axis. Solving the following problems will provide practice in the mathematical analysis of these important circuits.

1. Express the impedances of the following networks in both complex rectangular and polar coordinates and draw a phasor diagram of each.

a. A 0.1 μF capacitor in series with a 27 kΩ resistor at 60 Hz.
b. A 100 pF capacitor in series with a 1.3 kΩ resistor at a frequency of 1 MHz.
c. A 33 nF capacitor in parallel with a 5.6 kΩ resistor at 400 Hz.
d. A 0.00015 μF capacitor in series with a 500 kΩ resistor at 1 kHz.
e. A 27 nF capacitor in parallel with a 1 MΩ resistor at 2.2 kHz.
f. A 100 μF capacitor in series with a 10 Ω resistor at 50 Hz.
g. A 1 μF capacitor in series with a 2.7 μF capacitor and a 180 Ω resistor at 400 Hz.
h. An 0.047 μF capacitor in parallel with a 27 nF capacitor. A third parallel branch contains a 5.6 kΩ resistor. The source frequency is 400 Hz.

2. Calculate the source current and phase angle in the circuits of Problem 1 if the following are the source potential differences. Use the source potential difference as the reference in all cases.

a. 63 V	b. 8.5 μV
c. 14 V	d. 160 V
e. 0.46 V	f. 4.5 V
g. 45 V	h. 12 V

3. Calculate the potential difference across each component in Problem 1, (a), (b), (d), (f), and (g).

4. Use the impedance method to check your answer for the current supplied by the source in Problem 1, (c), (e), and (h).

D. APPLICATIONS

D.1 ELECTROLYTIC CAPACITORS

The design and production of physically small, high-capacitance capacitors is second only to the invention of the transistor in making it possible to produce the miniature electronic units that are the symbol of our technological age. Today, most high-capacitance components are either aluminum or tantalum electrolytic capacitors. They are called *electrolytic* capacitors because a conductive electrolyte is used as one of the capacitor plates. Depending on the type of electrolytic capacitor, the electrolyte can be in the form of a solid, a gel, a liquid, or a paste. The most common variety, the aluminum electrolytic capacitor shown in Figure 15.37, provides a basis for understanding how this class

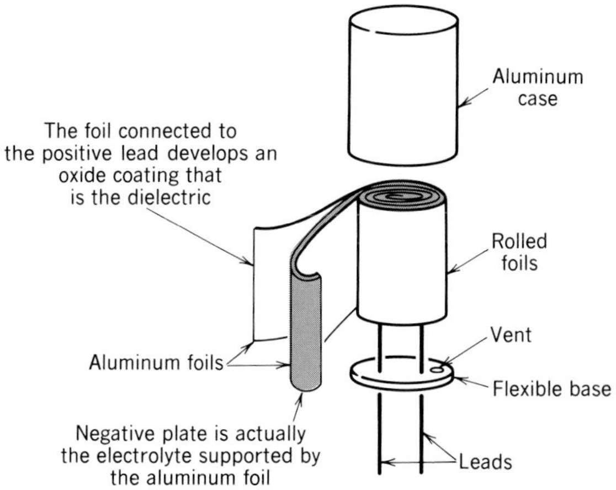

Figure 15.37 Structure of a typical aluminum electrolytic capacitor.

of capacitor operates. When it is manufactured, the aluminum electrolytic capacitor consists of an electrolyte paste sandwiched between two aluminum foils. There is no dielectric between the two foils at this point; in fact, there is a fairly good conductive path between them. At a final point in the manufacturing process, a *forming current* is made to flow between the two foils. This is a direct current that causes oxygen to be released from the electrolyte at the surface of the foil connected to the positive lead of the capacitor. As this oxygen is released, it forms a very thin layer of aluminum oxide on the surface of the foil, as shown in Figure 15.37. This oxide layer acts as the dielectric in the capacitor. Since the dielectric layer is very thin, the resulting capacitance is very high.

D.1.1 ALUMINUM ELECTROLYTIC CAPACITORS

Except for the tantalum electrolytics discussed in the next section, aluminum electrolytic capacitors provide the highest capacitance to volume ratio of any existing capacitor type. In addition, aluminum electrolytics also provide the lowest cost per microfarad of any capacitor type. There are, however, a number of disadvantages and problems in their use. The most important point to remember is that most aluminum electrolytics are polarized. That is, one of the capacitor leads is the positive lead, the other, the negative lead. The negative lead must always be maintained at a more negative potential than the positive capacitor lead during operation. If the polarity is reversed for any reason, serious damage, including bursting of the capacitor case, can result from the large quantities of gas produced. Some special-purpose electrolytic capacitors are manufactured in such a way as to be non-polarized, but this is always noted on the case. In general, one or both electrolytic capacitor terminals are marked to show polarity.

In addition to reversed polarity, a number of other malfunction conditions can cause the production of gas within an electrolytic capacitor. For this reason, larger-sized units are fitted with blow-out plugs or gaskets that permit built-up gas pressure to escape. After a gas buildup has been vented, the punctured plug will also permit the electrolyte to dry out. As this drying occurs, the equivalent series resistance of the capacitor increases, eventually making the component useless. Since the electrolyte is no longer conductive, the unit acts like an open circuit.

Aluminum electrolytic capacitors are almost always housed in cylindrical aluminum cans and are either single ended, as shown in Figure 15.38*a*, with foil connections made via wire leads, solder lugs, or screw terminals, or in axial-lead form, as shown in Figure 15.38*b*. The case sizes are not standardized and vary greatly depending upon the capacitance and the manufacturer. They range from tiny units 0.011 m high and 0.005 m in diameter to 0.3 m high and 0.1 m in diameter. A once popular form was the chassis-mounted cylindrical case containing two or three capacitors with separate positive leads and a common negative lead that was connected to the chassis. These capacitors were a standard part in radios and television receivers, and are still fairly common.

Aluminum electrolytics are commercially available in standard values from 1 μF to many thousand μF and in working voltages from 3 to 800 V. Remember that the working voltage of a capacitor is the recommended *maximum* potential difference between the plates, and that the capacitor will function properly at lower potential differences. For example, a 50 μF, 450-V capacitor can readily be used in a circuit where the potential difference between the capacitor plates is on the order of 35 V. However, the 450-V component will be larger than a 50 μF, 50-V capacitor, which would work equally well. In general, the size of an aluminum electrolytic capacitor depends on its capacitance and its working voltage rating. The higher the capacitance or voltage, the larger the component. This

Figure 15.38 Aluminum electrolytic capacitor case styles.

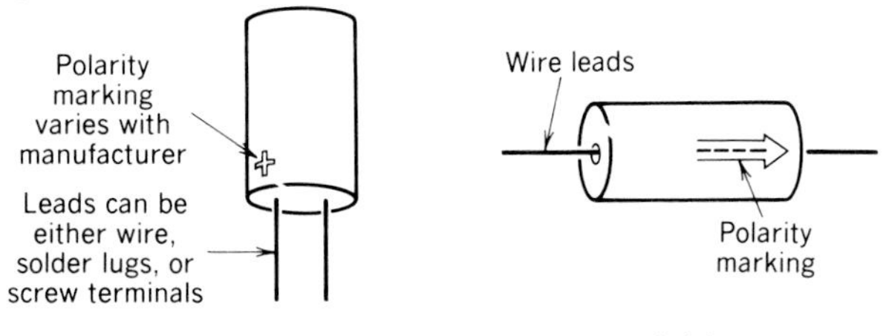

usually means that capacitances greater than 120 μF are limited to working voltages of 100 V or less in order to produce components that will fit into modern electronic units.

Another disadvantage of aluminum electrolytics is that it is fairly difficult to manufacture them to low tolerance ranges. Tolerances of −10 and +80 or +100 percent are among the most common and are acceptable in many circuits. Thus, an aluminum electrolytic capacitor nominally marked 10 μF can have an actual capacitance as low as 9 μF and as high as 20 μF. Temperature changes and the frequency of applied ac potential differences also cause the actual capacitance of an operating unit to differ from its nominal value. Special units are available for use in timing circuits. These capacitors provide ±10 percent tolerances but are more expensive.

One of the characteristics of electrolytic capacitors of all types is a measurable current between the capacitor plates when a dc potential difference is applied. Called the *"dc leakage current,"* this current is due to tiny breaks in the dielectric layer that provide conduction paths between the capacitor foils. Not to be confused with the equivalent series resistance, these leakage paths have resistances on the order of several tens to several hundreds of megohms for plastic film, glass, ceramic, and mica capacitors.

Properly functioning aluminum electrolytics, on the other hand, can possess leakage paths with dc resistances of less than 1 MΩ. The actual amount of dc leakage current depends on the total resistance of the leakage paths in the dielectric and on the dc potential difference applied to the capacitor. Figure 15.39 shows an equivalent circuit for an aluminum electrolytic. R_{ESR} represents the equivalent series resistance, while the resistor in parallel with the capacitor provides an equivalent for the current paths through the dielectric. The inductor, L_{eq} represents the inductance of the capacitor leads. This inductance is too small to be measured at the operating frequencies at which electrolytic capacitors are generally used. Applying higher than rated dc potential differences to an aluminum electrolytic may cause local heating along the current paths, burning away additional dielectric material and eventually short-circuiting the foils.

Aluminum electrolytics, like chemical cells, show signs of chemical activity even when not in use. Al-

Figure 15.39 The equivalent circuit of an electrolytic capacitor.

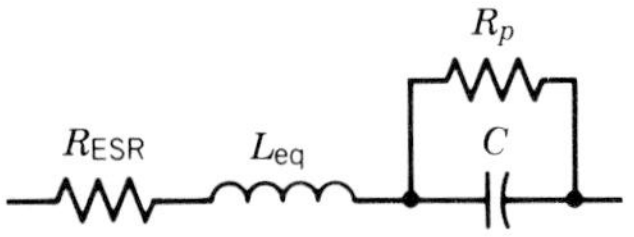

though not as serious a problem as it once was, aluminum electrolytic capacitors tend to deteriorate if stored for a long time, particularly if the storage temperatures are high. The reason for this is that the electrolyte tends to dissolve the aluminum oxide dielectric over a period of time. This process can normally be reversed by connecting the capacitor across a low-voltage dc source and passing a reforming current through the capacitor before using it in a circuit. Most modern aluminum electrolytics have been designed for shelf lives of 10 years or more if stored at room temperatures.

In summary, aluminum electrolytic capacitors are suitable for use in applications where high capacitance values are required in small cases and where relatively high leakage currents and excess capacitance over the nominal value can be tolerated. No special means are needed to control current surges since aluminum electrolytics can withstand sudden current in-rush and surge currents better than other electrolytic types.

The principal failure modes of aluminum electrolytic capacitors result in the capacitor acting either as a low resistance or short circuit, or as an open circuit with little or no capacitance. Unlike essentially stable components, such as inductors, aluminum electrolytic capacitors show gradual deterioration throughout their useful life. They will eventually fail due to the drying out of the electrolyte, even if other failures do not occur first. The drying out of the electrolyte causes a gradual drop in capacitance and increase in the equivalent series resistance (ESR). This occurs because the unit is not completely sealed, and the electrolyte slowly escapes. In addition to permitting a gradual failure due to drying out, the elastic seal can also permit the rapid failure of an aluminum electrolytic by permitting many of the commonly used circuit board cleaning chemicals to seep around the seal and into the case. For example, Freon®, which is a popular cleaning and degreasing chemical, can attack the internal structure of an aluminum electrolytic, causing it to fail within a few months. For this reason, only alcohol should be used to clean circuit boards containing aluminum electrolytics.

Poor circuit design or the failure of other components can cause conditions that produce failure of aluminum electrolytics. These failures occur because the capacitor is operated at potential differences, circuit currents, or temperatures outside its normal operating range. Depending on the conditions involved, either a gradual or a rapid failure of the capacitor can result. For example, applying a potential difference of 50 V across a capacitor with a recommended maximum working voltage of 10 V can result in what is referred to as a "catastrophic" failure. Failures of this type generally result in the explosion or bursting of the capacitor case or in fire damage. Overheating or fire is

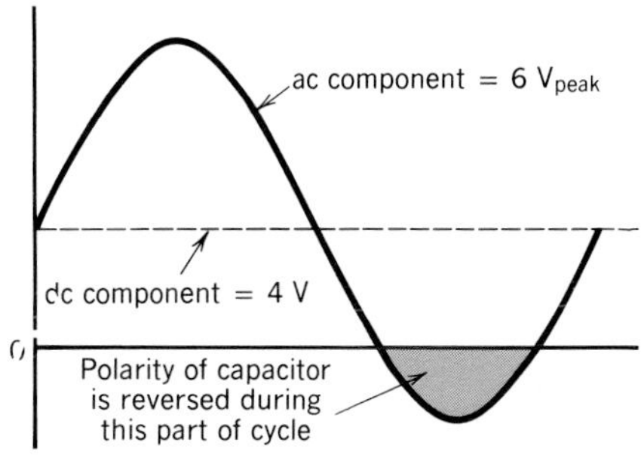

Figure 15.40 Applying a signal with an ac component amplitude greater than its dc component can result in electrolytic capacitor failure.

generally the result of the destruction of the dielectric brought about by applying an ac potential difference whose peak value is greater than the dc potential difference between the capacitor plates. As shown in Figure 15.40, this results in a reversal of polarity during parts of the ac cycle.

Special, low-ESR aluminum electrolytic capacitors are used in the switching power circuits found, among other places, in personal computers. These capacitors are subject to a great deal of electrical stress because of the high alternating currents and switching transients present in these circuits. When a capacitor of this type fails, it must be replaced with an equivalent low-ESR model or else the replacement component will fail, for no apparent reason, after a short time.

Another circuit that can cause the failure of aluminum or other electrolytic capacitors is the series circuit shown in Figure 15.41*a*. This arrangement is frequently chosen when the source potential difference is considerably higher than the recommended working voltage of available capacitors or when a capacitive voltage divider is required. In order to prevent too large a portion of the dc source potential from appearing across the capacitor with the greater leakage current, balancing resistors should be used in parallel with the identical capacitors, as shown in Figure 15.41*b*. The value of these balancing resistors depends on the construction of the capacitors and must not be too high or too low. If it is too high, the resistors will not act

Figure 15.41 Connecting electrolytic capcitors in series to obtain higher working voltages can lead to component failure unless balancing resistors are used as in (*b*).

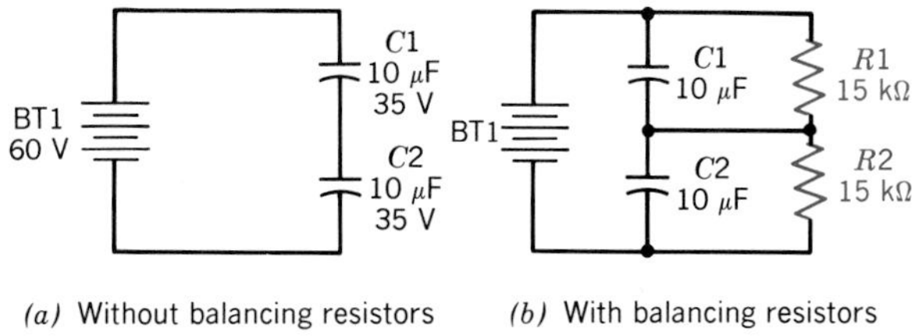

to balance the potential differences across the two capacitors. If the resistance value used is too low, the network will tend to act as a resistive divider. As a rule of thumb, values of $\frac{0.15}{C}$ or $\frac{0.2}{C}$ seem to work well, where C is the capacitance of one of the capacitors.

If used within their voltage and temperature ratings, modern aluminum electrolytic capacitors can be expected to deliver an average of 2000 hours or more of service life.

D.1.2 TANTALUM ELECTROLYTIC CAPACITORS

In an effort to produce high-value capacitors with characteristics superior to those of aluminum electrolytics, a number of capacitor types based on the use of oxides of the metal tantalum have been developed. There are three basic types of tantalum capacitors, each with different characteristics. The tantalum foil capacitor most closely resembles the aluminum electrolytic in construction. Two tantalum foils are chemically etched to increase their surface area, a process that is also used with some of the foils of aluminum electrolytics. One of the foils is then treated to produce a dielectric layer of tantalum pentoxide on its etched surface, and the two foils are rolled together and placed in a case. An electrolyte liquid such as ethylene glycol forms the contact between the negative foil and the dielectric layer. Since the dielectric layer is formed before the foils are wound, and the electrolyte is not required to produce oxygen, the case can be completely sealed. This means that there will be no electrolyte evaporation as there is in the case of aluminum electrolytic capacitors.

Although they are potentially the most versatile of the tantalum electrolytics and can provide higher operating voltages, tantalum foil capacitors appear to be less popular than the two other types. The reasons for this are probably the relatively large size and high ESR of tantalum foil capacitors when compared to other tantalum electrolytics. Also, tantalum foil units show a fairly large change in capacitance with temperature, and the higher working voltages, up to 450 V, in which they can be manufactured are less frequently used in modern solid-state circuits than was the case with tube-type units.

The most common tantalum electrolytic capacitors in use are the solid electrolyte units. They are used in low-voltage applications where stability, small size, light weight, and long shelf life are important factors. Computers and aircraft electronic equipment are typical applications. In fact, because they are manufactured with sealed cases, solid tantalums are the most widely used electrolytic capacitors in military electronic equipment.

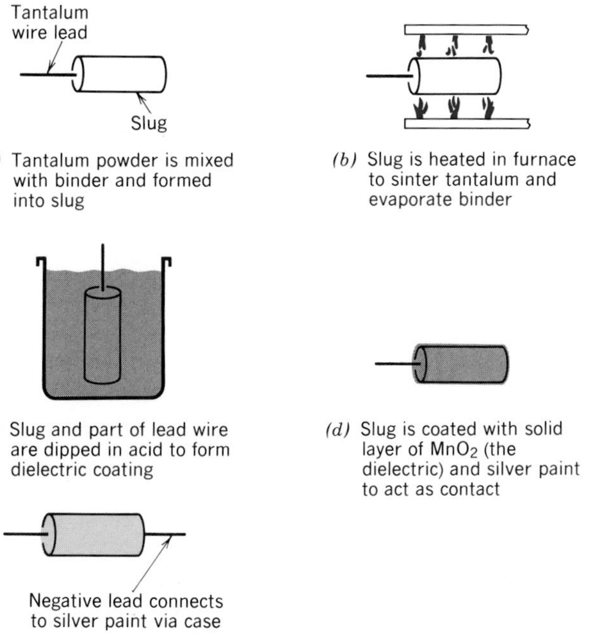

(a) Tantalum powder is mixed with binder and formed into slug
(b) Slug is heated in furnace to sinter tantalum and evaporate binder
(c) Slug and part of lead wire are dipped in acid to form dielectric coating
(d) Slug is coated with solid layer of MnO_2 (the dielectric) and silver paint to act as contact
(e) Slug is placed in sealed case

Figure 15.42 Steps in the manufacture of a typical solid tantalum electrolytic capacitor.

The solid tantalum electrolytic is constructed around a slug of tantalum powder, which is mixed with a binding compound and pressed into a pellet form. The pellet is then heated, causing the powder to form a porous mass after the binder has evaporated. The resulting pellet has a very large surface area for its size. The dielectric layer of oxide is formed on the entire surface of the pellet by dipping it in acid, and then the tantalum pentoxide layer is covered with a solid layer of manganese dioxide electrolyte and a layer of silver paint (see Figure 15.42). Notice that the manganese dioxide, the same electrolyte used in paste form in some chemical cells, is in dry form in the solid tantalum capacitor. Since there is no gas formed during operation, the whole unit can be sealed in its case.

The two most popular case styles for solid tantalum capacitors are the axial-lead metal cylinder style shown in Figure 15.43*a* and the axial-lead epoxy bullet shape shown in Figure 15.43*b*. The metal case is fa-

Figure 15.43 Common solid tantalum electrolytic capacitor case styles.

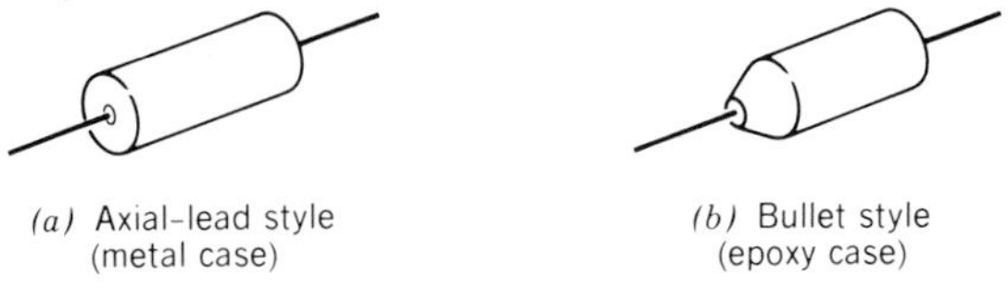

(a) Axial-lead style (metal case)
(b) Bullet style (epoxy case)

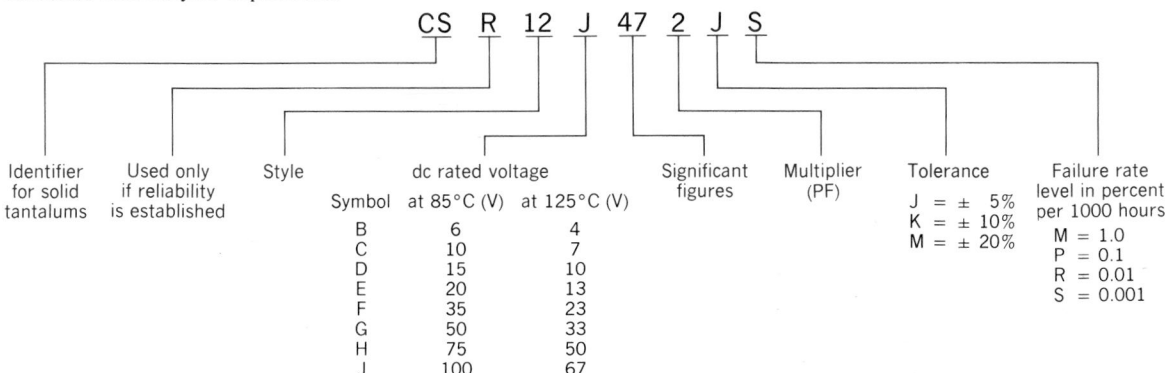

(a) Resembles film or ceramic capacitor *(b)* Dipped case style

Figure 15.44 Less common solid tantalum electrolytic capacitor case styles.

vored in military and aircraft equipment, while the cheaper epoxy case is more common in commercial and industrial applications for capacitors of 50 μF or less. Since it is not practical to produce solid tantalum electrolytic capacitors with working voltages much over 100 V or capacitances higher than around 680 μF, larger case styles are not needed. Less common case styles are those shown in Figures 15.44*a* and 15.44*b*. The style shown in 15.44*b* is the only one that is too small to provide enough space to print either a military specification number or the component capacitance and working voltage. Some manufacturers use a form of the color-coding scheme shown in Figure 15.45 to encode the essential information on the component. Of particular importance are the voltage and polarity

Figure 15.45 Color coding for dipped case solid tantalum electrolytic capacitors.

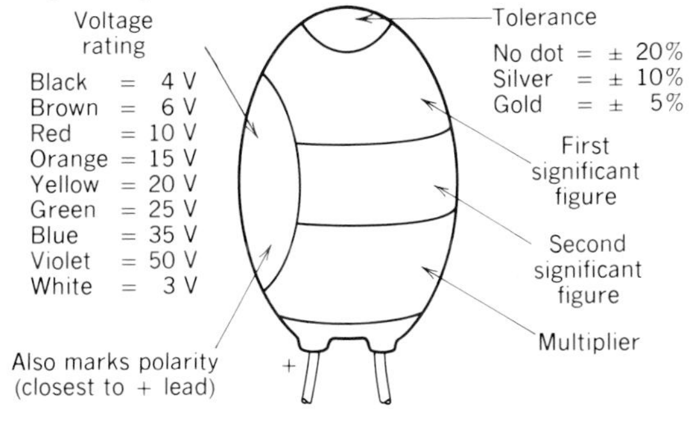

markings on the side of the case. Like aluminum electrolytics, most tantalum electrolytics are polarized, and the proper polarity must be observed when the component is connected in a circuit.

The most common military specification marking system for solid tantalum electrolytics is illustrated in Figure 15.46. It is similar to the system used for ceramic capacitors shown in Chapter 14. The two initial letters *CS* identify a solid tantalum electrolytic component, while the following *R* is used only when the component reliability has been established. Notice that the dc voltage ratings are given for two temperatures, 85° and 125°C. Such a high operating temperature is possible because of the stability of the solid tantalum electrolytic capacitor. Since the electrolyte material is solid and dry, the average capacitance variation is less than 10 percent of the nominal value over the entire temperature range from −55° to +125°C. In addition, this temperature stability makes it practical to produce solid tantalum electrolytes with tolerances of 10 and 5 percent.

There are a number of solid tantalum electrolytic characteristics that you should understand. First among these is the fact that the working voltages are rather low, ranging from about 6 to 100 V. Moreover, some parts distributors do not regularly stock components with working voltages over 50 V. Solid tantalum electrolytics are also more easily damaged by transients and reverse polarities than aluminum electrolytics. For example, a solid tantalum capacitor at room temperature can withstand a reverse voltage of 15 percent of its recommended dc working voltage for a brief period, but at higher temperatures, a reverse polarity condition of as little as 1 percent of the recommended working voltage can result in permanent failure of the capacitor.

Another characteristic of solid tantalum electrolytics is the low dc leakage current. This is one-tenth or less of that found in aluminum electrolytics. Leakage is due to tiny breaks in the dielectric layer, which

Figure 15.46 Military specification marking system for solid tantalum electrolytic capacitors.

CS R 12 J 47 2 J S

- CS — Identifier for solid tantalums
- R — Used only if reliability is established
- 12 — Style
- J — dc rated voltage
- 47 — Significant figures
- 2 — Multiplier (PF)
- J — Tolerance: J = ± 5%, K = ± 10%, M = ± 20%
- S — Failure rate level in percent per 1000 hours: M = 1.0, P = 0.1, R = 0.01, S = 0.001

dc rated voltage

Symbol	at 85°C (V)	at 125°C (V)
B	6	4
C	10	7
D	15	10
E	20	13
F	35	23
G	50	33
H	75	50
J	100	67

become filled with the manganese dioxide electrolyte. Leakage current depends on the surface area of the dielectric layer and its condition, but typically ranges from 1 μA to 20 μA at 25°C, and can be higher for a new capacitor than one that has been in service for some time. The reason for this improvement with age is that solid tantalum electrolytics have some self-healing ability. When a dc potential difference is applied to the capacitor, the leakage current is localized to the very small break areas in the dielectric. Although the total leakage current is low, the break areas in the dielectric film are small, and considerable heat is developed in the electrolyte in the break. This heat causes a chemical reaction in the manganese dioxide electrolyte, which changes it into a compound with a much higher electrical resistance, and this acts to insulate the break area in the dielectric layer.

Dielectric absorption is a problem that limits the use of solid tantalum electrolytics in some applications. This effect occurs because the dielectric material tends to retain energy for a period of time even after a capacitor is apparently fully discharged. If the leads of a charged solid tantalum electrolytic are shorted together until the potential difference has fallen to zero and then the short circuit is removed, a potential difference will gradually appear between the capacitor leads. In other words, some of the electrical energy stored in the capacitor dielectric is retained after discharge and is again converted into a potential difference when the discharging circuit is removed. Capacitors with dielectric absorption can produce difficulties in *RC* timing circuits, triggering circuits, and phase shift networks.

Solid tantalum electrolytic capacitors have two principal failure modes. The most critical of these is a massive short circuit through the dielectric layer. This generally occurs because impurities in the tantalum slug tend to move toward the contact area between the tantalum and the dielectric during operation. This results in the formation of breaks in the dielectric that are too large to be self-healing. When this happens, instead of insulating the break area, the heat produced tends to destroy more of the dielectric layer, causing an increase in the current flow and in the heat produced. This can lead to a dangerous thermal runaway situation similar to that found in ni–cad cells. Since short circuiting is a common failure mode, many designs place a low-value resistor in series with solid tantalum electrolytic capacitors to limit short-circuit currents that might cause fire or explosion.

A second common failure mode for solid tantalum electrolytics is due to open or intermittant internal connections. This condition is frequently the result of shock or vibration. Since there is no liquid or paste electrolyte

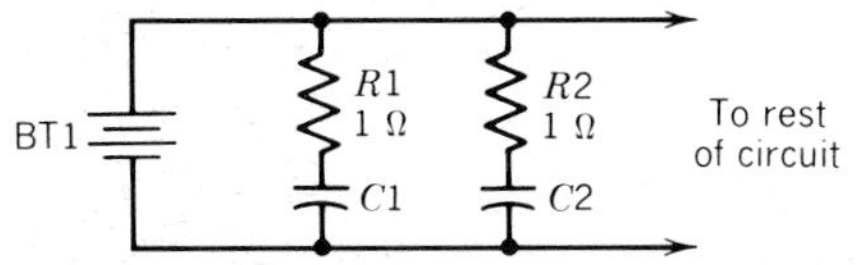

Figure 15.47 Using low-value resistors in series with tantalum electrolytic capacitors to limit surge currents.

to dry out, an open-circuit condition between the leads of a solid tantalum electrolytic is almost always the result of a mechanical failure.

Less common failure modes for solid tantalum electrolytic capacitors are a large change in capacitance, or Q, or a large increase in the leakage current. One common cause for these failures is the presence of heavy surge currents in the circuit. Where it is possible, small-value, current-limiting resistors are placed in series with solid tantalum electrolytics. This is particularly important when a number of capacitors are connected in parallel. If the series resistors shown in Figure 15.47 are not included, the appearance of a dielectric fault in one of the capacitors could result in a discharge of other capacitors through the fault. Depending on the circuit conditions, this can result in a thermal runaway instead of a self-healing condition in the fault area. As in the case of aluminum electrolytics, it is recommended that resistors be placed across solid tantalum electrolytic capacitors connected in series. This circuit, shown in Figure 15.48, is frequently used so that solid tantalums can operate in circuits with potential differences higher than 50 V. The value of the resistor used is generally around $\frac{0.15}{C}$ Ω.

The third type of tantalum electrolytic capacitor is referred to as the *wet-slug* type. Wet-slug tantalum capacitors were the first tantalum type developed, and, like the solid tantalums, are built around a porous tantalum pellet. Instead of using manganese dioxide as the electrolyte, gelled sulfuric acid serves as the negative capacitor plate. Since the acid is highly corrosive, the case and its seal must be complex. Although not as popular as solid tantalum electrolytics, wet-slug tantalums are used where the capacitance-to-size ratio of the components is the most important consideration.

Figure 15.48 As in the case of aluminum electrolytic capacitors, tantalum capacitors connected in series should have balancing resistors across them.

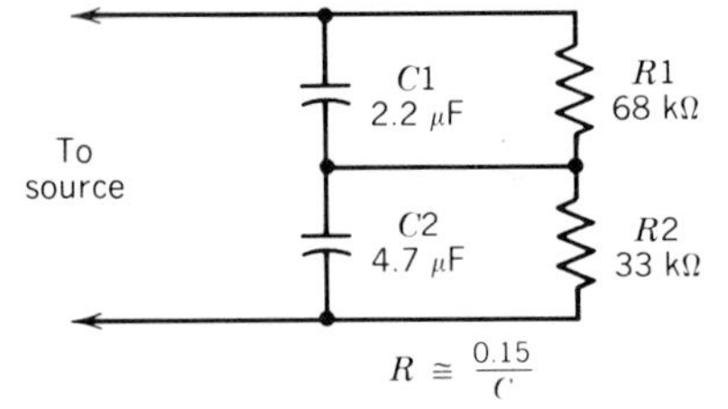

This type provides the highest capacitance per volume of any commonly used dielectric. It is also capable of operating at higher potential differences than the solid tantalum electrolytic. Units with working voltages up to 125 V are regularly stocked by distributors, as are lower-voltage components with capacitances up to 500 or 600 μF. Axial-lead, cylindrical metal cases seem to be the only case style used. Most frequently, the capacitance and working voltage are printed on the case, but unless the military specification number is included, it is difficult to distinguish wet-slug tantalums from solid tantalum types. The first two letters in the military specification number of a wet-slug tantalum are *CL* in place of the *CS* used for solid tantalums.

The most important drawbacks to the use of wet-slug tantalums are that (1) they are filled with a highly corrosive acid and (2) they can not tolerate reversal of polarity. Given the close packing of parts in modern electronic units, even the slightest leaking of the sulfuric acid electrolyte will cause considerable damage. This potential threat has slowed the acceptance of wet-slug tantalums in spite of recent improvements in case seal design. The wet-slug tantalum is also extremely sensitive to reversed polarity. Potential differences as low as 0.1 V with the wrong polarity will cause it to fail. In many applications, brief reversals of polarity during capacitor discharge or when a unit is first powered up can not be avoided, and wet-slug capacitors simply can not be used. A less critical drawback is the fact that wet-slug units are generally available only in tolerances of 20 percent. In other respects, such as leakage current, wet-slug tantalums resemble solid tantalum electrolytics.

From the description of its construction, it would seem that the primary failure mode of a wet-slug tantalum would be a loss of capacitance caused by the gradual "drying out" of the electrolyte. However, this does not appear to be the case. Standard authorities report that the majority of the wet-slug tantalum failures in the field are due to reversed polarity conditions. This failure mode frequently results in a short circuit across the capacitor.

D.2 VARIABLE CAPACITORS

In addition to the fixed capacitors discussed in the Applications sections of Chapter 14 and so far in this chapter, certain electronics units contain components whose capacitance can be changed over a certain range. For small components whose adjustment range is less than about 100 pF, the most frequently used term is *trimmer capacitor,* or simply *trimmer,* although the term *padder* is used at times. Larger units, or those with adjustment ranges greater than 100 pF are generally called *variable capacitors,* or *tuning capacitors.* These names are generally applied in a rather vague way, and often it is the function of a particular capacitor in a circuit that determines its name.

D.2.1 PARALLEL-PLATE, AIR-DIELECTRIC, VARIABLE CAPACITORS

The parallel-plate capacitor using air as its dielectric is particularly easy to turn into a variable component. At one time, the large, radio receiver tuning capacitor shown in Figure 15.49 was a common unit. As shown, it is composed of three parts: a frame, a set of stationary aluminum plates that are attached to the frame but electrically insulated from it, and a set of movable plates connected to the capacitor shaft. The shaft is secured to the frame by bearings and is free to turn, but a special brush arrangement provides electrical contact between the shaft and the frame. The movable plates connected to the shaft are called the *rotor,* while the stationary plates are referred to as the *stator.* By rotating the shaft, it is possible to change the amount of overlap between the interleaved rotor and stator plates. This controls the capacitance of the unit. The spacing between adjacent rotor and stator plates determines the maximum potential difference that can be applied across the capacitor. Since air can be ionized, arcing can occur if the potential difference across the capacitor is too large. For transmitter and other high-voltage circuits, the plate spacing is increased to prevent arcing. Since increasing the spacing would decrease the capacitance of the unit, a transmitting variable capacitor intended for use at high voltage generally has larger plates and more plates than receiver or low-voltage units. Figure 15.50*a* shows the basic schematic symbol for a variable capacitor.

There are a number of variations of the basic variable capacitor designed for special applications. One type found in radio receivers combines two electrically separate variable capacitors on a single shaft. This type of capacitor can be used to vary the capacitance of

Figure 15.49 The radio receiver variable capacitor was once a common electronic component.

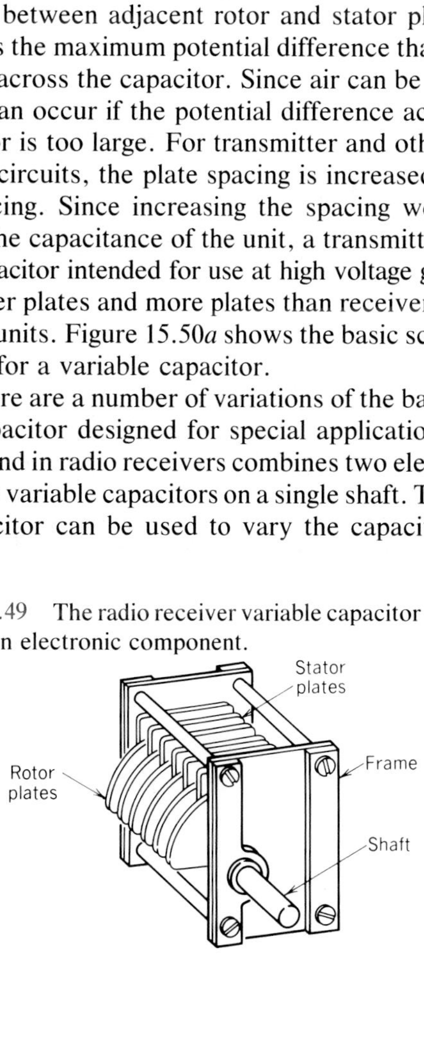

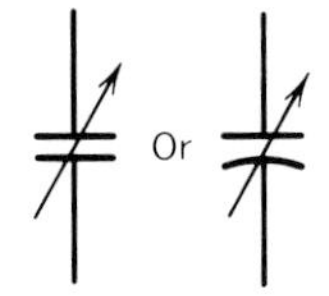

(*a*) Basic schematic symbol for a variable capacitor

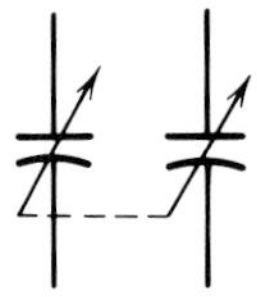

(*b*) Symbol for ganged variable capacitors

(*c*) Symbol for split-stator capacitor

Figure 15.50 Variable capacitor schematic symbols.

two separate circuits at the same time and is referred to as a *ganged capacitor*. The schematic symbol for a ganged capacitor is shown in Figure 15.50*b*. Note that the capacitances of the two ganged units with capacitances of 10 to 365 pF and 10 to 110 pF were frequently used to tune tube-type radio receivers.

One variation of the ganged capacitor is the split-stator capacitor whose schematic symbol is given in Figure 15.50*c*. The split-stator capacitor contains two electrically isolated groups of stator plates, which are interleaved with rotor plates that are electrically connected by the conducting shaft. A split-stator capacitor is shown in Figure 15.51*a*. When the large size of this form of split-stator capacitor would produce problems

Figure 15.51 Two forms of split-stator capactor.

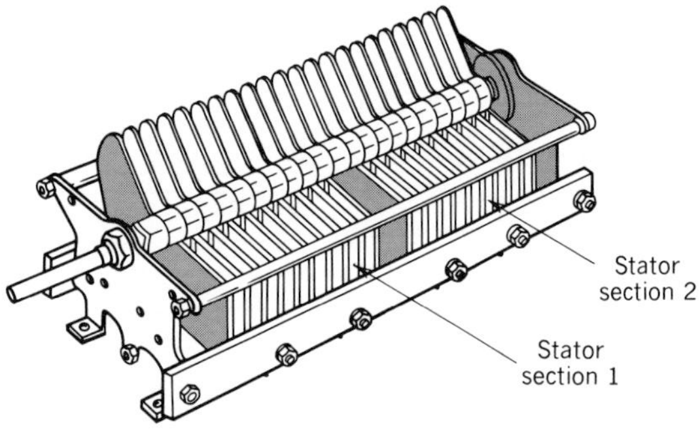

(*a*) Large, split-stator variable

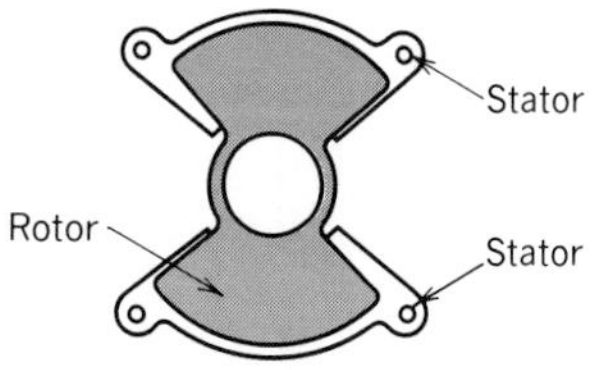

(*b*) When space is limited, a butterfly variable is used (rear view shown)

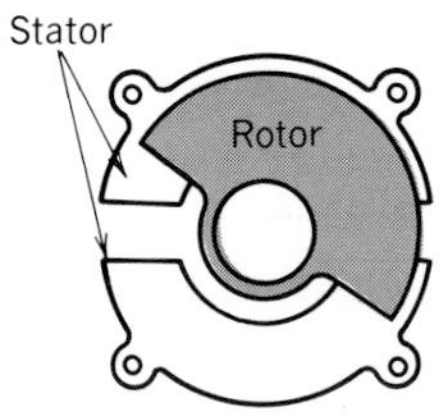

(*a*) Differential capacitor (rear view)

(*b*) Differential capacitor Schematic symbol

Figure 15.52 A differential capacitor and its schematic symbol.

in equipment design, the arrangement of rotor and stator plates shown in Figure 15.51*b* can be used. This type of capacitor is called a *butterfly capacitor*.

It is possible to confuse the butterfly capacitor with the differential capacitor, whose plate arrangement is pictured in Figure 15.52. The differential capacitor is used when it is necessary to decrease the capacitance in one circuit, while increasing it by the same amount in a second circuit, or for constructing a variable capacitive voltage divider. Figure 15.53 shows the schematic diagram of a divider. By considering the drawing of this type of capacitor, in Figure 15.52, you can see that rotating the shaft one-quarter turn in the clockwise direction will increase the overlapping between the rotor plates and lower set of stator plates, while decreasing the overlap between the rotor plates and the upper stator.

In addition to differences in plate spacing and in the construction of the air-dielectric types shown above, it was previously common to manufacture capacitors with the rotor plate shapes shown in Figure 15.54. Each of these shapes provides a different change in capacitance for a particular amount of rotation, but it is unlikely that you will run across any but the semicircular form (15.54*a*) in modern equipment.

Air-dielectric variable capacitors are less frequently used today, particularly in the higher capacitance ranges with maximum capacitances above 150 pF. In fact, the older 10- to 365-pF tuning capacitors found in every tube-type radio receiver are presently becoming rather hard to obtain. Smaller units, with capacitance ranges from 10 to 100 or 150 pF designed for infrequent circuit adjustment rather than constant tuning, are still readily available from distributors. Instead of the bulky and expensive air-dielectric variables, most small transistor radios use variable capac-

Figure 15.53 Using a differential capacitor as a variable capacitive voltage divider.

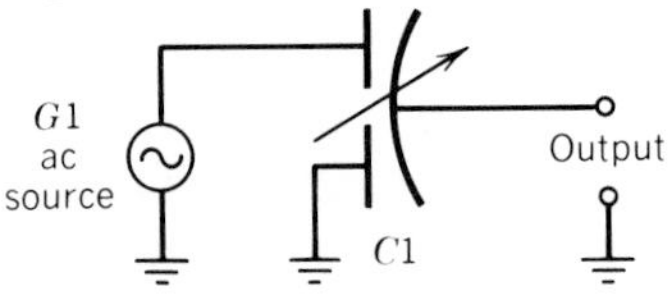

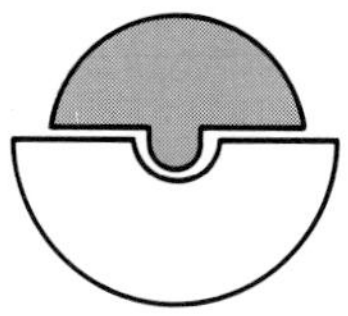

(a) Straight-line capacitance

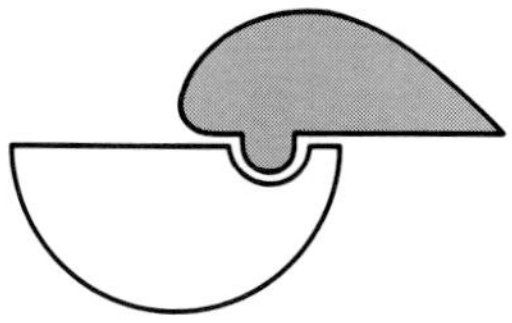

(b) Straight-line frequency

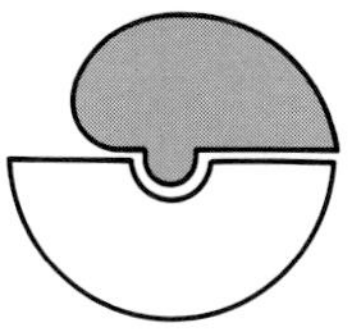

(c) Straight-line wave length

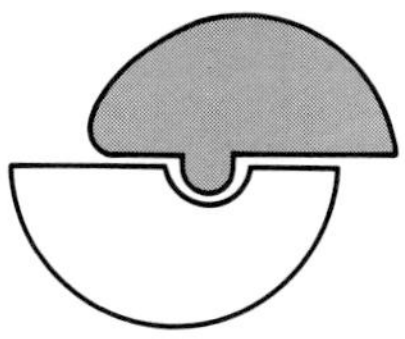

(d) Midline

Figure 15.54 Variable capacitor rotor plates were formerly manufactured in a variety of shapes for different purposes.

itors in which the air dielectric has been replaced by thin plastic sheets. These tuning capacitors are therefore much smaller than the air-dielectric variety.

In spite of its frequently fairly massive construction, the air-dielectric variable capacitor tended to fail because of damage received during equipment maintenance. Careless cleaning, in particular, would bend the rotor plates, causing them to contact the stator plates when the rotor and stator were fully meshed. Once bent, it is extremely difficult to straighten the plate again without introducing further bends and other short-circuit points.

Another common cause of component failure was the wearing out of the brass contact strip between the rotor and the frame. Poor contact between the rotor and frame produces noise or intermittant contact during capacitor adjustment. Short circuits or arcing because of the buildup of conductive dirt particles between the plates is another cause of failure.

D.2.2 TRIMMER CAPACITORS

The name *trimmer capacitors* is given to a group of small variable capacitors using air, mica, or ceramic materials as their dielectric medium. The air-dielectric trimmer shown in Figure 15.55 looks like a very small

Figure 15.55 Air-dielectric trimmer capacitors look like small air-dielectric variable capacitors, but lack the massive frame and bearings.

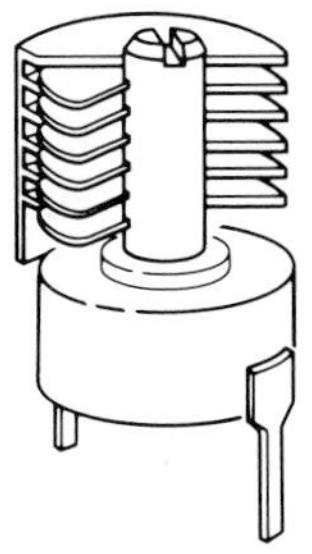

Table 15.2 Typical range of miniature air-dielectric trimmer capacitors

Unit	*Minimum C* (pF)	*Maximum C* (pF)
1	1.2	4.2
2	1.3	6.7
3	1.4	9.2
4	1.5	11.6
5	1.7	14.1
6	1.8	16.7
7	2	19.3
8	2.4	24.5

air-dielectric capacitor but lacks the massive frame and elaborate, smooth-acting, ball bearing shaft support of the radio receiver tuning capacitor. The bearings are not necessary because the trimmer capacitor is not intended to be used for constant adjustment. These units are designed to be set for a particular value and left in that position until the change of circuit characteristics through aging makes it necessary to adjust the trimmer again. Typical capacitance ranges are given in Table 15.2.

Where a limited change in capacitance is sufficient, a ceramic trimmer similar to that shown in Figure 15.56*a* is used. The construction is like that of a single rotor plate separated from one or two stator plates by a layer of ceramic dielectric. Although they are sensitive to capacitance changes because of moisture and temperature changes, ceramic trimmers are widely used in applications where variable capacitors under about 150 pF are required. In general, these capacitors are subject to the same failure modes as ceramic capacitors.

An alternative to the ceramic variable is the mica variable capacitor shown in Figure 15.56*b*. This type of capacitor is composed of interleaved aluminum plates and mica sheets. A screw adjustment controls the actual spacing of the plates and permits the capacitance of the unit to be varied with a great degree of resolution since a single turn of the screw can be made to produce only a small movement of the plates. Capacitors of this type are available with maximum capacitances of several hundred pF.

Figure 15.56 Ceramic and mica trimmer capacitors.

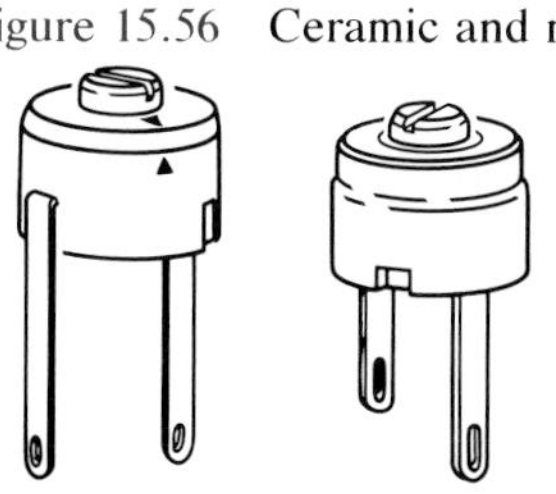

(a) Ceramic trimmer

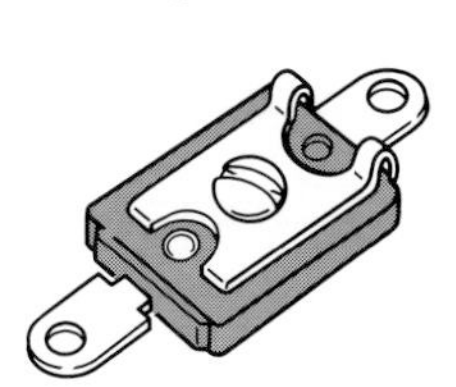

(b) Mica trimmer

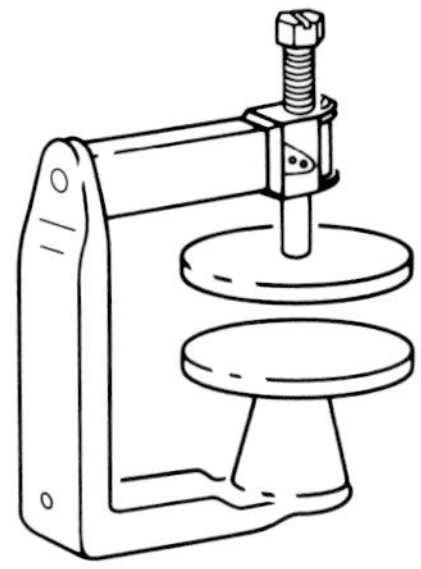

Figure 15.57 Adjustable air-gap parallel-plate trimmer.

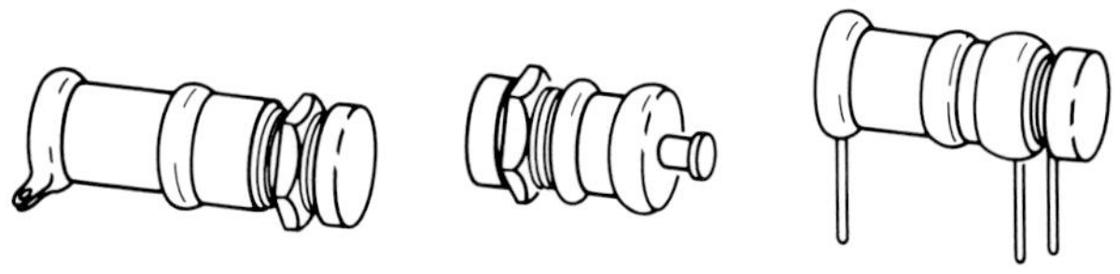

(a) Typical units

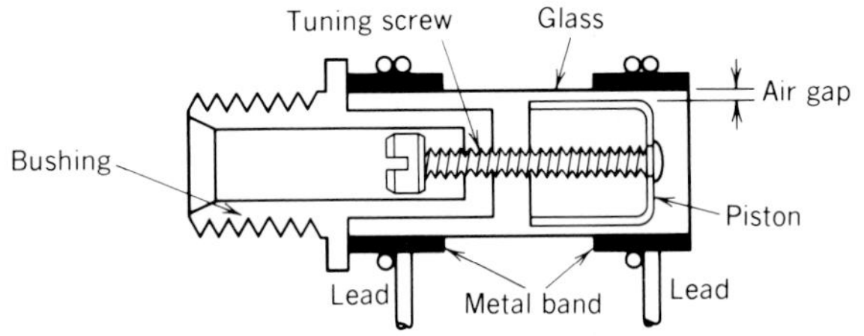

(b) Cutaway view (typical)

Figure 15.58 Piston-type trimmer capacitors.

Other, less frequently used trimmer capacitors are the air-gap, parallel-plate capacitors shown in Figure 15.57 and the piston type shown in Figure 15.58. Both these types provide capacitances of only a few pF at their maximum settings, but are capable of operating at very high potential differences.

With the exception of the ceramic trimmers, which have the same failure modes as ceramic capacitors in addition to those of the other trimmer types, physical damage during adjustment or equipment maintenance is the principal reason for trimmer capacitor failure. Other causes of failure are the buildup of dust between the plates of the air-dielectric types, which can lead to arcing or change in capacitance, and breakage of the glass bodies of the piston types.

D.3 TESTING CAPACITORS

Since short circuiting is one of the failure modes for most capacitor types, the practice of testing them with a multimeter set for resistance measurement has become common. The method itself is simple: It consists of measuring the resistance across the leads of the capacitor. In some cases, this method will also reveal open electrolytic capacitors and those with excessive leakage. If used carefully, and if circuit schematics are available, resistance checks can be used for troubleshooting capacitors in circuits.

The principal difficulty in using resistance checks for capacitors is in interpreting the results. Remember, regardless of the type of multimeter used, resistance measurement is performed by making the unknown resistance a part of a circuit that is powered by a source in the multimeter. Connecting the multimeter across a capacitor actually places a charge on the capacitor. When the leads are first connected to a properly functioning capacitor, the circuit current will be at its maximum. The circuit current is initially about the same as that which would flow if a resistor would be connected across the test leads. As the potential difference across the capacitor increases, the circuit current drops, so that the resistance indication of the meter increases to some steady-state value. This value is a measurement of the resistance that would produce a current equal to the leakage current of the capacitor. The time required to go from the initial to the steady-state resistance value is determined by the *RC* time constant of the capacitor and the internal resistances in the meter. Since these resistances are rather low, the resulting time constant for capacitors under 0.1 μF can be too short to register any significant change in the resistance indication. Particularly in the case of plastic, mica, glass, and ceramic capacitors of less than 0.01 μF, the indicator of an analog multimeter or the display of a digital multimeter may show no change at all. The reason for this is that the time constant of the circuit composed of the capacitor and the meter resistors is so short that the circuit has already reached its steady-state conditions before the analog meter indicator has had a chance to move or the digital meter has had a chance to calculate and display any values. In other words, the meter indication will remain on overrange for a digital meter or on infinity with an analog meter. But this is the same indication that would be obtained from an open circuit or an open-circuited capacitor. Also, this is the indication that would be obtained from an electrolytic capacitor in which the electrolyte has dried out or otherwise been lost.

A further difficulty in using a multimeter to test or troubleshoot capacitors and capacitive circuits results from the different characteristics of modern multimeter resistance measuring systems. The potential difference between the multimeter leads as well as the maximum current available are different for different multimeters. Even changing the range setting can vary the potential difference between the test leads in an unpredictable manner. In fact, some meters use current-limiting circuits so that the circuit current will always be considerably less than 1 mA. Such circuitry will tend to cause the potential difference to rise as the circuit current decreases, making it impossible to interpret the indications in any quantitative manner. The low potential differences involved also tend to hide many short-circuit conditions, which appear only when the capacitor dielectric is stressed at its normal operating potential difference.

When used to troubleshoot capacitor circuits, the resistance checking method can also lead to incorrect analyses because of the existence of circuit current paths in parallel with the capacitor being checked. These current paths may be as obvious as a parallel resistor or may be hidden as part of a semiconductor circuit. In both these cases, a multimeter will measure the resistance of the alternate path and provide an incorrect indication of a partially short-circuited or high-leakage current capacitor.

Finally, if you plan to use resistance measurements for troubleshooting circuits that contain tantalum capacitors, you must determine the polarity of your multimeter test leads. Certain analog multimeters applied the negative terminal of their internal source to the red lead for resistance measurements and the positive terminal of the internal source to the common lead. For most modern meters, particularly digital meters, the polarity is the opposite. The red lead is positive with respect to the common lead when the meter is set to measure resistance. An easy way to determine the polarity of the meter you will be using is to measure the potential difference between its leads when it is set to measure resistance, using a second meter. It is a good idea to record the polarity and the potential difference measurement between the leads at different range settings on a small piece of paper and tape it to the back of the meter for future reference. In this way you can avoid damaging tantalum capacitors or semiconductors, which can not tolerate reversed polarity or potential differences higher than their recommended maximum voltages. For example, a multimeter that uses a 9-V potential difference for resistance measurements should never be used in a digital circuit where the semiconductors operate at a 5-V level.

The most reliable way of troubleshooting circuits containing capacitors is to use an oscilloscope. By properly connecting the oscilloscope and applying power to the circuit under test, it is possible to observe the charge and discharge waveforms of the capacitor, or its effect on the waveform of the source potential. Laboratory experiments of this sort are provided in the Laboratory Manual accompanying this book. Usually, a combination of waveform observations using an oscilloscope and potential difference measurements with a multimeter will be sufficient to determine if a particular capacitor might be faulty.

Once a suspected capacitor has been removed from a circuit or otherwise isolated from the rest of the circuit, it can be tested by a number of methods. Recently, it has been possible to purchase relatively inexpensive digital capacitance meters that will measure capacitance with accuracies better than 0.5 percent. Some of these meters will also detect excessive capacitor leakage. Although they usually use dc rather than ac for their measurements, these devices are generally sufficient to detect most capacitor failures.

For a larger variety of problems, bridge devices can be used. Able to make measurements of capacitance, leakage, and dissipation factor with ac inputs at one or more frequencies and applied potentials, these units can spot capacitor failures. Bridges of this type frequently combine the ability to make inductance as well as capacitance measurements and are becoming more common on test benches.

D.4 REPLACEMENTS FOR FAULTY CAPACITORS

What to do after you have traced a circuit malfunction to a faulty capacitor is a topic seldom covered in elementary textbooks. In the case of resistors, which are fairly standardized components, it is usually an easy task to find an identical replacement component. In the case of inductors, the opposite condition exists. There is less duplication among manufacturers' lines, and in most cases, it will be necessary to replace a faulty component with one that is exactly the same type and has the same model number and manufacturer as the original. In the case of capacitor replacement, the situation is different. Depending on the equipment itself and the particular conditions of a maintenance program, it may be possible, sometimes even advisable, to replace a faulty component with one of slightly different characteristics. In certain types of equipment which are type regulated by a military or government agency, substitution is not permitted. Replacement capacitors, as well as any other replacement components, must be the same model and manufacturer specified in the unit parts list. This requirement is necessary to ensure continued certification of the unit. In industrial and consumer equipment, a degree of freedom is permitted. This freedom, however, must be used intelligently. For example, it is never correct to replace a faulty capacitor with a 50-V recommended working voltage with one that has a recommended working voltage of 25 V. Within limits, the major characteristics of the replacement component should always be the same as or within the tolerance range of the component that is being replaced. For example, some manufacturers make a 50 μF, 50-V aluminum electrolytic, others make a 47 μF, 50-V model with the same physical size. If the tolerance for this aluminum electrolytic is, as typical for general-purpose units, +50 percent, −10 percent at best, a 50 μF unit could be substituted for a faulty 47 μF capacitor. On the other hand, substituting a 47 μF capacitor for a faulty 50 μF one could lead to problems in some circuits.

There are a few general rules to follow when substituting capacitors for faulty units:

1. Determine if it is permitted to substitute a similar capacitor instead of an identical one for the faulty component. In military or federally regulated equipment such as aircraft radios, identical parts must be used. Certain computers and industrial devices that pass government or industry standards for radio interference or operation in hazardous areas must also use identical replacement parts. This information is usually contained in the maintenance manual accompanying the equipment.

2. If an identical replacement part is not available, and if use of similar parts is permitted, you must first be aware of the characteristics of the faulty part. You will usually need to look it up in the manufacturer's specification sheet. For example, is a faulty electrolytic capacitor one of the special low-ESR models used in modern switching power supplies?

3. Next, you will have to compare the characteristics of your proposed replacement with those of the original component. You will also have to use your knowledge of component types for this comparison, for example, aluminum electrolytics have a much greater tolerance for reversed polarity than tantalum types. Carefully note all the differences between the characteristics of the original component and the proposed replacement part.

4. Once you have determined the differences between the components, it is necessary to analyze the circuit to see if the differences actually matter in the particular application. In the previously used example, the difference between a 47 μF and 50 μF capacitor would not be significant in the power supply filter circuit. On the other hand, a 35-V capacitor could *not* be used if the original unit had a working voltage of 50 V. If the differences in the characteristics, even the minor ones such as the recommended temperature derating, will not affect circuit operation, the proposed replacement can be used.

Making this kind of decision depends heavily on general knowledge, experience, and common sense, but there are a few things to watch for.

1. Never replace a faulty component with a narrow tolerance with one that has a wider tolerance range. The faulty ±2 percent capacitor costs the manufacturer more than a ±10 percent unit, so there was probably a good reason for selecting it.

2. Never replace an NPO ceramic capacitor with anything but another NPO type. The zero temperature coefficient capacitor was probably used to prevent change in capacitance.

3. Never replace a Type I ceramic with a Type II.

4. Never replace a tantalum electrolytic with an aluminum electrolytic or vice versa in filter circuits. The characteristics of these two types are fairly different.

5. Older paper-dielectric capacitors can be replaced by plastic components if the capacitance and working voltages are similar.

6. Silver mica and polystyrene capacitors should always be replaced by identical units in tuned circuits.

7. Finally, when in doubt, call and ask the equipment manufacturer.

E. PROGRAMMED REVIEW

FRAME 1

With a certain capacitor in the circuit, a loss of source potential difference for 1 ms was found to have little effect on the circuit output. This is an example of the __________ characteristic of the capacitor.

a. Constant voltage. (2)
b. Any other answer, review Section B.1 and go on to Frame 2.

FRAME 2

If the capacitance of the capacitor described in Frame 1 was decreased so that the time constant it formed with the rest of the circuit was anything less than __________, the circuit output would probably be zero during the time that the power was interrupted.

a. 0.2 ms (3)
b. Any other answer, review Section B.1 and Figure 15.11.

FRAME 3

In an inductive circuit the __________ leads the __________, but in a capacitive circuit the __________ leads the __________.

a. Potential difference; current; current; potential difference. (5)
b. Any other answer, (4)

FRAME 4

Remember the two mnemonics: *eLi*—in an inductive circuit (L), the potential difference (e) leads the current (i); and *iCe*—in a capacitive circuit (C), the current (i) leads the potential difference (e). Go on to Frame 5.

FRAME 5

A series RC circuit is composed of a 100 Ω resistor and a 1 μF capacitor. The measured potential difference across the resistor is 2.44 V and the potential difference across the capacitor is 9.7 V. What is the phase angle between the circuit current and the source potential difference?

a. $-75.9°$ (6)
b. Any other answer, review the last part of Section B.2.

FRAME 6

Given the fact that the source frequency of the circuit in Frame 5 is 400 Hz, write the complex rectangular and polar form expressions for the circuit impedance.

a. $Z = 100 - j397.89$; $Z = 410.26 \angle -75.9°$ (7)
b. Any other answer, review Section B.3.

FRAME 7

Given the fact that the current in the circuit in Frame 5 is 24.4 mA, what are the magnitude and phase angle of the source potential difference?

a. 10 V; $-75.9°$ (8)
b. Any other answer, review Section B.3.

FRAME 8

In __________ circuits it is the current phasor that is taken as the reference, while in __________ circuits, it is the source potential difference.

a. Series; parallel. (9)
b. Any other answer, review Sections B.3 and B.4.

FRAME 9

Increasing the capacitance in a series RC circuit will *increase/decrease/have no effect on* the potential difference across the capacitor.

a. Decrease. (10)
b. Any other answer, review Figure 15.29.

FRAME 10

Increasing the source frequency in a series RC circuit will *increase/decrease/have no effect on* the potential difference across the resistor.

a. Increase. (11)
b. Any other answer, review Figure 15.29.

FRAME 11

Increasing the capacitance of the capacitor in a parallel RC circuit will *increase/decrease/have no effect on* the potential difference across the capacitor.

a. Have no effect on. (12)
b. Any other answer indicates a confusion of series and parallel RC circuits. Draw a parallel RC circuit and try Frame 11 again.

FRAME 12

In a parallel RC circuit $X_C = 159\ \Omega$ and $R = 100\ \Omega$. The polar coordinate expression for the total circuit impedance is __________.

a. $61.39 \angle -57.83°\ \Omega$ (13)
b. Any other answer, review Section B.5.

FRAME 13

The polar coordinate expression for the series equivalent impedance of X_C and R in Frame 12 is __________.

a. $61.39 \angle -57.83°\ \Omega$ (14)
b. $61.39 \angle 57.83°\ \Omega$, you forgot to convert to a current reference for the equivalent series impedance. Review Section B.5 and go on to Frame 14.
c. Any other answer, review Section B.5.

FRAME 14

Two effects that support the consideration of the dielectric effect as a molecular phenomenon are __________ and __________.

a. Dielectric charge absorption; the electret effect. (15)
b. Any answer not including these effects, review Section B.6 and go on to Frame 15.

FRAME 15

A certain parallel-plate capacitor has a capacitance of 18 pF. What will be its capacitance when a slab of glass ($K = 5$) is inserted between the plates?

a. 90 pF (16)
b. Any other answer, review Section B.6.

FRAME 16

An electrolytic capacitor is so called because one of its "plates" is formed by __________. The dielectric is a thin coating of __________.

a. An electrolyte; oxide. (17)
b. Any answer not incorporating these ideas, review Section D.1.

FRAME 17

Two causes of catastrophic failure in aluminum electrolytic capacitors are __________ and __________.

a. Reversal of polarity; exceeding the maximum working voltage. (18)
b. Any other answer, review Section D.1.1.

FRAME 18

The process of restoring the dielectric layer of an aluminum electrolytic capacitor is called __________.

a. Reforming. (20)
b. Any other answer, review Section D.1.1 and go on to Frame 19.

FRAME 19

The relatively short shelf life of aluminum electrolytic capacitors, in comparison with other capacitor types and resistors or inductors, makes it necessary to test the capacitors before using them as replacement parts. Reforming the dielectric layer by connecting a source of potential is a relatively easy task and should be done if necessary. Go on to Frame 20.

FRAME 20

When either aluminum or tantalum electrolytics are connected in series to increase their operating voltage, balancing resistors should be used. A correct value for use with two 39 μF tantalum electrolytics would be __________.

a. 3846 Ω, or 3.9 kΩ (21)
b. Any other answer, review Sections D.1.1 and D.1.2.

FRAME 21

The characteristic that limits the use of solid tantalum electrolytic capacitors in certain *RC* timing circuits is __________.

a. Dielectric absorption. (22)
b. Any other answer, review Section D.1.2 and go on to Frame 22.

FRAME 22

The two most common failure modes of solid tantalum electrolytic capacitors are __________ and __________.

a. Short circuit; open or intermittant internal connections. (23)
b. Any answer not incorporating these ideas, review Section D.1.2.

FRAME 23

The type of tantalum electrolytic capacitor that uses liquid sulfuric acid as its electrolyte is called the __________ type. This type is especially sensitive to damage caused by __________.

a. Wet slug; reversed polarity. (24)
b. Any other answer, review the last part of Section D.1.2.

FRAME 24

The principal parts of an air-dielectric variable capacitor are the __________, the __________, and the __________.

a. Rotor, stator; frame (order not important). (25)
b. Any answer that does not include all three, review Section D.2.1.

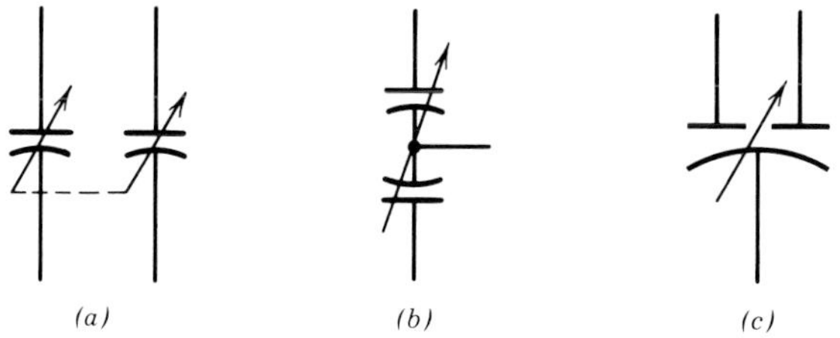

Figure 15.59 Figure for Frame 26.

FRAME 25

In an air-dielectric variable capacitor, the frame is electrically connected to the __________ plates, but is insulated from the __________ plates.

a. Rotor; stator. (26)
b. Any other answer, review Section D.2.1.

FRAME 26

Figure 15.59 contains schematic symbols for a __________, b __________, c __________.

a. (*a*) Ganged variable capacitors; (*b*) split-stator or butterfly variable capacitor; (*c*) differential variable capacitor. (27)
b. Any other answer, review Section D.2.1.

FRAME 27

Three principal types of trimmer capacitors include __________, __________, and __________.

a. Answer should name three of the following: air dielectric; ceramic; mica; piston; variable air gap. (END)
b. Any answer that does not name three types, review Section D.2.2.

F. PROBLEMS FOR SOLUTION OR RESEARCH

1. Figure 15.60 shows the schematic diagram of a power supply and a computer memory board. Capacitor $C1$ is intended to prevent the loss of data stored in the memory that occurs when the power supply potential difference falls below 1.84 V. If the internal resistance of the power supply is 12 Ω when a power outage occurs, what is the longest outage during which $C1$ will sustain the memory?

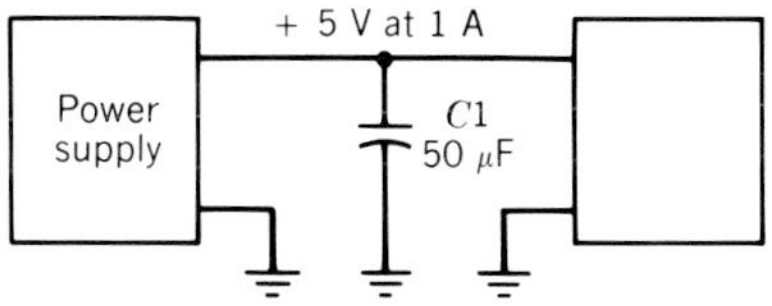

Figure 15.60 Figure for Problem 1.

2. Calculate the capacitive or inductive reactance and total impedance and phase angle in the following networks. Be sure to indicate the reference phasor for all phase angles.

a. An 8 H inductor in series with a 1000 Ω resistor at 60 Hz.
b. A 100 pF capacitor in series with a 1.5 kΩ resistor at 750 KHz.
c. A 50 μF capacitor in series with an 18 Ω resistor at 400 Hz.
d. A 27 mH inductor in parallel with a 330 Ω resistor at 1 KHz.
e. A 180 nF capacitor in parallel with a 270 nF capacitor at 10 KHz.
f. A 10 μF capacitor in parallel with a 1 H inductor at 50 Hz. (*Hint*: Use phasor diagrams if you have trouble with this.)

3. Use phasor methods to calculate the total impedance of circuit shown in Figure 15.61. (*Note*: Although you have not formally learned how to deal with circuits containing resistance, capacitance, and inductance, you already possess the mathematical tools and the methods necessary.)

a. Calculate the current in each branch and phase angle.
b. Using the current method, calculate the total current supplied by the source and its phase angle.
c. Check your answer to part (b) by using the impedance method.

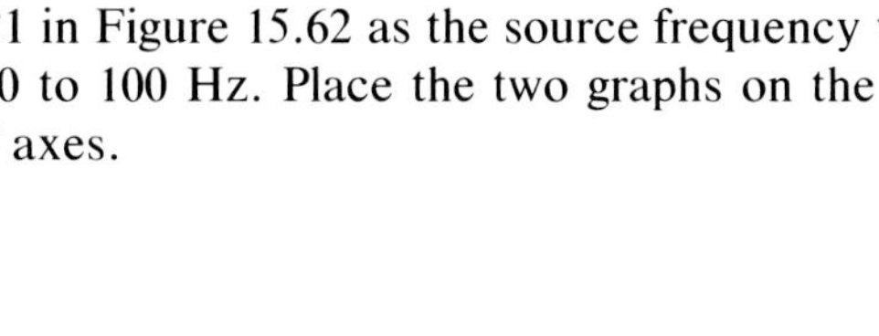

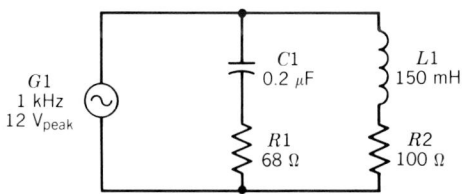

Figure 15.61 Circuit for Problem 3.

4. Draw graphs of the potential difference across $C1$ and $R1$ in Figure 15.62 as the source frequency varies from 0 to 100 Hz. Place the two graphs on the same set of axes.

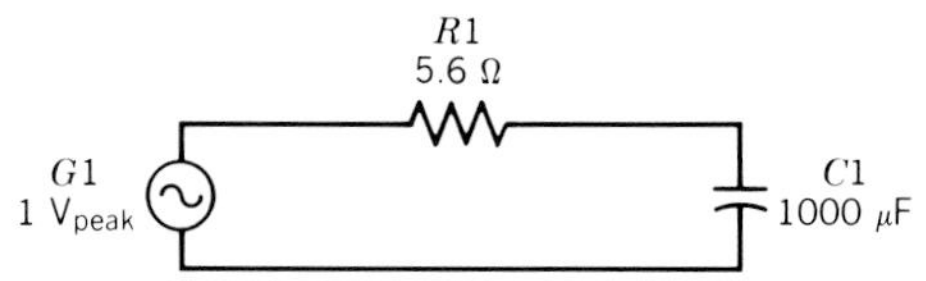

Figure 15.62 Circuit for Problem 4.

5. Complete variational analysis charts like that shown in Figure 15.63 for parallel *RC* and parallel *RL* circuits.

Figure 15.63 Figure for Problem 5.

Condition	*Impedance of C1 (L1) Branch*	*Current in C1 (L1) Branch*	*Circuit Current*	*Phase Angle between Source Potential and Circuit Current*
Source potential is increased				
Frequency is increased				
Frequency is decreased				
Value of *C*1 (*L*1) is increased				
Value of *C*1 (*L*1) is decreased				
Value of *R*1 is increased				
Value of *R*1 is decreased				

6. Obtain the schematic diagram for a modern communications receiver. Using colored highlight pens, mark the series and parallel *RC* networks. Predict the result of trying to test the capacitors in these networks using a multimeter set for resistance measurements.

CHAPTER 16

POWER IN RC AND RL CIRCUITS: PRACTICAL RC CIRCUITS

A. CHAPTER PREVIEW

1 In this chapter, you will learn about electric power in reactive circuits. After completing it, you will be able to calculate apparent, reactive, and true power in *RC* and *RL* circuits.

2 You will also learn to apply the methods of circuit analysis to the calculation of current, potential difference, and power in more complex circuits.

3 The lengthy Applications section of this chapter introduces a number of commonly used *RC* circuits. After completing this section, you will be able to recognize these networks, state their functions, and calculate their characteristics, including their Q.

4 The final part of the Applications section is devoted to the techniques of troubleshooting *RC* circuits.

B. PRINCIPLES

B.1 POWER AND REACTIVE POWER IN CAPACITIVE AC CIRCUITS

In Chapter 6, you learned that the power dissipated by the resistance in a dc circuit could be stated in terms of the circuit current and the resistance as $P = I^2R$, or in terms of the current and the potential difference across the resistance as $P = IE$, where I and E are the rms values of the current through and the potential difference across the resistance.

In a resistive circuit, such as that shown in Figure 16.1, both the circuit current and the potential difference across the resistance are constantly changing. According to Kirchhoff's voltage law, the potential difference supplied by source $G1$ is equal to the potential drop across $R1$. Likewise, referring to Kirchhoff's current law, the current into or out of the source is equal to the current through $R1$. This means that the instantaneous power supplied by $G1$ is all dissipated as heat in $R1$. The two graphs in Figures 16.2*a* and 16.2*b* show the product of the square of the instantaneous current i and the resistance and the product of the instantaneous circuit current i and the instantaneous potential difference. Because the current and the potential difference in a resistive ac circuit are in phase, the two power waveforms are identical. Expressing this mathematically, it is possible to write that for a resistive ac circuit,

$$P = i^2R = ie \qquad \text{FORMULA 16.1}$$

where p, i, and e are the instantaneous values of the power, current, and potential difference, respectively.

Notice that the power curve in the resistive circuit is always above the horizontal axis. In other words, the value of the power is always positive. This is because $-e \times -i = +p$, that is, the product of two negative values has a positive sign. This indicates that the power being delivered by the source is being dissipated in the circuit. As you will see in the following

Figure 16.1 A resistive load connected to an ac source.

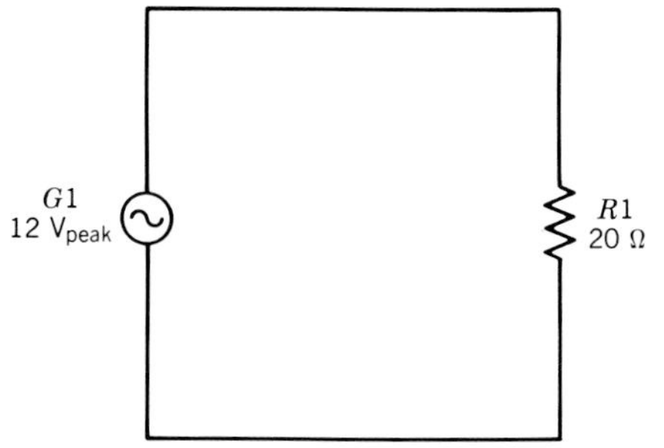

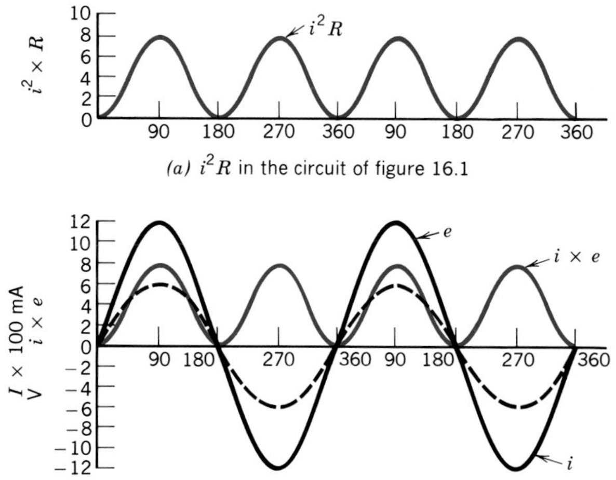

(a) i^2R in the circuit of figure 16.1

(b) $i \times e$ in the circuit of figure 16.1

Figure 16.2 Because the source potential difference and the circuit current are in phase in the circuit of Figure 16.1, i^2R and ei produce identical graphs.

discussion, this is not always the case. Also notice that the power waveform reaches its positive peak value twice during a single cycle of the source potential difference.

Recall from Chapter 6 that the *average* power P supplied by the source or dissipated in the resistance can be obtained by using the rms values:

$$P_{av} = I^2R = IE$$

When an ac potential difference is applied across a capacitive circuit, as in Figure 16.3, the conditions are different. In the circuit shown, the resistance is considerably smaller than the reactance of $C1$ and can therefore be ignored. Applying Kirchhoff's voltage law, since there is no other potential drop in the circuit, the source potential and the potential difference across the

Figure 16.3 When an ac source is connected across a capacitor, the source potential difference and the circuit current are not in phase.

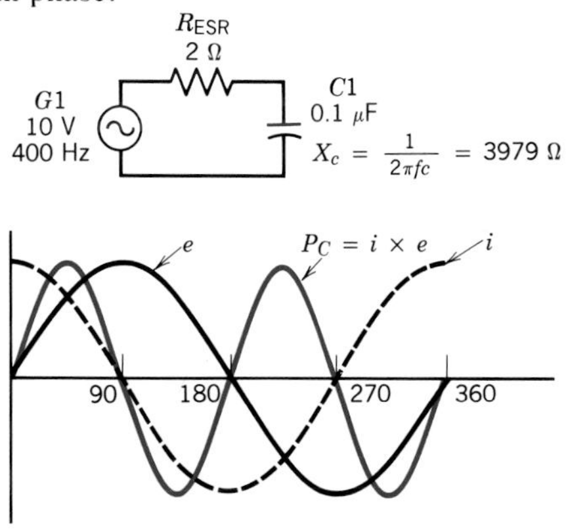

Note: waveforms not to scale

capacitor will be equal. This is really just another way of saying that since the circuit resistance is assumed to be nearly zero, the time constant of the circuit is practically zero. Since the phase angle between the current and the potential difference in this capacitive circuit is $\tan^{-1} \frac{-X_C}{R}$, the phase angle here between the circuit current and potential difference across the capacitor will be 90°. The circuit current and capacitor potential difference waveforms are shown in Figure 16.3. During the period between 0° and 90° of the waveforms shown, the current is decreasing, while the potential difference across the capacitor is increasing. Since both values are positive, the sign of their product, $i \times e$, is also positive. During this portion of the cycle, the source is delivering power to the circuit. But the circuit resistance is assumed to be zero, and so i^2R will also be zero, regardless of the value of i. It is clear that the power being delivered to the circuit is not being dissipated as heat, and ie does not equal i^2R. What actually happens to this power can be learned from the instantaneous power waveform in Figure 16.3. Between the 90° and 180° points on the axis, the potential difference across the capacitor is decreasing, and the circuit current has changed direction. The sign of the product of the instantaneous potential difference and the circuit current will now be negative, or $P = -i \times e$. This means that the capacitor is now providing power to the circuit and the source. Or, to put it a different way, the power stored in the electric field in the capacitor is now being returned to the source. Since no power has been dissipated, the amount of power returned is the same as the amount put in by the source during the period of time between the 0° and 90° points in the cycle.

During the time between 180° and 270° of the cycle, both the current and the potential difference across the capacitor have the same polarity. Since this polarity is the opposite of that during the part of the cycle between 0° and 90°, which was assumed to be the positive direction, both e and i now are negative. The product of e and i, however, is positive, indicating that the source is again providing power to the circuit. Finally, during the portion of the graph between 270° and 360°, the circuit current is in a positive direction while the potential difference is negative. Their product is again negative.

Looking at the shape of the $i \times e$ waveform for this circuit, you can see that it resembles a sine wave with twice the frequency of the potential difference waveform. The shaded area under the waveform during its positive segments, as shown in Figure 16.4, represents the total power delivered to the capacitor by the source, while the shaded areas between the axis and the negative segments represent the total power returned to the source by the capacitor. As you can see, the shaded areas above and below the axis are equal, so that over a complete cycle of the ac source, a purely capacitive circuit uses no power. In the real world, this is not a very useful statement. Even if the capacitive reactance of a real circuit is much larger than its resistance and the circuit can be considered purely capacitive, it is still important to know how much power is being alternately stored in and then given back by the capacitor. This power is called *reactive* power, and its average value can be calculated by using the rms values of the potential difference across the capacitor and the circuit current.

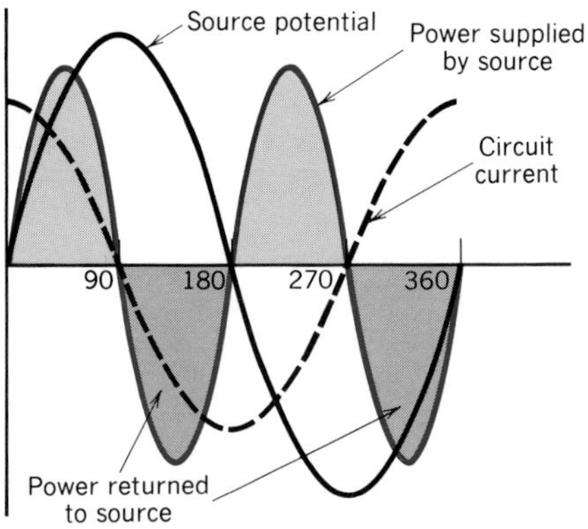

Figure 16.4 The total power delivered to the capacitor is returned to the source over the complete cycle.

$$\text{Reactive power} = P_r = IE_C \quad \text{FORMULA 16.2}$$

To prevent confusion with the power dissipated by a resistor in a circuit, reactive power is not measured in watts. Rather, reactive power is measured in *vars,* short for *volt-ampere reactive*. Note that the potential difference referred to in Formula 16.2 is the potential difference across the capacitor. It is true that in this case the potential difference across the capacitor is the same as the potential produced by the source. But this is an exception and is only true because the circuit resistance is so small. In general, reactive power must be calculated by considering the potential difference across the reactance.

EXAMPLE:
An ac capacitive circuit has a peak current of 2.4 A. The peak potential difference across the capacitor is 70 V, while the ESR of the capacitor and the resistance of the leads are low enough so that the circuit can be considered purely capacitive. What is the circuit power? ■

SOLUTION:
Since the circuit is purely capacitive, the circuit power is reactive power and can be calculated using Formula 16.2. Remember to first compute the rms values of the circuit current and the capacitor potential difference:

$$E_c = 0.707e_{C\ \text{peak}} = 49.49\ \text{V}_{\text{rms}}$$
$$I = 0.707i_{\text{peak}} = 1.7\ \text{A}_{\text{rms}}$$

The reactive power is:

$$P_r = IE_C = 84.13 \text{ vars}$$ ■

Recall that when the difference in phase is ignored in an RC circuit, the magnitude of the circuit current is related to the source potential difference by the formula

$$i = \frac{e}{\sqrt{R^2 + X_C^2}}$$

In a purely capacitive circuit $R = 0$, so this becomes

$$i = \frac{e}{X_C}$$

Multiplying both sides by 0.707 to change to rms values produces $I = \dfrac{E}{X_C}$. Now this expression can be solved for E: $E = IX_C$. Since $E = E_C = E_s$ in a purely capacitive circuit, the term IX_C can be substituted for E_c in Formula 16.2:

$$P_r = Ie_c = I(IX_C) \quad \text{or}$$
$$P_r = I^2X_C \qquad \text{FORMULA 16.3}$$

Notice that this useful formula resembles the formula for the power dissipated in a resistance, $P = I^2R$, except for the use of the capacitive reactance X_C instead of the resistance R.

EXAMPLE:
The frequency of the source in the previous example was 400 Hz. What is the capacitance of the capacitor? ■

SOLUTION:
At first glance it may look as though you do not have enough information to solve this problem, but in fact you do. You have already found that the rms circuit current is 1.7 A_{rms} and that the reactive power is 84.1 vars. This permits you to use Formula 16.3 to calculate the capacitive reactance

$$P_r = I^2X_C$$
$$84.13 = (1.7)^2X_C \quad \text{or} \quad X_C = 29.11\ \Omega$$

Combining this with the formula for capacitive reactance

$$X_C = \frac{1}{2\pi fC}$$
$$29.11 \times 2\pi f = \frac{1}{C}$$
$$C = 397.9\ \mu\text{F}$$ ■

Remember, the power in a purely capacitive circuit is P_r, reactive power, and is measured in vars.

$$P_r = IE_c = I^2X_C$$

Also, the reactive power is not dissipated but is returned to the source. Finally, in a purely capacitive circuit, the source potential and the potential difference across the capacitor are equal.

B.2 REACTIVE POWER, TRUE POWER, AND APPARENT POWER IN *RC* CIRCUITS

Although capacitor ESR and circuit resistance are low enough to be ignored in comparison with the capacitive reactance in some circuits, there are many in which a series or parallel resistor or other resistive network results in an actual dissipation of power in the circuit. In this type of circuit, a distinction must be made between the reactive power, that is, the power alternately stored in the capacitor and returned to the circuit, and the power that is dissipated as heat in the circuit resistances. The power dissipated by circuit resistance is called the *true* or *active* power. It is expressed in watts and can be calculated from the rms value of the circuit current and resistance:

$$P_{\text{true}} = P = I^2R$$

Alternately, since the rms value of the potential drop across the resistance $E_R = IR$, it is also possible to write

$$P_{\text{true}} = P = IE_R$$

where E_R is the potential drop across the resistor. Notice that careful attention has to be paid to the subscripts following E.

Consider an ac series circuit with both resistance and capacitance, as shown in Figure 16.5. Applying Kirchhoff's voltage law to this circuit, you can see that the source potential difference is equal to the sum of

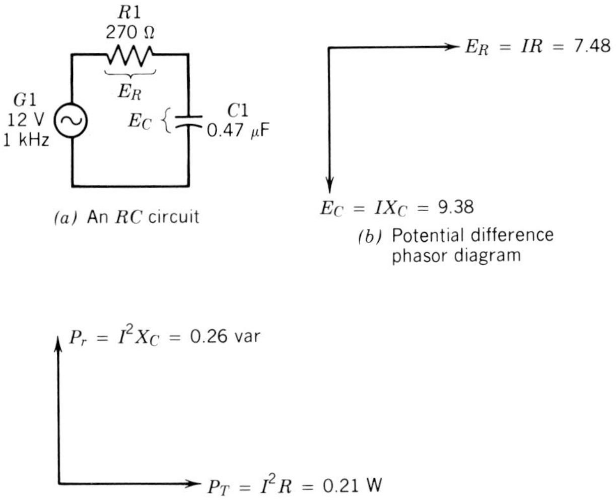

(a) An RC circuit

(b) Potential difference phasor diagram

(c) Circuit power

Figure 16.5 A circuit containing both capacitance and resistance exhibits both reactive and true power.

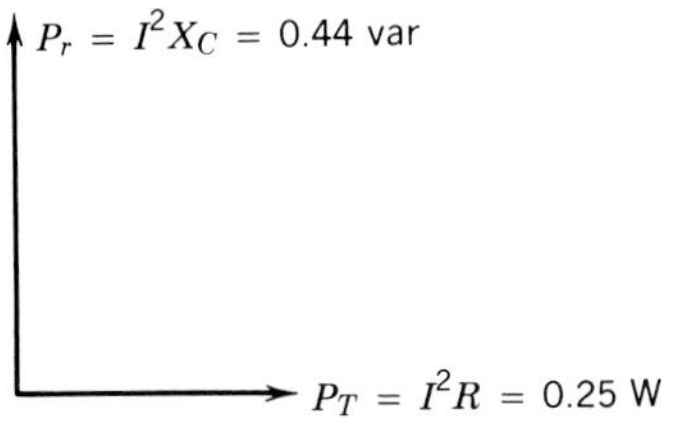

Figure 16.6 Phasor relationship of the true and reactive power in example.

the voltage drop across the resistor and the potential difference across the capacitor:

$$E_s = E_R + E_C$$

The phase relationship between these potential differences is shown in Figure 16.5*b*. Using the relationships

$$P_r = I^2X_C \quad \text{and} \quad P = I^2R$$

it is also possible to show the phase relationship between the reactive and true power in the circuit, as in Figure 16.5*c*.

EXAMPLE:
A 400 Hz source is connected to a series circuit consisting of a 10 μF capacitor and a 22 Ω resistor. The peak circuit current is found to be 150 mA. What is the true power, the reactive power? ■

SOLUTION:
Since the rms value of the current is used in the true and reactive power formulas, it is calculated first

$$I = 0.707I_{\text{peak}} = 0.707 \times 0.15 = 0.106 \text{ mA}$$

The true power, $P = I^2R = 0.25$ W. The reactive power is

$$P_r = I^2X_C = I^2 \times \frac{1}{2\pi fC} = 0.44 \text{ var}$$

The power values are shown in their phase relationship in Figure 16.6. ■

The sum of the reactive and true power in a circuit is referred to as the *apparent* power, P_a. (Sometimes P_s or S is used instead.) Apparent power is measured in volt-amperes or V-A to distinguish it from both the reactive and true power. Since the reactive and true power cannot be added directly because of the phase difference, they must be added by phasor methods. The simplest way to do this is to consider the two power values as complex rectangular components of the apparent power. In mathematical terms

$$P_a = P + jP_r \qquad \text{FORMULA 16.4}$$

Substituting $P = I^2R$ and $P_r = I^2X_C$ in this formula produces another handy relationship

$$P_a = I^2R + jI^2X_C \quad \text{or} \quad P_a = I^2(R + jX_C) \qquad \text{FORMULA 16.5}$$

The apparent power magnitude and the phase angle it makes with the reference phasor can then be obtained by converting $R + jX_C$ into polar form:

$$P_a = I^2 \sqrt{R^2 + X_C^2} \angle \tan^{-1} \frac{X_C}{R} \qquad \text{FORMULA 16.6}$$

Notice that the term $\sqrt{R^2 + X_C^2}$ is the impedance of the entire *RC* circuit, so the above formula can be summarized as

$$P_a = I^2Z \angle \tan^{-1} \frac{X_C}{R} \qquad \text{FORMULA 16.7}$$

Notice that unlike the reactive power, which is the power stored in the capacitor, and the real power, which is the power dissipated by the resistor, the apparent power is the power used by the entire circuit. It is also the power supplied by the source.

EXAMPLE:
A 10 kHz ac source providing a potential difference of 24 sin $2\pi ft$ volts is connected in a circuit as shown in Figure 16.7. What is the apparent circuit power? ■

Figure 16.7 Using Formula 16.3 to calculate apparent power.

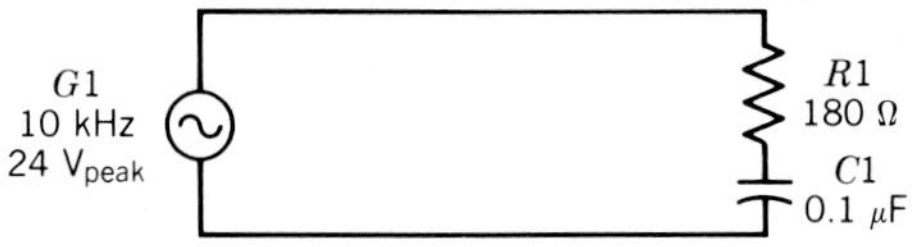

SOLUTION:
Formula 16.3 can be used to calculate the apparent power. Since the resistance is given in the diagram, it is necessary to calculate the capacitive reactance to obtain the impedance:

$$X_C = \frac{1}{2\pi f C} = 159.2\ \Omega$$
$$Z = \sqrt{R^2 + Z^2} = 240.3\ \Omega$$

The rms circuit current I can be found by dividing the rms value of the source potential difference by the circuit impedance

$$I = \frac{E}{Z} = \frac{0.707e_{\text{peak}}}{Z} = \frac{16.968}{240.3} = 70.6\ \text{mA}$$

So

$$P_a = (0.0706)^2 \times (240.3)\ \angle\tan^{-1}\frac{159.2}{180}$$
$$P_a = 1.2\ \angle 41.5^\circ\ \text{V-A}$$

■

Except for the fact that both impedance and branch currents provide difficulties, the apparent power in a parallel circuit can be calculated using the same logic. Consider the circuit of Figure 16.8. The same circuit component values have been chosen for comparison purposes. There are several ways of calculating the apparent power, but it is easiest to use the relationships

$$P_a = I_t^2 Z_t \quad \text{and} \quad I_t = \frac{E}{Z_t}$$

where I_t, E_t, and Z_t are the *total* rms current, potential difference, and impedance of the circuit. Substituting the expression for I_t produces

$$P_a = \frac{(E_t)^2}{(Z_t^2)} \times Z_t = \frac{E_t^2}{Z_t}$$

Now the total impedance of the parallel circuit Z_t is equal to the product of the impedances of the two branches divided by their sum:

$$Z_t = \frac{Z_{R1}\, Z_{C1}}{Z_{R1} + Z_{C1}}$$

A phasor diagram of the impedances of $R1$ and $C1$ based on the source potential difference as the reference phasor is shown in Figure 16.9. Using the methods of rectangular complex and polar coordinates,

Figure 16.8 Calculating apparent power in a parallel circuit.

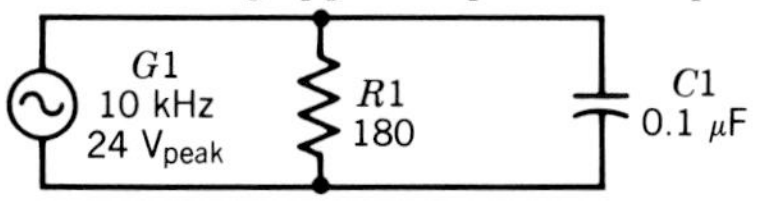

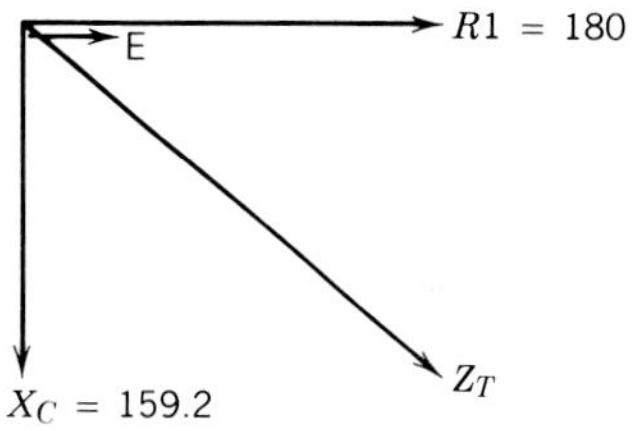

Figure 16.9 The impedances of Figure 16.8 shown in a phasor diagram referenced to the source potential difference.

$$Z_t = \frac{Z_{R1}\, Z_{C1}}{Z_{R1} + Z_{C1}}$$
$$= \frac{180\ \angle 0^\circ \times 159.2\ \angle -90^\circ}{180 - j159.2}$$
$$= \frac{28656\ \angle -90^\circ}{240.3\ \angle -41.5^\circ}$$
$$Z_t = 119.25\ \angle -48.5^\circ$$

Now it is possible to solve for P_a

$$P_a = \frac{E_t^2}{119.25\ \angle -48.5} = \frac{(0.707E_{\text{peak}}\ \angle 0)^2}{119.25\ \angle -48.5}$$

Notice that the reference phasor here is the potential difference rather than the current. This is because in a parallel circuit the same potential difference is applied across both branches, while the current in the capacitive branch leads the current in the resistive one. Solving for P_a,

$$P_a = 2.41\ \angle +48.5^\circ\ \text{V-A}$$

Remember that in a series RC circuit, the current is the reference phasor, and that the potential difference across a capacitive component lags the current by 90°, so that E_r is drawn on the reference axis and E_c is drawn on the $-j$ axis. In a parallel RC circuit, the source potential difference is the reference phasor, and the current in a purely capacitive branch is drawn on the positive j axis, while the current through a resistive branch is drawn along the reference phasor.

B.3 POWER AND REACTIVE POWER IN INDUCTIVE AC CIRCUITS

You may have noticed that the presentation of inductive ac circuits in Chapter 12 left out the consideration of power. This was done for three reasons. First, so that the presentation of power in inductive ac circuits could be compared to power in capacitive circuits.

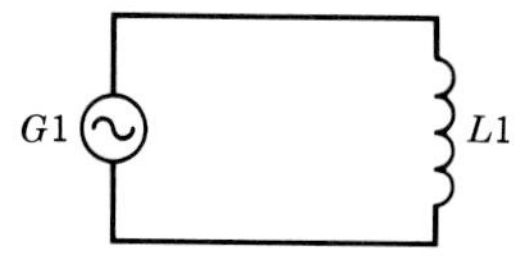

(a) AC applied to a pure inductance

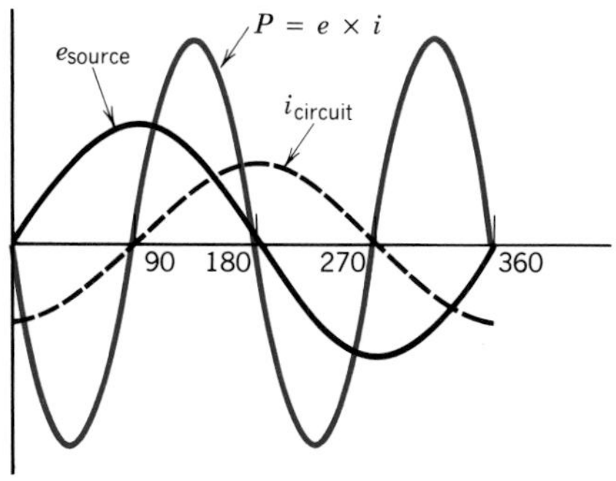

(b) Potential difference and current waveforms

Figure 16.10 AC power in inductive circuits.

Second, because it is easier to deal with ac power calculations after developing some experience with the rectangular complex and polar coordinate systems. Finally, most of the terms, formulas, and concepts used to describe power in *RC* circuits can also be applied to *RL* circuits.

Recall that when an ac potential difference is applied to a pure inductance, as shown in Figure 16.10*a*, a potential difference is developed across the inductance, but the circuit current lags the potential difference by 90°. The Kirchhoff's voltage law equation for this circuit, assuming that the total circuit resistance is small enough to be ignored in comparison with the inductive reactance, shows that the instantaneous potential difference developed by the source is equal to the potential difference across the inductance: $e_s = e_L$. The potential difference and current waveforms are shown in Figure 16.10*b*. During the period between 0° and 90° the instantaneous potential difference across the inductance is increasing from zero to its peak positive value. The instantaneous circuit current is derived from the collapse of the magnetic field that was built up around the inductor previous to the time chosen as 0° on the graph. As discussed in Chapter 12, the polarity of this current is opposite that of the increasing potential difference. During the portion of the graph between 0° and 90°, the instantaneous power $P = -i \times e$ is negative. That is, power stored in the magnetic field around the inductor is being returned to the circuit. In the next part of the cycle, from 90° to 180°, both the potential difference across the inductor and the circuit current are positive. The instantaneous power is also positive, which means that power is again being stored in the magnetic field. At the 180° point on the graph, the polarity of the potential difference is reversed, and between this point and the 270° mark, the power stored in the field is returned to the circuit. During the final quarter cycle, both the instantaneous potential difference and current are negative in polarity, so the instantaneous power P is positive, since $P = -e \times -i = +P$.

As in the case of the graph of the instantaneous power in a purely capacitive circuit, this graph is a sinusoid with twice the frequency of the potential difference. Also, since there is no circuit element that dissipates power as heat, the power returned to the circuit is the same as the power provided by the source. This is shown by the fact that the area above the axis under each positive section of the power curve is equal to the area between the axis and the negative sections of the power curve.

The power alternately stored in the magnetic field and returned to the circuit is called *reactive power* as in the case of the capacitive circuit. Its average value can be calculated using the same formula, with the exception that the rms value of the potential difference across the inductor E_L is substituted for the potential difference across the capacitor E_c:

$$\text{Reactive power} = P_r = IE_L \qquad \text{FORMULA 16.8}$$

Reactive power, whether capacitive or inductive, is measured in vars.

EXAMPLE:
The peak current in the circuit shown in Figure 16.11 is 1.2 A and the ac potential difference supplied by the source is 38.2 sin 377*t* volts. The resistance of the inductor and its leads is less than 10 percent of the inductive reactance, and so can be ignored. What is the circuit power? ■

SOLUTION:
Since the circuit resistance is so low that it can be ignored, the circuit can be considered a purely inductive circuit. The circuit power is reactive power and can be calculated with Formula 16.8. First, compute the rms values of the circuit current and the potential difference across the inductor:

$$I = 0.707 i_{peak} = 0.85 \text{ A}$$

$$E_L = 0.707 e_{peak} = 0.707 \times 38.2 = 27 \text{ V}$$

Figure 16.11 Computing power in a purely inductive circuit.

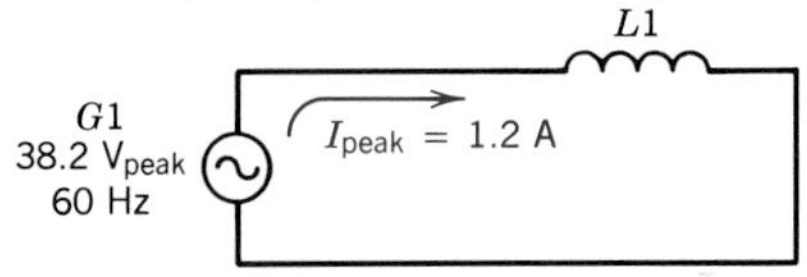

The reactive power is

$$P_r = IE_L = 2.95 \text{ vars}$$ ■

As in the case of a capacitive circuit, the magnitude of the circuit current in an inductive circuit is related to the source potential difference by the formula

$$i = \frac{e}{\sqrt{R^2 + X_L^2}}$$

In a purely inductive circuit $R = 0$, so this can be simplified to $i = \frac{e}{X_L}$, if the phase angle difference between the instantaneous current and potential difference is not taken into consideration. One way to eliminate the phase relationship is to use the rms values of the circuit current and the potential difference across the inductor, producing

$$0.707 i_{\text{peak}} = \frac{0.707 e_{\text{peak}}}{X_L} \quad \text{or} \quad I = \frac{E_L}{X_L}$$

FORMULA 16.9

Solving this expression for E gives

$$E_L = IX_L$$ FORMULA 16.10

Substituting this formula for E_L in Formula 16.8 gives

$$P_r = I^2 X_L$$ FORMULA 16.11

This formula is the equivalent of Formula 16.3, which was used for purely capacitive circuits.

EXAMPLE:
What was the inductance of the circuit in the previous example? ■

SOLUTION:
Having been given the source frequency as a part of the statement of the previous example, and calculated the power and circuit current, Formula 16.11 can be used to calculate the inductance, since $X_L = 2\pi fL$. Substituting,

$$P = I^2 X_L = I^2 \times 2\pi f L$$

$$22.95 = (0.85)^2 \times 377 \times \text{L}$$

$$L = 84.26 \text{ mH}$$ ■

B.4 REACTIVE POWER, TRUE POWER, AND APPARENT POWER IN *RL* CIRCUITS

As in the case of a series *RC* circuit, the presence of a resistance in a series *RL* circuit means that a certain amount of the power supplied by the source is dissipated as heat in the resistance. Using rms values, the power dissipated in the resistance, or true power, is $P = I^2R$. Since the resistance, the potential drop across the resistance, and the current are related by the expression $R = \frac{E_r}{I}$, it is also possible to write

$$P = \frac{I^2 E_r}{I} = IE_r$$

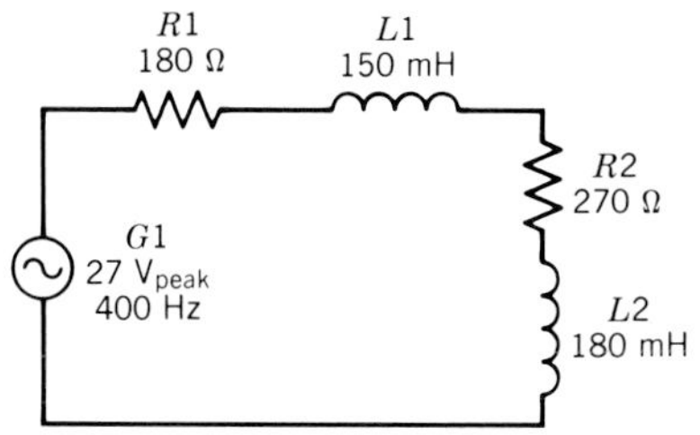

Figure 16.12 A series *LR* circuit with multiple components.

In the series *RL* circuit shown in Figure 16.12, the effective circuit current I can be calculated by $I = \frac{E_s}{Z}$. Since there are two inductances and two resistances involved, it is necessary to add them. Using complex rectangular coordinates,

$$R1 = 180 + j0$$

$$R2 = 270 + j0$$

$$X_{L1} = 0 + j377$$

$$X_{L2} = 0 + j452.4$$

$$Z = 450 + j829.4$$

Converting this into polar form provides a value for the magnitude of the circuit impedance as well as the impedance phase angle.

$$Z = 943.6 \angle 61.5^\circ$$

The magnitude of the circuit current, then, is

$$I = \frac{0.707 e_{\text{peak}}}{Z} = 0.0202$$

and the true power and reactive power are

$$P = I^2 R = 0.184 \text{ W}$$

$$P_r = I^2 X_L = 0.338 \text{ var}$$

Since the circuit current is considered the reference in a series circuit, the phase relationship of the current, potential difference, and true and reactive power is as shown in Figure 16.13.

The apparent power in the circuit is the phasor sum of the true and the reactive power. Or, in other

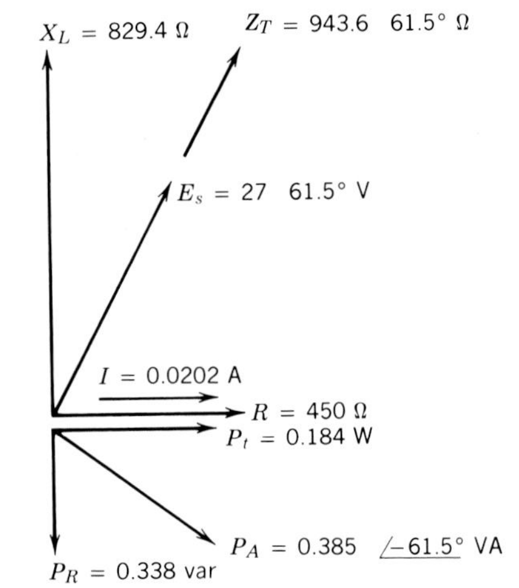

Figure 16.13 The phase relationships of the current, potential difference, impedance, and power in the circuit of Figure 16.12.

words, the true and reactive power are components of the apparent power:

$$P_a = P - jP_r$$

substituting the above values:

$$P_a = 0.184 - j0.338$$

The magnitude and phase angle of the apparent power can therefore be obtained by converting into polar form:

$$P_a = 0.184 - j0.338 = 0.385 \angle -61.5^\circ$$

In a parallel inductive circuit the branch currents and phase angles differ, so it is usually easier to calculate the apparent power of the entire circuit and then to resolve this into true and reactive components. Since the source potential difference is used as the reference phasor in a parallel circuit, the phasor diagram will resemble that shown in Figure 16.14*b*. The apparent power in the circuit of Figure 16.14*a*, for example, could be calculated by obtaining the phasor sum of the apparent power of each branch. Unless the apparent power in each branch is specifically required, however, this method usually requires more arithmetic work than calculating the total impedance of the circuit and using

Figure 16.14 A parallel *RL* circuit and its phasor diagram.

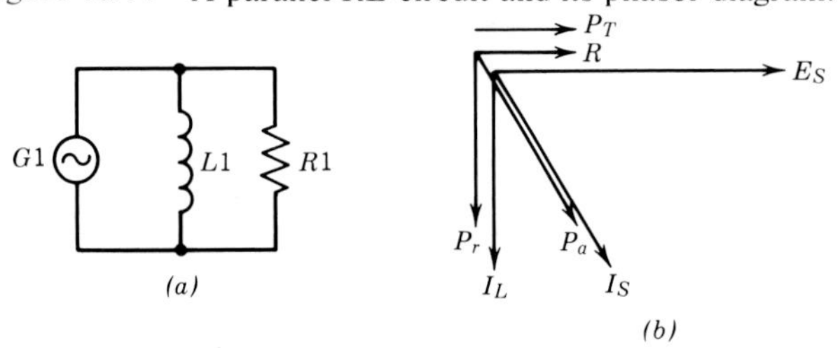

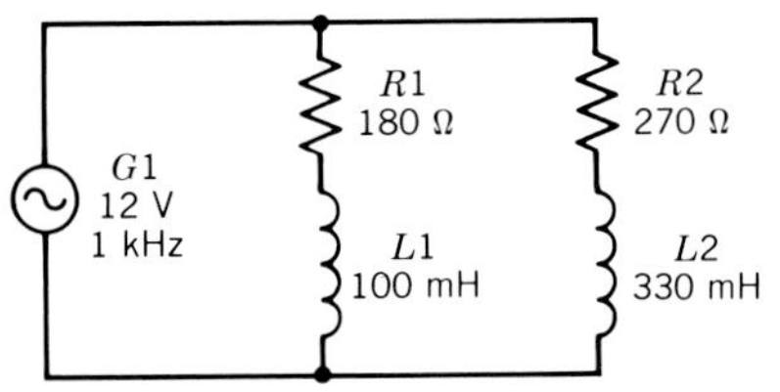

Figure 16.15 A series–parallel *RL* circuit for power calculations.

the relationship

$$P_a = \frac{E_s^2}{Z_t}$$

EXAMPLE:
Calculate the real, reactive, and apparent power in the circuit of Figure 16.15. ■

SOLUTION:
Since the series of calculations necessary to solve this problem is rather lengthy, it is a good idea to outline the steps that will be followed before beginning. First, the impedance of each branch in the parallel circuit will be calculated. Then, the total impedance of the circuit can be found and the apparent power in the circuit can be calculated using

$$P_a = \frac{E_s^2}{Z}$$

The true and reactive components of the apparent power can then be obtained.

The impedance of the *R*1*L*1 branch, in polar coordinates, is

$$Z_{R1L1} = 180 + j628.32 \quad \text{or} \quad 653.6 \angle 74^\circ$$

while that of the *R*2*L*2 branch is

$$Z_{R2L2} = 270 + j2073.45 \quad \text{or} \quad 2091 \angle 82.6^\circ$$

Using the product-over-the-sum formula,

$$Z_{\text{total}} = \frac{Z_{R1L1} Z_{R2L2}}{Z_{R1L1} + Z_{R2L2}}$$

$$= \frac{653.6 \angle +74^\circ \times 2091 \angle +82.6^\circ}{(180 + j628.32) + (270 + j2073.45)}$$

$$= \frac{653.6 \angle +74^\circ \times 2091 \angle +82.6^\circ}{450 + j2701.77}$$

Converting the denominator to polar coordinates produces

$$\frac{653.6 \angle +74^\circ \times 2091 \angle +82.6^\circ}{2738.99 \angle +80.5^\circ}$$

Performing the multiplication and division indicated gives

$$Z_T = 498.97 \angle +76.1°$$

Therefore, the apparent power is

$$P_a = \frac{E_s^2}{Z} = \frac{(12)^2}{498.97 \angle +76.1°} = 0.29 \angle -76.1° \text{ V-A}$$

Since the apparent power is composed of true and reactive power components, these can be obtained by converting the apparent power into its complex rectangular form:

$$0.29 \angle -76.1° = 0.0697 - j0.282$$

In other words,

$$P = 0.0697 \text{ W} \quad \text{and} \quad P_r = -0.282 \text{ var}$$ ■

B.5 POWER FACTOR

Figure 16.16 shows four diagrams illustrating the phase relationship between the true, reactive, and apparent power in series and parallel *RC* circuits and series and parallel *RL* circuits. In a somewhat different form, these diagrams are referred to as *power triangle* diagrams, and diagrams showing the reactive components of an impedance are sometimes referred to as *impedance triangle* diagrams. Notice that the angle between the reference phasor and the apparent power is labeled θ in each case. From the diagrams you can see that the true power in each case is

$$P = P_a \cos \theta \qquad \text{FORMULA 16.12}$$

The reactive power is

$$P_r = P_a \sin \theta \qquad \text{FORMULA 16.13}$$

If the product of the rms values of the total circuit current and the source potential difference are substituted for P_a in the first of these two formulas, a commonly used relationship is obtained:

$$P = IE \cos \theta \qquad \text{FORMULA 16.14}$$

Notice that θ is not only the angle between the reference phasor and the graphical representation of the apparent power, it is also the phase angle between the circuit current and the source potential difference. A bit of thought will show why this is true. If the representation of the apparent power makes an angle of θ with the reference phasor, then the product $I \times E$ does so as well. Since the current is the reference quantity in a series circuit, that is, the current is expressed in polar form as $I \angle 0°$, the potential difference

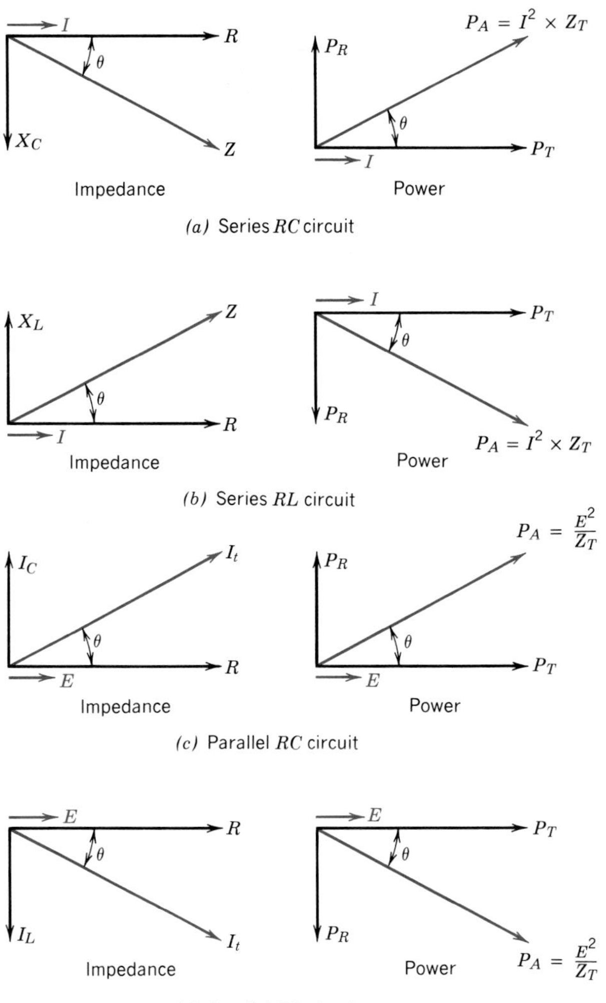

Figure 16.16 Impedance and power triangle phasor diagrams.

must have the form $E \angle \theta°$ for the product of I and E, the apparent power, to form an angle of θ with the reference phasor. Similarly, in a parallel *RC* or *RL* circuit, where the source potential difference is the reference phasor, that is, the source potential difference is expressed in polar form as $E \angle 0°$, the circuit current must have the form $I \angle \theta°$ for the product of I and E to form an angle of θ with the reference phasor.

If Formula 16.12 is solved for cos θ, the resulting equation is one that is widely used in the field of industrial technology:

$$\cos \theta = \frac{P}{P_a}$$

The quantity cos θ is called, the *power factor* of the circuit and serves as a basic measure of the amount of power that is actually doing some sort of useful work in a circuit. For example, when a large number of

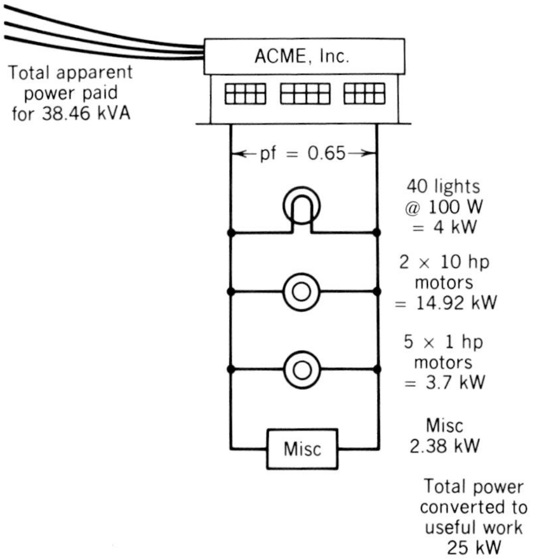

Figure 16.17 A practical demonstration of the importance of power factor in industrial applications.

motors are connected to the power mains in a factory, the resulting circuit has a large inductive component due to the motor coils. This means that the phase shift between the mains potential difference and the resulting current, the phase angle θ, can become large. Cos θ then is significantly less than 1. Since it is the true power and not the apparent power that is being turned into mechanical energy by the motors, only a fraction of the power input to the factory is actually being used to drive machinery. On the other hand, the factory must pay the power company for the apparent power measured by the power meters at the point of connection to the power lines. Therefore, a phase angle difference between the source potential and the current will result in greater operating expense. Just how a power factor of anything but $\cos\theta = 1$ can result in additional operating expense can be shown in the practical example of Figure 16.17. Here it is shown that a certain amount of true power, 25 kW, must be delivered to the machinery and lighting in a small factory. This represents the power used by 40 lights of 100 W each, two 10-hp motors, five 1-hp motors, and several other electrically operated devices. If the power factor of the resulting system is 0.65, corresponding to a phase angle θ of $0.65 = \cos^{-1}\theta = 49.5°$, then the apparent power input into the machinery and other equipment is

$$P_a = \frac{P}{\cos\theta} = \frac{25 \times 10^3}{0.65} = 38{,}461.5 \text{ V-A}$$

Although serious enough, this is not the whole story. If the distribution system is a 440-V ac service, as is common in industrial applications, the line current for a power factor of 0.65, or 65 percent, as it is usually stated, is

$$I = \frac{P_a}{E} = 87.4 \text{ A}$$

instead of the value it would be at a power factor of 1, or 100 percent,

$$I = \frac{25 \times 10^3}{440} = 56.8 \text{ A}$$

This much higher current in the 65 percent power factor system means considerably greater losses due to power dissipation in distribution lines, not to mention the huge expense because the larger current would require heavier cables and more massive circuit breakers and switches. Moreover, the fact that one of its customers has a low power factor reduces the power factor of the entire distribution system. Utility companies are quick to return the cost of this to the guilty customer by charging higher rates to those with a power factor less than a certain fixed value. Normally, these higher rates are applied if the power factor, $\cos\theta$, is less than 0.85.

Fortunately, it is possible to "correct" the power factor of a circuit, that is, to reduce the phase angle between the source potential difference and the circuit current.

EXAMPLE:

Figure 16.18 represents the 120-V ac distribution system of a student's room. If all the devices shown are operating, what is the power factor of the circuit? ■

SOLUTION:

The total impedance of the circuit is obtained by first combining the purely resistive branches and then in-

Figure 16.18 Power distribution system in a student's room.

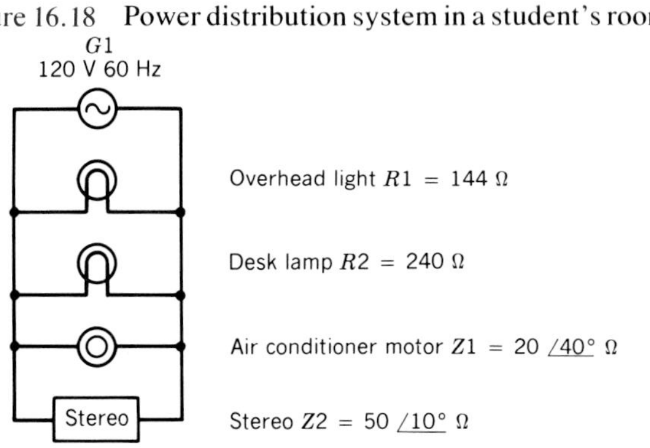

cluding the *RL* branches individually:

$$R_{R1R2} = \frac{144 \times 249}{144 + 240} = 90$$

$$Z_{R1R2Z1} = \frac{Z \times R_{R1R2}}{Z_1 + R_{R1R2}}$$

$$= \frac{20 \angle +40^\circ \times 90 \angle 0^\circ}{(15.32 + j12.9) + (90 \times j0)}$$

$$= \frac{1800 \angle +40^\circ}{105.32 + j12.9} = \frac{1800 \angle +40^\circ}{106.11 \angle 6.98^\circ}$$

$$= 16.96 \angle +33.02^\circ$$

$$Z_{R1R2Z1Z2} = \frac{16.96 \angle +33.02^\circ \times 50 \angle +10^\circ}{(14.22 + j9.24) + 49.24 + j8.68)}$$

$$= \frac{848 \angle +43.02^\circ}{63.46 + j17.92}$$

$$= \frac{848 \angle +43.02^\circ}{65.94 \angle +15.77^\circ} = 12.86 \angle +27.25^\circ\ \Omega$$

The phase angle between the current and source potential difference is +27.25°, and the power factor, cos θ is 0.889. ■

C. EXAMPLES AND COMPUTATIONS

C.1 PRACTICE IN AC CIRCUIT ANALYSIS

With the exception of the important material on circuits that include resistance, capacitance, and inductance, or *RCL* circuits, covered in the next chapter, you have by now learned most of the theoretical material necessary to analyze the behavior of almost any circuit that is made up of components in which electrical currents obey Ohm's law. This excludes circuits containing semiconductor components such as diodes and transistors, a number of nonlinear devices such as special-purpose resistors, and any components in which conduction takes place through a liquid, a gas, or in a vacuum, such as a radio tube.

There are two principal reasons for analyzing the behavior of ac circuits and networks. The first of these is to understand the function of these circuits and networks in electronic equipment. The second reason, related to the first, is to predict the theoretical values of certain electrical quantities such as potential difference, phase, and impedance, so that they can be compared to measured values in the process of troubleshooting.

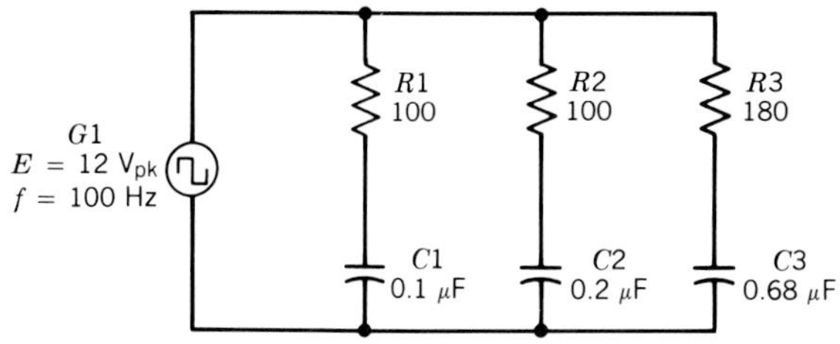

Figure 16.19 A problem that illustrates the advantage of using a computer program for *RL* and *RC* circuit calculations.

Unfortunately, the process of analyzing a parallel circuit with several branches or a series circuit with several reactances and resistances quickly becomes a tedious exercise in arithmetic, even when a calculator is used. For example, figuring out the rms value of the potential difference across *R*2 in Figure 16.19 is within the range of your present abilities, but it would be a long process. The potential difference for several of the sinusoidal components of the square wave and their phase angles would have to be calculated and then added together using phasor methods. If this circuit was suspected of malfunctioning it might be quicker to replace some or all of the components than to compute the theoretical value of the circuit current or potential differences for comparison with actual measurements.

In order to help make ac circuit analysis a practical tool, Program 16.1 has been included. Although it is longer than the other programs in this book, it can be made to fit into a very limited computer memory by leaving out all REM statements and by shortening other printed directions and comments. The program is crudely written, and could be simplified and shortened considerably if your BASIC uses ELSE and AND statements in IF . . . THEN . . . commands.

The program operates by calculating the rms current through each branch of a parallel circuit to provide potential difference or power computations for the branch. Note that a series circuit is treated as a parallel circuit with only one branch. Total circuit impedance, and true, reactive, and apparent power are calculated by summing the real and reactive components of each branch current to provide the value and phase angle of the circuit current. Since the source potential difference is known, the impedance and power can be calculated. Sufficient instructions have been included in the program to permit you to run it without reference to this book. Enter the program, save it on tape or disk, and solve the following sample problems to check your entry.

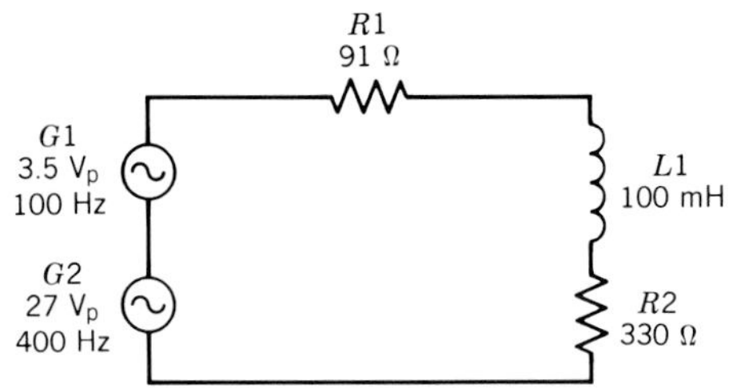

Figure 16.20 Circuit for the example of computer solution of multiple source problems.

EXAMPLE:
Calculate the power dissipated by the resistances in the circuit shown in Figure 16.20. ■

SOLUTION:
The circuit shown in this diagram is a fairly simple series circuit, except for the fact that there are two sources involved. Since the problem involves the dissipation of power in the resistances, it should be clear that each source can be considered separately and that the true power dissipated by the resistors is the sum of the power dissipated due to each source acting alone. Using Program 16.1,

$$P_T \text{ (at 100 Hz)} = 0.014 \text{ W}$$
$$P_T \text{ (at 400 Hz)} = 0.638 \text{ W}$$
$$P_T = 0.652 \text{ W}$$ ■

EXAMPLE:
Calculate the true, reactive, and apparent power in each branch in Figure 16.21. ■

SOLUTION:
A problem of this sort is tedious and is therefore ideally suited to solution by computer program. For the $L1R1$ branch $P_T = 0.08$ W, $P_r = -0.503$ var, and $P_a = 0.509 \angle -81°$ V-A. For the $L2R2$ branch, $P_T = 0.264$ W, $P_r = -0.565$ var, and $P_a = 0.623 \angle -65°$ V-A. For the $LR3$ branch, $P_T = 0.51$ W, $P_r = -0.59$ var, and $P_a = 0.78 \angle -49.3°$ V-A. The values for the $R4$ branch are $P_T = 3.24$ W, $P_r = 0$, $P_a = 3.24 \angle 0°$ V-A. Notice that the signs of the apparent power phase angles have to be checked by consulting Figure 16.16. ■

Figure 16.21 Complex parallel RL circuit for computer solution.

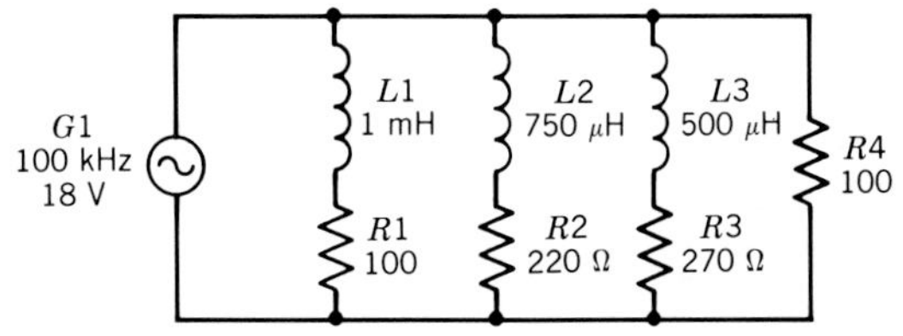

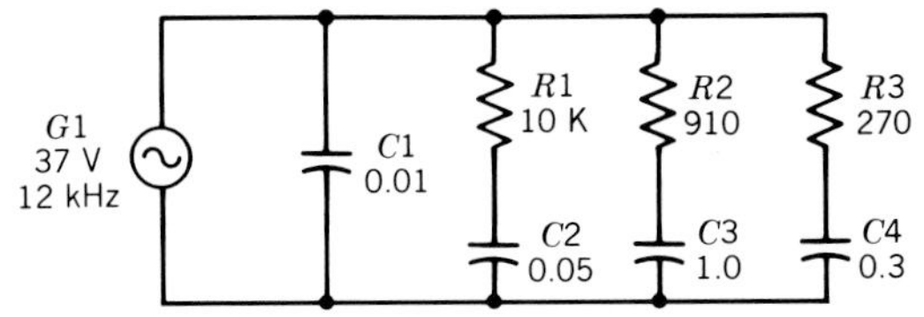

Figure 16.22 Using Program 16.1 to aid in the checking of component maximum characteristics.

EXAMPLE:
In cases where frequent problems of component failure occur, it is wise to check that the circuit conditions do not exceed recommended component operating characteristics and that the equipment designers have chosen component values that include an adequate safety margin. Use Program 16.1 to check the capacitor working voltage and resistor dissipation values in Figure 16.22. ■

SOLUTION:
Using Program 16.1, you can calculate that the peak potential difference across $C4$ will be $1.414 \times 31.58 = 44.65$ V, considerably above its operating potential difference. The true power dissipated in the $R1C2$ branch is 0.128 W, which is well below the 1-W rating of $R1$. On the other hand, the 1.47 W dissipated in the $R2C3$ branch and the 1.38 W dissipated in the $R3C4$ branch are above the 1-W resistor rating. ■

Using Program 16.1 should not be considered a substitute for the ability to analyze a circuit or to solve problems using pencil and paper or a calculator. On the other hand, the following troubleshooting exercises can be solved more economically using computer methods. Remember to consult Figure 16.16 to adjust the signs of the phase angles.

1. A series RL circuit composed of $R1$, 180 Ω, $R2$, 100 Ω, and $L1$, 0.01 H, is connected across a 12-V peak, 10 kHz source. What is the power factor of the circuit? Draw a phasor diagram of the circuit current and source potential difference.

2. Draw a graph of the apparent power in the circuit of Problem 1 as the source frequency varies from 5 kHz to 20 kHz.

3. Study the effect on the magnitude of the apparent power of the circuit in Problem 1 when the value of $L1$ is varied from 0.001 to 0.1 H. Use Program 16.1 and draw a graph of your results. Is the change in apparent power linear?

PROGRAM 16.1

```
10 PRINT "PROGRAM TO AID IN"
20 PRINT "SOLUTION OF RL AND"
30 PRINT "RC NETWORKS. COPY-"
40 PRINT "RIGHT S.L. ROSEN,"
50 PRINT "1985.": PRINT
60 PRINT "DO YOU NEED"
70 INPUT "AN EXPLANATION (Y OR
     N)"; A$
80 IF A$ = "N" GOTO 380
90 PRINT "GIVEN THE SOURCE"
100 PRINT "POTENTIAL DIFFER-"
110 PRINT "ENCE AND COMPONENT"
120 PRINT "VALUES, THIS PROGRAM"
130 PRINT "PRINTS REACTANCE, IM-"
140 PRINT "PEDANCE, CURRENT, VOLT-"
150 PRINT "AGE, AND POWER VALUES"
160 PRINT "FOR SERIES AND PARA-"
170 PRINT "LLEL RC AND RL CIRCUITS."
180 INPUT "TYPE Y TO GO ON"; A$
190 IF A$ = "Y" THEN GOTO 210
200 GOTO 90
210 PRINT: PRINT "IF THE CIRCUIT CON-"
220 PRINT "SISTS OF SEVERAL"
230 PRINT "BRANCHES, EACH OF"
240 PRINT "WHICH IS CONNECTED"
250 PRINT "ACROSS THE SOURCE,"
260 PRINT "IT IS A PARALLEL"
270 PRINT "CIRCUIT. IF THERE"
280 PRINT "IS ONLY ONE CURRENT"
290 PRINT "PATH, IT IS A SERIES"
300 PRINT "CIRCUIT. FOR SERIES-"
310 PRINT "PARALLEL CIRCUITS,"
320 PRINT "USE EQUIVALENTS TO"
330 PRINT "CHANGE THEM TO SERIES"
340 PRINT "OR PARALLEL."
350 INPUT "TYPE Y TO GO ON"; A$
360 IF A$ = "Y" THEN 380
370 GOTO 210
380 PRINT: PRINT "IS THE CIRCUIT SERIES
     (S)"
390 INPUT "OR PARALLEL (P)"; T$
400 IF T$ = "S" THEN GOTO 430
410 IF T$ = "P" THEN GOTO 430
420 GOTO 210
430 PRINT "IF THE CIRCUIT CONSISTS"
440 PRINT "OF RESISTORS AND CAPA-"
450 PRINT "CITORS, TYPE C. IF IT"
460 PRINT "CONSISTS OF INDUCTORS"
470 INPUT "AND RESISTORS, TYPE I"; B$
480 IF B$ = "C" GOTO 510
490 IF B$ = "I" GOTO 510
500 GOTO 430
```

PROGRAM 16.1 continued

```
510 IF T$ = "S" THEN B = 1: GOTO 600
520 REM SOME COMPUTERS WILL NOT
     ALLOW
530 REM LONGER VARIABLES, AND SO
540 REM CIRCUITS WITH MORE THAN
550 REM TWENTY COMPONENTS CAN NOT
560 REM BE ENTERED
570 PRINT "THE NUMBER OF BRANCHES"
580 PRINT "IN PARALLEL WITH THE"
590 INPUT "SOURCE IS"; B
600 IF B$ = "C" THEN B$ = "CAPACITOR"
610 IF B$ = "I" THEN B$ = "INDUCTOR"
620 PRINT "IS THE SOURCE VALUE"
630 PRINT "GIVEN IN PEAK (P) OR"
640 INPUT "RMS (R)"; R$
650 PRINT "ENTER THE SOURCE"
660 PRINT "POTENTIAL DIFFERENCE"
670 INPUT "E (SOURCE) IN VOLTS ";ES
680 IF R$ = "P" THEN ES = .707 *ES
690 PRINT "WHAT IS THE FREQUENCY"
700 PRINT "OF THE SOURCE IN"
710 INPUT "HERTZ"; F
720 FOR N = 1 TO B :REM ONE BRANCH
730 PRINT "HOW MANY RESISTORS"
740 PRINT "ARE IN SERIES"
750 IF T$ = "S" GOTO 770
760 PRINT "IN BRANCH NO. "; N
770 INPUT D
780 IF D = 0 GOTO 850
790 FOR J = 1 TO D
800 PRINT "THE VALUE OF R"; J ;
810 INPUT "IN OHMS IS ";RJ
820 REM CALCULATE BRANCH
     RESISTANCE
830 D(N) = D(N) + RJ
840 NEXT J
850 REM CALCULATE AND ADD BRANCH
860 REM REACTANCES
870 PRINT "HOW MANY ";B$;"S"
880 PRINT "ARE THERE"
890 IF T$ = "S" THEN GOTO 910
900 PRINT "IN BRANCH NO. ";N
910 INPUT G
920 IF G = 0 THEN GOTO 1010
930 FOR K = 1 TO G
940 PRINT "THE VALUE OF"
950 IF B$ = "INDUCTOR" THEN B2$ = "L"
960 IF B2$ = "L" THEN B3$ = "IN
     HENRIES"
970 IF B2$ = "L" THEN GOTO 1000
980 IF B$ = "CAPACITOR" THEN B2$ =
     "C"
```

PROGRAM 16.1 continued

```
990   IF B2$ = "C" THEN B3$ = "IN
        MICROFARADS"
1000  PRINT B2$ K B3$ " IS"
1010  PI = 3.14159
1020  IF G = 0 THEN GOTO 1070
1030  INPUT X(K): IF B2$ = "C" GOTO 1050
1040  G(N) = G(N) + 2*PI*F*X(K): GOTO 1060
1050  G(N) = G(N) + 1/(2*PI*F*X(K)*10^-6)
1060  NEXT K
1070  Z(N) = SQR((D(N))^2 + (G(N))^2)
1080  IF B2$ = "L" THEN T = -1
1090  IF B2$ = "C" THEN T = 1
1100  IF G = 0 THEN HP (N) = 0: GOTO 1120
1110  HP (N) = ATN(T*G(N)/D(N))
1120  PH(N) = 180*HP(N)/PI
1130  I(N) = ES/Z (N)
1140  XI (N) = I (N)*SIN(HP(N))
1150  IF G = 0 THEN RI (N) = I (N): GOTO
        1170
1160  RI (N) = I (N)*COS (HP(N))
1170  PRINT "DO YOU NEED THE
        POTENTIAL"
1180  PRINT "DIFFERENCE (RMS) ACROSS"
1190  PRINT "ANY COMPONENT";
1200  IF T$ = "S" GOTO 1220
1210  PRINT "IN THIS BRANCH"
1220  INPUT "(Y OR N)"; A5$
1230  IF A5$ = "Y" GOTO 1260
1240  IF A5$ = "N" THEN GOTO 1640
1250  GOTO 1170
1260  PRINT "IS THE COMPONENT A"
1270  INPUT "RESISTOR Y OR N"; A5$
1280  IF A5$ = "Y" GOTO 1310
1290  IF A5$ = "N" GOTO 1400
1300  GOTO 1260
1310  PRINT " TYPE THE VALUE OF"
1320  PRINT "THE RESISTOR ";
1330  INPUT "IN OHMS"; V
1340  PRINT "E "; V " OHM = " I (N) *V
1350  PRINT "DO YOU NEED ANOTHER"
1360  PRINT "POTENTIAL DIFFERENCE"
1370  PRINT "ACROSS A RESISTOR?"
1380  INPUT "Y OR N"; A5$
1390  IF A5$ = "Y" GOTO 1310
1400  PRINT "DO YOU NEED THE RMS"
1410  PRINT "POTENTIAL DIFFERENCE"
1420  PRINT "ACROSS A "; B$
1430  INPUT "Y OR N"; A5$
1440  IF A5$ = "N" GOTO 1640
1450  IF B2$ = "L" GOTO 1550
1460  PRINT "TYPE THE VALUE OF"
1470  PRINT "THE "; B$; " IN UF"
1480  INPUT V
1490  PRINT "E = " I (N) *
        1/(2*PI*F*(V*10^-6))
1500  PRINT "DO YOU NEED ANOTHER?"
1510  INPUT "Y OR N"; A5$
1520  IF A5$ = "N" GOTO 1640
1530  IF A5$ = "Y" GOTO 1460
1540  GOTO 1500
1550  PRINT "TYPE THE VALUE OF "
1560  PRINT "THE "; B$ " IN HENRIES"
1570  INPUT V
1580  PRINT "E = "; I (N) *2*PI*F*V
1590  PRINT "DO YOU NEED ANOTHER?"
1600  INPUT "Y OR N"; A5$
1610  IF A5$ = "N" GOTO 1640
1620  IF A5$ = "Y" GOTO 1550
1630  GOTO 1590
1640  IF T$ = "S" THEN GOTO 1810
1650  PRINT "DO YOU NEED POWER"
1660  PRINT "CALCULATIONS ";
1670  IF T$ = "S" THEN GOTO 1690
1680  PRINT "THIS BRANCH ";
1690  INPUT "(Y OR N)"; A5$
1700  IF A5$ = "Y" THEN GOTO 1720
1710  IF A5$ = "N" THEN GOTO 1810
1720  PRINT "THE TRUE BRANCH POWER"
1730  PRINT "IS "; (I(N))^2*D(N); " W."
1740  PRINT "THE BRANCH REACTIVE
        POWER"
1750  PRINT "IS "; (I(N))^2*G(N); " VAR."
1760  PRINT "THE MAGNITUDE OF THE"
1770  PRINT "APPARENT POWER IN"
1780  PRINT "BRANCH NO. "; N;
1790  PRINT " IS "; (I(N))^2*Z (N)
1800  PRINT "AT A PHASE ANGLE OF ";
        PH(N)
1810  NEXT N
1820  REM ADD REAL AND REACTIVE
        CURRENTS FOR ALL BRANCHES
1830  FOR J = 1 TO N
1840  XI = XI + XI (J): RI = RI + RI (J)
1850  NEXT J
1860  IF T$ = "P" THEN GOTO 1900
1870  IF B2$ = "C" THEN GOTO 1890
1880  J$ = "-":GOTO 1930
1890  J$ = "+":GOTO 1930
1900  IF B2$ = "C" THEN GOTO 1920
1910  J$ = "-":GOTO 1930
1920  J$ = "+"
1930  PF = (180/PI)*ATN(T*XI/RI)
1940  PT = ES*SQR((RI)^2 + (XI)^2)
1950  ZT = ES^2/PT
1960  PRINT "CIRCUIT IMPEDANCE = ";
1970  PRINT ZT " OHMS"
```

PROGRAM 16.1 continued

```
1980 PRINT "CIRCUIT APPARENT ";
1990 PRINT "POWER = "; PT ; " V-A."
2000 PRINT "PHASE ANGLE = ";
2010 PRINT J$ PF ; " DEGREES"
2020 PRINT "CIRCUIT REACTIVE ";
2030 PRINT "POWER IS ";
        PT*SIN(ATN(T*XI/RI)) ; " VAR."
2040 PRINT "CIRCUIT TRUE POWER ";
2050 PRINT "IS "; PT*COS(ATN(T*XI/RI)) ;
        " WATT"
2060 PRINT "POWER FACTOR = ";
2070 PRINT 100*COS(ATN(T*XI/RI)) " PER
        CENT"
2080 END
```

4. Repeat Problems 1, 2, and 3, substituting a 0.1 μF capacitor for the 0.01 H inductor.

5. Three inductive loads are connected in series across a 120-V, 60 Hz, ac power line: $L1$ = 0.01 H with an internal resistance of 10 Ω, $L2$ = 2 H with an internal resistance of 150 Ω, and $L3$ = 0.68 with an internal resistance of 120 Ω. Compute true, reactive, and apparent power of the circuit.

6. If the three inductors of Problem 5 are connected in parallel across the 120-V, 60 Hz ac line, what will be the true, reactive, and apparent power in each branch?

7. What is the power factor of each branch in Problem 6?

8. Graph the potential difference across $C1$ in Figure 16.23 as the source frequency varies from 500 Hz to 5 kHz.

9. Figure 16.24 represents the series connection smoothing inductors $L1$ and $L2$ with their internal resistances of $R1$ and $R2$, respectively, and a load $R3$. Observe the effect of this filter by calculating the amount of 60 Hz power dissipated by $R3$ with and without the filter. What is the difference in the amount of 60 Hz power dissipated by $R3$ with the filter in place?

10. What would be the reduction in the amount of 60 Hz power if only the filter composed of $L2$ and its resistance $R2$ was used?

Figure 16.23 Graphing the output of a filter circuit.

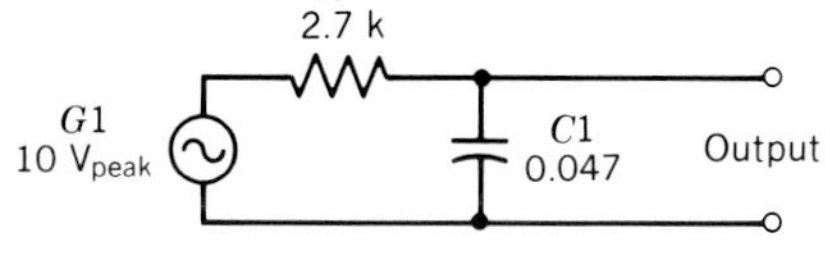

Figure 16.24 A dc power supply with 60 Hz noise and a noise reduction filter composed of two coils.

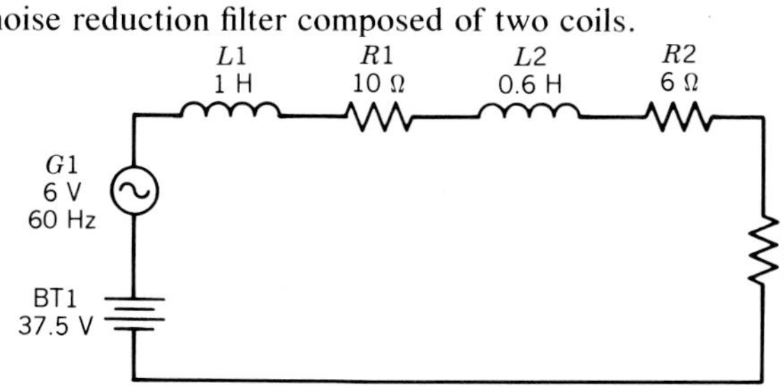

C.2 DECIBELS

Two common applications of networks containing resistors and reactive components are filtering, where only certain components of a complex waveform are passed on to the load or the next stage of an electronic unit, and impedance matching, where maximum power transfer between two stages or circuits is ensured by matching the impedance of the output of one stage to the input impedance of the following stage or circuit. These functions are illustrated in Figures 16.25*a* and 16.25*b*. In order to judge the effectiveness of a filter or impedance-matching network, it is convenient to compare power, voltage, or current conditions with and without the network. The normal way of making comparisons of this sort in electronics is to use measurement units based on Briggsian, or base 10 logarithms. These units are called decibels, abbreviated dB.

The use of decibels arose from the fact that the human ear is not a linear device. At low sound power levels the ear can distinguish relatively small changes in the power level of a sound, but when the power is greater, it requires a much greater change in power to be detected by the ear. The minimum change in power level that can be detected by the ear is the decibel. It is defined in terms of a power ratio by the formula

$$\text{dB} = 10 \log_{10} \frac{P1}{P2} \qquad \text{FORMULA 16.15}$$

where P_1 and P_2 are two power levels. The denominator is the reference value, so if the power in a load increases from a reference level of 1 W to 2 W, the

Figure 16.25 Networks composed of resistors and reactances are frequently used as filters or for impedance matching.

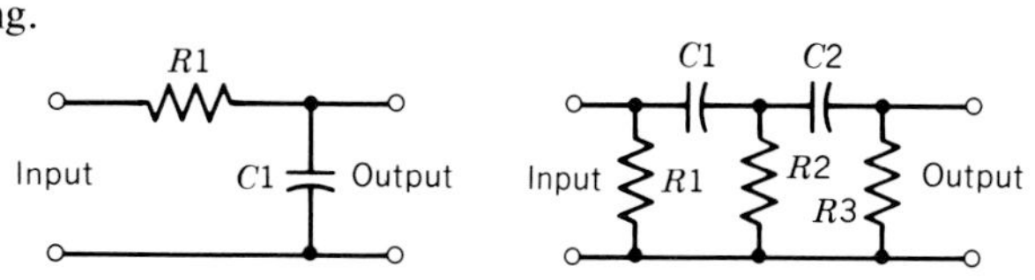

(*a*) An *RC* network used to remove high frequency signals from output.

(*b*) An *RC* impedance matching network

power increase is

$$dB = 10 \log_{10} \frac{2}{1}$$
$$= 10 \times 0.301 \quad \text{or} \quad \text{about 3 dB}$$

Often, you will see statements like "this amplifier provides a power increase at 30 dB." This statement is more meaningful if the reference power level is known. Although many different reference levels are used, the most popular is the 1-mW reference level. Based on a standard telephone industry signal level, it is noted by referring to dB ratios based on it as dBm ratios. The zero level, or reference, is defined in terms of the power dissipated in a 600 Ω resistive load by an rms potential difference of 0.775 V, or

$$P_{\text{reference}} = \frac{E^2}{R} = \frac{0.775^2}{600} = 0.001001$$

Notice that this provides a reference accurate to 0.1 percent of 1 mW.

EXAMPLE:
A power output stage develops a potential difference of 3.5 V across its 600 Ω load resistor. What is the power ratio of the stage in dBm? ■

SOLUTION:
The power dissipated in the load resistor is $\frac{E^2}{R}$, or $\frac{(3.5)^2}{600} = 20.42$ mW, so the power ratio referenced to a 1 mW level is

$$\text{dBm} = 10 \log \frac{P1}{P2} = 10 \log 20.42$$

A calculator is used to compute 10 log 20.42:

Enter number	(2)(0)(.)(4)(2)
Select $\log_{10}$	(log)
The display should indicate	1.3100557
Multiply by 10	(×)(1)(0)(=)
The display now reads	13.100557

The power ratio of the output stage, rounding off, is 13.1 dBm. ■

Notice that if the power being compared is less than the reference value, the dB or dBm ratio value is negative. This is usually interpreted as a power loss.

EXAMPLE:
A certain circuit produces a power output of 18 μW with a standard power input. What is the power ratio of this circuit? ■

SOLUTION:
The power ratio is

$$P\,(\text{dBm}) = 10 \log \frac{P1}{1 \times 10^{-3}} = 10 \log \frac{18 \times 10^{-6}}{1 \times 10^{-3}}$$
$$= 10 \log (0.018)$$

Using a calculator, dBm = −17.45. This ratio is also expressed by saying that the circuit produces a "loss" or "attenuation" of 17.45 dBm. Another common phrase is that the output is "17.45 dBm down." ■

A number of electronic equipment manufacturers use a reference level of 6 mW in place of the 1 mW reference level. In this case, the unit is generally abbreviated as dB.

EXAMPLE:
What would the power output ratio be in the previous example if a 6 mW reference had been used? ■

SOLUTION:
The power ratio is

$$P_{\text{dB}} = 10 \log \frac{P1}{P2} = 10 \log \frac{18 \times 10^{-6}}{6 \times 10^{-3}}$$
$$P_{\text{dB}} = 10 \log 3 \times 10^{-3}$$
$$= -25.23 \text{ dB}$$ ■

One of the most useful features of power ratio values is that a series of them can be added to provide a value for the power increase or attenuation of a number of circuits. Consider the block diagram shown in Figure 16.26, which gives the gain or loss of each stage in dBm. The effect upon an input signal is therefore

Figure 16.26 Block diagram of the stages in a signal source.

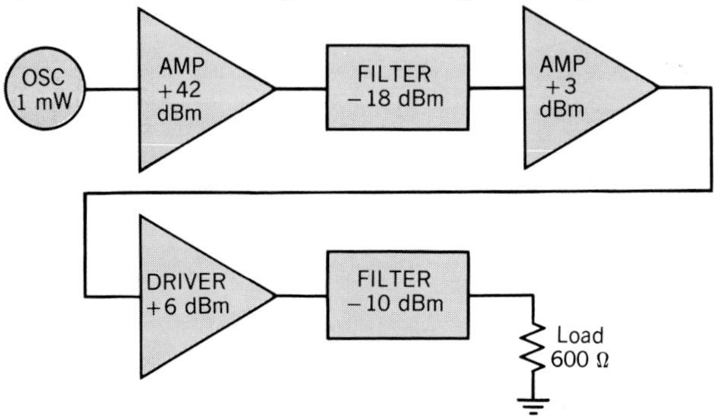

+42 − 18 + 3 + 6 − 10 = +23 dBm. The power output of this circuit into its 600 Ω load would be:

$$\text{dB} = 10 \log \frac{P1}{P2} \quad \text{or} \quad 23 = 10 \log \frac{P1}{P2}$$

dividing both sides by 10 and taking the inverse log or antilog

$$\log^{-1} 2.3 = \frac{P1}{1 \times 10^{-3}}$$

$$P1 = 0.1995 \quad \text{or} \quad \text{about } 0.2 \text{ W}$$

Practice your understanding of decibel power ratios by solving the following problems.

1. Calculate the power gain or loss in dBm for each of the power outputs into a 600 Ω load.

a. 56 mW	e. 0.56 W
b. 1.8 W	f. 0.001 W
c. 6.7 μW	g. 10 μW
d. 850 μW	h. 43 μW

2. The following power inputs or outputs have been measured across circuits whose theoretical power loss or gain is known. Provide the unknown quantity or quantities.

a. P_{in} = 0.001 W, gain = 6 dBm, P_{out} = ?
b. P_{in} = ?, loss = 26 dB, P_{out} = 1 W
c. P_{in} = ?, gain = 3 dB, P_{out} = 0.001 W
d. P_{in} = ?, gain = 16 dBm, P_{out} = ?
e. P_{in} = 6 mW, loss = 8 dB, P_{out} = ?
f. P_{in} = ?, loss or gain = ? dBm, P_{out} = 6 μW
g. P_{in} = 5 W, loss or gain = ?, P_{out} = 3 W

3. A certain unit is composed of the following stages:

Stage 1: Oscillator, output 8 μW
Stage 2: Buffer, gain 0 dB
Stage 3: Amplifier, gain 12 dB
Stage 4: Driver, gain 18 dB

Draw a block diagram of the unit and calculate its output power.

4. The power output of a certain audio amplifier is 16 W, but the available speaker is only rated at 10 W. Calculate the attenuation factor in dB of an attenuator unit necessary to reduce the amplifier output to a safe level for the speaker.

C.3 DECIBELS AND POTENTIAL DIFFERENCE AND CURRENT RATIOS

The fundamental relationships between the logarithms of numbers have been frequently used to simplify calculations by changing multiplications and divisions into additions and subtractions. The particular relationships are

$$\log(a \times b) = \log a + \log b \qquad \text{FORMULA 16.16}$$

$$\log(a/b) = \log a - \log b \qquad \text{FORMULA 16.17}$$

$$\log a^n = n \log a \qquad \text{FORMULA 16.18}$$

The use of logarithms in pencil-and-paper calculations is limited by the fact that using tables takes nearly as long to obtain the answer as it does to perform the calculations without the use of logarithms. Before the invention and widespread use of calculators, technicians and engineers relied on the slide rule, a mechanical device for multiplication and division that operated by adding logarithm values. The modern scientific calculator makes it easy to find the values of logarithms or antilogarithms, but it also makes the use of logarithms unnecessary in most cases.

The relationships given in Formulas 16.16 through 16.18 are still used in calculations involving logarithmic functions, such as inductor and capacitor charge and discharge values and decibel ratios.

EXAMPLE:
A certain electronic equipment manufacturer claims that a Type 1 filter provides an attenuation of 24 dB, but does not list the reference value. When a 100 Ω load is connected to the output terminals, the potential difference across it is 0.0446 V. What reference value is this manufacturer using, assuming that the claim of a 24 dB attenuation is correct? What would the attenuation ratio be in dBm? ■

SOLUTION:
Using Formulas 16.15 and 16.17, it is possible to solve for $P1$, the reference power

$$\text{dB} = 10 \log \frac{P2}{P1}$$

Applying Formula 16.17,

$$\text{dB} = 10(\log P2 - \log P1)$$

$$= 10 \log P2 - 10 \log P1$$

but

$$P2 = \frac{E^2}{R}$$

so

$$-24 = 10 \log \frac{E^2}{R} - 10 \log P1$$

$$-24 = 10 \log(1.989 \times 10^{-5}) - 10 \log P1$$

$$-24 = -47.01 - 10 \log P1$$

$$23.01 = -10 \log P1$$

or

$$P1 = \log^{-1} -2.301 \qquad P = 0.005\ \text{W}$$

The manufacturer's reference is 5 mW. If a 1 mW reference level had been used, the power ratio would be

$$\begin{aligned}\text{dBm} &= 10 \log \frac{P2}{0.001} \\ &= 10 \log \frac{E^2}{R} - 10 \log 0.001 \\ &= 20 \log E - 10 \log R - 10 \log 0.001 \\ &= -27.01 - 20 + 30 \\ &= -17.01 \quad \text{or} \quad \text{about 17 dBm} \quad ■\end{aligned}$$

Decibel ratios can also be used to describe the relationship between two potential differences or two currents, where the resistances or impedances involved are the same. The formulas involved can easily be obtained from Formula 16.15.

$$\text{dB} = 10 \log \frac{P1}{P2}$$

Since $P1 = \frac{E_1^2}{R}$, and $P2 = \frac{E_2^2}{R}$, this can be rewritten as

$$\text{dB} = \frac{\frac{E_1^2}{R}}{\frac{E_2^2}{R}}$$

Multiplying the fraction by $\frac{R}{R}$ produces

$$\text{dB} = 10 \log \frac{E_1^2}{E_2^2}$$

Using Formula 16.17, this can be written as

$$\text{dB} = 10 \log E_1^2 - 10 \log E_2^2$$

Using Formula 16.18, this can be rewritten as

$$\begin{aligned}\text{dB} &= 20 \log E_1 - 20 \log E_2 \quad \text{or} \\ \text{dB} &= 20 (\log E_1 - \log E_2)\end{aligned}$$

But this is the same as

$$\text{dB} = 20 \log \frac{E_1}{E_2} \qquad \text{FORMULA 16.19}$$

Similarly, it can be shown that

$$\text{dB} = 20 \log \frac{I_1}{I_2} \qquad \text{FORMULA 16.20}$$

These ratios are frequently used to specify the potential difference or current gain, otherwise called the *amplification* of a circuit or electronic unit. For example, an amplifier circuit with an input potential difference of 1 mV and an output of 5 V has an amplification of

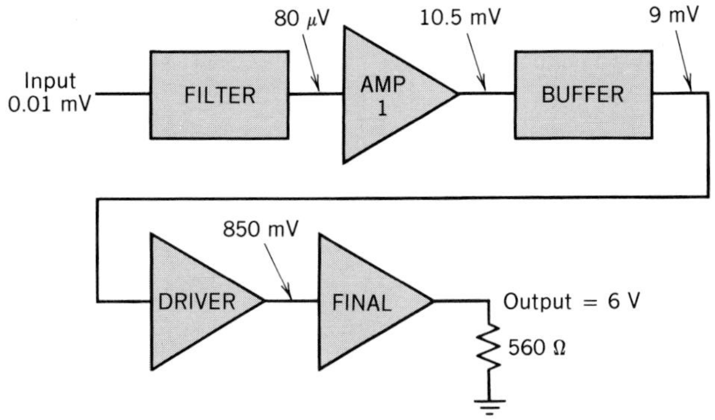

Figure 16.27 Block diagram of an electronic unit for Problem 2.

$$\text{dB} = 20 \log \frac{E_1}{E_2} \quad \text{or} \quad 20 \log \frac{5}{1 \times 10^{-3}}$$

$$\text{dB} = 73.98 \quad \text{or} \quad \text{about 74 dB}$$

Use decibel ratios and logarithmic relationships to solve the following problems.

1. Solve for the unknown quantity in the following:

a. $5 \log X + \log X = 10$, $X = ?$
b. $3 \log y - 2 \log y = 1.62$, $y = ?$
c. $\log\left(\frac{X}{4}\right) = 0.04$, $X = ?$
d. $\log(9X) = 2.716$, $X = ?$
e. $\log (A^4) = 0.163$, $A = ?$
f. $\log \left(\frac{A^3}{16}\right) = -0.04$, $A = ?$

2. A certain electronic unit is composed of stages, as shown in Figure 16.27, which gives the potential differences measured between ground and the output of each stage. Calculate the voltage gain or loss of each stage in dB.

3. The effective input signal to a certain amplifier is 18 mV across a 50 Ω load and the power output is 3.5 W across a 50 Ω load. Calculate the voltage and power gains of the amplifier.

4. Calculate the unknown quantity in each group.

a. $V_{in} = 4$ mV, dB, = ?, $V_{out} = 3.5$ V
b. $P_{in} = 1.64$ mV, dB = +8, $P_{out} = ?$
c. $I_{in} = ?$, dB = −3, $I_{out} = 6$ A
d. $V_{in} = 18$ V, dB = −30, $V_{out} = ?$
e. $I_{in} = 8.6\ \mu$A, dB = 17.9, $I_{out} = ?$
f. $P_{in} = ?$, dBm = ?, $V_{out} = 6.3$ to a 600 Ω load
g. $P_{in} = 0.006$ mW (600 Ω load), dB = 19, I_{out} to 600 Ω load = ?

D. APPLICATIONS

D.1 TYPES OF PRACTICAL *RC* CIRCUITS

For a number of reasons, including component physical size and cost, the use of *RC* networks is somewhat more common than the use of *RL* networks in electronic units. Depending on the source waveform and frequency, and on the values selected for capacitance and resistance, the *RC* circuit can be made to perform a number of functions. Capacitive networks fall into three general categories, depending on the function of the capacitor. These categories are coupling, bypassing, and waveshaping.

Capacitive coupling circuits make use of the dc blocking and high capacitive reactance at low frequency of capacitors to transfer higher frequency ac signals from one circuit or stage to another. This is shown in Figure 16.28. Often, impedance matching to provide maximum power transfer is also a function of the coupling network. Sometimes, the coupling network is designed to provide a certain amount of phase shift as well, to compensate for the effect of the previous stage or circuit.

Capacitive bypass circuits make use of the fact that capacitive reactance is low at high frequencies. Some bypass circuits are designed to provide a low-reactance path around certain components of relatively high resistance. This is shown in Figure 16.29, where *R*1 is needed to limit the dc current to the amplifier stage input and *C*1 is used to provide a low-reactance path around the resistor for the ac input signal. Most frequently, however, a low-impedance network or bypass capacitor is used to remove the high-frequency components of an ac signal from a point in a circuit by providing a bypass path to ground. In Figure 16.30, the high-frequency noise that might be produced on the dc supply wiring is bypassed to ground by *C*1.

Figure 16.28 Capacitive coupling makes use of the the characteristics of dc blocking and low impedance for high-frequency signals of capacitors.

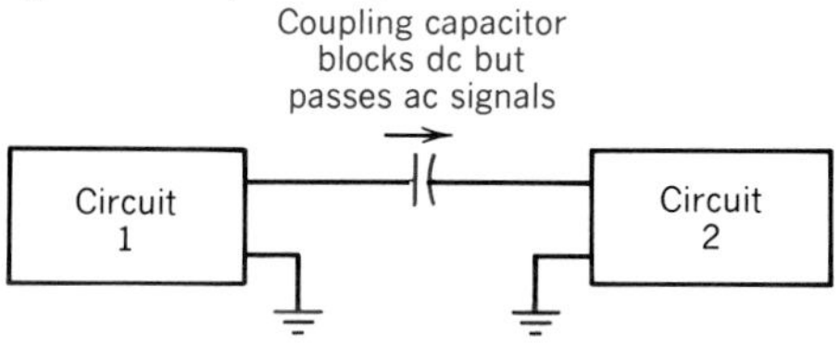

Figure 16.29 One application of a bypass capacitor is to provide a low-impedance path for high-frequency signals between circuits.

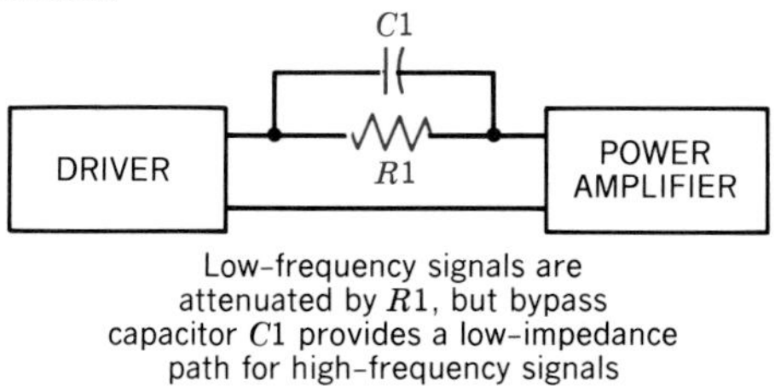

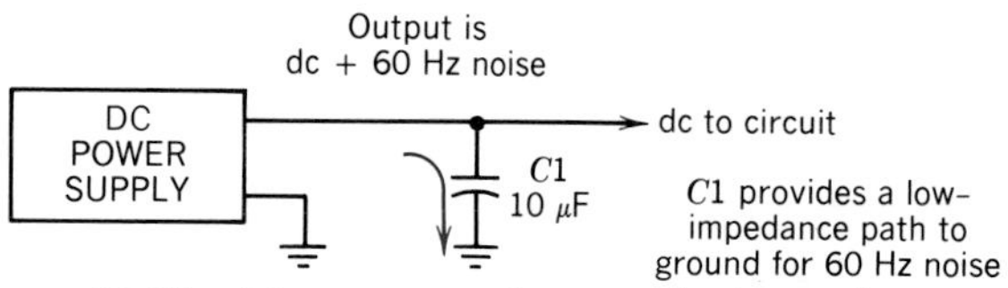

Figure 16.30 A bypass capacitor can also be used to remove high-frequency noise from a point in a circuit.

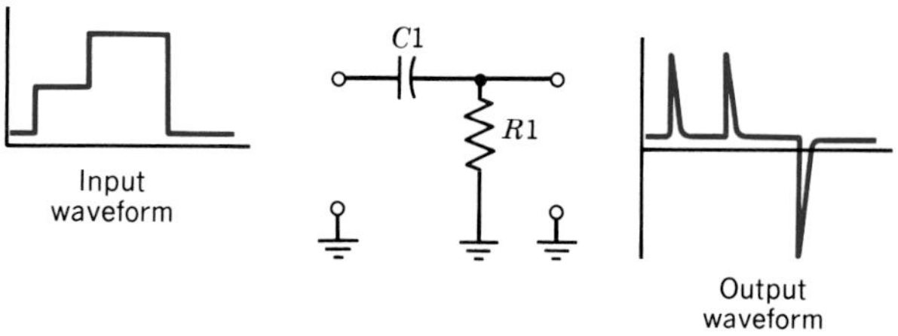

Figure 16.31 By choosing the values of capacitance and resistance carefully, it is possible to design a network that will produce a brief output pulse when the input changes its voltage level.

By choosing the design and *RC* time constant of a network, it is possible to significantly change the waveform of an input signal when necessary. For example, the circuit shown in Figure 16.31 provides a brief pulse each time the input signal changes its voltage level.

D.1.1 THE COUPLING CAPACITOR NETWORK (HIGH-PASS FILTER)

The circuit shown in Figure 16.32 consists of a coupling capacitor *C*1 and a resistor *R*1 across which the network output is taken. If the source potential difference is kept constant and the source frequency is increased, it is possible to draw a graph relating the output potential difference to the source frequency. This has been done in Figure 16.33. The shape of this curve shows that a dc or low-frequency source will produce relatively little output potential difference. This is understandable if you temporarily disregard the phase shift caused by *C*1 and consider this circuit as similar to the voltage divider shown in Figure 16.34. Recall that in a series circuit, the largest resistance will have

Figure 16.32 An *RC* network used as a high-pass filter.

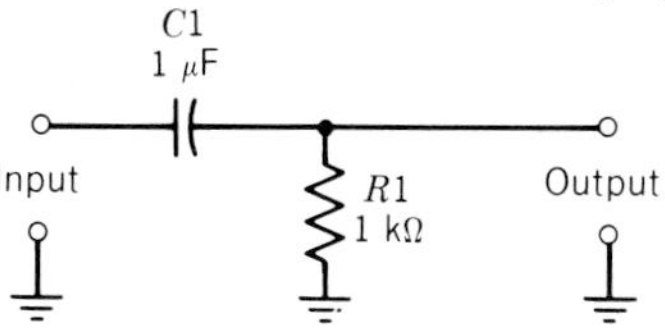

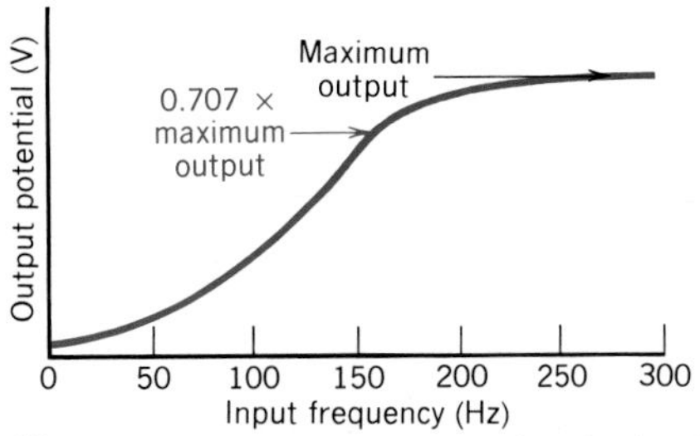

Figure 16.33 A rough graph can be sketched relating the output of the high-pass filter of Figure 16.32 to the input frequency.

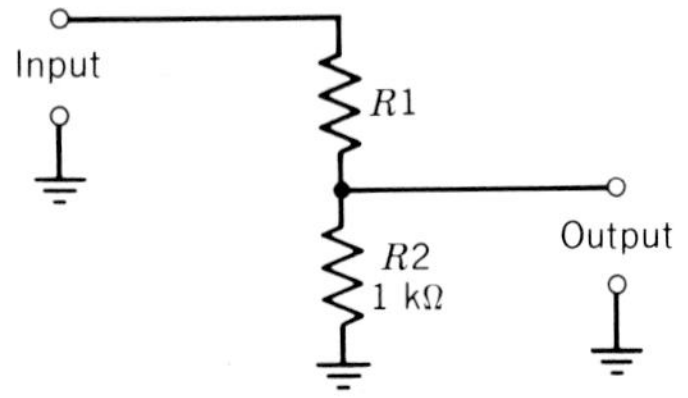

Figure 16.34 The operation of the high-pass filter of Figure 16.32 can be analyzed by referring to the operation of a voltage divider.

the largest potential difference across it. In Figure 16.34, resistor $R1$ represents the opposition to the circuit current caused by the capacitive reactance of $C1$. The resistance of this resistor will therefore decrease as the input frequency increases. $R2$ represents the resistance of $R2$ in Figure 16.32 and remains 1000 Ω, regardless of the opposition to circuit current and the voltage drop across the capacitor. The potential difference across $R2$, which is the network output potential, increases as the source frequency is made higher. In terms of the output, this means that the circuit of Figure 16.32 will provide a low output when the source provided is a single low-frequency sine-wave source. If the source waveform is complex, containing both low- and higher-frequency components, only the higher-frequency components will appear across the output. In effect, low-frequency signals are filtered out by the network. This network is therefore called a *high-pass filter* since it passes only high-frequency input signals.

The frequency for which the rms output potential difference of a filter is 0.707 times the maximum output rms potential difference is called the *cutoff frequency* of the network and is abbreviated f_c. The potential difference across the resistor will be $0.707E$ when the potential difference across the capacitor is equal to the voltage drop across the resistor. In other words, at the cutoff frequency the capacitive reactance is equal to the resistance, or

$$\frac{1}{2\pi f_c C} = R$$

Solving for the cutoff frequency,

$$f_c = \frac{1}{2\pi RC} \qquad \text{FORMULA 16.21}$$

A high-pass filter like that shown in Figure 16.32 is considered to pass all frequencies or waveform components above its cutoff frequency and to filter out or block all frequencies or components below its cutoff frequency.

EXAMPLE:

Engineer Vardis is using an electric guitar amplifier that is picking up some 60 Hz interference from various power leads, and the result is a serious hum. A pictorial diagram of the system is shown in Figure 16.35. Disregarding the impedances of the guitar and the amplifier, can you help Vardis design a simple filter using a 1 μF capacitor that will solve this problem? ■

SOLUTION:

The 60 Hz noise that is being picked up by the wires between the guitar and the amplifier has a lower frequency than the normal output of the guitar. For this reason, a high-pass filter is used. On the other hand, it is important not to change the waveform of the signal to the amplifier too much, or the sound quality might be changed. A high-pass filter with a cutoff frequency f_c of 60 Hz is chosen. Using Formula 16.21,

$$f_c = \frac{1}{2\pi RC}$$

since $C = 1\ \mu\text{F}$

$$60 = \frac{1}{2\pi \times R \times 1 \times 10^{-6}} \quad \text{or}$$

$$R = 2652.6\ \Omega \quad \text{or} \quad 2.7\ \text{K}$$

Figure 16.35 Pictorial diagram of a sound system showing how 60 Hz hum may be induced in sound circuits.

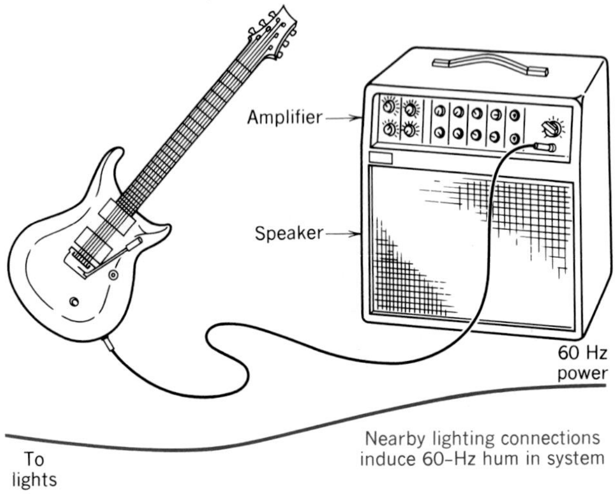

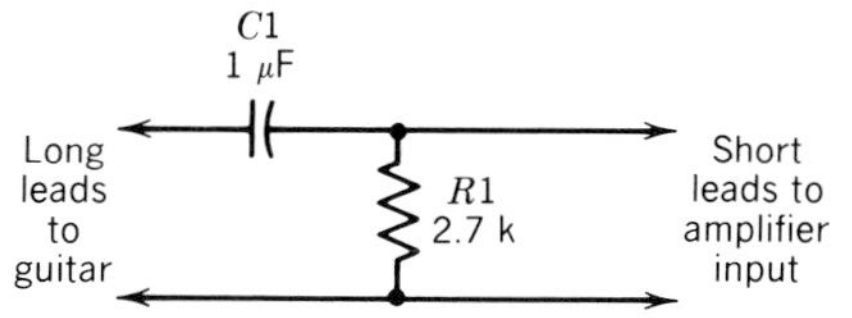

Figure 16.36 Installing a simple high-pass filter will eliminate most of the 60 Hz hum (it will also affect the tonal quality of the sound).

in standard values. This filter would be installed as shown in Figure 16.36. ■

D.1.2 THE LOW-PASS *RC* FILTER OR BYPASS CIRCUIT

When the connection of the resistor and capacitor is reversed, as shown in Figure 16.37, the output is taken across the capacitor. Since the capacitor offers a high reactance to a dc or low-frequency source input, a high potential difference will be developed across the capacitor when the input frequency is low. A high-frequency input, on the other hand, sees a very low reactance across the capacitor and develops little potential difference across the capacitor. If the source potential difference is kept constant while the frequency of the source is increased, the graph relating the output potential difference to the frequency of the source will resemble that shown in Figure 16.38.

As in the case of the high-pass filter, the action of this circuit can be compared to that in a voltage divider if the phase shift caused by the capacitor is ignored. In the case of the low-pass filter, as shown in Figure 16.39, the output potential difference is the voltage drop across R_{X_C}, which decreases as the frequency is

Figure 16.37 An *RC* low-pass filter.

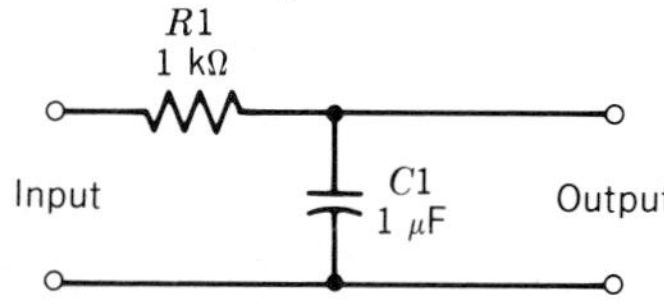

Figure 16.38 A rough graph relating the output of the low-pass filter of Figure 16.37 to the input frequency.

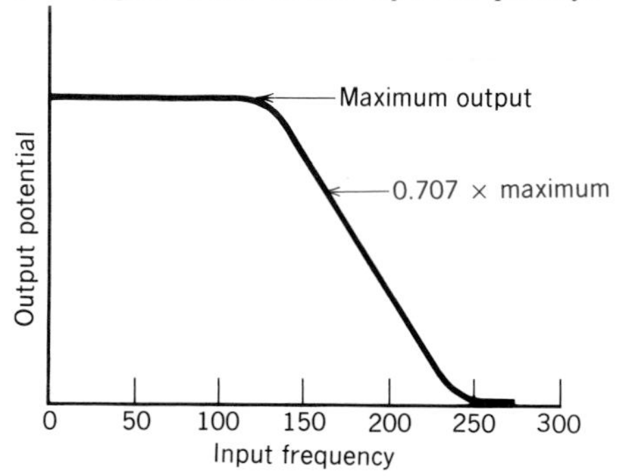

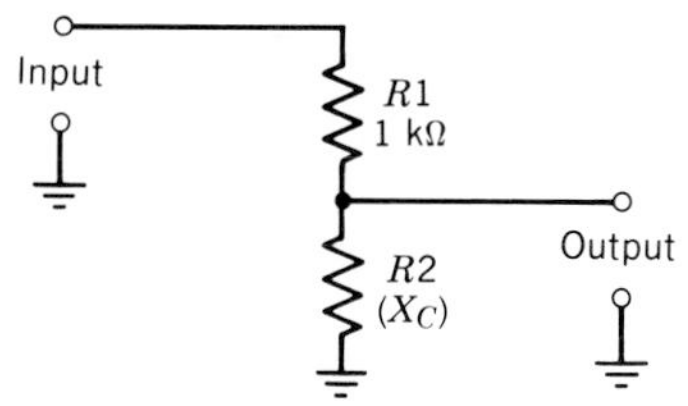

Figure 16.39 The operation of a low-pass filter can be understood in comparison with a voltage divider.

increased. The definitions and formula for the cutoff frequency f_c of a low-pass filter are the same as those for the high-pass filter given previously, except that the filter is considered to permit all frequencies or waveform components *less than* its cutoff frequency to appear as the output signal and to block or bypass to ground all frequencies or waveform components higher than the cutoff frequency.

EXAMPLE:

You have found that high-frequency disturbances from a nearby amateur radio transmitter are entering your computer via the power line. Design a low-pass *RC* filter to eliminate this problem using a resistor of 1 Ω to limit the power dissipated. Show how the network would be connected. ■

SOLUTION:

In order to bypass the higher-frequency noise while not reducing the 60 Hz power, a cutoff frequency f_c of 120 Hz is selected for the bypass filter. From Formula 16.21,

$$f_c = \frac{1}{2\pi RC} \quad \text{or} \quad 120 = \frac{1}{2\pi \times 1 \times C}$$

Solving for the value of *C*,

$$C = \frac{1}{2\pi \times 1 \times 120} = 0.00132 \quad \text{or} \quad \text{about } 0.13\ \mu\text{F}$$

Standard values of 0.15 or 0.1 μF could be used as shown in Figure 16.40. ■

Low-pass, or bypass, filters are very common in electronic units, particularly where digital circuits are involved. There are two reasons for this. First, many of the solid-state components used in digital circuits

Figure 16.40 A low-pass filter suitable for the power input of a small computer.

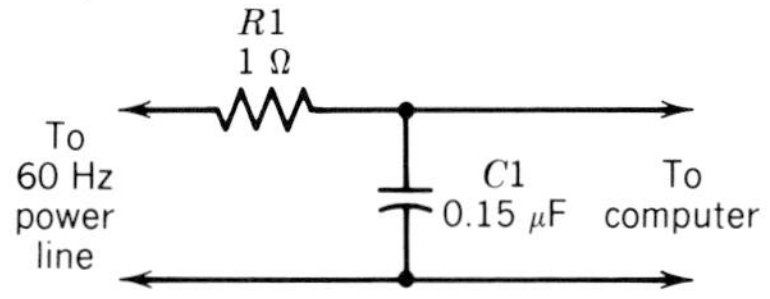

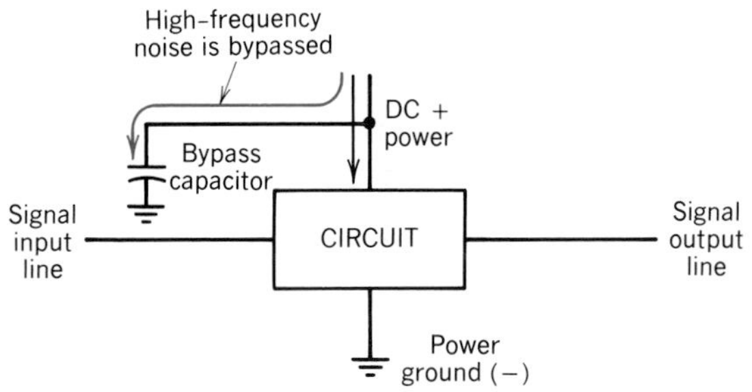

Figure 16.41 Installing a bypass capacitor across the dc power input to a circuit prevents noise from entering the circuit or from being produced on the dc power lines.

are sensitive to disturbances or transients in their dc operating power. Such transients can easily cause improper operation or even destroy the components. Second, because digital circuits almost always involve high-speed switching, disturbances and transients are produced by the digital circuit components themselves. In order to keep the transients produced by one component from affecting others, a bypass capacitor is normally connected across the DC+ and ground connections at each solid-state component. The effective bypass circuit resembles that shown in Figure 16.41.

As a rule of thumb, the value of a bypass capacitor is chosen so that at the highest frequency to be allowed into the load, the reactance of the bypass capacitor is $\frac{1}{20}$ of the load resistance. In other words, at f_c

$$X_C = \frac{R_L}{20} \qquad \text{FORMULA 16.22}$$

Another way of saying this is that at the lowest frequency to be bypassed, the resistance of the load must be at least 20 times greater than the reactance of the capacitor.

EXAMPLE:

A certain integrated circuit contains four separate switching devices. When the operating potential difference is 5 V dc, each switching device dissipates 2 mW. It is desired to place a capacitor across the circuit input to bypass any ac noise on the 5-V line. A cutoff frequency of 60 Hz has been selected. What should be the value of the bypass capacitor? ■

SOLUTION:

In order to use Formula 16.22, it is necessary to calculate the resistance of the integrated circuit. Since it contains four switching devices, each of which dissipates 2 mW, the total power dissipation of the package with an input of 5 V dc is 8 mW. Using a basic expression for the power in the integrated circuit,

$$P = \frac{E^2}{R} \qquad 0.008 = \frac{25}{R} \quad \text{or} \quad R = 3125\ \Omega$$

The capacitive reactance at 60 Hz then should be

$$X_C = \frac{R}{20} = 156.25 \quad \text{or} \quad \text{about } 156\ \Omega$$

Since $X_C = \frac{1}{2\pi f C}$, multiplying both sides by C and dividing by X_C provides a solution for C:

$$C = \frac{1}{2\pi f X_C}$$

Substituting,

$$C = \frac{1}{2\pi \times 60 \times 156} = 0.000017 \quad \text{or} \quad 17 \times 10^{-6}$$

$$C = 17\ \mu\text{F}$$

In practical circuits, it is rarely necessary to provide a frequency cutoff as low as 60 Hz for use with integrated circuits. Capacitances of 0.1 μF are used to provide effective bypassing at a minimum frequency of around 10 kHz at each integrated circuit. Since there are a number of such bypass capacitors connected to the dc supply line, effective bypassing is obtained. ■

D.1.3 PHASE SHIFTING WITH AN *RC* CIRCUIT

In certain electronic units, it is necessary to adjust the phase relationship between the sine-wave input to a stage and its sine-wave output. In other applications, it is necessary to provide two output voltages separated by a phase difference of between 0° and 90°. For these purposes, the circuit shown in Figure 16.42 can be used. The values of the capacitor and resistor are chosen to provide the amount of phase shift required. The relationship among the input potential difference, the potential difference across the capacitor, and the voltage drop across the resistor is given by the phasor diagram of Figure 16.43. The angle θ between the input

Figure 16.42 Selection of resistor value permits the *RC* network to be used for providing a calculated amount of phase shift.

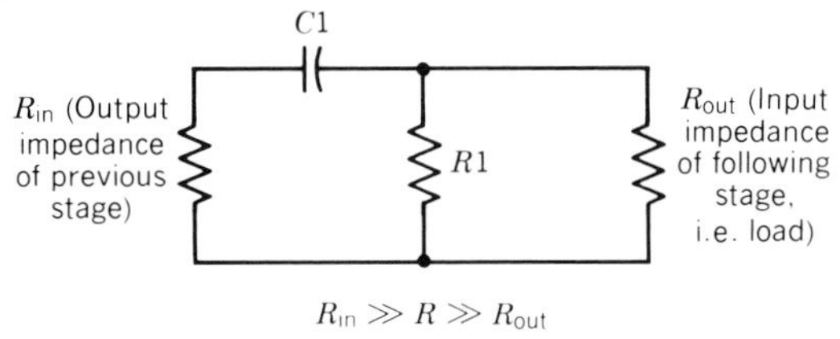

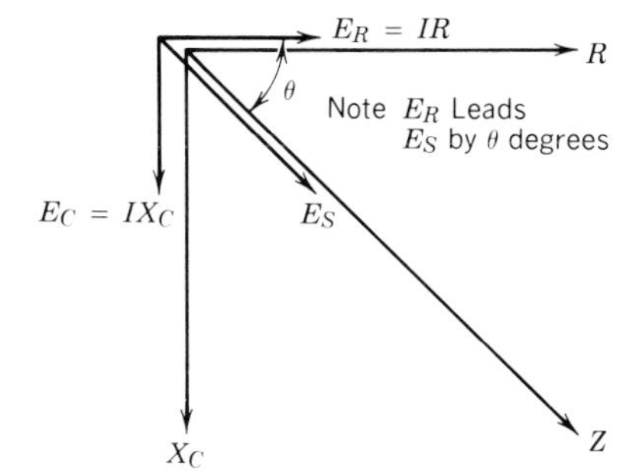

Figure 16.43 Phasor relationships among X_C, R, and Z; E_C, E_R, and E_s in the circuit of Figure 16.42.

potential difference and the current is

$$\theta = \tan^{-1}\frac{-X_C}{R}$$

Therefore, the potential difference across the resistor, that is, the output potential of the phase shifter, will lead the input potential difference by an angle of θ. In order to prevent inaccuracies in the amount of phase shift obtained, the resistance value chosen should be much greater than the output impedance of the source, but much less than the impedance of the load as shown in Figure 16.42.

Although it closely resembles a high-pass filter, the phase shift circuit differs in that it is designed to operate at one specific frequency and to provide a certain amount of phase shift at that frequency. The potential difference produced across the resistor can be changed by selecting different values of capacitance and resistance. It is the ratio of X_C to R that determines the phase shift angle.

EXAMPLE:

A stage in an electronic unit requires two input signals, a 1 kHz sine-wave source signal and a reference signal that leads the source signal by 30°. Draw the schematic diagram of the required phase shifter and calculate one set of possible values for the components. ■

SOLUTION:

Figure 16.44 shows the connection of a phase shift network between the source and load circuits. Since the impedance of the source circuit is 50 Ω and that of the load is 47 kΩ, it is relatively easy to choose a phase shift resistance value that will be greater than 20 times the source impedance (that is, the Thevenin impedance of the source network) and less than $\frac{1}{20}$ of the load impedance. A value of 2 kΩ would be a reasonable initial choice. Since

$$30° = \tan^{-1}\frac{-X_C}{R} \quad \text{or} \quad \tan 30 = 0.577 = \frac{-X_C}{2000}$$

so

$$X_C = 1154 = \frac{1}{2\pi f C}$$

Solving for C,

$$C = 0.1379\ \mu\text{F}$$

A 0.15 μF capacitor would provide the approximate phase shift required. If greater precision is required, the resistance could be recalculated:

$$\tan 30 = 0.577 = \frac{-X_C \text{ of a } 0.15\ \mu\text{F capacitor}}{R}$$

or,

$$0.577R = \frac{1}{2\pi \times 1000 \times 0.15 \times 10^{-6}}$$

$$0.577R = 1061.033$$

$$R = 1838.9$$

The network would consist of a 1.8 kΩ resistor and a 0.15 μF capacitor. ■

Figure 16.44 Calculating the component values for a phase shift network that will provide a phase shift of 30° at 1 kHz.

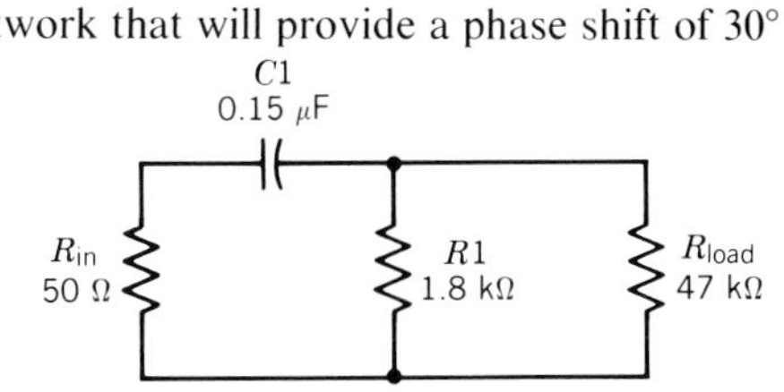

D.1.4 *RC* WAVESHAPING NETWORKS: THE DIFFERENTIATOR

The circuit shown in Figure 16.45 closely resembles the high-pass filter and the phase shifter shown in the earlier section, but the component values have been chosen to provide a specific output. When the source potential difference is a repetitive function, for example, a square wave or triangle wave, and the *RC*

Figure 16.45 Proper selection of the component values produces a differentiator network.

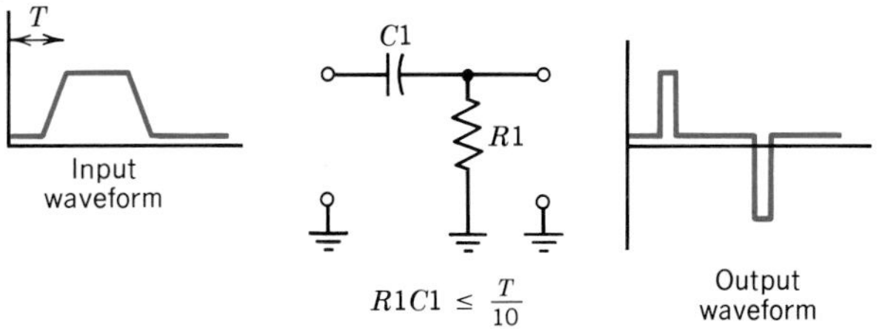

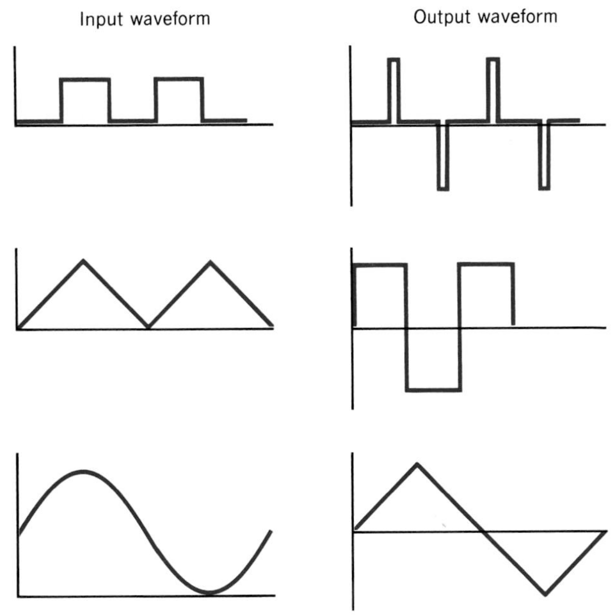

Figure 16.46 Differentiator output with standard waveform inputs.

time constant of the network is small when compared to the period of the input, the network acts as a differentiator. A differentiator is a network that produces an output potential difference that is directly proportional to the rate of change of the source potential. Figure 16.46 shows the differentiator output waveform for some standard wave shape inputs.

In order to obtain good differentiation, the *RC* time constant of the differentiator network should be less than one-tenth of the input signal period or

$$T = \frac{1}{f} \geq 10RC \qquad \text{FORMULA 16.23}$$

As in the case of the phase shift network, the resistance value chosen for the *RC* differentiator should be large in comparison with the Thevenin equivalent impedance of the source circuit and small in comparison with the load impedance.

EXAMPLE:

A source potential difference shown in Figure 16.47*a* is used as the input to the differentiator circuit shown in Figure 16.47*b*. Sketch the waveform of the differentiator network output. ■

SOLUTION:

Since the time constant of the *RC* network is about one-tenth of the period during which the input voltage rise takes place, the circuit will act as a differentiator. Initially, the source potential difference is zero, so the differentiator output is also zero. Between time $t = 0$ and $t = 1$ ms, the rate of change of the source potential

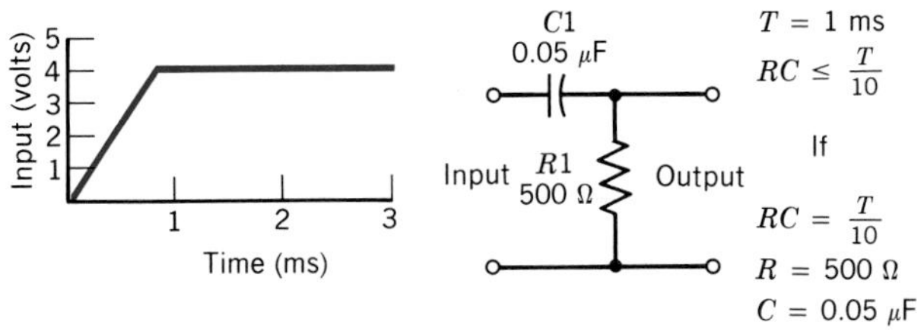

(*a*) Differentiator input waveform (*b*) Differentiator circuit

Figure 16.47 Example of differentiator action.

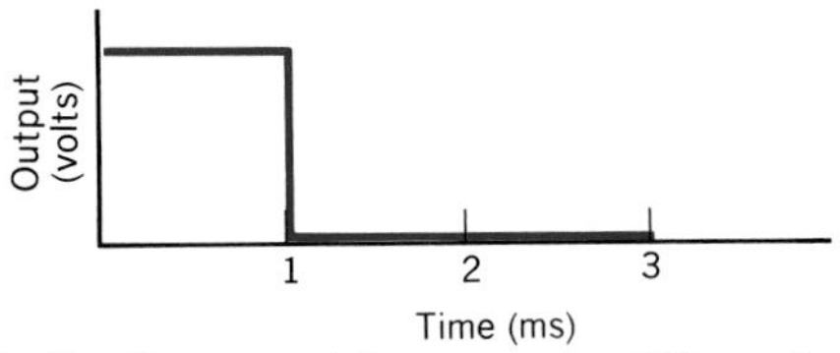

Figure 16.48 Output of the example differentiator circuit shown in Figure 16.47.

difference is $\frac{\Delta V}{\Delta t}$, or $\frac{5}{1}$. During this period, the differentiator output is constant. After $t = 1$ ms, the rate of change of the source potential difference is again zero, so the differentiator output will also be zero. A sketch of the output waveform is shown in Figure 16.48. ■

D.1.5 *RC* WAVESHAPING NETWORKS: THE INTEGRATOR

When the *RC* time constant of the *RC* network shown in Figure 16.49 is 10 or more times greater than the period of the source potential difference, the output potential difference is proportional to the area between the input waveform graph and the horizontal axis. The mathematical term for this summation process, illustrated in Figure 16.50, is *integration*, and the *RC* network that performs this function is called an *integrator*. Integrators are used in a number of different applications in electronic units, such as "stretching" input pulses, as in Figure 16.51*a*, smoothing sign waves that are modulated by ripple as in Figure 16.51*b*, and "summing" a rapidly changing input over a period of time as shown in Figure 16.51*c*. Since integration is mathematically the opposite of differentiation, the result of the application of the source waveforms is exactly the

Figure 16.49 When the *RC* time constant of this network is 10 or more times greater than the period of the input signal, this circuit functions as an integrator.

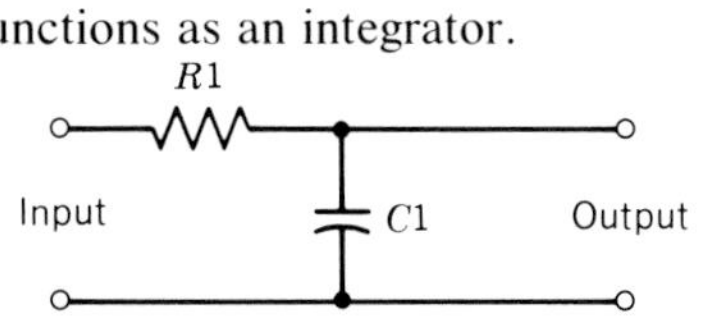

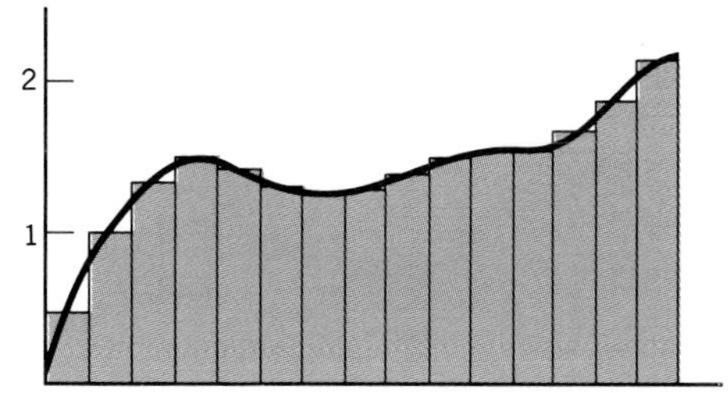

(a) Input function averaged over short periods of time

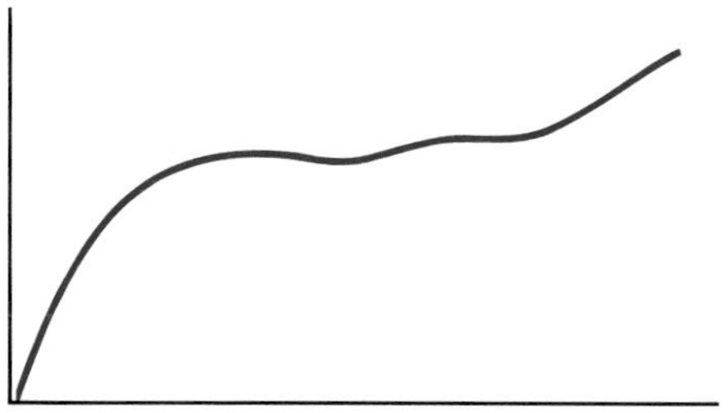

(b) The integrated function

Figure 16.50 The process of integration consists of "summing" (adding) the average values of the input function measured during short periods of time. The effect is to "smooth" the input waveform.

opposite of the illustration of differentiation previously shown. In order for an *RC* network to function effectively as an integrator, the *RC* time constant of the network must be 10 or more times greater than the period of the repetitive source potential difference. In mathematical terms,

$$RC = > 10\,T \qquad \text{FORMULA 16.24}$$

$$RC = > \frac{10}{F} \qquad \text{FORMULA 16.25}$$

Figure 16.51 Applications of integrator circuit.

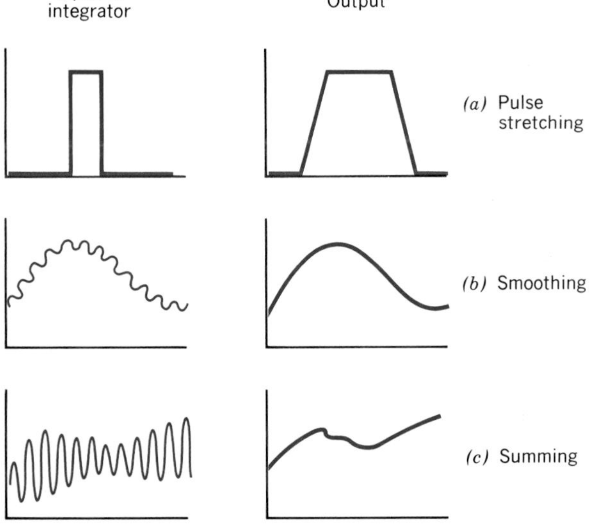

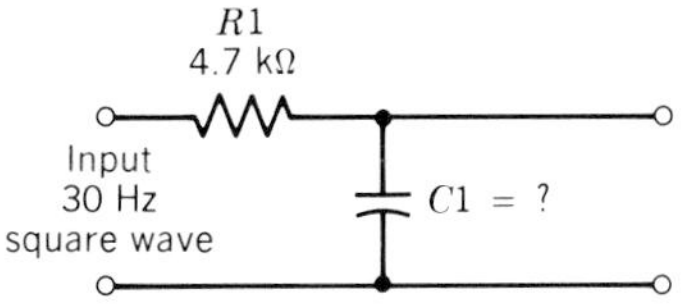

Figure 16.52 Example of integrator circuit component calculations.

The integrator network functions best when the resistance of any load connected to its output terminal is quite high. A load resistance much higher than that of the network resistor is necessary to prevent reduction of the circuit time constant.

EXAMPLE:
The input to the integrator shown in Figure 16.52 is a 30 Hz square wave. What is the minimum value of C_1 that will ensure proper circuit function? ■

SOLUTION:
Using Formula 16.25,

$$RC = \frac{10}{F} \quad \text{or} \quad 4.7 \times 10^3\, C = \frac{10}{30}$$

Solving, $C = 70.9\ \mu F$. Selecting a standard value, C_1 should be 68 μF. ■

D.2 *Q* IN CAPACITIVE CIRCUITS

The quality factor *Q* is rarely referred to in capacitive or in *RC* circuits, in contrast with *RL* circuits discussed in Chapter 12, or the *RCL* circuits covered in the next chapter. In the case of properly functioning, modern capacitors, the *Q* of a capacitor at normal operating frequencies tends to be high. Where capacitors, resistors, and inductors are combined in a circuit, the circuit *Q* is practically determined by the resistors and inductors.

It is, however, possible to calculate the *Q* of a capacitor or *RC* network by substituting the capacitive reactance X_C for the inductive reactance X_L in Formulas 13.3 and 13.4.

In the case of a properly functioning, nonelectrolytic capacitor, the leakage current is quite low, so the equivalent circuit of a capacitor connected directly across an ac source is a capacitor in series with a resistance representing its ESR. The equivalent series resistor R_{ESR} is shown in series with a pure capacitance. For this circuit

$$Q = \frac{X_C}{R_{ESR}} = \frac{1}{2\pi f C R_{ESR}} \qquad \text{FORMULA 16.26}$$

EXAMPLE:
What is the Q of a 10 nF capacitor with an equivalent series resistance of 0.3 Ω connected across a 10 kHz source? ■

SOLUTION:
Using Formula 16.26,

$$Q = \frac{1}{2\pi f C R_{ESR}}$$

$$= \frac{1}{2\pi \times 1 \times 10^4 \times 0.01 \times 10^{-6} \times 0.3}$$

$$Q = 5305.2$$ ■

When a resistance is connected in series with the capacitor, this resistance is added to the ESR of the capacitor and Formula 16.26 becomes

$$Q = \frac{X_C}{R + R_{ESR}} = \frac{1}{2\pi f C(R + R_{ESR})}$$ FORMULA 16.27

EXAMPLE:
What is the effect on the Q of the 10 nF capacitor in the previous example if a 2 Ω resistor is added in series with the capacitor? ■

SOLUTION:
Using Formula 16.27,

$$Q = \frac{1}{2\pi f C(R + R_{ESR})}$$

$$Q = \frac{1}{2 \times \pi \times 1 \times 10^4 \times 0.01 \times 10^{-6} \times 2.3}$$

$$= 691.97$$

The Q of the circuit is reduced to 692. In other words, the Q is decreased by a factor of $\frac{2.3}{0.3}$ or 7.66. ■

As in the case of a parallel RL circuit, the Q of a parallel RC circuit can be calculated by reactance:

$$Q = \frac{R_t}{X_C}$$ FORMULA 16.28

In practical applications, however, if the branch parallel to that containing the capacitor has an impedance 10 times or more than that of the branch containing the capacitor, the circuit can be considered a series circuit. For example, in the circuit shown in Figure 16.53a, R_p can be ignored for the purpose of calculating the circuit Q. In Figure 16.53b, however, the resistance of branch 2 must be included in Q calculations.

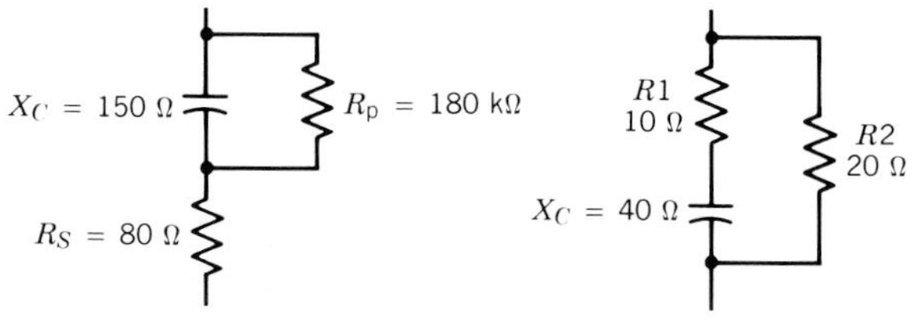

(a) R_p can be ignored for the purposes of calculating circuit Q

(b) Both series and parallel resistors must be taken into account to calculate Q

Figure 16.53 Calculating Q in RC circuits.

EXAMPLE:
Calculate the circuit Q in Figure 16.53b. ■

SOLUTION:
Branch 1 consists of a 10 Ω resistor and a capacitive reactance of 40 Ω, branch 2 of a 20 Ω resistor. Using complex rectangular coordinates,

$$Z_1 = 10 - j40 \qquad Z_2 = 20 + j0$$

Converting to a potential difference reference:

$$Z_{total} = \frac{Z_1 Z_2}{Z_1 + Z_2} = \frac{(10 - j40)(20 + j0)}{30 - j40}$$

Converting to polar coordinates for the division and multiplication,

$$Z_{total} = \frac{41.23 \angle -75.96° \times 20 \angle 0°}{50 \angle -53.13°}$$

$$Z_{total} = \frac{824.6 \angle -75.96°}{50 \angle -53.13°} = 16.49 \angle -23°$$

$$Q_{\text{of the circuit}} = \frac{Z_{total}}{X_C} = \frac{16.49}{40} = 0.41$$

Notice that no phase angle is given since Q is a pure number and not a phasor quantity. ■

D.3 TROUBLESHOOTING RC CIRCUITS

Although it is possible to use an ohmmeter to test for completely short-circuited capacitors, RC circuit troubleshooting generally requires additional equipment as well as more sophisticated techniques.

There are two major catagories of troubleshooting tests: in-circuit tests, which are made to determine which components could be the cause of a unit or circuit malfunction, and out-of-circuit tests, which are made to confirm the results of in-circuit testing or to check the condition of components before they are used as replacements for faulty components. The troubleshooting of RC networks, like all troubleshooting of complex circuits, should begin with an analysis of the fault conditions. The maintenance manual will sometimes help to isolate the trouble to a particular group of components. When no maintenance manual is available, circuit tracing techniques can be used. Although too involved for a complete discussion in this book, circuit tracing consists of providing a set of known inputs to a unit and then measuring or otherwise observing the resulting output of each stage of the unit.

Once a circuit fault has been isolated to a particular *RC* network or to a circuit containing several *RC* networks, a number of in-circuit checks should be performed to try to isolate the problem to a particular component. A working knowledge of circuit analysis and recalling the principal failure modes of the components involved can help you greatly. Too many technicians still rely on a few ohmmeter measurements followed by massive parts replacement to correct problems. This was not as likely to cause serious problems in the days of vacuum tubes and larger components, since neither the potential difference of an ohmmeter nor the heat of unsoldering would result in damage. In modern solid-state circuits, however, careless application of even low potential differences or excessive heat are likely to cause damage.

CAUTION

WHEN USING A MULTIMETER SET IN ITS OHMS FUNCTION TO CHECK FOR SHORTED CAPACITORS, USE THE "LO OHMS" SETTING OR OTHER LOW CURRENT RANGE. FAILURE TO DO SO MAY DAMAGE SEMICONDUCTOR DEVICES IN CIRCUITS CONNECTED TO THE CAPACITOR BEING CHECKED.

Paying careful attention to the unit schematic diagram, so that it is clear what each particular measurement means, ohmmeter checks can be performed to test for open resistors or shorted capacitors. Of course, it is necessary to remove all power from the unit and to discharge all capacitors before making resistance checks. If a dual-trace oscilloscope is available, it will also be possible to compare calculated with observed signal phase shifts.

Once a suspect component is identified, out-of-circuit tests should be performed to verify the in-circuit tests. Rather than remove the component completely from the printed circuit board to which it is soldered, it is frequently sufficient to unsolder only one of the leads to permit out-of-circuit tests. When the only test equipment available is a multimeter and a dc source, out-of-circuit capacitors can be checked for short circuits and excessive leakage. Out-of-circuit electrolytic capacitors can also be checked for open circuits between the foil and lead wire.

Short circuits are spotted by measuring the resistance of the capacitor. Except for electrolytic types, the resistance of a capacitor should be over range for most types, even on the highest resistance range. All electrolytics and some large nonelectrolytic types will show an apparently low resistance (for a capacitor) of 100 kΩ to 2 MΩ when the meter leads are first touched to the capacitor. This resistance reading will then increase at a rate determined by the capacitance of the capacitor and the meter potential difference. This behavior in electrolytic capacitors can be considered an initial indication that the unit is neither open-circuited nor short-circuited.

A better indication of the condition of an out-of-circuit capacitor can be obtained by using a capacitor tester of the sort shown in Figure 16.54. It is generally better to completely remove the capacitor from the circuit board when a tester of this type is used. The extra work is rewarded by a better analysis of the failure since actual capacitance and leakage at full-rated working voltage can be measured.

A short- or open-circuit condition, excessive leakage current, or out-of-tolerance value require the capacitor to be replaced. Select a suitable replacement capacitor and perform the same out-of-circuit tests which the component removed from the unit failed. This extra step has two functions. First, it ensures that you have correctly tested the component that was removed from the unit. Second, in the case of electrolytic capacitors, it checks that the dielectric layer is formed. Sometimes it will be necessary to reform an electrolytic capacitor after it has been stored for a long period of time.

Figure 16.54 A commercial capacitor tester (Courtesy Sencore, Inc.).

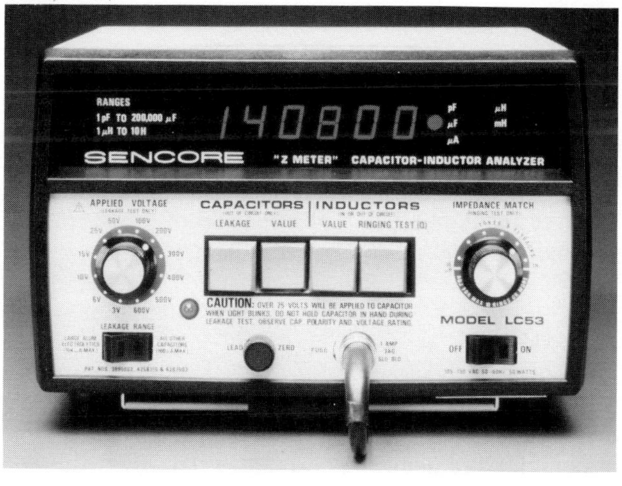

After soldering a replacement component into a unit, further in-circuit tests should be made to determine if the fault has been corrected, if possible, before turning on unit power. If such tests can not be performed, try to analyze the circuit to see if the failure of the replaced component was caused by an abnormal condition existing in another part of the network or unit.

Finally, if your part replacement restored the unit to correct function, allow the unit to operate for a time, to "burn in" the new part and to make sure that the failure of the original component was not due to an intermittent failure in some other component.

E. PROGRAMMED REVIEW

FRAME 1

In a circuit containing both resistance and reactance, the power that is dissipated in the resistances is called ___________, while the power temporarily stored in the magnetic or electric field of the reactance is called ___________. The phasor sum of these is the ___________.

a. True power; reactive power; apparent power. (2)
b. Any other answers, review Sections B.1 and B.2.

FRAME 2

In a series capacitive circuit, the current is 0.01 A and the capacitive reactance is 200 Ω. The reactive power is ___________ (give unit; degrees).

a. 0.02 var; +90° (4)
b. Any other answer, (3).

FRAME 3

Recall that the reactive power in a capacitive circuit P_r is defined as I^2X_C, in other words, the square of the current times the capacitive reactance. In a series circuit, the current is the reference phasor, and the capacitive reactance has a phase angle of −90°. P_r has an angle of +90°. Try Frame 2 again.

FRAME 4

The true power in a series capacitive circuit is 6.5 W, and the reactive power is 3.8 vars. Write an expression in complex rectangular coordinates that gives the apparent power. Apparent power is measured in ___________, abbreviated ___________.

a. $P_A = 6.5 + j3.8$; volt-amperes; V-A. (5)
b. Any other answer, review Section B.2.

FRAME 5

The total impedance of a parallel capacitive circuit is $180 + j270\ \Omega$ and the potential difference is $10\ \angle 0^\circ$ V. What is the magnitude and phase angle of the apparent power?

a. 0.308 V-A $\angle +56.3^\circ$ (6)
b. Any other answer, review Section B.2.

FRAME 6

The current in a series *RL* circuit is 0.03 A, and the potential difference across the inductor is 17.8 V. What are the magnitude of the reactive power and its phase angle?

a. 0.534 $\angle -90^\circ$ var (8)
b. Any other answer, review Section B.3 and go to Frame 7.

FRAME 7

Remember that the phase angle of the reactive power in a series *RL* circuit is −90°. The phase angle of the reactive power in a parallel *RL* circuit is also −90°. Go on to Frame 8.

FRAME 8

In a parallel capacitive circuit, the phase angle of the reactive power is ___________. The reference phasor is the ___________.

a. +90°; source potential difference. (9)
b. Any other answer, review the power triangles in Figure 16.16.

FRAME 9

The apparent power in a certain circuit is 37.39 $\angle -16.5^\circ$ V-A. How much power is actually being dissipated by the circuit resistance?

a. 35.85 W (10)
b. Any other answer, review Section B.5 and go on to Frame 10.

FRAME 10

What is the reactive power in the circuit of Frame 9?

a. 10.6 var $\angle -90^\circ$ (11)
b. You have still not mastered two basic relationships:

$$P = P_a \cos \theta \quad \text{and} \quad P_r = P_a \sin \theta$$

Try Frame 9 again.

FRAME 11

The oscilloscope trace of the potential difference source in a series circuit shows a peak value of 24 V. The trace of the potential difference across a 56 Ω resistor in the circuit shows 5.6 V with a waveform lagging the source potential by 30°. What is the true power consumed in the circuit?

a. 1.039 W (12)
b. You forgot to obtain the rms values of the potential difference and the current. Try Frame 11 again.
c. Any other answer, review Section B.5.

FRAME 12

In a distribution system, the true power dissipated is 4.34 kW. The phase angle between the source potential and the circuit current is 16.5°. What is the apparent power in the circuit?

a. 4.53 kV-A (13)
b. Any other answer, review Section B.5.

FRAME 13

Power comparisons in electronics are frequently made in terms of base 10 logarithms. The comparison unit is the ____________.

a. Decibel. (14)
b. Any other answer, review Section C.2 and go on to Frame 14.

FRAME 14

A certain manufacturer of attenuation networks claims its products provide an attenuation of −24 dBm. What is the power output of a unit, if this claim is true?

a. 4 μW (15)
b. Any other answer, review Sections C.2 and C.3.

FRAME 15

A certain radio receiver claims that its first stage produces a voltage gain of 17 dB. What will the voltage output of this stage be if the input is 4 μV?

a. 28.3 μV (16)
b. Any other answer, review Section C.3.

FRAME 16

The frequency for which the rms output potential difference of a filter is 0.707 times its maximum output is called the ____________, abbreviated ____________.

a. Cutoff frequency; f_c (17)
b. Any other answer, review Section D.1.1 and go on to Frame 17.

FRAME 17

At the cutoff frequency of an L-section high- or low-pass RC filter, the capacitive reactance is ____________. This permits the cutoff frequency to be expressed in terms of the capacitance and resistance as ____________.

a. Equal to the resistance; $f_c = \dfrac{1}{2\pi RC}$. (18)
b. Any other answer, review Section D.1.1.

FRAME 18

In choosing the correct value of a bypass capacitor, the value of the load resistance must be taken into consideration. If the load resistance is 10 kΩ and the source frequency is 100 Hz, the correct maximum capacitor value is ____________ μF.

a. 3.2 (19)
b. Any other answer review Section D.1.2.

FRAME 19

What is the correct value of the resistance to use in a 43° phase shift network if the capacitive reactance is 2.4 kΩ?

a. 2581 Ω (20)
b. Any answer not within round-off range of 2581, review Section D.1.3.

FRAME 20

An *RC* waveshaping network that produces an output that is proportional to the rate of change of its input potential difference is called a ________.

a. Differentiator. (21)
b. Any other answer, review Section D.1.4 and go on to Frame 21.

FRAME 21

An *RC* waveshaping network frequently used for "stretching" short duration signal pulses is called an ________.

a. Integrator (END)
b. Any other answer, review Section D.1.5.

E. PROBLEMS FOR SOLUTION OR RESEARCH

1. Calculate the true, reactive, and apparent power in the circuit of Figure 16.55.

a. What is the power factor (pf) of the circuit?
b. What is the Q of the circuit at its source frequency of 1.2 kHz?
c. What is the power dissipated by $R3$?

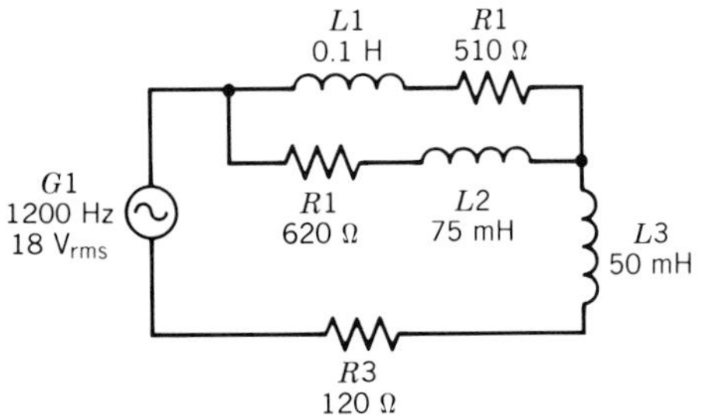

Figure 16.55 Circuit for Problem 1.

2. Write the complex rectangular coordinate expression for the impedance of each branch of the circuit shown in Figure 16.56.

a. What are the true, reactive, and apparent power in each branch?
b. Calculate the total circuit impedance.
c. Use the circuit impedance to calculate the circuit current and the true, reactive, and apparent power in the circuit.
d. Compare the power figures obtained in part (c) with the sum of the branch powers. Are they equal? (*Hint:* Remember to use phasor methods to add the power figures obtained in part (a).

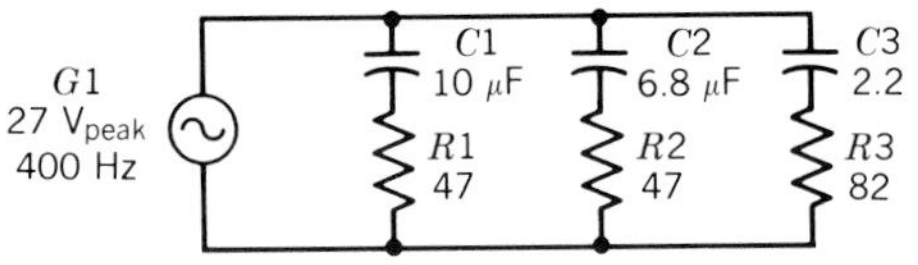

Figure 16.56 Circuit for Problem 2.

3. Calculate the true, reactive, and apparent power in the circuit shown in Figure 16.57.

a. What is the power factor of the circuit?
b. Calculate the power dissipated by each resistor.
c. Calculate the potential difference across each capacitor.

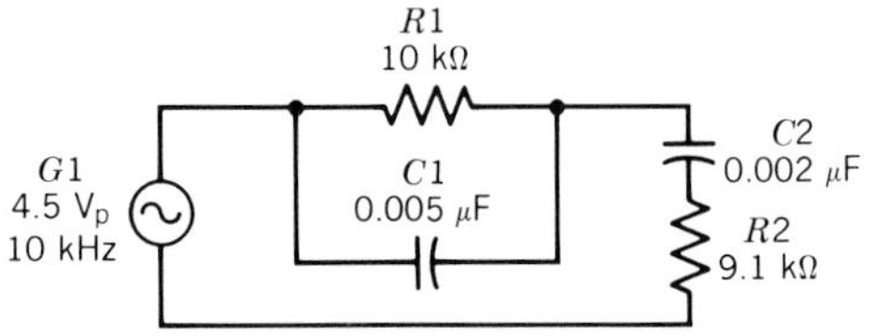

Figure 16.57 Circuit for Problem 3.

4. Calculate the power dissipated by $R3$ in the circuit of Figure 16.58.

a. What is the power dissipation in $R1$ with $G2$ shorted?
b. What is the potential difference across $L2$ with $G1$ shorted?

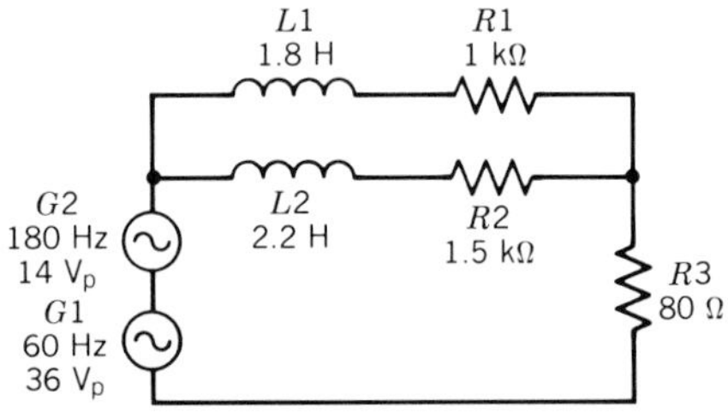

Figure 16.58 Circuit for Problem 4.

5. A square wave with a peak amplitude of 5 V and a period of 1 ms is applied to a series circuit consisting of a 0.1 μF capacitor and a 270 Ω resistor. What is the power dissipated in the resistor? (*Hint:* Consider the square wave as the product of at least six sine-wave inputs added together.)

6. A triangle waveform with a peak potential of 5 V and a period of 1 ms is applied to the circuit of Problem 5. What is the power dissipated in the resistor? Is there more power provided by a square-wave generator than a triangle-wave generator?

7. Repeat Problems 5 and 6 using a circuit composed of a 0.1 H inductor and a 2.7 kΩ resistor.

8. Calculate the power factor for each of the component sine-wave frequencies in Problems 5, 6, and 7. What is the effect on the power factor for an increase in source frequency in a series *RC* circuit? In a series *RL* circuit?

9. Repeat Problems 5 through 8 for a parallel rather than a series combination of the components.

10. Obtain schematic diagrams of such standard electronic units as television receivers, communications receivers, and small personal computers. Use a yellow highlighter to mark the bypass capacitors and any *RC* networks. Try to analyze the functions of the *RC* networks.

CHAPTER 17 RCL AND TUNED CIRCUITS

A. CHAPTER PREVIEW

1 Studying the first section of this chapter will enable you to analyze series, parallel, and series–parallel circuits that combine inductance, capacitance, and resistance in various arrangements.

2 You will also learn to identify the surprising effects produced by the combination of inductance and capacitance in a circuit. Some of these effects are caused by a condition called *resonance*. You will learn about the effects of resonance in series, parallel, and complex circuits.

3 After completing this chapter, you will be able to predict circuit values based on the quality factor, or Q, of a resonant circuit and on the characteristic known as *bandwidth*.

4 The Examples and Computations section provides practice in the analysis of complex RCL and resonant circuits.

5 In the Applications section of this chapter, you will cover important material on practical tuned circuits, which serves as an introduction to passive filter circuits.

B. PRINCIPLES

B.1 SERIES RCL CIRCUITS

A circuit containing resistance, capacitance, and inductance, that is, an *RCL* circuit, will not be any more difficult to analyze or troubleshoot than an *RC* or *RL* circuit if you keep three basic facts in mind:

1. The current through a resistor is in phase with the potential difference across the resistor.

2. The current through an inductance *lags* the potential difference across the inductance.

3. The current into and out of a capacitance *leads* the potential difference across the capacitance.

Notice that the second and third of these ideas express exactly opposite effects. This can be most easily understood by looking at an actual circuit. Figure 17.1 shows a series circuit combining a source, an inductor, a capacitor, and a resistance. Since the current is chosen as the reference in a series circuit, the potential difference across the capacitor will lag the reference phasor, while the potential difference across the inductor will lead the reference phasor. This is shown by the phasor diagram in Figure 17.2. Notice that the potential difference across $C1$ is larger than either the potential difference across the inductor or the resistor. This is true because the reactance of the capacitor is greater than either the reactance of the inductor or the resistance of the resistor.

Figure 17.1 A series circuit containing inductance, capacitance, and resistance.

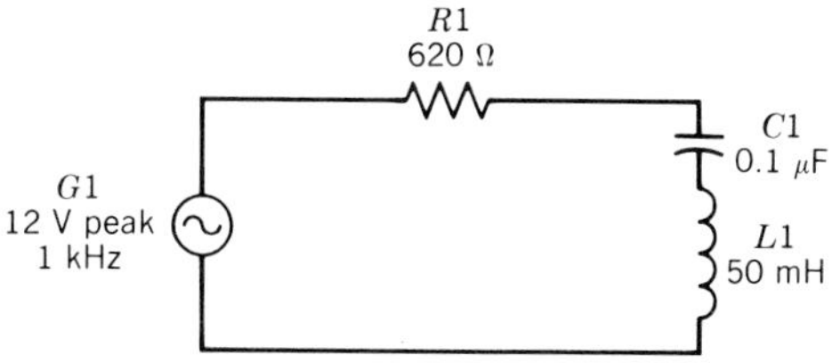

Figure 17.2 Phase relationship of the potential differences across $R1$, $L1$, and $C1$ in Figure 17.1.

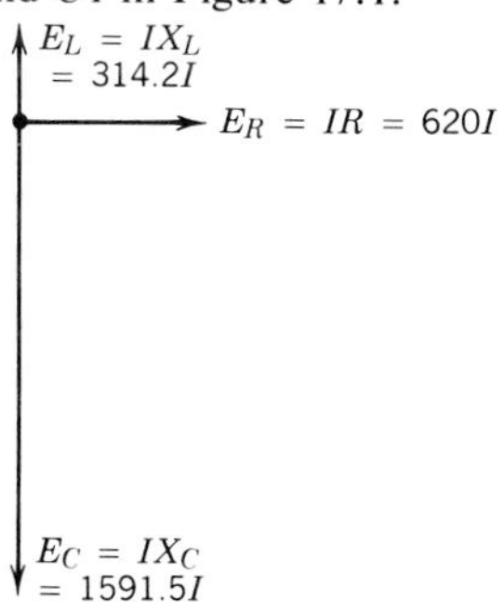

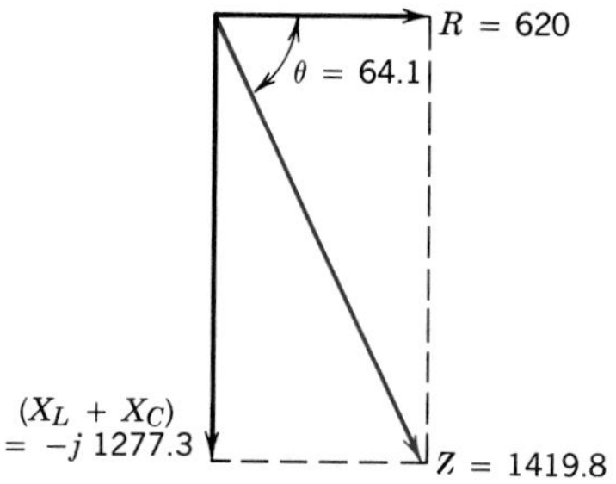

Figure 17.3 Phasor diagram of the resistance and reactance in the circuit of Figure 17.1.

The phasor diagram of the resistance and circuit reactances is shown in Figure 17.3. The total circuit impedance will then be the phasor sum of the resistance and capacitive and inductive reactances. Using complete rectangular coordinates,

$$Z_t = R + X_L + X_C$$

or

$$R = 620 + j0$$
$$X_L = 0 + j314.2$$
$$X_C = 0 - j1591.5$$
$$Z_t = 620 + j(-1591.5 + 314.2)$$
$$620 - j1277.3$$

Notice that the reactive term of the circuit impedance, $-j1277.3$, is the difference between the capacitive reactance and the inductive reactance, and that it has the sign of the larger reactance, the capacitive reactance in this case.

In mathematical terms, the general formula for the impedance of a series *RCL* circuit is

$$Z_t = R + j(X_L - X_C) \qquad \text{FORMULA 17.1}$$

From Figure 17.3 you can see that θ, the phase angle between the reference and the impedance phasor, is

$$\theta = \tan^{-1}\frac{X_L - X_C}{R} \qquad \text{FORMULA 17.2}$$

It is frequently necessary to express Z_t in polar coordinates for purposes of computation. This expression can be obtained either from the complex rectangular form or directly by using the formula

$$Z_t = \sqrt{R^2 + (X_L - X_C)^2} \quad \angle \tan^{-1}\frac{X_L - X_C}{R}$$

FORMULA 17.3

In the case of the circuit shown in Figure 17.1, the

polar form of the impedance is

$$Z_t = 1419.8 \angle -64.1^\circ$$

Once the impedance of the series circuit has been calculated, the circuit current can be obtained from $I = \frac{E}{Z_t}$. Using rms values,

$$I = \frac{0.707(12) \angle 0^\circ}{1419.8 \angle -64.1^\circ}$$

$$= 0.005975 \quad \text{or} \quad 5.98 \angle 64.1^\circ \text{ mA}$$

The reason that a phase angle other than zero is assigned to the current is that the above calculation used the source potential difference rather than the current as the reference. Since the phase angle between the source potential and the circuit current is known, it is possible to change the reference:

$$I_{\text{rms}} = 5.98 \angle 0^\circ \text{ mA} \quad \text{and} \quad E_{\text{rms}} = 8.484 \angle -64.1^\circ \text{ V}$$

This retains the same phase relationship between the current and source potential while using the current as the reference phasor.

It is now possible to observe one of the surprising effects of combining inductance, capacitance, and resistance in a circuit. Using the rms value for the current, the rms voltage drops across $C1$, $L1$, and $R1$ can be calculated:

$$E_{C1} = IX_C = I \times \frac{1}{2\pi fC} = 9.52 \text{ V}$$

$$E_{L1} = IX_L = I \times 2\pi fL = 1.88 \text{ V}$$

$$E_{R1} = IR = 620I = 3.71 \text{ V}$$

Note that the sum of these voltage drops is 15.11 V, but the rms value of the source potential difference is only $0.707 \times 12 = 8.484$ V! The circuit seems to violate Kirchhoff's voltage law.

Happily, this violation of the voltage law is not real, as a closer examination of what occurs during a single cycle in an *RCL* circuit will show. Consider the single cycle of the circuit current between points *A* and *B* in Figure 17.4*a*. Starting at point *A*, the circuit current is falling from its maximum value to zero. Since the potential difference across the capacitor lags the circuit current by 90°, the capacitor is receiving a charge during this time, as shown in Figure 17.4*b*. At any time during this interval, the product of the instantaneous value of the circuit current and the potential difference across the capacitor is positive, as shown in Figure 17.4*c*. This means that the capacitor is storing energy. The shaded area between the horizontal axis and the curve, which is the integral of the product of the potential difference and circuit current with respect to

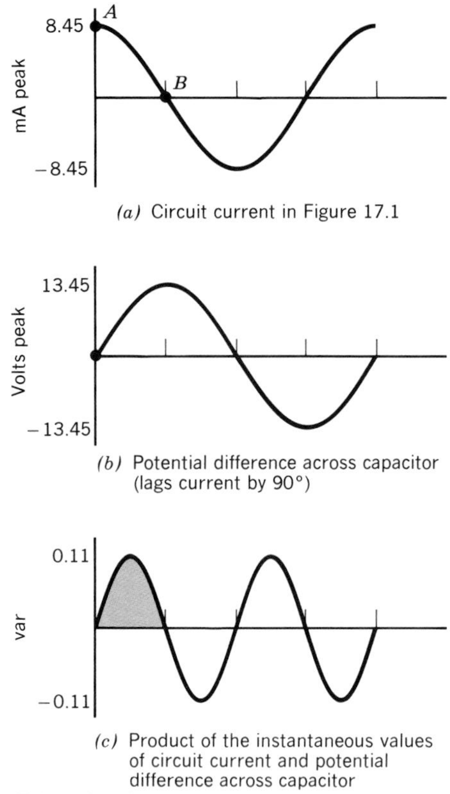

Figure 17.4 Circuit current and component potential differences in a series *RCL* circuit.

time, represents the amount of energy stored at any moment.

In an *RC* circuit, the energy being stored in the capacitor would have to come from the source. In an *RCL* circuit, however, this is not true. During the first quarter cycle following point *A*, when the circuit current is dropping, the magnetic field around the inductor is collapsing. This means that the inductor is acting as a second power source in the circuit during this period. This is shown by the fact that the potential difference across the coil (disregarding the resistance of the coil) leads the circuit current by 90° as shown in Figure 17.5*b*. The product of the instantaneous values of the circuit current and the potential difference across the coil results in the curve below the horizontal axis shown in Figure 17.5*c*. The shaded area below the horizontal axis represents the amount of power returned to the circuit during the first quarter cycle. Comparing Figures 17.4 and 17.5, you can see that the amount of power stored in the capacitor is greater than the amount of power returned to the circuit by the inductor. The difference is the amount of power supplied to the capacitor by the source, which is in addition to the amount dissipated by the resistor $R1$ in Figure 17.1.

During the second 90° of the cycle shown in Figure 17.4*a*, $C1$ discharges from its maximum to zero, as

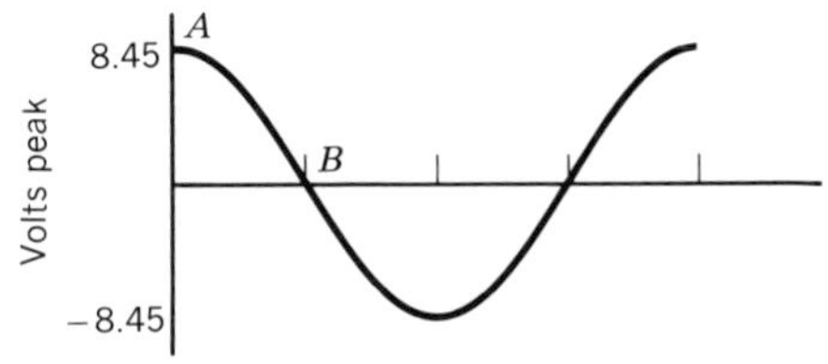

(a) Circuit current in Figure 17.1

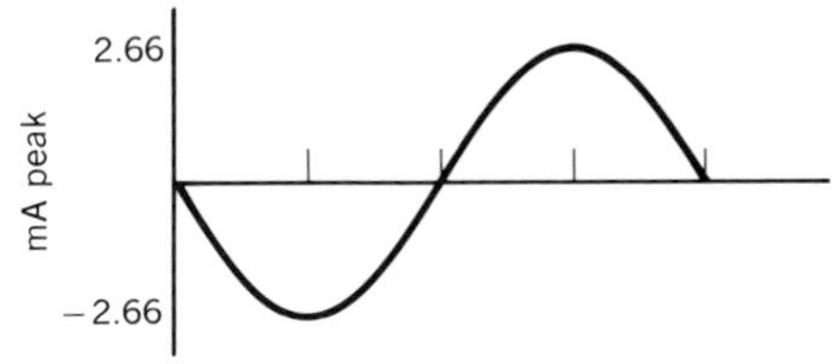

(b) Potential difference across inductor (leads current by 90°)

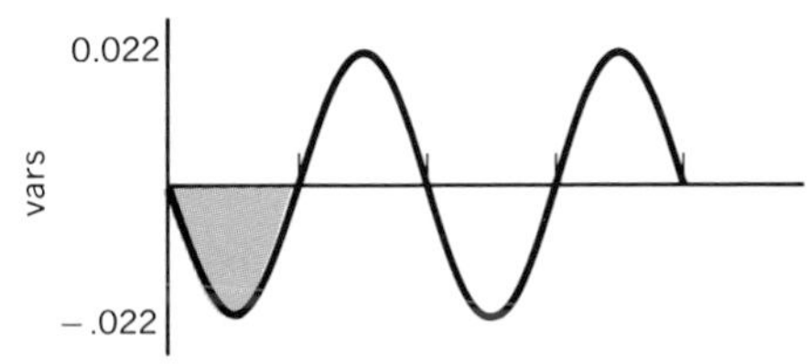

(c) Product of the instantaneous values of circuit current and potential difference across inductor

Figure 17.5 Circuit current and potential difference across the inductor in a series *RCL* circuit.

shown by the graph of the potential difference across *C*1 in Figure 17.4*b*. The product of the potential difference across the capacitor and the circuit current will be negative as in Figure 17.4*c*. This means that *C*1 is supplying power to the circuit. The inductor, on the other hand, is now drawing power from the circuit, as the magnetic field builds up around it, since the product of the circuit current and the potential difference across the capacitor is positive in sign. Again comparing Figures 17.4 and 17.5, you can see that the amount of power being stored in the magnetic field around *L*1 is less than the amount of power returned to the circuit by the capacitor. This additional power is dissipated in the circuit resistance and, in practical circuits, in the internal resistance of the source.

A similar interchange of power between the capacitor and the inductor takes place during the third and fourth 90° of the cycle. This explains the seeming violation of Kirchhoff's voltage law, since at any instant of time, only one of the reactive circuit components is acting as a load, the other is acting as a source. At a specific instant of time t, therefore, the Kirchhoff's voltage law equation for the circuit of Figure 17.1 is

$$e_s = -e_r \pm (e_L - e_C)$$

The symbol ± is used to denote the fact that the difference between the potential difference across the inductor and capacitor can be either a voltage rise or a voltage drop. In addition to the instantaneous values of potential differences, the rms values can be used if attention is paid to the phase angles. If the rms value of the current is used to obtain values for the potential differences across *C*1 and *L*1, and if these values are added to the potential difference across *R*1, then the sum of the potential drops in the circuit will be equal to the rms value of the source potential difference. (Bear in mind that the potential differences across *C*1 and *L*1 have phase angles of −90° and +90°, respectively.

EXAMPLE:

A series *RCL* circuit is connected across a 450 kHz ac source with a peak potential difference of 24 V as shown in Figure 17.6. The inductor is found to be burned out. Should it be replaced by a component with the same characteristics? What about the capacitor? Is it being operated within its rating? ■

SOLUTION

A burned-out component can be the result of a number of things, such as abnormally high current or a component forced to operate at a point above its normal working voltage. To see if the latter cause is the case here, the peak potential difference across *L*1 can be calculated. To do this, the circuit impedance and circuit current are obtained first. Using Formula 17.2 for the impedance,

$$Z_t = \sqrt{R^2 + (X_L - X_C)^2} \,\Big/ \tan^{-1}\frac{(X_L - X_C)}{R}$$

$$Z_t = \sqrt{(120)^2 + \left(2\pi f L - \frac{1}{2\pi f C}\right)^2} \,\Big/ \tan^{-1}\frac{X_L - X_C}{R}$$

$$Z_t = \sqrt{14400 + (28274.3 - 17683.9)^2} \,\angle \tan^{-1} 88.25$$

$$Z_t = 10591.2 \,\angle 89.4^\circ$$

Figure 17.6 A series *RCL* circuit for troubleshooting calculations.

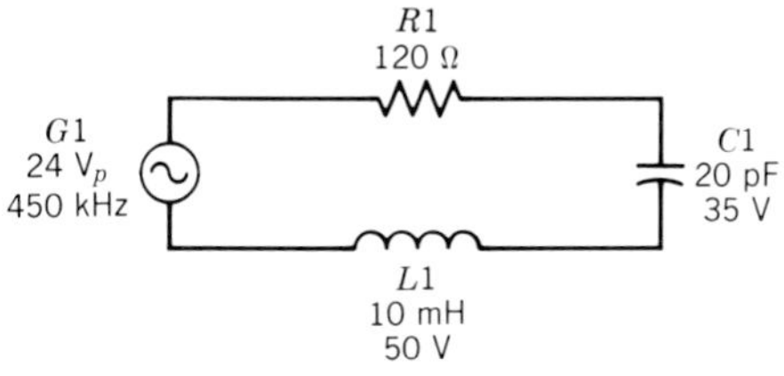

The rms value of the circuit current is given by

$$I = \frac{E}{Z} \quad \text{or} \quad I = \frac{0.707 \times 24}{10591.2} = 1.6 \text{ mA}$$

Since the current is taken as the reference, the phase angle of the current is considered 0°, the source potential is considered to be 24 $\angle 89.40°$ V. The rms potential difference across the inductor in normal operation is therefore

$$E_{L1} = IX_L = 45.24 \angle 90° \text{ V}$$

and the peak potential difference is

$$45.24 \times 1.414 = 63.97 \angle 90° \quad \text{or} \quad 64 \text{ V}$$

Clearly, an inductor rated at 50 V is not sufficient. In the case of the capacitor,

$$E_{C1} = IX_C = 28.3 \angle -90° \text{ V}$$

but the peak potential is 28.3 × 1.414 = 40 V, again above the rated working voltage. ■

This example is typical of series *RCL* circuits, where the potential difference across the reactive components can be much higher than the potential difference supplied by the source. In Section B.4, you will see that this increase in potential is related to the quality factor, or Q, of the circuit. Unfortunately, you will also learn that any attempt to connect a load across a reactive component in order to use this increased potential difference has the effect of reducing it drastically. This is referred to as "loading the *RCL* circuit."

If the circuit current and phase angle in a series *RCL* circuit are known, there are a number of ways to calculate the power in the circuit. Since the only circuit component that actually dissipates power is the resistor, (it is assumed that the resistance of the inductor, the *ESR* of the capacitor, and the internal resistance of the source are small in comparison with the reactances), the formulas

$$P = I^2R \quad \text{and} \quad P = \frac{E^2}{R}$$

could be used for the true power dissipated. However, if the source potential difference, circuit current, and phase angle are known, the true, apparent, and reactive power is easy to calculate:

$$P = IE \cos \theta$$
$$P_a = IE$$
$$P_r = IE \sin \theta$$

EXAMPLE:
Calculate the true, apparent, and reactive power in the circuit of Figure 17.6.

SOLUTION:
The true power, that is, the power dissipated in the resistance, is

$$P = IE \cos \theta$$
$$= 1.6 \times 10^{-3} \times (0.707 \times 24) \times 0.01 = 0.27 \text{ mW}$$

The apparent power is

$$P_a = IE = 1.6 \times 10^{-3} (0.707 \times 24) = 0.027 \text{ V-A}$$

The reactive power is

$$P_r = IE \sin \theta = 1.6 \times 10^{-3} \times (0.707 \times 24) \times 0.99$$
$$= 0.0268 \text{ var}$$
■

B.2 PARALLEL *RCL* CIRCUITS

The circuit shown in Figure 17.7 is the simplest form of parallel *RCL* circuit. In spite of this, it is fairly common to find practical circuits that function in the same way as the circuit shown. This is the case when the series resistance of the inductor and the ESR of the capacitor are both small when compared to either the reactance of $L1$ or $C1$ or to the resistance of $R1$. Recalling that the source potential difference is the same across each component, and that it is the reference in a parallel circuit, the current in each branch can easily be calculated. For the resistive branch:

$$I_{R1} = \frac{E}{R} = \frac{0.707 \times 16}{33} = 0.343 \text{ A} \angle 0°$$

In the branch containing $C1$,

$$I_{C1} = \frac{E}{X_{C1}} = \frac{0.707 \times 16}{\frac{1}{2\pi fC}} = 0.142 \text{ A} \angle 90°$$

In the branch containing $L1$,

$$I_{L1} = \frac{E}{X_{L1}} = \frac{0.707 \times 16}{2\pi fL} = 0.45 \text{ A} \angle -90°$$

Since each of the branches is a pure reactance or a pure resistance, the phase shift of the current in each of them is known and can be assigned without further calculation.

By converting these polar notations into complex rectangular form, the total circuit current can be ob-

Figure 17.7 A parallel *RCL* circuit in its simplest form.

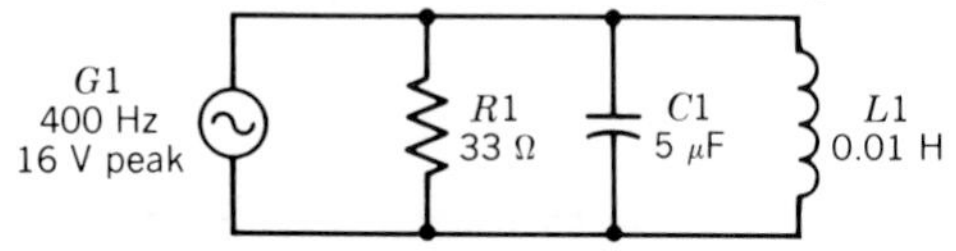

tained by a simple matter of addition:

$$\begin{aligned} I_{R1} &= 0.343\ \angle 0^\circ &&= 0.343 + j0 \\ I_{C1} &= 0.142\ \angle 90^\circ &&= 0 + j0.142 \\ I_{L1} &= 0.45\ \angle -90^\circ &&= 0 - j0.45 \\ \hline I_T & &&= 0.343 - j0.308 \end{aligned}$$

Changing this value for I_T into polar coordinates will provide the rms value of the current and the phase angle. Using the rectangular to polar coordinate function of a scientific calculator,

$$I_T = 0.461\ \angle -41.9^\circ$$

Using the polar coordinate values for the source potential difference and the current, the impedance of the parallel network can be calculated from

$$Z = \frac{E}{I} = \frac{0.707 \times 16\ \angle 0^\circ}{0.461\ \angle -41.9^\circ} = 24.54\ \angle 41.9^\circ$$

It is interesting to note that if this impedance is converted into complex rectangular coordinates,

$$24.54\ \angle 41.9^\circ = 18.27 + j16.39$$

and the result can be considered as the complex rectangular notation for a *series RL* circuit that is the equivalent of the parallel circuit of Figure 17.7. At a frequency of 400 Hz, the series inductance is $X_L = 2\pi f L$, or

$$L = \frac{X_L}{2\pi f} = 0.00652 = 6.52 \text{ mH}$$

The schematic diagram of this series circuit is shown in Figure 17.8. Remember, however, that all this equivalency means is that to the 400-Hz source, the circuit of Figure 17.8 would result in the same total current and phase angle as that shown in Figure 17.7.

The apparent, true, and reactive power of the entire circuit can be calculated in the same way as for the series *RCL* circuit discussed in Section B.1. The apparent power is

$$P_a = EI = 11.31\ \angle 0^\circ \times 0.461\ \angle -41.9^\circ = 5.21\ \angle -41.9^\circ \text{ V-A}$$

Figure 17.8 A series *RL* circuit that is the equivalent of the parallel *RCL* circuit of Figure 17.7 (as far as the source is concerned).

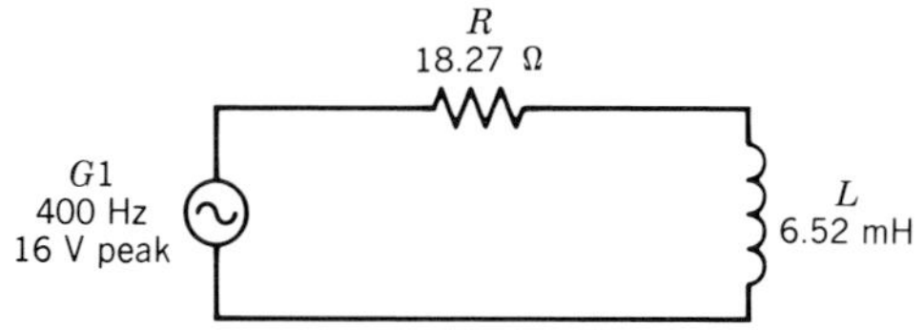

The true power is

$$P = EI \cos\theta = 3.88 \text{ W}$$

while the reactive power is

$$P_r = EI \sin\theta = -3.48 \text{ var}$$

An alternate way of calculating circuit power would be to use the formula

$$P = \frac{E^2}{R} = 3.88 \text{ W}$$

to calculate the true power. The reactive power is the phasor sum of the capacitive and inductive power,

$$P_{L1} = \frac{E^2}{X_{L1}} = \frac{(0.707 \times 16)^2}{25.13} = -5.09 \text{ var}$$

$$P_{C1} = \frac{E^2}{X_{C1}} = \frac{(0.707 \times 16)^2}{79.58} = +1.61 \text{ var}$$

The phasor sum is $+j1.61 - j5.09 = -j3.48$, or -3.48 var. (The negative sign here, as in the solution to the $EI \sin\theta$ above, means that the phase angle of the power is in the fourth quadrant, as shown in Figure 17.9.) The apparent power can then be obtained by converting the complex rectangular expression of its components into rectangular form:

$$P_a = 3.88 - j3.48 = 5.21\ \angle -41.9^\circ \text{ V-A}$$

EXAMPLE:
The parallel *RCL* network shown in Figure 17.10*a* is connected to a 455 kHz source with $E = 4.2$ V. Draw an equivalent series circuit and calculate the true power dissipated in its resistance. ■

Figure 17.9 Phasor diagram of the power in the circuit shown in Figure 17.7.

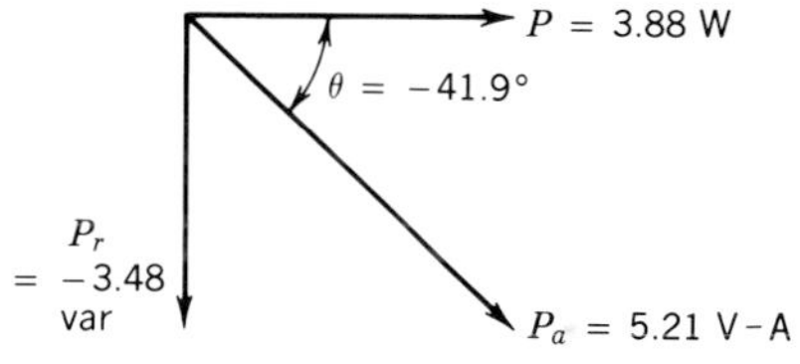

Figure 17.10 A parallel *RCL* network and its series equivalent.

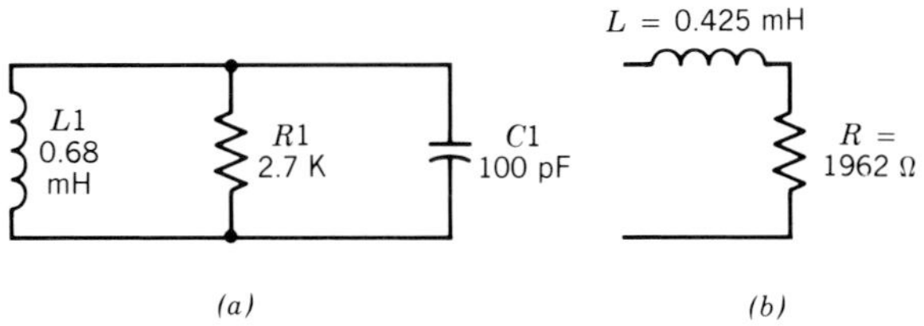

SOLUTION:
The solution to this problem requires the impedance of the parallel network to be calculated. This can be done by determining the reactance of $L1$ and $C1$, calculating the sum of the currents through each branch, and using the relationship $Z = \frac{E}{I}$ to calculate the impedance.

$$X_{L1} = 2\pi fL = 1944 \angle +90^\circ$$

$$X_{C1} = \frac{1}{2\pi fC} = 3498 \angle -90^\circ$$

Since the resistance of $R1$ is 2700 Ω.

$$I_{R1} = \frac{E}{R_1} = 1.55 \angle 0^\circ \text{ mA}$$

$$I_{C1} = \frac{E}{X_C} = 1.2 \angle +90^\circ \text{ mA}$$

$$I_{L1} = \frac{E}{X_L} = 2.16 \angle -90^\circ \text{ mA}$$

The total network current is therefore $1.55 - j0.96$ mA or, in polar form, $1.82 \angle -31.8^\circ$ mA. Now,

$$Z = \frac{E}{I} = \frac{4.2 \angle 0^\circ}{1.82 \times 10^{-3} \angle -31.8^\circ}$$

$$= 2308 \angle +31.8^\circ \ \Omega$$

Converting this value into complex rectangular coordinates provides the resistance and reactance of the equivalent series network:

$$2308 \angle +31.8^\circ = 1962 + j1216$$

In other words, the equivalent network is inductive and has a reactance (rounded off) of 1216 Ω. Since $X_L = 2\pi fL$,

$$L = \frac{X_L}{2\pi f} = \frac{1216}{2\pi f} = 0.425 \text{ mH}$$

The resistance in series with this inductor is 1962 Ω, as shown in Figure 17.10*b*. The only power dissipated in the network when it is connected to the specified source is

$$P = 6.49 \text{ mW}$$

As a check, the true power can also be calculated from

$$P = IE \cos \theta$$

$$= 4.2 \times 182 \times 10^{-3} \times \cos 31.8^\circ$$

$$= 6.49 \text{ mW}$$

■

B.3 SERIES–PARALLEL *RCL* CIRCUITS

Although many networks can be analyzed as though they were either series or parallel *RCL* networks, many others require circuit simplification by means of the substitution of equivalents or other methods before they can be analyzed. Consider the circuit shown in Figure 17.11*a*. The basis of this circuit is a π filter composed of $C1$, $L1$, and $C2$, connected between a source $G1$ and a load resistor $R1$, as shown in Figure 17.11*b*. This particular network was once the most common *RCL* network and was used to eliminate 60-Hz noise from the high-voltage power supplies of most radio and television receivers. The example shown disregards any dc output of the source and considers only the ac noise component.

With the aid of a calculator to speed the conversion between the polar and complex rectangular coordinate systems, the method of equivalent circuits can be used to obtain the total impedance of the network as well as any other circuit values that might be required. If only the total network impedance or circuit current is required, the order in which the components are combined to form equivalents is not important. On the other hand, if you need to calculate the current through one or more branches or the potential difference across one or more components, it is best, when possible, to begin the process of replacing series or parallel arrangements with equivalents at the circuit output or point furthest from the source. Then, working back toward the source in an orderly manner will make it easier to calculate branch currents and potential differences, as shown in this example.

The first step in the substitution of equivalents should begin with combining $R1$ and $C2$ into a single impedance. At a frequency of 60 Hz, the capacitive reactance of an 8 μF capacitor is

$$X_C = \frac{1}{2\pi fC} = 331.6 \ \Omega$$

Using the product-over-the-sum formula, the parallel resistance and capacitance can be combined into a single impedance. Notice that since it is the potential difference across both components that is the same, the potential difference is the reference, and the phase angle of the capacitive reactance is -90°. The impedance of $R1$ and $C2$ is

$$Z_{eq1} = \frac{Z_{R1}Z_{C2}}{Z_{R1} + Z_{C2}} = \frac{100 \angle 0^\circ \times 331.6 \angle -90^\circ}{100 - j331.6}$$

The denominator of this fraction is given in complex rectangular form since it is the sum of Z_{R1} and Z_{C2}.

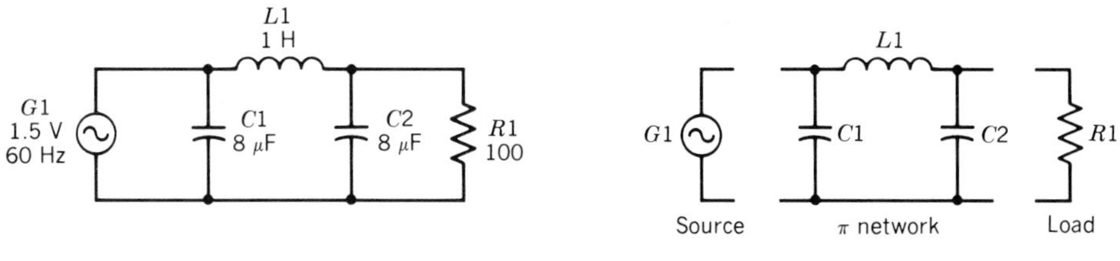

(a) Power supply filter circuit (b) Parts of the power supply filter

Figure 17.11 A common series–parallel *RCL* circuit.

Converting it to polar form produces

$$Z_{eq1} = \frac{100 \angle 0^\circ \times 331.6 \angle -90^\circ}{346.4 \angle -73.2^\circ}$$

Performing the multiplication of the numerator and dividing gives

$$Z_{eq1} = \frac{33160 \angle -90^\circ}{346.4 \angle -73.2^\circ} = 95.73 \angle -16.8^\circ$$

In other words, the parallel combination of $R1$ and $C2$ can be replaced by an impedance whose polar form is $95.73 \angle -16.8^\circ$ Ω. The original circuit with $C2$ and $R1$ replaced by Z_{eq1} is shown in Figure 17.12*a*. The complex rectangular notation is used in the diagram, in addition to the polar form, so that the equivalent of $L1$ and Z_{eq1} can be calculated easily. Notice that Z_{eq1} could also be represented as a 91.6 Ω resistor in series with a capacitor with a reactance of 27.7 Ω at 60 Hz. Since $X_C = \dfrac{1}{2\pi f C}$, the capacitance would be

$$C = \frac{1}{2\pi f X_C} = 95.8\ \mu\text{F}$$

The inductive reactance of $L1$ at 60 Hz is $X_{L1} = 2\pi f L = 377 \angle 90^\circ$ Ω. Combining this with $Z_{eq1} = 91.6 - j27.7$ by phasor addition gives the impedance of Z_{eq2}, which combines both Z_{eq1} and $L1$ into a single equivalent impedance Z_{eq2}:

$$\begin{aligned} Z_{eq1} &= 91.6 - j27.7 \\ + X_{L1} &= + j377 \\ \hline Z_{eq2} &= 91.6 + j349.3 = 361.1 \angle 75.3^\circ \end{aligned}$$

In other words, Z_{eq1} and $L1$ could be replaced by a single impedance Z_{eq2}. Or, if desired, Z_{eq2} can be considered as a 91.6 Ω resistor in series with an inductor with an inductive reactance of 349.3 Ω at a frequency of 60 Hz. This would be a 0.93 H inductor. The original circuit with Z_{eq2} substituted for $L2$, $C2$, and $R1$ is shown in Figure 17.12*b*.

The final step in calculating the impedance connected to the 60 Hz source is to calculate the equivalent of $C1$ and Z_{eq2}. In polar form, Z_{eq2} is $361.1 \angle 75.3^\circ$.

The equivalent impedance of $C1$ and Z_{eq2} is given by

$$Z_{eq3} = \frac{X_{C1} \times Z_{eq2}}{X_{C1} + Z_{eq2}}$$

Since the capacitive reactance of an 8 μF capacitor has been previously calculated, this equation becomes

$$Z_{eq3} = \frac{331.6 \angle -90^\circ \times 361.1 \angle 75.3^\circ}{(0 - j331.6) + (91.6 + j349.3)}$$

Notice that the expressions for X_{C1} and Z_{eq2} are written in complex rectangular form in the denominator for the purpose of addition. Adding the two terms in the denominator produces

$$Z_{eq3} = \frac{331.6 \angle -90^\circ \times 361.1 \angle 75.3^\circ}{91.6 + j17.7}$$

Figure 17.12 Simplifying an *RCL* circuit by the method of equivalents.

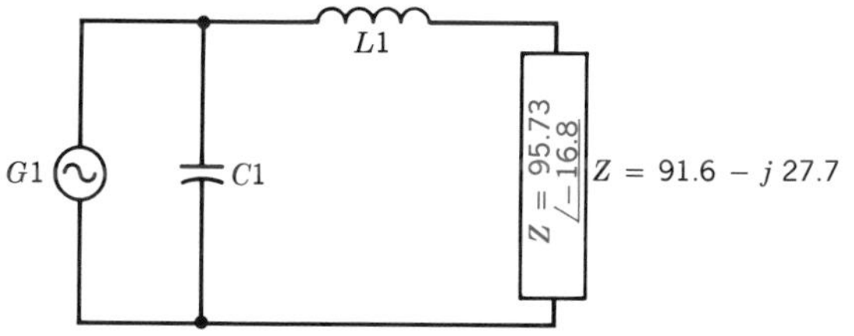

(a) C2 and R1 replaced by $Z_{eq\,1}$

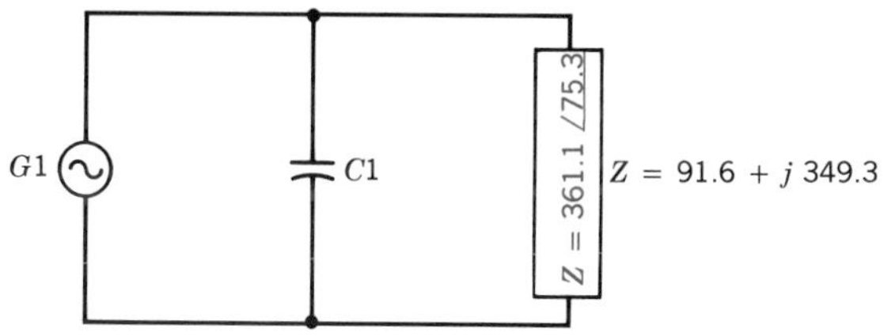

(b) L1 and $Z_{eq\,1}$ replaced by $Z_{eq\,2}$

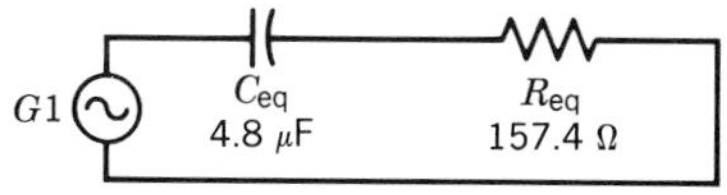

(c) C1 and $Z_{eq\,2}$ replaced by an equivalent series circuit

Converting the denominator to polar form,

$$Z_{eq3} = \frac{331.6 \angle -90^\circ \times 361.1 \angle 75.3^\circ}{93.3 \angle 10.9^\circ}$$

With all the terms in polar form, the indicated multiplication and division can be carried out:

$$Z_{eq3} = \frac{119740.8 \angle -14.7^\circ}{93.3 \angle 10.9^\circ}$$

$$Z_{eq3} = 1283.4 \angle -25.6^\circ$$

The total circuit impedance is $1283.4 \angle -25.6^\circ$ Ω, or, in complex rectangular form,

$$1157.4 - j554.5\ \Omega$$

As far as the source is concerned, therefore, the load resistor and π filter network could be replaced by a 157.4 Ω resistor in series with a capacitor with a reactance of 554.5 Ω at 60 Hz. Solving, $X_C = \frac{1}{2\pi f C}$, the value of C would be 4.8 μF. The equivalent circuit is shown in Figure 17.12*c*.

Once the total impedance of the circuit is known, the circuit current can be calculated from $I_t = \frac{E}{Z}$. Using the potential difference as the reference,

$$I_t = \frac{E}{Z_{eq3}} = \frac{1.5}{1283.4 \angle -25.6^\circ}$$
$$= 1.17 \angle +25.6^\circ \text{ mA}$$

The phase angle is 25.6°, with the current leading the source potential. Although it requires time to perform all the calculations of equivalents, this method is easy to understand.

In summary, the steps in using the method of equivalents to calculate the total impedance of a series parallel network are:

1. Start by combining the reactances or resistances of the two components furthest from the source, using

$$Z_{eq} = Z_1 + Z_2$$

for series impedances or

$$Z_{eq} = \frac{Z_1 Z_2}{Z_1 + Z_2}$$

for parallel impedances.

2. If necessary, convert from polar to complex rectangular notation or the reverse and combine the impedance of the previously calculated equivalent impedance with the reactance or resistance of the next component.

3. Repeat step 2 until all the components have been combined into a single impedance. This is the impedance of the entire circuit.

4. Use the relationship

$$I_{total} = \frac{E_{source}}{Z_{total}}$$

to calculate the total current supplied by the source, if required.

In most cases, calculations with series–parallel *RCL* circuits of the type shown in Figure 17.11*a* are performed to find the theoretical value of the potential difference across the load and the phase angle of this potential difference compared to the source potential. Since the source potential difference is known in Figure 17.12*b*, you can calculate the current through Z_{eq2}. Using the source potential difference as the reference phasor,

$$I_z = \frac{E_s}{Z_{eq2}} = \frac{1.5 \angle 0^\circ}{361.1 \angle 75.3^\circ} = 4.15 \angle -75.3^\circ \text{ mA}$$

This computation can be checked by calculating the current in the $C1$ branch and adding it to I_Z. If the calculations are correct, the phasor sum should be the same as the circuit current previously computed.

$$I_{C1} = \frac{E}{Z_{C1}} = \frac{1.5 \angle 0^\circ}{331.6 \angle -90^\circ} = 4.5 \angle 90^\circ \text{ mA}$$

Putting both I_Z and I_{C1} in complex rectangular form and adding them produces

$$I_{C1} = 4.5 \angle 90^\circ = 0 + j4.5 \text{ mA}$$
$$I_Z = 4.15 \angle -75.3^\circ = 1.05 - j4.0 \text{ mA}$$
$$I_{C1} + I_Z = 1.05 + j0.5 \text{ mA}$$

In polar form, this is $1.16 \angle 25.4^\circ$, a value close enough to the previously calculated $1.17 \angle 25.6^\circ$ to provide a check. The differences are due to rounding off in the calculations.

Now that the current in the Z_{eq2} branch is known, it can be used to compute the potential drop across $L1$ in Figure 17.11*a*:

$$E_{L1} = I_Z \times X_L$$
$$= (4.15 \times 10^{-3} \angle -75.3^\circ) \times (377 \angle 90^\circ)$$
$$= 1.56 \angle 14.7^\circ$$

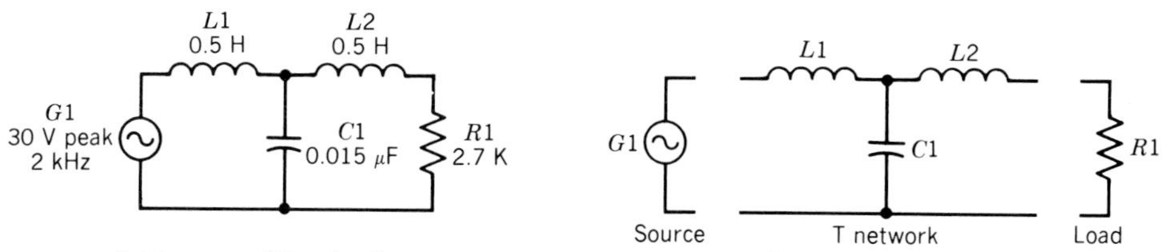

(a) Low-pass filter circuit (b) Parts of the low-pass filter

Figure 17.13 A T filter for analysis by current method.

in rectangular form this is $1.5 + j0.4$. Subtracting E_{L1} from the source potential difference,

$$E_s - E_{L1} = (1.5 + j0) - (1.5 + j0.4)$$
$$= 0 - j0.4$$

or in polar form, $0.4 \angle -90^\circ$ V. In other words, the potential difference across the output ($R1$) has an rms value of 0.4 V and lags the input source potential difference by 90°.

Although the method of equivalents shown above is easier to use, if the current in a particular branch or the potential difference across a component is required, it is better to use the method based on the calculation of branch currents. This method combines the method of equivalents with the calculation of branch currents and provides information more directly than the method of equivalents. Consider the circuit shown in Figure 17.13*a*. Like the circuit shown in Figure 17.11, this is another fairly common filter circuit designed to eliminate higher-frequency components from the potential difference developed across a load ($R1$). The essential parts of the circuit, the source, T network, and load, are drawn in Figure 17.13*b*. As in the case of the equivalent method, it is best to begin calculations with the branch that is farthest from the source. In this case the series combination of $L2$ and $R1$. Calculating the reactance of $L2$ at the source frequency, it is possible to write the impedance of this branch in complex rectangular coordinates without further calculation

$$X_{L2} = 2\pi f L2 = 6283\ \Omega \angle 90^\circ$$

The impedance of $R1$ and $L2$ is

$$Z_{R1,L2} = 2700 + j6283$$

or in polar notation

$$Z_{R1,L2} = 6838.6 \angle 66.7^\circ$$

The reactance of the next branch, consisting only of C_1 is

$$X_{C1} = \frac{1}{2\pi f C} = 5305\ \Omega \angle -90^\circ$$

The impedance of the branch in complex rectangular notation is therefore

$$Z_{C1} = 0 - j5305$$

Instead of using the product-over-the-sum formula to calculate the impedance of $C1$ in parallel with $L2$ and $R1$, a little trick is used. The trick consists of assuming the existence of some convenient potential difference with the same frequency as the source across the two branches. This is shown in Figure 17.14. Notice that the rest of the circuit, consisting of $L1$ and the source is ignored. If the potential difference chosen is 10 V, the currents in the two branches would be

$$I_{C1} = \frac{E}{Z_{C1}} = \frac{10 \angle 0^\circ}{5305 \angle -90^\circ} = 0.00189 \angle 90^\circ$$

and

$$I_{R1,L2} = \frac{E}{Z_{R1,L2}} = \frac{10 \angle 0^\circ}{6838.6 \angle 66.7^\circ} = 0.00146 \angle -66.7^\circ$$

Converting $I_{R1,L2}$ and I_{C1} to complex rectangular coordinates and adding them:

$$\begin{array}{lcl} I_{C1} & = & 0 + j0.00189 \\ I_{R1,L2} & = & 0.00058 - j0.00134 \\ \hline I & = & 0.00058 + j0.00055 \end{array}$$

Now, this supposed current can be converted to polar form and substituted into the formula $Z = \frac{E}{I}$ to calculate the impedance of $C1$, $L2$, and $R1$:

$$Z_{C1,L2,R1} = \frac{10 \angle 0^\circ}{0.000799 \angle 43.5^\circ} = 12516 \angle -43.5^\circ$$

Figure 17.14 Calculating the impedance of two parallel branches by assuming a potential difference and then calculating the branch currents.

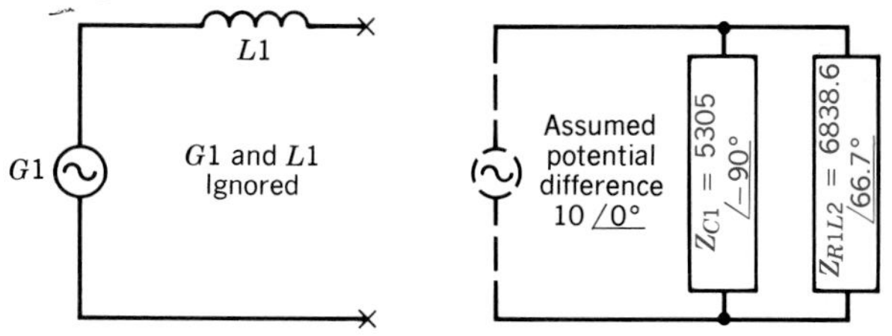

or, in complex rectangular form:

$$9079 - j8615$$

The reactance of $L1$ is in series with $Z_{C1,L2,R1}$, so it can be added to give the total impedance of the circuit:

$$\begin{aligned} Z_{C1,L2,R1} &= 9079 - j8615 \\ X_{L1} &= \quad\; 0 + j6283 \\ \hline Z_{\text{total}} &= 9079 - j2332 \end{aligned}$$

or in polar form

$$Z_{\text{total}} = 9374 \angle -14.4^\circ$$

In circuits of this type, as in the case of the power supply filter shown before, it is frequently necessary to determine the potential difference across the load, the current through it, and the phase angle. First, the total circuit current must be calculated. Since the peak, rather than the rms value of the source potential difference, is given, the current is

$$I_T = \frac{0.707E_{peak}}{Z_t} = \frac{21.21 \angle 0^\circ}{9374 \angle -14.4^\circ}$$

$$I_T = 2.26 \angle 14.4^\circ \text{ mA}$$

The voltage drop across $L1$ then is

$$E_{L1} = I_T X_{L1} = 2.26 \times 10^{-3} \angle 14.4^\circ \times 6283 \angle 90^\circ$$
$$= 14.2 \angle 104.4^\circ$$

In complex rectangular form, this is $E_{L1} = -3.35 + j13.75$. Subtracting this value from E_s produces the potential difference across the $C1$ and the $L2$, $R1$ branches. This is

$$E_{L2,R1} = (21.21 + j0) - (-3.53 + j13.75)$$
$$= 24.74 - 13.75$$

or, in polar form

$$28.3 \angle -29.1^\circ$$

Now the current through the L_2,R_1 branch is

$$I_{L2,R1} = \frac{E_{L2,R1}}{Z_{L2,R1}} = \frac{28.3 \angle -29.1^\circ}{6838.6 \angle 66.7^\circ}$$
$$= 0.00414 \angle -95.8^\circ \text{ A} \quad \text{or} \quad 4.14 \angle -95.8^\circ \text{ mA}$$

Since the load resistance is 2.7 K, the potential difference across it is $E = IR$, or $11.2 \angle -95.8^\circ$ V

The steps involved in a branch current analysis are different from those followed in the method of equivalents. They are:

1. Identify components grouped in series and calculate the impedance of all series strings.

2. Starting with the two parallel branches farthest from the source, calculate the total impedance of the two branches by assuming a potential source of some convenient value. Calculate the branch currents and add them. Use $Z = \frac{E}{I}$ *to calculate the impedance of the two branches.*

3. Proceeding toward the source, add the impedance of any component or branch in series.

4. Repeat steps 2 and 3 until the impedance of the entire circuit has been calculated.

5. Calculate circuit and branch currents and potential drops across components as required.

B.4 SERIES RESONANT CIRCUITS

Among the curious effects present in *RCL* circuits, the effect called *resonance* is at once the most surprising and the most useful. Resonance, whether in a series, parallel, or series–parallel circuit, is defined as the condition that exists when the capacitive and inductive reactance of a circuit are equal. In the series circuit shown in Figure 17.15, an inductor $L1$ and capacitor $C1$ are connected in series across a signal generator whose frequency can be varied. The small resistance $R1$ shown in the circuit represents the resistance of the inductor winding plus the ESR of the capacitor. Figure 17.16 is a graph showing the effects of increasing the source frequency on both the capacitive and inductive reactance of the components. At low frequencies, the inductive reactance is also low, but the capacitive reactance is quite high, as shown in the phasor diagram in Figure 17.17*a*. At high frequencies, on the other hand, the capacitor has a low reactance, while the inductive reactance is large. This is shown in the phasor diagram of Figure 17.17*c*. Calculating the circuit impedance at the low frequency of 50 Hz,

$$Z_{\text{low f}} = \sqrt{R^2 + (X_L - X_C)^2} \bigg/ \tan^{-1}\frac{(X_L - X_C)}{R}$$

$$= 2869 \angle -89.9^\circ$$

Figure 17.15 A series resonant circuit composed of $L1$ and $C1$. The resistor $R1$ represents the series coil resistance of $L1$ and ESR of $C1$.

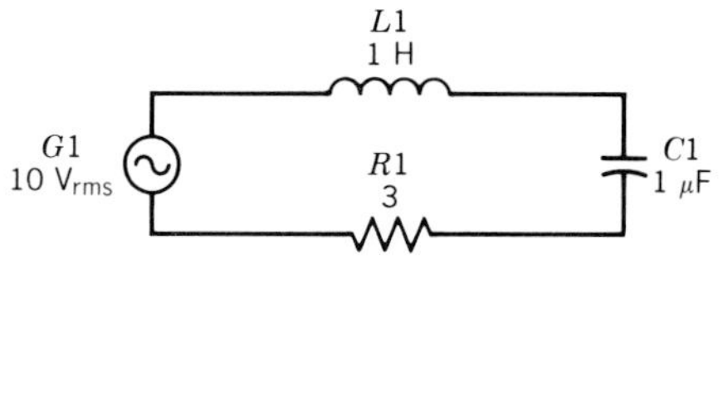

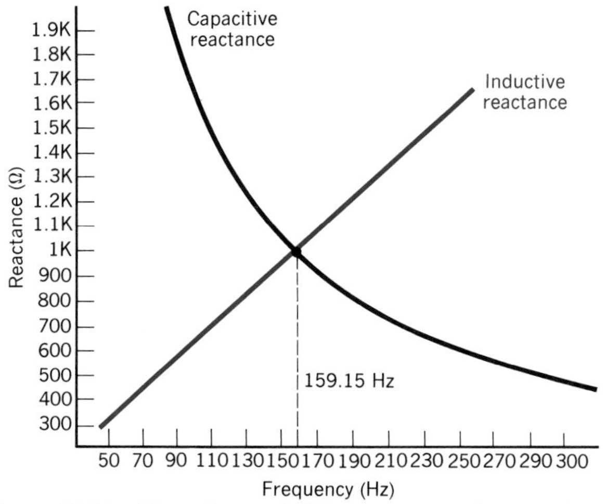

Figure 17.16 The effects of different source frequencies on the capacitive and inductive reactances of $C1$ and $L1$ in Figure 17.15.

At a source frequency of 159.15 Hz, however, the capacitive and inductive reactances are equal, as seen in Figures 17.16 and 17.17*b*. When these values are used to calculate the impedance at 159.15 Hz, the result is

$$Z = \sqrt{R^2 + (X_L - X_C)^2} \angle \tan^{-1}\frac{X_L - X_C}{R}$$

$$= R1 \angle 0^\circ = 3\ \Omega \angle 0^\circ$$

In other words, the only impedance in the circuit at a source frequency of 159.15 Hz is the resistance of the wire forming the inductor and the ESR of the capacitor. This effect is called *resonance*.

Since the circuit impedance is low when the source frequency is at the frequency of circuit resonance, the circuit current will be quite large:

$$I = \frac{E}{R} = \frac{10}{3 \angle 0^\circ} = 3.3 \angle 0^\circ \text{ A}$$

Figure 17.17 Phasor diagrams of the reactances in the circuit of Figure 17.15 with three different source frequencies.

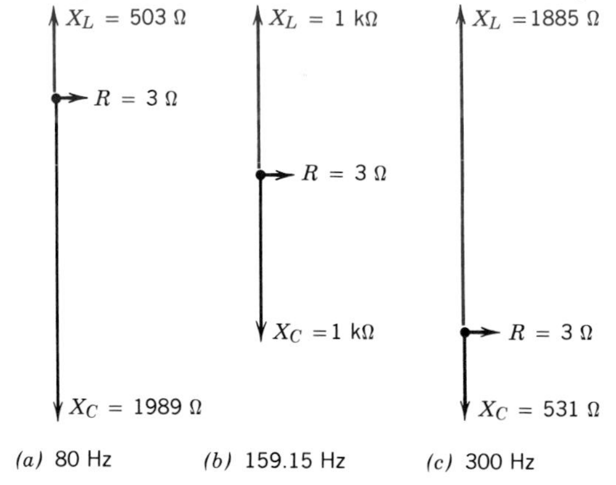

Even a low source potential difference can produce a large circuit current at resonance. Also note that the phase angle is zero. That is, the source potential difference and circuit current in a series circuit are in phase when the source frequency is at the circuit resonant frequency.

It is a simple matter to find the formula relating the capacitance and inductance of a circuit to its frequency of resonance or, as it usually is called *resonant frequency*. At the resonant frequency, f_r, the inductive and capacitive reactances are equal, or

$$2\pi f_r L = \frac{1}{2\pi f_r C}$$

Multiplying both sides by $2\pi f_r C$,

$$4\pi^2 f_r^2 LC = 1$$

Isolating the f_r term:

$$f_r^2 = \frac{1}{4\pi^2 LC}$$

Now, if the square root of both sides is taken,

$$\sqrt{f_r^2} = \sqrt{\frac{1}{4\pi^2 LC}}$$

$$f_r = \frac{1}{\sqrt{4\pi^2 LC}} \quad \text{or}$$

$$f_r = \frac{1}{2\pi\sqrt{LC}} \qquad \text{FORMULA 17.4}$$

This formula is somewhat cumbersome if it is the frequency and either the inductance *or* capacitance that is known and the value of the other component is required. On the other hand, it is a frequently used formula, and is easy to derive if forgotten.

EXAMPLE:
Calculate the resonant frequency of the series *RCL* circuit shown in Figure 17.18. What is the circuit current at resonance? ■

SOLUTION:
Using Formula 17.4, the resonant frequency of the circuit is given by

$$f_r = \frac{1}{2\pi\sqrt{LC}}$$

$$= \frac{1}{2\pi\sqrt{8 \times 10^{-6} \times 3.2 \times 10^{-3}}}$$

$$= 994.7 \text{ Hz}$$

Remember when using this formula to express the ca-

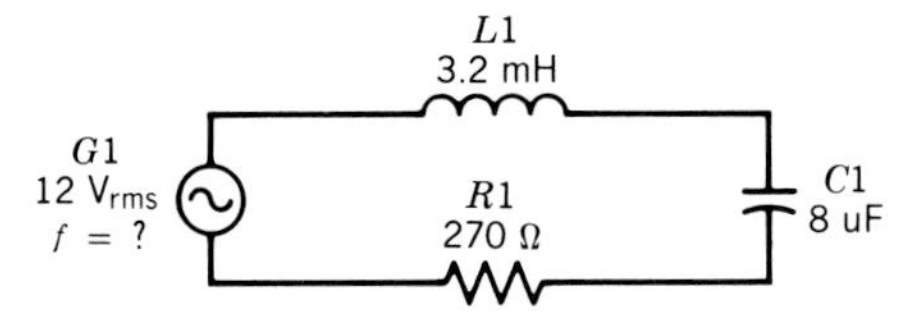

Figure 17.18 A series resonant circuit.

pacitance in farads and the inductance in henries. The circuit current is

$$I = \frac{E}{Z} = \frac{12}{270} = 0.044 \text{ A}$$ ■

Notice that the value of the resistance has no effect on the resonant frequency. It does, however, have an effect on the circuit current and on the potential difference across each of the components at resonance or at any other frequency. This can be seen from an examination of the circuit quality factor, Q. In Chapter 16 you learned that the reactive power stored in the magnetic field around an inductor is I^2X_L and the electric field in a capacitor is I^2X_C. Comparing the reactive power in the circuit shown in Figure 17.15 with the true power dissipated in the resistor, you can see that this ratio is equal to the circuit quality factor Q in a series circuit:

$$\frac{I^2X_L}{I^2R} = \frac{X_L}{R} = Q \qquad \text{FORMULA 17.5}$$

At resonance, the capacitive reactance is equal to the inductive reactance, so that Formula 17.5 could also be written for a series circuit as

$$\frac{I^2X_L}{I^2R} = \frac{X_L}{R} = Q \qquad \text{FORMULA 17.5}$$

As mentioned earlier, circuit Q is usually defined in terms of the inductive reactance in a circuit. In addition to considering Q in a series circuit as the ratio of the reactive power to the true power, it can also be considered the ratio of the potential difference across the inductor to the potential difference across the circuit resistance. Since $Q = \frac{X_L}{R}$, multiplying the right side of this equation by $\frac{I}{I}$ gives

$$Q = \frac{IX_L}{IR} = \frac{E_L}{E_R} \qquad \text{FORMULA 17.7}$$

Figure 17.19*a* is a graph showing how the circuit current in an *RCL* circuit varies as the source frequency changes from a frequency below the resonant frequency to a frequency above resonance. This type of graph is generally called a *resonance curve*. The circuit graphed is shown in Figure 17.19*b*. Comparing Figure 17.19 with the graph and circuit of Figure 17.20 shows the effect of raising the circuit resistance. Notice that the resonance curve in Figure 17.20*a* is shallower than the one in Figure 17.19*a*, and that the peak value of the circuit current at resonance is lower. Further increasing the circuit resistance will flatten the resonance curve further. When the resistance is large compared to either the inductive or capacitive reactance at resonance, the circuit current is determined by the resistance, and resonance effects are minimized.

The bandwidth of an *RCL* circuit is a measure of the range of frequencies around the resonant frequency

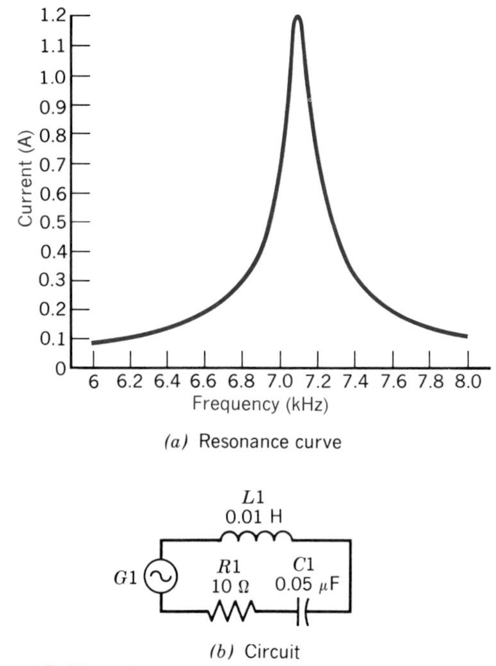

Figure 17.19 Effect of resistance on a resonance curve. Case 1, $R = 10\ \Omega$.

Figure 17.20 Effect of resistance on a 20-resonance curve. Case 2, $R = 100\ \Omega$.

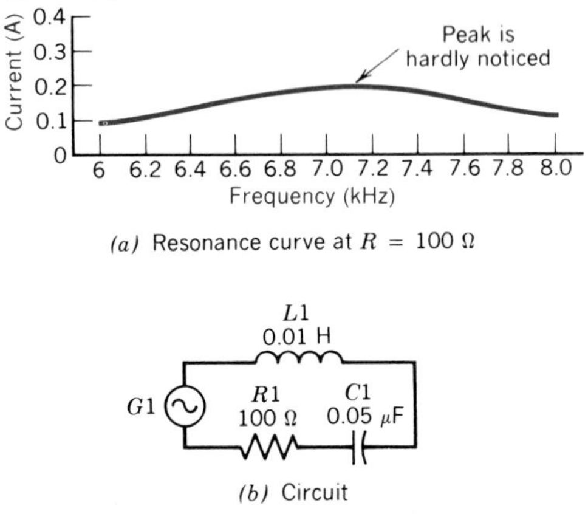

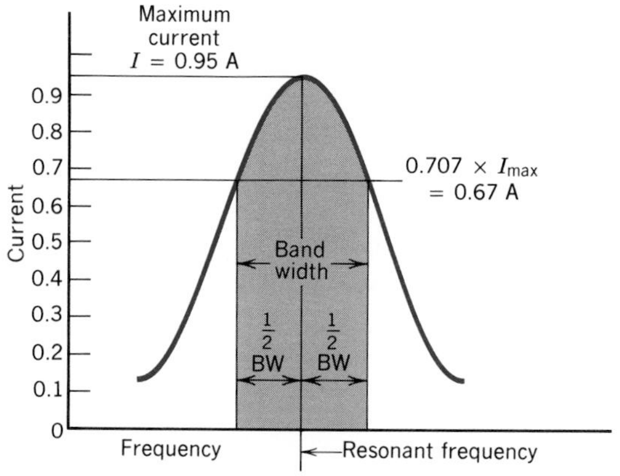

Figure 17.21 The bandwidth is the range of frequencies in a series resonant circuit for which the circuit current is at least 0.707 times the maximum current obtained when the circuit is at resonance.

at which the circuit current is at least 0.707 times the maximum circuit current that occurs at the resonant frequency. The bandwidth, which is sometimes also called the *passband* in a series resonant circuit, is shown in Figure 17.21. Notice that exactly half the bandwidth in the figure lies above the resonant frequency and half lies below it.

EXAMPLE:
Is the source frequency in the circuit of Figure 17.22 in the passband of the circuit? ■

SOLUTION:
In order to determine if the source frequency is within the passband, compare the circuit current at resonance with the current at 55 kHz. At resonance, the inductive and capacitive reactances are equal and cancel each other, so the only opposition to the circuit current is the resistor $R1$. ($R1$ is assumed to combine the various series resistances in the circuit, such as the resistance of $L1$, the ESR of $C1$, and the resistances of the leads and source.) Since the rms value of the source potential difference is given,

$$I = \frac{E}{R} = \frac{12}{20} = 0.6 \text{ A}$$

Figure 17.22 Series *RCL* circuit for bandwidth calculation example.

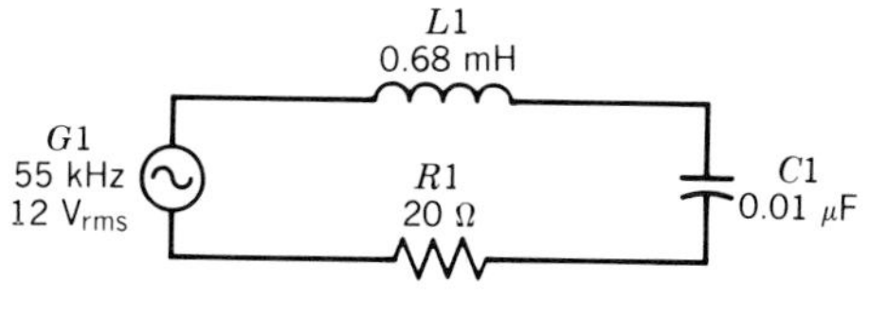

In other words, at resonance, the circuit current will be 0.6 A. The resonant frequency of the circuit is

$$f_r = \frac{1}{2\pi\sqrt{LC}} = 61{,}033.135 \text{ Hz} \quad \text{or} \quad \text{about 61 kHz}$$

Since 55 kHz is below the resonant frequency, the circuit current will be less than the current at resonance, and the capacitive reactance will be greater than the inductive reactance. At a source frequency of 55 kHz, the inductive reactance is $X_L = 2\pi fL = 234.99$, or about 235 Ω. The capacitive reactance is

$$X_C = \frac{1}{2\pi fC} = 289.36 \quad \text{or} \quad \text{about 289.4 } \Omega$$

The impedance of the circuit is

$$Z = \sqrt{R^2 + (X_L - X_C)^2} = \sqrt{400 + 2959.4} = 57.96$$

or about 58 Ω. The circuit current at 55 kHz is

$$I = \frac{E}{Z} = \frac{12}{58} = 0.206 \quad \text{or} \quad \text{about 0.21 A}$$

Comparing the two values, $\frac{0.21}{0.6}$ is 0.35, which is about half of 0.707. In other words, the 55 kHz source does not operate within the passband of the circuit. ■

Although it is possible to use the method of calculating the circuit currents at different frequencies and comparing these to the current at resonance, such computations would be too lengthy for practical use in finding the bandwidth of a circuit. Fortunately, there is a much simpler way of determining the passband of a resonant circuit.

Since the width of the passband depends on a comparison of the circuit reactance and its resistance, it is also possible to use the quality factor Q to determine the bandwidth of a circuit since it is also based on a comparison of reactance and resistance. In fact, the definition of the bandwidth (BW, or Δf) of a circuit has been chosen so that

$$\text{BW or } \Delta f = \frac{f_r}{Q} \qquad \text{FORMULA 17.8}$$

where Δf is the bandwidth of the circuit, f_r is its resonant frequency, and Q is the quality factor of either the capacitor or inductor. (Either can be used since the capacitive and inductive reactances are the same at resonance, but it is more common to use the inductive reactance in the calculation of Q.)

EXAMPLE:
Use Formula 17.8 to determine if the 55 kHz source of Figure 17.22 is within the passband of the circuit. ■

SOLUTION:
Using Formula 17.8 makes it unnecessary to calculate the circuit current. The resonant frequency is

$$f_r = \frac{1}{2\pi\sqrt{LC}} = 61{,}033 \quad \text{or} \quad \text{about 61 kHz}$$

The Q of the inductance is found by using $Q = \frac{X_L}{R}$.

$X_L = 2\pi fL = 260.6$, or about 261 Ω, so $Q = \frac{261}{20} = 13.05$. Rounding off and substituting in Formula 17.8,

$$\text{BW} = \frac{f_r}{\text{Q}} = \frac{61000}{13} = 4692.3 \text{ Hz}$$

Recalling that half the passband lies above the resonant frequency and half below it, $\frac{\text{BW}}{2}$ is subtracted from the resonant frequency: $61000 - 2346.15 = 58{,}653.85$ Hz, or about 58.7 kHz. This is the lowest frequency in the passband. As you can see, it is higher than the 55-kHz source frequency. ■

In situations where several inductors, capacitors, or resistors are combined into a single *RCL* circuit, either the circuit current method or the method based on Q can be used to calculate the bandwidth. Remember, however, to base your calculations on the total resistance, capacitance, and inductance in the circuit. In the circuit shown in Figure 17.23, for example, in order to use the circuit current method to determine if the source frequency is within the circuit passband, it would be necessary to calculate the reactance of all the capacitors and inductors.

Figure 17.23 Example of a series *RCL* circuit with several components of each type.

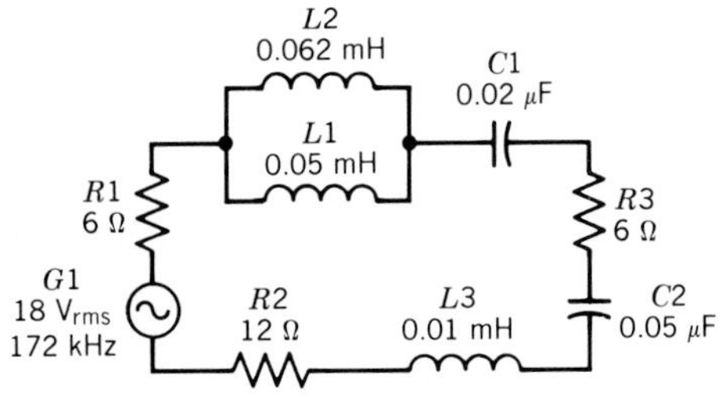

EXAMPLE:
Determine whether or not the source frequency is within the passband of the circuit shown in Figure 17.23 using both the circuit current and Q methods. ■

SOLUTION:
At resonance, the total inductive reactance of the circuit is canceled by the total capacitive reactance, so the circuit current can be obtained by dividing the source potential difference by the sum of the circuit resistances, or,

$$I = \frac{E}{R1 + R2 + R3} = \frac{18}{24} \quad \text{or} \quad 0.75 \text{ A}$$

The circuit impedance at the source frequency can be obtained by combining the inductive and capacitive reactances with the resistance. $L1$ and $L2$ in parallel have a combined inductance of

$$L_{L1 + L2} = \frac{L1L2}{L1 + L2} = 0.028 \text{ mH}$$

Adding the value of $L3$ produces a total circuit inductance of 0.038 mH. At 176 kHz, the inductive reactance is $X_L = 2\pi fL = 41.06$, or 41.1 Ω. The total capacitive reactance can be obtained by adding the capacitive reactances of $C1$ and $C2$ using the product-over-the-sum formula, or, since the two capacitive reactances are in series, X_{C1} and X_{C2} can be calculated separately and then simply added. This method is preferred since it requires fewer steps if a calculator is used.

$$X_{C1} = \frac{1}{2\pi fC_1} = 46.3\ \Omega$$

$$X_{C2} = \frac{1}{2\pi fC_2} = 18.5\ \Omega$$

$$X_{C1} + X_{C2} = 64.8\ \Omega$$

The impedance of the circuit is

$$Z = \sqrt{R^2 + (X_L - X_C)^2} \quad \text{or}$$

$$Z = \sqrt{576 + 561.7} = 33.7\ \Omega$$

The magnitude of the current at the generator frequency is

$$I = \frac{E}{Z} = \frac{18}{33.7} = 0.53 \text{ A}$$

Since 0.707 times the circuit current at resonance, that is, 0.707×0.75, is equal to 0.53 A, the frequency of the generator is within the passband of the circuit.

Using the method of passband range calculation with Formula 17.8 is actually more complicated than the current method in problems of this type since the resonant frequency of the circuit has to be calculated. The total circuit inductance was calculated to be 0.038 mH in the previous part of this exercise. The total capacitance, using the product-over-the-sum formula is

$$C_{\text{total}} = \frac{C1C2}{C1 + C2} = 0.0143\ \mu\text{F}$$

The resonant frequency of the circuit is

$$f_r = \frac{1}{2\pi\sqrt{LC}} = 215{,}904 \quad \text{or} \quad \text{about } 216 \text{ kHz}$$

The circuit Q is

$$\frac{X_L}{R} = \frac{2\pi fL}{24} = 2.15$$

The bandwidth is

$$\text{BW} = \frac{f_r}{Q} = \frac{216{,}000}{2.15} = 100{,}465 \quad \text{or} \quad 100 \text{ kHz}$$

Since $\frac{\text{BW}}{2}$ is about 50 kHz, it is clear that the generator frequency of 172 kHz is within the passband of the circuit. ■

From the previous examples, you can now see that a high Q is not necessarily desirable in a tuned circuit. In fact, in certain cases it is necessary to include a fairly high resistance in a series-tuned circuit so that a wide range of source frequencies will provide nearly equal outputs. One example of this is a circuit with a complex waveform source. As you will recall, a complex periodic waveform can be thought of as the result of adding a series of sine waveforms of different frequencies and amplitudes. Unless the bandwidth of a series *RCL* circuit is wide enough to provide adequate circuit current at a number of the harmonic frequencies involved, the waveform will be distorted by the circuit.

So far, this discussion of series-tuned circuits has considered only the circuit current at resonance. The potential difference across the various components has not been mentioned at all. You have seen how the cancellation of the inductive and capacitive reactance in a series *RCL* circuit leads to unexpectedly high circuit currents. The effects associated with the potential differences across the components are equally unexpected and quite important if you are involved with the troubleshooting or design of tuned circuits.

In addition to aiding in the calculation of bandwidth, circuit Q is also used to calculate the potential difference across the reactive components in the circuit. For example, the potential difference across the inductance in a series *RCL* circuit is $E_L = IX_L$. But $I = \frac{E_s}{R}$ at resonance, so it is possible to write that at resonance,

$$E_L = \frac{E_s X_L}{R}$$

where E_s is the rms value of the source potential difference. Recalling that $\frac{X_L}{R} = Q$, the above equation can be rewritten as

$$E_L = \frac{E_s X_L}{R} = QE_s \qquad \text{FORMULA 17.9}$$

Notice that this formula assumes that the resistance of the coil itself is small when compared to either the inductive reactance or the circuit resistance. When this is the case, the phase angle of E_L is $+90°$. In a similar way, it can be shown that the potential difference across the capacitor at resonance is

$$E_C = \frac{E_s X_c}{R} = QE_s \qquad \text{FORMULA 17.10}$$

The phase angle of the potential difference across the capacitor, with the ESR assumed to be small, is $-90°$.

Taken together, Formulas 17.9 and 17.10 illustrate the curious fact that the potential difference across the reactive components in a series *RCL* circuit can be considerably higher than the potential difference supplied by the source. This means that the working voltages of the components used in resonant circuits must be selected to withstand these high potential differences. For example, a circuit Q of 50, although considered fairly high, is quite common. If the source produces an rms potential difference of 12 V, the rms potential difference across the circuit capacitance will be $E_c = QE_s$, or 600 V. The peak potential difference across the capacitor will be even higher than this: $E_{C\,\text{peak}} = 1.414 \times 600 = 848.4$ V. As you can see, most of the physically smaller electrolytic capacitors, as well as some paper and plastic types, can not be used in this circuit due to low working voltages, even though the source potential difference is a modest 12 V. Also note that since the inductive and capacitive reactances cancel each other at resonance, the full source potential difference is developed across the circuit resistance:

$$E_R = IR \qquad \text{FORMULA 17.11}$$

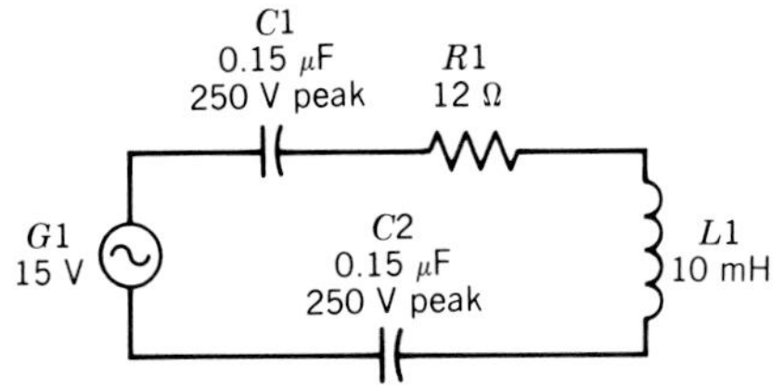

Figure 17.24 A resonant circuit for component potential difference calculations.

EXAMPLE:
Calculate the potential difference across each component in the resonant circuit shown in Figure 17.24. Are the capacitors operating within their recommended peak voltages? ■

SOLUTION:
There are a number of ways to solve this commonly encountered problem. It would be possible to calculate the impedance of the circuit and the circuit current. From this, the potential differences across each component could be derived. It is easier, however, to use the fact that the source frequency is the resonant frequency of the circuit. Since the two series capacitors have the same value, their equivalent is $0.5 \times 0.15 \times 10^{-6}$, or 0.075 μF. This frequency is

$$f_r = \frac{1}{2\pi\sqrt{LC}}$$

$$= \frac{1}{2\pi\sqrt{0.075 \times 10^{-6} \times 10 \times 10^{-3}}}$$

$$= 5811.5 \quad \text{or} \quad \text{about } 5812 \text{ Hz}$$

The inductive reactance of the circuit $X_L = 2\pi f_r L = 2 \times \pi \times 5812 \times 10 \times 10^{-3}$; $X_L = 365.17$, or about 365 Ω. The circuit Q then is

$$\frac{X_L}{R} = \frac{365}{12} = 30.4$$

Using this value of Q, the rms potential difference across the inductor is $Q \times E_s = 456$ V, and the peak potential is 1.414 times this, or 644.8 V. The peak potential difference across the equivalent capacitor is the same, 644.8 V, and since there are two series capacitors of identical value, the potential difference divides equally across them. The peak potential difference across each capacitor is 322.4 V, a value considerably higher than the peak rating of 250 V. The full source potential difference appears across the resistor:

$$E_{R\ \text{peak}} = 1.414 E_s = 21.21 \text{ V}$$ ■

The Q of the circuit of the previous example is considered to be high since the circuit resistance is one-tenth or less of the capacitive or inductive reactance at resonance. In other words, $Q = \frac{X_L}{R}$ or $\frac{X_C}{R}$ is greater than or equal to 10.

This provides another way of looking at Q. Since E_C or $E_L = QE_S$, it is also possible to write $\frac{E_C}{E_S} = Q$ and $\frac{E_L}{E_S} = Q$. These equations show that the circuit Q is equal to the ratio of the potential difference across either the capacitance or the inductance at resonance to the potential difference supplied by the source. But $\frac{E_L}{E_S}$ or $\frac{E_C}{E_S}$ is also referred to as the *voltage gain* of the circuit. That is, if little or no current is drawn, taking the output of a series resonant circuit across either of the reactive elements provides a multiplication of the source potential by Q. Remember, however, that loading the circuit will result in a serious reduction of the circuit Q.

The voltage gain of a series resonant circuit can be expressed in decibels. Remembering Chapter 16, it is possible to write

$$\text{Voltage gain} = 20 \log \frac{E_L \text{ or } E_C}{E_S}$$

$$= 20 \log Q \qquad \text{FORMULA 17.12}$$

EXAMPLE:
Express the voltage gain of the resonant circuit shown in Figure 17.25 in decibels. ■

SOLUTION:
Although the circuit is identified as resonant, the source frequency is not given and will have to be calculated, regardless of the method used to solve the problem. The source frequency is

$$f_r = \frac{1}{2\pi\sqrt{LC}}$$

$$= \frac{1}{2\pi\sqrt{1 \times 10^{-9} \times 1 \times 10^{-3}}} = 159154.94$$

Figure 17.25 Circuit for the calculation of voltage gain in a series resonant circuit.

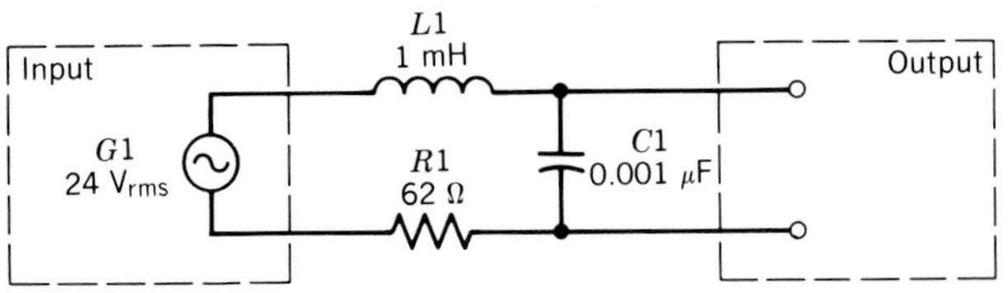

or about 159 kHz. At this frequency, the capacitive reactance is

$$X_C = \frac{1}{2\pi f C} = 1000\ \Omega$$

(rounding off). The Q of the circuit is $\frac{X_C}{R}$, or 16.13, and, using Formula 17.11, the voltage gain in decibels is

$$\begin{aligned} \text{dB} &= 20 \log Q \\ &= 20 \times 1.21 = 24.2 \text{ dB} \end{aligned}$$

Notice that it was not necessary to calculate the potential difference across the capacitor, although this could have been done using Formula 17.10.

$$\begin{aligned} E_c &= QE_s \\ &= 16.13 \times 24 \\ &= 387.1 \text{ V rms} \end{aligned}$$

■

In closing the discussion of voltage gain in series resonant circuits, it is interesting to point out that although the voltage gain is directly proportional to Q, the bandwidth of a tuned circuit (BW or Δf) is inversely proportional to the Q of the circuit. This statement is actually a formal way of presenting the information in Figures 17.19*a* and 17.20*a*.

B.5 PARALLEL RESONANT CIRCUITS

If an inductor and a capacitor are connected across an ac source as shown in Figure 17.26, the resulting circuit is called a *parallel-tuned circuit*. If the resistance of the inductor and the ESR of the capacitor are low, and the source can be varied from low to high frequencies, a number of curious effects will be noticed. At low frequencies, the capacitive reactance will be quite high, and the current in the branch containing the capacitor will be small. The inductive reactance, on the other hand, will be low, so the current through the inductive branch will be considerably larger. Since this is a parallel circuit, the source potential difference is the reference, and the phasor diagram of the current through each branch at a frequency of less than 100 Hz will be as shown in Figure 17.27*a*. With the inductor resistance and capacitor ESR low enough to be ignored, the current through the inductive branch is 180° out of phase with the current through the capacitive branch. The

Figure 17.26 A parallel-tuned circuit.

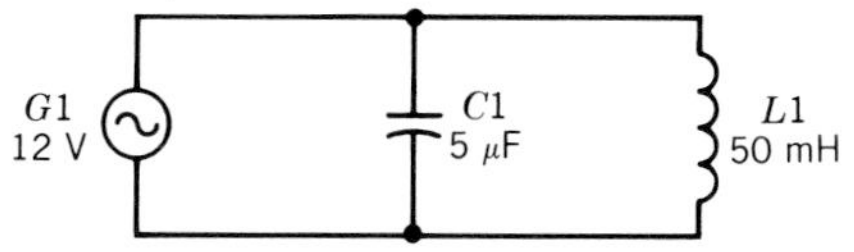

(*a*) Phasor diagram of the branch currents at 80 Hz (*b*) Phasor sum of the branch currents at 80 Hz

Figure 17.27 Branch and total currents in Figure 17.26 at a source frequency of 80 Hz.

(*a*) Phasor diagram of the branch currents at 600 Hz (*b*) Phasor sum of the branch currents at 600 Hz

Figure 17.28 Branch and total currents in Figure 17.26 at a source frequency of 600 Hz.

total circuit current is the phasor sum of the two branch currents. This sum is represented by the phasor shown in Figure 17.27*b*. At a high source frequency, the capacitive reactance will be lower than the inductive reactance, so there will be more current in the branch of the circuit containing the capacitor than in that containing the inductor. At a frequency of 600 Hz, the current phasors in each branch are shown in Figure 17.28*a*, and the total circuit current in both branches is shown in 17.28*b*.

As in the case of the series resonant circuit, there will be some source frequency at which the capacitive and inductive reactances of the circuit of Figure 17.26 will be equal, in other words,

$$2\pi f_r L = \frac{1}{2\pi f_r C}$$

Solving for f_r,

$$f_r^2 = \frac{1}{4\pi^2 LC} \quad \text{or} \quad f_r = \frac{1}{2\pi\sqrt{LC}}$$

This is the same as the formula used to calculate the resonant frequency of a series *RCL* circuit.

EXAMPLE:

Calculate the resonant frequency of the parallel circuit shown in Figure 17.29. ■

Figure 17.29 The resonant frequency of a parallel-tuned circuit is calculated in the same way as the resonant frequency of a series-tuned circuit.

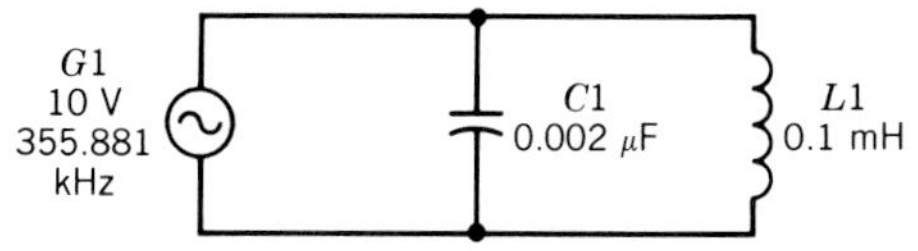

SOLUTION:
Using Formula 17.4, the resonant frequency is

$$f_r = \frac{1}{2\pi\sqrt{0.1 \times 10^{-3} \times 0.002 \times 10^{-6}}}$$
$$= 355{,}881 \text{ Hz}$$

For practical purposes, this could be rounded off to 356 kHz, but the equality of the inductive and capacitive reactance at the resonant frequency is best shown if the full, six-digit value is used. At a source frequency of 355,881 Hz,

$$X_L = 2\pi fL = 223.6\ \Omega$$
$$X_C = \frac{1}{2\pi fC} = 223.6\ \Omega$$

The ability to use Formula 17.4 to calculate the resonant frequency of a parallel-tuned circuit is only one of the similarities of series- and parallel-tuned circuits. On the other hand, there are also some surprising differences between them. ■

For example, the current in a series-tuned circuit is maximum at the resonant frequency. At that frequency, the only opposition to current in the series resonant circuit is the resistance of the coil, the capacitor ESR, or any pure resistance in series with the reactive components. The current in a parallel-tuned circuit reflects a much different situation. Using the circuit values given in Figure 17.29, the current through the branch containing the inductor is

$$I_{L1} = \frac{E_s}{X_{L1}} = \frac{10}{223.6 \angle +90^\circ} = 44.7 \text{ mA} \angle -90^\circ$$

and the current through the branch containing the capacitor is

$$I_{C1} = \frac{E_s}{X_{C1}} = \frac{10}{223.6 \angle -90^\circ} = 44.7 \text{ mA} \angle +90^\circ$$

From the phasor diagram shown in Figure 17.30, you can see that the sum of these two branch currents is zero. That is, there is no current supplied by the source,

Figure 17.30 Phasor diagram of the currents in the capacitor and inductor branches of the circuit shown in Figure 17.29.

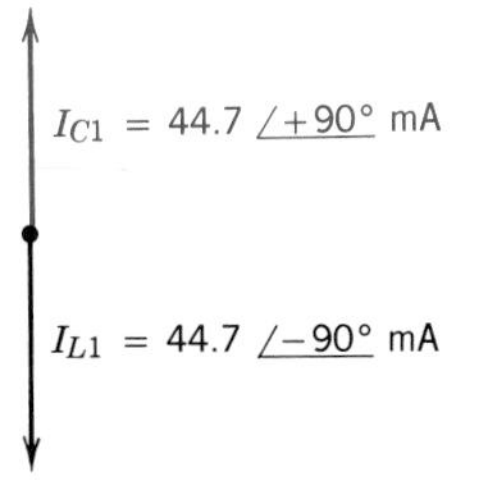

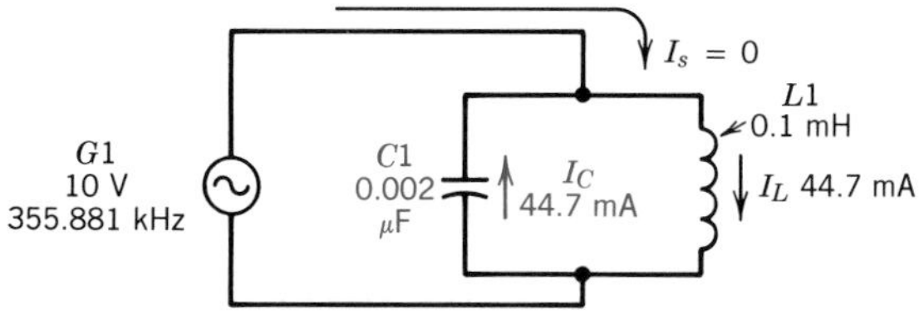

Figure 17.31 In a resistanceless parallel resonant circuit operating at its resonant frequency, no current is supplied by the source, even though the branch currents are not zero.

in spite of the fact that there is a current of 44.7 mA in each of the branches.

At first glance, this seems impossible. How can there be a current in both the capacitive and inductive branches of the circuit but not in the source or the leads from the source? Applying Kirchhoff's current law to the circuit of Figure 17.29 provides the answer. Remember that the currents in the inductive and capacitive branches are 180° out of phase. As shown in Figure 17.31, no current is provided by or returned to the source. Instead, there is an interchange of energy and a current between the inductor and capacitor. From the point of view of a source at resonance, the parallel-tuned circuit acts like a very high impedance. Some texts refer to the impedance of a resistanceless parallel-tuned circuit at resonance as being "infinite." However, since truly resistanceless circuits do not exist under normal conditions, it would be better to compare a parallel-tuned circuit operating at resonance to an open circuit.

Without any resistance in the current path between the inductor and capacitor, the interchange of electrical energy between the capacitor and inductor could continue indefinitely, without any loss or without drawing any energy from the source. Since it provides for energy storage, a parallel-tuned circuit at its resonant frequency is commonly called a *tank*. The idea conveyed by this is that the energy is stored as though in a storage tank.

Notice that the tank circuit itself functions as a series circuit at the resonant frequency, as shown in Figure 17.32. Looked at apart from the rest of the

Figure 17.32 Isolating the tank from the rest of the circuit shows that it acts as a series circuit.

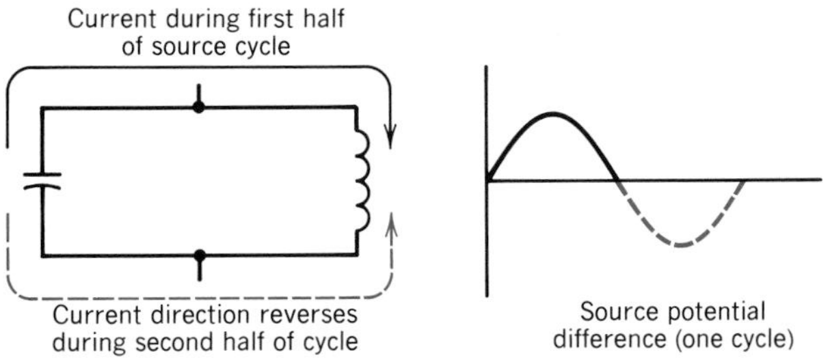

circuit, the current in the tank flows in a clockwise direction during one-half of the source cycle and counterclockwise during the other half-cycle. From the point of view of the tank itself, therefore, the tank current is in phase, that is, it describes a closed loop around the tank. This concept is important because it shows that a resistance in either branch of the parallel circuit will serve to dissipate the energy stored in the tank, and will also affect the Q of the circuit. Another important difference between series- and parallel-tuned circuits is the characteristic resonance curve of each type. In the case of the series-tuned circuit, it is the graph of the relationship between the source frequency and potential difference that is of greatest interest. For the parallel-tuned circuit, it is the graph of the relationship between the source frequency and the circuit impedance that is considered to be characteristic. Figures 17.33*a* and 17.33*b* show the characteristic impedance curve of an ideal parallel-tuned circuit compared to an actual circuit. Note that the ideal circuit has a very sharp impedance rise at the resonant frequency. The graph of the circuit current, which has been sketched on the graph, shows a sharp drop. The practical circuit, on the other hand, shows a broader increase in circuit impedance. The current curve, which is sketched on Figure 17.33*b*, shows a less abrupt drop in the circuit current at resonance. Notice that in the practical circuit at resonance, the circuit impedance reaches its maximum at some finite value, rather than continuing off the graph as in the ideal circuit. Also, the circuit current in the practical circuit does not drop to zero as it does in the case of the ideal circuit.

Figure 17.33 Comparison of an ideal (resistanceless) and a practical parallel-tuned circuit.

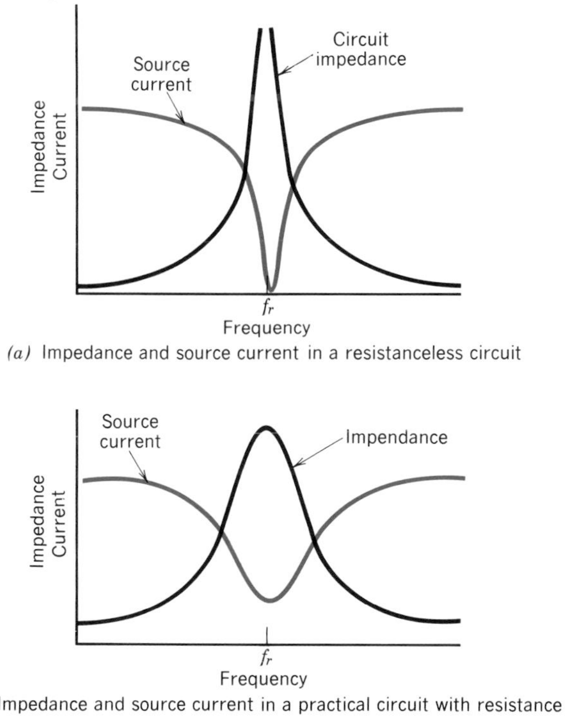

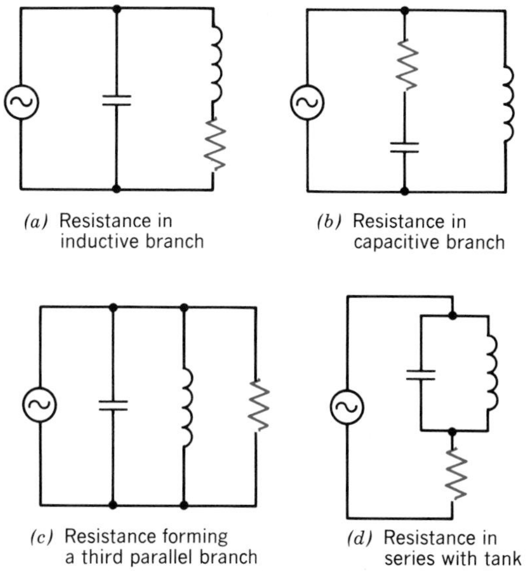

Figure 17.34 Resistances too large to be ignored can occur in one or more of four different places in a parallel-tuned circuit.

The difference between the ideal and practical circuits shown in Figure 17.33 are due to the effect of resistance in the practical circuit. Resistance that is too large to be ignored can appear in one or more of four different places in a parallel-tuned circuit, as shown in Figures 17.34*a* through 17.34*d*. In certain cases, this resistance is an inherent part of a circuit component, such as the resistance of the wire forming an inductor, while in other cases, one or more resistors have been added to obtain specific circuit characteristics.

Most often, the resistance of the inductor must be included in circuit calculations, as shown in Figure 17.34*a*. Small resistances may also be included in the capacitor branch of a circuit to limit the current in the branch and prevent capacitor heating, as shown in 17.34*b*. The presence of resistance in either or both branches of a parallel-tuned circuit means that the branch currents are not exactly 180° out of phase at resonance. The resistance will change the phase angle of the branch that it is in by forming a series *RC* or *RL* circuit in that branch. Consider the circuit shown in Figure 17.35,

Figure 17.35 A parallel resonant circuit with resistances in both the capacitive and inductive branches.

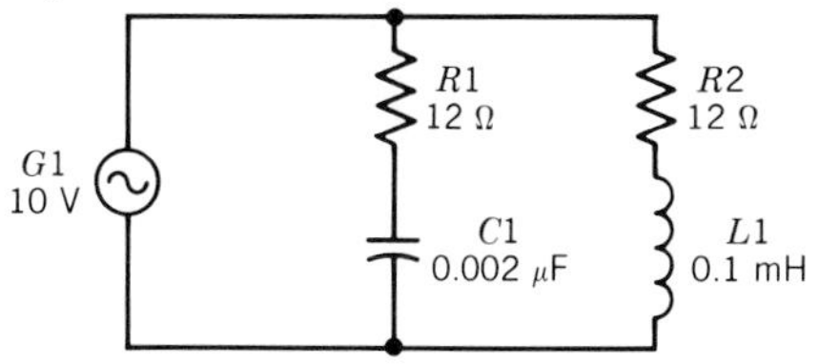

for example. This circuit duplicates that of Figure 17.29, except for the inclusion of $R1$ and $R2$. As you will see in the Applications section, the loading of a parallel-tuned circuit can have an effect on the resonant frequency, but in the case shown, the resistances of $R1$ and $R2$ are considerably less than the reactances of $C1$ and $L1$ at the resonant frequency. In this case, Formula 17.4 can be used. Since the formula does not consider resistive components, the resonant frequency

$$f_r = \frac{1}{2\pi\sqrt{LC}}$$

is the same as that for the circuit of Figure 17.28, that is, 355,881 Hz. At this frequency, the inductive and capacitive reactances are equal, and are 223.6 Ω at phase angles of $\angle -90^\circ$ for the capacitive reactance and $\angle +90^\circ$ for the inductive reactance. The impedance of the branch containing $R1$ and $C1$, in complex rectangular coordinates, is therefore,

$$Z_{R1C1} = 12 - j223.6$$

and the branch current can be calculated after converting the impedance to polar coordinates:

$$I_{R1C1} = \frac{E_s}{Z_{R1C1}} = \frac{10}{223.9 \angle -86.9^\circ} = 0.0447 \angle +86.9^\circ$$

Since the inductive and capacitive reactances and $R1$ and $R2$ are equal, the branch currents are also equal, except for their phase angle, as in the case of the ideal parallel resonant circuit. Usually, the resistance in the capacitive branch of a parallel circuit can be ignored since it is composed only of the ESR of the capacitor. The resistance in the inductive branch, however, is often substantial. Regardless of which branch the resistance is in, from the phasor diagram of the branch currents in Figure 17.36, you can see that the sum of the two branch currents will not be zero. Since the two currents are not separated by a phase angle of 180°, they will not cancel each other and there will be a circuit current. The two branch currents can be converted to complex rectangular form for addition

$$I_{R1C1} = 0.0447 \angle +86.9^\circ = 0.0024 + 0.0446$$

$$I_{R2L1} = 0.0447 \angle -86.9^\circ = 0.0024 - j0.0446$$

The sum of the two branch currents is $0.0048 + j0$, or 4.8 mA $\angle 0^\circ$. Although it is smaller than either of the branch currents, there will be a circuit current of 4.8 mA delivered by the source. Notice that this source current is in phase with the source potential difference.

The impedance of the parallel-tuned circuit is given by

$$Z_t = \frac{E}{I} = \frac{10}{0.0048 \angle 0^\circ} = 2083\ \Omega$$

Although the formula used in this calculation is considered the definition of the impedance of the circuit on the basis of some rather extensive algebra, it is possible to derive a simple, easy-to-use formula relating the impedance of a circuit of this type with the capacitance, inductance, and total resistance of the tank. Since it is the ability to use this formula, rather than the way in which it is derived, that is important, only the formula itself is shown:

$$Z_t = \frac{L}{CR} \qquad \text{FORMULA 17.13}$$

where R is the sum of the resistances in the tank circuit. In the circuit of Figure 17.35, this formula could be used to find out the circuit impedance without calculating the circuit current or knowing the source potential difference:

$$Z_t = \frac{L}{CR} = \frac{0.1 \times 10^{-3}}{0.002 \times 10^{-6} \times 24} = 2083\ \Omega$$

The same result is obtained as with the use of the potential difference divided by the circuit current. Remember, however, that Formula 17.13 is only true when the source frequency is the resonant frequency of the circuit.

Another version of Formula 17.13, which relates the impedance to only the inductive reactance of the circuit, is also possible. If $X_L = 2\pi fL$, and $X_C = \frac{1}{2\pi fC}$, then

$$L = \frac{X_L}{2\pi f} \quad \text{and} \quad C = \frac{1}{2\pi f X_C}$$

But, at resonance, $X_L = X_C$, so it is possible to write

$$L = \frac{X_L}{2\pi f} \quad \text{and} \quad C = \frac{1}{2\pi f X_L}$$

Substituting these expressions for L and C in Formula

Figure 17.36 When there are resistances in the tank circuit, the phasor sum of the branch currents is not zero.

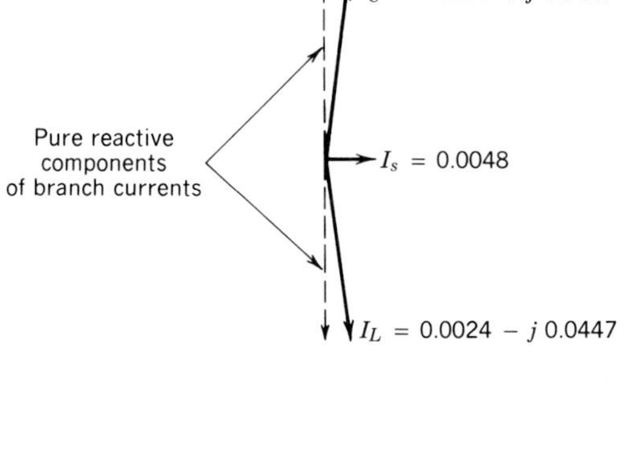

17.13 produces

$$Z_t = \frac{L}{CR} = \frac{\dfrac{X_L}{2\pi f}}{\dfrac{R}{2\pi f X_L}}$$

When this expression is multiplied by $\dfrac{2\pi f X_L}{2\pi f X_L}$ the result is

$$Z_t = \frac{X_L^2}{R} \qquad \text{FORMULA 17.14}$$

Used to calculate the impedance of the circuit shown in Figure 17.34, Formula 17.14 gives

$$Z_t = \frac{X_L^2}{R} = \frac{(2\pi f L)^2}{R} = \frac{(223.6)^2}{\text{R}} = 2083\ \Omega$$

This is the same value obtained through the other two methods.

Regardless of the method used to obtain its value, the impedance of a parallel-tuned circuit at resonance has a phase angle of 0°. In other words, the impedance does not produce a phase shift between the circuit current and potential difference and acts like a pure resistance to the source.

EXAMPLE:
Calculate the impedance of the parallel-tuned network shown in Figure 17.37 at resonance. ■

SOLUTION:
Since the resonant frequency of the network is not required, Formula 17.13 should be used.

$$Z_t = \frac{L}{CR} = \frac{0.1}{2 \times 10^{-6} \times 76} = 657.9\ \Omega$$ ■

Since parallel-tuned tank circuits are common in several types of electronic units, Formulas 17.13 and 17.14 can provide quick solutions to circuit analyses.

Figure 17.37 Calculating the impedance of a parallel-tuned network.

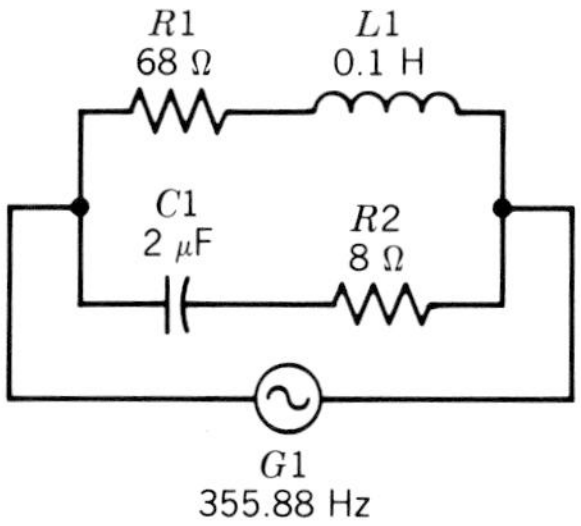

Remember that although the Q of a series RCL circuit is most frequently calculated by using $Q = \dfrac{X_L}{R}$, it can also be defined as the ratio of the energy stored in the reactive components of the circuit compared to the energy dissipated in the circuit resistances, in other words, $Q = \dfrac{E_L}{E_s}$, for a series circuit. In a parallel-tuned circuit, the energy stored in the reactances is proportional to the current circulating in the tank circuit, while the power dissipated in the circuit resistance is proportional to the circuit current, that is, the current provided by the source. Thus, for a circuit such as that of Figure 17.34,

$$Q = \frac{I_{\text{tank}}}{I_{\text{source}}} \qquad \text{FORMULA 17.15}$$

This formula provides a useful way of finding the Q of the tank circuit if the source and tank currents have to be calculated also. In the circuit of Figure 17.35, for example, $I_{\text{tank}} = 0.0447$ A and $I_{\text{source}} = 0.0048$ A, so

$$Q = \frac{I_{\text{tank}}}{I_{\text{source}}} = \frac{0.0447}{0.0048} = 9.3$$

Formula 17.15 is also particularly useful in complex parallel resonant circuits where the branch component values may be the result of several substitutions of equivalent rather than actual components.

Another useful expression for the Q of a parallel-tuned circuit at resonance can be found by going back to the definition of circuit Q. In the type of circuit shown in Figure 17.37, all the storage of power and all power dissipation take place in the tank circuit. The power stored in the tank circuit is the reactive power in either the capacitor or the inductor,

$$P_r = I^2X_L \quad \text{or} \quad I^2X_C$$

where I is the current in the tank circuit. The power dissipated is the true power dissipated by the total resistance of the tank. $P = I^2R$, where I is the tank current and R is the total resistance of the tank network. So

$$Q = \frac{P_r}{P} = \frac{I^2X_L}{I^2R} = \frac{X_L}{R}$$

Notice that this is the same formula used to obtain the Q of a series-tuned circuit. This is true because the tank circuit shown in Figure 17.37 acts as a series circuit to the circulating tank current. Using this formula to calculate the Q of the tank produces the same value as Formula 17.15:

$$Q = \frac{X_L}{R} = \frac{223.6}{24} = 9.3$$

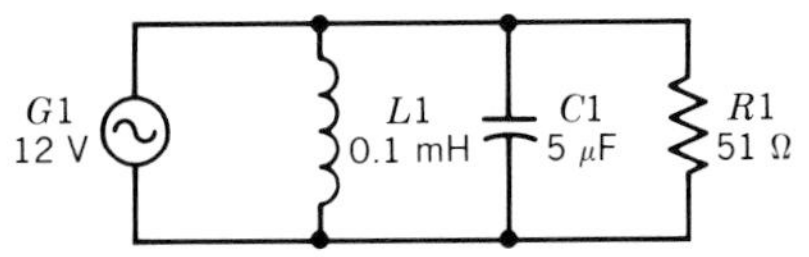

Figure 17.38 A parallel-tuned *RCL* circuit can also be formed by placing a resistor in parallel with an inductor and a capacitor.

A third possible location for a resistance in a parallel resonant circuit is in a separate branch in parallel with the capacitor and inductor branches. This is shown in Figure 17.38. Networks of this type are fairly common and the resistance $R1$ can function either as a load or to control the impedance or the Q of the tank circuit. Examining the schematic diagram, you can see that $R1$ provides a path in which the current will not be canceled by the combination of currents that have been phase shifted by reactive components. This means that there will always be a source current of at least $I = \frac{E_s}{R1}$ provided by the source, even when the source frequency is the same as the resonant frequency, and the currents in the $C1$ and $L1$ branches of the circuit cancel each other. Because of the presence of $R1$, the drop in the circuit current near the resonant frequency of the tank will not be as deep or as narrow. Because the parallel resistor makes the dip in the circuit current, or "null" of the parallel resonant circuit more gradual, the resistor is sometimes referred to as a *damping* resistor. The same term is also applied to a resistor placed in either the capacitor or inductor branch of a tank circuit.

The simplest way to calculate the total circuit current and impedance of a circuit like that of Figure 17.38 is to calculate each branch current separately and then to add them. Note that if there are no series resistances in the capacitor and inductor branches, the circuit current at resonance will be the same as the current through the parallel resistor, or 0.24 A in the circuit shown. Since the capacitive and inductive reactances of $C1$ and $L1$ cancel at resonance, the impedance of the entire circuit at the resonant frequency will be $R1 \angle 0°$, or 51 Ω, resistive. For calculating the Q of this circuit, it is possible to use Formula 13.4, which was used to calculate Q in a parallel RL circuit, $Q = \frac{R}{X_L}$, where R is the resistance in parallel with the inductor. In the case of the circuit shown in Figure 17.38, for example

$$f_r = \frac{1}{2\pi\sqrt{LC}} \quad \text{or} \quad 7117.6 \text{ Hz}$$

and

$$Q = \frac{R}{X_L} = 11.33$$

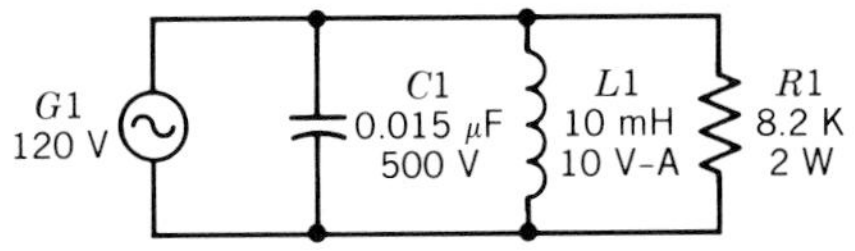

Figure 17.39 A parallel-tuned circuit for the calculation of component working voltages and power dissipations.

EXAMPLE:
Give the resonant frequency, circuit Q, and the current provided by the source at resonance in the circuit of Figure 17.39. Are any of the components operating beyond their ratings? ■

SOLUTION:
The resonant frequency of the circuit is

$$f_r = \frac{1}{2\pi\sqrt{LC}} = 12{,}994.9 \text{ Hz} \quad \text{or} \quad \text{about } 13 \text{ kHz}$$

At resonance, the currents in the $C1$ and $L1$ branches of the circuit cancel, so the current provided by the source is

$$I = \frac{E}{R_1} = \frac{120}{8200} = 0.0146 \text{ A} \quad \text{or} \quad 14.6 \text{ mA}$$

Since there are no resistances in either the $C1$ or $L1$ branches of the circuit, the Q can be determined by $Q = \frac{R}{X_L}$, the formula for the Q of a parallel RL circuit. The inductive reactance is $X_L = 2\pi fL = 816.8$ Ω, and

$$Q = \frac{8200}{816.8} = 10.039 \quad \text{or} \quad 10$$

For the final part of this example, note that the working voltage or power dissipation has been given. You have previously seen that the voltage ratings of components can easily be exceeded in a series resonant circuit. In this case, however, the 500-V rating of the capacitor is well above the peak potential difference across it, which is 1.414 × 120 × 169.68, or about 170 V. The 2-W rating of $R1$ is also sufficient since the power dissipated is I^2R or 1.75 W. For $L1$, however, the recommended power dissipation of 10 V-A is exceeded since the reactive power is

$$P_r = \frac{E^2}{X_L} = \frac{14400}{816.8} = 17.63 \text{ vars.}$$

There is no true power dissipated by $L1$ so both the apparent and reactive power is 17.63 V-A. ■

Another method used for calculating the current provided by a source at resonant frequency to a parallel resonant circuit is to combine the resistance and the impedance of the branch containing the inductance into a single impedance. This is done by using the product-over-the-sum formula,

$$Z_t = \frac{Z_1 Z_2}{Z_1 + Z_2}$$

The branches containing the parallel resistance and the inductor can then be replaced by a single branch with an impedance of Z_t. If Z_t is expressed in complex rectangular coordinates, the real term will be the value of the resistance, and the *j* term will provide the value of the inductive reactance of the equivalent branch. From the inductive reactance and the source frequency, the value of the inductor can be obtained, if required.

EXAMPLE:
Calculate the circuit current, the *Q* of the tank circuit, and the tank current in the circuit shown in Figure 17.40 by combining *L*1 and *R*1 into a single equivalent branch. ■

SOLUTION:
Since a parallel circuit is involved, the source potential difference is the reference phasor, and the inductive reactance phasor will be at $\angle +90°$. At a frequency of 159.155 Hz, the resonant frequency of the circuit, the inductive reactance of a 1-H inductor is 1000 Ω. Therefore, the impedance of the *L*1 branch is 0 + *j*1000, and the impedance of the *R*1 branch is 10,000 + *j*0. Combining the two impedances using the product-over-the-sum method,

$$\frac{(10{,}000 + j0)\,(0 + j1000)}{(10{,}000 + j0) + (0 + j1000)} = \frac{(10{,}000 + j0)\,(0 + j1000)}{10{,}000 + j1000}$$

Converting to polar form for multiplication and division produces

$$\frac{10{,}000\,\angle 0° \times 1000\,\angle +90°}{10049.9\,\angle +5.71°} = 995.035\,\angle +84.29°$$

This resultant impedance can then be converted into complex rectangular coordinates as 98.99 + *j*990.

From this you can see that the *R*1 and *L*1 branches of the circuit can be replaced by an equivalent branch containing a 98.99 Ω resistance in series with an inductance with an inductive reactance of 990 Ω at the resonant frequency. If practical component values are needed, the original 1-H inductor would be used and placed in series with a 100 Ω resistor. This equivalent circuit is shown in Figure 17.41*a*. The circuit current at resonance can be calculated by obtaining the current through the equivalent branch and resolving it into reactive and resistive components. The reactive component of the current through the equivalent branch will be canceled by the current in the capacitive branch as shown in the phasor diagram of Figure 17.41*b*, while the resistive component will represent the current supplied by the source. Since the impedance of the equivalent circuit rounds off to 995 Ω, the current through the branch is

$$I = \frac{E}{Z} = \frac{18\,\angle 0°}{995\,\angle +84.3°} = 0.0181\,\angle -84.29°\text{ A}$$

The value of the reactive and resistive components of the current can be obtained by converting this to complex rectangular components,

$$I = 0.0018 - j0.018$$

The resistive component is 0.0018, or 1.8 mA, which is the source current. This can be checked by comparing it to the source current in the original circuit shown in Figure 17.40, where

$$I = \frac{E}{R} = \frac{18}{10{,}000} = 1.8\text{ mA}$$

The *Q* of the circuit is the same as the *Q* of the equivalent series branch, so

$$Q = \frac{X_L}{R} = \frac{990}{98.99} = 10$$

This figure can also be checked by comparing the *Q* of the original parallel combination of *L*1 and *R*1,

$$Q = \frac{R}{X_L} = \frac{10{,}000}{1{,}000} = 10$$

Figure 17.40 Combining an inductive and resistive branch to form an equivalent branch.

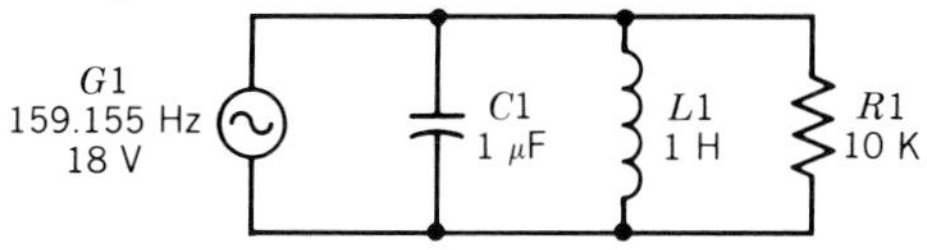

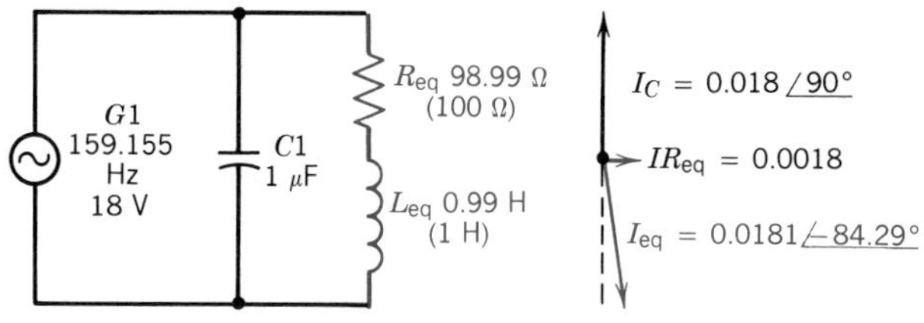

(*a*) Equivalent circuit of Figure 17.40

(*b*) Phasor diagram of currents in *C*1 and $R_{eq}L_{eq}$ branches

Figure 17.41 Combining the *L*1 and *R*1 branches of the circuit in Figure 17.40 into a single branch.

Once the circuit Q is known, the tank current can be calculated by using Formula 17.15:

$$Q = \frac{I_{\text{tank}}}{I_{\text{source}}} \quad \text{or} \quad 10 = \frac{I_{\text{tank}}}{0.0018}$$

$$I_{\text{tank}} = 0.018 \text{ A}$$

Notice that this is the same value obtained for the reactive component of the current in the equivalent circuit. ■

This example shows that in the type of circuit shown in Figure 17.42, either the equivalent branch or direct parallel circuit calculation methods can be used. In the circuit shown in Figure 17.43, however, parallel circuit calculation methods can not be used directly. This is a very common circuit form, where $R1$ represents the resistance of the inductor and $R2$ is a damping resistor included to reduce the circuit Q and broaden the resonance null.

Finally, a damping resistor can be added in series with an RCL parallel network, as shown by $R2$ in Figure 17.44. As you can see from the schematic diagram, resistor $R2$ will act to reduce the source potential difference across the parallel-tuned circuit composed of $L1$, $C1$, $R1$, and $R3$, by the quantity $I_{\text{source}} \times R2$. In this way it serves to reduce both the source and tank currents, without affecting the Q of the RCL tank. The inclusion of $R1$ and $R3$, on the other hand, *increases* the value of the source current, and *lowers* the Q of the tank.

Since some of the same component values used in the circuit of Figure 17.40 are also used in the circuit of Figure 17.44, the resonant frequency and the in-

Figure 17.42 In this type of circuit either equivalent branch or direct parallel circuit calculation methods can be used.

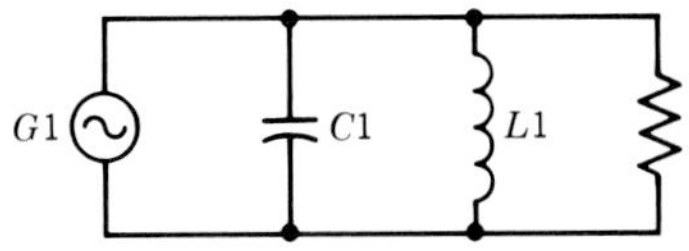

Figure 17.43 In this very common circuit type, direct parallel circuit calculation methods can not be used.

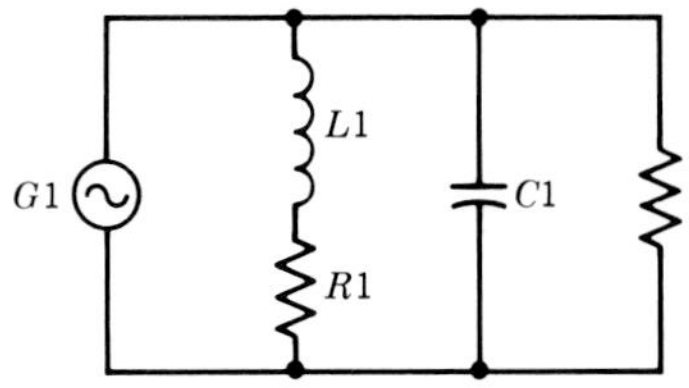

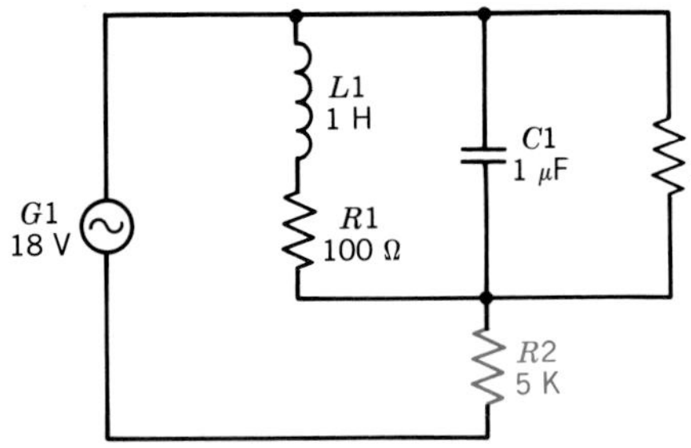

Figure 17.44 Adding a damping resistor ($R2$) in series with a parallel resonant circuit.

ductive and capacitive reactances will be the same:

$$f_r = \frac{1}{2\pi\sqrt{LC}} = 159.155 \text{ Hz}$$

$$X_L = 2\pi f L = 1000 \ \Omega$$

$$X_C = \frac{1}{2\pi f C} = 1000 \ \Omega$$

The tank circuit of Figure 17.44 has two resistances, $R1$, which can be thought of as the equivalent resistance of $L1$, and $R3$, which is a parallel damping resistor. The source current and circuit Q can be calculated if the $L1R1$ and $R3$ branches are combined into a single equivalent branch. The impedance of the $L1R1$ branch can be written in complex rectangular coordinates as

$$Z_{L1R1} = 100 + j1000$$

since the inductive reactance of $L1$ is 1000 Ω at the resonant frequency. The impedance of the $R3$ branch is

$$Z_{R3} = 10{,}000 + j0$$

The impedance of the equivalent branch will be

$$Z_{\text{eq}} = \frac{(100 + j1000)\,(10{,}000 + j0)}{(100 + j1000) + (10{,}000 + j0)}$$

Adding and converting to polar coordinates produces

$$Z_{\text{eq}} = \frac{1004.99 \angle{+84.3^\circ} \times 10{,}000 \angle{0^\circ}}{10{,}149 \angle{+5.65^\circ}}$$

$$= \frac{10{,}049{,}900 \angle{+84.3^\circ}}{10{,}149 \angle{+5.65^\circ}}$$

$$Z_{\text{eq}} = 990.24 \angle{+78.65^\circ}$$

Converting the equivalent impedance to complex rectangular coordinates will provide the values of the resistance and inductive reactance in the equivalent circuit

$$Z_{\text{eq}} = 194.88 + j970.87$$

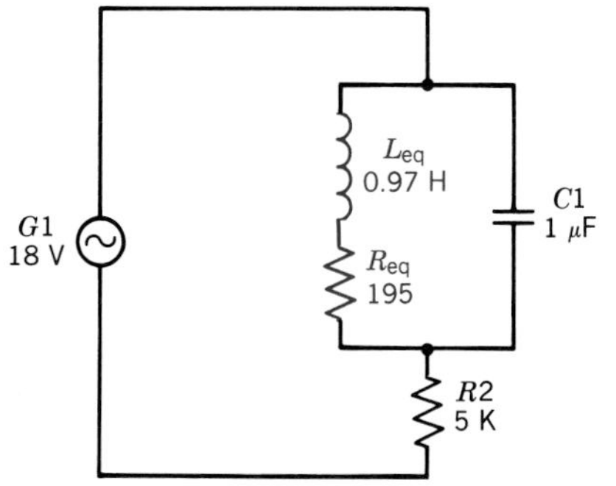

Figure 17.45 The circuit of Figure 17.44 with the $L1R1$ and $R3$ branches combined into a single equivalent branch.

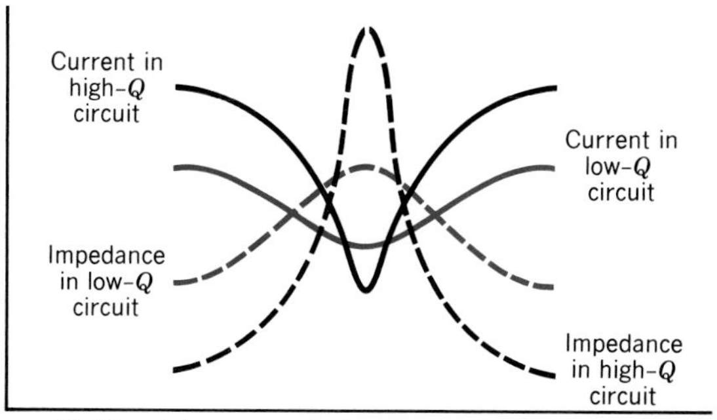

Figure 17.46 A lower tank circuit Q means flatter and wider impedance and circuit current curves.

The actual value of the inductance would be 0.97 H. Using practical components, the equivalent circuit would be composed of a 200 Ω resistor in series with a 1 H inductor. Figure 17.45 shows the circuit with the $L1R1$ and $R3$ branches replaced by an equivalent branch with the rounded-off theoretical component values rather than practical values, so that greater accuracy can be obtained in the calculations of the Q of the tank circuit. The Q can be directly obtained from the complex rectangular coordinate expression of the equivalent branch circuit impedance, since the only tank circuit resistance is the 195 Ω equivalent resistance. Therefore,

$$Q = \frac{X_L}{R} = \frac{971}{195} = 4.98 \quad \text{or} \quad \text{about } 5$$

Notice that $R2$, the series resistor, does not have any effect on the tank Q since it is not a part of the tank. At resonance, the inductive and capacitive reactances cancel, and the opposition to the source current in the circuit is provided by the series combination of R_{eq} and $R2$. The source current at resonance is therefore

$$I = \frac{E}{Z} = \frac{E}{R_{eq} + R2} = \frac{18}{5195} = 0.00346 \text{ A}$$

If only the Q of the tank circuit in Figure 17.44 had been required to solve a problem or perform a troubleshooting analysis, a simpler approach could have been used. For example, if the source current had been measured and the tank current had been required to calculate the reactive power $L1$, the formula

$$Q = \frac{X_L}{R1 + \dfrac{X_L^2}{R3}} \qquad \text{FORMULA 17.16}$$

could have been used to obtain the Q of the tank circuit. Solving

$$Q = \frac{971}{100 + \dfrac{971^2}{10{,}000}} = \frac{971}{100 + 94.3} = 4.99$$

This formula provides the same results, within the range of inaccuracies caused by rounding off, as the equivalent circuit method. Note, however, that if there is a series resistance in the capacitor branch of the tank circuit, Formula 17.15 can not be used. Once the Q of the tank circuit and the source current are known, the tank current can be obtained with Formula 17.14, $Q = \dfrac{I_{tank}}{I_{source}}$.

As in the case of the series-tuned circuit, the greater the resistance in a reactive branch of a parallel resonant tank, the lower the Q of the tank circuit. A low-Q tank circuit means that the resonance curve of both the source current and circuit impedance will be flatter and broader, as shown in Figure 17.46. The bandwidth (BW or Δf) of a parallel resonant circuit is therefore defined in a way similar to the bandwidth of a series-tuned circuit. The bandwidth is defined, as shown in Figure 17.47, as the range of frequencies for which the impedance of the tank circuit is 0.707 times its maximum value or greater. The bandwidth can also be defined in terms of the source current, as shown in Figure 17.48. Since this current can be measured directly, this definition is used more frequently than the definition based on impedance. As in the case of a series resonant

Figure 17.47 In a parallel resonant circuit, the bandwidth is defined as the range of frequencies for which the tank circuit impedance is equal to or greater than 0.707 times its maximum value.

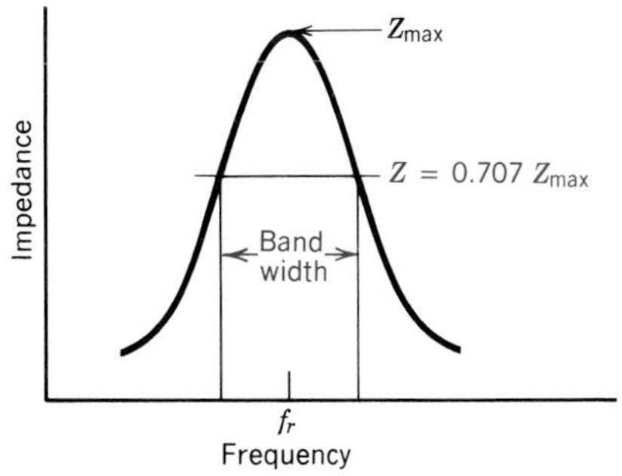

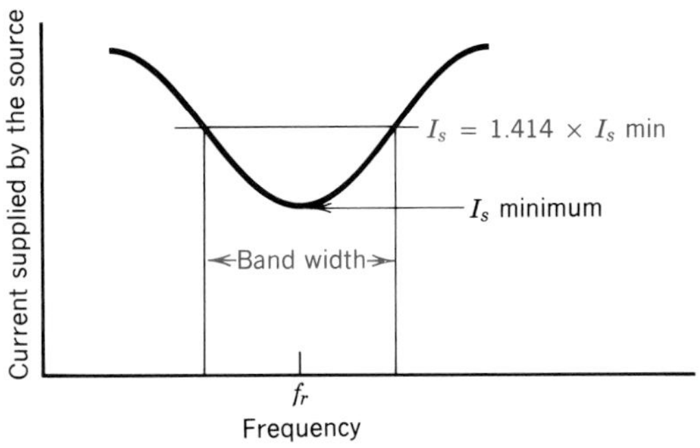

Figure 17.48 The bandwidth of a parallel resonant circuit can also be defined in terms of the source current.

circuit, bandwidth is related to Q, in circuits where Q is 10 or greater, by the formula

$$\text{BW } (\Delta f) = \frac{f_r}{Q}$$

where f_r is the resonant frequency of the tank.

EXAMPLE:
Determine the bandwidth of the circuit shown in Figure 17.49. ■

SOLUTION:
The solution to this problem begins with determining the resonant frequency of the circuit and the inductive reactance at this frequency. The resonant frequency is

$$f_r = \frac{1}{2\pi \sqrt{LC}} = 23{,}215 \text{ Hz}$$

At this frequency, the inductive reactance is

$$X_L = 2\pi f L = 145.9\ \Omega$$

Using Formula 17.16, the value of the circuit Q can then be found:

$$Q = \frac{X_L}{R2 + \dfrac{X_L^2}{R3}} = \frac{145.9}{8 + \dfrac{(145.9)^2}{3300}} = 10.06$$

Figure 17.49 Calculating the bandwidth of a parallel-tuned circuit.

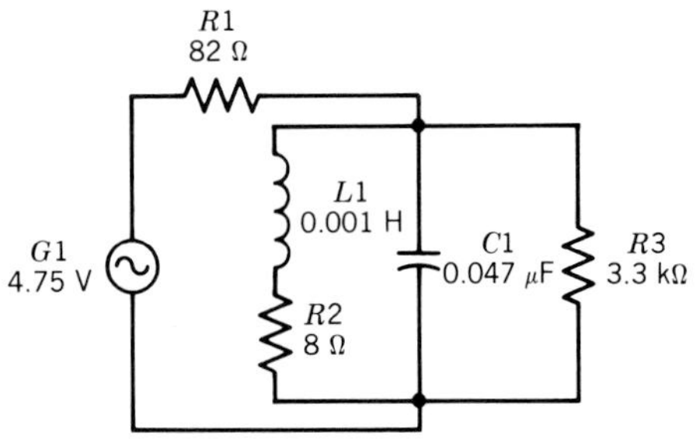

or about 10. The bandwidth is

$$\text{BW } (\Delta f) = \frac{fr}{Q} = 2321.5 \text{ Hz}$$

Notice that the value of $R1$ does not figure into any of the calculations since neither the total circuit impedance nor the source current are required. ■

The characteristics of a parallel resonant or parallel-tuned circuit at resonance are summarized as follows:

1. *From the point of view of the source, the impedance of the circuit is a maximum and is equivalent to a pure resistance at the resonant frequency.*
2. *The source current is at its minimum and is in phase with the source potential difference.*
3. *For frequencies above and below resonance, the tank circuit impedance is no longer purely resistive but includes a reactive component. At the resonant frequency, the inductive and capacitive reactance of the tank are equal in magnitude and 180° apart in phase.*
4. *Above its resonant frequency, a parallel-tuned circuit behaves capacitively; below resonance, it behaves inductively.*

B.6 COMPARISON OF SERIES-TUNED AND PARALLEL-TUNED CIRCUITS

It is rather easy to confuse the characteristics of series- and parallel-tuned circuits since some of these characteristics are identical, while others are quite different. In order to help keep these characteristics in mind, study Tables 17.1 and 17.2, which compare these characteristics for ideal series and parallel circuits at resonance and at frequencies other than the resonant frequency.

C. EXAMPLES AND COMPUTATIONS

C.1 MATHEMATICAL ANALYSIS AS AN EXPLANATION OF CIRCUIT BEHAVIOR

In most of this book, the behavior of electronic components and circuits has been explained in terms of physical principles such as potential difference and the drift of electrons. Only once before, in the discussion of what happens when nonsinusoidal waveforms are applied to reactive components, has it been necessary to base the explanation of what happens in a circuit

Table 17.1 Comparison of Tuned Series and Parallel Tuned Circuit Characteristics at Resonance

Property at Resonance	*Series Network*	*Parallel Network*
Resonant frequency (f_r)	$\frac{1}{2\pi\sqrt{LC}}$	$\frac{1}{2\pi\sqrt{LC}}$
Impedance	Minimum ($Z = R$)	Maximum ($Z = X_L Q$)
I_{source} or I_{total}	Maximum (I_{total})	Minimum (I_{source})
Inductive current (I_L)	I_{total}	$Q \times I_{source}$
Capacitive current (I_C)	I_{total}	$Q \times I_{source}$
E_L	$Q \times E_{source}$	E_{source}
E_C	$Q \times E_{source}$	E_{source}
Phase angle (θ)	Zero degrees	Zero degrees
Angular difference between E_L and E_C	180 degrees	Zero degrees
Angular difference between I_L and I_C	Zero degrees	180 degrees
Bandwidth (bw)	$\frac{f_r}{Q}$	$\frac{f_r}{Q}$
Quality (Q)	$\frac{X_L}{R}$ or $\frac{E_L}{E_{source}}$	$\frac{R}{X_L}$ or $\frac{I_{tank}}{I_{source}}$
Apparent power (P_A)	$E_{source} \times I_{total} \times \cos\theta$	$E_{source} \times I_{source} \times \cos\theta$

Table 17.2 Comparison of Series Tuned and Parallel Tuned Circuit Characteristics at Frequencies Other Than the Resonant Frequency

	Above Resonant Frequency		*Below Resonant Frequency*	
Property	*Series*	*Parallel*	*Series*	*Parallel*
Resistance ($X_L - X_C$)	X_L greater	I_C greater	X_C greater	I_L greater
Impedance (Z)	High	Low	High	Low
Phase Angle (θ)	Lagging I	Leading I	Leading I	Lagging I
How circuit reacts to the source	Inductive	Capacitive	Capacitive	Inductive

on a mathematical analysis. It was shown, you will remember, that a nonsinusoidal waveform such as a square wave could be considered as the combination of a dc level and a number of sine waves of different amplitude and frequency. In other words, a mathematical analysis was used both to predict current and potential difference values and to "explain" the observed effects.

Although less extreme than viewing a square wave as made up of different sine waveforms, there are certain combinations of reactive components that require mathematical analysis to explain their behavior. The parallel connection of two series resonant circuits shown in Figure 17.50 is an example of such a circuit. For the sake of simplicity, the coil resistances of the inductors and the equivalent series resistances of the capacitors in both branches are assumed to be equal and are represented by R_{eq1} and R_{eq2}. Notice that the values of $L1$ and $L2$ and $C1$ and $C2$ are different. This means that the resonant frequencies of the two branches will be different. The frequency of the $L1C1$ branch will be

$$f_{r1} = \frac{1}{2\pi\sqrt{L1C1}} = 10{,}382 \text{ Hz}$$

The resonant frequency of the $L2C2$ branch will be

$$f_{r2} = \frac{1}{2\pi\sqrt{L2C2}} = 27{,}705 \text{ Hz}$$

Figure 17.50 Two series resonant circuits connected in parallel.

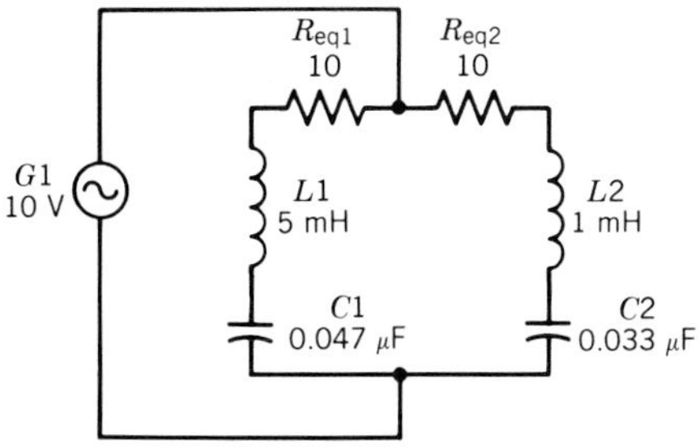

At resonant frequency f_{r1}, 10.382 kHz, the inductive and capacitive reactances of the $L1C1$ branch cancel since $X_L = +j326.2\ \Omega$ and $X_C = -j326.2\ \Omega$. The impedance of the $L1C1$ branch at this frequency is therefore 10 Ω and is resistive in nature. At a source frequency of 10.382 kHz, the impedance of the $L2C2$ branch is the phasor sum of the resistance and the inductive and capacitive reactance. At this frequency, $X_{L2} = 65.2\ \Omega$, but $X_{C2} = 464.5\ \Omega$. In complex rectangular form

$$Z_{L2C2} = 10 + j(X_{L2} - X_{C2}) = 10 - j399.3$$

or, in polar form,

$$Z_{L2C2} = 399.4 \angle -88.6^\circ$$

From the phase angle of the resulting impedance, you can see that the $L2C2$ branch of the circuit acts capacitively when the source frequency is the resonant frequency of the $L1C1$ branch. The source current at the resonant frequency of this branch will be the current through the 10 Ω impedance of the $L1C1$ branch plus the current through the $L2C2$ branch. Expressed mathematically,

$$I = \frac{E}{10} + \frac{E}{399.4 \angle -88.6^\circ}$$
$$= 1 \angle 0^\circ + 0.025 \angle +88.6^\circ$$

Expressing the two branch currents in complex rectangular form for addition,

$$I = (1 + j0) + (0.0006 + j0.025) = 1 + j0.025.$$

In polar terms, the current delivered by the source at 10,382 Hz is 1.0 A at a phase angle of 1.4°.

At the resonant frequency of the $L2C2$ branch, 27.705 kHz, the inductive and capacitive reactances of the $L2C2$ branch will be

$$X_{L2} = 2\pi fL = +j174.1\ \Omega \quad \text{and}$$

$$X_{C2} = \frac{1}{2\pi fC} = -j174.1\ \Omega$$

At that frequency, then, the inductive and capacitive reactances will cancel, and the branch impedance will be 10 Ω resistive. The impedance of the $L1C1$ branch at a frequency of 27.705 kHz is the phasor sum of R_{eq2} and the inductive and capacitive reactances. At 27.705 kHz,

$$X_{L1} = 2\pi fL1 = 870.4 \angle 90^\circ\ \Omega \quad \text{but}$$

$$X_{C1} = \frac{1}{2\pi fC1} = 122.2 \angle -90^\circ\ \Omega$$

The impedance of the $L1C1$ branch in rectangular form is

$$Z_{L1C1} = 10 + j(870.4 - 122.2) = 10 + j748.2$$

or, in polar form, $748.3 \angle 89.2^\circ$. From the fact that the impedance phase angle is positive, you can see that the $L1C1$ branch acts inductively when the source frequency is the resonant frequency of the $L2C2$ branch. The source current at a source frequency of 27.705 kHz is

$$I = I_{L2C2} + I_{L1C1}$$

or

$$I = \frac{E}{R_{eq2}} + \frac{E}{748.3 \angle 89.2^\circ}$$
$$= \frac{10}{10 \angle 0^\circ} + \frac{10}{748.3 \angle 89.2^\circ}$$
$$= 1 \angle 0^\circ + 0.0134 \angle -89.2^\circ$$

Converting to complex rectangular coordinates for addition gives

$$I = (1 + j0) + (0.0002 - j0.0134)$$

Rounding off, $I = 1.0 - j0.013$, or, in polar terms, $1.0 \angle -0.74^\circ$.

If the source current is graphed as a function of the source frequency, as in Figure 17.51, it will be seen that the two resonant frequencies are associated with peaks in the value of the source current. This is because the impedance of one of the two branches is at a minimum at its resonant frequency, so that the current through that branch will be at a maximum.

Also notice that there is a distinct drop in the circuit current between the two peaks, in this case, when the source frequency is at 14,756 Hz. The current

Figure 17.51 Source current as a function of frequency in the circuit of Figure 17.49. The central null is best explained by the formulas used to predict resonant circuit behavior.

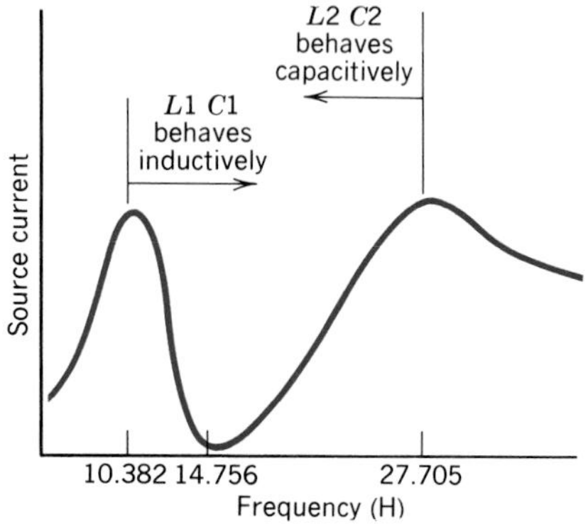

supplied by the source through the $L1C1$ branch at this frequency is

$$I_{L1C1} = \frac{E}{Z_{L1C1}} = \frac{10}{10 + j(463.6 - 229.5)}$$
$$= \frac{10}{10 + j234.1}$$

Converting to polar form for division,

$$I_{L1C1} = \frac{10 \angle 0^\circ}{234.3 \angle +87.6^\circ} = 0.043 \angle -87.6^\circ$$

Through the $L2C2$ branch,

$$I_{L2C2} = \frac{10 \angle 0^\circ}{10 + j(92.7 - 326.8)}$$
$$= \frac{10 \angle 0^\circ}{10 - j234.1}$$
$$= \frac{10 \angle 0^\circ}{234.3 \angle -87.6^\circ} = 0.043 \angle 87.6^\circ$$

In complex rectangular form, $I_{L2C2} = 0.0018 + j0.043$. Adding I_{L1C1} and I_{L2C2},

$$I_{\text{source}} = (0.0018 - j0.043) + (0.0018 + j0.043)$$
$$= 0.0036 + j0 \text{ A}$$

Notice that the two reactive branch currents cancel, exactly as they did in a parallel resonant circuit, and the current supplied by the source is 0.0036 A *in phase* with the source potential difference.

Comparing this value with the source current at two arbitrarily chosen frequencies, one above the resonant frequency of the $L2C2$ branch and one below the resonant frequency of the $L1C1$ branch, reinforces the notion that this circuit is behaving like a parallel resonant circuit at a frequency of 14,756 Hz. At a source frequency of 30 kHz, the current in the $L1C1$ branch is $0.00014 - j0.012$ and in the $L2C2$ branch, $0.12 - j0.32$. To save space, the steps in the calculations of the branch currents are not shown. The sum of the two branch currents is $0.12 - j0.332$, or 0.35 A at a phase angle of $\angle -70.13^\circ$ in polar form. At 9 kHz, the current in the $L1C1$ branch is $0.012 + j0.11$ and in the $L2C2$ branch it is $0.00044 + j0.02$. The sum of the branch currents at a source frequency of 9 kHz is $0.0124 + j0.13$, or 0.13 A at a phase angle of $\angle 84.55^\circ$. Both these values contrast sharply with the source current of 0.0036 A at 0° at a source frequency of 14,756 Hz.

The explanation of this third resonant frequency is actually given in Figure 17.51. As is shown there, for frequencies above the $L1C1$ resonant frequency, this branch of the circuit behaves inductively, while the $L2C2$ branch, for frequencies below its resonant frequency, behaves capacitively. Granting this, it should not be hard to imagine that there is some frequency between the resonant frequencies of the $L1C1$ and $L2C2$ branches at which the inductive reactance of the $L1C1$ branch operating above its resonant frequency is numerically equal to the capacitive reactance of the $L2C2$ branch operating below its resonant frequency. At this frequency, the entire circuit will operate as a parallel-tuned circuit, and its impedance will be maximum. Through the use of involved algebraic calculation, or more easily, by using calculus, a formula for this third resonant frequency can be derived. It is

$$f_P = \frac{1}{2\pi \sqrt{(L1 + L2) \dfrac{C1C2}{C1 + C2}}} \qquad \text{FORMULA 17.17}$$

Examining this formula leads to another curious observation. The term $L1 + L2$ is the total inductance of the two branch inductances in series, while the term $\dfrac{C1C2}{C1 + C2}$ would be the total capacitance of the branch capacitors connected in series.

As in the case of parallel-connected, series-tuned circuits, the series connection of two parallel-tuned circuits, as shown in Figure 17.52, possesses a third resonant frequency at which it operates as a series-tuned circuit. For the sake of simpler calculations, the coil and capacitor equivalent series resistances are assumed to be low enough to be ignored. In this case, you can see that the current supplied by the source will be zero at two frequencies: The resonant frequency of the $L1C1$ tank and at the resonant frequency of the $L2C2$ tank. The tank circuit made up of $L1$ and $C1$ has a resonant frequency of

$$f_r = \frac{1}{2\pi \sqrt{LC}} = 10{,}382 \text{ Hz}$$

At this frequency the inductive and capacitive react-

Figure 17.52 Two parallel-tuned circuits connected in series.

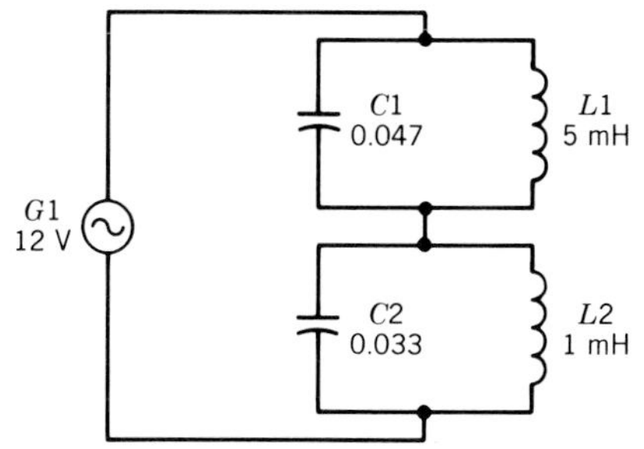

ances are

$$X_{L1} = 326.2 \angle +90^\circ \ \Omega \quad \text{and}$$
$$X_{C1} = 326.2 \angle -90^\circ \ \Omega$$

This means that the currents in the $L1$ and $C1$ branches are 180° apart and cancel at this frequency. In other words, there is no source current, and the impedance of the tank is "infinite." The same holds true for the tank circuit composed of $L2$ and $C2$ at its resonant frequency of 27,705 Hz. At this frequency,

$$X_{L2} = 174 \angle +90^\circ \ \Omega \quad \text{and} \quad X_{C2} = 174 \angle -90^\circ \ \Omega$$

The currents in the $L2$ branches are 180° out of phase, and so the sum of the currents is zero.

From Table 17.2, you can see that a parallel circuit operating above its resonant frequency acts capacitively, while a parallel circuit operating below its resonant frequency acts inductively. At a source frequency of 18 kHz, for example, the impedance of the $L1C1$ tank is

$$Z_{L1C1} = \frac{X_{L1}X_{C1}}{X_{L1} + X_{C1}} = \frac{565.5 \angle +90^\circ \times 188.1 \angle -90^\circ}{0 + j377.4}$$

Converting the denominator to complex rectangular components and performing the indicated multiplication and division,

$$Z_{L1C1} = \frac{106370.55 \angle 0^\circ}{377.4 \angle +90^\circ} = 281.9 \angle -90^\circ \ \Omega$$

Since the phase angle is negative, at this frequency the $L1C1$ tank is acting capacitively, and its equivalent circuit (at this source frequency) would be a 0.0314 μF capacitor. At this frequency, the $L2C2$ tank has an impedance of

$$Z_{L2C2} = \frac{X_{L2}X_{C2}}{X_{L2} + X_{C2}}$$
$$= \frac{113.1 \angle +90^\circ \times 267.9 \angle -90^\circ}{0 - j154.8}$$

Performing the indicated multiplication and division, the impedance of the $L2C2$ tank is

$$Z_{L2C2} = \frac{30299.49 \angle 0^\circ}{154.8 \angle -90^\circ} = 195.7 \angle +90^\circ \ \Omega$$

Here, the positive phase angle indicates a tank circuit that is acting inductively. The equivalent of the $L2C2$ tank at a source frequency of 18 kHz would be a 1.73-mH inductor.

The total circuit impedance at a source frequency of 18 kHz can be obtained by adding Z_{L1C1} and Z_{L2C2} after converting them to complex rectangular coordinate form.

$$Z_{L1C1} = 281.9 \angle -90^\circ = 0 - j281.9$$
$$Z_{L2C2} = 195.7 \angle 90^\circ = 0 + j195.7$$
$$Z_{\text{total}} = 0 - j86.2$$

or, in polar coordinates

$$Z_T = 86.2 \angle -90^\circ$$

The source current is, therefore,

$$I = \frac{E}{Z} = \frac{12 \angle 0^\circ}{86.2 \angle -90^\circ} = 0.14 \angle 90^\circ \text{ A}$$

The frequency at which the inductive reactance of the $L2C2$ tank has the same magnitude as the capacitive reactance of the $L1C1$ tank can be found by using the formula

$$f_s = \frac{1}{2\pi \sqrt{(C1 + C2)\left(\dfrac{L1L2}{L1 + L2}\right)}}$$

FORMULA 17.18

As in the case of Formula 17.17, examination of this formula reveals a curious fact. The term $C1 + C2$ is the total capacitance of the two circuit capacitors, while the term $\dfrac{L1L2}{L1 + L2}$ gives the equivalent inductance of the two circuit inductors.

Using Formula 17.18 to solve for the third resonant frequency of the circuit shown in Figure 17.52,

$$f_s = \frac{1}{2\pi} \sqrt{(0.047 \times 10^{-6} + 0.033 \times 10^{-6}) \times \left(\frac{0.001 \times 0.005}{0.006}\right)}$$
$$f_s = 19{,}492.4 \text{ Hz}$$

This calculation can be checked by calculating the circuit impedance at this frequency. Since there are no resistances in the circuit, the circuit impedance should be zero at this frequency. The impedance of the $L1C1$ tank at a source frequency of 19,492.4 Hz is

$$Z_{L1C1} = \frac{X_{L1} \times_{C1}}{X_{L1} + X_{C1}} = \frac{612.4 \angle +90^\circ \times 173.7 \angle -90^\circ}{438.7 \angle +90^\circ}$$
$$= \frac{106373.88 \angle 0^\circ}{438.7 \angle +90^\circ} = 242.5 \angle -90^\circ$$

The impedance of the $L2C2$ tank is

$$Z_{L2C2} = \frac{X_{L2} \times_{C2}}{X_{L2} + X_{C2}} = \frac{122.5 \angle +90^\circ \times 247.4 \angle -90^\circ}{124.9 \angle -90^\circ}$$
$$= \frac{30306.5 \angle 0^\circ}{124.9 \angle -90^\circ} = 242.6 \angle +90^\circ$$

From this you can see that the two impedances are about equal (except for the small difference due to

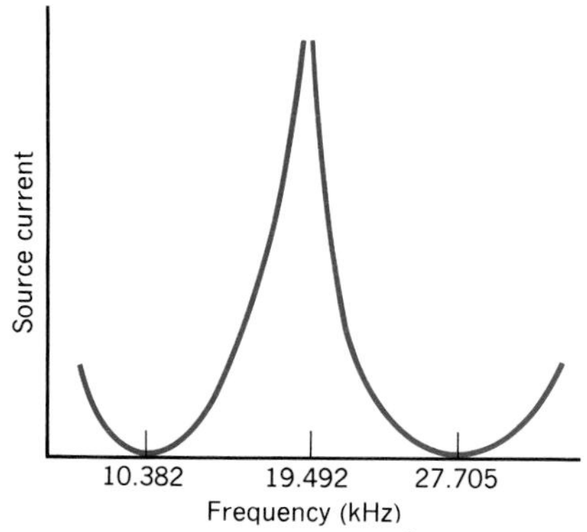

Figure 17.53 Series-connected parallel-tuned circuits produce a series-tuned current peak at a third resonant frequency.

rounding off) and opposite in phase, so that the circuit impedance will be practically zero at f_s, the series resonant frequency. Figure 17.53 is a sketch of the circuit current at frequencies near the three resonant frequencies. Notice that the curve is not symmetrical. In the laboratory exercises for this chapter, you will see that the current-versus-frequency curves for complex *RCL* circuits can be quite unsymmetrical.

C.2 USING THEVENIN'S AND NORTON'S THEOREMS TO ANALYZE RESONANT CIRCUITS

The warning about the use of Kirchhoff's voltage law included earlier in this chapter also applies to other circuit analysis techniques. But you should not assume that because these methods of analysis have to be used carefully that they are not true for circuits involving reactive components or resonance. Kirchhoff's voltage law is true for the series resonant circuit shown in Figure 17.54. The sum of the voltage rises and voltage drops around the closed loop is zero, if attention is paid to the phase of the voltage drops and rises. In Figure 17.54, the circuit Q is

$$Q = \frac{X_L}{R1} = \frac{3162.3}{270} = 11.7$$

Recall from Formulas 17.9 and 17.10 that

$$E_L = QE_s \quad \text{and} \quad E_C = QE_s$$

$$E_L = 117 \angle 90° \quad \text{and} \quad E_C = 117 \angle -90°$$

At resonance, the entire potential difference of the source appears across the series resistance, so $E_{R1} =$ 10 V. Writing the Kirchhoff's voltage law equation produces

$$0 = -10 \angle 0° + 10 \angle 0° + 117 \angle 90° + 117 \angle -90°$$

Adding by phasor methods shows that the equation

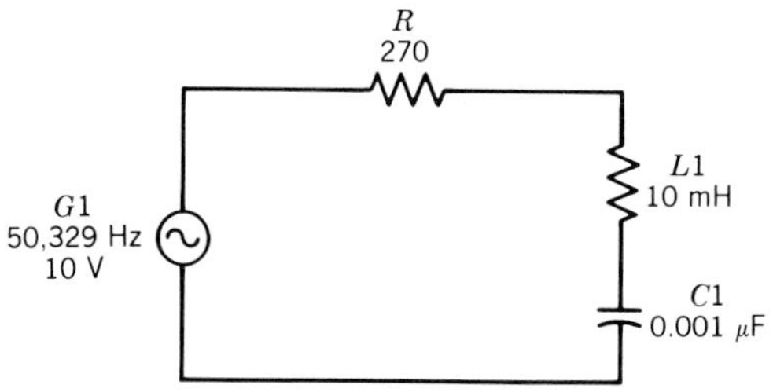

Figure 17.54 Applying Kirchhoff's voltage law to a resonant circuit.

balances. In other words, Kirchhoff's voltage law is correct for reactive circuits if the phase angles of the potential drops and rises are taken into account. Similarly, it can be shown that Kirchhoff's current law is valid for parallel circuits with reactive components.

Since most of the circuit analysis techniques you have learned for dc networks are based either directly or indirectly on Kirchhoff's laws, it should not be difficult to accept the fact that these techniques can be redefined for use with ac sources and reactive components. Two important analysis methods that can be applied are Thevenin's and Norton's theorems. Thevenin's theorem, for example, can be redefined to apply to networks with ac sources and impedances instead of resistances. In the circuit shown in Figure 17.55*a*, the current through $R2$ and the potential difference across it can be easily calculated if $G1$, $R1$, and $C1$ are replaced by a Thevenin equivalent source and series impedance. The same steps given for the calculation of the Thevenin source potential and series resistance in Chapter 8 can be used if impedance is substituted for resistance. The steps are shown in Figures 17.55*b* through 17.55*d*. In 17.55*b*, two terminals are placed to divide the circuit into source and load networks. In 17.55*c*, the load network has been removed and the potential difference across the terminals is calculated by determining the current in the $R1C1$ branch. This is obtained by $I = \frac{E}{Z}$, where Z is the combined impedance of $R1$ and $C1$. Since there is no circuit current through $L1$ in Figure 17.55*c*, it does not affect the potential difference across the terminals. The series impedance of $R1$ and $C1$ is $270 - j530.5$, or in polar form, $595.26 \angle -63°$, and

$$I = \frac{0.707\ (30) \angle 0°}{595.26 \angle -63°} = 0.0356 \angle 63°$$

The potential difference across $C1$, which will be the same as the potential difference across the network terminals, is

$$E_{C1} = I \times X_c = 0.0356 \angle 63° \times 530.5 \angle -90°$$
$$= 18.9 \angle -27° \text{ V}$$

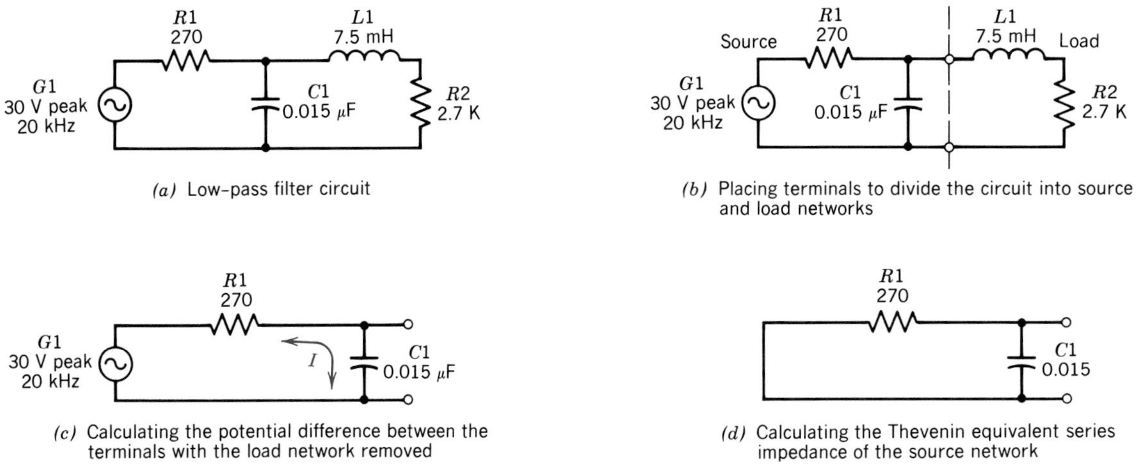

(a) Low-pass filter circuit

(b) Placing terminals to divide the circuit into source and load networks

(c) Calculating the potential difference between the terminals with the load network removed

(d) Calculating the Thevenin equivalent series impedance of the source network

Figure 17.55 Applying Thevenin's theorem to ac circuits containing inductors and capacitors.

This is the rms value and phase angle of the Thevenin source. The value of the Thevenin equivalent series impedance is calculated using the network shown in Figure 17.55*d*. First, the resistance of *R*1 and the reactance of *C*1 are combined

$$Z_{R1C1} = \frac{Z_{R1}Z_{C1}}{Z_{R1} + Z_{C1}} = \frac{143235 \angle -90^\circ}{270 - j530.5}$$

Converting to polar form for division,

$$Z_{R1C1} = \frac{143235 \angle -90^\circ}{595.26 \angle -63^\circ} = 240.63 \angle -27^\circ$$

which in complex rectangular form is $214.4 - j109.2$. This, then, is the impedance of an equivalent Thevenin series impedance that can be substituted for *R*1 and *C*1.

The Thevenin equivalent circuit is therefore a series combination of a source producing a potential difference of 18.9 V at a phase angle of -27° and an impedance of 240.63 Ω, producing a capacitive phase shift of -27°. Figure 17.56 shows the Thevenin equivalent circuit with the load network reconnected to the terminals. Adding the resistance of *R*2 and the impedance of *L*1 produces a total series circuit impedance of

$$2914.4 + j833.3 = 3031.2 \angle 15.96^\circ \quad \text{or} \quad 3031.2 \angle 16^\circ$$

Figure 17.56 The load network reconnected to the Thevenin equivalent.

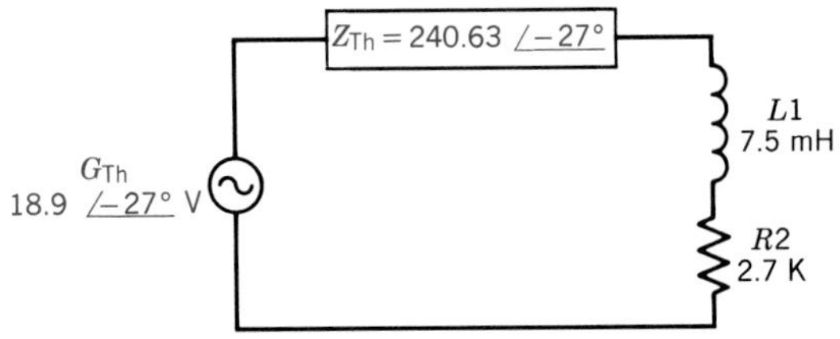

The current through *L*1 and *R*2 is

$$I = \frac{E}{Z} = \frac{18.9 \angle -27^\circ}{3031.2 \angle +16^\circ} = 0.00624 \quad \text{or} \quad 6.24 \text{ mA}$$

at a phase angle of $\angle -43^\circ$. The voltage drop across *R*2 is therefore $I \times R$, or 16.85 V at a phase angle of $\angle -43^\circ$.

The circuit shown in Figure 17.55*a* can also be analyzed using Norton's theorem, after dividing the circuit into source and load networks as in Figure 17.55*b*. This permits the calculation of the Norton source current by replacing the load with a short circuit and calculating the current in the short. As you can see from Figure 17.57*a*, this is quite simple. The short circuit effectively removes *C*1 from the circuit, leaving only *R*1. The current through the short is

$$I = \frac{0.707 \times 30 \angle 0^\circ}{270 \angle 0^\circ} = 0.07856 \quad \text{or} \quad 78.56 \text{ mA}$$

The parallel impedance of the Norton equivalent is obtained by means of the same calculation used for the series Thevenin impedance. The Norton impedance is $240.63 \angle -27^\circ$ Ω. The Norton equivalent circuit with the load network reconnected is shown in Figure 17.57*b*. The current through the load network composed of *L*1 and *R*2 is

$$I_{\text{load}} = I_{\text{source}} \times \frac{Z_{\text{Th}}}{Z_{\text{Th}} + Z_{\text{load}}}$$

$$= \frac{0.07856 \times 240.63 \angle -27^\circ}{2914.4 + j833.3}$$

Converting the denominator to polar coordinates and performing the division,

$$I_{\text{load}} = \frac{18.904 \angle -27^\circ}{3031.2 \angle 16^\circ} = 0.00624 \angle -43^\circ$$

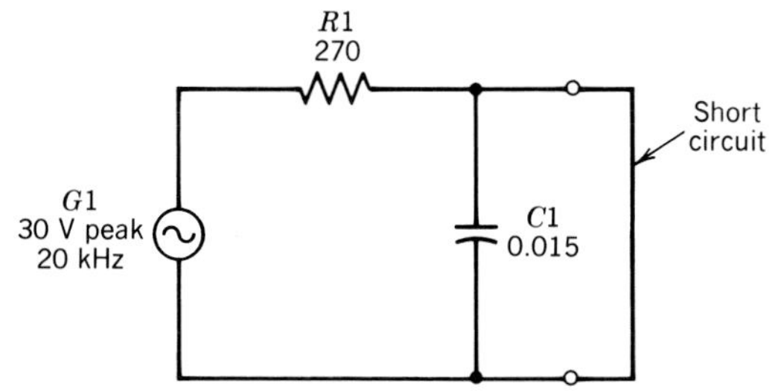

(a) Replacing the load network with a short circuit to calculate the current of the Norton equivalent source

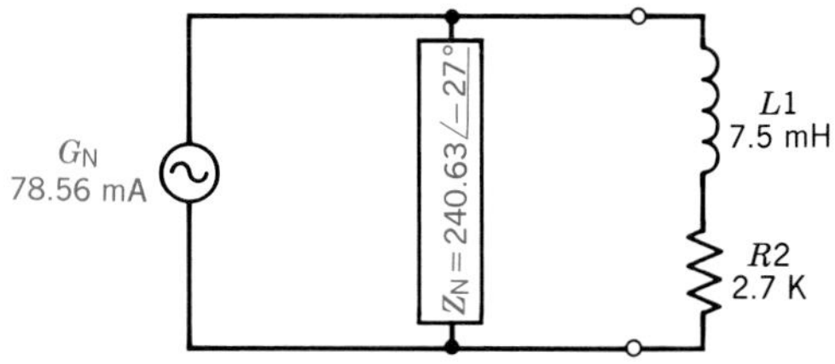

(b) Load network reconnected to the Norton equivalent

Figure 17.57 Applying Norton's theorem to the circuit of Figure 17.54 *a*.

or 6.24 $\angle -43°$ mA. This is the same answer obtained using Thevenin's theorem.

D. APPLICATIONS

D.1 PRACTICAL SERIES RESONANT CIRCUITS

Series resonant circuits are widely used in electronic units and can be adapted for a number of applications depending on how the circuit output terminals are arranged. In practice, series resonant circuits are also easier to troubleshoot than parallel circuits and are found in applications where the effects of loading are less noticed. As you can see from Figures 17.58*a* through 17.58*c*, it is possible to observe the effect of each component in a series-tuned circuit with an oscilloscope, if care is taken not to create short circuits by faulty grounding, as shown in Figure 17.58*d*. Also, a portable (ungrounded) multimeter can be used to measure the potential difference across each component, as shown in Figures 17.59*a* and 17.59*b*.

WARNING

THE POTENTIAL DIFFERENCES ACROSS COMPONENTS IN SERIES CAN REACH DANGEROUS LEVELS EVEN WHEN THE SOURCE POTENTIAL DIFFERENCE IS LOW. USE EXTREME CAUTION TO PREVENT INJURY OR EQUIPMENT DAMAGE WHEN MAKING MEASUREMENTS AROUND TUNED CIRCUITS.

Figure 17.58 Observing the phase shifts due to individual components in series resonant networks in equipment.

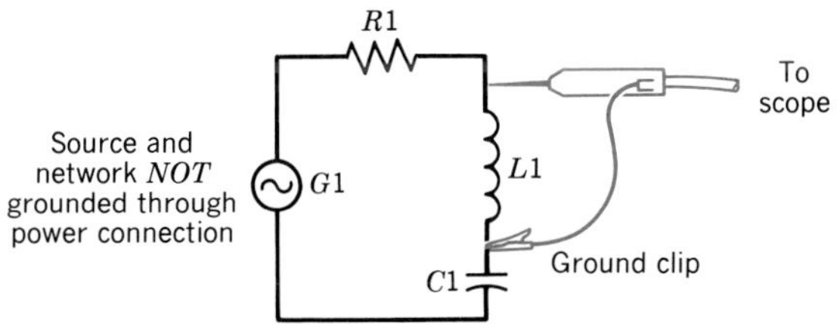

(a) Source and network *UNGROUNDED*, oscilloscope *GROUNDED*, scope probe and ground lead can be connected directly across each component

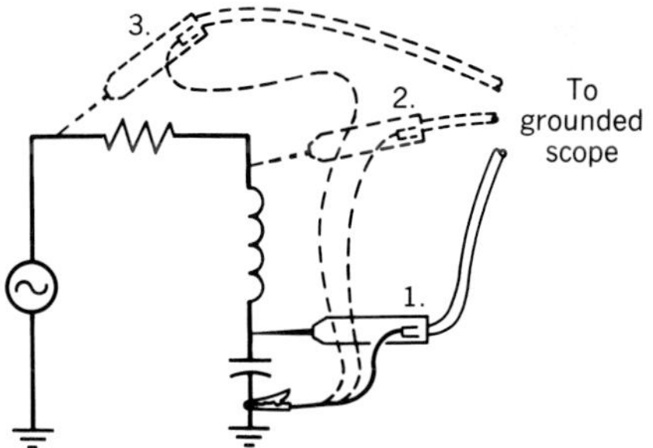

(c) If both source and oscilloscope are grounded, connect the probe ground clip to the circuit ground and make observations across groups of components

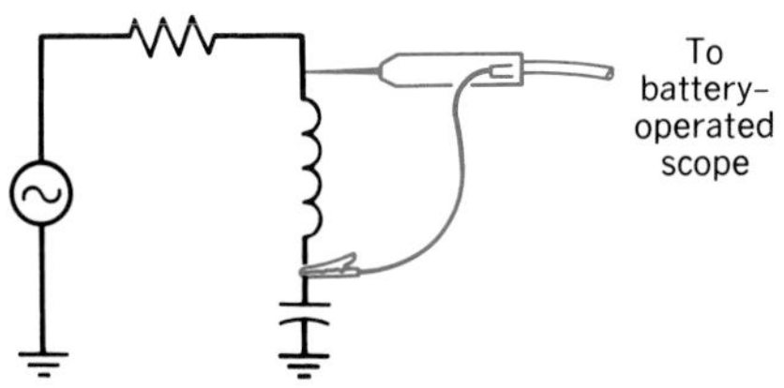

(b) If an *UNGROUNDED, BATTERY-OPERATED* oscilloscope is used, scope probe and ground lead can still be connected across each component, even if source or circuit are grounded.

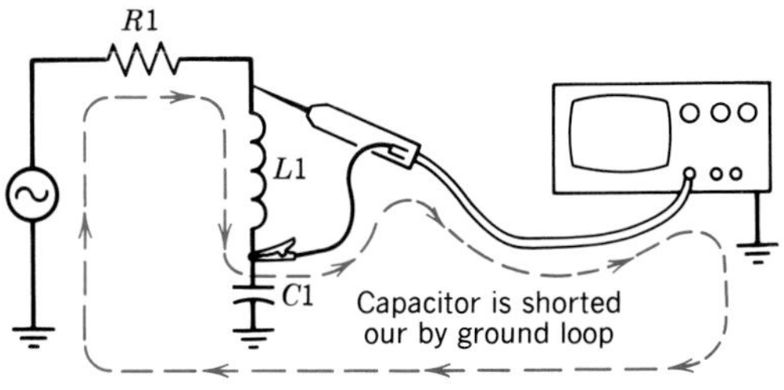

(d) *INCORRECT* method scope power ground provides a current path which shorts out *C*1.

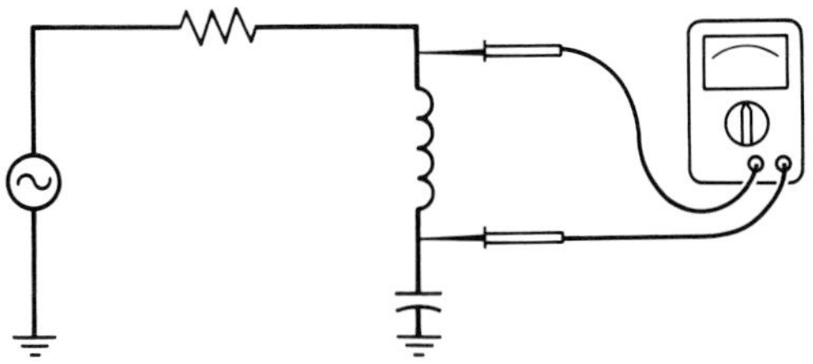

(a) Correct: Ungrounded, battery-operated meter can be used to measure potential regardless of circuit grounding.

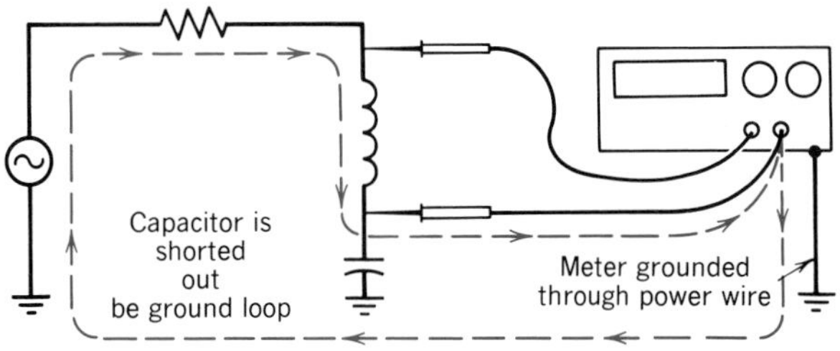

(b) Incorrect: A grounded meter can produce a ground loop that shorts out part of the series circuit

Figure 17.59 Caution is also required when using a meter to measure potential differences across components in a grounded series-tuned circuit.

Observing the phase shifts with an oscilloscope or measuring potential differences with a reasonably accurate rf voltmeter will reveal a large number of fault conditions such as excessive capacitor leakage and component value change, if the input potential difference is sinusoidal. First, measure the input frequency with a frequency counter or an oscilloscope; then calculate the expected potential difference and phase shift across each component in the series string. Comparing the calculated and observed values will usually point to the faulty component.

When troubleshooting series *RCL* circuits, it is often a good idea to calculate the Q of the circuit. If the Q is less than 10, resonance effects will be hard to observe and, in practical circuits, the resonant frequency may be shifted from that predicted by the formula

$$f_r = \frac{1}{2\pi \sqrt{LC}}$$

Heavy loading, that is, drawing excessive current from the circuit, can also result in a change of resonant frequency. This subject will be considered in greater detail in Section D.2.

The output of a series resonant circuit is most frequently obtained in one of three ways. In the circuit shown in Figure 17.60, the output is the potential difference appearing across the series resistance. When the input frequency is the resonant frequency, the total impedance of the circuit is at its minimum. This means

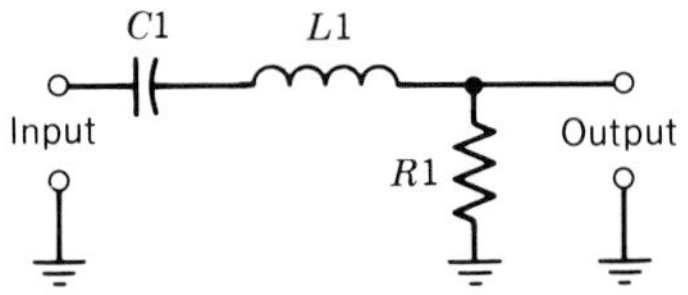

Figure 17.60 Taking the output of a series resonant circuit across the circuit resistor. This arrangement provides the highest output current.

that the current through the circuit resistor will be at its maximum, as will the potential difference of the output. For frequencies other than the resonant frequency of the circuit, the circuit current is less than its maximum, and the output potential difference is lower. Accordingly, such a circuit can be used to provide an output when the input signal is within a selected frequency band. This circuit is also able to furnish a greater output current than the other two to be discussed without a change in resonant frequency due to excessive loading.

In the circuit shown in Figure 17.61, the output is taken across a resistor placed in parallel with the inductive and capacitive components of the series resonant circuit. The effect of this arrangement is the opposite of that shown in Figure 17.60. Here, at resonance, the potential differences across $L1$ and $C1$ are equal in magnitude but 180° apart in phase, so that they cancel each other. The potential difference across output resistor $R2$ is therefore zero at resonance. At input frequencies other than the resonant frequency, the potential differences across $L1$ and $C1$ do not cancel completely, and the difference of the two appears across the output resistor $R2$. Resistor $R1$ is needed to limit the circuit current when the input is at the resonant frequency. A series-tuned circuit arranged in this manner is used to provide output at all but a narrow band of frequencies. In other words, it acts as a bandstop circuit.

When the voltage gain across the reactive components in a series resonant circuit is desired, the output is taken across a resistor in parallel with the circuit capacitor, as shown in Figure 17.62. This arrangement provides the highest output potential difference at res-

Figure 17.61 When the output is taken across the inductor and capacitor, the potential difference across the output resistor will be at a minimum when the input is at resonance.

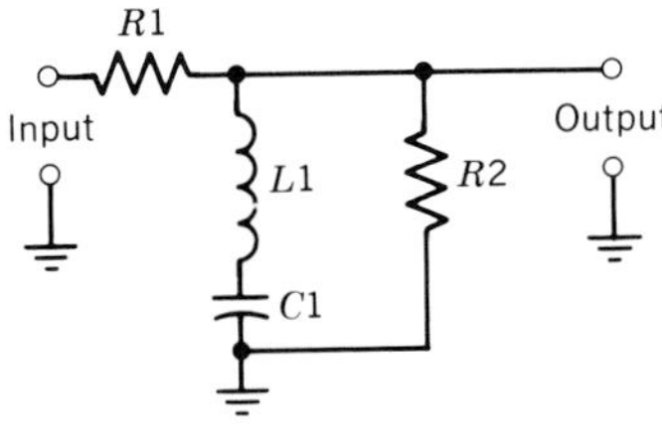

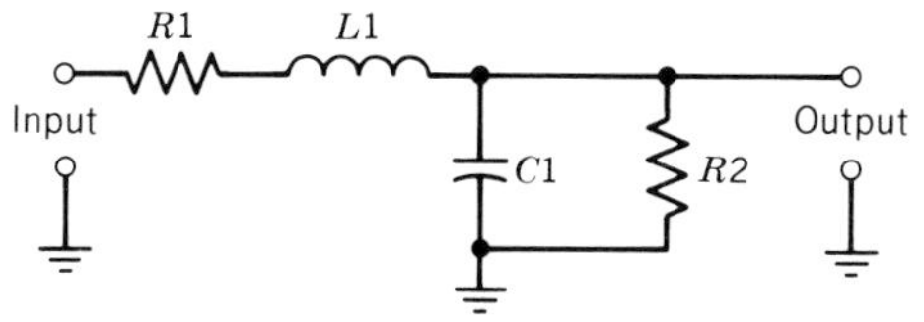

Figure 17.62 When the output is taken across a resistor in parallel with the capacitor, a voltage gain is obtained.

onance of the three circuits shown here but can not provide as much output current as the circuit shown in Figure 17.60.

D.2 PRACTICAL PARALLEL RESONANT CIRCUITS

The parallel resonant tank circuit is probably the most important single circuit used in electronic communications equipment. A parallel resonant tank, for example, acts as the frequency-determining network for most oscillators. Parallel resonant circuits are harder to troubleshoot than series resonant circuits because the inductor and capacitor are in parallel, and it is not possible to examine the potential difference of phase shift across each of them independently. The easiest way to check the operation of a parallel-tuned tank at resonance is to place a small value resistor in series with the tank as shown in Figure 17.63. A dual-trace oscilloscope can then be used to compare the source potential difference with the potential difference across the added resistance. If the input frequency is the resonant frequency, the source potential and that across the resistor will be in phase. An incorrect frequency or change in component value will cause the resistor potential difference to lead or lag the source potential. (See Table 17.2 for help in interpreting the cause of a phase shift.)

Increases in capacitor ESR or changes in the value of circuit resistances can be found by calculating the half power points of the circuit and comparing these

Figure 17.63 Placing a small resistance in series with a parallel resonant makes it possible to compare source potential difference and circuit current phase.

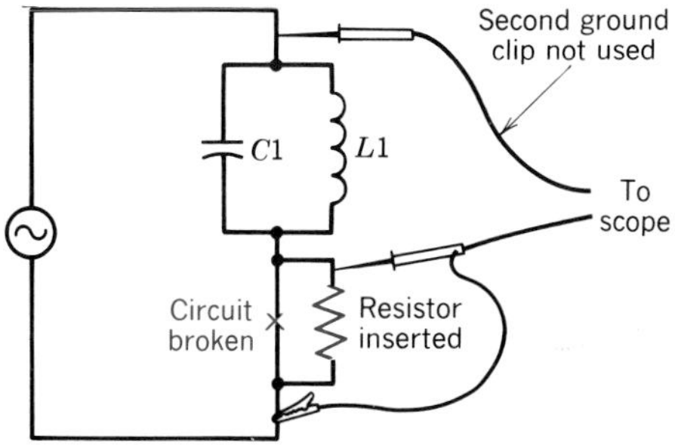

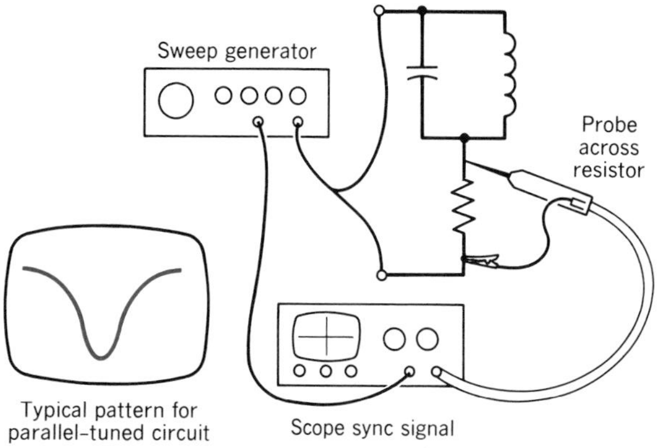

Figure 17.64 Using a sweep generator to check tuned circuit characteristic curves.

values to those measured. Usually, a sweep generator, one whose output frequency is constantly varied from a set lower limit to a set upper limit, is used. If the sweep generator is also connected to the oscilloscope, the characteristic of the circuit can be drawn on the oscilloscope display, as shown in Figure 17.64. Sweep generator testing can also be applied to series-tuned circuits to provide a display of the circuit characteristic curve.

Since parallel resonant circuits are often used as frequency-determining networks in oscillators and other units, stability of operation is important. It has been found in actual experience that tank circuits that store less than twice as much energy as they dissipate during each cycle tend to operate poorly and are unstable. On the other hand, if the Q, that is, the ratio of the energy stored to the energy dissipated, becomes too large, the operation of the tank becomes inefficient. This occurs because the amount of energy circulating between the magnetic field and the electric field in the tank is larger than necessary and various heating losses become serious. In practice, tank circuits are designed so that the ratio of the energy stored to the energy dissipated over a single cycle is about two. This works out to a circuit Q of about 4π or about 12.5. Inductor, capacitor, and resistor values are chosen to provide this value in addition to the correct resonant frequency.

Another important characteristic of tank circuits that involves their practical performance is circuit loading. Earlier examples have shown how a resistor, in this case a load resistor, can be placed in either of the branches of the tank, or in parallel with the tank, to form a third branch. A load resistor can also be placed in series with the tank. In addition to these possibilities of resistive coupling, tank circuits are frequently inductively coupled to the tank coil by means of a coupling coil as shown in Figure 17.65. Regardless of how the output of the tank circuit is obtained, the

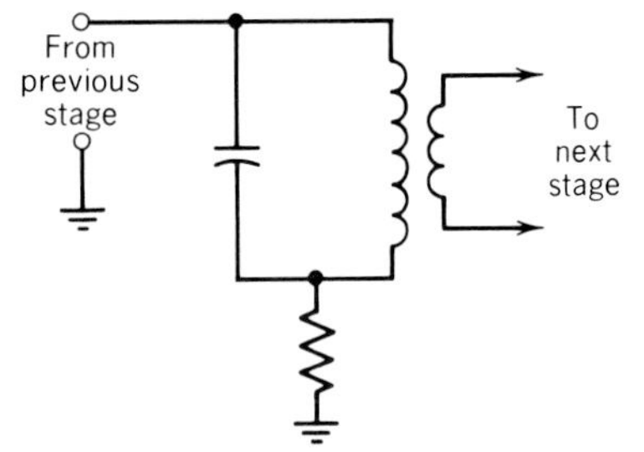

Figure 17.65 Tank circuit output is frequently obtained by means of a coupling coil or link. The coupling coil is generally wound on top of the inductor.

fact that electric power is removed from the tank produces the effect of an increase in tank resistance. As long as the parallel-tuned circuit Q remains above 10, the loading does not seriously affect the phase angle between the source potential difference and the source current, nor is the resonant frequency changed. As long as the circuit Q is above 10, the phase angle between the current in the capacitor branch and the inductor branch of the tank will be larger than 168.6°, which is fairly close to the theoretical value of 180° that exists in the tank composed of a pure inductance and pure capacitance. As the value of the circuit Q decreases below 10, the phase angle decreases rapidly.

In a parallel resonant circuit with heavy loading, or when the circuit Q is less than 10, it is usually necessary to use a modified form of Formula 17.4 to calculate the resonant frequency of the tank. When the Q of the tank is less than 10, or when the tank is heavily loaded, the practical, rather than theoretical, resonant frequency is given by the formula

$$f_r = \frac{1}{2\pi}\sqrt{\frac{1}{LC} - \frac{R^2}{L^2}} \qquad \text{FORMULA 17.19}$$

Formula 17.4,

$$f_r = \frac{1}{2\pi\sqrt{LC}}$$

can be used to calculate the resonant frequency of the tank as a first guess. Using this frequency, the inductive reactance of the inductor and the circuit Q can be calculated. If this results in a value for Q of 10 or less, the resonant frequency should be recalculated using Formula 17.19. This second value will provide better results if you are comparing calculated with measured values in troubleshooting.

Formula 17.19 provides another piece of interesting information about low-Q tank circuits. From the expression inside the square root sign, it is possible to show that the quantity $\frac{CR^2}{L}$ must be less than one. Otherwise, the quantity inside the square root sign will be zero or negative, resulting in an indeterminate resonant frequency. That is, there will be no frequency at which the inductive and capacitive branch currents cancel.

D.3 FILTERS

A *filter* is a network consisting of a number of impedances grouped together in such a way as to have a definite frequency characteristic. By this it is meant that a filter is designed to transmit; that is, to provide a low-impedance path between its input and output terminals for a certain range of input frequencies, but to provide a high-impedance path for other input frequency ranges. The range over which the filter provides a low-impedance path is called the *passband*, while the range of frequencies blocked by the filter is called the *attenuation band*. In Chapter 16, a number of simple *RC* filter circuits were discussed, including high-pass, low-pass, and bandpass filters. One of the most important characteristics of any filter is the input frequency at which its attenuation starts to increase rapidly, that is, the input frequency at which the filter impedance begins to increase rapidly. This is called the *cutoff frequency*, and is abbreviated f_c. The cutoff frequency of a filter is generally defined as the frequency at which the filter output drops more than 3 dB below its maximum.

Commonly used filter designs can include resistors, capacitors, and inductors in various configurations, although *RC* and *LC* combinations seem the most popular. The actual design of filter circuits is too complex to be covered in depth in this book, but the following sections should enable you to recognize some of the more common component configurations of the two principal design categories and to act as an aid to troubleshooting. Regardless of their seeming complexity, all passive filters, that is, those filters that do not contain amplifying devices such as transistors, are made up of *RC*, *RL*, *LC*, and *RCL* networks, and so can be analyzed using the methods you have learned in this and in previous chapters. If you can recognize basic filter types in a schematic diagram of a unit, you should be able to calculate their theoretical output for a given measured input potential difference and frequency.

Basic filter configurations are the L or "half section," shown in Figure 17.66, which consists of one series and one parallel or shunt arm; the T-section filter, shown in Figure 17.67, which consists of two series arms and one shunt arm; and the π-section filter, shown in Figure 17.68, consisting of one series arm

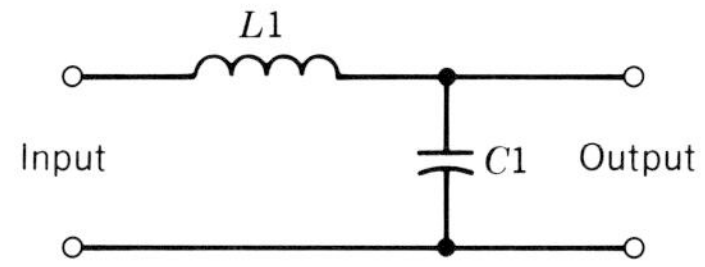

Figure 17.66 The L or "half section" filter.

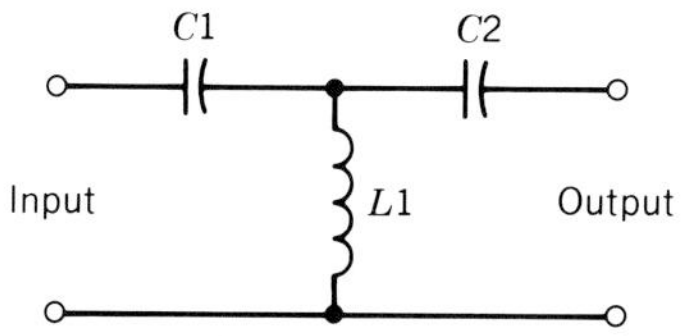

Figure 17.67 A T section filter.

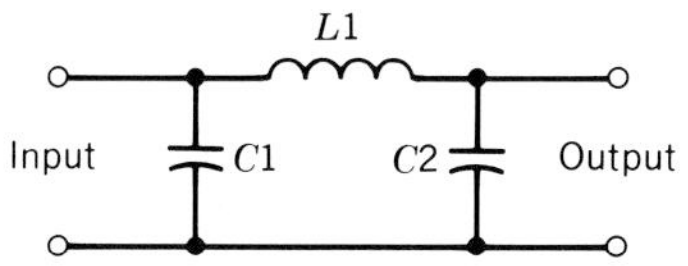

Figure 17.68 A π section filter.

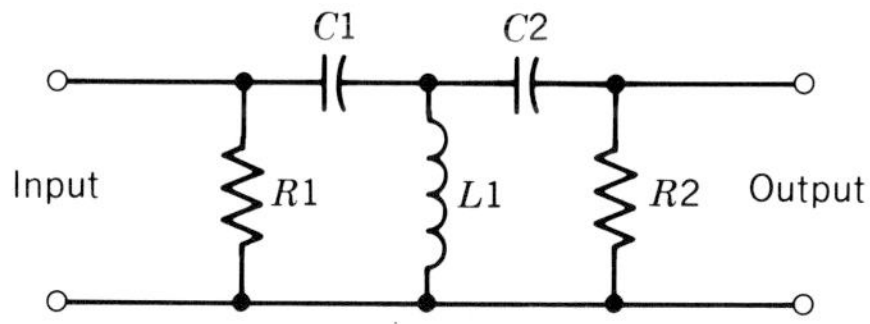

Figure 17.69 A T section filter with terminating resistances.

and two shunt arms. In some applications, several filter sections of the same type are joined to increase the attenuation of unwanted frequencies. Frequently, resistors of the same value are placed across input and output terminals of a filter, as in Figure 17.69. These resistors are called *terminating resistances*, or more simply, *terminations*. The value of the termination is generally determined by the input and output impedances of the circuits between which the filter network is connected.

D.3.1 CONSTANT *K* LOW-PASS FILTERS

A low-pass filter provides a low-impedance path between its input and output terminals for input signals below the cutoff frequency f_c. A constant K filter is

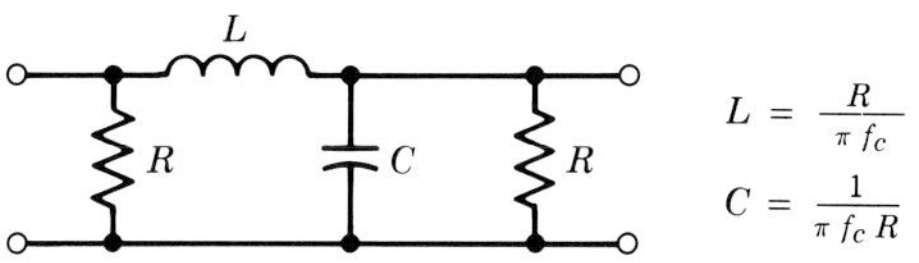

Figure 17.70 An L section, constant K, low-pass filter with terminations.

one of the two principal categories of filter. It is defined as a filter in which the impedance of the series arm or arms and the impedance of the shunt arm or arms are chosen so that their product is equal to the square of some constant. In mathematical terms, if Z_1 is the impedance of the series arm of the filter, and Z_2 is the impedance of the shunt arm,

$$Z_1 \times Z_2 = k^2 \qquad \text{FORMULA 17.20}$$

In this type of filter k^2 is equal to the square of the value of the termination resistors. An L-section circuit, including the termination resistances, is shown in Figure 17.70. For this type of circuit, the cutoff frequency is found by using the formula

$$f_c = \frac{1}{\pi \sqrt{LC}} \qquad \text{FORMULA 17.21}$$

Figure 17.71 shows the configurations of the T- and π-section low-pass filters providing the same attenuation factors as the L section of Figure 17.70. In some cases, resistors are substituted for either the inductors or the capacitors, particularly when the input signals cover only a narrow frequency band. The values of the inductors and capacitors for a particular cutoff frequency are easy to calculate. They are

$$L = \frac{R}{\pi f_c} \quad \text{and} \quad C = \frac{1}{\pi R f_c} \qquad \text{FORMULA 17.22}$$

A graph of the output of a constant K low-pass filter is shown in Figure 17.72. Note that the decrease in output is gradual. This is one of the characteristics of constant K filters.

D.3.2 *m*-DERIVED LOW-PASS FILTERS

A more complex form of low-pass filter circuit is called the "*m*-derived" type, which exists in two forms, either series or shunt. In this type of low-pass filter, the in-

Figure 17.71 T and π section constant K low-pass filters with terminating resistors.

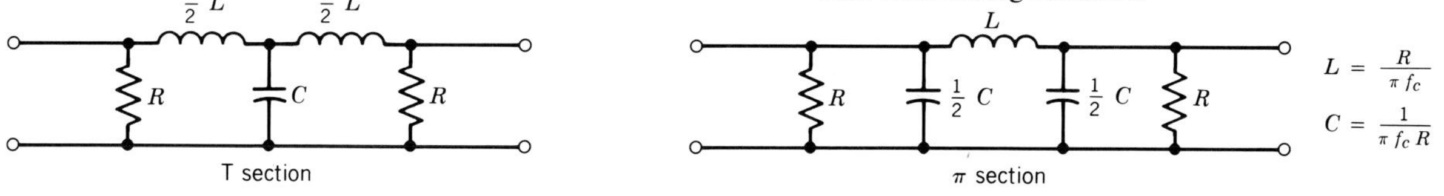

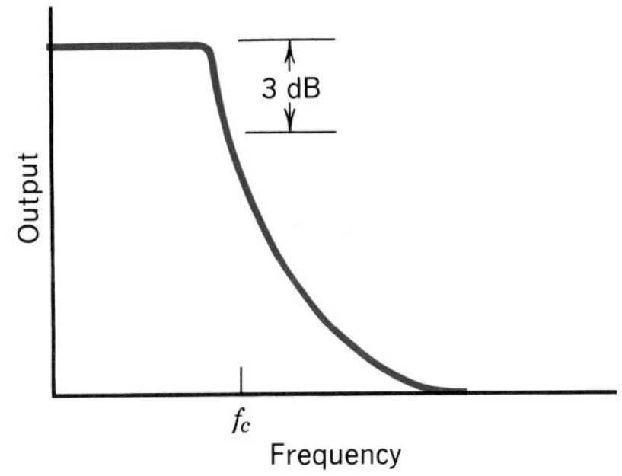

Figure 17.72 Output characteristic of a constant K low-pass filter (theoretical).

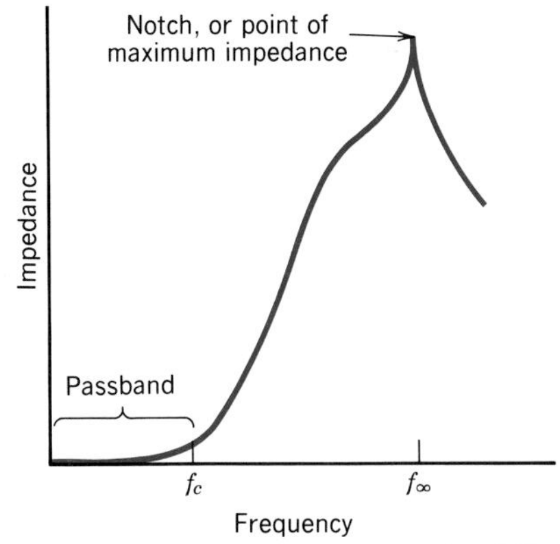

Figure 17.73 The impedance of an m-derived filter increases sharply between f_c and f_∞.

crease in impedance above the cutoff frequency is more rapid than in the constant K filter, and the impedance for unwanted input frequencies is greater. Depending on its configuration, the m-derived low-pass filter includes one or more series or parallel resonant networks that are tuned to a frequency above the cutoff frequency. This frequency, called the "frequency of infinite attenuation," is abbreviated f_∞. The impedance graph of an m-derived filter shown in Figure 17.73 shows that there is a sudden increase in impedance between f_c and f_∞. The steepness of the rise in the m-derived filter impedance curve means that this type of filter will provide a sharper cutoff of its passband than the constant K filter. The m-derived filter gets its name from the design factor m, which is used to calculate the value of f_∞ for a given value of f_c. the equation used is

$$f_\infty = \frac{f_c}{\pi\sqrt{1 - m^2}} \qquad \text{FORMULA 17.23}$$

Generally, m is made equal to some factor around 0.6, which provides a value for f_∞ of about $1.25f_c$. Decreasing the value of m will bring f_c and f_∞ closer together, thereby increasing the sharpness of the increase in the impedance above f_c. Figure 17.74 shows some configurations for m-derived low-pass filters. In all cases, the cutoff frequency f_c is

$$f_c = \frac{1}{2\pi\sqrt{LC}} \qquad \text{FORMULA 17.24}$$

D.3.3 HIGH-PASS FILTERS

The definition of a high-pass filter is a network that provides a low-impedance path between its input and output terminals for frequencies above its cutoff frequency, but which shows a relatively high impedance for frequencies below cutoff. As in the case of the low-pass filter, high-pass filters of both the constant K and m-derived varieties are found.

Three configurations of the constant K high-pass filter are shown in Figure 17.75, and the characteristic

Figure 17.74 m-derived low pass filters.

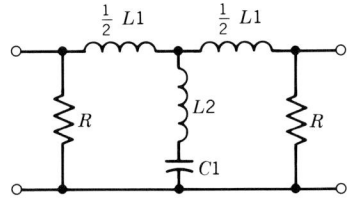

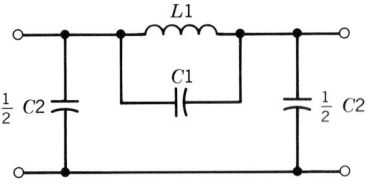

Figure 17.75 Three configurations of constant K high-pass filters.

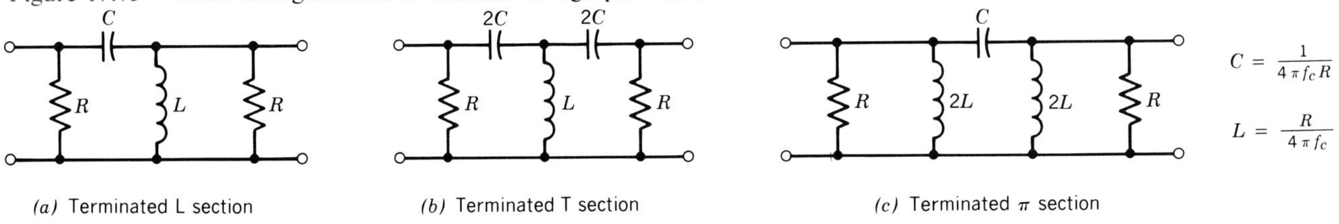

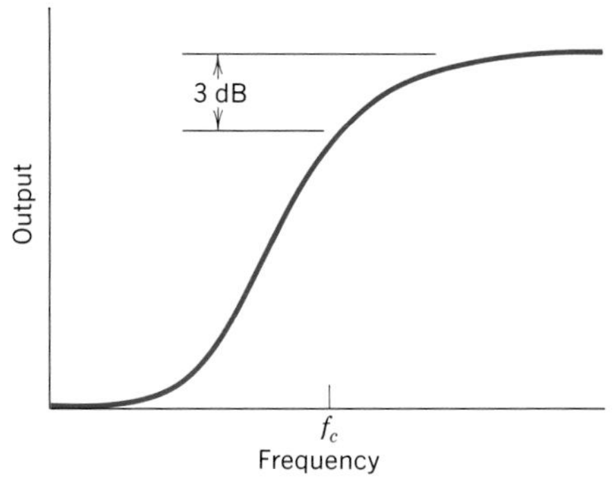

Figure 17.76 Output characteristic of a constant K high-pass filter.

curve is shown in Figure 17.76. The same gradual change in impedance exhibited by the constant K low-pass filter is also seen here. The formula for the cutoff frequency, however, is different. For the constant K high-pass filter it is

$$f_c = \frac{1}{4\pi \sqrt{LC}} \qquad \text{FORMULA 17.25}$$

Both series and shunt m-derived high-pass filters are used (see Figure 17.77). In these filters, the frequency of infinite attenuation is related to the cutoff frequency by the formula

$$f_\infty = f_c \sqrt{1 - m^2} \qquad \text{FORMULA 17.26}$$

The cutoff frequency can be found using

$$f_c = \frac{1}{\pi \sqrt{LC}} \qquad \text{FORMULA 17.27}$$

Generally, a design factor m of 0.6 is used, although smaller values can be used to move the frequency of infinite attenuation closer to the cutoff frequency, thereby making the impedance curve steeper. A typical m-derived high-pass filter characteristic curve is shown in Figure 17.78.

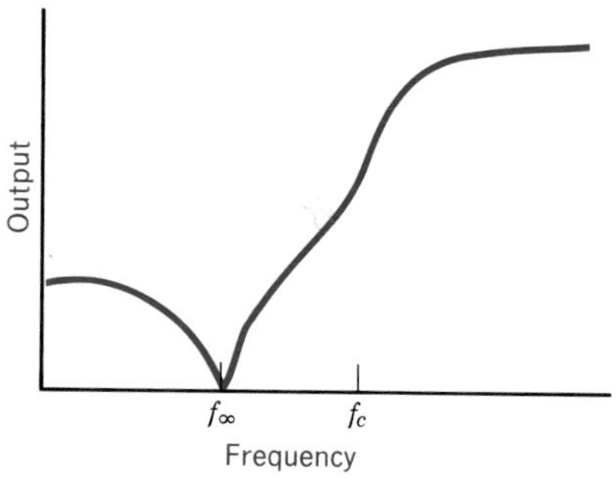

Figure 17.78 A typical m-derived high-pass filter characteristic curve.

D.3.4 BANDPASS AND BAND REJECTION FILTERS

Figure 17.79 shows the schematic diagram of a constant K bandpass filter and its characteristic curve. As the name implies, the bandpass filter provides a relatively low-impedance path for a frequency range of input signals and a high-impedance path for input frequencies not in this range. The circuit shown in Figure 17.80 along with its characteristic curve, acts in the opposite manner. It is a band rejection or bandstop filter and is capable of providing a high impedance for a particular band of frequencies while allowing any input not within the stop or rejection band to pass with little loss in amplitude.

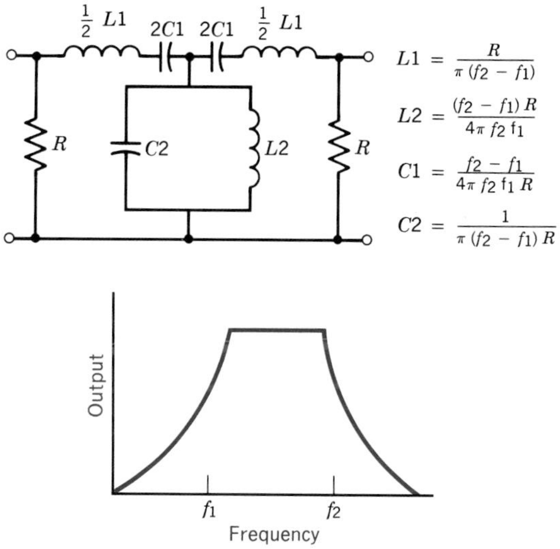

Figure 17.79 A constant K bandpass filter and its characteristic curve.

Figure 17.77 Representative series and shunt m-derived high-pass filters.

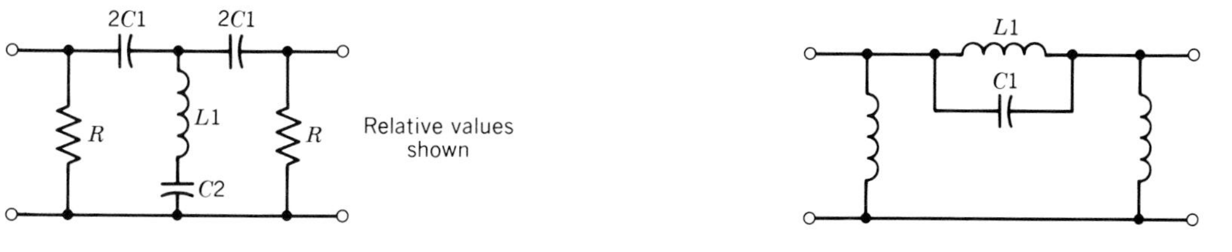

(a) Terminated T section series m derived

(b) Unterminated π section shunt m derived

$$L1 = \frac{(f2 - f1)\,R}{\pi\,f1\,f2}$$

$$L2 = \frac{R}{4\pi\,(f2 - f1)}$$

$$C1 = \frac{1}{4\pi\,(f2 - f1)\,R}$$

$$C2 = \frac{f2 - f1}{\pi\,f1\,f2\,R}$$

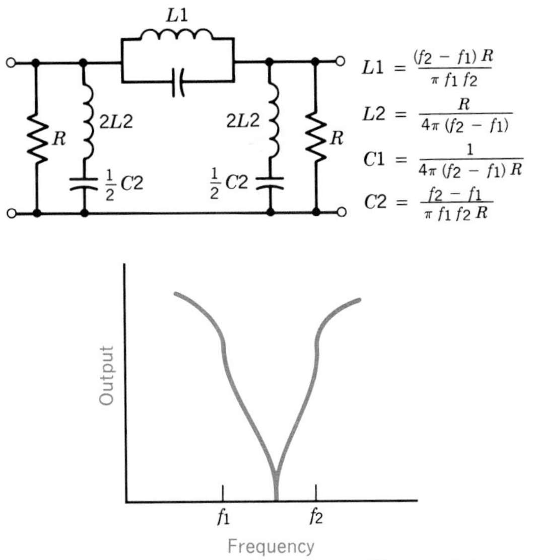

Figure 17.80 A constant K bandstop filter and its characteristic curve.

Bandpass and bandstop filters can be designed as L, T, or π sections and either as constant K or m derived, but the complexity of the filter itself can result in problems of operation at certain frequencies. Moreover, the fact that several tuned circuits are involved in the circuit means that a greater amount of input power is wasted due to losses in inductor resistance and capacitor ESR. For these reasons, and also because active components are generally cheaper than the precision inductors and capacitors needed in complex filters, filter networks built around such active devices as operational amplifiers are now becoming more common than passive component bandpass and band rejection filters.

D.3.5 TROUBLESHOOTING FILTER CIRCUITS

The most common failure modes of filter circuits are those that cause the filter to fail completely. Filters tend to perform properly or not at all. Any open- or short-circuited condition usually leads to one of the two following cases:

a. An open circuit that produces a no-output condition.

b. A short-circuited component that causes either a no-output or reduced output condition.

In most cases, a check for continuity with an ohmmeter will reveal any open-circuited components. Capacitors can be checked with an in-circuit type of capacitance checker for proper capacitance. Any short-circuited capacitor should be uncovered by these continuity and capacitance checks.

If an inductor is suspected of being short circuited, the dc resistance can be measured with an ohmmeter; but where the dc resistance is less than 1 or 2 Ω, the phase shift produced by the inductor can be checked by removing it from the circuit and checking it with a signal generator and oscilloscope.

CAUTION

WHEN CHECKING COMPONENTS SUSPECTED OF BEING SHORT CIRCUITED WITH A SIGNAL GENERATOR AND AN OSCILLOSCOPE, BE SURE TO KEEP THE GENERATOR OUTPUT AT A LOW LEVEL AND INCLUDE A RESISTOR IN SERIES WITH THE COMPONENT TO PREVENT DAMAGE TO THE GENERATOR.

Another failure mode is the change in a component value that affects the filter cutoff frequency, passband, or attenuation characteristics. Usually, all three of these are affected by a change in component value. This kind of failure can be quite difficult to isolate to an individual component using simple techniques.

One method of detecting which component in a filter has changed its value is to disconnect the filter from the circuit. If the filter cutoff is not known, it can be calculated using the analysis methods or formulas given in this chapter. Then a passband check can be made with an oscilloscope and signal generator, preferably a sweep generator, if one is available. Use the generator to simulate the input to the filter and observe the output with the oscilloscope. If the output differs markedly from the calculated values, compare the observed phase shifts across each component at a single input frequency with the calculated values. Where sufficient spare parts are available, it is sometimes useful to build up an identical filter using parts that are known to be good, for comparison purposes.

E. PROGRAMMED REVIEW

FRAME 1

A series RCL circuit contains a 1.2 kΩ resistor, a capacitor with a reactance of 750 Ω, and an inductive reactance of 200 Ω. In complex rectangular coordinates, the circuit impedance is _____.

a. $1200 - j550$ (3)

b. $1200 + j550$ (2)

c. Any other answer, review Section B.1.

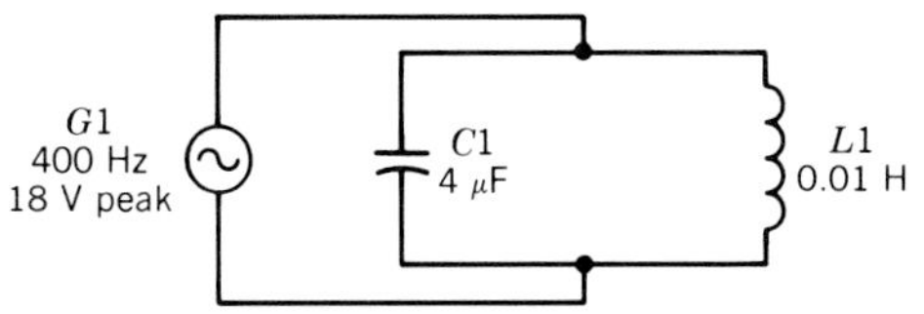

Figure 17.81 Circuit for Frame 5.

FRAME 2

The correct answer is 1200 − $j550$. Remember that inductive reactance is written as a $+j$ quantity and capacitive reactance is a $-j$ quantity. Since the reactive components are 180° apart in phase, its total reactive component is $j200 - j750$, or $-j550$. Go on to Frame 3.

FRAME 3

If a multimeter is used to measure the ac potential difference across each component in a series *RCL* circuit, and the readings are added, the result will be *higher/lower/the same as* the source potential.

a. Higher. (5)
b. Any other answer, (4).

FRAME 4

Did you forget that Kirchhoff's voltage law is only true for series *RCL* circuits if the phase angles of the potential differences are taken into account? Your answer should have been *higher*. Review Section B.1 and go on to Frame 5.

FRAME 5

In polar coordinates, the reactances of X_L and X_C in the circuit of Figure 17.81 are

X_L = __________ and X_C = __________

a. $X_L = 25.13 \angle +90° \ \Omega$
$X_C = 99.47 \angle -90° \ \Omega$. (6)
b. Any other answer, review Section B.2.

FRAME 6

The currents through the $L1$ and LC branches of the circuit in Figure 17.81 are (express in polar coordinates)

I_{L1} = __________ and I_{C1} = __________

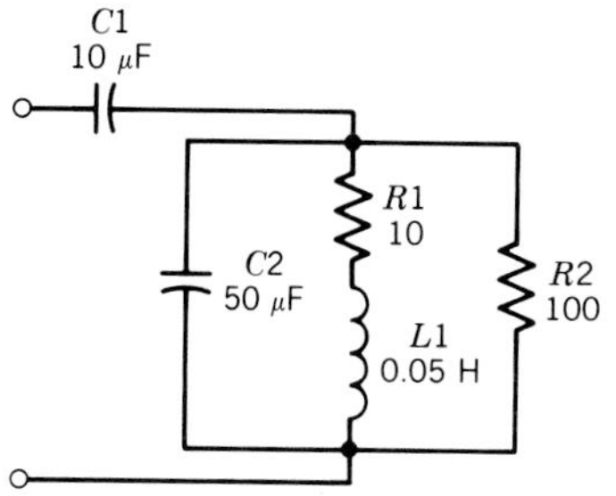

Figure 17.82 Circuit for Frame 8.

a. $I_{L1} = 0.51 \angle -90°$ A;
$I_{C1} = 0.13 \angle +90°$ A. (8)
b. Any other answer, go to Frame 7.

FRAME 7

Remember that the potential difference across both components is 18 V peak, or $0.707 \times 18 = 12.73 \ V_{rms}$. The current through the inductor is $I = \frac{E}{X_L}$ and the current through the capacitor is $I = \frac{E}{X_C}$. Go on to Frame 8.

FRAME 8

The input terminals of the network shown in Figure 17.82 are connected to a 100 Hz source. The equivalent impedance of the network is __________ Ω (in complex rectangular form).

a. 51.11 − $j165.9$ (9)
b. Any other answer not within round-off range of 51.1 − $j165.9$, review Section B.3.

FRAME 9

When using the current method to calculate the impedance in Figure 17.82, the impedance of the $C2$, $R1L1$, and $R2$ branches can be determined by calculating the branch __________. This is easily done if you assume the existance of a convenient __________ across the parallel branches.

a. Currents; potential difference. (10)
b. Any other answers, review Section B.3.

FRAME 10

The maximum rms circuit current in the circuit shown in Figure 17.83 is __________ at a phase angle of

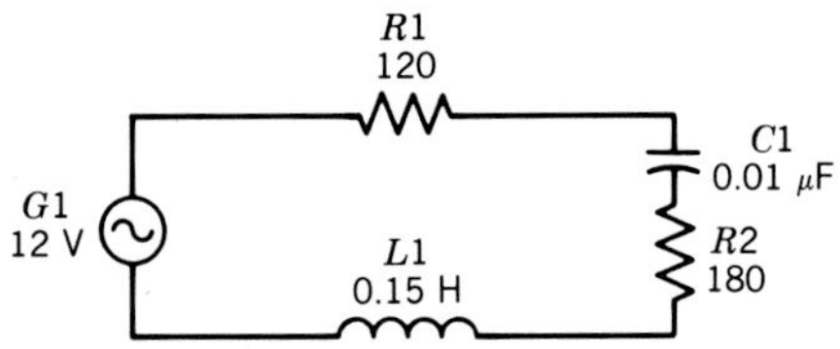

Figure 17.83 Circuit for Frame 10.

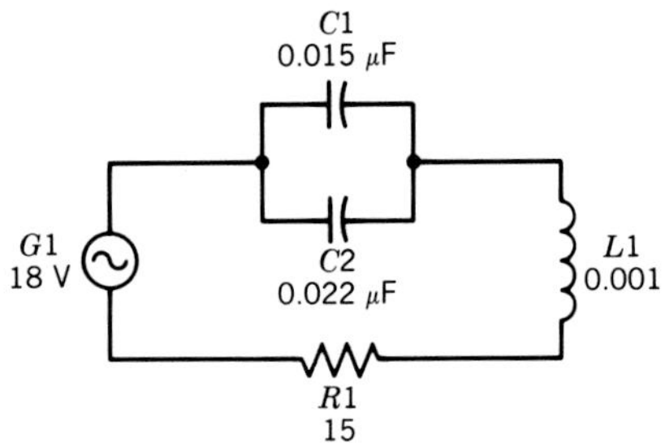

Figure 17.84 Circuit for Frame 12.

__________. This occurs when the source frequency is __________. At this frequency, the peak potential difference across the capacitor is __________.

a. 0.04 A; 0°; 4109.4 Hz; 218.9 V (11)
b. Any answer not within round-off values of those given above, review Section B.4.

FRAME 11

Is a source frequency of 3,930 Hz within the passband of the circuit of Figure 17.83?

a. No. (12)
b. If your answer was yes, check to see that you divided the calculated circuit bandwidth in half before subtracting; remember, half the bandwidth lies above the resonant frequency, and half below. For other problems, review Section B.4.

FRAME 12

What are the highest and lowest frequencies in the passband of the circuit shown in Figure 17.84?

a. 27,358.6 Hz; 24,971.2 Hz (13)
b. Any answers not within round-off accuracy of 27,358.6 and 24,971.2, review Section B.4.

FRAME 13

The output of the circuit shown in Figure 17.84 is taken across L1. What is the voltage gain of the circuit in dB?

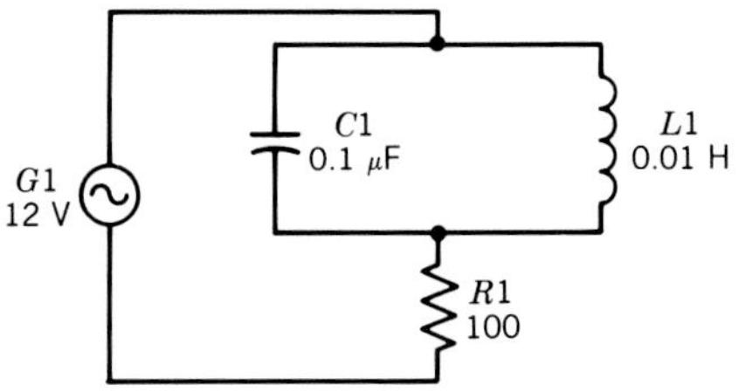

Figure 17.85 Circuit for Frame 15.

a. 20.8 dB (14)
b. Any answer not within round-off accuracy of 20.8 dB, review the last example in Section B.4.

FRAME 14

A tank circuit formed of an ideal 0.1 μF capacitor and an ideal 0.01 H inductor is placed in series with a 100 Ω resistor across a 12-V ac source. What is the current supplied by the source when it is at the resonant frequency of the tank?

a. Zero (16)
b. Any other answer, try drawing the circuit. It should resemble Figure 17.85. If you still cannot understand that the source current will be zero when the source frequency is at the resonant frequency of the tank, review Section B.5. Go on to Frame 15.

FRAME 15

When the source is at the resonant frequency, the currents in the inductive and capacitive branches of the circuit shown in Figure 17.85 are __________° apart.

a. 180 (16)
b. Any other answer, review Section B.5 and return to Frame 14.

FRAME 16

If the resistance of the inductor in Figure 17.85 is 27 Ω, what is the total current provided by the source when it is operating at the resonant frequency of the tank?

a. 3.15 mA (17)
b. Any answer not within round-off range of 3.15 mA, review Section B.5, especially the discussion of Formula 17.14.

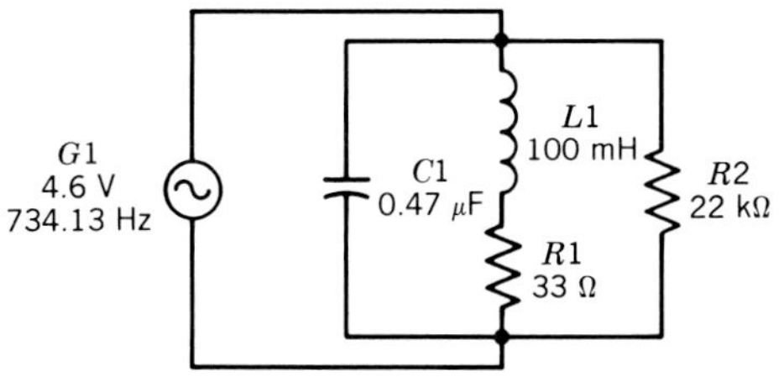

Figure 17.86 Circuit for Frame 18.

FRAME 17

A resistor added to reduce the Q of a parallel resonant circuit or to limit the source current at frequencies off resonance is called a __________ resistor. The Q is reduced when the resistor is placed __________ or __________.

a. Damping; in one of the branches of the tank; in parallel with the tank. (18)
b. Any other answer, review Section B.5.

FRAME 18

The Q of the tank circuit shown in Figure 17.86 is __________.

a. 10.81 (19)
b. Any answer not within round-off range of 10.81, review Section B.5, Formula 17.16.

FRAME 19

Above its resonant frequency, a parallel-tuned circuit behaves __________; below its resonant circuit, it behaves __________.

a. Capacitively; inductively. (20)
b. Wrong order, review Section B.5 and go on to Frame 20.

FRAME 20

The potential difference across $R1$ in Figure 17.87 will be at a maximum for two frequencies. They are __________ Hz and __________ Hz. At a third frequency, between these two, the potential difference across $R1$ will be a __________.

a. 103,821.2 Hz; 277,053.2 Hz; minimum. (21)
b. Any other answer, review the example in Section C.1.

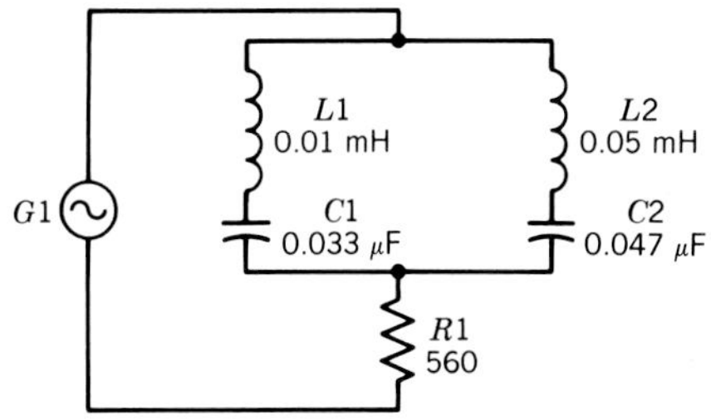

Figure 17.87 Circuit for Frame 20.

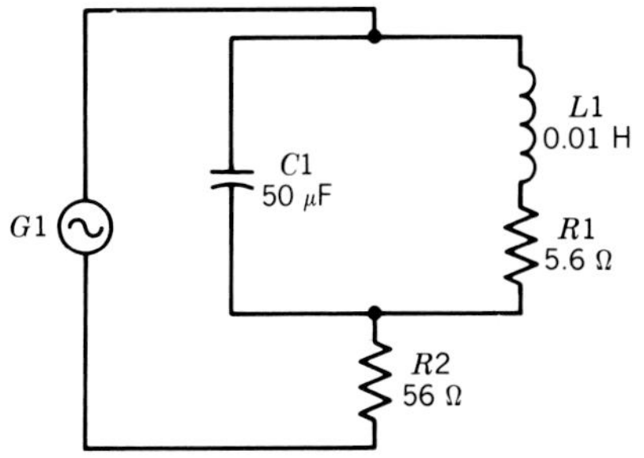

Figure 17.88 Circuit for Frame 22.

FRAME 21

In addition to exercising caution when making potential difference measurements across the components in series resonant circuits, it is necessary to avoid accidental __________ when using line-operated test equipment.

a. Short circuits or ground loops. (22)
b. Any answer that does not include one of these, review Section D.1 and go on to Frame 22.

FRAME 22

What are the resonant frequency and the Q of the circuit shown in Figure 17.88?

a. f_r = 206.7 Hz, Q = 2.32 (23)
b. Any answer not within round-off range of the above, review Section D.2.

FRAME 23

The range of frequencies over which a filter provides a low-impedance path between its input and output terminals is called its __________; the range of frequencies blocked by the filter is called its __________.

a. Passband; attenuation band or stopband. (24)
b. Any other answer, review Section D.3.

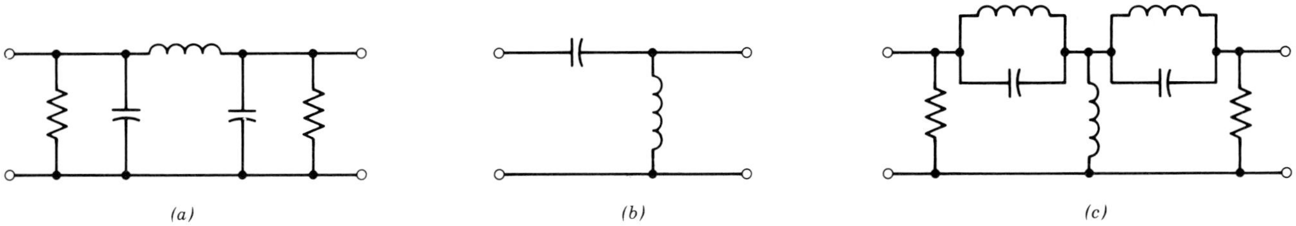

Figure 17.89 Circuits for Frame 25.

FRAME 24

The cutoff frequency f_c of a filter is generally defined as that frequency at which the filter output __________.

a. Drops more than 3 dB below its maximum. (25)
b. Any other answer, review Section D.3.

FRAME 25

Match the filter types listed below with the schematics in Figure 17.89.

1. L-section high pass
2. T-section shunt *m*-derived high pass
3. π section low pass

a. 1, b; 2, c; 3, a (END)
b. Any other answers, review Section D.3.

E. PROBLEMS FOR SOLUTION OR RESEARCH

1. A series *RCL* circuit consists of a 15 mH coil with an internal resistance of 1.3 Ω, a 12 μF capacitor, and a 27 Ω resistor.

a. Write the complex rectangular expression for the circuit impedance at a source frequency of 60 Hz.

b. What is the potential difference across each of the components at this frequency? (*Hint*: Remember that the coil combines both inductance and resistance.)

c. What is the circuit impedance at an input frequency of 400 Hz?

d. What are the true, reactive, and apparent power in the circuit at an input frequency of 400 Hz?

2. Calculate the source current in the circuit of Figure 17.90. Are the given power, voltage, or current ratings of any of the components exceeded?

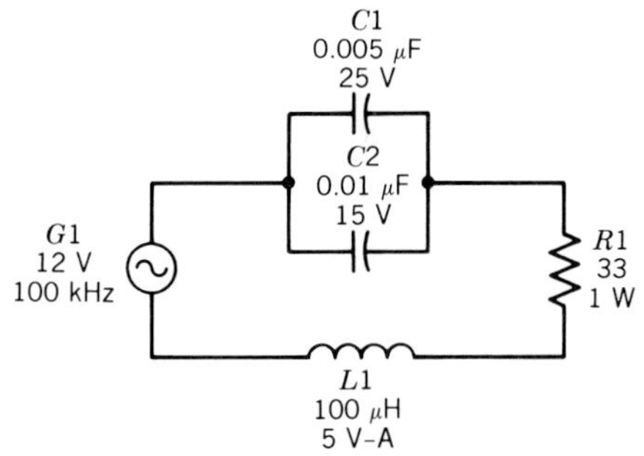

Figure 17.90 Circuit for Problem 2.

3. Calculate the circuit current and the current in each of the branches in the circuit shown in Figure 17.91.

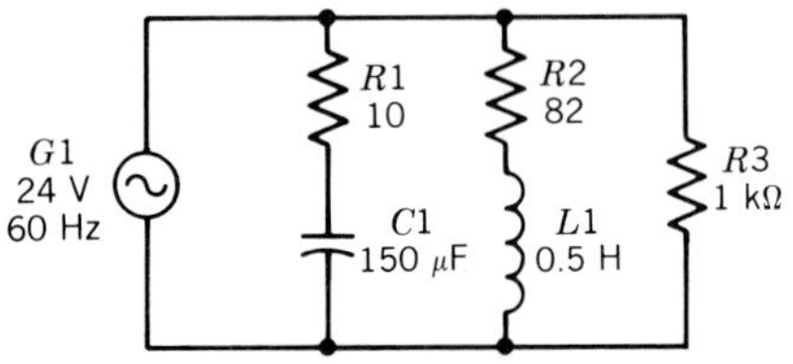

Figure 17.91 Circuit for Problem 3.

4. Find the source current in the series-parallel circuit shown in Figure 17.92. What is the current through *L*2?

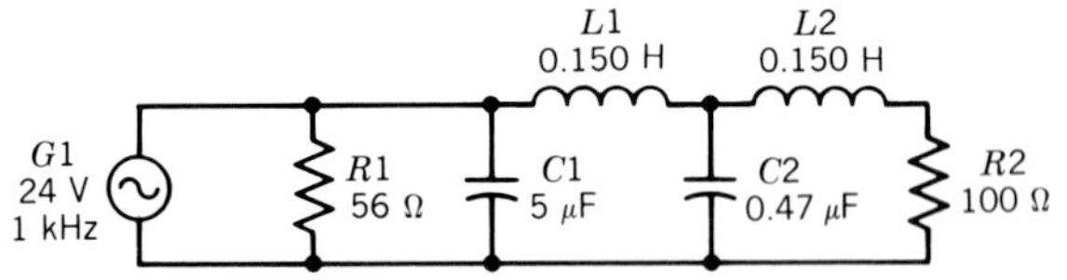

Figure 17.92 Circuit for Problem 4.

5. A 1 mH coil with an internal resistance of 10 Ω and a 0.001 μ capacitor are connected in series. What additional resistance must be connected in series to limit the circuit current to 10.5 mA, if the source is a 5-V, 200 kHz sine-wave generator?

6. What are the resonant frequency and bandwidth of the circuit shown in Figure 17.93? Will the given maximum values be exceeded for any of the components at resonance?

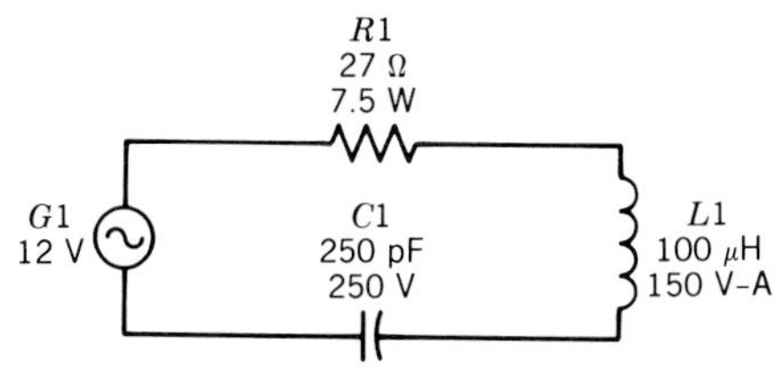

Figure 17.93 Circuit for Problem 6.

7. What is the minimum resistance that would have to be added to the series-tuned circuit shown in Figure 17.94 so that a source frequency of 16.8 kHz would be in the passband? What would be the minimum power dissipation of the resistor?

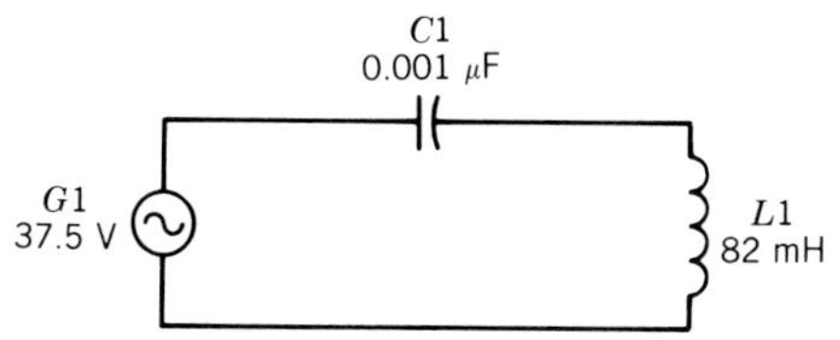

Figure 17.94 Circuit for Problem 7.

8. Design a series resonant circuit with a resonant frequency of 1.3 kHz and a bandwidth of 30 Hz around a 0.68 μF capacitor. Draw the circuit showing component values and recommended ratings.

9. What is the resonant frequency in the circuit shown in Figure 17.95?

a. What is the current through *R*1 when *G*1 is at its resonant frequency?

b. What is the *Q* of the tank circuit?

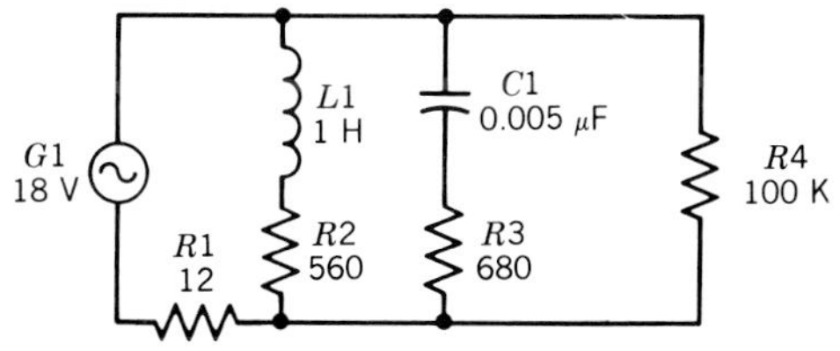

Figure 17.95 Circuit for Problem 9.

10. Design an *RCL* tank circuit that will draw practically no current from its source when the source frequency is between 500 and 100 Hz, but will draw appreciable current above and below this range. Draw a schematic of the circuit showing component maximum values.

11. Use the relationships given in Figure 17.75 to design a constant *K*, T-section high-pass filter that will remove the annoying, low-frequency hum from the output of a public address amplifier. The filter will be inserted between the 8 Ω speaker and the 8 Ω amplifier output, and should be resistor terminated. Design the cutoff frequency at 100 Hz.

12. The output of a power supply has a large 60 Hz component. Using the component value relationships given in Figure 17.71, design a constant *K*, π-section, low-pass filter for the output of the supply that has an output impedance of 4.7 kΩ. Cutoff should be 45 Hz.

13. Obtain the schematic diagram of a modern, multiband communications diagram of a modern, multiband communications transceiver. Identify the series- and parallel-tuned circuits found in it, as well as any passive filter types that you might recognize. Try to calculate the resonant frequencies of the circuit.

14. Look up the formulas for deriving the component values of Butterworth and Chebyshev filters. Try to design and build one or more filters of each type.

GLOSSARY

As with any other introductory text, this book uses many technical terms in special or limited senses. The following glossary has been included to provide short definitions of these terms, particularly where a different sense than that given in common technical dictionaries is intended.

A

Action. Action, in reference to switches, is the type of motion that actuates the switch. For example, slide, push, toggle, and rotary action switches.

Actual value. The measured value of a component is its actual value.

Acute angle. An angle of less than 90°.

Aging. A capacitance decrease of 10 to 15 percent during the first thousand hours of operation of a Class II ceramic capacitor.

Algebraic notation. The sequence of instructions used by most calculators. Numbers and signs are entered in the same order in which an algebraic expression is written.

Alkaline cell. A chemical cell using manganese dioxide and powdered zinc as its active metals. The electrolyte contains potassium hydroxide, commonly called lye.

American wire gauge. Abbreviated AWG, this system assigns gauge numbers to standard wire diameters. Larger gauge numbers represent smaller-diameter wires.

Ammeter. A device that measures electric current.

Ampere. The basic unit of electric current. One ampere signifies a drift of 6.25×10^{18} electrons past a point in a circuit in one second.

Ampere-hour rating. A manufacturer's specification of the amount of current that can be obtained from a type and size of cell. It is obtained by connecting a sample cell to a circuit and measuring the current produced while keeping track of the time until the end voltage is reached.

Amplification. An increase in signal voltage, current, or power provided by a circuit. Amplification is frequently measured in dB or dBm.

Amplitude. The maximum positive value of a potential difference or current waveform as shown by its maximum height above the x axis on a graph or oscilloscope trace.

Amplitude modulation. A means of mixing two signals so that the instantaneous value of the lower-frequency signal determines the amplitude of the higher-frequency signal.

Analog meter. A meter in which a pointer is made to move across a numbered scale to indicate the magnitude of the measured quantity. Also called an *electromagnetic meter.*

Analog signals. Signals that can assume any value between some maximum and some minimum value, as opposed to digital signals, which assume one of two specific values.

Angle. The geometrical shape that results when two lines are drawn to a common point called the *vertex.*

Angle velocity or angular velocity. The angular velocity of a sine waveform with a frequency of f is defined as $2\pi f$.

Apparent power. Symbolized as P_a or P_s, the apparent power in a circuit is the phasor sum of the true and reactive power.

Armature. A hinged or pivoted metal bar attracted by the magnetic field of the coil in a relay.

Assembly or parts blowup. A type of diagram that shows each component or part of a unit connected to its actual place on a main assembly by a dotted line.

Attenuation. A reduction in signal voltage, current, or power provided by a circuit. Attenuation is frequently measured in dB or dBm.
Attenuator probes. Special oscilloscope probes containing components that reduce the amplitude of the input signal to the oscilloscope. $\times 5$ and $\times 10$ attenuator probes are common.
Audio-frequency generator. A signal generator producing sine-wave signals up to as high as 100 kHz.
Audio taper. A standardized, nonlinear type of potentiometer used as a volume control in audio circuits.
Autotransformer. A special form of transformer that consists of a single winding.
Axis. A numbered line used in a graph or in the Cartesian coordinate system.
Ayrton or universal shunt. A meter shunt circuit that enables resistance switching and uses higher value resistors than a simple shunt arrangement.

B

Bandstop circuit or band rejection circuit. A tuned *RCL* circuit designed to have a high impedance at a particular range of frequencies.
Bandwidth or passband. The range of frequencies of a series *RCL* circuit at which the current is at least 0.707 times the maximum current at resonance. Bandwidth is similarly defined in terms of impedance in a parallel *RCL* circuit.
BASIC. A conventional way of entering commands into a computer, or programming. An operating language used by many small computers.
Battery. A combination of chemical source cells, usually packed in a single container.
Bayonet base. A type of lamp base using two tiny prongs to retain the lamp in its socket.
Bilateral. A characteristic of certain electronic components. These components provide the same opposition to current in either direction.
Bleeder resistor. The resistor whose value is fixed by calculating 10 percent of the total current supplied in a practical voltage divider. Also, a resistor used for filter capacitor discharging in a power supply.
Block diagram. An electronic or electrical diagram that uses labeled rectangles to symbolize circuits. Only generalized signal paths between the blocks are shown.
BNC. A type of coaxial cable connector widely used for test equipment and electronic units. A modified form of this connector type is called TNC, and is used in high-vibration applications.
Bounce. Faulty switch contact resulting from the recoil of switch parts.
Branch. A branch is defined in circuit analysis as the portion of a network between two junctions.
Brushes. Carbon rods or bars that are used to contact the rotating part of a motor or generator.
Bypass network. An electronic network designed to provide a low-impedance path around certain components.

C

C/10 charge rate. Recharging a secondary cell at the current that can be drawn from a fully charged cell for 10 hours. This rate is usually sufficient to restore a fully discharged cell to 100 percent of its rated service capacity in 14 to 16 hours.
Cable. The term *cable* is used both for heavy conductive wire and for groups of wires formed into a single package.
Candelabra base. A term referring to the screw-in type bases used in most electric light bulbs.
Capacitance. Along with resistance and inductance, capacitance is one of the three principal electrical properties. It is defined as the ratio of the charge stored to the potential difference in a system composed of two conductors separated by a nonconducting dielectric material.
Capacitive reactance. The opposition to an alternating current in a circuit due to the presence of a capacitor.
Capacitor. An electronic component consisting of two conductors separated by a dielectric material. A capacitor is able to store a certain amount of electrical charge.
Carbon composition resistor. A resistor made of a carbon core material.
Carbon–zinc cell. The Leclanché primary cell. The active metals are zinc and manganese dioxide; the electrolyte is a paste solution of ammonium chloride, zinc chloride, starch, and water.
Cartesian coordinate method. Also called the "method of rectangular coordinates," this method is a means of graphing variables and showing how they are related.
Catastrophic failure. The failure of an electronic component accompanied by a bursting or explosion.
Cathode-ray tube or CRT. A device in which a beam of electrons is made to produce a spot of light on a phosphor screen. CRTs are used in television receivers, oscilloscopes, and computer monitors.
Ceramic capacitor. A capacitor using a fired, ceramic material as its dielectric. Class I ceramic materials are very stable; Class II materials are inexpensive and permit construction of physically small capacitors.
Charging by contact. Producing an electrical charge on an object by touching it with a charged object.
Charging by induction. A means of producing an electrical charge on an object by bringing a charged object near one side while touching the other side to ground.
Choke. Another term for an inductor.
Circuit analysis techniques. A set of mathematical techniques used to calculate potential differences or currents in complex circuits.

Circuit breaker. A component designed to provide circuit protection similar to that of a fuse and to be resettable, like a switch.
Circular mils. A measurement related to the cross-sectional area of a wire. It is obtained by squaring the wire diameter in mils (thousandths of an inch.)
Closed circuit. A continuous, conductive path for charge carriers between an area of high potential and an area of lower potential.
Coax or coaxial cable. A two-path cable formed of an inner conductor, plastic insulation, a conductive metal braid which acts as the second conductor, and an outer sheath of insulation.
Coefficient. The coefficient of a variable, more properly called the numerical coefficient, is the number by which a variable is multiplied in a term.
Coefficient of coupling. A number less than 1 that represents the percentage of the flux of one coil that is linked to a second coil.
Common. The meter terminal connected to the most negative point of measurement. The common terminal is usually marked with a minus sign and color-coded black.
Common or Briggsian logarithms. Logarithms using 10 as the base.
Common pole or pole. The switch terminal connected to or disconnected from any other switch terminal by operation of the switch.
Complementary angles. Two angles whose sum is 90°.
Complex conjugate. The complex conjugate of a complex number is formed by changing the sign of the j term. For example, the complex conjugate of $a + jb$ is $a - jb$.
Complex number notation or complex rectangular form. A way of expressing an impedance or similar quantity in the form $a \pm jb$, where $j = \sqrt{-1}$.
Compound. A material made up of two or more different atoms bound together by electrical forces.
Conductance. A quantity defined as the reciprocal of resistance.
Conduction band. The range of energies possessed by the conduction electrons in a material.
Conduction electron. An electron that has absorbed additional energy and is no longer found in the valence or lower energy levels. Such an electron is free to drift through a material and can be thought of as belonging to the mass of material rather than to a particular atom.
Conductor. A material possessing many conduction electrons at normal temperatures and pressures.
Constant-current device. An electronic component that acts to keep circuit current at a constant level.
Constant-voltage device. An electronic component that acts to keep the potential difference between two points in a circuit constant.
Constant-voltage transformer. Power transformers designed to maintain a constant potential difference across their secondaries in spite of minor, short-term variations in their primary potential difference.
Contact resistance. The actual resistance between a pair of switch contacts that are supposed to be in contact in a relay or switch.
Continuity checking. Testing for a low-resistance current path (closed circuit) between two points.
Conventional current. The assumption that current is from a positively charged area to a less positively charged or negatively charged area.
Coordinates. The x and y values of a particular point in the Cartesian coordinate graphing system.
Copper losses. Transformer power losses due to the resistance of the primary and secondary windings.
Core losses. Transformer power losses due to less than perfect coupling between the primary and secondary windings or electric currents in the core.
Corona. The ionization of the air between transformer windings or between windings and the core.
Cosine. The ratio of the length of the side adjacent to an angle to the length of the hypotenuse in a right triangle is the cosine of the angle.
Coulomb. The unit of charge presently used in electricity and electronics. It is the charge possessed by 6.25×10^{18} electrons.
Counter EMF The potential difference induced across a conductor when a magnetic field expands or collapses. Not to be confused with the potential difference that causes the magnetic field.
Coupling network. An electronic network designed to pass a signal from one circuit to another.
Current. Current is defined as the movement of electric charges from one area to another due to an electric field.
Current electricity. The effects associated with the movement of electrical charge carriers, usually electrons, in an electric field.
Cutoff frequency. The frequency at which the impedance of a particular filter begins to increase or decrease rapidly.
Cycle. A complete, single unit of a recurrent or periodic waveform.

D

D'Arsonval or PM/MC meter. The most popular form of analog meter in use today. This movement uses a fixed magnet and a moving coil.
dBm. A power ratio based on a logarithmic scale and a power input of 0.001 W.
dc Blocking transformer. A coupling transformer used to pass an ac signal from one circuit to another, but to isolate the two circuits as far as dc potential differences are concerned.

dc Leakage current. A small direct current leakage through a capacitor due to breaks in the dielectric material. Leakage current is generally found in electrolytic capacitors.
Decibel or dB. A measurement unit based on a base 10 logarithmic scale. The decibel is the minimum sound power difference detectable by the human ear.
Decimal point. Also called the "radix," the decimal point is used to mark the separation of the units place and the tenths place in decimal notation.
Decimals. A system of fractional notation using the place value of numbers to the right of a decimal point.
Δ–Y equivalency theorem. A statement of the fact that for every Δ- or π-shaped network, there is an equivalent Y- or T-shaped network that can be substituted without resulting in an overall change in circuit characteristics.
Dendrites. Thin crystals of conductive material that form in secondary cells. The crystals can cause short circuits between the cell plates.
Dependent variable. In an equation with two variables, the dependent variable is that whose value is given as a function of the other variable. Conventionally, y is the dependent variable, and an equation is given as $y = \mathcal{F}(x)$.
Determinants, method of. A method of solving simultaneous equations.
Diamagnetic material. A material repelled by either pole of a magnet. No strongly diamagnetic material is known.
Dielectric. A nonconducting material that is readily polarized by an electric field. Dielectric materials are used to separate the conductive surfaces in capacitors.
Dielectric breakdown voltage. The potential difference between two capacitor plates at which the dielectric between the plates is pierced or ionized and becomes conductive.
Dielectric charge absorption. A phenomenon that occurs with certain dielectrics. When these dielectrics are used in a capacitor that is charged and then fully discharged, a renewed potential difference will be observed across the capacitor after a period of time.
Dielectric coefficient or constant. A measure of the ability of a material to act as a dielectric in a capacitor.
Dielectric rupture or breakdown. The piercing or ionization of a dielectric when it is subjected to too high a potential difference.
Difference. The result when one number is subtracted from another. For example, in $8 - 5 = 3$, 3 is the difference.
Differentiator. An electronic network whose output is proportional to the rate of change of its input signal.
Digital multimeter or DMM. A piece of test equipment that uses semiconductor devices to measure and display a quantity in numeric form. Neither a pointer nor a scale are used. DMMs measure potential difference, current, and resistance.
Digital signals. In contrast to analog signals, digital signals are at one of two values, either maximum or minimum, and change from one value to the other quickly.
Dimensional analysis. A method of checking a formula or calculation based on the substitution of the measuring units for the unit symbols in a formula.
Dip relay. A relay built into a small package with contacts brought out of the case by two rows of pins.
Direct current, or dc source. A source that produces an electric field that does not periodically change direction.
Discharging. The draining off of an electric charge stored in a capacitor or the electric power stored in a cell.
Distributed load. An electrical circuit load, such as a wire, that does not have its resistance situated in a particular place. When drawn as a single resistance symbol in a schematic diagram, it is called a *lumped load*.
Dividend. The number being divided in a division. For example, in $\frac{8}{4} = 2$, 8 is the dividend.
Divisor. In a division, the number you are dividing by is the divisor. For example, in $\frac{8}{4} = 2$, 4 is the divisor.
Double-precision numbers. As used in BASIC, numbers with up to 16 significant figures or digits.
DPDT switch. A double-pole, double-throw switch, that is, a switch with two common poles, either of which can be connected to one of two switch terminals.
DPST switch. A double-pole, single-throw switch, that is, a switch with two common poles. Each pole can be connected to or disconnected from another switch terminal.
Dry circuits. A technical term for circuits with very low current, on the order of a few microamperes.
Duty factor. The duty factor of a pulse is the ratio of the pulse width to the period of the pulse. Multiplying the duty factor by 100 to turn it into a percentage produces a number called the duty cycle of the pulse.

E

Eddy currents. Eddy currents are circulating electric currents in the cores of coils and transformers. These currents lower component efficiency.
Effective or rms value. The effective or rms (root mean square) value of a sinusoidal current is defined as the alternating current that will produce the same

heating effect in a resistive load as a direct current with a value of 0.707 times the peak ac value.
Electrets. Certain waxes, plastics, and resins that are capable of producing an electric field in a way similar to that in which a magnet produces a magnetic field.
Electric field. The change in the quality of space around a charged object caused by an electrical charge.
Electrodynamometer. A versatile type of meter that uses a combination of fixed and moving coils. Meters of this type can measure alternating or direct current, power, and power factor.
Electrolyte. The ionized liquid, paste, or gel used in chemical cells and electrolytic capacitors.
Electrolytic capacitor. A capacitor that uses a thin film of gas as its dielectric.
Electromotive force or emf. A term generally used to mean the same thing as potential difference or voltage.
Electron. Subatomic particle with negative electrical charge. Movement of these particles is the cause of most electrical effects.
Electron pair bonding or covalent bonding. A form of bonding between two or more atoms that occurs when valence electrons are shared among the atoms.
Electroscope. A mechanical device used for detecting or measuring electrical charge.
Electrostatic unit of charge (esu). A unit of electrical charge formerly used in physics. The esu is based on distance and the force exerted on a test charge.
Electrovalent or ionic bond. A form of compounding in which a number of outer, or valence, orbit electrons are transferred from one atom to another. Electrical charge difference then holds the two atoms together.
Electrum. The Greek word for amber, a hard substance formed by petrified pine sap. An active triboelectric material.
Element. A basic substance made up of atoms of only one type.
End-voltage. The potential difference selected by manufacturers at which a secondary cell should be recharged and a primary cell should be discarded.
Energy. In a scientific sense, energy is the ability to do work.
Engineering notation. A method for writing numbers that is similar to scientific notation. In engineering notation, any number can be expressed as a number greater than or equal to 1 and less than 1000, times 10 raised to a positive or negative whole number that is exactly divisible by 3.
Equation. A formula using an equals sign.
Equivalent circuit. A simpler circuit that can be substituted for a more complex arrangement without affecting other portions of the original circuit.
Equivalent series resistance (ESR). The resistance of the leads and internal connections in a capacitor.
EVM or TVM These abbreviations for "electronic voltmeter" or "transistor voltmeter" identify an analog multimeter equipped with semiconductor devices used to amplify the measured quantity and indicate its value on an analog scale.
Exponent. A mathematical method of indicating that a number called the base is to be multiplied by itself. For example, in $A^3 = A \times A \times A$, 3 is the exponent and A is the base.
Expression. Any meaningful collection of numbers, symbols, and signs for mathematical operations.

F

Failure mode analysis. An aid to troubleshooting that takes into consideration the probability of component failures of various kinds.
Fall time. The time it takes a pulse with decreasing amplitude to drop from 90 to 10 percent of its peak value.
Faraday's law. Faraday's law is a mathematical expression of the relationship between the voltage across the ends of a conductor being moved through a magnetic field, the strength of the field, the length of the conductor, and the speed and direction of the motion: $E = Blv \sin \theta$.
Fast-acting fuse. A fuse designed to burn out quickly when small current overloads are present.
Fast-charge rate. The recharging rate that will restore a lead-acid cell to 95 percent of its full charge in 30 minutes. Recharging at the fast-charge rate can result in damage to a cell.
Ferrite. A magnetic core material made of powdered iron alloy and epoxy. The particles of iron alloy are small, so core losses are minimized.
Ferromagnetic. Another term for "strongly paramagnetic," that is, strongly attracted by either pole of a magnet.
Field intensity. Field intensity is the magnetomotive force per unit length of a solenoidal coil.
Filament. The wire portion of an incandescent bulb, which is electrically heated and caused to glow.
Film resistor. A resistor formed by coating an insulating core with a resistive material, which may be either a carbon or metal film.
Filter. A filter is a network consisting of a number of impedances grouped together in such a way as to have a definite frequency characteristic.
Fixed capacitor. A fixed capacitor is an electronic component designed to provide a single value of capacitance in a circuit. In a properly functioning capacitor, this value is within a tolerance range of a marked nominal value.
Fixed resistor. A resistor with a specific nominal value.
Float charging rate. The recharging rate that will re-

store 100 percent of the service capacity of a secondary cell in about 16 hours.

Floating. Condition that exists when a point of electrical connection is completely isolated from ground.

Forming current. A small direct current used to produce the gas layer in an electrolytic capacitor when it is initially manufactured or to restore the gas layer when the capacitor has been unused for a time.

FOR-NEXT loop. A BASIC command structure that results in a program loop or repetition of a number of instructions.

Fourier analysis. A means of analyzing any periodic waveform as the sum of a dc component and a number of sinusoids with frequencies that are multiples of the frequency of the waveform being analyzed.

Free-running oscilloscope. An oscilloscope with a horizontal section that is allowed to operate without any trigger or synchronizing signal from the vertical section. This type of oscilloscope is not generally used in industrial applications.

Frequency. The number of cycles a recurrent or periodic waveform passes through in one second.

Frequency meter/counter. Also called a frequency meter or frequency counter, or just counter, it is a device for measuring the frequency of a periodic waveform, the time between two pulses, or counting a number of pulses.

Frequency of infinite attenuation. A frequency near that of the cutoff frequency in a *m*-derived filter. The filter impedance shows a sudden increase between these two frequencies.

Frequency response curve. A graph used to show how the transfer of power in an audio-frequency transformer is affected by frequency.

Function. One variable is a function of another when there is a specific mathematical relationship between the two variables.

Function generator. A signal source capable of producing sine, square, triangle, and pulse wave shapes of variable frequency and amplitude.

Fundamental. The base sine-wave frequency of any waveform. Whole number multiples of this frequency are called *harmonics*.

Fuse. A fuse is defined as a purposely weakened portion of a circuit designed to burn out when forced to pass excessive current.

G

Gas discharge tube. A glass tube containing a gas under low pressure. When two conductive plates in the tube are connected to a source of electrical energy, some of the gas in the tube is ionized. The recapture of electrons by ionized atoms results in the production of a glow.

General-purpose fuse. The form of fuse to use where extremely rapid action is not needed. The general-purpose fuse will support a current of 110 percent of its rated value for at least 4 hours and withstand a 135 percent overload for at least 1 hour.

Given or known quantities. Values that are stated or understood and do not have to be calculated.

Graph. A graph is a drawing that represents the numerical value or values of a variable.

Grounding. The process of connecting a charged object or part of an electric circuit to the earth, which serves as a reservoir of charge carriers.

Ground state. The condition of an electron in a shell or energy level closest to the atomic nucleus.

H

Harmonic distortion. A characteristic of audio transformers resulting in distortion of the output waveform.

Heat-shrink tubing. A thin, flexible tubing that can be shrunk to fit by the application of heat.

High-pass filter. An electronic network designed to provide a low impedance to high-frequency signals and high impedance to frequencies below a certain cutoff value.

Hook-up wire. A commonly used, plastic insulated, stranded wire.

Horsepower (hp). Scientifically defined as the power necessary to lift 550 pounds a distance of one foot in one second.

Hydrometer. A device used to measure the specific gravity of the electrolyte solution in a secondary cell. Such measurements accurately determine the amount of available energy in the cell.

Hypotenuse. The longest side in a right triangle. This will always be the side opposite the right angle.

Hysteresis loss. A measure of the electric power wasted in the movement of magnetic domains in an iron coil core.

I

Ideal current source. A concept used in circuit analysis, an ideal current source is assumed to provide its rated current regardless of the load connected to it. In order to do so, it must have an "infinite" internal resistance.

Ideal voltage source. A concept used in circuit analysis, an ideal voltage source is assumed to provide its rated potential difference regardless of the current drawn. In order to do so, it must have no internal resistance.

Imaginary numbers. In mathematics, numbers involving the square root of a negative number.

Immediate or command mode. A mode of operation of BASIC in which a single command is entered and acted on immediately.
Impedance. The phasor sum or resultant of the reactance and resistance of a circuit.
Impedance-matching transformer. An electronic component designed to provide efficient power transfer from one circuit to another by matching the output impedance of the first to the input impedance of the second.
Independent variable. In an equation with two variables, the independent variable is that named in the function statement. Conventionally, x is the independent variable and an equation is given as $y = \mathcal{F}(x)$
Inductance. Along with resistance and capacitance, inductance is one of the three basic electrical characteristics. Inductance is the opposition to a change in current through a conductor, and is based on magnetic effects.
Inductive kick. The high-voltage surge brought about by a rapid collapse of the magnetic field around a coil.
Inductive reactance. The opposition to the change in the current through a conductor due to magnetic effects. Inductive reactance depends on the configuration of the conductor and upon the rate of change of the current through it.
Inductor. A component designed to provide a specific amount of inductance (opposition to the change in current) in a circuit. In some usages, this term is used for coils designed for use at frequencies below 20 kHz.
Infant failures. Component failures during the initial period of operation.
Infinite decimal. A decimal number that can be carried out to any number of decimal places.
Insertion loss. A combination of the core and copper losses in a transformer.
Insulation resistance. Also referred to as insulation test voltage, this transformer characteristic refers to the maximum potential difference permitted between any winding and the core or between any two windings.
Insulator. A material possessing few conduction electrons at normal temperatures and pressures.
Integrator. An electronic circuit whose output is the integral or "sum" of its input signal.
Intrinsic value. The numerical value of a digit without regard to its place value in a decimal number. The intrinsic value of the digit 8 in 387 is 8, not 8×10.
Ion. An atom that has given up or gained a number of electrons so that the positive electrical charge of the protons in the nucleus is no longer balanced by the negative charge of the electrons in the surrounding shells.
Isolation transformer. A transformer with a 1:1 turns ratio used to provide isolation between the circuit connected to its secondary and the mains service or other source connected to the primary.

J

j**.** In electronics, an operator which is $\sqrt{-1}$.
Joule. A unit of energy. The energy used when a force of one newton operates through a distance of one meter.
Junction. A point in a circuit or network at which three or more components are connected.

K

Kirchhoff's current law. Kirchhoff's current law is one of the basic methods of circuit analysis. It states that at any node or junction in a circuit, the sum of the currents entering the node or junction is equal to the sum of the currents leaving.
Kirchhoff's voltage law. One of the basic methods of circuit analysis. Kirchhoff's voltage law states that around a loop or mesh in a circuit, the sum of the potential drops and potential rises is zero.
Knife switch. A kind of switch that is operated by the movement of a conductive blade.

L

Lag. One sine wave is said to lag a second of the same frequency if it reaches its positive peak less than 180° after the second waveform.
Laser. A device that emits a beam of coherent light by causing a large number of high-energy state electrons to drop suddenly into lower energy levels.
Lead. One sine wave is said to lead a second of the same frequency if it reaches its positive peak less than 180° before the second.
Leading zeros. The zeros immediately to the right of the decimal point in decimal number less than 1. Leading zeros are not considered significant digits.
Leclanché or dry cell. A primary cell in which the electrolyte is in paste form. The common carbon–zinc cell is still called a Leclanché cell in Europe.
LED. A light-emitting diode; a semiconductor device that produces light when connected to a source of electrical energy. Unlike an incandescent lamp, heating effects are not used for the production of light in a LED.
Left-hand rule for generators. Also called Fleming's rule, this rule is a way of remembering the relationship among the forces in a generator. To use it, point the thumb in the direction of the conductor motion and the first finger in the direction of the magnetic field or flux. The middle or center finger, held at right angles to the other two, then points in the direction of the electron drift through the conductor.

Lenz's law. This law is a special application of the law of conservation of energy. It states that an induced current is accompanied by a magnetic field that acts to oppose the action that produces it.
Limit. A value that the graph of a mathematical function approaches without actually reaching.
Linear. A form of meter scale in which equal sized divisions represent the same change in value, no matter where they are on the scale.
Linear component. A component in which the opposition to current remains constant regardless of the amount of current or the potential difference.
Linear function. A mathematical function whose graph is a straight line.
Lines of force. Imaginary lines drawn to map the intensity and shape of an electric or magnetic field.
Lissajous pattern. A complex pattern on an oscilloscope used to compare the frequency and phase of two input signals.
Lithium cell. One of a group of cell types using some form of lithium as an active metal. Various electrolytes are used.
Load. A device or circuit component that converts the drift of electric charge carriers into some form of work.
Lodestone. A natural magnetic material.
Logarithm. The power to which a base number must be raised to produce an arbitrary number N is called the "logarithm of N." If N is the arbitrary number and b is the base, then $N = b^x$, where x is the logarithm of N to the base b.
Logarithmic curve. The graph of an equation that contains two variables that are related by a logarithmic function. For example, $y = 3 - \log z$.
Loop, or mesh. In circuit analysis, a loop or mesh is defined as a complete path traced through a network, without backtracking, back to the beginning point.
Low-level relay. A relay with switch contacts especially designed for switching very small currents.
Low-pass filter. An electronic network designed to provide low impedance to low-frequency signals and a substantially higher impedance to high-frequency signals.

M

Magnet or transformer wire. A solid copper, enamel-insulated wire frequently used for winding coils.
Magnetic circuit breaker. A circuit breaker that is actuated by the magnetic field produced by a current overload in a circuit.
Magnetic flux density. Also called flux density and magnetic induction, this quantity represents the strength of the magnetic field at a particular point or through a small area at a right angle to the direction of the field.
Magnetic lines of force. Imaginary lines used to map the shape and intensity of a magnetic field.
Magnetic poles. The two points of greatest magnetic activity on a magnet.
Magnetizing by induction. Magnetizing a piece of material by holding it in a strong magnetic field.
Magnetomotive force. Magnetomotive force is an analog of the electric field quantity, emf. It is defined as the product of the number of turns in a coil and the current through it.
Maximum power transfer theorem. A principle that states that the maximum source power is transferred to a load when the resistance (impedance) of the load is equal to the internal resistance (impedance) of the source network.
Megohmmeter. A device used for measuring insulation resistance at high potential differences.
Memory effect. A condition that can occur in ni–cad cells. If a cell is repeatedly discharged only slightly, it may become impossible to use the full rated service capacity. It is as though the cell "remembered" its earlier discharge level and refused to provide further power.
Mercury cell. A primary cell using mercuric oxide and powdered zinc as its active metals. The electrolyte is gelled potassium hydroxide (lye).
Metal fatigue. The formation of tiny cracks in a wire due to bending or vibration. Metal fatigue is frequently responsible for breaks in wire.
Meter loading. The effect of connecting a meter to a circuit for potential difference or current measurements.
Mica. A naturally occurring mineral used as a capacitor dielectric.
Mil. A mil is 0.001 inch.
Millman's theorem. A network theorem stating that a network composed of any number of ideal current sources connected in parallel and parallel resistors can be replaced by an equivalent circuit composed of a single ideal current source and a parallel resistor.
MIL SPEC. Military specifications. A set of specifications and definitions issued by the U.S. government that includes descriptions of electronic component types, nomenclatures, and requirements.
Minuend. In a subtraction, the number from which you are going to subtract a quantity.
Miss. The failure of a pair of relay contacts to complete a circuit when the coil is energized.
Molecule. A single unit composed of two or more atoms bound together by electrical forces.
Momentary action switch. A switch that returns to its initial position as soon as the actuator is released.

Moving-iron meter. Not to be confused with the moving-magnet type, the moving-iron meter movement uses a fixed coil and a pair of iron vanes to produce an accurate meter that can be used to measure alternating or direct currents.
Moving-magnet meter. A type of indicating meter that uses a moving magnet and a fixed coil. Still used in applications where cost is important and accuracy is not required. Also called a polarized iron meter.
Multimeter. A piece of test equipment able to measure potential difference, current, and resistance.
Multiplicand. In a multiplication, the number that is multiplied by the multiplier, for example in $3 \times 2 = 6$, 3 is the multiplicand.
Multiplier. The multiplying number in a multiplication. For example, in $3 \times 2 = 6$, 2 is the multiplier.
Mutual induction. The ability of the magnetic field around a conductor to induce a potential difference across or a current in a second conductor.

N

Natural, or Naperian logarithms. Logarithms using the mathematical constant ϵ as a base.
$\epsilon = 2.71828. . .$
Negative angle. An angle resulting from the clockwise rotation of a line segment.
Neon lamp. A lamp that produces light due to the ionization of a gas.
Network. An arrangement of components. A network need not form a closed circuit.
Network graph. A method of symbolizing a network to emphasize the interconnection of its components.
Network theorem. In general, a network theorem is a way of redrawing a circuit so that Ohm's and Kirchhoff's laws can be applied to it.
Neutron. A subatomic particle with a mass close to that of a proton and no electric charge. Neutrons are found in the nucleus of atoms. They act to keep the nucleus together.
Nicad cells. Nickel–cadmium, or ni–cad cells, are secondary cells using metallic cadmium and nickelic hydroxide as the active metals. A water solution of potassium hydroxide is the electrolyte.
Node. A point in a circuit at which two or more components are connected.
Nominal value. The marked value of a component.
Nonlinear function. A mathematical statement whose graph is not a straight line.
Norton's theorem. A method of substituting an equivalent circuit composed of a current source and parallel resistor for a network of sources and resistors, no matter how they are interconnected.
Nucleus. The central part of an atom. The region in which the protons and neutrons are found.
Nuisance failure. The burning out of a fuse for any reason other than its intended function of protecting electronic circuits.
Null. The source current in a parallel *RCL* circuit at resonance.

O

Obtuse angle. An angle of more than 90° but less than 180°.
Ohms-per-volt rating. A way of specifying the sensitivity of a meter. This rating specifies the amount of resistance that must be connected in series with the meter to produce full-scale indication when a potential difference of one volt is applied to the series combination.
Open circuit. In general, an open circuit is a path that is very difficult or impossible for charge carriers to follow from a point of higher to a point of lower potential.
Orthogonal system. A set of three vector quantities that are always at right angles to each other.
Overrange. The indication used by a digital meter to indicate that the input quantity is too large to be measured. Frequently, a higher scale must be selected.

P

Parallel circuit. A method of circuit connection in which there are at least two different current paths or branches.
Parallel-tuned circuit or tank. A parallel *RCL* circuit.
Paramagnetic material. A material attracted by either pole of a magnet. Materials can be either strongly or weakly paramagnetic.
Passive filter. A filter composed of inductors, capacitors, and resistors.
Peak-to-peak value. The difference between the maximum positive and maximum negative values of a single cycle of a recurrent or periodic waveform as shown on its graph.
Percent regulation. A power transformer characteristic used to indicate how much the secondary potential difference will change under varying load conditions.
Period. The time necessary to complete a single cycle of a recurrent or periodic waveform.
Permanent magnet. A magnetized material that tends to retain its magnetic properties in the absence of an external magnetic field.
Permeability. The permeability of a material is the amount of magnetic field intensity required to produce a particular flux density in the material. Permeability,

like resistivity, is a characteristic of a material and is independent of size or shape.
Permittivity. Permittivity is an electric field quantity that measures the degree of ease with which an electric field can pass through a material.
Persistance. The time during which the dot on a cathode-ray tube phosphor screen glows after the electron beam has moved on.
Phasor method. A method of symbolizing a sine wave as a vector quantity possessing a length (its peak or rms amplitude) and an angle (its phase angle as compared to a reference sine wave).
Phosphor. A material that produces visible light when struck by electrons.
Pictorial diagram. A pictorial diagram is a line drawing or photograph of a piece of electronic equipment. Names of component parts; part numbers or reference designators may be included.
Place value. The numerical value of a digit in the decimal number system that is determined by the position of the digit. The value of the digit 8 in 387 is 8×10, or 80.
Planté cell. The Planté cell, named after its inventor, is a lead-acid secondary cell closely resembling the cells used in a modern automobile battery.
Plotting. The process of calculating variable values and marking them on a graph.
Polar coordinate system. A manner of specifying the end point of a vector or any point on a plane by giving the length of a vector and the angle it makes with a reference axis.
Polarization. The process of forming gas bubbles inside a chemical cell. The bubbles interrupt the current path through the cell and result in early failure of the cell.
Potential. The potential energy of an electron in an electric field.
Potential difference or voltage. The difference between the potential energies of an electron at different points in an electric field or electric circuit.
Potential energy. The energy possessed by an object by virtue of its position in a field.
Potential gradient. A term that refers to the fact that the potential difference in an electric field varies smoothly and continuously between points at different potentials.
Potential or voltage rise. In circuit analysis, an increase in the potential energy of an electron as it moves between two points in a circuit.
Potentiometer. A three-terminal variable resistor.
Power. Power is the rate at which work is done.
Power dissipation. In electronics, the amount of electric power converted into heat as an electric current passes through a resistance.
Power factor. The ratio of the true power to the apparent power in an ac circuit.
Power relay or contactor. A relay designed for switching currents of 10 A or more.
Primary. The coil of a transformer that is connected to an ac source.
Primary cell. A source that furnishes electrical energy to a circuit. A primary cell is discarded when its output falls below a certain level.
Probe compensation. Adjustment of a variable control on an oscilloscope probe to prevent waveform distortion due to the probe.
Probes. The connection devices used to connect circuit points with the input jacks of an oscilloscope.
Product. The name given to the result when two numbers are multiplied. For example, in $4 \times 2 = 8$, 8 is the product.
Programmable calculator. A calculator that can be set up to do a certain series of calculations automatically.
Prompt. A particular character or sign used by a computer to signal that it is ready to receive information or commands.
Proton. Subatomic particle with a positive electrical charge equal to the negative charge of the electron. Protons are found in the nucleus of atoms.
Pull-in or response time. The time required for an energized relay to complete a contact.
Pulse generator. A signal source which provides pulses that can be varied in frequency, duty cycle, and amplitude.
Pulse width. The pulse width of a pulse is defined as the time between two successive points at which the pulse amplitude reaches 50 percent of its peak amplitude.
Pushbutton switch. A switch actuated by a short-distance thrust of the actuating button.
Pythagorean theorem. A statement of an essential characteristic of right triangles drawn on plane surfaces: that is, the sum of the squares of the lengths of the sides is equal to the square of the length of the hypotenuse.

Q

Q or quality factor. An important characteristic of components and circuits, Q provides a comparison of the reactive and resistive effects of the component or circuit at a particular frequency.
Quadrant. One of the four quarters of the number plane defined by the two axes in a Cartesian graph.
Quotient. The result when one number is divided by another. For example, in $32 \div 8 = 4$, 4 is the quotient.

R

Radian. An angle that when placed with its vertex at the center of a circle, produces an arc equal to the radius of the circle. To three significant figures, 1 Radian = 57.3°.

Radio-frequency choke. A component used primarily to prevent the distribution of high-frequency ac signals along dc power or low-frequency signal lines.

Radio-frequency coil. An inductor designed for use at frequencies above 20 kHz.

Radio-frequency transformer. A transformer designed to operate at frequencies higher than 20 kHz.

Random failure. A component failure that occurs after the burn-in or initial period of operation is over.

Range multiplier. A resistor placed in series with a current-measuring meter to enable it to make potential difference measurements.

Reactive power. The amount of power that is alternately stored in circuit reactances and then given back in an ac circuit.

Reciprocal. The reciprocal of a quantity is the result obtained when that quantity is divided into 1. If X is a quantity, its reciprocal is $\frac{1}{X}$.

Rectangular coordinates. Another term for the Cartesian coordinate system which uniquely identifies any point on a plane by giving its X and Y coordinate values.

Rectifier. A device that converts an ac input into a dc output.

Recurrent or periodic waveforms. Waveforms composed of a basic shape that is repeated without change.

Reed relay. A form of relay using a thin magnetic material reed as its moving part.

Reference designator. A combination of letters and numbers used to uniquely identify a component or subassembly. Component type or subassembly function are generally implied by the letters used.

Reference junction. In a Kirchhoff's current law analysis, the reference junction is selected as the reference point for potential difference calculations.

Reflex angle. An angle of greater than 180°.

Relative permeability. Used to simplify calculations, relative permeability is defined as the permeability of a material divided by the permeability of free space.

Relay. An electrically operated switch that uses the magnetic field produced by an electric current to operate a mechanical action that opens or closes pairs of electrical switch contacts.

Release time. The time required for a relay to go from its energized to its unenergized or "relaxed" state after the coil current has been shut off.

Reluctance. The magnetic analog of resistance. Defined as the amount of magnetomotive force necessary to produce a unit of magnetic flux in a particular closed core.

Reset delay. The time delay between the opening of a circuit breaker and the time that an automatic reset is attempted.

Resistance. The opposition to the drift of electrons in a particular piece of material of a certain length and thickness is the resistance of that piece of material. Resistance is measured in units called ohms (Ω).

Resistivity. Resistivity is the measurement of how well the atoms of a material block the drift of the electrons that make up an electric current.

Resistor. A component designed to provide a specific resistance in a circuit.

Resonance. The condition in an *RCL* circuit when the capacitive and inductive reactances are equal.

Resonance curve. A form of graph that shows how the current or impedance in an *RCL* circuit varies with changes in the source frequency.

Resonant frequency. The source frequency at which the capacitive and inductive reactances in an *RCL* circuit are equal.

Retrace. The period of time during which the oscilloscope beam moves back across the screen from right to left after tracing out a waveform. Frequently, the luminosity of the spot on the screen is reduced during retrace. This is referred to as "retrace blanking."

Reversal of polarity. If one of the cells in a battery is at a lower charge level than the others, it may begin to recharge with opposite polarity while the other cells are functioning normally. Reverse polarity recharging produces large quantities of hydrogen gas, which may explode.

Reverse Polish notation. A system of entering numbers and functions used by a few modern calculators. The system is said to perform calculations with fewer steps. Less popular than the algebraic system.

rf Generator. A signal generator producing sine-wave signals from 100 kHz to 500 MHz or higher.

Rheostat. A two-terminal variable resistor with a rotary actuator.

Right-hand rule for motors. A way of remembering the relationship among the forces involved in motor operation. To use this rule, point the first finger in the direction of the magnetic field or magnetic flux, and the middle finger, bent to form a right angle with the first finger, in the direction of the current. The thumb then points in the direction of the force or thrust on the conductor.

Rise time. The time it takes a pulse with increasing amplitude to go from 10 to 90 percent of its peak value.

Rotary switch. Any switch actuated by a twisting motion of a shaft.

Rounding off. The process of reducing the number of

significant figures or places in a number in order to simplify calculation or to reflect the correct level of accuracy in measurements.

S

Saturation. In iron core coils, saturation refers to the condition that occurs when the magnetizing force produced by the coil current is so great that changes in this current cannot significantly increase the magnetic flux in the core.

Scalar quantity or scalar. A quantity with only a magnitude, in contrast to a vector, which has both a magnitude and a direction associated with it.

Schematic diagram. An electrical diagram that uses symbols to represent component functions. The symbols are connected with solid lines representing current paths.

Scientific notation. A method of writing numbers using a mathematical shorthand. Any number can be expressed as a number greater than or equal to 1 or less than 10, times 10 raised to a positive or negative whole number.

Sealed lead-acid or gelled acid cell. A lead-acid cell using a gelled rather than liquid electrolyte. The active metals are lead and lead oxide.

Secondary. The winding or coil of a transformer that is connected to a load.

Secondary cell or accumulator. A chemical cell that can be restored to nearly its initial condition by passing an electric current through it. This process is called recharging.

Self-healing. The property of some capacitor dielectric materials to heal or repair small gaps in the dielectric.

Self-induction or induction. The electrical effects produced when the magnetic field around a conductor expands or collapses.

Semiconductor. One of a group of materials in which the conduction and valence energy levels are close together. In its natural state, there are few conduction electrons present in a semiconductor, but it is relatively easy for valence electrons to absorb enough additional energy to enter the conduction band.

Sensitive relays. Relays requiring very little coil power for operation. On the order of 100 mW or less is required to operate a sensitive relay.

Sensitive switch. A sensitive switch has an actuator that is not directly connected to the contact mechanism but acts as a trigger. When the trigger is operated, the switch action is rapidly carried out by a spring mechanism.

Series circuit. An electrical circuit in which there is only one current path, without branches or loops.

Series–parallel circuit. A method of circuit connection in which certain of the components are connected in series, forming a single current path, while other components are in parallel, providing multiple current paths.

Shelf life. Defined as the amount of time a component can be kept in storage without loss of its operating characteristics.

Shells or energy levels. Specific paths around an atomic nucleus in which electrons may be found. Both terms are used since each path corresponds to a particular amount of energy possessed by an electron found in it. For a particular atom, a higher energy level corresponds to a path further away from the nucleus.

Shorting stick. A shorting stick is an insulated rod with a grounded, conductive cable attached to one end. It is used to discharge large capacitors charged to dangerous potential differences.

Shunt. A resistance placed in parallel with another component, frequently a meter.

Signal generator or oscillator. A commonly used signal source that produces a sine-wave output whose frequency and amplitude can be varied over a specific range.

Signed numbers. Numbers prefixed by either a positive (plus) or negative (minus) sign. The plus sign is frequently omitted and is understood. for example, 8 means +8.

Significant figure or significant digit. A number considered to result from an accurate measurement or a mathematical computation.

Silver oxide cell. A primary cell similar to the mercury cell, except that the active metals are silver oxide and powdered zinc. Electrolyte is a gelled form of potassium hydroxide.

Similar triangles. Two triangles whose corresponding angles are equal.

Simplified schematic diagram. A diagram that uses symbols for component functions. Some circuit details are deliberately left out to stress essential parts or illustrate operating principles.

Sine. The ratio of the length of the side opposite an angle to the length of the hypotenuse in a right triangle is the sine of the angle.

Single-precision numbers. Six-digit whole numbers and seven-place decimals in BASIC.

Sinusoid. An alternate name for the graph of a sine or cosine function.

Slope. The steepness of a line on a two-axis graph.

Smoothing. The term used for the reduction of the ac component of a combined ac and dc signal or power supply.

Source. A device that supplies electrical energy to a circuit. The source produces an electric field and supplies charge carriers at a high potential level.

Spaghetti. Flexible plastic tubing used to insulate bare wire.
SPDT switch. A single-pole, double-throw switch, that is, a switch with one common pole that is connected to either of two other switch terminals depending on the position of the switch actuator.
Spectrum analyzer. A device that displays the amplitudes and frequencies of the components of a complex waveform.
Spin. A quality of electrons used to explain magnetic effects.
SPST switch. A single-pole, single-throw switch, that is, a switch with one common pole that is connected to or disconnected from a second terminal by switch operation.
Square. The square of a number is the result when a number is multiplied by itself.
Square root. The square root of a number N is a number that when multiplied by itself, produces N.
Static charge. The condition in which either an excess or deficiency of electrons exists in an object, giving it a net electrical charge.
Static electricity. The effects associated with the existence of an excess or deficiency of electrons in an object.
Steady-state condition. The current and potential difference conditions existing in a circuit after changes due to circuit switching have disappeared.
Step-down transformer. A transformer with more turns in its primary winding than in its secondary. The potential difference across the secondary will be less than the potential difference applied to the primary.
Step-up transformer. A transformer with more turns in its secondary winding than in its primary. The potential difference across the secondary will be greater than the potential difference applied to the primary.
Stranded wire. A wire made up of a number of conductor strands twisted together. Stranded wire is stronger and more flexible than solid wire.
Subscript. A number, printed below the line and following a letter symbol. For example, in E_1 and I_2, the 1 and 2 are subscripts.
Subtrahend. In a subtraction, the number which is subtracted.
Superposition theorem. A method of analyzing circuits with multiple sources by considering the effects of each source individually and combining the results.
Supplementary angles. Two angles whose sum is 180°.
Sweep generator. A signal generator whose output varies continuously in frequency between two limits.
Switch. In general, any device used to open or close an electrical conduction path.
Synthesizer. Also called an arbitrary waveform synthesizer, a synthesizer is a signal source capable of reproducing any complex periodic signal within its frequency range.

T

Tangent. A trigonometric quantity equal to the length of the side of a triangle opposite an angle divided by the length of the adjacent side.
Taut band. A modification of the basic design of the D'Arsonval meter using ribbonlike bands to support the moving coil instead of pivots.
Temperature coefficient of a capacitor. The rate of change of capacitor value caused by changes in temperature. The coefficient is usually given in parts per million per degree centigrade.
Temporary magnet. A magnetized material that loses its magnetic properties quickly in the absence of an external magnetic field.
Term. A term is any constant, variable, or combination of constants and variables separated from other terms by plus or minus signs.
Thermal circuit breaker. A circuit breaker that is actuated by the heat produced by a current overload.
Thermal-magnetic circuit breaker. A circuit breaker that uses both heat and magnetic field actuation.
Thermal runaway. A dangerous condition in ni–cad cells that lower their resistance during recharging. This can, in turn, cause the development of heat, which will result in a further lowering of resistance and production of more heat. Eventually, the cell can explode.
Thermocouple. The junction point of two wires made of different materials. There is always a potential difference across a thermocouple junction, which depends on the material of the wires and on the temperature.
Thevenin's theorem. A method of substituting an equivalent circuit composed of a single ideal voltage source and a series resistor for a network of sources and resistors, no matter how they are interconnected.
Time constant. The time in seconds required for the potential difference across a capacitor connected to a dc source to reach 63.2 percent of its steady-state value, or the time required for the current through an inductor to reach 36.8 percent of its steady-state value.
Time-delay (slow blow) fuses. Time-delay fuses are designed to withstand heavy current overloads for a brief period of time but to burn out if the overload time is fairly long.
Tinning. The process of coating a copper conductor with a thin layer of tin or solder alloy.
Toggle switch. A sensitive switch operated by flipping a bat-shaped actuator.
Tolerance. The permitted actual value range for a component value. Expressed in percent of nominal value.

Total magnetic flux. Defined as the total strength of the magnetic field surrounding a magnet or current-carrying conductor.
Trailing zeros. Zeros to the right of the significant figures or digits in a number.
Transformer. An electronic component, operating by means of magnetic effects, that transforms an ac input at one potential difference and current into an ac output at a different potential difference and current.
Transient state. The current and potential difference conditions existing because of changes produced by switching a circuit.
Triboelectricity. The general term for the electrical effects produced by the contact or rubbing together of different materials.
Trickle charge rate. The trickle charge rate is that which recharges secondary cells at a current equal to the current that can be obtained when discharging a fully charged cell for 500 hours. It is the rate recommended for keeping stand-by cells at full service capacity.
Trigonometry. The division of mathematics that deals with triangles that contain a right angle (an angle of 90°).
Trimmer capacitor. Also called a trimmer or padder, a trimmer capacitor is a variable capacitor designed for infrequent adjustment.
Trimmer potentiometer. A three-terminal variable resistor designed for infrequent adjustment.
Trip delay. The time delay between the beginning of an overload condition and the time at which a circuit breaker opens the circuit.
Trip free. A term used to characterize a circuit breaker in which the tripping mechanism is always free to operate and open the circuit, even if the actuating push-button or lever is held in the ON position.
True power. Also called the active power, it is the power that is dissipated in the resistances in an ac circuit.
True rms meter. A meter that actually measures the rms value of a sine waveform at a large number of instants and then combines these samples to obtain a true rms value for display.

U

Unknown quantity. A value that has to be calculated using a formula.

V

Variable capacitor. A variable capacitor is an electronic component designed to provide a capacitance value that can be varied within a specific range.
Variable resistor. A resistor whose value can be varied over a specific range.
Variational analysis. A method of relating the results of a component failure to the observed changes in current or potential difference in the failed circuit.
Vector quantity. A quantity, like current, that has both a magnitude and a direction associated with it.
Voltage divider. A series arrangement of resistors designed to provide specific potential differences.
Voltage drop. The change in the potential difference between two points in a circuit and the ground reference.
Voltage gain. The ratio of the potential difference across either the inductor or the capacitor to the source potential difference in a resonant circuit.
Voltaic pile or voltaic battery. A source composed of stacking alternating disks of different metals separated by spacers soaked in an ionized solution. Invented by Alessandro Volta.
VOM or volt-ohmmeter. A battery-powered device using an analog meter for potential difference, current, and resistance measurements. The meter is driven directly in the VOM; no electronic components such as transistors are used.
VTVM or vacuum tube voltmeter. An older form of EVM that used vacuum tubes as the amplifying device. VTVMs seldom measured current. They were usually used for potential difference and resistance measurements.

W

Watt. The power exerted when an energy of one joule operates for one second. It is also the amount of work done when a potential difference of one volt moves a charge of one coulomb past a point in one second.
Wattmeter. A device used to measure the amount of power used in a circuit.
Waveform. The graph of a current or potential difference function with respect to time.
Wheatstone bridge. A form of resistor bridge circuit used for resistance measurements.
Wire. A single conductive path made of a length of solid metal or a number of metal strands twisted together.
Wire-wound resistor. A resistor composed of a coil of wire wound around a cylindrical form made of insulating material.
Wire wrap. A means of connecting wires used in electronics.
Wiring or interconnect diagram. A diagram that uses squares or rectangles to represent the various parts of a unit or system and is detailed only in the specification

of wires, connectors, and connection points. Wire colors and gauge numbers of wires are usually included.

Work. Work is done when a force moves an object some distance in the direction of the force.

Working voltage. The suggested peak potential difference that should ever be applied across a capacitor.

Z

Zinc chloride cell. An improvement of the carbon–zinc, or Leclanché cell. Only zinc chloride is used in the electrolyte. This provides better performance than the ammonium chloride and zinc chloride mixture used in carbon-zinc cells.

ANSWERS TO SELECTED PROBLEMS

CHAPTER 1

C.3 p. 11 (Addition of decimals)
a. 55.049 c. 47.774 e. 10.442 g. 0.185

C.3 p. 11 (Subtraction of decimals)
a. 3.193 c. 0.015 e. 2.072 g. 91.87

C.3 p. 11 (Multiplication of decimals)
a. 287.64 c. 0.0078 e. 9.8209
g. 0.000 004 75

C.3 p. 12 (Division of decimals)
a. 32.65 c. 1.65 e. 0.25 g. 1.25

C.4 p. 12 (Decimal equivalents of fractions)
a. 0.25 c. 0.375 e. 0.09375 g. 0.125
i. 0.53125 k. 0.333

F.1 p. 18

Fraction	*Decimal*	*Fraction*	*Decimal*
$\frac{1}{32}$	0.03125	$\frac{5}{16}$	0.3125
$\frac{1}{16}$	0.0625	$\frac{1}{3}$	0.3333
$\frac{3}{32}$	0.09375	$\frac{1}{2}$	0.5
$\frac{1}{8}$	0.125	$\frac{9}{16}$	0.5625
$\frac{5}{32}$	0.15625	$\frac{5}{8}$	0.625
$\frac{3}{16}$	0.1875	$\frac{3}{4}$	0.75
$\frac{7}{32}$	0.21875	$\frac{15}{16}$	0.9375

F.2 p. 18
a. 0.7071 c. 0.244186 e. 0.3333 . . .
g. 1.4144 . . . i. 2.072 k. 0.186062
m. 159.23567

CHAPTER 2

C.1 p. 29 (Addition of signed numbers)
a. 21.67 c. −80.75 e. 7.29 g. −38
i. 0.522

C.1 p. 30 (Subtraction of signed numbers)
a. 218 c. −19 e. −10 g. 0.083
i. −2.706

C.1 p. 31 (Multiplication and division of signed numbers)
a. −1 c. −0.522 e. 6.75 g. −544
i. −804.685 k. 16.67 m. 152.52
o. −189.75

C.2 p. 31 (Exponential form)
c. $8^2 = 8 \times 8 = 64$
e. $d^2 = d \times d = 5 \times 5 = 25$

C.3 p. 32 (Writing out numbers expressed in scientific notation)
a. 60,200 c. 0.0199 e. 0.000 000 00456
g. 70.7

C.3 p. 32 (Writing numbers in scientific notation)
a. 8.32×10^1 c. 3.3333×10^2 e. 6.2×10^7
g. 2.1×10^1

C.3 p. 32 (Decimals in scientific notation)
a. 3.75×10^{-3} c. 9.98×10^{-10}
e. 3.3333333×10^{-1}

C.4 p. 33 (Converting numbers to engineering notation)
a. 1.8×10^3 c. 250×10^{-6}
e. -6.93×10^{-3} g. 627×10^{-3}
i. 365.2×10^{-3} k. 6.5×10^{-9} m. 1×10^3

F.1 p. 40 (Addition)
a. -2 c. $-432{,}494$ e. 7.573
g. -56.848 i. 10,155

F.2 p. 40 (Subtracting signed numbers)
a. 15.27 c. -22 e. 0.056 g. -0.866
i. -5.53

F.3 p. 40 (Multiplying signed numbers)
a. -300.773 c. 0.01428 e. -324.77445
g. -0.9984 i. -5790727 k. 0.000 015

F.4 p. 40 (Dividing signed numbers)
a. 0.733 c. -0.31944 e. -4.39
g. 96.8889 i. 19.119 k. 928.4

F.5 p. 41 (Decimals to scientific notation)
a. 8.643×10^{7} c. 1.3×10^{-6}
e. 4.1116×10^{1} g. 9.001×10^{1}
i. 2.06×10^{-1} k. 8.92×10^{4}

F.6 p. 41 (Scientific notation to decimal form)
a. 310,000,000 c. 1762 e. 0.000 000 628
g. 0.000 092 9 i. 43,050 k. 840,000
m. 93,000,000,000 o. 16,370

F.7 p. 41 (Convert to engineering notation)
a. 1.001×10^{3} c. 100×10^{-3}
e. 430×10^{6} g. 142×10^{-6} i. 30×10^{-3}
k. 45×10^{-9} m. 300×10^{3}
o. -475.3×10^{-3}

F.8 p. 41 (Engineering to decimal notation)
a. 3200 c. 1,000,000,000 e. 0.00456
g. 0.00475 i. 640,000,000,000,000
k. 8,060,000 m. 0.000 000 00125
o. 0.000 000 008

F.9 p. 41 (Scientific to engineering notation)
a. 1.04×10^{3} c. 6.73×10^{-3}
e. 1.07×10^{-18} g. 36.05×10^{-9}
i. 8.35×10^{6} k. 240×10^{3}
m. 189×10^{-12} o. 62×10^{-6}

F.11 p. 41 0.5 C positive

F.13 p. 41
c. 6 nanoseconds e. 5.42 microamperes
g. 5 megohms i. 750 milliwatts
k. 18 megohms m. 1 millivolt
o. 173 microseconds q. 40 milliamperes
s. 0.1 millivolt or 100 microvolts

F.15 p. 41 Discussion should include the notion that there are two kinds of electrical charge, but there seems to be only one gravitational "type."

CHAPTER 3

B.7 p. 55 (Interpreting meter deflections)
a. 5.2 c. 0.62 e. 275 g. -1.6
i. 0.15

C.1 p. 56 (Metric prefixes)
c. 3 nanoseconds, 3 ns e. 3 centimeters, 3 cm
g. 8 microseconds, 8 μs
i. 3.3 microamperes, 3.3 μA
k. 6.72 megavolts, 6.72 MV
m. 900 ohms, 900 Ω
o. 8.85 picoseconds, 8.85 ps
q. 62 kilohms, 62 kΩ
s. 1.3 megawatts, 1.3 MW

C.2 p. 58 (Significant figures)
a. 2 c. 4 e. 4 g. 2 i. 1 k. 5

C.2 p. 59 (Rounding off)
a. 67.3; 67 c. 1880; 1900 e. 0.0134; 0.013
g. 284; 280 i. 155,000; 160,000
k. 25,000; 25,000 m. 0.109; 0.11
o. 1.01; 1.0

C.3 p. 60 (Addition and subtraction)
a. 6.00×10^{4} c. 2.2×10^{-1} e. 1.93×10^{6}
g. 77 or 7.7×10^{1} i. 6.307×10^{1} or 63.07
k. 8.6×10^{-3}

C.4 p. 60 (Multiplication of exponentials)
a. 43×10^{5} c. -300×10^{4} e. -6.47
g. 1.3 i. 4.2×10^{-3} k. -7.9×10^{-6}

C.4 p. 61 (Division of exponentials)
a. 6.1×10^{2} c. 6.8×10^{-1} e. 3.9×10^{-5}
g. -3.3×10^{1} or -33

F.1 p. 76
a. 8.72; 8.7 c. 5.57; 5.6 e. 1.35; 1.4
g. 1.14; 1.1 i. 1,250,000; 1,300,000
k. 73.2; 73

F.2 p. 77
a. 67.7 c. -3.00×10^{3} e. 1.01×10^{-2}
g. 1.79×10^{-1} i. -1.65×10^{2}
k. 1.41×10^{3}

F.3 p. 77
a. -7.22×10^{4} c. -4.60×10^{-3}
e. 1.29×10^{5} g. -1.22×10^{-2}
i. 1.11×10^{8} k. 5.82×10^{-2}

F.5 p. 77 31.25 mA.

CHAPTER 4

C.1 p. 90
a. $Q = 12$ c. $X = 7$ e. $R = 5$
g. $H = 0.0793$ i. $X = -1.5$

C.1 p. 91
a. $Y = 1$ c. $X = 3$ e. $C = -46.8$
g. $J = 8$ i. $Y = 4.29$

C.1 p. 92
a. $X = 0.89$ c. $B = -0.4$ e. $D = 1.33$
g. $E = 0.314$ i. $Z = 2.667$

F.1 p. 98
14 V; 0 V

F.5 p. 99 Any individual cell could be replaced by an open circuit in Figure 4.42. No cell could be replaced by a short.

F.7 p. 99
a. 0.534 m c. 0.45 M^3 e. 169 in.
g. 60 in.^{2} i. 12.3 L

F.8 p. 100
a. $A = 2.1875$ c. $A = 42$ e. $j = 8.5$
g. $Z = 2.42$ i. $P = 0.1667$ k. $P = 7.2$

F.9 p. 100
c. $a = 3b - 1$ e. $a = \frac{3}{2Q} - 3.5$ g. $E = \frac{P}{I}$
i. $C = \frac{1}{2\pi FX}$

CHAPTER 5

C.1 p. 110 (Ohm's law table)
a. $R = \frac{E}{I}$, 3000 Ω c. $E = IR$, 0.40 V
e. $I = \frac{E}{R}$, 4.0 A g. $I = \frac{E}{R}$, 3.6 mA
i. $R = \frac{E}{I}$, 621 Ω k. $E = IR$, 150 V
m. $R = \frac{E}{I}$, 3.9 kΩ o. $E = IR$, 50 V

C.2 p. 111 (Variational analysis)
a. $2I$ c. $\frac{1}{4}E$ e. $\frac{1}{16}E$ g. same
i. same

C.3 p. 113 (Reciprocals)
a. 0.01 c. 5.56 e. 0.11 g. 0.0100 Ω
i. 10^3 Ω

C.3 p. 113 (Reciprocals)
a. 6 c. $\frac{1}{2Z}$ e. $J = 1$

F.1 p. 122
a. Ohm's law; resistance c. longer
e. less . . . than g. resistivity i. increase

F.3 p. 122 The resistance will not change, the current will be 0.3 A.

F.5 p. 123
a. 0.12 A c. 200 Ω

F.7 p. 123 Resistivity is a characteristic of a type of material; resistance is a property of a particular piece of material. A multimeter measures resistance in its ohmmeter function.

F.9 p. 123 Refer to Figure 5.6

F.11 p. 123 Answer might include (a) continuity checking for broken wires (b) short-circuit checks and (c) poor connections.

CHAPTER 6

C.1 p. 135 (Squares and square roots)
a. 26.2 c. 9.87 e. +0.707; −0.707
g. +3.65; −3.65 i. +0.137; −0.137
k. 8.48 m. 1730 o. 48

C.1 p. 135 (Y^x key problems)
a. 1.73 c. 1.00 e. 24 g. 0.0772
i. 0.399 k. 1.32 m. 82.8 o. 2.80

C.3 p. 136 (Ohm's law problems)
a. 5 A c. yes, $V_{R2} = 1.5$ V, $V_{R3} = 2.5$ V, $V_{R4} = 5$ V e. yes, 12 V g. 6.5 A
i. $R1 = 0.6$ V, $R2 = 4$ V, $R3 = 2$ V, $R4 = 2$ V, $R5 = 2$ V

F.1 p. 156 One hundred bulbs use 6 kW of power, at 120 V, this is equivalent to a current of 50 A. Using a 200 percent factor, the wire must carry at least 100 A. AWG 0 should be used.

F.2 p. 156
a. 42.9 c. 210 e. 0.624 g. 0.229
i. 7.12 k. 5.20 m. 512 o. 0.437
q. 0.00130 s. 12

F.3 p. 156 15 (2.5, 3.33, 3.99, 5, 6, 6.67, 7.5, 10, 12.5, 15, 16.67, 20, 25, 30, and 40 Ω).

CHAPTER 7

C.2 p. 174 (Angles)
1. Point 0

2a. πR c. 270° e. $\frac{\pi}{3}R$ g. 144°
i. 1440°

C.3 p. 176 (2 × 2 determinants)
a. $I_1 = 2.15, I_2 = 3.63$ c. $I_1 = -3, I_2 = 1.7$
e. $X = -2, Y = 4$ g. $I_1 = 4, I_2 = 2.4$
i. $I_1 = 2, I_2 = -8$

C.3 p. 179 (Answers by determinants)
a. $I_1 = 2.5$ A, $I_2 = 2.167$ A c. $I_1 = 0.3$ A, $I_2 = 0.25$ A e. $I_1 = 0.111$ A, $I_2 = 0.0256$ A

C.4 p. 181 (Tolerance calculations)
a. 8262 Ω to 7938 Ω c. 1.782 V to 1.318 V
e. 1.067 Ω to 1.065 Ω g. 13 H to 7 H

3 p. 181 $I_{max} = 1.142$ A, $I_{min} = 0.927$ A, $P_{150\,\Omega\,(max)} = 0.701$ W

4a. p. 181. 3.85% c. 7.35% e. 6.67%
5. p. 181 2%

F.1 p. 196
$V_{R3} = 1.06$ V, $I_{R3} = 0.106$ A

F.2 p. 196
a. $I_1 = 2.5$ A, $I_2 = 3$ A, $I_3 = 0.5$ A, $I_4 = 2$ A, $I_5 = 2.5$ A c. $I_1 = 0.192$ A, $I_2 = 0.046$ A, $I_3 = -0.003$ A, $I_4 = -0.108$ A, $I_5 = 0.127$ A
e. $I_1 = 0.69$ A, $I_2 = 2.38$ A, $I_3 = 3.07$ A

F.3 p. 196 Figure 7.78 is easier with current law.

CHAPTER 8

C.1 p. 213 (Simultaneous equations on a computer)
1. p. 213 a. $X = -9$, $Y = 7$ c. $I_1 = 0.84$, $I_2 = 0.44$ e. no unique answer
g. $X = 0.667$, $Y = 0.333$ i. $X = 1.94$, $Y = -1.76$, $Z = 1.63$
2. p. 214 $I_1 = 0.491$ A, $I_2 = 0.31$ A, $I_3 = 0.207$ A $E_{R1} = 4.91$ V, $E_{R3} = 2.17$ V, $E_{R5} = 0.618$ V
3. p. 214 $E_{R1} = 0.0$ V, $E_{R2} = 0.0$ V, $E_{R3} = 5$ V, $E_{R4} = 5$ V, $E_{R5} = 3.75$ V, $E_{R6} = 1.25$ V
5. p. 214 About 5 V. No, other resistors could be at fault.

C.2 p. 215 (Δ–Y on a computer)
1. p. 215 $I = 1.315$ A
3. p. 215 0.0977 V
5. p. 215 $I = 0.496$ A

C.3 p. 216 (Comparison of methods)
1. p. 216 I_{R1}, $I_{R2} = 33.1$ mA, $E_{R1} = 0.331$ V, $E_{R2} = 0.397$ V, $I_{R3} = 44.6$ mA, $E_{R3} = 1.472$ V, $I_{R4} = 66$ mA, $E_{R4} = 0.528$ V, $I_{R5} = 54.5$ mA, $E_{R5} = 1.472$ V, I_{R6}, $I_{R7} = 1.667$ mA, $E_{R6} = 0.01667$ V, $E_{R7} = 0.01133$ V
3. p. 216 $I_{R2} = 0.433$ A, $E_{R2} = 4.33$ V

F.1 p. 227 $R_A = 1302.26\ \Omega$, $R_B = 1441.79\ \Omega$, $R_C = 2070.26\ \Omega$
3. p. 227 $I_{R2} = 0.0392$ A
5. p. 227 $I_N = 0.3$ A, $R_N = 2.31\ \Omega$
6. p. 227 a. $I_1 = 0.228$, $I_2 = 0.554$
c. $X = 13.35$, $Y = -4.467$, $Z = 0.560$
e. $I_1 = 5.06$, $I_2 = 18.61$, $I_3 = 10.85$
g. $I_1 = 2.35$, $I_2 = -0.035$, $I_3 = -1.79$
9. p. 227 Refer to Figure 8.40. b. Calibrate against a known resistor.

CHAPTER 9

C.1 p. 240 (Functions)
1. p. 240 a. $14X$, 3 c. a_0, a_1X_1, a_2X_2
e. $\frac{X}{5}, \frac{X-Y}{7}$ g. $(X + Y + 7)$
2. p. 240 a. 7, 3 c. 8, −1, 8 e. $\frac{1}{3}, \frac{1}{7}, 9$
g. $-a_0, +a_1, -a_2, +a_3$
3. p. 240 a. $X + 2Y$ c. $2(X - Y)$
e. $8(X - 2)$ g. $X - 4Y$
i. $16\left(\frac{X+Y}{3}\right)$

C.3 p. 245 (Trigonometric functions, sines)
a. 0.588 c. 0.342 e. −0.643 g. −0.225
i. −0.259 k. 0.00 m. −0.0523 o. 1.00

C.3 p. 246 (Cosines)
a. 0.866 c. 0.500 e. 1.00 g. −1.00
i. 0.00 k. 1 m. 0.766 o. 0

C.3 p. 247 (Inverse trigonometric functions)
a. 90° c. 60.0° e. 20.7° g. 0°
i. −7.00° k. 0° m. 109° a. 1.02 R
c. 0.314 R

F p. 259

F.1 p. 259 9 turns

F.3 p. 259 The product of the number of turns and the coil current should be 1.13, or 11.3 mA for 100 turns of wire.

F.5 p. 259 $\mu = 0.0125$ or 1.25×10^{-2} $\mu_r = 9944$

CHAPTER 10

C.1 p. 270 (Resolving vectors)
a. $X = 4.33$, $Y = 2.5$ c. $X = -3.65$, $Y = 1.63$
e. $X = 4.86$, $Y = 7.57$ g. $X = 22.88$, $Y = -79.78$ i. $X = -4.5$, $Y = 7.79$
k. $X = 1.17$, $Y = 0.486$ m. $X = -0.647q_1$, $Y = 2.414q_1$

C.1 p. 271 (Pythagorean theorem)
a. 5 c. 4.24 e. 1.414 g. 15.97
i. 8.54 k. hypotenuse = 1.414, adjacent = 1

C.1 p. 272 (Rectangular to polar coordinates)
a. 5, 36.87° c. 19.65, 75.26° e. 5, 233.1°
g. 3.16, 296.6° i. 5

C.2 p. 274 (Computations with sine waves)
1. p. 274 $f = 40$ Hz, $t = 0.025$ s, $I_{\text{p-to-p}} = 1.184$ A, $I_{\text{average}} = 0.377$ A, $I_{\text{rms}} = 0.419$ A
3. p. 274 7.07 V_{peak}, 5 V_{rms}
5. p. 274 371.1 $V_{\text{p-to-p}}$
7. p. 274 a. 254.6 V_p c. 3.185 V
e. 1158.75 g. 38.22 V_{average} i. 0.91

C.3 p. 276 (Computations with pulse widths)

Figure	*a*	*c*	*e*
Period	40 ms	1 ms	0.2 s
Frequency	25 Hz	1000 Hz	5 Hz
Peak	3 V	10 V	2 V
Peak-to-peak	6 V	15 V	2 V
Average	1.91 V		
rms	2.12 V		
Duty factor	X	0.2	0.25
Duty cycle	X	20%	25%

F.1 p. 296 169.73 V

F.5 p. 297 Still does not distinguish between no trigger and bad generator output.

F.7 p. 297 Notice the 0, 10, 90, 100 divisions. Use the variable VOLTS/DIV potentiometer to adjust the height of the pulse so that it fills the area between the 0 and 100 divisions. Count the horizontal axis divisions between the points at which the trace crosses the 10 and 90 percent divisions.

CHAPTER 11

C.1 p. 320
a. $3.62 \sin(\theta + 13.96°)$ c. 0°
e. $7.53 \sin(\theta + 61.36°)$ g. No unique answer.
$4 \sin \theta$ and $2 \sin (\theta + 180°)$ are one example.

F.4 p. 330
A, 6.02; *C*, 8.14; *E*, 6.32

F.6 p. 330
a. $17.24 \sin(\theta + 27.65°)$ c. $23.18 \sin(\theta + 270°)$
e. $6.22 \sin \theta$

F.7 p. 330
Small radio TV repair shop: af and rf signal generators; perhaps a function generator.

Custom music system plant: af signal generator, perhaps an af sweep generator.

Mobile microwave maintenance: rf signal generator, sweep generator.

Computer repair facility: pulse generator, function generator.

Aircraft electronics equipment manufacturer: all types.

Arcade game repair shop: function generator.

CHAPTER 12

C.1 p. 348 (Logarithms and antilogarithms)
a. 0.5563025 c. 5.146128 e. 6309.5734
g. 0.0024788 i. 3.6553227 k. 0.3467369
m. 7.3890561

C.2 p. 349 (Solving logarithm problems)
a. About 0.1 s c. 28.86 H e. 91.79 mA

F.1 p. 360
a. 2.4281348 c. 1 e. 10 g. 1.7466342
i. 3.5389506 k. 1.0087882

F.2 p. 360
a. 5.590987 c. 1 e. 2.7182818
g. 4.0217739 i. 8.1487348 k. 1.0038072

F.3 p. 360
$\log \epsilon = 0.4342945$; yes $\dfrac{\log N}{\log \epsilon} = \ln N$

F.5 p. 360
About 9.6 turns.

F.7 p. 360
$L = 0.153$ H, $Q = 0.577$

F.9 p. 361
The total circuit current will be the result of adding the components of the current in the two branches. The current in the *R*2 branch will be $42.4 \sin(2\pi ft)$ mA. In the *L*1*R*1 branch it will be $24.7 \sin(2\pi ft - 77.44°)$ mA. The result is $i = 53.32 \sin(2\pi ft - 26.52°)$ mA.

CHAPTER 13

C.2 p. 381 (Transformer calculations)
1. 60 V 3. 663 turns 5. 24:1, 0.24
7. 400 turns

C.3 p. 382 (Polar coordinates)
a. $3.75 \angle 30°$ A c. $10 \angle 0°$ A
e. $68 \angle -45°$ mA g. $i \angle -34°$
i. $65 \angle 90°$

C.3 p. 384 (Polar to rectangular, rectangular to polar forms)
1 p. 384 a. $10.39 + j6$ c. $1.19 - j2.06$
e. $5.17 - j4.34$ g. $0 - j36$
i. $-2.82 + j7.75$
2 p. 384 a. $18 \angle 0°$ c. $20 \angle -36.87°$
e. $5 \angle 53.13°$ g. $8.15 \angle -146.5°$
i. $10.36 \angle 74.89°$

C.3 p. 385 (Imaginary numbers)
a. $j3$ c. $j5.45$ e. $j3.16a\sqrt{b}$
g. $j2.459\sqrt{c + d}$ i. $\dfrac{1}{j1.73\sqrt{M}}$ k. $j3$

C.3 p. 386 (Expressing phasors)
a. $56 + j180$ c. $X_L = 2.65$, $R = 4.59$, $Z = 4.59 + j2.65$ e. $37.2 + j45.53$

F.2 p. 398
a. $5.6 + j0$ c. $160.2 - j92.5$
e. $3.72 - j4.13$ g. $0 - j12$
i. $-1.18 - j0.21$

F.3 p. 398
a. 5 $\angle 53.13^\circ$ c. 10.98 $\angle 146.89^\circ$
e. 20.47 $\angle 61.56^\circ$ g. 8.16 $\angle -62.65^\circ$

F.4 p. 398
a. 180 + j156.19; 238.32 $\angle 40.95^\circ$
c. 1200 + j942.48; 1525.87 $\angle 38.15^\circ$
e. 2700 + j1922.7; 3314.6 $\angle 35.46^\circ$

F.5 p. 398
Inductor alone, Q = 4.90.

Inductor with series resistor, Q = 0.77.

Inductor with parallel resistor, Q = 0.90.

F.7 p. 398
a. 41.67 mA
b.

Fundamental	*416.67 Hz*
$F \times 3$	1250
$F \times 5$	2083.33
$F \times 7$	2916.67
$F \times 9$	3750
$F \times 11$	4583.33
$F \times 13$	5416.67
$F \times 15$	6250
$F \times 17$	7083.33

c.

Frequency (Hz)	*Current (μA)*
416.67	304
1250	33.8
2083.33	24.3
2916.67	12.4
3750	7.5
4583.33	5.02
5416.67	3.60
6250	2.7
7083.33	2.1

CHAPTER 14

C.1 p. 417 (Capacitor problems)
1a. 4.7 μF c. 0.01667 μF e. 282.8 nF
g. 15.55 nF i. 0.0545 μF
3. p. 417 11.59 μF
5. p. 417 a. 220 nF c. 1.8 nF e. 48.71 pF
g. 1 μF a. 0.0018 s c. 0.0015 s
e. 0.6 s

C.1 p. 418 (Time constant problems)
1. p. 418 3.93 V, 6.07 μA
3. p. 418 Up to 59.4 ms
5. p. 418 59.61 μA

C.2.1 p. 420 (Addition and subtraction of phasors)
a. 20.57 + j11.2, 23.42 $\angle 28.57^\circ$
c. 10.62 − j3.6; 11.2 $\angle -18.73^\circ$
e. 14.62 − j14.7; 20.73 $\angle -45.2^\circ$
g. −6.42 − j10.4; 12.22 $\angle -121.69^\circ$
i. 24.98 − j28.51; 37.91 $\angle -48.78^\circ$

C.2.2 p. 421 (Multiplication and division of phasors)
1a. 62.23 $\angle 78^\circ$ c. 89.76 $\angle -90^\circ$
e. 6 $\angle -16^\circ$ g. 1.67 $\angle -4.71^\circ$
i. 12.77 $\angle -60^\circ$
3. 16.48 $\angle 40^\circ$ V

C.2.3 p. 422 (Multiplication and division in polar form)
a. −16 + j28 c. 26.64 + j0
e. 11.41 + j28.52 g. 546.84 + j0
i. −26.97 + j39.04

C.2 p. 423 (Using phasors in problems)
1. p. 423 i = 12.1 $\angle -18.29^\circ$ mA peak
3. p. 423 10.73 $\angle -87.27^\circ$ mA; 0.511 − j10.72 mA
5. p. 423 0.702 $\angle -0.49^\circ$
7. p. 423 373.33 $\angle -26^\circ$ Ω

F.1 p. 435
a. 14.12 $\angle 24.93^\circ$ c. 364.58 $\angle 29.42^\circ$
e. 0.25 $\angle -51.58^\circ$ g. 85 $\angle 21.2^\circ$
i. 50.58 $\angle 11.65^\circ$

F.2 p. 435 0.001 C; 10 V
a. R = 227.48 Ω

F.4 p. 435 2.21 ms
a. 2.405 V

F.5 p. 435 0.037 $\angle -68.3^\circ$ A

CHAPTER 15

C.1 p. 454 (Review)
1. p. 454 a. 1.8 $\angle 19.44^\circ$ c. 83 $\angle 0^\circ$
e. 13.35 $\angle -90^\circ$ g. 33.02 $\angle -54.87^\circ$
i. 180087 $\angle -1.78^\circ$ k. 91000 $\angle 0^\circ$
2. p. 454 a. 8.49 + j8.49 c. 0 + j243.5
e. 27.7 + j16 g. 0 − j68000 i. 3.14 + j0
3. p. 454 a. 270 + j377; 463.7 $\angle 54.4^\circ$ Ω
c. 10000 + j13,436.6; 16,749.4 $\angle 53.34^\circ$ Ω
e. 0.6 + j1885; 1885 $\angle 89.98^\circ$ Ω
4. p. 454 a. 0.259 $\angle -54.4^\circ$ A
c. 0.896 $\angle -53.34^\circ$ mA e. 1.06 $\angle -89.98^\circ$ μA
5. p. 454 a. 1,115 $\angle 21.7^\circ$ Ω; 1036 + j412.3 Ω
c. 260.1 $\angle 89.45^\circ$ Ω; 2.5 + j260 Ω
e. 0.392 $\angle 38.44^\circ$ Ω; 0.307 + j0.244 Ω

6. p. 454 a. $0.108 \angle -21.7^\circ$ A
c. $33.4 \angle -89.45^\circ$ mA e. $7.65 \angle -38.44^\circ$ μV
7. p. 454 $i_{L1} = 88.7 \angle -84.55^\circ$ mA;
$0.00842 - j0.0883$, $i_{L2} = 40.45 \angle -86.69^\circ$ mA;
$0.00234 - j0.0403$, $i_{L3} = 466.67 \angle 0^\circ$ mA;
$0.4667 + j0$,
$i_{\text{tot}} = 0.4775 - j0.1286 = 0.495 \angle -15.1^\circ$ A

C.2 p. 455 (Impedance in capacitive circuits)
1. p. 455 a. $27{,}000 - j26{,}525.8$;
$37849.9 \angle -44.49^\circ$ c. $5078.9 \angle -24.91^\circ$;
$4606.4 - j2139.2$ e. $2679.4 \angle -89.85^\circ$;
$6.94 - j2649.4$ g. $180 - j545.26$;
$574.2 \angle -71.73^\circ$
2. p. 455 a. $1.66 \angle 44.49^\circ$ mA
c. $2.76 \angle 24.91^\circ$ mA e. $0.1717 \angle 89.85^\circ$ mA
g. $78.37 \angle 71.73^\circ$ mA
3. p. 455 a. $E_r = 44.82 \angle 0^\circ$ V;
$E_C = 44.03 \angle -90^\circ$ V b. $E_r = 5.33 \angle 0^\circ$ μV;
$E_C = 6.53 \angle -90^\circ$ μV d. $E_r = 68 \angle 0^\circ$ V;
$E_C = 144.3 \angle -90^\circ$ V f. $E_r = 1.35 \angle 0^\circ$ V;
$E_C = 4.30 \angle -90^\circ$ V g. $E_r = 14.11 \angle 0^\circ$ V;
$E_{2.7\,\mu\text{F}} = 11.55 \angle -90^\circ$ V, $E_{1\,\mu\text{F}} = 31.18 \angle -90^\circ$ V

F.1 p. 469 $t = 275$ μs

F.3 p. 469
a. $I_{R1C1} = 10.62 \angle 85.12^\circ$ mA,
$I_{R2L2} = 8.95 \angle -83.94^\circ$ mA
b. $2.497 \angle 42.23^\circ$ mA

CHAPTER 16

C.1 p. 484 (Using computer)
1. p. 484 power factor = 40.7%
5. p. 487 $P_t = 3.64$ W, $P_r = 13.19 \angle +90^\circ$ var,
$P_a = 13.69 \angle +74.56^\circ$ V-A.
7. p. 487 Branch 1 = 93.56%, branch 2 = 19.5%, branch 3 = 42.39%
9. p. 487 Without filter 0.3 W, with filter 0.0113 W; difference = 0.2887 W

C.2 p. 489 (Decibels)
1. p. 489 a. 17.48 dBm c. −21.74 dBm
e. 27.48 dBm g. −20 dBm
2. p. 489 a. 0.00398 W c. 0.0005 W
e. 0.95 mW g. loss = −2.22 dB
3. p. 489 8 mW

C.3 p. 490 (Logarithmic relationships)
1. p. 490 a. $X = 46.4159$ c. 4.386
e. 1.0984
2. p. 490 Filter, 18.062 dB; amp no. 1, 42.362 dB; buffer, −1.339 dB; driver, 39.5 dB; final, 16.97 dB
3. p. 490 Voltage gain = 57.33 dB; power gain = 57.33 dB

F.1 p. 502 $P_t = 0.198$ W, $P_r = 0.343$ var, $P_a = 0.396$ V-A
a. pf = 50.043 b. $Q = 1.731$
c. $P_{R3} = 0.0581$ W

F.3 p. 502 $P_T = 0.465$ mW, $P_R = 0.5035 \angle -90^\circ$ mvar, $P_a = 0.685 \angle 47.27^\circ$ mV-A
a. pf = 67.86% capacitive
b. $P_{R2} = 0.422$ mW, $P_{R1} = 0.043$ mW
c. $E_{C2} = 1.71 \angle -90^\circ$ V, $E_{C1} = 0.686 \angle -90^\circ$ V

F.5 p. 502 $P_t = 1.864 \times 10^{-3}$ W (using 7 components)
$E_n = \dfrac{2\text{ V}}{n\pi}$ where $n = 1, 3, 5, 7, \ldots.$

E_n	*f (Hz)*	P_t *(V-A)*	*pf (%)*
$E_1 = 3.18$	1000	5.24×10^{-4}	16.7256
$E_3 = 1.06$	3000	4.28×10^{-4}	45.36
$E_5 = 0.6366$	5000	3.139×10^{-4}	64.69
$E_7 = 0.455$	7000	2.24×10^{-4}	76.49
$E_9 = 0.354$	9000	1.62×10^{-4}	83.6543
$E_{11} = 0.289$	11000	1.20×10^{-4}	88.14
$E_{13} = 0.245$	13000	9.22×10^{-5}	91.07

F.7a.
$L = 0.1$ H
$R = 2.7$ kΩ

pf	*n*	*f*	E_n	P_t
97.398	1	1000	3.18	1.78×10^{-3}
81.995	3	3000	1.06	1.398×10^{-4}
65.18	5	5000	0.6366	3.187×10^{-5}
52.32	7	7000	0.455	1.04×10^{-5}
43.087	9	9000	0.354	4.307×10^{-6}
36.39	11	11000	0.289	2.05×10^{-6}
31.39	13	13000	0.245	1.09×10^{-6}

F.7 p. 503 b.
$L = 0.1$ H
$R = 2.7$ kΩ

pf	*n*	*f*	E_n	P_t
97.398	1	1000	2.026	7.21×10^{-4}
81.995	3	3000	0.225	6.30×10^{-6}
65.18	5	5000	0.0811	5.17×10^{-7}
52.32	7	7000	0.0414	8.685×10^{-8}
43.087	9	9000	0.025	2.15×10^{-8}
36.39	11	11000	0.01675	6.88×10^{-9}
31.39	13	13000	0.012	2.63×10^{-9}

CHAPTER 17

F.1 p. 548

a. $28.3 - j215.4$ b. $E_{\text{coil}} = 0.641 \angle 77.05^\circ$ V, $E_{\text{capacitor}} = 24.42 \angle -90^\circ$ V, $E_{\text{resistor}} = 2.983 \angle 0^\circ$ V

c. $Z = 28.3 + j4.54$ or $28.66 \angle 9.11^\circ\ \Omega$

d. $P_t = 19.83$ W, $P_r = 3.18 \angle +90^\circ$ var, $P_a = 20.1 \angle +9.11^\circ$ V-A

F.3 p. 548

$I_{R3} = 0.024 \angle 0^\circ$ A, or $0.24 + j0$,

$I_{R1C1} = 1.18 \angle 60.51^\circ$ A, or $0.58 + j1.03$,

$I_{R2L1} = 0.117 \angle -66.48^\circ$ A, or $0.047 - j0.107$,

$I_{\text{total}} = 0.867 + j0.923$, or $1.27 \angle 46.8^\circ$ A

F.5 p. 548 $R = 109.96$ or about $110\ \Omega$

F.7 p. 549 $R = 799.34$ or about $800\ \Omega$, 1.76 W

F.9 p. 549 2250.8 Hz

a. $I_{R1} = 0.291 \angle 0.013^\circ$ mA b. $Q = 4.36$

F.11 p. 549 $R = 8\ \Omega$, $L = 6.4$ mH, $C = 99.5\ \mu$F, use 200 μF capacitors, since a value of $2C$ is required.

TABLE OF TRIGONOMETRIC FUNCTIONS

Angle	Sine	Cosine	Tangent	Angle	Sine	Cosine	Tangent
0	0	1	0	38	.615661	.788011	.781286
1	.0174524	.999848	.0174551	39	.629321	.777146	.809784
2	.0348995	.999391	.0349208	40	.642788	.766045	.8391
3	.052336	.99863	.0524078	41	.656059	.75471	.869287
4	.0697565	.997564	.0699268	42	.669131	.743145	.900404
5	.0871558	.996195	.0874887	43	.681998	.731354	.932515
6	.104528	.994522	.105104	44	.694658	.71934	.965689
7	.121869	.992546	.122785	45	.707107	.707107	1
8	.139173	.990268	.140541	46	.71934	.694658	1.03553
9	.156434	.987688	.158384	47	.731354	.681999	1.07237
10	.173648	.984808	.176327	48	.743145	.669131	1.11061
11	.190809	.981627	.19438	49	.75471	.656059	1.15037
12	.207912	.978148	.212557	50	.766044	.642788	1.19175
13	.224951	.97437	.230868	51	.777146	.62932	1.2349
14	.241922	.970296	.249328	52	.788011	.615662	1.27994
15	.258819	.965926	.267949	53	.798636	.601815	1.32704
16	.275637	.961262	.286745	54	.809017	.587785	1.37638
17	.292372	.956305	.305731	55	.819152	.573577	1.42815
18	.309017	.951057	.32492	56	.829038	.559193	1.48256
19	.325568	.945519	.344328	57	.838671	.544639	1.53987
20	.34202	.939693	.36397	58	.848048	.529919	1.60033
21	.358368	.933581	.383864	59	.857167	.515038	1.66428
22	.374607	.927184	.404026	60	.866026	.5	1.73205
23	.390731	.920505	.424475	61	.87462	.48481	1.80405
24	.406737	.913546	.445229	62	.882948	.469471	1.88073
25	.422618	.906308	.466308	63	.891007	.45399	1.96261
26	.438371	.898794	.487733	64	.898794	.438371	2.0503
27	.453991	.891007	.509525	65	.906308	.422618	2.14451
28	.469472	.882948	.53171	66	.913546	.406737	2.24604
29	.48481	.87462	.554309	67	.920505	.390731	2.35585
30	.5	.866025	.57735	68	.927184	.374607	2.47509
31	.515038	.857167	.600861	69	.93358	.358368	2.60509
32	.529919	.848048	.624869	70	.939693	.34202	2.74748
33	.544639	.838671	.649408	71	.945519	.325568	2.90421
34	.559193	.829038	.674509	72	.951057	.309017	3.07768
35	.573577	.819152	.700208	73	.956305	.292372	3.27085
36	.587785	.809017	.726543	74	.961262	.275637	3.48742
37	.601815	.798636	.753554	75	.965926	.258819	3.73205

(continued on next page)

Angle	*Sine*	*Cosine*	*Tangent*
76	.970296	.241922	4.01078
77	.97437	.224951	4.33148
78	.978148	.207912	4.70463
79	.981627	.190809	5.14456
80	.984808	.173648	5.67128
81	.987688	.156435	6.31375
82	.990268	.139173	7.11537
83	.992546	.121869	8.14434
84	.994522	.104528	9.51437
85	.996195	.0871558	11.43
86	.997564	.0697567	14.3006
87	.99863	.0523359	19.0812
88	.999391	.0348994	28.6363
89	.999848	.0174523	57.2904
90	1	0	∞
91	.999848	−.0174526	−57.2892
92	.999391	−.0348996	−28.6362
93	.99863	−.0523359	−19.0812
94	.997564	−.0697567	−14.3006
95	.996195	−.0871558	−11.43
96	.994522	−.104528	−9.51437
97	.992546	−.121869	−8.14434
98	.990268	−.139173	−7.11537
99	.987688	−.156434	−6.31376
100	.984808	−.173648	−5.67128
101	.981627	−.190809	−5.14456
102	.978148	−.207912	−4.70463
103	.97437	−.224951	−4.33148
104	.970296	−.241922	−4.01078
105	.965926	−.258819	−3.73205
106	.961262	−.275637	−3.48741
107	.956305	−.292372	−3.27085
108	.951057	−.309017	−3.07768
109	.945519	−.325568	−2.90421
110	.939693	−.34202	−2.74748
111	.933581	−.358368	−2.60509
112	.927184	−.374607	−2.47509
113	.920505	−.390731	−2.35585
114	.913546	−.406737	−2.24604
115	.906308	−.422618	−2.14451
116	.898794	−.438371	−2.0503
117	.891007	−.453991	−1.96261
118	.882948	−.469472	−1.88073
119	.87462	−.48481	−1.80405
120	.866025	−.5	−1.73205
121	.857167	−.515038	−1.66428
122	.848048	−.529919	−1.60033
123	.838671	−.544639	−1.53986
124	.829038	−.559193	−1.48256
125	.819152	−.573576	−1.42815
126	.809017	−.587785	−1.37638
127	.798636	−.601815	−1.32704
128	.788011	−.615661	−1.27994
129	.777146	−.629321	−1.2349
130	.766045	−.642788	−1.19175
131	.75471	−.656059	−1.15037

Angle	*Sine*	*Cosine*	*Tangent*
132	.743145	−.669131	−1.11061
133	.731354	−.681999	−1.07237
134	.71934	−.694659	−1.03553
135	.707107	−.707107	−1
136	.694658	−.71934	−.965689
137	.681999	−.731354	−.932515
138	.669131	−.743145	−.900404
139	.656059	−.75471	−.869287
140	.642788	−.766045	−.8391
141	.62932	−.777146	−.809784
142	.615662	−.788011	−.781286
143	.601815	−.798636	−.753554
144	.587785	−.809017	−.726542
145	.573577	−.819152	−.700208
146	.559193	−.829038	−.674509
147	.544639	−.838671	−.649407
148	.529919	−.848048	−.624869
149	.515038	−.857167	−.600861
150	.5	−.866026	−.57735
151	.48481	−.87462	−.554309
152	.469472	−.882948	−.53171
153	.45399	−.891007	−.509525
154	.438371	−.898794	−.487733
155	.422618	−.906308	−.466308
156	.406737	−.913546	−.445229
157	.390731	−.920505	−.424475
158	.374607	−.927184	−.404026
159	.358368	−.933581	−.383864
160	.34202	−.939693	−.36397
161	.325568	−.945518	−.344328
162	.309017	−.951057	−.32492
163	.292372	−.956305	−.305731
164	.275638	−.961262	−.286746
165	.258819	−.965926	−.267949
166	.241922	−.970296	−.249328
167	.224951	−.97437	−.230868
168	.207912	−.978148	−.212557
169	.190809	−.981627	−.19438
170	.173648	−.984808	−.176327
171	.156435	−.987688	−.158384
172	.139173	−.990268	−.140541
173	.121869	−.992546	−.122785
174	.104528	−.994522	−.105104
175	.0871558	−.996195	−.0874887
176	.0697563	−.997564	−.0699266
177	.0523361	−.99863	−.0524079
178	.0348996	−.999391	−.0349209
179	.0174526	−.999848	−.0174553
180	0	−1	0
181	−.0174526	−.999848	.0174553
182	−.0348996	−.999391	.0349209
183	−.0523363	−.99863	.0524081
184	−.0697653	−.997564	.0699266
185	−.0871558	−.996195	.0874887
186	−.104528	−.994522	.105104
187	−.121869	−.992546	.122785

Angle	*Sine*	*Cosine*	*Tangent*
188	−.139173	−.990268	.140541
189	−.156434	−.987688	.158384
190	−.173648	−.984808	.176327
191	−.190809	−.981627	.19438
192	−.207912	−.978148	.212556
193	−.224951	−.97437	.230868
194	−.241922	−.970296	.249328
195	−.258819	−.965926	.267949
196	−.275637	−.961262	.286745
197	−.292372	−.956305	.305731
198	−.309017	−.951057	.324919
199	−.325568	−.945519	.344328
200	−.34202	−.939693	.36397
201	−.358368	−.933581	.383864
202	−.374607	−.927184	.404026
203	−.390731	−.920505	.424475
204	−.406737	−.913546	.445229
205	−.422618	−.906308	.466307
206	−.438371	−.898794	.487733
207	−.45399	−.891007	.509525
208	−.469472	−.882948	.53171
209	−.48481	−.87462	.554309
210	−.5	−.866025	.577351
211	−.515038	−.857167	.600861
212	−.529919	−.848048	.624869
213	−.544639	−.838671	.649407
214	−.559193	−.829038	.674508
215	−.573576	−.819152	.700208
216	−.587785	−.809017	.726542
217	−.601815	−.798636	.753554
218	−.615661	−.788011	.781285
219	−.62932	−.777146	.809784
220	−.642788	−.766045	.839099
221	−.656059	−.754709	.869287
222	−.669131	−.743145	.900404
223	−.681998	−.731354	.932515
224	−.694659	−.71934	.965689
225	−.707107	−.707107	.999999
226	−.71934	−.694659	1.03553
227	−.731354	−.681998	1.07237
228	−.743145	−.669131	1.11061
229	−.75471	−.656059	1.15037
230	−.766045	−.642788	1.19175
231	−.777146	−.629321	1.2349
232	−.788011	−.615662	1.27994
233	−.798635	−.601815	1.32704
234	−.809017	−.587785	1.37638
235	−.819152	−.573576	1.42815
236	−.829038	−.559193	1.48256
237	−.838671	−.544639	1.53987
238	−.848048	−.529919	1.60034
239	−.857167	−.515039	1.66428
240	−.866026	−.5	1.73205
241	−.87462	−.48481	1.80405
242	−.882948	−.469472	1.88073
243	−.891007	−.45399	1.96261
244	−.898794	−.438371	2.0503
245	−.906308	−.422618	2.14451
246	−.913546	−.406737	2.24604
247	−.920505	−.390731	2.35585
248	−.927184	−.374607	2.47509
249	−.933581	−.358368	2.60509
250	−.939693	−.34202	2.74748
251	−.945518	−.325568	2.90421
252	−.951057	−.309017	3.07769
253	−.956305	−.292372	3.27085
254	−.961262	−.275637	3.48741
255	−.965926	−.258819	3.73205
256	−.970296	−.241922	4.01078
257	−.97437	−.224951	4.33148
258	−.978148	−.207912	4.70464
259	−.981627	−.190809	5.14456
260	−.984808	−.173648	5.67128
261	−.987688	−.156435	6.31374
262	−.990268	−.139173	7.11535
263	−.992546	−.121869	8.14436
264	−.994522	−.104528	9.51437
265	−.996195	−.0871558	11.43
266	−.997564	−.0697563	14.3007
267	−.99863	−.0523363	19.081
268	−.999391	−.0348992	28.6365
269	−.999848	−.0174523	57.2904
270	−1	0	∞
271	−.999848	.0174526	−57.2892
272	−.999391	.0349	−28.6359
273	−.99863	.0523359	−19.0812
274	−.997564	.0697567	−14.3006
275	−.996195	.0871554	−11.4301
276	−.994522	.104528	−9.51437
277	−.992546	.121869	−8.14434
278	−.990268	.139173	−7.11535
279	−.987688	.156434	−6.31376
280	−.984808	.173648	−5.67128
281	−.981627	.190809	−5.14457
282	−.978148	.207912	−4.70463
283	−.97437	.224951	−4.33148
284	−.970296	.241922	−4.01078
285	−.965926	.25882	−3.73204
286	−.961262	.275637	−3.48741
287	−.956305	.292372	−3.27085
288	−.951057	.309017	−3.07769
289	−.945519	.325568	−2.90421
290	−.939693	.34202	−2.74748
291	−.933581	.358368	−2.60509
292	−.927184	.374607	−2.47509
293	−.920505	.390731	−2.35585
294	−.913546	.406737	−2.24604
295	−.906308	.422618	−2.14451
296	−.898794	.438371	−2.0503
297	−.891007	.453991	−1.96261
298	−.882948	.469471	−1.88073
299	−.87462	.48481	−1.80405

(continued on next page)

Angle	*Sine*	*Cosine*	*Tangent*
300	−.866025	.5	−1.73205
301	−.857168	.515038	−1.66428
302	−.848048	.529919	−1.60033
303	−.838671	.544639	−1.53986
304	−.829038	.559193	−1.48256
305	−.819152	.573576	−1.42815
306	−.809017	.587785	−1.37638
307	−.798636	.601815	−1.32704
308	−.788011	.615661	−1.27994
309	−.777146	.629321	−1.2349
310	−.766045	.642787	−1.19175
311	−.754709	.656059	−1.15037
312	−.743145	.669131	−1.11061
313	−.731354	.681999	−1.07237
314	−.71934	.694659	−1.03553
315	−.707107	.707107	−1
316	−.694659	.71934	−.965689
317	−.681998	.731354	−.932515
318	−.669131	.743145	−.900404
319	−.656059	.75471	−.869286
320	−.642788	.766045	−.839099
321	−.629321	.777146	−.809784
322	−.615662	.788011	−.781286
323	−.601815	.798635	−.753555
324	−.587785	.809017	−.726543
325	−.573576	.819152	−.700208
326	−.559193	.829037	−.674509
327	−.544639	.838671	−.649408
328	−.52992	.848048	−.62487
329	−.515039	.857167	−.600861
330	−.5	.866026	−.57735

Angle	*Sine*	*Cosine*	*Tangent*
331	−.48481	.87462	−.554309
332	−.469472	.882948	−.53171
333	−.453991	.891007	−.509526
334	−.438371	.898794	−.487732
335	−.422618	.906308	−.466307
336	−.406737	.913546	−.445229
337	−.390731	.920505	−.424474
338	−.374607	.927184	−.404026
339	−.358368	.933581	−.383864
340	−.342021	.939693	−.363971
341	−.325568	.945519	−.344328
342	−.309017	.951057	−.32492
343	−.292372	.956305	−.305731
344	−.275638	.961262	−.286746
345	−.258819	.965926	−.267949
346	−.241922	.970296	−.249328
347	−.224951	.97437	−.230868
348	−.207912	.978148	−.212556
349	−.190809	.981627	−.19438
350	−.173648	.984808	−.176327
351	−.156434	.987688	−.158384
352	−.139173	.990268	−.14054
353	−.12187	.992546	−.122785
354	−.104529	.994522	−.105105
355	−.0871562	.996195	−.0874891
356	−.0697567	.997564	−.069927
357	−.0523363	.99863	−.0524081
358	−.0349	.999391	−.0349212
359	−.0174523	.999848	−.0174549
360	0	1	0

INDEX

A

Ac circuit analysis, 483–487
Accumulator, 64
Accuracy, in calculators, 13
Ac/dc selector, 299
Action, 551
Active power, defined, 475
Actual value, 551
Acute angle, 551
Addition:
  of decimals, 10–11
  in engineering or scientific notation, 59–60
  of signed numbers, 29
Aging, 551
Algebraic expression, 239
Algebraic notation, 551
Alkaline cell, 67–68, 551
  effect of temperature on, 68
Alternating current, 266
Amber, 1
American wire gauge (AWG), 115–116, 551
Ammeter, 46, 551
Amp or AMP, 45
Ampere, 45, 551
Ampère, 234–235
Ampere-hour capacity, effect of temperature on, 66
Ampere-hour rating, 65, 551
Amplification, 551
Amplitude, 273, 551
Amplitude modulation (AM), 307, 551
Analog meter, 46–49, 52–55, 551
Analog signals, 363, 551
Analysis:
  branch current in RCL circuits, 513–514
  as explanation of circuit behavior, 530–535
  nodal, 166–167
Angle, 171–174, 551
  acute, 171
  multirotation, 172
  negative, 173
  obtuse, 171
  positive, 173
  reflex, 171
  right, 171
Angle or angular velocity, 302, 551
Angles:
  complementary, 172
  supplementary, 172
Antenna coils, 390
Antilogarithm, 348
Apparent power, defined, 476, 551
Arabic number system, 9, 57
Arctangent, 272
Arithmetic, using decimals, 10–12
Armature, 551
  relay, 249–251
Array, definition, 175
Assembly blowup, 80, 551
Atom, 3
  modern theory, 3–6
  weight, 4
Atomic theory, 3–6
Attenuation, 551
  high-frequency, 368
Attenuation band, 540
Attenuator probes, 552
Audio-frequency generator, 552
Audio taper, 552
Autoranging meter, 50, 106
Autotransformer, 391–392, 552
Average value, in ac measurements, 299
Axis, 168, 240, 269–270, 552
Ayrton or universal shunt, 217–218, 552

B

B (magnetic induction or magnetic flux density), 234–236
Banana plug and jack, 314–315
Band stop circuit of band rejection circuit, 552
Bandwidth or pass band, 516–519, 552
Base, 31
  of logarithm, 347
BASIC, 13, 33, 552
  engineering and scientific notation in, 62–63
Battery, 83
  definition, 64, 552
  schematic symbol, 83
Bayonet base, 552
Bench mat, conductive, 36
Bilateral component, 204, 552
Bleeder resistor, 552
Block diagram, 82, 552
Blowup, parts, 80
BNC connectors, 315–316, 552
Bobbin, 250
Bohr, Neils, model of atom, 4–5
Bond:
  electron pair or covalent, 6
  electrovalent or ionic, 6
Bounce, 552
Branch, 552
  definition, 160
Branch current analysis, or RCL circuits, 513–514
Breaker, circuit, 247–249
Bridge:
  balanced, 219–220
  Wheatstone, 219
Bridge circuit, 218–220
  solution, 177–179
Bridge method of resistance measurement, 105
Briggsian logarithms, 347
Brushes, 265, 552
Burn-in, 392, 500
Button cells, 68
Bypass network, 552

C

C/10 charge rate, 552
Cable, 114, 119–120, 552
  coaxial, 119–120
  ribbon, 119

Calculations:
  inductance, 348–349
  tolerance, 179–181
Calculator:
  engineering and scientific notation using, 61–62
  features, 8
  four-function, 8
  programmable, 8
  scientific, 8
  square root, 134–135
  types, 7–9
  use in inductance calculations, 348–349
  use in signed number calculations, 29–31
Calculus, integral, 366
Candelabra base, 552
Capacitance, 401–405, 552
  nominal, 424
  of parallel-plate capacitor, 403–404
Capacitive reactance, 441–451, 552
Capacitor, 552
  in ac circuits, 441–451
  aging, 428
  aluminum electrolytic, 455–458
    balancing resistors, 457–458
    case style, 456
    dc leakage current in, 456
    failure modes, 457
    low esr, 457
    shelf life, 456–457
    working voltage, 456
  axial lead, 424
  bathtub case, 424
  calculations using calculator, 407–408
  case shapes, 424–425
  ceramic, 426–428
    case styles, 427
    chip, 427
    class I, 427–428
    class II, 427–428
    failure modes, 428
    feed through, 427
  characteristics, 423–430
  chip, 424
  coding, 430–431
  as constant voltage device, 437–441
  coupling, 491–493
  cylindrical, 424
  in dc circuits, 405–409
  dielectric absorption, 460
  discharging, 405
  disk ceramic, 425, 427
  "dog bone," 425
  electrolytic, 424, 455–461
    blow-out plugs, 456
    general, 455
    non-polarized, 455–456
  equivalent series resistance (ESR), 426, 406
  fixed, 424–430
    definition, 424
  function of dielectric, 451–453
  glass, 429
    damage to, 429
  ground or outer foil, 430
  high-voltage disk, 425
  lead style, 424
  maximum voltage, 425
  mica, 425
  MIL SPEC coding, 430–431
  NPO, 426, 428
  operation, 401–405
  padder, 461
  paper or plastic, 429–430
    failure modes, 430
  parallel-plate, 423
    air-dielectric variable, 461–463
  in parallel RC circuits, 450–451
  postage stamp, 425
  radial lead, 424–425
  recommended working voltage, 425
  rules for replacement, 465–466
  schematic symbol, 402
  single-ended, 424
  solid tantalum electrolytic,
    case styles, 458–459
    characteristics, 459–460
    color code, 459
    failure modes, 460
    MIL SPEC coding, 459
    wet slug, 460–461
  square case, 424
  tantalum electrolytic, 458–461
    foil, 458
    slug-type, 458–461
  temperature coefficient, 426
  tester, 499
  testing with bridge, 465
  testing with capacitance meter, 465
  testing with multimeter, 464–465
  time constant in RC circuits, 409–411
  tolerance, 425–426
    of electrolytics, 426
  trimmer, 461, 463–464
    ceramic, 463
    mica, 463
    parallel-plate, 464
    piston-type, 464
  tuning, 461
  types, 423–430
  variable, 424, 461–464
    butterfly, 462
    differential, 462
    failure modes, 463
    ganged, 461–462
    rotor, 461
    rotor plate shapes, 462–463
    split-stator, 462
    stator, 461
    types, 461
  working voltage, 425
Capacitors:
  calculations with, 416–418
  in parallel, 414
  in series, 414–415
Carbon composition resistor, 552
Carbon-zinc cell, 66–67, 68, 552
Cartesian coordinates, 240–241, 552
Cathode-ray tube, 33–34, 552
Catastrophic failure, 552
Cell, chemical, 63–73
  gelled lead-acid, 70–71
  lead-acid, 69–70, 71–72
  Leclanché, 82
  nickel-cadmium, 72–73
  Planté, 69–70, 71–72
  primary, definition, 64
  schematic symbol, 82
  secondary, definition, 64
Ceramic capacitor, 552
Charge:
  measurement, 22–23
  static, 24
  surface, 26
Charging:
  by contact, 24–25, 552
  current, definition, 69
  by induction, 25–26, 552
Chemical activity, atomic explanation, 5–6
Chemical cell, 63–73
  for standby power, 64
  used with generators, 64
Choke, 552
CHS (change sign), 61
Circuit, 28
  analysis, 159–167
  analysis techniques, 552
  breaker, 247–249, 553
    hydraulic damping, 248
    magnetic, 248–249
    thermal, 247–248
    thermal, sensitivity to temperature, 248
    thermal-magnetic, 248–249
    trip-free, 247
  bridge, 218–220
  bypass, 493–494
  closed, 28, 44, 553
  comparison of series tuned and parallel tuned, 530
  dry, 250
  equivalent, 85–88
  grounding, 88–89
  magnetic, 237
  parallel, 84
  parallel RCL, 508–510
  parallel resonant, 521–530
  parallel tuned, 521–530
  practical parallel resonant, 539–540
  practical series resonant, 537–539
  RC phase shifting, 494–495
  resonant and Thevenin's and Norton's theorems, 535–537
  series, 83
  series-parallel, 85, 133
  series-parallel RCL, 510–514
  series RCL, 505–508
  series resonant, 514–521
  series tuned, 514–521
  steps for solution of series-parallel, 512, 514
Circular mil, 114, 553
Closed circuit, 28, 44, 553

Coax, or coaxial cable, 119–120, 315, 553
Code, color, 186–188
Coefficient, 239, 553
 of coupling, 553
Coil, 233
 formulas, 338
Collection of terms, 91–92
Color code, solid tantalum electrolytic, 459
Columbus, Christopher, 230
Command mode, 13
Common, 553
 logarithms, 347, 553
 pole, 553
Compass, 230–231
Complementary angles, 553
Complex conjugate, 422, 553
Complex number notation, 385–386, 553
Complex rectangular form, 382, 553
Component:
 electromagnetic, 247–256
 failure due to static electricity, 34
 linear, 204
Compound, 3, 553
Computations:
 with sine waves, 273–274
 with square waves and pulses, 275–277
Computer:
 Δ-y equivalency theorem using, 214–215
 operating language, 13
 solving simultaneous equations on, 211–213
 square root computations on, 136
 in study of electronics, 13
 used as calculator, 13
Conductance, 102, 136, 553
 definition, 112
Conductances, in parallel, 231–133
Conduction band, 125, 553
Conduction electron(s), 43, 553
Conductor, 553
 atomic theory, 7
 definition, 103
 effect of temperature, 108
Conjugate, complex, 422
Connectors:
 BNC, 315–316
 TNC, 315–316
 UHF, 315
Constant, 239
Constant current device, 553
Constant voltage device, 553
Constant voltage transformer, 553
Contactor, 250
Contact resistance, 553
Continuity checking, 107–108, 553
Conventional current, 2, 553
Conversion of units, 58
Coordinates, 269, 553
 Cartesian, 240–241
 computation, 418–423
 exponential form, 418
 polar, 272, 381–382
  division, 420
  multiplication, 420
 rectangular, 272, 382
  addition, 418–419
  division, 422–423
  multiplication, 421–422
  subtraction, 419
 trigonometric form, 418
Copper losses, 553
Core:
 ferromagnetic, 338
 losses, 377, 553
Corona, 553
Cosine, 270, 553
 defined, 245–246
Coulomb, 45, 553
 balance, 21, 231
 Charles, 21
 unit of charge, 23
Counter, 304–307
Counter emf (cemf), 336, 553
Coupling, 371–372, 334
 coefficient, 371–372
 network, 553
CRT, 33–34
Current, 44, 553
 alternating, 266
 in capacitive ac circuits, 448–450
 definition, 42
 direct, 42
 direction, 46
 directly proportional to potential difference, 111
 electricity, 553
 forming, 455
 induced, 262
 through inductor, 338–341
 inversely proportional to resistance, 111
 law, 166–167
 maximum in wires, 139
 measurement in circuits, 299–301
 measuring with multimeter, 50
 path in schematic diagrams, 81
 produced by sources in parallel, 85
 steady-state, 45
Curve, logarithmic, 339
Cutoff frequency, 492, 540, 553
Cycle, 553
 of waveform, 267

D

D'Arsonval or PM/MC meter, 553
dBm, 488, 553
Dc blocking transformer, 553
Dc leakage current, 554
 in aluminum electrolytic capacitors, 456
Dc source, 46
Decibel, 487–490, 554
 defined, 487
 potential difference and current, 489–490
Decimal, 9–13, 554
 addition, 10–11
 arithmetic, 10–12
 derived from fraction, 12–13
 division, 11–12
 infinite, 12
 multiplication, 11
 place, 10
 places required, 13
 point, 10, 554
 subtraction, 11
Deep discharge of ni-cad cells, 73
Deflection, 47, 53
Degree, definition, 171
Δ-y equivalency theorem, 199–203, 554
 using computer, 214–215
Dendrites, 554
 formation, 70
Density, magnetic flux (B), 234–236
Dependent variable, 554
Descartes, Rene, 240
Designator, reference, 79–80
Determinants, 175–179, 554
Diagram:
 block, 82
 interconnect or wiring, 80–81
 pictorial, 79–80
 schematic, 81–82
 types of electrical, 79–82
Diamagnetic material, 231, 554
Dielectric, 402–403, 554
 breakdown, 402–403, 404
 breakdown voltage, 554
 charge absorption, 452, 554
 coefficient, 453, 554
 constant, 453
 function in capacitor, 451–453
 rupture or breakdown, 554
Difference, 554
Differentiation, 444
Differentiator, 495–496, 554
Digit, 9
 significant, 32, 57–58
Digital multimeter or DMM, 554
Digital signals, 365, 554
Dimensional analysis, 92, 554
Diode, light-emitting (LED), 14, 140
DIP relay, 554
Direct current, 42
 source, 46, 554
Direction, current, 46
Discharging, 554
Dissipation, 126
Distributed load, 159–160, 554
Dividend, 12, 554
Divider, voltage, 220–222
Division:
 of decimals, 11–12
 of signed numbers, 30–33
Divisor, 12, 554
DMM, 49–50
Domain, magnetic, 232, 236
Double-precision number, 63, 554
DPDT switch, 554
DPST switch, 554
Drift, 43
Dry cell, 66
Dry circuit, 250, 554
Dummy load, 316

Duty cycle, 275
Duty factor, 275, 554

E

e (ε), 347
e, 50–51
E, 50
Eddy currents, 377, 554
Effective or rms value, 554
  of sine wave, 274
Electrets, 452–453, 555
Electric charge, loss, 24
Electric current:
  as flow of electrons, 2
  Franklin's definition, 2
Electric field, 4, 21–22, 43, 555
  definition, 21
  and magnetic field, 261
  mapping, 21–22
Electrical characteristics, due to energy levels, 7
Electrical effects, due to charged particles, 7
Electricity:
  current, 24
  derived from Greek *electrum,* 1
  as fluid, 1–2
  static, 23–26
Electrodynamometer, 555
Electrolyte, 555
  in cells, 65
  in lead-acid cells, 69–70, 71–72
Electrolytic capacitor, 555
Electromagnet, 236
Electromagnetic components, 247–256
Electromotive force, 27, 555
Electron, 555
  absorption and reradiation of energy, 13–15
  drift, 43–45
  free, or conduction, 7
  and light, 7
  movement, 2
    in atom, 6–7
    as source of electrical effects, 6–7
  as package of energy, 7
  pair bonding, or covalent bonding, 555
  pump, 64
  valence, 6–7
  weight compared to proton, 4
Electroscope, 555
  construction of, 25
Electrostatic units, 23, 555
Electrovalent, or ionic bond, 555
Electrum, 555
Element, definition, 3, 555
Emf, 27
End voltage, 65, 555
Energy, 555
  absorption and reradiation, 13–15
  in atomic theory, 3–4
  definition, 1
  energy level, 4–7
  requirements for use, 1
  state, 14–15
Engineering notation, 32–33, 555
  arithmetic, 59–62
Envelopes, conductive, 34–35
Equation, 45, 89–92, 555
  definition, 90
  differential, 342
  solution, 90–92
Equations, simultaneous, 164–165, 174–179
  solving with computer, 211–213
  solving by substitution, 165–166
Equipotential surface, 401
Equivalent, Norton, 207–210
Equivalent, Thevenin, 206–207
Equivalent circuit, 555
  failure mode analysis, 94–95
  in series-parallel circuit, 133
Equivalent series resistance (ESR), 497, 555
Error, parallax, 54–55
Esu, 23
EVM, or TVM, 49, 51, 555
Exponent, 31–32, 59–62, 555
Exponentials, 31, 42
Expression, algebraic, 239, 555

F

Failure mode anlaysis, 94–95, 555
Fall time, 555
Farad, 402
Faraday, Michael, 231, 334, 402
Faraday's law, 263–264, 555
Fast-acting fuse, 555
Fast-charge rate, 555
Fast charge rate of lead-acid cell, 72
Ferrite, 555
Ferromagnetic, 231, 555
Field:
  gravitational, 125
  magnetic, 229–239
Field intensity, 555
Figure, significant, 57–58
Filament, 14, 140–141, 555
Film resistor, 555
Filter, 352, 540–544, 555
  bandpass and band rejection, 543–544
  Butterworth, 549
  constant K low-pass, 541
  Chebyshev, 549
  cutoff frequency, 540
  high-pass, 491–493, 542–543
  L or half section, 540–541
  low-pass, 493–494
  m-derived low-pass, 541–542
  π section, 540–541
  T section, 540–541
  troubleshooting, 544
  types, 540–541
Fire bow, 14
Fixed capacitor, 555
Fixed resistor, 555
Fleming's rule, 262
Float charge rate of lead-acid cell, 72
Float charging rate, 555–556
Floating, 224, 556
Flux (total magnetic flux), 234
Flux density, 335
Fluxmeter, 234–235
Force:
  lines, 21–22
  magnetic lines, 229–230
  magnetomotive, 236
  produced by charged objects, 21
Forming current, 455, 556
Formula, 45, 89–94
FOR-NEXT loop, 556
Fourier analysis, 365–369, 556
Fractions, changing to decimals, 12–13
Franklin, Benjamin, 1
  explanation of electrical effects, 1–2
  problems caused by his theories, 2
Free electron, 17
Free-running oscilloscope, 556
Frequency, 268, 556
  cutoff, 492, 540
  measurement, 304–307
  of infinite attenuation, 542, 556
  resonant, 515
  response curve, 389, 556
  spectrum, 268
  vibrating reed meter, 304
Frequency meter/counter, 304–307, 556
  functional block theory, 304–306
  operating modes, 305–306
  operation, 305–306
  time base circuit, 305–306
Function, 170, 556
  cosine, 245–246
  generator, 556
  graphing, 240–242
  linear, 242
  mathematical, 239–242
  sine, 242, 243–244
  trigonometric, 242–246
Fundamental, 317, 367, 556
Fuse, 142–146, 556
  common sizes, 143–144
  fast-acting, 144–145
  general purpose, 145, 556
  mounting, 146
  reasons for failure, 143–144
  slow-blow (time-delay), 145–146

G

Galvani, Luigi, 63
Gas discharge tube, 556
Gelled acid cell, 70–71
Generator:
  ion, 37
  left-hand rule, 262
  output, 264–266
Generator effect, 262
Geometry, 171
Gilbert, William, 230–231
Given or known quantitiy, 89, 556
Graph, 167–170, 556
  network, 159–161
Gravitational field, 125
Ground:
  isolated, 88

reference, 88–89
state, 5, 6, 556
symbol, 88
Grounding, 25, 88–89, 556

H

Hall effect, 234
Harmonic, 317, 367, 368
distortion, 390, 556
Heat:
and light, 14
shrink tubing, 556
Heater, electric, 139–140
Henry, Joseph, 337
High-pass filter, 556
Hook-up wire, 118, 556
Horsepower, 125, 556
Hydraulic analogy, 16
Hydraulic damping, 248
Hydrometer, 71, 556
Hypotenuse, 556
defined, 243
Hysteresis loss, 556

I

Ideal current source, 556
and Millman's theorem, 210–211
Ideal source, schematic symbol, 203
Ideal voltage source, 556
Imaginary numbers, 384–385, 556
Immediate or command mode, 13, 557
Impedance, 346–347, 363, 445, 557
matching transformer, 378–380, 557
Incandescent bulb, 14
Independent variable, 557
Induced current, 262
Inductance, 337–338, 557
calculations, 348–349
mutual, 371–372
unit, 337
Inductances:
in parallel, 344–345
in series, 344
in series-parallel, 345–346
Induction, 336–337
mutual, 333–335
Inductive:
circuit, square waves and pulses, 365
kick, 557
reactance, 337, 343–344, 557
voltage surges, 341
Inductor, 350–357, 557
in ac circuits, 341–342
air gap, 353–354
audio-frequency, 350–352
applications, 352
failure modes, 351–352
coil Q, 353–354
core, 350, 354–357
eddy currents in, 350
encapsulated, color code, 353
ferrite, 355–357
ferrite beads, 356–357
ferrite cores, 352–353, 356–357
frequency response, 354
hysteresis loop, 355
hysteresis loss, 355
metal-encased, 350–351
MIL SPEC, 350–351
open-frame, 350
potential difference and current, 338–341
powdered iron core, 355–357
power, 350–352
practical, types, 350
radio-frequency, 352–353
failure modes, 353
rf choke, 352–353
saturable reactor, 353–354
saturation, 353
set-screw core, 355–356
swinging choke, 353–354
Infant failure, 392, 557
Infinite decimal, 12, 557
Insertion loss, 557
Instantaneous value, 45
Insulation, 118–119
resistance, 557
Insulator, 7, 557
definition, 103
Integrator, 496–497, 557
Intensity, magnetic field (H), 236
Interconnect diagram, 80–81
Interface network, 223–225
International system of units, 33, 42, 557
Intrinsic value, 9, 557
Ion, 64, 557
definition, 6
generator, 37
movement, 7
Isolation transformer, 557

J

j, 364, 382–384, 557
Joule, 55, 557
per second, 125
Junction, 557
definition, 159
reference, 167

K

Key, change sign, 61
Kirchhoff, Gustav, 162
Kirchhoff's current law, 166–167, 557
Kirchhoff's laws, 162–167
in ac circuits
solving equations, 174–179
Kirchhoff's voltage law, 162–166, 557
in capacitive circuits, 442
seeming violation, 506–507
Knife switch, 147–148, 557

L

Lag, 557
Lamps, 139–142
base styles, 142
bulb shapes, 142
incandescent, 140–142
failure mode, 140
heat build-up, 141
life expectancy, 141
metal deposits in, 141
neon, 141–142
life expectancy, 142
operating voltage, 141–142
surge currents in, 141
table of standard types, 142
types, 140
Language for computers, 13
Laser, 14–15, 557
Lead-acid cell, 69–70, 71–72
charging, 71–72
compared to ni-cad, 73
maintenance of, 71–72
specific gravity of electrolyte in, 71
Leader line, 79
Leading zeros, 557
Leclanché cell, 66–68, 557
Leclanché, Georges, 65–67
LED, 14, 557
Left-hand rule for generators, 262, 557
Left-hand rule for magnetic field around wire, 232–233
Left-hand rule for north pole of coil, 233–234
Lenz's law, 264, 336, 558
Light:
bulb, 14
caused by absorption and reradiation of energy, 13–15
and heat, 14
Lightning protection, 35–36
Limit, 558
Line, leader, 79
Linear, 558
component, 204, 558
function, 170, 558
Linearity of component, 204
Lines of force, 558
Lissajous figures, 291–293
Lissajous pattern, 558
Lithium cell, 69, 558
Load, 44–45, 558
definition, 42
distributed, 159–160
lumped, 160
Lodestone, 229–231, 558
Logarithm, 347–349, 487, 558
as used in inductance calculations, 348–349
Logarithmic curve, 339, 558
Loop, or mesh, 558
definition, 160
Loudspeaker (speaker), 307
Low-level relay, 558
Low-pass filter, 558
Lumped load, 160

M

Magnesia (Greece), 229
Magnet:
permanent, 230
temporary, 230
wire, or transformer wire, 117, 558
Magnetic:
biasing, 252–253

Magnetic (*Continued*)
  circuit, 237
  circuit breaker, 558
  circuits, Ohm's law for, 237
  field, 229–239
    and electric field, 261
    intensity (H), 236
    left-hand rule, 232–233
    around wire, 232–233
  force due to, 231
  flux density (B), 234–236, 558
  induction (B), 234–236
  lines of force, 229–230, 558
  poles, 229–231, 558
  shield, 236–237
Magnetism, 229–232
  theory, 230–232
Magnetizing by induction, 230, 558
Magnetomotive force $\mathcal{F}$, 236, 558
Mat, antistatic, 36
Mathematical analysis, as explanation of circuit behavior, 530–535
Maximum power transfer theorem, 222–223, 558
Measure, radian, 173
Mechanical biasing, 252
Megohmmeter, 393, 558
Memory effect, in ni-cad cells, 73, 558
Mercuric oxide (mercury) cells, 68–69, 558
Metal fatigue, 117, 558
Meter, 46–55
  circuit loading, 325
  crossed-coil movement, 322–323
  D'Arsonval or PM/MC movement, 323–324
  dynamometer, 322
  electrodynamic, 322–323
  electrodynamometer, 322–323
  loading, 558
  maintenance, 324–325
  moving iron, 321–322
  moving magnet or polarized iron, 320–321
  sensitivity, 326–327
  shunt, 216–218
  single-element dynamometer, 322
  suspensions, 324
  taut-band, 324
  thermocouple, 299–301
  true rms, 299–301
  types of electromagnetic, 320
  zero adjustment, 324
Metric prefixes, 33, 55–57
Metric system, 33, 42, 55–57
Metric units, conversion of, 92–94
Mho, 112
Mica, 558
Microammeter, 47, 51
Mil, 114, 558
Milliammeter, 47, 51
Millman's theorem, 210–211, 558
MIL SPEC, 558
Minuend, 11, 558
Mirror segment, on meter, 55
Miss, 558
MKS system, 51
Mnemonics, for color code, 187
Molecule, 3, 558
Momentary action switch, 558
Motors, right-hand rule, 261
Movement, as definition of work, 1
Moving iron meter, 558–559
Moving magnet meter, 559
Multimeter, 46, 48–55, 559
  digital, 49–50
Multiplicand, 11, 559
Multiplication:
  of decimals, 11
  in engineering or scientific notation, 60–61
  of signed numbers, 30
Multiplier, 11, 218, 559
Mutual inductance, 559
  calculations, 381

N

Naperian logarithms, 347–348
Natural logarithms, 347, 559
Negative angle, 559
Negative charge, Franklin's definition, 2
Negatively triboelectric, 23
Neon lamp, 559
Network, 559
  coupling capacitor, 491–493
  definition, 159
  differentiator, 495–496
  graph, 159–161, 559
  integrator, 496–497
  interface, or resistance matching, 223–225
  theorem, 199–211, 559
    Δ-Y equivalency, 199–203
    Norton's theorem, 207–210
    superposition, 204–206
    Thevenin's theorem, 206–207, 209–210
  waveshaping, 495–497
Neutron, 4, 559
Newton, 55, 125
  -meter, 55
Ni-cad cell, 72–73, 559
  effect of temperature, 73
Nodal analysis, 166–167
Node, 159, 559
Nominal capacitance, 424
Nominal value, 559
Nonlinear function, 170, 559
North pole:
  left-hand rule for coil, 233–234
  of magnet, 230–231
Norton equivalent, 207–210
  and Thevenin's theorem, 209–210
Norton's theorem, 207–210, 559
  method of using, 208–209
  in resonant circuits, 535–537
Notation:
  algebraic in calculator, 8
  complex number, 385–386
  engineering, 32–33
  keystroke, explanation, 9
  Reverse Polish, 561
  scientific, 31–32, 42
Nucleus, 4, 559
Nuisance failure, 559
  in fuses, 144
Null, 526–559
Null detector, 219
Number:
  double-precision, 63
  imaginary, 384–385
  real, 384
  signed, 28
  single-precision, 63
  system, Arabic, 57
Numerical coefficient, 239

O

Obtuse angle, 559
Oersted, Hans, 231
Offset, 366
Ohms adjust control, 105, 106
Ohm's law, 102, 103–104
  in ac circuits, 301–303
  calculations, 109–110, 136–137
  for magnetic circuits, 237
  wheel, 110
Ohms-per-volt rating, 559
Open circuit, 28, 559
Operator, 382
Orthogonal system, 261, 559
Oscilloscope, 277–293
  attenuator probes, 284
  beam finder, 279
  cathode-ray tube (CRT), 278
  coupling selector, 280
  dangers of grounding, 297, 537
  display section, 278–280
  dual-trace, 278
  dual-trace, triggered, 285–288
  focus circuit, 278–279
  free-running, 277
  frequency measurements, 291–293
  functional blocks, 277–278
  grounding, 297
  horizontal section, 281–283
  input attenuator circuit, 280–281
  intensity circuit, 279
  Lissajous figures, 291–293
  mode control, 285–286
  observing waveforms, 288–290
  probe compensation, 284–285
  probes, 283–285
  purpose, 277
  retrace, 282
  retrace blanking, 282
  scale or graticule brightness control, 280
  sec/div control, 282
  slope control, 287
  sweep generator, 282
  synchronized, 277
  time and period measurements, 290–291
  trace rotation circuit, 279–280
  trigger controls, 287
  use with series resonant circuits, 537–538
  vertical position control, 281
  vertical section, 280–281

voltage measurements, 289–290
volts/div control, 280–281
Overrange, 559

P

Parallax error, 54–55
Parallel circuit, 559
Parallel resonant circuit, 521–530
characteristics, 530
Parallel-tuned circuit or tank, 521–530, 559
Paramagnetic material, 231, 559
Parts blow-up, 80
Passband, defined, 517
Passive filter, 559
Peak-to-peak value, 559
Percent regulation, 559
Period, 559
of waveform, 267
Permanent magnet, 230, 559
Permeability μ, 237–239, 559
relative (μ_r), 238
Permittivity, 402, 560
Persistance, 282, 560
Phase, 316–318
difference, 318
shifting circuit (RC), 494–495
Phasing dots or marks, 372
Phasors, 318–320
addition, 319
leading and lagging, 319
subtraction, 320
method, 560
Phosphor, 14, 34, 560
Photosphere, 13
Pi (π), 13
measure, 173
Pictorial diagram, 79–80, 560
function, 80
Pin plugs and jacks, 314–315
Place value, 9–10, 560
Planté, Gaston, 65
Planté cell, 69–72, 560
compared to sealed lead-acid cell, 70–71
Plastic, conductive, 35
Plotting, 168, 560
Point of reference, for voltage drops, 161
Polar coordinate system, 272, 381–382, 560
Polarity diagram, 163
Polarization, 560
in cells, 67
Poles, magnetic, 229–231
Positive charge, Franklin's definition, 2
Positively triboelectric, 23
Pot, *see* Potentiometer
Potential, 27, 43, 125, 560
drop, 161–162
energy, 27, 560
gradient, 27–28, 43, 560
in capacitor, 402
rise or voltage rise, 161–162, 560
Potential difference or voltage, 560
across inductor, 338–341
of cells, 65
definition, 27
measuring, 50–52
measuring in non-dc circuits, 299–301
in reference to ground, 88–89
in resonant circuits, 519
Potentiometer, 191–192, 560
multiturn, 192
control, 192
trimmer, 191–192
Power, 125, 560
in ac circuits, 303–304
with capacitance, 473–477
with inductance, 477–481
apparent, 476
dissipation, 126, 560
and size of resistors, 188
electric, 125–128
factor, 323, 481–483, 560
defined, 481
law, 126–127
calculations, 137
measuring, 127–128
ratios, 487–488
reactive, 474–481
defined, 474
relay, or contactor, 560
triangle, 481
true, defined, 475
Powers, fractional, 134–135
Prefixes, metric, 33, 55–57
Primary, 560
cell, 64–69, 560
winding, 373
Probe, 560
Probe compensation, 560
Product, 560
Programmable calculator, 560
Programmed review, instructions, 15
Prompt, 560
Proton, 4, 560
Protractor, 171
Pull-in or response time, 560
Pulse:
fall time, 277
generator, 560
rise time, 277
width, 275, 560
Pulses:
computations with, 275–277
in inductive circuits, 365
Pushbutton switch, 560
Pythagoras, 270
Pythagorean theorem, 270–271, 560

Q

Q, 560
in capacitive circuits, 497–498
of resonant circuits, 516
in series and parallel RL circuits, 369–371
symbol for charge, 23
Quadrant, 240–241, 270, 560
Quantity, vector, 46
Quantum mechanics, 4
and free electrons, 7
Quotient, 12, 560

R

Radian, 173, 561
measure, 302–303
Radical sign, 134
Radio frequency:
choke, 561
coil, 561
transformer, 561
Random failure, 393, 561
Range, 47, 51
multiplier, 213, 561
Rating, ampere-hour, 65
RC circuits:
delay, 411
parallel, 411, 450–451
phase shift, 494–495
practical, 491–497
series-parallel, 411–413
solving problems, 454–455
troubleshooting, 498–499
RCL circuits, 505–544
loading, 508
parallel, 508–510
series, 505–508
series-parallel, 510–514
steps for solution, 512, 514
Reactance:
capacitive, 441–451
inductive, 337, 343–344
Reactive power, 474, 561
Real numbers, 384
Recharging, 64
Reciprocal, 112–113, 561
Rectangular coordinates, 272, 561
Rectifier, 323, 561
Recurrent or periodic waveforms, 561
Reed relay, 561
Reference designator, 79–80, 561
in schematics, 81
Reference junction, 561
Reflex angle, 561
Relative permeability (μ_r), 238
Relative permeability, 561
Relay, 249–256, 561
arcing, 255
armature, 249–251
function, 250
response time, 251
case styles, 253–254
causes of failure, 254–256
common operating voltages, 250
contact resistance, 255
crystal-can type, 253
DIP, 254
definition, 249
FORM A contact, 251
FORM A reed contact, 252
FORM B contact, 251
FORM C contact, 251
FORM C reed contact, 252
general purpose, 250
low-level, 250
magnetic biasing, 252–253
mechanical biasing, 252
mercury-wetted contacts, 253

Relay (*Continued*)
- miss in, 255
- power, 250
- reed, 251–253
- sensitive, 250
- solid-state, 255–256
- temperature effects, 255–256
- thermal, 249

Release time, 561
Reluctance ℜ, 237
Reluctance, 561
Reset delay, 561
- in circuit breakers, 248

Resistance, 102, 103–105, 561
- effect of temperature, 108–109, 111–112
- measurement, 105–108
  - by bridge method, 105
  - using Ohm's law, 105
  - comparison method, 106
  - flowchart, 107
- and resistivity, 104–105
- of switch contacts, 148

Resistances:
- in parallel, 130–132
- in series, 128–130

Resistivity, 102, 103, 104, 561
- and resistance, 104–105

Resistor, 182–192, 561
- adjustable, 190
- bleeder, 221, 411
- carbon composition, 184–185
  - failure modes, 185
- film, 185
- fixed, 182–189
  - types, 183–185
- in inductive ac circuits, 341–342
- MIL SPEC coding, 189
- potentiometer, 191–192
- power dissipation and size, 188
- reasons for use, 182–183
- rheostat, 190–191
- schematic symbol, 182, 190
- as shunt, 216–218
- standard color code, 186–188
- standard values, 185–186
- terminating, 541
- variable, 183, 189–192
- wire-wound, 183–184

Resolving vector quantities, 269–273
Resolving velocity vector, 263
Resolution (in potentiometers), 191–192
Resonance, 514–515, 561
- curve, 516, 561

Resonant circuit:
- frequency, 515, 561
  - of tank with low Q, 540
- potential difference in, 519
- series, 514–521

Retrace, 561
Reversal of polarity, 73, 561
Reverse Polish Notation, 561
Reverse-reading technique, 322
Rf generator, 561
Rheostat, 190–191, 561
Right-hand rule for motors, 261, 561
Rise time of pulse, 277, 561
RL circuits:
- composite ac and dc sources, 363–365
- power, 479–481
- Q, 369–371
- review, 454

Rms value, 274
- use of uppercase, 301

Rotary switch, 561
Rotor, 461
Rounding off, 13, 42, 57–59, 94, 561–562
Rules, for rounding off, 58–59
Rutherford's theory of atom, 3–4

S

Saturation, 353, 562
Scalar, 269, 562
Scales:
- linear, 53
- multiple, 52–54
- nonlinear, 53
- reading analog, 52–55

Schematic:
- diagram, 81–82, 562
  - simplification, 160
  - symbols, 81
- simplified, 81

Scientific notation, 42, 562
- arithmetic, 59–62

Sealed lead-acid cell, 70–71, 562
Secondary, 562
- cell, or accumulator, 69–73, 562
- winding, 373

Self-healing, 562
Self-induction, 336–337, 562
Semiconductor, 7, 562
- effect of temperature, 108

Sensitive:
- relays, 562
- switch, 562

Series-aiding:
- cells, 83
- coils, 372

Series circuit, 562
Series-opposing:
- cells, 83–84
- coils, 372

Series-parallel circuit, 562
Service capacity, of cells in parallel, 85
Shelf life, 562
- of cells, 66

Shell, electron, or energy level, 4–7, 562
Shield, magnetic, 236–237
Shorting stick, 405, 562
Shunt, 47, 182, 216–218, 562
- Ayrton or universal, 217–218
- circuit, 216–218

S.I., 33, 42
Signals:
- analog, 363
- digital, 365

Signed numbers, 562
Significant digit, 57–58, 562
Significant figure, 57–58, 562
Siemens, 112
Signal generator or oscillator, 562
Signal sources, 307–316
- audio frequency, 307
- cables for, 314–315
- connectors, 315–316
- FM generator, 307–308
- function generator, 309–310
- markers, 308
- operation, 312–314
- oscillator, 307–308
- pulse generators, 310–311
- signal generators, 307
- sweep generator, 307–309
- synthesizers, 312
- types, 307

Signed number, 28
- arithmetic with calculator, 29–31

Significant digit, 32
Signs, neon, 14
Silver oxide cell, 68–69, 562
Similar triangles, 562
Simplified schematic, 81, 562
Simultaneous equations, 164–165
- solving with computer, 211–213
- solving with determinants, 175–179
- substitution method, 174–175

Sine, 270, 562
- defined, 243–244

Sine wave:
- analysis, 380
- average value, 273
- effective value, 274
- peak-to-peak value, 273

Sine waves:
- computations, 273–274
- phase relationships, 316–320

Single-precision number, 63, 562
Sinusoid, 299, 562
Slide rule, 7
Slope, 169, 562
Smoothing, 352, 562
Solder, 118
Soldering iron, grounded, 37
Solenoid, 233
Solid wire, 116–117
- strength, 117–118

Source, 43–44, 562
- composite AC and DC in RL circuits, 363–365
- definition, 42
- grounding, 88–89
- ideal current, 203–204
- ideal voltage, 203
- parallel connection, 84–85
- series connection, 82–84
- series-parallel connection, 85–87
- signal, 307–316

South pole of magnet, 231
Spaghetti, (insulation), 118, 563
SPDT switch, 563
Spectrograph, 18
Spectrum, 18
- analyzer, 563
- frequency, 268

Spin, 563
electron, 231
SPST switch, 563
Square, 133–136, 563
root, 133–136, 563
waves,
computations, 275–277
in inductive circuits, 365
Static:
charge, 24, 563
discharge, 36
electricity, 23–26, 33–37, 563
applications, 33–34
danger to components, 34
prevention, 34–37
Stator, 461
Steady-state:
condition, 563
current, 45
in inductor, 333
Step-down transformer, 375, 563
Step-up transformer, 375, 563
Stranded wire, 116, 563
table, 118
Subscript, 89, 563
Substitution, method of, 89
Substitution method for solving equations, 165–166
Subtraction:
of decimals, 11
in engineering or scientific notation, 59–60
of signed numbers, 29
Subtrahend, 11, 563
Superposition theorem, 204–206, 563
Supplementary angles, 563
Surface charge, 26
Surge, inductive voltage, 341
Sweep generator, 539, 563
Switch, 146–154, 563
action, 147
basic operation, 147–149
break-before-make, 150, 152–153
contact bounce, 151
contact resistance, 148
detent, 152
double pole, 147
double throw, 147
ideal characteristics, 148
index, 151–152
insulation resistance, 149
knife, 147–148
lighted pushbutton, 150
make-before-break, 150, 152–153
momentary action, 149–150
pole, or common pole, 147
progressive-shorting, rotary, 153
pushbutton, 149–150
normally-closed (PBNC), 149–150
normally-open (PBNO), 149–150
rotary, 151–154
schematic symbols, 152–153
section or gang, 151–152
sensitive, 148–149
single pole, 147
single throw, 147
slide, 150–151
toggle, 150–151
use in lamp circuit, 148
voltage rating, 149
Symbols, in diagrams, 81
Synthesizer, 563
System:
Arabic number, 57
definition, 80
metric, 55–57

T

Tangent, 271–272, 563
Tank, 522
Taper, in potentiometers, 191
Taut band, 563
Temperature, effect on cells, 66
Temperature coefficient, of capacitors, 426, 563
Temporary magnet, 230, 563
Term, 239, 563
Termination, 541
Tesla, 234
Technology, basic considerations, 1
Theorem:
network, 199–211
superposition, 204–206
Thermal circuit breaker, 247–248, 563
Thermal-magnetic circuit breaker, 563
Thermal runaway, 563
in ni-cad cells, 73
Thermocouple, 563
meter, 299–301
Thevenin equivalent, 206–207
and Norton's theorem, 209–210
Thevenin's theorem, 206–207, 209–210, 563
in RC circuits, 411–413
method of using, 206–207
in resonant circuits, 535–537
Time constant, 563
in LR circuit, 340–341
Time delay (slow blow) fuses, 563
Tinning, 118, 563
TNC connectors, 315–316
Toggle switch, 563
Tolerance, 563
definition, 179–180
Total magnetic flux, 564
Trailing zero, 57–58, 564
Transformer, 335, 564
defined, 373
effect, 372–376
primary winding, 373
secondary, 373
step-down, 375
step-up, 375
wire, 117
Transformers:
antenna, 390
audio:
case styles, 390
characteristics, 389–390
dc ratings, 389
frequency range, 389
frequency response, 389
harmonic distortion, 390
insertion loss, 390
interstage, 389–390
shielding, 390
autotransformers, 391–392
calculations, 381
causes of stress, 393
center-tap, 387
constant voltage, 388
copper losses, 378
core losses, 377
corona, 388
dc blocking, 390
eddy currents, 377
efficiency, 376–378
electrostatic shield, 389
failure modes, 392–393
if, 390
impedance matching, 378–380, 389–390
insulation resistance, 388
insulation test voltage, 388
isolation, 392
magnetic failure, 394
MIL SPEC designation, 386
percent regulation, 389
power, 387–389
characteristics, 388–389
dual primary, 388
operating frequency, 387–388
for vacuum tube circuits, 387
real or practical, 376–378
regulation factor, 388–389
rf, 390–391
antenna impedance matching, 391
shielding, 389
surge conditions, 389
troubleshooting, 393–394
types, 386–387
Transient state, 564
in inductor, 333
Transistor voltmeter, 49
Transposition, 91–92
Triangles, similar, 242–243
Triboelectricity, 23–24, 43, 63, 564
Trickle charge rate of lead-acid cell, 72, 564
Trigonometry, 564
Trimmer:
capacitor, 564
potentiometer, 564
Trip delay, in circuit breakers, 248, 564
Trip-free circuit breaker, 247, 564
Troubleshooting, definition, 1
filters, 544
RC circuits, 498–499
resistance measurements, 107–108
True power, 475, 564
True rms measurements, 299–301
True rms meter, 564
Tube, cathode-ray, 33–34
Tubing, heat-shrink, 118
Tuning, 355
TVM, 49

U

UHF connectors, 315
Unit analysis, 92
U.S. customary units, conversion of, 92–94
Units, International system of, 33
Unknown, 89, 564

V

Vane, 321
Var, 474
Variable, 239
  capacitor, 564
  dependent, 170, 240
  independent, 170, 240
  resistor, 564
Variational analysis, 95–96, 564
  exercises, 111–112
  of series and parallel circuits, 137–139
Vector, 46, 261, 564
  resolving, 269–273
Vertex, 171
Volt, defined, 51
Volta, Alessandro, 51, 63
Voltage, 27
  -controlled generator (VCG), 309
  -controlled oscillator (VCO), 308
  divider, 183, 220–222, 564
    similar to filter, 491–492
    troubleshooting, 221–222
  drop, 161–162, 564
  gain, 520–521, 564
  rise, 161–162
Voltaic pile or battery, 63, 564
Voltmeter, range, 51
Volt-ohmmeter, 48
VOM, 48, 51, 564
  connection, 49
VTVM, 564

W

Watt, 564
Wattmeter, 127–128, 564
Waveform, 242, 266–269, 564
  amplitude modulated sine wave, 266–267
  applications, 268
  cycle, 267
  frequency, 268
  period, 267
  recurrent or periodic, 266-269
  sawtooth, 266
  sine wave, 266, 268
Waveshapes, *see* Waveform
Wear-out failures, 393
Weber, 234
Wheatstone bridge, 219, 564
Wire, 114–119, 564
  aluminum, 117
  hook-up, 118
  insulation, 118–119
  power dissipation, 139
  wrap, 117, 564
Wire-wound resistor, 564
Wiring diagram, 80–81, 564
Work, definition, 1, 565
  in relation to charge carriers, 21
Working voltage, 565
Wrist straps, grounded, 36

Z

Zero, trailing, 57–58
Zinc chloride cell, 67, 565